"Value-packed, accurate, and comprehensive..."
—*Los Angeles Times*

"Unbeatable..."—*The Washington Post*

LET'S GO:
FRANCE

is the best book for anyone traveling on a budget. Here's why:

No other guidebook has as many budget listings.

In Paris, we found 40 hotels or hostels for under $20 a night. In the countryside we found hundreds more. We tell you how to get there the cheapest way, whether by bus, plane, or thumb, and where to get an inexpensive and satisfying meal once you've arrived. There are hundreds of money-saving tips for everyone plus lots of information on student discounts.

LET'S GO researchers have to make it on their own.

Our Harvard-Radcliffe researchers travel on budgets as tight as your own—no expense accounts, no free hotel rooms.

LET'S GO is completely revised every year.

We don't just update the prices, we go back to the places. If a charming café has become an overpriced tourist trap, we'll replace the listing with a new and better one.

No other budget guidebook includes all this:

Coverage of both the cities and the countryside; directions, addresses, phone numbers, and hours to get you there and back; in-depth information on culture, history, and the people; listings on transportation between and within regions and cities; tips on work, study, sights, nightlife, and special splurges, city and regional maps; and much, much more.

LET'S GO is for anyone who wants to see France on a budget.

Books by Let's Go, Inc.

Let's Go: Europe
Let's Go: Britain & Ireland
Let's Go: France
Let's Go: Germany, Austria & Switzerland
Let's Go: Greece & Turkey
Let's Go: Israel & Egypt
Let's Go: Italy
Let's Go: London
Let's Go: Paris
Let's Go: Rome
Let's Go: Spain & Portugal

Let's Go: USA
Let's Go: California & Hawaii
Let's Go: Mexico
Let's Go: New York City
Let's Go: The Pacific Northwest, Western Canada & Alaska
Let's Go: Washington, D.C.

LET'S GO:

The Budget Guide to

FRANCE

1993

Rebecca Knowles
Editor

Patrick J. LaRivière
Assistant Editor

Written by
Let's Go, Inc.
a wholly owned subsidiary of
Harvard Student Agencies, Inc.

PAN BOOKS
London, Sydney and Auckland

Helping Let's Go

If you have suggestions or corrections, or just want to share your discoveries, drop us a line. We read every piece of correspondence, whether a 10-page letter, a tacky Elvis postcard, or, as in one case, a collage. All suggestions are passed along to our researcher/writers. Please note that mail received after May 5, 1993 will probably be too late for the 1994 book, but will be retained for the following edition. Address mail to:

Let's Go: France
Let's Go, Inc.
1 Story Street
Cambridge, MA 02138

In addition to the invaluable travel advice our readers share with us, many are kind enough to offer their services as researchers or editors. Unfortunately, the charter of Let's Go, Inc. and Harvard Student Agencies, Inc. enables us to employ only currently enrolled Harvard students.

Published in Great Britain 1993 by Pan Books Ltd
Cavaye Place, London SW10 9PG
9 8 7 6 5 4 3 2 1

Published in the United States of America
by St. Martin's Press, Inc.

LET'S GO: FRANCE.
Copyright © 1993 by Let's Go, Inc.,
a wholly owned subsidiary of Harvard Student Agencies, Inc.
Maps by David Lindroth, copyright © 1993, 1992, 1991, 1990, 1989, 1986
by St. Martin's Press, Inc.

ISBN: 0 330 32692 9

Let's Go: France is written by the Publishing Division of
Let's Go, Inc., 1 Story Street, Cambridge, Mass. 02138

Let's Go® is a registered trademark of Let's Go, Inc.

Printed and bound in the United States of America
on recycled paper with biodegradable soy ink.

Acknowledgments

If I never again see a half-timbered house or a cobblestone street or a Caféteria Flunch or an affable proprietor, it will be none too soon. Indeed, I have enjoyed this job, this lifestyle, this book I call *Let's Go: France*. Why, what better way to put off the real, sane world than to sit in an office with **crazy-man Zach S.**, ever-laughing **Cecily M.**, and ever-working Pat. But alas, I must go now and travel around that crazy hexagon we call France, carrying this creation everywhere I go so that people will see my bold-faced name on the preceding page and will at once bow down in prayer, offer me gifts, rooms, food, wine, a frigging job.... Of course, I did not take this job for the fame and fortune it promised me—but, aaaah, what fame and fortune I have found. The lights, the glitter.

If I have done nothing right this summer—and I do wonder—at least I hired the best gosh-darned staff *Let's Go France* has ever seen. Like Paris, **Patrick La Rivière** slakes the human thirst for perfection. He worked linguistic and other wonders, turning a doll-drum G.I. into a veritable Pulitzer Prize deserving opus, and putting up with my post-workout perspiration and pathetic-joke cackles. Working phenomenal hours with phe-nomenal patience, he made the days fly by faster than a rolling "O." I can't say enough about him. As for the researchers, well, they truly made the France book easy as peach pie to edit. Researcher extraordinaire **Jon Glass** discovered the beauty of Australia, sang Queen hits on the sticky stages of southern eateries, put a couple towns on the map, and all he brought back home was a case of Southern Fried Chicken Pox (oh, and colorful copy that kept us rolling with laughter). Despite immediately being pickpock-eted while she was at church, **Marina Harss** made the transition from glamorous Paris to grungy North country with style. **Jared Hohlt** had a flu here, a broken backpack there, but still metaphorically flew down the west coast offering us magnanimous copy and meticulously detailed directions. No west coast traveler will ever get lost again. Blond wonder **Elizabeth Hoyt** astounded us with her adventurous spirit, copious copy, discerning eye, and unrivaled ability to attract **heavy-breathing balding accordion players.** She also devotedly saw us through the final stages of putting this baby to bed. With the eye of a skeptic and heart of a romantic, **Keven McAlester** made us laugh, made us cry, made us write bad checks.(which we did, many times, to the poor, broke researcher!). How he found the post-graduation energy to whiz his way through a high-ly demanding itinerary, I'll never know. Central France will never be the same again, not since **David McMurry** trekked, now naked, now clothed in purple-polka-dotted regalia, through the region, always managing to send us perfect copy. I await the day when this charming and hard-working cynic is old, plump, and grey, and sitting, sip-ping Perrier water on a Petit Train at a quaint little spa town. Taskmaster **Chris Caps** exuded abnormal competency, faithfully reordering, rewording, revamping, and remapping, this purple pineapple of a book; **Mark T.** passed, with flying colors, the computer tests I administered every 30 stupid seconds. **Pete D.**, once my editor, al-lowed me to be hired. Hey, Pete, I never thought of it that way. Thanks! And **Bart S.** kicked proverbial ass. Ooops, exsqueeze the language—it's late

And now, as I write this cheez-doodle 30 minutes before the book deadline, I yearn achingly, longingly, lovingly, to thank those who have made me happy recently. First, I'd like to thank the Academy. Stewart W., because of you, I did not have to eat Ramen noodles every day. Thanks for the room! Allison, Kath, Maye, Nell, and Sandra—I love you guys, even though I don't write, or call, or visit.... Katie B., Ellen M., Mikaela M., and Becky W.—the WWC—I admire you more than you know. Thanks Yelena, Debbie, Dana, and Richelle, for always making me laugh. Andy B., Mark L., and Drew C., from dog tracks to cigar-smoking to Studs-watching, I'll miss you. Betsie R., thanks for all your help and advice. Aimee L., you're a treat. Mike W., thanks for ev-erything. Wes H., keep on smilin'. Maybe now we can take that trip we've been saving up for. All the office staff, I love you folks-each and every one of you, and you and you and you and you and, oops, not you. And the France Room, aaah, *mais oui*: Qu'est-ce que je peux dire? Handstands, flowers on the nose, that little lace number Pat loves, constant giggles from Cecily's corner, Zach and his human-flesh menu reader, socks on the ears, eating bunny-meat, afternoon cookies, phosphorescence, effervescence, and the crazyBec file. The wonders of stress. Fluffy: old dogs never die, they just keep on living and living and living dammit. Mom, Dad, John, Larry: I love you. Send money soon.

—RDK

What *is* the name of that "built-in sharpener" box of 64 Crayola crayons? The obvious "Crayola 64," the catchy "Color Cart," or the to-the-point "Tub o' wax"? There are few jobs in this world where such an apparently trifling question would necessitate an office-wide APB. Fortunately, I had one of them. To say that this was the best job I have ever had would be to understate it. To say that I was surrounded by brilliant, motivated, interesting people would be similarly inaccurate.

Of these more-than-brilliant, overmotivated, impossibly interesting people, there are a few I must single out. First, Becca, who proves that a little insanity can take you far. Thank you for having faith in the prose and character of this subdued Montrealer, whose closest ties to France lie with a handful of distant ancestors, and a slightly twisted, Québecois version of the tongue. Your sharp wit and affable demeanor kept me laughing all summer; your spontaneity kept me worried. I wish you a long, successful life—hopefully someday you'll settle down with a red-hair-and-freckles Irishman of your choice in a quaint and secluded half-timbered house. Office mates and friends Zach and Cecily taught me more than I've ever learned from two people. From Cecily I learned how to see every work in the MFA in under an hour, everything I ever wanted to know but was afraid to ask about Bohemia, and, most importantly, that things are never so bad that you can't laugh (and I mean *never*). From Zach, that brutal merchant of prose, I learned what it means to be well-educated, what it means to be a thinker, and, not insignificantly, that Napoleon's most private scepter floats imperially in a jar at some sterile lab in New York City. I'll miss you both next year. Managing editor, travel companion, and friend Chris Caps edited with a precision that Freud would have found most intriguing. If this book is at all consistently formatted, it's his fault. My pedaling pals, Nicole and Carolyn, provided indispensable company for many tours of the Boston area. Pete K., I look forward to more caffeine- and beer-only weekends in the future.

Mike, Win, Zeid, Leah, Tony, and Mariah made life in that adorable rhomboid we call Somerville eventful and enjoyable, even through nightly battles with a miserably uncooperative sink. Adam, Marc, Mrs. Hirsch—who the hell blew up that train anyway? Amy K. filled my mailbox with limpid letters and ran up my phone bill with captivating conversation. The Khetanis's wonderful hospitality (and stellar food) made my first 4th of July a memorable (albeit damp) one. Suzannah saved me from Ramen more than once. Thank you all. And Mom, Dad, and Michelle, thank you for the support, love, and *tourtière*—all three kept me going through the summer. And while not knowing a word of the language when you dropped off at a French kindergarden many years ago was somewhat traumatic at the time, the experience has clearly proved fruitful. Thank you. And who knows, maybe someday I'll actually set foot in France. But why go when you can just write about it?

—P.J.L.

The greatest acknowledgment for the creation of this book goes to the nine researcher-writers who made it all happen: let this tome stand as a monument to your crusades. Here in Cambridge, Becca Knowles deserves moundsa moundsa praise for convincing me that the cliff of madness from which she so oft teetered was, in fact, a solid rock of "normal competency." Your love of pain will serve you well. Pat La Rivière refused simply to play straight man to Becca's antics, adding his own, all the while shepherding copy into my ever-fattening drawers and nurturing my new-found love for late-night *poutine*. *Let's Go: France* is deeply indebted to Zach Schrag and Cecily Morgan of *Let's Go: Paris* for masterfully painting the canvas of Paris in their two favorite media: blood and paint.

And now for the personal acknowledgments: to Pete Deemer, for hiring me in the first place; to July, Blythe, Mark, and Tim for surviving it all with me; to Andrew Kaplan, whose literary and visual aesthetic never failed to astound me; to the rest of the office (Your Name Here); to roommates and friends outside the office (Your Name Here); and, most importantly, to Let's Go's very own, the man who taught me to love phone codes, to never tolerate irrational bureaucracy, and to never quit until I'd answered the right question, Ian Watson. You have changed my life forever.

I'd like to dedicate my work to my enormous family (again, Your Name Here), in exchange for all the times I *couldn't* come home this summer, but in the final analysis, all of the work I ever did on this book, and all the work I ever implored Becca and Pat to do, came out of a dedication to you, the reader of this book. I hope you have a wonderful time. Send me a postcard.

—CC

About Let's Go

A generation ago, Harvard Student Agencies, a three-year-old non-profit corporation dedicated to providing employment to students, was doing a booming business booking charter flights to Europe. One of the extras offered to passengers on these flights was a 20-page mimeographed pamphlet entitled *1960 European Guide*, a collection of tips on continental travel compiled by the HSA staff. The following year, students traveling to Europe researched the first full-fledged edition of *Let's Go: Europe*, a pocket-sized book with tips on budget accommodations, irreverent write-ups of sights, and a decidedly youthful slant.

Throughout the 60s, the series reflected the times: a section of the 1968 *Let's Go: Europe* was entitled "Street Singing in Europe on No Dollars a Day." During the 70s *Let's Go* evolved into a large-scale operation, adding regional European guides and expanding coverage into North Africa and Asia. In the 80s, we launched coverage of the United States, developed our research to include concerns of travelers of all ages, and finetuned the editorial process that continues to this day. The early 90s saw the introduction of *Let's Go* city guides.

1992 has been a big year for us. We are now Let's Go, Incorporated, a wholly owned subsidiary of Harvard Student Agencies. To celebrate this change, we moved from our dungeonesque Harvard Yard basement to an equally dungeonesque third-floor office in Harvard Square, and we purchased a high-tech computer system that allows us to typeset all of the guides in-house. Now in our 33rd year, *Let's Go* publishes 17 titles, covering more than 40 countries. This year *Let's Go* proudly introduces two new entries in the series: *Let's Go: Paris* and *Let's Go: Rome*.

But these changes haven't altered our tried and true approach to researching and writing travel guides. Each spring 90 Harvard University students are hired as researcher-writers and trained intensively during April and May for their summer tour of duty. Each researcher-writer then hits the road for seven weeks of travel on a shoestring budget, researching six days per week and overcoming countless obstacles in the quest for better bargains.

Back in Cambridge, Massachusetts, an editorial staff of 32, a management team of six, and countless typists and proofreaders—all students—spend more than six months pushing nearly 8000 pages of copy through a rigorous editing process. By the time classes start in September, the typeset guides are off to the printers, and they hit bookstores world-wide in late November. Then, by February, next year's guides are well underway.

A NOTE TO OUR READERS

The information for this book is gathered by Let's Go's researchers during the late spring and summer months. Each listing is derived from the assigned researcher's opinion based upon his or her visit at a particular time. The opinions are expressed in a candid and forthright manner. Other travelers might disagree. Those traveling at a different time may have different experiences since prices, dates, hours, and conditions are always subject to change. You are urged to check beforehand to avoid inconvenience and surprises. Travel always involves a certain degree of risk, especially in low-cost areas. When traveling, especially on a budget, you should always take particular care to ensure your safety.

You can't buy beans without francs.

You'll probably find that the country that gave us the words "gourmet," "couture" and "champagne" isn't cheap. And it's trés likely you might find yourself a little short on francs. Which is why there's Western Union Money Transfer.

With Western Union you can receive money from the States within minutes in many cities throughout France, including Paris, Nice, Lyon, Cannes, Eze, Beaulieu, Marignane, Marseilles and Montpellier. Simply call 331-40-23-95-79 in France, or 1-800-325-6000 in the United States for the locations nearest you.

And relax, we'll send your francs as far as you need, in case yours don't go far enough.

WESTERN UNION | MONEY TRANSFER®

Contents

List of Maps

LET'S GO: FRANCE

General Introduction

Temple of culture, cuisine, fashion, snobbery, and cheese, France consists of an extraordinary mosaic of tiny villages, walled medieval cities, seamy ports, and, of course, sophisticated Paris. Charles de Gaulle, World War II Resistance hero and French President during much of the post-war era, summed up the French spirit with the words, "France cannot be France without greatness." In the center of all this greatness, the crowded brilliance of Paris presents only one of France's many faces. In the north, the industry of Lille hangs close by the bubbly of the Champagne region. The cliffs and fertile countryside of Normandy posed for the impressionists and embraced an Anglo-American liberation, while Brittany and Corsica have clung passionately to distinct cultural identities. The Loire Valley blossoms with the architecture of the French Renaissance, while the snowcapped Alps illustrate the architecture of raw geological force. The Dordogne River Valley, dubbed "The Capital of Prehistory," shelters 20,000-year-old cave paintings, while the Côte d'Azur is so glorious it has nearly ruined itself.

Let's Go is a helpful companion that introduces the budget traveler to the many sides of that adorable hexagon we call France. Our researchers travel on a shoestring budget, so their concerns are the same as yours: how to travel, eat, drink in the sights, enjoy evenings, and sleep in the most economical way possible. We list the best of the least expensive accommodations and restaurants in each town. We suggest ways to cut costs at every corner, corners from every cost.

Let's Go also guides you through the maze of tasks that need to be performed before you go. This general introduction provides details about applying for passports and student IDs, suggestions on what to pack, how to secure an inexpensive flight, and procedures for sending mail and money overseas. We help you decide what kind of trip to take and whether to invest in a rail pass or hostel card. Finally, we provide capsule accounts of political and cultural history, cultural quirks, and culinary glories.

Let's Go: France divides the country—western Europe's largest—into 21 regions, roughly correlated to the historical provinces to which the French retain their allegiance, despite the reorganization of the country into *départements* during the Revolution. The chapters are arranged geographically in a spiral centered in Paris and circling outward in a counterclockwise arc. Each section begins with an introduction that tries to capture the flavor and texture of the countryside, luring you to untrammeled places—remote villages in the Pyrénées, lesser-known vineyards in Burgundy, secluded hill towns in the Dordogne, the rural interior of Brittany, and the rugged, wind-swept islands off France's shores.

Practical Information sections supply just that, to prepare you not only for the poetry but also for the reality of your destination. *Let's Go* will get you into and out of the town, and from the train and bus stations to the center of town. It also provides you a list of vital phone numbers and addresses, for everything from laundromats to horse rental.

With your purse in mind, a *ranked* list of accommodations follows, succeeded by a similar list of restaurants. Finally, each section concludes with a write-up of the town's sights, festivals, and nightlife and a description of possible daytrips into the neighboring countryside.

Use our guide as a starting point for your own explorations; the best discoveries may be those you make yourself. If *Let's Go* is indeed the Bible of the budget traveler, healthy skepticism may serve you better than blind faith.

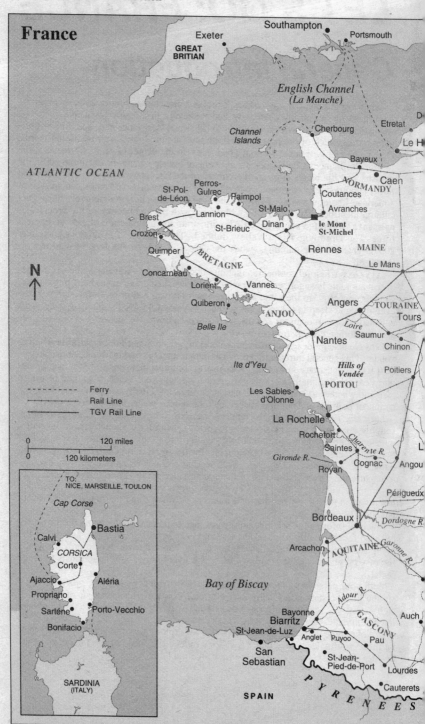

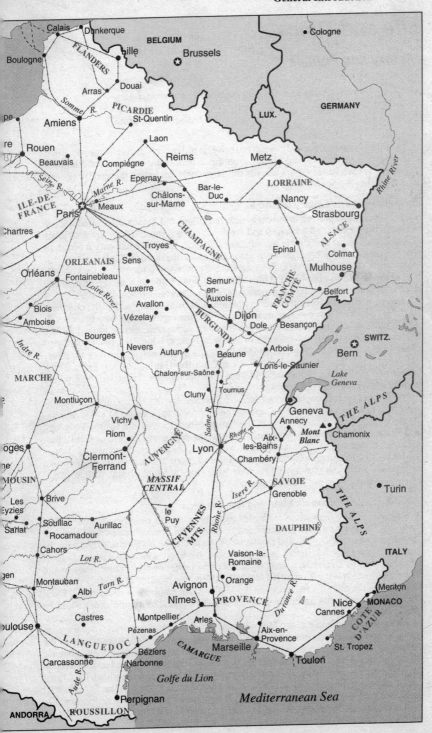

Life and Times

History and Politics

> You write to me that it's impossible; the word is not French.
>
> — Napoleon Bonaparte

The dimunitive emperor aptly captured the spirit of France's historical mosaic. Tiled with enlightened empires and bloody republics, flamboyant bourgeois and humble monarchs, French history often records the impossible becoming the very likely and soon thereafter the *fait accompli.*

Early History: The Legacy of Rome

In 1940, children playing in the caves near the village of Lascaux discovered a set of paintings produced by an advanced and creative people some 20,000 years ago. Little else is known about these early inhabitants of France, who have left only a few such relics to posterity. A more significant group, a Celtic tribe dubbed "Gauls" by the Romans, swept into France in 1000 BC, establishing permanent settlement in the lush valleys of the Rhône. A clan-based people, their tradition of rule by a strong, charismatic leader has served as a model for generations of self-absorbed French monarchs.

Centuries later, the Roman Empire, which had been diffusing across the continent since 500 BC, turned its eye (and its armies) toward the region that is now France, valuing it more as an international causeway than as a permanent settling ground. In 121 BC, the Empire established a colony in southern France, which served to guard precious trade routes connecting Spain and Italy. Gradually recognizing the region's inherent merits, the Romans sought to wrest it from the Gauls. The struggle, which culminated in a Roman victory in 52 BC, has been irreverantly chronicled in the wildly popular *Astérix* comic book series.

The Roman Empire could not last forever, however. By the 3rd century AD, its collapse was nearly imminent. The economic base of the empire began to erode as long-distance trade declined. Invasions by Barbarian tribes, such as the Goths, Visigoths, and Franks (who ultimately gave their name to the region and people of Gaul), hastened the disentanglement of the imperial web, as inhabitants clustered around powerful lords, swapping agricultural services for protection. The region fragmented into myriad self-sufficient manors and the next 1000 years of history brims with attempts, of varying success, to put it back together.

Charlemagne: Reconsolidation and Renaissance

Struggles among the various Barbarian tribes persisted for centuries, but the Franks soon saw the quickest path to preeminence. In 496, the Frankish chieftain **Clovis,** of the Merovingian family, allowed baptismal waters to drip on his forehead, and with the backing of the Catholic Church in Rome he was able to consolidate his power over all of Gaul. On this day, church and politics became bedfellows in France; they would share a pillow until the Revolution of 1789. Owing to a practice of dividing the kingdom among the ruler's sons, however, the Merovingian empire was soon erased. But it had demonstrated that amid the chaos of the Dark Ages, unity and order could be achieved.

Following the example of the Merovingians, another Frankish family—the Carolingians—soon rose to preeminence. In 687, the Carolinigans seized the remnants of the Merovingian territory, secured the French borders and began to extend their influence in the rest of the continent. By the year 800, the Carolingians controlled an area stretching from the Pyrénées to the Rhine and from the Mediterranean to Scotland. On Christmas Day in that year their most famous son, **Charlemagne,** knelt before Pope Leo III who crowned him Holy Roman Emperor. A new savior was born, to restore unity to Christendom. A commanding figure, with ceaseless intellectual curiosity, Charlemagne revived interest in the art and literature of the ancients, initiating what is now known as the Caroligian Renaissance. He insisted that Saint Augustine and Saint Jerome be read aloud to him as he dined, and sponsored attempts to preserve the decaying texts of Classical Greece.

Unfortunately, as with the Merovingians, familial infighting in the generations after Charlemagne weakened the empire. When a new wave of Barbarian tribes, this time consisting of Vikings, Hungarians and Seracens, pounced on Europe in the 10th century, France crumbled into feudal fragments once again.

The Medieval Period: The Birth of "France"

As the turn of the millenium approached, the map of France showed some 55 independent feudal lordships. In 987, the lords elected **Hugh Capet** to the throne of France, establishing the Capetian dynasty that would rule France for centuries. Capet's power, however, was essentially nominal. The territory he controlled personally was minimal, little more than the Ile de France—the swath of land cradling Paris. Yet he initiated a program of centralization, pulling together the lordships, often one by one, continually struggling against the centrifugal pull of the feudal system.

The feudal system was a complex societal structure, essentially a hierarchical pyramid erected from social, economic, military and political bricks. At the top stood the feudal lord, who controlled a huge tract of land, allotting part to warriors who promised him military service in return and another part to peasant farmers who contributed a part of their agricultural take. While clearly hierarchical, the system was far from tyrannical; in fact, the mutual, contractual nature of the feudal bond was one of its defining characteristics. The peasants enjoyed certain rights vis-a-vis the lord and owed him certain duties; they were not slaves and he was not an absolute ruler.

The preconditions for feudalism, however, slowly began to erode in the 11th century. The Barbarian threat that first urged peasants under the protective wings of feudal lords had subsided, and the European economy began to churn once again. New technology yielded agricultural surpluses on a regular basis and the roots of a market-based, capitalist economy found good soil. Long-distance commerce revived and towns sprang up at important commercial intersections.

The Capetians, meanwhile, corralled lordship after lordship into their fold. They convinced the territorial lords, who sensed their power waning as the economic base of feudalism slipped, that central authority could reinvest them with the control they desired. Perhaps more importantly, a series of astute marriages multiplied the land under the direct control of Paris. During his 43-year reign, from 1180 to 1223, **Phillipe II Auguste** singlehandedly married into the Artois, Valois, and Vermandois families and conquered Normandy and Anjou back from England. The unification of France neared completion. As historian André Maurois writes, "in the course of two centuries the Duke of Ile de France had become the King of France."

Noise from across the Channel soon disrupted this centralizing program, however, for when the last Capetian, **Charles IV,** passed away in 1328, **Edward III** of England staked his claim to the French throne. The dispute crescendoed in 1337, with the start of the Hundred Years War, a conflict that actually stretched for 116 years, until France emerged victorious in 1453.

Throughout this costly war, and despite some pillowfighting, the church and the state remained close, although the state soon emerged ascendant. Yet even amid the backhanded political manipulations necessary for Paris to gain control over the Church in Rome, religion remained a central part of daily life in medieval and Renaissance times. The monarch derived his very political legitimacy from "divine right"—in a word, he was the Lord's parliamentarian. The sheer force of religion in this time became evident when nascent strands of Protestantism fomented strife across France in the late 16th century. Catholics and Protestants struggled in the wake of the St-Bartholomew's Day Massacre of 1572, where a wild Paris mob slaughtered some 2000 *Huguenots* (French Protestants). In 1589, **Henri IV,** a Protestant, acceded to the throne. Keenly aware of the difficulties this would cause for his rule, he converted to Catholicism, waving off the magnitude of the decision with a nonchalant, *"Paris vaut bien une Messe"* (Paris is certainly worth a mass). He did not fully abandon his Protestant kin, however; in 1598 Henri enacted the Edict of Nantes, guaranteeing them religious and political rights.

The Old Regime: Absolute Excess

The 17th century was the crowning achievement of the French monarchy, a period of burgeoning absolutism when the kings nearly drowned in their own splendor and ceremony. Henri IV was succeeded on the throne in 1610 by **Louis XIII,** whose reign is perhaps better remembered for his first minister—**Cardinal Richelieu.** Richelieu began to fashion the greatest absolutist state Europe had ever seen, a nation where sovereignty rested solely and entirely with the monarch. Indeed, only nine years after Richelieu's death, a French monarch, **Louis XIV,** could utter for the first time, "*L'etat, c'est moi"* (I am the state). The rise of this absolutist state strained the already taut social fabric of France, as Richelieu manipulated the nobility into submission, and teased the bourgeoisie with the promise of social advancement.

The power and glamor of the Old Regime culminated under Louis XIV, the Sun King, who rose to the throne as a five year-old in 1642 and ruled for 72 years. He built the capital at Versailles into a magnificent showcase for regal opulence and noble privilege, surrounding himself with exquisite luxuries and submissive nobles. Filling his day with minute rituals of ridiculous scope, from a multi-step awakening involving a legion of servants to an elaborate bedtime procedure, the Sun King glittered while his people starved. Nonetheless, France rose to greatness under his rule. He mustered military support for France in virtually every country in Europe, negotiating a delicate series of alliances. And he insured that French culture should come to dominate Europe, with Molière, Descartes and Pascal circulating almost as widely outside of France as within its borders.

Yet this ostensibly powerful regime was rife with contradiction. As part of the legacy of feudalism, the nobility was exempt from a number of important taxes that weighed heavily on the bourgeosie and the peasantry, and those nobles still living on territorial estates retained a number of terribly anachronistic privileges over the peasant farmers. But while the social structure of feudalism was thus preserved, its economic base had long before been undermined by the emergence of capitalism. The middle classes quickly recognized this inconsistency, which limited their social mobility, and sought to right it. The nobles refused to relinquish their privileges; the bourgeois refused to relinquish their demands; and the king vacillated. Something drastic seemed imminent.

The French Revolution: To Raze and Build Anew

The French Revolution began with a bankrupt monarch and ended with an enlightened dictator. It was not about rulers; it was about privilege. Its goal was two-fold, at once destructive and constructive: to tear down the vestiges of feudalism and to erect in its place a new society built on the tripartite ideal of *liberté, égalité, fraternité.*

The flamboyant lifestyle and vainglorious wars of the absolutist monarchs had strained the palace purse. By 1787, a financial crisis beset Versailles and **Louis XVI** called an Assembly of Notables to seek solutions. They suggested that an Estates General, an archaic French parliament, be called—the first time since Louis XIII had dismissed it in 1614. Debate ensued over the proper balance of power between the three estates (the clergy, nobility, and bourgeoisie). In frustration, the bourgeoisie broke away, and declared *itself* to be the National Assembly. The revolution against royal finances initiated by the nobles had given way to a bourgeois revolution against feudal privilege. The Paris mob soon joined in, skillfully manipulated by the bourgeoisie, and with the storming of the Bastille the revolution took on a violent character that would haunt it until its bittersweet end. On August 4, 1789, the revolution succeeded in its first goal, that of eradicating feudal privilege. In the Assembly on that hot summer night, preordained nobles rose one by one and renounced their hereditary feudal privileges. When the evening ended, the world had changed. Three weeks later, with the enactment of the Declaration of the Rights of Man, the revolutionaries began to build society anew on the ashes of the old order. The Declaration encoded the driving principles of *liberté, fraternité,* and *égalité.* The history of the tumultuous decade following the Revolution of 1789, and indeed of the entire 19th century, represents the attempt of

France to congeal these ideals in the form of a stable government. In many ways, this was not achieved until well into the 20th century.

In the years between 1789 and 1799, France saw a flip-flopping of regimes, the execution of the traitor-king Louis XVI, who continued to side with the disenfranchised nobles, and the rise of the Terror, a mass guillotining of perceived enemies of the state led by brutal merchant of death **Maximilien Robespierre** and his Committee of Public Safety. A confused and exhausted French people yearned for stability and welcomed gratefully the rise of a man they felt could achieve it: Napoleon. An accomplished general and unquestionable genius, **Napoleon Bonaparte** wielded the scepter of power selfishly but judiciously. He established a strong central bureaucracy and a system of law that still lies at the foundation of legal systems around the world. But he was not satisfied with ruling France alone, and soon initiated a series of military campaigns that nearly yielded him hegemony over the entire European continent. The harsh Russian winter of 1812 and the Battle of Waterloo in 1815 prevented this. In the wake of Napoleon's wars, European leaders, meeting at the Congress of Vienna, legislated a step backward in time, resetting the French borders to those of 1792, instating Louis XVIII, the late king's brother, to the throne.

The Nineteeth Century: Search for Stability

The 19th century continued the Revolution's quest for a stable regime. Caught in a cycle of revolution and reaction, the country swapped monarchy for dictatorship, for republic, for empire, and for republic once again in the course if 55 years. Where other countries would change governments in times of dissatisfaction, the Revolution had left France with a tradition of changing the *system* of government itself. It had also bequeathed France a polarized society of liberal urban-dwelling republicans and conservative rural peasants whose tug-of-war, in large measure, accounts for the instability of the 19th century. The century culminated with the founding of the Third Republic (the First being founded by the Revolution, the Second a mere parenthesis between 1848 and 1851), a seemingly stable regime that would endure until World War II.

As France neared the turn of the century, the nation brimmed with optimism, as did most of Europe. Science had unlocked many of nature's deepest secrets and its bedfellow technology had improved the quality of life and the capacity for production across the continent. Industrialization and urbanization had introduced many new social plights that challenged the Third Republic, and the regime's reluctant reforms lay the foundation for the contemporary welfare state. A belief in the notion of progress—that civilization was moving ever-forward toward a state of Utopian bliss unblemished by the poverty, hunger, and war that had plagued life in the 19th century—pervaded French society.

The Twentieth Century: Stability Lost and Found

The advent of **World War I** exploded this notion of progress. In the 19th century, European statesmen felt they had solved the problem of international conflict with their balance of power system, whereby any country moving to augment its power would be confronted by an alliance of other nations seeking to protect mutual interests. The system broke down in the early years of the 20th century, as the actions and negotiations of the Germans split Europe into two tripartite alliances: the Triple Entente (England, France, and Russia) vs. the Triple Alliance (Germany, Italy, and Austria-Hungary). The continent was a delicately balanced see-saw, and the slightest disturbance was sure to send some nation's metaphorical bottom slamming against the cold hard soil of defeat. A crisis in the Balkans provided just such a disturbance. War erupted and the continent was transformed into a maze of trenches and rubble. The entrance of the Americans in 1917 tilted the balance in favor of the French and British, and by 1918 Germany surrendered, admitting defeat. The war profoundly touched the French, who lost five million citizens and faith in the idea of civilization. In compensation, they demanded crippling reparations from Germany, a humiliation for the Germans that led in part to World War II.

The Great Depression struck at the very foundations of the Third Republic, and government after government rose and fell, as coalitions formed and dissolved. Socialists, communists, even fascists ran amok through the political system. The political scene was a swarm, a jumble; France was a country unprepared for the blow delivered by a newly militarized and antagonistic Germany. On June 14, 1940, German armies swept into Paris. The French government fled into exile in the small town of Vichy. A resistance movement was established by General **Charles de Gaulle** who, with the help of the Allies and especially the Americans, drove the Germans out of France. In October of 1946, the Fourth Republic was proclaimed, under the presidency of de Gaulle.

Similar institutionally to the Third Republic, the Fourth Republic suffered from the same shortcomings, particularly the lack of a strong executive to keep the country running if the legislature stalemated. In 1946, de Gaulle resigned out of frustration with the system, as well as to show how indispensable he was. Problems with the colonial empire plagued the regime and a 1958 revolution in Algeria triggered the collapse of the Fourth Republic. In 1958, de Gaulle returned to inaugurate the Fifth Republic, which has lasted to this day. Finally, the ideals of the Revolution have found stable form in a government that protects liberty and strives for equality, while remaining flexible enough to meet the complex demands of the 20th century. Legislative power is held by Parliament, which consists of a 317-member Senate and a 491-member National Assembly, both elected by universal suffrage. Executive power is held by the President, who is elected by popular vote for a seven-year term. The President appoints a Council of Ministers, headed by the Prime Minister, which manages the country and is responsible to Parliament. Depending on the composition of the Assembly, the balance of power lies alternately with the President or the Prime Minister, a system which prevents legislative deadlock.

Despite its strengths, the regime almost collapsed in 1968, when demonstrations by students and workers nearly paralyzed the country. For two weeks, students fought to alter the authoritarian French university system. Demonstrations gave way to riots and students took over the Sorbonne. Soon 10 million workers joined the hundreds of thousands of students, decrying low wages and slow social reform. The National Assembly was dissolved, but a new election returned the ruling Gaullists to power.

In 1969 de Gaulle resigned once again. Subsequent elections have brought **Georges Pompidou** and then **Valery Giscard d'Estaing** to the Presidency, as well as **François Mitterrand,** France's first Socialist President, who was elected in 1981. Within two weeks of taking office, Mitterrand had raised the minimum wage and instituted a mandatory fifth week of annual vacation. He continued to enact traditional socialist legislation, but an economic recession in 1983 forced him to advance a number of unpopular deflationary policies. Soon after, socialists suffered serious setbacks in local and European parliamentary elections. Symptomatic of recent social strife in France, the 1986 legislative elections saw the emergence of a new racist, ultra-rightist, ultra-nationalist party—the National Front (FN), headed by Jean-Marie Le Pen. He ran under the slogan, *"La France pour les français,"* (France for the French, with a very narrow interpretation of Frenchness.) Nonetheless, Le Pen only gained 10% of the vote that year. Two years later, in 1988, Mitterrand was reelected president and was joined by France's first woman Prime Minister, **Edith Cresson,** who stepped down in 1992.

In broader European politics, the French have been a major force in the development of the European Community. In January of 1992, France, along with 12 other EC member-nations, began a program of tariff reduction that will eventually allow goods and workers to pass freely from nation to nation. A recent agreement has also set Europe in motion towards monetary union, whereby all member countries would use a common currency, controlled by a single central bank. Some historians believe this "shared sovereignty" marks but the first step towards an ultimate political union. Some 1500 years after the collapse of the Roman Empire, and 1000 years after the dissolution of the Carolingian Empire, France is poised once again to mesh quietly into a larger European unit.

Art and Architecture

Ancient and Medieval

Some 20,000 years ago, prehistoric people, working with crude brushes by flickering torch light, executed the world's first painting in a dank cave near what is now Lascaux, France. What it was, precisely, that drove them to translate the reality of human existence into symbolic form is, of course, unknown. But this uniquely human urge to create has flourished in France, sculpted by, and in turn sculpting, the very course of the country's development.

France's classical forebears—the ancient Greeks and Romans—have left an impressive artistic legacy. In many ways, virtually all of Western art and architecture have developed either in sympathy with, or in reaction to, the Greek artistic idiom, which emphasized realism and the perfection of the human figure. As for Rome, the remains of some of the city's most ambitious architectural undertakings still dot the countryside of southern France, like the majestic triple-arched aqueduct that carried water to Nîmes (c. 100 BC). Still, if classical civilization left many themes and ideals for French art, the birth and death of Jesus Christ provided centuries worth of subject matter. No scene has been depicted more often in French art than the Crucifixion. No village or town, however small, lacks a grand cathedral or simple church.

With the rise of Charlemagne in the 9th century, art and architecture flourished across Western Europe, for the Emperor was a keen and generous patron. Under him, artists combined elements of the classical legacy with elements of the northern Barbarian tradition to achieve the first distinctively "Western" style. Almost exclusively religious, this was very much a symbolic art, focused on conveying feeling rather than representing what is seen. The idealized human figures and realistic scenes of Greek art ceded to ethereal depictions of another, more heavenly, reality.

Powerful symbols of religious omnipresence, the earliest churches in France are direct descendants of secular Roman basilicas. Dubbed **Romanesque** and characterized by round arches and massive, heavy walls, they reflect both the limitations of contemporary architecture and the uncertainty of a world that demanded solid, defensible structures. Romanesque churches, like the **Basilique St-Sernin** (1096) in Toulouse were designed to accommodate large crowds of worshipers. Typically, they map out Latin crosses, with vaulted naves to add grandeur. But while St-Sernin's thick walls and barrel vaults provide ample space, they let in very little light.

In the late 12th century, Abbott Suger, the bishop of St-Denis, solved this problem, by adding pointed arches and flying buttresses to the rebuilt **Church of St-Denis** (1144). In so doing he initiated the **Gothic** style of architecture which has become synonymous with the late Middle Ages. While the barrel-vaulted roofs in Romanesque structures rest on fortified pillars, Gothic structures utilize a system of arches that distributes weight outward rather than straight down. Flying buttresses counterbalance the pressure of the ribbed vaulting, relieving the walls of the roof's weight and allowing for the installation of more windows. As a result, the walls of Gothic churches seem to soar weightlessly, and light streams in through enormous stained glass windows. Noyon's and Laon's cathedrals in northern France embody the early Gothic style, characterized by simplicity in decoration. Although the architecture remained similar through the Gothic period, the high Gothic style of the later Middle Ages embodied extreme ornamentation as seen in the Paris, Amiens, and Chartres cathedrals.

Less immediately accessible are the other arts of the Middle Ages—manuscript illumination, tapestry weaving, and decorative arts—on view in various museum collections, notably the **Musée de Cluny** in Paris and the seminary in Bayeux. As the medieval period wore on, Christian themes continued to inform the day's art, but works of art slowly began to creep out of the cathedrals into more secular venues. Even in religious art, individual human beings, realistically portrayed, began to figure more prominently than before—witness the impressive Bibilical figures poised tirelessly on the portals of the Chartres cathedral.

Renaissance and Early Modern

The return of art into the realm of the human, coupled with a nostalgia for the classical past, strongly colored the art of the 15th-century **Renaissance,** centered in Italy. Although nation-states began to coalesce in this period, it was still hard to point to a distinctively French art. France was sandwiched, both geographically and artistically, between the Netherlands in the north and Italy in the south. In fact, François I, who ruled France from 1515 to 1547, was one of the greatest patrons of *Italian* art. Architecturally, François commissioned such buildings as the remarkable Château de Chambord and the Louvre palace, which combined a flamboyant French Gothic motif with aspects of Italian design. In 1528 he hired Italian artists to improve the original hunting lodge of **Fontainebleau.** The resulting Renaissance palace shows few traces of its medieval origins, when the architecture of castles and palaces had been almost purely functional, blending strong fortification with strategic location.

The ostentatious palaces of the 16th and 17th centries were anything but functional. As the French aristocracy began its migration away from Paris to the surrounding countryside, they demanded suitably lavish living quarters. Great châteaux sprung up in the Loire River Valley, providing escapes from the proverty of Paris as well as convenient access to the nobility's favorite hunting grounds. The exodus culminated with Louis XIV's move from Paris to **Versailles** in 1672, shifting the seat of the French government away from the ancient capital. Here Louis commissioned the world's largest royal residence, an exorbitantly beautiful palace that signaled the zenith of France's aristocratic excess and remains today a symbol of the all-powerful Sun King.

Under Louis, an indigenous French art finally flourished and, indeed, rose to European dominance. The center of Western art shifted decisively from Rome to Paris where, many would say, it has remained to this day. In the wake of the Scientific Revolution sealed by Isaac Newton in the late 17th century, art favored reason over faith. Concrete, secular art quickly overtook the tired symbolism of cathedral art. Georges de la Tour and the Le Nain brothers chose simple subjects for their paintings and made striking use of light and shadow. Nicolas Poussin elaborated the theory of the "grand manner," with its huge canvases and panoramic subjects taken from mythology and history. The French Royal Academy, founded in 1648, came to value this style above all others and all subsequent French painters had to contend with these weighty "academic" precepts. Drawing on the academic idiom, two 18th-century artists, Watteau and Boucher, developed an art best described as aristocratic, a fluffy and extravagant style since dubbed **Rococo.** The sugary creations of Fragonard are still more elaborate, depicting French nobles at work and play. Yet already, painters espousing middle class, bourgeois values began to eschew tradition. Chardin, for one, painted the common and the everyday with realistic, unsaccharine strokes.

This nascent style soon triumphed, as the bourgeois "victory" in the Revolution of 1789 threw flamboyant aristocratic art into disfavor. Revolutionary leaders called for a more austere and dignified art. The chief painter of the republic, Jacques-Louis David, looked to Rome for inspiration. Using art to foment national spirit in the newly born republic, David depicted such noble historic subjects as the death of Marat and the coronation of Napoleon. His *Oath of Horatii* (1784) uses an ancient subject—the swearing of an oath to defend Rome—to express contemporary Republican values. The Napoleonic period adopted David's **Neoclassicism** as its official style.

In reaction to David's staid compositions, the **Romantics** of the first half of the 19th century relied on vivid color and expressive brush strokes to create an emotional and subjective visual experience. Artists like Théodore Gericault and Eugène Delacroix took as their subject the exotic, the violent, the grotesque—anything to provoke spontaneous emotion while shunning classical harmony. Consider two of Géricault's titles: *Decapitated Heads* (c. 1818) and *Portrait of a Child Murderer* (1822-23). In his *Raft of the Medusa* (1819), Géricault depicts with agonizing clarity the still-suffering survivors of a shipwreck, floating hopelessly under an orange-fired sky. His gifted contemporary, Delacroix, while perhaps less gruesome than Géricault, nonetheless framed scenes of great emotional power. His dramatic *Liberty Leading the People* (1830) is a triumphant scene of the bare-breasted Lady Liberty ushering in the new republic.

Tradition did survive the powerful influence of the Romantics, however, transmitted in part by the work of Jean-Auguste Dominique Ingres, a student of David. Like his master, he chose rich historical subjects and dressed his figures in opulent materials while drawing attention to the sensual surface of the canvas.

The Modern

If the Revolution of 1789 ushered in a new bourgeois art, the Revolution of 1848 introduced a proletarian art. **Realist** painters like Gustave Courbet looked closely at, and indeed glorified, the "humble" aspects of peasant life. His *Burial at Ornans* (1850) uses the grand scale of history painting for a simple village scene, an approach which angered many conservative patrons of art. Courbet's somewhat abrasive personality did not help his work get accepted in salons; when his paintings were refused by the Universal Exposition of 1855, he set up his own Pavilion of Realism right outside. Fellow Realist Jean Millet invested peasants with grandeur through the value of their work and presented the idyllic simplicity of their lives; Honoré Daumier, best known for his lithographed caricatures, also painted vivid social commentaries. Simultaneously, another group of mid-19th-century painters, particularly Camille Corot and Théodore Rousseau, transformed the landscape painting, depicting rural subjects from direct observation and paying close attention to light and atmosphere. This new trend, when coupled with the realism of Courbet, soon gave birth to a movement known as Impressionism.

The **Impressionist** movement changed art forever through its revolutionary approach to artistic subject and visual experience. Treating color as an inherent property of light, not of objects, Edouard Manet, Claude Monet, and their successors painted outside, endeavoring to capture a moment of vision involving movement and the changing effects of light. Manet's *Olympia* (1863) symbolized the end of bourgeois societal dominance, by presenting a nude prostitute who did not seem to submit to the subjugating stare of the bourgeois observer. His *Le Déjeuner sur l'Herbe (Luncheon on the Grass)* (1863) depicting a picnic party composed of a nude woman and two men in contemporary clothing revolutionized the possibilities of subject matter and perturbed his contemporaries. Lighter and airier than Manet's, Monet's works include views of water and waterlilies *(nymphéas),* Rouen's cathedral, haystacks, and Norman seashores. His painting *Impression: Soleil Levant (Impression: Sunrise)* (1872), gave the movement its name. The Impressionists, once relegated to a "Salon des Réfusés," became a huge collective success and paved the way for all 20th-century Western art. Other important Impressionists include Camille Pissarro, Pierre Auguste Renoir, and Edgar Degas.

The inheritors of the Impressionist tradition share the label of **Post-Impressionism,** though they largely went their separate ways. Paul Cézanne worked in Aix-en-Provence and created still lifes and geometric landscapes (among them his *Mont Ste-Victoire,* 1885-87) with planes of orange, gold and green, as well as still lifes and portraits. His style, which attempted to deconstruct reality and reassemble it in a series of geometric planes, anticipates cubism. Georges Seurat's **Pointillisme** takes Impressionism a step further, using even tinier dots and further simplifying forms. Using large flat blocks of intense color, Paul Gauguin painted scenes from Brittany and Arles in the same primitive style he used to depict Tahiti and Martinique. In his own words, Vincent van Gogh "tried to express the terrible passions of humanity by means of red and green." His wavy, passionate strokes of color create an individual and deeply expressive view of the world.

Matisse, Dérain, and Braque exchanged the pale Impressionist palette for intensely bright colors; critics dubbed them **"Fauves,"** meaning "wild beasts." Inspired by the Fauves and other post-Impressionists, much of the art of the 20th century moved toward pure abstraction, an attempt to depict a more subtle reality than the simple "retinal" reality that had long dominated Western painting. Georges Braque went on to create the sharply geometric abstractions of the **Cubist** style along with Pablo Picasso, possibly the 20th century's greatest artist. Picasso's career, spanning many decades and movements, is chronicled at the Musée Picasso in Paris and at the older Musée Picasso in Antibes.

Similarly revolutionary trends in architecture have erected a number of controversial projects in Paris. The **Centre Pompidou,** hated by some and adored by others, was built in 1970 by Richard Rogers and Renzo Piano. With its innards (heating and plumbing pipes, electrical wires, and escalators) on the outside, the building houses a cultural center and modern art museum in its vast interior space. I.M. Pei's modernist glass pyramid, planted smack in the middle of the Louvre courtyard, was blocked for months while the conservative Finance Ministry took its time moving out of the offices in the Richelieu branch of the ancient palace. Conservatives have succeeded, however, in keeping towering urban architecture (except for the Montparnasse tower) out of Paris proper. Instead, skyscrapers cluster in the business and industrial suburb of La Défense, home to the new **Grande Arche,** a giant, hollowed-out cube of an office building aligned with the Arc de Triomphe, the smaller arch in the Tuileries, the place de la Concorde, and the Louvre.

The art and architecture of the late 20th century can not be easily labeled or even accorded the status of a movement; it revels instead in a chaotic mix of revolution and reaction, torn between further abstraction and a return to more concrete representation. For information on contemporary art in France, check out the numerous art magazines or the galleries around Les Halles, Bastille, or bd. St-Germain in Paris.

Partners in Crime?

Pablo Picasso and his poet friend Guillaume Apollinaire had been accused of many things in their lives—of excessive abstraction in their art, of decadent living—but in August of 1911 they found themselves accused of something far worse: stealing the *Mona Lisa.* At the time that the painting disappeared, the two had "acquired" statues also stolen from the Louvre. Fearing these might be uncovered in a search for the *Mona Lisa,* the two buddies packed the statues into a suitcase, intending to dump them in the Seine under the cover of night. They hesitated, however, and instead anonymously left the statues at a local newspaper. The police soon tracked the artists down and jailed them as suspects in the *Mona Lisa* case. Only through the efforts of local artists, who attested to the fine quality of the men's characters, were the two released.

Meanwhile, the *Mona Lisa* turned up two years later in the possession of a former Louvre employee. He had snuck it out of the museum under his overcoat, leaving behind only the frame and a fine left thumb print. Unfortunately, the museum recorded only its employees' right thumb prints. The joyful, albeit embarrassed, museum directors allowed the painting to be shown in its native Italy for a month, at which time they returned the smiling lady to her proper place on the Louvre wall.

Literature

Given the pride the French take in their literary heritage, one would think the Bible itself had been first penned in their noble tongue. On the contrary, it is impossible to speak of a French literature much before the 10th century, when the colloquial Latin spoken in Gaul first transmuted into a larval form of French. The very first text composed in this nascent French language—still much closer to Latin than modern French—was the *Serment de Strasbourg,* a contractual oath written on February 14, 842. As the language continued to develop in the 11th century, a plethora of literary forms emerged, from the *chansons de geste,* which were long epic poems celebrating heroic deeds in the age of Charlemagne, to the narrative romances set in a mystical land of fierce dragons and bearded sorcerers ruled by King Arthur. Indeed, writings in verse far outnumbered prose writings in this period, in part to retain the traditional rhythms of oral storytelling. These verse forms gathered increasing complexity in the two centuries before the Renaissance, stretching both in variety and in subtlety.

Still, the 15th-century **Renaissance** brought not so much a shift in form and style as a transformation of subject matter. The Italian humanist movement that had restored humanity as the focus of art and literature quickly swept into France. When coupled with the invention of the printing press around 1450, the result was a widely circulated literature addressing the very foundations of human nature. Meanwhile, the still unstandardized and somewhat unstable French language accorded prosaists a great deal of stylistic freedom. Indeed, the three greatest literary figures of the 16th century were all writers of prose: Rabelais, the moralist, Calvin, the reformer, and Montaigne, the humanist. While each profoundly affected the literary discipline, Montaigne in particular left to posterity the personal essay, a form he more or less invented. Through these essays, Montaigne initiated a literature of self-exploration to contend with his grief over the loss of a father and close friend; he sought to understand humanity through understanding a single man: himself.

While the 16th century's liberating approach to subject matter persisted into the 17th century, the freedom of style and language did not. The Académie Française, founded in 1635, gathered some 40 men to regulate and codify French literature, grammar, spelling and rhetoric. The rules and standards they set loosely at this time would soon solidify into rigid regulations. Hence was born the **"Classical"** age of French literature. Heralded by the moralizing animal fables of La Fontaine as well as the crystal clear poetry of Malherbe, the age yielded the three most influential dramatists in the nation's history: Corneille, Molière, and Racine. All three wrote in verse, and focused generally, and often quite sarcastically, on the elite in French society. Corneille penned *Le Cid*, a story of love, honor, and family set in Spain, criticized by the Académie for not conforming to its increasingly dogmatic standards. Racine's most important work, *Phèdre* (considered by some to be the greatest work in the French literary canon), recounts the tale of the incestuous love of Phèdre for her step-son Hippolyte. Finally, Molière, perhaps the most talented of the three, sacrificed a stable career in the family business—upholstery—for a try at the stage. In a country since overrun with furniture, and always craving good theater, it can not be denied that his decision was auspicious. His comedies of manners, including *Le Misanthrope, Le Bourgeois Gentilhomme (The Bourgeois Gentleman), Les Femmes Savantes (The Learned Ladies),* and *Le Docteur Malgré Lui (The Doctor in Spite of Himself)*, satirize the habits and speech of his time with a deadly wit matched by a faultless sense of comedy. In the realm of non-fiction, French thinkers like René Descartes initiated a skeptical philosophy of rationalism, whereby all of current knowledge was thrown into doubt, to be retrieved only by carefully constructed logic. In writing his *Discours sur la Méthode (Discourse on Method)*, he thought—therefore he was—and from this certain base of existence, he erected his complex philosophy.

The trend toward **Rationalism,** inherent, some say, in the French mentality, crescendoed in the 18th century, when thinkers came to believe that they could uncover a rational set of laws to explain human nature and human institutions, not unlike the laws Newton had found for the cosmos. No work captures the century's literary mood better than the *Encyclopédie,* compiled by Denis Diderot, a multi-volume work that sought to catalog, systematize, and rationalize the whole of human knowledge. Some of the period's greatest minds participated in the project: Voltaire, d'Alembert, Rousseau. Born amid this questioning, the century's creative literature bore a distinctly philosophical tone. Voltaire's *Candide* relates the story of young Candide who travels the world over, convinced that "all is the best in the best of all possible worlds," only to meet misfortune at every turn. In the end, the reluctant hero realizes that he must focus not on the world but on cultivating his own individual possibilities; the Voltairean philosophy is nicely encapsulated in the work's final line, *"Il faut cultiver notre jardin,"* (We must tend our own garden). Taking the skepticism of the age to its logical extreme, many thinkers began to question and criticize the French state itself, albeit quietly in most cases. One of the more vocal critics, Jean-Jacques Rousseau, introduced the concept of an implicit bond betwen the individual and society, whereby individuals sacrifice a measure of personal freedom in return for the protection of their interests by the state. Unfortunately, he felt, the inhabitants of Old Regime France had "negotiated" a very poor contract; some historians believe that his attacks on the state helped to launch the French Revolution. Nonetheless, while Enlightenment philosophers maintained an attitude of cynicism toward the world as it was, they had great faith in the power of reason to sort everything out. The violent and chaotic aftermath of the French Revolution struck a blow to this faith, and the 19th century opened rife with uncertainty.

Deeply influenced by German romantics like Goethe, the 19th century in France began with a new literary movement, in reaction to restictive literary precepts in the 17th century and the omnipresence of "reason" in 18th. Initiated by Mme. de Stael, François-René de Chateaubriand, and Benjamin Constant, and crystallized by Victor Hugo, the **Romantic** movement was colored by a preoccupation with the self, often conveyed through intensely lyric poetry. Reason was sacrificed to emotion, old standards to fresh approaches. For the first time, the novel flourished as a primary mode of literary expression, with the penning of masterpieces like Hugo's *Les Misérables,* which traces the fortunes and complex social interactions of Paris and the provinces in the 1830s. Still, 19th-century literature saw as many regime changes as the political sphere. Romanticism soon fell out of vogue, when writers grew tired of its sugary emotionalism and flowery lyrics. They now preferred to focus on the common, the everyday, the ordinary man and woman. Flaubert's *Madame Bovary* relates the life of the dreamy wife of bourgeois Dr. Bovary, detailing her hopes and wishes, both simple and extravagant. As a whole, **Realists** like Flaubert crafted exacting, almost scientific descriptions of scenes and characters. At the same time, in 1861, Charles Baudelaire published his infamous *Fleurs du Mal,* ushering in a new age of poetry that focused on the sordid world of modern Paris—the crowd, the wanderers, the prostitutes, the meaninglessness. As the century closed, a new movement known as **Symbolism** emerged, grounded in the experiments of Baudelaire, heralded by Paul Verlaine, Arthur Rimbaud, and brought to fruition by Stéphane Mallarmé and later Paul Valéry. Symbolists decried the concern of their predecessors for the world of appearances and of the senses. Through symbols and carefully crafted language, they felt they could probe a more profound reality, reaching into the subjective natural world and into the human psyche.

The complex psychological explorations of the Symbolists anticipated the subconscious and existential literature of the 20th century. As in art, 20th-century literature moved toward abstraction. The **Surrealist** poets, like André Breton and Paul Eluard, attempted to escape the mundane world of bourgeois life by looking to a more exciting, albeit ephemeral, world of dreams. At the turn of the century, the philosopher Henri Bergson introduced stunning and abstract notions of time, duration and memory, strikingly similar to those encoded mathematically in Einstein's 1905 Theory of Relativity. Inspired by Bergson, novelist Marcel Proust infused many of his own works with the philosopher's ideas. His monumental *A la Recherche du Temps Perdu (The Remembrance of Things Past),* explores upper-class life during the Belle Epoque, investigating the experience of time and memory as well as narrative means of rendering them.

Continuing the trend of profound psychological and ontological questioning, author/ philosophers Jean-Paul Sartre and Albert Camus explored the very foundations of human nature in treatises and works of fiction. Sartre's philosophy of **Existentialism,** introduced in his tome *L'Etre et le Néant (Being and Nothingness),* holds that existence has no inherent meaning or value—at each moment of existence, he claimed, a human must reforge a personal set of values and meanings. Thus it is not being which matters, but becoming. Camus, weaving with Sartre's existential threads, initiated a literature of the absurd. In works such as *L'Etranger (The Stranger)* and *La Peste (The Plague),* he confronted the fundamentally bizarre experience of being a human being, particularly of being a human being who must interact with other human beings.

While Sartre and Camus preserved somewhat traditional literary styles, experimental writing in the 50s and 60s produced the **Nouveau Roman** (the New Novel), which challenged the reader by abandoning conventional narrative techniques and embracing subject matter previously considered too trivial and mundane. Among its best known exponents are Alain Robbe-Grillet and Nathalie Sarraute. The latter presents character dialogue with an emphasis on *sous conversation* (what people think as they converse), as opposed to actual dialogue. If you're interested in the latest French writing (in French), check the lists of best sellers in the weekly magazine *Livre* or look for reviews in the literary section (usually weekly) of a national newspaper.

The French, of course, remain fiercely proud of their literary and linguistic heritage. Still active, the Académie Francaise occasionally pronounces official changes to the grammar, spelling, or usage of the French language. And just last summer, concerned that the growing significance of English throughout the world posed a threat to France's cultural heritage, the French National Assembly added a line to the constitution. In case anyone asks, French is now in fact the official language of France.

Food

> The French will only be united under the threat of
> danger. No one can simply bring together a country
> that has 265 kinds of cheese.
>
> —Charles de Gaulle

De Gaulle, in fact, underestimated France's culinary diversity. It produces over 400 kinds of cheese. The aristocratic tradition of extreme richness and elaborate presentation known as *haute cuisine* originated in the 12-hour feasts of Louis XIV at Versailles but is preserved today only in family homes and humble country restaurants that pride themselves on their traditions. In their work and writings, great 19th-century chefs made food an essential art of civilized life. To learn about the skills involved, leaf through the *Larousse Gastronomique,* a standard reference for chefs first compiled in the 19th century. The style made famous in the U.S. by Julia Child is *cuisine bourgeoise,* high quality French home-cooking. A glance through her books, *Mastering the Art of French Cooking I & II,* should give you a list of dishes to try while in France.

Both *haute cuisine* and *cuisine bourgeoise* rely heavily on the *cuisine des provinces* (provincial cooking, also called *cuisine campagnarde,* or country cooking), which creates hearty peasant dishes using refined methods.

The trendy *nouvelle cuisine,* consisting of tiny portions of delicately cooked, artfully arranged ingredients with light sauces, became popular in the 1970s; since then, its techniques have been integrated with heartier provincial fare. Though *le fast-food* and *le self-service* have hit France with a vengeance, most French people still shop daily, make the effort to create fine meals, and take the time to enjoy them.

The French breakfast *(petit déjeuner)* is usually light, consisting of bread *(pain)* and sometimes *croissants* or *brioches* (buttery breads almost like pastries) and an espresso with hot milk or a hot chocolate *(chocolat).* Many people still eat the largest meal of the day *(déjeuner)* between noon and 2pm. Most shops, businesses, and government agencies close for two hours during this time; even Paris has four rush hours—morning, evening, and two in the middle of the day as people hurry home and back.

Dinner *(dîner)* begins quite late, and often goes on for hours as revelers extend their meals into the early morning. Traditionally, the complete French dinner includes an *apéritif,* an *entrée* (appetizer), *plat* (main course), salad, cheese, desserts, fruit, coffee, and a *digestif* (after-dinner drink, typically a cognac or other local brandy, such as *calvados* in Normandy). There are five major *apéritifs—kir,* white wine with *cassis,* a black currant liqueur *(kir royale* substitutes champagne for the wine); *pastis,* a licorice liqueur diluted with water; *suze,* fermented *gentiane,* a sweet-smelling mountain flower that yields a wickedly bitter brew; *picon-bière,* beer mixed with a sweet liqueur; and *martini.* The French *always* take wine with their meals. You might hear the story of the famous actor/director who dared to order a coke with his 1500F meal; he was promptly kicked out of the restaurant by the head chef. Of him, it was said, *"Il manque du savoir vivre"*— he doesn't know how to live.

Most restaurants offer a *menu à prix fixe* (fixed-price meal) that costs less than ordering *à la carte* and includes appetizer *(entrée),* such as *pâté, crudités* (raw vegetables), or *jambon* (ham); a main course *(plat)* such as chicken *(poulet),* duck *(canard),* veal *(veau),* lamb *(agneau),* or pork *(porc),* and cheese *(fromage)* and/or dessert.

Bread is served with every meal. It is perfectly polite to use a piece of bread to wipe your plate (in extraordinarily refined circles, French diners may push their bread around their plates with a fork). French etiquette dictates keeping one's hands above the table, not in one's laps. Elbows must not rest on the table. If you want to try eating in true French manner, hold your fork in your left hand, your knife in the right, and scoop food onto your fork with the sharp edge of the knife (not with the dull edge—that's British). Mineral water is ubiquitous; order sparkling water *(eau pétillante* or *gazeuse)* or flat mineral water *(eau plate).* Ice cubes *(glaçons)* are rare. To order a glass of tap water, ask for *une carafe d'eau.*

Finish the meal with espresso, which comes in lethal little cups. When *boisson comprise* is written on the menu, you are entitled to a free drink (usually wine) with the meal. You will often see the words *service compris* (service included), which means the tip is automatically added to the check *(l'addition).* Otherwise you should tip 15%.

For an occasional 90F spree you can have a marvelous meal, but you needn't pay dearly to eat well. It's easy to find satisfying dinners for under 60F or to assemble inexpensive meals yourself with staples such as cheese, *pâtés,* wine, and bread. The government controls the prices of bread, so you can afford to indulge with every meal.

When in France, do as the French do: go from one specialty shop to another to assemble a picnic, or find an outdoor market *(marché).* A *charcuterie,* the French version of the delicatessen, offers cooked meats, *pâtés,* and sausages. *Crémeries* sell dairy products, and a street-corner *crémerie* may stock over 100 kinds of cheese. A *boulangerie* sells breads, including the *baguette* (the long, crisp, archetypal French loaf). Be sure to try the many other types of bread the bakeries carry; get there in the morning while goods are still warm. A *pâtisserie* offers pastry and candy, and a *confiserie* stocks candy and ice cream (though the distinction between these two kinds of stores is somewhat unclear). You can buy your fruits and vegetables at a *primeur.* For the adventurous carnivore, a *boucherie chevaline* sells horse-meat (look for the gilded horse-head over the door); the timid can stick to steaks and roasts from a regular *boucherie.*

Like most things American, the *supermarché* has invaded France. Look for the small foodstore chains such as **Casino, Prisunic** and **Monoprix.** *Epiceries* (grocery stores) also carry staples, wine, produce, and a bit of everything else. The open-air markets, held at least once a week in every town and village, remain the best places to buy fresh fruit, vegetables, fish, and meat. Competition here is fierce, and prices low.

Each region has delightful local specialties. Look in the regional introductions for typical fare.

Cafés in France, as in most of southern Europe, figure pleasantly in the daily routine. When choosing a café, remember that you pay for its location. Those on a major boulevard can be much more expensive than smaller establishments a few steps down a sidestreet. Prices in cafés are two-tiered, cheaper at the counter *(comptoir)* than in the seating area *(salle).* Both these prices should be posted. Coffee, beer, and (in the south) the anise-flavored *pastis* are the staple café drinks, but there are other refreshing options. Consider the cool *perrier menthe,* a bottle of Perrier mineral water with mint syrup. *Citron pressé* (lemonade)—*limonade* is a soda—and *diabolo menthe* (peppermint soda) are other popular non-alcoholic choices. Cafés also offer Coke, but be prepared to pay twice what you would in the U.S. If you order *café,* you'll get espresso; for coffee with milk, ask for a *café crème.* (The term *café au lait* has been rendered derogatory.) If you order a *demi* or a *pression* of beer, you'll get a pale lager on tap. You can also order bottled imported beer: Heineken is popular in Paris, and Pelforth, a dark beer, is the southern choice. A glass of red is the cheapest wine in a café (4-6F), with white costing about twice as much; southerners prefer rosé to white. Tips are not expected in cafés—except for the really fancy ones in the big cities.

Cafés are not suited to cheap meals, but snacks are usually quite economical. A *croque monsieur* (grilled ham-and-cheese sandwich), a *croque madame* (the same with a fried egg), and assorted omelettes cost about 15F. A more popular choice is a salad. Try the *salade niçoise,* the French version of a chef's salad, or a *chèvre chaud,* a salad with delicious, warm goat cheese.

Wine

Wine is an institution in France and is served at almost every occasion. The character and quality of a wine depend upon the climate, soil, and variety of grape from which it is made. Long, hot, and fairly dry summers with cool, humid nights create the ideal climate. Soil is so much a determining factor that identical grapes planted in different regions yield very different wines. **White wines** are produced by the fermentation of red grapes carefully crushed to keep the skins from coloring the wine. **Rosés** allow some of the red juice from the skin to seep in; and **reds** come from the fermentation of the juice, skins, and sometimes stems of black grapes.

The major wine-producing regions are distributed throughout the country. The Loire Valley produces a number of whites, with the major vineyards at Angers, Chinon, Saumur, Anjou, Tours, and Sancerre. Normandy produces *calvados,* an apple brandy distilled from cider, in the area near Caen. Cognac, farther south on the Atlantic coast, is famous for the double-distilled and blended spirit of the same name.

Centered on the Dordogne and Garonne Rivers, the classic Bordeaux region ("Those who know choose Bordeaux") produces both the red and white wines of Pomerol, Graves, and the sweet Sauternes. *Armagnac,* similar to *cognac,* comes from Gascony, while Jurançon wines come from vineyards higher up the slopes of the Pyrénées. Southern wines include those of Languedoc and Roussillon on the coast and Limoux and Gaillac inland. The vineyards of Provence on the coast near Toulon are recognized for their rosés. The Côtes du Rhône from Valence to Lyon in the Rhône Valley are home to some of the most celebrated wines of France. Burgundy is especially famous for its reds, from the wines of Chablis and the Côte d'Or in the north, to the Mâconnais and Beaujolais in the south. Alsatian whites tend to be spicier and more pungent. Many areas produce sparkling white wine; the only *true* bubbly is bottled in a region of Champagne centered around Reims.

France passed the first comprehensive wine legislation in 1935, and since then the *Appellation d'Origine Contrôlée* regulations (AOC or "controlled place of origin" laws) have ensured the quality and fine reputation of French wines. All wines are categorized according to place of origin, alcohol content, and wine-making practices; only about 16% of French wines are deemed worthy of the top classification. Categories include *Vins Délimités de Qualité Supérieure* (VDQS or "restricted wines of superior quality") and *Vins de Pays* (country wines).

One way to discriminate among the bewildering range of wines in France is to examine the varieties of grapes that go into their production. Burgundies are made from *Pinot Noir* and other grapes, while Bordeaux wines come from different mixtures of four varieties of grape, with *cabernet-sauvignon* the dominant variety. Whites are often made from *chardonnay* or *chenin blanc* grapes.

When shopping for a fairly expensive wine, study the label carefully. The majority of wines are matured by shippers who buy young wines from the growers and mix them to achieve the desired blend. In general, the label will indicate a product's region but not its specific grower. Look for the term *mis en bouteille au domaine* (or *au château)* to ensure the wine was estate-bottled. Though these wines tend to be much cheaper, only the connoisseur can differentiate between a mixed wine and a château-bottled wine.

While many distributors (both small producers and the great châteaux offer tastings, or *dégustations),* these do not mean free beverage services. If you decide to sample wines, make it clear that you intend to buy something you like. If you clearly show no intention to buy a bottle, the proprietor will become enraged by your ulterior motives. Remember that winegrowers are in the business of selling produce, not providing free drink to poor backpackers. Besides, tasting often means just a glass of red and a glass of white, so it's probably not worth going out of your way for a single glass.

Sports, Recreation, and Holidays

The French are crazy about tennis (the French Open is in early June), skiing, sailing, windsurfing, and many other **sports.** The whole populace keeps tabs on the rugby and soccer teams, among the world's best. If you're in France in May or June of the correct year, be prepared to discuss the fortunes of the *footballers* in the quadrennial World Cup. Le Mans is a 24-hour car race on the second weekend of June. The Tour de France, a three-week bicycle race in July, traverses most of France. Check the itinerary to see if the participants will cycle past one of your stopovers.

The French are also serious **vacationers;** government-mandated vacation time is upwards of a month, not counting national holidays. Recreational activities are likely to be readily available in even the smallest French town.

France blossoms with **festivals** throughout the year. In summer, almost every town celebrates a local *fête* that may include carnivals, markets, and folk dancing. The Cannes Film Festival, the Nice Jazz Parade, the Avignon Drama Festival, and the festivities in Aix-en-Provence occur in May, June, July, and August, respectively. In addition, there are at least 100 smaller events every year, such as the Paris Festival du Marais from mid-June to early July. For a comprehensive listing by region of all festivals (music, dance, film, jazz, folklore, puppetry, *son et lumière,* theater, and literature) write for the English brochure *Festive France,* available from any branch of the **French Government Tourist Office.**

Try to be somewhere special for **Bastille Day** on July 14, a sort of French independence day commemorating the fall of the Bastille on July 14, 1789; it's the one day each year when Parisians indulge in berserk but harmless pyromania. May 1, **La Fête du Travail** (French Labor Day), marks a socialist celebration all over the country. For **Jeanne d'Arc Day** (the 2nd Sun. in May), Orléans has a commemorative celebration. The **Feux de St-Jean** is a rural bonfire holiday combining John the Baptist's Day (June 24) with the ancient Celtic summer solstice observance.

Banks, museums, and other public buildings close on the following **public holidays:** January 1, Easter Monday, May 1 (Labor Day), May 8 (Victory in Europe Day), Ascension Day (the 40th day after Easter, a Thurs.), Whit Monday (the 7th Mon. after Easter), July 14 (Bastille Day), August 15 (Assumption Day), November 1 (All Saints' Day), November 11 (Armistice Day), and December 25 (Christmas). When a holiday falls on a Tuesday or Thursday, the French often also take off the Monday or Friday, a practice known as *faire le pont* (to make a bridge). Note that banks close at noon on the day, or the nearest working day, before a public holiday.

Also keep in mind that most food stores close on Monday, though they remain open on Sunday mornings. Smaller stores (including groceries, shops, and even some banks) and government offices often close for lunch between noon and 2pm. Some stores and smaller businesses also close for a few weeks in July or August; they will post on their doors the names of similar stores open in the area. Almost all museums close on Tuesday.

Climate

The following information is drawn from the International Association for Medical Assistance to Travelers (IAMAT)'s *World Climate Charts.* In each monthly listing, the first two numbers are the average daily maximum and minimum temperatures in degrees Celsius; the numbers in parentheses represent the same data in degrees Fahrenheit.

	Jan.	April	July	Oct.
Bastia	11/6 (52/42)	18/11 (65/52)	28/19 (82/60)	20/11 (68/52)
Bordeaux	9/2 (48/36)	17/6 (63/43)	25/14 (77/57)	18/8 (64/46)
Boulogne-sur-Mer	6/2 (43/36)	12/6 (54/43)	20/14 (68/57)	14/10 (57/50)
Brest	9/4 (48/39)	13/6 (55/43)	19/12 (66/54)	15/9 (59/48)
Lourdes	10/1 (50/33)	17/6 (63/42)	25/14 (77/57)	18/8 (65/46)
Lyon	5/-1 (41/30)	16/6 (61/43)	27/15 (81/59)	16/7 (61/45)
Nantes	8/2 (46/36)	15/6 (59/43)	24/14 (75/57)	16/8 (61/46)
Nice	13/4 (55/39)	17/9 (63/48)	27/18 (81/64)	21/12 (70/54)
Paris	6/1 (43/34)	16/6 (61/43)	25/15 (77/59)	16/8 (61/46)
Strasbourg	3/-2 (37/28)	16/5 (61/41)	25/13 (77/55)	14/6 (57/43)

Weights and Measures

1 millimeter (mm) = 0.04 inch	1 inch = 25mm
1 meter (m) = 1.09 yards	1 yard = 0.92m
1 kilometer (km) = 0.62 mile	1 mile = 1.61km
1 gram (g) = 0.04 ounce	1 ounce = 25g
1 liter = 1.06 quarts	1 quart = 0.94 liter

Language

The imposition of the northern *langue d'oïl,* the dialect that evolved into modern French, was critical in forging the political unity of the nation and in creating the image of a monolithic national culture that still persists. France is largely a one-language country, though a few region-specific languages do exist. Breton (a Celtic tongue) in Brittany, Alsatian in Alsace, Occitan in Languedoc, Catalan in Roussillon, Corsican in Corsica, and Basque in the Pyrenees are all spoken with various degrees of frequency and are the source of a fierce regional pride that has recently begun to challenge the hegemony of French in the public school system. As France gradually adapts to an ever-increasing number of tourists, you will find more and more multi-lingual signs in airports, train stations, and major tourist sites. In most towns, the tourist office staff speaks passable English, and at sites where the guided tours are in French, there is often a printed English translation available. In large cities and heavily touristed areas, hotelkeepers and waiters know enough English for essential transactions. See the *Let's Go* Glossary in the Appendix for more help.

Planning Your Trip

US$1 = 4.96F	1F = US$0.20
CDN$1 = 4.17F	1F = CDN$0.23
UK£1 = 9.56F	1F = UK£0.10
IR£1 = 8.97F	1F = IR£.11
AUS$1 = 3.57F	1F = AUS$0.28
NZ$1 = 2.66F	1F = NZ$0.38

A Note on Prices and Currency

The information in this book was researched in the summer of 1992. Since then, inflation will have raised most prices at least 10%. The exchange rates listed were compiled on August 18, 1992. Since rates fluctuate considerably, confirm them before you go by checking a national newspaper.

For a successful trip, plan ahead. Research places you'd like to visit, ways to get there, and what to do along the way. Travel is a large industry in France; you will be surprised by how much information is available. Write to the organizations listed in *Let's Go* and request specific information.

No matter how you do it, remember that traveling shouldn't be a chore. When every city seems to have 1001 points of historical interest, and none of your trains connect with one another, it's easy to forget that a trip is supposed to be *fun.* Avoid letting cathedrals and museums blur into boredom—take a break from the routine of traveling. Go running on the backroads, have a picnic in the park, watch street artists, or spend the afternoon sipping a *citron pressé* while trying to decipher the local newspaper.

Remember that traveling during the off-season cuts costs. Fall wine harvests, skiing in the Alps, and springtime in Paris are some of the enticements of non-summer travel. Airfares are lower, and flying standby is simple (except around major holidays). You also don't have to compete with hordes of summer tourists flocking to establishments and driving up prices. Off-season travel does, however, have its drawbacks. Winters in France are usually mild, but the frequent rain and overcast skies can dampen more than just your spirits. The same holds true for autumns in France. Many hostels and some hotels close down, and museums and tourist offices keep shorter hours. If you do travel in summer, remember that France goes on vacation in July and August. Getting anywhere during peak weekends is difficult. You should reserve seats on trains and try to book accommodations in advance.

Useful Organizations and Publications

Research your trip early. The government and private agencies listed below will provide useful information.

French Government Services

The French government is well aware of the benefits of tourism for the country's economy, and will gladly provide prospective visitors a panoply of pamphlets and an inundation of information.

French Government Tourist Office: Write for information on any region of France, festival dates, and tips for travelers with disabilities. **U.S.,** 610 Fifth Ave., New York, NY 10020; 645 N. Michigan Ave., #630, Chicago, IL 60611; 9454 Wilshire Blvd. #303, Beverly Hills, CA 90212 (tel. nationwide (900) 990-0040, costs 50¢ per minute). **Canada,** 1981 av. McGill College, #490, Montréal, Qué. H3A 2W9 (tel. (514) 593-4723); 30 St-Patrick St., #700, Toronto, Ont. M5T 3A3 (tel. (416) 593-6427). **Australia,** B&P building, 12th Fl., 12 Castlereagh St., Sydney, NSW 2000 (tel. (02) 231 52 44). **New Zealanders** should contact this branch. **U.K.,** 178 Piccadilly, London W1V OAL (tel. (1) 629 1272). **Irish** residents should consult this branch.

Cultural Services of the French Embassy, 972 Fifth Ave., New York, NY 10021 (tel. (212) 439-1400). General information about France including culture, student employment, and educational possibilities.

French Consulates

While not laden with colorful brochures, the French consulate in your home country can supply you with important legal information concerning your trip, arrange for necessary visas, and direct you toward a wealth of other information about tourism, education, and employment in France. Write or call for more information.

U.S., Consulate General: 3 Commonwealth Ave., Boston, MA 02116 (tel. (617) 266-1680); **Visa Section,** 20 Park Plaza, Statler Bldg., 11th floor, Boston, MA 02116 (tel. (617) 482-3650 for a recording of general information, (617) 482-2864 for specific inquiries). There are 12 branch offices across the U.S.; contact the Consulate General to locate the branch nearest you. **Canada,** 1, place Ville Marie, #2601, Montréal, Qué. H3B 4S3 (tel. (514) 878-4381). **U.K.,** 21 Cromwell Rd., London SW7 2DQ (tel. (071) 581 5292). **Visa Section,** 6A Cromwell Pl., London SW7 2EW (tel. (071) 823 9555). **Irish** citizens should address inquiries to this consulate. **Australia,** 31 Market St., 20th Fl., Sydney, NSW 2000 (tel. (02) 261 5931 or (02) 261 5779). **New Zealanders** should address inquiries to this consulate.

Travel Services

A number of organizations exist that can help travelers research trips, book flights, acquire railpasses, and secure student ID cards.

Council on International Educational Exchange (CIEE)/Council Travel, 205 E. 42nd St., New York, NY 10017 (tel. (212) 661-1414). Administers programs and distributes information on study, work, voluntary service, and professional opportunities abroad. Administers ISIC, FIYTO, and ITIC cards. Publishes the biannual *Student Travels* (free, postage US$1), a new travel magazine for college students. Among CIEE's books are *Work, Study, Travel Abroad: The Whole World Handbook* (US$12.95 plus US$1.50 postage), *Going Places: The High School Students's Guide to Study, Travel, and Adventure Abroad* (US$13.95 plus US$1.50 postage), and *Volunteer! The Comprehensive Guide to Voluntary Service in the U.S. and Abroad* (US$8.95 plus US$1.50 postage). Budget travel subsidiaries of CIEE include **Council Travel** and **Council Charter.** Council Travel sells Eurail and individual country passes, guidebooks, travel gear, discounted flights, ISIC, FIYTO, ITIC cards, and HI memberships. 205 E. 42 St., New York, NY 10017 (tel. (212) 661-1450); 729 Boylston St., Boston, MA 02116 (tel. (617) 266-1926); 1093 Broxton Ave., Los Angeles, CA 90024 (tel. (310) 208-3551); 1153 Dearborn St., Chicago, IL 60610 (tel. (312) 951-0585); 28A Poland St., London W1V 3DB, UK; 1, rue St-Augustin, 75002 Paris, France. Council Charter, 205 E. 42 St., New York, NY 10017 (tel. (800) 800-8222) operates charter and scheduled flights to most major European cities, which can be purchased through any Council Travel office in the U.S.

Let's Go Travel Services, Harvard Student Agencies, Inc., Thayer Hall-B, Harvard University, Cambridge, MA 02138 (tel. (617) 495-9649). Sells railpasses, American Youth Hostel memberships (valid at all HI youth hostels), International Student and Teacher ID cards, YIEE cards for nonstudents, travel guides and maps (including the *Let's Go* series), discount airfares, and a complete line of budget travel gear. All items are available by mail; call or write for a catalog.

Rail Europe Inc., 226 Westchester Ave., White Plains, NY 10604 (tel. (800) 438-7245, in NY, NJ, CT call (914) 682-5172). Sells all Eurail products in addition to 26 national and regional European Rail and Rail n' Drive passes. Also available are point-to-point tickets, reservations and hotel vouchers for Best Western hotels.

Travel CUTS (Canadian Universities Travel Service), 187 College St., Toronto, Ont. M5T 1P7 (tel. (416) 979-2406). Offices throughout Canada; in London, 295-A Regent St. W1R 7YA (tel. (071) 255 1944). Sells discounted transatlantic flights, the ISIC, International Youth Card, and also runs the Canadian Work Abroad Programme. Sells the Eurailpass/Youthpass. Arranges adventure tours and work abroad. Their newspaper, *The Canadian Student Traveler,* is free at all offices and on campuses across Canada.

Educational Travel Centre (ETC), 438 N. Frances St., Madison, WI 53703 (tel. (608) 256-5551). Flight information, HI (AYH) membership cards, railpasses. Write or call for a free copy of their travel newspaper, *Taking Off.*

International Student Exchange Flights (ISE Flights), 5010 E. Shea Blvd., #A104, Scottsdale, AZ 85254 (tel. (602) 951-1177). Budget student flights on major regularly scheduled airlines. International Student Exchange ID cards, *Let's Go* series, traveler's checks, International Youth Hostel guide books, and railpasses.

International Student Travel Conference (ISTC): In the U.S., they are represented by CIEE. In Canada: Travel CUTS (see address above). In the UK: London Student Travel, 52 Grosvenor Gardens, London WC1 England (tel. (071) 730 3402). In Australia: STA/SSA, 222 Faraday St., Melbourne, Victoria 3053, Australia (tel. (03) 347 69 11). In New Zealand: Student Travel, 2nd Floor, Courtenay Chambers, 15 Courtenay, Wellington (tel. (04) 85 05 61). Issues ISICs.

STA Travel, a worldwide youth travel organization. Offers bargain flights, railpasses, accommodations, tours, insurance, and ISICs. Ten offices in the U.S., including 17 E. 45th St., New York, NY 10017 (tel. (212) 986-9643 or (800) 777-0112) and 7202 Melrose Ave., Los Angeles, CA 90046 (tel. (213) 934-8722). In the UK, STA's main office is at 74 and 86 Old Brompton Rd., Lon-

don SW7 3LQ England (tel. (071) 937 9921 for European travel; (071) 937 9971 for North American). In New Zealand they're at 10 High St., Auckland (tel. (09) 309 9995).

Publications

Forsyth Travel Library, 9154 W. 57th St., P.O. Box 2975, Shawnee Mission, KS 66201 (tel. (913) 384-3440 or (800) 367-7984). A mail-order service that stocks a wide range of city, area, and country maps, as well as guides for rail and ferry travel in Europe. Sole North American distributor of the Thomas Cook *European Timetable* for trains, covering all of Europe and Britain (US$24.95, postage $4). Write for free catalog and newsletter.

John Muir Publications, P.O. Box 613, Sante Fe, NM 87504 (tel. (505) 982-4078 or (800) 888-7504). Publishes more than 12 books by veteran traveler Rick Steves. These include *Europe through the Back Door,* revised winter 1992 (US$16.95), which offers good advice, especially on traveling light and avoiding tourist traps. *2-22 Days in Europe* (US$12.95) provides a 3-week itinerary for those who want to see the essential Europe. *Mona Winks* (US$14.95) provides a good-humored, self-guided tour of Europe's top museums.

Press and Information Division of the French Embassy, 4101 Reservoir Rd. NW, Washington, DC 20007 (tel. (202) 944-6048). Write for information about political, social, and economic aspects of France. The service also provides a bi-weekly newsletter, *News from France,* as well as *France Magazine.*

Superintendent of Documents, U.S. Government Printing Office, Washington, DC 20402-9325 (tel. (202) 783-3238). Publishes helpful booklets including *Your Trip Abroad* (US$1), *Safe Trip Abroad* (US$1), and *Health Information for International Travel* (US$5).

Wide World Books & Maps, 1911 N. 45th St., Seattle, WA 98105 (tel. (206) 634-3453). Useful, free catalog listing the most recent guidebooks to every part of the world.

Documents

Remember to file all applications several weeks or even months before your planned departure date. A backlog at any agency could spoil even the best-laid plans.

Passports

You need a valid passport to enter France and to re-enter your own country. Apply well in advance. Most offices suggest that you apply in the winter off-season for speedy service. Be sure to record your passport number in a separate, safe place, and photocopy the pages with your photograph and visas in case of loss or theft. Leave a copy with someone at home. These precautions will help prove your citizenship and facilitate the issuing of a new passport if needed. Notify your home country's nearest embassy or consulate and the local police immediately if your passport is lost or stolen. Registering with the nearest embassy or consulate is wise if you intend an extended stay in France. Some consulates can issue new passports, given proof of citizenship, within two days. In an emergency, ask for an immediate temporary passport.

Bring two extra pieces of identification when traveling abroad. A second proof of citizenship can be anything from your birth certificate to a driver's license. Keep these items separate from your passport. A few extra passport-type photos can also come in handy if you lose your passport or decide to apply for a visa.

U.S. citizens over age 18 may apply for a 10-year U.S. passport at one of the several thousand Federal courts or U.S. post offices that accept passport applications, or at any one of the 13 Passport Agencies, which are located in Boston, Chicago, Honolulu, Houston, Los Angeles, Miami, New Orleans, New York, Philadelphia, San Francisco, Seattle, Stamford, and Washington, DC. Those under 18 can obtain a five-year passport. Parents must apply in person for children under age 13. If this is your first U.S. passport, if you are under 18, or if your current passport is more than 12 years old or was issued before your 18th birthday, you must apply in person. Otherwise, you can renew by mail for US$55.

For a U.S. passport you must submit the following documents: (1) a completed application form; (2) proof of U.S. citizenship, which can be a certified birth certificate, naturalization papers, or a previous passport; (3) identification bearing your signature and either your photo or personal description, e.g., an unexpired driver's license or passport; and (4) two identical, recent, passport-sized photographs. If you are renewing by mail, your old passport will serve as both (2) and (3); do not forget to enclose it with your application. To obtain or renew a passport when ineligible for application by mail, bring items (1-4) and US$65 (under 18 US$40) in the form of a check (cashier's, traveler's, certified, or personal) or money order. Passport agencies will accept cash in the exact amount, but post offices and courts may not. Passport Services also requests that you write your birth date on your check.

Processing usually takes three to four weeks (longer through a court or post office), but it's best to apply several months early. If you are leaving within five working days, the passport office can provide urgent service, but you must have valid proof of your departure date (e.g., an airline ticket) and arrive early at the office. Abroad, a U.S. consulate can usually issue new passports, given proof of citizenship. For more details, call the U.S. Passport Information's 24-hour recording (tel. (202) 647-0518) or write the passport agency nearest you.

Canadian citizens may present their passport application in person at one of the 26 regional offices (addresses are in the telephone directory) or mail it to the Passport Office, Department of External Affairs, Ottawa, Ont. K1A 0G3. Passport applications are available from passport offices, post offices, and most travel agencies. Passport requirements include (1) a completed application; (2) original documentary evidence of Canadian citizenship; and (3) two identical photographs, both signed by the holder and one certified by a "guarantor" from an approved list who has known you for at least two years. Children may be included on a parent's passport; they also need proof of Canadian citizenship. The fee is CDN$35 and may be paid in cash, money order, certified check, or bank draft. Expect a five-day wait if applying in person and three weeks if applying by mail. A Canadian passport is valid for five years. For more information, consult the booklet *Bon Voyage, But...*, available free from the Passport Office. Canadian citizens residing in the U.S. should apply at the nearest Canadian diplomatic mission.

There are two types of **British** passport. The **Visitor's Passport** is available over-the-counter at main post offices; you must bring two photos and identification. It is valid for travel to Western Europe for one year and costs £7.50. For a **Full British Passport,** you may apply by mail or at any one of the passport offices in London, Liverpool, Newport, Peterborough, Glasgow, and Belfast. You need a completed application, your birth certificate and marriage certificate (if applicable), and two identical copies of recent photos signed by a guarantor. The fee is £15 for a 10-year adult passport (5 years if under 16). A spouse who does not have a separate passport, and children under 16, may be included on one person's passport. The application process averages four to six weeks.

Irish citizens should pick up an application at a local guard station or request one from one of the two passport offices. If you have never had a passport, you must send your birth certificate, the long application, and two identical pictures to Passport Office, Setanta Centre, Molesworth St., Dublin 2 (tel. (01) 711 633) or Passport Office, 1A South Mall, Cork, County Cork (tel. (021) 272 525). To renew, send your old passport, the short form, and the photos. Passports cost £45 and are valid for 10 years.

Australian citizens must apply for a passport in person at a local post office, where an appointment may be necessary, through a passport office, or through an Australian diplomatic mission overseas. A parent may file for an applicant who is under 18 and unmarried. With your application you must turn in proof of citizenship, proof of your present name, two photographs, and other forms of identification. Proof of citizenship can be an Australian passport valid for more than two years and issued after November 22, 1984, a birth certificate, or a citizen certificate from the Department of Immigration. The photographs (45mm by 35mm) must be identical, not more than six months old, and signed as instructed in the application. Other ID includes driver's license, credit card, rate notices, etc. Application fees are adjusted every three months; call the toll free information service for current details (tel. 13 12 32 or (008) 02 60 22). There is also a departure tax when a citizen over 11 years old leaves the country.

New Zealanders must contact their local Link Centre, travel agent, or New Zealand Representative for an application which must be completed and mailed to the New Zealand Passport Office. Evidence of identity and New Zealand citizenship and two certified passport-sized photos must accompany your application. The fee for a passport is NZ$56.25, NZ$110 if overseas. For children under 16 the fee is NZ$25.30, NZ$49.50 overseas. The application process normally requires three weeks, but the office will speed up processing in an emergency. For more information, write to New Zealand Passport Office, Documents of National Identity Division, P.O. Box 10-526, Wellington (tel. (04) 474 8100).

Visas

A visa is an endorsement or stamp placed in your passport by a foreign government allowing you to visit their country for a specified purpose and period of time. Visas are currently required of **all** visitors to France, except those from EC member countries, the U.S., Canada, New Zealand, Andorra, Austria, Czechoslovakia, Cyprus, Finland, Hungary, Iceland, Japan, Republic of Korea, Liechtenstein, Malta, Monaco, Norway, Poland, San Marino, Sweden, and Switzerland. Note that Australia is distinctly absent from this list. A visa is required for *anyone* planning to stay more than three months (see below). It must be obtained from the French consulate *in your home country*. For more details write to R. Woods, Consumer Information Center, Box 100, Pueblo, CO 81002, for *Foreign Entry Requirements* (US50¢).

Requirements for a long-stay visa vary with the nature of the stay: work, study, or *au pair.* Apply to the nearest French Consulate at least three months in advance. For a **student visa,** you must present a passport valid until at least 60 days after the date you plan to leave France, an application with references, a passport photo, a letter of admission from a French university or a study abroad program, a notarized guarantee of financial support for $600 per month, and a fee which fluctuates according to the exchange rate (currently US$57). To obtain a **work visa,** you must first obtain a work permit. After securing a job and a work contract from your French employer, your employer will obtain this permit for you and will forward it with a copy of your work contract to the consulate nearest you. After a medical checkup and completion of the application, the visa will be issued on your valid passport. Note, however, that it is illegal for foreign students to work during the school year, although they can receive permission from their local *Direction départementale du travail et de la main-d'oeuvre étrangère* to work in summer (see below). For an *au pair* stay of more than three months, an **au pair's visa** is required and can be obtained by submission of a valid passport, two completed application forms, two passport photos, a fee (varies betwen US$15-25), a medical certificate of good health completed by a Consulate-approved doctor, two copies of the *au pair's* work contract signed by the *au pair,* and proof of admission to a language school or university program. (An *au pair* is someone who lives abroad with a family and receives a small stipend for doing household chores and taking care of the children. See Au Pair Positions, below, for more info.)

In addition to securing a visa, if you are staying longer than 90 days in France—for one of the above three reasons or any other—you must obtain a **carte de séjour** (residency permit) once in France. Report to the local *préfecture* of the *département* in which you are residing. You must present a valid passport stamped with a long-stay visa, a medical certificate, six (yes, six) application forms completed in French, six passport photos, a letter of financial guarantee, and, if you're under 18, proof of parental authorization. Be prepared to jump through hoops, bark like a dog, and stand in line, perhaps repeatedly. Bring your Proust.

Student, Teacher, and Youth Identification

The **International Student Identity Card (ISIC)** (US$15) is an internationally recognized proof of student status. If you have a student ID from a school in France or from your home country, it will usually qualify you for the same discounts on train and theater tickets and on admission to museums, historical sites, and festivals. The ISIC offers other benefits including lower fares on many forms of local and international transportation—it's essential if you plan to use student charter flights or clubs. The card incorporates the International Union of Students card. If you purchase the card in the U.S., it also provides you with US$3000 medical/accident insurance and US$100 per day for up to 60 days in case of in-hospital illness. The **International Teacher Identity Card (ITIC)** (US$16) offers identical discounts in theory, but because of its

Always travel with a friend.

Get the International
Student Identity Card,
recognized worldwide.

For information call toll-free **1-800-GET-AN-ID**.
or contact any Council Travel office. (See inside front cover.)

 Council on International Educational Exchange
205 East 42nd Street, New York, NY 10017

recent introduction, many establishments are unfamiliar with the card and are reluctant to honor it.

To apply for either, submit the following to one of the student travel services listed above: (1) current, dated proof of student or teacher status (a photocopy of your school ID showing this year's date, a letter on school stationery signed and sealed by the registrar, or a photocopied grade report); (2) a 1 1/2 x 2-inch photo with your name printed in pencil on the back; (3) proof of your birthdate and nationality. The card is valid from September 1 through December 31 of the following year. If you are about to graduate, you can still get a card by proving student status during the same calendar year. You cannot purchase a new card in January unless you were in school during the fall semester.

If you're not a student but are under age 26, inquire about other youth discounts. The **Federation of International Youth Travel Organizations (FIYTO)** issues the **International Youth Card** to anyone under age 26; it is also available from a number of the travel services listed above. The card is internationally recognized and gives you access to over 8000 discounts on international and intra-European transport, accommodations, restaurants, cultural activities, and tours. Applications must include proof of age, a passport-sized photo and a certified check or money order for US$15. For further information and an application, write to FIYTO, Islands Brygge 81, DK-2300 Copenhagen S, Denmark (tel. (45) 31 54 60 80).

International Driver's License

An International Driving Permit (essentially a translation of your driver's license into 9 languages) is not usually required to drive in France, but is recommended if you don't speak French. Most rental agencies will not ask to see the permit but will want to see a valid driver's license. The permit is available at any branch of the **American Automobile Association** or at the main office, AAA Travel Agency Services, 1000 AAA Drive (mail stop 100), Heathrow, FL 32746. The AAA toll-free national number is (800) 222-4357. For more information, contact your local AAA. It is also available from the **Canadian Automobile Association (CAA),** 60 Commerce Valley Dr. E., Markham, Ont. L3T 7P9 (tel. (416) 771-3170). You will need a completed application, two recent passport-sized photos, a valid U.S. (or Canadian) driver's license (which must always accompany the International Driving Permit), and US$10. You must be over 18 to apply.

If you are going to drive, buy, or borrow a car that is not insured, you will need an **International Insurance Certificate,** or **green card,** to prove you have liability insurance. Inquire at the AAA. If you are renting or leasing, you must get the green card (and the coverage too, if your insurance does not apply abroad) from the rental agency or dealer.

Money

Currency and Exchange

The basic unit of currency in France is the franc, also divided into 100 centimes, and issued in both coins and paper notes. The smallest unit of French currency is the five-centime piece. The new franc, equal to 100 old francs, was issued in 1960.

When changing money, be it cash or traveler's checks, it pays to compare rates. Banks often offer the best rates, but usually charge a commission which can be as much as US$4. Large, local banks or national ones, such as **Crédit Agricole** or **Crédit Lyonnais,** have competitive rates and charge the smallest commission. Avoid exchanging money at hotels, airports, train stations, restaurants, or speciality stores; their convenient hours and locations allow them to offer less favorable exchange rates. To minimize losses, exchange fairly large sums at one time, though never more than is safe to carry around. Banks are open only on weekdays; be sure to procure enough cash to carry you through weekends, holidays, and side trips in isolated areas. In large cities, many post offices will exchange foreign currency; look for the *Change* sticker. Before leaving home, convert US$50 or so into French bills; this will save you time at the airport.

Traveler's Checks

Carrying around large amounts of cash, even in a moneybelt, is risky. Traveler's checks are the safest and least troublesome means of carrying funds. Several agencies and many banks sell them, usually for face value plus a 1% commission. American Express and Visa are the most widely recognized, though other major checks are sold, exchanged, cashed, and refunded with almost equal ease. Each agency provides refunds if your checks are lost or stolen, and many provide additional services. (Note that you may need a police report verifying the loss or theft.) Inquire about toll-free refund hotlines, emergency message relay services, and stolen credit card assistance when you purchase your checks.

You should expect a fair amount of red tape and delay in the event of theft or loss of traveler's checks. To expedite the refund process, keep your check receipts separate from your checks and store them in a safe place, or with a traveling companion. To help identify which checks are missing, record check numbers when you cash them and leave a list of check numbers with someone at home. When you buy your checks, ask for a list of refund centers. American Express and Bank of America have over 40,000 centers worldwide. Keep a separate supply of cash or traveler's checks for emergencies.

Finally, consider purchasing traveler's checks in francs. While U.S. citizens can easily exchange dollars for francs in France, New Zealanders and Australians may have difficulty exchanging their currencies. Dealing with double exchange rates (such as Canadian to U.S. dollars and then U.S. dollars to francs) can be expensive. In smaller French cities and towns, as in stores and restaurants, it is often easier to exchange checks in francs. In addition, you avoid the hassle of worrying about exchange rates. Most banks will cash French franc traveler's checks commission free (be sure to ask, however, *before* you give them your money). Depending on fluctuations in the value of the French franc, you may either gain or lose money by buying them in francs in advance.

American Express (tel. in the U.S. and Canada (800) 221-7282, in the UK (088) 52 13 13, collect to the U.S. from anywhere else in the world (801) 964-6665; in France, call toll-free (19) 05 90 86 00). Available in 7 currencies, commission-free for members of AAA. **Check for Two,** a pricey new option, allows for double signing with a travel partner. American Express has 22 offices in France, each of which will cash their checks commission-free, as well as providing a mail-holding service (see Keeping in Touch) and assistance with lost travel documents, temporary IDs, and airline, hotel, and car rental reservations. Call and ask for their cute booklet, *Traveler's Companion,* which gives full addresses for all their travel offices, as well as stolen check hotlines for each European country. AmEx maintains a Global Assist hotline for travel emergencies (tel. (800) 554-2639 or collect (202) 783-7474).

Bank of America (tel. in the U.S. (800) 227-3460, collect from elsewhere (415) 624-5400). Checks in US$ only. 1% commission. Checkholders get access to a Travel Assistance hotline (tel. in the U.S. (800) 368-7878, collect from elsewhere (202) 347-7113). Hotline offers services including free legal and medical assistance, urgent message relay, lost document services, translator/interpreter referral, and up to US$1000 advance to a medical facility to ensure prompt treatment (tel. (01) 629 7466).

Visa (tel. in the U.S. and Canada (800) 227-6811, in the U.K. (0800) 89 5078 toll-free; collect the U.S. from anywhere else in the world (415) 574-7111). Checks available in 13 currencies. Commission depends on individual bank.

Barclays Bank (tel. in the U.S. and Canada (800) 221-2426; in the U.K. (202) 671 212; from elsewhere call collect (212) 858-8500). 1% commission. Checks in U.S. and Canadian dollars, British pounds, and German marks.

Citicorp (tel. in the U.S. and Canada (800) 645-6556, collect from elsewhere (813) 623-1709). Checks available in U.S. dollars, British pounds, German marks, and Japanese yen at banks throughout the U.S. 1-2.5% commission. Checkholders are automatically enrolled for 45 days in Travel Assist Hotline (tel. (800) 523-1199), a slightly abridged version of Europe Assistance Worldwide's Travel Assist program.

MasterCard International (tel. in the U.S. (800) 223-7373, collect from anywhere else in the world (212) 974-5696). Traveler's checks available in 11 currencies at many banks and from **Thomas Cook** (tel. same as Mastercard). 1% commission.

Credit Cards

Credit cards in Europe do everything they do in America—and more. For one, major credit cards—**American Express, Mastercard,** and **Visa** are the most welcomed—instantly extract cash advances from banks and teller machines throughout Western Europe, in local currency (albeit with hefty interest charges). Nearly 800 banks in France, indicated by the sticker *CB/VISA ou EC,* will allow you to withdraw money at a teller with a Visa or AmEx card. Additionally, Visa cash machines proliferate in France. American Express cards work in ATMs at **Credit Lyonnaise** banks, as well as at AmEx offices and major airports. All such machines require a **Personal Idenitification Number (PIN),** which credit cards in the United States do not carry; ask American Express, Mastercard, or Visa to assign you one before you leave home. Keep in mind that Mastercard and Visa have aliases here (Eurocard and Carte Bleue, respectively); some cashiers may not know this until they check their manual.

Credit cards are also invaluable in an emergency—an unexpected hospital bill or ticket home or the more prosaic loss of traveler's checks—which may leave you temporarily without other resources. Try to pay for large purchases abroad by credit card: the credit card company gets a better exchange rate than you would have. Furthermore, credit cards offer an array of other services, from insurance to emergency assistance—these depend completely, however, on the issuer. Some even cover car rental collision insurance. If a family member has a credit card, an additional card can be effortlessly issued in your name, with bills (and an increased annual fee) going to your loved ones.

In addition, **American Express** cardholders can cash up to US$1000 in personal checks (US$5000 for gold card holders) at any of the AmEx offices in France. With someone feeding money into your account back home, this can be one of the easiest and cheapest ways to send money overseas. Call **American Express Travel Service** (tel. (800) 221-7282) for more information, as well as their *Traveler's Companion* booklet which lists full-service offices worldwide.

Cash Cards

Cash cards—popularly called ATM cards—are widespread within Europe, and in the last year huge advances have been made in the extension of the **Cirrus** network to Europe. Cirrus currently operates over 600 machines in France. Look for the red and blue **Credit mutuel** logo and the ATM network name **minibank 24.** Call (800) 424-7787 for more information. We recommend this option highly, since overseas cash-card withdrawals get similarly favorable exchange rates as credit cards, without the ruinous interest charges. The **PLUS** network, unfortunately, can not be accessed in France. Many French tourist offices have lists of money-machine addresses throughout France.

Sending Money Abroad

The easiest way to get money from home is to use the American Express personal check service described above. Otherwise, money can be wired abroad through international money transfer services operated by **Western Union** or **American Express.**

American Express offers a MoneyGram service by which US$100-10,000 may be sent abroad. MoneyGrams sent from the US to France arrive in 10 minutes at the designated AmEx office. It costs US$45 to send US$500 and US$70 to send US$1000. The money is disbursed in traveler's checks (in American funds). For more information, call the American Express MoneyGram Customer Service toll-free number: (800) 543-4080. This service operates only between American Express offices proper, not their representatives, and is available for non-card holders. Not every office in France can receive MoneyGrams; check carefully.

Western Union offers a convenient service for cabling money abroad to any of 15 cities in France. In the U.S., call Western Union any time at (800) 325-6000 to cable money with your **Visa** or **MasterCard.** No money orders are accepted. It costs US$65 to send US$500 and $75 for $1000. The cabled money is handled by Citibank in France and can be retrieved with proper identification. It should arrive, in francs, within 2-5 business days. A new direct money service is available to send money to any of three offices in Paris within 15 minutes (US$40 to send US$500, US$50 for US$1000).

Don't forget to write.

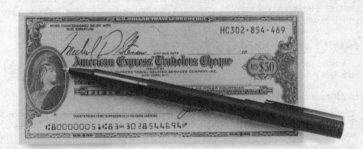

Now that you've said, "Let's go," it's time to say, "Let's get American Express® Travelers Cheques." Because when you want your travel money to go a long way, it's a good idea to protect it. So before you leave, be sure and write.

If you're staying in France long enough to have a personal bank account, a cheaper alternative may be to **cable money** from bank to bank. Tell your home bank by mail or telegram the amount you need and the name and address of the receiving bank, together with the destination account number. Give the same information to a friend or family member who is sending you money from their own account. Transfer can take up to a few days; the fee is usually a flat US$20-30. Outside an American Express office, avoid trying to cash checks in foreign currencies; they usually take weeks and a US$30 fee to clear.

In emergencies, U.S. citizens can have money sent via the State Department's **Citizens Emergency Center,** Department of State, 2201 C St. NW, Washington, DC 20520 (tel. (202) 647-5225; at night and on Sundays and holidays (202) 647-4000). For a fee of about US$25, the State Department will forward money within hours to the nearest consular office, which will then disburse it according to instructions. The center serves only Americans in the direst of straits abroad and prefers not to send sums greater than US$500. The quickest way to have the money sent is to cable the State Department through Western Union or to leave cash, a certified check, a bank draft, or a money order at the department itself.

Value-Added Tax

Value-Added Tax (in France, abbreviated TVA) is a varying sales tax levied especially in the European Economic Community. The French rate is 18.6% on all goods except books, food, and medicine. There is a 33% luxury tax on such items as video cassettes, watches, jewelry, and cameras.

If you spend more than 2000F (4200F for EC members) in a particular store, you can participate in a complex over-the-counter export program for foreign shoppers that exempts you from paying TVA. Ask the store for an official *formulaire de détaxe pour l'exportation* (detax invoice) and a stamped envelope. At the border, show the invoices and your purchases to the French customs officials, who will stamp the invoices. If you're at an airport, look for the window labeled *douane de détaxe,* and be sure to budget at least an hour for the intricacies of the French bureacracy. On a train, find an official (they won't find you) or get off at a station close to the border. Then send a copy back to the vendor. With this official T.V.A.-exempt proof, they will refund the agreed amount. The refunds are sent to your bank account and not to your address, a process which may take as much as six months.

Health and Insurance

A little prevention and a lot of precaution should prevent you from falling ill—or into debt—while you tour.

Health

The simplest prescription for staying healthy while traveling is to eat well, keep clean, and avoid excessive exertion. All food, including seafood, dairy products, and fresh produce, is normally safe in France. The water is chlorinated and also safe, but in parts of the country, the bacteria differ from those found in North American water and may cause mild-to-severe diarrhea. While Europe offers many fine sights, its bathrooms don't necessarily merit such frequent visits. Relying on bottled mineral water during the first couple of weeks is a sensible precaution. When traveling in the summer, especially in the south, take precautions against **heatstroke** and **sunburn:** drink plenty of liquids, wear sunscreen, and stay inside in the middle of the day. To minimize the effects of **jet lag,** you must "reset" your body clock. Don't consume tea, coffee, alcohol, or large meals the day of your flight. This way, you clear your natural body clock and can reset it once in Europe. Set your watch to the time of your destination and come "morning," eat breakfast. You should be acclimatized to the new time zone by the end of the first day or two.

Although no special immunizations are necessary for travel to France, be sure that your **inoculations** are up-to-date. Typhoid shots remain good for three years, tetanus for 10. *Health Information for International Travel* (US$5) provides U.S. Public

Health recommendations and other hints; write the Superintendent of Documents (address under Useful Publications above).

Travelers with **contact lenses** should bring an extra pair, or at least a copy of their prescription. Since the pressurized atmosphere of an airplane can dehydrate soft lenses, clean them just before leaving, and don't drink coffee or alcohol or read for long periods of time while on the plane. Bring along adequate supplies of your cleaning solutions, and don't let them get overheated in luggage. Foreign brands with familiar names may have different formulations than your brand. For heat disinfection you'll need outlet and low-watt voltage adapters.

Travelers with a chronic medical condition requiring regular treatment should consult their doctors before leaving. All travelers should carry an ample supply of appropriate **medicines,** since matching a prescription with a foreign equivalent may be difficult. Always carry up-to-date prescriptions (in legible, preferably typewritten form, including the medication's trade name, manufacturer, chemical name, and dosage) and/or a statement (with a translated version) from your doctor, especially if you use insulin, syringes, or any narcotic drug. Keep all medicines and syringes in your carry-on luggage.

If you have a medical condition that cannot be easily recognized (e.g., diabetes, allergies to antibiotics, epilepsy, heart conditions), you should obtain a **Medic Alert identification tag.** This internationally recognized tag indicates the nature of the condition, and provides the number of Medic Alert's 24-hour hotline, through which medical personnel can obtain information about the member's medical history. Lifetime membership, which includes the price of a steel tag, costs US$35; contact Medic Alert Foundation International, P.O. Box 1009, Turlock, CA 95381-1009 (tel. (800) 432-5378, emergency (209) 634-4917).

At night and on Sundays, the local *commissariat de police* will supply the address of the nearest open *pharmacie* (drugstore) and that of a doctor on duty. The *pharmacie de garde* is also noted in newspapers and on the doors of pharmacies in town. For an ambulance, look in the phone book under *ambulances municipales. Let's Go* lists emergency numbers in most practical information listings.

If illness does strike, few areas of France are so isolated that you will have to worry about finding competent medical attention. Before you go, obtain a directory of English-speaking physicians worldwide from the **International Association for Medical Assistance to Travelers (IAMAT),** a non-profit organization established to provide medical care to travelers by doctors trained in Europe or North America. There is no charge for membership, although a donation is appreciated as IAMAT relies wholly on voluntary contributions. It charges for medical services according to a set payment schedule. Members are guaranteed qualified medical assistance from English-speaking physicians and are entitled to an ID card, an international directory of IAMAT physicians, a chart detailing advisable immunizations for 200 countries and territories, and charts noting areas at risk for malaria and and other diseases. It also tells members how to take preventive measures for a number of infectious diseases. A person donating at least US$25 will also receive a packet of 24 World Climate Charts reporting climate, recommended seasonal clothing, and sanitary conditions of water, milk, and food in 1440 cities around the world in addition to the regular information package. They also publish the pamphlets *How to Adjust to the Heat, How to Adapt to Altitude,* and the moving *How to Avoid Traveler's Diarrhea.* For more information, contact IAMAT in the United States at 417 Center St., Lewiston, NY 14092 (tel. (716) 754-4883) or in Canada at 40 Regal Rd., Guelph, Ont. N1K 1B5 (tel. (519) 846-0102). American, Canadian, and British embassies and consulates, and American Express offices can also help you find English-speaking doctors. You may also be able to find a good doctor in the emergency room of a university hospital. As a last resort, go to the largest city nearby and hope that someone at the hospital speaks English.

Insurance

Beware of unnecessary insurance coverage—your current policies might well extend to many travel-related concerns. For instance, your **medical insurance** policy may cover costs incurred abroad. University term-time medical plans often include insurance for summer travel. Medicare's foreign travel coverage is limited and is valid only in Canada and Mexico. Canadians are protected by their home province's health insurance plan; check with the provincial Ministry of Health or Health Plan Headquarters. Your **homeowners' insurance** (or your family's coverage) often covers theft during travel. Homeowners are generally covered against loss of travel documents (passport, plane ticket, railpass, etc.) up to about US$500.

Claims can only be filed against your home medical or homeowner's insurance upon return to your home country and must be accompanied by the proper documents (i.e., police reports and/or doctor's statements) written in English if possible, and all relevant receipts. Note that some of the plans listed below offer cash advances or guaranteed transferrals, so it is not always necessary to use your own vacation cash to pay doctor bills. Full payment in cash before check-out (and sometimes even before treatment) is virtually the rule at most European hospitals. If your coverage doesn't include on-the-spot payments or cash transferrals, then budget for emergencies.

When purchased in the U.S., the **ISIC,** International Student Identification Card, provides you with US$3000 worth of accident insurance plus US$100 per day for up to 60 days of in-hospital sickness coverage as long as the card is valid. **CIEE** offers an inexpensive Trip-Safe package that extends coverage of medical treatment and hospitalization, accidents, and even charter flights missed due to illness. ISIC also provides a 24-hour traveler's assistance line for legal and financial aid. American Express cardholders receive automatic car-rental and flight insurance on purchases made with the card.

A number of agencies offer insurance against theft, loss of luggage, trip cancellation/interruption, and medical emergencies; rates average around US$6 per $100 of coverage. Consult your local yellow pages or a travel agency to find an agency that suits you.

Travelers with Specific Needs

Senior Travelers

The freedom of retirement affords many seniors the opportunity to travel, while an assortment of discounts on transportation, tours, and museums helps make it affordable. Write the Superintendent of Documents (see Useful Publications, above) for a copy of *Travel Tips for Older Americans* (US$1). The following organizations offer information, assistance, and discounts to seniors.

American Association of Retired Persons (AARP), Special Services Department, 601 E St. NW, Washington, DC 20049 (tel. (800) 227-7737; for travel information, (202) 434-2277). For an annual membership fee of $8, anyone 50 or over and their spouses can receive benefits from AARP Travel Services and get discounts on hotels, motels, car rental, and sightseeing companies.

Elderhostel, 75 Federal St., 3rd Fl., Boston, MA 02110 (tel. (617) 426-7788). Weeklong educational workshops in over 40 countries in the Americas and Europe cover a variety of subjects. US$1500-5000 fee includes room, board, tuition, and extracurricular activities. You must be 60 or over to enroll; companions must be 50 or over.

Gateway Books, 13 Bedford Cove, San Rafael, CA 94901 (tel. (415) 454-5215). Publishes Gene and Adele Malott's *Get Up and Go: A Guide for the Mature Traveler* (US$10.95). Offers recommendations of places to visit and general hints for the budget-conscious senior.

National Council of Senior Citizens, 1331 F St. NW, Washington, DC 20004 (tel. (202) 347-8800). Information on discounts and travel abroad.

Pilot Industries, Inc., 103 Cooper St., Babylon, NY 11702 (tel. (516) 422-2225). Publishes *The International Health Guide for Senior Citizen Travelers* (US$4.95) and the newly revised *Senior Citizen's Guide to Budget Travel in Europe* (US$5.95).

Travelers with Disabilities

The French Tourist Board provides free handbooks and access guides to travelers with disabilities, but these directories can be misleading since they are not compiled by other travelers with disabilities. Accurate information about ramps, the width of doors,

the dimensions of elevators, and so on, remains difficult to secure. The best method is to directly ask restaurants, hotels, railways, and airlines about their facilities.

All TGV high-speed trains can accommodate wheelchairs, and guide dogs are transported free. Other trains have a special compartment and an escalator for boarding. It is worth writing to the train station at your destination to alert the conductor of your needs. In Paris, travel by metro is facilitated by seats reserved for the disabled, although many stations have stairs rather than escalators or elevators. The new RER network, which complements the metro coverage of Paris, operates a number of stations with lift access and others with flat/ramped access.

If you bring a seeing-eye dog into France, you must carry a rabies vaccination certificate issued in your home country or a certificate showing there have been no cases of rabies in your country for over three years.

The American Foundation for the Blind, 15 W. 16th St., New York, NY 10011 (tel. (800) 232-5463 or (212) 620-2147). Call from anywhere in the continental U.S. Mon.-Fri. 8:30am-4:30pm EST. Information, travel books, and ID cards (US$10) for the blind. Write for an application.

L'Association des Paralysés de France, Délégation de Paris, 22, rue du Père Guérion, 75013 Paris (tel. 44 16 83 87). Publishes *Où ferons-nous étape?* (180F), which lists French hotels and motels accessible to persons with disabilities.

Disability Press, Ltd., Applemarket House, 17 Union St., Kingston-upon-Thames, Surrey KT1 1RP, U.K. Publishes the *Disabled Traveler's International Phrasebook* (£1.75), listing useful phrases in 8 languages, including French.

Federation of the Handicapped, 211 W. 14th St., New York, NY 10011 (tel. (212) 206-4200). Leads tours as well as an annual summer trip for its members. Annual membership US$4.

The Guided Tour, 613 West Chelterham Ave., #200, Melrose Park, PA, 19126 (tel. (215) 782-1370). Year-round full-time travel program for developmentally and learning-disabled adults as well as separate trips for those with physical disabilities.

Mobility International, USA (MIUSA), P.O. Box 3551, Eugene, OR 97403 (tel. (503) 343-1284, voice and TDD). MIUSA has information on travel and exchange programs, accommodations, organized tours, and study abroad. They recently updated and expanded their *A World of Options for the 1990s: A Guide to International Educational Exchange, Community Service and Travel for Persons with Disabilities.* Travel information and referral network for members. In the U.K., contact Mobility International, 228 Burough High St., London SE1 1JX.

Pauline Hephaistos Survey Projects, 39 Bradley Gardens, West Ealing, London W13 8HE. *Access Guides* to Paris, Jersey, and the Channel Ports, detailing ease of access relating to traveling, accommodations, hotels, and points of interest (£4 each). The guides are researched by people with disabilities.

Wings on Wheels, c/o Evergreen Travel Service, 19505L 44th Ave. W., Lynnwood, WA 98036 (tel. (800) 435-2288 or (206) 776-1184, in WA (800) 562-9298). Provides services for travelers with disabilities. Charters buses with on-board wheelchair-accessible facilities and runs White Cane Tours for the blind as well as tours for deaf travelers and slow walkers.

Gay and Lesbian Travelers

In general, the French public is unperturbed by gay people living openly, especially in the capital. Gay life continues to be rather discreet outside Paris, with more openness in Nice, Lyon, Marseille, Toulouse, and Nantes.

Indispensable to the gay or lesbian traveler in France is the encyclopedic *Guide Gai 1993*, which lists support groups, hotels, clubs, and restaurants across the country that cater to an either uniquely homosexual, or mixed gay and straight, clientele (45F). From the same publishers comes Paris' weekly journal, *Gai Pied Hebdo*, which is distributed nationally. The best of the gay and lesbian monthly magazines are *Gay International, Gay Men,* and *Lesbia. Illico* is available free in bars and other gay meeting places. Well-regarded Parisian **bookstores** include **Les Mots à la Bouche,** 6, rue Ste-Croix de la Bretonnerie, 75004 Paris (tel. 42 78 88 30) which carries the city's most extensive collection of gay and lesbian literature including novels, essays, books on art, and magazines in French, English, German, and Italian. **Ecoute Gaie,** a gay **hotline** based in Paris, takes calls on Monday through Friday from 6pm until 10pm (tel. 48 06 19 11).

For more general travel information, consult **Ferrari Publications,** P.O. Box 37887, Phoenix, AZ 85069 (tel. (602) 863-2408), which publishes a number of travel books for gay people, including *Places of Interest* (US$12.95), *Places for Men* (US$12.95), *Places of Interest to Women* (US$10) and *Inn Places: USA and Worldwide Gay Accommodations* (US$14.95). The *Spartacus International Gay Guide* (US$27.95) provides information about gay bars, restuarants, hotels, bookstores, and hotlines throughout the world; it is very specifically for men. Order the guide from 100 East Biddle St., Baltimore, MD 21202 (tel. (301) 727-5677) or c/o Bruno Lutzowstrasse, P.O. Box 30 13 45, D-1000 Berlin 30, Germany (tel. +49 (30) 25 49 82 00).

Traveling with Children

A car is almost indispensable when traveling with children. In the culinary domain, don't fight the siren song of *le hot dog* or *le croque monsieur* (a grilled ham-and-cheese sandwich) if your kids don't take to the subtleties of *haute cuisine.* France also offers great ice cream (if you don't buy it in supermarkets), and older children may enjoy a *demi-panaché* (shandy) made half-and-half with beer and an otherwise uninspiring carbonated lemonade *(limonade;* for true mix-it-yourself lemonade, ask for *citron pressé).* Not all restaurants have highchairs, but French servers are generally less put out by children than their North American counterparts. Young diners are especially welcome in informal cafeterias, *café-restaurants,* and *brasseries.* The French habit of family roadside picnics is another convenience you'll enjoy.

Paris has much to offer children, and traveling with your kids gives you a chance to enjoy it all. **The Jardins du Luxembourg** have a *guignol* (puppet show), pony rides, go-carts, a carousel, boats to rent and sail on the ornamental ponds, and swings with attendants who, for a tip, will push the swings while you vanish into a café. The gardens also maintain some of the few lawns in Paris that children may play on. In the summer, there is an amusement park in the **Tuileries.** **Les Invalides** will fascinate older kids with its full-scale dioramas of Napoleon's battles. The **Jardin des Plantes** and the Paris **Zoo** are also fun, and even the most clichéd sights such as the Eiffel Tower and the

bateaux mouches (tour boats on the Seine) rejuvenate jaded travelers when seen with children.

Outside Paris, watch for village *fêtes,* which usually have a few rides. Châteaux (in the Loire Valley and elsewhere) and medieval walled towns like **Carcassonne** and **Avignon** are a child's fairytale dreams realized in stone. Children may also enjoy exploring crypts and catacombs, if they don't mind getting the creeps.

For bedtime stories before or during your trip, follow the 12 little girls around the sights of Paris in Hugo Bemelmans's *Madeleine* picture books. *Crin blanc* and *Le ballon rouge,* both by Albert LaMorisse, are two powerful stories that exemplify a peculiarly French sentimentality regarding early childhood. *Le petit prince,* by Antoine de St-Exupéry, is a great story for kids with allegorical meaning for Mom and Dad. Works by Marquis de Sade make captivating reading for the whole family. The well-known *Tintin* and *Astérix* comics appeal to a wide range of ages, and the hardbound copies are both travel- and child-proof (well, almost).

Lonely Planet Publications, 115 Filbert St., Oakland, CA 94607 (tel. (510) 893-8555) publishes Maureen Wheeler's *Travel with Children* (US$10.95, U.S. postage US$1.50). If you plan to camp with very young children, consult *Backpacking with Babies and Small Children* (US$8.95) and *Sharing Nature with Children* (US$6.95), both published by Wilderness Press, 2440 Bancroft Way, Berkeley, CA 94704 (tel. (800) 443-7227).

Specific Diets

While you should have little trouble finding tastefully prepared vegetables in France, they are often cooked with salt, butter, or sugar. **Vegetarians** will have trouble eating cheaply in restaurants, since *menus à prix fixe* almost always feature meat or fish. Ordering a salad may prove cheaper (if you don't eat eggs, be careful of green salads with eggs in them). *Viande* refers only to red meat. If you don't eat pork, chicken, fish, eggs, or dairy products, you should clearly state this to the server. **Kosher** food certainly exists in France, a country with one of Western Europe's largest Jewish populations, although tracking it down may prove difficult. It may be near impossible to find an expressly kosher restaurant or deli in rural regions, but such outlets certainly exist in larger cities, such as Lyon and Marseilles. In Paris, kosher delis and restaurants abound in the 3rd and 4th *arrondissements,* home to many of the city's Jews, particularly on rue des Rosiers and rue des Ecouffes. **Halal** food is equally difficult to come by outside of the Muslim districts of larger cities. Although the natural foods movement began in Europe, American-style health food merchandising has not caught on outside of large cities, and you may have to search long and hard for tofu and tahini. Health food stores are *diététiques* or *maisons de régime.* Health food products are sometimes referred to as *produits à santé.*

North American Vegetarian Society, P.O. Box 72, Dolgeville, NY 13329 (tel. (518) 568-7970) publishes pamphlets of interest to vegetarian travelers. In the U.K., contact **Vegetarian Society of the U.K.,** Parkdale, Dunham Rd., Altrincham, Cheshire WA14 4QG (tel (061) 928 07 03), for further infomration.

Sephor-Herman Press, Inc., 1265 46th St., Brooklyn, NY 11219 (tel. (718) 972-9010). Sells *The Jewish Travel Guide* (US$11.50), which lists kosher restaurants, synagogues, and other Jewish institutions in over 80 countries. In the U.K., it is sold by Jewish Chronicle Publications, London EC4A IJT, U.K.

Alternatives to Tourism

If the often madcap, city-swapping pace of tourism loses its appeal, you might consider a longer stay in France; through study, work, or volunteering you can gain a deeper appreciation for the France which extends beyond cathedrals and cafés.

Useful Publications

The Council on International Educational Exchange, 205 E. 42nd St., New York, NY 10017 (tel. (212) 661-1414), publishes a wide variety of books on work, study and volunteering abroad. (See listing above under Travel Services for a list of publications.)

The **Institute of International Education (IIE)**, 809 UN Plaza, New York, NY 10017-3580 (tel. (212) 883-8200). Publishes a number of useful books, including *Basic Facts on Foreign Study* (free), and the very thorough, annual *Academic Year Abroad* (US$39.95, postage US$ 3), and *Vacation Study Abroad* (US$31.95, postage US$3). You can call or write IIE for information, or visit their reference library (open by appointment). They also publish *Financial Resources for International Study,* available from Peterson's Guides, P.O. Box 2123, Princeton, NJ, 08543-2123 (tel. (800) 338-3282), which lists over 600 foundations providing money to undergrad, grad and post-grad students. Finally, they distribute several books published by the **Central Bureau for Educational Visits and Exchanges** in the UK, including *Study Holidays* (£8.95 including UK postage, £10.40 including postage to mainland Europe, and £13.95 including airmail postage worldwide), Working Holidays (£8.95, £10.45, and £13.95), and *Home from Home* (£7.99, £9.49, and £11.99), an annual guide to homestays, termstays and exchanges. Write to the Central Bureau directly at Seymour Mews House, Seymour Mews, London W1H 9PE, England (tel. (071) 486 5101).

Vacation Work Publications, 9 Park End St., Oxford OX1 1HJ, England (tel. (0865) 241 978). Distributes books on work and volunteer opportunities, including *Directory of Summer Jobs Abroad* (£7.95), *Work Your Way Around the World* (£9.95), *The Au Pair and Nanny's Guide to Working Abroad* (£7.95), *International Directory of Voluntary Work* (£8.95), and *Emplois d'Eté en France* (£6.95).

Study

If you choose your program well, study in France can be one of the best ways to acquaint yourself with the country and its people. Research your options well, however, as programs vary considerably in academic quality, living conditions, and expense. A good place to begin investigating study abroad programs is **CIEE's** *Work, Study, Travel Abroad: The Whole World Handbook. Basic Facts on Study Abroad,* put out by the IIE, CIEE, and NAFSA: The Association of International Educators, a free brochure that covers the nitty-gritty of foreign study, from visas to tax returns. **UNESCO** publishes *Study Abroad* (US$24, postage US$2.50), available from Unipub Co., 4611-F Assembly Dr., Lanham, MD 20706 (tel. (800) 274-4888). For free pamphlets on various fields of study in France, contact the **Cultural Services** of the **French Embassy.**

Language instruction is a booming business in France; semester- and year-abroad programs are run by American universities, independent international or local organi-

zations, and divisions of French universities. The **tourist office** in Paris maintains a list of member language schools.

Alliance Française, Ecole Internationale de Langue et de Civilisation Française, 101, bd. Raspail, 75270 Paris Cedex 06 (tel. 45 44 38 28; fax 45 44 89 42). Mo. Notre-Dame-des-Champs, St-Placide, or Rennes. Offers language courses at various levels, a business course, teacher training, and refresher courses.

Institut Catholique de Paris, 21, rue d'Assas, 75270 Paris Cedex 06 (tel. 42 22 41 80). Mo. St-Placide. Semester-long and summer classes at all levels, including business French and courses for teachers of French.

Cours de Civilisation Française de la Sorbonne, 47, rue des Ecoles, 75005 Paris (tel. 40 46 22 11). The **Sorbonne** has been giving its French civilization course since 1919. Academic year course which can be taken by the semester; four-, six-, and eight-week summer programs with civilization lectures and language classes at various levels; and a special course in commercial French during the academic year and a four-week session for high-level students during the summer. You can also take the *Cours de Civilisation* through the **American Institute for Foreign Study (AIFS),** 102 Greenwich Ave., Greenwich, CT 06830 (tel. (800) 727-2437), which also arranges accommodations and meals in Paris for its students. In addition the AIFS administers programs in Cannes and Grenoble.

Eurocentres, another of the many hats worn by Council Travel. Long and short intensive courses, holiday courses, and teacher refresher courses at centers in Paris (13, passage Dauphine, 75006 Paris, tel. 43 25 81 40); La Rochelle (10ter, rue Amelot, 17000 La Rochelle, tel. 46 50 57 33); and Amboise (9, Mail Saint-Thomas, BP 214, 37402 Amboise-Cedex, tel. 47 23 10 60). Call or write the nearest Council Travel office for information on centers worldwide.

AzurLingua, 25, bd. Raimbaldi, 06000 Nice (tel. 93 62 01 11). Learn French in style—on the Riviera. Learning in a small classroom setting at a variety of levels and with varying degrees of intensity. Some packages include accommodations, meals, and activities.

While it is tempting (and comforting) to meet and talk to other Americans, you may regret it later. If your French is already extremely competent, enrollment in a **French university** may be more rewarding than a language or civilization class filled with English-speakers. Enrolling yourself directly can sometimes cost three or four times less than going through an American university's program, but it might be more difficult to receive academic credit at your home university. The French educational system is structured to prepare students for a series of standard examinations that must be passed to earn degrees. They operate on a full-year schedule (no semesters here) and entrance requirements are rigorous. Most French universities require at least a *baccalauréat* degree or its putative equivalents (British A-levels or two years of college in the United States) for admission. For details on application procedures, contact the cultural services office at the nearest French consulate or embassy.

Founded in 1955 to improve the living and working conditions of its members, the **Centre Régional des Oeuvres Universitaires et Scolaires (CROUS),** can be of tremendous assistance to foreign students. The regional center is at 39, av. Georges-Bernanos, 75231 Paris Cedex 05 (tel. 40 51 36 00). CROUS of Paris also publishes brochures, *Guide Infos Etudiants,* listing addresses and information on every aspect of student life in Paris. Pick up the helpful guidebook *Je vais en France* (free), available in French or English, from any French embassy or consulate.

Work

Finding work in France is extremely difficult. Because of high unemployment, the French government has become wary of hiring foreigners. Before you can obtain a work permit through normal channels, your employer must convince the Ministry of Labor that there is no French citizen capable of filling your position. Even when a foreigner is considered, EC members have priority. Long-term employment is difficult to secure unless you have skills in high-demand areas such as medicine, computer programming, or teaching. If you have the appropriate skills or educational background, you might investigate positions with US firms, government agencies, or non-profit organizations that hire Americans for work abroad.

With the exception of *au pair* jobs, it is illegal for foreign students to hold full-time jobs during the school year. Students registered at French universities may get work permits for the summer with a valid visa, a student card from a French university, and proof of a job. Check the fact sheet *Employment in France for Students,* put out by **Cultural Services of the French Embassy,** which provides basic information about work in France and also lists the government-approved organizations through which foreign students must secure their jobs. **CIEE** operates a reciprocal work program with France and is the only U.S. organization so approved. If you are a degree-seeking college or university student, a resident U.S. citizen, and have an intermediate level knowledge of French (at least 2 years of college French), CIEE will issue you a three-month work permit for US$125. Under this system, you do not need a job prior to obtaining a work permit. CIEE will provide information on accommodations and job-hunting but will not place you in a job. Jobs available are mostly short-term, unskilled work in hotels, shops, restaurants, farms, and factories. Wages should cover food, lodging, and basic living expenses. Complete information and application are enclosed in their *Work Abroad* brochure.

A number of firms publish guides that can lead you through the complicated process of finding work abroad.

CIEE: Their *Work, Study, Travel Abroad: The Whole World Handbook* (US$12.95, postage US$1.50), available in bookstores, from any Council Travel office, or from CIEE's New York headquarters, is a comprehensive guide to overseas opportunities which includes a work-abroad section with listings by country. The handbook also includes a section on long-term employment. For more detail specific to France, consult *CIEE's Emplois d'Eté en France* (US$13.95, postage US$1.50). Also available from CIEE is *Working in France: The Ultimate Guide to Job Hunting and Career Success à la Française* (US$12.95 plus US$1.50 postage).

Peterson's, P.O. Box 2123, Princeton, NJ 08543 (tel. (800) 338-3282), publishes the *1992 Directory of Overseas Summer Jobs* (US$14.95 plus US$4.75), which lists 50,000 openings worldwide, volunteer and paid.

World Trade Academy Press, 50 E. 42nd St., #509, New York, NY 10017 (tel. (212) 697-4999), publishes a *Directory of American Firms Operating in Foreign Countries* (look it up in the library—it costs an awe-inspiring US$195), and the more manageable *Looking for Employment in*

Foreign Countries (US$16.50). It also publishes excerpts of listings of American firms in specific countries for about $10-15.

Addison Wesley, 1 Jacob Way, Reading, MA 01867 (tel. (800) 447-2226) makes available another general guide, *International Jobs: Where They Are, How To Get Them* (US$12.95).

Once in France, a good place to start your job search is the **American Chamber of Commerce,** 21, av. George V, 75008 Paris (tel. 47 23 80 26). The *Membership Directory of the French-American Chamber of Commerce* is available from its office at 509 Madison Ave., #1900, New York, NY 10022 (tel. (212) 371-4466). It is quite expensive, so go through the directory at the office. The **Agence Nationale Pour l'Emploi,** 4, rue Galilés, 93198 Noisy-le-Grand Cedex (tel. 49 31 74 00) has specific information on employment. You could also visit the **Centre d'Information et de Documentation Jeunesse (CIDJ),** 101, quai Branly, Paris 75015 (tel. 45 66 40 20), a government-run information clearinghouse on French law, camping, touring, sports, employment, careers, and long-term accommodations. Part-time jobs and housing listings are posted at 9am on the bulletin boards outside. Pamphlets available include *Cours d'été pour étrangers en France, Placement au pair en France,* and *Tourisme en France.* (Open Mon.-Fri. 9am-7pm, Sat. 10am-6pm.) Alternatively, check help-wanted columns in newspapers, especially *Le Monde, Le Figaro,* and the English-language *International Herald Tribune.* **The American Church,** 65, quai d'Orsay, 75007, Paris, posts a full bulletin board of potential job and housing opportunities.

A number of programs offer practical experience to people with technical and business skills. The **International Association for the Exchange of Students for Technical Experience (IAESTE)** program, a division of the Association for International Practical Training (AIPT), is an internship exchange program for science, architecture, engineering, agriculture, and math students who have completed at least two years at an accredited four-year institution. There is a non-refundable US$75 fee. Apply to the IAESTE Trainee Program, c/o AIPT, 10 Corporate Ctr., Suite 250, 10400 Little Patuxent Parkway, Columbia, MD 21044 (tel. (410) 997-2200). Applications are due December 10 for summer placement.

Summer positions as **tour group leaders** are available with **Hostelling International, American Youth Hostels (AYH),** P.O. Box 37613, Washington, DC 20013-7613 (tel. (202) 783-6161). You must be over age 20 and are required to take a nine-day training course (US$295, room and board included; in Washington, DC US$395). You must lead a group in the U.S. before taking one to Europe. The **Experiment in International Living (EIL),** P.O. Box 676, Kipling Rd., Brattleboro, VT 05302 (tel. (800) 451-4465 or (802) 257-7751), requires leadership ability and extensive overseas experience (minimum age 24). Applications are due in late November for summer positions. CIEE also has group leader positions available; contact its International Voluntary Projects division.

Au Pair Positions

And then there is the old standby—*au pair* work. Positions are reserved primarily for single women aged 18 to 30 with some knowledge of French; a few men are also employed. The *au pair* cares for the children of a French family and does light housework five or six hours each day (1 day off per week) while taking courses at a school for foreign students or at a French university. Talking with children can be a great way to improve your French, but looking after them may be extremely strenuous. Make sure you know in advance what the family expects of you. *Au pair* positions usually last six to 18 months; during the summer the contract can be as short as one to three months, but you may not be able to take courses. You'll receive room, board, and a small monthly stipend (around 1300F). Be sure to acquire a visa *long séjour* before arriving in France.

The Cultural Services of the French Embassy (see Tourist Offices above) offers a detailed information sheet on *au pair* jobs. Organizations offering placement include **L'Accueil Familial des Jeunes Etrangers,** 23, rue du Cherche-Midi, 75006 Paris (tel. 42 22 50 34 or 42 22 13 34) and **Centre d'Echanges Culturels Internationaux (CECI),** B.P. 30 171, 69406, Lyon, Cedex 3 (tel. 77 27 00 91).

Volunteering

If you have the financial freedom to forgo a salary, volunteering can provide a wonderful opportunity to meet people and might even secure you room and board in exchange for your work. *Volunteer! The Comprehensive Guide to Voluntary Service in the U.S. and Abroad* is co-published by CIEE and the Commission of Religious Volunteer Agencies. It offers advice on choosing a voluntary service program and lists over 200 organizations in fields ranging from health care and social work to construction. Write to CIEE (US$8.95, postage US$1.50).

CIEE also offers placement in international **work camps** in the U.S., Europe, Africa and Asia each summer. Volunteers from throughout the world live and work together on a two- to four-week community project. A working knowledge of French is required for projects in France, and participants must be at least 16. The camp provides room and board; the application fee is US$135. Write to CIEE International Voluntary Projects (address above).

Volunteers for Peace, a work camp organization, publishes an annual *International Workcamp Directory* to workcamps in 37 countries, primarily in the former USSR and Europe (US$10 postpaid). They also publish a free newsletter. Write to VFP, 43 Tiffany Rd., Belmont, VT 05730 (tel. (802) 259-2759). Placement is quick; volunteer reservations are generally confirmed within three weeks. There is a US$125 registration fee for camps in Western Europe. **Service Civil International/International Voluntary Service—USA** runs workcamps throughout France that aim to advance international peace. Contact them at Rte. 2, Box 506, Crozet, VA 22932 (tel. (804) 823-1826). Apply well in advance. The registration fee for placement in camps is US$75. Many French organizations run *vacances en chantier,* workcamps involving building and restoration. You should know some French before embarking on a project run by a French organization. Write to **Club du Vieux Manoir,** 10, rue de la Cossonnerie, 75001 Paris (tel. 45 08 80 40), which works to protect the environment and restore churches, castles, fortresses, and other historical French monuments. The club offers summer- and year-long programs. Anyone 15 or over (14 for some programs) is eligible, and the application fee is 60F. If you are 17 or over and work during the off-season, your room and board

are free after a 15-day trial period. **REMPART,** 1, rue des Guillemites, 75004 Paris, organizes similar projects, mostly for participants 18 and over. Programs cost anywhere from nothing to 90F per day. **Compagnons Bâtisseurs,** Maison de la Solidarité, 6, av. Charles de Gaulle, 81100 Castres (tel. 63 35 89 33), an international volunteer association, renovates and converts local buildings into facilities for the economically underprivileged and those with mental and physical disabilites. Work includes heavy physical labor, but extensive experience is not necessary. Terms run two to three weeks, June to October. Volunteers prepare their own food (cooking facilities provided) and sleep in provided tents or barracks. Apply two months in advance.

If working on an archeological dig interests you, the **Archaeological Institute of America** publishes *The Archaeological Fieldwork Opportunities Bulletin* (Members US$8.50, nonmembers US$10.50, postage US$3) listing international fieldwork projects. Contact the AIA at 675 Commonwealth Ave., Boston, MA 02215 (tel. (617) 353-9361). Also contact the Cultural Services of the French Embassy for possible positions in France as **camp counselors.**

There are a variety of resources available to those interested in **teaching English** in a foreign school. The U.S. State Department **Office of Overseas Schools,** Rm. 245 SA-29, Department of State, Washington, DC 20522 (tel. (703) 875-7800) maintains a list of elementay and secondary schools abroad and agencies which arrange placement for Americans to teach abroad.

International Schools Services, 15 Roszel Rd., P.O. Box 5910, Princeton, NJ 08543 (tel. (609) 452-0990) publishes a free newsletter, *NewsLinks;* call or write to get on the mailing list. Their Educational Staffing Department, which coordinates placement of teachers in international and American schools, publishes the free brochure *Your Passport to Teaching and Administrative Opportunities Abroad.* The *ISS Directory of Overseas Schools* (US$34.95) is distributed by **Peterson's, Inc.,** 202 Carnegie Center, Princeton, NJ 08543 (tel. (800) 338-3282).

Packing

Pack light. Lay out everything you think you'll need, pack only half of it, and take more money. Remember that you can buy almost anything you'll need in Europe, and that the more luggage you carry, the more alien you'll feel.

Decide what kind of luggage is best suited to your trip. A **backpack** is ideal if you plan to cover a lot of ground and want to hike or camp often. If you intend to stay mainly in cities and towns, consider a light **suitcase.** For unobtrusive travel, choose a large **shoulder bag** that zips or closes securely. This may also be the best choice for hitchhikers because it's less intimidating to drivers than a large backpack. Whenever you can, store your luggage in secure lockers while you see the sights; bring a small **daypack** to carry your *Let's Go,* lunch, map, rain poncho, and camera.

Pack solid, dark-colored clothes that won't show the wear they'll surely receive and are not obtrusively American (leave the Clemson t-shirts in the drawer). If they're loose and wearable in layers, they will be more versatile. Dress neatly and conservatively—you'll fare better when dealing with locals. Sturdy cotton-blend pants or a skirt are cooler for summer and look more polished than jeans, although jeans (carefully ironed, of course!) are very chic among French students. Also remember that you should dress neatly when visiting any house of worship, whether or not services are being held. Many churches in France will not allow visitors with bare shoulders to enter (no flip flops or tube tops, *Mon Dieu!*). Taking clothes that you can wash in a sink and that dry quickly and wrinkle-free will save you laundromat visits.

France is generally warm in the summer with temperatures in the 70s (around 25°C) in the north, 80s (30°C) in Paris, and 90s (35°C) in the south. Early and late summer, however, can be quite cool, particularly in Paris and the north where rain is common. Even in mid-summer, the evenings can be windy and cold, and hot weather doesn't really hit Paris until mid-July. Winters are mild, averaging about 40°F (5°C) during the day, though some regions (predictably, mountainous areas and the North) are considerably colder. Lightweight cottons or blends are a must in summer, but don't forget a sweater or jacket for unexpected cold weather. Light wool clothing is good for autumn and will carry you through winter as well except in the north and in the mountains. You'll need **rainwear** in all seasons, and if you plan to camp, it's worth paying a little more for a lightweight poncho that unbuttons to form a groundcloth.

Avoid taking electrical appliances, but if you must, remember that electricity in most European countries is 220 volts AC, twice as much as in North America and enough to fry any of your appliances. In France, as in most of Europe, sockets accommodate mainly two-pin round plugs; get an adapter. If the appliance is not dual voltage, you'll also need a **converter** (US$15-18). But remember that you can use these converters only in areas with AC current. You can buy adapters and converters when you get to Europe, or order them in advance from the **Franzus Company,** Murtha Industrial Park, P.O. Box 142, Beacon Falls, CT 06403 (tel. (203) 723-6664). The company also distributes an illuminating pamphlet called *Foreign Electricity Is No Deep Dark Secret.*

The following is a **checklist** of some items you should definitely squeeze in the corners of your pack: needle and thread, string, a pocket knife, a plastic water bottle, safety pins, rubber bands, a small flashlight, a cold-water soap (Dr. Bronner's Castile Soap, available in camping stores, claims to work as everything from clothes detergent to toothpaste), a bath towel, bags that seal shut (for damp clothing, soaps, or messy foods), a notebook and pens or pencils, a pocket French-English dictionary or phrasebook, and a (non-ticking!) travel alarm clock. Waterproof matches and English-language maps might be useful as well. If you take expensive **cameras** or equipment abroad, it's best to register everything with customs at the airport before departure. Buy a supply of film before you leave; it's more expensive in France. Unless you're shooting with 1000 ASA or more, airport security x-rays should not harm your pictures. It never hurts, however, to buy a lead pouch, available at any camera store. Either way, pack your film in the carry-on luggage, since the x-rays employed on checked baggage are much stronger. To avoid x-rays altogether, you can have your film and camera hand-inspected at most American airports, although French airports may be less accommodating. If you're bringing a laptop or notebook **computer,** be sure to have both computer and floppy discs hand-inspected, lest stray x-rays wipe out your as yet un-

published *chef-d'oeuvre*. Officials may ask you to turn it on, so be sure the batteries are fully loaded. A final warning: lost baggage is common, and not always retrieved. Be sure to keep all valuables and an extra day's clothes in your carry-on.

Getting There

From North America

Budget air travel began inauspiciously with Icarus, whose no-frills flight to the center of the solar system was fatally turbulent. Survival rates have risen dramatically since then, but air travel has become immensely more complicated. Use the following suggestions as a base for research, but above all, plan ahead and shop around.

Making reservations far in advance gives you access to cheaper fares and a wider choice of dates. Also, try to be flexible. Direct, regularly scheduled flights are notoriously expensive. If possible, leave from a travel hub—such as New York, Atlanta, Dallas, Chicago, Los Angeles, San Francisco, Seattle, Montréal, Toronto, and Vancouver—where greater competition yields cheaper flights. A similar flexibility in destination is advisable. Fares to cities only 100km apart may differ by as many dollars. Flying to London is usually the cheapest way across the Atlantic, though special fares to other cities—such as Amsterdam, Luxembourg, or Brussels—can cost even less. Off-season travelers will enjoy lower fares and face much less competition for inexpensive seats, but you don't have to travel in the dead of winter to save; peak season rates begin on either May 15 or June 1 and run until about September 15. "Midweek" (Mon.-Thurs.) flights run about US$30 cheaper each way. It is generally advisable to fix a return date when purchasing your ticket. Traveling with an "open return" ticket can be pricier than fixing a return date and paying to change it. Purchasing a one-way ticket invites the same danger.

Begin by calling **student travel organizations** such as Council Travel, Travel CUTS, or Let's Go Travel (see Useful Organizations above). They cut special deals for students not available to regular travel agents, and are often significantly cheaper. If you are not eligible for their fares, look for a knowledgeable, sympathetic travel agent. Consulting several is a good idea; some travel agents won't be eager to help you find the cheapest option, since budget flights earn them only a small commission. Another option is the Sunday travel sections of *The New York Times* and other newspapers, where fare brokers advertise incredibly cheap but erratic fares. Seniors can also get excellent deals; many airlines offer senior-traveler club deals or airline passes, and discounts for seniors' companions as well.

Commercial Airlines

Flying with a commercial airline is usually the most expensive option, but will reward you with a commensurate level of flexibility, reliability, and comfort. The industry is extremely variable: in 1992 prices on commercial flights from the East Coast to Paris ranged from $200-$1000 round-trip. Plan for a ball-park figure of $800-900, $500-700 in the off-season. Look into smaller carriers such as Icelandair, Virgin Atlantic, and Martinair Holland which may undercut the fares of large airlines. Most airlines offer price cuts for advance purchase; a small number have **standby** and **three-day advance purchase** youth fares. Check with individual carriers for information on restrictions and availability.

Charter Flights

Charter flights make the most economic sense, especially in the high season. You can book charters up until the last minute, but most flights during the summer fill up months in advance. Later in the season, companies have trouble filling their planes and either cancel flights or charge special fares. Charter flights allow you to stay abroad for as long as you like and often allow you to mix and match arrivals and departures from different cities. Once you have made your reservations with a charter company, however, flexibility flies away. You must choose your departure and return dates when you

book the flight, and if you cancel your ticket within 14 to 20 days of departure, you will lose some money.

Be aware, however, that charter flights are often inconvenient and require long layovers. Also, ask a travel agent about your charter company's reliability, since such companies reserve the right to cancel flights until 48 hours before departure.

Council Charter is among the oldest and most reliable charter-flight companies and offers flights to most major European cities with a variety of gateways in the U.S.. Tickets can be purchased at any Council Travel office, or through Council Charter in New York. Call (800) 800-8222. Also try **DER Tours** (tel. (800) 782-2424); and **Travel Avenue,** (tel. (800) 333-3335 or (312) 876-1116). In Canada, try **Travel CUTS** (see Useful Organizations above).

Discount Clubs and Ticket Consolidators

Last-minute discount clubs and fare brokers offer savings on European travel, including charter flights and tour packages. Organizations that act as clearing houses for unsold airline, charter, and cruise tickets include **Access International** (tel. (800) 825-3633 or (212) 465-0707); **Discount Travel International** (tel. (215) 668-7184; US$45 membership); **Last Minute Travel Club** (tel. (800) 527-8646 or (617) 267-9800); **Last-Minute Travel Connection** (tel. (708) 498-9216 or (900) 446-8292) for last-minute travel opportunities; **Moment's Notice** (tel. (212) 486-0503, hotline (212) 750-9111); **Unitravel Corporation** (tel. (800) 325-2222); and **Worldwide Discount Travel Club** (tel. (305) 534-2082; US$50 membership). Clubs generally charge a yearly subscription fee of $30-50; fare brokers like Access International do not. Both sell empty seats on commercial carriers and charters from three weeks to a few days before departure. Study their often Byzantine contract—you may prefer not to stop over in Luxembourg for 11 hours.

For the truly flexible budget traveler, **Airhitch** (tel. (212) 864-2000) lets you choose a date range in which you want to travel and a number of possible destitations; you are then placed with 90% certainty in a vacant spot on a flight in your date range to one of your destinations. While Airhitch's prices are ostensibly low (one-way flights to Europe from New York cost US$169), this is by no means a convenient or reliable means of travel. Be sure to read all the fine print.

Courier Flights

Go-getters who don't mind traveling light might consider flying to Europe as a **courier.** A company hiring you as a courier will use your checked luggage space for freight, leaving you with only the carry-on allowance. Fares vary wildly, depending on proximity to departure date, but are usually standby level or lower—often dramatically lower. Most courier companies offer single round-trip tickets only, leaving from New York with fixed-length stays (usually short). **Now Voyager** (tel. (212) 431-1616) couriers fly to Paris from New York. **Courier Travel Service,** (tel. (800) 922-2359 or (516) 374-2299), and **Halbart Express** (tel. (718) 656-8189) advertise similar opportunities. Check the travel section of a major newspaper for other courier companies. For more information, write or call for the *Courier Air Travel Handbook* (US$10.70; Thunderbird Press, 5930-10 W. Greenway Bd., Suite 112H, Glendale AZ 85306; tel. (800) 345-0096).

From Europe

By Plane

If charters to your ultimate destination are booked and commercial flights are too expensive, you can always fly to London and connect with an intra-European flight. **Council Travel** offers rates of around US$75-95 between London or Amsterdam and Paris. In London, check newspapers, travel agencies, and student travel organizations for bargain charter flights. The **Air Travel Advisory Bureau,** Strauss House 41-45, Goswell Road, London EC1V 7DN (tel. (071) 636 2908) puts travelers in touch with the cheapest carriers for free. Also contact **STA Travel** or a **CIEE** office for information about inexpensive flights throughout Europe.

EUROPE BY YOURSELF

WITH THE YOUTH & STUDENT TRAVEL SPECIALISTS

FROM PARIS TO

		✈ return	🚄 return
Amsterdam	FFR	910	488
Berlin	FFR	1480	1121
Rome	FFR	1100	1008
Madrid	FFR	1580	1042
Moscow	FFR	2900	-
New York	FFR	2450	-
Sydney	FFR	8425	-
Bangkok	FFR	5385	-

FROM ROME TO

		✈ return	🚄 return
Athens	$	310	200
Cairo	$	540	
Istanbul	$	370	220

FROM LONDON TO

		✈ return	🚄 return
Athens	£	133	265
Rome	£	120	170
Venice	£	150	157

ACCOMMODATION WORLDWIDE

Paris	$ 30
London	$ 30
Amsterdam	$ 28
Athens	$ 18
Madrid	$ 32
Florence	$ 21
Rome	$ 21
Venice	$ 23

Prices are valid for summer '92

CtS YOUTH & STUDENT
TRAVEL CENTRE

PARIS V°	20, rue des Carmes - Tel. (00331) 43250076 **Metro Maubert Mutualitè**
LONDON	44 Goodge Street, W1P 2AD - Tel. (004471) 5804554/6375601 Metro Goodge Street
LONDON	220 Kensington High Street, W8 7RA - Tel. (004471) 9373265 Metro High Street Kensington
ROME	via Genova, 16 - Tel. (06) 46791
ROME	corso Vittorio Emanuele II, 297 - Tel. (06) 6872672/3/4
ROME	Air Terminal Ostiense - Tel. (06) 5747950
FLORENCE	via dei Ginori, 25/R - Tel. (055) 289721/289570
MILAN	via S. Antonio, 2 - Tel. (02) 58304121
NAPELS	via Mezzocannone, 25 - Tel. (081) 5527975/5527960
VENICE	Dorso Duro Ca' Foscari, 3252 - Tel. (041) 5205660/5205655

You may also want to consider special student fares offered within Europe, which can be competitive with ferry ticket prices. See a student travel organization such as CIEE about this option. Finally, check on special deals offered by national airlines if you fly with them across the Atlantic. For continental travel, some of the lowest fares can be found on Eastern European airlines. Note that baggage limitations for intra-European flights are lower than those for flights to and from North America (20kg (44 lbs.) as opposed to 32kg (70 lbs.)).

By Train or Bus

Trains will take you to France from nearly anywhere on the continent. **BIJ tickets** (Billet International de Jeunesse) remain one of the cheapest options for travelers under 26. They cut up to 25% off regular second-class rail fares on international routes and are valid on the vast majority of trains. When you buy a BIJ ticket, you specify both your destination and route and have the option of stopping anywhere along that route for up to two months.

You can buy BIJ tickets in the U.K. or on the Continent. They are available from **Eurotrain** outlets as well as other student travel agencies. Eurotrain consists of nine student organizations in Europe; in England, it is located at 52 Grosvenor Gardens, London SW1W OAG (tel. (071) 730 8518).

Bus travel in Europe is significantly more comfortable than in North America, although trains remain the landlubber's preferred form of transportation. Amsterdam, Athens, Istanbul, London, Munich, and Oslo are centers for private lines that offer long-distance rides across Europe and, of course, to France.

By Ferry

Many ferries link France with England and Ireland. **Sealink Stena Lines** and **P&O European Ferries** offer extensive service across the English Channel. Sealink ferries leave from Dover, take about one and a half hours, and are the most frequent (at peak times every 75min.). Standard foot passenger fare is about £20, with savings up to 50% on certain return packages. Alternate routes between England and France include

Southhampton to Cherbourg (4 1/2hr., night service 6hr.) and Newhaven to Dieppe (3 per day, 4hr.). **P&O European Ferries** operates the fastest crossing by ship—just 75 minutes from Dover to Calais. Other convenient channel crossings include Portsmouth to Le Havre and Cherbourg, and Dover to Oostende and Zeebrugge in Belgium (3 3/4-4 1/4hr.). Le Havre has the fastest road connections to Paris, and Cherbourg is ideal for a scenic route through Normandy to Brittany. **Brittany Ferries** run from Plymouth or Cork to Roscoff, from Portsmouth to St-Malo/Caen, and from Poole to Cherbourg. Standard foot passenger fare from all Dover routes is about £20, with substantial savings available on fixed-period returns. **Irish Ferries** offers ferry service between Cherbourg or Le Havre to Rosslare in Ireland, and to Le Havre from Cork. Irish Continental is rather expensive (price varies between £50-100 depending on season), but Eurailpass holders travel free.

Traveling by **catamaran** is quicker (50min.), but you should book in advance. **Hoverspeed** departs for Calais or Boulogne from Dover. Service is suspended in rough weather, so you may find yourself waiting for a ferry instead. Hoverspeed also offers combination rail/bus and hovercraft service to and from London, Paris, Brussels, Amsterdam, and points in southwestern France. Hoverspeed operates a new summer service to and from London, Lourdes, and Andorra. Students under 26 travel at youth rates. For information, write **Travelloyd,** 8 Berkeley Sq., London SW1, or the British Rail Travel Centre, 4-12 Lower Regent St., London SW1Y 4PQ.

By late 1993 travelers will have the option of tunneling beneath the Channel when the Chunnel, the undersea road-and-rail connection, opens to passenger service. It has yet to be decided which side of the road motorists will use.

Once There

Helpful People

Tourist Offices

All large cities in France have an **Office de Tourisme.** Smaller French towns that attract a significant number of visitors have a tax-supported office called the **Syndicat d'Initiative** to provide information on the town and the surrounding area. Since these offices have the same purpose and France is in the process of merging these bureaucratically different offices, *Let's Go* lists both as "Tourist Offices." Don't hesitate to use them: they can be invaluable sources of up-to-date information unavailable in any guide book.

Consulates

If anything serious goes wrong—arrest, theft, death of a companion, etc.—make your first inquiry to your country's consulate in France. The distinction between an embassy and a consulate is significant: an embassy houses the offices of the ambassador and his or her staff; you won't gain access unless you know someone inside. All facilities for dealing with nationals are in the consulate, and when you call the numbers listed below for information, you should ask to be connected with the consulate. If your passport gets lost or stolen, your status in France is immediately rendered illegal—go to the consulate *as soon as possible* to get a replacement. A consulate is also able to lend (not give) up to 100F per day (interest free), but you will be forced to prove you are truly desperate with no other source of money. The consulate can give you lists of local lawyers and doctors, notify family members of accidents, and give information on how to proceed with legal problems, but its functions end there. Don't ask the consulate to pay for your hotel or medical bills, investigate crimes, obtain work permits, post bail, recite poetry, or interfere with standard French legal proceedings. Consulates are generally found only in the very largest cities, such as Paris, Marseille, and Lyon; *Let's Go* lists consulates in the Practical Information sections of relevant cities. Travelers should be aware that consulates other than those of their native country are often willing to help out in case of emergency.

Transportation

By Plane

Two airlines serve major French cities and resorts: **Air France** and **Air Inter.** A third airline, **U.T.A. (Union des Transports Aériens)** offers limited service within France. Although Air Inter and U.T.A. both offer a wide range of discounts, domestic air travel in Europe is rarely an inexpensive option.

By Train

European trains retain the charm and romance their North American counterparts lost long ago. France has a vast rail network to accommodate its 15,000 daily departures, and its national rail company, the **Société Nationale de Chemins de Fer (SNCF),** is generally efficient. Off the main lines between cities and large towns, however, service is both less frequent and less convenient. Consequently, be prepared for long waits and obscure timetables. Buses fill in shorter gaps in the system, and recently a few unprofitable SNCF train routes have been replaced with SNCF buses, which also honor railpasses.

Overnight trains may save you money on accommodations, but spend a few extra dollars for a berth in a *couchette* (bunkbed) car. Bring your own food and drink—it's expensive in the diner cars, and the water from the bathroom faucets is not suitable for drinking. Be mindful of safety as trains are hardly theft-proof: lock the door of your compartment if you can, and keep valuables on your person.

French **timetables** are complicated but well-organized. They consist of three periods, designated by colors, which depend on the expected volume of passenger traffic. Red (peak) periods generally fall on important long weekends and tickets are accordingly more costly. Individual days are generally divided into white (peak) and blue (off-peak) hours; again, prices vary accordingly. Every major railroad station in France carries schedules and provides train information at computer tellers, via various representatives at the station, or most commonly, on poster timetables. You can purchase the complete **SNCF timetable** at newsstands in the stations. SNCF representatives in the U.S. provide material on France Railpasses and Eurailpasses, as well as a booklet of French and European fares. Thomas Cook publishes the incredibly useful *European Timetable,* with schedules for routes all over Europe, available from Forsyth Travel Library.

Point-to-point tickets can be purchased in France or from a travel agent in North America. They are "open" tickets, specifying only points of departure and arrival, not specific dates or seat assignments. As such, if you purchase your ticket in France, remember to validate it in one of the orange ticket punches (with signs marked "compostez votre billet") at the entrance to the platforms. This stamps the date on the ticket making it valid for that day of travel. If you break your journey with a stop along the way, you must validate your ticket again after the stopover. Always keep your ticket with you, as you may have to present it during your trip and when you finally leave the train.

Reservations, for which you will be charged a moderate fee, are recommended for longer trips on all international trains, though you can usually find a seat on shorter journeys. It is always advisable to make reservations when traveling during red periods, if you want to have a seat. The **TGV** *(train à grande vitesse)* serves major cities and is faster and more comfortable than normal express trains ("express" or "rapide"); *it always requires a reservation even if you have a railpass.* The reservation fee (about US$8) is waived for Eurailpass holders.

A number of special discounts can be applied to point-to-point tickets purchased in France. The **Carrissimo,** available for 12-25 yr. olds traveling alone or with up to 3 friends all under the age of 26, offers discounts of 50% on blue period trips for the traveler and 3 friends or fewer, or 20% discounts during the white period. (Valid for one year. 190F for 4 trips, 350F for up to 8 trips.) The **Carte Vermeille,** (230F), entitles travelers over 60 up to 50% off first- or second-class tickets for unlimited trips in blue periods. It can be obtained at larger rail stations (valid for 1 yr.). A second option, sold for 130F, entitles senior travelers to identical discounts on 4 trips (also valid for 1 yr.). The Carte Vermaille and Carrissimo are sold only in Europe.

Once in Europe, those under 26 may also purchase **BIJ tickets,** available at Eurotrain and Wasteels offices, which cut up to 25% off regular second-class rail fares on international routes. In Paris, **Eurotrain** is located at 3, bd. des Capucines, 75002 (tel. 44 71 30 00), and at the Student Travel Center (STC), 20, rue des Carmes, 75005 (tel. 43 25 00 76). Most major cities have Eurotrain or Wasteels offices. Check at STC's Travel Services Desk or at any office in Europe for addresses and information.

If you are planning to rack up many miles on French or European trains, you might consider investing in a **railpass.** Ideally, a railpass allows you hop an any train in France or Europe (depending on the pass), go wherever and whenever you want, and change your plans at will. You can ride the TGV or regular trains during peak periods and hours at no extra charge (other than the mandatory reservation fee). The handbook that comes with your railpass is designed to tell you everything you need to know, including a timetable for major routes, a map, and details on ferry discounts. In practice, of course, it's not so simple. You must still stand in line to pay for seat reservations, for supplements, and for *couchette* reservations, and to have your pass validated when you first use it. More importantly, railpasses don't always pay off. Find a travel agent with a copy of the *Eurailtariff* manual (or call Rail Europe at (800) 438-7245), add up the second-class fares for the major routes you plan to cover, deduct 5% (the listed price includes a commission), deduct 30% if you are under 26 and eligible for BIJ, and compare. The ostensible convenience of a railpass might prove expensive.

With a **France Railpass**, travelers can ride for four days within a one-month period (US$175 1st class, US$125 2nd class). The days of use need not be consecutive. Up to five additional days can be purchased (each US$38 1st class, US$27 2nd class). Included is a pass for the Paris Métro, covering the city's buses, subways, and RER trains for one day. You also get free transfer from Orly or Roissy-Charles de Gaulle Airports to Paris and back. You can buy the railpasses in North America at offices of Rail Europe or from travel agents. France passes cannot be purchased or used by residents of

France. If your itinerary includes Britain as well, you might consider purchasing a **BritFrance Railpass**. The pass is good for rail travel in France and Great Britain for 5 days within a 15-day period for US$335, first class or US$249, second class. A second option allows for 10 days of travel within a one-month period for US$505, first class, or US$385, second class. If you are under 26, a Youthpass, providing second-class travel through the BritFrance Railpass will cost you US$199 for the first option and US$299 for the second. All BritFrance Railpasses include one round-trip hovercraft crossing of the English Channel. For those bit by the travel bug early in life, consider the **Kiwi** pass, which yields 50% discount off tickets for children under 16. The trips must begin during the white or blue period. Up to 4 adults traveling with the child also receive 50% discounts. The Kiwi pass is sold at French rail stations only.

For travel across the continent, five flavors of **Eurailpass** exist. The basic **Eurailpass** is valid for unlimited rail travel in Western European countries, including the Republic of Ireland, but not Great Britain or Northern Ireland. You can travel first class for periods ranging from 15 days (US$460) to three months. If you are under 26, you also qualify for the **Eurail Youthpass,** good for one month (US$508) or two months (US$698) of second-class travel. The **Eurail Flexipass** allows you to travel on specific days within a two-month period: five days for US$298, 10 days for US$496, or 15 days for US$676. The **Eurail Youth Flexipass** offers those under 26 the same options for US$220, US$348, and US$474, respectively. Finally, the **Eurail Saverpass** allows two or more people traveling together at all times (3 or more from April 1-Sept. 30) to travel first class for fifteen days for US$390 per person. You must get your Eurailpass or Eurail Youthpass in North America. Purchase them from a travel agent, CIEE, the Educational Travel Center, or from Let's Go Travel Services. Rail Europe (tel. (800) 438-7245) sells all passes, point-to-point tickets, and reservations for European rail travel.

By Bus

In France, buses usually serve tour groups or fill in gaps in train service. When buses and trains cover the same routes, the bus is usually slightly cheaper and slower. For routes and fares, check at the local tourist office or bus station (*gare routière,* often next to the railway station). **Europabus, Eurolines,** and **Miracle Bus** provide inexpensive transportation to major cities in Europe and beyond. *Let's Go* lists important bus connections and fares to most cities and towns in the Practical Information sections.

By Car

Although a single traveler will almost never save by **renting** a car, groups of four usually will; even groups of two or three might find renting cheaper than a railpass, unless traveling unusually long distances. Expect to pay at least US$200 per week for a four-seater, excluding taxes (28%) and deposit. Parking in cities can be expensive and gas costs at least US$3 per gallon.

If you want a car for longer than three weeks, **leasing** becomes more economical than renting. Beware, though, that along with the economy of leasing come several potential pitfalls, such as hidden servicing expenses. Some tourists have found that a purchase/resale plan is cheaper than renting for long vacations. You must arrange the deal before you go; contact the American Automobile Association or the Canadian Automobile Association for advice.

Nearly all car-rental companies require renters to be over age 20 and have a major credit card. Several U.S. firms offer rental and leasing plans in France. Send for their catalogs. Compare prices carefully; they vary substantially between firms. Also, make sure that rental prices include the T.V.A. tax. Some companies are **Auto-Europe,** P.O. Box 1097, Camden, ME 04843 (tel. (800) 223-5555); **Europe by Car, Inc.,** 1 Rockefeller Plaza, New York, NY 10020 (tel. (800) 223-1516); and **Kemwel Group,** 106 Calvert St., Harrison, NY 10528 (tel. (800) 678-0678). **France Auto Vacances,** 420 Lexington Ave., New York, NY 10170 (tel. (800) 234-1426) has a three-week minimum and offers a $50 rebate to students; CIEE also offers discounted rental and leasing plans to students and faculty members.

If you know before you go that you will need to rent a car, it's a good idea to make arrangements in advance to ensure availability, though making arrangements once in

France is also relatively simple. **Avis, Hertz, Solvet, Budget,** and **Europcar** operate agencies all over the world, the last two generally being the least expensive. **Europcar** has an office at 145 av. Malekoff, 75016 Paris (tel. 45 00 08 06). The **French National Railroad (SNCF)** offers a train-plus-car rental package available in about 200 cities. Many firms in the U.S. and France rent campers (sometimes called "motor caravans"), which can also be economical when the cost is split among several people.

For the adventurous and well-informed, **purchasing** a car in Europe and selling it back at the end of the vacation can provide the continent's cheapest wheels. *How to Buy and Sell a Used Car in Europe* (US$4.95 plus 75¢ postage) contains useful tips; write to Gil Friedman, P.O. Box 1063, Arcata, CA, 95521 (tel. (707) 822-5001).

Once you have a car, you'll have to adjust to the French road system. The speed limit on *autoroutes* is 130kph, or 80mph. Somewhat slower are the *Routes Nationales* that run through towns. For a synopsis of **French driving regulations,** write to the French Government Tourist Office. Cars drive on the right side of the road in France. You should be especially aware of the *priorité à droite:* cars approaching from the right have the right of way, no matter what the relative size of the roads. While an international driving permit is not required to drive in France, it can aid in smoothing over difficulties with police officers and provides an additional piece of identification.

Michelin makes good **road maps,** available in book stores and kiosks. The large map #989 is especially useful. The suggested roads, drawn in yellow, supposedly bypass congested areas. Refer to the sections on Documents and Formalities and Health and Insurance above for information concerning **international driver's licences** and **auto insurance.**

By Bicycle

Cycling is an excellent way to explore the countryside, and French roads, with a wealth of well-paved minor routes, are generally fine. Ride in the morning or evening when it's cool and you'll have the road to yourself. Michelin maps, available in most bookstores, mark the main roads in red, secondary roads in yellow, and local roads in white. Cyclists should avoid major *autoroutes* (marked in red with a dotted line), and

heed the round road sign bordered in red with a diagram of a bike; this means bikes are forbidden. Bikers may also want the larger-scale, more expensive maps (21-52F) from the **Institut Géographique National (IGN)**, 107, rue la Boétie, 75008 Paris (tel. 45 63 48 01; Mo. St-Philippe du Roule or Franklin D. Roosevelt). Experienced cyclists recommend a front bag with a transparent pocket for maps, as well as panniers, which can hold a sleeping bag. At about US$35-66, the best bike helmets are cheaper and more pleasant than critical head surgery or a well-appointed funeral; they are available in most sports and bicycle-speciality shops.

When purchasing a bike, mail-order items will probably be cheapest, but you may want to check a local biking club or store for advice. A good mail-order outfit is **Bike Nashbar,** 4111 Simon Rd., Dept. LG3, Youngstown, OH 44512 (tel. (800) 627-4227). French treads and rim sizes differ from English sizes, but spare parts in English sizes have become available in many towns. Even so, if you plan a long ride, carry one or two extra inner tubes *(chambres à l'air),* a spare tire, a few spokes taped to the body, and a pump. You can also buy an excellent bicycle in France and have it shipped back home, but make sure you get one fitted for export. French parts are even harder to find in the U.S. than American ones are in France.

Outstanding touring regions include the Loire Valley (especially the route west of Tours to Villandry and Ussé), Normandy, Brittany, Provence, the Vosges, the Massif Central, and the somewhat mountainous Jura. In the Pyrénées and the Alps, you (and your bicycle) can catch a lift up the mountain on a train and then cycle down. For touring information, first consult the tourist bureau annexed to most French embassies. The **Fédération Française de Cyclotourisme,** 8, rue Jean-Marie Jégo, 75013 Paris (tel. 45 80 30 21; Mo. Corvisart), is a non-profit, member-supported liaison between 3000 cycle-touring clubs. Although they are not a travel agency or tourist information bureau, they are friendly and will advise foreign cyclists on a limited basis. (Include 3 reply coupons for an airmail response.) In late 1992, they are expected to publish a booklet of general information available in English.

Most **airlines** will accept a boxed bike as one of your two pieces of luggage, provided that the total baggage weight does not exceed the given limit (32kg (70 lbs.) for flights to and from North America, 20kg (44 lbs.) for intra-European flights). You can also count a bicycle as an extra piece of luggage on transatlantic flights; it will cost about US$85. Some airlines supply bike boxes; you can also obtain one at bike shops, which often give away old cartons. Carry a wrench to the airport and know how to make adjustments on the spot if necessary. (You might be asked to remove the handlebars, for instance.)

Bikers will find it convenient to fly into **Orly** airport in Paris, since you can assemble your bike in the airport and ride it into the city on the *piste cyclable,* a bike path that avoids heavy traffic the first few km. If you arrive at the Roissy-Charles de Gaulle airport, you can take the Roissy Rail commuter train into Paris. Bikes are not allowed on the Métro, though this may not be rigorously enforced.

Once in France, you can easily combine biking with **train** travel. For information in advance, write to SNCF for the brochure *Guide du train et du vélo.* Regardless of how far you go, it will cost about 42F to register a bicycle as baggage for transport. The SNCF provides cartons (about 15F) to protect the bike in transit. Bicycles are easily damaged, so all removable parts, such as headlights, should be taken off the frame or padded and taped. Look for the SNCF advertisements that say *"Dans certains trains votre vélo peut voyager avec vous, gratuitement."* On trains thus advertised (sometimes called *trains omnibus),* your bike travels with you, and you save the registration fee. On other trains, your bike may arrive up to 48 hours after you. You can also **rent bicycles** in many of the larger towns, and it is usually possible to get a serviceable 10-speed model. *Let's Go* lists bike rental outlets in the Practical Information sections.

By Thumb

> *Let's Go* strongly urges you to consider seriously the risks before you choose to hitch. We do not recommend hitching as a means of travel.

Hitching in France takes patience, as the country ranks among the worst in Europe for hitchhikers. Hitchhikers will have more luck if they try to look neat and respectable, if they stand rather than sit, if they carry a destination sign, and if they travel light. Service stations and the stopping areas near toll booths are places where drivers can stop and get back on the road safely. Truckers may offer long rides, but find gas stations, weigh stations, and roadside restaurants easier to stop at than on the roadside. It is illegal for truckers to pick up more than two passengers at one time.

It is not safe to hitch alone in France. Women should always hitch in pairs. Two men may have difficulty securing a ride. Always refuse rides in the back of a two-door car. Don't lock the door, and keep your luggage handy—don't put it in the trunk if you can avoid it. In an emergency try opening the car door; this may be enough of a surprise to slow the driver down. If you feel uneasy about the ride for any reason, get out at the first opportunity or firmly demand to be let out.

You may be able to find rides (or hitching companions) by checking message boards in student travel offices or in student gathering places. **Allostop Provoya,** 84, passage Brady, 75010 Paris (tel. within Paris 42 46 00 66, outside Paris 47 70 02 01), with offices in many major cities, brings together drivers and riders to share expenses. Telephone or write a few days in advance if you can. For passengers, the service costs 220F for eight trips within a two-year period. Single trip rates depend on the distance traveled, but fall between 27 and 67F. In either case, gas and tolls are extra.

By Boat

France has more than 11,000km of navigable rivers, canals, lakes, and sea coast. To float through the countryside or take better advantage of your time at the seaside, contact the **Syndicat National des Loueurs de Bateaux de Plaisance,** Port de la Bourdonnais, 75007 Paris (tel. 45 55 10 49). They'll set you up anywhere in the country with boats ranging from dinghies and canoes to yachts. For information on waterways suitable for canoeing, contact the **Fédération Française de Canoe-Kayak,** BP 58-94340 Joinville Le Pont (tel. 48 89 39 89).

By Foot

If you have more time than money and prefer countryside to cityscape, try hiking France's extensive network of long-distance footpaths. The **Fédération Française de la Randonnée Pédestre,** 8, av. Marceau (enter at 9, av. George V), 75008 Paris (tel. 47 23 62 32), sells topographical maps *(topo-guides)* with itineraries for 40,000km of footpaths. Huts or mountain hostels, which usually serve meals, are located along many of the suggested routes. The member organizations of the federation organize group trips through the countryside.

Proper **hiking gear** is essential. Lightweight non-leather hiking boots are lighter, more comfortable, less expensive, and just as rugged as the old-fashioned thick leather ones. You will also need a sweater, water-proof poncho, long pants, shorts, and a comfortable pack with a hip belt. You may also want to carry a light butane or white gas stove and a mess kit. Remember that high altitudes and hot sun make mid-day trekking unsafe; bring sunscreen, a hat, and plenty of water.

For more information about hiking, contact the **Club Alpin Français,** 24, ave. de Laumière 75019 Paris (tel. 42 02 68 64). The club runs 180 centers across France, including two in the Alps that provide instruction in Alpine technique. The following books may also help you plan your journey: *Walking in the Alps* (Hunter, US$9.95); *Hiking and Walking Guide to Europe* (Passport Books, US$7.95); and *Walking in France* (Oxford Illustrated Press, US$9.95).

Accommodations

Just one night in an overpriced, undercleaned hotel or worse still, on a city park bench, will dampen even the most spirited vacation. Plan carefully when it comes to accommodations, and be flexible. If you arrive in a town without an advance reservation, your first stop should be the nearest phone booth or the local tourist office. Tourist offices across France distribute extensive accommodations listings free of charge and will also reserve a room for a small fee. *Let's Go* is not an exhaustive guide to budget accommodations, but most of the places will be happy to refer you somewhere else when full. Unless otherwise noted, we list hostel prices per person, prices elsewhere per room.

Hotels

French hotels can be a bargain. The French government publishes a comprehensive guide that classifies hotels with a star system: 4L (luxury), 4, 3, 2, and 1. Most hotels in *Let's Go* are one-star or unclassified establishments, though two-star establishments offering inexpensive rooms are sometimes included. As a general rule, French hotels charge by the room and not by the number of people staying in it, so two traveling together can sleep less expensively than one. Most rooms come with double beds. Expect to pay at least 90F for singles. If your room has no shower, you'll generally have to pay for a hall shower (10-25F) or, especially in small hotels, go without. Many North Americans are surprised to discover a strange toilet-like apparatus located in all bathrooms. This is called a *bidet*. A *bidet* is a somewhat archaic device intended for the cleansing of the more private body parts. No matter how desperate you are, do not use your *bidet* as a toilet. You will cause yourself much embarrassment and force your unfortunate proprietor to spend a few hours bleaching the bowl and cleaning out the pipes. Another distinctly French practice to keep in mind when looking at hotels is that the French call the ground floor the *rez-de-chaussée,* and start numbering with the first floor *above* the ground floor *(premier étage).*

Many hotels serve a *petit déjeuner obligatoire* (obligatory breakfast), which costs 15-25F. Since local cafés serve croissants and coffee for less, you should opt out of breakfast if you can. Beware of hotels, usually in heavily touristed areas, that require *demi-pension* (one obligatory meal with each night's stay).

If you plan to visit a popular tourist area, especially during a festival, it is advisable to write ahead for reservations. Most hotels will confirm reservations only upon receipt of a check—not a credit card number—for the first night's rent. Include an International Reply Coupon for a prompt reply.

Hostels

Especially in the summer, Europe is overrun by young, budget-conscious travelers. Hostels are the hub of this gigantic student subculture, providing innumerable opportunities to meet people from across the globe, find new traveling partners, trade stories, and learn about places to visit. A night in an *auberge de jeunesse* averages 40 to 80F, with breakfast (usually not obligatory, and often included) averaging an additional 12 to 15F. Only camping is cheaper. Accommodations usually consist of bunk beds in single-sex dormitories, and most hostels either serve evening meals or have kitchen facilities you can use. Quality varies widely; some hostels are extremely well-kept and well-situated; others are in run-down barracks far from the center of town.

Hostel life has its drawbacks: many stays might include an early curfew (usually 10-11pm, in Paris midnight-2am), lack of privacy, prohibitions against smoking and drinking, a 10am-5pm lockout, a three-day limit to your stay, and hordes of vacationing school-children. But the prices compensate for these inconveniences, and many hostels fill quickly in July and August. Lockout and curfew times are often flexible—many hostels leave a back door open most of the night. Some hostels accept reservations—it's worth calling ahead—but always arrive early if you can.

For sanitary reasons, hostels often prohibit sleeping bags, instead requiring **sheet sleeping sacks,** which they rent or sell. You can make your own by folding a sheet lengthwise and sewing the long side and one end. You can also get a sleeping sack before you go from some of the travel organizations listed above for an extravagant US$14-16.

As of summer 1992, the **International Youth Hostel Federation (IYHF)** has officially changed its name to **Hostelling International (HI)**, with the result that all signs, membership cards, and other products relating to the association will henceforth bear the HI initials and logo, as well as the symbols of the relevant national hosteling association.

Prospective hostelers should become members of the official youth hostel association in their country; all national associations are part of **Hostelling International (HI).** To stay in an HI hostel, you must be a member. While international agreement strongly recommends securing membership in your home country, you don't absolutely have to become a member in advance: if you show up at an HI hostel but have not joined a national youth hostel association, the hostel should issue you a blank membership card with space for six validation stamps. Each night you'll then pay a nonmember supplement (equal to one-sixth of the membership fee) and earn one Guest Stamp; get six stamps and you're a member. Membership purchased in France costs about 100F, but if you've lived there for a year, it costs 70F. Most student travel agencies sell HI cards on the spot. or you can contact one of the national hostel organizations listed below. The **HI** card costs US$25 (over 54 US$15, under 18 US$10, family US$35). Also ask about the *Guide to Budget Accommodations, Vol. 1: Europe and the Mediterranean*, which sells for about US$11 and lists up-to-date information on HI hostels.

Hostelling International headquarters, 9 Guessens Rd., Welwyn Garden City, Herts, AL8 6QW, England (tel. (707) 33 24 87), is mainly responsible for international policy matters. Direct general inquiries to one of the following national associations: In France, the **Fédération Unie des Auberges de Jeunesse (FUAJ),** 27, rue Pajol, 75018 Paris (tel. 46 07 00 01; Mo. La Chapelle); in the U.S., contact **American Youth Hostels,** 733 15th St. NW, Suite 840, Washington DC 20005 (tel. (202) 783-6161); in Canada, **Hostelling International—Canada,** Suite 608, 1600 James Naismith Dr., 6th Floor, Gloucester, Ottawa, Ont. K1B 5N4 (tel. (613) 748-5638); in England and Wales, **Youth Hostels Association of England and Wales (YHA),** Trevalyn House, 8 St. Stephen's Hill, St. Alban's, Herts AL 1 2DY (tel. (727) 552 15); in Ireland, **An óige,** 39, Mountjoy Sq., Dublin 1 (tel. (01) 363 111); in Scotland, the **Scottish Youth Hostel Association (SYHA),** 7 Glebe Crescent, Sterling FK8 2JA (tel. (0786) 511 81); in Northern Ireland, **Youth Hostel Association of Northern Ireland (YHANI),** 56 Bradbury Pl., Belfast BT7 1RU (tel. 0232) 324 733); in Australia, **Australian Youth Hostels Association (AYHA),** Level 3, 10 Mallett St., Camperdown, NSW 2050 Australia (tel. 61 2 5651699); and in New Zealand, **Youth Hostels Association of New Zealand (YHANZ),** P.O. Box 436, 173 Gloucester St., Christchurch, 1, New Zealand (tel. (643) 79 99 70).

In many cities and towns, rooms are available in **Foyers de Jeunes Travailleurs et de Jeunes Travailleuses,** residence halls founded for young workers with jobs in cities far from home. They are usually single-sex dorms with single rooms and a bathroom in the hall. They accept foreign travelers if there's space available, and offer the advantages of hostels without the disadvantages (lockout, curfew). The *foyers* offer a fairly good deal to the single traveler, and they almost always have room because tourists don't know about them.

Student Accommodations

Short-term student housing is available in summer in the dormitories of most French universities. Contact the **Centre Régional des Oeuvres Universitaires et Scolaires (CROUS)** (address above). Travelers interested in summer housing and students interested in year-long accommodations can also contact the **Cité Internationale Universitaire de Paris,** 19, bd. Jourdan, 75690 Paris Cedex 14 (tel. 45 89 68 52). *Foyers* (youth residence halls) are a good bet in Paris. These single-sex dormitories require a three-day minimum stay. You can also find a bed through the **Accueil des Jeunes en France (AJF),** a central booking organization for youth accommodations in Paris.

Camping

Camping liberates you from hostel regulations and drab hotels. Campgrounds dot the French countryside, many nestled by peaceful lakes, rivers, or even the ocean. However, be aware that the vacationing French often arrive at campgrounds burdened with trailers, radios, and a great deal of cooking paraphernalia, leaving little space between sites. In August, you might have to arrive well before 11am to ensure yourself a spot.

French campgrounds, like hotels and restaurants, are classified by a star system. Three- and four-star sites are usually large, grassy campgrounds with hot showers, bathrooms, a restaurant or store, and often a lake or swimming pool nearby. Some campsites will ask for your passport, but resist giving it to them, and try to substitute a less vital piece of identification. The **International Camping Carnet** (membership card) is one highly acceptable substitute, and will save you a lot of time and money if you intend to do much camping (see below). You may also choose to camp unofficially in fields or forests, at your own risk; simply be discreet, polite, and, if within sight of a farmhouse, ask permission. Respect the environment and don't ever light a fire.

Purchase your equipment before you leave. American packs are generally more durable and comfortable, and less expensive, than European ones. As a rule, prices go down in the fall as old merchandise is cleaned out. **Backpacks** come with either an external frame or an internal X- or A-shaped frame. If your load is not extraordinarily heavy and you plan to use the pack mainly as a suitcase, choose an internal-frame model. It's more manageable on crowded trains and when hitching, and it's less likely to be mangled by rough handling. Make sure your pack has a strong, padded hip belt, which transfers much of the pack's weight from delicate shoulders to more powerful legs. A good pack costs US$100-300.

Your **sleeping bag** need not be made of down; a good synthetic fiber is almost as warm and dries much more quickly. A sleeping bag is rated according to the lowest temperature in which it can be used. A three-season bag (spring, summer, fall) keeps you warm even in temperatures that dip below freezing and will cost at least US$110 for synthetic or US$135 for down. A bag for more casual use, however, will cost about US$40. At about US$10-15, an **ensolite pad** (much warmer than foam rubber) is a real bargain, offering crucial protection from cold, damp, and often rocky ground. Therm-A-Rest (US$40) is a hybrid ensolite pad and air mattress that virtually inflates itself. Regular air mattresses start at US$50. Good **tents** are expensive (at least US$95 for a 2-person), but are a sound investment. Often you can find a model from the previous year at a drastically reduced price. A **tarpaulin** rigged between two trees will keep you from getting completely soaked in a downpour, but only experienced campers should rough it with just a tarp. For cooking, **campstoves** come in a variety of sizes, weights, and fuel types, but none is truly cheap (US$40-125). Consider using GAZ, a form of bottled propane gas widely available in France that connects easily to an economically priced cooking unit. The following organizations provide camping information or supplies.

Campor, 810 Rte. 17N, P.O. Box 997-LG92, Paramus, NJ 07653 (tel. (800) 526-4784). Offers name-brand equipment at attractive prices.

L.L. Bean, 1 Casco St., Freeport, ME 04033 (tel. (800) 221-4221, customer service (800) 341-4341). A well-established firm that sells camping equipment and outdoor clothes. Publishes a quarterly catalog. Always open.

National Campers and Hikers Association, Inc., 4804 Transit Rd., Bldg. 2, Depew, NY 14043 (tel. (716) 668-6242). Issues the **International Camping Carnet,** required by some European campgrounds. The US$30 fee includes membership in the association. Short bibliography of travel guides for campers and a list of camping stores in major European cities.

Recreational Equipment, Inc. (REI), Sumner, WA 98302 (tel. (800) 426-4840). Long-time outdoor equipment cooperative favorite. Lifetime membership (not required) US$10. Sells *Europa Camping and Caravanning* (US$13), an encyclopedic catalog of campsites in Europe.

A good general book is *Camp Europe by Train* (US$13), available from the Forsyth Travel Library. If you plan to camp extensively, you should buy the *Guide Officiel Camping/Caravaning,* which provides good maps and lists both ordinary campsites, and *terrains à la ferme* (farm sites). It is available from the **Fédération Française de Camping et de Caravaning,** 78, rue de Rivoli, 75004 Paris (tel. 42 72 84 08). Michelin publishes a similar, but much less comprehensive guide, *Camping Caravaning,* geared to car-camping and designed to accompany the Michelin 1:200,000 scale maps.

Gîtes d'Etape

Gîtes d'etapes are rustic rural accommodations, designed for cyclists, hikers, and other ramblers. They tend to be removed from cities or towns, located in areas where one might hike, sail, or ski, and they consist of furnished lodgings in farmhouses, cottages, and even campgrounds. *Gîtes* generally do not offer meals, and often lack a permanent staff. If you plan to bed down in one of the more isolated ones in the off-season, you may even have the place to yourself. Don't even think about bringing a car to a *gîte*—you won't make it past the front door. For further information, contact the **Fédération Nationale des Gîtes de France,** 35, rue Godot-de-Mauroy, 75009 Paris (tel. 47 62 20 20).

Alternative Accommodations

For a more pastoral experience, look for **logis** and **auberges de France,** hotels and restaurants roughly comparable to country inns. They serve excellent food and charge reasonable prices for comfortable rooms, although generally more than the cheapest hotel. A list of them is available by writing **La Fédération Nationale des Logis de France,** 25, rue Jean Mermosz, 75008 Paris (tel. 43 59 86 67).

Servas is an international cooperative system of hosts and travelers established to help build world peace and understanding by providing opportunities for personal contacts among people of diverse cultures and backgrounds. Travelers are invited to stay in hosts' homes in over 100 different countries. Travelers are expected to contact their hosts in advance and to be willing to fit into the household routine. Homestays are of a two night duration. Prospective travelers must apply and pay a membership fee of US$55 plus a US$25 deposit for up to five host lists. The host lists provide a short self-description of each host member. To apply, write to US Servas, Inc., 11 John St., #407, New York, NY 10038 (tel. (212) 267-0252).

Also try **Amicale Culturelle Internationale,** a non-profit organization that offers placements to visitors as paying guests in French families everywhere in France on a full-board basis, and in Paris and its suburbs on a half-board basis. Write them at 27, rue Godot-de-Mauroy, 75009 Paris (tel. 47 42 94 21). **Accueil France Famille** is a

similar organization; its address is 5, rue François Coppée, F-75015 Paris (tel. 45 54 22 39).

Monasteries are ideal for those seeking a few days of peaceful contemplation. Reservations must be made well in advance. For a list of monasteries, *Guide des Monastères* (about 100F), write to **La Procure,** 3, rue de Mézières, 75006 Paris (tel. 45 48 20 25).

Security

A few precautions will see you safely through your travels more effectively than constant paranoia. First of all, take as few valuables as possible; flashy jewelry and big cameras will only draw attention to yourself. Keep all valuables with you whenever you leave your room, even if it has a lock, as others may have a pass-key. At night, sleep with valuables on your person; laying your pack alongside the bed won't deter thieves.

Keep your money, passport, and other important documents with you in a pouch or **moneybelt** at all times. **Neck pouches** worn under the shirt prove the most theft-resistant. Look for packs that have zippers designed to accept combination locks. If you are forced by circumstances to sleep outside, or simply can't carry everything with you, store your gear in sturdy lockers or at the baggage check at a bus or train station. However, since these lockers are sometimes broken into, always carry essential documents with you. Be aware that most lockers have time limits of a few days and are cleared out regularly; you will have to pay extra to reclaim your belongings.

Pickpockets are fast, practiced, and professional. Pros can unzip a bag in just a few seconds, so wear yours with the opening against your body. Threading a safety pin or keyring through both zippers on a pack makes it difficult to open quickly and prevents it from slipping open accidentally. Thieves often work in pairs, one providing a distraction and the other grabbing your wallet or purse. Some street children will do anything to distract you, even pretend that they are being molested. In busy areas, walk quickly and purposefully. Thieves in *métro* stations may try to grab your bag as you walk through the turnstile or as you board the subway, just before the doors close.

Photocopy all **important documents** such as your passport, identification, credit cards, and traveler's checks serial numbers. Keep one set of copies in a separate, secure place in your luggage, and leave another set at home. Although copies can seldom substitute for originals, at least you'll have the relevant information. If you are robbed, check your surroundings carefully. Thieves may throw away your wallet after taking the cash, and you might be able to retrieve non-cash items such as credit cards. Report the theft to the police station in the area where it occurred. Be insistent; a police report may be necessary to claim stolen traveler's checks. To replace a stolen passport, head for the nearest American consulate.

Traveling Alone

Traveling with other people can be emotionally taxing; at one time or another you may want to strike out on your own. There are many possible rewards, including a sense of adventure, freedom to go where and when you want, and the chance to reflect on your experiences without the stress of another person. The following safety precautions apply to all travelers, but people traveling alone should be particularly attentive.

Be sure that someone knows your itinerary, and check in with that person reasonably often. Steer clear of empty train compartments, and avoid bus and train stations and public parks after dark. When on foot, stick to busy, well-lit streets. Ask the managers of your hotel, hostel or campground for advice on specific areas, and consider staying in places with a curfew or night attendant.

Some cheap accommodations may entail more risks than savings. Forgo dives and city outskirts; remember that centrally located accommodations are usually safest. Never tell anyone that you're traveling alone.

Women Travelers

Women exploring any area on their own inevitably face additional safety concerns. In all situations it is best to trust your instincts; if you'd feel better somewhere else, don't hesitate to move on. You may want to consider staying in *foyers* or religious organizations that offer rooms for women only. Stick to centrally located accommodations and avoid late-night treks or metro rides. Remember that hitching is *never* safe for lone women, or even for two women traveling together. Foreign women in France are frequently beset by unwanted and tenacious followers. Try to exercise reasonable caution without falling prey to the notion that all French men are best avoided. To escape unwanted attention, follow the example of local women; the less you look like a tourist, the better off you'll be. In general, dress conservatively, especially in the more rural provinces. If you spend time in cities, you may be harassed no matter how you're dressed. Look as if you know where you're going, and ask women or couples for directions if you're lost or if you feel uncomfortable. Your best answer to verbal harassment is no answer at all. In crowds, you may be pinched, squeezed, or otherwise harassed. Wearing headphones or a conspicuous wedding band may help prevent such incidents. If you are propositioned directly, a loud *"Non!"* or *"Laissez-moi tranquille!"* (lehsay mwah trahnKEEL; "leave me alone") is best, with no further explanation. Seek out a police officer or a female passerby before a crisis erupts, and don't hesitate to scream for help *("Au secours";* oh suhKOOR). *Always* carry a *télécarte* and change for the phone and enough extra money for a bus or taxi. Carry a whistle on your keychain, and don't hesitate to use it in an emergency. For additional tips and suggestions, consult *The Handbook for Women Travellers* (£7) published by Piatkus Books, 5 Windmill St., London W1 1P 1HF, U.K. (tel. (071) 631 0710). If the tragic occurs, **SOS Viol,** the national **rape hotline,** answers calls (in French) from Monday through Friday, 10am to 6pm; in August, Wednesday through Monday, 10am to 6pm (tel. (1) 05 05 95 95).

All this should not discourage women from traveling alone. Don't take unneccessary risks, but don't lose your spirit of adventure either. A series of recent travelogues by women outline their sojourns; check a good library or bookstore for these and other books: *Nothing to Declare: Memoirs of a Woman Traveling Alone* and *Wall to Wall: From Beijing to Berlin by Rail* by Mary Morris (Penguin); *One Dry Season* by Caroline Alexander (Knopf); *Tracks* by Robyn Davidson (Pantheon); and, *The Road Through Miyama* by Leila Philips (Random House/Vintage).

Drugs

Possession of drugs in France can end your stay abruptly. Never bring any non-prescription drugs across any border, since drug laws and the severity with which they are enforced vary considerably among different countries (e.g., between Holland and France). Even prescription drugs, particularly insulin, syringes, or narcotics, should be accompanied by a statement from a doctor and left in original labeled containers. In France, police may legally stop and search anyone on the street. It is not uncommon for a pusher to increase profits by first selling drugs to a tourist and then turning that person in to the authorities for a reward. If you are arrested, your home country's consulate can visit you, provide a list of attorneys, inform family and friends, and tell you bedtime stories, but they cannot get you out of jail. You're virtually on your own if you become involved, however innocently, in illegal drug trafficking. Write the Bureau of Consular Affairs, Public Affairs #5807, Department of State, Washington, DC 20520 (tel. (202) 647-1488) for more information and the pamphlet *Travel Warning on Drugs Abroad.*

Keeping in Touch

Mail

Between major cities in France and North America, air mail takes five to ten days and is fairly dependable. From France, send mail from the largest post office in the area. Surface *(par eau* or *par terre)* mail is considerably cheaper, but takes one to three months to arrive. It's adequate for getting rid of books or clothing you no longer need.

You must complete a customs form to send any package over 1kg (2kg for letter-post rate) via air mail *(par avion* or *poste aérienne).*

When mailing to France, you can save your recipient the cost of postage for a response by enclosing an **International Reply Coupon** (available at post offices for about US$1) for a response by surface mail; send two for airmail.

Air-mailing a 25g (about 1 oz.) **letter** from France to the U.S. or Canada costs about 4F. **Postcards** *(cartes postales)* are slightly less. Special delivery is called *avec recommandation,* and express mail *exprès postaux.*

You can **receive mail** in France through the **Poste Restante** system. In major cities, the central post office handling Poste Restante is open long hours and on weekends. Almost all post offices function as Postes Restantes. To specify a particular post office, you must know its postal code—*Let's Go* lists postal codes for the central post office in the Practical Information section of every city. To ensure the safe arrival of your letter, address it: LAST NAME (in capitals), first name; Poste Restante; R. P. *(Recette Principale);* Postal code, city name, FRANCE. You will have to show your passport as identification and pay about 3F for every letter received. You can forward mail from most post offices to other French Postes Restantes.

American Express also receives and holds mail for its clients for up to 30 days, after which it is returned to the sender. If you want to have it held longer, just write "Hold for x days" on the envelope. The envelope should be addressed with your name in capital letters, and "Client's Mail" should be written below your name. Most big-city American Express offices provide this service free of charge if you have their traveler's checks, but some require that you be an AmEx cardholder. The free booklet *Traveler's Companion* contains the addresses of American Express offices worldwide, and can be obtained from any American Express office or by calling customer service at (800) 221-7282 (allow 6-8 weeks for delivery).

Post offices are usually open weekdays until 7pm (they stop changing money at 6pm) and on Saturday mornings. Avoid long lines by purchasing stamps at local *tabacs* or from the yellow coin-operated vending machines outside major post offices.

Telephones

Almost all French pay phones accept only **télécartes;** in outlying districts and cafés and bars, some phones are still coin-operated. You may purchase the card in two denominations: 40F for 50 *unités,* and 96F for 120 *unités,* each worth anywhere from six to 18 minutes of conversation, depending on the rate schedule. The *télécarte* is available at post offices and most metro stations and *tabacs.* The best places to call from are **phone booths** and **post offices.** If you phone from a café, hotel, or restaurant, you risk paying up to 30% more.

You can make **intercontinental calls** from any phone booth or post office. The postal clerk will assign you to a phone from which you can usually dial direct, and will collect your money when you complete your call. One of the cheapest options is to dial directly overseas from a phone booth, and ask to be called back (the number should be written on a sticker inside the booth, prefaced by *ici le);* this technique is much cheaper than calling collect or via credit card. A better alternative is AT&T **USA Direct** service, which allows you to be connected instantly to an operator in the U.S. Simply dial 19, wait for the tone, then dial 0011. Rates run about US$1.75-2 for the first minute plus about US$1 per additional minute. Calls must be made either collect (US$5.75 surcharge) or billed to an AT&T calling card (US$2.50); the people you are calling need not subscribe to AT&T service. For more information call (800) 874-4000. **Canada Direct, Australia Direct,** and **New Zealand Direct** are similar to USA Direct, though not as extensive. For information in Canada, call (800) 561-8868; in Australia, dial 0102; and in New Zealand, dial 018.

If your itinerary is unplanned and you don't want to be constrained by mailstops or the expense of phone calls, you might also consider **Overseas Access,** a telephone checkpoint service offered by EurAide. In its Munich office, an American staff relays messages to and from family, business, or other travelers. As a member, you can call the Munich office for news from home (US$15 initial registration, US$15 per week or US$40 per month). If you buy a Eurailpass from them, the initial registration fee is waived. In the U.S., contact EurAide, Inc., P.O. Box 2375, Naperville, IL 60567 (tel. (708) 420-2343). In Germany, contact Bahnhofplatz 2, 8000 München 2 (tel. (089) 59 38 89).

Telephone rates are reduced Monday through Friday 9:30pm-8am, Saturday 2pm-8am, and Sunday all day for calls to the Common Market and Switzerland; Monday through Friday noon-2pm and 8pm-2am, and Sunday afternoon to the U.S. and Canada; Monday through Saturday 9:30pm-8am and Sunday all day to Israel.

A brief **glossary:** A call is *un coup de téléphone* or *un appel;* to dial is *composer;* a collect call is made *en PCV* (pay-say-vay); a person-to-person call is *avec préavis.* Emergency or collect calls do not require coins or a télécarte.

A brief **directory:**

Operator *(Téléphoniste):* tel. 10.

International Operator: tel. 19 33 11.

Directory information *(Renseignements téléphoniques):* tel. 12.

International information: 19 33 12 + country code (Australia 61; Ireland 353; New Zealand 64; U.K. 44; U.S. and Canada 1).

Direct long-distance calls within France: To call from the Paris region to elsewhere in France, dial 16 + the number. To call the Paris area from elsewhere in France, dial 1 + the number. Within the Paris area, just dial the number; do the same to make a call to a region outside of Paris from a region outside of Paris.

Direct international calls from France: tel. 19 + country code (listed above) + area/city code + the number.

Direct international calls to France: international dialing prefix (Australia 0011; Ireland 16; New Zealand 00; U.K. 010; U.S. and Canada 011) + 33 + 1 (only if calling Paris) + the number.

AT&T operator: 19 00 11.

Fire: 18.

SAMU (Ambulance): 15.

Police Emergency: 17.

Customs: Returning Home

Unless you plan on hauling back a BMW or a barnyard animal, don't be alarmed by customs procedures. First off, visitors have an allowance of what they can bring into France. Anything exceeding the allowance is charged a duty. Among other things, if you are bringing into France more than 200 cigarettes, 2 liters of wine, 1 liter of alcohol over 38.8 proof, or 50g of perfume, you must declare such items. All travelers must declare articles acquired abroad; only the truly profligate budget traveler must pay duties; time may be spent in better ways than collecting receipts from duty-free shops.

Before leaving, **U.S. citizens** should record the serial numbers of expensive (especially foreign-made) items that will accompany you abroad. Have this list stamped by the Customs Office before you leave. U.S. citizens may bring in US$400 worth of goods duty-free every 30 days; the next US$1000 is subject to a 10% tax. Duty-free goods must be for personal or household use and cannot include more than 100 cigars, 200 cigarettes (1 carton), and 1 liter of alcohol. You must be 21 or older to bring liquor into the U.S. These items may not be shipped. Non-prescription drugs and narcotics, many foods, plant and animal products such as sea monkeys or Chia pets, pornography, lottery tickets, and harmful items (including, say, pop rocks, Soft Hits 8-track tapes, or asbestos) may not be imported into the U.S. Similar restrictions apply in many other countries; Australia is reputedly extra stringent with pop rocks. Write for the brochure, *Know Before You Go* (50¢), item 477Y, R. Woods, Consumer Information Center, Pueblo, CO 81009. To avoid problems when carrying prescription drugs, make sure the bottles are clearly marked, and have the prescription ready to show the customs officer. *Travelers' Tips on Bringing Food, Plant, and Animal Products into the United States* is available from the Animal and Plant Health Inspection Service, U.S. Department of

Agriculture, 6505 Belcrest Rd., Attn: Public Information, Washington, DC 20250. They also provide information on restrictions in the wildlife trade.

While in Europe, you can mail unsolicited gifts back to the U.S. duty-free if they're worth less than US$50. Mark the package "unsolicited gift" and indicate the nature of the gift and its retail value. Again, you may not mail liquor, tobacco, or perfume into the U.S. If you send back a parcel worth over US$50, the Postal Service will collect the duty plus a handling charge when it is delivered. To mail home personal goods of U.S. origin, mark the package "American goods returned."

Before departure, **Canadian citizens** should identify or list the serial numbers of all valuables on a Y-38 form at the Customs Office or point of departure; these goods can then be reimported duty-free. Once every year after a seven-day absence, you can bring in goods up to a value of CDN$300. After any two-day absence, you can bring in goods up to a value of CDN$100. These two allowances may not be claimed on the same trip. Duty-free goods may not include more than 50 cigars, 200 cigarettes, 1kg of tobacco, or 1.1 liters of alcohol. The minimum age to import tobacco is 16; the age for liquor varies by province. Anything above the duty-free allowance is charged a 20% tax. Shipped items will be taxed at a higher rate and may not include alcohol or tobacco products. You can send gifts up to a value of CDN$40 duty-free, but again, you cannot mail alcohol or tobacco. Canadians traveling to or from Europe via the U.S. should also note that pain-killers containing codeine—available over-the-counter in Canada—are illegal in the U.S. For more information, get the pamphlet *I Declare,* available from the Revenue Canada Customs and Excise Department, Communications Branch, Mackenzie Ave., Ottawa, Ont. K1A 0L5 (tel. (613) 957-0275) or *Bon Voyage, But...* from External Affairs, Ottawa, Ont., K1A OG2 (tel. (613) 993-6435).

Returning **British citizens** are allowed an exemption of up to £32 of goods. This includes not more than 200 cigarettes; 100 cigarillos; 50 cigars; 250g tobacco; and 2 liters of wine plus 1 liter of alcohol over 22% by volume, or 2 liters of alcohol not over 22% by volume. Allowances are about 50% higher for goods obtained tax- and duty-paid in the European Community. You must be 17 or over to import liquor or tobacco.

Irish citizens may import a maximum of IR£34 per adult traveler duty-free (IR£17 per traveler under the age of 15). Travelers above the age of 17 may bring in 200 cigarettes or 100 cigarillos or 50 cigars or 250g of tobacco, and 1 liter of alcohol over 44 proof or 2 liters of alcohol under 44 proof. You may import as much currency into Ireland as you wish. For more information, write Division 1, Office of the Revenue Commissioners, Dublin Castle, Dublin 1 (tel. (01) 679 27 27).

If you are an **Australian citizen** over 18 years of age, you can bring 250g of tobacco (equivalent to 250 cigarettes) and 1 of alcohol back into the country duty-free. The duty-free allowance is AUS$400 (under 18 AUS$200). Goods above the limit will be taxed and must be carried into the country with you. You may not import or export more than AUS$5000 (or the foreign equivalent) without filing a special form with customs. You may mail back personal property; mark it "Australian goods returned" to avoid duty. Consult the brochure *Customs Information for All Travellers,* available at an Australian Consulate or offices of the Collector of Customs.

Citizens of **New Zealand** may bring in NZ$700 worth of duty-free goods as long as the goods are intended for personal use or as unsolicited gifts. Travelers 17 or older are allowed 200 cigarettes (1 carton) or 50 cigars or 250g of tobacco or a mixture of all three not to exceed 250g. You may also bring in 4.5 liters of beer or wine and 1.125 liters of liquor. The *New Zealand Customs Guide for Travelers* and *If You're Not Sure About It, DECLARE IT* are both available from any customs office. For more information, contact **New Zealand Customs,** P.O. Box 29, Auckland (tel. (9) 773 520).

Paris

Paris slakes the human thirst for perfection. If Paris did not exist, we would have to invent it. If we did not exist, Paris would not really care. In Greek mythology, Paris was the capricious mortal who dared defy the gods in his quest for the most beautiful of all things beautiful. Paris's pride lives on in the image of today's Parisians as they stride down the streets, finely dressed, long noses raised into the butter-scented air, lips pursed for the ever-ready reply, *"Bah; ch'ai pas, moi"* ("Dunno"), and the mandatory accompanying shrug. And Paris lives on in the impeccably arranged shop windows, in shoppers' relentless persistence to select the perfect assortment of fresh produce, in the *boulanger's* floured-hand pat on the end of a raw *baguette* before sending it into the oven....Walter Benjamin proclaimed Paris the capital of the 19th century. Indeed, to modern Parisians, Paris remains no less than the nucleus of human civilization, an incarnation of the mythological longing for luxury, indulgence, romance, and beauty.

Thousands world-wide have left their native lands to come to Paris in search of an allegorical contentment denied them at home. Think of Wilde and Joyce, the Hemingways and the Fitzgeralds, Gertrude Stein and Milan Kundera. Read the works of James Baldwin and William Wharton to see how the hypnotic spirit of this city courses through their writings. Because everyone dreams about Paris before actually strolling through the twisting medieval streets and the *grands boulevards,* no one is at a loss for words to speak of it, but few have anything original to say. And yet, its heartbreaking beauty is entirely artificial, composed of monuments to order, improve, please, and transcend. Your own first visit to Paris may feel like an odd sort of homecoming. Or, you may be painfully aware all along that you are just a visitor, a pasty out-of-place foreigner with wrinkled jeans, big hair, and broken French. Place aside your expectations, your inhibitions, and discover a Paris of your own creation. Build a little world for yourself out of the romantic Seine, the regal architecture, the delicious finery that hangs in shop windows, and the population of exuberant locals. Paris loves lovers; so hug it and kiss it and call it your very own.

Originally home to the Parisii on the Seine, the city was named Lutetia (Lutèce) by the conquering Romans in 52 BC. In 987, when Hugh Capet, count of Paris, became King of France, he brought prestige to the tiny medieval town by naming it his capital. King Philippe Auguste (1180-1223) consolidated the crown's possessions and established the basic segregation of functions that still characterizes the city: political and ecclesiastical institutions on the Ile de la Cité, academic on the Left Bank, and commerce on the Right Bank. Over the centuries, the city expanded outward in concentric ovals, swallowing up whole villages, now called *arrondissements.*

Baron Haussmann's redesign of the city in the mid-19th century was superficially intended to facilitate military movement within the city, thus enabling a firm resistance to foreign invasion. But construction of the *grands boulevards* through ancient residential neighborhoods ripped apart the social fabric of the city; only the bourgeoisie and the aristocracy could afford homes in the new Paris, and lower income groups were pushed into the suburbs. The layout and physical organization of the city have been created to facilitate social interaction, yet the persistence of winding medieval passages and small districts with unique reputations have tempered the kind of alienation one expects from an immense, modern city. Great altars of space such as the Place de la Concorde and striking monuments like the Arc de Triomphe glorify the concept of public space while innumerable alleys and courtyards preserve privacy. Parisians believe that *la politesse* keeps life civilized. But they also believe in their right to say and do what they want behind closed doors and, on a number of occasions throughout the centuries, in the streets. Paris saw continental Europe's first mass revolution in 1789 and has since witnessed the violent comings and goings of two Empires, a monarchy, four Republics, and two military occupations, not to mention the furious civil riots of 1968 and the more recent student protests of 1986 and 1987.

Intellectual and cultural life has always flourished here, but Paris is also a European political center. The city is a frequent choice for international conferences, and Presi-

Paris

1 Accueil Central de France:
  127 Champs Elysée
2 Transalpino: 16, rue La Fayette
3 American Express: 11, rue Scribe
4 Post Office: 52, rue du Louvre

5 Musée Marmottan
6 l'Arc de Triomphe
7 Sacré-Coeur
8 Musée d'Art Moderne
  de la Ville de Paris
9 Grand Palais
10 Petit Palais
11 Opéra Garnier
12 Place Vendôme
13 Comedie Française
14 Palais Royal
15 Orangerie
16 St-Eustache
17 Centre National d'Art et
   Culture George Pompidou
18 Hôtel de Ville
19 Musée Picasso
20 Musée Carnavalet

21 Place des Vosges
22 Opéra Bastille
23 Sainte Chapelle and Palais de Justice
24 Notre Dame
25 St-Germain-des-Prés
26 Musée de Cluny
27 Sorbonne
28 Panthéon
29 Palais du Luxembourg
30 Musée d'Orsay
31 Musée Rodin
32 Les Invalides

33 Tour Eiffel
34 Cité Internationale
   de l'Université de Paris
35 Louvre

dent Mitterrand has been among the staunchest supporters of European unification. Modern Parisian politics focus around the issues of immigration and minority communities. Paris once presided over an empire embracing Algiers, Hanoi, and Port-au-Prince, and the city has been adopted by many of its former subjects. Its universities and art and music institutes draw students from the world over. Many of these cultures are quite visible, especially in the variety of North African and Caribbean restaurants, bakeries, *patisseries,* markets, houses of worship, and culturally ramshackle neighborhoods (especially in the 10th, 19th, and 20th *arrondissements),* which have the air of a Middle Eastern city. The last decade has seen an influx of Vietnamese and Chinese immigrants, and a growing interest in Eastern culture. These populations, however, constitute a strict cultural minority in largely homogeneous Paris. Racism and exclusion are as stubbornly rooted here as elsewhere in the world. The popular candidacy (for everything from mayor to chair of the European Parliament) of Jean-Marie Le Pen—proponent of expelling all immigrants and their offspring—and paranoid rumors of Arab, African, Jewish, and homosexual conspiracies supply the sad proof of this continuing prejudice. Unlike many major cities, Parisian poor live outside the city instead of in inner city slums. Northern suburbs witness frequent riots and demonstrations led by discontented minority groups. As even Parisians will attest, Paris is rapidly becoming a city for the rich, and, even worse, for the tourists.

Like New York or London, Paris is regarded with suspicion by country folk. The province and the capital are especially divided in France due to the centralizing policies of a government that has often ignored the welfare of the rest of the country. Decentralization has been the overall trend since the war, but Paris still monopolizes one quarter of France's manufacturing sector, and the bulk of the country's luxury and service trades, such as fashion, jewelry, furnishing, higher education, banking, insurance, law, and government.

Many visitors from abroad or even from the French provinces have returned with stories of the Parisians' xenophobia and snobbery. Even Emerson must have felt snubbed to have written, "Paris is terribly derisive of absurd pretensions—but not its own." These tall tales of Parisian discourtesy may come true if you address people in English without the prefatory *"Parlez-vous anglais, Madame/Monsieur?"* Although some Parisians have the somewhat annoying habit of answering all queries in English, even the simplest of efforts to speak fractured French will be appreciated. Be lavish with your *Monsieurs, Madames,* and *Mademoiselles*—unlike English, French demands use of titles when addressing strangers—and greet everyone with a friendly *bonjour* or *bonsoir.* Following these simple rules of etiquette may reward you with the music of an entire staff of a *boulangerie* singing in chorus, *"Merci, Monsieur/Madame. Au revoir."* When you do encounter rude locals, consider their point of view. Every summer, tourists more than double the city's population. Many do not speak French and are unwilling to accept the challenge of dealing with people who do not understand them. Parisians definitely have a soft spot for those who wish to share their love of France and French culture, but Paris is not about to pamper you.

Hemingway called Paris a moveable feast, a city with a foretaste so irresistible that once you swallow, you will carry memories of the experience around with you forever after. It is also something of a giant all-night *patisserie,* a collection of delights able to satisfy individuals of every inclination. Seductive and addictive, arch and sassy, Paris still exudes a *joie de vivre* that seems to jet from the Seine into the city's famous sewers and infect everything it passes. Don't let intimidation keep you from seeing and doing what you want. A surrender to Paris can be the sweetest of all possible defeats. For more detailed coverage of Paris and its surroundings than we can provide here, consult the new *Let's Go:Paris 1993.*

Practical Information

Note: In Paris addresses, "Mo." indicates the nearest metro stop.

Getting There

By Plane

Roissy-Charles de Gaulle

Most transatlantic flights land at **Aéroport Roissy-Charles de Gaulle,** 23km northeast of Paris. As a general rule, Terminal 2 serves Air France (info. tel. 43 20 14 55; arrivals tel. 43 20 12 55; departures tel. 43 20 13 55), and most other carriers operate from Terminal 1 (info. tel. 48 62 22 80).

The cheapest and fastest way to get into the city from Roissy-Charles de Gaulle and vice versa is by the **Roissy Rail** (tel. 43 46 14 14) bus-train combination. Take the free shuttle bus from Aérogare 1 arrival level gate 28, Aérogare 2A gate 5, Aérogare 2B gate 6, or Aérogare 2D gate 6, to the Roissy train station. From there, the **RER B3** (one of the Parisian commuter rail lines) will transport you to central Paris. If you are going to transfer to the metro, be sure to buy an RER ticket that includes metro transfer, and get off at **Gare du Nord** or **Chatelet-Les Halles**, which double as RER and metro stops. Conversely, to go to Roissy-Charles de Gaulle from Paris central, take the RER B3 to "Roissy," and change to the shuttle bus (10min. bus ride, 25-35min. on the RER, 31F with metro transfer).

Alternatively, **Air France Buses** run to the Arc de Triomphe/pl. d'Etoile (Mo. Charles de Gaulle/Etoile) at av. Carnot (every 15min. from 5:40am to 11pm, 40min., 48F, group of 3 passengers 112F, group of 4 140F), and the pl. de la Porte de Maillot/Palais des Congrès (Mo. Porte de Maillot), near the agence Air France (every 20min, 5:40am-11pm, 40min., same prices). For recorded information about either of these buses, call 42 99 20 18. Air France buses also run to and from a spot near the Gare Montparnasse, 113, bd. du Vaugirard (Mo. Montparnasse-Bienvenue; departure every hr. to the airport 7am-9pm; departure every hr. from the airport 6:30am-7:30pm; 45min.; 64F, group of 3 passengers 144F, group of 4 170F). Call 43 23 82 20 for recorded info.

The **RATP** (tel. 43 46 14 14) runs city buses from Roissy-Charles de Gaulle into Paris. **Bus #350** plies between the airport and Gare du Nord and Gare de l'Est (every 15min. from 5:30am-11pm, 50min., 30F). **Bus #351** goes to pl. de la Nation (every 30min. from 6am-8:30pm, 40min., 30F). Unless your hotel is near one of these terminals, you'll wind up having to take the metro anyway. **Taxis** take at least 50min. to the center of Paris and cost about 210F during the day, 290F at night.

Orly

Aéroport d'Orly (tel. 49 75 15 15), 12km south of the city, is used by charters and many continental flights. From Orly Sud gate H or Orly Ouest arrival level gate F, take the shuttle bus (every 15min. from 5:40am-11:15pm) to the **Pont de Rungis/Aéroport d'Orly** train stop where you can board the **RER C2** for a number of destinations in Paris. (35min., 25F; call RATP at 43 46 14 14 for info.).

Air France Buses run to and from Montparnasse, 36, rue de Mienne, 6ème (Mo. Montparnasse-Bienvenue) and the downtown Invalides Air France agency (tel. 43 23 82 20 or 43 23 97 10, every 12min., 32F, group of 3 passengers 83F, group of 4 103F). In addition the RATP runs **Orlybus** to and from metro and RER stop Denfert Rochereau. Board at Orly Sud gate H platform 4 or Orly Ouest level O door D (every 10-15min. from 6am-11pm, 25min., 21F). **Taxis** from Orly to the center cost at least 170F during the day, considerably more at night. Allow at least 45 minutes for the trip.

Le Bourget

Paris's third airport, **Le Bourget** (tel. 48 62 12 12) is notable only because Charles Lindbergh landed there after his historic transatlantic flight. Nowadays, Le Bourget is used for charter flights, generally within France. Should you land at Le Bourget, take **Bus #350** (every 15min. from 6:10am-11:50pm, 2 metro tickets) to Gare du Nord or

Gare de l'Est. **Bus #152** also makes these stops, and, for the same price, will take you to Porte de la Villette, where you can catch the metro or another bus.

By Train and Bus

Each of Paris's six train stations is a veritable community of its own, with resident street people and police, cafés, restaurants, *tabacs,* and banks. Locate the ticket counters *(guichets),* the platforms *(quais),* and the tracks *(voies),* and you will be ready to roll. Each terminal has two divisions: the *banlieue* and the *grandes lignes.* **Grandes lignes** depart for and arrive from distant cities in France and other countries—each of the six stations serves destinations in a particular region of France or Europe (see below). Trains to the **banlieue** serve the suburbs of Paris and make frequent stops. Within a given station, each of these divisions has its own ticket counters, information booths, and timetables; distinguishing between the two before you get in line will save you hours of frustration. All train stations are reached by at least two metro lines, with the metro station cleverly bearing the same name as the train station. For train information, call the SNCF at 45 82 50 50; for reservations, call 45 65 60 60 or use the minitel 3615 SNCF (see Communications, below; reservations and minitel both open daily 8am-8pm). The SNCF line may seem perpetually busy—visiting a local travel agency will let you buy your tickets or make your reservations with more personal attention and little to no fee. There is a free telephone with direct access to the stations on the right-hand side of the Champs-Elysées tourist office.

A word on safety: though full of atmosphere, each terminal also shelters its share of thieves and other undesirables. Gare du Nord, for example, becomes rough at night, when drugs and prostitution take over; Gare d'Austerlitz can be similarly unfriendly by moonlight. As in all big cities, be cautious in and around stations; the unsuspecting may be invited out for a drink only to be doped up and ripped off. In each train station metro stop, you will encounter friendly looking people who will try to sell you a metro ticket at exorbitant prices. Do not purchase anything in the stations except from uniformed personnel. Above all, do not change cash or buy anything from these con artists. Any money you hand over will never be seen again.

Gare du Nord: Trains to northern France, Britain, Belgium, the Netherlands, Scandinavia, the Commonwealth of Independent States, and northern Germany (Cologne, Hamburg). To: Brussels (10 per day, 3hr., 211F); Amsterdam (6 per day., 6hr., 339F); Cologne (6 direct, 6 indirect per day, 5-6hr., 406F); Boulogne (11 per day, 2 1/2hr., 153F); Copenhagen (1 direct, 3 indirect per day, 16hr., 1183F); London (by train and boat, 7hr., return within 5 days 602F, within 2 months 502F).

Gare de l'Est: To eastern France (Champagne, Alsace, Lorraine), Luxembourg, parts of Switzerland (Basel, Zürich, Lucerne), southern Germany (Frankfurt, Munich), Austria, and Hungary. To: Zürich (7 per day, 6hr., 357F); Munich (4 direct, 4 indirect per day, 9hr. direct, 584F); and Vienna (3 per day, 15hr., 898F).

Gare de Lyon: To southern and southeastern France (Lyon, Provence, Riviera), parts of Switzerland (Geneva, Lausanne, Bern), Italy, and Greece. To: Geneva (5 per day, 3 1/2hr., 287F plus 16-80F TGV reservation); Florence (4 per day, 11-12hr., 612F); Rome (3 per day, 14-16hr., 575F); Lyon (12 per day, 2hr., 250F plus 16-80F TGV reservation); Nice (8 per day, 7hr., 443F plus 16-48F TGV reservation); Marseille (10 per day, 5hr., 368F plus 16-48F TGV reservation).

Gare d'Austerlitz: Trains to the Loire Valley, southwestern France (Bordeaux, Pyrénées), Spain, and Portugal. See Gare Montparnasse for TGV service to southwestern France. To Barcelona (3 per day, 11-14hr., 485F) and Madrid (5 per day, 12-16hr., 578F).

Gare St-Lazare: To Normandy. To: Caen (10 per day, 2 1/2hr., 150F).

Gare Montparnasse: To Brittany, and the TGV to southwestern France. To: Rennes (15 per day, 2-2 1/2hr., 199F plus 32-80F TGV reservation).

Most buses to Paris arrive at **Gare Routière Internationale,** 3, av. Porte de la Villette, 19*ème* (tel. 40 38 93 93; Mo. Porte de la Villette). Some buses, however, have more bizarre ports of call. The **City Sprint** bus (tel. 42 85 44 55), operating in conjunction with Hoverspeed from England, drops its passengers in front of the Hoverspeed offices, three blocks from Gare du Nord at 135, rue Lafayette (Mo. Gare du Nord). For information about buses to other European countries, call **International Express Eurolines Coach Station** at 40 38 93 93.

By Thumb

Competition for rides is fierce. If you treasure your safety and sanity more than money, you'll take a train or bus out of Paris. Hitchhikers don't wait at a *porte* (city exit); traffic is too heavy for cars to stop safely.

Toward the east: Metz, Strasbourg, Munich. The *Autoroute de l'est* A4 is accessible from the metro to Porte de Charenton after a walk along bd. Massena. This is reportedly the worst highway on which to hitch.

Toward the north: Lille, Brussels, Cologne, Hamburg, Berlin, Scandinavia. Mo. Porte de la Chapelle is next to the *Autoroute du nord* A1.

Toward the west: Rouen, Caen, Cherbourg, Mont St-Michel, St-Malo. Hitchhikers take the metro to Porte de St-Cloud and walk up bd. Murat toward pl. de la Porte d'Auteuil, where *Autoroute de Normandie* A13 begins.

Toward the south: A number of *autoroutes* are accessible from Mo. Porte d'Orléans. **Southeast** A6: Lyon, Marseille, Cannes, Nice, Monaco, Switzerland, Italy, Barcelona. **Southwest** A10: Orléans, Bordeaux, Madrid, Galicia, Portugal. A11 branches off A10 toward Brittany: Chartres, Le Mans, Rennes.

A sign clearly stating the destination, ornamented by the letters "S.V.P." *(s'il vous plaît)* helps ingratiate hitchhikers. Hitchers also sometimes ask customers at gas stations or truck stops if they are going their way.

Ride Sharing

For a more formal "hitch," many try **Allostop-Provoya,** 84, passage Brady, 10*ème* (tel. 42 46 00 66; Mo. Strasbourg-St-Denis). They will try to match you with a driver going your way. The cost is 67F per ride and, for rides longer than 500km, 18 *centimes* per km given to the driver. (Round-trip 134F. 8 trips over 2 years 220F.) Also available from Allostop is **Eurostop International** membership, valid in 76 cities in Switzerland, Germany, Spain, France, Hungary, Italy, Holland, Belgium, and Canada, which entitles you to a 25% reduction on ride-sharing services. If your home country is one of the nine listed above, you must purchase your card there. At Allostop-Provoya, you can also buy train and bus tickets to points throughout Europe. They sell BIJ/Eurotrain tickets and, via a bus company, arrange special weekend tours in Europe. (Open Mon.-Fri. 9am-7:30pm, Sat. 9am-1pm and 2-6pm.)

Getting Around

Orientation

Coursing from east to west through the very heart of modern Paris, the Seine River played midwife to the city's birth on an island—the Ile de la Cité—some 2300 years ago. The Ile de la Cité and neighboring Ile St-Louis remain near the geographical and sentimental center of the city, while the Seine splits Paris into two large expanses—the renowned Left Bank (to its south) and the Right Bank (to its north). But since Haussmann's reconstruction of Paris in the mid-19th century, the city has been further divided into 20 *arrondissements* (districts), which spiral clockwise from the Louvre (1*er*) to the Porte de Vincennes (20*ème*). Originally much like independent villages, the *arrondissements* retain some of their erstwhile atmosphere. The first four *arrondissements* comprise most of what is thought of as central Paris. Across the Seine, the 5th and 6th, making up the well-known Latin Quarter, provide an interesting mix of both collegiate bohemia and seasoned glamour. The wealthiest Parisians live in the 7th, 8th, and 16th. Wander through for a glimpse of unabashed luxury. The 18th cradles Montmartre, the highest point in Paris and a one-time artists' haven. Many of the other outer *arrondissements*—especially the 19th and 20th—are largely low income residences, populated in large part by immigrants from Northern and Western Africa. The 15th, 14th, and 11th on the Left Bank are somewhat tamer residential corners of Paris. Such citified compactness renders walking tours a breeze—a stroll from the Arc de Triomphe to pl. de la Bastille, for example, passes most major monuments and takes about two hours. Paris **addresses** usually include the number and street, *arrondissement,* and nearest metro stop. The **postal code** of Paris addresses is formed by affixing the two-digit *arrondissement* number to 750. Thus, the postal code of an address in the 8*ème* (eighth) is 75008.

Maps

A map of Paris is essential if you plan to do any serious strolling. By far the best guide to Paris is a *Plan de Paris par Arrondissements,* which includes a detailed map of each *arrondissement,* all the bus lines, a wealth of miscellany, and an essential index of streets and their nearest metro stops. Editions Coutarel offers the most basic, red-covered *plan* at 30F. Others run as high as 150F, but unless you plan to drive in Paris, don't pay more than 50F. All such *plans,* marketed by several different companies, are found at most bookstores, *papeteries* (stationery stores), and kiosks. Unfortunately, the metro map in these guides is often out of date. Make sure to pick up a free updated one in any metro station: it also includes bus lines and the RER suburban system. McDonald's distributes decent maps with seven suggested walking tours of various quarters. Most importantly, the map indicates the location of every McDonald's in the city.

Métro

Inaugurated in 1888, the Paris Métropolitaine (metro) is one of Europe's oldest and most efficient subway systems, able to whisk you within walking distance of nearly any spot in the city. All trains run frequently, and connections *(correspondances)* are easy. A disabled metro train is a rare sight. The first trains start running at 5am; the last leave the end-of-the-line stations (the *"portes de Paris,"* i.e., Porte d'Orléans, Porte de Clignancourt, etc.) for the center of the city near 12:15am. One exception is the last train leaving from Porte de Balard, which does not travel the length of the line to Porte de Charenton but goes only as far as République. In the other direction, however, the train runs the whole route from Porte de Charenton to Porte de Balard. For the exact departure times of the last trains from the *portes,* check the poster in the center of each station called *"Principes de Tarification"* (Rate Guidelines).

Free metro maps are available in most stations, display maps are posted in all stations, and all have a *plan du quartier*—a detailed map of the surrounding neighborhood. Connections to other lines are indicated by orange *"correspondance"* signs, and the exits by blue *"sortie"* signs. All metro lines are numbered, but referred to by their final destination. Transfers to other lines are free if made in the same station, but it is not always possible to reverse direction on the same line without exiting the station and using another ticket.

The entire subway and bus system is under the direction of **RATP (Régie Autonome des Transports Parisiens).** In addition to the metro, RATP also runs the **RER** (Réseau Express Régional), the local suburban train system, which passes through central Paris. Within the city, the RER travels much faster than the metro. For information on the services of RATP, contact their main office at 53ter, quai des Grands-Augustins, 6*ème* (tel. 43 46 14 14; Mo. St-Michel; open daily 6am-9pm). You can also stop by the **Bureau de Tourisme RATP,** pl. de la Madeleine, 8*ème* (tel. 43 46 14 14; Mo. Madeleine; open Mon.-Sat. 7:30am-7pm, Sun. and holidays 6:30am-6pm). An English-speaking representative is usually available at both offices. RATP can also be reached round the clock through Minitel: 3615 RATP. (See Communications, below.)

Most train lines are well-traveled at night, and Parisian women often travel alone, though their familiarity lends them a confidence you may lack. Although violent crime on the metro is relatively uncommon, use common sense. Avoid empty cars. At night, many people choose to ride in the first car, where the conductor is only a door away. Stay away from the most dangerous stations (Barbès-Rochechouart, Pigalle, Châtelet, Trocadéro, and Anvers). Despite the excellent neighborhoods in which some of these stops are located, they are often frequented by thieves and other troublemakers looking to prey on the tourist or the wealthy. Be careful in the long, empty corridors of larger stations.

All metro lines are inaccessible to those in **wheelchairs,** and only the stations "Gare de Lyon" and "Chatelet-Les Halles" have access points for people in wheelchairs, and these only for the RER trains. People who are blind or deaf can get a metro staff person

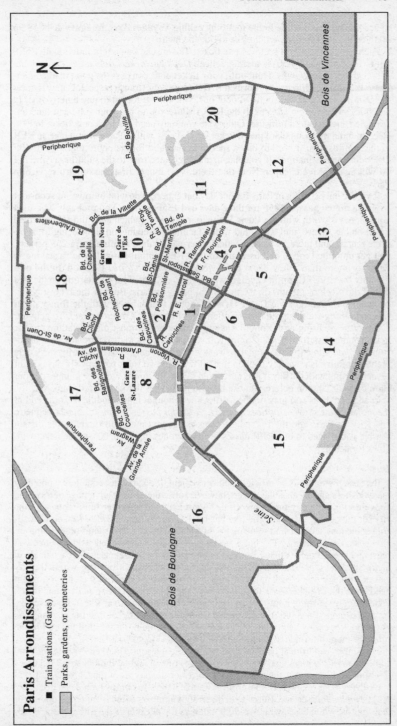

Paris Arrondissements

- ■ Train stations (Gares)
- ▨ Parks, gardens, or cemeteries

to accompany them while in the metro by calling **Voyages Accompagnés** at 49 59 96 00 three days before they would like to ride the metro.

Each trip on the metro requires one ticket. Tickets can be bought individually (6F), but a *carnet* of 10 (36F50) is more practical. *Don't buy tickets from anyone except the people in the ticket booths.* **Hold onto your ticket** until you pass the point marked *Limite de Validité des Billets;* a uniformed RATP *contrôleur* (transit inspector) may request to see it on any train. If caught without one, you will be forced to pay a hefty fine. In addition, any *correspondances* to the RER require you to put your validated (and uncrumpled) ticket into a turnstile. Otherwise you may need to buy a new ticket to exit. Keep in mind that a standard metro ticket is valid only within Paris. If you take an RER to the suburbs, you'll need to buy a special ticket valid for the entire journey (10-40F depending on destination). If you plan to make repeated trips to the suburbs, a *carnet* of 10 will again prove cheaper. Note that there is no longer first-class metro service in Paris.

If you're only staying in Paris for one day but expect to do a lot of traveling, consider buying a **metro pass.** At 85F for three days and 135F for five, you probably won't get your money's worth with the **Paris Visite** tourist tickets, which are valid for unlimited travel on bus, metro, and RER, and which facilitate discounts on sightseeing trips, bicycle rentals, and more. A more practical saver-pass is the **Formule 1;** for 25F per day, you get unlimited travel on buses, metro, and RER within Paris. If you're staying in Paris for more than a few days, get a weekly *(hebdomadaire)* **Coupon Jaune** or a monthly *(mensuel)* **Coupon Orange,** which allow unlimited travel (starting on the first day of the week or month) on the metro and buses in Paris. Both of these must be accompanied by the ID-style **Carte Orange** (not to be confused with the flimsy paper *Coupon Orange,* although Parisians often refer to both as *Carte Orange).* To get your *Carte Orange,* bring an ID photo (taken by machines in most major stations) to the ticket counter, ask for a *Carte Orange* with a plastic case, and then purchase your handsome *coupon jaune* (57F) or equally swanky *coupon orange* (201F). Finally, the **Carte Hebdomadaire** is a weekly coupon that allows you two rides per day, six days out of seven, starting with the day it was purchased (37F). Be sure to write the number of your carte on your coupon before you use it. Also remember that these cards have specific start and end dates and may not be worthwhile if bought in the middle or at the end of the month or the week. *All prices quoted here are for passes in zones 1 and 2* (the metro and RER in Paris and the immediate suburbs). If you intend to travel to the distant 'burbs, you'll need to buy RER passes for more zones (up to 5). Ask at the ticket windows for details.

Bus

Because the metro is so efficient and convenient, the Paris bus system is ignored by many visitors and locals alike. Buses, however, offer the distinct advantage of traveling above ground, thereby providing prime sightseeing and a greater familiarity with the city for the cost of one ride. The free bus map *Autobus Paris-Plan du Réseau* is available at the tourist office and some metro information booths. The routes of each line are also posted at each stop. The buses no longer take the same tickets as the metro; you must buy special tickets that cost exactly the same as metro tickets and are available in metro stations, *tabacs,* and from the bus drivers themselves. Most trips within the city and nearest suburbs cost 1 ticket; if your journey takes you out of the city you might need more than 1 ticket—ask the driver. Enter the bus through the front door and punch your ticket by pushing it into the cancelling machine by the driver's seat. If you have a *coupon orange,* flash it at the driver, but **do not** insert the ticket into the machine. As on the metro, *contrôleurs* may ask to see your ticket; hold onto it until the end of the ride. For more information, call the RATP office (tel. 43 46 14 14).

Most buses run from about 7am to 8:30pm, although some (marked *Autobus du Soir)* continue until 12:30am, and others *(Noctambus)* run all night. Night buses (3 tickets, 4 if you use 2 buses) start their runs to the *portes* of the city from the Châtelet stop and leave every hour on the half hour from 1:30 to 5:30am. **Bus maps** include an inset map of the *Noctambus* service. Buses with three-digit numbers come from or are bound for the suburbs, while buses with two-digit numbers travel exclusively within Paris. Buses with numbers in the 20s come from or are bound for Gare St-Lazare, in the 30s Gare de l'Est, in the 40s Gare du Nord, in the 70s Châtelet/Hôtel de Ville (with exceptions), in the 80s Luxembourg (with exceptions), and in the 90s Gare Montparnasse.

For more detailed diagrams of all bus routes, consult the *Plan de Paris par Arrondissements* (see Maps, above). The pamphlet printed by the RATP, *Paris Bus Métro RER,* lists several bus routes that pass through interesting neighborhoods and by the main sights of Paris (available at metro stops). It also lists directions to major museums, churches, and monuments. Some routes pass by enough sights to make them mini-tours in themselves. Buses worth riding from start to finish include:

Bus #20: From Gare St-Lazare to the Opéra, Montmartre-Poissonière, République, Bastille (50min.). A trip down the *grands boulevards.* Open platform in back.

Bus #21: From Gare St-Lazare to the Opéra, Palais Royal, the Louvre, the Pont Neuf, St-Michel, Gare du Luxembourg, Porte de Gentilly (40min.).

Bus #52: From Opéra to Concorde, Charles-de-Gaulle-Etoile, Auteuil, Pont de St-Cloud (50min.).

Bus #67: From Pigalle to Carrefour de Châteaudun, Louvre, Châtelet, Hôtel-de-Ville, Jussieu, pl. d'Italie, Porte de Gentilly (45min.).

Bus #82: From Gare du Luxembourg to Gare Montparnasse, Ecole-Militaire, Champs-de-Mars, Tour Eiffel, Porte Maillot, Neuilly (45min.).

Bus #83: From pl. d'Italie, along bd. Raspail, Gare des Invalides, pl. des Ternes (50min.). A glimpse of some of Paris's finest real estate and great views of the quais. Open platform in back.

Bus #95: From Tour Montparnasse past St-Germain-des-Prés, the Louvre, Palais Royal, the Opéra, and to Montmartre, near Sacré-Coeur (50min.).

Bus #96: From Montparnasse past St-Michel, the Palais de Justice on the Ile de la Cité, Châtelet, Hôtel-de-Ville, Oberkampf, Ménilmontant, Porte des Lilas (50min.).

Taxi

Taxi trips within Paris are not compatible with budget travel. Rates vary according to time of day and geographical area, but they're never cheap. Tarif A, the basic rate, is in effect in Paris proper from 7am to 7pm (2F62 per km). Tarif B is in effect Mon.-Sat. 7pm to 7am, Sundays, and during the day from the airports (4F08 per km). Tarif C, the highest, is in effect from the airports from 7pm to 7am (5F48 per km). In addition, there is a base fee (*prix en charge*) of 11F, and stationary time (such as at traffic lights and traffic jams) costs 108F per hour. All taxis have lights on top indicating the rate being charged, so you can check to see that the driver is playing it straight. Make sure the meter is on when you start the ride. A 15% tip is customary (round up to the nearest 5F). If you must take a taxi, try picking one up at a train station or waiting at a stand (*arrêt taxis, tête de station*), usually found near bus stops. Calling a radio-cab (**AR-TAXI,** tel. 42 41 50 50, **Taxis Radio Etoile** tel. 42 70 41 41, or **Taxis G7** tel. 47 39 47 39) is far more expensive, since you must pay for the distance the cab drives to pick you up. Technically, taxis cannot refuse to take a fare if their roof light is on, but can refuse to take more than three people. Illegal overcrowding of cabs can bring heavy fines upon the driver. If you have a **complaint,** write to Service des Taxis de la Préfecture de Police, 36, rue des Morillons, 75015 (tel. 45 31 14 80). If you expect to file a complaint, ask the driver for a receipt.

Bicycle

With its narrow, congested streets overrun by ill-tempered drivers, the center of Paris is not the place for a leisurely afternoon pedal. A few intrepid souls, tourists and locals, still venture out into the city *en vélo*. The parks, especially the Bois de Boulogne and the Bois de Vincennes, are well-suited to two-wheeled exploration. The metro cannot accommodate bikes, but local trains list specific times when they allow bicycles on board for free. **Mountain Bike Trips** (tel. 48 42 57 87) runs popular bike tours in English through Paris for 118F. The daily tours leave from 6, pl. Etienne Pernet, 15*ème* (Mo. Félix Faure). Ask for information at Y&H Youth Hostel or the Three Ducks Hostel. **Paris-Vélo,** 2, rue de Fer-à-Moulin, 5*ème* (tel. 43 37 59 22; Mo. Censier) rents bikes for 90-140F per day (depending on the model) or 1000-2000F per week, with a 1000F deposit (including accident insurance). Try to book in advance and ask for any accessories you'll need. (Open Mon.-Sat. 10am-12:30pm and 2-7pm.) The **Bicyclub de France,** 8, pl. de la Porte-Champerret, 17*ème* (tel. 47 66 55 92; Mo. Porte de Champerret), also rents bikes at similar rates. (From 17F per hr., 400F for the first week, 200F for each subsequent week. Deposit includes insurance that covers you but not the bike. Open daily 9am-7pm; Sept.-June Mon.-Fri. 9am-7pm, Sat. 9am-1pm and 2-7pm.)

Mopeds and motorcycles are no longer leased in the city, but you can rent a scooter from **Mondial Scooter,** 20bis, av. Charles de Gaulle (tel. 46 24 63 64; Mo. Porte Maillot) in Neuilly-sur-Seine from 145F per day or 800F per week, with a 2500F deposit.

Car

Paris is, at best, difficult to drive in. Parisian drivers are notorious for their *"système D"*—D for *débrouiller* (doing whatever works), which includes driving on the sidewalk in traffic jams, ignoring any lane markings that might exist, and passing in small streets at high speeds. *Priorité à droite* gives the right of way to the car approaching from the right, regardless of the size of the streets, and Parisian drivers make it an affair of honor to take this right even in the face of grave danger. Drivers are not allowed to honk their horns within city limits unless they are about to hit a pedestrian, but you will see how often this rule is broken. The legal way to show discontent is to flash the headlights, for which you should be on the lookout in case a law-abiding driver refrains from honking until just before impact. If you do not have a map of Paris with the one-way streets marked, the city will be almost impossible to navigate. Street parking is hard to locate (although Parisians do park on sidewalks, corners, etc.), and garages are expensive.

Possibly the best excuse for renting a car in Paris is to escape from the city into the provinces. Renting a car for a group of three or four may be even cheaper than buying train tickets. Foreigners need a passport, a license of at least two years, and a credit card to rent in Paris; an international license is not required. None of the agencies in Paris will rent to drivers under 21. The best deal in town is at **ACAR,** 77, rue de Lagny, 20*ème* (tel. 43 79 54 54; Mo. Porte de Vincennes). A two-door SEAT Mirabella costs 218F per day, first 100km free plus 1F15 per additional km; insurance costs 35F. A weekend with 1000km and insurance included is 710F. A week with unlimited mileage and insurance included is 1820F. (Open Mon.-Fri. 8am-12:30pm and 2-7pm, Sat. 8am-12:30pm and 2-6pm.) **Inter Touring Service,** 117, bd. Auguste Blanqui, 13*ème* (tel. 45 88 52 37; Mo. Glacière), rents Renault 4s for 145F per day plus 1F50 per km, insurance included, or 1820F per week, distance and insurance included. (Open Mon.-Sat. 8:30am-6:30pm.) **Autorent,** 98, rue de la Convention, 15*ème* (tel. 45 54 22 45; Mo. Boucicaut), and 3-5, av. Jean Moulin, 14*ème* (tel. 49 92 55 06; Mo. Alésia), rents Fiat Pandas for 199F per day plus 2F40 per km.

Tourist Offices

Though packed in the summer, the following offices are usually able to keep the wait down to an hour at most. Lines are worse in the afternoon. They all stock the requisite reams of brochures, maps, and pamphlets, as well as information on special seasonal events. Tourist offices will help you find a room in a one-star hotel for 15F, two-star for 20F, three-star for 35F, and hostels for 5F. They will also help you reserve rooms in other parts of the country, though no more than seven days in advance, for a 23F minimum charge. All the offices exchange money at decent rates with no commission; they are a sensible option when banks are closed.

Bureau d'Accueil Central: 127, av. des Champs-Elysées, 8*ème* (tel. 47 23 61 72). Mo. Charles-de-Gaulle-Etoile. Helpful English-speaking staff. Mobbed in summer but remarkably efficient. Open daily 9am-8pm. There are 5 smaller *Bureaux d'Accueil,* also operated by the *office de tourisme,* located in the following train stations and at the Eiffel Tower: **Bureau Gare du Nord,** 10*ème* (tel. 45 26 94 82). Mo. Gare du Nord. Open Mon.-Sat. 8am-10pm, Sun. 1-8pm; Nov.-Easter daily 8am-8pm. **Bureau Gare de L'Est,** 10*ème* (tel. 46 07 17 73). Mo. Gare de l'Est. Open Mon.-Sat. 8am-10pm; Nov.-April Mon.-Sat. 8am-1pm and 5-8pm. **Bureau Gare de Lyon,** 12*ème* (tel. 43 43 33 24). Mo. Gare de Lyon. Open Mon.-Sat. 8am-10pm; Nov.-April Mon.-Sat. 8am-1pm and 5-8pm. **Bureau Gare d'Austerlitz,** 13*ème* (tel. 45 84 91 70). Mo. Gare d'Austerlitz. Open Mon.-Sat. 8am-10pm; Nov.-April Mon.-Sat. 8am-3pm. **Bureau Tour Eiffel,** Champs de Mars, 7*ème* (tel. 45 51 22 15). Mo. Champs de Mars. Open May-Sept. daily 11am-6pm.

In addition, both international airports run tourist offices where you can make same-day hotel reservations (with deposit equal to 12% of room rate) and receive information about Paris.

Orly, Sud: Near gate H; **Orly, Ouest:** Near gate F (tel. 48 84 32 63). Both open daily 6am-11:45pm.

Roissy-Charles de Gaulle: Near gate 36 arrival level (tel. 48 62 22 81). Open daily 7am-11:30pm.

Also try the following:

Maison de la France: 8, av. de l'Opéra, 1*er* (tel. 42 96 10 23). Mo. Palais-Royal. A friendly and well-staffed agency that provides tourist information on all of France. If you're planning to tour the rest of the country, come here to get maps and sightseeing brochures; this information will save you countless trips to tourist offices in other cities. Prices for hotels and campgrounds but no reservations. Also free tourist literature and information by mail. Open Mon.-Fri. 9am-7pm.

Tourist Information: tel. 47 20 88 98. A tape-recorded message in English gives the major events in Paris. Updated weekly. Call 47 20 94 94 for French and 47 20 57 88 for German.

Budget Travel

Accueil des Jeunes en France (AJF): 119, rue St-Martin, 4*ème* (tel. 42 77 87 80; Mo. Rambuteau), across from the pedestrian mall in front of the Pompidou Center. Open Mon.-Sat. 9am-6pm. Also 16, rue du Pont Louis-Philippe, 4*ème* (tel. 42 78 04 82; Mo. Hôtel-de-Ville or Pont-Marie), near the Hôtel de Ville. Open Mon.-Fri. 9:30am-6:30pm. Also 139, bd. St-Michel, 5*ème* (tel. 43 54 95 86; Mo. Port-Royal), in the Latin Quarter. Open March-Oct. Mon.-Fri. 9am-6pm. Another in Gare du Nord arrival hall next to Agence de Voyages SNCF (tel. 42 85 86 19). Open June-Sept. daily 8am-10pm; Oct. and March-May Mon.-Fri. 9:30am-6:30pm. The Gare du Nord office only books accommodations. The other offices will give you free maps, sell ISIC cards (45F), and make room reservations in *foyers* in Paris, London, or Spain (72-85F per night). Reduced-price student train and bus tickets, budget weekend holidays in Europe, and meal vouchers for Paris youth hostels. The office across from the Pompidou Center can be used as a mailing address but is so ridiculously crowded that it pays to try one of the other branches—all friendly, centrally-located, English-speaking, and, well, crowded.

Office de Tourisme Universitaire (OTU): 39, av. G. Bernanos, 5*ème* (tel. 43 36 80 27). Mo. Port-Royal. A French student travel agency. Crowded and English-speaking. The same reduced train and plane tickets for students under age 26 that are sold at any travel agent in Paris, but more crowded. Bring an official form of ID. Also sells ISIC (45F), HI card (70F), Carte Jeune (70F), and BIJ tickets. Open Mon. 11am-6:45pm, Tues.-Fri. 10am-6:45pm. **CROUS** next door (tel. 40 51 36 00) has information on student housing, employment, university restaurants, transubstantiation, and health care.

Council Travel: 51, rue Dauphine, 6*ème* (tel. 43 26 79 65). Mo. Odéon. Also at 16, rue de Vaugirard (tel. 46 34 02 90; Mo. Odéon) and at 31, rue St-Augustin, 2*ème* (tel. 42 66 20 87; Mo. Opéra). English-speaking travel service for young people. Books international flights. Sells student train tickets, guidebooks, and ISIC cards (45F). BIJ/Eurotrain tickets. If you have lost your CIEE charter flight ticket, go to the Opéra office and they will telex the U.S. to authorize a substitute, for which you will pay a penalty depending on your flight. All open Mon.-Fri. 11am-1pm and 2-6:45pm, Sat. 11am-1pm and 2:30-5pm.

Council on International Educational Exchange (CIEE) and Centre Franco-Américain Odéon: 1, pl. de l'Odéon, 6*ème* (tel. 46 34 16 10). Mo. Odéon. CIEE's Paris office. See Travel Services under Useful Organizations in the General Introduction for information on CIEE'S services. Open Mon. and Thurs.- Fri. 2-6pm, Tues. 9:30am-12:30pm.

Embassies and Consulates

U.S.: 2, av. Gabriel, 8*ème* (tel. 42 96 12 02 or 42 61 80 75; Mo. Concorde), off pl. de la Concorde. **Consulate** at 2, rue St-Florentin (tel. 42 96 12 02, ext. 2613), 3 blocks away. Passports replaced for US$42 (under 18 US$27), or the equivalent in francs. Open Mon.-Fri. 9am-4pm. Closed for both American and French holidays.

Canada: 35, av. Montaigne, 8*ème* (tel. 47 23 01 01). Mo. Franklin-Roosevelt or Alma-Marceau. **Consulate** at 16, rue d'Anjou (same phone), around the corner from the embassy. New passport CDN$25, or the equivalent in francs. Open Mon.-Fri. 9-11:30am and 2-4pm.

U.K.: 35, rue du Faubourg-St-Honoré, 8*ème* (tel. 42 66 91 42). Mo. Concorde or Madeleine. New passport 158F (must be paid in francs). **Consulate** at 16, rue d'Anjou, around the corner. Visa bureau open Mon.-Fri. 9am-noon.

Australia: Embassy at 4, rue Jean-Rey, 15*ème* (tel. 40 59 33 00). Mo. Bir-Hakeim. New passport 400F. Open Mon.-Thurs. (Fri. in an emergency) 9:15am-noon and 2-5pm.

New Zealand: Embassy at 7ter, rue Léonard-de-Vinci, 16*ème* (tel. 45 00 24 11). Mo. Victor-Hugo. New passport 400F (must be paid in francs). Open Mon.-Fri. 9am-1pm and 2:30-6pm.

Ireland: 12, av. Foch, 16*ème* (tel. 45 00 20 87). Mo. Dauphine. Not a consulate, but in an emergency call this number for instructions.

Money

When looking to change money in Paris, try to approach the event with the spirit of competition. Not every change bureau offers the same rates and most do not charge commission. Don't be fooled by what seems like fantastic rates. Make sure that no strings (like having to sell your soul or exchange at least 15,000F worth of currency) apply. The best rates in town are unquestionably found around the Opéra on rue de Scribe (close to American Express), rue Auber, and rue de la Paix. The American Express office and currency exchanges on the Champs Elysées are almost always crowded, especially on summer afternoons. Many post offices will change cash and American Express traveler's checks at competitive rates and without commission; bureaus at train stations and airports tend to offer less favorable rates. Most banks are open 9am-noon and 2-4:30pm, but not all exchange currency. Check before you get in ' line. For more general information, consult the Money section of the General Introduction.

American Express: 11, rue Scribe, 9*ème* (tel. 47 77 77 07). Mo. Opéra or Auber. Across from the back of the Opéra. No commission on AmEx traveler's checks, 5F20 commission on all other transactions. Mediocre exchange rates. Cardholders can cash a personal check from a US bank account; bring your passport. Mobbed during the summer, especially Mon. and Fri.-Sat. They will hold mail for you free if you have their card or traveler's checks; otherwise 5F per inquiry. Open Mon.-Sat. 9am-5pm.

Change Automatique, 66, av. des Champs-Elysées, 8*ème*. Mo. George V. An automatic machine that accepts 5, 10, or 20 dollar bills and 50 or 100 German mark, 50 or 100 Swiss franc, and 50,000 or 100,000 Italian lire notes. Rates and commission posted above "insert bill" slot. Not the best rates in town. Open 24 hrs.

At Train Stations: Remember these offices offer less than attractive rates intended for impatient travelers. **Gare d'Austerlitz,** 13*ème* (tel. 45 84 91 40). Open daily 7am-9pm. **Gare de Lyon,** 12*ème* (tel. 43 41 52 70). Open daily 7am-11pm. **Gare de l'Est,** 10*ème* (tel. 46 07 66 84). Open Mon.-Fri. 9am-6:30pm, Sat. 9:30am-5:30pm. **Gare du Nord,** 10*ème* (tel. 42 80 11 50). Open daily 6:15am-11:30pm. **Gare St-Lazare,** 8*ème* (tel. 43 87 72 51). Open daily 7am-9pm.

At Airports: Also not the best place to change your currency. Exchange just enough to get to Paris and change the rest within the city. **Orly-Sud:** open daily 6am-11:30pm. **Roissy-Charles de Gaulle:** open daily 6am-11:30pm.

Lost American Express Traveler's Checks: tel. (19) 05 90 86 00.

Lost American Express Cards: tel. 47 77 72 00.

Lost Visa Cards: tel. 42 77 11 90.

Communications

Post Office: 52, rue du Louvre, 75001 Paris, 1*er* (tel. 40 28 20 00). Mo. Châtelet-Les-Halles. Open 24 hrs. All **Poste Restante** mail is held at this office unless otherwise specified. Only urgent telegrams and calls. No bulk mailings or packages over 2kg outside of normal business hours. Complete telephone book collection. Long lines Sat. and Sun. Fax service on 3rd floor. For postal information, call 42 80 67 89. The only other **branch office** with extended hours is at 71, av. des Champs-Elysées, 8ème (tel. 43 59 55 18). Mo. George V. Open Mon.-Sat. 8am-10pm, Sun. 10-11am and 2-8pm. Many more branches throughout the city. Inquire at your hotel or hostel for the nearest one, or look for PTT signs. Generally open Mon.-Fri. 8am-7pm, Sat. 8am-noon. Lines longest noon-2pm.

Telephones: As soon as you arrive in Paris, buy a *télécarte,* available at ticket windows in all SNCF stations, metro stations, post offices, or at *tabacs.* Fifty-unit card 40F, 120-unit card 96F. Local calls cost 1 unit; long distance more. Few phones still accept coins, and the *télécarte* will save you from having to feed the phone frantically while you talk. Pick up the receiver, insert your card, close the shutter covering your card, wait for a dial tone, and dial. The digital display tells you how much credit you have left. Refer to the Keeping in Touch section of the General Introduction for details on placing international calls. To call from the Paris region to elsewhere in France, dial 16 + the number. To call the Paris area from elsewhere in France, dial 1 + the number.

Telegrams in English: tel. 45 33 44 11. Operators not fluent in English, but they get the job done. Telegrams to U.S., Canada, and the U.K. 76F70 for 1st 15 words; 25F each additional 5 words. To Australia and New Zealand 81F for 1st 15 words; 21F each additional 5 words. Same price whether sent from post office or telephone, but must have address in Paris to send by phone. Telegrams within France can be sent by Minitel 3656 (see below); same rates as to U.S., Canada, and U.K. The United States, Australia, and the U. K. no longer deliver telegrams: if you send a telegram to one of these countries, the French will call the nearest post office immediately, but from there, it will be delivered by standard mail. It's cheaper and quicker to just use the telephone.

Minitel: This service is not essential if you are only passing through Paris. It is, however, fun to play with this computer system that not only provides telephone numbers, addresses, and professions of French telephone subscribers, but also offers newspapers on screen (including the *International Herald Tribune),* shopping, phone sex, the weather, and train schedules. There are several coin-operated Minitels (2F per min.) for public use at the Bibliothèque Publique Information at the Centre Pompidou. Directory information in English: 3614 ED.

Emergency, Health, and Help

Police Emergency: tel. 17.

Police: Each *arrondissement* of Paris has its own *gendarmerie* and it is to them that you should take all your non-emergency concerns. Call the operator (tel. 12) and ask where your local branch is.

Fire: tel. 18.

Emergency Medical Assistance: Ambulance (SAMU): tel. 15. For house calls, call 45 67 50 50 at any time.

Hospitals: Hospitals in Paris are numerous and efficient. They will generally treat you whether or not you can pay in advance. Settle with them afterward and don't let your financial concerns interfere with your health care. Unless your French is really great, you'll have best luck at one of the anglophone hospitals. **Hôpital Américain de Paris:** 63, bd. Victor Hugo, Neuilly (tel. 46 41 25 25). Mo. Sablons or bus #82. In a suburb of Paris. Employs English-speaking personnel, but much more expensive than French hospitals. You can pay in U.S. dollars. If you have Blue Cross-Blue Shield, your hospitalization is covered as long as you fill out the appropriate forms first. They can also direct you to the nearest English-speaking doctor and provide dental services. **Hôpital Franco-Britannique de Paris:** 48, rue de Villiers, Levallois-Perret (tel. 47 58 13 12). Mo. Anatole-France. Considered a French hospital and bills like one. Has some English-speakers and a good reputation.

Poison Control: tel. 40 37 04 04.

All-Night Pharmacies: Les Champs Elysées, in the Galerie des Champs, 84, av. des Champs-Elysées, 8ème (tel. 45 62 02 41). Mo. George V. Open 24 hrs. **Drugstore St-Germain,** 149, bd. St-Germain, 6ème (tel. 42 22 80 00). Mo. St-Germain-des-Prés or Mabillon. Open daily 9am-2am. Also, every *arrondissement* should have a *pharmacie de garde,* which, if not open 24 hrs., will open in case of emergencies. The locations change, but your local pharmacy can provide the name of the nearest one.

Alcoholics Anonymous: 3, rue Frédéric Sauton, 5ème (tel. 46 34 59 65). Mo. Maubert-Mutualité. A recorded message in English will refer you to several numbers you can call for help. Daily meetings. Open 24hrs.

Birth Control: Mouvement Français pour le Planning Familial, 10, rue Vivienne, 2*ème* (tel. 42 60 83 20). Mo. Bourse. Open Tues. and Thurs. noon-3pm.

Emotional Health: Services and aid for the needy in Paris are provided by a number of organizations. Try calling **SOS Crisis Help Line: Friendship,** tel. 47 23 80 80. English-speaking. Support and information for the depressed and lonely. Open daily 3-11pm. For more personalized counseling (for anything from pregnancy to homesickness), go to the services based at the **American Church,** 65, quai d'Orsay, 7*ème* (Mo. Invalides or Alma-Marceau): the **International Counseling Service (ICS)** and the **American Student and Family Service (ASFS).** These 2 groups share the same staff and provide access to psychologists, psychiatrists, social workers, and a clerical counselor. Payment is usually 250-300F per session, but if you are truly in need, the fee is negotiable. The ICS keeps hours in the morning (Mon.-Sat. 9am-1pm), the ASFS in the afternoon (Mon.-Fri. 2-7pm). The office is staffed irregularly July-Aug. but will respond if you leave a message on their answering machine. Call for an appointment (tel. 45 50 26 49 for both) at the American Church.

Gay and Lesbian Services: Paris is not a haven for gays and lesbians. Homosexuality is tolerated but still draws attention and sometimes harassment. See the section on Gay and Lesbian travelers in the Travelers with Specific Needs section of the General Introduction for useful publications and hotlines.

Rape Crisis: SOS Viol, tel. 05 05 95 95. Call from anywhere in France for counseling, medical and legal advice, and referrals. Open Mon.-Fri. 10am-6pm.

STD Clinic: 43, rue de Valois, 1*er* (tel 42 61 30 04). Mo. Palais Royal. Testing and treatment for sexually transmitted diseases. Free consultations, blood tests, and injection treatments. Syphilis tests free. Plasma and chlamydia tests usually around 175F each. AIDS tests are generally 145F. Tests are not given anonymously, but the clinic does not require ID to establish that the name you give is genuine. If you need a doctor, it's best to call for an appointment (also free). English spoken. Open Mon.-Thurs. 9am-7pm, and Fri. 9am-6pm.

HIV Testing: 218, rue de Belleville 20*ème* (tel. 47 97 40 49). Mo. Télégraphe. Free and anonymous. Open Mon.-Fri. 4-7:30pm, Sat. 9:30am-noon. Also at 3-5, rue de Ridder 14*ème* (tel 45 43 83 78). Mo. Plaisance. Open Mon.-Fri. noon-6pm; Sept.-July Mon.-Fri. noon-7:30pm, Sat. 9:30am-noon.

Drug Problems: Hôpital Marmottan, 17-19, rue d'Armaillé, 17*ème* (tel. 45 74 00 04). Mo. Argentine. You're not always guaranteed an English-speaker. For consultations or treatments, open Mon.-Sat. 9:30am-7pm; Aug. Mon.-Fri. only.

Other

Lost Property: Bureau des Objets Trouvés, 36, rue des Morillons, 15*ème* (tel. 45 31 14 80; Mo. Convention). You can visit or write to them describing the object and when and where it was lost. No information given by phone. Open Mon.-Fri. 8:30am-5pm; Sept.-June Mon., Wed., and Fri. 8:30am-5pm, Tues. and Thurs. 8:30am-8pm.

Bookstores: See Shopping below.

Public Libraries: Bibliothèque Publique Information, in the Centre Pompidou, 4*ème* (tel. 44 78 12 33). Mo. Rambuteau, Hôtel de Ville, or Châtelet-Les-Halles. Many books in English. Record and video listening room. Novels are arranged alphabetically by century on the 1st floor (entrance to the library on the 2nd floor), so you'll have to hunt for those in translation. Guide books and books about France and Paris abound. Books cannot be checked out. Open Mon.-Fri. noon-10pm, Sat.-Sun. 10am-10pm. If you just need a quiet place to read or write, the historic **Bibliothèque Mazarine,** 23, quai de Conti, 6*ème* (tel. 43 54 89 48; Mo. Pont-Neuf), provides handsome old volumes and perfect silence. If you plan to visit frequently, apply for a *carte d'entrée* (bring ID and 2 photos). Open Mon.-Fri. 10am-5:45pm. Closed Aug. 1-15. Free to the public.

Language Courses: Refer to the Study section of the General Introduction for a selection of language schools based in Paris.

Catholic Information Center: 6, pl. du Parvis Notre-Dame, 4*ème* (tel. 46 33 01 01). Information about religious activities, prayer, and pilgrimages. Open Mon.-Fri. 9am-noon and 2-6pm.

American Church in Paris: 65, quai d'Orsay, 7*ème* (tel. 47 05 07 99). Mo. Invalides or Alma-Marceau. As much a community center as a church. Bulletin boards with notices about jobs, rides, apartments, personals, etc, both in the lobby and downstairs. *Free Voice,* a free English-language monthly specializing in cultural events and classifieds, is published here; submit your ad with 60F by the 20th of the month before. Interdenominational services Sun. at 11am, followed by a 1/2-hr. coffee break and, during the school year, by a filling, friendly luncheon at 12:30pm (45F, students

30F). International counseling service. Come here for advice (tel. 45 50 26 49). Church open Mon.-Sat. 9am-10:30pm, Sun. 9am-8pm. Free student concerts Oct.-May Sun. at 6pm. Hosts meetings for AA, AL-ANON, ACOA and FAACTS (workshops for people affected by AIDS, ARC, or HIV positive status).

Synagogue: Union Libéral Israélite de France, 24, rue Copernic, 16ème (tel. 47 04 37 27). Mo. Victor-Hugo. The multilingual, ever-jovial M. Ogorek presides over a welcoming staff. Sixty-min. services Fri. at 6pm and 90-min. services Sat. at 10:30am, mostly in Hebrew with a little French. English-speaking rabbi stays after the service to chat. Call for information about the large High Holy Days celebrations and religious groups. Secretariat open Mon.-Fri. 9am-noon and 2-5pm.

Weather: Allo Météo, five-day recorded forecasts. Preferable to call from touch-tone phones. **Paris,** tel. 36 65 02 75; **Ile de France,** tel. 36 65 00 00; **France,** tel. 36 65 01 01; **mountain regions** (choice of northern Alps, southern Alps, Pyrénées, and Massifs), tel. 36 65 04 04; **marine conditions,** tel. 36 65 08 08. All in French. You can also check out a map of the day's predicted weather at the corner of Rapp and Université in the 7ème, posted by **Météorologie nationale.**

Laundromats: Ask your hotel or hostel for the location of the closest one. The average price is 28F per wash, detergent included, and 2F per 6min. dry. Most laundromats are open 8am-10pm; last wash 9pm.

Public Baths: 8, rue des Deux Ponts, 4ème (tel. 43 54 47 40). Mo. Pont-Marie. Shower 4F80, with soap and towel roughly 10F80. For the same price you can also rub-a-dub-dub at 42, rue du Rocher, 8ème (tel. 45 22 15 19; Mo. St-Lazare), and at 40, rue Oberkampf, 11ème (tel. 47 00 57 35; Mo. Oberkampf). They are clean, respectable, and quite popular in summer. All open Thurs. noon-7pm, Fri. 8am-7pm, Sat. 7am-7pm, Sun. 8am-noon.

Sports Hotline: ALLO SPORTS, tel. 42 76 54 54. The helpful operators on this line can tell you everything you've ever wanted to know but were afraid to ask about being active in Paris. Open Mon.-Thurs. 10:30am-5:30pm, Fri. 10:30am-4:30pm.

Swimming Pools: The mayor's office runs 26 well-kept municipal pools, many of which have adjoining gyms. Admission 9F80, under 16 and over 65 4F90. For more information, and a list of pool hours, pick up the brochure *Les Piscines à Paris,* free from the Hôtel de Ville or any *mairie,* which lists all the public pools and some private ones as well. **ALLO SPORTS** (see above) also has information.

Publications About Paris

On those heartbreaking and rare occasions when *Let's Go* falls just short, consult the following guides. *Alison Landes's Pariswalks,* (New Republic Book Company, 110F), leads you on four walks around the Latin Quarter and one around pl. des Vosges in the Marais, explaining odd street names and relating historical anecdotes all the while. Although the prose is perhaps too cute and the suggestions often ignore the privacy of the occupants of interesting houses, the paths are well-chosen and fun. *Gault Millau* is a well-respected guide to Parisian eateries. Patricia Wells's *The Food Lover's Guide to Paris* (US$13, about 100F in France) lists most of the city's greatest and most famous restaurants, cafés, bakeries, cheese shops, *charcuteries,* wine shops, etc. Gourmets may not share all of Wells's opinions (and budget travelers may not be able to verify them), but the guide is generally reliable. All of the above are available at **Gibert Jeune** and other Parisian bookstores.

Your most important printed resource will invariably be a map (see Maps above). The Office du Tourisme publishes a monthly booklet entitled *Paris Sélection* that highlights exhibitions, concerts, suggested walking tours, and other useful information (free). Similarly, the **Mairie de Paris** publishes the monthly *Paris le Journal* (10F) with articles and listings about what's on, touristically and culturally, around the city (available at the Mairie's salon d'acceuil, 29, rue de Rivoli; tel. 42 76 42 42, and at most *arrondissement mairies).* Some *arrondissements* (like the 16ème) publish their own magazines.

The weeklies (published every Wed.) *Pariscope* (3F), *Officiel des Spectacles* (2F), and *7 à Paris* (7F) list current movies, plays, exhibits, festivals, clubs, and bars. While *Pariscope* is the most comprehensive, the articles and reviews in *7 à Paris* reflect *branché* (literally, plugged in) Parisian tastes. The Wednesday edition of *Le Figaro* includes *Figaroscope,* a supplement about what's on in Paris. The *Free Voice,* a monthly newspaper published by the Cooperative for Better Living at the American Church, (65, quai d'Orsay, 7ème; Mo. Invalides), is available there for free and at many student centers. *France-USA Contacts* (FUSAC to those in the know), printed twice monthly and available free from English-speaking establishments (bookstores, restaurants, travel agencies) throughout Paris lists job, housing, and service information for English speakers. See the section on Gay and Lesbian travelers in the General Introduction for publications of special interest.

To look like a true Parisian on the metro, disappear behind a copy of *Le Monde* (7F), the city's most respected newspaper, decidedly centrist in outlook, albeit with a few socialist leanings. *Le Figaro* (6F) tends to fall more toward the conservative end of the spectrum and offers more diverse coverage than *Le Monde*. *La Libération* (6F) writes from the left. *France Soir's* (5F) sports coverage is good but the rest of its efforts tend toward the McPaper view of the world. *L'Equipe* (6F), the sports and automobile daily, offers coverage and stats on most sports you can think of and some that you cannot. Those homesick for the *Washington Post* and the *New York Times* can get the best of both in the *International Herald Tribune* (8F50).

Accommodations

There are three basic types of Parisian accommodations suitable to the budget traveler: hostels, *foyers,* and hotels. If you arrive in Paris in high season (Easter, May-June, and Sept.-Oct.) without a reservation, you will probably spend most of your first day looking for accommodations, ruin your initial impression of this glorious city, and end up settling for something mediocre either too far from the city center or priced beyond your daily budget. If life delivers you in Paris with this unfortunate fate, don't start madly calling random hotels (although those near the place de la Bastille and place de la République occasionally have space in summer), and try not to get frustrated by the insanely bureaucratic and confusing system that makes budget accommodations shopping such a bundle of joy. You can try to visit the establishment itself. Start with hostels, *foyers* and hotels that don't accept reservations. The earlier you show up anywhere—and the earlier you call—the better. Hostels and *foyers* tend to vacate early in the morning and hotel guests often check out mid-morning. You may, however, have more luck if you visit one of the accommodations booking centers associated with hostels and *foyers* (see Hostels and Foyers below). The **Office du Tourisme** on the Champs-Elysées or one of its other bureaus should be able to find you a room, although the lines may be long and its selections are not among the cheapest in Paris. Hotels usually accept Mastercard and Visa, sometimes American Express; hostels generally do not accept credit cards.

If you plan to stay in Paris for a longer period of time, consider renting an apartment. Call, fax, write, or visit **Allô Logement Temporaraire,** 4, pl. de la Chapelle, 18ème (tel. 42 09 00 07; fax 46 07 14 41; Mo. Chapelle). This helpful, English-speaking association charges a 100F commission for each month of rental if the rental exceeds 5000F. For less expensive apartments, the maximum commission is 600F. In addition, there is an annual membership fee of 250F. When you call or write, be sure to leave a phone or fax number where you can be reached easily. Vacancies come and go very quickly. (Open Tues.-Sat. noon-8pm.) To avoid commissions, try the bulletin boards in the **American Church** (see Practical Information). Or, look in any of the English-French newsletters like *Free Voice* or *France-USA Contacts,* also available at the American Church. Short-term rentals, usually more expensive per month than longer rentals, can be difficult to procure, especially in winter months. Make sure to sign a contract with your leaser detailing the finances of the transaction, such as the deposit, phone charges, utilities, etc.

Hostels and Foyers

There are only two hostels in Paris that require HI membership; they can sell you a one-night membership for 19F, but it is easier to buy full membership at home. To get a same-day room, call the HI hostel itself or else try calling **FUAJ (Fédération Unie des Auberges de Jeunesse) Centrale Sans Frontières,** 8, bd. Jules Ferry, 11*ème* (tel. 43 57 02 60; fax 40 21 79 92). It can also reserve you a room in a budget hotel with which it is affiliated. For room reservations in the hostels, the Centrale often caters only to groups.

The rest of the dorm-like accommodations in Paris are either non-HI hostels or *foyers*. *Foyers*, many of which are full-time dorm residences during the academic year, have their own characters, rules, and prices. Some cater to rowdy students of all genders, while others are quiet and just for women. Check for availability of rooms by calling ahead or arriving early in the morning. A better option may be to visit or call the **Accueil des Jeunes en France (AJF).** Its main office is at 119, rue St-Martin, 4*ème* (tel. 42 77 87 80; Mo. Rambuteau; open Mon.-Sat. 9:30am-6pm). Other offices are at 139, bd. St-Michel, 5*ème* (tel. 43 54 95 86; Mo. Port-Royal; open Tues.-Sat. 10am-12:30pm and 1:30-6:15pm); and Gare du Nord, 10*ème* (tel. 42 85 86 19; open June 1-Sept. 4 daily 7:30am-10pm). Even in the busiest months, the AJF guarantees you "decent and low-cost lodging with immediate reservation" for the same day only. You must pay the full price of the *foyer* room when you make your reservation, even before seeing the room. AJF can also help you find a hotel room. Often, however, it cannot find you a room for the full duration of your stay; you may have to use AJF more than once. Individuals must pay a fee of 10F per reservations.

All prices listed below are per person.

Auberge de Jeunesse "Jules-Ferry" (HI), 8, bd. Jules Ferry, 11*ème* (tel. 43 57 55 60). Mo. République. About 100 beds in this wonderfully located hostel. Clean, large rooms. Slightly crowded. Noisy party atmosphere, and jovial management. No groups accepted, but most spaces fill by 8am. Adequate kitchen facilities. 4-day max. stay. Reception open 6am-2am. 2- to 6-bed rooms 72F per person. Showers and breakfast included. Sheets 14F. To reserve, send an HI voucher well in advance. Also books rooms in hostels around France, runs sightseeing tours of Paris, and sponsors group excursions to cities around Europe. Call 43 57 02 60; fax 40 21 79 92 for information.

Auberge de Jeunesse "Le d'Artagnan" (HI), 80, rue Vitruve, 20*ème* (tel. 43 61 08 75; fax 43 61 75 40). Mo. Porte de Bagnolet. The epitome of a mega-hostel. Seven-floor college dorm-type complex with 420 beds. Rooms are designed for maximum space utilization, with luggage storage compartments under mattresses and showers hidden behind closet doors. Bar. Several microwaves. Friendly English-speaking staff. 3-day max. stay. Reception closes noon-2:30pm in summer. Rooms closed for cleaning 10am-2:30pm. 3- to 8-bed rooms 82F. Sheets 16F. Wash 15F, dry 5F. Lockers 5F. Good chance of finding a room since they limit groups to 150 beds. Call ahead. Reservations accepted only for groups; arrive early.

Maisons des Jeunes Rufz de l'Avison, 18, rue J.-J. Rousseau, 1*er* (tel. 45 08 02 10). Mo. Louvre or Palais Royal. From the Louvre metro stop (not to be confused with "Musée du Louvre"), take rue du Louvre away from the river, turn left onto rue St.-Honoré, and then turn right onto rue J.-J. Rousseau. During the academic year, this is a private residence hall for male university students, but in summer it is filled with tourists of both sexes. Some rooms may be open during the school year as well. Reserve by mail with one night's payment, or arrive early. 3-day min. stay. Reception open 7am-2am. No curfew. Doubles, triples, and quads 95F per person. Shower and breakfast included. No credit cards accepted.

Centre International de Paris (BVJ). A relatively luxurious chain of youth hostels. **Paris Louvre,** 20, rue Jean-Jacques Rousseau, 1*er* (tel. 42 36 88 18; fax 42 33 40 53). Mo. Louvre. 200 beds in spacious, dormitory-style rooms. Lunch or dinner for 50F. Groups that book into this one have to pay for one meal a day. **Paris Opéra,** 11, rue Therese, (tel. 42 60 77 23; fax 42 33 40 53), 1*er*. Mo. Pyramides. 68 beds in bigger rooms with fewer beds, and a more subdued atmosphere than Louvre. **Paris Les Halles,** 5, rue du Pélican, (tel. 40 26 92 45; fax 42 33 40 53), 1*er*. Mo. Palais Royal. 55 beds. Cramped rooms, less common space, and toilets and showers on alternate floors. **Paris Quartier Latin,** 44, rue des Bernardins, 5*ème* (tel. 43 29 34 80; fax 42 33 40 53) Mo. Maubert. 138 beds. Beautifully designed with a modern decor, with large, spotless, but more densely packed rooms. All these hostels are open 6am-2am. Families not allowed. Singles available in all except Paris Louvre. Rooms available at 2:30 pm. 100F per person, including breakfast and showers. Singles in Paris Opéra, 110F. Individual reservations not accepted—call or show up the same day.

Hôtel des Jeunes (MIJE): "Le Fauconnier," 11, rue du Fauconnier (tel. 42 74 23 45; Mo. St-Paul or Pont-Marie); "Le Fourcy," 6, rue de Fourcy (tel. 42 74 23 45; Mo. St-Paul or Pont-Marie); "Maubisson," 12, rue des Barres (tel. 42 72 72 09; Mo. Hôtel de Ville or Pont-Marie). All in the 4*ème*. These stellar foyers are all located in former aristocratic residences *(hôtels particuliers)* of the Marais district, close to the sights and to one another. **Le Fauconnier** *is* luxury in modern hostelry. Rooms with 2, 4 and 8 beds are fairly spacious. **Le Fourcy** surrounds a large courtyard, ideal for meeting travelers from around the world. Rooms are smaller, but the atmosphere is friendly. Lively **Maubisson,** the smallest of the three, has newer and even smaller rooms. All 3 give priority to groups of 10 or more (but no group discounts). Individuals cannot make reservations at all, whereas groups can reserve up to one year in advance. There are no age specifications or limits to time of stay for groups, but individuals must be between 18 and 30 years old and can stay no longer than 7 days. Lockout noon-4pm. Curfew 1am-6am. 105F per person, showers and breakfast included (showers are always in the room, toilets down the hall). Lockers 2F. Within walking distance of all three hostels is the Restaurant la Table d'Hôtes, 16, rue du Pt. St-Louis-Phillipe, where you can get 3 courses for 40F provided you're staying at one of the hostels and you show up at 12:30pm, 6:30pm, or 7:30pm. Also try **Residence Luxembourg,** 270, rue St-Jacques, 5*ème* (tel. 43 25 06 20). Mo. Luxembourg. Singles 95F with breakfast. Reception open 24 hrs. No curfew. Open July to Sept. for ages 18-25, though some exceptions are made.

Paris Quartier Latin, 44, rue Bernardins, 5*ème* (tel. 43 29 34 80). Mo. Maubert-Mutualité. A BVJ hostel offering 138 luxuriously modern rooms and tons of space. Beds 100F per person in doubles, triples or quads; 10F more for a single. Breakfast and shower included. No reservations, so arrive early, like 8am.

Young and Happy (Y&H) Hostel, 80, rue Mouffetard, 5*ème* (tel. 45 35 09 53; fax 47 07 22 24). Mo. Censier-Daubenton. An average but clean youth hostel ideally located in the heart of the raucous student quarter on the rue Mouffetard. Lockout 11am-5pm. Curfew 1am. Rooms with 2-4 beds 85F per night, sheets and shower included. Reservations accepted with one night s deposit.

Foyer International des Etudiantes, 93, bd. St-Michel, 6*ème* (tel. 43 54 49 63), across from the Jardin du Luxembourg. Mo. Luxembourg. With wood floors, large windows, beautiful desks, and excellent facilities, this is top notch. Accepts women only for long stays between Oct. and June. July-Sept. it accepts men as well as women for a min. of 5 days. TV lounge, piano, kitchenettes on each floor (bring your own equipment), irons, hair dryers. International students galore, and a friendly director. Reception open Sun.-Fri. 6am-1:30am, Sat. all night. Singles 140F. Doubles 98F per person. Showers and breakfast (July-Sept. only) included. Written reservations should be made 2 months in advance and followed by 100F if confirmed. Call ahead or arrive around 9:30am to check for no-shows.

UCJF (Union Chrétienne de Jeunes Filles) or YWCA, 22, rue Naples, 8*ème* (tel. 45 22 23 49). Mo. Europe or Villiers. Accepts women ages 18-24 for a 3-day min. stay June-Sept. only. Light, airy rooms, with old wood floors and low-set beds. From Sept.-May, caters women ages 18-24 for longer stays and requires half-pension of breakfast and dinner (1900-2260F per month). All guests must pay a 30F membership fee before enrolling and a 100F processing fee. Reception open Mon.-Fri. 9am-6:30pm, Sat.-Sun. 9:30am-2:30pm. Curfew 12:30am. Singles 105F. Doubles and triples 82F per person. Showers and breakfast included. Sheets 30F (or bring your own). Self-service meals in cafeteria for roughly 40F. If you're staying for a week, *forfait semaine* is a good idea: 5 breakfasts, 5 dinners and 7 nights for 620F (single) or 540F (double or triple). Make at least a phone reservation.

Hôtel Ste-Marguerite, 10, rue Trousseau, 11*ème* (tel. 47 00 62 00). Mo. Ledru Rollin. Affiliated with the Jules Ferry hostel. 240 beds. Small but airy rooms, with real mattresses, an atmosphere of happy chaos and youthful idealism. Most rooms 2-6 beds; those on the courtyard especially pleasant. Small showers. Some bathrooms in hall, others in rooms. There is a safe for valuables. Room downstairs to eat in or just hang out in. Vending machine sells beer for 5F. Need we say more? 90F per person. Same day reservations available through Jules Ferry. Otherwise, show up at 8am to get a room.

Maison Internationale des Jeunes, 4, rue Titon, 11*ème* (tel. 43 71 99 21; fax 43 71 78 58). Mo. Faidherbe-Chaligny. Well-located, exceptionally clean and tranquil with a garden in the back. Mostly bright rooms with 2-8 beds for ages 18-30 (exceptions made), with especially beautiful new duplexes. Some family housing. Three-day max. stay. They'll find you another place if they're full. Reception open 8am-2am. Lockout 10am-5pm. Curfew 2am. Quiet hours 10pm-8am. Coed bathrooms. Single sex by room, but exceptions made for traveling buddies, couples, and consenting groups. 110F. Showers and breakfast (served 8-9am) included. Bring your own sheets or rent them for duration of your stay, 15F.

Résidence Bastille (AJF), 151, av. Ledru Rollin, 11*ème* (tel. 43 79 53 86). Mo. Voltaire. Recently renovated, airy rooms with wood bunks. 167 beds; rooms for 2-4 people. Triples and quads have bathrooms in the room; doubles use older hall bathrooms. Hair dryers in hall. Less crowded, subdued but friendly multilingual staff. Limited to ages 18-35. Reception open 7am-12:30pm and 2pm-1am. Curfew 1am. 105F. Showers, breakfast, and sheets included. No reservations, so arrive early in the morning.

Centre International du Séjour de Paris: CISP "Ravel," 6, av. Maurice Ravel, 12ème (tel. 43 43 19 01; fax 43 44 45 30). Mo. Porte de Vincennes. On the edge of the city. Large and professional in its services, with numerous facilities, this hostel caters primarily to groups. Imposing and professional reception desk. Ravel has large rooms (most of which have 4 beds or fewer; 216 beds total), a bar, restaurant, and access to the municipal pool next door (50% reduction for guests, 15F). Some rooms available for guests with disabilities. 3-day max. stay (flexible). Reception open daily 6:30am-1:30am. Singles 136F, with ISIC 125F80. 2- to 5-bed dorms 116F, with ISIC 107F80. 8- to 12-bed dorms 93F, with ISIC 87F10. Breakfast included. Reservations accepted no more than 36 hrs. in advance. Self-service restaurant open 7:30-9:30am, noon-1:30pm, and 7-8:30pm.

F.I.A.P. Jean-Monet, 30, rue Cabanis, 14ème (tel. 45 89 89 15). Mo. Glacière. From the metro, follow your nose down bd. St-Jacques, hang a left at the first stree. (rue Ferrus), and then a right onto rue Cabanis. An international student center with 507 beds, most of which are full during the summer with visiting American tour groups. Comfortable and well-furnished rooms are impeccably maintained and come equipped with toilet and shower. The center offers a disco and jazz concerts at night (free) and stacks of tourist information, as well as a game room, laundry room, and a cheap cafeteria (54F for a full meal). April-Sept. 3-day max. stay. Doubles 150F per person. Quads 130F per person. Eight-bed rooms 110F per person. Reservations required.

Aloha Hostel, 1, rue Borromée, 15ème (tel. 42 73 03 03), on a tiny sidestreet across from 243, rue de Vaugirard. Mo. Volontaires. The outgoing management welcomes the hordes of weary backpackers that swarm here with tons of cheer and a cheap Heineken or two. The paint is peeling, but the kitchen facilities let you save more francs for beverages. Lockout 11am-5pm. Sunny and pleasant 4-bed rooms 75F per person. Reservations accepted with one night s deposit.

Three Ducks Hostel, 6, pl. Etienne Pernet, 15ème (tel.48 42 04 05). Mo. Commerce. Turn 180 degrees when you come out of the metro, and take a right onto the rue du Commerce. The hostel is to the right of the church about 50m down the street. The dismal plastic flooring, dark rooms (4-, 6-, and 8-person rooms) and portable toilets are offset by the pleasant leafy courtyard, where the young raucous guests eat their dinners and then drink and sing late into the night. One-week max. stay. Lockout 11am-5pm. Curfew 1am. 85F. Small kitchen. Reservations accepted with one night s deposit. Mountain bike tours of Paris begin here.

Hotels

Of the three classes of Parisian budget accommodations, hotels may be the most practical for the majority of travelers. There are no curfews, no school groups, and total privacy—features hostels and *foyers* usually can't offer. Most importantly, hotels routinely accept reservations, which will save you hours of bed-searching. Budget hotels in Paris are not significantly more expensive than their hostel/*foyer* counterparts. Larger groups (of 3 and 4) may actually find it more economical to stay in a hotel.

Remember that these budget hotels are not miniature Waldorfs. Don't expect a brightly colored bus to pick you up at the airport or a uniformed cleaning staff to make your bed daily, change your towels and leave you souvenir bars of soap. Many hotels listed in this section have only a few rooms in any category (e.g., single with shower). Request what you like, but you may be disappointed when you arrive. Most hotels are happy to change your room on the second day if they could not accommodate your wishes on the first, especially if you plan to stay at least one week.

Appreciate the individual charm of these hotels as yet another aspect of your immersion in a foreign culture. Remember that there are usually rules against bringing food into your rooms. Parisian law forbids hanging laundry from windows or over balconies to dry. Respect other guests' need for quiet at night.

Generally, if you book a room without a shower, you will have to go to the reception desk and pay 10-20F for the key to the hall shower. Many North Americans are surprised to discover a strange toilet-like apparatus located in all wash-closets. This is called a *bidet*. A *bidet* is a somewhat archaic device intended for the cleansing of the more private body parts. No matter how desperate you are, do not use your *bidet* as a toilet. This would be dumb, uncouth, not a smooth move...and you will force an unfortunate proprietor to spend a few hours bleaching the bowl and cleaning out the pipes.

Reservations

> *Do not* reserve for more nights than you might possibly need. If you decide to leave Paris before you intended, or if you simply want to switch hotels, don't expect to get back all your money. Every year, *Let's Go* receives many letters from readers complaining that hotel managers would not refund the nights that went unused. If in doubt, reserve for just one night; you can usually extend your stay once you get to the hotel.

Make reservations at least two weeks in advance; a number of hotels claim that they are fully booked two months in advance for the summer. To guarantee that you have a room waiting when you arrive, the following process is advised:
1.) Call or write to the hotel asking for a reservation for a specific date and kind of room (single, double, with bathroom, shower, etc.).
2.) If you write, enclose an International Reply Coupon, so that the hotel need not bother with postage expenses (sold at post offices).
3.) When you receive positive confirmation, send *des arrhes* (a deposit) for one night. Most large banks will make out international money orders in French currency. A cheaper option is to send a signed traveler's check in francs. Without a deposit, most hotels will not honor a reservation for more than an hour or so, the time it might take to arrive after calling from a payphone somewhere in Paris.
4.) Call one or two days in advance to confirm (or cancel) and inform the manager of your intended arrival time.

Try your best to honor your reservation. Budget hotels cannot afford to hold a room, turn away potential guests, and then swallow the losses if you decide you don't want it.

Rive Gauche (Left Bank)

It used to be that the *"gauche"* in *"Rive Gauche"* signified a secondary, lower class status. Now it suggests an alternative, possibly even exclusive lifestyle. Thus, the Left Bank remains the traveler's first choice for accommodations. A higher concentration of inexpensive restaurants and fashionable cafés and bars puts the Left Bank closer to the nightlife. And although conveniently close to the major sights, it escapes the daily flood of tourists to the Louvre and the Pompidou Center across the River.

Fifth Arrondissement: Le Quartier Latin

Always crowded, always lively, but not always cheap, the Latin Quarter tempts the traveler with an exhilarating flourish of Parisian pizzazz, luring even the most world-weary into the streets. Spiritually focused on the **Sorbonne,** the Latin Quarter has been a center for Parisian and international students for decades. The western boundary of the fifth, bd. St-Michel overflows with cafés, movie theaters, boutiques, and bookstores. As you head southeast from this busy thoroughfare, hotel prices gradually diminish. Farther east, the neighborhood around pl. de la Contrescarpe, at the center of the fifth, is less commercial, more intimate, and cheaper still.

Hôtel d'Esmeralda, 4, rue St-Julien Le Pauvre (tel. 43 54 19 20, fax. 40 51 00 68). Mo. St-Michel. Right next door to Shakespeare and Co. A charmingly well-kept establishment tucked into a small street overlooking the Seine on one side and a flowery park on the other. The cozy wooden interior complements the homey atmosphere and friendly, multilingual staff. Reserve at least a month ahead during the summer. Singles 130F, with shower 290F. Doubles with shower 290F. Triples with shower and toilet 490F. Quads with shower and toilet 550F. Breakfast 40F.

Hôtel des Carmes, 5, rue des Carmes (tel. 43 29 78 40; fax 43 29 57 17), off the bd. St-Germain. Mo. Maubert-Mutualité. Located on a quiet street, this amicable hotel offers clean, well-furnished rooms with an orange decor. Singles with bath and toilet 256F. Doubles with bath 412F. Two-bed triples with bath 546F. Reservations accepted with one night s deposit. Breakfast included.

Hôtel de Médicis, 214, rue St-Jacques (tel. 43 29 53 64) Mo. Luxembourg. Don t despair when you see the entrance; the hotel cuts corners to keep the prices down, but the rooms are in much better shape than the lobby. A young and energetic clientele frequents this hotel. Singles 75F. Doubles 140-160F.

Hôtel des Grandes Ecoles, 75, rue Cardinal Lemoine (tel. 43 26 79 23). Mo. Cardinal Lemoine. If you re comtemplating going all-out on a hotel in Paris, this is the place to do it. Built around a verdant and flowery garden, where guests breakfast in warm weather, this charming ivy-covered establishment maintains impeccably clean and tastefully decorated rooms to the delight of its faithful guests, many of whom return year after year. Doubles 280-330F, with shower and toilet 420-550F. Breakfast included. Reserve well in advance; deposit required.

Hôtel des Alliés, 20, rue Berthollet (tel. 43 31 47 52; fax 45 35 13 92). Mo. Censier Daubenton. Off bd. Port Royal. Not quite as scenic or centrally located as other hotels in the 5th, but a fantastic bargain of clean and comfy rooms. Singles 120F. Doubles 160F, with shower and toilet 270F. Triples available for a 30% supplement on the double rate. Showers 15F. Breakfast 25F. Reservations accepted with one night s deposit.

Hôtel Gay Lussac, 29, rue Gay Lussac (tel. 43 54 23 96), at rue St-Jacques. Mo. Luxembourg. The affable owner loves Let s Go readers and provides carefully cleaned sunlit rooms with sculpted plaster ceilings in an old but well-preserved hotel on a noisy street. Tour groups may limit available space. Singles 200F. Doubles (with two beds) 280F. Triples 320F. Showers 10F. Breakfast included. Reservations accepted with one night s deposit.

Grand Hôtel du Progres, 50, rue Guy Lussac (tel. 43 54 53 18). Mo. Luxembourg. An English- and German-speaking receptionist welcomes guests with open arms. Breakfast room complete with piano and a miniature library. Clean, bright rooms with lovely windows. Top floors, with charming eaved rooms, look out over the Panthéon. Singles 136-200F, with shower and toilet 295F. Doubles 220-275F, with shower and toilet 310F. Triples with shower and toilet 310F. Showers 15F. Breakfast included. A very steep *non-refundable* deposit required for a reservation: 300F for one person, 400F for two people, 600F for three people.

Hôtel de Nevers, 3, rue de l Abée de l Epée (tel. 43 26 80 83), off rue Gay Lussac. Mo. Luxembourg. Run by a sprightly retired couple, this six-story hotel offers clean rooms, renovated bathrooms, a view of the Panthéon and peace and quiet. Some beds are rather saggy. Singles 140F. Doubles with one bed and shower 230F, with shower and toilet 260F. Doubles with two beds 230F, with shower and toilet 320F. Showers 15F. Breakfast 25F. Reservations accepted with one night s deposit.

Sixth Arrondissement: St-Germain-des-Prés

One of the greatest people-watching arteries in the world, Boulevard St-Germain enlivens St-Germain-des-Prés, a neighborhood that has turned the sidewalk café into an art form. Jean-Paul Sartre whiled away the hours in Aux Deux Magots and Le Flore, but such cafés now belong mostly to the beautiful people. Budget hotels are sparse in this chic neighborhood, which stretches from the Seine to the bd. Montparnasse.

✘ **Hotel Nesle,** 7, rue Nesle (tel. 43 54 47 02), off rue Dauphine. Mo. Odéon. The impeccably clean rooms with wooden rafters and funky Egyptianesque frescoes, the warm, outgoing management, the gaggle of geese in the rose garden and the outrageously low price of 125F, including breakfast and shower, make this charming little hotel in the heart of the 6th *arrondissement* without doubt the best place to stay on the Left Bank. Singles 125F. Doubles 150F. Reserve 3-4 days in advance, or show up early.

✘ **Hotel St-Michel,** 17, rue Git le Coeur (tel. 43 26 98 70), near pl. St-Michel, just steps away from the Seine. Mo. St-Michel. Large, comfortable rooms with bright floral prints. Friendly management. Curfew 1am. Singles 170F, with shower and toilet 300F. Doubles 170F, with shower 265F, with shower and toilet 300F. Shower 12F. Breakfast 25F.

Hotel Stella, 41, rue Monsieur le Prince (tel 43 26 43 49). Mo. Odéon or Luxembourg. While the office can be a steam bath during the summer, the wood-trimmed bedrooms are pleasant and breezy. Singles with shower and toilet 178F. Doubles with shower and toilet 238F. No reservations accepted; just come early.

Hotel Petit Trianon, 2, rue de l'Ancienne Comédie, (tel. 43 54 94 64), tucked away in the busy corner of rue Dauphine and rue St-André-des-Arts. Mo. St-Germain-des-Prés. Centrally located, but somewhat worn. Singles 160F. Doubles with shower 250F, with shower and toilet 350F. Showers 25F. Reserve at least one week ahead with one night s deposit.

Seventh Arrondissement: The Eiffel Tower

Hotels galore cluster around the western edge of the 7th *arrondissement,* all proudly advertising that the Eiffel Tower is indeed visible from their rooms. But don't stay in the seventh for the view or for the party atmosphere. A civil servant heaven, filled with traveling businesspeople, the seventh proffers slightly pricier, spatially challenged rooms.

Hôtel de la Paix, 19, rue du Gros Caillou (tel. 45 51 86 17). Mo. Ecole Militaire, up av. Bosquet and left on rue de Grenelle. The only true budget accommodations in the 7th and it shows. Soft mattresses, old carpets, and peeling paint, but fairly clean and lively as a spring chicken. Self-proclaimed "shareholder" Noël will greet you in French, English, or Japanese. Check-out at noon. Baggage storage. Reception open 9am-9pm. Key gets you in after doors lock at 10pm. Check-out at noon. Singles 125F, with shower 183F. Doubles with shower 235F, with shower and toilet 302F. Twins with shower and toilet 267F. Triples with shower and toilet 390F. Showers 15F. Breakfast (7-10:30am in the lobby) 28F. Reservations recommended. Deposit required depending on time of arrival.

Hôtel Muguet, 11, rue Chevert (tel. 47 05 05 93). Mo. Ecole-Militaire (off av. de Tourville) or Latour-Maubourg (off av. de la Tour Maubourg). Space...the final frontier...room enough for you and your extended family in these 43 enormous rooms and in the high, firm, silky spread covered beds. Clean, with nice wood paneling. Check-out at noon. Singles 200F, with tub or shower 230F, with tub or shower and toilet 300F. Doubles 230F, with tub or shower 270F, with tub or shower and toilet (and small sitting room) 350F. Showers 15F. Breakfast (7-9:30am) 30F. Call first for reservations and confirm in writing with the 1st night deposit. Closed in Aug.

Hôtel du Palais Bourbon, 49, rue de Bourgogne (tel. 45 51 63 32 or 47 05 29 26; fax 45 55 20 21), down the road from the Palais Bourbon. Mo. Cambres des Députés, Varenne, or Invalides. Mme. Claudon has been fostering the family atmosphere in this 33 room hotel for 23 years. On-going renovations are producing ultra-modern, ultra-slick bathrooms. Direct line telephones in each room and high ceilings in some. Have breakfast or work in the beautiful salon full of elegant tables. English spoken. Reception open 24 hrs. Singles 200-227F, with shower 239F, with shower and toilet 339F, with tub and toilet 403-430F. Showers 12F. Breakfast (7-9:30am) included. Reservations recommended—call and confirm by letter or fax with credit card number.

Fourteenth Arrondissement: Montparnasse

Renowned for its nightlife, this commercial district just south of the Latin Quarter attracted artists and literati in the 1920s. Picassso and his contemporaries abandoned their traditional haunt of Montmartre for this livelier, more central location. Today, areas closest to the fashionable bd. du Montparnasse maintain their glamor while adjoining neighborhoods have become residential and calm. Be prepared for an abundance of sex-shops and sleazy nightlife at the Northern end of av. du Maine (Mo. Gaîté).

Hôtel Plaisance, 53, rue Gergovie (tel. 45 42 11 39). Mo. Pernety. From the metro, take a right onto rue Raymond Losserand, and then a left onto rue de Gergovie. Institutional, but adequately clean and comfortable hotel on a quiet street in a working-class neighborhood. Some rooms have frayed drapes and bedspreads but are more-or-less livable. Singles 100F, with shower and toilet 210F. Doubles 150F, with shower and toilet 240F. Showers 20F. Breakfast 20F.

Hôtel de Blois, 5, rue des Plantes (tel. 45 40 99 48). Mo. Mouton-Duvernet. From the metro, swing right onto rue Brezin, cross av. du Maine, continue on rue Sablière, and take your first right onto rue des Plantes. Unquestionably one of the best deals in Paris, considering that these rooms, decked-out with full bathrooms, televisions, telephones, and a Laura Ashley decor, would go for twice the price if there were an elevator in the hotel. But who cares when the stairs are so well maintained? The gracious proprietress, a real jewel compared to the majority in Paris, offers tourist advice and travel directions to her appreciative guests. Doubles 250-300F with bath. Triples 320F. Breakfast 25F.

Hôtel du Midi, 4, av. René-Coty (tel. 43 27 23 25). Mo. Denfert-Rochereau. A large, professionally run hotel, with rooms that recall a Holiday Inn. Antique-style headboards doubling as closets frame the queen-size beds. All rooms come with TV, telephone and a spotlessly clean bathroom. Doubles from 200-320F. Breakfast 26F.

Hôtel du Parc, 6, rue Jolivet (tel. 43 20 95 54). Mo. Montparnasse-Bienvenue. A large, modern hotel decked out with a marble interior and self-opening doors. Uncoordinated decor but comfortable rooms that'll make you feel like a privileged budget traveler. Doubles 210F, with bath 320F, with bath and toilet 380F. Breakfast 20F.

Fifteenth Arrondissement

The expansive Parc des Expositions, just outside of the Porte de Versailles at the southern end of the 15th, attracts execs throughout the winter months. In summer, the hotels go scrambling for business, and tourists can sometimes even bargain on the price of breakfast when their fellows have swamped the more central *arrondissements*.

✘ **Hôtel l Ain,** 60, rue Olivier de Serres (tel. 45 32 44 33). Mo. Convention. From the metro, take a left onto rue de la Convention, and then a right onto rue Olivier de Serres. On a quiet residential street. Adequately clean rooms with whitewashed walls and plaid bedspreads lie up just one flight of stairs. Singles 140F. Doubles 200F, with shower 240F, with shower and toilet 320F. Triples 360F with shower and toilet. Reservations accepted with 1st night deposit.

Practic Hôtel, 20, rue l Ingenieur Keller (tel. 45 77 70 58). Mo. Charles Michels. From the metro, walk toward the river on av. Emile Zola, take a right onto rue des Peignot, and a left onto rue Ingenier Keller. A cozy family-run hotel with absolutely spotless rooms with sturdy wood furnishings and sparkling tiled bathrooms. About half the rooms have TVs. Doubles 240F with toilet but no shower, 300F with full bath and shower. Triples 400F with bath and shower. Breakfast 28F. Reservations accepted with one night deposit.

Hôtel Mont Blanc, 11, bd. Victor (tel. 48 28 16 79). Mo. Porte de Verailles. From the metro, walk right down Bd. Victor. Clean hallways and flowered wallpaper. During the winter it fills with visitors to the exposition hall across the street but is likely to have vacancies in the summer. Singles 150F. Doubles 240F with shower. Triples 300F with shower. Breakfast 25F. Reservations accepted with one night deposit, but just call ahead during the summer.

Rive Droite (Right Bank)

Since most bargain hunters head first for the Left Bank, this side of the Seine is more likely to yield vacancies. In general, hotel prices here rise with proximity to the Louvre and the Opéra. Exceptions do exist, but supermarkets and inexpensive restaurants are fewer-and-farther-between than in the Left Bank.

First Arrondissement

You won't regret staying in the fashionable first, but your wallet might. Fortunately, a number of small family hotels still offer clean rooms at reasonable prices. Although the first is one of the safest areas of Paris, shun Mo. Châtelet or Les Halles at night (unless of course you enjoy the company of muggers and drug dealers). If your hotel is near Mo. Châtelet-les-Halles, try taking a different metro line or stopping at the next station down the road.

✘ **Hôtel de Lille,** 8, rue du Pelican (tel. 42 33 33 42). Mo. Palais Royal. Walk down rue St. Honoré until you turn left onto rue Croix des Petits Champs. Take the first right and you are on rue du Pelican. Clean and pleasant. Unbeatable location in a quiet street wicked close to the Louvre. Singles 160F. Doubles 190-240F. Showers 30F.

✘ **Hôtel Saint-Honoré,** 85, rue St.-Honoré (tel. 42 36 20 38 or 42 21 46 96; fax 42 21 44 08). Mo. Louvre, Châtelet-Les-Halles. From Mo. Louvre, take rue du Louvre (away from the river) and turn right onto rue St-Honoré. Most of the rooms have been renovated recently. Pleasant atmosphere, friendly staff, young clientele. In summer, confirm your reservations by phone or fax the night before, or by telephone as soon as you arrive in Paris. Singles or doubles 150-180F, with shower and toilet 280F. Triples or quads with shower and toilet 330-400F. Showers 15F. Breakfast 19F.

Hôtel Lion d'Or, 5, rue de la Sourdière (tel. 42 60 79 04; fax 42 60 09 14). Mo. Tuileries or Pyramides. Slightly worn, but clean. Singles 180F, with shower 220F. Doubles 220F, with shower 280F, with bath and toilet 360F. Showers 20F. Extra bed 40%. Breakfast 25F. For stays of more than 4 days, 5% discount; larger discounts for longer stays.

Hôtel du Palais, 2, quai de la Mégisserie (tel. 42 36 98 25). Mo. Châtelet. The location by the Seine, at the corner of place du Châtelet and quai de la Mégisserie, gives all rooms in the hotel (except on the top floor) splendid views of the Châtelet square or the Ile de la Cité. Clean, comfortable, and recently renovated rooms. Telephone in every room. Singles on the top floor 180F. Doubles on the top floor 230F. Singles with shower, 280F, with shower and toilet 320F, with bath and toilet 350F. Doubles with shower 320F, with shower and toilet 350F, with bath and toilet 380F. One quint 550F. Extra bed 70F. Breakfast, served in your room, 25F.

✘ **Hôtel de Rouen,** 42, rue Croix des Petits Champs (tel. or fax 42 61 38 21). Mo. Louvre or Palais Royal. From the Palais Royal metro, place yourself on rue St. Honoré with the Palais Royal on your left; walk straight ahead and turn left onto the rue Croix des Petits Champs. Renovated in 1991, with shiny bathrooms and new carpeting and wallpaper. A phone in every room, but overseas calls must be made from the lobby. Singles or doubles 180F, with shower 240F, with shower and toilet and TV 290F. Triples with shower and toilet 290F. Quads with shower and toilet 350F. Extra bed free. Breakfast downstairs or in your room 20F.

Second Arrondissement

Although it is not blessed with many major sights of its own, the second *arrondissement* is within easy walking distance of the Marais, the Centre Pompidou, the Louvre, the Palais Royal, Notre-Dame, and more. Many little restaurants and hotels, often quite cheap, are to be found in this mostly working-class area, making it an excellent choice as a place to stay. Though the rue St-Denis, at the eastern end, is a center of prostitution and pornography, it is more unpleasant than unsafe, and its seediness does not spill over very far into neighboring streets.

Hôtel Sainte-Marie, 6, rue de la Ville Neuve (tel. 42 33 21 61; fax 46 06 33 30). Mo. Bonne Nouville. Simple but clean; decidedly superior to many other hotels in the same price range. Phone in every room. No elevator. Singles 150F, with shower and toilet 205F. Doubles 160-180F, with shower and toilet 220-240F. Showers 15F. Breakfast 20F.

Hôtel La Marmotte, 6, rue Léopold Bellan (tel. 40 26 26 51). Mo. Sentier. Pristine rooms. Firm beds. Friendly managers. Singles 160F, with shower and toilet 240F. Doubles 180F, with shower and toilet 260F. Showers 15F. Breakfast 20F.

Hôtel Tiquetonne, 6, rue Tiquetonne (tel. 42 36 94 58). Mo. Etienne-Marcel. Near the intersection of rue St-Denis and rue de Turbigo. Other hotels in Paris are more welcoming, but rooms are clean. Singles 120F, with shower and toilet 190F. Doubles with shower and toilet 220F. Showers 22F. Breakfast 22F.

Hôtel Zora, 4, rue Léopold Bellan (tel. 45 08 18 75). Mo. Sentier. Poorly lit and somewhat worn, but clean, adequate rooms still make this a decent option. Unless you speak Serbo-Croatian, you may have difficulty making yourself understood. No deposit required. Singles 120F, with shower and toilet 220. Doubles 160F, with shower and toilet 220F. Showers 20F.

Hôtel Bonne Nouvelle, 17, rue Beauregard (tel. 40 08 42 42, for reservations 45 08 87 71; fax 40 26 05 81). Mo. Strasbourg-St-Denis or Bonne Nouvelle. Cozy, clean hotel with a TV and phone in every room. Singles and doubles with toilet and bath or shower 245-300F. Triples with toilet and bath 375F. One triple/quad with toilet and bath 475F. Breakfast 25F. They require a one-night deposit only if you're arriving after 3pm.

Hôtel Chénier, 1, rue Chénier (tel. 42 33 92 32; fax 45 08 57 73). Mo. Strasbourg-St-Denis. Clean, comfortable, and recently renovated. Phone in every room. All rooms with toilet. No elevator. Singles with shower 220F, with bath 300F. Doubles with shower 250F, with bath 300F, with bath and TV 330F. Triples with shower or bath 450F. Quads with bath 500F, with bath and TV 530F.

Hôtel Vivienne, 40, rue Vivienne (tel. 42 33 13 26; fax 40 41 98 19). Mo. Bourse, Richelieu-Drouot, or Montmartre. From the Bourse metro, walk down rue Vivienne toward bd. Montmartre. This place isn't just comfortable, clean, and well-lit...it's actually kind of *plush.* Friendly staff, firm beds, TV, and phone in every room. Elevator. Singles or doubles with shower 330F, with shower and toilet 390F, with bath and toilet 410-420F. Smaller singles with shower 330F, with shower and toilet 370F, with bath and toilet 410F. Breakfast 40F. Extra bed 30F (free for kids).

Third and Fourth Arrondissements: Le Marais

Absolutely *the* place to live in the 17th century, the labyrinthine Marais has regained its chic, thanks to extensive renovations in the past 30 years. The one-time palatial mansions have metamorphosized into exquisite museums, as interesting for their collections as for their aristocratic elegance, and the tiny twisting streets have adopted fashionable boutiques and galleries. Fascinating and lively quarters, the third and fourth *arrondissements* shelter some terrific accommodations at reasonable rates. Prices tend to drop as you head north through the fourth and into the third.

Grand Hôtel des Arts et Métiers, 4, rue Borda, 3*ème* (tel. 48 87 77 00; fax 48 87 66 58). Mo. Arts et Métiers. From the metro, take rue de Turbigo a few meters toward the Place de la République, turn left onto rue Montgolfier, then take the first right onto rue Borda. Central location; peeling paint and wallpaper compensates. There is a kitchen for guests with babies, and a fridge downstairs for all guests. Reception open 24 hrs. Singles 130-160F, with toilet 220F. Singles or doubles with shower 250F, with toilet and shower 280F. Showers 20F.

Hôtel Bretagne, 87, rue des Archives, 3*ème* (tel. 48 87 83 14). Mo. République, Temple, or Filles du Calvaire. From the République metro, walk down rue (not *boulevard* du Temple), then turn left onto rue de Bretagne, and right onto rue des Archives. A clean and pleasant hotel with a fancy mirrored entrance staircase. Wide spread in room prices and quality. Reception open 24 hrs. Singles 140F, with bath, toilet, and TV 290F. Doubles 180F, with bath, toilet, and TV 340F. Triples 400F, with 3 separate beds and bath, toilet, and TV 600F. Showers included. Breakfast 25F.

Hôtel Picard, 26, rue de Picardie, 3*ème* (tel. 48 87 53 82). Mo. République or Filles du Calvaire. From the République metro, walk onto rue Beranger and then turn right onto rue de Franche-Comté, which becomes rue de Picardie. Ever-friendly, ever-jovial proprietor and his polyglot daughter. Anyone armed with *Let's Go* gets a 10% discount. The family that runs this place actually *likes* American students, who make up the vast majority of their clientele. Charming, clean little rooms. Singles 200F, with shower 250F, with bath and toilet 320F. Doubles 240-260F, with shower 320F, with bath and toilet 390F. Triples 360F. Showers 15F. Breakfast 25F. Extra bed 90F.

Henri IV, 25, place Dauphine, 4*ème* (tel. 43 54 44 53) Mo. Cité. The last outpost of cheap accommodations on the Ile de la Cité offers clean, average-sized rooms. Includes friendly management, as well as one of the best locations in Paris. The biggest disadvantage is that the toilets are located outside, accessible only by a little staircase that curls around the building. Singles 185F. Doubles 210F. Reserve way ahead.

Hôtel Practic, 9, rue d'Ormesson, 4*ème* (tel. 48 87 80 47). Mo. St-Paul or Bastille. Smallish, relatively clean rooms, with damp bathrooms and a pleasant location next to a cobblestone square in the Marais. Singles 100-135F, with shower 180F, with shower and toilet 250F. Doubles 190-200F, with shower 220F, with shower, and toilet 295F. Extra bed 80F. Showers 15F. Breakfast 20F. Prices lower off season.

✗ **Grand Hôtel du Loiret,** 8, rue des Mauvais Garcons, 4*ème* (tel. 48 87 77 00; fax 48 04 96 56). Mo. Hôtel de Ville. Modest, fairly clean rooms in a well-located hotel, just blocks from the Hôtel de Ville. The helpful management speaks some English. Singles and doubles 160F, with shower 210F. Showers 15F. Breakfast 15F.

Hôtel de la Herse d'Or, 20, rue St-Antoine, 4*ème* (tel. 48 87 84 09). Mo. Bastille or St-Paul. Built around a freshly painted, clean courtyard protected by a glass roof. Rooms are a little worn. The area is reasonably quiet, but tell them you're a light sleeper and they'll give you one of the rooms in the back. Phone in every room. Singles 150F, with toilet and shower 200F. Doubles 200, with toilet and shower 250F, with toilet and bath 270F. Triples with shower and toilet 375F. Breakfast 25F. Extra bed (in doubles only) add 50%.

Hôtel de Nice, 42 bis, rue de Rivoli, 4*ème* (tel. 42 78 55 29; fax 42 78 36 07). Mo. Hôtel de Ville. This recently redecorated hotel is a rare find in the world of budget accommodations. Courteous management presents elegant rooms, an elevator (not large enough for wheelchairs), and a delightful lounge that will make you forget you're on a budget. On the 6th floor is a particularly nice room, that can be rented as a triple (400F) or a double (350F), complete with a beautiful view of the Seine (including Notre-Dame). Phone in every room. Singles and doubles 220F, with toilet and shower 320-350F. Triples 270F, with bath and toilet 400. Breakfast 27F. Showers free.

✗ **Hôtel Andréa,** 3, rue St-Bon, 4*ème* (tel. 42 78 43 93). Mo. Châtelet or Hôtel de Ville. Clean, comfortable rooms with plenty of light. Phone in all rooms, TV in rooms with shower. It's just as well that they have an elevator (not wide enough for wheelchairs), since the common showers are only on the first floor. Singles 170F, with toilet and shower 275F. Doubles 180F, with toilet and shower 290-330F. Extra bed 60F. Showers 15F. Breakfast 25F.

Ninth Arrondissement

The ninth bridges some of Paris's wealthiest and most heavily touristed quarters—the second and the eighth—as well as the less tantalizing and less affluent tenth and eighteenth. There are plenty of hotels here, but many in the northern half of the area are used for the local flesh trade. Avoid the Anvers, Pigalle, and Barbès-Rochechouart metro stops at night; use the Abbesses stop instead. The southern half of the quarter, though no glamorous hot spot, provides several worthwhile accommodations not too far away from the sights and sins of Paris. A few nicer, but not-so-cheap hotels are available near the more respectable and central bd. des Italiens and bd. Montmartre.

Hôtel des Trois Poussins, 15, rue Clauzel (tel. 48 74 38 20). Mo. St-Georges. Managed by the wonderful Desforges family, this hotel has a lovely courtyard, clean rooms, and editions of *Let's Go* dating from 1982. No children under 15. Singles 140-150F. Doubles with shower 220-230F. Showers 15F. Breakfast 20F.

Hôtel d'Espagne, 9-11, cité Bergère (tel. 42 46 73 30; fax 48 00 95 69). Mo. Montmartre. Not elegant, but it has high ceilings and is relatively clean, with decent beds and lighting. Helpful reception; some English spoken. Telephones in every room; TVs in some. Singles with toilet 150F. Doubles with shower and toilet 300F, with bath and toilet 320F. Triples with shower and toilet 420F. Quads 510F. One common shower 10F. Breakfast 22F. Reservations recommended.

Hôtel Beauharnais, 51, rue de la Victoire (tel. 48 74 71 13). Mo. le Peletier. Demure, sunny rooms with flowered wallpaper and wooden frame beds. All have a telephone. Singles with shower 280F, with shower and toilet 300F. Doubles with shower and toilet 320F. Triples with shower and toilet 420F. Breakfast 25F.

Tenth Arrondissement

In response to the voluminous traffic that pours through the Gare de l'Est and the Gare du Nord, a flock of inexpensive hotels has roosted in the tenth. In fact, supply often exceeds demand, making this crowded corner of Paris a decent turn if you've struck out everywhere else. Bear in mind that the ever-swelling cost of living in Paris has driven many of the city's poor to the outer *arrondissements,* often resulting in large crowds and visibly depressed areas. In addition, these hotels are far from the primary sights and nightlife, so you'll be forced to use taxis once the metro stops running. Anyone traveling alone might want to look elsewhere; areas near the train stations are often far from safe. Exercise special caution in the area stretching west from pl. de la République along rue du Château d'Eau.

✗ Palace Hôtel, 3, rue Bouchardon (tel. 42 06 59 32). Mo. Strasbourg/St-Denis. A family affair with an assembly of children and pets around the reception desk. Small, cheerful rooms, many facing an attractive, plant-filled courtyard. Quiet back-street location. Singles 100F. Doubles 130F, with bath and toilet 250F. Triples 180F, with shower and toilet 280F. One 2-room quad 230F. Breakfast 20F. No reservations.

Cambrai Hôtel, 129bis, bd. de Magenta (tel. 48 78 32 13; fax 48 78 43 55). Mo. Gare du Nord. Clean and airy rooms with high ceilings. Firm beds and large-ish, clean showers. Telephones in every room, and just a step away from the Gare du Nord. Singles 110F, with shower 188F. Doubles 160F, with shower 208F. Triples 315F, with shower 330F. 2-room suite for 4 335F, with shower 352F. Showers 20F. Breakfast included.

Hôtel Mêtropole Lafayette, 204, rue Lafayette (tel. 46 07 72 69). Mo. Louis Blanc. Small, somewhat dark rooms, offset by nice, firm beds. Very clean, with friendly reception. Singles 110F, with shower 150F. Doubles 130F, with shower 180F, shower and toilet 200F. Triples with shower 230F, shower and toilet 250F. Showers 25F. Breakfast 15F.

Hôtel des Familles, 216, faubourg St-Denis (tel. 46 07 76 56). Mo. Gare du Nord. A little dark and modest looking, but decent with big beds to play in and and nice showers to sing in. Singles 120-150F, with shower 200F. Doubles 180F, with shower 200F. Triples 234F, with shower 286F. Quads 286F, with shower and toilet 325F. Showers 17F. Breakfast 18F.

Eleventh Arrondissement: The Bastille

The eleventh is the hip and happening quarter of Paris, the new Bohemia, the new hang-out of the young, the eclectic, and the electric. Just don't count on the sumptuous glamor of the steadfast fifth or sixth in this area charged with an intriguing mix of youthful vibrance and working-class joviality, and try to avoid place de la République at night, when prostitutes and pickpockets come out to play. This might be difficult, however, since the reasonably cheap hotels, many of which consider July and August the off-season, line the streets surrounding the place de la République and place de la Bastille. Others dot the more interior streets of the eleventh. All are likely to have space. Five metro lines converge on République; three cross over at Bastille.

Hôtel Baudin, 113, av. Ledru-Rollin (tel. 47 00 18 91; fax 48 07 04 66). Mo. Ledru-Rollin. A real find: 20 big clean rooms with patterned bedspreads. Only a few blocks from the Bastille and direct line phone in every room. Check-out at noon. Singles 120F. Doubles 170-200F, with shower 230F, with tub and toilet 270F. Extra bed 100F. Shower 20F. Breakfast 25F. Call to reserve and confirm in writing.

Hôtel de Vienne, 43, rue de Malte (tel. 48 05 44 42). Mo. Oberkampf or République. From Mo. Oberkampf, exit at Crussol and take rue de Malte. Peaceful, floral papered rooms with firm mattresses and clean bathrooms. Direct line phone and comfortable, family atmosphere. Singles 100F, bigger bed 125F. Doubles 150F, with shower 210F. No hall showers. Breakfast 30F. Call and confirm in writing (with 1st night's deposit) to reserve. Closed in Aug.

Hôtel Rhetia, 3, rue du Général Blaise (tel. 47 00 47 18). Mo. Saint-Ambroise, St-Maur, or Voltaire. From Mo. St-Maur, walk left onto rue St-Maur, turn right onto Lacharrière. A quiet neighborhood, not too far from the Bastille. Well lit, tastefully decorated rooms overlooking the happy park. Reception open Mon.-Fri. 7:30am-10pm, Sat.-Sun. and holidays 8am-10pm. Singles 160F, with shower or tub and toilet 200-220F. Doubles 180F, with shower or tub and toilet 220F. Triples 220F, with shower or tub and toilet 260F. Showers 10F. Breakfast included; served Mon.-Fri. 7:30-9am, Sat.-Sun. and holidays 8-9:30am. Call to reserve and confirm in writing with first night's payment.

Hôtel de Belfort, 37, rue Servan (tel. 47 00 67 33). Mo. Père Lachaise, St. Maur, or Voltaire. From Mo. Père Lachaise, take rue du Chemin Vert. Turn left onto rue Servan. Not exactly chic, but the patterned blankets are homey and the bathrooms, although worn, are as modern as they come. Breakfast served in a cool *cave*, staff will greet you in multiple languages, including English, and the Lizard King's tomb is a stone's throw away. 100F per person per night for a bed in a double, triple, or quad, with shower, toilet, phone, and TV—most excellent! Otherwise: Singles with shower, toilet, and TV 300F. Doubles 190-220F, with shower, toilet, and TV 320F. Twins with shower, toilet, and TV 350F. Triples with shower, toilet, and TV 420F. Extra bed 100F. Hall showers included. Breakfast 30F. Call to reserve 24 hrs. ahead, confirm.

Camping

Campgrounds near Paris can offer a welcome respite from the commotion of the city. In high season, however, they become terribly crowded. Many campers are East Europeans trying to see Paris on the smallest of budgets; staying at a campground might enable you to make some friends from the East. Note that any money you save may evaporate because of the cost of commuting to Paris. If you're determined to join the crowd and pitch your tent, contact the **Camping Club International de France,** 14, rue Bourdonnais, 1er (tel. 42 36 12 40; Mo. Châtelet-Les Halles), or the tourist office at 127, av. des Champs-Elysées, 8ème (tel. 47 23 61 72; Mo. Charles de Gaulle-Etoile). Either can provide more extensive listings and information.

Camping du Tremblay (TCF), bd. des Alliés, 94507 Champigny-sur-Marne, Val de Marne (tel. 43 97 43 97). Take RER line A2 (direction: "Boissy-St-Leger") 20min. from Gare d'Austerlitz, get off at the Joinville-Le-Pont station (about 10F) and take bus 108N (5F50) directly to the site. On the banks of the Marne River, 14km east of Paris along the A4. 17F per person, 13F per tent and car. Open daily 7am-8pm.

Camping Choisy-le-Roi, 125, av. de Villeneuve-St-Georges, Choisy-le-Roi (tel. 48 90 92 30). Take RER line C to Choisy-le-Roi. From the station, you can take bus #182 (5F50). Or walk across the bridge, take av. Villeneuve-St-Georges immediately to the right, and follow the signs (20min. from the station). An attractive site in a gritty suburb. Modern showers, toilets, and washing facilities. Wheelchair access. 20F per person, 20F per tent, 8F per car.

In an Emergency...

If you have had the most unfortunate bad luck to arrive in Paris without reservations, spent the whole day searching everywhere for accommodations to no avail, know no one in the city and don't want to take a night train somewhere else, only to try Paris again (with the added security of a reservation!)—despair not. There are plenty of options for the resourceful trooper. An excellent first choice would be to check your bags at the train station, hop on the metro and venture to one of the many all-night discos in Paris. Your day full of hassled hotel searching may not leave you with much desire for dancing but at least at a disco you'll be guaranteed shelter (though not quiet) throughout the night. Who knows? You might even meet someone who can help you out. Or, try one of the (less abundant) all-night restaurants (see All Night Restaurants in Food listings). These joints are often frequented by traveling souls who, at the very least, can provide companionship throughout the night. Of course, you can always try one of the more luxurious hotels in Paris, which, because of their larger size, are more likely to have beds, but be warned, the damage you'll do your budget might make you more miserable than exhaustion after a night in a happening club.

The **Armée de Salut (Salvation Army),** 76, rue de Rome, 8ème (tel. 43 87 41 19; Mo. St-Lazare), offers up to two weeks of free shelter to the destitute. (Open Mon.-Fri. 8:30am-noon and 1-5pm.) They have various facilities for men and women, including the **Cité de Refuge Hommes et Femmes,** 12, rue Cantagrel, 13ème (tel. 45 83 54 40; Mo. National or Chaveleret; open daily 5am-midnight). Keep in mind that these are social services for the homeless, *not* budget accommodations. Unless you're truly desperate, don't disturb them.

Every night, swarms of sleeping bags carpet the **Gare du Nord** and the **Gare de l'Est.** Exercise extreme caution! Many of these "campers" are homeless people who may be somewhat resentful of the bountiful collection of supplies in a traveler's backpack. Similarly, police will often rouse sleepers from these dirty, uncomfortable makeshift beds and send them out into the street. If you decide, against the strongest caution to the contrary, to risk these dangers, make sure that whatever you do (men and women alike), you never stretch out alone, and store your bags in a locker.

If all your money has been lost or stolen, and you can't get any more mailed from home, try visiting your home consulate. (See Embassies and Consulates in the Practical Information above.)

Most importantly, if you feel threatened or endangered at any time during your stay in Paris or anywhere else in France, your first call should be to the police. They can be reached from any phone by dialing 17; no coins are needed.

Food

Chefs in Paris serve one of the world's most finicky audiences—Parisians. You see, Parisians do not simply eat—they eat well, they eat often, and they eat at length. Fortunately, they do not necessarily eat expensively. In a city with some of the world's most fabulous restaurants, you can spend as much as you care to, but Parisians seldom spend more than 100F on a meal. You can eat satisfactorily for 50F, enjoyably for 65F, superbly for 90F, and unforgettably for 130F. The restaurants of Paris are a diverse lot; don't hesitate to try one of the many wonderful Vietnamese, North African, or Middle Eastern restaurants that dot the city, where you can find superbly prepared food at prices lower than many comparable French restaurants. Otherwise, crunch a *croque monsieur* or a plate of quiche at a sidewalk café. Or absorb the best of both realms at a bistro, a wonderfully pretentious café/restaurant hybrid. For a light meal accompanied by excellent wine, hit one of Paris's many wine bars, cozy places that seem to sidestep the tourist onslaught. Above all, be bold, be adventurous, and splurge at least once: you may never get another chance to slurp snails by the Seine.

Restaurants

The world's first restaurant was born in Paris over 200 years ago. Ironically its purpose was not to indulge its clientele with delicious foods and wines, but rather to restore (from the French verb *restorer)* over-fed party-goers (most of Parisian high society throughout history) to a state of physical health. Restaurants were a social respite from the high-calorie world of soirées, balls, and private dinner parties. Here, one could be in a social atmosphere and eat nothing. Instead, one was served a single glass of a ghastly brew made from concentrated meat and vegetable products.

Happily, the only similarity between Parisian restaurants today and their primordial ancestors is that they remain highly social milieus. Below we list a number of restaurants, organized by *arrondissement;* although most serve informal meals, we include several splurges for special occasions. If exploring restaurants on your own, avoid the telltale signs of an unsatisfying meal, such as an advertised "tourist special," a menu in any language but French, or any place that offers you raw vegetables *crudités*—often just a mound of carrot shreds—as an entree on a *prix-fixe* menu.

A word on fast food: if you go to Paris and eat at McDonalds, you should probably be shot, hit hard on the head many times, reprimanded, and doomed to eat large fries and a coke for the rest of your life. But ahhh, it is indeed true that fast food is cheap food, and cheap food is good. Chains include **Quick, Free Time, La Brioche Dorée, Tout Chaud, La Croissanterie,** and a couple unknown American chains called **McDonald's** and **Burger King.** Possibly more interesting are the self-service cafeterias *(les selfs)* that litter the business areas of town. Certainly more interesting is **Fauchon,** 30, pl. de la Madeleine, 8*ème* (Mo. Madeleine), behind Eglise de la Madeleine. A shrine for the worship of fine cuisine for years and a must for window shoppers seeking the apex of visual gluttony. Nothing is cheap, but everything is delicious and authentically French. Head for the cafeteria downstairs, not the outrageous restaurant upstairs. *(Plats du jour* (50-70F) served 11am-2pm. Pastries 16F. Open Mon.-Sat. 8:15am-7pm.)

Rive Gauche (Left Bank)

Fifth Arrondissement: Le Quartier Latin

A rainbow of ethnic restaurants compete for customers through rock-bottom pricing along the **rue Mouffetar,** which undisputably constitutes the culinary heart of the 5th *arrondissment.* Spreading from the "Mouf," traditional and ethnic restaurants spill down through the rue Descartes, all the way to the bd. St-Germain, attracting not only locals, but large crowds of tourists in search of a cheap and filling meal. The specialty on the Mouf is the enormous *shwarma* sandwich, which comes with a side of crispy fries for only 22F; it can be bought at any of the numerous sandwich stands that line the sidewalks.

L'Apostrophe, 34, rue de la Mont Ste. Geneviève. Mo. Maubert-Mutualité. Tiny, unpretentious French restaurant situated on a lovely street that winds its way down the hill from the Panthéon. Somewhat garishly decorated with huge candles made to seem even larger by the collection of wax drippings that adorn their sides. Three *menus:* 49F served until 8pm, 59F until 9pm, and 75F until closing. Open Tues.-Sat. noon-2pm and 7-10pm.

Chez Lena et Mimille, 34, rue Tournefort (tel. 47 07 72 47). Mo. Censier Daubenton. Truly *cares* about its food. Elegant but pricey traditional French cuisine served in this small pink restaurant. In warmer months try the terrace which overlooks an exquisite tree-lined *place.* Soak up French *joie de vivre* when the festive sing-along begins. Open noon-2pm and 6-8pm. Reservations recommended in nice weather.

Restaurant Perraudin, 157, rue St-Jacques. Mo. Luxembourg or Maubert-Mutualité. Family-style bistro where individual coffee filters perched atop the coffee cups invoke a bygone era of simple, affordable dining. Order the chef s daily suggestions, or try old favorites like *sautée d agneau aux flageolets* (sauteed lamb with white beans, 55F). Come early; this place gets crowded. Appetizers 25F, main dishes 50-60F. Open Tues.-Fri. noon-2:15pm and 7:30-10:15pm, Sat. and Mon. 7:30-10:15pm.

Le Clos Descartes, 10, rue Descartes. Mo. Maubert-Mutualité. A miniscule restaurant in the heart of the Latin Quarter, that melts the best *raclette* around, including potatoes, *charcuterie,* and as much melted, runny raclette-cheese as you can scoop on top.

Café Le Volcan, 10, rue Thouin. Mo. Cardinal Lemoine. A boisterous restaurant with a young clientele at home in a plain brick-floored interior. The 55F *menu* includes appetizer, main dish, dessert; at lunch they throw in a glass of wine as well. Open daily noon-2:30pm and 7-11:30pm.

Sixth Arrondissement: St-Germain des Prés

Tiny restaurants with rock-bottom *prix-fixe menus* jostle each other for space and customers in this *arrondissement.* The streets around the rue de Buci, including rue Dauphine and rue du Seine, offer excellent bargain restaurants as well as expansive and rambling daily street markets, where you can pick up anything from a whole roasted chicken and fries to fresh yogurts and cheeses. The **rue Grégoire de Tours** takes the cake for highest density of cheap restaurants and makes a great place to start if you feel like doing a little menu browsing. Farther west, toward the St-Germain-des-Prés area and closer to the 7th *arrondissment,* cheap restaurants fade fast and are replaced by immaculately elegant and horrifically overpriced watch-and-be-watched cafés and restaurants.

Orestias, 4, rue Gregoire de Tours, off bd. St-Germain (tel. 43 54 62 01). Mo. Odéon. *Menu* has copious first and second courses as well as cheese or dessert for only 44F at lunch *and* dinner. Both the food—grilled meats, fries, green beans—and ambience are supremely average, but you can't eat more for less anywhere in the area. Open daily 11:30am-11:30pm.

Così, 54 rue du Seine, off rue de Buci. Mo. Odéon. Strains of *Così Fan Tutte* emanate from this hip sandwich shop. Superb sandwiches stuffed with curried turkey, goat cheese, and tomato and basil salad go for 30-40F. More than mere sandwiches, these suckers are creations. Respectable wines go for 12F per glass. Open daily noon-11pm.

Le Petit Vatel, 5, rue Lobineau. Mo. St-Germain-des-Prés or Mabillon. Eat delicious, inexpensive meals at plastic tables adorned with simple bouquets of daisies. A 64F *menu* includes rotating daily specialties like *lapin au vin blanc* (rabbit in white wine sauce), and vegetarian stews. Take-out available. Open Mon.-Sat. noon-3pm and 7pm-midnight, Sun. 7pm-midnight. Closed one week in Aug.

Restaurant Des Beaux Arts, 11, rue Bonaparte, across from the Ecole des Beaux Arts. Mo. St-Germain-des-Prés. Extremely popular with the locals, this place features friendly service, a simple decor and festive frescoed walls. Renowned food writer A. J. Liebling learned to eat here as a "student" in the 1920s. The 67F *menu* (wine or beer included) includes *lapin à la moutarde* (rabbit with mustard sauce) and *maquereau aux pommes à l huile* (mackeral with apples in oil) as well as a daily vegetarian dish. Open daily noon-2:30pm and 7-10:45pm.

Seventh Arrondissement

Contrary to what you might expect, the military and ministerial seventh actually offers affordable food. Don't expect great variety—*crêpes* and traditional meat dishes are the order of the day—but the standards are well executed. To buy your own bread, cheese, wine, and meat, invade the **rue Cler** between rue de Grenelle and av. de la Motte-Picquet. *Fromagers, boulangers,* and *bouchers* sell their tasty wares side-by-side; fruit and vegetable stands abound. The seventh is also a good place to indulge in that 100F-plus *menu* meal that you promised to do at least once in Paris.

La Pie Gourmande, 30, rue de Bourgogne. Mo. Varenne or Chambre des Députés. Families, jean-clad friends, and civil-servants mix happily in this comfortable *crêperie.* Sit at the counter or one of the floral-clothed tables and unwind to the sound of sizzling *galettes* (*crêpe* cousins; 35-45F) and *crêpes* (for dessert; 18-35F). Open Mon.-Fri. 11:30am-3pm.

Sampieru Corsu, 12, rue de l Amiral Roussin, 15*ème.* Mo. Cambronne. A short hike from the 7th, but worth the worn shoe leather. Run by a Marxist Corsican separatist. Simple tables that you might share with other visitors. You are expected to pay according to your means, though the suggested price for the simple, but copious, three-course *menu* is 36F (beer or wine included). Give a little extra for the artist on nights when entertainment is offered. Open Mon.-Fri. 11:45am-1:45pm and 7-9:30pm.

Au Babylone, 13, rue de Babylone. Mo. Sèvres-Babylone. Jovial atmosphere—a faithful local clientele as French as Pépé le Pew. Classy red tablecloths match the classic French food. An 80F *menu* includes appetizer, steak or *plat du jour,* and drink or dessert. A la carte appetizers 12-20F, main dishes 45-60F (try the *gigot d'agneau*—45F), desserts 15-18F. Open Sept.-July Mon.-Sat. 11:30am-2pm.

CROQ 100WICH, 23, av. de la Motte Picquet, Mo. Ecole Militaire or Latour-Maubourg. A quick bite at the lunch counter or to go: Filling sandwiches (15-22F) or warm quiche (16F). Salads look small but taste big—*la salade paysanne* is chock full o'potatoes, chicken, bacon, olives and other good stuff. Vegetarian options. Open Mon.-Fri. 9am-8pm, Sat. 9am-5pm.

La Croque au Sel, 131, rue St. Dominique. Mo. Ecole Militaire. Good country cuisine in a charming restaurant with brightly painted windows and nifty ceramic lamps. Eat excellent *pavé de boeuf émincé* (roast beef) smothered in *sauce croque au sel* as one-third of the 68F *menu.* Salads 30-40F, main dishes 60-70F, desserts 20-30F. The difference between the 68F and the 98F *menus* is, as the waiter explains, more choice and 30F. Open Mon.-Fri. noon-2pm and 7-10:30pm, Sat. 7-10:30pm.

Fourteenth Arrondissement: Montparnasse

Montparnasse consists of that area where the fashionable sixth *arrondissement* meets the commercial fourteenth. Center of expatriate life in the 1920s, it provided a surplus of cafés and restaurants for the Hemingway/Stein crowd. In the same period it saw an explosion of *crêperies* introduced by an influx of Breton immigrants, carrying the recipe for their notorious thin pancakes. Montparnasse remains rife with expensive cafés and restaurants. In recent years, however, the area has become a favorite of tourists rather than artists.

Restaurant au Rendez-Vous des Camioneurs, 34, rue des Plantes (tel. 45 40 43 36). Mo. Alesia. A low-key establishment, which puts more emphasis on the food than on decor, offering honest traditional fare at unbeatable prices. The 60F *menu* includes such delights as stuffed grape leaves and *civet de lapin* (rabbit stew). Open Mon.-Fri. 12:45-2:45pm and 6-9:30pm.

Le Jerobam, 72, rue Didot. Mo. Plaisance. An authentic, comfortable French restaurant serving superb traditional fare at unbeatable prices. 65F lunch *menu* includes delectably prepared dishes such as *Tagine de Poisson aux olives et citron confit* (a fish stew with preserved lemons and olives). Dinner *menu* 85F. Open Tues.-Sat. noon-2pm and 7-10pm, Mon. noon-2pm.

Crêperie St-Malo, 53, rue de Montparnasse. Mo. Edgar Quinet. The most appealing of the *crêperies*. A 49F *menu* includes a meat *crêpe*, a dessert *crêpe,* hard cider and coffee for 49F. Open Mon.-Sat. noon-2:30pm and 6-10:30pm.

Aquarius Café, 40, rue Gergovie (tel. 45 42 10 29). Mo. Pernety. A beautifully serene vegetarian restaurant, where light wood tables and an exceptionally friendly staff enhance a politically correct meal. The famous "mixed grill" includes tofu sausages, cereal sausages, wheat pancakes, wheat germ, brown rice, and vegetables in a mushroom sauce for 65F. Positively yummy desserts 30-40F. Open July-Sept. Mon.- Sat. noon-2:30pm and 6:30-10pm.

Restaurant Le Berbère, 53, rue Gergovie. Mo. Pernety. A serious selection of Moroccan specialties, including a hearty *couscous* with chicken or beef for just 42F. Be sure to save enough room to attack the glorious dessert tray at the end, which supports an amazing array of fantastic sugar creations. For 20F, I wouldn't kick the honey-laden baklava out of *my* bed. Open Mon.-Sat. noon-2pm and 7-10pm.

Thirteenth Arrondissement
It's Chinatown, Jake. Many choices.

Rive Droite (Right Bank)

First and Second Arrondissements: Around the Louvre and Les Halles
The first and second *arrondissements* attract the kind of diner who enters a restaurant not because of how it feeds, but because of how it looks, darling. Thus an unfortunate number of obscenely overpriced restaurants cater to the tidal waves of tourists and businesspeople who wash over the area. Fast-food establishments, hardly a satisfying alternative, fill the void of inexpensive restaurants. Despite the many laughably high prices, realize that excellent bargains do exist (many for lunch only); they are lauded and frequented by a loyal French clientele.

L'Incroyable, 26, rue de Richelieu or 23, rue de Montpensier, 1er. Mo. Palais-Royal. This intimate restaurant serves up a three-course *menu* at an *incroyable* 58F (in the evening 68F). *Foie de veau* 55F, *confit de veau* 70F. Choose between the terrace and quaintly decorated interior. Open Tues.-Fri. 11:45am-2:15pm and 6:30-9pm, Sat. and Mon. 11:45am-2:15pm. Closed in late Dec. and the first three weeks of Jan.

Au Petit Ramoneur, 74, rue St-Denis, 1er. Mo. Les Halles. Bounteous food in a solid, working-class ambience. The restaurant's location is convenient if you're visiting St-Eustache or Les Halles. Sit on the terrace and watch businessmen in suits darting into gaudily lit sex stores where they watch videos or buy flavored toys. 61F *menu* includes appetizer, main course, salad and a 1/2-liter of wine. Open Mon.-Fri. 11:30am-2:30pm and 6:30pm-9:15pm.

Crémerie Louvois, 5, rue Louvois, 2ème. Mo. Quatre-Septembre. Quick service, good simple food, low prices. A 3-course *menu* for 48F (2 courses for 42F). A small glass of red wine only 3F. Open Mon.-Sat. 11:30am-2:45pm. Closed in Aug.

Ma Normandie, 11, rue Rameau, 2ème. Mo. Pyramides. Down from the Bibliothèque Nationale on the pl. Louvois. A crowded restaurant with a jovial, laid-back atmosphere. A 51F lunch *menu* promises *service rapide* to a largely business crowd. The regulars clamor for *couscous* on the days they have it. The 105F dinner *menu* offers a variety of meat selections. Open Mon.-Sat. 11:30am-3:30pm.

L'Epi d'Or, 25, rue J.-J. Rousseau, 1er. Mo. Les Halles. Expensive, but girlfriend, it's worth it. The dignified interior is adorned with linen tablecloths and polished wood. Service is polite, the clientele refined. *Onglet à l'échalotte* (flank steak) 80F, heavenly *entrecôte Bordelaise* 95F, steak *tartare* 90F. Open Mon.-Fri. noon-2:30pm and 7:30-11:30pm, Sat. 7:30-11:30pm.

Lescure, 7, rue de Mondovi, 1er. Mo. Concorde. Animated ambience has accompanied hearty French cuisine for over 70 years in this popular restaurant. 98F *menu* (includes three courses and wine) offers a wide selection and huge servings. Open Mon.-Fri. noon-2:15pm and 7-10pm, Sat. noon-2:15pm. Closed in Aug.

Country Life, 6, rue Daunou, 2*ème*. Mo. Opéra. Vegetarian *haute cuisine* in a charming, wooded health food store. 58F buffet includes soups and salads as well as hot and cold entrees. Restaurant open Mon.-Fri. 11:30am-2:30pm. Store open Mon.-Thurs. 10am-6:30pm, Fri. 10am-3pm.

Third and Fourth Arrondissement: Le Marais

Bargains do exist in this residential neighborhood, but you'll have to look hard. Avoid the area immediately surrounding Les Halles—better food at better prices awaits just a few blocks from the underground shopping mall. **Rue des Rosiers,** running through the heart of the 4th *arrondissement,* is the focal point of the city's Jewish population. Here you'll find superb kosher delicatessens and excellent Middle Eastern *patisseries,* although the prices aren't as low as you would expect. The area remains lively on Sunday, when many other districts shut down.

La Dame Tartine, 2, rue Bisemiche, 4*ème*. Mo. Rambuteau. From the ample terrace, watch the sculptures in the Stravinsky fountain bob about. The restaurant itself has an atmosphere almost as lively as the fountain. A mostly young crowd. Good value for your money—main courses 20-36F. Open daily noon-11:30pm.

L'Arbre Aux Sabots, 3, rue Simon Leclerc, 4*ème*. Mo. Rambuteau. The decor (a lot of Klimt, some temporary art exhibits), and a good location near Beaubourg may explain why this restaurant attracts such an artsy crowd. It can't hurt that the *menu* is a bargain: 65F for 3 courses of reasonably good food plus 1/4-liter of wine. A la carte, mixed fish with wine sauce is 70F, *emincé* of fowl with liqueur 65F. Open Mon.-Fri. noon-midnight.

La Taverne, 5, place de la Republique, 3*ème*. Mo. Republique. Beer lovers unite. This Belgian cuisine, which takes the merits of beer seriously, features mussels cooked in, um, beer, (54F, plus 20F if you take a side order of *pommes frites),* and, aaaahhh, beer fondue. Open daily 9am-2am.

Chez Marianne, 2, rue des Hospitaliers St-Gervais, 4*ème*. Mo. St-Paul. Nearly every Israeli specialty and many Eastern European ones served here. Known for falafel, blini, pirogi, and *gâteau de fromage,* a delicious treat rather different from what Americans call cheesecake. Popular and friendly. Sit in a cozy dining room and order 4, 5, or 6 specialties (50F, 60F, or 70F) from options such as chopped liver, tabouli, or hummus. Falafel 30F. Take-out available. Open Sat.-Thurs. 11am-midnight.

Le Bourgeois Gentilhomme, 75, rues des Archives, 3*ème*. Mo. Arts et Métiers. Pleasant neighborhood restaurant, serving reasonable food at good prices. A 3-course *menu* costs 62F. A la carte: fowl with lemon (57F), beef *Bourgeois Gentilhomme* (68F), and duck in honey sauce (94F). Open Mon.-Fri. noon-2:30pm and 7:30-9:30pm.

Les Arcades, 4, rue Charlot, 3*ème*. Mo. Filles du Calvaire. A small restaurant frequented mainly by people from the neighborhood. 58F *menu* includes a wide choice of 3 courses plus 1/4-liter of wine. Prices a la carte are not much higher: chicken with olives costs 40F, and a steak is 50F. Open Mon.-Sat. 8am-2am.

Eighth Arrondissement: Champs-Elysées

You should know better than to expect inexpensive restaurants amid embassies and salons of *haute couture.* The eighth *arrondissement* is the *Michelin* diner's dream come true. Many of Paris's finest and most famous restaurants have assembled in this posh neighborhood. Alas, *Let's Go* diners might want to drift back to the first or second *arrondissements* for a bargain meal after strolling through the eighth's famous *grands boulevards.* Of course, resourceful city that it is, Paris does in fact offer a few select affordables amid this pantheon of opulence.

L'Aubergade, 122 rue la Boétie. Mo. Franklin D. Roosevelt. Chaos may reign a few steps away on rue la Boétie, but you will find peace through the stained glass doors here. Lacy tablecloths, arched mirrors, and a luscious dessert table will entice you to linger, as will the 55F lunch *menu:* a filling salad and meat or fish dish. Also 75F and 120F *menus.* Open Mon.-Fri. 10am-3pm and 6-11:30pm, Sat. 6-11:30pm.

Persepoliss, 66, av. des Champs-Elysées in the basement of Galerie Point Show no. 69. Mo. Franklin D. Roosevelt. Sweep aside the door beads, and a tacky bronze-esque wall hanging, as well as generous portions of Persian specialities, will greet you here. A 37F *menu* includes a meat dish accompanied by a heaping plate of rice. *Menus* at 42F, 59F and 79F get progressively more elaborate; try the *gheymeh polo* (47F). Open Mon.-Sat. 11am-3pm and 7-11:30pm.

Dynastie Thai, 101, rue La Boétie. Mo. St. Philippe du Roule. An acknowledged top choice among Paris's Asian restaurants. Take advantage of the bargain weekday menu to sample exquisitely prepared Thai cuisine in an ambience *de luxe. Menu* 90F, weekdays only. Open daily noon-2:30pm and 7-11:30pm.

Ninth and Tenth Arrondissements

Heading north from the Marais, the elegant mansions yield to affordable places, terrific deals that only locals know about.

Hit by the projectile force of the city's skyrocketing prices, much of ethnic Paris has found itself in these outer quarters of the city. As a result, wondrous delicacies from former French colonies spill forth from this quarter. Shuffle north of the overpriced Opéra area for the best bargains. Try to venture out in groups, as not all areas are wildly safe. In particular, be aware of the Pigalle area of the ninth and the place de la République southern end of the tenth.

Taverne Kronenbourg, 24, bd. des Italiens, 9*ème.* Mo. Richelieu-Drouot. Cheery waiters serve up healthy portions of heavy Alsatian favorites, including plenty of *choucroûte,* in a huge comfortable café atmosphere perfectly designed for optimal people-gazing. 79F and 170F *menus.* Open daily noon-1am.

Paris-Dakar, 95, rue du Faubourg St-Martin, 10*ème.* Mo. Gare de l'Est. Run by a Senegalese family, this place is heralded as "the most African of all African restaurants." Brochettes and curries abound and *Tiep Bou Dieone*—the "national dish of Senegal"—is recommended. 59F lunch *menu.* Open daily noon-4pm and 7pm-midnight.

Casa Miguel, 48, rue St-Georges, 9*ème.* Mo. St-Georges. This self-proclaimed bastion of communism holds strongly to its ideology of asking each to pay according to her means. Dinner or lunch is still 5F (unless you're an oppressive capitalist) for plentiful portions of simple (and not fantastic) fare of *couscous,* macaroni, or the like. Go for the lively, friendly atmosphere, and go early—it fills with students. Open Mon.-Sat. noon-1pm and 7-8pm, Sun. noon-1pm.

Au Boeuf Bourguignon, 21, rue de Douai, 9*ème.* Mo. Pigalle. The checkered tablecloths and movie posters contribute to the happy atmosphere. Cheerful French family presents 3-course 92F and 160F *menus,* drinks included. Clearly the *boeuf bourguignon* comes highly recommended. Open Mon.-Sat. noon-3pm and 6:30-10:30pm.

Eleventh Arrondissement: La Bastille

The little *quartier* surrounding the place de la Bastille and the recently added Opéra de la Bastille is the place St-Michel of the 1960's. In this rising neighborhood, Paris's young and trendy brush elbows with the old-fashioned French working class, creating a surprising mélange of social backgrounds. The result is a wonderfully vibrant place to dine and explore. Don't wander too far away from the pulsating heart of all this activity, the place de la Bastille itself, as neighborhoods here change as quickly as the fashions.

A la Banane Ivoirienne, 10, rue de la Forge-Royale. Mo. Daidherbe-Chaligny. Run by a gregarious Ivoirian emigré who wrote his doctoral thesis on his country's booming banana industry, this cheerful *endroit* serves delicious West African specialties, such as *attieke,* made from cassava, and *aloko,* from bananas. Entrees 49-80F. *Menu* 89F. Open Tues.-Sat. 7pm-midnight.

Au Petit Keller, 13, rue Keller. Everyone seems to be a regular in this traditional, working-class bistro in the heart of the vibrant Bastille district. A 60F *menu* includes filling and wholesome food and beer or wine. *Gâteau de riz* (rice cake) is the house specialty. Open Mon.-Fri. noon-2:30pm and 7-9pm.

Occitanie, 96, rue Oberkampf. Mo. St-Maur. Specialties form the south of France. *Formules express* 46-55F offer varying combinations of salads, wine, tabouli and the *plat du jour. Entrées* 30-50F, *plats* 45-92F. Open mid-August to mid-July Mon.-Fri. noon-2pm and 7-10:30pm, Sat. 7-10:30pm.

Au Trou Normand, 9, rue Jean-Pierre Timbaud. Mo. Oberkampf. With its orange tablecloths and unbelievably low-priced no-fuss French food, this place is an institution. The lunch crowd has clearly been here before. Not huge portions. Appetizers 9-13F, *plats du jour* 29-39F, tasty desserts 9-13F. Open Mon.-Fri. noon-2:30pm and 7:30-11pm, Sat. 7:30-11pm. Closed Aug.

Sixteenth Arrondissement

The affluent sixteenth *arrondissement* is not a mecca for cheap eat seekers. If you're visiting this corner, heading back to the student quarter for a less expensive meal may be well worth the trip. The standard *croques monsieur* and sandwiches are available here, but if you wish to indulge a little, visit **Les Chauffeurs,** 8, chaussée de la Muette (Mo. La Muette). The checkered tablecloths will make you feel at home no matter where you're from, but the scenes of Paris sketched on the walls will remind you that we're not in Kansas anymore. A local professional crowd packs in at lunch for the 59F lunch *menu* and 16F bottles of wine. (Open daily noon-2:30pm and 7-11pm.)

Seventeenth Arrondissement

For shopping in the western part of the seventeenth, near the Arc de Triomphe, the **rue Poncelet** (Mo. Ternes), is the best bet, not only for its daily morning market, but also for the dozens of *charcuteries, fromageries, bûcheries,* and *boulangeries* that line the sidewalks. Toward the Place de Clichy and environs, the **Marchée des Batignolles,** a covered market (open Mon.-Sat. 7am-12:30pm and 4-7:30pm), presents choice offerings, with a variety of meat, cheese, and fruit and vegetable stands. For a quick and gargantuan *shwarma* sub (with fries and a drink for 27F) amble up to the nameless Turkish joint at 76, av. Clichy (Mo. Place de Clichy; open Mon.-Sat. 11am-10pm). Parisians from all over the seventeenth float in through the door of **Paul,** a bakery at 4, rue Poncelet (Mo. Ternes), following the overpowering scent that wafts from its crusty loaves. Even if you're not in the area, this place merits a special pilgrimage. (Open Mon. and Wed.-Sat. 6:30am-7:30pm. Sun. 6:30am-1pm.)

Eighteenth Arrondissement: Montmartre

The 18th abounds with charming, cheap-ish places to eat. The trick is to stay away from the place du Tertre and walk down the *butte* to more interesting, cheaper, and less touristy places. Go in groups, because this area at night (especially close to the places Pigalle, Anvers, and Blanche) can be, if not dangerous, at least unpleasant, especially for women.

La Villa des Poulbots, 10, rue Dancourt. Mo. Anvers. Sumptuously elegant and scrumptiously cheap. Plush velvet chairs and tapestried walls. The 41F, 68F, 95F, and 120F *menus* let you dine like royalty on a peon's budget. Specialties: *magret* (breast) of duck, seafood lasagna, chicken in banana sauce. Outdoor seating as well. Open Tues.-Sun. noon-3pm and 6-9pm.

Au Grain de Folie, 24, rue la Vienville. Mo. Abbesses. A vegetarian restaurant for one and all, with a vast array of dishes from *couscous* to salads to every kind of cheese. On a quiet street. Dinner a la carte about 100F; also 65F and 100F *menus.* Open Tues-Sun. noon-3pm and 7:30-11:30pm, Mon. 7:30-11:30pm.

Le Refuge des Fondues, 19, rue des Trois Frères. Mo. Abbesses. Hey, you want selection, you go somewhere else. You want fondue, well, alright, maybe we can help you out. A whopping two main dishes: *fondue bourgignonne* (meat fondue) and *fondue savoyarde* (cheese fondue). The 80F *menu* includes appetizer, fondue, dessert, and half *pichet* (jug) of wine. Open Tues.-Sun. noon-2:30pm and 7-9:30pm, Mon. 7-9:30pm.

Nineteenth and Twentieth Arrondissements: Eastern and Northeastern Paris

The nineteenth and twentieth don't merit a special trip, but if you're staying or sightseeing in the area, a few good options present themselves. **Aux Arts et Sciences Réunis,** 161, av. Jean-Jaurès (tel. 42 40 53 18; Mo. Ourcq) offers outstanding tradtional Southwestern fare, a neigborhood clientele, and a Clemenceau-mustached *patron.* *(Menu* with 3 courses and wine for only 55F; open May-July Mon.-Fri. 6am-9pm, Sat. 8am-2pm; Sept.-June also open Sat. until 9pm. Closed in Aug.) Another goodie is Tai-Yien, 5, rue de Belleville (tel. 42 41 44 16; Mo. Belleville). A big and simple "food factory," with excellent Chinese dishes. (Open daily 10am-2am. Take-out available.)

Sweets

Indulge your fickle foreign sweet-teeth on some real ice cream with one of Paris's renowned *glaces,* which are lighter, wetter, and less creamy than their American counterparts, or work off all those cardio-funk exercise classes with a sinfully exquisite French pastry at any number of *patisseries.*

Berthillon, 31, rue St-Louis-en-l'Ile, 4ème, on the Ile-St-Louis. Mo. Cité or Pont Marie. Quite simply the best ice cream in Paris; unfortunately it's also the most expensive. Every imaginable flavor. Open Sept.-July Tues.-Sun. 10am-8pm.

Mandarine, 6, Place du Marché Ste. Catherine, 4ème. Mo. St-Paul. A small café in a cobblestone square at the heart of the Marais. Superb ice cream from the legendary Berthillon (see above). Two (large) scoops 32F; pastries 32F. Take-out service: two (smaller) scoops 18F. Open Fri.-Wed. 11am-midnight in good weather and 3pm-midnight in bad weather.

Peltier, 66, rue de Sèvres, 7ème. Mo. Vaneau or Duroc. Also: 6, rue St-Dominique, 7ème. Mo. Solférino. This delectable sweet-tooth haven concocts the not overly rich, but oh-so-gooey *tarte au chocolat,* with a gold drop in the middle (16F). Homesick travelers will appreciate the sight of Peltier's "normally shaped" bread (24-32F). Open Mon.-Sat. 9:30am-7:45pm, Sun. 8:30am-7pm.

Maison du Chocolat, 4, bd. de la Madeleine, 9ème. Mo. Madeleine. Every imaginable kind of chocolate: bonbons, blocks, milk chocolate, dark chocolate. Plus delicious ice cream and sorbets. A place *not* to be missed.

L'Arbre à Canelle, 57, passage de Panoramas, 2ème. Mo. Rue Montmartre or Bourse. Cakes and tarts baked fresh every morning and served in a pleasant *galerie*—a little less elegant, but rather more animated. Tarts 26-30F; salads 39-54F. Open Mon.-Sat. 10:30am-6:30pm.

Cafés

> *The hours I have spent in cafés are the only ones I call living, apart from writing.*
>
> —Anaïs Nin

Cafés entered Parisian society in 1675 when **Le Procope** opened its doors to an eager coffee-drinking, cigarette-smoking crowd that included such luminaries as Volatire, Montesquieu, Diderot, and Rousseau. Parisian café culture means first finding a favorite place and making it yours, a home away from home. Next, cultivate the correct etiquette. Learn to nurse a tiny espresso for hours, to stare at passers-by without lowering your eyes if they stare back, to flaunt the title of an intimidating tome while pretending to read, to buy round after round of beer as a lively conversation spins off into the night. Cafés near monuments charge monumental prices for minimal atmosphere. The best seats in the theater of Parisian culture are the cafés on fashionable thoroughfares, such as the Champs-Elysées, bd. St-Germain, bd. Montparnasse, or rue de la Paix. To be sure, they charge exorbitant prices (coffee 14-25F), but an intriguing crowd passes the sidewalk tables, providing hours of entertainment for the price of one cup.

More casual crowds frequent the more dilapidated, hidden spots where coffee is only 8F and the use of *argot* (slang) makes eavesdropping an educational challenge. Make sure the prices posted outside correspond to your budget, and be picky before you relax. Prices are usually much lower if you stand at the bar *(comptoir* or *zinc)* rather than sitting down. If you order *un café,* expect a little cup of potent espresso. Referring to a coffee with milk as *"café au lait"* is an immediate two strikes against your social reputation; refer to it as *"un crème, grand"* or *"un crèmr petit. "*

Café Costes, 4-6, rue Berger, pl. des Innocents, 1er. Mo. Les Halles. Opened in 1905, Philippe Starck's strikingly modern café is a fashionable people-watching spot between Les Halles and Beaubourg. Coffee 16F, sandwiches 26-40F. Open daily 8am-2am.

Le Flore, 172, bd. St-Germain, 6ème, next door to Les Deux Magots. A favorite stomping ground of Jean-Paul Sartre, who even penned his masterpiece *L'être et le Néant (Being and Nothingness)* while sipping coffee here. Apollinaire, Picasso, and André Breton also sipped their brew in this shiny, happy atmosphere. Coffee 22F. Open daily 7:30am-1:30am.

Café de la Paix (tel. 40 07 30 12), at the corner of av. de l'Opéra and, rue de la Paix, *2ème*. Mo. Opéra. This institution on the rue de la Paix (the most expensive piece of property on French Monopoly) has served a wealthy clientele ever since its founding in 1862. Stop by if think you can tolerate a 26F Coke on the terrace. Open daily 10am-1am.

Les Deux Magots, 6, pl. St-Germain-des-Prés, *6ème* (Mo. St-Germain-des-Prés). Sartre's second choice and Simone de Beauvoir's first—the two first spotted each other here. A home to Parisian literati since its opening in 1875, the two Magots is now a favorite of Parisian youth. Before you enter, buy your Roland Barthes and Jacques Derrida at **La Lune,** the *hyper-chic* bookstore across the street, and brood over them as you drink your espresso. Coffee 22F. Open daily 8am-2am.

La Coupole, 102, bd. du Montparnasse, *14ème* and **Le Séléct,** 99, bd. du Montparnasse, *6ème*. Both Mo. Vavin. Two of the most famous cafés in Paris, these animated and oh-so-chic establishments have served political exiles (Lenin and Trotsky), musicians (Stravinsky and Satie), writers (Hemingway, Breton, Cocteau), and artists (Picasso and Eisenstein). So...who are you? Coffee 12F. Both open daily 8am-2am.

La Closerie des Lilas, 171, bd. de Montparnasse, *6ème*. Mo. Vavin. Hemingway adored this lovely flower-bedecked café (a scene in *The Sun Also Rises* takes place here), as did the Dadaïsts and Surrealists before him. Picasso stopped by here weekly to hear Paul Fort recite poetry. Exquisite decor. Coffee 24F. Open daily 10:30am-2am.

Salons de thé

Less crowded and less famous than cafés, *salons de thé* are just as much a ritual of *savoir vivre*—knowing how to live. Here, sample a fresher, more extensive offering of light meals and exquisite pastries.

Christian Constant, 26, rue du Bac, *7ème*. Mo. Rue du Bac. On one of the tastiest streets in Paris, this tearoom offers over 30 types of tea as well as 5 varieties of sugar. Modern chic rather than elegantly refined, but the desserts and chocolate transcend mere prose (Opéra 18F). Fresh jams and jellies line the windows. Open Mon.-Sat. 8am-8pm.

Le Loir Dans la Théière, 3, rue des Rosiers, *4ème*. Mo. St-Paul. The name means "the dormouse in the teapot," an allusion to the Mad Hatter's tea party in *Alice and Wonderland*. A unique, comfortable atmosphere somewhere between an upper-crust *salon* and bohemian student lodgings. Tea 20F, coffee 10-12F. Homemade cakes 35-45F. Sunday brunch 100F. Open Mon.-Sat. noon-11pm; Sun. 11am-11pm.

Thé-Troc, corner of rue de Nemours and rue de Jean-Pierre Timbaud, *11ème*. Mo. Parmentier. Call it the alternative *salon de thé*—non-smoking, environmentally conscious, with windows chock full o' teas, spices, Asian figurines, as well as records, comics, and T-shirts, all on sale inside. Natural and perfumed teas 13-18F. Open Mon.-Fri. 9am-noon and 2-8pm, Sat. 10am-1pm and 4-8pm.

René Saint-Ouen's salon de thé, 111, Bd. Haussmann, *8ème,* corner of rue d'Argenson. Mo. Miromesnil. Specializes in bread sculptures—bikes, horses, dogs, ducks, etc. Grab an edible Eiffel Tower for 45F.

Marais Plus, 20, rue des Francs Bourgeois, *3ème*. Mo. St-Paul. This teahouse has a pleasant, cultured feel to it, perhaps because it is the annex of a bookstore, or perhaps because it is surrounded by fine old buildings in the Marais. Fresh pastry 33F, coffee 15F, tea 23F. Open daily 10am-7pm.

A Priori Thé, 35-37, Galerie Vivienne, *2ème*. Mo. Bourse or Palais Royal. Classy place to have a meal or just sip tea. Shielded from the city noise because it's tucked away in a pleasant *galerie* (see Sights). You can get to the *galerie* from 6, rue Vivienne, 4, rue des Petits Champs, or 5, rue de la Banque. Single-course meals in the 75-85F range. Tea 22F. Open Mon.-Sat. noon-7pm, Sun. 1-6pm. Tea service starts at 3pm.

Wine Bars

Although wine bistros have existed since the early 19th century, the modern wine bar emerged only a few years ago with the invention of a machine that pumps nitrogen into the open bottle, thus protecting the wine from oxidation. Rare, expensive wines, exorbitant by the bottle, have become somewhat affordable by the glass, but this is still not the place for pinching pennies. Expect to pay 20-80F for a glass of high-quality wine; your entire meal (and you should do more than drink a glass) will run about 200F. With restraint, lunch verges on affordable.

Try to go with a friend who knows wine, a helpful guide book, or an open mind and inquisitive tongue. The owners personally and carefully select the wines which constitute their *caves* (cellars) and are usually available to help out less knowledgeable patrons. Over 100-strong, the wine shops in the **Nicolas** chain are reputed for having the world's most inexpensive cellars, though Nicolas himself owns the fashionable and expensive wine bar **Jeroboam,** 8, rue Monsigny, 2ème (tel. 42 61 21 71; Mo. Opéra). Enjoy your bottle or glass with a full meal or a *tartine* (cheese and/or *charcuteries*—French equivalent of cold cuts—served on *pain Poilâne* or *pain de campagne).* And don't hesitate to ask the waiters for advice on which wine best complements your order.

Jacques Mélac, 42, rue Léon Frot, 11ème. Mo. Charonne. *The* Parisian family-owned wine bar. Also an excellent bistro, frequented by a friendly crowd. Stop by in Sept. when owner Mélac harvests his own vines and convinces some women to crush them with their feet. Call for exact date. *Tartines* from 16F, wine from 15F per glass. Open Aug. 15-July 15 Mon., Wed., and Fri. 9am-7pm, Tues. and Thurs. 9am-10pm.

Au Sauvignon, 80, rue des Sts-Pères, 7ème. Mo. Sèvres-Babylone. This wine bar offers a sublime sampling of Beaujolais (especially in early Nov.) and Alsatian wines. Caricatures praising the owner and his wines coat the walls. Wine from 25F a glass. Open Sept.-July Mon.-Sat. 9am-11pm.

Le Val d'Or, 28, av. Franklin D. Roosevelt, 8ème. Mo. St-Philippe-du Roule. Just steps away from the Champs-Elysées. Wonderful wines from all across France, including a magnificent selection of Beaujolais in Nov. Wine 25-80F (10-15F per glass at counter). Excellent home-made quiche and pastries (30-50F). Open Mon.-Fri. 8am-9pm, Sat. 8am-6pm.

Le Bar du Caveau, place Dauphine, 1er. Mo. Cité. Stylishly dressed Parisians make a point of meeting for a liquid lunch at this traditionally brass and wood saloon where they can sample glasses from the vast selection of heavenly wines (14-35F) over a plate of grilled goat cheese and Poilane bread (40F). It s not cheap, but it is worth every *sou.* Open Mon.-Sat. 10am-8pm.

University Restaurants

Anyone with a student ID can buy meal tickets at each restaurant from 11:30am to 1:30pm and from 6 to 8pm. (Tickets 18F40, *carnet* of 10 100F.) University restaurants are often crowded with students, thus providing a good opportunity to meet some local friends. For more information, including summer and weekend schedules, stop at **CROUS,** 30, av. Georges Bernanos, 5ème (tel. 40 51 36 00; Mo. Port-Royal). The following University Restaurants are most convenient but the list is not nearly exhaustive. In addition, all the following, except Citeaux, Grand Palais, and C.H.U. Necker are also *brasseries,* open between lunch and dinner for sandwiches and drinks.

Bullier, 39, av. Georges Bernanos, 5ème. Mo. Port-Royal.

Censier, 31, rue Geoffroy St-Hilaire, 5ème. Mo. Censier Daubenton. Closed for dinner.

Châtelet, 10, rue Jean Calvin, 5ème. Mo. Censier Daubenton.

Assas, 92, rue d'Assas, 6ème. Mo. Port-Royal or Notre-Dame-des-Champs. Closed for dinner.

Mabillon, 3, rue Mabillon, 6ème. Mo. Mabillon.

Grand Palais, cours de la Reine, 8ème. Mo. Champs-Elysées Clemenceau.

Citeaux, 45, bd. Diderot, 12ème. Mo. Gare de Lyon.

C.H.U. Pitié-Salpe-Trière, 105, bd. de l'Hôpital, 13ème. Mo. St-Marcel.

Dareau, 13-17, rue Dareau, 14ème. Mo. St-Jacques.

C.H.U. Necker, 156, rue de Vaugirard, 15ème. Mo. Pasteur.

Dauphine, av. de Pologne, 16ème. Mo. Porte Dauphine.

All Night

You'll have to look far and wide for a moonlight eatery in the City of Lights. What you find might not be altogether sumptuous, and it may be significantly overpriced. Don't expect a variety of options. **Le Poule au Pot,** 9, rue de Vauvilliers, 1er (Mo. Les

Halles) serves decent French food at steep prices. (Open Tues.-Sat. 7pm-6am, Sun. 7pm-4am.) **The Front Page,** 56-58, rue St-Denis (Mo. Chatelet-Les-Halles), brings a piece of The Village to Paris. (Open daily 11:30am-5:30am.) **Feri's,** 76, rue Mazarine, 6*ème* (Mo. Odéon) offers take-out sandwiches (15-30F), croissants (5-10F), and salads (10-25F). (Open daily 11am-6am.) Fine for a light snack, the **Ancienne Comédie,** 10, rue de l'Ancienne Comédie (Mo. Odéon) bakes bread and pastries. (Open Mon.-Sat. 8am-8am, Sun. 9pm-6:30am.)

Shopping for Food

The ultimate in fine food elegance preens at **Fauchon,** 28, pl. de la Madeleine, 9*ème* (tel 47 42 60 11; Mo. Madeleine), where mouth-watering windows display tarts, *pâtés,* and meats seemingly too beautiful for human consumption. Don't touch the merchandise—one of the ever-attentive staff will pick your fancies off the shelves for you. The café/cafeteria downstairs can actually be affordable with pastries for 17-30F and perfectly prepared plates of *taboulie* or *terrine* for 30-50F. You must buy something at Fauchon, if only to parade your black-and-white shopping bag around Paris during the rest of your stay. (Open Mon.-Sat 9:40-7pm.) **Hédiard,** 21, pl. de la Madeleine (tel. 42 66 44 36) sells fine teas, spices, and fruits under a classy red and black awning. (Open Mon.-Sat. 9:30am-9pm.) Their neighboring *cave* offers a fine selection of wines.

Some of the city's best pastries and chocolates are at **Patisserie Le Nôtre,** 44, rue du Bac, 7*ème,* and 44, rue d'Auteuil, 16*ème.* **Alleosse,** 13, rue Poncelet, 17*ème,* stocks an immense and exquisite selection of cheeses, and the **Charcuterie Coesnon,** 30, rue Dauphine, 6*ème,* carries traditional homemade sausage and prepared foods. The market (**Monoprix, Prisunic,** and **Uniprix**) is a wonderful and cheap place to do your shopping. The **Nicolas** chain sells wines at inexpensive prices, but do not always carry the widest selections. Look for small neighborhood stores—the ones where bottles are covered in five-year-old layers of dust—to unearth some truly incredible deals. Browse through Patricia Wells's *A Food Lover's Guide to Paris* (available in bookstores) for a candid discussion of the city's most tantalizing restaurants, *patisseries, fromageries, charcuteries,* cafés, wine bars, and *salons de thé.*

Sights

Sightseeing in Paris is redundant: the whole city is a sight. Even the city's design, largely the product of urban planner and architect Baron Georges-Eugène Haussmann, deserves your attention. Commissioned by Napoleon III to make the city more resistant to attack, Haussmann widened the major streets in order to facilitate movement of the military. The result was the metamorphosis of Paris from an intimate medieval city to a bustling modern metropolis. His "assaults" on the city included leveling hills (there were seven before Haussmann; now only Montmartre and Parc des Buttes Chaumont remain), expanding the system of sewers, widening existing streets, and building new thoroughfares to make the city both more accessible and more monumental. Catering to the decadent 19th-century bourgeoisie, his grandiose projects left thousands homeless as beautiful new streets were blasted through existing dwellings. The entire area surrounding today's place de l'Opéra was a tranquil residential neighborhood before 1850. As its name implies, Montparnasse was a hill. Note the discrepancy between the façades on different sides of some streets: in widening the *avenues,* Haussmann often obliterated the buildings on one side while keeping those on the other side intact. Haussmann's major triumphs are the city's primary axes, emanating from the Châtelet: bd. St-Michel on the Left Bank, extending to bd. de Sébastopol on the Right Bank, and bd. St-Germain. Rue de Rivoli, with its splendid arcades is Paris's main east-west axis and may well be the most beautiful street in the city. To appreciate the city's transformation, consider that before 1850, the widest residential street was 12m from building to building. Indeed, there are historians who maintain that without Baron Haussmann, Paris would still be the world's largest medieval city. Beaudelaire sighed, *"Le vieux*

Paris n'est plus. La forme d'une ville change plus vite que le coeur d'un mortel." (Old Paris exists no longer. Alas, the form of a city changes faster than the heart of a mortal.)

Probably the biggest mistake you can make while sightseeing around Paris is to rely too heavily on itineraries. Stake out on your own, and try to understand the source of Paris's monumental-mystical-magical reputation. The tides of Parisians washing past are as intriguing as the magnificent façades of centuries-old buildings. Look around you to understand the quirks of the Parisians—their fashions, their spirits, their expressions, their conversations, their pain, their hopes, their fears, their needs, their desires, their . Wander into a café and observe this parade as it marches past. On a sunny day, kick back in one of Paris's parks. They are an integral part of city life, frequented by Parisians of all classes, tourists, bums, and dogs as refuge from the traffic and the noise of city life. Each park has its *habitués* (regulars) who come to play *boules* or *pétanque* (a sport with metal balls loosely akin to horeshoes), to feed their feathered friends, and to philosophize.

Wander around Paris as a Parisian. Leave your maps and tour guides at home. Explore and experience each twist of each little *rue*. Revel in the age-old tradition, made famous by the likes of Baudelaire, of the art of *la flânerie,* aimless strolling and observation. Your strongest memories will come from discoveries made on your own; not just in the Louvre or Notre-Dame, but also at a street market, on the *quais* of the Seine, or from a curbside seat at a café. Keep in mind that Paris was built for Parisians, not for late-capitalist tourists and their photo albums. Modern Parisians love their city, and they even regard themselves sightseers as they walk (seldom ride) from place to place. Make an effort to consider the city not through a camera, but through the eyes of a proud resident. Look at churches as houses of worship, at the Arc de Triomphe as commemorating Napoleon's *Grande Armée,* at the Eiffel Tower as the showpiece of a 19th-century world's fair, and at the Panthéon as France's tribute to its greatest luminaries. Parisians consider the most beautiful sight to be La Seine, whose banks see countless friendships, romances, break-ups, and pensive strolls. Les Invalides, place de la Bastille, place de la Concorde, and so on, are all spots of ineffable pride for the French; try to avoid yelling in English, gawking at elderly veterans, and generally behaving like Chevy Chase on vacation. Parisian churches are places of worship (even Notre-Dame); be as quite as possible (especially during a service), respect areas that are cordoned off for prayer, and observe the appropriate dress code (no shorts, low necklines, or bare shoulders).

Seine Islands

Ile de la Cité

If any one location could be called the sentimental and physical heart of Paris, the capital of the capital, it is this sliver in the river. Possessing a long and varied history, the Ile de la Cité was first inhabited by a primitive Gallic tribe of hunters, sailors and fisherfolk called the Parisii. After the Roman conquest of 52 BC, the island became the center of the Empire's Lutèce colony. In the early 6th century, Clovis crowned himself king of the Franks and adopted the embattled island as the center of his domain. During the Middle Ages, the island began to acquire the features for which it is best-known and loved today: Notre-Dame and Ste-Chapelle. As the industrial revolution lured workers into Paris, the narrow streets surrounding these buildings came to house more and more of the city's poor, until these slums were destroyed by Haussmann. The Baron left the buildings of the Middle Ages intact, but so altered the area around them that they were demoted from functioning elements in the urban fabric to anachronistic relics. Now the island sinks under the weight of countless tour buses whose passengers spill into the souvenir shops to buy the only berets you're likely to see in Paris.

The Cathédrale de Notre-Dame de Paris (Mo. Cité) was begun in 1163 but not completed until 1361. After the Revolution, the building fell into disrepair and was even used to shelter livestock. But Victor Hugo's 1831 novel, *Notre-Dame de Paris (The Hunchback of Notre Dame)* inspired thousands of citizens to push for restoration. The modifications by the architect Eugène Viollet-le-Duc (including the addition of the spire, the gargoyles and a statue of himself admiring his own work), remain highly controversial. Is Notre-Dame as we see it today a medieval building, or a product of the 19th century? Nonetheless, in 1870 and 1940, thousands of Parisians attended masses here to pray for deliverance from the invading Germans—both times without immediate success. But ultimately the calls were answered, most poignantly on August 26, 1944, when Charles de Gaulle braved sniper fire to give thanks for his victory from the altar of Notre-Dame.

Today, thousands of visitors float in sweeping torrents past the doors of the cathedral, overlooking one the most glorious aspects of the entire structure: the **façade**. Break away from the line of marching souls to admire the delicate, intricate curves that adorn the three central wooden portals. Highly symbolic, the carvings were designed to instill the fear of God and desire for righteousness in a population of which less than ten percent was literate. The central and especially picturesque **Porte du Jugement** expounds on the Damned and the Saved. In the 1790s, Revolutionaries attacked and decapitated the stone images of the kings of France above the doors. The heads were found in 1977 and were installed in the Musée de Cluny (see Museums). Replicas of the heads now crown the royal bodies.

Once you pass inside, you ll be overawed by the soaring light and seeming weightlessness of the walls. The magical verticality is created by the spidery flying buttresses which support the vaults of the ceiling from outside, allowing the walls to be opened up to stained glass. The effect is increased by a series of subtle optical illlusions, including the use of smaller pillars to surround the bigger ones, diminishing their apparent size. The most spectacular feature of the interior, and certainly the cathedral's biggest draw, is the enormous stained-glass **rose windows** that dominate the north and south ends of the transept. Free **guided tours** of the cathedral are an excellent way to acquire a deeper understanding of its history and architecture; inquire at the information booth to the right as you enter. (Tours in English Wed. noon. Tours in French Mon.-Fri. noon, Sat.-Sun. 2pm. Free.) The cathedral s **treasury** (to the south of the choir) contains a rather humdrum assortment of robes and sacramental cutlery from the stately and artistic period of 1949. (Open Mon.-Sat. 10am-6pm, Sun. 2-6pm. Admission 15F, students 10F, children under 17 5F.)

Outside again, visit the haunt of the cathedral s most famous fictional resident, the Hunchback of Notre Dame, with a hair-raising climb into the two **towers.** The perilous and claustrophobic staircase emerges onto a spectacular perch, where weather-worn gargoyles survey a stunning view of the city's heart. The climb generally deters the bus-bound tourists, and you may even have the towers relatively to yourself if you come early. Continue on (if you can face the stairs again) to the south tower, where a dwarf-sized door gives access to the 13-ton bell. (Open daily Aug. 10am-6:30pm; Sept. and April-July 9:30-11:30am and 2-5:30pm; Oct.-March 10am-4:30pm. Admission 31F, senior citizens and students 17F, children under 17 6F.)

Far below the cathedral towers, in a cool and dark excavation beneath the pavement of the *Parvis* (the square in front of the cathedral), the **Archeological Museum,** pl. du Parvis du Notre Dame (tel. 43 29 83 51), shelters an archeological dig of the remarkably preserved Roman village that once covered the island. Discovered in 1965 by construction workers digging for an underground parking garage, the ruins admit visitors for a self-guided tour as well as an exhaustive display on the history of the Ile de la Cité through dioramas and accompanying text (in both English and French). (Open daily 10am-6pm. Admission 25F, senior citizens and students 14F, children under 17 6F.)

The Palais de Justice, spanning the western side of the island, harbors numerous tribunals where you can see the law in action, as Paris's district courts have clustered here since the 13th century. All trials are open to the general public, but don t expect a *France v. Dreyfus* every day. *Chambre 1* of the *Cour d Appel* witnessed the conviction of Maréchal Pétain after his involvement in the Vichy France government of World War II. Even if your French is not up to legal jargon, the cool sobriety of the interior, along with the lawyers archaic yet stylish black robes, makes a quick visit interesting and worthwhile, especially since it s free. (Trials Mon.-Fri. 1:30pm until the day s agenda is completed, around 5pm.) Criminal cases are the most interesting; ask for the location of the criminal courtrooms (Mon.-Fri. 1:30-4pm).

At the heart of the Palais, **Ste-Chapelle** remains one of the foremost examples of 13th-century French architecture, though its imprisonment in the middle of the 19th-century Palais de Justice obscures its medieval flavor. Crowded into an interior courtyard, the beautiful exterior is lost to view; the random passerby sees no more than the iron steeple, a 19th-century addition. The church was begun in 1241 to house the most precious of King Louis IX s possessions, the crown of thorns from Christ s Passion. Although the crown—minus a few thorns that St-Louis gave away as political favors—has been moved to Notre Dame, Ste-Chapelle still remains a masterpiece. A blissfully dark and serene interior and domed roof mark a room of golds, reds and blues in the lower chapel. In the upstairs chapel, reserved for royalty and their court, an overwhelming array of stained glass windows lights the church with a hue of fine wine. Check weekly publications for the occasional concerts here, or ask at the information booth at the gate; tickets 75-155F. (Open daily 9:30am-6:30pm. Admission 25F, students and senior citizens 14F, children under 17 6F. Combined ticket for the Chapelle and the Conciergerie 40F.)

The Conciergerie, one of Paris's most infamous prisons, lurks ominously around the corner of the Palais from the entrance to the Chapelle, jealously brooding over the souls and memories of the prisoners who died here during the Revolution. The northern façade, visible in its entirety from the shores of the Right Bank, is that of a gloomy medieval fortress. Don t pause too long at the heavy-handed guard room at the entrance, but instead flit along the *"Rue de Paris,"* the corridor leading from the entrance. It is named for the prisoners destination—*"M. Paris"*—as the Revolutionary guillotine was familiarly known. Past the enormous Great Hall, stairs lead to facsimiles of prisoners cells. Further down the hall is a room that once served as Robespierre s cell, now converted into a display of his letters, as well as an actual guillotine from 1836. Marie-Antoinette s cell has been converted to a chapel, but a rather homey and unsatisfying replica can be found upstairs. The Conciergerie is still used as a temporary prison for those awaiting trial in the Palais de Justice. (Open daily 9:30am-6pm; Oct.-March 10am-5pm. Admission, including guided tour in French 25F, students and seniors 14F, under 17 6F. Combined ticket to the Conciergerie and Ste-Chapelle 40F.)

As you leave Ile de la Cité from its western tip, you'll walk over the oldest bridge in Paris, ironically named **Pont Neuf,** or "New Bridge." Completed in 1607, the bridge's radical design eschewed that of the usual domestic residences lining its sides. Although not of particular architectural interest, the bridge does have individual gargoyle capitals on its supports, which can be viewed by hanging one's head over the edge, or better yet, from below while taking a *bateau-mouche* trip down the river (see Entertainment).

Ile St-Louis

A short walk across the Pont St-Louis will take you to **Ile St-Louis,** among the city's most charming and elegant neighborhoods. Some of the most privileged of Paris's exceedingly privileged elite, including the Rothschilds and Pompidou's widow, now call this scrap of land home. At night, Ile St-Louis comes alive with the glow of cast-iron lamps, outlined against the shadows of the Seine. Sweeping arcs of light from *bateaux-mouches* highlight the 17th-century *hôtels* on the *quais* and the 19th-century buildings on either side of the island.

Begin anywhere on this island and follow the *quais* around the perimeter for beautiful views on every side, including a postcard-perfect Notre Dame (flying buttresses and all). Try to get a peek at the beautiful interior courtyards filled with flowers, plants, and fountains. Follow steps down to the newly-renovated lower *quais,* a traditional hideout for couples and daydreamers alike. Women should not explore the lower *quais* alone at night. Walk down the central **Rue St-Louis-en-l'Ile.** This is the "main drag" of Ile St-Louis, filled with an appealing array of gift shops, art galleries and traditional French restaurants. The **Hôtel Lambert,** at No. 2, has hosted such luminaries as Voltaire. The humble exterior of **Eglise St-Louis-en-l'Ile,** at the corner of rue St-Louis-en-l'Ile and rue Poulletier, disguises the airiest of rococo interiors, magnificently decorated with gold leaf, marble, and graceful statuettes. (Open to the public Mon.-Sat. 9am-noon and 3-7pm.) On either side of rue St-Louis-en-l'Ile, small quiet residential streets lead back to the *quais.*

Rive Gauche (Left Bank)

Fifth Arrondissement: Quartier Latin (Latin Quarter)

Only one part of the Rive Gauche deserves a bohemian reputation: *Le Quartier Latin*. The Romans built some of the area s ancient streets, but the *Latin* in the *Quartier s* name refers to the language of scholarship and daily speech heard here until 1798. Traditionally home base to many Parisian schools and scholars, the *Quartier* has changed greatly in the last 20 years, imperiling its youthful and scholarly ambience. After the student uprisings of May 1968, the University of Paris was decentralized, and in one blow, the *Quatier* lost many of its inhabitants. Then a tidal wave of tourist gold swept over the area and crushed many of its small booksellers and cafés. Much of the area now resembles any other Parisian commercial center.

The boulevard St-Michel, with its fashionable cafés, restaurants, bookstores and movie theaters, courses with student life. **Place St-Michel,** at the northern tip of this grand avenue, offers a microcosm of the entire quarter—-the beautiful fountain, the students, and the street people (modern descendants of the bohemians of yore). At the intersection of bd. St-Germain and bd. St-Michel, 6, pl. Paul Painlevé, the **Hôtel de Cluny** (Paris s 2nd-oldest residential bulding still standing, built in 1330 and modified to its present Gothic flamboyant style in 1510), is now home to the **Musée de Cluny,** one of the worlds finest collections of medieval art, jewelry, architecture, and tapestry (see Museums).

Farther south on bd. St-Michel, the **place de la Sorbonne** (Mo. Cluny-La Sorbonne; RER Luxembourg), a square lined with cafés, lounging students, and bookstores, is the focus of student life in the Latin Quarter. At the eastern end of the square stands the **Sorbonne,** 45-7 rue des Ecoles, one of Euope s oldest universities. Founded in 1253 by Robert de Sorbon as a simple dormitory for theology students, the Sorbonne became the administrative quarters for the University of Paris by the end of the 13th century. All the original buildings have been destroyed and rebuilt, the last time being 1885, except for the Ste-Ursule-de-la-Sorbonne (the main building), commissioned in 1642 by Cardinal Richelieu. The Cardinal, himself a Sorbonnard, lies buried inside, his hat suspended above him by a few threads hanging from the ceiling. Legend has it that when Richelieu is freed from Purgatory, the threads will snap and the hat will tumble down. The public is only admitted to the chapel, which occasionally hosts art exhibits (open Mon.-Fri. 9am-5pm). Behind the Sorbonne is the considerably less exclusive **Collège de France,** an institution created by Francis I in 1530 to contest the university s supreme authority. Outstanding courses, given over the years by such cerebral celebs as Henri Bergson, Paul Valéry, and Milan Kundera, are free and open to all. Check the schedules which appear by the door in September. (Courses run Sept.-May. For more information, call 43 29 12 11.)

The Panthéon, its proud dome visible from any point in the Latin Quarter, towers over the highest point of the Left Bank (tel. 43 54 34 52; Mo. Cardinal Lemoine, RER Luxembourg). The Panthéon is only the latest church to be built on this hill dedicated to Ste-Geneviève, the first being a shrine built by Clovis in 508 to the saints Peter and Paul, in celebration of his victory over Alaric at the Battle of Vouillé. The current structure was begun in 1754, when Louis XV created it as a sign of his gratitude to Ste-Geneviève for helping him recover from a grave illness. The Revolution converted the church into a mausoleum of heroes, designed to rival the royal crypt at St-Denis. In the **crypt,** you ll find the remains of Voltaire, Rousseau, Victor Hugo, Emile Zola, Jean Jaurès, and Louis Braille decaying peacefully in their stone tombs, which can be viewed from behind locked iron gates at each of their niches. From the crypt, a twisting staircase winds upward to the roof and dome, where you can get an up close view of a horrifyingly garish set of neoclassical frescoes proclaiming the glory and justice of France, plus a disappointing view of the surrounding neighborhood. The interior is an extreme example of neoclassical architecture, replete with austere Corinthinian columns and expansive heights. As part of the Revolutionary transformation of the church to its new secular calling as mausoleum, the 42 tall windows of the exterior were walled over and all symbols of Christian worship were removed. During 1993 the interior of the church will be undergoing renovations, and so will most likely be open only sporadically to visitors; call ahead to find out when you can visit the interior. One ticket provides entry to both. (Crypt and dome open daily 10am-5:45pm. Admission 25F, students 14F, children 17F.)

East of the Panthéon, at the intersection of rue de Navarre and rue des Arènes, rest the remains of the **Arènes de Lutèce,** a 100m x 130m oval Roman amphitheater, built to accommodate 15,000 spectators (far surpassing the needs of the still-tiny colony of Lutetia). If an average walk in the park bores you, stroll through the nearby **Jardin des Plantes** (tel. 40 79 30 00; Mo. Jussieu; main entrance 57, rue Cuvier). The 45,000 square meter park, opened in 1640 by Guy de la Brosse, Louis XIII s personal doctor, was originally intended for the sole purpose of growing medicinal plants to promote His Majesty s health. It has since been converted into a conglomeration of museums, including a natural history museum, a mineral museum, an insect gallery, a hedge maze, an arboretum, a tropical-flower greenhouse, and best of all, a full-fledged zoo. A walk through the park is, of course, free, but the many museums charge admission. (See Museums. Zoo open Mon. and Wed.-Sat. 10am-5pm, Sat.-Sun. 11-6pm. Admission 25F, students and ages 6-16 13F.)

Walking west along the Seine back toward pl. St-Michel, stop to rest in the beautiful **Jardin des Sculptures en Plein Air,** quai St-Bernard, a lovely collection of modern sculpture on a long stretch of green along the Seine. Avoid this place at night; exhibitionists frequent this park to show tourists their own special parts of Paris. Across the street is the **Institut du Monde Arabe (Institute of the Arab World)** (see Museums). Just next door to the institute, **La Tour d Argent,** 15, quai de la Tournell (Mo. Maubert), is Paris s most prestigious, most expensive restaurant.

Sixth Arrondissement: St-Germain-des-Prés

Less frenzied and more sophisticated than its neighbors, the sixth *arrondissement* combines the vibrancy of the Latin Quarter to the east with the fashionable cafés, restaurants, and movie theaters of Montparnasse to the south. This area has long been the focus of literary Paris, and it remains less ravaged by tourists than other, more monumental quarters. Join the locals at one of the famous cafés on the bd. St-Germain, former haunts of the likes of Sartre and Apollinaire, and watch the hordes of well-dressed Parisians scope each other out.

The **Palais de l Institut de France,** pl. de l Institut, broods over the Seine beneath its black and gold topped dome. This one time college (1688-1793) and prison (1793-1805) now holds the prestigious **Académie Française,** which, since its founding by Richelieu in 1635, has assumed the tasks of constantly purging the sacred French language of dastardly foreign influence and compiling the official French dictionary. Having already registered its adamant disapproval of *le weekend*, *le parking*, and other "Franglais" profanities, the academy recently triumphed with the passing of a constitutional amendment making French the official language of France.

To see what local art students are up to, walk around the **Ecole des Beaux Arts,** 14, rue Bonaparte (Mo. St-Germain des Prés), at quai Malaquais. France s most acclaimed art school presents periodic exhibits of student work; check Parisian publications for exhibit information.

The **Eglise St-Germain des Prés,** pl. St-Germain Des Prés (Mo. St-Germain des Prés), showing the wear of its many centuries, is officially the oldest standing church in modern-day Paris, dating from 1163. Parts of the church were repeatedly torn down and rebuilt at several stages during its lifetime, resulting in a mélange of Romanesque, gothic and baroque features.

Two blocks to the south on rue Bonaparte, the awesome **Eglise St-Sulpice** (Mo. St-Sulpice) contains Delacroix frescoes in the first chapel on the right, a stunning *Virgin and Child* by Jean-Baptiste Pigalle in one of the rear chapels and an enormous Chalgrin organ, among the world s largest and most famous with 6588 pipes. Like other examples of regional Gothic architecture, its fortress-like outer bulk conceals a serene, vaulted interior space. (Open daily 7:30am-7:30pm.)

The **Jardin du Luxembourg** is the closest spot to nirvana on this side of paradise. Parisians use their park well, sunbathing, contemplating, writing, romancing, strolling, or just gazing at the luscious rose gardens. Thanks to the 12,000 citizens who defended this park against Haussman s wretched intentions to carve a street through it, you can still sail a toy boat on the pond, ride a pony, attend the *grand guignol* (see Theater under the Entertainment section), shoot hoops, or simply soak up Paris in its favorite garden.

Inside the park, the **Palais du Luxembourg** was commissioned in 1615 by Marie de Medici, who aked for an Italianate palace to remind her of her native Tuscany. The palace was handed its current purpose, as the meeting-place for the largely impotent French Senate, in 1852. The president of the Senate lives in **Petit Luxembourg**, a gift from Marie de Medici to her nemesis, Cardinal Richelieu. The **Musée du Luxembourg** (tel. 42 34 20 00), next to the palace on rue de Vaugirard, displays temporary exhibitions.

Seventh Arrondissement: Faubourg St-Germain

Architectural 18th-century Paris lives on in the seventh *arrondissement*. For several centuries, the **Faubourg St-Germain**, roughly between the Invalides and rue des Saints-Pères around the boulevard St-Germain, was the city's most fashionable place to live. Within its hallowed precincts, financiers and noblemen built terribly grand *hôtels particuliers*, set back from the street behind high gates and elegant *cours d'honneur* (central courtyards). Many of these mansions are today ministeries and embassies.

Some *hôtels* remain closed to the socially meek, like, for example, the **Hôtel Matignon**. It is the official residence of the French Prime Minister, but unless Pierre invites you in, it's off-limits. The neighboring **Hôtel Biron**, at number 77, rue de Varenne, was built by Gabriel in 1728. The state made it an artists' residence in 1904; sculptor Auguste Rodin rented a studio on its ground floor in 1908. When the Ministry of Education and Fine Arts evicted all tenants in 1910, Rodin offered to donate all of his works to make a museum—on the condition that he be able to spend his last years at Biron, where the museum was to be founded. Despite fierce debate, the state agreed to accept Rodin's gift, today called the **Musée Rodin** (see Museums).

Across the street stands the more famous rue de Bellechasse resident, the **Musée d'Orsay** (see Museums). The Gare d'Orsay, the train station in which the museum is housed, takes its name from the nearby *quai*. The façade borrows from the monumental grandeur of the Louvre, but the glass and metal roof heralded the arrival of the modern era when the building was completed in 1900. For forty years, the Orsay was the main station for departures to the French southwest, but the platforms were too small for long trains and the station was given over to other activities. After several incarnations, it opened as the Musée d'Orsay in 1986.

The Palais Bourbon, 33, quai d'Orsay, challenges the Madeleine across the river for colonnaded supremacy of the place de la Concorde axis. Napoleon had the present façade erected in 1807, but the *hôtel* itself was built in 1722 for the Duchess of Bourbon, daughter of Louis XIV and Mme. de Montespan. Allegorical sculpture abounds on the palace, but the high iron gates and Uzi-toting police planted every few meters tend to be distracting. They guard the **Assemblée Nationale,** the French legislature, which meets inside. French-speaking politicophiles may want to observe the assembly in session (if you are neither, you won't understand and you won't care). (The Assembly sits Oct.-Dec. and April-June, although the session may stretch longer. Call 40 63 64 80 for the starting time of a particular day's meeting—the Assembly meets most weekday afternoons.)

The Esplanade des Invalides, a happy combination of benches, trees, and grass, stretches down to the river. And this is no ordinary Parisian grass: not only do people venture to sit on it, but they'll even dare to engage in exuberant games of soccer. Of course, it's really just there to give you an unobstructed view of the fabulously huge **Hôtel des Invalides,** 2, av. de Tourville (Mo. Invalides or Latour-Maubourg or St-François Xavier). In 1670, war-monger Louis XIV, decided to "construct a royal home, grand and spacious enough to receive all old or wounded officers and soldiers." The building accepted its first wounded in October of 1674, and veterans still live in the Invalides today. Jules Hardouin-Mansart finished the adjacent **Eglise St-Louis** and, in 1706, the imposing dome, which has been called superior to St. Paul's in London and

St. Peter's in Rome—it now houses Napoleon's remains. (See Museums for a description of the Invalides and Napoleon's tomb.)

At the opening of his impressive iron monument in 1889, Gustave Eiffel scrawled on the fan of an adoring spectator, "France is the only country in the world with a 300m flagpole." His contemporaries were unimpressed. Today, the railroad bridge cut in half and planted on end that is the **Tour Eiffel** (Mo. Bir-Hakeim) pierces the Paris skyline, symbolizing the City of Lights to the world. Judges chose the tower for the centerpiece of the 1889 World's Fair, held to celebrate the centennial of the French Revolution. Shockwaves of dismay reverberated around the city before the construction site at the end of the Champs-de-Mars even opened. Guy de Maupassant, Alexandre Dumas, *fils,* Charles Garnier, and Sully Prudhomme joined countless other artists in condemning it as "the useless and monstruous Eiffel Tower." Maupassant allegedly ate his lunch in the two-and-a-half-acre expanse beneath it because it was the only place in Paris where he could avoid seeing it. The condemnation was not altogether surprising: with its metal girders and boldly modern look, the tower was a triumph of engineering not aesthetics, seemingly cementing the split between science and art. Eiffel patiently responded to his critics by saying that his engineer's sense of beauty was delighted primarily by design that served a purpose, and that the grand curves of the tower would possess the beauty of wind resistance. The then-tallest structure in the world would be a monument to modern engineering and industry, comparable to the pyramids of Egypt. Seeing the Eiffel Tower, even for the umpteenth time, is inevitably breathtaking. The Tower is huge and, well, towers over its surroundings. It's also a soft brown, not the metallic steel gray that most visitors anticipate. And despite the 18,000 pieces of iron, 2,500,000 rivets, and 9,100,000 kilograms of sheer weight that compose the world's largest Gallic symbol, the Eiffel Tower appears surprisingly elegant, with many of the girders taking on a spidery, web-like elegance. This is especially true at night, when lines of light follow the delicate skeleton, turning it into a brilliant lace-like, lofty apparition—a modern counterpart to the heaven-reaching spires of Notre-Dame. Maybe.

The tower has three "floors," or landings, which protrude from its steel web. The cheapest way to get up the tower is to walk up the first two floors (8F). This approach also gives you an unbeatable, step-by-step tour of the Tower's complex structure. But you can't go to the Eiffel Tower and not go all the way. The third floor/summit/tip-top is accessible only by elevator. Tickets can be bought from the *caisse,* when open, or from the coin-operated dispenser in the east corner. (2nd-3rd floor elevator 17F, kids 4-11 7F, under 4 free. Ticket good for the day, when the 3rd floor is open). No matter what height you find yourself at, survey the city. Excellent aerial photographs point out significant landmarks and accompanying blurbs, in English, fill in the history. Try it at night—even the most blasé will be impressed by the beautiful, illuminated iron structure and the lights of Paris—its buildings, its traffic, its river—down below. (Tower open daily July 4-Sept. 6 9am-midnight; Sept. 7-March 20 9:30am-11pm; March 21-July 3 9am-11pm. Stairs open July 4-Sept. 6 daily until 11pm; Sept. 7-May 22 Sun.-Thurs. until 6:30pm; May 23-July 3 Sun.-Thurs. until 6:30pm, Fri.-Sat. until 11pm. Admission to stairs and 3rd-floor elevator as above. By elevator to first floor 17F, ages 4-11 8F; to 2nd floor 34F, ages 4-11 16F; to third floor 51F, ages 4-11 23F; under 4 free to all levels.)

For an area dedicated to the God of War, the **Champ de Mars** teems with a remarkable amount of peace and happiness. A green flower-embroidered carpet stretching from the Ecole militaire to the Eiffel Tower, the park is a veritable kid's heaven: jungle gyms, monkey bars, wood trains, and even abbreviated cement soccer fields line the southwest side. This does not prevent anyone from picking up a game of *foot* (soccer) in front of obscure Egyptian statues. The park's name comes from its original function as a drill ground for the neighboring Ecole Militaire. Napoleon III chose the field for the Great Exhibition of 1867, the crowning glory of his regime. An enormous glass pavilion sheltered the displays, which were visited by 15 million people from all over the world, as well as by almost every crowned head of Europe. Other expositions followed in 1878, 1889 (for which the Eiffel Tower was built), 1900, and 1937, using the field as a combination fairground/construction site. After the 1900 Exhibition, the Municipal

Council seriously considered parceling off the Champ de Mars for development, but was persuaded that this dense city needed all the open space it had.

The Ecole Militaire was created by Louis XV at the urging of his mistress, Mme. de Pompadour, who wanted to transform "poor gentlemen" into educated officers. In 1784, a 15-year-old Corsican named Napoleone Bonaparte arrived and within weeks presented the school's administrators with a comprehensive plan for its reorganization. Its architectural and spiritual antithesis, **UNESCO (United Nations Educational, Scientific, and Cultural Organization)** stands in the shape of a "Y" across the street at 7, place de Fontenoy. (Mo. Ségur.) Nine appropriately international pieces of art decorate the building and garden: ceramics by Miró and Artigas, a nameless painting by Picasso, a Japanese garden, and an angel from the façade of a Nagasaki church destroyed by the atom bomb, among them. (UNESCO open Mon.-Sat. 9am-6:30pm. Bookstore open Mon.-Sat. 9:15am-12:45pm and 2:15-5:45pm. Variable times for temporary exhibits. Free.)

Fifteenth Arrondissement

The museums, the shopping districts, the famous concert halls and opera houses are elsewhere, but the fifteenth possesses the most important sight of them all: the true Paris, where people simply go about their daily lives. Just breathing the air, drinking in a café among dedicated patrons, and watching children play in a nearby park is the kind of irreplaceable Parisian experience that you can't find on the Champs Elysées. For the best people-watching around, pop out of the metro Convention, where pretentious cafés stake their claim on each corner.

La Tour de Montparnasse (Mo. Montparnasse-Bienvenüe) dominates the neighborhood's northeast corner. The steel monstrosity was built by an American company in 1973 and indeed looks like it was left behind by a group of Manhattan skyscrapers on a field trip. An elevator whisks visitors to the observatory on the top floor (merely the 59th) for an indecent 34F, students 28F, from which you can see the only *real* tower of Paris, M. Eiffel's. (Open daily 9:30am-11pm; Oct.-March 10am-10pm.)

L'Institut Pasteur, 28 rue Dr. Roux (Mo. Pasteur) is a Montparnasse mecca for bovinophiles and infectious disease afficionados alike. Founded by Louis Pasteur, a champion of the germ theory, in 1887-89, the Institute gained fame in 1983 for the isolation of the AIDS virus. The museum offers an exhaustive run-down of Pasteur s medical and artistic accomplishments, a tour of his laboratory equipment and living quarters, and a visit to the crypt currently housing the scientist's corpse. (Tours in French with photocopied translations in English. Admission 12F, students 6F.)

Fourteenth Arrondissement: Montparnasse

One of the most heterogeneous areas of Paris, the fourteenth draws immigrants from remote provinces in France, Europe, the United States, and even just the other side of the Seine. In the early 20th century, floods of Bretons fleeing their failed crops poured out of the Gare Montparnasse. Picasso, Gauguin, Whistler, and others set up *ateliers* here, and an equally august set of writers—such as Hemingway, Sartre, de Beauvoir—found themselves stuck to the cafés of the bd. de Montparnasse, which later became the center of the literary pretenders and general hangers-on. The fourteenth remains a conglomoration of different styles: business and tourism around Montparnasse, residential toward Mo. Denfert-Rochereau, and poor-student-dormitory in the Cité Universitaire.

Boulevard Montparnasse remains devoted to people-watching as well as to *crêpes,* the renowned Breton invention. Around this chic thouroughfare, the intersection of the sixth, fourteenth, and fifteenth *arrondissements* has become one of the capital s most modern business centers, though dominated by the architecturally tragic **Tour de Montparnasse** (see 15th *arrondissement).*

The Cimitière Montparnasse, 3, bd. Edgar Quinet (Mo. Edgar Quinet) is less than romantic. Shrouded by the black pall of the Tour Montparnasse, bisected by a through street, too crowded by tombs to have grass, piled with heaps of beer and mineral water bottles, the cemetery is better left to the dead. Armed with a free *Index des Celebrités* (the detailed map available just left of the main entrance), determined sightseers thread their way through the unimportant to pay their respects to writers Baudelaire, de Maupassant, Beckett, Julio Cortázar (whose slab sports a scultped smiley face), Sartre and de Beauvoir (who share a grave); car manufacturer André Citroën; composer Saint-Saens; artist Man Ray; and non-traitor Alfred Dreyfus. (Open Mon.-Fri. 7:30am-6pm, Sat. 8:30am-6pm, Sun. 9am-6pm. From Nov. 6-March 15 closing times 1/2 hour earlier. Free.)

Les Catacombs, 1, pl. Denfert-Rochereau (Mo. Denfert-Rochereau), crowds in five to six million lesser Parisians. These subterranean tunnels were originally excavated to provide stone for building the city. By the 1770s, much of the Left Bank was in danger of caving in, and the quarry was converted to a mass grave to relieve the unbearable stench emanating from cemeteries around Paris. Near the entrance to the ossuary reads the ominous caution, "Stop! Beyond Here Is the Empire of Death." In 1871, some of the last *communards* tried to hide in the passages, only to be hunted down and shot by torchlight. During WWII, the resistance set up headquarters among these old and loyal Parisian bones. Bring a sweater, a flashlight, and a friend for support. (Open Tues.-Fri. 2-4pm, Sat.-Sun. 9-11am and 2-4pm. Admission 15F, students 10F.)

Parc Montsouris, offers a sunny, sublime return to the land of the living. Doubling as an arboretum, the park offers sanctuary to hundreds of rare and unusual trees, all well-labeled and cared for, along with an amazing variety of birds, ducks and geese who splash contendenly in the artificial lake (whose designer killed himself after the water mysteriously drained at the park s opening ceremony). Across the bd. Jourdan, hundreds of thousands of students rage the night away in the **Cité Universitaire,** a 40 hectare rompus park containing no less than 44 different dormitories, with students from no less than 122 countries worldwide.

Rive Droite (Right Bank)

First Arrondissement: The Louvre and Les Halles

The 1st arrondissement has one of the highest concentrations of interesting sights-per-acre in the world. Hugging the side of the Seine, the Louvre occupies about a seventh of the *arrondissement.* The Jardin des Tuileries, the Palais Royal, the Place Vendôme, and Les Halles round out the lineup of all-stars.

The **Palais du Louvre** is Paris's single largest building, the largest palace in Europe, the largest museum in the Western Hemisphere, and probably the most recognized symbol of art and culture in all history (for a full description of the building and its treasures, see Museums).

Le Jardin des Tuileries extends to the western foot of the Louvre. The views from the elevated terrace by the river, and along the central path of the park, are spectacular. Catherine de' Medici, yearning for the public promenades of her native Italy, had the gardens built in 1564; in 1649 André le Nôtre (designer of the Gardens at Versailles) imposed his preference for straight lines and sculptured trees upon the landscape of the Tuileries. Once he had completed his work, the gardens were made public and have since become one of the most popular open spaces in Paris. Along with the gardens, Catherine ordered the **Palais des Tuileries,** which stretched along the west end of the Jardin du Carrousel, forming the western wall of the Louvre. Long after most of the Louvre had been converted into an art museum, the Tuileries remained the royal residence. Napoleon III, the last French monarch, was chased out in 1870. Nine months later, a vengeful Communard official packed the palace with gunpowder, tar, and oil and destroyed the symbol of monarchal rule. The park opens at 7am on weekdays, and on weekends and holidays at 7:30am. From the last Sunday of March to the Saturday preceding the last Sunday of September, closing time is 10pm; for the rest of the year it is 8pm. Don't tempt fate by trying to remain in the Tuileries after the gates are locked. If you manage to survive the large hounds that patrol the grounds, you might enjoy less luck with muggers. Flanking the end of the Tuileries farthest from the Louvre, the **Jeu de Paume** and the **Orangerie** museums pale a little in the shadow of their grandaddy to the east, but the Orangerie's splendid modern collection and the Jeu de Paume's temporary exhibits still place them among the city's finest (see Museums).

The Place Vendôme, three blocks north along the rue de Castiglione from the Tuileries, was begun in 1687 according to plans by Jules Hardouin-Mansart, who convinced Louis XIV and a group of five financiers to invest in a proposed ensemble of private mansions and public institutions. Due to a lack of funds, the theatrical and ostentatious Place Vendôme remained no more than a series of empty façades until 1720. Many of the buildings were gutted in the 1930s; again, their uniformly dignified façades were protected, and Place Vendôme, as it exists today, is little more than a series of 17th-century façades masking 20th-century offices. Under renovation in 1992, the *place* should be more beautiful than ever by 1993.

The **column** in the center of the square has acted as a barometer reflecting French regime fluctuations for some 200 years. Originally, the square held a 7m statue of Louis XIV in Roman costume. The statue was destroyed by Revolutionaries in 1792. In 1805, the aristocratic Place Vendôme was reborn when Napoleon erected a central column modeled after Trajan's column in Rome. Cast from 1,250 Austrian and Russian bronze cannon captured in battle, the column showed a series of soldiers and military heroes; the emperor glowered at the top. Through various revolutions and restorations, the statue of Napoleon was replaced, in turn, by the white flag of the ancient monarchy, by a renewed Napoleon in military garb, by a classical Napoleon modelled after the original, and, finally, by the Red Flag of the Commune. Soon after this last addition, a committee headed by the artist Gustave Courbet toppled the entire war-like victory column, but four years later, Napoleon enjoyed a postmortem last laugh when the original column was recreated at Courbet's expense.

Today, the entire *place* shimmers with opulence; here are well-known bankers, perfumers, jewelers, and the Parisian branch of IBM. Supposedly, Rothschild, rather than lend his "needy" friends money, would simply allow them to stroll with him around pl. Vendôme for a few minutes. The next morning the fortunate souls would be certain of credit at the most prestigious banks. Chopin died at no. 12; Hemingway drank at no. 15; the **Ritz Hotel.** no. 11 and 13, identified by the proud flag, is the Ministry of Justice. At street level, to the left of the entrance, is The Meter, the mother of all rulers, as it was once the world standard for that unit of measurement. Nowadays meters are defined using krypton 86 radiation, but this 1848 unit is a pretty reliable source.

Palais Royal. Further east, across rue de Rivoli from the Louvre is the Palais Royal. Constructed in 1639 as Cardinal Richelieu's *Palais Cardinal,* it became a *Palais Royal* when Anne of Austria, regent for Louis XIV, set up house there. Louis-Philippe d'Orléans, whose son became King Louis-Philippe, inherited the palace in 1780. Strapped for cash, in 1784 he built and rented out the elegant buildings that enclose the palace's formal garden, turning the complex into the 18th century's version of a shopping mall. It had boutiques, several restaurants, prostitutes, and—in lieu of a multi-screen cinema—theaters, wax museums, and puppet shows. On July 12, 1789, on the eve of the Revolution, 26-year-old Camille Desmoulins leaped on a café table and urged his fellow citizens to arm themselves. The enthusiastic crowd filed out, and were soon skirmishing with cavalry in the Tuileries garden. In the second half of the 19th century, the Palais recovered as a center of luxury commerce, preserving a serene aristocratic flavor amid the "commercialism" of Haussman's boulevards and the new, modern department stores.

Today, the galeries of the venerable buildings contain small shops and a few cafés, with a splendid view of the palace fountain and flower beds. The levels above the cafés and shops, as well as the older parts of the palace, are occupied by government offices. For couples with a large height disparity, the *colonnes de Buren* are a popular place to kiss—they are a set of striped pillars and stumps that completely fill the *cour d'honneur* (the main courtyard). Planted there in 1986, Daniel Buren's columns created a storm of controversy comparable to the one that greeted the Louvre pyramids. On the southwestern corner of the Palais Royal, facing the Louvre, the **Comédie Française** is home to France's leading dramatic group. The theater was built in 1790 by architect Victor Louis, who created the other buildings and was likewise sponsored by the Duc de Chartres.

Les Halles. (Mo. Les Halles, Châtelet-Les Halles.) In the second half of the 19th century, Emile Zola, father of French literary naturalism, proclaimed the huge food market of Les Halles *"le ventre de Paris"* (Paris's belly). After 1135, when Louis VI built two wooden buildings here to house a bazaar, Les Halles (pronounced LAY AHL) was the site of the largest market in Paris. The Les Halles Zola described received a much-needed facelift in the 1850s and 60s, with the construction of large iron and glass pavilions that sheltered the vendors stalls. One hundred years later, the Les Halles market had again slipped into disrepair. This time, however, the authorities decided to solve the problem merely by shooing the vendors off to a suburb near Orly.

Most Parisians adored the elegant pavilions and wanted to see them preserved. But planners insisted that only by destroying the pavilions could they create a needed transfer point between the metro and the new RER; demolition began in 1971. Architects Claude Vasconi and Georges Penreach have since replaced the pavilions with a subterranean shopping mall, the **Forum des Halles.** Some 200 boutiques (the most fashionable of which have floated to the uppermost levels) are crammed into the complex, along with a swimming pool and several museums (see Museums). Watch your wallet inside Les Halles, and stay above ground at night.

St-Eustache (Mo. Les Halles, Châtelet les Halles), is the large Gothic/Renaissance church visible from all over Les Halles, right next to the Turbigo exit of the Les Halles metro. Construction began in 1532 and dragged on for over a century. The church was finally consecrated in 1632, with its façade incomplete. In 1754, with the neoclassical trend that swept the nation, the unfinished façade was knocked down and replaced with the Roman façade that it has today—terribly incongruous with the rest of the building, but entirely appropriate for the Roman saint in question. Perhaps the best way to take in the architecture and the stained glass is to attend one of the organ concerts organized in June and July. The organ at St-Eustache is one of the best in Paris; classical music lovers will not want to miss the experience of its thrilling baritone. For information on the organ festival, check *Pariscope,* call 45 22 28 74, or read the posters in front of the church. Tickets go for 120F, or 80F for students. (Church open Mon.-Sat. 8:30am-7pm, Sun. 8:15am-12:30pm and 3pm-7pm. Guided tours in French at 3pm on Sun.; daily at 2pm in June and July. Mass Mon.-Fri. 10am and 6pm; Sat. 6pm; Sun. 8:30am, 9:45am, 11am, and 6pm. On Sun., the 11am mass is with the choir and organ and the 6pm is with the organ.)

Second Arrondissement: La Bourse

Galerie Vivienne and Galerie Colbert, near the Palais Royal, are the finest examples of 19th-century Parisian *galeries,* covered pedestrian streets, lined with cafés, restaurants, and quaint boutiques. An entrance at 4, rue des Petits Champs reveals Galerie Colbert, a long passage with a glass ceiling and faux-marble columns. Make a U-turn at the end of the passage into the galerie Vivienne, filled with little boutiques and a number of large display windows belonging to the Bibliothèque Nationale.

The **Bibliothèque Nationale,** 58, rue de Richelieu (tel. 47 03 81 26) competes with the British library for the title of largest library in Western Europe. Its collection of 12 million volumes includes two Gutenberg Bibles and countless first editions from the 15th century to the present. Ever since 1642, the law has stipulated that every book published in France must be archived here. Foreigners are not allowed into the library stacks, unless they can prove they need publications unavailable elsewhere in Paris. For plebes who are denied stack privileges, there are temporary exhibitions: if your French is up to it, call 47 03 81 10 to ask what's being shown. Opening hours vary depending on the exhibition.

The **Bourse des Valeurs (stock exchange),** 4, place de la Bourse (Mo. Bourse), is housed in a sober building with an unmistakably financial air. The exchange was founded in 1724; the present edifice was begun in 1808. The only way you can visit the interior is by going on one of the **guided tours** offered at least twice a day (be ready to show your passport as you enter). You get a little lecture about stock markets, complete with computerized audio-visuals, then a look at the trader's pit (which is pretty tame compared to London or New York). Unless markets fascinate you and your grasp of French financial vocabulary is fairly good, this probably isn't worth the 10F and the 45 minutes.

Third and Fourth Arrondissements: The Marais

The third and fourths *arrondissements* are called *le Marais* (the "swamp") because of the area's distinguishing quality of dampness before 13th-century monks drained it. With Henry IV's construction of the Place des Vosges at the beginning of the 17th century, the area became the center of fashionable living. Leading architects and sculptors were kept busy building the *hôtels particuliers* that still dot the Marais—discretely elegant mansions nestled between large courtyards in front and gardens in the rear. Under Louis XV, the center of Paris life moved out of the Marais, to the faubourgs St-Honoré and St-Germain, and construction of *hôtels* in the Marais slackened considerably. The 19th and early 20th centuries were not kind to the old Marais. Many *hôtels* were destroyed or allowed to fall into disrepair. Narrow, medieval streets were widened at great architectural cost. Recently the government has shown a greater interest in conservation. Part of the Marais was declared a historic neighborhood and protected from further destruction. In addition, museums such as the Musée de la Chasse, the Musée Picasso, and the Musée Cognacq-Jay have moved into and restored old *hôtels*.

Les Archives Nationaux (National Archives) are housed in the Hôtel Soubise, the Hôtel Rohan, and a few other old residences. The courtyard of the **Hôtel Soubise,** built between 1705 and 1709, provides a classic example of 18th-century aristocratic architecture. If you choose to visit the Museum of French History (see Museums), you can see the very rich—some would say gaudy—interior decorations, executed between 1730 and 1745. The building's towered gate at 58, rue des Archives, is the only surviving portion of a mansion that was built in 1380. The unusual angle between the gate and the road was chosen to facilitate the entrance of litters and carriages. **Hôtel de Rohan,** one of the most famous *hôtels* in the Marais, reposes at no. 87, rue Vieille du Temple. It was built between 1705 and 1708 for the Bishop of Strasbourg. During temporary exhibitions, you are allowed to visit the richly decorated interior of the palace (but only if you pay 10F or so for the temporary exhibit); otherwise, just tour the large, impressive courtyard.

The nearby **rue des Quatre Fils** illustrates the city's piecemeal efforts to widen the streets in the Marais. The 17th-century gate of no. 16 used to stand forward of where it is now. The hotel was destroyed, and the gate moved backwards and stuck onto a newer building. At no. 18, a modern building with three arches occupies part of the courtyard of a 17th-century *hôtel*. Behind it, you can see the inner façade of the older building, which was spared by the street-widening policy.

The rue Vielle-du-Temple, which runs along the east side of the Hôtel Rohan, is lined with several stately residences. On the **Rue de Sévigné** (Mo. Chemin Vert), a small street worth passing through on your way to the Place des Vosges or the Eglise St-Paul-St-Louis, the **Hôtel Carnavalet** houses an enlightening museum of Parisian history (see Museums). Even if you don't visit the museum, it's worth looking at the gate and courtyard of the building. The statue in the middle of the courtyard is Louis XIV; it used to be in front of the Hôtel de Ville.

Much of the fourth *arrondissement* was left untouched by Haussman's modernization; with its mish-mash of different social strata and political inclinations, it will give you a sense of the old Paris, where aristocratic families lived next door to (or even downstairs from) the same workers who made their furniture or baked their bread.

The **Hôtel de Lamoignon,** 24, rue Pavée (Mo. St-Paul), is one of the finest *hôtels particuliers* in the Marais. When it was built in 1584 for Diane de France, daughter of Henri II, the *hôtel* consisted only of the section immediately in front as you enter the courtyard. The noble façade, with its two-story Corinthian pilasters, is the first example in Paris of the "colossal" style of decoration. Charles de Valois added the wing at left; the buildings of the small courtyard to the right date from 1968. Through a door in the 1968 half-courtyard you can enter the **Bibliothèque Historique de la Ville de Paris**. (Open Mon.-Sat. 9:30am-6pm.) To see the gardens of the *hôtel*, which are closed to the public, exit onto rue Pavée and turn right on rue des Francs Bourgeois.

Place des Vosges (Mo. Chemin Vert, St-Paul), Paris's oldest remaining public square and perhaps its most charming, provides one of the city's most pleasant strolls. In 1605, Henri IV planned the square, specifying that all the buildings be constructed "according to the same symmetry," which explains the unusual unity of the square's architecture. All 36 buildings have arcades on the street level, each surmounted by two stories decorated with pink brick and capped by a steep, slate-covered roof. Louis XIII married Anne of Austria in the square, assuring it a most fashionable status. Madame de Sevigné (born at no. 1bis), Cardinal Richelieu (no. 21), Molière, Racine, and Voltaire filled the grand parlors with their wit and philosophy. Mozart played his first concert here at the age of seven. Even when the majority of the city's nobility moved across the river to the faubourg Saint-Germain, the *place* remained among the most elegant spots in Paris. Théophile Gautier and Alphonse Daudet lived at no. 8; at no. 6, romantics will not want to miss the former residence of Victor Hugo, now an excellent museum with displays on his life, his work, and his contemporaries (see Museums). During summer weekends, these arcades teem with an array of talented musicians, playing and singing a variety of mostly classical music, from harp medleys to Mozart arias. Come here at dusk for a romantic stroll, amid iron lamps and gracious silhouettes of the townhouses.

The Hôtel de Sens, 1, rue du Figuier (Mo. Pont Marie), was built between 1474 and 1507 for Tristan de Salazar, the archbishop of Sens, with its military features reflecting both de Salazar's life as a soldier and the violence of the day. The turrets were designed to survey the streets outside, while the square tower at the far left corner of the courtyard served as a dungeon.

Since the 13th century, when King Phillipe-Auguste politely requested that the Jewish population living in front of Notre-Dame move to the Marais (then outside of city limits), this quarter has been the Jewish center of Paris. The area around rue des Rosiers and rue des Ecouffes still forms the spine of the Jewish community, with two synagogues and dozens of kosher restaurants and delis. At 17, rue Geoffroy de l'Asnier, the solemn 1956 **Mémorial du Martyr Juif Inconnu** (Memorial to the Unknown Jewish Martyr; Mo. St-Paul) commemorates the Parisian Jews who died at the hands of the Nazis and their French collaborators. The crypt downstairs has an eternal flame over human ashes brought back from concentration camps and the Warsaw ghetto. (Open Sun.-Thurs. 10am-1pm and 2-6pm, Fri. 10am-1pm and 2-5pm. Admission free.) Upstairs, the **Centre de Documentation Juive Contemporaine** (Jewish Contemporary Documentation Center) has a small Holocaust museum (entry 12F) and a library with more than 400,000 documents relating to the Nazi era. The center, open Monday through Thursday from 2 to 5:30pm, frequently organizes temporary exhibitions.

The Hôtel de Ville (Mo. Hôtel de Ville), Paris's grandiose city hall, dominates a large square with refreshing fountains and Victorian-style lamp posts. The present edifice is little more than a century old, but Paris municipal government has been housed on this site ever since 1357. In 1533, a new building was designed by Boccadoro in a Renaissance style that recalled the Châteaux of the Loire. On May 24, 1871, despairing insurgents of the Paris Commune set Boccadoro's Hôtel de Ville on fire with the help of several barrels of petroleum. The fire lasted no less than eight days, at the end of which nothing remained but the frame. The building of a virtually identical Hôtel de Ville began in 1872 on the same spot and still stands, governing Paris from within its splendiferous walls. The only way to visit the interior of the building is to take a guided tour. The tours are in French and leave from the Information Office on 29, rue de Rivoli (open Mon.-Sat. 9am-6pm), every Monday (except for public holidays) at 10:30am. The Information Office also holds temporary exhibits in its lobby. The **Place Hôtel de Ville** outside has been used as a meeting-place for angry or unemployed workers and as a site for hundreds of picturesque tortures, book-burnings, and executions. In 1789, the first Paris Commune was declared here, and later copy-cats declared the July Monarchy and the Second Republic on the same spot. The Third Republic, for a change, was proclaimed from a balcony of the Hôtel de Ville.

The Tour St-Jacques (between 39 and 41, rue de Rivoli) stands strangely alone in the center of its own park. The flamboyant Gothic tower is the only remnant of the 16th-century Eglise St-Jacques-la-Boucherie, which was destroyed in 1802. The meterological station at its top continues a long scientific tradition that began with Pascal's experiments to determine the weight of air, performed here in 1648.

In the western section of the fourth, strollers stumble upon the startling **Centre Pompidou,** visible from afar (impossible to miss, in fact), with its famous inside-out architecture. Here it is: the most famous, roaringly idiosyncratic blemish in the uniformity of the city, even beating out the newer additions of the Louvre Pyramide and the Opéra Bastille. (For a fuller description of the center, see Museums.) In the afternoons and early evenings, the vast cobblestoned *place* in front of the center is extraordinarily animated. Street performers, peddlers, and pickpockets try their hand at raking in the crowd's money. Late at night when the tourists have left, the square can get fairly dangerous because of the number of drunk men who hang around, occasionally picking fights. On your right as you look at the Pompidou façade, an exuberant modern fountain, aptly named the **Fontaine Stravinski,** spurts and splashes amidst an array of brightly colored shapes, representing the atonal compositions of Russian composer Igor Stravisnsky that shook the music world eighty years ago.

Eighth Arrondissement: The Champs-Elysées and the Arc de Triomphe

Almost as elegant as its neighbor to the southwest, the 16th, the 8th *arrondissement* is home to Haussmann's *grands boulevards,* plus the grandest street of all, the **avenue des Champs-Elysées.** Salons and boutiques of **haute couture** pepper fashionable streets with world-famous names, like the rue de Faubourg St. Honoré. Embassies crowd around the **Palais de l'Elysée,** state residence of the French president. The whole area bustles and it should; within a very few blocks, the 8th provides you with all the resources necessary to dine exquisitely, dress impeccably and accessorize magnificently. You can indulge your esoteric music tastes, satisfy your *penchant* for sweets, and tuck away a ticket for a winter flight to Rio with minimum effort (and maximum expenditure). Most importantly, the pleasantly pretentious 8th and its tree-lined streets provide you the opportunity to show it all off.

The Arc de Triomphe, looming gloriously above the Champs-Elysées in pl. Charles de Gaulle, moves every heart not made of stone (Mo. Charles de Gaulle-Etoile). The world's largest triumphal arch, and an internationally recognized symbol of France, this behemoth was commissioned in 1806 by Napoleon in honor of his Grande Armée. The monument was completed in 1836, 21 years after the defeat of The Little Corporal's great army. The victorious Prussians marched through its opening in 1871, followed in 1919 by an Allied celebration parade headed by Maréchal Foch, then by the Nazis goose-stepping through in 1940. Finally, in 1944, the Free French and the Yanks sidled majestically through to liberate the war-torn city. The Tomb of the Unknown Soldier has rested beneath the arch since November 11, 1920; there, an eternal flame is rekindled every evening at 6:30pm, when veterans and small children lay wreaths decorated with blue, white, and red.

Rather than risk an early death by crossing the traffic to reach the Arc, use the underpasses on the even-numbered sides of both the Champs-Elysées and av. de la Grande-Armée. Climb 205 steps up a winding staircase to the *entresol* and then dig deep for the 29 more that take you to the musée. (Or tackle the lines at the elevator.) The real spectacle lies just 46 steps higher—the *terrasse* at the top of the Arc provides a terrific view of the gorgeous av. Foch and the sprawling city. (Observation deck open daily 10am-5:30pm. Admission 31F, students 18-25 and seniors 17F, ages 7-17 6F, 6 and under free. Expect lines even on weekdays and buy your ticket before going up to the ground level.)

The avenue des Champs-Elysées is perhaps the most famous street in the world. No one can deny that this ten-lane wonder, flanked by exquisite cafés and luxury shops and crowned by the world's most famous arch, deserves its reputation. LeNôtre planted trees here in 1667 to extend the Tuileries vista, extending the work begun under Marie de Medici in 1616. It was only under the Second Empire, after considerable repair, that this became the asphalt den of luxury that it is today. Of course, you'll probably see more foreigners than Parisian aristocrats. Tourists and French film stars share the turf at **Fouquet's,** an outrageously expensive café/restaurant near the Arc de Triomphe. Paris's answer to Hollywood's Sunset Strip, this stretch of the Champs-Elysées bears golden plaques with names of favorite French entertainers. Street performers move in at night. Six big avenues radiate from the Rond Point des Champs-Elysées. Av. Montaigne runs southwest from the point and shelters houses of *haute couture*—join the models who prance with their photographers, directors, and reflector panel holders on the trottoir.

Like two big toes at the foot of the Champs-Elysées, the **Grand Palais** and the **Petit Palais,** face one another on av. Winston Churchill. Built for the 1900 World's Fair, both illustrate the art nouveau style, with the glass over steel and stone composition of the Grand Palais recalling a giant greenhouse. The **Petit Palais** is now a permanent museum (see Museums), while the Grand Palais (tel. 42 89 54 10) hosts temporary exhibits. At the same time the palaces were built, the **Pont Alexandre III** was sent across the river, providing a noble axis with the Invalides (see 7th *arrondissement).*

The **Place de la Concorde** (Mo. Concorde), Paris's largest and most infamous public square, forms the eastern terminus of the Champs-Elysées. Constructed between 1757 and 1777 to provide a home for a monument to Louis XV, the vast area soon became the place de la Revolution, the site of the guillotine that severed 1,343 necks. Louis XVI, Marie Antoinette, Charlotte Corday (Marat's assassin), Lavoisier, and other celebrated heads rolled into baskets and were held up to cheering crowds. In an ironic twist, even Robespierre, the brutal merchant of death himself, lost his head here in 1794. After the Reign of Terror, the square was optimistically renamed. The gargantuan, rose granite **Obélisque de Louqsor** was a gift offered by Mehemet Ali, Viceroy of Egypt, to Charles X in 1829. Paris's oldest monument dates back to the 13th century BC and recalls the deeds of Ramses II. In 1944, the *place* was the site of a tank battle as the French 2nd Armored Division closed in on the German headquarters nearby.

Directly north of the Place, like two sentries guarding the gate to the Madeleine stand the **Hôtel Crillon** (on your left) and the **Hôtel de la Marine** (on your right). Architect Gabriel built the impressive colonnaded façades between 1757 and 1770. The businesses along rue Royale boast their own proud history. **Christofle** has been producing works in gold and crystal since 1830. World-renowned **Maxim's** restaurant (no. 3) won't even allow you a peep in through the windows of what was once Richelieu's home.

The **Madeleine,** formally called Eglise Sainte-Marie-Madeleine, is the commanding building ahead. This architectural orphan was begun in 1764 at the command of Louis XV and modeled after a Greek temple. Construction was halted during the Revolution, whose leaders alternately considered using the edifice as a bank, a theater, or a courthouse. In 1806, at the height of his power, Napoleon consecrated the partially completed building as a Temple of Glory. Completed as a church in 1842, the structure is distinguished by its four ceiling domes, which light the interior in lieu of windows, as well as by its 52 exterior Corinthian columns, and its noticeable lack of even one cross. (Open daily 8am-6:15pm. Occasional organ concert.) Stretching out just below the Madeleine, roughly parallel to the Champs-Elysées, is the **rue de Faubourg St. Honoré.** Head west from rue Royale to rue Boissy d'Anglas where you can stare at the lavish, sparkly, refined, colorfully outrageous and oh-so-French decorated windows of **Hermès** (no. 24). Other boutiques cluster nearby.

Square Louis XVI, on rue Pasquier, below bd. Haussmann, includes the improbably large **Chapelle Expiatoire.** A cemetery, affiliated with the Madeleine, was opened on the site in 1722; the victims of the guillotine, Louis and Marie among them, were buried there. Although the royal remains were removed to Saint-Denis in 1815, Charlotte Corday (Marat's assassin) and Philippe-Egalité (Louis XVI's cousin who voted for the king's death, only to be beheaded himself) remain buried on either side of the staircase. Statues of the expiatory ex-king and queen, displaced crowns at their feet, stand inside the Chapelle. (Open daily April 1-Sept. 30 10am-6pm; Oct. and Feb. 1-March 31 10am-5pm; Nov. 1-Jan. 31 10am-4pm.)

The **Parc Monceau** borders on the elegant bd. de Courcelles. Whereas the Jardin du Luxembourg emphasizes show over relaxation, the Parc Monceau serves as a bucolic setting for children to play and parents to unwind in the shade. The Rotonde de Monceau, at the north end of the park, is a remnant of the Farmers-General wall of the 1780s. Designed to enforce customs duties rather than to keep out invaders, the wall and its fortifications reflected their creator's tastes in ornament more than the latest advances in military engineering. An array of architectural follies—a pyramid, a covered bridge, a pagoda, and picturesque Roman ruins—make this one of Paris's most pleasant spots for a *déjeuner sur* bench. Frolicking on the grass is forbidden. (Open daily April 1-Oct. 31 7am-10pm; Nov. 1-March 31 7am-8pm. Gates begin closing 15min. earlier.)

The Ninth Arrondissement: L'Opéra

Charles Garnier's grandiose **Opéra** (tel. 42 66 50 22)is the most extravagant creation of the Second Empire: an outpouring of opulence and meaningless allegory. It did not actually open until 1875, five years after the Empire's collapse. The interior of the Opéra demonstrates the fabric of 19th-century bourgeois social life, with its grand staircase, enormous golden foyer, vestibule, and five-tiered auditorium—all designed so that audience members could watch each other as much as the action onstage. The interior is adorned by Gobelin tapestries, gilded mosaics, a 1964 Chagall ceiling, and the six-ton chandelier that fell on the audience in 1896. Since 1989, when the new Opéra de la Bastille was inaugurated, most operas have taken place there; Garnier's hall is now used mainly for ballets. There is also a program of films on dance. Schedules for all performances and films are available in the entrance hall. Visits cost a hefty 28F, 15F for ages 10-16, and they include all public parts of the theater, except for the auditorium on performance days, and also the library and museum which holds documents about costumes and objects tracing the history of opera and dance. Whether it's worth the money depends largely on your interest in theater and late 19th-century extravagance. (Opéra open for visits Mon.-Sat. 10am-4:30pm. Tickets for the ballet start at 30F; for the opera 50F; for the movies 60F. Rush tickets at reduced prices available at the box office 15 minutes before each performance. To reserve seats, call 7-14 days ahead at 47 42 53 71, between noon and 6pm.)

Directly across from the Opéra is the **Café de la Paix,** dating from the 19th century, which caters to the after-theater crowd and anyone else who doesn't mind paying 30F for an espresso. West from this area along boulevard Haussmann, toward Mo. Chaussée d'Antin and Trinité, you'll find the largest clothes shopping area in Paris, including two of Paris's largest department stores, **Printemps** and **Galeries Lafayette** (see Shopping).

The area north of rue Châteaudun is a quiet and mostly residential, with a large student population and many small, well-priced, ethnic restaurants. Further north, at the border of the 18th *arrondissement* is **Pigalle,** an area famous the world over, not only as home to the **Moulin Rouge** cabaret and many popular discotheques (see Entertainment), but also as the center of much of the city's prostitution and hub of its sex shop industry. Tourists, especially women, should never walk around here alone at night and should always be wary of pickpockets.

Tenth Arrondissement

The **Gare du Nord** (Mo. Gare du Nord) is generally encountered out of necessity rather than curiosity, but it is worth a look. Jacques-Ignace Hittorf created the enormous station in 1863, in the midst of the great reconstruction of Paris. The platforms are covered by a vast *parapluie* (umbrella), as Napoleon III called the glass and steel heaven that creates the giant vault of the train station. Across from the station, a fringe of *brasseries* and cafés caters to the thousands of travelers who pass through here every day. Nearby is the **Marché St-Quentin,** 85, bd. Magenta, a massive, elegant construction of iron and glass, built in 1866 with a transparent ceiling as glorious as, if smaller than, that of Gare du Nord. Inside you can find an enormous variety of goods, from flowers to fresh produce and skinned rabbits for your delectable *lapin Schragois à la moutard* (Open Tues.-Sat. 8am-1pm and 3:30pm-7:30pm, Sun. 8am-1pm.)

The **Gare de l'Est** was constructed on a smaller scale than its neighbor du Nord, but conforms to the same neoclassical style in which all six of Paris's train stations were originally built. Directly across from the station, the Place du 11 Nov. 1918 opens into the **Boulevard de Strasbourg,** a hopping thoroughfare, as crowded with cafés, shops, fruit stands and people as St. Petersburg's Nevsky Prospect.

Close by, the small **Rue de Paradis** offers a quaint and prosperous little area bordered by shops displaying fine china and crystal. The beautiful (and expensive) objects mark the road to the **Baccarat Co.** headquarters and the **Baccarat Museum,** housed in an 18th-century building at 30-32 rue Paradis (see Museums). Farther up the street, at 18, rue de Paradis, the art gallery **Le Monde de l'Art** displays a variety of exhibits, housed in what was once the headquarters of the Boulanger china company (see Museums).

Going south on the **rue du Faubourg St-Denis,** one must dodge a crowd of Parisians assembling their dinners in a very active market area. At the end of the Fg. St. Denis, the majestic **Porte Saint-Denis** (Mo. Strasbourg/St. Denis) welcomes the visitor into Paris's inner city. Built in 1672 to celebrate the victories of Louis XIV, it is an imitation of the Arch of Titus in Rome. In the Middle Ages, this was the site of a gate in the city walls, but the present arch, characterized by André Breton as *"très belle et très inutile"* (very beautiful and quite useless) served only as a ceremonial marker and a royal entrance on the old road to St-Denis.

The **Place de la République** (Mo. République), at the meeting point of the 10th, the 3rd and the 11th *arrondissements,* is a good place to avoid at night, when prostitutes and swindlers are ubiquitous. In the center a monument to the Republic of France celebrates the victories of the 23 years of republican rule between 1789 and its erection in 1880. A bit further east lies the **Canal Saint-Martin,** 4.5km long and connecting the Canal de l'Ourcq to the Seine. The canal has several locks, which can be traveled by boat on one of the **canauxrama** trips (see Entertainment). One can also walk along the tree-lined banks, trying to sidestep the many joggers. Again, be careful in this area after dark.

Sixteenth Arrondissement

Every city has a 16th, be it called Park Avenue or Pall Mall. The names, languages, and architectural styles change but the atmosphere generated by a concentration of old money is the same the world over. Magnificent buildings of the style found all over Paris stand majestically in the 16th, façades clean, balcony grilles intricate, and flower baskets bursting with color. An abundance of older ladies (for they are definitely ladies), wearing far too much or far too little make-up, floats serenely above the urban fray, devotedly exercising their compact dogs. History continues to loom large in this area, full of old aristocratic families who have held on to their heritage. Some of these families refuse to allow their children to sing *La Marseillaise* in the home because it was to this same tune that their ancestors were beheaded during the Revolution. Not surprisingly, this sumptuous neighborhood remains the nucleus of the city's conservative politics, fashion, and culture. Much social life here revolves around a uniquely French institution called a *rallye,* an exclusive group of children and young adults whose parents pay for the privilege of having their children *sortent* (go out) with other grand families of their class. Other less wealthy families crowd into small apartments to establish the residency that will allow them to send their children to the city's finest schools.

Avenue Foch, one of Haussmann's finest creations, runs from l'Arc de Triomphe (see 8th *arrondissement)* to the Bois de Boulogne. Lined on either side by trees and parks, this is one of Paris's grandest boulevards. Not all mansions are created equal, however—those on the south side are even more prohibitively expensive because they receive better sun. **Rue Bugeaud,** leading south from the avenue, runs through the impossibly beautiful **Pl. du Chancelier Adenauer.**

Palais de Chaillot (Trocadéro). Catherine des Medici had a château on the heights of Chaillot. Napoleon wanted to erect a residence for his son, but was interrupted by Waterloo. In the 1820s, the duc d'Angoulême built a fortress-like memorial to his victory at Trocadéro in Spain. In 1878, this was replaced by the Palais du Trocadéro, which in turn yielded to the present structure prior to the 1937 World's Fair. Architect Jacques Carlu's radical design features two curved wings with a gap where a central hall might be expected. Today the Palais houses the **Musées du Cinéma Henri-Langlois, de l'Homme, de Marine, et National des Monuments Français** (see Museums) as well as the **Théatre National de Chaillot** and the **Cinémathèque Française** (see Entertainment). The large terrace provides the best view of the Eiffel Tower and the Champ de Mars, right across the Seine. Beneath the Palace, the **Jardins du Trocadéro** bask with cooling fountains and much green grass, to the delight of frisbee-throwers, carousel-riders, and roller skaters. Manet and Debussy lie in the nearby **Cimetière de Passy.**

Passy (or **La Muette**), the region to the immediate south and southwest of the Trocadéro, has been known historically for its restorative waters, its châteaux, and its grand houses. The marks of its famous residents linger. Visit the homes of a famed novelist and of a revered statesman by entering the **Maison de Balzac** and the **Musée Clemenceau** (see Museums). Jean-Jacques Rousseau lived on rue Raynouard and Benjamin Franklin, remembered by street and statue, built France's first lightning rod nearby. Northwest of the La Muette Métro lies the former site of the Château de la Muette, from whose lawn the first manned balloon lifted off in 1783. Walk through the **Jardin de Ranelagh,** where kids (and the young at heart) will enjoy the old-style carrousel (5F) On the other side of the park, the **Musée Marmottan** offers an exquisite collection of impressionist paintings and medieval illuminations (see Museums).

Bois de Boulogne

Spreading its leafy umbrella over 846 hectares at the western edge of Paris, the **Bois de Boulogne** (Mo. Porte Maillot, Sablons, Pont de Neuilly, Porte Dauphine, or Porte d'Auteuil) is a popular place for walks, jogs, and picnics. Napoleon III created the park in 1852, remembering with fondness the parks of London, where he spent years in exile. Although the police have recently cleaned out many of the drug dealers and prostitutes who once did business in the park, it's still a bad idea to come here for a romantic, moonlight stroll.

The Jardin d'Acclimatation, an amusement park at the northern end of the Bois (Mo. Sablons) is designed to appeal to kids—there's also the **Musée en Herbe,** an art museum designed especially for children. (Open daily 10am-6:30pm. Ticket office closes 45min. before park. Admission to the Jardin 9F, under 3 accompanied by parents free.) **Pré Catelan** is a manicured park whose paths wind through neatly clipped grass and lovely old trees. Inside the Pré Catelan, the **Jardin de Shakespeare** features all of the plants mentioned by the bard, grouped by play—thus there is a collection of Scottish highland vegetation in the *Macbeth* area, a Meditteranean section for *The Tempest,* etc. (Pré Catelan open 7:30am-8pm in summer, shorter hours in winter. Shakespeare garden open daily 3-3:30pm, 4:30-5pm. Entrance to Shakespeare garden 3F; ages under 10 1F50.)

The manicured islands of the **Lac Inférieur** (Mo. Porte Dauphine) can be reached by rented rowboat only. Boats accommodate up to 5 people. (Boathouses open late Feb. to early Nov. Mon.-Fri. 9am-6pm, Sat.-Sun. 9am-7pm. Boat rentals 48F per hour, 200F deposit.) **Bicycles** can be rented across the street from the boathouse at the northern end of the Lac Inférieur and in front of the entrance to the Jardin d'Acclimatation. (Rentals Mon.-Fri. 1-6:30pm, Sat.-Sun. 9:30am-7pm; Sept.-Jun. Wed. 1-6:30pm, Sat. and Sun. 9:30am-7pm. 27F per hour. Leave your passport or driver's license as deposit.)

Eighteenth Arrondissement: Montmartre and Sacré Coeur

Soaring above Haussman's flattened city, the heaven-kissing hill of Montmartre has a long and bloody history. The Romans decapitated St-Denis here in 272; legend has it that he and two other martyred bishops picked up their heads and carried them north to their final resting point, 7km away, where the Eglise St-Denis now stands; thus the name *Montmartre* (Hill of the Martyrs), which this area has borne ever since. Until the 19th century, Montmartre remained a farming area, covered with vineyards and wheat fields. The last of these vineyards is still operational. The wheat was processed in Montmartre's famous windmills, of which the Moulin de la Galette is one of the last remaining examples.

The Paris Commune essentially began here in the wee hours of March 18, 1871, on the heels of a conflict between the French army and the Parisian National Guard. After the Commune, the narrow streets and sharp corners of Montmartre attracted such notable Bohemians as Gustave Charpentier, Toulouse-Lautrec, and Eric Satie, and performers like "La Goulue" and Aristide Bruant. A generation later, in its last moment of glory before the devestation of WWI, Montmartre welcomed Picasso, Modigliano,

Utrillo, and Apollinaire into its artistic circle. Montmartre's heyday has since passed. Most of the places which were once so alive with art and conversation are merely shells for touristic tomfoolery. Still, come at dusk to watch the lights of Paris turn on below, and gape at the famous gas lamps that trace the line of the steps up the hillside.

For the classic approach to Sacré-Coeur, climb up the switchbacked stairs leading up from the **Square Willette.** At night, crowds of students and tourists mingle in the square to enjoy guitar music and sing and smoke and drink wine. (If you do come at night, use the Abbesses metro.) A funicular offers a ride up for one metro ticket (6F), but unless you're truly exhausted, it may not be worth the wait or the price—the (free) climb up is not particularly taxing, and offers a splendid view of the receding metropolis below. The famous narrow cobblestone stairs of the rue Foyatier, just to the west (to your left as you look uphill), offer a more romantic climb, as well as an escape from the crowds and street peddlars on the white marble steps of the central park.

The **Basilique du Sacré-Coeur (Basilica of the Sacred Heart),** 35, rue du Cheval de la Barre (tel. 42 51 17 02; Mo. Anvers, Abbesses, Château-Rouge), crowns the very top of the *butte* Montmartre like an enormous, puffy, white meringue. Its onion dome is visible from almost any corner of Montmartre and from much of the city down below. The style is pseudo Romanesque-Byzantine (mostly just strange). Climb the 112m bell tower for the highest point in Paris (yes, you *can* go higher than the Eiffel Tower) and a view that stretches as far as 50km on clear days. The crypt is open (for a price) and contains displays on the Basilica's history. (Basilica open daily 7am-11pm. Free. Dome and crypt open daily 9am-7pm; in winter 9am-6pm. Admission to dome 15F, 8F reduced; to crypt 10F, 6F reduced.)

Behind the basillica is the **Place du Tertre,** the central square of the *butte.* Crowded with overpriced restaurants and souvenir shops, this area caters to the unwieldy masses of tourists that congregate here. A conglomeration of portrait and landscape painters offer souvenir sketches, often more of service to the artist's pocket than to any higher Art. At 21, pl. du Tertre, the **tourist office** (tel. 42 62 21 21) gives free annotated maps and information about the area (open daily 10am-10pm; Oct.-March 10am-7pm).

Moving away form the crowded pl. du Tertre you'll find narrow, winding streets, hidden walled gardens, sharp corners, and whimsical clues to the way life used to be when Montmartre was a center of Bohemian life and artistic extravagance. The area west of the *place,* including the rue des Abbesses, rue des Trois Frères, and rue Lepic, is littered with pleasant restaurants, antique stores, and *boulangeries.* Cobblestone roads twist around, moving down the hill; many of the 18th-century residences hide charming gardens behind their iron gates. The definitive hangouts of the Belle Epoque lurk along the boulevard de la Rochechouart: the **Moulin Rouge,** for example, immortalized by the paintings of Toulouse-Lautrec and the music of Offenbach. **Place de Pigalle** has some discothèques, trendy nightspots for Parisian and foreign youth (see Entertainment). Other than that, it is the home of a large portion of Paris's seedy "sexshop" industry, where one can indulge in a little voyeurism, be it live or electronic. Women should never venture into this area alone at night.

Eastern Paris

As it courses eastward, rue de Rivoli transforms into rue St-Antoine, which runs to the **place de la Bastille.** A tower marks the spot where, on July 14, 1789, rioters freed from the infamous prison a whopping seven social misfits and petty criminals who were living relatively comfortably. The symbol of despotism was destroyed by the revolution; only the ground plan of the prison remains on its original site, marked by a line of stones. Intended to be the largest in the world and to entertain over 960,000 spectators per year, the **Opéra Bastille,** 120, rue de Lyon (Mo. Bastille) was conceived as a "People's Opera House." Inaugurated on July 14, 1989, it charges unusually low prices for performances of the highest caliber (see Entertainment.) The flocks of students lounging on the steps in front of the oddly appealing metal and glass structure are tugging the youthful, artistic center of Paris away from the Latin Quarter and into this up-and-coming neighborhood. The new Bohemia has thankfully not entirely lost its former working-class personality and offers a well-blended array of the young set amidst some of Paris's more garrulous and crotchety old inhabitants.

The **Cimetière Père-Lachaise,** on boulevard de Ménilmontant (Mo. Père-Lachaise), encloses the remains of Balzac, Colette, Corot, Danton, David, Delacroix, La Fontaine, Haussmann, Molière, and Proust within its peaceful, winding paths and elaborate sarcophagi. Foreigners inhumed here include Chopin, Jim Morrisson, Sarah Bernhardt, Gertrude Stein, Modigliano, and Oscar Wilde. Napoleon created the cemetery in 1803, but Parisians were reluctant to bury their dead in a site which, at the time, was quite far from the city. To increase the cemetery's popularity, Napoleon ordered that the remains of a few famous figures be dug up and reburied in Père-Lachaise, and now it is an all-star to match Westminster Abbey. The most adored grave has to be that of **Jim Morrison.** Within a radius of at least 100m of the Lizard King, graffiti on all the tombs points in his direction. French Leftists pay homage to the **Mur des Fédérés** (Wall of the Federals), where 147 *communards* were executed and buried after the suppression of the Commune. (Open Mon.-Fri. 8am-6pm, Sat. 8:30am-6pm, Sun. 9am-6pm; Oct.-March Mon.-Fri. 8am-5:30pm, Sat. 8:30am-5:30pm, Sun. 9am-5:30pm.)

The **Bois de Vincennes** has never been quite as fashionable or as formal as its sister, the Bois de Boulogne, but is commensurately more peaceful. The **Parc Zoologique de Paris,** 53, av. de Saint-Maurice (Mo. Porte Dorée), is considered the best zoo in France. The zoo was something of a novelty when it opened in 1934 because it was designed to give the animals space to roam outside. (Open Mon.-Sat. 9am-6pm, Sun. 9am-6:30pm; winter Mon.-Sat. 9am-5pm, Sun. 9am-5:30pm. Admission 35F, ages 6-16, students age 16-25 and over 60 20F, under 6 and disabled free. Ticket office closes 1/2hr. before zoo. Train tour 10F, under 10 8F. Departs from the restaurant.) The **Château de Vincennes** was home away from Louvre for every French monarch from Charles V to Henri IV. The 52m **donjon** (keep) was built between 1360 and 1370, a striking piece of medieval architecture and an impressive hide-out for any king. The **Ste-Chapelle** was founded as a church in 1379. (Château open daily 9:30am-7pm; Oct.-April 10am-5pm. Guided visits, 10 per day, are the only way to get inside these places. In French, but guides have written English translations. Admission 25F, students under 26 and seniors 14F.)

Museums and Galleries

Having played host to a good deal of history and a great many artists, it seems only natural that Paris should have gathered up a little of what was left behind. Every institution, artistic movement, ethnic group, and custom seems to have a museum devoted to its history, art, and memorabilia. For listings of the often excellent temporary exhibits, consult the bimonthly *Le Bulletin des Musées et Monuments Historiques,* available at the tourist office. *Musées et Monuments, Paris,* published by the tourist office, provides not only phone numbers, addresses, and hours, but also describes the museums and indexes them by theme and *arrondissement. Pariscope, 7 à Paris,* and *L'Officiel des spectacles* also list museums with hours and temporary exhibits.

Most students, children, and senior citizens are eligible for reduced admission rates at almost all Parisian museums. Frequent museum-goers, especially those ineligible for these ticket discounts, may want to invest in a **Carte Musée,** which grants entry into 65 Parisian museums as well as others in the suburbs and environs. The card is available at all major museums and Métro stations (1 day 55F, 3 days 110F, 5 days 160F).

Not as well-known among tourists as museums, **galleries** are extremely popular among Parisians. These more intimate exhibits generally feature only one or two showrooms, so they can be easily enjoyed in a half hour or so. Most of the city's 200 galleries specialize in one type of art, such as *naïf* painting, modern sculpture, or sketches of Parisian scenes. The highest concentration is in the Marais; in a casual stroll through the third and fourth *arrondissements,* you're sure to pass by dozens. St-Germain-des-Prés's galleries are small and enticing. For a complete list, pick up a free poster in any gallery.

Must See

The Louvre

The Building

Construction of the Louvre, 1er (tel. 40 20 50 50; Mo. Palais-Royal/Musée du Louvre), began in 1200, and still isn't finished. The original Louvre was a fortress built by King Phillipe-Auguste. When Charles V extended the city walls, the fortress sat quite useless in the middle of the city, so Charles converted the austere defensive structure into a residential château. Later monarchs destroyed his palace in favor of more modern and more grandiose structures. But in 1672, Louis XIV, sick of Paris, abandoned the Louvre in favor of Versailles. With the departure of the royal court, the buildings fell into a state of disrepair. Then in 1725, the Academy of Painting inaugurated annual *Salons* in the halls to show its members' paintings. In 1793, the Revolution made the exhibit permanent, creating the first Louvre Museum. Napoleon, who had vastly increased the museum's collection with art plundered from the nations he had vanquished, added the **Arc de Triomphe du Carroussel** to commemorate his victories of 1805.

As for the glass **pyramid** in the middle of the courtyard, it made its appearance in 1989. The previous entrances, ill-equipped for handling large crowds, were further hobbled by an extremely inefficient welcoming service. Architect I. M. Pei's remarkable proposal, which was at first met with intense disapproval, is now acknowledged to be a stroke of genius. He moved the main entrance to the central Cour Napoléon, but left the great space unspoiled by putting most of the entrance underground. This **Hall Napoléon** is illuminated by sunlight streaming through the pyramid overhead. Mitterrand's Grand Louvre project continues with construction to incorporate the Richelieu wing into the museum, which will double the area and make the Louvre the largest museum in the world.

The Museum

The **Musée du Louvre** is enormous. Don't try to cover the entire museum in two hours; the most satisfaction you're likely to derive is the pride in saying you saw the *Mona Lisa* through a forest of golf hats. Spending a full day in the museum is more likely to dull your powers of perception than to sharpen your appreciation of the art. Try to take in a few galleries over the course of several days. The extra admission charges are a small price to pay for the satisfaction. Better yet, come on a Monday or Wednesday evening, when there are more paintings than people.

Though best known for its European paintings, the Louvre displays some 400,000 works, divided into seven categories: Oriental antiquities, Greek and Roman antiquities, Egyptian antiquities, objets d'art, painting, drawing, and sculpture. (East Asian works are in the Guimet, and works after the mid-19th century in the Orsay or Pompidou.) The Greco-Roman works include such icons as the *Venus de Milo,* and the *Winged Victory of Samothrace.* Michelangelo's *Slaves* writhe in the sculpture section. But the paintings are the real stars. Early Renaissance masterpieces like Mantegna's *Crucifixion* provide a sharply classical contrast to Leonardo's atmospheric *Virgin of the Rocks.* Among the French works, the movie-screen-sized canvases of neoclassicist Jacques-Louis David steal the show. Under the old regime, he painted *The Oath of the Horatii* to inspire his countrymen to virtuous deeds like those of the sons of Horatius, who vowed to die for their fatherland. The *Brutus,* which shows an anguished father who has ordered the execution of his own sons for treason against the republic, foreshadowed David's political career as a Jacobin during the Terror.

(Museum open Mon. and Wed. 9am-10pm, Thurs.-Sun. 9am-6pm. Ticket office closes 45min. before the museum. Admission 31F, ages 18-25 16F, ages under 18 free. Sun., ages over 18 16F, ages under 18 free. If you are buying full-priced tickets, save up to 30min. by using one of the automatic ticket machines. Tours in English, Wed.-Sat. every 1/2hr. 10-11:30am and 2-3:30pm, 30F. Meet at the "Acceuil Groupes" area. Recorded tours of 25 masterpieces—available in English—25F.)

The Musée d'Orsay

The **Musée d'Orsay**, 1, rue de Bellechasse, 7*ème* (tel. 40 49 48 14; RER Musée d'Orsay; Mo. Solférino), comes as close to museum perfection as is humanly, or institutionally, possible. Much more than a display of Impressionist paintings, it is an aesthetic and educational experience. Sheltered within the historic renovated *Gare d'Orsay,* once the train station which served southwestern France, it offers a survey not only of the successes in 19th-century French art, but also its failures. The Orsay has arranged its exhibits chronologically, highlighting the development of contrasting artistic styles throughout the second half of the 19th and the early years of the 20th centuries. Even the complete artistic novice can find his or her bearings in the Orsay— this may well be the most user-friendly museum in the world.

The Salon paintings in the right side of the ground floor present a telling description of the Academic tradition against which the Impressionists were rebelling. Alexandre Cabanel's *Naissance de Vénus* (Birth of Venus; 1863) epitomizes the state of accepted Academic painting before the onset of modernism. A student at the Ecole de Beaux Arts, Cabanel received the prestigious Prix de Rome and was elected to the Academy after his painting's huge success in the Salon of 1863. The painting itself—so symbolic of the flawless technique, the balanced composition, the historical or mythological subject, which one needed to receive a commission or show at the all-important salon— was bought by Napoléon III. The result, to modern eyes (and to the eyes of contemporaries like Manet and Monet), is not only artificial and schematic, but utterly absurd.

Across the hall from Cabanel's *Vénus,* Edouard Manet's *Olympia* (1863), arguably the first "modern" painting, caused an uproarious scandal when exhibited at the 1865 salon. Manet had taken the format of Titian's *Venus of Urbino* (1538), *the* standard for female nudes in Western art, and twisted it to fit his modern vision. Manet's painting reversed the role of spectator and subject. Whereas Cabanel's *Vénus* seems entirely passive and vulnerable to the spectator's gaze, *Olympia* stares back, well aware of her nudity and rebuffing the bourgeois observer for his voyeurism. This was pornography, cried the critics, not art. Moreover, they criticized its realism for being ugly: Olympia's hands and feet are too big, she is too thin and too muscular, and her skin is not of the correct (lily white) color. The painting invalidated the concept of art as Beauty, while opening the road to the modern, with its acknowledgement of "Art for art's sake."

Upstairs, on the top floor, the Impresionism celebration begins in earnest. The glass-topped arcade of the station, roofing in this area, provides the perfect setting for viewing Impressionist works; the radiance of soft light, filtered through heavy metal grill-work, highlights the interplay of colors on paintings like Monet's *Gare St-Lazare* and Renoir's *Le Bal du Moulin de la Galette.* On the one hand, Impressionism was an aesthetic movement, breaking with the Academy's program of flawless surface, monumental themes, and invisible brush strokes—insisting that Art could be made just as easily with swift brushstrokes, broken surfaces, and ordinary themes, and most of all, that paintings ought to capture the spirit and sensations of a moment. On the other hand, Impressionism was a movement seeking to capture the new rhythm of bourgeois life—no longer expressible through the tired channels of traditional French painting. Works like Monet's *La rue Montorgueil Fête de 30 juin 1878* illustrate the boulevards of Haussman's new Paris and the faceless crowds that had become a fact of the modern city.

Moving right along, we come to the "Post-Impressionists," a blanket title for a series of highly individualistic artists and artistic movements which, in their experiments with light, color, and planar geometry, anticipated the 20th century's movement to cubism and abstract art. Van Gogh, for example, experimented with dazzling, at times lurid intensities of color and distorted perspectives to create his highly personal, spiritual views of the world around him; Cézanne, preoccupied by form, space, color, and their inter-relation, painted his famous still-lifes, portraits, and landscapes, experimenting with soft colors and shifting geometric planes to create a reconstructed definition of the painting surface.

The Impressionism exhibits end in a lovely third-floor café and terrace which overlooks the Seine and the Right Bank. The middle floor, and last stage of the visit, presents an array of Belle Epoque sculpture, painting, and decorative art. Don't miss the fascinating *art nouveau* exhibit, with its strangely vegetal furniture and whimsical flowing forms. For more information on anything you've seen, visit the *Salle de Consultation* (Documentation room; upstairs from the café), where a serene atmosphere provides a perfect setting to relax and read about the planning of the museum. Remarkable computers have on-line access to information about any painting, complete with a video replica. (Museum open Tues.-Wed. and Fri.-Sun. 9am-6pm, Thurs. 9am-9:30pm; Sept 21-June19 Tues.-Wed. and Fri.-Sat. 10am-6pm, Thurs. 10am-9:45pm, Sun. 9am-6pm. Last tickets sold 5:15pm, 9pm on Thurs. Admission 31F, ages 18-25, ages over 60, and everyone on Sun. 16F, under 18 free. Nursery facilities. Guided tours Tues.-Sat. 11:30am, Thurs. also at 7pm; in summer a tour at 2pm is added; 90min., 30F.)

Centre Pompidou

Often referred to as the Palais Beaubourg, the Centre National d'Art et de Culture Georges-Pompidou, 4*ème,* has inspired architectural controversy ever since its inauguration in 1977 (tel. 42 77 12 33, recorded information in French on the week's events 42 77 11 12; Mo. Rambuteau, Hôtel de Ville, or Chatelet-Les Halles; Wheelchair accessible: enter through the back, on Rue Beaubourg). Chosen from 681 competing designs, Richard Rogers and Renzo Piano's dazzlingly shameless building-turned-inside-out bares its circulatory system to all passers-by. Piping and ventilation ducts in various colors run up, down, and sideways along the outside (blue for air, green for water, yellow for electricity, red for heating). Framing the structure like a cage are the huge steel bars which carry all of the building's weight, opening an expansive display space inside.

The Pompidou center attracts more visitors per year than any other museum or monument in France—more than Versailles, and more than the Louvre and the Eiffel tower combined. The views from the escalator (which is bolted to the building's façade) and from the fifth-floor terrace are as dizzying as from the Arche de la Défense, but without the cost. An English-language tour of the building leaves every day at 4pm (50F, ages under 26 25F).

The Musée National d'Art Moderne, the center's main attraction, houses a rich selection of 20th-century art, from fauves and cubists to Pop and conceptual art. The captioning leaves something to be desired, and not everything is translated into English. The entrance to the museum is on the 4th floor, which is particularly strong on modernism: Matisse, Derain, Picasso, Magritte, Braque, Kandinsky, and Yves Klein. The lower level of the museum (which can only be reached by a small escalator from the floor above) houses work from the 1960s to the present. (Museum open Mon. and Wed.-Fri. noon-10pm, Sat.-Sun. 10am-10pm. Admission 28F, ages under 26 18F, ages under 18 free. On Sundays 10am-2pm everybody gets in for free. Prices for temporary exhibits varies with show. Buy your tickets downstairs; they are not available at the museum entrance.)

Most visitors are unaware that displaying art is only one (and perhaps the least important) of the four functions of the Centre Pompidou. The open-stack **Bibliothèque Publique d'Information** (tel. 42 77 12 33), a free, non-circulating library, is open to anyone who walks in (entrance on the second floor), and has a large selection of English books, a computer room, a lounge with the latest international newspapers, a stereo center, and a language lab. (Open Mon. and Wed.-Fri. noon-10pm, Sat.-Sun. 10am-10pm.) The third permanent department of the center, the **Centre de Creation Industrielle (CCI),** studies the relationships between humanity, architecture, and technology. Although the resources of the center are closed to the public, its gallery is open to visitors for 16F. Finally, the **Institut de la Recherche et de la Coordination Accoustique/Musique (IRCAM)** is an institute of musical research housed (appropriately enough) next to the Stravinsky fountain (over the little Japanese bridge). Except in summer, the institute organizes concerts: for inquiries, call 42 60 94 27. A fifth floor restaurant and café round out the center's offerings. (Restaurant and café open Sun.-Mon. and Wed.-Thurs. noon-3pm, Fri.-Sat. noon-3pm and 7-11:30pm.)

The Invalides Museums

The Invalides complex (*7ème*, Mo. Invalides, Latour-Maubourg, Varennes) guards a series of museums, revolving around French history and above all, France's martial glory. Pacifists beware: the **Musée de l'Armée** (tel. 45 55 37 70 Mon.-Fri., 45 55 37 68 Sat.-Sun. and holidays) celebrates centuries of French military history, examining heroes ranging from Napoleon to de Gaulle, with lesser Generals sandwiched in between. (Open daily 10am-6pm; Oct.-March 10am-5pm.) Upstairs, the **Musée des Plans-Reliefs,** gathers a collection of a hundred models of fortified cities, some of them enormous. The same ticket admits you to **Napoleon's Tomb,** lovingly placed under Jules Hardouin-Mansart's royal dome. Finished in 1861, Napoleon's tomb itself is actually six concentric coffins, made of materials ranging from mahogany to lead. This riot of bombast delighted Adolph Hitler on his visit to Paris in 1940. (Open daily 10am-7pm; Sept. and April-May 10am-6pm; Oct.-March 10am-5pm.) On your way out, peer across the glass partition into the **Eglise St-Louis des Invalides,** also known as the Eglise des Soldats. Berlioz's Requiem was first played on this organ. Famous standards (battle flags) have always decorated the church, although the collection was depleted when the Hôtel governor burned 1400 of them upon learning of the enemy arrival in Paris on March 30, 1814. (Church open daily, in theory, April-Sept. 10am-6pm; Oct.-March 10am-5pm). A ticket valid for two days (30F, kids 7-18, students under 30, and EEC seniors 20F) admits you to the Musée de l'Armée, Napoleon's Tomb, the Eglise des Soldats, and the Musée des Plans Reliefs.

One of the least celebrated, but most worthwhile parts of the Invalides is the **Musée de l'Ordre de la Libération,** 51 bis, bd. de Latour-Maubourg (47 01 35 15). Charles de Gaulle founded the order on November 16, 1940, to recognize individuals and organizations—civilian and military—and cities which distinguished themselves in the liberation of France and its Empire. Quiet and uncrowded, the museum tells the story of those who fought for the liberation of France, believing, like de Gaulle, Grandmaster of the Order, that although France had lost a battle, she had not lost the war. (Open Mon.-Sat. 2-5pm. Admission 10F.)

Musée Rodin

The Musée Rodin, 77, rue de Varenne *7ème* (tel. 47 05 01 34), Mo. Varenne, inside and outside the elegant 18th-century Hôtel Biron ranks among the top attractions in Paris. Auguste Rodin (1840-1917) is undoubtedly France's most famous sculptor; during his lifetime, his artistic style placed him among the country's most controversial artists. Many think of Rodin as a sculpting Impressionist (Monet was a close friend and admirer); almost all today acknowledge him as the father of modern sculpture. Just inside the gates of the garden in front of the museum sits Rodin's most famous sculpture, *Le Penseur (The Thinker,* 1880-1904), meant, some believe, to represent Dante contemplating his *Inferno.* The tautness of the musculature, the intensity of the facial concentration, and the tension of coiled energy coordinate to present a remarkable portrait of a human being actively engaged in thinking. On the other side of the garden, *Les Bourgeois de Calais (Burghers of Calais),* recall a near-tragic moment in the Hundred Years War. England's King Edward III had offered to hang the mayor of Calais and several prominent residents rather than slaughter all the city's inhabitants; the burghers decided to sacrifice their lives for their townsfolk, and their heroism prompted the impassioned and successful 11th-hour intervention of Edward's French wife, Phillipine. As with *Le Penseur,* Rodin sculpts the moment of peak tension, grossly exaggerating the size and contortions of the hands and feet for dramatic effect. Beyond the Burghers stands Rodin's largest and most intricate work, *La Porte d'Enfer (The Gates of Hell),* whose tormented souls are drawn directly from the pages of Dante's *The Divine Comedy.*

Most of Rodin's smaller sculptures are displayed inside the *hôtel.* Conceived as a model of Dante's Paolo and Francesca, *Le Baiser* freezes in white marble two intertwined lovers. A similar work is *Paolo and Francesca,* also portraying the doomed lovers. In this and in *La Main de Dieu (the Hand of God),* Rodin experiments with the contrast between rough and smooth sculpture. Only a heart of steel could resist feeling the somber elegance of suffering portrayed in *La Douleur (Suffering), Le Cri (The*

Shriek), La Pleureuse (The Weeper), and *Le Désespoir (Despair).* The rose-filled gardens behind the museum, decorated with lesser-known Rodin sculptures, offer a perfect place to relax after touring the museum. Also included are several works by Camille Claudel, Rodin's muse, apprentice, and lover. (Museum open Tues.-Sun. 10am-5:45pm; Oct.-March Tues.-Sun. 10am-5pm. Last admission 1/2hr. before closing. Admission, good for museum and park 21F, under 18, students, seniors, and Sun. 11F. Park open Tues.-Sun. 10am-7:45pm; Sept. and April-June 10am-5:30pm; Oct.-March 10am-4:45pm. Last admission 1/2hr. before closing. Admission to park alone 4F.)

Musée de Cluny

The Hôtel de Cluny, 6, Pl. Paul-Painlevé, *5ème* (tel. 43 25 62 00), not only houses one of the world s finest collections of medieval art, jewelry and tapestries, but is itself a perfectly preserved medieval manor, built on top of restored Roman ruins. Most visitors to the museum rush right upstairs to Room XIII on the second floor to gawk at the *La dame à la licorne* (Lady and Unicorn) cycle, consisting of six oversize tapestries dating from the end of the 15th century. Art historians agree that five of the tapestries depict the senses. The sixth tapestry, *Mon seul desir* (My Only Desire) shows the Lady giving up her jewelry, or overcoming her wordly senses, for her lover.

Also upstairs you'll find an entire room (room XVI) devoted to medieval royal jewelry and crowns. The gold rush continues down the corridor in Room XIX with an enormously rare and valuable gold altarpiece, a finely worked ornament from Basel, Switzerland. Downstairs, the *Gallerie des Rois,* Room VII, proudly displays a set of 21 stone heads of Judean and Israelite kings, dating from 1210 to 1230. These heads (attached to statues) sat atop Notre Dame s portals until the revolutionaries of 1793 separated them from their bodies, mistaking them for statues of the French kings. On Friday afternoons, the museum sponsors concerts of medieval chamber music performed on original instruments (Fri. at 1pm—call ahead to confirm the time. Free with admission to the museum. Museum open Wed.-Mon. 9:30am-5:15pm. Admission 17F, students 9F. Sunday admission 9F.)

La Villette

The **Parc de la Villette** (tel. 42 78 70 00, Mo. Porte de la Villette), is a highly successful urban renewal project in the northeastern corner of the nineteenth *arrondissement,* 150 acres large and growing. President Mitterrand inaugurated the project in 1985; the principal architect is Philippe Starck, although his collaborators include the avant-garde American architect Peter Eisenmann and French philosopher Jacques Derrida. Several major sights beckon the curious. Perched on La Villette's northern end, the **Cité des Sciences et de l'Industrie** (tel. 40 05 80 00) is the largest science museum in France, dedicated to making science more accessible to the layperson. A series of ingenious interactive displays make learning something unavoidable. While there, sit under the stars at the complex's **planetarium.** If traveling with children, inquire about the special programs and demonstrations for the younger set. (Museum open Tues.-Sun. 10am-6pm. One-day "Cité-Pass" tickets 45F, under 25 35F, under 7 free. If you're planning to see a movie at the Géode, buy a combined ticket—see below.) The submarine *Argonaute,* now parked in front of the Cité, served for 25 years in the French navy until it was decommissioned in 1982. (Open Tues-Fri. 10am-6pm, Sat-Sun. 10am-7pm. Children under 3 not admitted. Covered by Cité-Pass.) **La Géode** (tel. 40 05 80 00), the enormous floating golf ball in front of the Cité, shows Omnimax movies on a 1000 square meter hemispheric screen inside. Consult *Pariscope* to learn what's playing. (Showings Tues.-Sun. on the hour every hour from 10am to 9pm. Mon. also during French school holidays, last showing at 7pm. Get your ticket early; they sell out. Admission 50F, students and ages under 18 37F. Combined tickets for Cité, and Géode, available only at Géode ticket booth, are 85F full, 72F reduced. No reduced-price tickets from 1-7pm on weekends and holidays.) If you have time, wander through the rest of the park, which encompasses a number of thematic gardens, a shakin', rattlin', and rollin' theatre, called the **Cinaxe,** and a concert hall.

Try to See

Musée du Jeu de Paume (Museum of the Tennis Court) (tel. 42 60 12 69), 1er. Mo. Concorde. The Jeu de Paume is one of two buildings in the Tuileries that overlooks the place de la Concorde; when you have your back to the Louvre, it's the one on your right. Originally constructed under Napoleon III as a court on which to play *jeu de paume*, an ancestor of tennis, the Jeu de Paume was converted in 1909 into a display area, mostly for art exhibits. Between 1947 and 1986, the building housed an Impressionist collection which has subsequently been transferred to the Musee d'Orsay. Since June 1991, the Jeu de Paume has been a gallery of contemporary art. Open Tues. noon-9:30pm, Wed.-Fri. noon-7pm, Sat.-Sun. 10am-7pm. Admission 30F, students, teachers, ages 13-18, and seniors 20F, under 13 free.

Musée de l'Orangerie, (tel. 42 97 48 16), 1er. Mo. Concorde. The Orangerie is the other building in the Tuileries that overlooks the place de la Concorde; when you have your back to the Louvre, it's the one on your left. Displayed here is a small collection of Impressionist painting. Though less spectacular than the Orsay, this museum is also less crowded, so you can admire the Cézannes, Renoirs, Matisses, Picassos, and other greats in comfort. The crown jewel of the Orangerie's collection is Claude Monet's *Les Nymphéas* (The Water Lilies), occupying two rooms of the underground level. Open Wed.-Mon. 9:45am-5:15pm. Admission 26F, ages 18-25 and over 60 14F, Sun. 14F.

Musée Marmottan, 2, rue Louis-Boilly (tel., 42 24 07 02), 16ème. Mo. La Muette. The erstwhile *hôtel* of the collector Jules Marmottan will captivate you with a small but exquisite Impressionism collection. The lower level displays some 100 Monet canvases, donated by Michel Monet, the artists' son, including *Impression: Soleil Levant,* the painting that gave its name to the movement. Of course, Mssrs. Renoir, Pisarro, and Gauguin also figure prominently. Open Tues.-Sun. 10am-5:30pm. Admission 30F, students 15F, under 8 free.

Musée National des Arts Asiatiques (Musée Guimet), 6, pl. d'Iéna (tel. 47 23 61 65), 16ème. Mo. Iéna or Boissière. The largest collection of Asian art in the western world. Musée open Wed.-Mon. 9:45am-5:15pm. Admission 26F, students and seniors 14F. When temporary exposition is showing 32F, students and seniors 20F, grants admission to everything. A few steps away, its annex, the **Hôtel Heidelbach-Guimet,** 19, av. d'Iéna. is devoted to Buddhist pieces from China and Japan. Open same hours as Musèe Guimet. Admission to one permits entry to the other.

Why Not?

Musée des Arts Africains et Océaniens, 293, av. Daumesnil, 12ème (tel. 43 43 14 54), on the western edge of the Bois de Vincennes. Mo. Porte Dorée. One of the capital's best non-Western museums, it houses a terrific collection of several millennia of African and Pacific art. The tropical fish aquarium downstairs is immensely popular with Parisian families and school children. Open Mon.-Fri. 10am-noon and 1:30-5:20pm, Sat.-Sun. 12:30-5:50pm. Last admission 30min. before closing. Aquarium and superb temporary exhibits open daily 10am-5:20pm. Admission to museum and aquarium 17F, students and seniors 9F, under 18 free. With temporary exhibit 23F, students and seniors 15F, under 18 free.

Musée des Arts Décoratives, 107, rue de Rivoli, 1er (tel. 42 60 32 14). Mo. Palais Royal. Enter through a side door of the Louvre building. The definitive collection of interior decoration. Tapestries, china, paintings, and furniture from the late Middle Ages to the avant-garde fill 5 stories. Tastes have changed considerably, which means that you won't find everything beautiful or even interesting, but there are some highlights, including the medieval tapestries (2nd floor) and the Haentschel room in the 20th-century collection (1st floor). Open Tues.-Sat. 12:30-6pm, Sun. noon-6pm. Admission 23F, under 25 14F, under 5 free.

Maison de Balzac, 47, rue Raynouard, 16ème (tel. 42 24 56 38). Mo. Passy. Honoré de Balzac (1799-1850), one of France's greatest novelists, lived here from 1840-47, penning the last part of *la Comédie Humaine.* The house gives a feel for Balzac's entire life with portraits of his family, samples of his work, and caricatures of him amid his fellow 19th-century literati. Starting in April 1993, a temporary exhibition will explore the theme of Balzac and Russia, including his Ukrainian wife. Open Tues.-Sun. 10am-5:40pm. Admission 12F, students and big families 6F50, seniors free. When temporary exhibition is showing 25F, reduced rate 18F.

Musée Bourdelle, 16, rue Antoine Bourdelle, 15ème (tel. 45 48 67 27). Mo. Montparnasse Bienvenue. Even people who don't yet appreciate the raw aggressive style of the sculptor Antoine Bourdelle (1861-1929), friend and contemporary of Auguste Rodin, will become die-hard fans after spending the afternoon wandering the rooms of Bourdelle's studios-turned-museum. Unfortunately, the lack of space, especially in the miniscule garden where the sculptures are literally piled on top of each other, makes the display crowded at best, and some of the works seem lost in the shuffle of hundreds of figures. Open Tues.-Sun. 10am-5:40pm. Admission 12F, students 6F50, Sun. free.

Musée Carnavalet, 23, rue de Sévigné, 3*ème* (tel. 42 72 21 13). Mo. Rivoli or Carnavalet. Housed in a 16th-century *hôtel,* the former residence of the Marquis de Sévigné, this is Paris's main display of its own history. A must for any francophile; it traces the history of the city from prehistory, through a step-by-step chronology of the Revolution, to the present. See Sights section of 3rd *arrondissement* for comments on the museum's entrance courtyard. Open Tues.-Sun. 10am-5:40pm. Admission 16F, Sun. free. Temporary exhibits extra.

Musée du Cinéma Henri-Langlois, 16*ème* (tel. 45 53 74 39), in the Palais de Chaillot. Mo. Trocadéro. The history of sound and light in film starting with magic lanterns and shadow theaters. You can only see the Musée by 1-hr. tour, however, and it is conducted in French. Open Wed.-Mon. for tours at 10am, 11am, 2pm, 3pm, and 4pm. Tours canceled if fewer than 8 people. Admission 22F, students and seniors 14F.

Musée Clemenceau, 8, rue B. Franklin, 16*ème* (tel. 45 20 53 41), through a small courtyard. Mo. Passy. The 4 rooms in which Georges Clemenceau (1841-1929), Prime Minister, *Président du Conseil,* Minister of War (1917-20) and hero to the French people, lived for 35 years have not been changed since his death: the yellowed calendars are all hauntingly torn off at November 24, 1929. Open Tues., Thurs., Sat.-Sun., and holidays 2-5pm. Admission 20F, students and seniors 12F.

Musée Cognacq-Jay, 8, rue Elzevir, 3*ème* (tel. 42 74 33 66). Mo. St-Paul, Chemin Vert or Rambuteau. The city of Paris acquired this collection of Enlightenment fine art and decorative art, which belonged to Ernest Cognacq and his wife, Marie-Louise Jay, upon the death of M. Cognacq in 1929. Since 1990, the museum has been housed in the 16th-century Hôtel Denon, which the city of Paris rescued from decay for this purpose. Highlights include works by Watteau, Tiepolo, and Canaletto. The layout of the museum is very professional. Works are grouped together in a natural and uncrowded manner; some of the rooms combine furniture and paintings to produce a "total" picture of a wealthy 17th-century household. Open Tues.-Sun. 10am-5:40pm. Admission 12F.

Cristalleries Baccarat, 30-32, rue Paradis, 10*ème* (tel. 47 70 64 30). Mo. Gare de l'Est. The building at 30-32, rue Paradis houses both the Baccarat crystal company headquarters and the Baccarat museum (on the 2nd floor). Since its founding in 1764, Baccarat has become one of the most prestigious and expensive crystal makers, producing chandeliers, vases, and table finery for kings, czars, and shahs. The museum houses an array of every imaginable crystal object, including a life-size chandelier-woman at the entrance. Open Mon.-Fri. 9am-6pm and Sat. 10am-noon and 2pm-5pm. Free.

Palais de la Découverte (Palace of Discovery), in the Grand Palais, entrance on av. Franklin D. Roosevelt 8*ème* (tel. 43 59 18 21 (answering machine); groups 40 74 80 15). Mo. Champs-Elysées-Clemenceau. More central, less flashy than the Cité des Sciences; a poke and prod sort of place. Open Tues.-Sat. 9:30am-6pm, Sun. 10am-7pm. Admission 20F, students, seniors and kids under 18 10F. Planetarium show 13F extra, students, seniors, and kids under 18 9F; call for times.

Musée des Egouts de Paris (Museum Paris's Sewers), actually inside the sewers, at the corner of the quai d'Orsay and the place de la Résistance, 7*ème* (tel. 47 05 10 29). Mo. Pont de l'Alma. In *Les Misérables,* Victor Hugo wrote, "Paris has beneath it another Paris, a Paris of sewers, which has its own streets, squares, lanes, arteries, and circulation." This unique museum details the history of the City of Light's fascinating subterranean avenues: each Parisian street over 20m wide has at least one sewer tunnel beneath it—if you stretched out the entire network, it would reach from Paris to Istanbul. Take a self-guided tour with a French, English, German, and Spanish pamphlet, or one of the impromptu tours with a real live *égoutier* (sewer worker). Open Sat.-Wed. 11am-6pm; winter Sat.-Wed. 11am-5pm. Last ticket sold 1hr. before closing. Admission 22F, students and kids under 10 17F. Closed for 3 weeks in Jan.

Musée Grevin, 10, bd. Montmartre, 9*ème* (tel. 47 70 85 06). Mo. Montmartre. This wacky wax museum is rather light fun, a soft and sticky look at the last few centuries. See Marie Antoinette in jail, or Michael Jackson in mid-moonwalk. Open daily 10am-7pm; Oct.-May 1-7pm. Admission 48F, ages 6-14 34F.

Musée Grévin, level "-1" of Forum des Halles, near the Porte Berger, 1*er* (tel. 40 26 28 50). Mo. Châtelet-Les Halles. A subsidiary of the larger Grévin wax museum in the 9th *arrondissement,* it presents a fascinating spectacle of Paris in its "Belle Epoque" (1885-1900). A terrific sound and light show recreates the turn of the century through wax figures of Hugo, Verne, Renoir, Pasteur, Eiffel, and many others. Unfortunately, the show relies so heavily on the French voice-over that if you don't have a good grasp of the language, it's really not worth your time. Open Mon.-Sat. 10:30am-7:30pm, Sun. and holidays 1-8pm. Ticket office closes 45min. before museum. Admission 38F, ages 6-14 28F, under 6 free.

Musée Gustave Moreau, 14, rue de La Rochefoucauld, 9*ème* (tel. 48 74 38 50). Mo. Trinité. This museum is a gem; located in the house of the 19th-century symbolist painter Gustave Moreau, it contains thousands of his drawings and more paintings than the walls can hold. Open Wed.-Mon. 10am-12:30pm and 2-5pm. Admission 17F, students and children 9F.

Musée de l'Histoire de France, 60, rue des Francs-Bourgeois, 3*ème*. Mo. Hôtel de Ville or Rambuteau. Housed in part of the Hôtel Soubise, this museum contains reams of important French documents, including Napoleon's will, a letter by Jeanne d'Arc, and *the* Edict of Nantes. Only true Francophiles need enter. Open Wed.-Mon. 1:45-5:45pm.

Musée de l'Homme (Museum of Man), 16*ème* (tel. 45 53 70 60), in the Palais de Chaillot. Mo. Trocadéro. A painted cart from Sicily, a chock-full-o'-stuff Turkish store, a 3m cylindrical drum from the New Hebrides, and the requisite polar bear leading into an Inuit exhibit. It's a small world, after all. Open Wed.-Mon. 9:45am-5:15pm. Admission 25F, students, seniors, big families 15F, disabled and children under 6 free.

Musée Jacquemart-André, 158, bd. Haussmann, 8*ème* (tel. 45 62 39 94). Mo. St- Philippe-du-Roule. Closed for renovation in 1992 but expected to re-open by 1993. Works from the Italian Renaissance (Donatello bronzes, Della Robbia's terra-cottas) and the French 18th century (Fragonard) join pieces by Rembrandt, Rubens, and Watteau under Tiepolo's fresco. Open Sept.-July Wed.-Sun. 1:30-5:30pm. Admission 10F.

Musées du Jardin des Plantes, 5*ème*. The Jardin des Plantes (see Sights, 5th *arrondissement*) confines 3 main museums within its grounds. The **Musée d'Histoire Naturelle (Museum of Natural History)** features a collection of dinosaur and human skeletons. (Open Mon. and Wed.-Fri. 10am-5pm, Sat.-Sun. 11am-6pm. Admission 18F, students 12F.) An insect museum, the **Galerie d'Entomologie,** buzzes with excitement over the *Titanus Gigantus,* an 18cm-long brown and black beetle monster from South America, and its closest cousins. Fortunately, they're all dead. (Open Wed.-Mon. 1-4:45pm. Admission 12F, students 8F.) Finally, the **Musée de Minéralogie (Museum of Mineralogy),** devotes itself to the finest in fine gems, and their most splendid artistic uses. (Open Mon. and Wed.-Fri. 10am-5pm, Sat.-Sun. 11am-6pm. Admission 25F, students 16F.)

Musée de la Marine (Museum of the Navy), 16ème (tel. 45 53 31 70), in the Palais de Chaillot. Mo. Trocadéro. A bevy of bitty boats. 'Nuff said. Open Wed.-Mon. 10am-6pm and on holidays. Tickets issued until 5:30pm. Admission 28F, seniors, ages 5-12, and big families 14F, under 5 free.

Les Martyrs de Paris, porte du Louvre of the Forum des Halles, 1*er.* Mo. Les Halles. A macabre museum of torture and cruelty, with a heavy emphasis on the medieval. Realistic waxwork representations of people being branded, burned, and abused in ways you never have dreamed of, while signs in English and French fill in the historical details. Heavy Metal fans will be delighted to see a model of the "Iron Maiden" torture machine from Nuremberg Castle. Shares a ticket booth with the wax figure-laden **Rock 'n' Roll Hall of Fame,** right next door. Both open daily 10:30am-6:30pm. Admission 40F, students 29F. Martyrs of Paris and Rock 'n' Roll Hall of Fame, 66F, students 48F.

Musée de la Mode et du Costume (Museum of Fashion and Clothing), in the Palais Galliera, 10, av. Pierre 1*er*-de-Serbie, 16*ème* (tel. 47 20 85 23). Mo. Iéna. With over 12,000 ensembles in its possession, the Musée mounts temporary exhibitions showcasing fashion throughout the past three centuries. Open Tues.-Sun. 10am-5:40pm, when an exhibition is on. Admission 30F, students and seniors 20F.

Institut du Monde Arabe (Institute of the Arab World), 23, Quai St-Bernard, 5*ème* (tel. 439 78 01 97). Mo. Jussieu. One of Paris newest museums, harboring an exhaustive cross-cultural collection of Arab art and a display on Arab history. A delightful café on the 9th floor overlooks the Seine. Museum open Tues.-Sun. 1-6pm. Cafeteria open Tues.-Sun. 11am-4pm. Admission 40F, students 20F, under 18 free. 90-min. tour included with the full ticket price, Tues.-Fri. at 3pm, Sat.-Sun. at 2:30 and 6:30pm.

Galerie Le Monde de l'Art, 18, rue Paradis, 10*ème* (tel. 42 46 43 44). Mo. Gare de l'Est. The airy and light-filled interior of this gallery is decorated with beautiful tiles, holdovers from the days when the building served as headquarters for the Boulanger China Company. The exhibits themselves rotate through this small gallery every few months and usually highlight modern dissident artists (ex-Soviets, Cubans, and others). Open Mon. 2-7pm, Tues.-Sat. 1-7pm. Free.

The Musée de la Monnaie de Paris, 11, quai de Conti, 6*ème* (tel. 40 46 55 33). Mo. Pont.-Neuf. This is *the* unmissable Parisian collection for the numismatists among you! (Anybody? Anybody?) Open Tues.- Sun. 1-6pm. Admission 15F, Students 10F.

Musée National des Monuments Français (National Museum of French Monuments), 16*ème* (tel. 47 27 35 74), in the Palais de Chaillot. Mo. Trocadéro. Why go to the provinces when you can have the provinces come to you? Just about everything in this warehouse-like structure is a copy of something elsewhere in France, from the angels at Chartres to the cave paintings at Les Eyzies. Open Wed.-Mon. 9:30am-5pm. Admission 17F, students 18-25, seniors, and on Sun. 9F. Conferences explaining parts of the museum free with admission Wed. at 1 and 3pm. Some parts of museum closed until March 1993.

Musée Nissim de Camondo, 63, rue de Monceau, 8ème (tel. 45 63 26 32). Mo. Villiers or Monceau. Inspired by the Petit Trianon in Versailles, the building now houses a fine collection of 18th-century art and antiques, dedicated by the last descendant of the great Camondo family to his son Nissim, who was killed in 1917. Open Wed.-Sun. 10am-noon and 2-5pm. Admission 18F, students under 25 and seniors 12F.

Musée du Petit Palais, also called the Palais des Beaux-Arts de la Ville de Paris, av. Winston Churchill, 8ème (tel. 42 65 12 73). Mo. Champs-Elysées-Clemenceau. A display of sparkling gems from ancient art through 19th- and 20th-century painting and sculpture, starring Cézanne, Monet, Renoir....Also hosts temporary exhibits. Open Tues.-Sun. 10am-5:40pm. Permanent collection admission 15F, students, big families 8F50 each, seniors free. Temporary exhibits admission roughly 35F, students, seniors, and big families 20F each.

Musée Picasso, 5, rue de Thorigny, 3ème (tel. 42 71 25 21). Mo. Chemin Vert. In France there is a hefty tax on inherited wealth. When the great Cubist Pablo Picasso died in 1973, his heirs opted to pay this tax in artwork rather than money, which is why the French government owns the collection in this museum. Many of the works are of minor significance, but the collection as a whole is fascinating, thanks largely to the tasteful and informative layout of the museum. It illustrates the artist's development through the several stages in his career, grouping works together by period. Alongside Picasso's paintings and sculptures are works by various artists who influenced him, including Braque, Cézanne, and (anonymous) African and Oceanean sculptors. Open Thurs.-Mon. 9:15am-5:15pm, Wed. 9:15am-10pm. Admission 21F. Wheelchair access.

Musée de La Poste, 34, bd. de Vaugirard, 15ème (tel. 42 79 24 24). Mo. Montparnasse. O.K., so a museum dedicated to the history of the French postal system since the year 1820 may not be the reason you came to Paris, but it does deliver a pleasant surprise once you re in the city. Most impressive are the several thousand stamps, every one produced by the post office since 1817, which adorn the walls of an entire floor. Also of note are the various failed mailbox designs on display. Open daily 10am-4pm. Admission 19F, students 9F.

Musée Salvador Dalí (Espace Montmartre), 11, rue Poulbot, 18ème. Mo. Anvers, Blanche, Pigalle. Right off the Place du Tertre, on the Rue Poulbot, this space dedicated to the "Phantasmic world of Salvador Dalí" is chock full of drawings and sculptures by the Spanish surrealist. Don't miss the bronze sculptures of the famous droopy clocks, which express the fluidity and irregularity of time. The museum is well laid out, with good explanations, interesting lighting, and slightly ridiculous "space-music" in the background. Open daily 10am-7pm. Admission 35F, students 25F.

Musée des Techniques, 292, rue St-Marti, 3ème (tel. 40 27 23 31). Mo. Réamur-Sébastopol or Arts et Métiers. In 1794, French revolutionaries decided to create a national collection of new technology to be housed in the 12th-century priory, Saint Martin-des-Champs. The museum has become an often-quaint record of progress over the past 2 centuries. Here you can find Volta's original battery, Foucault's original pendulum, vintage cars and airplanes, wooden telescopes and brass models of the solar system, as well as a roomful of 18th-century automata—activated on the 1st Wed. of each month at 2:30pm. Open Tues.-Sun. 10am-5:30pm; closed public holidays. Admission 20F, Sun. 10F.

Maison de Victor Hugo, 6, Place des Vosges, 4ème (tel. 42 72 16 65). Mo. Chemin Vert. This small museum, dedicated to the "father of the French romantics," is housed in the historic Place des Vosges in the building where Hugo lived from 1832 to 1848. Contains many of his posessions, love letters, photographs, and even some graphic art he executed himself. *Les Miz* fans should make a point of seeing the drawing of Cosette that became the musical's logo, displayed in one of the blue rooms on the 1st. floor. Open Wed.-Sun. 10am-5:40pm. Admission 12F, students 6F50.

Musée du Vieux Montmartre, 12, rue Cortot, 18ème (tel. 46 06 61 11), behind the pl. du Tertre. Mo. Camarck Caumartin. Dedicated to the political, artistic, cultural, and religious past of the *butte* Montmartre and sheltered in a 17th-century house that has hosted the likes of Renoir and Utrillo. Open Tues.-Sun. 11am-6pm.

Entertainment

Paris after dark—you've heard a lot about it. The sun has set over the City of Lights and now you wait for things to happen. The city has much to offer, but don't expect the whole shebang of glamorous options to fall into your lap. The hottest spots in town change at the flight and fancy of elite Parisian party-goers. "In" spots are usually tough to find and frequented by a moderately exclusive crowd that will not go out of its way to accommodate newcomers. Meeting a local may be your only chance to enter a highly private culture that loves to disappear behind unbreathably smoky air to stomp, shimmy, sing, or mellow out until dawn. Although nightclubs, jazz *caves,* theater, and even opera don't have to cost an arm and a leg, they grow more expensive in geometric proportion to their exclusivity. Look for exceptions.

The first thing to do is to buy an entertainment weekly; the best are the glossy magazine **Pariscope** (runs Wed.-Tues., 3F) and the Entertainment section in the Thursday **Figaro** (Paris's major newspaper, 6F). These publications, used by hip-hop Parisians, give listings of everything, from theater and films to concerts, discothèques, and late-night bistros. Look here for your Godard festival, your tango party, your free Mozart requiem. Even if you don't understand French, you should be able to decipher the listings of times and locations.

Fortunately, the most traditional Parisian entertainment—*la flânerie,* strolling, observing other passers-by—is free. Hit the streets, walk around, seek out your own adventures. Parade along the banks of the Seine or weave your way through the Latin Quarter—and join the many Parisians doing so already. The area around Beaubourg (the Pompidou Center) fills with fire-eaters, sword-swallowers, Chilean guitar bands, and other performers. Around place St-Germain, you'll find throngs of people parading by in the latest fashions and a few bars where unlimited jazz comes with the price of one drink. At Ile St-Louis you'll find more refined tourists, strolling the banks of the Seine. To see a movie or to linger in the more fashionable cafés, wander around Montparnasse, the touristy Champs-Elysées, and the streets radiating from bd. St-Michel, bd. St-Germain, and bd. Sébastopol.

Keep in mind that several sections of Paris have developed entertainment businesses of a different sort. The areas around Pigalle, Gare St-Lazare, and Beaubourg fill nightly with prostitutes and drug dealers. Everyone, men and women alike, should avoid the Bois de Boulogne after dark.

Cinema

Paris is famous the world over for a movie scene that rivals—and some say, surpasses—that of New York. Movies, which the French call *cinéma,* are a national obsession, more an activity than a passive form of entertainment. Sitting in the dark need not be a vacation from the Parisian experience. After all, cinema was invented here, by the Lumière brothers. Auguste and Louis Lumière showed their first moving picture (featuring a train and workers returning home) on Dec. 28, 1895, in the basement of the Grand Café on 14, bd. des Capucines. Although proud of the short movie, Louis claimed that "the cinema is an invention without a future"; obviously, he was wrong.

Lines are often long. Before the feature comes the *séance*—a collection of commercials and previews which roll for as much as a half hour—during which a vendor with a basket of chocolate, ice cream, and cookies will pass your way. These are expensive, but part of the experience. Make sure you tip the man or woman who points you to your seat (about 2F); most foreigners are not aware that they are expected to tip ushers and often encounter hostility when they don't.

The entertainment weeklies list show times and theaters. Film festivals are listed separately. The notation "V.O." (for *version originale*) after a non-French movie listing means that the film is being shown in its original language with French subtitles. "V.F." (for *version française*) means that it has been dubbed. If you're in Paris during its annual (short) hot spell, make sure the movie theater advertises *"climatisé."* If not, you'll regret it. Most cinemas grant students a 10F discount off the regular 35-50F admission on weekdays and sometimes before 5pm on weekends. Many theaters lower their prices by several francs on Mondays.

In addition to the latest European and American big-budget features, Parisian cinemas screen classics from all countries, avant-garde and political films, documentaries, and little-known or forgotten works. In the 1940s, French critics discovered the wonderful crime films being made in Hollywood and elevated them to an art form with the fancy title *film noir.* And ever since the New Wave crested in the early '70s, French interest in

American movies has been phenomenal; in fact, many American films play here that have not been shown in U.S. cinemas for years.

You will find that French have an odd taste in Hollywood fare; Mickey Rourke is an icon here, as is Rosanna Arquette, and, of course, master *auteur* Jerry Lewis. French audiences show far more respect for film directors than their American counterparts. Feature films play in the grand theaters on the Champs-Elysées, bd. St-Germain, bd. Montparnasse, and bd. St-Michel. Artsier flicks roll in the little theaters on the side streets of the Left Bank. The options below are some of the most interesting, most unusual, and most popular theaters in Paris.

Cinémathèque Française, at the Musée du Cinéma in the Palais de Chaillot, on av. Albert de Mun at av. Président Wilson, 16*ème* (tel. 47 04 24 24). Mo. Trocadéro. Answering machine lists all shows. A must for serious film buffs. This government-supported theater shows 1-2 films per day, many of them classics, near-classics, or soon-to-be classics. Foreign films almost always shown with French subtitles. Expect long lines. Screenings also at the Palais de Tokyo just down the street. Open Tues.-Sun. Last show 9pm. Admission 22F.

Le Grand Rex, 1, bd. Poissonière, 2*ème* (tel. 42 36 83 93). Mo. Bonne-Nouvelle. This 2800-seat behemoth is the largest theater in Paris. Well worth a visit just to experience the phenomenon of "privatized" viewing amid thousands. Primarily first-runs. Unique atmosphere. Last showing around 9:30pm. Admission 45F, students 31F.

La Géode, 26, av. Corentin-Coriou, 19*ème* (tel. 40 05 80 00). Mo. Corentin-Coriou, in La Villette. Mostly scientific documentaries on this huge hemispherical screen. A 3-D sound , light, and comfortable chair extravaganza. Shows daily, on the hour, 10am-9pm. Admission 45F, students 35F (Mon.-Fri. only).

La Pagode, 57bis, rue de Babylone, 7*ème* (tel. 47 05 12 15). Mo. St-François-Xavier. No tremendous screen, and not even Dolby sound, but the intimate *salle chinoise* and the oriental architecture make this Paris's most charming cinema. A *salon de thé* serves up delicious (if pricey) goodies for the pre-show wait. Current films, usually in the original language. Admission 45F, students 35F.

Le Cosmos, 76, rue de Rennes, 6*ème* (tel. 45 44 28 80). Mo. St-Sulpice. Once the actual property of the Soviet Union, with appropriately Soviet films—Russian, Armenian, Georgian, etc.—this theater has responded to the "end of the cold war" by expanding to generally artsy, foreign film festivals. Admission 35F, students 25F.

L'Entrepôt, 7-9, rue Francis-de-Pressensé, 14*ème* (tel. 45 43 41 63). Mo. Pernety. Organizes a wide variety of week-long festivals, sometimes with director-debates. Two branches: **Les Trois Luxembourg,** 67, rue Monsieur-le-Prince, 6*ème* (tel. 46 33 97 77; Mo. Odéon), with 3 screens; and **Le St-Germain-des-Prés,** pl. St-Germain-des-Prés, 6*ème* (tel. 42 22 87 23; Mo. St-Germain-des-Prés), a big, beautiful theater. Both project high-quality independent, classic, and foreign films. Open noon-midnight. Admission 35F, students 28F.

Action Ecoles, 23, rue des Ecoles, 5*ème* (tel. 43 25 72 07; Mo. Maubert); **Action Rive Gauche,** 5, rue des Ecoles, 5*ème* (tel. 43 29 44 40; Mo. Maubert), both on a large street parallel to bd. St-Germain; and **Action Christine,** 4, rue Christine, 6*ème* (tel. 43 29 11 30; Mo. Odéon), off rue Dauphine. Superb, innovative festivals, from Marilyn Monroe to the Marx Brothers. Admission 38F, students 28F.

Racine Odéon, 6, rue de l'Ecole de Médicine (tel. 43 26 19 68). Mo. Odéon. Mostly film festivals of such greats as Godard and Truffaut. Very studenty crowd. Admission 38F, students 28F (Mon.-Thurs. only).

Theater

Theater in Paris is not limited to Molière, Corneille, and Racine. The classics are there if you want them, but so are modern masterworks by Beckett and Genet, Broadway-type comedies and musicals, experimental plays, and political satires. Aside from the intimate *café-théâtres, cafés chansonniers,* and the Las Vegas-style *revues,* theater in Paris takes two main forms: the national theaters, such as the Comédie Française, and the private theaters, which concentrate on newer and more experimental works. Theater tickets typically start at 130F, but there are usually a few tickets from 20 to 80F. Some theaters sell standby tickets a half-hour before the performance. Most theaters close at least for August. *Pariscope* prints complete listings of current shows.

Plays and concerts are often quite expensive, but discounts exist for most events. The Number One Best Place to get reduced-rate theater tickets is at the **Kiosque-Théâtre,**

1**5**, place de la Madeleine, 8*ème* (Mo. Madeleine), which sells tickets at half-price the day of the show. (Open Tues.-Sat. 12:30-8pm, Sun 12:30-4pm). For more advanced planning, the student organization **COPAR** (Service des Activités Culturelles), whose ticket agency is at 39, av. Georges Bernanos, 5*ème* (tel. 40 51 37 13), Mo. Port-Royal, sells discounted tickets and publishes a monthly list of plays. The agency also sells reduced-priced concert tickets, even in summer. Any student ID is accepted. (Open Sept.-July Mon.-Fri. 9am-4:30pm). Another useful service for theater, concert, and festival tickets is **Alpha FNAC: Spectacles** at 136, rue de Rennes, 6*ème* (tel. 45 44 39 12; Mo. Montparnasse-Bienvenue); 26, av. de Wagram, 8*ème* (tel. 47 66 52 50; Mo. Charles de Gaulle-Etoile); and Forum des Halles, 1-7, rue Pierre Lescot, 1*er* (tel. 42 61 81 18; Mo. Châtelet-Les Halles). The *Carte Alpha* (50F for 1 year) or Carte FNAC (100F for 3 years, students 50F) entitles you to discounts of up to 40% on classical music and theater tickets. (Open Tues.-Sat. 10am-7pm.) Finally, contact the theater itself—many offer last minute rush tickets and can give you updates on availability.

National Theaters

Supported by the French government, the national theaters are the brightest stars of Parisian theater. With the advantages of giant auditoriums, superb acoustics, veteran actors, and, in some cases, several centuries of history, these companies stage superlative and extremely popular productions. Although modern pieces appear occasionally, expect Molière, Racine, Goethe, and Shakespeare (all in French). Reserve 14 days ahead.

La Comédie Française, 2, rue de Richelieu, 1*er* (tel. 40 15 00 15). Mo. Palais Royal. Founded by Molière, this is the granddaddy of all French theaters. Guaranteed pomp and prestige. Open Sept. 15-July. Box office open daily 11am-6pm. Admission 45-195F. 20F rush tickets available 1/2hr before show. Come 1 1/2hr. ahead to wait in line.

Théâtre National de Chaillot, in the Palais de Chaillot, pl. du Trocadéro, 16*ème* (tel. 47 27 81 15). Mo. Trocadéro. Mostly plays but occasional musicals as well. 1000 seats. Box office open Mon.-Sat. 11am-7pm, Sun. 11am-5pm. Admission 140F, ages under 25 and over 60 100F. Student standby tickets 70F.

Odéon Théâtre de l'Europe, 1, pl. Odéon, 6*ème* (tel. 43 25 70 32). Mo. Odéon. Eclectic programs run the gamut from classics to avant-garde. 1042 seats. Also **Petit Odéon,** 82 seats. Open Sept.-July. Box office open daily 11am-6:30pm. Admission 30-150F, Petit Odéon 48F.

Théâtre Nationale de la Colline, 15, rue Malte-Brun, 20*ème* (tel. 43 66 43 60). Mo. Gambetta. 760 seats. Also **Petit Théâtre,** 200 seats. Open Sept.-July. Box office open daily 11am-7pm. Admission 110-140F, ages under 25 and over 60 75F.

Private Theaters

Although private theaters don't carry the reputations or historical baggage of the national theaters, some stage outstanding productions. Poor showings are much more common than in the national theaters; check the reviews before investing in a seat.

Athénée-Louis Jouvet, 4, sq. de l'Opéra, 9*ème* (tel. 47 42 67 27). Mo. Opéra or Auber. 687 seats. Hard-to-find and unremarkable exterior, but a magnificent 18th-century interior and outstanding classical productions. Closed June-Sept. Box office open Mon.-Sat. 11:30am-6pm. Admission 80-110F.

Théâtre Mogador, 25, rue Mogador, 9*ème*. Mo. Trinité. For info, call 48 74 33 74; for reservatons call 48 78 75 15. With 1792 seats, one of the largest theaters in Paris. Grandiose comedies and musicals on a colossal stage. Closed June-Sept. Box office open daily 11am-7pm. Admission 80-240F.

Théâtre de la Ville, 2, pl. Châtelet, 1*er* (tel. 42 74 22 77). Mo. Châtelet. 1000 seats. Excellent productions of all sorts, with a heavy emphasis on the musical. Box office open Tues.-Sat. 11am-8pm, Sun.-Mon. 11am-6pm. Admission 70-120F, students 60-85F.

Théâtre Renaud-Barrault, 2bis, av. Franklin D. Roosevelt, 8*ème* (tel. 42 56 60 70). Mo. Franklin D. Roosevelt. 920 seats. Also **Petite Salle** (tel. 42 56 08 80), 150 seats. Large stage allows for some outlandish musicals and comedies. Open Sept.-July. Box office open Tues.-Sat. 11am-6pm, Sun. noon-5pm. Admission 120-200F, students and seniors 80F.

Théâtre de la Huchette, 23, rue de la Huchette, *5ème* (tel. 43 26 38 99). Mo. St-Michel. 100 seats. Tiny theater whose productions of Ionesco's *La Cantatrice Chauve (The Bald Soprano)*, and *La Leçon (The Lesson)* are still popular after 33 years. Shows Mon.-Sat. Box office open Mon.-Sat. 5-9:30pm. Admission 100F, students 70F; for both shows 130F, students 90F. No discounts Sat.

Jardin Shakespeare du Pré Catelan, at the end of the Bois de Boulogne (tel. 42 71 44 06). Take bus #244 from Porte Maillot. Summertime Shakespeare in French. Tickets at the door or at FNAC. Shows start 7:30pm Fri. and Sat., 5pm Sun. Buses won't be running after the show, *but do not walk.* Take a taxi to Porte Maillot. Admission 80-120F.

The Sweeney, 18, rue Laplace, *5ème* (tel. 46 33 28 12). Mo. Maubert Mutualité. This Irish pub hosts the Gare St-Lazare players, an English speaking, Chicago-based theater company under the direction of Bob Mayer. 1-hr. productions Sun. and Mon. at 8pm. Admission 25F. Call for more information.

Experimental Theater Wing Studio, 14, rue Letelier, *15ème.* Mo. Emile-Zola. 6-year-old extension of New York University's theater program. Interesting and unusual productions in English. Prices vary with performance.

Lucernaire Centre National d'Art et d'Essai, 53, rue Notre-Dame-des-Champs, *6ème* (tel. 45 44 57 34). Mo. Notre-Dame-des-Champs. 130 seats. Plays by classic authors like Chekhov, Tennessee Williams, and St. Exupéry. Box office open 2-7pm or call for reservations 9am-5pm. Admission 140F, reduced price 71F.

Café-Théâtres

Continuing the European showtime tradition, *café-théâtres* deliver caustic, often political satire through skits and short plays. Puns and double-entendres galore; those who aren't up on French slang and politics may miss most of the fun. Despite the name, not all *café-théâtres* have tables with waiter service.

Au Bec Fin, 6, rue Thérèse, *1er* (tel. 42 96 29 35). Mo. Palais Royal. Usually 2 different shows per night in this tiny place (60 seats). Dinner and 1 show from 220F. Dinner and 2 shows from 300F. Shows at 7pm, 8:30pm, and 11:30pm. Auditions sometimes open to the public (40F). Admission for show only 75F, students (Sun.-Fri.) 60F. Two shows 115F.

Le Point Virgule, 7, rue Sainte-Croix-de-la-Bretonnerie, *4ème* (tel. 42 78 67 03). Mo. Hôtel-de-Ville. Often features gay subject matter. Reservations suggested, available 24 hrs. Mon.-Fri., 2 shows, 130F; 3 shows, 150F. Admission 75F, students 50F. Open 3pm-midnight.

Théâtre de l'Arlequin, 13, passage du Moulinet, *13ème* (tel. 45 89 43 22). Mo. Tolbiac. Experimental and classic works—and much uncanned laughter. Shows Tues.-Sat. at 8:30pm. Admission 45-75F.

Chansonniers

The *chansonnier* is the musical cousin of the *café-théâtre.* In the spirit of old Paris, the audience is invited to sing along to French folk songs. Again, the better your French, the better you'll follow the proceedings. Admission usually includes one drink (but only one).

Au Lapin Agile, 22, rue des Saules, *18ème* (tel. 46 06 85 87). Mo. Lamarck-Coulaincourt. Picasso and his friends used to hang out here during the heyday of Montmartre. Get here before 7pm for a good seat. Usually crowded with tourists. Shows at 9pm. Open Tues.-Sun. until 2am. Admission and 1st drink 100F, students 75F. Subsequent drinks 32F.

Caveau de la République, 1, bd. St-Martin, *3ème* (tel. 42 78 44 45). Mo. République. A more Parisian crowd fills the 100 seats. Tickets sold 6 days in advance from 11am. Shows Tues.-Sat. at 9pm. Matinées on Sun. at 3:30pm. Admission 150F, students 80F. Closed Sun. and Mon. night.

Guignols

These renowned traditional puppet shows entertain adults and children alike. For your badly-needed dose of slapstick humor, try *the* classic *guignol,* the **Guignol du Parc Choisy,** 149, av. de Choisy, *13ème* (tel. 43 66 72 39; Mo. Pl. d'Italie; Wed., Sat.-Sun., and holidays at 3:30pm; admission 10F). Or try the **Marionettes du Luxembourg** in the Jardin du Luxembourg (tel. 43 26 46 47; Mo. Odéon; Wed., Sat., Sun., at 3pm; admission 20F) The puppets speak French, but you'll have no problem understanding their outrageous antics. And even if you miss the joke, seeing rows of school-children roar with laughter is as amusing as the show itself. Look in *Pariscope* for schedule changes and for other parks with *guignols*.

Cabarets

Contrary to popular tourist belief, Parisian cabarets (officially called *revues)* are not exclusively for foreigners. The big names—the Moulin Rouge and the Folies Bergère—are frequented by as many cameras as people, but some of the less-publicized cabarets lure Parisians as well; stampedes of well-shod locals unwind at **The Crazy Horse** after work. Although the complete dinner package is forbiddingly expensive, you might be able to watch from the bar while hanging on to your cash.

Le Bal du Moulin Rouge, pl. Blanche, 9*ème* (tel. 46 06 00 19). Mo. Blanche. The most famous of them all, this *revue* celebrated its centennial in 1989. Unfortunately, tourists—of the money-burning-a-hole-in-their-pocket variety—have replaced Toulouse-Lautrec and his leering disciples, who carefully selected their models from the girls on stage. Shows daily at 10pm and midnight. Reserve by phone 10am-7pm. Dinner and show from 640F, just the show 445F.

Crazy Horse Saloon, 12, av. George V, 8*ème* (tel. 47 23 32 32). Mo. Alma-Marceau. More Parisians, fewer tourists; more flesh, less glamour. Shows Sun.-Thurs. at 9pm and 11:35pm, Fri.-Sat. at 8pm, 10:30pm, and 12:50am. Reserve by phone 11am-6pm. Seats 195F-520F, seats and 2 drinks 390F-520F, seats and 1/2 bottle of champagne 450F-580F.

Les Folies-Bergère, 32, rue Richer, 9*ème* (tel. 42 46 77 11). Mo. Cadet or rue Montmartre. Over 60 dancers and musicians in the music hall which Manet immortalized with his strangely disturbing *Bar aux Folies-Bergère*. Show Tues.-Sun. at 9:30pm. Reservations at box office daily 11am-6pm or by phone 11am-6:30pm. Seats 98F-399F.

Classical Music, Opera, and Dance

The spirit of French socialism has made classical music, opera, and dance available to even the most constricted budget traveler. The internationally renowned **Orchestre de Paris,** playing in the Salle Pleyel, 252, rue du faubourg St-Honoré, 8*ème* (tel. 45 43 96 96), Mo. Ternes, delivers first-class performances under the baton of music director Semyon Bychkov. Its season runs September through May; call or stop by for the concert calendar (tickets 50-250F). Guest orchestras and ballet companies normally perform in the superb 2300-seat **Théâtre Musical de Paris,** pl. du Châtelet, 1*er* (tel. 42 33 00 00), Mo. Châtelet. Acoustics are magnificent, and tickets run 70-300F; call for a recorded schedule.

The huge postmodern **Opéra de la Bastille,** pl. de la Bastille, 11*ème* (Mo. Bastille), opened its doors on July 14, 1989, the bicentennial of the French Revolution. Its 1992-93 season features such delights as Tchaikovsky's *Swan Lake* (yes, the ballet), Mozart's *The Marriage of Figaro,* Arthur Honegger's *Jeanne d'Arc au Bûcher,* and Bizet's *Carmen.* (50-560F tickets go on sale at the site 14 days before performance. Call 43 43 96 96. Wheelchair accessible—call 44 73 13 73 to make arrangements at least 15 days before the show.) Meanwhile, the old **Opéra Garnier,** pl. de l'Opéra, 9*ème,* (Mo. Opéra), hosts the Ballet de l'Opéra de Paris and visiting ballet troupes, as well as occasional operas and concerts by foreign companies and orchestras. (Tel. 40 17 35 35 for information, 47 42 53 71 for reservations. 30-350 tickets available at the box office 14 days before performance, Mon.-Sat. 11am-6:30pm).

Free concerts are often held in churches and parks, especially when summer festivals scatter music throughout the city. These events are extremely popular; get there early if you want to breathe. Check any of the entertainment weeklies and the Alpha FNAC offices (see Entertainment introduction) for concert notices. *Pariscope* has day-by-day concert listings in its "Musique" section. **AlloConcerts** maintains a 24-hour hotline that provides information (in French) on free open-air concerts in the parks (tel. 42 76 50 00). The **American Church,** 65, quai d'Orsay, 7*ème* (tel. 47 05 07 89), Mo. Invalides or Alma Marceau, sponsors free concerts (Oct.-June Sun. at 6pm). **Eglise St-Merri** is also known for its free concerts, which take place Saturdays at 9pm and Sundays at 4pm, except in August; contact Accueil Musical St-Merri, 76, rue de la Verrerie, 4*ème* (tel. 42 76 93 93), Mo. Châtelet or Hôtel de Ville.

Other churches, such as **Eglise St-Germain-des-Prés,** 3, pl. St-Germain-des-Prés, 6*ème,* Mo. St-Germain-des-Prés; **Eglise St-Eustache,** rue du Jour, 1*er,* Mo. Les Halles;

and **Eglise St-Louis-en-l'Ile,** 19, rue St-Louis-en-l'Ile, 4*ème,* Mo. Pont Marie, stage frequent concerts that are somewhat expensive (70-100F for students), but feature fantastic acoustics and unbeatable atmosphere. For information about all church concerts, call 43 29 68 68. **Ste-Chapelle** hosts concerts a few times per week in summer (sometimes free on Sun.). Contact the box office at 4, bd. du Palais, 1*er* (tel. 46 61 55 41), Mo. Cité, open daily 1:30-5:30pm. (Admission 110F, students 65F.) Weather permitting, Sunday concerts take place in the bandshell of the **Jardin du Luxembourg** (tel 42 37 20 00). Infrequent concerts in the Musée d'Orsay are free with a museum ticket.

Jazz

Some critics mourn that Paris is no longer the jazz center it once was. Although the big names find it more profitable to play the huge summer festivals in southern France and in Switzerland, Paris still nourishes dozens of interesting clubs. Not only do many fine, lesser-known American musicians play here, but the variety of music—including African, Antillean, Brazilian—is astounding. For the most complete listings, pick up a copy of the monthly *Jazz Magazine* or check in one of the entertainment weeklies.

New Morning, 7-9, rue des Petites-Ecuries, 10*ème* (tel. 45 23 51 41). Mo. Château d'Eau. 500 seats. All the greats have played here. Open Sept.-July from 9:30pm (times vary—check *Pariscope).* Admission around 110F.

Le Petit Opportun, 15, rue des Lavandières-St-Opportune, 1*er* (tel. 42 36 01 36). Mo. Châtelet. Relaxed and unpolished, featuring some of the best modern jazz around. The tiny 60-seat club is so popular that it ought to seat 500. Come early. Open daily, Sept.-July. Shows start around 11pm and the bar is open till 3am. First drink 100F, 50F thereafter.

Au Duc des Lombards, 42, rue des Lombards, 1*er* (tel. 42 33 22 88). Mo. Châtelet. French jazz groups, with the occasional American singer or soloist. Great ambiance—dark and smoky—and an enthusiastic clientele. Call for prices. First drink about 60F. Open every night from 10:30pm.

Le Petit Journal St-Michel, 71, bd. St-Michel, 5*ème* (tel. 43 26 28 59). Mo. Luxembourg. A crowded, intimate establishment. New Orleans bands and first-class performers play in this Parisian center of the "Old Style," classic big-band jazz. Music Sept.-July Mon.-Sat. 10pm-2:30am Obligatory first drink 100F, 40F thereafter.

Slow Club, 130, rue de Rivoli, 1*er* (tel. 42 33 84 30). Mo. Châtelet. Was Miles Davis's favorite jazz club in Paris. Big bands, traditional jazz, and Dixieland in a wonderful old-time setting. Expect dancing and a 30-something crowd. Open Tues.-Thurs. 9:30pm-2:30am, Fri. 9:30pm-3:30am, Sat. 9:30pm-4am. Weekday cover 65F, weekend cover begins at 95F. Women and students 5F less during the week. Drinks from 18F.

Caveau de la Huchette, 5, rue de la Huchette, 5*ème* (tel. 43 26 65 05). Mo. St-Michel. The one-time tribunal, prison, and execution rooms here were used by Danton, Marat, St-Juste, and Robespierre during the Revolution. Now just a traditional jazz hotspot. Maxim Saury often whistles Dixie. Crowded on weekends. Open Sun.-Thurs. 10pm-2:30am, Fri. 9:30pm-3am. Sat. 9:30pm-4am. Must be over 18. Cover Sun.-Thurs. 55F, students 50F. Fri. and Sat. cover 60F. Drinks from 35F.

Théâtre Dunois, 28, rue Dunois, 13*ème* (tel. 45 84 72 00). Mo. Chevaleret. A newly renovated theater with 200 seats; specializes in American avant-garde jazz. The bar serves drinks from 15-40F. Cover 80F. Open daily 10pm-2am.

Jazz O' Brazil, 38, rue Mouffetard, 5*ème* (tel. 45 87 36 09). Mo. Monge. Excellent samba guitarists and new groups. Try the house drink *caitirissa* (lime juice and vodka). Open daily 9:30pm-2am. No cover. Drinks 55F.

Chica, 71, rue St-Martin, 4*ème* (tel. 48 87 73 57). Mo. Châtelet. Primarily an excellent Brazilian restaurant (first courses 45F, main dishes 90F). Devoted clients reserve tables downstairs in the *cave* for late night samba action. Live bands tune up at midnight. Fruit drinks 45F. Open Tues.-Thurs. and Sun. 8pm-2am, Fri.-Sat. 8pm-4:30am.

Discos and Rock Clubs

Paris is not Barcelona, Montreal, or Buenos Aires; you won't find entire streets filled with young people waiting and struggling to get into discos. Instead, the clubs are small, private, and nearly impossible to sniff out unless you're a native. Many Parisian clubs are officially private, which means they have the right to pick and choose their clientele; the management can evaluate prospective customers through peepholes in the handle-less front doors. Parisians tend to dress up more than Americans for a night on the town; haggard backpackers might be wise to try a bar instead. In general, word of mouth is the best guide to the current scene. Some of the smaller places in the Latin Quarter admit almost anyone who is sufficiently decked out. To access one of the more exclusive places, you need to accompany a regular. Many clubs reserve the right to refuse entry to unaccompanied men. Women often get a discount or get in free, but don't go alone unless you're looking for lots of amorous attention.

The French dance any way they please and often alone. The music is often mediocre at best, with fast-paced disco and new wave pop. Weekdays are cheaper and less crowded so you'll have a better chance of moving, but most of the action (by force of inevitable body contact) happens on weekends.

Les Bains, 7, rue de Bourg l'Abbée, 3ème (tel. 48 87 01 80). Mo. Réaumur-Sébastopol. Ultra-selective and ultra-expensive, but worth it—if you can get in past the fearless bouncers. Prince established the joint's reputation with a surprise free concert a few years ago. Lots of models and super-attractive people dressed to those proverbial nines. Admission 140F (includes 1 drink), second drink 100F. Can you stand a third? Open Tues.-Sun. midnight-6am.

La Locomotive, 90, bd. Clichy, 18ème (tel. 42 57 37 37). Mo. Blanche. Shaped like a huge choo-choo, this place has already had its heyday. Nonetheless, it's still a reasonably popular choice among Parisians who couldn't force their way into Les Bains. Major physical contact: a pick-up scene. Tues.-Thurs. and Sun. first drink 60F, Fri.-Sat. 100F. Second drink 50F. Open Tues.-Sun. 11pm-5am.

Le Palace, 8, rue du faubourg Montmartre, 9ème (tel. 42 46 10 87). Mo. Montmartre. Huge (up to 2000 people per night), funky disco with multi-level dance floors, each with separate bars and different music. American cocktails and occasional rock concerts. Its reputation as the hottest club in Paris no longer holds. Top-40 hits and happy high-school students hoping to hook up. Some older people as well. Cover Tues.-Thurs. 100F; Fri.-Sat. 130F; Sun. 130F for men, free for women. Cover includes 1 drink, subsequent drinks 85F. Open Tues.-Thurs. and Sun. 11pm-6am., Fri.-Sat. 11pm-10am. The British owners also run **Le Central,** 102, av. des Champs-Elysées, 8ème. Mo. George V. Same prices, with older clientele and a higher percentage of foreigners.

Scala de Paris, 188bis, rue de Rivoli, 1er (tel. 42 60 45 64). Mo. Tuileries. Not as well known or trendy as some of the other clubs, but becoming more and more popular as the others decline. Youngish (18-24) crowd dances to house and techno. Lots of foreigners. Cover Sun.-Thurs. 80F, free for women; Fri. 80F for all; Sat. 90F for all. Open daily 10:30pm-dawn.

Le Balajo, 9, rue de Lappe, 11ème (tel. 47 00 07 87). Mo. Bastille. Formerly the favorite stage of Edith Piaf. Founded in 1936 by Jo France, hence the *Bal à Jo.* Jammed with a youthful crowd in love with excitement. Cover and first drink 110F. Open Thurs.-Mon. 10pm-dawn.

Flash Back, 18, rue des Quatre Vents, 6ème (tel. 43 25 56 10). Mo. Odéon. Two levels of unusual secluded lounges and a small dance floor complete with mirrored walls and a shiny disco ball. Tuesday nights are retro—70s and early 80s tunes. Comfortable, easy atmosphere among Paris's beautiful youth. Cover 65F, women free Sun.-Thurs. Drinks 65F. Open Mon.-Sun. 11pm-6am.

Also popular in France are clubs that specialize in **Brazilian samba** and **African music:**

Chez Félix, 23, rue Mouffetard, 5ème (tel. 47 07 68 78). Mo. Monge. Eat on the top level; sway to the excellent Brazilian beat in the *caves.* Music 11pm-dawn. Tues.-Sat. obligatory first drink 100F, 50F thereafter. Open Sept.-July Tues.-Sat. 8pm-5am.

La Plantation, 45, rue Montpensier, 1er (tel. 42 97 46 17). Mo. Palais-Royal. A friendly place playing mostly African, Antillean, and salsa music. Dress well. M. Yaffa, the owner, is dedicated to improving race relations. Doesn't pick up 'til 2am. Cover and first drink 90F, 2nd drink 50F. Open Tues.-Sun. 11pm-dawn.

Le Tchatch au Tango, 13, rue au Maire, 3ème. (tel. 42 72 17 78). Mo. Arts et Métiers. Crowd dances to Antillean, African, Salsa, and Zouk music. Regulars all know each other. Wed. is salsa night; Fri., Sat., and the eves of holidays, they play mostly Zouk. Cover: Wed. 50F, Fri. 40F, Sat. and eves of holidays 60F. Drinks 25-40F. Open Wed., Fri., Sat., and eves of holidays, 11pm-5am.

Bars

Almost as common as cafés, the bars are places for heavier drinking and heavier socializing. Expect to meet new people and engage in absurd conversation. Law dictates a price increase after 10pm, but no one really ventures out to drink before then.

Le Bar sans Nom, 49, rue de Lappe, 11*ème*. Mo. Bastille. There's nothing cooler than this bar—cavernous, deep crimson, and packed with the hippest of the hip. Beer 20F. Cocktails 44F. Open daily 8pm-2am.

La Micro Brasserie, 106, rue de Richelieu, 2*ème*. Mo. Richelieu-Drouot. Possibly the best beer in Paris. You can choose from over 60 kinds, but the best deals are on the beers they brew themselves. Try the reddish Morgan—and that's an order! Food served as well. Beer before 10pm, 11-14F; after 10pm, 20F. Between 5 and 7:30pm, buy one beer and get another one free. Open Sun.-Mon. 7am-2am, Fri.-Sat. 7am-9pm. Visit the brewery downstairs on Tues. and Thurs. 10am-8pm without paying extra.

Le Violon Dingue, 46, rue de la Montagne Ste-Geneviève. Mo. Maubert-Mutualité. Reminiscent of an American frat party with its American waiters, stuffed interior, and cheap, fast-flowing beer. Bottled beer starts at 25F, on tap 32F. Cocktails from 30F. Open daily 6pm-2am.

Polly Magoo, 13, rue St-Jacques, 5*ème*. Mo. St-Michel. When the Violon Dingue closes at 2am, Polly's gets going. Super friendly, amazingly lively crowd often bubbles over into the street, providing nights of endless amusement and adventure. Beer 18-35F. Open noon-4am.

Pub St-Germain-des-Prés, 17, rue de l'Ancienne Comédie, 6*ème*. Mo. Odéon. Perhaps the largest and least interesting pub in Europe, this mammoth bar is a long-time favorite of American students. 100 types of whisky. 450 different types of bottled beer, 24 on tap. The three underground rooms, with cheesy renditions of American pop music are the most fun. Beers and cocktails start at a whopping 75F per bottle. Open 24hrs.

Gay and Lesbian Entertainment

While not London or Berlin, Paris has a lively and venerable gay/lesbian scene. There is a particular concentration of restaurants, cafés, and bars between the Métro stops Rambuteau and Hôtel-de-Ville. The gay discos scattered throughout Paris change more rapidly than *hétéro* spots, so check *Gai Pied* (summer guide 50F from kiosks) for up-to-date information and an English introduction. *Lesbia's* ads are a good gauge of what's hot, or at least what's open (22F from kiosks).

Club 18, 18, rue du Beaujolais, 1*er* (tel. 42 97 52 13). Mo. Bourse. A happy, hopping place with a mirrored dance floor. Mostly men, but friendly to women as well. Cover 40-50F. Open daily 11pm-dawn.

La Champmeslé, 4, rue Chabanais, 2*ème* (tel. 42 96 85 20). Mo. Opéra. Intimate women's bar in a relaxed atmosphere. Comfortable couches, dim lighting, and an eclectic assortment of music for dancing or hanging out. Come Thurday night for the wild cabaret show. Few men. No cover. Drinks from 25F. Open Oct.-Aug. Mon.-Sat. 6pm-2am.

Le Boy, 6, rue Caumartin, 9*ème* (tel. 47 42 68 05). Mo. Havre-Caumartin. Young crowd. 50F cover includes one drink. Open daily 11pm-dawn.

Le Bar Central, 33, rue Vieille du Temple, 4*ème* (tel. 42 72 16 94). Mo. Hotel de Ville. Small and crowded, this friendly bar is a favorite among locals and tourists alike. Mostly men. Drinks from 20F. Open daily 4pm-2am.

Le Swing, 42, rue Vieille du Temple, 4*ème* (tel. 42 72 16 94). Mo. Hôtel de Ville. Bar with 50s decor and happy hour 9-11pm. Cocktails from 50F. Open Mon.-Sat. noon-2am, Sun. 2pm-2am.

Le Piano Zinc, 49, rue des Blancs Manteaux, 4*ème* (tel. 42 74 32 42). Mo. Rambuteau. Campy downstairs piano bar with Liza-Minnelli-Judy-Garland-style decor is very crowded. Lots of physical contact. Mostly men. Drinks from 15F; after 10pm, drinks 35-65F. Open daily 6pm-2am.

Le Petit Prince, 12, rue de Lanneau, 5*ème* (tel. 43 54 77 26). Mo. Maubert-Mutualité. Superb dining in this casual restaurant for gay men and women. Menus 85 and 110F. Delicious white-chocolate mousse 18F. Make reservations. Open daily 7:30pm-12:30am.

Au Petit Cabanon, 7, rue Sainte-Apolline, 3*ème* (tel. 48 87 66 53). Mo. Strasbourg-St-Denis. Classic French cuisine for women. 120F *menu*. Open Sun.-Wed. noon-2pm, Thurs.-Sat. noon-2pm and 8pm-midnight.

Dumb Fun

Every evening after sunset until midnight (1am on Sat.), Paris literalizes its reputation as the City of Light. Bright, often colored, lights flood the Arc de Triomphe (Mo. Etoile), Notre-Dame (Mo. St-Michel), the Tour Eiffel (Mo. Bir-Hakeim), pl. de la Concorde (Mo. Concorde), the Hôtel de Ville (Mo. Hôtel-de-Ville), and the Panthéon (Mo. Luxembourg). In summer, the historic buildings of the Marais (Mo. St-Paul) and some of the buildings and gardens of Montmartre (Mo. Abbesses) are also illuminated.

The French have invented a new art form: take an impressive building, add a light show, superimpose a recorded message about the glorious history of the building, the region, or the country, *et voilà:* **son et lumière.** It's as tacky as it sounds, but that's half the fun. Check the three entertainment weeklies for listings.

A ride on the **bateaux-mouches** (tel. 42 25 96 10) river boats may seem like goofy fun until you actually try it. The high embankments on both sides of the river obscure everything but the tops of the highest buildings. If that doesn't deter you, imagine one-and-a-half hours of continuous sight-commentary in five languages and dozens of tourists straining their necks to peer over the next person. Convinced? (If not, boats leave every 1/2hr. from 10am-11pm from the right-bank pier near pont d'Alma. 30F, under 14 15F.) Another option is **Vert Galant** boats (every 1/2-hr. from 10am-noon and 1:30-6:30pm from the Pont Neuf landing, 35F, ages under 10 20F.) The **Canauxrama** (tel. 42 39 15 00) boat tours of Paris actually get good reviews. The shortest (3hr.) tour leaves at 9:15am from Bassin de la Villette, 9bis quai de la Loire, 19*ème* (Mo. Jaurès) and at 2:30pm from Port de l'Arsenal facing 50, quai de la Bastille, 12*ème* (Mo. Bastille). (80F, students 65F, under 12 45F.) Day-long trips to the countryside leave the Bassin de la Villette at 8:30am Thursday through Tuesday. (190F. Reserve ahead.) The **Batobus** (tel. 47 05 50 00) makes frequent stops along both sides of the river from April to September. A spin on this ridiculous form of transportation costs 10F. (Day pass 50F.) Buy tickets on board.

Festivals and Other Seasonal Events

The French love of celebration is most evident in Paris, where the slightest provocation brings masses of people into the streets to drink, dance, and generally lose themselves in the spirit of the *fête* (festival) or *foire* (fair). The gatherings in Washington on July 4, or in Times Square on New Year's Eve, pale before the assemblages of humanity on hand for Bastille Day fireworks, the arrival of the New Year, or political demonstrations. The **tourist office,** 127, av. des Champs-Elysées, 8*ème*, (tel. 47 23 61 72; Mo. Etoile), has a booklet in English that lists all the celebrations that take place in Paris each month. The English information number (tel. 47 20 88 98) reports a weekly summary on current festivals. *Pariscope* lists *fêtes populaires* for the coming week. You can also get a listing of festivals from the **French National Tourist Office** (see General Introduction).

March and April

Foire du Trône, Neuilly Lawn of the Bois de Vincennes. Mo. Porte Dorée. A gigantic amusement park with roller coasters, pony rides, fortune-tellers, funhouses, and enough caramel apples, *barbe à papa* (cotton candy), doughnuts, and waffles to keep the most gluttonous junk-food junkie smiling for days. Jammed on warm weekends. End of March-May. Open 2pm-midnight.

May

Festival de Versailles (tel. 30 21 20 20, *poste* 234). Ballet, operas, concerts, and theater. Prices vary radically from one event to another. Late May-late June.

Festival de Musique de St-Denis (tel. 42 43 72 72). Music in the Basilique. Late May-late June.

Festival de Paris, 38, rue des Blancs-Manteaux, 4*ème* (tel. 40 26 45 34). A harmonic convergence of some of the greatest orchestras and choruses. Mid-May to late June. Admission 50-500F.

Foire du Trône continues.

June

Fête de la Musique. On June 21, the city celebrates the first day of summer with major rock concerts and bodacious partying in all the big *places*. Latin Quarter fills with anyone who can blow a horn, carry a tune, or watch others do so. Dancing all night. Free and obvious to anyone who goes out.

Fête du Cinéma, June 28. One movie ticket allows you to go from theater to theater until your head spins with movies.

Festival du Marais, 68, rue François Minon, 4*ème* (tel. 45 23 18 25). Mo. St-Paul. Classical and jazz music, theater, and exhibits. Many events are outside, in courtyards, or in renovated Renaissance buildings in the Marais. The classical concerts tend to be expensive, but other events are free. Early June-early July.

Festival Foire St-Germain (tel. 43 29 12 78). Antique fair in pl. St-Sulpice, concerts in the Mairie du 6*ème*, sports events in the Jardin du Luxembourg. All events free. Two weeks in mid-June.

Musique en Sorbonne, at the Sorbonne Grand Amphithéâtre, 47, rue des Ecoles, 5*ème* (tel. 42 62 71 71). Everything in classical music from chamber groups to grand operas. Late June-early July. Admission 60-140F.

Fêtes du Pont Neuf (tel. 42 77 92 26). Mo. Pont-Neuf. The bridge is closed to traffic and opened for dancing, music, street artists, and minstrels. A weekend in late June.

Festival de la Butte Montmartre, 14bis, rue Ste-Isaure, 18*ème* (tel. 42 62 46 22). Experimental drama, dance, and jazz performances. Master classes in jazz and acting. Mid-June to mid-July.

Foire du Trône, Festival de Musique de St-Denis, Festival de Paris, and **Festival de Versailles** continue.

July

July 14 is Bastille Day. Big-time celebrations nationwide. *Vive la République,* and pass the champagne. The day starts with the army parading down the Champs-Elysées and ends with fireworks over the Arc de Triomphe, at Montmartre, the Parc Montsouris, and the Palais de Chaillot. Traditional street dances are held on the eve of Bastille Day at the tip of the Ile St-Louis (the Communist Party always throws its gala there), the Hôtel de Ville, pl. de la Contrescarpe, and of course, pl. de la Bastille, where it all began. Dancing continues the next night. Unfortunately, the entire city also becomes a nightmarish combat zone of leering men cunningly tossing firecrackers (sometimes ignited inside bottles) under the feet of unsuspecting bystanders (and into the metro). Check the newspapers a few days before to see where the main *bals* will take place.

End of the Tour de France (4th Sunday in July). Thousands of spectators turn out along the Champs-Elysées to watch the finish of the month-long bicycle race, which attracts as much attention in France as the World Series does in the U.S. Get there early and expect a huge crowd.

Festival Estival, 20, rue Geoffroy-l'Asnier, 4*ème* (tel. 48 04 98 01). Opera, chamber music, and recitals in churches, palaces, and concert halls throughout the city. Early July to mid-Sept. Admission 25-40F.

Festival de l'Orangerie de Sceaux. In the Orangerie of the Château de Sceaux (tel. 46 60 07 79). A mixture of chamber music, popular music, and piano recitals. Performances late July-early Oct. Sat.-Sun. at 5:30pm. Admission 60-110F.

Versailles Display (tel. 39 50 71 81) Spectacular fountain effects every Sun. starting the first Sun. in July from 4-6pm. Runs through Aug.

Festival du Marais, Musique en Sorbonne, and **Festival de la Butte Montmartre** continue.

August

Festival Estival, Festival de Musique de Sceaux, and **Versailles Display** continue.

September

Festival d'Automne (tel. 42 96 12 27), in the Pompidou Center and other museums and churches. Drama, ballet, expositions, and chamber music concerts. Late Sept.-Dec.

Fête de l'Humanité, parc de la Courneuve (Mo. Porte de la Villette, then special buses). The annual fair of the French Communist Party—like nothing you've ever seen. A million people converge to hear debates, ride roller-coasters, and collect Marxist-Leninist leaflets. (*Humanité* is the newspaper of the French CP.) Communist parties from all over the world distribute literature and sell their native food and drink. Entertainers in recent years have included Charles Mingus, Marcel Marceau, the Bolshoi Ballet, and radical theater troupes. A cross between the Illinois state fair, the Republican Convention, and Woodstock; you don't have to be a Communist to enjoy it. Second or third week of Sept.

Festival de l'Ile-de-France (tel. 47 39 28 26). Gala celebratory concerts in the churches and monuments of the larger Paris area. Late Sept.-late Dec.

Festival Estival, Festival de Sceaux and **Festival de Montmartre** continue.

October

Festival de Jazz de Paris, 5, rue Bellart, 15ème (tel. 47 83 33 58). There's so much jazz in Paris that this is hardly necessary, but it makes things official. Everybody on the European circuit (Nice, Antibes, Montreux, etc.) should be here. At the Théâtre Musical de Paris and the Théâtre de la Ville. Late Oct.-early Nov.

Fête des Vendanges à Montmartre, rue Saules, 18ème. Mo. Lamarck-Caulaincourt. The celebration of the harvest of the vineyards on Montmartre. Though not France's best-known wine-producing region, Montmartre still bottles enough wine to merit a day of celebrating its accomplishments. The first Sat. in Oct.

Festival d'Art Sacré, 4, rue Jules Cousin, 4ème (tel. 42 77 92 26). Sacred music at churches around Paris (including Notre-Dame) by the Radio France Philharmonic Orchestra and the Choir of Cologne. Early Oct.-Dec.

Festival d'Automne, Festival de l'Ile de France, and **Festival de Sceaux** continue.

November

Armistice Day (Nov. 11). Military parade from the Arc de Triomphe to the Hôtel des Invalides.

Festival Internationale de la Guitarre (tel. 45 23 18 25). Concerts in many Parisian churches. Mid-Nov. to mid-Dec.

Concours international de Danse de Paris (tel. 45 22 28 74). Week-long dance competition in mid-Nov.

Festival d'Automne, Festival d'Art Sacré, Festival de Jazz de Paris, and **Festival de l'Ile-de-France** continue.

December

Christmas Eve. At midnight, with the celebration of the Christmas Eve Mass, Notre-Dame becomes what it only claims to be the rest of the year: the cathedral of the city of Paris. Thousands of people fill the church. Many of the neighboring cafés stay open late for those who want to start celebrating Christmas early. Children's entertainment continues until the end of school vacation.

New Year's Eve. When the clock strikes midnight, the Latin Quarter explodes: strangers embrace, motorists find people dancing on their hoods, and for an hour bd. St-Michel transforms into a pedestrian mall, much to the dismay of the cops who still attempt to direct traffic. A similar scene occurs on the Champs-Elysées.

Festival d'Automne continues.

Shopping

In a city where everything is a "sight," where even walking becomes entertainment, where eating is a religion, one can only imagine what pleasures await the shopper—looking, walking, and eating all at the same time. Strolling down any major boulevard, you may become painfully aware that Parisians dress well. The essence of Parisian style, however, embodies the utmost simplicity and never goes out of fashion.

While Paris is not a bargain-hunter's paradise, even some of the hautest of the city's *haute couture* boutiques join in the twice-yearly *soldes* (major sales) that sweep the city in January and late June/early July. Remember that almost all stores in Paris are closed on Sunday.

Today's swankiest shopping districts are scattered all around Paris. Probably the most famous of these areas surrounds the exquisite **rue du faubourg St-Honoré,** which runs northwest through the 8*ème*. Gawk at the obscenely expensive scarves and bags at **Hermès** (#24), the outlandish solid knits at **Sonia Rykiel** (#70), the untouchables at **Yves Saint Laurent** (#38), and the high-fashion design of the Japanese **Ashida** (#34). **Karl Lagerfield, Pierre Balmain,** and **Gianni Versace** boutiques cluster in the area. Nearby, the streets projecting from the **place de la Victoire** 1*er* and 2*ème* harbor another galaxy of *haute couture*. Running southwest from the Rond Point des Champs-Elysées, **avenue de Montaigne** shelters the houses of **Christian Dior** (#32), **Chanel** (#42), **Valentino** (#17-19), and **Nina Ricci** (#39). **Pierre Cardin** appears on a regal house in place François 1*er*. The windows in **place Vendôme** and along **rue de la Paix** (north to the Opéra) glitter with the designs of **Cartier, Van Cleef & Arpels,** and other offerings from the jewelry overlords of Paris.

Across the river on the Left Bank, boutiques tend to be smaller and occasionally less expensive, but no less stunning. A slew of shops (including **Sonia Rykiel, Kenzo,** and **Claude Montana**) display their goods in large open windows along the streets of rue Bonaparte, rue du Four, rue de Grenelle, rue de Rennes, and rue de Sèvres. Write your wish list on bd. St-Germain, but hunt around for better bargains around rue de Seine and the top of bd. St-Michel. A little farther east, boutiques in the Marais and the Bastille tend more towards the funky and the trendy.

A unique Parisian shopping phenomenon is the *magasin du troc,* a large store that re-sells clothes bought and returned at the more expensive stores. Don't expect dirt cheap prices, but given the retail prices of Chanel and Dior, the bargains are astonishing. Try **Troc Mod,** 230 av. du Maine, 14*ème* (tel. 45 40 45 93; Mo. Alesia; open Tues.-Sat. 11am-7:30pm; Sept.-July Tues.-Sat. 10am-7:30pm); **Troc'Eve,** 25, rue Violet, 15*ème* (tel. 45 79 38 36; Mo. Dupleix; open Tues.-Sat. 10am-7pm); or **Réciproque,** possibly the king of the genre with three outlets at 95, 101, and 123 rue de la Pompe, 16*ème* (tel. 47 04 30 28; Mo. Pompe; open Tues.-Sat. 10am-6:45pm). For the lowest prices on the newest **shoe fashions,** try the side streets surrounding place de la République and rue des Saints-Pères in the 7*ème*.

Or check it all out at one of Paris's many department stores—a number group together on the *grands boulevards* around the Opéra and the Gare-St.-Lazare, 9*ème* (Mo. Opéra or Havre-Caumartin). **Galeries Lafayette** 40, bd. Haussmann (tel. 42 82 34 56; in English tel. 42 82 36 40; open Mon.-Sat. 9:30am-6:45pm), offers the ultimate in high-quality deparment store shoping with designer labels galore. Neighbor **Printemps,** 64 bd. Haussmann (tel. 42 82 50 00), challenges for the title of finest of the fine in *grands magasin* shopping. As elegant as the Galeries Lafayette, it claims to be the "most Parisian Department Store" (open Mon.-Sat. 9:35am-7pm). Along the Right Bank, **La Samaritaine,** 19, rue Monnaire 1*er* (tel. 40 41 20 20; Mo. Pont Neuf; open Mon.-Wed. and Fri.-Sat. 9:30am-7pm, Thurs. 9:30am-10pm), and the **Bazar de l'Hôtel de Ville,** 52, rue Rivoli, 4*ème* (tel. 42 74 90 00; Mo. Hôtel de Ville; open Mon.-Tues. and Thurs.-Sat. 9:30am-7pm, Wed. 9:30am-10pm), carry everything you think you want and certainly tons you know you don't. **Tati,** 13 place de la République, 4*ème* (tel. 48 87 72 81; Mo. République), is the original bargain basement store (bermudas 20-80F, dresses 80-150F, T-shirts 15-40F, nightgowns 40-60F; open Mon. 10am-7pm, Tues.-Fri. 9:30am-7pm, Sat. 9:15am-7pm). For **souvenirs** such as perfume, watches, pens, and beauty products, at a 30-40% discount, try **Honoré,** 316, rue St-Honoré, 1*er* (tel. 42 60 49 00; Mo. Tuileries; open Mon.-Sat. 9:45am-6:45pm). Of course, every Pierre, Jacques, and Jean-Guy peddles them on most streets.

The most famous English bookseller is **Shakespeare and Co.,** 37, rue de la Bucherie, 5*ème* (Mo. St-Michel), across the Seine from Notre-Dame. Run by George Whitman (alleged great-grandson of Walt), this cozy shop seeks to reproduce the atmosphere of Sylvia Beach's original establishment (at 8, rue Dupuytren and later at 12, rue de l'Odéon), gathering-place for expatriate American writers in the 1920s, beat-niks Allen Ginsberg and Lawrence Ferlinghetti, and most importantly, the first *Let's Go* writer. (Open daily noon-midnight.) For a more extensive selection, especially of American literature, and a wider display of guidebooks, seek out **Brentano's,** 37, av. de l'Opéra, 2*ème* (tel. 42 61 52 50; Mo. Opéra; open Mon.-Fri. 10am-7pm, Sat. 10am-noon and 2-7pm). The **Village Voice,** 6, rue Princesse, 6*ème* (tel. 46 33 36 47; Mo. Mabillon), has a terrific contemporary science-fiction section and a decent collection of feminist literature. (Open Mon. 2-8pm; Tues.-Sat. 11am-8pm.) **W.H. Smith,** 248, rue de Rivoli, 1*er,* (tel. 42 60 37 97; Mo. Concorde), has the best selection of magazines and British literature and a pleasant but pricey English tea room upstairs. (Open Mon.-Sat. 9:30am-7pm.) **Gibert Jeune,** 5, pl. St-Michel near the Seine (tel. 43 25 70 07; Mo. St. Michel) is *the* bookstore near bd. St-Michel. It is also a good bet for French classics. **Les Mots à la Bouche,** 6, rue Ste-Croix-de-la-Bretonnerie, 4*ème* (tel. 42 78 88 30; Mo. Hôtel-de-Ville), is a serene bookstore with French and English titles, magazines, post-cards, and newsletters of interest to both gay men and lesbians. (Open Mon.-Sat. 11am-11pm.) **La Librairie des Femmes,** 74, rue de Seine, 6*ème* (tel. 43 29 50 75; Mo. Odéon), one-time home of feminist collective MLF, is a comfortable place to browse women's literature. (Open 10am-7pm. In late July and August, sometimes closed between 12:45and 2pm.)

Non-Europeans making large purchases in a single store are eligible to receive a refund of the Value Added Tax (V.A.T.), a tax (about 15%) that is automatically added to all luxury goods sold in the European Community. See the Money section of the General Introduction for details.

Markets

Although the days when the eagle-eyed might spot Rembrandt's smudged signature in the corner of a 5F painting are long gone, the wise shmoozer can still strike good bargains in Paris's galaxy of flea markets. For produce, market shopping is still *de rigueur* (the norm). Locals line up early at neighborhood markets, roving markets, and covered markets to buy only enough fruits and vegetables for each day's meals. Snag the free booklet *Les Marchés de Paris,* available from any *mairie,* for a complete list of the city's markets. Also, be aware that in any of these markets, especially the flea markets, more thieves than merchants may have their eyes on your wallet.

A Paris flea market is a world unto itself, complete with vendors selling food, antiques, second-hand clothing (not to be confused with the stalls of pricier vintage clothing), and random assortments of desirable junk—books, records, and car, cleaning and hair supplies. Arrive early for the most interesting wares. Come prepared to bargain; dealers quote prices higher than what they expect to receive. The **Marché aux Puces de St-Ouen,** 17*ème* (Mo. Porte de Clignancourt; Sat.-Mon. 8am-8pm) is the largest flea market in Paris and one of the largest in Europe. The market at the **Porte de Vanves,** 14*ème* (Mo. Porte de Vanves; Sat.-Sun. 7am-7:30pm), is also enjoyable and one of the cheapest. The **Marché du Temple,** Carreau du Temple, 3*ème* (Mo. Hôtel-de-Ville), sells new clothes at wholesale prices in a beautiful building. (Open Tues.-Sun. 9am-noon.)

Each neighborhood has its own **street market** which convenes two or three days each week. (Hours vary slightly, but generally run between 7am and 1:30pm; ask a local shopkeeper for details.) Merchants set up their stands with impeccable attention to detail that surprises even the pickiest of shoppers. The covered food market, **Marché St-Martin,** 33, rue du Château d'Eau, 10*ème,* is consistently excellent. (Open Tues.-Sat. 8:30am-1pm and 4-7:30pm, Sun. 8am-1pm.) In general, markets in the 18th, 19th, and 20th *arrondissements* such as the **Algerian market,** rue de la Goutte d'Or, offer a tantalizing supply of spices and prepared foods of Asian and Northern African origins. Prices here tend to be the lowest in Paris for bulk buying.

Place Louis Lépine, on the Ile de la Cité, 4*ème* (Mo. Cité), blooms with color as the **Marché aux Fleurs** carpets the small square (Mon.-Sat. 8am-7:30pm). On Sunday from 8am to 7pm, the colors literally come alive as the plants are replaced by hundreds of birds for the **Marché aux Oiseaux.** Be careful; they bite.

Stamp and postcard collectors congregate every Thursday, Saturday, Sunday, and holiday from 10am to nightfall at the **Marché aux Timbres,** on av. Gabriel at av. Marigny, 8*ème* (Mo. Champs-Elysées-Clemenceau). If you're looking for antique books, prints, or posters, check out the *bouquinistes* stalls which line the Right Bank of the Seine from the Louvre to the Hôtel de Ville and the Left Bank, from quai de Conti to quai de Montebello. Paris's largest auction house is the **Hôtel Drouot,** 9, rue Drouot, 9*ème* (tel. 42 46 17 11; Mo. Richelieu-Drouot), where everything from collectors'

Let's Go 1993

PLACE
STAMP
HERE

RENAULT EURODRIVE
650 First Avenue
New York, NY 10016

Place
Stamp
Here

LET'S GO Travel

Harvard Student Agencies, Inc.
Harvard University
Thayer B
Cambridge, MA 02138 U.S.A.

pieces to odd lots of toilet plungers goes on the block almost every day. (Open Sept.-July Mon.-Sat. 11am-6pm.)

Near Paris

La Défense

Paris has laws governing the size and shape of buildings within the city limits; these were instituted to prevent repeating the architectural mistakes of the 1960s (ugly tower blocks that are not only aesthetic disasters, but also contribute to traffic congestion). La Défense, just outside city limits, forms a sharp contrast to this regimentation. Clustered around the Grande Arche (a 35-story office block in the shape of a hollowed cube), the headquarters of 14 of France's top 20 corporations vie to outdo each other with sleek modern design. Shops, galleries, trees, and a liberal sprinkling of sculpture make the large pedestrian esplanade a pleasant place for a stroll. Major roads run underneath the esplanade, and you'll feel less oppressed by pollution and cars here than you ever will in central Paris.

The proliferation of office towers in the area began in 1956, as part of a scheme to expand office space for Paris without drastically altering the city center. Originally, the planners intended to limit buildings to certain heights and styles to create a unified complex. But by the late 1960s and early 70s, companies were allowed to build distinctive *gratte-ciels* (skyscrapers), "Manhattan-style." This haphazard building threatened the dignity and grandeur of the *axe historique,* the straight-line urban swath of road stretching across the Pont de Neuilly, the avenue Charles de Gaulle, the avenue de la Grand Armée, through the Arc de Triomphe, then down the avenue des Champs Elysées and the place de la Concorde all the way to the Louvre itself. President Mitterrand received 424 projects in his contest for a monumental building to anchor the axis, eventually choosing the plan of previously unkown Danish architect Otto von Spreckelsen for its "purity and strength."

The Grande Arche de la Défense, Spreckelsen's winning design, now towers over the metro/RER stop bearing its name. It was inaugaurated on the French Republic's bicentennial—July 14, 1989. The walls are covered with a white marble that shines blindingly in the (rare) sunlight. Its undeniably modern design blends rakishly into the centuries-old architectural context of the *axe historique,* though it is aligned 6 degrees off the axis. As you approach the Grand Arche and walk around its perimeter, it seems to shift from a two-dimensional square to a starkly three-dimensional cube. For an unparalleled view and an entirely modernist aesthetic experience, go to the top. But first go to the **Info Défense booth** (tel. 47 74 84 24; open daily 10am-7pm; located near the arch, in front of the shell-shaped CNIT building). There you can ask for a brochure that entitles you to a 20% discount on the ticket to the arch, as well as the handsome *Guide to Works of Art in the La Défense District* (available in English). Tickets for the roof of the arch are sold at a booth near the elevator shaft. (Ticket office open Sun.-Thurs. 9am-8pm, Fri.-Sat. 9am-9pm; roof closes one hour after ticket office. Tickets 40F, ages under 18 30F.)

Even if you don't want to go through the roof, it's still worth climbing the steps to admire the view of the Arc de Triomphe across the river. Visible on the left as you walk down toward Paris is the **CNIT building,** the oldest building at La Défense, a hoary old survivor from 1958. The **Colline de l'Automobile,** an auto museum (scheduled to open in late 1992) that includes a dome-shaped cinema is on your right. Near here, plans are underway to construct the **Tour sans fin** (tower without end)—a 400m tower that will be the tallest skyscraper in Europe. The brightly colored play-dough-like sculpture at the place de La Défense by **Joan Miró** looks remarkably like one of his anthropomorphic paintings come to life. Across the place, **Alexander Calder's** linear, spidery red steel sculpture provides a fitting counterpart.

Just past the little lawn in front of you is a white tube called the **galerie art 4** (tel. 49 00 15 96; open Wed.-Mon. noon-7pm). Call to find out about their temporary exhibits and their tours of La Défense, available in French only for 20F. Originally known as

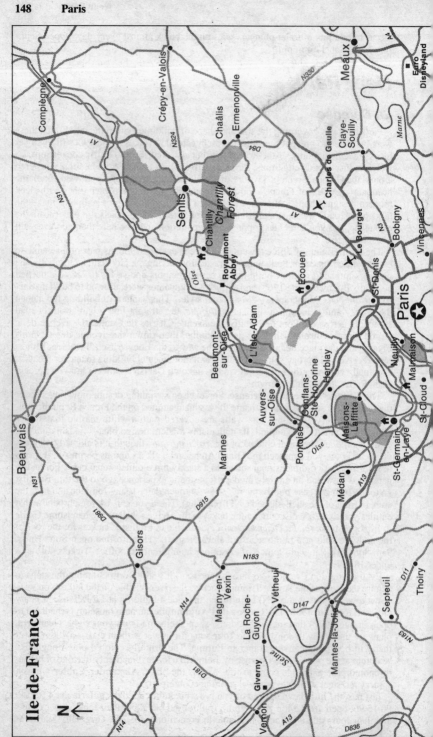

Ile-de-France

N←

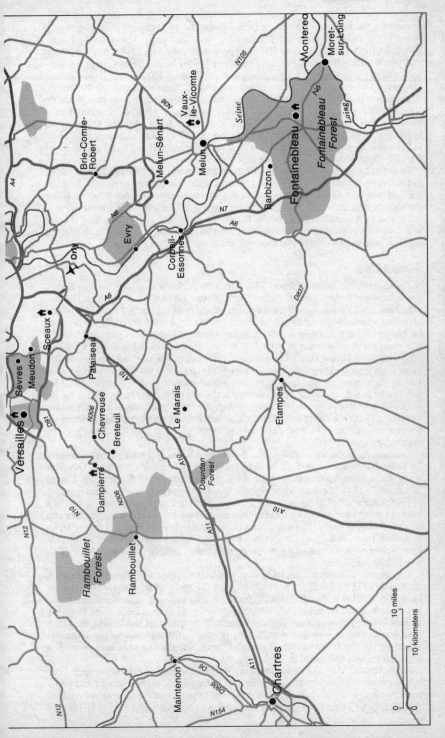

Corbevoie, the area was renamed La Défense after the 1870 siege of Paris; the bronze statue to the right of galerie art 4 honors the city's defenders. The statue by Louis-Ernest Barrias was selected over 100 other proposals, including one by Auguste Rodin.

If you want to eat or shop in La Défense, head to the huge **4 Temps shopping center**—one of the largest shopping malls in Europe, home to 200 stores, 3 levels, 20 restaurants, 9 cinemas, and 50,000 daily passers-through. You can enter from the Grande Arche metro stop, from doors behind the Miró sculpture, or from next to the Colline de l'Automobile. (Shops open Tues.-Sat. 10am-8pm, Mon. 11am-8pm. Supermarkets—*hypermarchés*—open Tues.-Sat. 9am-10pm, Mon. 10am-10pm.) A good bet among the restaurants in the mall is **Le Bistrot d'Edmond** (tel. 47 73 73 88). Located at place de la Patinoire, level 1, it's a large place with a vaguely rural feel and a two-course *menu* for 72F. (Open Mon.-Sat. 7:30am-10pm.)

To get to La Défense from Paris you can take the metro or RER. The RER is faster, but the metro is cheaper—La Défense counts as zone 2 for the metro but zone 3 for the RER. If you do take the RER, be sure to buy the more expensive ticket before going through the turnstile—a normal metro ticket may get you into the RER station in Paris, but it won't get you out at La Défense. Though La Défense is eerily impressive at night when the area is deserted one really needs a car to appreciate it as trains have stopped running, and a taxi would be quite expensive.

Versailles

The magnificent palace of Louis XIV, Versailles perfectly embodies the Sun King's absolute power and his famous statement, *"L'Etat, c'est moi"* (I *am* the State). Shunning Paris for its association with the power struggles of his youth, Louis XIV turned his father's hunting lodge (20km from Paris) into his royal residence, built and decorated mainly by Le Vau, Le Brun, and le Nôtre, the team stolen from Vaux-le-Vicomte. The court became the center of noble life, as more than a thousand of France's greatest aristocrats vied for the king's favor here. In turn, Louis was able to keep the nobility away from Paris and their provincial power-bases and under his watchful eye in what Harold Nicholson called a "vast and glittering concentration camp." Busy wrestling for roles in the Sun-King's wake-up *(levée)* and bed-going *(coucher)* rituals, such as the inestimable privilege of passing the king his shirt, the French aristocracy had no time for subversion. Ever the clever politician, he also successfully destroyed their financial independence by forcing them to pay crippling taxes, which he used to support his own extravagant expenditures.

Entrance A, on the right hand side in the North Wing as you enter, is the main entry for individual visitors. Lines can be long, especially on summer afternoons. This door leads to the **State Apartments of the King** and **Queen** and the **Galerie des Glaces** (the famed Hall of Mirrors). Most of these rooms are presently a self-guided museum of French history, full of portraits and engravings of the French aristocracy. Invest in a guide of some kind; without explanation, the symbolic freight of the architecture and artwork will pass you by. Cassette guides (25F) last roughly one hour and require an ID as deposit (open 9am-5pm). The written guide by Danile Meyer, a curator of the château, is the best and includes comments on the gardens and the Trianons. At 50F, it's a worthwhile investment.

The general admission ticket starts your visit in the **Musée de l'Histoire de France,** created in 1837 by Louis-Philippe to celebrate the glory of his country. Against the backdrop of richly textured walls hang portraits of the men and women, aristocrats and artists, generals and ministers who shaped the history of France. Each of the **Drawing Rooms** in the **State Apartments** is dedicated to a mythological god—Hercules, Marx, Mercury, and the ever-present Apollo, among others. Although less brilliant than you would expect, the gilt wood is still splendid, fresh from the five-year, seventy-million dollar restoration that ended in 1989.

Framed by the **War** and **Peace Drawing Rooms,** the **Hall of Mirrors** reflects Louis's ostentation like no other room in the palace. Originally, the hall was a dark, somewhat gloomy passageway, until Mansart (of roof fame) added the mirrors and doubled the light. In an ironic twist, modern Germany was born here in 1871, as William of

Prussia became Kaiser William I of Germany beneath the ceiling depicting Louis XIV, once-conqueror of the Rhine. Forty-eight years later, the Germans were forced to sign the ruinous Treaty of Versailles in the same room. Although many of the mirrors are old and cloudy, nothing quite compares to the visual impact of standing at one end of the Hall and gazing down past the mirror-filled arches, the gold figures, and the countless chandeliers. Each mirrored panel was the largest that 17th-century technology could produce; the ensemble represented an unbelievable, stunning extravagance.

(The château is open Tues.-Sun. 9am-6:30pm; Oct.-April Tues.-Sun. 9am-5:30pm. Last admission 1hr. before closing. Admission to State Apartments and Hall of Mirrors 31F, ages 18-25, over 60 and Sun. 16F, under 18 free. For general information, call 30 84 76 76 or 30 84 74 00.)

Guided tours, which allow you to bypass the long lines, begin at Entrance D. These tours are the only way to visit many of the most interesting parts of the castle. The admission ticket that you purchase at Entrance D allows you to bypass Door A and enter at the uncongested A2. (If the guards give you trouble, explain that the people at cash register D told you to enter there. You should not have to wait in the A line if you already have a ticket.) Seven tours of different parts of the château are offered; only three are given in English, and the English of the tour guides is of variable quality. Don't miss a tour of the **Opera and Chapel,** offered a few times a day. Other tours are fairly uninspiring and will appeal only to French-aristocracy addicts. Expect empty rooms with limited decoration—Versailles was completely sacked during the Revolution and only a tiny portion of its original glory has been restored. (Tours of the Apartments offered Tues.-Sun. 10:15am-4:15pm; Opera and Chapel 10:45am-4pm. Tours last 1hr. and cost 20F each, under 18 15F. Brace yourself for some tortured English accents and very odd translations. Check at Entrance D for specific times, mandatory reservations, and tickets. Tours leave from entrance F, across the courtyard.)

The immense expanse of park behind the château is currently under restoration to return it to its appearance in the days of Louis XIV. Even with work in progress and crowds of tourists, the gardens at Versailles are a breathtaking sight, an appropriately lavish buffer between the Sun King's huge palace and the rest of the world. Come in the evening to see the immense château unsullied by other visitors. You will experience the entire panorama of Versailles as it was originally conceived—a single work of art, bringing together all artistic and natural media as a backdrop for the aristocrats esconsed beneath its rigid, controlled beauty.

Directly in front of the château, the **Latona Parterre** holds the **Fountain of Latona,** one of the most extraordinary fountains alive with baroque transformation. Latona, mother of Diana and Apollo, is seen shielding her children from the attack of peasants, whom Jupiter is turning into frogs. Past the Latona group lies the **Tapis Vert (Green Carpet),** the central strip of grass linking the château to the much-photographed **Fountain of Apollo.** Pulled by the vigorous prancing of four horses, Apollo/Sun God/Louis XIV (as God of the Arts—the greatest of all patrons) rises out of dark water to enlighten the world with his questionable taste. Don't forget to look back up at the château from the Apollo Fountain. The culmination of any visit to the gardens must be the **Fountain of Neptune,** the largest of all the fountains, with 99 water-jets. (Gardens open sunrise-sundown. Mon.-Sat., free; May-Sept. 18F on Sun.)

The Trianons, cozy palaces designed to give the royal family some privacy, prove that even kings and queens need a break. Built by Mansart, the single story, marble-decorated **Grand Trianon** was intended as a meeker château in which, if need be, the king could reside alone with his family. (Open Tues.-Sun. 11am-6:30pm; Oct.-April Tues.-Fri. 10am-12:30pm and 2-5:30pm, Sat.-Sun. 10am-5:30pm. Last admission 1/2hr. before closing. Admission 17F, ages 18-25, ages over 60, and Sun. 9F, under 18 free.) All but four rooms of the **Petit Trianon,** built for Louis XV and Mme. de Pompadour, are under renovation and closed to the public. (Same hours as Grand Trianon. Admission 12F, ages 18-25, over 60, and Sun. 7F, under 18 free). **Le Hameau (the Queen's Hamlet),** is a collection of Normandy cottages built so Marie-Antoinette could play peasant, to the great disgust of the people who actually fit that description.

Brave the crowds on Sundays May through September to see (and hear) the **Grandes Eaux Musicales,** the only time when the fountains are in full operation. A *grande per-*

spective is offered between 11:15 and 11:35am; the best time to circulate among the fountains is between 3:30 and 5pm when the fountains spout and appropriately inspirational music plays. (Admission to park during *Grandes Eaux* 18F.)

The **Grand Fête de Nuit,** a theatrical musical and firework extravaganza that imitates the huge fêtes that Louis XIV threw, is held at the Neptune Fountain rain-or-shine on Saturday nights in July and September. Call the Tourist Office at 39 59 36 22 for exact dates and ticket info. Tickets are on sale at the tourist office and certain agencies within Paris. Enter at 2, bd. de la Reine. (Shows last 80min. 50-170F, reduced rates for children. Doors open 90min. before show; access at 2, bd. de la Reine.)

Reach Versailles by RER Line C5 to Versailles Rive Gauche station from one of the downtown Paris stations (roughly every 20min., 35min). From Mo. Invalides, the ticket there is 8F, the ticket back is 12F—they will frequently only allow you to purchase a one-way ticket. Buy your RER ticket *before* going through the turnstile to the platform, despite the fact that your metro ticket will get you through-your metro ticket won't let you exit the station in Versailles. From Invalides, take trains whose four letter label begins with V.

Chartres

Stunning **Cathédrale de Chartres,** spared by bureaucratic inefficiency after being condemned during the Revolution, survives today as one of the most sublime creations of the Middle Ages. In 876, Charlemagne's grandson, Charles the Bald, made a gift to Chartres of the *Sancta Camisia,* the cloth believed to have been worn by Mary when she gave birth to Christ. Pilgrims have flocked to the cathedral ever since to see the sacred relic and perhaps benefit from its supernatural powers. Disaster struck in 1194 when the third fire in two hundred years burned all but the enormous crypts, the new west tower, and the Royal Portal. When they discovered that Mary's relic (hidden in the crypt by three loyal priests who stayed with it, sweating out the fire) had emerged like the phoenix unsinged by the flames, the villagers took it as a sign of not only Mary's love but her desire for a more fitting cathedral. Clerics took advantage of the miracle to solicit funds on a grand scale and building proceeded at a furious pace: the bulk of the cathedral was completed by 1223 and consecrated in 1260. Arguably the finest example of Gothic architecture in the world, the stained-glass windows soon gained fame for their clarity and beauty, as did the magnificent sculptures adorning each of the main portals.

Few cathedrals rival Chartres in size and majesty and fewer reward time spent as generously. A masterpiece of finely crafted detail—architecture, sculpture, and glass— the cathedral is an extraordinary fusion of Romanesque and Gothic architectural elements. Built in a record-breaking 29 years (compared to 163 years for Notre Dame de Paris), the cathedral stands as one of the most unified and harmonious of medieval buildings. The famous twin-steepled silhouette is visible miles from the town, rising up above the flat wheat fields that surround Chartres and reminding viewers of a time when the Church controlled every aspect of the daily routine and the tallest buildings in existence were its cathedrals. The famous 12th-century statues of the Royal Portal present an assembly of Old Testament figures at the height of late Romanesque sculpture. The ones in the central bay, attributed to the "Master of Chartres" are especially beautiful: their elongated figures have a stillness and elegance that invites visitors to leave the earthly behind as they enter the divine space of the cathedral.

Most of the glass dates from the 13th century. During both World Wars, town authorities dismantled over 3000 square meters of glass and stored them piece by piece until the end of hostilities. The merchant sponsors of each window are recorded permanently in the lower panels, providing a valuable record of daily life during the 13th century. The famous "Blue Virgin" window, an object of pilgrimage and one of the few pieces of 12th-century glass to survive the fire, is visible at the first window of the choir, on the right. Note the contrast between the jewel-like brilliance of the windows that have been cleaned and the murkiness of the ones that have not. Bring binoculars if you can; many of the stories told by the stained glass will appear only as a technicolor puddle without magnification.

World-renowned tour guide Malcolm Miller, an authority on Gothic architecture, has brought the cathedral to life for English-speaking visitors for the past 35 years. Miller composes each tour individually to explain the cathedral's colorful history, as well as the fascinating symbolism in different segments of its windows and sculpture. If you can, take both of his tours the day you are there. They are worth it, and Miller is careful to discuss different aspects of the cathedral on each one. You may want to invest in a 29-35F guide (pretty pictures included) as well. (1 1/4-hr. tours run April-Jan. Mon.-Sat. at noon and 2:45 pm. Admission 30F, students 20F. Try to avoid Sat. and Tues.—busy days in the high season. Private tours available on request; call 37 28 15 58.)

Climb the north tower, **Tour Jehan-de-Beauce,** named after its architect and completed in 1513, for a magnificent view of the cathedral roof, the flying buttresses, and the city below. The tower itself is a wonderful example of flamboyant Gothic, a late medieval style named after the flame-like nature of its decoration. Built to replace a wooden steeple that repeatedly burned down, it provides a fascinating counterpart to its more sedate neighbor (and predecessor by three centuries), the octagonal steeple built just before the 1194 fire. (Open April-Sept. Mon.-Fri. 9:30-11:30am and 2-5:30pm, Sat. 9:30-11:30am and 2-4:30pm, Sun. 2-4:30pm; Nov.-Feb. Mon.-Sat. 10-11:30am and 2-4pm, Sun. 2-4pm. Admission 20F, students, seniors, and big families 13F, under 6 free.)

The cathedral is open daily in summer from 7:30am to 7:30pm and in winter from 7:30am to 7pm. No casual visits are allowed on Sat. 5:45 to 7pm or Sun. 9 to 10:15am and 10:45am to noon because of religious services. If you want the true Chartres experience, however, try attending one of these services. Call the tourist office (see below) for information on concerts in the cathedral, as well as the annual student pilgrimage in late May and other festivals throughout the year.

The town of Chartres provides a refreshing change from the grand boulevards and cosmopolitan atmosphere of Paris. The charming *vieille ville* (old town) has the cobblestone staircases, gabled roofs, timbered houses, and iron lamps of a traditional French village. Old streets, named for the trades once practiced there—rue de la Poissonerie being home to the fishmongers—run into one another. Charming stone bridges cross the Eure River, providing an ideal spot for photographs. Although the town is surrounded by flat wheat fields, Chartres is built on a hill, and some of the best views of the cathedral are found by walking down along the well-marked tourist circuit. Maps are available from the **tourist office** (tel. 37 21 50 00), opposite the cathedral's main entrance. They will help you to find accommodations in Chartres or in the surrounding area (20F fee). They also carry a list of restaurants and oodles of delectable brochures. For 35F, one or two people can use a headphone guide (in English, French, or German) to see the old city. (Tour lasts 90min.-2hr. and is worth it. Available while the office is open.) The tourist office staff speaks excellent English, as well as other languages. (Open Mon.-Fri. 9:30am-6:45pm, Sat. 9:30am-6pm, Sun. 10:30am-noon and 2-6pm; Oct. and March-May Mon.-Sat. 9:30am-6pm, Sun. 10:30am-noon and 2-6pm; Nov.-Feb. Mon-Fri. 9:30am-6pm, Sat. 9:30am-5pm.)

La Galerie du Vitrail (Gallery of Stained Glass), 17, rue du Cloître Notre-Dame (tel. 37 36 10 03), provides information on the cathedral's stained glass and showcases contemporary pieces. Films (8-25min.) on the history and production of stained glass and Chartres in the Middle Ages are shown free upon request in English, French, or German. (Open Tues.-Sun. 9:45am-7pm; Nov.-March Tues.-Sat. 9:45am-1pm and 2-6:30pm. Free.) The **Centre Internationale du Vitrail,** 5, rue du Cardinal Pie (tel. 37 21 65 72), hosts temporary exhibitions on stained glass, both historical and contemporary. The 12th-century barn in which it is housed was once used to store wine and grains received by the clergy from surrounding farmers. Note the 14th-century wood rafters and the 12th-century vaulting downstairs. (Open 9:30am-7pm; Oct.-March 10am-12:30pm and 1:30-6pm.)

The pleasant **auberge de jeunesse (HI),** 23, av. Neigre (tel. 37 34 27 64), is 2km north of the train station. Follow the signs past the cathedral and over the river by Eglise St-André. Comfortable four- to eight-bed rooms run 59F per night for HI members; others pay an additional 19F for a guest stamp. It is five minutes from all conveniences, and has a spectacular view of the cathedral. Toilet seats aren't guaranteed, but rejoice in the nice, new mattresses. Sleeping bags are allowed. (Reception open daily Sept. 30 to late Dec. 8-10am and 6-11pm; Feb.-March 6-10pm. Lockout 10am-6pm. Curfew 11:30pm in summer, 10:30pm in winter. Sheets 16F. Breakfast included.)

For **food,** try sandwich or *brasserie* fare in rue de Cygne or Place Marceau, open-air pedestrian areas with musicians and great atmosphere. **La Passacaille,** 30-32, rue Sainte-Même offers filling pizza (28-53F) in a tasteful green, peach, and mural surrounding. (Open June-Aug. daily 11:30am-10:30pm; rest of the year around meal-times.) **Le Pélage,** Place Châtelet serves ample portions of standard meat and potatoes fare (49-60F; *menus* at 68F50 and 79F50; open daily Mon.-Sat. noon-2pm and 7-11:30pm).

Chartres is accessible by frequent **trains** from Gare Montparnasse (1hr., round-trip 122F. In Paris call 45 82 50 50 for info; in Chartres call 37 28 50 50. Many trains run only on certain days or occasions—make sure you aren't caught waiting in vain.)

Fontainebleau

The château **Fontainebleau** has been a glorified hunting lodge for nearly 500 years, presenting a radically different architectural statement from the unity of Vaux-le-Vicomte and Versailles. Kings of France have lived on these grounds since the 12th century, though the present structure was built in 1528 for François I, who wanted to be closer to the "red and black furred animals" he so loved to kill. The building remained intact during the Revolution, and Napoleon declared it a state residence once again, refurnishing many apartments to suit his own sumptuous neoclassical style.

The Grands Appartements, the standard visitors' circuit, provides a lesson in the history of French architecture and decoration. Guides available in English make the whole visit more meaningful: 15F will get you a pamphlet about the château and some of the gardens or one describing the Grands Appartements alone; 25F buys the glossy booklet with more complete descriptions. In the **Gallery of François I,** arguably the most famous room at Fontainebleau, muscular figures by Mannerist artist Il Rosso tell mythological tales of heroism and bravado, brilliantly illuminated by light flooding in from courtside windows. The ensemble of the decorative scheme in each room, successfully incorporating furniture and paintings from different eras and styles, overwhelms the eyes. (Grands Appartements open Wed.-Mon. 9:30am-12:30pm and 2-5pm. Admission 26F, students, seniors, and Sun. 14F, children under 18, teachers with ID, unemployed, and art students with ID free. No tickets sold and no entry permitted after 11:45am and 4:15pm. Ticket valid all day. 90-minute guided tours available in French and possibly English on Wed. and Sat.-Sun, 30F, reduced rate 20F. Call 64 22 27 40 for details.)

The same ticket admits you to the **Musée Napoléon,** a collection of paraphernalia including His tiny shoes, His tootbrush, His field tent (the most elaborate you've ever seen) and His son's toys. (Hours same as Grands Appartements. No entry permitted after noon and 4:30pm).

The **Musée Chinois de l'Impératrice Eugénie,** also in the château, offers a welcome respite from the sometimes crowded apartments upstairs. These four rooms were remodelled in 1863 by the Empress to house the collection which she called her *"Musée chinois"* (Chinese museum), a gathering of Far Eastern decorative art—porcelain, jade, and crystal. (Open same hours as château. No entry after 12:15pm and 4:45pm. Admission 12F, students, seniors and Sun. 7F.)

Underkept and fairly unimpressive, the gardens at Fontainebleau still make for a pleasant stroll. If you throw some bread into the **Etang des Carpes,** the hundreds of carp that live in this pond, once they wake up, will battle to the death for the last soggy crumb. You can cruise around the pond in a rented boat. (Boat rental May 23-Aug. 31 daily 10am-12:30pm and 2-6pm; Sept. Sat.-Sun. 2-6pm. 35F per 1/2hr., 55F per hr., 50F deposit may be requested. 4 people max. per boat.) Quieter and more refined are the **Jardin Anglais** and the **Jardin de Diane,** where peacocks flaunt their feathers. (Gardens open daily sunrise-sunset. Jardin Anglais and de Diane open variably.)

The **Forêt de Fontainebleau** is a thickly wooded 20,000-hectare preserve with hiking trails and the famous rocks used for training alpine climbers. Fans of 19th-century art will recognize the thick hardwoods and sandstones made famous by painters of the Barbizon school.

Euro Disneyland

It s a small world after all; it s a small, small world. Although Disney owns land equal to one-fifth the area of Paris, the theme park itself doesn t even rank the size of an *arrondissment.* From the gate it takes only ten minutes to walk to the farthest point inside the park, a disappointment for visitors used to the vast reaches of Florida's Disneyworld. On the other hand, this Disney park is the most technologically ripping yet, and the special effects make the park a worthwhile daytrip from Paris.

Try to get there on a weekday, on a Tuesday or Thursday in particular, the least frenetic days of the week. Otherwise, you can expect to spend most of your time fighting to keep your place in line against the characteristically line-cutting French. Devious architecture hides the true length of the lines; a line just emerging from a building may look short, but there are probably 90 minutes worth of people coiled up inside. Save the bigger rides for the evening; the park closes at midnight, so you'll still have plenty of time to ride all of your favorite *manèges* several times over.

There are a total of 14 rides (of which nine are relatively sedate and suitable for small children and families), 20 other attractions, such as dance shows and car displays, as well as a grand total of 58 stores, boutiques and restaurants, not to mention the plethora of food stands throughout the park. In particular, Pirates, Big Thunder Mountain, and Star Tours are not to be missed.

The park can roughly be divided into five areas. **Main Street,** the first area you ll encounter after the gate, is where you ll find City Hall and many stores. Maybe a Gap if you look hard enough. Up Main Street, the **Château de la Belle au Bois Dormant** contains a stupendous high-tech smoke-breathing *dragon* in the dungeon. Exiting out the back of the château, you fall immediately into **Fantasyland,** a small world designed for small people. Although the rides are tame, they all merit a spin. One attraction to occupy your time while shunning lines is **Alice s Labyrinth,** a peculiar hedge maze, replete with squirting fountains and a bong-smoking caterpiller sitting on a purple spotted 'shroom——now how did that ever get into a children s story?

Off to the left, **Adventureland** awaits both the intrepid explorer and the weary parent with a mix of themes from adventurous countries, whose only link is that they re all southern regions: Egypt, West Africa and the Caribbean. **Pirates** presents 15 minutes of uncannily lifelike swashbucklers and a fantastic water-dungeon set, where you occasionally get sprayed with the bilge water as your lifeboat rushes through. In **Frontierland, Thunder Mesa**—a towering sunset colored reproduction of a New Mexican desert mesa—encloses the park s most breath-taking ride (and its only roller coaster), **Big Thunder Mountain. Discoveryland** thrusts you into the future. Fasten your seatbelt on **Star Tours,** a Star Wars theme flight simulator that dizzies passengers with a combination of a high-tech video display and fast dips and turns. **Visionarium** pieces together footage from nine different cameras to create a 360-degree film about the desire to fly.

Besides the rides, Disney also puts on three daily special events: a **Disney character parade,** including a myriad of elaborate floats with Snow White s castle, a fire-breathing dragon, and live doves; a night time **electrical parade** (for the best view of the parades stand to the left at the top of Main Street near the pseudo rotary—that s where the special effects on the floats are timed to go off); and a fantastic **fireworks** show, set against the background of the château (for the times of these events check the daily entertainment schedule available at City Hall).

The easiest way to get to EuroDisney is to take the RER A4 from Paris. Get on the train at Mo. Gare de Lyon or Chatelet-Les Halles in the direction Marne-La-Vallée to the last stop, Marne-La-Vallée/Chessy. Before hopping on the train check the illuminated electric boards hanging above the platform to make sure there is a light next to the Marne-La-Vallée stop, otherwise the train won t end up there. Trains depart every 30 minutes and take 50 minutes to get there. The trip costs 27F50 going out from Paris, and 31F coming back (the return ticket includes a metro trip). Last train to Paris leaves Disney at 12:20am.

Tickets are available at the fifty windows located to the left after passing through the pink hotel which surrounds the front of the park. You can also buy them at the Paris tourist office on the Champs-Elysées (see orientation and practical information for Paris), which is definitely the way to get tickets if you plan on coming on a weekend. (Open daily 9am-midnight. Open 8am-midnight for those staying in the resort hotels. Admission 225F, under 12 150F. Hours subject to change during the winter.

Vaux-le-Vicomte

The Château de Vaux-le-Vicomte may seem like a hut compared to Versailles or Fontainebleau, but its fascinating history and compact grace makes it one of the most famous palaces in the country. This diminutive masterpiece (designed by Le Vau, decorated by Le Brun, and landscaped by Le Nôtre) arose from the wealth and stature of Fouquet, Louis XIV's Minister of Finance. Unfortunately, the château's excessive grandeur hastened its haughty owner's downfall. Apparently, young King Louis XIV, received here for a feast in 1661, became furious at being outdone by his minister and stripped Fouquet of all his power, condemning him to life in prison. Astonished with the magnificence of Vaux, prototype of the classical style, the king appropriated Vaux-le-Vicomte's artists (and eventually some of its works) before beginning the construction of Versailles, where the style would reach full maturity. Although Vaux-le-Vicomte itself remains unfinished, many of the rooms display exquisite decor. Fouquet's audacity is revealed by the recurrence of script Fs and squirrels, his symbol. Outside, Le Nôtre's trimmed shrubs, shaved lawns, and strategic pools produce a kind of embroidered tapestry exuding classical harmony. The same ticket admits you to the **équipages,** former stables which now house a carriage museum.

The crowds here are wonderfully sparse, probably because it's so hard to reach. If you're with other people, consider renting a car. Take Autoroute A4 or A6 from Paris and exit at "Val-Maubée" or "Melun," respectively. Head toward Meaux on N36 and follow the signs. Or take a one of the frequent trains from Paris's Gare de Lyon to Melun, 6km from the château (45min., round-trip 61F). From there, it's a 90-minute hike or an expensive taxi ride. (From 66F from the station. Pick a cab up at the station, call 64 52 51 50 from Vaux to get back.). Biking is tough—the highway has many trucks and no shoulders. Taxi drivers will tell prospective hikers that Vaux is 10km from Melun; don't believe them. Your persistence in getting here may be best rewarded on Saturday evenings from May to September, when the candlelit château seems private and homey. The fountains in Le Nôtre's abundant gardens are turned on April-October every second and last Saturday of the month from 3 to 6pm. (Château (tel. 60 66 97 09), open April-Oct. Mon.-Sat. 10am-12:30pm and 2-5:30pm, Sun. and holidays 10am-6pm; Feb.-March, Nov. 1-29, and Dec. 19-Jan. 4 Mon.-Sat. 11am-12:30pm and 2-4:30pm, Sun. and holidays 11am-5pm. *Equipages* are open the same hours, and remain open during lunch and for 1/2hr. after the château closes. Gardens open the same hours as the *équipages,* except on Sun. when they remain open an additional 1/2-hr. Admission to château, gardens, and *équipages* 42F, under 16 and students with ID 34F, under 6 free. All parts of the estate open May-Oct. Sat. 8:30-11pm on candle-lit evenings; admission 55F, reduced rate 46F. Gardens always open; admission 20F.)

Normandie (Normandy)

Normandy, whose jagged coastline, gently sloping valleys, and elaborate cathedrals provided inspiration for the impressionists, has had a separate history from the rest of France. Seized by Vikings in the 9th century, Normandy was officially recognized as independent in 911, when the French king acknowledged the domination of the Norsemen (a name later corrupted to "Normans"). The great age of Norman independence, during which the Normans continued to expand their territory, lasted from the 10th to the 13th century. During this period, the Normans also created their greatest architectural monuments, a string of mammoth ornate cathedrals.

During the Hundred Years War, the English invaded and overpowered the fierce Norman resistance. The English troops, led by the Duke of Bedford and aided by French traitors, succeeded in capturing Joan of Arc after a great victory on September 8, 1430. Charged with heresy and sorcery, Jeanne was confined in Rouen3s Tour Jeanne d'Arc (which still stands today), condemned to be burned at the stake on May 30, 1431 at the age of 19. Although the British were eventually overthrown, they left behind a profound mark on the customs, crafts, and cuisine of the area, an imprint that remains to the present day. The British did not attempt another invasion until D-Day, June 6, 1944, when they returned with American and Canadian allies to wrest Normandy from German occupation.

The Norman ports of Le Havre, Dieppe, Caen, and Cherbourg welcome travelers arriving by ferry from England and Ireland or by hovercraft from England. Within Normandy, only major towns are connected by rail; buses fill in the gaps between smaller towns. SNCF buses are covered by railpass; all other bus companies are not. Since many memorable spots lie off the main roads, a bike or car helps for extended touring. Cyclists should note that the roads are hilly and that the coastal winds blow roughly west to east.

Gustave Flaubert once wrote, "All of us Normans have a drop of cider in our veins. It's a bitter, fermented drink which sometimes bursts the gut." The province's traditional *cidre* comes both hard *(brut)* and sweet *(doux)*. *Calvados,* apple brandy aged 12 to 15 years, ranks with the finest, most potent cognacs. Although the *calvados* on supermarket shelves pales in comparison to what you might be served in cozy Norman restaurants, you may be able to buy the real stuff from the farmers themselves. *Galettes*—thin whole wheat pancakes stuffed with vegetables, cheese, or meats—and *crêpes* are ubiquitous, filling, and usually inexpensive. The famous pure white and pure brown cows of Normandy supply a large percentage of the nation's dairy products. Try the creamy, pungent *camembert* cheese, but be sure it's ripe (soft in the middle).

Rouen

Best known as the city where Joan of Arc was burned and Emma Bovary was bored, Rouen is no provincial town. From the 10th through the 12th century, Rouen (pop. 400,000) witnessed a flowering of Gothic architecture while enjoying great power and prestige as the capital of the Norman empire, which controlled much of France and England. But Rouen's most famous legends revolve around the life and death of Joan of Arc. Held prisoner here by the English after her great campaign across France, she was interrogated and tried for heresy by the French clergy. Joan stood firm for three months and was sentenced to life imprisonment. Still not satisfied, the English pressed for a heavier punishment, and in May 1431, Joan burned at the stake in Rouen's pl. du Vieux Marché, today a busy marketplace.

Not all of Rouen's prisoners were so unlucky. Legend has it that in the 12th century, a fierce dragon with a voracious appetite for human flesh terrorized the population of Rouen. A local felon was "elected" to fight the beast. He succeeded in vanquishing Rouen's habitual menace and earned his freedom. Archbishop Ouen, later canonized,

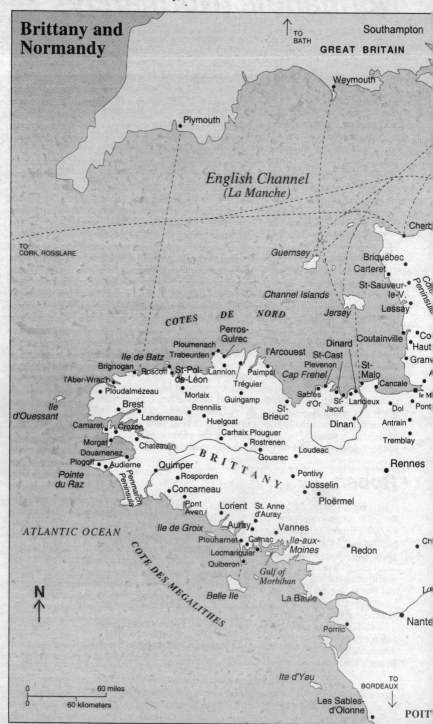

Brittany and Normandy

Southampton

GREAT BRITAIN

TO BATH

Weymouth

Plymouth

English Channel
(La Manche)

Cherb

TO CORK, ROSSLARE

Guernsey

Briquébec
Carteret
St-Sauveur-
le-V.
Lessay

Coutainville

Channel Islands

Jersey

COTES   DE   NORD

Perros-
Gulrec
Ploumenach
Trebeurden
Ile de Batz
Brignogan
Roscoff
St-Pol-
de-Léon
l'Aber-Wrac'h
Ploudalmézeau
Lannion
Paimpol
Tréguier
Morlaix
Guingamp
Brennilis
Huelgoat
Carhaix Plouguer
Rostrenen
Gouarec
Loudeac

l'Arcouest

Dinard
St-Cast
Plevenon
Cap Frehel
Sables
d'Or
St-
Jacut
Landieux
St-
Malo
Cancale

Coutainville

Co
Haut
Granv

le M

Dol
Antrain
Tremblay

Dinan

*Ile
d'Ouessant*

Brest
Landerneau
Camaret
Crozon
Morgat
Douarnenez
Plogoff
Audierne
*Pointe
du Raz*
Chateaulin

St-
Brieuc

Pont

Rennes

Quimper
Rosporden
Concarneau
Pont
Aven
Lorient
St. Anne
d'Auray
Auray

BRITTANY

Pontivy
Josselin
Ploërmel

Ile de Groix
Plouharnet
Locmariquier
Quiberon
Carnac
Vannes
*Ile-aux-
Moines*

Redon

Ch

ATLANTIC OCEAN

COTE DES MEGALITHES

Belle Ile

*Gulf of
Morbihan*

La Baule

Lo

Nante

Pornic

N

Ite d'Yeu

TO
BORDEAUX

Les Sables-
d'Olonne

POIT

0   60 miles
0   60 kilometers

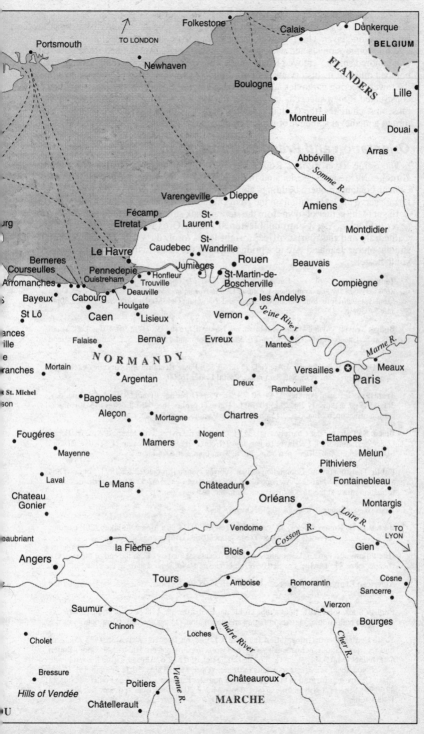

decreed that one prisoner be liberated each year to honor the accomplishment of the brave dragon-slayer. This practice continued until the end of the Revolution.

While impressionists and writers such as Victor Hugo, who dubbed Rouen the "city of a hundred spires," enjoyed Rouen in the 19th century, American and German troops bombed much of its history away in the 20th. Nonetheless, visitors continue to admire the towers, leering gargoyles, and gables that embellish Rouen's skyline today. The reconstructed Rouen succeeds in showing tourists a good time with its wealth of great museums, churches (the Gothic cathedral, currently under renovation, promises to return to a medieval splendor of white stone), and architecture.

Orientation and Practical Information

The Seine River divides Rouen into two parts—the **Rive Droite** and the **Rive Gauche.** Most sights are located in the old city on the Rive Droite, while the Rive Gauche contains modern buildings along wide avenues. Frequent trains from Paris St-Lazare serve the train station on the Rive Droite.

To get to the center of town from the station, walk straight down rue Jeanne d'Arc for several blocks. A left onto cobblestoned rue du Gros Horloge leads to pl. de la Cathédrale and the tourist office; a right leads to pl. du Vieux Marché. Continue straight on rue Jeanne d'Arc to a bridge crossing the Seine to the Rive Gauche and the youth hostel.

Tourist Office: 25, pl. de la Cathédrale (tel. 35 71 41 77), opposite the cathedral. Accommodations service 15F. The comprehensive guide *Le P'tit Normand* covers the Rouen area (46F). Open Mon.-Sat. 9am-7pm, Sun. 9:30am-12:30pm and 2:30-6pm; Oct.-March Mon.-Sat. 9am-12:30pm and 2-6:30pm.

Budget Travel: Voyage Wasteels, 111bis, rue Jeanne d'Arc (tel. 35 71 92 56). BIJ tickets. Youth railcards. Cheap flights. Open Mon.-Fri. 9am-12:30pm and 1:30-7pm, Sat. 9am-12:30pm and 1:30-6pm.

Post Office: 45, rue Jeanne d'Arc (tel. 35 08 73 66). **Poste Restante** and **currency exchange.** Open Mon.-Fri. 8am-7pm, Sat. 8am-noon. **Postal Code:** 76000.

Trains: rue Jeanne d'Arc (tel. 35 98 50 50). To: Paris (1 per hr., 70 min., 95F); Lille (3 per day, 3hr., 154F); Caen (every 2hr., 2hr., 107F); Le Havre (1 per hr., 1hr., 64F). **Lockers** 15-30F. Information office open Mon.-Sat. 7:15am-7pm, Sun. 9am-noon and 2-7pm.

Buses: SATAR, rue des Charrettes (tel. 35 71 23 29), by the river off rue Jeanne d'Arc. To Dieppe (2 per day, 2hr., 58F), Le Havre (6 per day, 2 1/2hr., 72F50), and Fécamp (1 per day, 21/2hr., 61F50). Information office open Mon.-Fri. 8:30am-6pm, Sat. 8am-noon.

Public Transportation: Completion of new subway system is projected for 1993. For now, hop a bus. **Le Bus,** rue Jeanne d'Arc, one block from the river (tel. 35 52 52 00). 4F50 per ticket. Information office at the train station open Mon.-Sat. 6:30am-8pm.

Taxis 67, rue Thiers (tel. 35 88 50 50). Open 24 hrs.

Bike Rental: Rouen Cycles, 45, rue St-Eloi (tel. 35 71 34 30). Mountain bikes 120F per day, 320F per week. Deposit 2000F. Open Tues.-Sat. 8:30am-12:15pm and 2-7:30pm.

Hitchhiking: To Paris or Caen, hitchers report success taking bus #12 to the end of the line. For Dieppe, #2 or 8 to Déville. For Le Havre, autoroute du Havre, which starts in the center of town.

American Express: 1-3 pl. Jacques-Lelieur (tel. 35 98 19 18). Open Mon.-Fri. 8:45am-noon and 1:30-6pm.

English Bookstore: ABC Bookshop, 11, rue des Faulx (tel. 35 71 08 67), has cheap paperbacks and a large collection of classics in fiction and non-fiction. Open Tues.-Sat. 10am-6pm.

Youth Center: Centre Information Jeunesse (CIJ), 84, rue Beauvoisine (tel. 35 98 38 75), helps find accommodations, permanent housing, and work. (Open Mon.-Fri. 10:30am-6:30pm.) **Rouen Cité Jeunes (MJC),** 11, pl. du Général de Gaulle (tel. 35 71 17 07), upstairs from the restaurant, can tell you about activities and events in Rouen. (Open Mon.-Thurs. 10am-8:30pm, Fri. 10am-7pm.) **Centre d'Information et d'Orientation pour les Etudiants,** 40, rue de Fontenelle (tel. 35 89 50 99), helps primarily in finding jobs. (Open Mon. 1:30-5:30pm, Tues.-Fri. 9am-12:30pm and 1:30-5:30pm.)

Laundromat: 79, rue Beauvoisine. Between the train station and the *centre ville*. Wash 14F. Dry 2F per 7 min. Open daily 7am-9pm.

Crisis Lines: S.O.S. Viol. Toll-free call; tel. 05 05 95 95 daily 10am-6pm for victims of rape. **S.O.S. Amitié,** tel. 35 60 52 52. Available 24 hrs. **S.O.S. Médecins,** tel. 35 03 03 30. 24-hr. medical assistance.

Hospital: Hôpital Charles Nicolle, 1, rue de Germont (tel. 35 08 81 81). Also **Hôtel Dieu,** 51, rue de Lecat (tel. 35 89 81 30).

Ambulance: 1, rue de Germont (tel. 35 88 44 22). **Emergency: SAMU** tel. 15.

Police: 5-6, rue Brisout de Barneville (tel. 35 63 81 17). **Emergency:** tel. 17.

Accommodations and Camping

Finding a room in Rouen is more difficult in the off-season than in the summer. As a number of Parisians commute to work here, accommodations are tight during the week. The cheaper lodgings are on the quiet side streets, particularly those between the train station and the Hôtel de Ville. Ask the tourist office or call 35 74 18 68 for information on university **CROUS** lodgings, which, though cheap, are usually available only on weekends from June through September.

Auberge de Jeunesse (HI), 118, bd. de l'Europe (tel. 35 72 06 45), on the Rive Gauche, 5km from the station. Take bus #12 from the station. Or walk straight across the river on rue Jeanne d'Arc and its extensions, av. Jacques Cartier and Av. de Bretagne, to the newly constructed bd. de l'Europe (1/2hr.). Clean, modern 6-bed rooms with decent showers. Kitchen facilities. HI card required. Reception open 7-10am and 5-11pm. Lockout 10am-5pm. Curfew 11pm. 53F50 includes breakfast. A 100F refundable deposit gets you sheets and a locker key.

Hôtel Normandya, 32, rue du Cordier (tel. 35 71 46 15), between Tour Jeanne d'Arc and rue Beauvoisine. Attractive bright rooms run by an owner who loves *Let's Go* travelers. Singles and doubles 80-100F, with shower 130F. Breakfast 18F.

Hostellerie du Vieux Logis, 5, rue de Joyeuse (tel. 35 71 55 30), off rue Louis-Ricard. Elderly proprietor keeps the worn velvet rooms cozy. Located in a quiet area that overlooks the spires of Rouen, and decorated with Victorian simplicity. Call ahead if you plan to arrive late. No one accepted after 10pm. Partake of the 6-course 60F *menu* downstairs even if you're not staying. Singles 90F. Doubles 100F. Breakfast 15F.

Hôtel St-Ouen, 43, rue des Faulx (tel. 35 71 46 44), across from Eglise St-Ouen. Spacious rooms kept by a friendly owner and her shaggy dog. Singles 70-95F, doubles 100-105F. Showers 16F. Breakfast 17F.

Hôtel de La Rochefoucauld, 1, rue de La Rochefoucauld (tel. 35 71 86 58), 1 block to the left of the station. 25 good-sized rooms in a convenient location for travelers with huge backpacks. Singles 90F, with shower 130F. Doubles 120F, with shower 140F.

Hôtel du Palais, 12, rue Tambour (tel. 35 71 41 40), off rue du Gros Horloge. Clean, large, and pink rooms in a central location. Singles and doubles from 110F, with shower from 130F. Showers 10F. Breakfast 20F.

Camping: Camping Municipal de Déville, rue Jules Ferry in Déville-les-Rouen (tel. 35 74 07 59), 4km from Rouen. Take bus #2 from the station. Attractive sites with squeaky clean bathrooms. Hot showers. 26F per person, 5F per tent or car. Open March-Oct. Ask at CIJ (see Youth Center) for a comprehensive list of area campgrounds.

Food

The **pl. du Vieux-Marché** presents a mouth-irrigating range of fish, cheese, and fresh produce (Tues.-Wed. and Fri.-Sun. 7am-12:30pm). Local specialties include duck *pâté, canard au sang* (pressed duck), *sole normande,* and *tripe à la normandaise.* Locals take their lunches in the busy streets north of pl. du Vieux Marché, where frugal students and flashy businesspeople are both well-served. Grocery stores carry *calvados* (apple liqueur) at cheaper rates than specialty shops. Try **Monoprix,** 67, rue du Gros Horloge (open Mon.-Sat. 9am-7pm) or **Marché U,** at rue de Cercle next to pl. du Vieux-Marché (open Mon.-Sat., 9am-12:30pm and 3-7:30pm). For the ferocious *calva-*

dos of yore, you might just want to wait to buy directly from the farmers in the Norman countryside.

Le Marmite, 3, rue de Florence (tel. 35 71 75 55), near the Vieux-Marché. Seafood and other local delights served in a bright and elegant dining room. The 95F, 3-course dinner *menu* reduces to 70F during lunch hours. Make reservations on weekends. Open Tues.-Sun. noon-2pm and 7-10pm.

Les Flandres, 5, rue des Bons-Enfants. French favorites like *cordon bleu* and *pâté de campagne* served unpretentiously. Simple, filling *menu,* 55F; *plats du jour* 35F. Open Mon.-Fri. noon-1:30pm and 7:30-9:15pm, Sat. noon-1:30pm.

La Petite Flambée, 24, rue Cauchoise, just off pl. du Vieux-Marché. Pink and white crêperie with outdoor seating. *Crêpes* (10-28F) and *galettes* (10-45F). Open Tues.-Fri. noon-3pm and 7-10pm, Sat.-Sun. 7-10pm.

Natural Vital, 3, rue du Petit Salut, off pl. de la Cathédrale. Vegetarian hot meals. 60F will get you a *plat du jour,* choice of drink (try carrot orange juice) and dessert. Also a well-stocked health food store. Restaurant open Tues.-Sat. noon-3pm. Store open Tues.-Sat. 8:30am-7pm.

Pizzeria du Drugstore, 2, rue Beauvoisine. Three-tiered restaurant above a drugstore. 54F lunch *menu* includes pizza, dessert, drink, and coffee. Open Mon.-Sat. noon-3pm and 7-11pm.

Rouen Cité Jeunes (MJC), 11, pl. du Général de Gaulle (tel. 35 71 17 07) and pl. des Faïenciers (tel 35 72 26 51). Cafeteria food has never seemed so appealing. 29F self-service *menu,* plus 3F for admittance card. Call ahead in summer as only one of the two cafeterias is usually open. Open Mon.-Fri. 11:30am-1:30pm.

Sights and Entertainment

The majority of Rouen's historical sights and museums fit in a walking tour of the Rive Droite. From rue Jeanne d'Arc, turn left onto the pedestrian **rue du Gros Horloge.** Built into a bridge halfway down the street, the **Gros Horloge** tells the time with charmingly specious imprecision. Climb the belfry to see the 14th-century clockwork and the rooftops of Rouen's medieval timber-frame houses. (Open April-Oct. Thurs.-Mon. 10am-noon and 2-6pm, Wed. 2-6pm. Free. Closed for repairs in 1992.)

At the end of the rue du Gros Horloge lies the **Cathédrale de Notre Dame.** Built between the 12th and 16th centuries, it incorporates nearly every intermediate style of Gothic architecture. The façade that fascinated Monet is now black with soot, but the half-completed renovations already show signs of eventually returning it to its pre-industrial hue. To the left rises the 12th-century **St. Romanus Tower.** To the right, the spire-less 17th-century **Tour de Beurre** was purportedly financed through dispensations granted to those who wanted to eat butter rather than fast during Lent. The cathedral, whose central tower is the tallest in France (151m), is illuminated nightly during July and August (Sept.-June Sat., Sun., and holidays).

Set just behind the cathedral, the 15th-century **Eglise St-Maclou** provides a striking contrast to its larger neighbor. Whereas Notre Dame de Rouen is remarkable for its hodgepodge of architectural styles, St-Maclou—built within a relatively short span of 80 years—displays an extraordinarily uniform Gothic flamboyance. Beyond the church, a small passageway at 186, rue de Martainville leads to the **Aitre St-Maclou.** This cloister served as the church's charnel house and cemetery during the great plagues of the later Middle Ages. Appropriately, the wooden beams of the inner courtyard bear a gory 15th-century frieze of the *danse macabre.* Today, in a happier incarnation, the building houses Rouen's Ecole des Beaux-Arts. (Open daily 9am-6pm. Free.) A few blocks from Notre Dame and St-Maclou, lies Eglise **St-Ouen,** once the abbey of a Benedictine monastery. Begun in 1318, the Hundred Years War put a damper on its construction, postponing the completion of this pure example of French Gothic architecture, with its towering vaults second in height only to those of Beauvais, until the 16th century. Enter on the south side, through the Marmouset Portal. (Open Wed.-Mon. 10am-12:30pm and 2:30-6pm.) Renovations to the façade proceed slowly.

Towards the *centre ville* and behind the pockmarked (from heavy bombardment) and gargoyled **Palais de Justice,** an 11th-century synagogue, known simply as the **Monument Juif** (Jewish Monument) was recently uncovered during excavation. Unfortunately, you must call the tourist office at least three days in advance in order to take their guided tour in French. (Sun. 11am; Oct-April Sat. 2pm. Admission 26F; under 25 and over 60, 22F.) On the other side of rue Jeanne d'Arc and pl. du Vieux Marché is the site of **Eglise Jeanne d'Arc,** a massive, vaulting structure meant to resemble an upturned boat. Its stained-glass windows were recovered from Eglise St. Vincent, destroyed during WWII. Next to the church is a 65m cross marking the spot where the Maid of Orleans was burned at the stake. The **Tour Jeanne d'Arc,** near the station on rue du Donjon, is the last remaining tower of the château which confined her. The display inside contains materials relating to the trial. (Open Wed.-Mon. 10am-noon and 2-5:30pm. Admission 6F, students free.)

While its many churches occupy most visitors' itineraries, Rouen also claims a number of notable museums. The centrally located **Musée des Beaux Arts,** just off rue Jeanne d'Arc at rue Thiers, has collections of the works of Rouen's native artists Jacques Emiles Blanche and Géricault, as well as other European masters and French artists from the 16th through 20th centuries such as Monet, Sisley, Renoir and Caillebotte. (Open Thurs.-Mon. 10am-noon and 2-6pm, Wed. 2-6pm. Admission 11F, students free.) Next to the Musée des Beaux Arts on rue Jacques-Villon, the **Musée de Ferronnerie Le-Secq-des-Tournelles** (Ironworks Museum) fills a 15th-century church with a frighteningly archaic collection of hardware—grillwork, locks, keys, and other household objects, dating from the 3rd to the 19th century. (Open Thurs.-Mon. 10am-noon and 2-6pm, Wed. 2-6pm. Admission 11F, students and children free.) Uphill from the Musée des Beaux Arts at 198, rue Beauvoisine (follow rue Thiers to its intersection), the **Musée des Antiquités** in Cloître Ste-Marie, 198, rue Beauvoisine (tel. 35 98 55 10), houses a refined collection of Gallo-Roman, Merovingian, and Renaissance relics, mostly from local sources. (Open Mon. and Wed. 10am-5:30pm, Sun. 10am-noon and 2-6pm. Admission 10F, students free.)

Novelist **Gustave Flaubert** grew up at 51, rue de Lecat, next door to the Hôtel-Dieu hospital (which bears the same address). Now the fascinating **Musée Flaubert et d'Histoire de la Médecine** (tel. 35 08 81 81), the building houses a few of Flaubert's prosaic possessions. The museum's prize, however, is its collection of gruesome and frighteningly pre-anesthesia-age medical "instruments" (including a battlefield amputation kit and gallstone-crushers-and-removers) used by Flaubert *père,* a renowned physician. (Open Tues.-Sat. 10am-noon and 2-6pm. Free guided tours in French every 1/2hr.) On a small bay of the Seine, 15 minutes out of town, **Croisset,** where Flaubert wrote *Madame Bovary,* is of interest only to hardcore fans. Dramatist **Pierre Corneille's** home is at 4, rue de la Pie, off pl. du Vieux Marché. (Open Thurs.-Mon. 10am-noon and 2-6pm, Wed. 2-6pm. Admission 2F, students free.)

Share a cup or a glass at the preppy watering hole, **Café le Leffe,** pl. des Carmes (open 7am-1am), named for the Belgian beer which students from all over France seem to adore, or at **La Rotonde,** 61bis, rue St-Sever. The **Night-On,** 8, rue de l'Ancienne Prison (tel. 35 70 60 60), is a popular mainstream place to do the hustle. (Open Fri.-Sat. 11pm-4am. Cover 80F.) For a more sedentary evening, try **Le Scottish,** 21, rue Verte (tel. 35 71 46 22), which hosts a weekend jazz concert on an outdoor terrace (café open 10:30am-2am).

Local students frequently trek out to **Exo 7** (tel. 35 72 28 92), a disco/club 6km south of Rouen which often stages excellent live concerts. The only reliable way to get there is by taxi (50F one way), but bus #5 runs part-way. Call ahead to confirm show times and prices, which vary depending on the evening's entertainment.

Throughout October, Rouen celebrates the students' return with the **Festival d'Eté de Seine Maritime.** The impressive program offers an unusual range of events including classical and baroque music, theater, and water ballet. For tickets and information, call 35 70 04 07, or write to Festival d'Eté, Hangar 23, Port Automne, bd. Emile Duchemin, 76000 Rouen.

Near Rouen

From Rouen to Le Havre, the Seine snakes through 58,000 hectares of protected forests, apple orchards, and grassy fields. Today, many exceptional ruins as well as functional abbeys founded by Benedictine monks during the 17th century still dot this undisturbed part of the Norman countryside ideal for walking, biking, fishing, and camping.

Frequent service by SATAR **buses** covers the Seine in the direction of Le Havre. Buses #30A and 30B stop at most of the small villages along the way. The ride to Le Havre costs 69F50 (120F round-trip) and takes three hours. Buses run every 1-2 hours, and schedules are available at the *gare routière* in Rouen (tel. 35 71 23 29). You can stop at any of the remote villages along the way and get back on the next bus.

In addition to its therapeutic natural setting, the park offers visitors a chance to see a number of abbeys and churches less blackened and blistered than their urban counterparts. Nearest Rouen, in **St.-Martin de Boscherville**, sits the 12th-century **Abbaye St.-Georges** whose rounded arches and pyramidal towers are a masterpiece of Romanesque architecture. Recent excavations have uncovered Gallo-Roman paintings. (14F from Rouen by bus.) The abbey is a mere ten-minute walk from the bus stop; follow the signs. (Open April-Sept. Mon.-Fri. 8am-noon and 1-6pm, Sat.-Sun. 9am-noon and 2-7pm. Admission 15F, students 12F.)

In nearby **Jumièges**, about 4km off the D982, the stunning ruins of a once-majestic 11th-century Romanesque church, the **Ancienne Abbaye Notre Dame,** interrupt half-forgotten landscape. (Open 9am-7pm; Sept. 16-Oct. and April-June 15 Mon.-Fri. 9am-noon and 2-5pm, Sat.-Sun. 9am-noon and 2-6pm; Nov.-March Mon.-Fri. 10am-noon and 2-4pm, Sat.-Sun. 10am-noon and 2-5pm. Admission 25F; ages 18-25 and over 60, 14F.) You will probably have to walk the 4km from **Yainville,** the closest bus stop (24F). The only buses serving this region (still #30A and 30B) go all the way to Jumièges once per day (27F50); the area is not served by train.

About 10km farther down D982 in the tiny village of **St-Wandrille** is the **Abbaye St-Wandrille** (tel. 35 96 23 11). The monks still live, work, and perform their devotions according to 1200-year-old Benedictine traditions. Daily offices are sung in Gregorian chant. (Mon.-Sat. at 9:25am and 5:15pm, Sun. at 10am and 5pm). An amusing monk leads guided tours of the cloister and other buildings twice per day (15F). The bus fare to St-Wandrille from Rouen is 35F50.

A picturesque campground lies adjacent to an outdoor recreational center at **Base de Plein Air et de Loisirs Jumièges-le-Mesnil** (tel. 35 37 93 84; open March-Oct. 12F50 per person, 13F per tent, 6F50 per car). Jumièges's **Camping Municipal** (tel. 35 37 24 15) is 3km down the hill on the main road from the ruins of the Abbaye. (Open May-Aug. 6F80 per person, 3F40 per tent, 3F40 per car.) For information on activities and fishing licenses, contact Centre Administratif du Parc, 2, Rond-Point Marbec, 76580 Le Trait (tel. 35 37 23 16).

Caudebec-en-Caux is a few km beyond St-Wandrille in the heart of the Parc de Brotonne, still on the #30A and 30B bus lines (35F50). An extensive network of hiking trails penetrates the forested hills behind the rather ordinary town. The Caudebec **tourist office,** rue Thomas Basin (tel. 35 96 20 65), is up rue des Boucheries. (Open July-Aug. Mon.-Sat. 9am-12:15pm and 2-6pm, Sun. 2-6pm; Sept. and Easter-June Sat. night and Sun. only.) When it's closed, bring your inquiries to the *mairie* (tel. 35 96 11 12), a palatial building by the river and past the miniature golf course. An adequate **campground** awaits 1km beyond the town hall by the riverside (tel. 35 96 26 38; open mid-April to Sept. 8F25 per person, 7F per tent and car). On the last Sunday in September, Caudebec hosts the **Festival du Cidre,** the region's largest folk festival. The town awakens with dancing in the streets and liberal cider consumption. (Every 2 years, to be held in 1994.)

Near the intersection of the N182 and the N138 in the Risle Valley, and 16km from Rouen, the religious community of **Notre-Dame du Bec-Hellouin** (tel. 32 44 86 09) harbors a 15th-century tower and Benedictine cloister. The abbey opens to the public only during guided visits (Mon.-Fri. at 10am, 11am, 3pm, 4pm, and 5pm, Sat. at 11am, 3pm, and 4pm, Sun. at noon, 3pm, 3:30pm, and 4pm; Oct.-May daily at 11am, 3:15pm, and 4:30pm.) There is a noon mass daily. Take the daily train from Paris to Evreux (1hr. 15 min.) and catch a bus from there.

Giverny

Halfway between Rouen and Paris, the small village of **Giverny** would have fallen off the map by now had Claude Monet not decided to purchase a small garden here. Sixty-seven years after his death in 1926, the then-impoverished painter surely would not recognize today his quaint pink and green house and his small, tangled garden. Landscapers now tend the famed impressionist flora for six months a year, and the house witnesses a barrage of tourists to rival that of Versailles. The Japanese-style bridge and water lilies are indeed quite beautiful, but the site has been methodically converted into a tourist trap of the first degree, called the **Musée Claude Monet** (tel. 32 51 28 21). The steep admission fees now finance six months of continuous blooms, something Claude, who spent nearly as much time writing rent-forgiveness letters to his landlord as he did painting, might well find incredible. The most famous paintings have been scattered around the world's great museums, but with a little imagination, it's possible to disregard the tourists and appreciate the inspiration of Monet's water lilies, which the master not only painted, but even addressed by name. (House and garden open April-Oct. Tues.-Sun. 10am-noon and 2-6pm. Admission 30F, students 20F. To garden only, 20F.)

Thanks to their popularity, Giverny and the lilies are easily accessible by public transportation. The train station of **Vernon,** across the river and 6km from the museum, lies along the Rouen-Paris St-Lazare train line. Trains leave from Rouen to Vernon (every 2 hr., 40 min., 49F) and from Paris St-Lazare (every 2 hr., 45 min., 59F). To get to Giverny, rent a **bike** from the station (44F per half day, 55F per day, 1000F deposit), or take a **bus** from the front of the station (3 per day each way, 10 min., 10F, round-trip 16F). If you're not burdened by a frenzied itinerary, climb up the valley into the **Forêt de Vernon,** alongside Giverny, to see some of the beautiful poppy-covered countryside and more Norman cows. The Vernon **tourist office**, 36, rue Carnot (tel. 32 51 39 60) distributes maps of the most rewarding hiking trails in the area. (Open Tues.-Sat. 9:30am-12:15pm and 2:30-6:30pm, Mon. 2:30-6:30pm.) Frequent signs lead the way from the Vernon station to the tourist office and to Giverny. Finally, the **Musée de Vernon,** 12, rue du Pont (tel. 32 21 28 09) exhibits an eclectic collection. Besides the predictable series on Giverny (only one is a Monet), this converted mansion houses a display of archaeological relics found near Vernon and a room devoted to animal art. (Open Tues.-Sun. 2-6pm. Admission 15F, students free.)

Although hotel beds in Vernon do not conform to the constraints of a tight budget, the excellent **Auberge de Jeunesse (HI)** (tel. 32 51 66 48) has immaculate and modern four-person rooms with bathrooms and kitchen. The walk along the green banks of the river takes 20 minutes. The hostel is only one block from the Seine, at 28, av. Ile de France. (Reception open daily 7-10am and 6:30-10:30pm. No lockout. Members only, 40F. Breakfast 15F. Open April-Sept. Reservations recommended at least a few days in advance.) You can also **camp** behind the hostel on the wide lawn (22F per person).

Coast: Upper Normandy

Along the white cliffs of the fertile Alabaster coast, the road from Dieppe to Le Havre passes through choice Norman countryside. A leisurely ramble on any of the side roads leads to a number of Grade-A coastal towns that nestle among the precipitous cliffs along the English Channel. White cows pasture contentedly on the farms sprinkling the green valleys inland. Hitchhikers report the going easier on the inland D925, where local farmers chat with passers-by and may offer samples of their home brew, than along the coast. Trains frequently connect the larger towns of Dieppe, Fécamp, and Le Havre, but do not stop at any other towns along the upper coast. Cycling is best for exploring, though the **CNA (Compagnie Normande d'Autobus)** and **Car Gris** bus services will shuttle you up and down the steep hills more efficiently. Buses run infrequently on Sundays.

Accessible by CNA bus from Fécamp or Dieppe (Mon.-Sat. 4 per day, 20 min., 14F40), the small village of **Varengeville** sequesters treasures of the long-gone aristocracy. A right off Varengeville's main road leads to the **Parc Floral des Moutiers** (tel. 35 85 10 02). Planted in 1900, these brilliant gardens rival Giverny in their bewildering variety and color. (Open Easter-Nov. daily 10am-noon and 2-6pm, Sun. 2-7pm. Admission 30F, children 10F.) One km farther, a beautiful 12th-century Romanesque church, surrounded by the 13th- to 15th-century **Maritime Cemetery,** perches at the end of a rocky outcrop of coastal cliffs. Co-founder of cubism, Georges Braque, who is buried in the church's cemetery, designed its stained-glass windows to replace those destroyed in the war. Just outside the eastern edge of Varengeville lies the **Manoir d'Ango** (tel. 35 85 12 08), a 16th-century château with a striking Byzantine-style tower where the lords frittered away their time raising and breeding pigeons. (Open April to mid-Nov. daily 10am-7pm. Admission to house and gardens 30F, students 25F, children ages 7-12 20F.)

A bit farther inland, toward Rouen, lies a tranquil beech-tree forest. Guy de Maupassant was born August 5, 1850, in the nearby **Château de Miromesnil,** (don't pronounce the "s"), which his mother rented for three years to ensure him a noble birth. Call ahead (tel. 35 04 40 30) and ask to be guided by Count Bertrand de Vogüé, the château's present inhabitant, who leads delightful tours in French or English. (Open May-Oct. 15 Wed.-Mon. 2-6pm. Admission 25F, children 15F.)

The churches, ports, and beaches of **Fécamp,** a small coastal city (pop. 22,000) two-thirds of the way from Dieppe to Le Havre, reflect its significance as a religious, commercial, and recreational center. Legend says that a few drops of Christ's blood, preserved by Joseph of Arimathea and his uncle Nicodemus in a hollow fig-tree trunk, washed up here during the 6th century and caused a spring to gush forth. Fécamp subsequently became an important destination for religious pilgrimages. A museum and chapel marking this source has been constructed at 2, rue de Précieux Sang. (Open daily 9:30am-noon and 2-7pm. Admission 5F.) The spring itself is at 12, rue de l'Aumône.

Ten minutes away at the foot of the walking street **rue Jacques Huet,** is Fécamp's massive 11th-century **Abbatiale de la Trinité,** with its 127m nave as long as that of Notre Dame de Paris, and its 70m tower at the transept-crossing. Inside the nave sits the relic of the *Précieux Sang*—the fig trunk that carried the blood. (Open daily 9am-7pm. Guided tours in French leave from the front of the abbey July-Aug. Mon.-Sat. at 11am and 3pm.)

From the 16th century through the French Revolution, Fécamp's Benedictine monks used an elixir of regional plants and oriental spices as a healing agent. A local wine merchant rediscovered the recipe and in 1880 built the distillery **Palais Benedictine,** 110, rue Alexandre Le Grand (tel. 35 28 00 06), christening the liqueur after the monks who invented it. (Guided tours of the factory, daily 10am-6pm; Sept.-Nov. and April-June 10am-noon and 2-5:30pm; Dec.-March 10:30am and 3:30pm. Admission 24F, children 12F. Admission includes a sample.)

Fécamp also has a regional art museum and a maritime museum. **Le Musée Centre-des-Arts,** near the Abbey at 21, rue Alexandre-Legros (tel. 35 28 31 99), displays regional art and objects such as earthenware, furniture, paintings, and architectural relics. (Open Wed.-Mon. 10am-noon and 2-5:30pm. Admission 20F, students 10F.) Across town on the beach, the **Musée des Terre-Neuvas et de la Pêche,** 27, bd. Albert Ier (tel. 35 28 31 99), recounts the trials and adventures of local cod fishers who crossed the sea to fish on Newfoundland's Grand Banks. (Open daily 10am-noon and 2-6:30pm; Sept.-June Wed.-Mon. 10am-noon and 2-5:30pm. Admission 20F, students 10F.) The admission ticket for either of these two museums also admits you to the other.

La Maison de Tourisme, 113, rue Alexandre Le Grand (tel. 35 28 51 01), dispenses free maps and books rooms. (Open daily 9am-12:15pm and 1:45-6pm, Nov.-April Mon.-Sat. 9am-12:15pm and 1:45-6pm.) Another branch is conveniently located off pl. St-Etienne at pl. Bellet (tel. 35 28 20 51). All buses stop at the **train station** (tel. 35 28 24 82), on bd. de la République or up the steps on av. Gambetta, which extends from the beach to the center of town. You can pick up schedules at the **bus station,** 8, av. Gambetta (tel. 35 28 16 04), behind Eglise St-Etienne. **Auto-Car Gris** serves Le Havre via Goderville (6 per day, 1 1/2hr., 37F) or via Etretat (6 per day, 11/2hr., 43F).

Compagnie Normande d'Autobus (tel. 35 84 21 97) runs to Rouen via Yvetot (1 per day, 2 3/4hr., 58F) and to Dieppe via St-Valéry-en-Caux (3 per day, 2 1/2hr., 58F). Trains run to Dieppe via Rouen (3 per day, 2hr., 94F); Le Havre (4 per day, 1 1/2hr., 39F); Paris (7 per day, 2 1/2hr., 137F); and Rouen (6 per day, 1 1/4hr., 57F). (Station open Mon.-Sat. 5:15-6:30am, 9am-12:15pm and 1:20-8:05pm, Sun. 7:45am-9pm.)

Fécamp's **Auberge de Jeunesse (HI),** above the town on rue du Commandant Roquigny (tel. 35 29 75 79), looks like a cement block outside but feels like a rustic mountain cabin inside. Turn right from the train station, cross the bridge, and go left onto Quai Guy-de-Maupassant, then take a right into the doorway marked "Sente aux Matelots," where thankful sailors began their climb to the the Chapelle above. You lucky dogs only have to ascend halfway; the hostel is to the left on rue du Commendant-Roquigny. (39F per person. HI card required. Camping 22F. Breakfast 16F. Sheets 15F. Kitchen facilities. Open May-Sept.) Ask at the tourist office for a list of hotels and their prices. One of the cheapest and friendliest is the **Hotel Martin,** 18, pl. St-Etienne (tel. 35 28 23 82). Conveniently located up the hill from the train station on the other side of Eglise St-Etienne, the hotel has cozy rooms upstairs from a restaurant even the locals recommend; its 78F, four-course *menu* comes served on platter-sized plates. (Singles and doubles from 90F, with shower from 110F.) Less appealing but closer to the train station, the **Hôtel Moderne de la Gare** (tel. 35 28 04 04), 3, av. Gambetta, has clean rooms. (Singles and doubles 95-115F, with shower 140-150F. Breakfast 23F.) **Hôtel de l'Univers** (tel. 35 28 05 88) 5, pl. St-Etienne features an ultra-space-saver shower in each room which swivels into its own fitted nook. (Singles 150-180F. Breakfast 25F.) Across town from the pl. St-Etienne and across the port from the hostel, the **Camping de Reneville** (tel. 35 28 20 97) roosts above a beautiful landscape over the beach. (Two people, tent, and car 32F. Small store. Laundry machines 20F.) If the Restaurant Martin (see Hôtel Martin) is too busy, try **Les Arcades,** 27, Pourtour du Marché (tel. 35 28 15 88), just two blocks from Eglise St-Etienne. Its 48F, four-course *menu* offers fish and mussels, a well as more earthly delights like beef and turkey. Try the superb 69F *menu* at **Le Mogador,** 7, rue du Vicomte, a rare treasure for excellent Norman seafood (open March-Sept. daily noon-11pm).

Those traveling along Normandy's coast should not forego the chance to visit the small but splendid resort of **Etretat.** Made famous by a series of Monet's paintings, Etretat's soaring white cliffs, the **Falaise d'Amont** and the **Falaise d'Aval,** are flanked by natural arches which extend like flying buttresses into the blue-green sea. The portals they create inspire the town's motto, *Mes portes sont toujours ouvertes.* ("My doors are always open.") A walk around the base of the Falaise d'Aval (possible only at low tide) reveals that the whole cliff has been honeycombed with block houses and gun emplacements now plastered with seaweed and barnacles. The steep hike up the cliffs from the beach brings breathless visitors to the **Chapelle des Marins** (sailors' chapel). The **tourist office,** pl. de la Mairie (tel. 35 27 05 21), provides free help with accommodations, a useful map of cliff foot paths, and a tide table that indicates the best times to explore the base of the cliffs. (Open daily 10am-7pm; Sept. 15-Nov. 11 and March 15-June 15 daily 10am-noon and 2-6pm; Nov. 11-March 15 Fri. 3-5pm, Sat. 10am-noon and 3-5pm, Sun. 10am-noon.) Hotel prices are as steep as the cliffs; ask the tourist office for a list of *chambres d'hôtes,* where families receive guests in their private homes. (Singles and doubles start at about 140F.) The **Hôtel de la Poste,** 6, av. Georges V (tel. 35 27 01 34), welcomes the weary with luxurious rooms and an expensive restaurant downstairs. (Singles 130F, with shower 200F. Doubles 150F, with shower 250F. Breakfast 25F.) The neon-lighted **Hôtel l'Escale,** pl. Maréchal Foch (tel. 35 27 03 69), offers small, but adequate rooms for 160F, with shower 220F; breakfast is 25F. The immaculate washrooms and flat, uninspired sites of Etretat's **campground** (tel. 35 27 07 67) lie inland 1km from town on rue Guy de Maupassant. (Gate closed 10pm-7:30am. Adults 10F, children 5F25. 10F per car and per tent. Open April-Sept.) For a healthful and inexpensive meal, try the filling salads (40-50F) at **le Pichet,** 51, rue Notre-Dame. (Open daily noon-2:30pm and 7-9:30pm; Sept.-June Sat.-Thurs. noon-2:30pm and 7-9:30pm.)

Dieppe

In 1030, the Vicomte Gosselin d'Arques de Cigare traded the port of Dieppe, along with five salt marshes and five farm houses, to the Abbey of Mont Ste-Catherine-les-Rouen in exchange for five thousand smoked herrings each year. Centuries later, Oscar Wilde, along with a deluge of British sun-seekers, found solace in the chalky white cliffs and pebbly beaches of this resort on the Channel. With its busy port, seaside relief, and thriving pedestrian district rebuilt after taking a beating during WWII, Dieppe is now one of the largest passenger ports in France and certainly worth more than five thousand fish. Much smaller and more inviting than Calais and Boulogne, the town is connected to England only by **Sealink** ferries. Those arriving by boat should get their francs on board; there is no currency exchange in Dieppe on Sunday or Monday.

Orientation and Practical Information

Dieppe is accessible by direct train from Rouen or from Paris's Gare St-Lazare. Service is most frequent on Sundays, when SNCF reduces the round-trip fare and when Parisians venture to sunbathe en masse. Sealink runs ferries from its terminal in the center of Dieppe to Newhaven. Their terminal is conveniently close to the center of town. **Grande Rue,** across from the terminal, is the main commercial street. The beach is two blocks to the right as you walk down Grande Rue from the ferry port. To get to the main train station, walk about ten minutes along quai Duquesne away from the terminal and the beach. The tourist office on Pont Jehan Ango is between the terminal and the station.

Tourist Office: Pont Jehan Ango (tel. 35 84 11 77), right next to Sealink's passenger terminal. Multilingual staff books rooms for 20F. The *Dieppe/Sealink* brochure lists hotel and restaurant prices, and also contains a map of the city. Open daily 9am-12:30pm and 1:30-7pm; Sept. 15-April Mon.-Sat. 9am-noon and 2-6pm.

Post Office: 2, bd. Maréchal Joffre (tel. 35 06 99 20). **Poste Restante. Currency exchange.** Open Mon.-Fri. 8am-6pm, Sat. 8am-noon. **Postal Code:** 76200.

Trains: bd. G. Clemenceau (tel. 35 84 28 92 for info.; tel. 35 98 50 50 for reservations). To: Paris St-Lazare via Rouen (8 per day, 2 1/2hr., 108F); Rouen (10 per day, 1hr., 47F); Caen (change at Rouen, 130F); Le Havre (change at Rouen, 97F). Ticket office open daily 6am-8pm. **Lockers** 5-10F. Information office open Mon.-Sat. 9am-12:30pm and 1:30-6:30pm.

Buses: Compagnie Normande d'Autobus (tel. 35 84 21 97), next to the train station. To Rouen (4 per day, 1 3/4hr., 58F40) and Fécamp (2 per day, 2hr., 62F). Buy tickets from the driver. Information office open Mon.-Sat. 9am-noon and 2-6pm. **Société des Transports Urbains Dieppois** (yes, **STUD**), 1, pl. Ventabren (tel. 35 84 49 49), runs buses throughout Dieppe and to the hostel and campgrounds. 5F90 for one ticket, 38F for 10 tickets *bleues*.

Ferries: Sealink, quai Henri IV, *gare maritime* (tel. 35 84 80 54). To Newhaven (4 per day, Jan.-April 3 per day; 3hr.; 260F one-way, students 220F, ages 4-14 140F, bicycles free). Information office open daily 9:30am-2pm and 3-6pm.

Laundromat: 48, rue de l'Ecosse. 16F wash, 5F per 10 min. dry. Open daily 7am-9pm. Stock up on 10F and 2F coins.

Hospital: av. Pasteur (tel. 35 06 76 76).

Ambulance: Charles, 14bis, rue Thiers (tel. 35 84 24 02). **Emergency: SAMU,** tel. 15.

Police: Bd. G. Clemenceau, next to the train station (tel. 35 84 87 32). **Emergency:** tel. 17.

Accommodations and Camping

Without a reservation, it will be tough to find a room here in summer. Start early in the day, call two or three days ahead, or try the tourist office's booking service.

Auberge de Jeunesse (HI), rue Louis Fromager (tel. 35 84 85 73). Closed for renovations in much of 1992, the hostel will most likely be open by summer 1993. Take bus #1 (direction "Les Bruyères") from in front of the station; ask the driver to drop you at the *auberge*. If walking, turn left outside the station, turn right on rue de la République, and then make a sharp left on rue Gambetta. Climb the hill, and bear right onto av. Jean Jaurès. Turn left on rue Fromager, and cross through the parking lot. The hostel will be on the right (25 min.). Some 3-4 person rooms. No lockout. Members only. 39F. Breakfast 15F. Kitchen facilities. Call ahead to determine renovation status.

Hôtel de la Jetée, 5, rue de l'Asile Thomas (tel. 35 84 89 98), near the beach. Large, sunny rooms, many with an ocean view and firm new mattresses. Delightfully amusing proprietor gestures enough to overcome any language barriers. Plenty of bathrooms and showers. 1- to 6-person rooms 115-160F. Breakfast 19F, with croissants 24F.

Chez Fanfan, Chemin de la Falaise (tel. 35 84 16 84), just behind Notre-Dame de Bonsecours. From the bus stop in front of the station, take bus #1 (direction: "4 Poteaux") or #8 (direction: "Puys") to the cliff top. Striking view overlooking the harbor. Plain singles and doubles 150-190F. Breakfast 25F. Restaurant and bar downstairs.

Hôtel au Grand Duquesne, 15, pl. St-Jacques (tel. 35 84 21 51). Decent rooms and proprietors. Singles and doubles 130F, with shower 160F. Breakfast 20F.

Camping: The wholesome **Camping Vitamin** (tel. 35 82 11 11) lies on the coast a few km from downtown Dieppe on chemin des Vertus. Take bus #2 (direction "Val Druel") or bus #10 (direction "St-Aubin-sur-Scie") from the station to Vasarely. Bar, café, swimming pool. 15F per person, 20F per tent. Showers included. Open year-round. The less luxurious but more economical **Camping Pré-St-Nicholas,** route de Pourville (tel. 35 84 11 39), rests atop a cliff 3km west of the city. Take bus #3 (direction "Golf") or bus #11 (direction "Pourville") from the station to the campground. Or walk the 25-min. climb from the station. 10F50 per person, 5F40 per tent. Rustic cold showers.

Food

Stay away from the touristy, overpriced neighborhood around the Sealink terminal, and look for the local fish specialties: *sole dieppoise, harengs marinés* (marinated herring), *soupe de poisson* (fish soup), and *marmite dieppoise* (a fish and shellfish chowder). Unlike Calais and Boulogne, which bombard British visitors with *friteries,* Dieppe offers authentic fare at decent prices. Near the hostel, **Restaurant Relais Gambetta,** 95, av. Gambetta (tel. 35 84 12 91), serves traditional *menus* from 58F (open Tues.-Sun. noon-2:30pm and 7-9:30pm). Make reservations. In town, **Les Ecamias,** 129, Quai Henri IV (tel. 35 84 67 67) offers a 55F three-course *menu* including salmon, ray (fish), and *filet dieppoise* (closed Mon.). **Crêperie,** 22, rue de la Morinière, off Grande Rue, flips a mouth-watering selection of *galettes* for 22-39F. Choose one of the internationally dubbed *galettes,* such as the *Irlandaise* (39F), made with *coquilles St-Jacques,* whiskey and cream (open Wed.-Mon. 11:30am-2pm and 6-10pm). **Bar-Pizzeria de L'Europe,** 57-61, rue d'Ecosse, serves a varied array of dishes from lasagna (34F) to *escargots* (28-42F; open daily noon-1:30pm and 7:30pm-12:30am). Always an attractive option for hardcore budget travelers, the **supermarkets** on rue Duquesne and near the hostel on rue Gambetta have...food!

Sights

Most of Dieppe's summer visitors come to roast on the long pebbly **beach,** bordered by protective cliffs to the west and the port to the east. Climb those same cliffs to find the 15th-century **château** (tel. 35 84 19 76), now the civic museum with a celebrated ivory collection, a sampling of impressionist paintings, and an exhibit of George Braque's prints. (Open daily 10am-noon and 2-6pm; mid-Sept. to May Wed.-Mon. Admission 12F, children 8F.)

In town, Dieppe's **Eglise St-Jacques** offers a cool stone refuge from the sun. Inside, the English influence reflects back to the 14th century in the flat vaults and the chapels. The entire structure was begun in 1182 and ravaged so often that it wasn't completed until 1543. German warplanes renewed the bombardment four centuries later. A somber reminder is the **Canadian Cemetery** in nearby Hautot-Sur-Mer, where each identified gravestone bears an individual poem or inscription. Turn right out of the hostel, walk 15 minutes, and then turn right at the cross and sign.

In even-numbered years, Dieppe takes two weeks in September to celebrate the **International Kite Festival.** 1994 will mark the eighth such event. Write Dieppe Capitale du Cerf-Volant, Les Tourelles, Bd. de Verdun, 76200, Dieppe, or call 16 32 90 04 95. Dieppe also hosts a **herring festival** during the second weekend in November.

At night, locals head for beer at the **Cambridge Arms Pub,** 2, rue de l'Epée. (Open Tues.-Sun. 9pm-2am; Oct.-March Tues.-Sun. 9pm-1am.) The more energetic may prefer **Djin's Club** (tel. 35 82 33 60), Dieppe's only disco, at the **Casino,** 3, bd. de Verdun. (Open Tues.-Sat. 10pm-4am. Admission Thurs.-Fri. 60F, Sat. 80F, Tues.-Wed. 50F.)

Le Havre

Whether you approach Le Havre (pop. 200,000) by land or sea, the smog and glut of the refineries, warehouses, and factories that line the docks of France's largest transatlantic port will overwhelm you. Most cruise ships from North America stop here, as do car ferries from Rosslare and Cork in Ireland and Portsmouth in England.

Although he renamed the city "Bouville" ("Mudville") in his novel *La Nausée,* Jean-Paul Sartre thoroughly enjoyed pre-war Le Havre's pastel-colored *vieille ville* and smoky port cafés. Bombed to rubble during WWII, Le Havre has since become an experiment in French civic design. The rebuilding of the city was entrusted to architect Auguste Perret, the "magician of concrete," whose designs produced sprawling complexes, sharply geometric war monuments, and a spartan church. Perret's **Eglise St-Joseph,** with its cavernous interior and 107m steeple, exudes an appealing gloom. The **Musée des Beaux Arts-André Malraux,** on bd. J.F. Kennedy (tel. 35 42 33 97), houses a well-displayed collection of canvases by Ernest Boudin and Norman impressionists, as well as many works by Dufy, Pissarro, Monet, Sisley, and others. (Open Wed.-Mon. 10am-noon and 2-6pm. Free.) The huge white structure resembling an overturned toilet in l'Espace Oscar Niemeyer, pl. Gambetta, is actually the **Maison de la Culture du Havre** (tel. 35 21 21 10). Whatever its shape may imply, it contains a state-of-the-art theater and cinema, which admits students to showings of classic and new films for only 20F. Unfortunately, the theater and cinema are closed mid-June through August. Note the gossamer pedestrian suspension bridge that arches gracefully above the basin in front of the Maison de la Culture, suggesting ever-so-slightly that modern urban planning has its merits.

Orientation and Practical Information

Le Havre sprawls at the mouth of the Seine River, bordered by beach on one edge and piers on the other. The large avenues of bd. de Strasbourg and rue de Paris intersect at **pl. de l'Hôtel de Ville.** Straight down av. Foch, across from bd. de Strasbourg, is the port and the beginning of a rocky stretch of **beach.**

The train station lies east of the center of town and is an easy walk down bd. de Strasbourg. The P&O European ferry terminal lies on the southern side of town. To get to the tourist office from here, take bus #3 from Perrey or walk down rue de Paris for about 10 minutes. The Irish Ferries terminal lies much farther to the southeast. The long walk takes you through a dangerous neighborhood; take the ferry's bus that runs between the terminal and the station (5F50). Those arriving by ferry should change money on board as the terminal itself has no currency exchange.

Tourist Office: Inside the Hôtel de Ville (tel. 35 21 22 88). Turn left from the station onto bd. de Strasbourg, and walk for about 10min., or take bus #1, 3, 4, 5, 6, or 12 from outside the train station. Accommodations service 5F. Open Mon.-Sat. 8:45am-12:15pm and 1:30-7pm; Nov.-March 8:45am-12:15pm and 1:30-6:30pm.

American Express: 57, quai Georges V (tel. 35 42 59 11). Open Mon.-Fri. 8:45am-noon and 1:30-6pm.

Post Office: rue Jules-Siegfried (tel. 35 42 45 67). **Poste Restante. Currency Exchange.** Open Mon.-Fri. 8am-7pm, Sat. 8am-noon. **Postal Code:** 76600.

Trains: cours de la République (tel. 35 43 50 50). Information office open Mon-Sat. 8:30am-6:30pm. Ticket office open Mon.-Sat. 5:15am-8:15pm, Sun. 5:15am-9pm. To: Paris St-Lazare (12 per day, 2 1/2hr., 139F); Rouen (12 per day, 1hr., 63F); Fécamp (3 per day, 1hr., 39F). **Luggage storage** (23F) open daily 5:15am-8:40pm.

Buses: bd. de Strasbourg (tel. 35 26 67 23), across from the train station. **CNA.** To: Rouen (4 per day, 2 1/2hr., 72F50) via St-Romain, Bolbec, Lillebonne, Caudebec, and Duclair. **Bus Verts** runs to Caen (3 per day, 2 1/2hr., 108F50), Deauville, and Honfleur via Pont Route de Tancarville. **Car Gris** serves Fécamp (via Etretat, 4 per day, 1 1/2hr., 43F; via Goderville, 4 per day, 1 1/2hr., 37F90). Information office open Mon.-Fri. 8am-noon and 2-5:15pm.

Public Transportation: Bus Océane, 115, rue Jules Lecesne (tel. 35 19 75 75) and at the kiosk, pl. de l'Hôtel de Ville, next to the tourist office. Frequent service. 5F50 per trip; 15F *Ticket Ville* allows one day's unlimited travel within the city; *carnet bleu* (37F) covers 10 trips. Most bus service stops after 9pm.

Ferries: P&O European Ferries, quai de Southampton (tel. 35 21 36 50). Bus #3 from the train station or the Hôtel de Ville. To Portsmouth, England (3 per day; 6hr., 7hr. at night; 270F, ages over 60 250F, children 130F). Reductions for night travel in July and Aug. You can reserve cabins on both day and night ferries. Ticket and information office open Mon.-Sat. 7am-noon and 2-11:30pm. **Irish Ferries,** quai du Môle Central (tel. 35 53 28 83). Take bus #4 from the Hôtel de Ville or the train station to stop "Marceau." To Rosslare or Cork, Ireland. (Alternates destinations. June 1-June 30, July 1-July 9, Aug. 15-Aug 31, Sept. 1-Sept 30, 3 per week, 22hr., 625F, students 588F; July 10-Aug. 14, 3 per week, 836F, students 798F; Oct.-May, 2 per week, 413F, students 357F. Eurailpass valid.)

Taxis: Radio-Taxis, at the train station, (tel. 35 25 81 81).

Laundromat: 23, rue Jean de la Fontaine, near the *gare maritime.* 14F per wash, 2F per 6 min. dry.

Women's Center: Foyer des Jeunes Femmes, 29, rue du Mont Joly (tel. 35 24 02 95).

Hospital: Centre Hospitalier du Havre, 29, av. Pierre Mendés France, Montivilliers (tel. 35 55 25 25).

Medical Emergency: SAMU, tel. 15. Central Ambulance, tel. 35 21 33 33.

Police: Rue de la Victoire (tel. 35 21 77 00). **Emergency:** tel. 17.

Accommodations, Camping, and Food

Avoid walking alone at night in Le Havre, especially around the areas near the station and the port.

Union Chrétienne des Jeunes Gens, 153, bd. de Strasbourg (tel. 35 42 47 86; look for the triangular neon sign). Close to the train station. A centrally located YMCA *foyer* for French workers that usually has room. Dorm-like facility with English-speaking staff. Bare rooms. Cafeteria serves breakfast and lunch Mon.-Sat. (*plats du jour* 30-35F). Call ahead or show up at 5pm to book a room. Reception open daily 7am-10:30pm. Singles 45F. Doubles 38F per person.

Hôtel Jeanne d'Arc, 91, rue Emile-Zola (tel. 35 41 26 83), off rue de Paris across the bridge from the tourist office, in the center of town. A homey atmosphere, with banistered landings, heavy dining-room tables, and big showers. Rooms are light and clean. Singles from 105F. Doubles from 115F. Breakfast 17F50.

Hôtel Séjour Fleuri, 71, rue Emile-Zola (tel. 35 41 33 81). Pleasant hotel with comfortable but small rooms. Singles and doubles 100-130F, with shower 145F. Breakfast 20F.

Camping Municipal du Havre (tel. 35 46 52 39). From the station, take bus #1, 8, or 11 (all stop running around 9pm) to pl. Jenner and walk the last 20 min. to the northeast corner of the park. Hot showers, ping-pong, and a nearby grocery store accessorize this wooded site. 1-2 people, tent, and car 41F. Gates closed 11pm-6:30am. Open April 15-Sept. 30.

The small streets between rue de Paris and quai Lamblardie frame a haven of neighborhood restaurants. **Le Tilbury,** 39, rue Jean de la Fontaine, serves an elegant 72F *menu* and a delicious 3-course 52F luncheon. (Open Tues.-Fri. noon-1:30pm and 7-10pm, Sat. 7-10pm, Sun. noon-1:30pm.) At **Le P'tit Comptoir,** rue Jean de la Fontaine at av. Faidherbe, by the port, sailors and executives rub elbows over the hearty 56F and 78F *menus* (open daily 10am-2pm and 7-10pm). Down the street, **Restaurant La Salamandre,** 33, rue Jean de la Fontaine, serves varied *crêpes* and *galettes* (8-40F) (open Tues.-Sat. noon-2pm and 7-11pm). The **Maison des Jeunes et de la Culture,** 2, av. Foch (tel. 35 42 66 97), across from the beach and 10 minutes from the Hôtel de Ville, is a three-tiered rumhouse of activity. The second-floor restaurant is lively and offers a 30F *plat garni* (open Mon.-Fri. 12:30am-2:30pm, Sat. 11:30am-1pm). The first-floor cafeteria stocks daily newspapers (open Sept.-July Tues.-Sat. noon-8pm, Mon. noon-2pm), and mounts a *cabaret de jazz* one Friday each month from September through May at 8:30pm. On the third floor, expositions of modern art and photography are free to the public. Take bus #2 from the Hôtel de Ville to "Porte Océane."

Coast: Lower Normandy

In contrast to Normandy's working port cities—like Dieppe, Le Havre, Cherbourg, and even Fécamp—the cities along the Fleurie Coast are decidedly playful. Communities of casinos and beach umbrellas dot the wide sandy stretches between Honfleur and Cabourg. Doubling as resort towns and thalassotherapy centers (Deauville for cellulite, Trouville for neurological problems), these coastal towns have served as weekend destinations for Paris's healthy and ailing elite since the mid-19th century. Today they cater to a more international crowd, which means the tourist office staff won't turn up its nose at your miserable French. Of course, such hospitality doesn't come cheap. This is a resort town, darling. You'll find no such thing as a budget hotel and certainly no free lunches, although the beach is *compris*.

Consider, therefore, making the hostel or a cheap hotel in **Caen** your touring base. **Bus Verts du Calvados** (tel. 31 44 77 44 in Caen, 31 89 28 41 in Honfleur, and 31 88 95 36 in Deauville) serves the entire region from Caen to Le Havre and west to Bayeux. Bus #20 runs along the coast. The region is divided into zones and the fare varies with the number of zones crossed; one zone costs 4F50. Tickets are sold for a minimum of two-zone travel. Be sure to ask about youth reductions, and consider a *Carte Liberté* if you will be traveling extensively in the region. It allows unlimited travel for 3 days (100F) or 7 days (207F), but is not accepted on the InterNormandie buses between Le Havre and Honfleur. It secures reductions at some museums and free use of Caen's city buses. Remember that weekend service is infrequent.

Honfleur manages to shun the Fleurie coast's resort town image; of course, technically it is not even on the Fleurie coast. Twenty km north of the coast via the Corniche Normande, Honfleur first served a purpose during the Hundred Years War when its proximity to the English Channel made it an important military port. When the war ended, municipal leaders decided to rebuild the devastated town, and to add a new church to the urban landscape. As the town's masons were occupied with the general reconstruction, Honfleur's many shipbuilders undertook the church project, completing the remarkable ceiling of the wooden **Eglise Ste-Catherine** as they would have the hull of an overturned ship. (Open daily 9am-noon and 2-6pm.) During the 16th and 17th centuries, the town witnessed the embarkation of several important voyages of discovery, most notably Samuel de Champlain's journey leading to the 1608 founding of Québec City. During the 19th century, Honfleur was seen in a new light, as the paintings of Eugène Boudin and the Ferme St-Siméon became popular. Today, visitors flock to the **Musée Eugène Boudin,** at pl. Erik Satie off rue de l'Homme de Bois (tel. 31 89 54 00), to see an impressive collection of Boudin's work and that of his contemporaries. (Open Wed.-Mon. 10am-6:30pm; Sept. and March 16-June Wed.-Mon. 10am-noon and 2-6pm; Oct.-March 15 Mon. and Wed.-Fri. 2:30-5pm, Sat.-Sun. 10am-noon and 2:30-5pm. Admission 35F, students 28F.) Those visiting Honfleur during Pentecost will see the **Fêtes des Marins:** on Sunday, all the town's boats line up in the estuary to receive a blessing. The following day sailors, townspeople, and children carrying model ships make the age-old pilgrimage to the **Chapelle-Notre-Dame-de-Grâce,** where mariners have given thanks since the 11th century.

The **tourist office,** 33, pl. Arthur-Boudin (tel. 31 89 23 30), is a short walk from the bus station on rue de la Ville. (Open Mon.-Sat. 9am-12:30pm and 2-6:30pm, Sun. 10am-noon and 3-5pm; Nov.-Easter Mon.-Sat. 9am-noon and 2-5pm.) Ask for a list of **chambres d'hôtes**, whose prices range from 120-200F per night. Otherwise the only tenable option is the seaside **Le Phare campsite** (tel. 31 89 10 26), about 300m from the *centre ville* at the end of rue Haute. (Reception open 8:30am-12:30pm and 2-7:30pm. 20F per adult, 12F per child, 30F per tent or car. Open April-Sept.) Honfleur's other campsite, **La Briquerie** (tel. 31 89 28 32) is 3km from town. Take the bus (9F40) to Equemauville. (23F per adult, 12F per child, 22F per tent or car. Open April-Sept.)

Restaurant prices mirror hotel prices: expensive. **Le Goéland,** 21, rue de la Ville, near the bus station, serves *galettes* and a delicious 68F *menu* including such house specialties as almond trout, marinated mussels, and escalloped duck (open Feb.-Nov. daily noon-10pm). Look at Honfleur's many **boulangeries** for a loaf of tough-crusted Normandy bread.

South of Honfleur, **Deauville** and **Trouville** mark the northern edge of the Fleurie coast. Twin cities which continue to attract an international elite to their broad, gorgeous beaches and grand casinos, they are particularly well-known to equestrians; Deauville's annual yearling auctions are world-famous. The two racetracks clamor from June to August (admission 22F, Sun. 33F). Consult one of the **tourist offices** for schedules. Deauville's is at pl. de la Mairie (tel. 31 88 21 43). Cut diagonally left on rue Désire-Le-Hoc from the train station. (Open Mon.-Sat. 9am-12:30pm and 2-7pm, Sun. 10:30am-1pm and 3:30-6pm.) To get to Trouville's tourist office, 22-36, bd. F. Moureaux (tel. 31 88 36 19), take a right over the bridge from the train station and turn left onto the main *rue*. (Open May-Sept. daily 9am-12:15pm and 2-6:30pm.) **SNCF trains** (tel. 31 83 50 50) run to Paris (2 per day, 2hr., 137F) and to Caen (2 per day, 2hr., 58F), although from October to May, service is limited to weekends. **Bus Verts** (tel. 31 88 95 36) also stops at the train station.

Restaurants and hotel prices are exorbitant. Even *chambres d'hôtes* generally cost 200F per night. But **Les Charmettes,** 22, rue de la Chapelle, two blocks from Trouville's beach (tel. 31 88 11 67), offers linoleum hallways and pretty rooms with street and ocean views. (Singles 120F, with shower 160F. Doubles 150F, with shower 180F. Breakfast 25F.) Those who plan ahead can reserve space at Trouville's **Camping Hamel,** 55, rue des Soeurs de l'Hôpital (tel. 31 88 15 56). Follow rue d'Agnesseau and rue d'Estimauville from the *place* at the foot of the bridge. (9F per person, 4F per tent or car. Open April-Sept.) Ask at the tourist office about other area campgrounds.

The seaside resorts west of Deauville are less pretentious and more inviting. **Houlgate** has a casino right in the middle of town and a 1.5 km sandy beach, perhaps the most attractive in the area. An enjoyable hour's walk east along the beach toward Deauville takes you to the **Vache Noire cliffs,** named for the black color of the exposed crumbling limestone containing fossil deposits of ancient crustaceans. A tide table is available at Houlgate's **tourist office** (tel. 31 24 34 79), next to the town hall on bd. des Belges. (Open Mon.-Sat. 10am-noon and 2:30-5pm.) There is an **annex** (tel. 31 24 62 31) just off the beach next to the casino (open Mon.-Sat. 10:30am-1pm and 2:30-5:30pm; Sept.-June Sat.-Sun. same hours). Hotel prices tend to rise with the temperature in July and August. As usual, ask for a list of *chambres d'hôtes* at the tourist office, but it's hard to beat **Hôtel Mon Castel,** 1, bd. des Belges (tel. 31 24 83 47). Between the tourist office and the beach, the hotel has spacious rooms, kept clean and bright by its friendly and energetic owners. (Singles and doubles 150F, with shower 175F. Breakfast 28F.) Overlooking Houlgate beach is **Camping de la Plage,** rue Henri Dobert (tel. 31 91 61 25). (16F per adult, 9F50 per child, 9F50 per tent, 8F50 per car. Open April-Sept.) **Club Oasis,** on the beach, rents windsurfers in July and August. The very excellent restaurant at **Hôtel Mon Castel** delights with 55F, 80F, 105F, and 150F *menus* featuring Norman seafood specialities. (Open daily noon-2pm and 7-9pm.) Locals cling like barnacles to **La Maison du Coquillage,** 37, rue des Bains, for heaping platters of stuffed oysters and mussels, sole *à la normande,* lobster, and crab. (Three-course *menus* from 70F. Open daily 11am-10pm.)

Still farther down the coast, Cabourg, the port from which William the Conqueror set sail for England in 1066, has since evolved into a tourist destination of imperial proportions, having been a favorite vacation spot of Napoleon III and Empresse Eugénie. Marcel Proust, after whom the town named its seaside promenade, spent many summers penning his *A la Recherche du Temps Perdu* at Cabourg's beachfront **Grand Hôtel.** The **tourist office,** Jardins du Casino (tel. 31 91 01 09), lies immediately in front of the hotel at the edge of its gardens. (Open daily 9am-7pm; Sept.-June Mon.-Sat. 9:30am-12:30pm and 2-6:30pm, Sun. 10am-12:30pm and 2:30-6pm.) Across the Dives River, the Dives-Cabourg **train station** (tel. 31 91 00 74) serves Paris-St-Lazare (2 per day, 2hr., 167F) and Deauville (2 per day, hr., 22F), although from October to mid-June trains run only on weekends. **Bus Verts** frequents Cabourg year-round. Check any of the seven stops for schedules to Caen, Houlgate, Honfleur, Deauville, Trouville, and Le Havre. Buy your ticket from your driver. Rent **bikes** at the train station (55F per day, 1000F deposit) or at the **Bureau de Bains** (tel. 31 91 27 00) on the beach side of the Grand Hôtel (3-speeds only; 80F per day, 400F per week, 1000F deposit; open April-Sept. daily 9am-7pm).

The **Hôtel au Bon Coin**, 23, av. du Commandant Bertaux-Levillain (tel. 31 91 03 64), across from the "8 mai" bus stop, is easily the best hotel deal in town, offering nondescript rooms at agreeable prices. (Singles and doubles 110F, with shower or bath 140-180F. Breakfast 25F.) **Camping Plage,** rue Charles de Gaulle (tel. 31 91 05 75), has prices in keeping with its perks; beach-front location and laundry, tennis, and restaurant facilities. (27F per adult, 17F per child, 47F per tent and car. Open April to mid-Nov.) The smaller **Oasis Camping**, rue Charles de Gaulle (tel. 31 91 10 62), farther down the road from Camping Plage, is an adequate alternative. (16F per adult, 11F per child, 24F per tent or car. Open April to mid-Sept.) For a satisfying meal after a day in the sun, try **Le Champagne,** pl. du Marché (tel. 31 91 02 29), with three-course *menus* starting at 60F, *à la carte* 40-70F. (Open daily noon-2pm and 7-9pm; Sept. to mid-June open Tues.-Sat. noon-2pm and 7-9pm.) Many pizzerias and *crêperies* flank av. de la Mer, but lobsters (50F), oysters (30F for 6 and 40F for 12), and tortoises (30F) lurk two blocks away at **L'Ecailler du Romantique,** 8, av. Piat. (Take-out window open daily 10am-3pm or call 31 24 10 92 from 10am-10pm to order. Prices nearly double if you eat in the restaurant.)

Caen

"One moment it was there; the next, the whole town—parks, churches, shops—dissolved into a pile of dust." So gasped an American soldier to reporters in 1944. Gutted in World War II, the capital of Lower Normandy has reemerged as a vivacious and proud city of 113,000 and a major rail and ferry hub. Norman politics have focused around Caen ever since William the Conqueror based his duchy here from 1035 to 1087. The red flag with two gold lions that still flies above the castle was the standard of the Dukes of Normandy and was later incorporated into the English flag by the Plantagenet kings. Today, Caen is placid but politically aware, tinged with an air of scholarship by the cafés, bookstores, and students encircling the château.

Orientation and Practical Information

Caen is served frequently by trains from Paris's St-Lazare. The station and the youth hostel are on the south side of the Orne River, far enough from the *centre ville* that you will probably want to take the bus (5F50); you might even consider a day pass (14F). (Remember that the Bus Verts *carte liberté* grants access to Caen's city buses.) All of the buses leaving from immediately in front of the train station stop in the vicinity of Eglise St-Pierre and the *centre ville*. Try to get a map at the CTAC kiosk before heading into the city. From the station, the parallel av. du 6-juin and rue St-Jean run northwest to the *centre ville*.

Tourist Office: pl. St-Pierre (tel. 31 86 27 65), by the Eglise St-Pierre. Accommodations service (12F). Proffers itineraries covering all of Lower Normandy's "cider routes" as well as other rural biking routes in the region. Free town map (the more detailed one costs 21F). Guided tours of the city (July-Aug. 2 per day, 35F, children 20F). **Currency exchange.** Open Sat. 9am-7pm, Sun. 10am-12:30pm and 3-6pm; mid-Sept. to May Mon. 10am-noon and 2-7pm, Tues.-Sat. 9am-noon and 2-7pm. **Information booth** at train station open June-Aug. Mon.-Fri. 9am-1pm and 2-6pm.

Post Office: pl. Gambetta (tel. 31 39 35 93) **Currency Exchange. Poste Restante.** Open Mon.-Fri. 8am-7pm, Sat. 8am-noon. **Postal Code:** 14000.

Trains: pl. de la Gare (tel. 31 83 50 50). To: Paris (17 per day, 2hr., 148F); Rouen (4 per day, 1 1/2hr., 107F); Cherbourg (8 per day, 1 1/2hr., 90F); Rennes (2 per day, 3hr., 158F); Tours (6 per day, 3 1/2hr., 162F). **Lockers** (5-10F, 3-day max.). Information office open Mon.-Sat. 7:30am-7:30pm. Station open daily 5am-9:30pm.

Buses: To the left of the train station (tel. 31 44 77 44). This is the central terminal for the **Bus Verts,** which covers the Calvados region from Le Havre to Carentan. To: Bayeux (2 per day, 1hr., 32F90); Le Havre (2 per day, 2 1/2hr., 108F10); Deauville (3-4 per day, 1hr., 47F); Falaise (2 per day, 1hr., 37F60). Office open Mon.-Fri. 7am-7pm Sat.-Sun. 9am-6pm. **City Buses: CTAC** (tel. 31 84 42 76). Information booth outside station. One ticket 5F50, unlimited 1-day travel 14F, *carnet* of 10 44F.

Ferries: Brittany Ferries: B.P. 109 (tel. 31 36 36 00), in Ouistreham, 13km north of Caen. To Portsmouth, England (April-Dec. 3 per day, Jan.-March 1-2 per day, 6hr., Aug. 8-30 290F, May 29-Aug. 7 and Aug. 31-Sept. 13 and weekends through Oct. 190F, Sept. 14-May 28, 150F). These one way fares allow you to return to France within 60hr. at no extra cost. Bus Verts links Ouistreham to Caen's *centre ville* and train station. **English Bookstore:** 3 shelves in a corner at **FNAC,** Centre Paul Doumer on rue Doumer. Open Mon. 2-7pm, Tues.-Fri. 10am-7pm, Sat. 9:30am-7pm.

Laundromat: Lavamatic, 103, bd. Maréchal-Lyantey, just a few blocks from the hostel. Wash 15F, dry 2F per 6min. Open daily 7:30am-8pm. **Women's Center: Foyer l'Oasis,** 18, rue de l'Oratoire (tel. 31 86 04 22).

Ambulance: SAMU (tel. 31 34 35 36). **Emergency:** tel. 15.

Hospital: Hôpital Clemenceau, av. Côte de Nacre (tel. 31 06 31 06).

Police: rue Jean Romain (tel. 31 30 45 50). **Emergency:** tel. 17.

Accommodations and Camping

In addition to the youth hostel, there are plenty of pleasant, reasonable hotels and student accommodations in Caen. In summer, the inexpensive hostel and university housing fill quickly, so call ahead and reserve if possible.

Auberge de Jeunesse (HI), Foyer Robert Reme, 68bis, rue Eustache-Restout (tel. 31 52 19 96). From the station, walk right, take a left up the hill at the end of the street and catch bus #5 or #17 (direction: "Fleury" or "Grâce de Dieu") to "Lycée Fresnel." A 25-min. walk from the station, 40min. from the *centre ville.* Clean and recently renovated hostel and workers' dormitory. Two- and four-person rooms have showers and kitchen facilities. Snack bar and adjacent restaurant. Reception open June-Sept. daily 7-10am and 5-10pm. Lockout 10am-5pm. Members only. 60F. Breakfast included.

Centre International de Séjour, (tel. 31 95 41 00), at the "la Cité" bus stop, 5km north of town in Hérouville-St-Clair. Take bus #15 from the station to "la Cité." Spacious, carpeted singles 95F, with shower 126F. HI members 74F, with shower 90F. Breakfast 15F.

University Housing: CROUS, 23, av. de Bruxelles (tel. 31 94 73 37), north of the château at "Bruxelles" bus stop. Reception open Mon.-Fri. 9am-12:15pm and 1:45-4pm. No curfew. Adequte singles 40F. Call ahead to inquire then confirm in writing, as phone reservations aren't accepted.

Hôtel de la Paix, 14, rue Neuve-St-Jean (tel. 31 86 18 99), off av. du 6 Juin. Well-located with a helpful proprietor. Comfortable singles 100F, with shower 140F. Doubles 110F, with shower 160F. Showers 20F. Breakfast 20F.

Hôtel Auto-Bar, 40, rue de Bras (tel. 31 86 12 48), off rue de Strasbourg one block from rue St-Pierre. Singles and doubles, 70-90F. Breakfast 17F50.

Hôtel St-Jean, 20, rue des Martyrs (tel. 31 86 23 35), next to Eglise St-Jean. Quiet setting with clean and modern rooms. Private parking. Singles and doubles with shower 130-160F. Breakfast 18F.

Camping: Terrain Municipal, rte. de Louvigny (tel. 31 73 60 92). Take bus #13 (direction: "Louvigny") to "Camping." Willow-shaded sights near the river. Reception open 8am-noon and 6-9:45pm, Sun. 8am-noon and 6-10pm. 9F per person, 5F per tent or car. Open May-Oct.

Food

Crêperies, brasseries, and ethnic restaurants all line the picturesque cobblestone streets of the **quartier Vaugueux** near the château. Nearby, pl. Courtonne stages the colorful morning market (Tues.-Sat.). Culinary daredevils should seek out *tripes à la mode de Caen*—stomachs of ox cooked in an earthenware pot with vegetables, herbs, and *calvados*.

> **La Petite Auberge,** 17, rue des Equipes-d'Urgence next to Eglise St-Jean. Excellent Norman-style *menus*. The 3-course 55F *menu* includes a warm goat cheese salad and oysters. Open Tues.-Sat. noon-2pm and 7-9pm, Sun. 7-9pm.

> **La Couscousserie,** 12, rue du Vaugueux. An extensive wine list accompanies a selection of meats and *couscous* (48-70F). Refined atmosphere in a picturesque house. Open Tues.-Sun. 8pm-midnight.

> **Au Petit Chef,** 40, rue de l'Oratoire. An inexpensive and popular *crêperie* with wide-ranging selections. *Crêpes* from 13F, *galettes* from 15F, omelettes from 19F. Open Mon.-Sat. 11am-2:30pm and 6:30-10:30pm.

> **La Toscane,** 17, rue Porte du Berger, just a block from La Couscousserie in the *quartier Vaugueux*. Enjoy pizza from 38F, pasta and salads from 48F in a cozy corner of the city. Open Mon.-Fri. noon-1:30pm and 7-11pm, Sat. 7-11pm.

Sights and Entertainment

Great prosperity under William the Conqueror in the late 11th century left Caen a legacy of fine Romanesque architecture. The emperor's reign coincided with the rekindled acceptance of Christianity by Norman dukes and the subsequent reopening of monasteries and erection of new churches across the region. To atone for the sin of marrying his cousin Mathilda, and to demonstrate his rapidly expanding hegemony, William ordered the construction of several ecclesiastical structures, most notably Caen's twin abbeys, begun in 1066. The first, **Abbaye-aux-Hommes,** off rue Guillaume le Conquérant, was founded as a down payment on William's bid for heaven. Rebuilt in the 18th century, the abbey served as a *lycée* (high school), and now functions as Caen's Hôtel de Ville. (Tours in French daily every hr. 9am-noon and 2-5pm. Admission 10F.) The smaller and less ornate **Eglise de la Trinité** of the **Abbaye-aux-Dames,** off rue des Chanoines (Mathilda's penance for her part in William's sin), has a Romanesque interior and two 16th-century towers. To visit the crypt, enter through the low doorway in the south transept. (Open daily 9am-noon and 2-6pm. Free guided visits, in French only, daily 2:30 and 4pm.)

Within the ruins of William's imposing **château** (open daily 6am-9:30pm; Oct.-April 6am-7:30pm) is the modern **Musée des Beaux Arts** (tel. 31 85 28 63), containing a few paintings by Perugino, Rubens, van Dyck, and Monet, as well as van der Weyden's outstanding *La Vièrge à l'Enfant,* and a collection of modern works. (Open Wed.-Mon. 10am-noon and 1:30-6pm; Sept.-May 10am-noon and 1:30-5:30pm. Free.) The **Musée de Normandie** (tel. 31 86 06 24), across the way, traces Norman peasant life through the years, focusing on the past two centuries of *cidre* and *calvados* production with a glance at lace- and candle-making. (Open Wed.-Fri. 10am-12:30pm and 1:30-6pm; April-Sept. Sat.-Mon. 9:30am-12:30pm and 2-6pm. Admission 10F, students 5F. Wed. free.)

Caen boasts seven noteworthy churches scattered throughout the city. In the shadow of the château stands **Eglise St-Pierre,** whose famous bell tower and detailed exterior illustrate the evolution of the Gothic style from the 13th through the 16th centuries. (Open daily 9am-noon and 2-6pm.) Straight down rue St-Pierre at the west end of the city stands **Eglise St-Etienne,** which dates from the 11th to the 13th centuries. The church blends the Romanesque and Gothic schools of architecture; its sober façade opens into a beautifully intricate interior. (Open daily 8:15am-noon and 2-7:30pm.)

Commemorating a later era of turbulence, the powerful **Mémorial: Un Musée pour la Paix** (tel. 31 06 06 44), presides over manicured lawns in the north of the city. This fascinating museum incorporates a unique array of actual footage, high-tech audio-visual aids, and displays from the pre-war years in Europe as well as the Battle of Normandy and the liberation of France. A spectacular futuristic tunnel details the accomplishments of Nobel Peace Prize laureates through innovative displays with drama and flair. The entire visit considers the demanding question, "Dictionaries have always defined a country in peace as a country which is not at war. Will the approaching 21st century be able to find any better definition?" From the *centre ville,* take bus #17 (direction: "Mémorial") to Mémorial. (Open daily 9am-10pm; Sept.-May 9am-7pm. Admission 45F.)

Caen's **Université,** founded in 1432 by England's Henry VI, lies north of the château, left along the ramparts to rue du Gaillon. Unlike most French universities, all the buildings concentrate within a clearly defined campus. The iron phoenix at the entrance symbolizes the university's rebirth after its destruction in 1944. The students make way for the plentiful tourists who wander the nearby paths of the expansive and bucolic **Jardin des Plantes** on pl. Blot (open 8am-sunset).

Caen's staid old streets pulsate by moonlight, especially those that wind around the château by the university. At the **Pub Concorde,** 7, rue Montoir Poissonnerie (tel. 31 93 61 29), the "century-and-a-half-club" samples 150 beers from around the world. (Open Mon.-Sat. 9pm-4am.) Locals frequent the **Retro Piano-Bar,** 9, rue Fresnel (tel. 31 44 09 19), for its mellow atmosphere, and nightly jazz concerts. (Open Tues.-Sat. 8:30pm-2am.) At **Le Chic,** 19, pl. Courtonne (tel. 31 94 48 72), a younger crowd shimmies to disco and house music. (Open Tues.-Wed. 10pm-1am, Thurs.-Sat. 10pm-4am. Cover with first drink 40F.) *Le Mois à Caen,* lists plays, concerts, and exhibitions for the month. Free copies are available at the youth hostel or at the student center, **CROUS,** 23, av. de Bruxelles (tel. 31 94 73 37). For a less sophisticated, albeit more colorful evening adventure, check out Caen's **Point Ball & Co.,** 57, av. de Tourville (tel. 31 95 08 08), where friends and strangers alike have good, not-so-clean fun stalking one another with paint guns. (Indoor and outdoor facilities. Open Mon.-Sat. 2pm-midnight, Sun. by reservation. Admission 110F, students 90F.) If you've lost your shirt at a coastal casino, you might browse the **Kilo Shop,** 21-23, rue Paul Doumer, where American-style clothing is sold by the kilogram. (100F per kg. Most shirts 12-40F, jeans 70F, jackets 120F).

Near Caen: Let's Go Bungy Jumping

When castles, beaches, churches, museums, spectacular views, wine tastings, weddings, deadlines, papers, boyfriends, or girlfriends get to be a drag, some people head to France's first bungy jumping facility for some (not-so-)cheap thrills. (First jump 480F, students 420F, additional jumps 250F; Nov.-March first jump 400F, students 350F, additional 250F. Includes 4 free photos; video of your jump 190F.) For information, write to A. J. Hackett-Bungy, Viaduc de la Soulevre, 14350 La Ferrière-Harang (tel. 31 67 37 38).

Getting to the site requires some planning. **Trains** run as close as Vire (8 per day from Paris, 3hr., 161F), as do Bus Verts **buses** (3 per day from Caen, 1hr., 65F80). From Vire, a taxi to the site costs about 100F. If driving, follow the RN175 from Caen. Make a left onto the D56, and follow it for 5km to the Viaduc de la Soulevre.

The newly renovated **Hôtel de France** (tel. 31 68 63 10), subsists entirely on the bungy industry and is the only hotel in **Le Bény Bocage,** the closest town to the site. (Bunks 100F per night, spacious doubles with bathroom 260F. Breakfast 25F.) The *restaurant gastronomique* below serves filling *menus.* **Camping** is also available; ask for information at the hotel.

Bayeux

Bayeux (pop. 15,000) is famous for its tapestry, an 11th-century linen embroidery nearly a football field long, depicting the Norman invasion of Britain in 1066. By a fortuitous error in German strategic planning, Bayeux suffered no damage from World War II bombings, and was one of the first cities to be liberated in 1944. Today, the city basks in the prosperity of its surrounding fertile farms and its burgeoning tourist trade. A beautifully preserved and ancient town, Bayeux also makes a convenient base for exploring the commemorative cemeteries of the surrounding area as well as the landing beaches of the allied invasion of Normandy on D-Day, 1944.

Orientation and Practical Information

Bayeux is on the Caen-Rennes and Paris-Cherbourg train lines. The station is about 10 minutes from the town center. Turn left onto the highway (bd. Sadi-Carnot) and then right, following the signs to the *centre ville*. Once there, continue up rue Larcher until it hits **rue St-Martin,** Bayeux's commercial avenue. On your right, **rue St-Jean** begins the pedestrian zone.

Tourist Office: 1, rue des Cuisiniers (tel. 31 92 16 26), in a 14th-century wooden building. From the cathedral, turn right onto rue Bienvenue, which becomes rue des Cuisiniers. Helpful English-speaking employees. You can book a room for the cost of a phone call. **Currency exchange** only when banks are closed. Open Mon.-Sat. 9:30am-12:30pm and 2-6:30pm, Sun. 10am-12:30pm and 3-6:30pm; mid-Sept. to May Mon.-Sat. 9:30am-12:30pm and 2-6:30pm.

Post Office: rue Larcher. **Poste Restante. Currency exchange.** Open Mon.-Fri. 8am-7pm, Sat. 8am-noon. **Postal Code:** 14400.

Trains: pl. de la Gare (tel. 31 83 50 50), 10min. from the center of town. To: Paris (5 per day, 2hr., 147F); Lille (5 per day, 5hr., 254F); Caen (12 per day, 20min., 28F). Ticket counters open daily 6am-8pm.

Buses: Bus Verts, pl. de la Gare (tel. 31 92 02 92), serves Port-en-Bessin and points west as well as Le Havre and other towns east, via Caen.

Bike Rental: At the station (tel. 31 92 80 50). 50F per day, 175F per week. 500F deposit. Open daily 8am-8pm. **Family Home,** 39, rue Général de Dais (tel. 31 92 15 22). Rusty 3-speeds 50F per day. 100F deposit. Open 7am-7pm. **English Bookstore: Maison de la Presse,** rue St-Martin, one block down from the tourist office. Carries some recent bestsellers and English language newspapers and magazines.

Laundromat: 10, rue Maréchal Foch. Open daily 8am-8pm.

Hospital: rue de Nesmond (tel. 31 51 51 51), next to the tapestry exhibit.

Ambulance: rue St-Jean (tel. 31 92 15 38). **Emergency:** tel. 15.

Police: av. Conseil (tel. 31 92 94 00). **Emergency:** tel. 17.

Accommodations, Camping, and Food

Inexpensive lodging exists, but plenty of tourists (especially July-Aug.) compete for limited spaces. Arrive early or reserve in advance.

Auberge de Jeunesse (HI)—Family Home, 39, rue Général de Dais (tel. 31 92 15 22). Follow the signs for the "Family Home" and "Auberge de Jeunesse" from the train station. Take a left off rue Larcher before the cathedral, then from the front of the cathedral turn left onto rue de la Juridiction, which intersects rue Gébnéral de Dais. The Family Home is to the right. A 16th-century residence converted into a labyrinth of rooms and *pensions*. All-you-can-eat 55F meal served nightly at 7:30pm. Expected completion of annex (a 15min. walk from the central hostel) by 1993. Reception open daily 7:30am-11pm. 73F, nonmembers 125F. Breakfast included. Bike rental 50F per day, 100F deposit. Reservations accepted and often necessary.

Centre d'Accueil Municipal, 21, rue des Marettes (tel. 31 92 08 19). From the station, follow the busy bd. Sadi Carnot to the left as it becomes bd. Maréchal Leclerc and bd. Fabien Ware. The *centre* is across from the Musée de la Bataille de Normandie. Big and modern with sterile singles only. 78F. Breakfast included. Reception open daily 7am-8pm.

Hôtel des Sports, 19, rue Saint-Martin (tel. 31 92 28 53), one block down from tourist office. Great location and beautiful modern rooms. Trendy, mirrored café below. Singles with shower 150F. Doubles with shower 170F. Breakfast 25F.

Hôtel Notre-Dame, 44, rue des Cuisiniers (tel. 31 92 87 24), next to the cathedral. Luxurious restaurant and *foyer* downstairs, neat comfortable rooms upstairs. Singles and doubles 130-140F, with shower 200-220F. Showers 20F. Breakfast 24F.

Hôtel de la Gare, pl. de la Gare (tel. 31 92 10 70). Cheap and near the station. Singles 85-90F. Doubles 100F. Students 50F per person. Breakfast 22F.

Camping: Municipal Camping, bd. Eindhoven (tel. 31 92 08 43), within easy reach of the town center and the RN13. Follow rue Genas Duhomme; continue straight on av. de la Vallée des Pres. 11F50 per person, 14F10 per tent and car. Open March-Nov.

The **Family Home** hostel serves a bountiful feast at 7:30pm. They choose the menu; you eat until you're stuffed. Call ahead to reserve if you're not staying there. Another fantastic restaurant is **Le Petit Normand,** 35, rue Larcher (tel. 31 22 88 66), where you can dine in a 16th-century building overlooking the cathedral. (*Menus* 49F, 90F, and 125F. Open Mon.-Sat. noon-2pm and 7-9:30pm, Sun. noon-2pm. Reservations advised.) On the other side of the cathedral, **Crêperie de la Notre Dame,** 8, rue de la Juridiction, folds surprisingly inexpensive *crêpes* (10-20F) and *galettes* (12-29F) to eat in or take out. (Open Mon.-Sat. 11:30am-4:30pm and 6:30-9pm.)

Sights

Measuring almost 70m in length but only 50cm in height, the celebrated **Tapisserie de Bayeux** illustrates in startling detail the entire story of the Battle of Hastings in 1066. William the Conqueror—known as William the Bastard before the battle—traded in his erstwhile nickname when he defeated his cousin Harold, then recognized as the King of England, and united the Duchy of Normandy and England under one throne. The tapestry, actually a linen embroidery probably commissioned by Odon de Conteville, Bishop of Bayeux and half-brother to William, was most likely intended to hang in the Bayeux cathedral. It is now presented, together with an excellent and detailed explanation of the Norman lifestyle and conquest, in the **Centre Guillaume le Conquérant,** a renovated seminary on rue de Nesmond (tel. 31 92 05 48). If you're having trouble telling the teams apart, note that the English are depicted with moustaches and the Normans are clean-shaven. (Exhibitions and audio cassette in French and English. Open daily 9am-7pm; Sept. 16-Oct. 15 and March 16-May 15 9am-12:30pm and 2-6:30pm; Oct. 16-March 15 9:30am-12:30pm and 2-6pm. Admission 25F, students 12F. Audio cassette 5F.)

A masterpiece of Norman design, Bayeux's impressive **Cathédrale Notre-Dame** stands near the Tapisserie de Bayeux. Gothic spires crown Romanesque towers, which rise over a small Roman temple, now an underground crypt. The cathedral's serene beauty is perhaps only compromised by the flouncy rococo awning over the pulpit. Informal guided tours are given in summer. (Open Mon.-Sat. 8am-7pm, Sun. 9am-7pm; Sept.-June Mon.-Sat. 8:30am-noon and 2:30-7pm, Sun. 9am-12:15pm and 2:30-7pm.) Across the street, the **Musée Baron Gérard** houses an interesting collection of paintings, including David's *Le Philosophe*, intently examining his finger, and a peaceful pastoral scene by Gustave Caillebotte. It also houses a display of Bayeux lace. (Open daily 9am-7pm; Sept.-Oct. 15 and March 16-May 9:30am-12:30pm and 2-6:30pm; Oct. 16-March 15 10am-12:30pm and 2-6pm. Admission 15F, students 8F.) Near the Centre d'Accueil and the British war cemetery, the **Musée Memorial de la Bataille de Normandie—1944,** bd. Fabian Ware (tel. 31 92 93 41) recalls the enormous manpower and losses of the Battle of Normandy through its large collection of uniforms, arms, and photographs. The exhibits include an excellent 40-minute film in English and French. (Same hours as Musée Baron Gérard. Admission 20F, students 10F.) If you plan to visit several museums in Bayeux, consider purchasing a discounted ticket for admission to the Tapestry, Battle of Normandy Museum, the Baron Gérard Museum, and the **Musée Diocésain d'Art Réligieux,** a small collection of ceremonial chalices, ecclesiastical dresses, and manuscripts. (Global pass to all museums, available at any museum; 50F, students 26F.)

Take time to stroll through Bayeux's high-walled streets for a peek at the lovely old houses. Note especially the turrets of 15th-century **Hôtel de Rubercy** at 5, rue Franche, still a private home. Explore the gardens of **Monastère St-Trinité,** 48, rue St-Loup, where Benedictine nuns have prayed since 1648.

In July and August, weekly organ and classical concerts resound in the Cathédrale (most are free). Ask at the tourist office for a schedule. In early July, the **Marché Médiavales** brightens the streets of Bayeux with costumed dancers, flame-blowers, artisans, and griffins-on-stilts.

Near Bayeux: The D-Day Beaches

Normandy's beaches have been gnawed and sculpted by the tireless waters of the English channel for thousands of years. But one tragic and glorious month left a cataclysmic mark like none before it. In June of 1944, over 1,000,000 Allied soldiers climbed from the English Channel onto these beaches, seeking to wrest France from the hands of the occupying Germans. The invasion bequeathed a glaring record to posterity—pockmarked façades and blown out stained glass in the cities, cannons and graves by the beaches—and made a more subtle mark on an entire generation of Normans, whose yards and streets served as battlefields for a summer. But it shifted the balance of the war in Europe decisively, and less than a year later Germany capitulated and Adolf Hitler was dead.

Preparations for the attack began at the Québec conference of 1943, when the Allied leaders decided to attempt a landing on the European continent. While using false intelligence reports to feed Hitler's suspicion that the attack would fall farther north at Calais, the British, American and Canadian authors of "Operation Overlord" instead planned a landing on the Normandy coast between the Cotentin peninsula and the Orne River. In the pre-dawn hours of June 6, 1944, the invasion began. Sixteen thousand American and British paratroopers tumbled from a clear moonlit sky. The American 82nd (All American) and 101st Airborne (Screaming Eagles) divisions were to cut the road and rail links between Paris and Cherbourg and to cover the beach landings in the west. The British 6th parachute brigade was to capture bridges over the Orne River and to protect the eastern flank of the invasion. Scattered across the dark and unfamiliar Norman countryside, the troops reeled in confusion at first, but after slow regrouping were able to execute their missions with surprising success.

A few hours later, on the heels of the paratroopers, 120,000 troops landed on the beaches codenamed Utah, Omaha, Gold, Juno and Sword. The most difficult landing was that of the 1st U.S. Infantry Division at Omaha Beach, where a rough sea and well-fortified enemy compounded the challenge of ascending a steep cliff face. In one of the day's most dramatic moments, 225 specially trained US Rangers scaled the sheer 30m cliffs at **Pointe du Hoc.** Having neutralized the key German position, the Rangers were left to defend it against enemy counterattack for two days and nights until Allied help arrived. By month's end over a million soldiers had crossed the sands of Normandy, and the battle raged on until August 21. On August 24, 1944, the Allied forces entered and liberated Paris.

Museums and cemeteries, scattered from Cherbourg to Caen, commemorate the devastating episode. At **Ste-Mère-Eglise** near Utah Beach, the **Musée C-47** (tel. 33 41 41 35) houses the plane that spilled paratroopers over the Ste-Marie district—one of whom was left dangling from the steeple of Ste-Mère's church when his parachute snagged. (Open daily 9am-7pm; Sept.-May 9am-noon and 2-7pm. Admission 15F, children 6F.) The town hall here displays the American flag that paratroopers of the 82nd division planted to mark the liberation of the village. The **Voie de la Libération** (Liberty Highway) begins at km "0," in front of the town hall; similar markers designate each kilometer of the U.S. Army's advance to Bastogne in Belgium.

At **Utah beach,** near **Ste-Marie-du-Mont,** an exhibition on the landing occupies a blockhouse near the American Commemorative Monument. A model of the operation shows how 836,000 soldiers, 220,000 vehicles, and 725,000 tons of equipment were brought ashore. (Open daily 9am-noon and 2-7pm; Sun. and bank holidays only off-season.)

Ten km north of Bayeux on D514 is **Arromanches,** a small town at the center of Gold Beach. Here the British built Port Winston in a day, on June 6, 1944, using retired ships and 600,000 tons of concrete towed across the Channel at 3km per hour and sunk in a wide semi-circle a mile out to sea. The enormous artificial harbor provided shelter while the Allies unloaded their supplies. The **Musée du Débarquement,** on the beach (tel. 31 22 34 31), houses fascinating relics and photographs of the British and Canadian landings. A film included in the price of admission is in French, but English cassettes are available. (Open daily 9am-6:30pm; Sept.-June 9-11:30am and 2-5:30pm. Admission 25F.) The **Musée à Pegasus Bridge** in Benouville tells the story of the British Parachute Brigades' operations on the Dives River. (Open daily 9am-7pm; Sept.-June 9:30am-12:30pm and 2-6pm. Admission 15F.) At **Colleville-St-Laurent,** 19km from Bayeux on the coast between Arromanches and Grandchamps, almost 10,000 American graves stretch over an achingly beautiful 200-acre coastal reserve.

Juno Beach, the landing site of the Canadian forces, lies east of Arromanches. The Canadian cemetery is located at **Bény-sur-Mer-Reviers,** and there are commemorative monuments at Bernières, Courseulles, and St-Aubin. The second British beach, **Sword,** continues east from Juno Beach. There are British cemeteries at **Hermanville-sur-Mer** and **Ranville.** Like their American counterparts, the British and Canadian paratroops spent the first hours of the June 6 invasion in confusion as they tried to organize at predetermined rallying points. War museums at **Benouville** and **Merville** recall the battles fought at twilight.

The best way to see the D-Day beaches is by car. The road that follows the coast, the D514, is narrow and tortuous, so hitchhiking and even cycling may be dangerous. **Bus Verts** (tel. 31 92 02 92 in Bayeux) serves **Port-en-Bessin** from Bayeux (bus #70; Mon.-Sat. 3 per day, 1/2hr., 14F10) and Arromanches (2 per day, 1/2hr., 14F10). Public buses may prove inconvenient if you plan to travel from beach to beach. Several inexpensive tour guides based in Bayeux arrange comprehensive visits to the sites. **Normandy Tours** (tel. 31 92 10 70) runs small flexible tours in both English and French for one to eight people (2 per day, 100F, students 90F; bus picks you up at your hotel). **Bus Fly,** 24, rue Montfiquet, Bayeux (tel. 31 22 00 08), includes all the beaches, the American cemetery, and the Musée du Débarquement entrance fee. The bus leaves from the Family Home, 39, rue Général de Dais, in Bayeux (daily 9am and 2pm; 120F, students 100F). Make reservations a day or two in advance for both tours.

Camping Reine Mathilde at Etreham, near Port-en-Bessin (tel. 31 21 76 55) 2.5km from the sea, 7km from Omaha Beach, and 9km from Bayeux is fully equipped—and densely packed. (20F per person, 20F per tent. Open weekends in May; daily from June to mid-Sept.) The tourist office of Bayeux can help you find accommodations in small *chambres d'hôte* along the coast.

Cotentin Peninsula

The northwestern arm of Normandy, the Cotentin Peninsula juxtaposes busy ports, picturesque resort towns, and small rural villages. Trains, TER buses, and STN buses connect most of the villages on weekdays (although Sunday bus service dwindles to a trickle), but, as in the rest of Normandy, an earnest local fascination with foreigners often results in rides for those who choose to hitchhike. Bikers will pass long stretches of fertile farmland dotted with herds of ruminating cows producing Methane gas as only they know how, but novices may end up spending more time pushing than pedaling, especially as the roads branch inland, toward the rugged Cotentin terrain.

Cherbourg

At the northern tip of the peninsula, Cherbourg, nicknamed *"Port de la Libération"* during World War II, is now a major port with numerous ferry and train connections. The ever ebbing and flowing tides of ferry passengers have sparked the development of an active nightlife featuring discos, casinos, and fine restaurants. Unfortunately, late-night pedestrians are not safe here, especially around the poorly lit canal and north of the train station. If your connection is after dark, stay in well-lit, crowded areas, especially if traveling alone. But, as Cherbourg offers nary more than rows of cement developments, the curious traveler will find little reason to linger here between connections.

All ferries to Britain and Ireland leave from the same **Gare Maritime** north of the Bassin du Commerce off Quai de l'Ancien Arsenal. **Irish Ferries** (tel. 33 44 28 96) sends ferries to Rosslare, Ireland. (Mid-June to Aug. 3 per week; Sept. and April to mid-June 2 per week; Oct.-March 1 per week; 17hr.; July 10-Aug. 14, 836F, students 798F; July 1-9 and Aug. 15-31, 545F, students 500F; June and Sept. 625F, students

588F; Oct.-May 413F, students 357F; Eurail valid.) **P&O European Ferries** (tel. 33 44 20 13) serves Portsmouth, England. (May 22-Sept. 27 4 per day; Sept. 28-Dec. 23 and April 2-May 21 3 per day; Jan. 2-April 1 1 per day; day trip 4hr., night trip 7hr.; July 16-Aug. 31 260-300F; Sept. 1-July 15 250-260F; one-way ticket price same as three-day excursion ticket.) **Brittany Ferries** (tel. 31 96 80 80) sails to Poole, England. (April-Dec. 1-2 per day, 4hr., 250-320F depending on time of year. One-way ticket price same as three-day excursion.) **Sealink** (tel. 33 20 43 38) ferries connect Cherbourg and Southampton. (June-Sept. 1-2 per day, 4-7hr., 360-500F depending on time of year, students 320-480F.)

The **train station** (tel. 33 57 50 50) lies at the base of the Bassin du Commerce, a 15-minute walk from the ferry terminal. From the terminal, follow quai de l'Ancien Arsenal and quai de l'Entrepôt to the southern end of the Bassin du Commerce and the busy av. François Millet. The front of the station is across the avenue and to the right. (Open daily 5:30am-8:15pm.) Trains run to Paris (7 per day, 3 1/2hr., 199F); Rouen (3 per day, 3hr., 168F); Caen (6 per day, 1 1/2hr., 86F); Bayeux (9 per day, 1hr., 69F); and Rennes (change at Lison, 3 per day, 4hr., 161F). Across the street from the station is **Autocars STN** (tel. 33 44 32 22), whose buses makes irregular runs to les-Pieux, Barfleur, Valognes, St-Lô, Ste-Mère-Eglise, and Coutances among other destinations (22-60F; open Mon.-Fri. 8:15am-12:15pm and 2-6:30pm).

The helpful Cherbourg **tourist office** (tel. 33 93 52 02), at the northern end of the Bassin du Commerce near the bridge **Pont Tournant,** has plenty of brochures on the Cotentin. (Open Mon.-Sat.. 9am-noon and 1:30-6pm; **annex** at the Gare Maritime open June-Sept. daily 9am-noon and 1:30-6pm.) The **post office** is on rue de l'Ancien Quai, a five-minute walk west from the Bassin du Commerce. Major banks such as **Crédit Lyonnais** and **Banque Nationale de Paris** are located on rue Gambetta, west of the Bassin du Commerce. On weekends, try the **Bureau de Change** at the ferry terminal. (Open daily 6-7:30am, 1:30-7pm, and 8:30-10:30pm.)

The **Auberge de Jeunesse (HI)**, av. Louis Lumière (tel. 33 44 26 31), is a good 15-minute walk from the train station. A converted elementary-school building, the hostel lies across the street from a slaughterhouse. Take bus #5 (direction: "Tourlaville") from behind the train station to the "Fleming" stop (every 1/2hr., last bus 7:20pm, 5F20), or walk right on the highway towards Tourlaville. Take a right at the first light after the round-about, onto av. Maréchal de Lattre de Tassigny, and the hostel is one block away on the left corner. (Reception open daily 8-10am and 6-11pm. Lockout 10am-6pm. Members only. 56F. Sheets 14F. Breakfast included.) **Hôtel Divette,** 15, rue Louis XVI (tel. 33 43 21 04), a five-minute walk from the train station one block west of the Bassin du Commerce, has a broad staircase and generous landings that open into spacious Victorian-style rooms. (Singles 95F, with shower 120-130F. Doubles 130F, with shower 150F. Showers 10F. Breakfast 16F.) Ask at the tourist office for a free list of B&B accommodations. Most offer singles beginning at 100-120F. In the Place du Théâtre, local vendors peddle fruit, cheese, and flowers in a huge **market** every Tuesday and Thursday morning.

If you have time between connections, visit the **Musée de la Libération** (tel. 33 20 14 12), perched atop the Montagne du Roule in the old citadel, about 1.5km from the center of town and behind the youth hostel. If the large collection of German and American weaponry, photos, and documents doesn't thrill you, the panoramic view of Cherbourg and its surroundings might justify the strenuous hike. (Open daily 9am-noon and 2-6pm; Oct.-March Wed.-Mon. 9:30am-noon and 2-5pm. Admission 5F, under 18 2F50.) A somber incestuous love story marks the **Château de Tourlaville,** a strikingly beautiful 16th-century castle built in the Italian Renaissance style, about 4km east of Cherbourg. Sixteenth-century siblings Julien and Marguerite de Ravalet lived here until Marguerite's vengeful husband exposed the liaison and had the pair publicly executed in Paris. Only the surrounding park and gardens are open to visitors. Take bus #4 (10F) and get off at "bd. Schuman."

In **Lessay's** fine Romanesque abbey, the resident monks still sing mass in Gregorian chant every Sunday and stage the **Holy Cross Fair** each September. Call the Lessay town hall (tel. 33 46 46 18) for more information. Lessay lies midway between Cherbourg and Coutances and is accessible by STN bus (2-3 per day, 1hr., 43F).

Coutances

Rising out of expanses of farmland southeast of Lessay, Coutances—with a 13th-century cathedral Victor Hugo called the most beautiful after Chartres—is a walled city-on-a-hill. The town survived the war practically unscathed and is worth a visit to hike through its steep stone streets and to imbibe the surrounding countryside.

The cathedral, completed in 1274, extends its spires some 77m into the air. Inside, 13th-century stained-glass windows depict the lives of St. Thomas à Becket, St. Blaise, and St. George. On the opposite side of the town hall from the cathedral is the **Musée Quesnel Morinière** (tel. 33 45 11 92) in the **Jardin des Plantes.** The museum houses a fairly interesting collection of 18th- and 19th-century paintings, as well as regional pottery and period costumes. (Open Wed.-Mon. 10am-noon and 2-6pm. Admission 10F.) Although the intricate formal garden may appear to be all that's worth seeing, check out the 18th-century 400-liter Norman cider press near the museum courtyard. (Open daily 9am-11:30pm; Oct.-March 9am-5pm; April-June 9am-8pm. Illuminated amid classical music July-Aug. Wed-Mon.) The 15th- and 16th-century **Eglise St-Pierre,** south of the cathedral, contains a unique baroque organ. (Open daily 8am-noon and 2-7pm.)

The **train station** (tel. 33 07 50 77) is a 15-minute walk downhill from the cathedral. (Open Mon.-Fri. 5am-8:30pm, Sat. 5:30am-8pm, Sun. 7:30am-10:45pm.) Trains run to Rennes (2 per day, 1hr., 94F); Caen (5 per day, 1 1/2hr., 72F); Paris (2 per day, 4hr., 188F); Granville (3 per day, 1hr., 36F); and Avranches (3 per day, 45min., 38F). **Buses** leaving from the train station connect Coutances with Cherbourg (2 per day, 2hr., 56F); Granville (1 per day, 45min., 32F); and St-Lô (2 per day, 1hr., 28F). Call **STN** (tel. 33 05 65 25) in St-Lô for departure times. Coutances's **tourist office** (tel. 33 45 17 79), blessed with brochures, is one block from the cathedral down rue Clemenceau. (Open Mon.-Sat. 10am-12:30pm and 2-7pm, Sun. 2-7pm; Sept. and June Mon-Sat. 10am-12:30pm and 2-6pm; Oct.-May Mon.-Fri. 10am-12:30pm and 2-6pm.) The tourist office organizes guided one-hour **tours** through the old city and cathedral (July-Aug. only, 5 per day, 15-22F). Nearby **Les Unelles** (tel. 33 45 23 72) is an abbey newly restored as a cultural center with a swimming pool. (Open Mon.-Fri. 9am-noon and 2:30-6:30pm, Sat. 9am-noon; Oct.-April Mon.-Fri. 9am-noon.)

The **Hôtel des Trois Pilliers,** 11, rue des Halles (tel. 33 45 01 31), run by a young couple, has small rooms but a fine location near the cathedral. (Singles and doubles 120F. Breakfast 25F.) The **Hôtel le Champ'Bord,** 8, rue du Lycée (tel 33 45 01 12), just around the corner has an equally friendly reception above a bar popular with local workers. (Singles and doubles 80F-100F, with shower 120-160F. Breakfast 20F.)

The **Hôtel de Normandie,** pl. du Général de Gaulle (tel. 33 45 01 40), has clean, comfortable rooms. (Singles 85F, with shower 135F. Doubles 120F, with shower 155F. Showers 15F. Breakfast 22F.) Downstairs, a sea of bright blue tablecloths wait under wooden-beamed ceilings, poised to uphold the restaurant's 50F and 70F *menus* of good Norman fare. (Open Tues.-Sat. noon-2pm and 6-11pm, Sun. noon-2pm.)

Coutances hosts a **Jazz Festival** each year in late May and sponsors performances in the Jardin des Plantes and in public squares around the town. In July and August, organ and classical concerts resound in the Cathédrale Notre-Dame on Saturday evenings, and on Wednesday through Friday afternoons at 4 and 6pm. Many are free or charge reduced rates for students. Contact the tourist office for information and schedules for all events.

Granville

Not until the 15th century did Granville make an appearance in the history books, when the English used "le Roc"—it sprawls over a rocky peninsula on the western coast of Normandy—as a base from which to battle the French at Mont St-Michel. The victorious French afterward decided to develop the city, now known chiefly as a resort. Austerely beautiful with its rugged cliffs and long stretches of smooth, white sand, Granville's distance from Paris keeps it happily less crowded and less expensive than other Norman resorts. Although it sells itself as a convenient base for exploring Mont-St-Michel and the Channel Islands, Granville is worth the trip solely for its own merits.

From the train station, go left and follow av. Maréchal Leclerc—less than a 10-minute walk downhill—to the *centre ville.* At the *place,* take a right onto cours Joinville (follow the rails); the **tourist office,** 4, cours Joinville (tel. 33 50 02 67) is just ahead next to the **post office.** (Tourist office open Mon.-Sat. 9am-1pm and 2-7:30pm, Sun. 10:30am-12:30pm; Sept.-June Mon.-Sat. 9am-12:30pm and 2-7pm.)

Peer through the narrow, twisting streets of the *haute ville,* crowned by the massive 15th-century **Eglise de Notre-Dame,** where classical concerts (30-50F) are often held on Saturday evenings. Stretch out and bake on the long, sandy public beach, or visit the **Jardin Public Christian Dior,** off av. de la Libération, a piece of oceanfront property donated by the fashion magnate a century ago. (Open daily 9am-9pm. Free.)

Granville can be reached by car via the D971; many hitchhikers report the going easy, as the roads leading into and out of the city are well-traveled during the day. **STN buses** (tel. 33 50 08 99) link Granville to Coutances (1 per day, 45min., 28F60) and Avranches (3 per day, 1hr., 27F90). The buses roll from the **train station** (tel. 33 57 50 50) on av. Maréchal Leclerc. (Open daily 9am-10pm.) Trains run to Paris (via Argentan; 3-4 per day, 4hr., 180F); Cherbourg (2 per day, 3hr., 105F); and Bayeux (2-3 per day, 1 1/2hr., 77F). There are **lockers** (3F, 3-day max.) in the station. From May through September boats leave daily for the Chausey Islands, an archipelago of anything from 52 to 365 islets (depending on the tide), with few inhabitants and beautiful **beaches** (1-3 per day, round-trip 78F.) For more information, contact **Vedette "Jolie France"** (tel. 33 50 31 81) at the *gare Maritime* or **Emeraude Lines,** 1, rue Lecampion (tel. 33 50 16 36). The latter also sails to Jersey (April-Sept. 1 per day, 260F same day round-trip) as does **vedettes Armoricaines,** *gare Maritime* (tel. 33 50 77 45; mid-April to Oct., 1 per day, 250F same day round-trip) and Sealink's Channiland, 3, rue Georges-Clémenceau (tel. 33 51 77 45; mid-April to Oct., 1 per day, 250F same day round-trip.) The tourist office has schedules and fares for all excursions.

Granville welcomes its share of loyal tourists in the summer, so don't expect solitude or a surplus of hotel rooms, especially on weekends. Call ahead if you can, especially to stay at the **Auberge de Jeunesse** (tel. 33 50 18 95), which shares quarters with the **Centre Regional de Nautisme** along the town's southern shore (follow the signs to the Centre). This place has unquestionably earned its HI four-tree rating. Five minutes from the *centre ville,* a restaurant, bar, outdoor patio, ping-pong, billiards table, and beach all await you. The sailing center also hosts summer camps, so you may have to share this treasure with temperamental teeny-boppers. (44F. Singles 78F. Breakfast 13F50. Meals 46F). You can also rent **windsurfers** here (70F per hr.) You'll pay more for the powder pink and baby blue striped wallpaper of **Hôtel Terminus,** pl. de la Gare (tel. 33 50 02 05), but its bright, clean rooms and convenient location across from the train station could make it worth your while. (Singles and doubles 95-135F, with shower 120-185F. Breakfast 19F.) The more sterile atmosphere of **Hôtel Michelet,** 5, rue Jules Michelet (tel. 33 50 06 55), is also appealing. The friendly and well-organized management will show you to your room, then point you toward the beach, just five minutes away. Book ahead in the summer. (Singles and doubles 90-100F, with shower 200F. Showers 15F. Breakfast 24F.) Everything in Granville shuts down at lunchtime, so resign yourself to eating in one of its many inexpensive restaurants. Near the hostel, **Chez Salvatore,** 13, rue St-Sauveur serves spaghetti (38F) and other pasta dishes. (Open noon-2pm and 7-10pm.) The beach's broad, flat rocks make perfect picnic perches.

A few small coastal towns dot the pristine countryside and gorgeous beaches near Granville: **Hauteville-sur-Mer** and **Coutainville** are particularly worth a visit. These towns are served by STN buses, but the schedules are so inconvenient that you will do better renting a **bike** at the train station (50F per day; open daily 8:30am-noon and 2-4:30pm). **Mopeds** go for 100F per day at **Action,** 11, rue Clément-Desmaison (tel. 33 50 04 13; open Tues.-Sat. 8:30am-noon and 2-6pm).

Avranches

Balanced on a hill in a northern corner of the bay of Mont-St-Michel, Avranches (pop. 9000) will appeal to diehard fans of the fortified island. On the western side of the city, the truly beautiful **Jardin des Plantes,** illuminated to the sounds of classical music every night from June to September, offers a sweeping view of the bay and the far-off island. The **Mairie d'Avranches** on pl. Littré (tel. 33 58 18 11), annually displays 10th- to 12th-century manuscripts, painstakingly illustrated by the Mont's Benedictine monks that detail all aspects of daily village and abbey life. Avranches managed to preserve the documents after they were moved to avoid destruction when the Mont's abbey was sacked during the French Revolution. (Open June-Aug. Mon. and Wed.-Sat. 10am-noon and 2-6pm. Admission 10F.)

For those less enamored of Mont-St-Michel, Avranches is still a pleasant if uninspiring place to pause on a tour down the Cotentin Coast. The central **tourist office,** on rue Général de Gaulle (tel. 33 58 00 22), is adjacent to the town hall. (Open daily 9am-8pm; Sept.-June daily 9am-noon and 2-6pm.) There is a smaller branch at the Jardin des Plantes (open July-Aug. daily 9am-7pm). The main tourist office shares its building with the **STN bus station** (tel. 33 58 03 07), which sends buses to and from Mont-St-Michel (July-Aug. 1 per day, 22F30, round-trip 42F80; Sept.-June 1 per week) and to Granville (29F). (Station open Mon.-Tues and Thurs.-Fri. 10:30am-12:15pm and 3:30-6:30pm, Wed. 10am-noon and 3:30-6:30pm, Sat. 9am-noon.) The Caen-Rennes train line passes through Avranche's **BF station** at the bottom of the hill. Destinations include Granville (2 per day, 15min., 31F), and Paris via Folligny (2 per day, 5hr., 194F).

Its **Auberge de Jeunesse (HI),** 15, rue du Jardin des Plantes (tel. 33 58 06 54), is a converted stone house near the gardens and across the street from the cathedral. There's no sign—look for the drive with the swinging white gates. It lets singles, doubles, and triples. (Reception open Mon.-Fri. 6-10pm. 50F per person. Sheets 20F. Breakfast included. Kitchen facilities. Meals ordered in advance 33F. Open year-round.) If the hostel's ten beds are full, try the popular **Hôtel de Normandie,** 2, Corniche St-Michel (tel. 33 58 01 33), on the end of the footpath from the station. The ivy-covered, white shuttered building offers cozy rooms with hilltop views of the patchwork Norman countryside. (Singles 100F. Doubles 130F, with shower 220F. Showers 25F. Breakfast 30F.) **Hôtel le Select,** 11, rue de Mortain (tel. 33 58 10 62), is clean with modern rooms. (Singles and doubles 100F, with shower 150F. Triples with shower 170F. Showers 15F. Breakfast 17F.) **Les Mares Camping,** rue de Verdun (tel. 33 58 05 45), next to the school to the south of the *centre ville,* has flat, unshaded sights enclosed by a wall and thick hedges. (10F per person, 10F per tent, 5F per car. Open April to mid-Sept.) Numerous cheap *brasseries* and restaurants surround the tourist office. **L'Express Bar,** rue des Fossés, has indoor and outdoor seating and lots of appetizing *galettes* for 8-20F served by a welcoming proprietor (open daily 9am-midnight).

Mont-St-Michel

No matter how many times you've seen it in pictures, your heart will flutter when you first glimpse Mont-St-Michel rising out of the water. Now connected to the mainland by a causeway, the abbey buildings represent an imposing tribute to monastic solitude. These days, you won't find much solitude, as the Mont is France's second-most visited attraction after Paris; try to get there in the morning; the crowds are as inevitable as the Mont is unforgettable.

Orientation and Practical Information

Because the Mont itself is isolated from the mainland, and the town proper is a tiny village, you should plan your visit carefully to avoid being stranded in a place where "budget hotel" is an oxymoron. Consider making Mont-St-Michel a daytrip, easily accessible from St-Malo, Avranches, or Pontorson. **Trains** continue no farther than **Pontorson,** where STN buses cover the remaining distance to the Mont (see listings below). The only break in the Mont's outer wall is the **Porte de l'Avancée.** Inside, the **tourist office** lies immediately to the left; to the right, the **Porte du Boulevard** and **Port du Roy** open onto the town's major thoroughfare, **Grand Rue.** All hotels, restaurants, and sights are on this one spiraling street, but try to sneak off via several inconspicuous stairwells and archways to explore Mont-St-Michel's less-visited corners.

Tourist Office: Boîte Postale 4, 50116 Le Mont-St-Michel (tel. 33 60 14 30), behind the stone wall to your left after you enter the city. Sells posters and books at lower prices than the shops at the abbey. Ask about organized 2-hr. hiking expeditions over the sand to the **Ile de Tombelaine** (April-June and Aug.-Sept. at low tide). Avoid the **currency exchange** here and elsewhere on the Mont. Ask for the useful tide table *Horaire des Marées*. Open Mon.-Sat. 9am-6pm; Sept.-June Mon.-Sat. 9am-noon and 2-6pm.

Post Office: Grand-Rue, near the Porte du Roi (tel. 33 60 14 26). Open Mon.-Fri. 9am-6pm, Sat. 9am-5pm; mid-Sept. to June Mon.-Fri. 9am-noon and 2-5pm. **Postal Code:** 50116.

Trains: The nearest train station is in Pontorson (tel. 33 60 00 35; open Mon.-Fri. 8:30am-noon and 1:30-8pm, Sat. 8:30am-noon and 2-6:30pm, Sun. 1:30-10pm). If coming by train from Paris, change at Rennes for Pontorson (2 per day, 4hr., 230F). You can also reach Pontorson from Paris by changing at Foligny (2 per day, 192F), or Caen (2 per day, 215F). The TGV from Paris (via Rennes) provides the fastest transportation of all (3-4 per day, 3hr., 230F plus 32F required reservation). Returning to Paris, note that the last train from Pontorson to Rennes leaves at around 7pm.

Buses: All buses leave from the Porte du Roy. Tickets available on board. **STN buses** (tel. 33 60 00 35 in Pontorson) link the Mont to Pontorson and from there to other cities in the region. The last STN bus leaves the Mont at 6:40pm. To: Pontorson (4 per day, 10min., 12F60, round-trip 20F). **STN** (tel. 33 50 08 99 in Granville, tel. 33 58 03 07 in Avranches), **SCETA** (tel. 33 50 77 89 in Granville), and **Courriers Bretons et Normands** (tel. 33 60 11 43) offer **bus service** connecting Pontorson to Dol, St-Malo, Rennes, Avranches, Granville, and Folligny. Buses run infrequently on weekends. **Bike Rental:** At the Pontorson **train station** for -day (44F), full day (55F), with a 500F deposit or a major credit card.

Luggage Storage: Leave your bags at the Pontorson train station (3F). Or, for 10F the bathroom attendant by the Porte Bavole will store your bags in a room nearby.

Police: Emergency: tel. 17.

Accommodations, Camping, and Food

If you're considering spending the night in the Mont-St-Michel area, plan ahead to reserve a room you can afford. Also realize that prices climb faster than the bay's famous tides; what's listed here may have doubled by 1993. St-Malo, Avranches, and Pontorson offer accommodations at more reasonable prices. Most of the listings below are in Pontorson (**postal code:** 50171), a small old Norman town.

Centre Duguesclin (HI), rue Général Patton (tel. 33 60 18 65), in Pontorson. From the train station, turn right onto rue du Tizon, take your first left (rue du Couesnon) and then a right onto rue St-Michel to the post office. Turn left, and behind the cathedral lies rue Hédou. Follow it to its end and take a right on rue Général Patton. The hostel is on your left, 1 block down (10min.). Spartan, dorm-style 6-bed rooms are bright and conducive to communal gathering. Fully equipped kitchen, outdoor clothesline. Reception open daily 10am-noon and 5-10pm. Lockout 10am-5pm. Members only. 40F.

Pleine-Fougères (HI), rue de la Gare (tel. 99 48 75 69), about 5km from Pontorson. Count on walking both ways; buses to the hostel run only in the morning and leave the town only in the afternoon. Reception open 9am-noon and 2-10pm. No curfew. Six-bed rooms in a pretty stone house. 40F. Breakfast 14F.

Hôtel de la Croix Blanche, rue Grande Rue (tel. 33 60 14 04), in Mont-St-Michel. Located in the thick of the souvenir shops and the seething throngs of visitors. Not unreasonable, especially for 2 or more people, considering its location. Small rooms; most command a memorable view of the coastline. Singles and doubles 170F, with shower 270F. Triples and quads 260F, with shower 300F. Breakfast 40F. Reserve at least 2 weeks in advance. Open Feb.-Nov.

Hôtel de France, 2, rue des Rennes (tel. 33 60 29 17), to the left of the train station in Pontorson. Rooms are worn but adequate, with low-slung beds skimming dark floorboards. The sheer vertical drop of the staircase will challenge any backpacker. Singles and doubles 75-110F. Triples and quads 140-150F. Showers 15F. Breakfast 20F.

Hôtel de l'Arrivée, pl. de la Gare (tel. 33 60 01 57), across from the station in Pontorson. Nicest rooms are above the bar, but all are comfortable. Reception open 8am-8pm. Singles and doubles 80-100F, with shower 145F. Triples 145F, with shower 175F. Quads 160F. Showers 15F. Breakfast 22F. Bar and restaurant downstairs.

Camping: Camping Pont d'Orson, cours de la Victoire (tel. 33 68 11 59; July-Aug. tel 33 60 00 18), near the hostel, 10min. from the station in Pontorson. Simple but adequate site by the river. 11F50 per person, 11F50 per tent, 5F per car. Hot showers included. Open April-Sept. **Camping du Mont-St-Michel,** B.P. 8, 50116 Le Mont-St-Michel (tel. 33 60 09 33). As close to the Mont as you will get (1.8km), at the junction of D275 and N776. Clean, pleasantly shaded sites. Best location for viewing the Mont at night, but fills fast. Great showers. Supermarket next door. 12F per person, 11F per car or tent. Reserve in advance. Open April-Sept. **Camping St-Michel,** rte. du Mont-St-Michel (tel. 33 70 96 90), by the bay in Courtils. A bit far from the Mont (9km), but the Granville bus stops 200m from the entrance. Buses go to the Mont at 10:30am and 5pm; ask the helpful proprietor for the return schedules. The sites are quiet and equipped with a common room and telephone. 11F per person, 5F50 per car or tent. Open April-Oct.

Overpriced and lackluster snack bars have infested the Mont, so watch out. Look for local specialties such as *agneaux pré-salé,* lamb raised on the salt marshes surrounding the island, and *omelette poulard,* a fluffy soufflé-like dish (about 35F). Ask for a recipe at the tourist office. One of the more attractive places, **La Sirène,** on the Grand-Rue, serves delicious *galettes* and omelettes (11-25F) in the middle of the action. (Open daily noon-10pm. Closed Thurs. evening in winter.) To eat in a room with a view, walk along the ramparts and take your pick of the restaurants; all sport terraces or glass walls. The **Restaurant de la Croix Blanche** serves filling 68F and 90F *menus* (open daily 11am-2pm and 5-10pm). Or, since restaurant prices compete with the Mont's spire for title of the highest peak in town, pack a picnic and eat in the abbey gardens near the top of the hill (a few flights below the entrance), or on the beach at low tide. Provisions are available at the **Shopi supermarket,** 5, rue Couesnon, in Pontorson. (Open Mon.-Thurs. 9am-12:30pm, Fri.-Sat. 9am-12:30pm and 2:30-7:15pm.)

Sights

The island monastery first came into existence in the 7th century, when a gigantic wave swamped the forest of Sissy, isolating the Mont from the mainland. In 708, the archangel St-Michel appeared three times in the dreams of the Bishop of Avranches, instructing him to build a place of worship on the barren and rocky island north of Pontorson. Over the centuries, the modest church expanded to its present size with only a few stones—buried by endless additions in various styles—remaining from the original oratory.

The additions began in 966, when a group of Benedictine monks made a pilgrimage to the Mont and were so inspired by its beauty and power that they began the construction of an even larger church on the original site. Its construction mostly completed by the 14th and 15th centuries, the Mont was used by French kings as a solitary fortress, starting in the time of the Hundred Years War. While its outer walls repelled English attacks, its inner walls still cloistered the Benedictines, who received religious pilgrims until 1789, when the Revolutionary government turned the island into a state prison. Mont-St-Michel remained under government control from then on, continuing to serve as a prison until Emperor Napoleon III recognized its historical significance; his patronage set in motion renovations that began after his fall from power. In 1874, Mont-St-Michel was classified as a national monument and topped by the crowning bronze statue of St-Michel.

Rather than wandering aimlessly through the abbey, invest in a comprehensive guide to the Mont. The *Michelin* guide, available from booths near the abbey, describes each of the buildings and discusses its history and architecture. For a simpler guide with more photographs, try Jean-Paul Brighelli's *Entre Ciel et Mer, le Mont-Saint-Michel,* (72F at the abbey bookstore, in French). In English and shorter, *All of Mont-Saint-Michel,* was written by the curator of the abbey, Nicolas Simonnet (45F at abbey bookstore).

Enter via the **Porte de l'Avancée,** and then through the **Porte du Roy** onto Grand-Rue, a winding pedestrian street full of souvenir stands and restaurants. A climb up several flights of stairs, places you at the **abbey** entrance, the departure point for all of the one-hour tours. (Tel. 33 60 14 14. Open daily 9:30am-6pm; Sept. 16-Nov. 10 and Feb. 16-May 14 9:30-11:45am and 1:45-5pm; Nov. 12-Feb. 15 daily 9:30-11:45am and 1:45-4:15pm. Tours in English daily at 10am, 11am, noon, 1:30pm, 2:30pm, 3:30pm,

4:30pm, and 5:30pm. Tours in French every 20min. Admission 32F, ages 18-25 and over 60 18F, ages 18 6F, Sun. 1/2-price. Call 33 60 14 14 for information.) For a special treat, take one of the more detailed *visites conférences.* These two-hour tours in French allow you to walk atop a flying buttress and crawl inside the pre-Roman crypts. (Daily at 10am and 2:30pm. No reservations necessary. Admission 49F, ages 18-25 and over 60 35F, under 18 21F.) Mass is still held daily at 12:15pm .

Constructed on the highest point on the island, the church balances directly above some frigid crypts. Passing through the refectory, a descent leads into the dark and astonishingly chilly church foundations where the walls are 2m thick at some points. **La Merveille,** an intricate 13th-century cloister housing the monastery, encloses a seemingly endless web of passageways and chambers. If you're not impressed with its architectural complexities, the mechanical simplicity of the Mont's treadmill will surely catch your attention. Prisoners held in the Mont during the French Revolution would walk here for hours, their foot labor powering the elaborate pulley system that carried heavy stones up the side of the Mont.

Bertrand Duguesclin, the governor of Pontorson, built the **Logis Tiphaine** in 1365 to protect his young wife Tiphaine, an astrologer, from the English while he was fighting in Spain. Today, the *logis* houses an interesting museum of well-preserved 15th-century furniture and other interesting paraphernalia including a 14th-century chastity belt. (Open daily 9am-6pm. Admission 20F, students 15F, under 12 10F.)

After the tour, escape down the ramparts and into the abbey garden, where you can reflect upon both the soaring stone buttresses that wrap around the entire island and the coasts of Normandy and Brittany. To avoid the asphyxiating crowds on the main street, descend to the **Porte du Bavole** via the ramparts.

Do not wander off too far on the sand at any time of day. The bay's tides are the highest in Europe, shifting every six hours or so. During high-tide days, or *mascarets,* the water recedes for 18km and rushes in at 2m per second, flooding the beaches along the causeway. While the tides were once said to rush in "faster than a horse at full gallop," the water now seldom moves faster than at a brisk walking pace. To see this spectacle, you must be within the abbey fortifications two hours ahead of time.

When darkness falls, Mont-St-Michel is lit up and becomes a glowing jewel, best seen from either the entrance to the causeway or across the bay in Avranches. The Mont is illuminated during all church festivals and feasts, on high-tide nights, and nightly from July to September (dusk-11pm). Those who like *son* with their *lumière* should visit in July and August, when **Les Heures Musicales du Mont-St-Michel,** take place in the abbey. (Admission 60F per concert, students with ID 35F.) Buy tickets at the door, or contact the tourist office in Avranches for more information (tel. 33 58 00 22) From mid-June through September, the **Les Imaginaires** night program animates the Mont's interior with a sound and light show. (Mon.-Sat. 10pm-midnight. Admission 60F, students 35F.) In early May, the Mont celebrates **St-Michel de Printemps,** during which costumed men and women parading throughout the Mont recapture the local Breton folklore and dance to medieval and Renaissance music.

Channel Islands

US$1 = 0.52 British pounds
CDN$1 = £0.44
AUS$1 = £0.38
NZ$1 = £0.28
IR£1 = £0.93
FRA1 = £0.10

£1 = US$1.92
£1 = CDN$2.28
£1 = AUS$2.61
£1 = NZ$3.54
£1 = IR£1.07
£1 = FRA9.56

With more sunny days per year than any other of the British Isles, the Channel Islands draw more than their fair share of tourists. Fortunately, much of the natural, rural beauty of Guernsey, Jersey, and Sark (the three main islands) remains unspoiled by high-rise hotels and posh tourist developments. A curious mélange of their French-English heritage, these islands display bilingual street signs and their inhabitants drink four o'clock tea but dine late. Sark is still "owned" by a *Seigneur* and run by the old French feudal customs.

Historically and politically, the Channel Islands are British. After King John lost the Duchy of Normandy to the French in 1204, the islands remained under the protection of the English crown and have remained so in spite of several French attempts to reclaim them. Residents fled Hitler to England and returned after the war with English affectations. In return for fealty to the British, the islands enjoy favorable trade regulations and almost complete autonomy. Jersey has its own elected State Assembly, as does the Bailiwick of Guernsey, a federation of Guernsey and the smaller islands that surround it. Although the British Parliament conducts all foreign policy and is responsible for the defense of the islands, Guernsey and Jersey negotiate their own trade agreements (they belong to the European Economic Community under a special provision which excludes them from levying the VAT). Low income taxes have attracted a menagerie of millionaires to both islands. Guernsey and Jersey issue their own currencies, of the same denominations and value as British sterling, but they operate a separate postal system, so you have to buy their stamps for postcards. All organizations accept British pounds, and some accept French currency as well. To avoid difficulties, exchange your francs upon arriving.

Many ferry companies offer reduced round-trip excursions fares to the islands from France and England, but extended stays can be expensive. The Channel Islands are on **British time,** one hour behind France.

Jersey

La Reine de la Manche (The Queen of the Channel), as the French call Jersey, is famed for sweaters, stamps, and package-tour holidays. Since Jersey does not impose the cumbersome Value-Added Tax, luxury goods are less expensive here than in either France or England. Avoid the built-up coast between St-Helier and Gorey. Instead, explore the cliff paths along Plemont and Bonley Bay, and relax on St-Ouen's *croissant*-shaped beach.

Getting There and Getting Around

Reaching Jersey from either France or England is not difficult, but it can be expensive if you stay more than three days. In July and August, be sure to book ferries as early as possible (at least a week in advance), since boats often fill well before departure. Most ferries leave France from the *gare maritime* in **St-Malo** and take roughly two hours to reach Jersey, with the exception of the **Condor Hydrofoil,** Commodore Travel, 28 Conway St. and Albert Quay (tel. 763 00 in St-Helier or 99 56 42 29 in St-Malo), which makes the voyage in 70 swift minutes from St-Malo (3-4 per day, 248F, ages 3-

14 149F; same-day return 275F, 165F; 3-day return 419F, 251F; period return 441F, 265F).

Emeraude Lines (tel. 99 40 48 40 in St-Malo, 665 66 in Jersey) sails the same route in two hours (2 per day, 225F, ages 3-14 135F; same-day return 260F, ages 3-14 156F; 3-day return 419F, ages 3-14 251F; period return: 450F, 270F). Emeraude Lines also sails between Granville in Normandy and Jersey (1-2 per day, 1hr., one-way 232F, ages 3-14 139F; same-day return 260F, 156F; 3-day return 400F, ages 3-14 240F; period return 422F, 253F). In addition, **Condor** runs ferries from the Channel Islands to Weymouth, England (1-2 per day, 3 1/2 hr., £40, ages 3-14 £20; 5-day return £60, £30).

Cycling is probably the best way to savor the natural beauty of Jersey, although the long hills of the coast might literally take your breath away. Hitchhiking may prove difficult, as most drivers are older tourists. **Bus travel** is dawdling but dependable. "Rover passes" buy unlimited bus travel (1 day £3, 3 days £7, 7 days £13).

St-Helier

The capital and only real city of Jersey, St-Helier subsists on tourism. Restaurants and B&Bs here tend to outprice the rest of the island, but bargains do exist. Stay for a night to recover from any lingering seasickness; then move on to the countryside.

Orientation and Practical Information

To reach the tourist office after docking, bear right at the end of Albert Pier; the tourist office lies about 100m down on the left. The main intersection of the city and pedestrian shopping district begin at the corner of Conway and King St.

Tourist Office: Weighbridge Station (tel. 780 00 or 247 79, for accommodations 319 58). Unusually helpful and knowledgeable staff. Free accommodations service. Map and guide *What's On: Jersey* (free). Open Mon.-Sat. 8am-8pm, Sun. 8am-2pm and 5-8pm, Nov.-April Mon.-Fri. 8:45am-5pm.

Currency Exchange: The major banks, Lloyds and Barclays, give the best exchange rates and charge the lowest commissions. Open Mon.-Fri. 9:30am-3:30pm. On Sun., the only places to exchange are the Roseville St. Pharmacy (open Mon.-Sat. 9am-9:30pm, Sun. 9:30am-1pm and 2-9:30pm). Also at the Condor docks at Albert Pier (open a few hr., around boat arrival and departure times). Neither posts competitive rates, andthey charge £3 and £5 commissions, respectively.

Post Office: Broad St. (tel. 262 62). You must use Jersey stamps on all mail. **Currency exchange. Poste Restante.** Philately shop with pretty stamps to show the folks back home. Open Mon.-Fri. 9am-5pm, Sat. 9am-noon. **Postal Code:** JE11AA.

Telephone Code: 534. Dial 19, followed by the country code (44) and 534 and then the number you're trying to reach.

Flights: Aurigny Air Services, Weighbridge Station (tel. 357 33). About 15 flights per day to Guernsey (£18.90). Bus #15 runs between the airport and St-Helier (every 15min., £1). Also to Cherbourg (tel. 33 22 91 32 in Cherbourg): £41.50, day return £60.

Buses: Weighbridge Station (tel. 212 01) is the hub of island bus transport. To: Gorey Village (every 30min., Sun. every 90min., 30min., £1), the zoo (every 1-2hr., last bus at 6:15pm, £1), St-Ouen's Bay (every hr., 40min., £1).

Ferries: Condor Hydrofoil, Commodore Travel, 28 Conway St. and Albert Quay (tel. 712 63). Runs the fastest boats to Jersey and to St-Malo (4-5 per day, 70min., £26.10, ages 3-14 £15.70) and to Guernsey (3-4 per day, £18.60, ages 3-14 £11.10). **Emeraude Lines,** Albert Quay (tel. 665 66), also runs between Jersey and St-Malo (1-2 per day, 2hr., £26, ages 3-14 £15.70), between Jersey and Guernsey (1-2 per day, 1hr., £18.60, ages 3-14 £11.10), and between Jersey and Sark (Mon.-Sat. 2 per day, 1hr., day return £20.70, ages 3-14 £12.40).

Bike Rental: Zebra, 9 Esplanade (tel. 365 56). A large selection (£4 per day, £20 per week, £15 deposit) as well as mountain bikes (£6 per day and £25 per week, £20 deposit). Open daily 8am-6pm. Farther along, **Kingslea,** 70 Esplanade (tel. 247 77), rents 3-speeds (£3 per day, £15 per week, £5 deposit). Also **moped rental** (must be over 18 years and have had driver's license for over 1 year; £10 per day, £50 per week, deposit £10). Open daily 8:30am-5:30pm.

Luggage Storage: Emeraude Lines Office, Albert Pier, £1 per bag per day. Open Mon.-Sat. 7:30am-6:30pm., Sun. 8am-noon and 2-6:30pm.

English Bookstore: 99 percent of Jersey's bookstores cater to English speakers; there should be no trouble finding reading material. **Jura Bookshops** at Broadstreet (across from the post office) and on Don Street in St-Helier carry copies of *Let's Go: Europe*. Open Mon.-Sat. 9am-9pm, Sun. 10am-5pm.

Laundromat: Sunshine Launderette, 77 New St. Closest to center of town. Wash and dry £3. Open Mon.-Sat. 8am-8pm. Last wash 6:30 pm, Sun. 9am-7pm. **Launderette,** 51 David Place, across from Royal Liver Friendly Society (no joke). Wash and dry about £3. Open daily 8am-6pm. Last wash 4:45pm. Bring plenty of £1, 20p and 50p coins.

Beach Guards: St-Ouen's Bay, tel. 48 20 32. **Plemont Bay,** tel. 48 16 36.

Hospital: General Hospital, Gloucester St. (tel. 590 00). Free clinic Mon.-Fri. 9:30am-11:30am; Oct.-April Mon., Wed., Fri. 9:30-11:30am. Prescription charge 90p per item.

Police: Rouge Bouillon, tel. 699 96.

Emergency: tel. 999 (no coins required).

Accommodations and Camping

Finding a room on your own in the summer is nearly impossible. The island has no youth hostel, and even the campgrounds fill early. The tourist office runs a free and fantastic accommodations service: when all the hotels and B&Bs are full, it makes public radio and TV appeals asking Jersey citizens to open up their homes to tourists. Many B&Bs will take only visitors who stay for a few days or even a week. If you arrive late in the day during July or August, be prepared to pay as much as £30. All the following accept reservations by phone but may also require written confirmation and/or deposit. Make reservations far in advance. Keep in mind that prices go down 20-40% during the off-season.

The Fairholme, Roseville St. (tel. 321 94). Friendly, family-run B&B about 100m from the beach and a 5-min. walk from the town center. Light, airy, and cheerful rooms. £21 per person with breakfast and shower, with dinner £26.

Bromley, 7 Winchester St. (tel. 239 48), near the city center off Val Plaisant. Even the garrets are spacious and comfortable in this B&B run by an Italian and French family. Pleasant dining room. £18 per person, with dinner £22.

Greenwood Lodge Hotel, Roseville St. (tel. 670 73), down the street from the beach and 5min. from town make this a great location. Decent rooms. Swimming pool. £19 per person, with shower £25, with dinner £23, with shower and dinner £28.

Sundowne, 6 Raleigh Ave. (tel. 250 32). A 10-min. walk from the center of town. Kind owners and nice rooms with big bath towels. £17.25 per person. Breakfast included. Evening meal £3.

Camping: Camping outside official sites is illegal. Most of the island's campgrounds have facilities and services such as convenience stores, TV and game rooms, swimming pools, and hot showers. Reservations are necessary. **Beauvelande Camp Site,** in St-Martin (tel. 535 75), off rte. A6 from St-Helier. Take bus #3, get off at St-Martin's Church, continue in the same direction, take the second right, and follow the signs; it's a 30-min. walk (last bus at 11pm). £4 per person includes tent and car. Excellent **bikes** £3 per day, £11 per week. Open July-Aug. **Rozel Camping Park** (tel. 567 97), south of Rozel Bay. From St-Helier, follow the A6 to St-Martin's Church and continue straight through the intersection along the B38—the campground is on the right. June-Sept. £4; April-May £3.10. Tent rental £1.90-8.65. Open April-Sept. 20. **St-Brelade's Camping Park** (tel. 413 98), off route A13, halfway between St-Aubin and St-Ouen's Bay. Quiet spot with inexpensive dinner and breakfast menus. £4.50 per person for small tents, £5.50 per person for large tents. Good behavior deposit £20 per person. Open May-Sept.

Food

Jersey's tourists support a thriving population of restaurants, mostly expensive. For two weeks in mid- to late May, the Jersey **Good Food Festival** provides a justification for gastronomic indulgence; prizes are awarded to the best chefs. Less expensive meal options include a large open **market,** held Monday to Saturday (7am-5:30pm) at Halkett Pl. For pub grub, try one of the many options in the harbor area.

Albert J. Ramsbottom, 90/92 Halkett Pl. Noisy, popular seafood restaurant shared by locals and tourists. Large portions of seafood scampi £4.75, chicken or tuna salad £3.95. Open Mon.-Sat. 11:30am-2pm and 5-10pm, Sun. 5-10pm.

Broadway Restaurant, 24 Esplanade. Silly cinematic names but excellent food. Efficient servers dispense Minelli or Streisand burgers £2.90-3.20. They're like butter. Just say yes to hardening arteries and chow on the deep-fried rings of fresh squid (£2.35). Open noon-2pm and 6-10pm.

The Waterfront, Chicago Pizza Restaurant, 10 Wharf St. Eat pizzas (£2.75-4) before large-screen music videos. Also delivers. Open daily noon-11pm.

Bilbo's Salad and Sandwich Bar, La Chasse, off Hill St. Excellent quiches, salads, and a long list of sandwiches served in a lively café. Spicy chicken *tikka* £4.50, other sandwiches from £1.50-10.95. Gollum. Open Mon.-Sat. 11am-11pm.

La Gondola, 35 Hill St. Inexpensive and ample portions of pasta (£3.90-4.40). Try Chicken Mexican (£5.50) for variety from the island's usual English fare. Open Wed.-Mon. 10am-3pm and 6-10:30pm, Tues. 10am-3pm.

Sights and Entertainment

While the city itself is not aesthetically pleasing, the efforts of the indefatigable tourist industry have produced many attractions for the visitor. The VAT-free status of Jersey's shopping lowers the prices of such travelers' staples as camera film, much cheaper here than in England or France, and gold jewelry. Stock up if you're running low on Mother's Day presents. The pedestrian shopping district begins at the corner of **Conway St.** and **King St.,** the city's main drag.

At low tide, you can walk from St-Helier's thin and grimy beach out to **Elizabeth Castle,** a Tudor fortress in the middle of the harbor. The castle is strong on anecdote but weak on visual impact. Helier himself, a pious, 6th-century hermit who later decapitated Vikings, brooded on **Hermitage Rock** at the castle's south side. (Open March-Oct. 9:30am-5pm. Admission £2, students, seniors, and children £1.)

Relics of Jersey history slumber beneath the fort in the **Jersey Museum,** 9 Pier Rd. The somewhat dull **Barreau Art Gallery** on the second floor features a Gainsborough charcoal sketch (considered one of the earliest representations of a Jersey cow), watercolors by Blampied for the first edition of Barrie's *Peter Pan,* and local oils of Jersey dating from the German occupation. (Open daily 10am-6pm. Admission £2, students, seniors, and children £1.)

Above the museum, disguised by the trees of **South Hill Battery Park,** and happily tucked away from sight atop St-Helier's only hill, **Fort Regent** has been converted to a sports and leisure center. You can lift weights, swim in the heated swimming pool, and participate in such dubious, though undoubtedly wholesome endeavors as the "Fort Apache totem pole building competition." (Open 9am-10pm. Admission £3, Sat. £2, after 5pm £1.25.)

In early August of each year, Jersey breaks out the **Battle of the Flowers,** an offering to those cruel gods of tourism. The streets overflow with onlookers as some 30 floats covered with hundreds of thousands of blooms spark sneezes up and down the main thoroughfare. Festivities continue throughout the week with bands and other entertainment. In days past, the procession of flower-decked floats culminated in an orgy of destruction as people tore the entries apart and pelted one another with petals. The tourist office has since decreed that winning floats must be preserved in the **Battle of the Flowers Museum** (in La Robelaine, Mont des Corvées St-Ouen), now full of mummified blooms. (Open March-Dec. daily 10am-5pm. Admission £1.50, seniors £1.25, children 70p.) You must get bleacher seats in advance for the Battle Parade (£5-12). For tickets, contact the **Jersey Battle of the Flowers Association,** Burlington House, St-Savior's Rd., St-Helier (tel. 301 78).

Other festivals run almost continuously between March and October. Check the tourist office for listings and exact dates. Weekend nights, hedonists find gratification in St-Helier, where nightlife is surprisingly diverse. **Thackery's** (called "Tack's") on the Esplanade, as well as **Café de Paris,** serve a well-dressed local clientele. **Lord's,** on Beresford St., and the **Red Lamp Pub,** Peter St., cater to a more casual crowd, and post more casual prices. Many of the bars in the pedestrian section and along Wharf St. and the Esplanade scream with laughter and music. More intimate entertainment rolls at the **Odéon,** Bath St. (tel. 241 66), and the **Ciné de France** (tel. 716 11), off St. Saviour's Rd, Jersey's most fashionable cinemas. (Admission £4 and £3.50, respectively.)

Jersey Countryside

Upon leaving St-Helier, the land assumes new character as rocky cliffs along the coast and hills and meadowed forests inland resist the overtures of tanning tourists. They, of course, are deposited along the beautiful beaches that dot the coast. The Rover **bus passes** make it easy to get around (£3 for 1 day, £7 for 3 days, £13 for 7 days of unlimited travel).

The massive and ruggedly beautiful 13th-century fort, **Mont Orgeuil Castle,** looks out across the Channel toward its erstwhile Norman attackers. The castle's key role in such major historical events as the English Civil War and World War II make it a worthwhile stop for history buffs. On the clearest days, the views from the lookout tower extend as far as Mont St-Michel. Otherwise, settle for the sailboats bobbing nearby in the harbor of **Gorey Village.** Restaurants, souvenir shops, and expensive hotels surround the bay below the castle. (Open late March-Oct. daily 9:30am-4:30pm. Admission £2, students, seniors, and children £1.) To reach Gorey Village by bike (about 10min. from St-Helier), follow the A6 out of St-Helier and turn right onto the B28, which winds its way to the castle. Routes A3 and A4 to Gorey Village are shorter, but not nearly as beautiful. Buses to Gorey Village depart every 30 minutes Monday to Saturday, every 90 minutes on Sunday (30min., £1).

On the way to Gorey Village along the B28, **La Hougue Bie** is an ancient pagan religious complex. At the base of a large hill lies the entrance to a 50m passage grave dating from around 3500 BC. Outside, the tomb is covered by a 60-ft. mound, capped by two medieval chapels.

To the north of La Hougue Bie on the B46 is author Gerald Durrell's **Jersey Zoo,** where Jambo the gentle silver-backed gorilla as well as many of his fellow endangered species (including lemurs and fruit bats) live in blissful security. (Open daily 10am-6pm. Last ticket issued at 5pm. Closes at dusk in winter. Admission £4.20, seniors £2.70, under 14 £2.20.)

During the German Occupation, the Channel Islands became one of the most heavily fortified areas in Western Europe as Hitler sent 30,000 troops here, an apparently symbolic endeavor to plant a German flag on British soil. The strategic value placed on the islands by the Allies becomes apparent when one considers that they remained in German hands until May 9, 1945. Today, bunkers and fortifications crop up frequently along the coastline and Jersey still celebrates "Liberation Day." An exhibit in the **German Underground Hospital,** Meadowbank, St-Lawrence, details the 1940 bombing of a fleet of potato lorries, which a German squadron mistook for military vehicles. (Open March-Nov. daily 9:30am-5:30pm. Admission £3.50, under 14 £1.50.) To reach the underground hospital from St-Helier, follow either the A1 or A2 out of town along St-Aubin's Bay, turn right onto the A11, and then continue straight onto the B99. Buses run every hour (15min., £1).

Jersey churches merit detours. In the **Fisherman's Chapel,** by the old parish church of St-Brelade, Norman murals still hang on the walls. From St-Helier, take the A1 west and turn right onto the B66. **St-Matthew's Church,** in Millbrook between St-Helier and Coronation Park on the A2, is known as the "Glass Church" for its Lalique stained-glass windows and altar. (Open to visitors Mon.-Fri. 9am-6pm, Sat. 9am-noon, Sun. for services.)

The terrain of the Jersey shore includes gently curving bays and harsh, rocky cliffs. Beautiful **St-Brelade's Bay** lays claim to the most popular **beach,** but **St-Ouen's Bay** grabs the title for the roughest and most spectacular surf. While swimming is ill-advised, you can watch the play of the tides—or that of the many surfers. **Anne Port** to the east is gentler, with smaller coves and rippling waters. All the beaches suffer from a strong undertow and swiftly rising seas; a list at the tourist board warns of danger spots.

Guernsey

Guernsey is one of the luckiest little islands in the world: it has a country all to itself. Guernsey and neighboring islands Sark, Herm, and Alderney make up an independent, self-governing unit, or Bailiwick, within the United Kingdom. Locals strive to distinguish themselves from the "British." For example, the English say "cheerio" instead of "good-bye"; Guernseyans, on the other hand, will wave you off with a "cheerie" (pronounced cheer-AY). Cheery, in fact, might well be the best word to describe Guernsey residents, an active and outgoing lot who revel in their island's wealth of natural amenities.

Western Guernsey is fringed with wide, sandy beaches. Ominous gray bunkers pepper the perimeter; the British built a few of these to defend themselves from the French, but most were commissioned by Hitler, to defend his little piece of Britain. The island's interior is a network of narrow roads, winding among grassy hills, wooded headlands, and cliffs. Cows and small cottages sprinkle the landscape, while looming manor houses lend an element of mystery to the pastoral scenery.

Getting There and Getting Around

From St-Malo in France, **Condor Hydrofoil** (tel. 72 61 21 in Guernsey) sails to Guernsey daily via Jersey (2-4 per day, 2 1/2hr., 285F, ages 3-14 171F; 3-day return 505F, ages 3-14 303F). Condor also sails to Guernsey from **Weymouth,** England (2-3 per day, 2 1/4hr., £36, ages 3-14 £18; 5-night return £55, ages 3-14 £27.50). **Emeraude Lines,** New Jetty White Rock, St-Peter Port (tel. 71 14 14), connects St-Malo to Guernsey (1 per day, 301F, ages 3-14 181F; 24-hr. return 279F, ages 3-14 167F; 72-hr. return 505F, ages 3-14 303F). **Aurigny Air Services,** South Esplanade, Guernsey (tel. 72 34 74), flies between Jersey and Guernsey nearly every half-hour (15min., £18.90).

Guernsey is only about 25 square miles. *Perry's Guide* (£2.25), with detailed maps and suggested walking paths for all the islands in the Bailiwick, is useful if you're planning to explore on foot or by bike. Pick it up at the tourist office or at bookstores around the island. Hitchhiking is almost impossible in St-Peter Port but reportedly easier away from the city. All buses leave from the terminal outside **The Picquet House** (tel. 72 46 77), which has maps and information on the extensive but notoriously unreliable bus system. An island-wide **Rover bus ticket** (see Buses below) will give you unlimited bus travel for a day. Cyclists will encounter steep hills.

St-Peter Port

Guernsey's capital, like its sister-city St-Helier, is a bustling but accommodating port city. St-Peter Port welcomed Victor Hugo when, in 1855, Emperor Napoleon III exiled him as a subversive intellectual whose very presence on French soil was liable to foment revolution. He remained here until 1870, penning his *Les Misérables* and *Les Travailleurs de la Mer* in a house that still stands. Make a housecall *chez* M. Hugo, and then climb the cobblestone streets to the older parts of the city for a most entrancing vista of St-Peter Port.

Orientation and Practical Information

Tourist Office: Crown Pier (tel. 72 35 52, for accommodations 72 35 55), at Victoria Pier. Free accommodations service. Pick up a map and tourist guide, *What's On: Guernsey.* Open Mon.-Sat. 9am-8pm, Sun. 10am-1:30pm and 6-8pm; Sept.-May Mon.-Sat. 9am-8pm.

Currency Exchange: Condor Ltd., White Rock Pier, exchanges cash only (8:15am-7pm) and is the only exchange open on Sun. **Thomas Cook,** High St. Open Mon.-Fri. 8:30am-5pm, Sat. 9am-4pm.

Post Office: Smith St. (tel. 72 62 41). **Poste Restante.** Open Mon.-Fri. 8:30am-5pm, Sat. 8:30am-noon. No postal code. Have your letter postmarked with an ornate collectors' stamp at the **Philatelic Shop** in front. Open Mon.-Fri. 8:30am-5pm, Sat. 8:30am-noon; Oct.-May Mon.-Fri. 9am-4pm.

Telephone code: 481. Dial 19, then the country code (44), followed by 481, and then the number you're trying to reach. All numbers in St-Peter Port are prefixed with the city code (7).

Flights: Aurigny Air Services, The Picquet House (tel. 72 34 74). Sells tickets for about 15 flights per day to Jersey (£18.90 one-way) and Cherbourg (£41.50). Take bus #C1 or C2 to the airport (25min.).

Buses: The Picquet House (tel. 72 46 77). Extensive service around the island with various scenic excursions in summer. Most fares 75-85p. **Rover passes** for unlimited travel (£3 for 1 day, £7 for 3 days, £12 for 5 days, £16 for one week).

Taxis: Central Taxi (tel. 72 30 47) under the clock tower. Operates Sun.-Thurs. 6am-12:30pm, Fri.-Sat. 24hrs. Also has **luggage storage** (£1 per bag per day).

Bike and Moped Rental: Moullin's Cycle Shop, St-George's Esplanade (tel. 72 15 81). 3-speeds and 5-speeds £3.50 for one day, £3 per additional day. Mountain bikes £5.50 for one day, £5 per additional day. Open Mon.-Sat. 9am-5:30pm. **Millard and Co.,** Victoria Rd. (tel. 72 07 77). 3-speeds £3.25 per day, £14.50 per week. Mopeds £7 per day, £30 per week. Motorcycles £12 per day, £40 per week. Open Mon.-Wed. and Fri.-Sat. 8:30am-12:45pm and 2-5:30pm, Thurs. 8:30am-12:30pm.

Sport Center: Beau Séjour Leisure Centre (tel. 72 72 11). Swimming, saunas, squash, roller-skating, and the only **cinema** in town. Tourist membership (£3 for 3 days) buys access to swimming, badminton, and table tennis from 9am to 5pm daily. Center open 9am-11pm daily, although hours for specific activities vary.

English Bookstore: Lots. **Buttons Bookshop,** 21 Smith St., carries copies of *Let's Go.* Open Mon.-Sat. 9am-5:30pm.

Laundromat: Albert Pier. Conveniently located. Wash and dry about £2. Bring 20p and 50p coins. Open daily 7am-midnight. Also at 59 Victoria Rd. Wash and dry £2.50. Open Mon.-Fri. 8am-9pm; Sat.-Sun. 8am-5pm. Last wash 7:30pm.

Hospital: Princess Elizabeth (tel. 72 52 41).

Police: tel. 72 51 11.

Emergency: tel. 999 (no coins required).

Accommodations and Camping

Guernsey strictly regulates its tourist industry; all guesthouses are graded in the official accommodations list available at the tourist office. As rooms are nearly impossible to find in July and August, call ahead for reservations. There are no youth hostels but plenty of campgrounds.

Friends Vegetarian Guest House, 20 Hauteville (tel. 72 11 46). In a house Victor Hugo, his family, and his mistress once occupied. Friendly proprietors serve vegetarian breakfast in a room with a great view of the port. Singles £15. Doubles £30. Triples £45. Open Easter-Oct.

Les Granges Manor, Ivy Gates (tel. 72 09 39). Take one of the many buses from town to the top of the Grange, then walk down the gravel drive. Elegant 17th-century home kept by a kind proprietor and his black labrador. £15 per person in one of 9 doubles or 2 singles. Breakfast included.

Cordier Hill Bungalow, Cordier Hill (tel. 72 30 41). A 15-min. trek up from the harbor, or take a bus to the top of the Grange. Clean rooms. Affable proprietors. £13.50 per person for the 1 single or 1 of 3 double rooms.

Forrester Arms, St-Georges Esplanade (tel. 72 35 83), close to the harbor. Small hotel run by a cordial manager. Doubles only, £14 per person. £16 for one person in a double room. Breakfast included.

Camping: Guernsey's 5 campgrounds are all accessible by bus from St-Peter Port, and most will rent equipment, especially if you book in advance. **Vaugrat Camp Site,** Les Hougues, rte. de Vaugrat (tel. 574 68), in St-Sampson (bus H1, H2, L, or K), is nearest. (£3.30 per adult, £2.50 per child, 75p per car. Rent a tent £8.75. Rents bikes for £3 per day, £13 per week.) Near St-Sampson, in Guernsey's northern interior, is **L'Etoile Site,** Hougue Guilimine (tel. 443 25), take bus J1 or J2 (£2.50 per adult, £1.25 per child; open June-Aug.); and **La Bailloterie,** (tel. 436 36), take bus J1 or J2 (£3 per adult, £1.50 per child; open June-Sept). In adjacent Castel (bus D or E) is: **Faux-quets Valley Farm** (tel. 554 60; £3.30 per adult, £1.65 per child; open mid-May to Sept. 14). Finally, there is camping in Torteval (bus C1 or C2) at **Laleur** (tel. 632 71; £3 per adult, £1.50 per child, 50p per car; open May-Sept.)

Food

Moderately priced restaurants cluster around Le Pollet and above Mill and Mansell St. Sip afternoon tea at the **Maison Carré** at the corner of the Commercial Arcade. (Tea with scone, butter, jam, and cream £2. Served until 4:30pm.) **Da Nello's,** 46 Le Pollet (tel. 72 15 52), lures frightening numbers of up-and-coming business people with its seafood, pasta, and meat. Make reservations. (Entrees £8.50 and up. Open daily noon-2pm and 6:30-10:30pm.) Those yearning for some home-style pretention should seek out **Partner's,** 41 High St., a popular, Americanized, yuppie-style restaurant with peach and pine green decor, which doles out burgers and vegetarian menus from £3. Get a seat in back with a harbor view. (Restaurant open daily noon-2pm and 6-10:30pm.) On the quay opposite the tourist office, **Valentino's** jumbles pizza, Mexican food, a salad bar, an upstairs harbor view, and courteous service. Buffalo wings are £3.95. (Open Mon.-Sat. noon-2pm and 6-11pm, Sun. 6-11pm. Delivers.) Down an after-dinner pint at the **Golden Lion Pub,** where guitar and song perfectly complement Guernsey's own **Pony Ale** (£1.10). **The White Hart** is the island's largest pub; beneath it, the **Golden Monkey** disco swings all night long.

Sights

St-Peter Port's buildings seem to grow in layers. Boutiques and restaurants occupy the ground level. Hotels follow, and the oldest residences occupy the top tier. Below the entire urban complex, the stately port shelters majestic yachts and humbler fishing vessels.

The **High Street** shop fronts, banks, and restaurants reflect Guernsey's prosperity. As in Jersey, prices tend to be lower than on the continent or in Britain because of the absence of the Value Added Tax. At the end of High St., turn uphill to face the **Old Town Church,** and behind it the **French Halles** where individual stalls sell fruits, vegetables, meat, fish, and local flowers. Steer straight ahead to the retail shop of the state dairy, where you can sample Guernsey milk, milk shakes, and yogurt.

The **Guernsey Traditional Market,** held most Thursday afternoons on Market St. (2-8pm in summer; 2-5pm in winter), sells local specialties. In the fish market, you may come across some ormer shells (from *oreille de mer,* "sea ear") for sale. Don't count on it, though, as the animal itself is becoming increasingly rare, sparking local concern, and is considered a delicacy. If you're really set on locating some specimens, try the **Aquarium.** (Open daily 10am-10pm; Oct.-April 10am-5pm. Admission £1.60, students £1, children and over 60 80p.)

The aquarium neighbors **La Veillette Underground Military Museum,** which details the hardships of Nazi-occupied Guernsey. (Open daily 10am-9pm; Nov.-Feb. Thurs., Sat.-Sun., and Tues. 10am-5pm. Admission £2.25, ages 5-15 £1.75, over 60 £1.) Both the museum and the aquarium are housed in tunnels built by Soviet and Eastern European prison laborers to hold fuel for U-boats. Look for the hammer and sickle chiseled into a wall of the second tunnel of the Aquarium. The **Castle Cornet** is a 13th-century complex of fortresses occupied and attacked by everyone from King John to the Nazis (tel. 72 16 57). (Open daily 10:30am-5:30pm. Admission £4, ages 5-15 £1.50, over 60 £1. Tours daily at 10:45am and 2:15pm.) The castle keep affords a 180-degree view of the town, the port, and neighboring islands. Below the keep, the **Maritime Museum** explores the history of navigation in Guernsey with fairly interesting videos and an addictive game in which you use radar to guide a ship to the harbor.

Heading straight inland, follow Hauteville to #38, Guernsey's most compelling attraction—the **Victor Hugo House** (now property of the city of Paris). Hugo spent 15 years and wrote some of his greatest works here, including *Les Misérables* and *Les Travailleurs de la Mer.* Exiled from France between 1855 and 1870, Hugo designed and decorated the interior; the home is preserved as the author left it. The house can only be visited by guided tours, which last 45 minutes and are conducted in French and English. (Open Mon.-Sat. 10-11:30am and 2-4:30pm. Admission £3, students £1.50, children and over 60 free.)

A statue of Hugo, cape and beard flowing, watches over the **Candie Gardens** on Candie St. Also in the gardens, the **Guernsey Museum and Art Gallery** showcases an exhibit on the archeological history of Guernsey with some interesting displays on the island's pre-Christian past. (Open daily 10:30am-5:30pm. Admission £2, students £1, children and over 60 75p.)

Elected representatives of the Bailiwick of Guernsey convene at the **Royal Court,** at the top of Smith St., on the last Wednesday of every month except August. The Queen sends a representative to the island's Parliament, but Guernsey writes its own laws and sets its own taxes. The island's only military obligation to England is to rescue the sovereign if he or she is captured and to help recover England if it is taken from the Crown. The court's proceedings betray Guernsey's unique and hybrid heritage, for although the court's non-partisan debates are completely in English, representatives must declare all votes in French.

Guernsey Countryside

Tiny bays ring the island of Guernsey, which has a different character on each side. The east coast, facing France, is fortified with cliffs to the south and castles to the north. Bolder sweeps of sand and rocky headlands mark the west coast. The best way to explore the countryside is by bike, but be warned that the southeast corner of the island has steep hills. Bus service, though extensive, is not very frequent, and hitchhiking is, as elsewhere, difficult, dangerous, and not recommended.

The archaic beauty of the island is most visible outside of St-Peter Port. The cliff path starting from Val des Terres south of St-Peter Port near the Aquarium begins quite tamely, but soon meets a steep incline. By the end, near Torteval, the cliffs are nearly deserted, and if you wander from the path, you'll be wading through shoulder-high ferns and brambles. Early birds get to see green **Fermain Bay** uncongested and explore the German fortifications with only the small sailboats bobbing at their moorings for company.

Legend has it that Guernsey witches based themselves in Perelle Bay at **Le Catriorc,** one of the island's many ancient *dolmens* (prehistoric stone monuments). The best place to make your flesh crawl is the **Dehus Dolmen,** a chambered tomb dating from 2000 BC, at the northern tip of the island, near the yacht marina in the Vale. Take the bus to Beaucette Marina from St-Peter Port. Although witchcraft has not made a popular resurgence on the island, as recently as 1914, one Mrs. Lake was accused of weaving a spell over one Mrs. Outin and her husband. The husband fell ill and died, as did all of Mrs. Outin's cattle.

An hour and a quarter by bike from St-Peter Port, you'll pass **Fermain Bay** and then reach **Telegraph Bay** and **St-Martin's Point.** If you don't have your own wheels, take the Jerbourg Road bus. One of the most beautiful spots on the island, St-Martin's Point shelters a small grove of evergreens which grow on a slope of land gently rolling down to the sea. Across Telegraph Bay, peculiar rocks called "peastacks" protrude at the island's southern tip. Follow the path from here along the cliff to the **Doyle Monument,** with its splendid view of the nearby isle of Herm.

Continuing around Jerbourg Point, you'll find **Moulin Huet Bay;** take your pick of the beaches here. As you continue around the bay to **Icart Point,** turn inland for tea with cream at the **Icart Tea Gardens,** one of the finest tea houses on the island. (Open daily 10am-5:30pm. Cream tea £1.50.) If you turn inland anywhere before Icart, you'll be near **St-Martin's,** the parish adjacent to St-Peter Port. *La Grandmère du Clim-*

quière, a stone figure dating from 700 BC, serenely guards the **St-Martin Parish Church Cemetery.** Leave an offering of flowers, or if you are a newlywed, placing coins on La Grandmère's head assures immediate and everlasting happiness.

Continuing inland toward the east, you'll soon come to the **German Underground Hospital** in **St-Andrew's.** It is preserved just as it was the day the Germans abandoned it: damp walls, rusty beds, and fetid atmosphere. (Open May-Sept. daily 10am-noon and 2-4pm; April and Oct. 2-4pm. Admission £1.80, under 14 80p.) Also in St-Andrew's is the bizarre **Chapel of Les Vauxbelets,** which claims to be the smallest chapel in Europe. It's just large enough for a priest and two parishioners. The exterior is decorated with shells and bits of broken china—one monk dedicated his life to building the chapel out of broken dishes sent to him by the faithful?!?! (Always open. Free.)

Rejoin the cliff path from the Occupation Museum (1.5km south of the chapel) and follow it to the end. In lovely **Torteval,** a few minutes from St-Peter Port, the public bar of the **Imperial Hotel** on Pleinmont St. serves superb pub grub for lunch (£3.50 for a ploughman sandwich) and decent dinners. Along the western coast, the grand sprawling expanses of the flat bays—**Roquaine, Vazon, Grand Havre**—are best seen at high tide. At low tide (as much as 40ft. below high tide), you can walk across to **Lihou Island,** between Roquaine and Perelle Bays, and see the ruins of the **Priory of St-Mary.** Be sure not to get stranded on Lihou, as the high tide covers the causeway and there are no accommodations on the island.

Although hotels are located on Sark and Alderney, a less expensive option is to make daytrips to these smaller neighbors of Guernsey. Automobiles are banned on the island of **Sark** and some of its laws date back to feudal times; the *Seigneur* still lives on and "rules" the island. The **Isle of Sark Shipping Company,** White Rock (tel. 72 40 59), offers full- and half-day tours of Sark. (Mon.-Sat. 3-6 boats; £15, children £7.50; cheaper if you leave before 8:30am.) You can share **Herm's** superb beaches with puffin colonies. The unusual **Shell Beach** is composed of tiny shell fragments. **Trident** runs day excursions from Guernsey (8-9 boats per day, £5, children £2.50).

Alderney (pop. 2000), the northernmost of the Channel Islands, is linked to Guernsey by **Condor Hydrofoils,** North Pier Steps (tel. 72 61 21).

Bretagne (Brittany)

This rugged peninsula, with cliffs gnawed by the sea into long crags and inlets, tugs away from mainland France, intent on its own direction. Unlike most of their compatriots, Bretons are a Celtic people whose ancestors crossed over from Britain to escape Anglo-Saxon invaders in the 5th and 6th centuries. They settled in the ancient Kingdom of Armor, converting its remaining inhabitants to Christianity and renaming it "Little Britain," or Brittany. Although the locals' frequent claim that they are Bretons first and French second may seem to hold little meaning in this era of fax machines and acid-washed denim, distinctive customs endure in many villages. The traditional costume of Breton women, the black dress and lace *coiffe* (an elaborate headdress), appears in museums, at reenacted folk festivals, and even at some markets. The lilting *Breizh* (Breton) is spoken energetically at the pubs and the ports in the western part of the province, and some children still learn the old Celtic tongue in school.

Bretons parade their cultural heritage in grand fashion during the village *pardons,* ancient church rites held on the Feast of the Assumption and on days honoring the most beloved of the region's several hundred local saints. Still considered days of repentance rather than displays for tourists, these festivals include a morning mass and an afternoon procession of costumed locals carrying banners, candles, and statues of the saints. The secular dances that follow tend to be set to modern music, but the lucky may hear ancient melodies played on traditional instruments. The best-known *pardons* take place at Tréguier in May, at Quimper's Festival de la Cornouaille between the third and fourth Sunday in July, at Ste-Anne-d'Auray in late July, at Perros-Guirec in mid-August, at Ste-Anne-La-Palud a week later, and at Josselin in early September. Also of note is Lorient's Festival Interceltique, held the first two weeks of August. For information, contact a tourist office in any large town.

Industrialization and modernization have come only in the post-war period to this relatively poor province, but they have come with a vengeance. Traditional vocations like farming and fishing have become increasingly difficult to pursue, and many younger people have emigrated to Paris and other cities throughout France. In the past, economic difficulties have fueled an active separatist movement. Recently, however, the French government has granted more autonomy to the local Breton leadership and has begun to support the preservation of Breton culture. In June 1979, under Giscard d'Estaing's administration, students were allowed to replace one language section of the *baccalauréat* exam with Breton. Mitterand made Brittany more easily accessible to the rest of France with his extensive road-building projects and the construction of TGV lines to Brest and Quimper. Discrimination against the Bretons, however, has not ended. One poster publicizing a recent Breton candidate for national office depicted a father telling his daughter that she can marry a man of any nationality, ethnic group, or race—just not a Breton.

However they may treat the Bretons, the rest of the French have great affection for the spectacular beaches and misted, almost apocalyptic headlands that line this province. If you dislike crowds, beware visiting in July and August. June is a perfect month to see Brittany, as the weather is mild, the restaurants and hotels open, and the towns not yet swarmed. Off-season, many of the coastal resorts such as St-Malo, Quiberon, and Concarneau essentially shut down, but the churches, cobblestones, beaches, and cliffs will seduce with their eerie and romantic solitude. Whatever the season, try to spend some time on the crowded but pristine islands off the mainland—Batz, Ouessant, and Bréhat, in particular—and in the smaller towns of the Argoat interior, where tourists are rarer and the Breton traditions less disturbed.

Both the Breton islands and the mainland lay claim to some inscrutable archeological treasures. Little is known of the neolithic people who settled here before the Gauls and erected the thousands of megalithic monuments visible today. The Romans, who conquered the area in 56 BC, decorated some of these monuments and incorporated them into their own rituals. Later, the Christian Bretons capped some standing stones with crosses or carved Christian symbols into them. *Menhirs* are large single stones weighing between 25 and 100 tons and pointing towards the heavens. Enormous *menhirs* usually stand alone, but some stand in circles to form *cromlechs* like the famous one at Er Lannic on a small island in the Gulf of Morbihan. *Dolmens,* smaller stones stacked to form roofed passages, may have been altars or tombs. The Merchant's Table in Locmariaquer, in the Gulf of Morbihan, is an impressive example.

The region's 1800-odd *crêperies* set their tables with more than just the famed regional specialty. *Galettes* of ground buckwheat flour *(sarrasin)* wrapped around eggs, mushrooms, seafood, or ham, precede dessert *crêpes* made of ground wheat flour *(froment)* and filled with chocolate, fruit, or jam. These are accompanied by *cidre brut* (the local cider) or by the sweeter *cidre doux,* while such delectable seafood dishes as *coquilles St-Jacques* (scallops), *saumon fumé* (smoked salmon), and *moules-marinières* (steamed mussels in a white wine-based broth) are served with *muscadet,* a dry white wine from the vineyards around Nantes. Brittany's *patisseries* display *kouign amann* (flaky sheets dripping with butter and sugar) and the custard-like *far breton.*

Getting to Brittany is hardly a problem; high-speed trains from Paris's Gare Montparnasse arrive in Rennes and Brest two and four hours later, respectively. Getting around Brittany is a different matter. The main train lines run between Rennes and Brest (passing through none of the scenic towns); between Rennes and Quimper; and between Nantes and Quimper. Smaller, less frequent trains and SNCF buses connect such towns as St-Malo, Dinan, Paimpol, Roscoff, Camaret, Concarneau, and Quiberon to the main lines, but not necessarily to each other. Private buses sometimes connect points that the train lines miss, but their prices are high, their departures infrequent (once or twice daily), and their hours inconvenient.

Cycling is the best way to travel, especially since the most beautiful sights are also the least accessible by public transportation. The terrain is relatively flat, though it gets a bit hillier in the Argoat region. Hikers can choose from a number of routes, including the long-distance footpaths ("Grandes Randonnées") GR341, GR37, GR38, GR380, and the spectacular GR34 along the northern coast. Tourist offices can help you coordinate your hiking or biking tour. Many people hitchhike along the major roads such as the D786 from Morlaix to St-Brieuc.

Rennes

In 1720, a drunken carpenter knocked over his lamp and set most of Rennes ablaze. Despite this misbegotten bonfire, which consumed all but the heart of the wood-heavy *vieille ville,* Rennes (pop. 250,000) has survived to become the administrative center of Brittany, though not its tourist center. Unlike other towns in the region, Rennes is most active during the school year, when 40,000 students—apparently oblivious to the lesson of the 18th-century carpenter—return to the bars and cafés and rouse the city from its summer slumber. The fetching but small old city warrants an afternoon's wander in any season, but those looking for deep insight into traditional Breton culture may find themselves itching to skip town. When planning your excursions, consult the tourist office, the Association Bretonne des Relais et Itinéraires (ABRI), and the Centre d'Information Jeunesse Bretagne.

Orientation and Practical Information

Rennes is two hours from Paris's Gare Montparnasse by TGV (3 1/2hr. by regular train), and accessible from Normandy via Caen. The **Vilaine River** cuts the city in two, with the station to the south and most of the sights and shopping to the north. From the front of the ultra-modern station, **av. Jean Janvier,** straight ahead, takes you to the river. To reach the tourist office, turn left along the river and walk five blocks to the Pont de Nemours. The *quais* that flank the Vilaine River are filled with shops and offices; popular bars and restaurants crowd the narrow streets behind the Cathédrale St-Pierre and pl. St-Germain.

Tourist Office: pont de Nemours (tel. 99 79 01 98). Exceptionally friendly staff. Camping booklets, hotel listings, and city maps (including a detailed map of the *vieille ville*). Open Mon.-Sat.

9am-7pm, Sun. 10am-1pm and 3-5pm; mid-Sept. to mid-June Tues.-Sun. 10am-12:30pm and 2-6:30pm, Mon. 2-6:30pm. **Annex** at the train station (tel. 99 53 23 23) open Mon.-Fri. 8am-8pm, Sat.-Sun. 9am-1pm and 2-6pm.

Post Office: 27, bd. du Colombier (tel. 99 31 42 72). **Branch office** on pl. de la République (tel. 99 79 50 71). **Currency exchange** with decent rates (1% commission). Open Mon.-Fri. 8am-7pm, Sat. 8am-noon. **Postal Code:** 35000.

Trains: pl. de la Gare (tel. 99 65 50 50; reservations 99 65 18 65), at the end of av. Jean Janvier. To: St-Malo (11 per day, 1hr., 61F); Nantes (8 per day, 2hr., 101F); Tours via Le Mans (8 per day, 3 1/2hr., 164F); Caen (3 per day, 3hr., 160F); Paris (3 per day, 3 1/2hr., 207F); TGV to Paris (9 per day, 2hr., 200F plus min. 16F required reservation). Information office open Mon.-Sat. 8am-7:30pm, Sun. 9am-7:30pm. **Lockers** 15-30F. Also, **bike rental** downstairs at the **luggage storage** window. (33F per 1/2-day, 44F per day; 1000F deposit; window open 8am-8pm.)

Buses: bd. Magenta (tel. 99 30 87 80), off pl. de la Gare. **TIV** (tel. 99 82 26 26) serves St-Malo (2 per day in summer, 6 per day in winter, 1 1/2hr., 47F; day excursion in summer 76F round-trip). **TAE** (tel. 99 50 64 17) goes to Dinard (4 per day, 1 3/4hr., 58F). **Courriers Bretons** (tel. 99 56 79 09), rolls to Mont-St-Michel via Pontorson (1-3 per day, 1 1/2hr., 56F). While not cheap, the **Pass 35** (260F) allows unlimited travel between Rennes, the destinations listed above, and some points beyond, including Cap Fréhel, Granville, and Fougères. Ask for a complete schedule of buses covered. Not covered by the Pass 35 are buses to Nantes (3 per day, 2hr., 86F); Vannes (2 per day, 2 3/4hr., 85F50); and Angers (2 per day, 3hr., 83F). Service to tiny local towns is more frequent on weekdays during the school year. Ticket windows open Mon.-Fri. 9am-6:30pm, Sat. 9am-noon.

Taxis: at the train station (tel. 99 30 79 79). 24hrs.

Car Rental: Hertz, 10, av. de Mail (tel. 99 54 26 52), which runs west from pl. Maréchal Foch at the town's western end. From 350F per day and 1800F per week. **English Bookstore:** This university town has dozens of 'em. The university bookstore **Librairie le Failler,** 8, rue Edith Cawell (tel. 99 78 10 05), off the pl. de Palais, is booked solid with literature, from Shakespeare (less than 30F) to Toni Morrison (80F). Open Tues-Sat. 9:15am-12:15pm and 1:30-7pm, Mon. 2-7pm. Rows and boxes of used English books fill a couple of corners at **F. Corre,** 18, rue Hoche (tel. 99 38 78 87). The amusing owner will guide you through mountains of French classics to reach them. Paperbacks about 15F. Open Tues.-Sat. 1:30-7pm.

Laundromat: Fluff and fold at 59, rue Duhamel just across from the train station. Wash 17F, dry 5F per 9min. Open daily 8am-10pm.

Hiking and Biking Information: Association Bretonne des Relais et Itinéraires (ABRI), also known as **maison de la Randonée,** 9, rue des Portes Mordelaises (tel. 99 31 59 44). Devoted to helping you discover Brittany on foot, on horseback, or by canoe, ABRI offers piles of invaluable information on Brittany's extensive network of GR (Grande Randonée) routes. Lists of *gîtes d'étape* (country residences now converted into hostels). Open Mon.-Sat. 9:30am-12:30pm and 2-6pm.

Institut Franco-Américain, 7, quai Châteaubriand (tel. 99 79 20 57). Arranges joint French-American activities. **American library** is open for public use and has over 5000 titles. Open Mon. and Thurs. 1-7pm, Tues.-Wed. 10am-noon and 1-7pm, Fri. 1-5pm, Sat. 9am-noon. Office on the 2nd floor open daily 9am-7pm. "Unofficial consulate" can help with problems or put you in touch with an embassy.

Youth Center: Centre d'Information Jeunesse Bretagne, Maison du Champ de Mars, 6, cours des Alliés (tel. 99 31 47 48), on the 2nd floor. Provides a comprehensive list of inexpensive hotels in Rennes as well as information on cycling, cultural events, work opportunities, and more for all of Brittany. Free babysitting service. Friendly staff. Open during school vacations and July 15-Aug. daily noon-6pm; other times of year Mon.-Fri. 10am-6pm, Sat. 10am-noon and 2-6pm.

Hospital: Hôpital de Pontchaillon, rue Henri le Guilaux (tel. 99 28 43 21).

Medical Emergency: SAMU, (tel. 99 59 16 16).

Police: rue d'Echange (tel. 99 65 00 22), off pl. St-Anne. **Emergency:** tel. 17.

Accommodations and Camping

Finding accommodations in Rennes shouldn't be a problem, except in early July during the Tombées de la Nuit festival. The spacious youth hostel is a 30-minute walk from the train station. In July and August, one university dorm sometimes remains open to student travelers for short stays. You may or may not be able to find someone who actually knows which dorm it is. (52F first night, 32F each additional night. To check availability, visit **CROUS**, 7, pl. Hoche or tel. 99 36 46 11; open Mon.-Fri. 8:30-11:30am and 1-4pm.) A number of small, moderately priced hotels lie to the east of av. Janvier between quai Richemont and the train station.

Auberge de Jeunesse (HI), 10-12, Canal St-Martin (tel. 99 33 22 33). From the train station, follow av. Jean Janvier straight to the canal where it becomes rue Gambetta. Head in this same, relatively straight, direction for about 5 blocks on rue Gambetta and Contour de la Motte, then take a left onto rue des Fossés. After one block, follow the diagonal rue de la Visitation, which ends across the street from pl. Ste-Anne. On the northern side of the *place* (to your right), rue St-Malo leads directly to the hostel. Bypass that 30-minute trek by taking bus #20 or #22, or #2 on weekends (direction: "Centre Commercial Nord") to "Pont de Legraverend." From the bus stop, continue following the river away from the station and *centre ville*. The youth hostel is a 5-min. walk, across the busy intersection and to the right. Great, newly renovated facility. Cafeteria and bar offer a variety of meals (mostly Italian) for 26F. Wash 16F. 25% discount coupons for local movies and 50% reduction passes for local buses and buses to Mont-St-Michel. Wowza showers! Reception open Mon.-Fri. 7:45am-11pm, Sat.-Sun. 8-10am and 6-11pm. Curfew midnight. Members only. Singles 100F. Doubles 71F per person. Triples and quads 61F per person. Breakfast included. Sheets 16F.

Hôtel de Léon, 15, rue de Léon (tel. 99 30 55 28), near the Vilaine River off quai de Richemont. Super location with big, well-kept rooms. Run by a warm couple that loves to discuss travel. The owner has done all the wacky, wild artwork himself. Singles 114F, with shower 160F. Doubles 124F, with shower 174F. Triples and quads 174F. Floor showers 16F. Breakfast 21F. Closed 2 weeks in July or August.

Hôtel Riaval, 9, rue Riaval (tel. 99 50 65 58). Turn right as you leave the train station, and immediately turn right again onto the stairs just past the gas station. Follow the path over the railroad tracks to the end; peaceful rue Riaval will be in front of you, branching off slightly to the left (about 5min.). Charming, despite location away from the *centre ville*. Clean, cozy, rooms and chatty owners. Top-floor rooms enjoy a view of the city. Singles and doubles 108F, with shower 140F. Triples 140F, with shower 160F. Showers 15F. Breakfast 20F.

Hôtel le Saint-Malo, 8, rue Dupont des Loges (tel. 99 30 38 21). Take av. Janvier from the train station and make a right onto rue Dupont des Loges, one block before the canal. Ongoing renovations have yielded bright, immaculate rooms, all with showers. Singles 145-170F. Doubles 160-190F. Breakfast 22F.

Hôtel le Magenta, 35, bd. Magenta (tel. 99 30 85 37). Across from the bus station and a 5-min. walk from pl. de la Gare. Bd. Magenta runs straight from the train station, a little to the left. Clean, capacious, and well-lit rooms on a busy street opposite the bus station. Reception at the bar open Mon.-Sat. 7am-9pm. Singles and doubles 120F, with shower 160F. Showers 20F. Breakfast 22F.

Camping: Municipal des Gayeulles, near Parc des Bois (tel. 99 36 91 22). Take bus #3 from rue de Paris, the southern border of the Jardin de Thabor, to "Parc les Gayeulles." Grassy, scenic, isolated site. 11F per person, 9F90 per site, 4F50 per car. Showers 5F. Open Easter-Sept.

Food

As in most of Brittany, *crêperies* are the cheapest places for a light meal; many of them scatter about the old quarter and on rue St-Melaine near the university and gardens. Take some fruit, bread, and cheese to a bench in the beautiful **Jardin du Thabor.** A covered **market** is held Monday through Saturday from 7am to 6pm in Les Halles, behind the post office. An open market is held in a different place every day; ask the tourist office or any local where it is. To escape the *crêpe* doldrums, try one of Rennes's Afghan, Indian, Pakistani, Spanish, or Italian restaurants.

Crêperie du Boulingrain, 25, rue St-Melaine. Formerly a prison, this place now serves a pickled sardine *galette* worth some jail time. The *boulingrain*, the restaurant's namesake, is a *crêpe* stuffed with apples, caramel, and almonds (28F). Open Mon.-Fri. 11:30am-2pm and 6:30-11pm, Sat.-Sun. 6:30-11pm. **Au Jardin des Plantes**, 32, rue St-Melaine. Lively crowd in a half-timbered house. Filling 3-course *menus* 47F and 82F. Open Mon.-Fri. noon-2pm and 7:15-10pm, Sat.-Sun. 7:15-10pm. **Auberge St-Sauveur**, 6, rue St-Sauveur (tel. 99 79 32 56). Exquisite cuisine and impeccably orchestrated service. Superb 98F and 153F *menus*. Open Mon.-Sat. 7-11pm. Reservations recommended.

Restaurant des Carmes, 2, rue des Carmes, off bd. de la Liberté. Popular joint with a wide selection of salads, pizzas, and meat dishes. 3- and 4-course *menus* 48F, 68F, and 86F. Open Tues.-

Sat. 11:30am-2pm and 7-10pm, Mon. 11:30am-2pm. Closed for a month in June-July at owner's discretion.

Crêperie des Portes-Mordelaises, rue des Portes Mordelaises, near pl. des Lices at the foot of a 15th-century tower, in an old and rustic corner of town. Try the goat cheese *galette* (28F). *Crêpes* 12-29F. Open Tues.-Sat. noon-2pm and 7-10:30pm, Sun. 7-10:30pm.

L'Escale, 178, rue St-Malo (tel. 99 59 19 55), near the youth hostel. Cross the bridge in front of the hostel and walk down rue St-Malo; the restaurant is on your right. Smoky and cozy with a local clientele. Bounteous and inexpensive red wine. *Galettes* 10-30F, *crêpes* 6-22F, entrees 20-50F. Open Sept.-July Tues.-Thurs. and Sat.-Sun. 7:30-10pm.

Sights and Entertainment

Rennes's skyline of bland modern buildings doesn't even merit a postcard. Instead, stroll through the narrow streets between pl. du Palais and Palais St-Georges, cluttered by medieval houses with overhanging upper stories designed to maximize space. If you long for American kitsch, go to pl. du Colombier, just off bd. de la Liberté, south of the old city and near the train station, for some quality shopping time at the new Rennes mall, complete with a McDonald's.

Entertainment in Rennes ranges from visiting rock groups at the Maison de la Culture to marionette performances of *Peter and the Wolf* at the rue de la Paillette. The pamphlet *Spectacles, informations* at the tourist office lists *everything,* even the blooming periods of Rennes's flowers, bushes, and trees. In early July, Rennes holds the festival **Les Tombées de la Nuit,** nine days of non-stop music, dance, party-'til-you-drop, theater, song, and mime by international performers who prowl the streets from noon to midnight. For information, write to the Office de Tourisme, Festival de TN, 8, pl. du Maréchal Juin, 35000 Rennes (tel. 99 79 01 98 or 99 30 38 01). The annual **Festival International des Arts Electroniques** brings candlelight to the canal and displays of electronic art and sculptures to the streets in June. Be sure to visit the startlingly green, well-kept **Jardin du Thabor** behind the Renaissance **Eglise Notre Dame** and the **Cloître Ste-Melanie.** To reach the gardens, follow the continuation of rue Jean Janvier across the river and turn right on rue Victor Hugo. (Open June-Sept. daily 7am-9:30pm.) The **Musée de Bretagne** and the **Musée des Beaux Arts** are housed in the same building at 20, quai Emile Zola, by the canal. The Musée de Bretagne provides an informative introduction to the region's history and traditions, with tools, costumes, and jewelry from prehistoric to present times. The Musée des Beaux Arts displays local landscapes as well as an interesting (if obscure) collection of art from the 14th century to the present. (Open Wed.-Mon. 10am-noon and 2-6pm. Admission covering both 15F, students with ID and families 7F50.) For a superb introduction to the area's history and ethnology, visit the **Ecomusée du pays de Rennes,** located on a former farm (Ferme de la Bintinais) at the edge of the city. Not only can you learn about Rennes's daily life since about 1600, but you can also picnic on the remaining 75 acres of fields and apple orchards. From pl. de la République, take bus #14 (Sundays, #1) to stop "Le Gacet." (Open April 1-Oct. 15 Wed.-Mon. 2-7pm; Oct. 16-March31 2-6pm.)

Summer visitors looking for stomping student nightlife may have to stick around until September. If a café or a drink is all you want, stay within the picturesque *vieille ville.* Dance off extra energy (or *crêpes)* at the popular **Le Pyms,** 27, pl. du Colombier (tel. 99 67 30 00; cover 80F, Sun.-Thurs. 60F; open daily 10:30pm-5am). Pink-pillared **L'Espace,** 43, bd. de la Tour d'Auvergne (tel. 99 30 21 95), is also worth a try. (cover Fri.-Sat. 80F, Sun.-Wed. 50F, Thurs. 60F; open daily 10:45pm-5am).

St-Malo ✓

To a 6th-century Welshman named St-Malo, the island was a refuge from marauding Angles and Saxons. To privateers and pirates, the growing city offered protection from English, Norman, and French invaders. To writer Châteaubriand, St-Malo's ever-changing shore provided Romantic inspiration. Today, the town and its past remain a source of pride to the *St-Malouin* people; witness only the city's motto: "Neither French, nor Breton, I am from St-Malo."

Although eighty percent of the city was destroyed in World War II, St-Malo has been marvelously reconstructed. Within the towering stone walls that enclose the entire island lies a web of cobblestone streets winding among 15th-, 16th-, and 17th-century buildings. Almost as impressive as the city's miles of ramparts are its miles of beach—warm brown sands that play host to hundreds of sunbathers and then disappear completely at high tide. While the summer onslaught of tourists slightly fetters its romantic spirit, St-Malo remains an independent and determined freebird.

Orientation and Practical Information

The old walled city (called *intra muros*) is the northernmost point of St-Malo, which has since fanned out along the coastline to the southwest and southeast. The *train station* is in the center of this fan. From the entrance to the station on the west side, turn right, cross bd. de la République, and follow av. Louis-Martin directly north to the tourist office (10min.). Various buses make the same trip (the stop is "Porte St-Vincent") including the red #2 and #3 and the purple #4, which run every 20 minutes from the stop on bd. de la République. (6F70).

Tourist Office: Esplanade St-Vincent (tel. 99 56 64 48), near the entrance to the old city. Busy staff. Request the indexed city map and a list of local campsites. Open Mon.-Sat. 8:30am-8pm, Sun. 10am-6:30pm; Sept.-June Mon.-Sat. 9am-noon and 2-7pm, Sun. 10:15am-12:15pm and 2:15-5:15pm.

Post Office: 1, bd. de la Tour d'Auvergne (tel. 99 56 12 05), at the intersection with bd. de la République. Open Mon.-Fri. 8am-7pm, Sat. 8am-noon. **Branch office,** pl. des Frères Lamennais in the *vieille ville* (tel. 99 40 89 90). Both open Mon.-Fri. 8:30am-6:30pm, Sat. 8:30am-noon; Sept. 17-May Mon.-Fri. 8:30am-12:30pm and 1:30-5:30pm, Sat. 8:30am-noon. **Currency exchange** at both offices. Poste Restante: address mail "Instance, Poste Restante; 35401 St-Malo Principal" for the main office. **Postal Code:** 35400.

Trains: pl. de l'Hermine (tel. 99 65 50 50; reservations in St-Malo 99 56 15 33). To: Paris-Montparnasse (3 per day, 5hr., 230F); Rennes (8-12 per day, 1hr., 58F); Caen via Dol (8 per day, 3 1/2hr., 131F); Dinan via Dol (8 per day, 1hr., 41F), TGV to Paris via Rennes (7-9 per day, 3 1/2hr., 230F plus 32F required reservation). Open Mon.-Fri. 5:30am-8pm, Sat. 6am-8pm, Sun. 7:30am-8pm. **Lockers** 30F for 72 hrs. **Luggage Storage** (30F per day per item) at ticket windows. **Bike rental** in July and Aug.

Buses: Information offices are in the pavilion opposite the tourist office. **Tourisme Verney** (tel. 99 40 83 83). To: Rennes (Mon.-Sat. 3 per day, 2hr., 46F); Dinan (3 per day, 1hr., 30F); Cancale (1-2 per day Mon.-Sat., 50min., 18F). Buses leave from the esplanade St-Vincent and stop briefly at the train station. Office open Mon.-Fri. 8:30am-noon and 1:45-6:15pm, Sat. 8:30am-noon; mid-Oct. to mid-June Mon.-Fri. 8:30am-noon and 2-6:30pm, Sat. 8:30-noon. **Courriers Bretons** (tel. 99 56 79 09). Day excursions to Mont St-Michel, 89F. To Cancale (3-5 per day, 1/2hr., 18F, seniors 8F). Office open Mon.-Fri. 8:30am-12:15pm and 2-6:15pm, Sat. 8:30am-12:15pm. Information on St-Malo **city buses** call 99 56 06 06. 6F80 per ticket (valid for one hour after use to include cost of return), *carnet* of 10 46F50.

Ferries: Voyages Pansart, esplanade St-Vincent (tel. 99 40 85 96), in the pavilion with the bus offices. Information and booking for all ferries. Ask about special excursions to Mont St-Michel, Quimper, Cap Fréhel, and Quiberon (90-150F). To Jersey (248F, 225F one day round-trip). Open Mon.-Sat. 8am-noon and 2-7pm, Sun. 8:30am-noon and 4-6:30pm; Sept.-June Mon.-Sat. 9am-noon and 2-7pm. **Brittany Ferries,** Gare Maritime du Naye. To: Portsmouth (1-2 per day, 8 1/2hr., 400F one-way or round-trip, bicycles 70F; Sept. 7-July 24, 330-360F, bicycles free; children always half price). **Emeraude Lines,** Gare Maritime de la Bourse (tel. 99 40 48 40). To: Jersey (1-2 per day, 1 1/4hr., car ferry one-way 225F, one day round-trip 260F, 72-hr. round-trip 419F; children one-way 135F, one day round-trip 156F, 72-hr. round-trip 251F), Guernsey (1-2 per day, 2 1/2hr., 301F, 72-hr. round-trip 505F; children 181F, 72-hr. round-trip 303F), and Dinard (8 or more per day, 10min., 20F, round-trip 30F; children 12F, round-trip 20F). Summer excursions to Cap Fréhel (115F, children 69F) and to Dinan, up the Rance estuary (same prices). **Lockers** available. **Condor Hydrofoil,** Gare Maritime (tel. 99 56 42 29). To Jersey (1-4 per day, 70min., 248F, 72-hr. round-trip 403F; children 3-14 143F, 72-hr. round-trip 242F), Guernsey or Sark (1-4 per day, 3 1/2hr., 285F, one day round-trip 301F, 72-hr. round-trip 505F; children 171F, one day round-trip 181F, 72-hr.round-trip 303F), and Weymouth (1-4 per day, 4hr., 500F, round-trip 900F; children 250F, round-trip 475F).

Bike Rental: Diazo, 47, quai du Duguay-Trouin (tel. 99 40 31 63). 3-speeds 50F per day, 250F per week, 500F or ID deposit. 10-speeds and mountain bikes 80F per day, 480F per week. Open Mon.-Sat. 9am-noon and 2-6pm.

Windsurfer Rental: Quai 34 Surf School, 7, rue Courtoisville (tel. 99 40 07 47). Walk along the Grande Plage until you see the signs. First rental 140F per hr., 180F per day. Further rental 80F per hr., 160F per day. Two-hr. personal lesson 175F. Open June-Aug. daily 9am-2pm.

Laundromat: 27, bd. de la Tour d'Auvergne, 3 blocks from the station down bd. de la République. Wash 18F, dry 2F per 7min.

Hospital: Centre Hospitalier Broussais, 2, rue Laennec (tel. 99 81 60 40).

Ambulance: 16, av. Waldeck-Rousseau (tel. 99 40 02 02 or 99 56 30 64). 24 hrs.

Police: pl. des Frères Lamennais (tel. 99 40 85 80). **Emergency:** tel. 17.

Accommodations and Camping

St-Malo is a the ultimate vacation spot, and everybody knows it. During July and August, reserve up to six months in advance to repose in the *vieille ville*. Arrive early to stay in the hostels. Do not sleep on the beaches—even if the water is 350m away when you lie down, it will dash you against the wall within six hours.

Auberge de Jeunesse/Centre de Rencontres Internationales (HI), 37, av. du Père Umbricht (tel. 99 40 29 80). You can avoid the 25-min. walk from the station by taking bus #5 (direction: "Paramet"); get off at the stop after the hostel flags on the left (last bus at 7:30pm). On foot, from the *front* of the station, follow bd. de la République to the right. After two blocks, turn right onto av. Ernest Renan. Follow it for 3 blocks, then turn left at the cemetery. Continue straight to av. Pasteur, which becomes av. du Père Umbricht (keep right). The youth hostel is on the left. Pretty, ivy-covered building, fronted by tennis courts and beautiful pink flowers, just 3 blocks from the beach. Sorrowful showers, but the new building has decent ones. Office open Mon.-Fri. 9am-noon, and 2-10pm, Sat.-Sun. open 24 hrs. No lockout. Members only. 61F. Modern doubles 71F. Breakfast included. Lunch or dinner 34F. Sheets 15F. Kitchen facilities. Next door, the **Foyer des Jeunes Travailleurs** has laundry facilities (20F), a pool table, and a higher ratio of French natives. May accept hostelers, if you're lucky. 57F.

Auberge de Jeunesse (HI), Maison l'Hermitage, 13, rue des Ecoles (tel. 99 56 22 00). Dignified stone mansion with beautiful grounds and a friendly staff, but a 40-min. walk from the *vieille ville*, 1/2-hr. from the station. 2- to 6-person rooms are highly coveted: be sure to call ahead. Take bus #5 (direction "Les Fontanelles") from av. Jean Jaurès to Petit Paramet. Reception open 24 hrs. 42F. 62F50 per person in 4-person bungalows with kitchens, 32F in dorm-style tents. Breakfast 13F.

Auberge Au Gai Bec (The Jolly Beak), 4, rue des Lauriers (tel. 99 40 82 16). Great location *intra muros,* and exceptionally affable owners. Small, but clean rooms, a steep staircase with plaster fishes on the walls, and a delicious restaurant downstairs, all inside this small building that served as a brothel during the WWII years. Singles and doubles 100F, with shower 160F. Triples and quads with shower 200F. Breakfast 25F.

Hôtel le Neptune, 21, rue de l'Industrie (tel. 99 56 82 15). 5min. to the beach, station, and the *vieille ville*. Clean rooms, with pitched ceilings on the top floor. Singles and doubles 115F, with shower 140F. Triples and quads with shower 180-200F. Breakfast 21F.

Hôtel Le Vauban, 7, bd. de la République (tel. 99 56 09 39). Slightly dark, but centrally located and cheap, with a 10% discount for *Let's Go* holders. Singles 100F. Doubles 120F. Triples 140F. Quads 160F. Showers included. Breakfast 20F.

Information on all municipal campgrounds is available at the tourist office, or call 99 40 71 11. **Camping de la Cité d'Aleth,** near promenade de la Corniche in St-Servan (tel. 99 81 60 91), is the closest and most scenic site, equipped with running water and hot shower. From July-Aug., you can take bus #1 to "Aleth." (11F60 per adult, 5F80 per child, 5F80 per car, 7F40 per tent.)

Food

Outdoor **markets** sprout from 8am to 12:30pm behind Eglise Notre-Dame-des-Grèves (Mon., Thurs., and Sat.); on pl. Bouvet in St-Servan and at the **Marché aux Légumes** *intra muros* (Tues. and Fri.); and on pl. du Prieuré, in Paramé (Wed. and

Sat.). **Intermarché,** bd. Théodore Botrel, stocks bags of *craquelins de St-Malo,* crunchy flour biscuits that melt in your mouth—not in your hands. (Open Mon.-Fri. 9am-12:30pm and 3-7:15pm, Sat. 2:30-7:30pm.) *Craquelins* are also available within the walls at the well-stocked **R. Cornu,** 4, pl. de Marché aux Légumes. Also *intra muros,* countless *crêperies* and seafood restaurants abound, especially along **rue Jacques-Cartier.**

> **Le Petit Malouin,** 6, rue de la Vieille Boucherie (tel. 99 40 87 44). Traditional *Brotonne* crêpes at good prices—a three-crêpe *menu* for 38F or 48F. Special student prices on lunch *menus* during the week. Good location in one of the *vieille ville*'s liveliest corridors. Open daily 11:30am-11:30pm.

> **Auberge Au Gai Bec,** 4, rue des Lauriers (tel. 99 40 82 16). Downstairs from the hotel. A busy restaurant with good French fare. Seafood specialities include *lotte bordelaise* (fish in red wine sauce, 72F) and *foie gras maison* (86F). Make reservations, or bide your waiting time at J-P Baquere's shop next door, where you can watch the *souffleur de verre* handcraft dishes, ornaments, and glass sculptures. (Open Tues.-Sat. noon-2pm and 7:30-10:30pm.)

> **Chez Ferhat,** 4, rue de la Vieille Boucherie. Same pleasant *rue* as Le Petit Malouin, but farther down on its own little *place.* Welcome relief from the crêpe onslaught. Healthy servings of chicken and lamb *couscous* (60F) and pitchers of *sangria.* Open Tues.-Sun. noon-3pm and 7-11pm.

> **Siam,** 39, rue de la République, near the train station. Thai food with a French twist, like *cuisse de grenouilles au basilic* (frogs' legs in basil sauce, 45F) and *caramel mou avec cacahuète enrobé de sésame* (peanut nougat in sesame sauce, 19F). *Menu* 69F. Open Sun.-Tues. and Thurs.-Fri. noon-2:30pm and 7:30-10:30pm, Sat. 7:30-10:30pm.

Sights and Entertainment

The best way to see St-Malo is to explore the ramparts—you'll have the old town at your feet on one side and a long stretch of sea on the other. The careful reconstruction of the 15th-, 16th-, and 17th-century slate and stone buildings is evident from from this vantage point. The WWII bombing raids burned all but the skeletal framework, and unconnected beams still poke out from the sides of some houses. The top of the Porte St-Vincent opposite the tourist office overlooks lively pl. Châteaubriand, where street musicians and dancers serenade café- and restaurant-goers. On the other side of the Hôtel de Ville, Porte St-Thomas looks out onto the **Fort National,** accessible only at low tide. Farther along, the **Tour Bidouane** marks the northern point of the old city. Climb down to the beach and continue along the stone walkway to **Le Grand Bé.** This small island holds the lonely grave of the Romantic pencil-pusher Châteaubriand, who asked to be buried near the crashing of the waves and the wind. The independent spirit of St-Malo and of Brittany flares up three yards behind him. On the plaque engraved with the words *"Un grand écrivain français a voulu reposer ici"* (a great French writer wanted to rest here), someone has drawn a line through the word *"français"* and scrawled above it *"Breton."* Don't set out for the island if the sea is within 10m of the submersible walkway; you may get dangerously stranded in the surf for a good six hours until the tide recedes. Châteaubriand was born at the **Hôtel de la Gicquelais** at 3, rue de Châteaubriand. If the tide keeps you from Chateaubriand's island, the **Piscine de Bon-Secours,** slightly farther along the beach from Tour Bidouane, is a tidal swimming pool, with simple barricades to distinguish its perimeter from the surrounding waters, and is a favorite summer hangout of the younger *St-Malouin* set.

Within the walls (literally), the **Musée de la Ville** (tel. 99 40 71 11), at the Hôtel de Ville near Porte St-Vincent, leads you through caches of maps, models, maritime documents, and other pirate paraphernalia. It ends in the turret, with a phenomenal panorama over St-Malo. (Open daily 10am-noon and 2-6pm; Nov.-March Wed.-Mon. 10am-noon and 2-5:30pm. Admission 18F, students 11F50.) Nearby, set into the wall at the **Aquarium** (tel. 99 40 91 86) and the **Exotarium** (tel. 99 40 86 21), house an eclectic array of both aquatic and land-lubbing reptiles. (Open daily 9am-11pm; mid-Sept. to June 9am-noon and 2-7pm. Admission to each 20F, students 15F. Admission to both buildings 35F, students 30F.)

While wandering aimlessly among the streets of old St-Malo is a treat, there are a few areas worth seeking and seeing. Not far from the Exotarium, intricate leaded windows adorn one domestic façade along rue Pelicot, and the last house before the traffic barricade exemplifies fortified residential architecture. Farther down, you will see **l'Escalier de la Grille** (though the *grille,* or gate, has been replaced with wooden doors), and to the right at 2, cours la Houssaye, lies the former residence of the Duchesse Anne de Bretagne, whose marriages to Louis XII and Charles VIII indirectly united Brittany with the rest of France. Gothic **Cathédrale St-Vincent** has also been extensively restored; the union of a dark, 12th-century nave with fiery, modern stained-glass windows creates an eerie effect. Note the tomb of Jacques Cartier who "discovered" Canada. (Open daily 8am-7pm; Sept.-May 8am-noon and 2-7pm.) Over 300 dolls and furnished doll houses fill the displays of the **Musée de la Poupée,** 13, rue de Toulouse (tel. 99 40 15 51). (Open July-Aug. daily 10am-1pm and 2-7pm. Admission 20F.)

Stop for a drink at the **Angelus Bis,** 3, rue des Cordeliers, a popular bar complete with circular red couches, Greek statues, and a large video screen (open 10pm-5am). The **Atrium,** on the chaussée du Sillon outside the Porte St-Vincent offers a chance to gamble at *la boule,* a roulette-like game (18 and over; cover 60F; open daily 10pm-5am.) From June to August, the annual **Festival Internationale de Musique Sacrée** profits from the exquisite acoustics of the cathedral with weekly concerts of choral and orchestral music.

Near St-Malo

St-Malo is a crowded but convenient base from which to explore the eastern segment of the Côte d'Emeraude and even Mont St-Michel. To the east, serviced by Tourisme Verney and Courriers Bretons buses, lies **Cancale,** famous for its oysters and the scenic **Pointe de Grouin.** For a detailed explanation of oyster cultivation, visit Cancale's **Musée de l'Huitre**, on route de la Corniche. (Open March-Oct.; guided tours in English at 10:30am and 2:30pm; in French at 11am, 3:15pm, 4:30pm, and 6pm. Admission 30F, students 15F; 6 oysters, wine, and bread 30F.) Thirty-six km southeast of St-Malo lies **Combourg,** about which Châteaubriand wrote, "It was in the woods of Combourg that I became what I am." If the prospect of becoming a cape-wearing Romantic poet doesn't deter you, visit the well-preserved **Château de Combourg** (tel. 99 73 22 95). Châteaubriand spent many childhood nights in the *Tour du Chat* (Cat's Tower), which was supposedly haunted by a previous inhabitant's wooden leg and a black cat intent upon using the limb as a scratching post. (Château open April-Oct. Wed. Mon. 2-5:30pm. Garden open April-Oct. Wed.-Mon. 9am-noon and 2-6pm. Admission 24F, students 18F.) Farther east, **Mont St-Michel** makes a convenient daytrip from St-Malo. Secure reservations a day in advance at any of the bus tour offices by the tourist office. Most cost 87F.

Accessible by bus or a 10-minute boat ride, **Dinard,** a resort town founded by an American, is the *très chic* haven for Brittany's Great Gatsby set. (Emeraude Lines runs 9:30am-6:15pm, from the *gare maritime* complex; 20F, round-trip 30F.) Watch pedal boats, windsurfers, and sailboats from Dinard's top-notch beach or swim in the Olympic-size swimming pool with heated sea water. The town itself sports some ugly highrises and amusement-park-type fast food stands, but it's worth a daytrip. Walk around both the **Pointe du Moulinet** and the **Pointe des Etetés,** where stone steps overgrown with rosebushes spiral up to mansions and viewpoints. Emeraude Lines also sails up the Rance to Dinan once a day with the tide (2 1/2hr., 83F, round-trip 115F); the boats stop in Dinard, but there's no time to get off.

Dinan ✓

Like much of Brittany, Dinan mired as the focus of a medieval tug-of-war between England and France. In fact, in 1364 its very fate turned on the outcome of a duel; the Frenchman Du Guesclin won; Sir Thomas of Canterbury yielded; and the English forces withdrew across the Channel. Today, Dinan boasts proudly—in French—of its reputation as the best preserved medieval town in Brittany. In the *vieille ville,* 66m above the Rance River, 15th-century houses line cobblestone streets. Precipitous paths to arouse the envy of mountain goats descend to the port, and a castle and museum round out the city's attractions. Tranquil Dinan is not for those seeking riotous fun and adventure, but it is a welcome respite from its more popular neighbors St-Malo and Dinard.

Orientation and Practical Information

To reach the tourist office, in the *vieille ville,* from the station bear left across pl. du 11 Novembre 1918 onto rue Carnot, then right onto rue Thiers, which brings you to a large rotary intersection, pl. Duclos. Climb the hill to the left on rue du Marchix, which becomes rue Ferronnerie. Turn left at the sign for the tourist office, cross the square, take rue Ste-Claire, and turn left onto rue de l'Horloge.

Tourist Office: 6, rue de l'Horloge (tel. 96 39 75 40). A granite-pillared 16th-century mansion beside a weeping willow. Helpful staff. Walking tours of the town July-Aug. daily at 10am and 3pm (25F, children 10F). Map and excellent guide to the town's sights (10F). Open Mon.-Sat. 9am-6:45pm, Sun. 9am-1pm and 2-4:45pm; Sept.-May. Mon.-Sat. 8:30am-12:30pm and 2-6pm.

Post Office: pl. Duclos (tel. 96 85 12 07). **Currency exchange.** Open Mon.-Fri. 8:30am-6:45pm, Sat. 8:30am-noon. **Postal Code:** 22100.

Trains: pl. du 11 Novembre 1918 (tel. 96 39 22 39, information 96 94 50 50). To: Rennes via Dol (6 per day, 2hr., 61F); St-Brieuc (3 per day, 1hr., 47); Paimpol (1 per day, change at St-Brieuc and Guingamp, 4hr., 83F); Morlaix (3 per day, 2 Sun., change at St-Brieuc, 2hr., 97F); St-Malo (7 per day, change at Dol, 1 1/4hr., 41F). Paris-Montparnasse via Rennes (9 per day, 5hr., 233F); TGV to Paris via Rennes (9 per day, 3 1/2hr., 226F plus 32F required reservation). Ticket office open Mon.-Tues. and Thurs. 5:30am-6:55pm, Wed. 5:30am-7:30pm, Fri. 5:50am-6:55pm, Sat. 6:20am-6:55pm, Sun. 8:30am-8:10pm.

Buses: CAT/TV (tel. 96 39 21 05), at the train station on the other side of the baggage office. Buses leave from pl. Duclos. July-Sept. service to St-Malo only (3 per day, 1hr., 30F50). Excursions to points along the northern coast, Mont St-Michel, and the Gulf of Morbihan in July and Aug. only. Information office open Mon.-Fri. 8am-noon and 2-6pm, Sat. 8am-noon. **TAE** (tel. 99 50 64 17). To Rennes (2-3 per day, 1hr., 46F) and Dinard (2-3 per day, 1/2hr., 26F).

Ferries: Emeraude Lines, quai de la Rance (tel. 96 39 18 04). May-Sept. 1 excursion per day downstream to St-Malo, return by bus (2 1/2hr. down by boat, 3/4hr. back by bus; 83F, ages 2-12 50F).

Bike Rental: B. P. Zoom, 30, rue Carnot (tel. 96 39 21 94). 10-speeds 45F per day; 500F or passport deposit. Open Tues.-Sat. 8:30am-12:30pm and 2-7pm.

Canoe and Kayak: Club de Canoë, port de Dinan across from rue du Quai (tel. 96 39 01 50). Kayaks 40F per hr., 70F per 1/2-day, 100F per day, 400F per week. Canoes for two 50F per hr., 80F per 1/2-day, 120F per day, 500F per week. Open Mon.-Sat. 2-5pm. Reserve for Sun.

Laundromat: 33, Grand'Rue, opposite the Eglise St-Malo. Wash 14F, dry 2F per 5min. Bring lots of 1F and 2F coins. Open Mon.-Sat. 8:30am-8pm.

Hospital: rue Châteaubriand (tel. 96 85 72 85), at Léhon.

Police: pl. Duguesclin (tel. 96 39 03 02). **Emergency:** tel. 17.

Accommodations and Camping

Dinan has many campsites, a comfortable youth hostel, and a few cheap hotels that often have room in the summer. Call ahead just to be sure.

Auberge de Jeunesse (HI) tel. 96 39 10 83. Moulin du Méen in Vallée de la Fontaine-des-Eaux. There's no bus to this wooded hideaway, but if you are arriving at night and call ahead, the hostel will arrange to pick you up at the station. If you're walking, turn left from the train station's main exit, turn left across the tracks, and follow the signs (1/2hr.). If coming from town, go down the very steep rue Petit Fort (not for those with wobbly knees or hearts), turn left onto rue du Quai, and walk about 15min. Follow the signs and look left. A wonderful, friendly place by a stream and weeping willows. Good facilities, including kitchen, common room, and gallery with temporary exhibits. Reception open daily 8-11am and 5-8pm. Lockout 11am-5pm. Curfew 11pm. Make arrangements if you want to stay out later. Members only. 43F. If the hostel is full, cots in a tent outside are only 20F. Sheets 15F. Hearty dinner 43F. Lockers 5F.

Hôtel du Théâtre, 2, rue Ste-Claire (tel. 96 39 06 91), around the corner from the tourist office in the *vieille ville.* Comfortable but poorly lit rooms, congenial owner, and crackerjack location. Singles and doubles 75-115F. Doubles with showers 145F. Breakfast 19F.

Hôtel-Restaurant de l'Océan, pl. du 11 Novembre 1918 (tel. 96 39 21 51), across from the station. Warm owner, clean rooms, and parking for bikes and cars. Singles and doubles 100F, with shower 130F. Triples and quads with shower 190F. Breakfast 21F.

Camping: The campground at the **youth hostel** is in a beautiful location (20F per night). The tourist office provides a list of other sites, the closest of which is the **Camping Municipal,** 103, rue Châteaubriand (tel. 96 39 11 96). If you face the post office in pl. Duclos, rue Châteaubriand is to your right. Convenient location, average grounds, but below-par shower and toilet facilities. 11F per person, 10F per site, 7F per car. Open May-Nov.

Food

Place du Champ and place Duguesclin in the *vieille ville,* site of the famous duel, now host the town's outdoor **market** (Thurs. 8am-noon), where you can safely buy a picnic of fruit and *"crêpes à emporter"* and dine *al fresco* in the beautiful Jardin Anglais behind the church.

Crêperie des Artisans, 6, rue du Petit Fort. Featured in the *New York Times.* A delightful owner serves a feast of two *galettes* and 2 *crêpes* under the warm wooden rafters or on the terrace. *Menus* 42-57F. Open daily noon-10:30pm; Sept.-June Tues.-Sun. noon-10:30pm.

La Kabylie, 48, rue du Petit Fort. If you're coo coo for *couscous,* try this place tucked into the steepest hill in Dinan. *Couscous* with your choice of meat 48-76F. Open daily noon-2pm and 7-11pm; Sept.-June Wed.-Sun. noon-2pm and 7-11pm.

Le Connétable, 1, rue de l'Apport, in the *vieille ville.* Reputedly the oldest *crêperie* in Dinan. Wonderful *crêpes* in a 15th-century dark-timbered house. *Crêpes flambées* (with Grand Marnier and kirsch) 20-22F. Best ice-cream cones in town 7-16F. Open daily noon-10:30pm. Next door, the **Viennoiserie des Porches** is a *pâtisserie* to die for. Try the *diplomate.*

Le Papillon, 27, rue du Quai (tel. 96 39 93 76), at the port. Airy English salon by the canal. Generous omelettes and hamburgers 42F. Grandma's apple pie 22F. Open mid-March to mid-Jan. daily 9:30am-midnight.

Bar au Prélude, 20, rue Haute-Voie. Moooove over cows, cause here comes the killer "beef kabab gargantua" at this popular night-spot-*cum*-restaurant. Or gobble down some turkey for 50F. Open Mon.-Sat. 6pm-1am.

Sights and Entertainment

The **Promenade des Petits-Fossés** begins near the post office and follows the looming ramparts to the 13th-century **Porte du Guichet,** the entrance to the formidable **Château de la Duchesse Anne.** Before you descend into the 14th-century *donjon,* pause to enjoy the antics of the **Jardin du Val Cocherel's** peacocks, roosters, and goats. (Open daily 8am-7:30pm. Free.) Inside the oval tower, the **Musée de Dinan** displays 18th-century multicolored statuettes and bas-reliefs and a selection of medieval and Roman weapons and artifacts. The nearby **Tour de Coëtquen** houses additional galleries with temporary exhibits, and a small but memorable collection of *gisants* (tomb sculptures). (Château and museums open June-Oct. 14 daily 10am-6:30pm; Oct. 15-Nov. 15 and March 16-May Wed.-Mon. 10am-noon and 2-6pm; Nov. 16-Dec. 31 and Feb. 7-March 15 Wed.-Mon. 1:30-5:30pm. Admission 20F, students 10F.)

As you reenter the *vieille ville* through porte St-Louis, a right onto rue Général de Gaulle will bring you to the **Promenade de la Duchesse Anne,** at the end of which stands the beautiful **Jardin Anglais.** In the garden, the 12th-century *Basilique St-Sauveur* flaunts the incongruous 17th-century addition of a three-tiered steeple whose sleek tiles bear an uncanny resemblance to an armadillo. The garden looks out over the Rance River, the viaduct, and the port below. At the far end, a path and a tiny staircase lead down to the river. Across the small Gothic bridge and under the viaduct, a winding path leads to the cloisters and ruined priory at **Léhon,** about 40 minutes away. You can also reach Léhon by road (about 3km). Take rue Châteaubriand from the post office and turn left at the sign.

From the port, reenter the walled city by **rue du Petit Fort,** which becomes **rue du Jerzval,** one of Dinan's prettiest (and steepest) roads. Interrupt your hike with visits to traditional artisans who continue to manufacture leather products, wood carvings, and ceramic statuettes according to time-honored traditions.

Back in the center of town, on Grand'Rue, **Eglise St-Malo** contains a remarkable polychrome organ, built by Englishman Alfred Oldknow in 1889. (For a schedule of organ concerts, contact the tourist office.) The flamboyant colors of stained-glass windows from the 1920s illuminate the church's interior. The second window from the rear on the right side commemorates the Dinan soldiers killed in World War I. The 15th-century **tower** on rue de l'Horloge commands a brilliant view of Dinan's jumbled medieval streets and the surrounding countryside. (Open June-Aug. Mon.-Sat. 10:45am-1pm and 3-6pm, Sun. 3-6pm. Admission 10F. Call the tourist office if you wish to climb the tower off-season.)

The last weekend in September brings the annual **Fête des Remparts,** complete with 6000 medieval costumes, *chevalier* (knight) combat, and the once-a-year chance to explore the inside of the town's otherwise forbidden ramparts. Night owls can quench their thirst year-round at the **Bar au Prélude** (tel. 96 39 06 95) with live music most evenings (open Mon.-Sat. 6pm-1am). A number of intimate, cozy bars hide along rue de la Cordonnerie (off rue de la Ferronnerie).

Côtes d'Armor (Northern Coast)

The northern coast's three principal geographic regions—the Côte d'Emeraude, the Côte de Granite Rose, and the Finistère—feature some of the most spectacular scenery in France. Conveniently located near the most worthwhile sites, youth hostels and *gîtes d'étape* range in quality from the rugged tent-camp near Cap Fréhel to the well-equipped hostel in Brest. (Motorists cannot stay in most *gîtes d'étape.*) The increasing presence of tourists hasn't marred the appeal of this region, but finicky weather might disappoint your expectations.

Transportation poses problems, but don't let it deter you. Get yourself a good set of schedules and be flexible.The Paris-Brest line brings frequent service to St-Brieuc, Guingamp, Plouaret, Morlaix, Landivisiau, and Landerneau, with connecting **trains** (or SNCF buses) running northward to selected destinations.

Tourisme Verney, located on esplanade St-Vincent in St-Malo (tel. 99 40 82 67), serves the Côte d'Emeraude in Dinard, St-Lunaire, St-Briac, Lancieux, Ploubalay, and St-Jacut. Eleven buses per day (9 on Sun.) ply as far as St-Briac on weekdays. In July and August, two buses continue to St-Jacut (15F per bicycle). **Companie Armoricaine de Transports (CAT)** has offices in St-Brieuc (tel. 96 33 36 60) and Lannion (tel. 96 37 02 40) and runs east to west from St-Brieuc to Le Val-André, Sables d'Or, Le Vieux-Bourg, and St-Cast. A second line links St-Brieuc and Paimpol (6 per day, 1 1/2hr., 35F50) with connections to Pointe de l'Arcouest and Lézardrieux. Consider CAT's **carte vacances** (90F for one week's unlimited travel, 160F for two weeks, 290F for one month) if you plan to travel extensively on CAT bus routes.

For the more physically ambitious, most train stations rent three- and ten-speed **bikes** (around 50F per day). Several hostels also rent bikes to HI members (roughly 40F per day). Tourist offices have information on local rentals, and many stock the *Guide Touristique Côtes-du-Nord* (5F), which lists all bike and car rental agencies in the region and provides a wealth of information on outdoor activities. Even the main roads, which pass through fields edged by Queen Anne's lace, are well-paved, scenic, and relatively flat. Many trains will carry your bike for free, and some bus companies charge only a small fee. If your budget permits, renting a **car** is without question the most convenient way to explore the region. Finally, the GR34, one of France's most famous Grande Randonée **footpaths,** snakes along the entire coast.

Côte d'Emeraude

From Dinard to St-Brieuc, the Brittany coast is fighting a losing battle with its millenia-old foe: the sea. Slightly sheltered from the relentless pounding which has sculpted the neighboring Côte de Granite Rose into eerie piles of giant pink rocks, the Côte d'Emeraude still presents a ruggedly dramatic face to the waves. But what were perhaps eons ago towering cliffs are now just very high, interrupted only by the telltale signs of erosion—long white stretches of soft sand. You've caught the region at a good time; a few *more* eons and it will be a fluvial plain. Hikers and bikers will be challenged by the coastal roads and paths, but at least you can drop your exhausted body on a golden beach at the end of the day, fickle weather permitting. As usual, the best way to get around the region, little served by public transportation, is by car or bike.

St-Brieuc is a great place to launch a tour of the Côte d'Emeraude and even the eastern part of the Côte de Granite Rose, but not for much else. It has a train station (most towns around here don't) and is a central hub for the buses which service the area. Frequent **trains** arrive from (and depart for) Paris as well as Rennes (12 per day, 1hr., 72F). The Paris-Brest line connects St-Brieuc to Morlaix (10 per day, 1hr., 64F); a separate line connects it to Dinan (2-3 per day, 49F). The station has **lockers** (15F, 3-day max.) and an info/reservation office (tel. 96 01 61 64; open Mon.-Sat. 8am-7:15pm, Sun. 8am-12:30pm and 2-7pm) as well as automatic ticket dispensers. **Buses** stop at the train station, and run from St-Brieuc to Cap Fréhel (1 per day direct, 1 1/2hr., 37F; 3 more to nearby Le Vieux Bourg, 1hr. 25min., 37F); to St-Cast (1 per day, 2hr., 37F); to Paimpol (6 per day, 1 1/2hr., 35F50); and to Lézardrieux (1 per day, 2hr., 37F).

St-Brieuc's **tourist office** is at 7, rue St-Gouéno (tel. 96 33 32 50). Follow the signs from the train station to the *centre ville* and then to the *office de tourisme,* an inconspicuous window-front down a sidestreet from the front of the post office. Around the corner from the tourist office, the 13th- to 14th-century **Cathédrale St-Etienne** merits a visit, as long as you're in the neighborhood.

If St-Brieuc seduces you into spending the night, the youth hostel, **Manoir de la Ville Guyomard (HI),** will make it a memorable one (tel. 96 78 70 70). It's a 35-minute walk from the station. Buses leave from Champ-de-Mars/pl. Duguesclin, two blocks down rue de la Gare toward the *centre ville* from the front of the station and to the right on rue du 71*ème* Régiment d'Infanterie. Take bus #3 (direction: "Les Villages") to the "Van Meno" or "Jean Moulin" stop (last bus around 7:30pm, 6F). On foot, follow rue du 71*ème* Régiment D'Infanterie to the left from rue de la Gare, continue as it becomes rue du Brest, then take a left onto rue de la Corderie, following the signs for *Ville Guyomard* toward the hostel. (Reception open daily 8am-11pm; Sept.-May 9am-noon and 2-7pm. 53F. Tent with cots 20F. Camping 20F. Breakfast 16F. Sheets 16F. Kitchen and laundry facilities. Make reservations.) The hostel rents **bikes** (40F per day, 200F deposit) and mountain bikes (70F per day, 50F per 1/2-day, 200F deposit) and organizes trips up the Côte d'Emeraude and the eastern Côte de Granite Rose.

Northeast of St-Brieuc, **Cap Fréhel** marks the northern point of the Côte d'Emeraude, a windswept peninsula whose tip drops 70m into the ocean below. A popular tourist stop, the Cap provides little solitude in summer, but if you're taking a few days to explore the area, you are bound to find plenty of less crowded, equally breathtaking nooks for rainy-day ramblings and naps in the sun (the weather here shifts frenetically). The Cap itself is served by **CAT buses** only once per day (37F from St-Brieuc), although the nearby Le Vieux Bourg sees more frequent service (3 per day from St-Brieuc, also 37F). Don't take the bus to the town of Fréhel—it's nowhere near the Cap. If your spirit is as rugged as the Cap's cliffs, you'll love the **Auberge de Jeunesse Plénevon (HI),** Kerivet, la Ville Hadrieux (tel. 96 41 49 98). Take a bus to the Cap and walk 20 minutes toward Plénevon on the D16. The building flaunts an office, kitchen, dining room, great high-pressure showers, and an attic with 15 mattresses laid neatly on the floor. But most of those "vacationing" here turn up their noses at such luxury, opting for the two tents beyond the bonfire pit outside. Even the employees sleep under the stars. (36F inside and out. Camping 20F. Breakfast 15F. Sheets 15F. Open May-Aug.) The hostel also rent **bikes** (same prices as St-Brieuc). If you ask at St-Brieuc, they may allow you to leave a rented bike at Cap Fréhel and vice-versa. If trolling the sea for supper allures you, ask at the hostel about the 15F **fishing excursions** that local fishers organize for travelers. The boats leave from Port St-Géran.

Along the entire edge of this peninsula, red-and-white striped markers guide ramblers along the GR34 hiking path. An easy walk southwest from the Cap leads to a breathtakingly beautiful and secluded little beach. Follow the GR34 east for a lovely 90-minute walk to the **Fort La Latte** (tel. 96 41 40 31), a 13th-century castle complete with drawbridges, a cannonball kiln, and a hair-raising view of both the Cap and St-Cast. (Open daily 10am-12:20pm and 2:30-6:30pm; Oct.-May Mon.-Fri. 2:30-5:30pm. Admission 13F.)

Across the bay to the southeast, the resort town **St-Cast-le-Guildo** is unfortunately close to Cap Fréhel, adding to the deluge of tourists which detract from the latter. But St-Cast does have a good if crowded beach, as well as some passable hotels if the woodsy hostel at the Cap is too rustic for you. The nearest **train station** (tel. 96 31 00 56) is in **Lamballe**. You can take a **CAT bus** from there to St-Cast (2 per day, 1hr., 29F), a slightly shorter (and cheaper) trip than from St-Brieuc (1 per day, 2hr., 37F). St-Cast's **tourist office** (tel. 96 41 81 52) is at pl. Charles-de-Gaulle. (Open Mon.-Sat. 9am-noon and 2-6:30pm.)

When it comes time to bed down, **Hôtel le Chrisflo,** 19, rue du Port (tel. 96 41 88 08), is nice for the price, with lots of seashell colors and fairly spacious rooms. (Singles and doubles 150F, with shower 180F. Breakfast 28F.) **Hôtel le Commerce,** le Bourg (tel. 96 41 81 37), will also let you sleep for cheap. (Singles 90F. Doubles 110F. Showers 20F. Breakfast 25F.) **Hôtel du Centre et des Plages,** 10, rue Frégate Laplace, has a flippin' *foyer,* but the smallish rooms are a little worse for the purse than those of the **Hôtel le Commerce.** (Singles with shower 130F. Doubles with shower 160F. Triples with shower 195F. Breakfast 28F.) **Camping Municipal de la Mare,** just to the west of the promontory on Plage de la Mare (tel. 96 41 89 19), has decent sites and showers (reception open 9am-noon and 2-7pm; 12F per person, 12F per tent, 6F per car). **Camping les Mielles,** three blocks from the main beach (tel. 96 41 87 60), is well-located and has modern shower facilities. (Reception open 9am-noon and 2:30-6:30pm. 15F per person, 30F per tent, 8F per car.)

East of St-Cast, the coast is dotted with small resorts. **St-Jacut** and **Lancieux** are particularly pleasant; both are accessible by Tourisme Verney **buses** from St-Malo and Dinard. Buses run hourly to Lancieux (45min. from St-Malo, 29F), continuing to St-Jacut in July and August only (2 per day, 37F from St-Malo).

Côte de Granite Rose

From Paimpol to Perros-Guirec to Trébeurden to Lannion, the unforgiving ocean surf has worn Brittany's coast down to a gentle slope, distinctive both for the dark pink color of the rocks and for their mutated shapes. In this area rich with artistic, musical, and religious tradition, your newly cultivated French accent will be worth next-to-nothing, as weighty Celtic names and accents are prevalent. Transportation, once again, might prove problematic, but the Paris-Brest train line hits Guincamp and Plouaret, while connecting trains stretch to Paimpol and Lannion. CAT buses fill in many gaps.

Paimpol to Tréguier

The bustling town of **Paimpol** (pop. 8000) anchors the eastern end of the Côte de Granite Rose. Historically a launching site for fishing expeditions to Newfoundland and Iceland, Paimpol now receives an annual deluge of visitors. Perhaps its greatest asset is geographical—this a perfect place from which to explore the spendiforous eastern section of the Côte de Granite Rose. (To explore west of Tréguier, either Lannion or Trébeurden makes a more convenient base.) **Trains** connect St-Brieuc to Guincamp (8 per day, 20min.) and then to Paimpol (4 per day, 3/4hr., 33F). A ticket from St-Brieuc to Paimpol via Guingamp costs 49F. Taking your bike is no problem; most of the choochoos on this line have a baggage car where you can stash it for free. Six **CAT buses** run daily direct from St-Brieuc to Paimpol (1 1/2hr., 33F50). The **post office** and **bank** are across the street from the train station. The port and *centre ville* are best reached by heading right from the station, then left at the lights. Visit the friendly **tourist office,** rue Pierre Feutren (tel. 96 20 83 16), in the city hall near the church of Notre Dame, for information on the surrounding area. From the train station, turn left, then right at the light; near the top of the hill, look for the sign and turn right again. From anywhere else in town, just walk toward the church. (Open Mon.-Sat. 9am-noon and 2-7:30pm, Sun. 9am-noon; mid-Sept. to June Mon.-Sat. 9am-noon and 2-5pm.)

Paimpol's **Auberge de Jeunesse/Gîte d'Etape (HI),** at Château de Keraoul (tel. 96 20 83 60), is 25 minutes from the station. Turn left onto av. Général de Gaulle, turn right at the first light and left at the next light (even if the signs point straight), and then follow the signs to "Keraoul." Take a left at the end of rue de Pen Ar Run. The hostel is at the second driveway on the right. An old manor house with rooms for 1 to 6 people and hardwood floors, the hostel is comfortable and convenient—no lockout, no curfew. (Members only. 40F. Breakfast 16F. Camping 22F. Lunch or dinner 43F. Sheets 16F.) Options in town include the **Hôtel Berthelot,** 1, rue du Port (tel. 96 20 88 66), where outrageously orange hallways connect clean, airy rooms. (Singles and doubles 120-160F, with shower from 200F. Breakfast 24F.) Down the street, the **Hôtel l'Origano,** 7bis, rue de Quai (tel. 96 22 05 49) has chosen a more muted color scheme. Clean and airy rooms here too, with pastel swans floating on all the bedspreads. (Singles and doubles with shower from 195F. Breakfast 25F.) Sunny and sprawling, **Camping Municipal de Cruckin,** near the plage de Cruckin (tel. 96 20 78 47), is the closest campground. From the tourist office, take a left onto rue de la Marne, another left onto av. du Général de Gaulle, then veer right and follow schizophrenic rue du Général Leclerc as it twists through four identity changes: Général Leclerc to Prof. Jean Renaud to Commandant Charcot to Commandant le Conniat. Rue de Cruckin branches off to your left from rue du Commandant le Conniat. (Reception open Tues.-Sat. 8-11am and 6-8pm, Sun. 10-11am, Mon. 8-9am and 5:30-7:30pm. 6F80 per person, 5F65 per site, 4F50 per car. Showers 5F65. Open mid-June to mid-Sept.) A block farther down rue Commandant le Conniat lies the more placid **Camping de Beauport** (tel. 96 22 09 87). (7F per person, 6F per site, 5F50 per car. Showers 5F. Open April-Sept.)

In Paimpol, the **plage de la Tossen,** a small sandy beach, provides the obligatory view of the bay. One km south of town, a 10m *menhir* looms over the Field of Grief. According to local legend, the rock fell to earth and is slowly sinking, its complete disappearance timed to coincide with the end of the world. Just east of Paimpol, near the campgrounds, along the D786 are the ivy-covered ruins of the **Abbaye de Beauport.** The abbey dates from 1202, when monks of the order of Prémontré escaped to Brittany from Normandy. (Open July-Aug. daily 9am-noon and 2-7pm. To visit at other times, call M. Lecalvez at 96 20 81 59. Admission 16F, students 11F.) Walk down the pebbled, primrose-bordered lane to the rear of the abbey for a view of marsh and the Bay of Poulafret. The path winding along the coast is the GR34, which can take you back to the Paimpol port. The first week of August brings the **Fête du Chant Marin,** with over 500 musicians and 100 old ships.

Six km north of Paimpol at the terminus of the D789, the peninsula ends with a dramatic flourish in the tumbling pink granite of the **Pointe de l'Arcouest.** The blue-green waters flowing around this archipelago of alternately bald and tree-laden islands are supposed to provide some of the world's best sea-kayaking. You can catch a **bus** here from Paimpol (10 per day, 15min., 13F, round-trip 22F). A five-minute boat ride from Arcouest, the footpaths crisscrossing the idyllic **Ile de Bréhat** have been worn as much by the island's many tourists as by its 500 inhabitants. The only motorized vehicles allowed here are those of the diminutive police and fire departments, as well as tractors. A ton of tractors mosey along, however—so many, that you have to wonder if non-farming families own them just to avoid the 3km walk from one end of the island to the other. **Les Vedettes de Bréhat** sends boats back and forth (15 per day; Oct.-May 5 per day, 31F round-trip, 30F round-trip for bikes). For 60F per day you can rent a bike on the island.

Back on the mainland, inland from Paimpol at the point of the Trieux River estuary, the little town of **Pontrieux** nestles snuggly in a green valley, the high hills along the inlet offering protection to the rows of boats docked below. Served by the Guingamp-Paimpol train line (4 per day, 1/2hr., 17F), Pontrieux is the best place from which to reach an even more elusive destination, the **Château de la Roche-Jagu** (tel. 96 95 62

35). Positioned high above the estuary with a sweeping view of the valley carved below, the 15th-century château offers tours of its interior and also hosts annual artistic expositions. (1992's exposition featured five centuries of maritime art from the Côtes d'Armor. Open 10am-7pm. Admission 30F, students 20F.) Like most places worth visiting in Brittany, it's a little out of the way, which makes the accompanying *gîte d'étape* all the more convenient. In a stone outbuilding adjacent to the château, the *gîte* has 19 beds and mattresses in its two-level attic. (30F. Showers included. Good kitchen facilities and a truly sweet caretaker. Make reservations.) Unfortunately, there's no bus service. Consider bringing a bike from Guingamp, or biking all the way. The St-Brieuc youth hostel organizes occasional trips up here. If you're on foot, expect the 5km walk to take over half an hour. From the Pontrieux train station go left along the river, cross the little bridge to the other side and turn right. This road (the D787) leads up hills and across fields to the château; you'll know it by the wide, tree-lined boulevard leading off to the right, the Côte d'Armor flags and the sign that says "Château Roche-Jagu."

On the coast again, **Lézardieux** is a quiet little town in which most shops and the tourist office delineate one rectangular, flower-lined, stone *place*. Some gather by the port below. The port's information office helps landlubbers. Shower-lubbers can lather up at the **showers** just across the parking lot. A **gîte d'étape** (tel. 96 22 90 68, for mandatory reservations 96 22 87 05), lies 7km north at Min ar Goas. Follow the signs off the D20 just before Lanmodez. (3-night max. in summer. 30F. Showers included. Meals 46F. Kitchen.) Bring pearls home to your pals from the oyster farm next door, or head to the point, the site of traditional Brotonne sailing regattas each summer.

Ten km west of Lézardrieux, the cathedral in **Tréguier** is the site of a *pardon* honoring St-Yves every May 19. One of Britanny's favorite saints, St-Yves was patron of both lawyers and the poor (go figure). A medieval song tells us that "Saint Yves was a Breton, a lawyer but not a thief, a thing which amazed the people." From Tréguier, the D8 continues 10km north to **Pointe du Château,** another of the coast's scenic promontories where house-sized rock formations (great for climbing) stand silhouetted against the Channel waters and, in summer, Brittany's stunning sunsets. On your way, stop at the oddly crooked Chapelle St-Gonéry in Plougrescéant. Farther west, stop at Port Blanc's chapel and at its point for yet another breathtaking view of the sea and coast. If you can't get a bed at the *gîte*, Tréguier's **Hôtel de l'Estuaire** (tel. 96 92 30 25) has singles and doubles from 105F. The town is served by the Guegan Voyages bus via Lézardrieux (2 per day, 20min., 14F). The line runs along the coast from Paimpol to Lannion (tel. 96 20 59 50).

Trégor: Perros-Guirec to Trébeurden

With their pink-rock buildings, the towns on the western corner of the Côte de Granite Rose don't copy-cat those of the eastern coast. Tréburden, Trégastel, Perros-Guirec, and others all do their best to attract summer crowds to the beaches which line this bit of coast, and with some success, so don't expect the whole *plage* to yourself.

Perros-Guirec is a popular and busy resort town with a harbor and two well-sheltered, sandy beaches. The **tourist office,** 21, pl. de l'Hôtel de Ville (tel. 96 23 21 15; open daily 9am-12:30pm and 1:30-7:30pm; Sept.-May Mon.-Sat. 9am-12:30pm and 2-6:30pm; **currency exchange** on Mon.) is across from the *mairie* where the buses stop. It distributes an English brochure detailing footpaths for exploring the area, the most celebrated of which is the **Sentier des Douaniers,** the route the customs collectors followed along the coast. The 5km hike leads through spectacular piles of bizarrely shaped rocks, such as those of the **Château du Diable,** where the waves have carved the stones into creepy bird and animal forms. The *sentier* ends in the adjacent town of Ploumanach. Between Ploumanach and Perros-Guirec rests the pink chapel **Notre Dame de le Clarté,** where a famous *pardon* takes place every August 15. Again, ask at the tourist office for information on any of the surrounding villages.

Perros-Guirec has few cheap hotels, but many campgrounds. Try **West-Camping,** 107, rue Gabriel Vicaire (tel. 96 91 43 82). (50F per 2 people and tent, 7F per car, 14F per extra person. Open June 15-Sept. 15.) **Camping la Claire Fontaine,** rue de Pont-Hélé (tel. 96 23 03 55), lets you pitch your tent at slightly lower prices (18F per person, 16F per tent, 6F per car; open June-Sept.). There are are two **gîtes d'étape** in the area.

Ask at the tourist office for details. You can rent **bikes** (50F per day, 250F per week, 500F deposit) or mountain bikes (100F per day, 430F per week, 1000F deposit) at **Perros 2 Roues,** 41, bd. Aristide Briand (tel. 96 91 03 33).

Near Perros-Guirec, the resort of **Trégastel** commands attention with the startling beauty of its rocks and its exquisite beaches. Avenue de la Grève Blanche leads from the D788 to the white shore; a path follows the cliff to sandy **plage de Coz-Pors,** passing a series of rocks worn by wind and sea into fantastic shapes. Local campgrounds include **Tourony** (tel. 96 23 86 61), which has a video-game room for campers who would rather not get *too* close to nature. (13F per person, 7F50 per car, 17F per tent. Open May-Aug.) The campground is on the D788 just across the bridge from Ploumanach. **Hôtel de la Corniche,** 38, rue Charles le Goffic (tel. 96 23 88 15), is a tidy, green-shuttered hotel with bright rooms. (Singles and doubles from 120F, with shower from 220F. Triples and quads 320F. Breakfast 30F. Open May-Sept.)

The D788, otherwise known as the "Corniche Bretonne," continues 11km south from Trégastel to **Trébeurden.** If possible, take a few detours off the main road to see megalithic monuments, the wild and natural beauty of Ile Grande, and miles of spectacular coastline. Trébeurden itself is a cross between a resort and a seaside wilderness. Its south-facing beaches, rare in this part of Brittany, are less crowded than those farther north in Perros-Guirec. From the beach, a series of footpaths twist among gnarled underbrush and towering rock formations to other more secluded caves and inlets. Ask for a map and other information at the tourist office, at the top of the hill on the D788 (tel. 96 23 51 64; open Mon.-Sat. 9am-7pm, Sun. 10am-12:30pm). In addition to CAT, **Car Verts buses** connect the town to Lannion. The office is at 1, rue de Kerganan (tel. 96 23 50 32) just down the hill from the tourist office, where all buses stop anyway (office open Mon.-Fri. 8:30am-12:30pm and 2-6:30pm).

Call ahead to reserve one of 18 beds at the **gîte d'étape** on **Ile Milliau.** Remember to pick up a tide table at the tourist office if you plan to get there on foot—the island is only accessible at low tide. *En plus,* there is no running water. Aaaah, to be at one with nature! It's possible to arrange a ferry *(bac)* when an uncooperative tide ebbs at inconvenient times. (Call the Gardiens de l'Ile, tel. 96 23 68 28.) Otherwise, the **Auberge de Jeunesse Trébeurden (HI)** (tel. 96 23 52 22), a pseudo-Frank Lloyd Wright-style cement block structure, is also a pleasant option. To get there, walk 2km north of the tourist office on the D788. If you're traveling by bus in summer, the drivers will often stop at the foot of the hostel's road if asked. (Reception open 8:30-10am and 6-8pm. Members only. 44F. Camping 21F. Breakfast 16F. Sheets 15F. Kitchen facilities.)

Nord Finistère

Like the venerable, wind-burned Bretons who keep its many lighthouses, Nord Finistère is hardy, aloof, perhaps a bit rough around the edges. Miles of barren, rocky shore gaze across a choppy English Channel. This northern peninsula of Brittany's westernmost *département* is, in a word, the Land's End. Still, the old keepers—and the peninsula—have soft sides. After tramping across miles of sharp and desolate coastline, you're likely to stumble across a warm and welcoming oasis of sand.

Morlaix

Where two smaller rivers join to form the Morlaix, the town of the same name rests picturesquely among the high green hills that flank the water's edge, a jumbled mass of steeply winding streets and occasional staircases under the shadow of the towering two-tiered aqueduct which dissects the *centre ville*. Its location made Morlaix an important port even before 1277, when it joined the duchy of Burgundy. In 1522, British invaders ransacked the town, but having celebrated their victory to drunken excess, were caught unawares by the city's avenging citizens who returned to reverse the earlier battle's decision. From this confrontation came the Morlaix's motto: *"S'ils te mordent, mords-les!"* (If they bite you, bite them back.)

Today Morlaix enjoys more amicable relations with 20th-century British invaders—the tourists who come via Brittany Ferries when the tide is too low to dock at Roscoff. The city is more regularly served by the Paris-Brest line; seven to nine daily **trains** run to St-Brieuc (1 hr., 64F) and other points east. Nine trains also connect Morlaix to Brest (3/4hr., 46F), and a set of trains travel to Quimper (87F) and Roscoff (28F). Call 98 80 50 50 or 98 31 51 64 for rail information. **Cycles Henri le Gall,** 1, rue de Callac (tel. 98 88 60 47), rents **bikes** (50F per day, ID deposit; all-terrain bikes 90F per day; ask about one-way rentals to neighboring towns; open Mon. 2-6pm, Tues.-Sat. 8:30am-noon and 1:50-7pm). The modern station also rents **bikes** (33F per 1/2-day, 44F per day, 33F per day after the 3rd day, 1000F deposit); go to the baggage check office to the right as you leave the front door of the station. (Open Mon.-Sat. 8am-7:30pm, Sun. 8am-12:30pm and 1-7:30pm.) **CAT buses** run once per day each way between Morlaix and Lannion (9am from Lannion to Morlaix, 5:35pm from Morlaix to Lannion, 37F). The buses stop at the train station in both towns (CAT in Lannion, tel. 96 37 02 40). **SCETA buses** also run from the Morlaix train station to Carhaix via Huelgot (1-3 per day, 11/2hr., 44F). Travelers under 26 years old can get a **billet jeune**—50% off the price of a regular round-trip SCETA ticket.

The helpful and multilingual **tourist office,** pl. des Otages (tel. 98 62 14 94), down the hill from the train station on the central *place-cum*-parking-lot next to the aqueduct, can give you a map of the city which includes a brief history, or a self-guided walking tour brochure (5F). (Open Mon.-Sat. 9am-12:30pm and 1:30-7:30pm, Sun. 10am-12:30pm; Sept.-June Tues.-Sat. 9am-noon and 2-6:30pm.) Look for the unique 16th-century oak construction of **La Maison de la Reine Anne,** rue du Mur. The apparently collapsed staircase in the left-hand corner of the house was so designed to connect the opposite walls by a narrow indoor bridge. (Open Mon.-Sat. 10:30am-noon and 2:30-6pm.) As if in homage to the ale which aided the town's ousting of its British invaders, Morlaix now brews its own beer. You can visit the Coreff brewery, the **Brasserie des Deux Rivières,** 1, pl. de la Madeleine, for free (Mon.-Wed., tours at 10:30am, 2pm, and 3:30pm). The tourist office has a list of Brittany pubs that serve the pure malt beverage.

Cheap restaurants are not hard to find in Morlaix. As for cheap accommodations, you get what you pay for. The **Auberge de Jeunesse (HI),** 3, route de Paris (tel. 98 88 13 63), offers a cavernous dining room and kitchen area, and pale dorm-style rooms. From the train station head straight forward down rue Gambetta. Where it starts to curve, go left down the steps, then farther down the endless set of steps (rue Courte). Turn left onto pl. Emile Souvestre. Follow rue Carnot, take a right onto rue d'Aiguillon, a left onto rue de Paris, and then another left onto route de Paris (20min.). The hostel is around the curve to the right. (Reception open 8-11am and 6-9pm. Lockout 10am-6pm. Curfew 11pm. Members only. 40F. Breakfast 16F. Sheets 15F.) For something more luxurious, try the hotel **Au Roy d'Ys,** pl. de Jacobins (tel. 98 88 61 19) where a marvelous old staircase spirals up three flights to welcoming, comfortable rooms overlooking the *place*. (Singles and doubles 105F. Triples 155F. Showers 10F. Breakfast 25F.)

There are plenty of interesting sites **near Morlaix** if you want to plan a few daytrips. In summer, the tourist office leads trips to the parish *closes* of **St-Thégonnec** and **Guimiliau,** two masterpieces of the distinctly Breton religious architecture which groups chapel, cemetery, charnel house, and Calvary into a single unit. Guimiliau's Calvary scene is especially impressive, mixing legendary Breton figures with the Biblical ones that wind around the foot of the cross. Head north to visit a different type of architectural ensemble, the **Tumulus de Barnenez,** an ancient Celtic burial site. Or go west to **Kerjean** to visit the 16th-century château whose architecture influenced that of all the Nord Finistère. (Open July-Aug. Sat.-Thurs. 10am-7pm, Fri. 10am-6pm; Sept. 1-15 Wed.-Mon. 10am-6pm. Admission 23F, students 16F. Free guided visits in English.) Fifteen km west of Morlaix, the **Chapel of Lambader** in tiny **Plouvorn** is reputed to be the quintessential Breton church. It holds a sound and light *spectacle* every year in late July or early August, complete with Breton costumes and a mass delivered in the ancient tongue. The Morlaix tourist office has information on all of these events.

Although not quintessential, Plouvorn's **Camping Municipal Lannorgant** (tel. 98 61 35 06) is worth the money. (32F for 1 or 2 people, tent, car, and hot water; 10F for extra person.) People without camping equipment (and, of course, without cars) can stay in one of the four area **gîtes d'étape.** All cost 30F per night. Ask at the tourist office in Morlaix for more information.

St-Pol-de-Léon, Roscoff, and Ile de Batz

Twenty-one km northwest of Morlaix, St-Pol-de-Léon is capital of the **Ceinture Dorée,** or "gilded belt," a rich agricultural region whose potato, cauliflower, and especially artichoke production nourishes both the area's population and its economy. The seaside town is equally well-known for its **Ancienne Cathédrale,** which enshrines St. Pol's bones as well as the skulls of 30-odd distinguished residents who, while their bodies were banned from the Cathedral due to plague scares, still managed to be at least partially buried with the favorite saint. (Open daily 9-11:45am and 1:30-6pm. Free guided visits in English.) St-Pol's pride is the magnificent belfry of its **Chapelle de Kreisker,** next to the train station on rue Cadiou. For 4F, you can crawl up 75m of tiny, circular stairs to glimpse a magnificent view of the coast and surrounding towns. Enter by the altar. (Open 10-11:30am and 2-6pm. Closed for renovations in 1992.) The **tourist office,** pl. de l'Evêché (tel. 98 69 05 69), is across the street from the Cathedral.

St-Pol's miniature **train station** (tel. 98 80 50 50; open Mon.-Sat. 9:35-11:40am and 12:45-6:45pm; Sun. buy tickets on the train) welcomes SNCF trains from Morlaix (5 per day, 1/2hr., 19F), as well as buses. To get to Brest, make a connection at the Morlaix train station or take a bus part-way along the far-western coast. **Les Cars du Kreisker,** 2, rue du Mun in St-Pol (tel. 98 69 00 93), is the only line that follows this remote route (2 per day Mon.-Sat., 1 1/2hr., 36F50; St.-Pol to Roscoff and vice-versa 4 per day, Mon.-Sat., 10min., 9F50). From the train station, follow bd. de la Gare to the left, then turn right onto rue Pen ar Pont which, through various incarnations of other street names, follows an approximately straight line past the post office and Kreiker's *gare routière* to the *centre ville.*

For non-campers, St-Pol is sorely lacking in accommodations, reasonably priced or otherwise—it has but 4 hotels. **Hôtel du Cheval Blanc,** 6, rue au Lin (tel. 98 69 01 00), a five-minute walk from the cathedral, lets pleasant, airy rooms. (Singles and doubles 110-140F. Showers 15F. Breakfast 30F.) There is a **gîte d'étape** in the town of Tréflaouénan, roughly 11km southwest of St-Pol via the D788 (contact the crêperie next to the *gîte,* "Moulin de Kerguidiff," tel. 98 29 51 20, or the Tréflaouénan city hall, tel. 98 69 97 81. 30F.) Campers, however, are in luck—both St-Pol's campgrounds are right on the beach. The municipal campground, Trologot (tel. 98 69 06 26), is open May 20 through September (7F per person, 5F per tent, 5F per car, showers 5F). Just down the road, the private campground **Ar Kleguer** (tel. 98 69 18 81) offers gorgeous sites on a wooded outcropping overlooking the beach, although if the sea is too cold you can use the campground's heated pool. (18F per person, 28F per tent, 8F per car. Hot showers included. Make reservations. Open April-Sept.) Follow the signs from the *centre ville* to both campgrounds. At rue Vezen Dan and rue des Minimes is the **Crêperie Ty Korn,** whose crisp 8-23F *crêpes* are local favorites. Hôtel Cheval Blanc also has a reasonably priced restaurant. **Briez Bar,** 16, pl. au Lin, is a favorite haunt of Breton locals.

In the 17th century, **Roscoff** (pop. 3700), 8km northwest of Morlaix, marked the beginning of the feared Pagan Coast. Lawless brigands lit bonfires along the rocky shore from Roscoff to Brignogan, beguiling hapless seafarers and pillaging their wrecks. These days, you can bronze yourself safely on Roscoff's sands, and depart unmolested from the harbor for the stunning Ile de Batz, whose **Auberge de Jeunesse** will save you from hotel tariffs that verge on piracy. While in Roscoff, don't miss the striking **Eglise de Notre Dame de Croas-Batz,** whose Renaissance belfry resembles the dripsand castles of Spanish architect Antoni Gaudí. Enveloping a monolith that juts into the ocean, the newly built **Jardin Exotique** is an inspiring collection of unusual flora piled neatly into a terraced garden. (Follow signs. Open daily 9am-noon and 2-5:45pm.)

Roscoff does have some affordable hotels, like **Hôtel les Arcades,** 15, rue Amiral Réveillère (tel. 98 69 70 45), in whose chic bar and seaside restaurant you'll find every Roscoff inhabitant and tourist under 30. After you grow weary of the nightlife, retire to a clean, adequate room upstairs. (Singles and doubles 120-130F, with shower 195F. Breakfast 29F.) If you're feeling rich, dine on the terrace or in the elegant restaurant overlooking the bay toward Ile de Batz (68F *menu).* Campers can stake out a piece of Roscoff at **Perharidy** campground (tel. 98 69 70 86; 9F per person, 6F per tent, 6F per car; open April-Oct.) or the private campground at **Manoir de Kerestat** (tel. 98 69 71 92). The **tourist office** (tel. 98 61 12 13) is located near the port. (Open March-Nov. Mon.-Sat. 9am-7pm, Sun. 9:30am-12:30pm.)

SNCF trains and buses run from Morlaix to Roscoff (5 per day, 1/2hr., 26F). **Les Cars du Kreisker**, 2, rue de Mun in St-Pol (tel. 98 69 00 93), go from Roscoff to Brest via Plonescat and other points west (2 per day each way, 1 1/2hr., 46F). **Brittany Ferries** (tel. 98 29 28 28) sails to Plymouth, England from Roscoff (up to 3 per day, 5-6hr., 360-400F, mid-Sept. to June 330F). Ferries also leave for Cork, Ireland (1 per week, 15hr., 435-625F); ask the tourist office for more details. You can rent **bikes** at the train station (50F per day, 44F per day after 3rd day, 1000F deposit).

Escape postcard stands and film vendors at the unspoiled **Ile de Batz** *(Enez Vaz* in Breton). A 15-minute ferry ride from the Roscoff port, its enticing old town of 750 inhabitants seems worlds apart, with few tourists and undiscovered beaches. Go, but keep it a secret. Protected by natural rock jetties, its rugged shoreline presides over an emerald seascape. As on the islands of Ouessant, Bréhat, and Groix, Breton farming and seafaring still exist here despite modest tourist incursions. A *pardon* honoring Ste-Anne takes place the last Sunday in July, with an open-air mass and a *fête.*

Vedettes de l'Ile de Batz (tel. 98 61 78 87) and **Compagnie-Maritime Armein** (tel. 98 61 77 75) both float frequent **ferries** to the island from Roscoff. You can buy tickets at the Roscoff tourist office or at the port. (July-Sept. 13 per day in each direction; Oct.-Feb. 8 per day; March-June 9 per day. Round-trip 24F. No bicycles.) Once on the island, you can rent bicycles at the dock from Monsieur Le Saôut (tel. 98 61 77 65) for 30F per 1/2-day, 45F per day, 25F after the last boat leaves. The **tourist office** (tel. 98 61 75 70) is at the dock. (Open Mon.-Fri. 10am-noon and 2-5pm, Sat. 10am-noon.)

To reach the island's gem of an **auberge de jeunesse (HI)** (tel. 98 61 77 69 from April-Sept., tel. 98 41 90 41 from Oct.-March), walk straight up the hill from the dock and follow the signs for AJ/Centre Nautique (5-10min.). Looking out on an expanse of water and rocks, this airy cabin in the pines has an upstairs loft lined with mattresses, bunks downstairs, and new kitchen facilities. The summer overflow crashes on cots in tents. (Reception open 8:30am-7:30pm, but leave your bags anytime. No lockout. 40F. Cots in tents 36F. Breakfast 16F. Dinner 43F. Canoeing, kayaking, windsurfing, and sailing lessons in July and Aug.)

You can buy food from the island's small grocery stores and *boulangeries.* In July and August, the **Crêperie Ty Yann** serves a 43F *menu* of three *crêpes,* cider, and coffee; it's just across from the hostel. (Open July-May 12:30-4pm and 7:15-10:30pm.)

Brest and Ile d'Ouessant

Situated on the southern side of Finistère's northern peninsula, Brest (pop. 220,000) has a natural harbor so ideal that in 1631, Cardinal de Richelieu designated it as France's major naval base. The city grew and prospered, its rue de Siam leading up from a harbor known to sailors around the world. Used by Americans to enter Europe during the First World War, Brest's ports were carefully watched and controlled by the Germans during the second. Consequently, Allied bombing pulverized most of the city's historical sites in 1944. The château is one building that survived; today it shelters the **Musée de la Marine,** a collection detailing the history of Brest and its rich maritime tradition. (Open Wed.-Mon. 9:15-11:30am and 2-5:30pm. Admission 22F.) For a glimpse of a rich maritime present, stop by the impressive **Océanopolis Brest,** port de Plaisance (tel. 98 34 40 40), Europe's first sea center and home to thousands of marine organisms and some cuddly seals. (Open daily 9:30am-7pm; Oct.-April Mon. 2-5pm, Tues.-Fri. 9:30am-5pm, Sat.-Sun. 9:30am-6pm. Admission 45F, ages 18-25 35F, under 17 25F.) From the stop across from and to the left of the train station, take bus #7 (every 1/2-hr. until 7:40pm, 6F) to Port de Plaisance. The **tourist office,** 8, av. Georges Clemenceau (tel. 98 44 24 96), across from the *mairie* on pl. de la Liberté, has a bevy of colorful brochures on the city and surrounding area, many in English. (Open Mon.-Sat. 9am-7pm, Sun. 10am-12:30pm and 2-6pm.) In the summer, the tourist office has an **annex** at the train station. (Open daily 10am-noon, 1-4:30pm, and 6:30-7:30pm.) The

post office lies directly across from the main tourist office. **Point-Passion-Plage** rents **windsurfers** (120F for 2hr., 260F per 5hr.), kayaks (90F for 2hr., 200F for 5hr.) and 2-seat canoes (160F for 2hr., 350F for 5hr.) at plage du Moulin Blanc (tel. 98 30 54 67), near the hostel.

The **Auberge de Jeunesse (HI)** is located next to an artificial beach at le Moulin Blanc, rue de Kerbriant (tel. 98 41 90 41), about 4km from the train station and right near Océanopolis. From the Port de Plaisance bus stop, take the first left and turn left again at the first street. (Reception open 8-9am and 5-8pm. Lockout 10am-6pm. Curfew 11pm. Members only. 63F. Breakfast included. Dinner 43F. **Bikes** 40F per day.) Alternatively, try **Hôtel Le Ponant**, 20, rue de la Porte (tel. 98 45 09 32). (Singles from 65F. Doubles 80F. Showers 10F. Breakfast 20F.) From the center of town, follow rue de Siam toward the water and cross the bridge to rue de la Porte.

For a good, cheap meal, go where the *brestois* go: tidy **Crêperie des Fontaines,** 44, rue Jean Macé, off rue de Siam, whose menu is more alluring than its plain, brown decor. (3-*crêpe menu* 40F, substantial salads 25-35F. Open Mon.-Fri. 9am-9:30pm, Sat. noon-2pm and 6-9:30pm.) Look snazzy when you go to visit **Le Tom,** a café frequented by *la jeunesse brestois.* Its at the end of av. Auguste Morvan, which starts to one side of the Mairie on pl. de la Liberté.

A pleasant 2 1/2-hour boat ride from Brest is windswept **Ile d'Ouessant** *(Ushant* in Breton), its green pastures dotted with gray sheep and white stone crosses. Fabled among sailors as the *Ile des Prêtresses* (Isle of Priestesses), this island's typically Breton division of labor often leaves the farming to its indefatigable women while men voyage with the merchant marine or in lobster boats. Ushant tradition dictates that women propose marriage.

Boats dock at **Port du Stiff** on the northeastern shore, and the main town of **Lampaul** is just a 45-minute southwestern stroll (or an 8F bus ride) across the island. You can rent a **bike** at the dock from one of the island's two rental agencies, **Savina** (tel. 98 48 80 44) and **Malgorn** (tel. 98 48 83 44), both of which send busloads of bikes (40F per day) and mountain bikes (70F per day) to meet the ferries (200F deposit). The boats from Brest and Le Conquet charge you to bring a bike to Ouessant (28F each way), so except for a regular bike it's not worth lugging it. In Lampaul, you'll find the **tourist office** (tel. 98 48 85 83) complete with maps. (Open Mon.-Thurs. and Sat. 9:45am-12:45pm, 2-4:30pm and 6:15-7:15pm, Fri. 9:45am-12:45pm, 2-4:30pm, and 7:15-8:15pm, Sun. 9:45am-12:45pm.)

At the **Ecomusée du Niou-Huella,** about 1km northwest of Lampaul, you can take a look inside a traditional Ouessantine home. Take the D81 uphill out of town and watch for the turnoff sign. The guide will show you the beam where slaughtered pigs were hung and the porcelain racks still lined with *faïencerie.* The stone house's ingeniously spare design includes a kitchen table that opens to reveal a *laverie* and well-positioned windows that keep the rooms bright from dawn to dusk. (Open daily 10:30am-6:30pm; Oct.-March 2-4pm; April-May 2-6:30pm. Admission 15F, tours in French included.) The **Musée des Phares et Balises** devotes an enlightening exhibit to the history of lighthouses and maritime signaling, with a collection of remarkable lenses. (Same hours as ecology museum. Admission 20F.)

There are three budget hotels on Ile d'Ouessant; all are located in Lampaul and have comparable prices. **Duchesse Anne** (tel. 98 48 80 25) has singles and doubles from 100-150F, **L'Océan** (tel. 98 48 80 03) from 140-180F, and **Roch ar Mor** (tel. 98 48 80 19) from 115-130F. You can **camp** at **Pen-ar-Bed** (tel. 98 48 84 65), 2km from the port (9F40 per person, 6F80 per tent).

From May to September, **Penn Ar Bed** (tel. 98 80 24 68 in Brest) ferries ply back and forth between Brest and Ouessant, stopping at **le Conquet,** at the western end of the peninsula. (1hr. between Brest and Le Conquet, 1hr. between le Conquet and Ouessant; ferries leave Brest at 8:30am, Ouessant at 5pm; 158F round-trip from Brest, 130F round-trip from le Conquet.) **Cars de St-Mathieu** (tel. 98 89 12 02) at Brest's *gare routière* information office (tel. 98 44 46 73) buses landlubbers west along the D789 from Brest to Le Conquet (daily at 7:30am from the Brest *gare routière,* 80min., 29F). In winter, the passage from Brest can get rough. Tickets are sold at both ports, but it's best to make reservations a day or two in advance with the Service Maritime Départemental (tel. 98 80 24 68).

Argoat Interior

Although *Argoat* (roughly pronounced ARE-gwaht) still means "wooded country" to Breton ears, centuries of clearing have made the rocky Argoat Interior one of the least forested regions in France. The Parc Régional d'Armorique, the rolling hills of the Monts d'Arée, and the one-car/two-cow villages bounded by pastures contain plenty of hydrangea bushes bursting with blue, pink, and purple, but precious few trees. The Argoat's relative baldness, however, scarcely diminishes its beauty. The one-hour bus ride along the D769 from Morlaix to Huelgoat provides a mere introduction to the area. Here in Brittany's interior, the people are friendlier, the prices lower, the scenery as remarkable as along the coastline, while the lifestyle remains refreshingly oblivious to the demands of a tourist economy.

The hilly terrain is better suited to walking than cycling. The **Fédération Française de la Randonnée Pédestre** has excellent topographical maps that include detailed hiking tours. The organization **ABRI** has designed routes that follow scrupulously marked trails from one *gîte d'étape* to the next (30F per night). These maps are available for 20-45F each at several tourist offices, including those at Morlaix and Huelgoat. As elsewhere in Brittany, public transportation is scarce outside of Huelgoat, and hitching is reportedly slow.

Huelgoat

A small town on a sparkling lake, Huelgoat (pop. 1745) sits among the curious grottoesand rocks of the **Parc Naturel Régional d'Armorique.** As such, the town's lush forest enjoys significant attention and protection; megaliths, parish closes, and the Arée Mountains are only a bike ride away. The tourist office sells a map (2F) indicating Huelgoat's best-known geological oddities. One footpath begins at the end of rue du Lac, where the lake empties into the Argent River. Twisting through piles of enormous granite boulders, the path leads to the **Grotte du Diable.** Descend the iron staircase into the dark, clammy chasm formed by overlying boulders. The footpath threads its way onto the **Roche Tremblante,** Huelgoat's greatest claim to fame. If you can't budge the 151-ton boulder, watch with shame as any local 10-year-old (wearing a tourist office armband) pushes on the precise point where the rock moves without effort. Other sights in the immediate vicinity include the **Chaos de Moulin** and the **Ménage de la Vierge,** two thought-provoking piles of rock.

The path **Allée Violette** (500m) leads you to the road from Carhaix, just past the bridge over the Argent. You may either turn right and head back into town or turn left and look for signs to the **Promenade du Fer-à-Cheval,** a half-hour stroll through more thick forests. As the paths end, you are once more on the main road to Carhaix. Turn left to head home, right to find the **Gouffre,** where the Argent River crashes into a deep cavity and disappears for some 150m. The **Allée du Clair Ruisseau** also starts on the D764 to Carhaix and leads to the **Mare aux Sangliers,** a pretty pond surrounded by more weird rock formations (about 600m from the road). A 6km jaunt brings you to **Locmaria-Berrien,** its sturdy 18th-century church surrounded by 17th-century oaks. Follow the directions to the *gîte d'étape.* Within 2km is the **Menhir de Kérampeulven,** an impressive solitary obelisk.

Huelgoat's center is on the eastern bank of the lake. All SNCF buses stop in pl. Aristide Briand, less than a minute's walk from both the lake and the **tourist office** which is behind the church on pl. de la Mairie (tel. 98 99 72 32). The staff distributes regional guides, maps (33F), and a book of hiking trails (75F). (Open daily 10am-1pm and 2-6pm; Sept 16-June 14 inquire at the *mairie* next door, open Mon.-Fri. 8:30am-noon and 1:30-5:30pm, Sat 8:30am-noon.) The **post office** is at 22, rue des Cieux. (Open Mon.-Fri. 9am-noon and 2-5:30pm, Sat. 9am-noon.) Huelgoat's **postal code** is 29690. For an

ambulance, call 98 99 73 96 or 98 99 75 35, and, as usual, in an **emergency,** dial 17. The police station is at route des Carrières (tel. 98 99 71 45).

You can usually find a room here in the summer, but call ahead to be safe. The pleasant, English-speaking owners of **Hôtel de l'Armorique,** 1, pl. Aristide Briand (tel. 98 99 71 24), across from the bus stop, practically give away their mid-sized, simple rooms with good mattresses. (Reception open daily 8am-1pm; off-season, closed Mon. Singles and doubles 90F. Triples 155F. Quads 165F. Quints 200F. Showers 18F. Breakfast 25F.) **The Hôtel du Lac,** 12, rue Général de Gaulle (tel. 98 99 71 14), is on the waterfront and offers decent but small rooms with soft mattresses. (Singles and doubles 95-140F, with shower 140-170F. Two-bed triples with shower 200F. Breakfast 25F. Nice restaurant serves 60-120F seafood and 29-52F pizza *menus.*) For those who like to rough it, the **Camping Municipal du Lac,** rue du Général de Gaulle, (tel. 98 99 78 80), 5 minutes from bus stop, is a sunny and well-tended lakeside location with hedges separating sites. (Reception open Mon.-Fri. 7:30-11:30am and 4-8pm, Sun. 8-11am and 4-7pm. 23F per person, 34F per 2 people, car and site included. Open June-Sept. 15.) A less convenient but more pleasant option is the **Camping de la Rivière d'Argent,** 3km from town on the way to Carhaix (tel. 98 99 72 50 or 98 99 70 56; 12F50 per person, 13F per site; open June-Sept.).

Huelgoat's **market** takes place on the first and third Thursday of the month from 8:30am to 5pm in pl. Aristide Briand and along rue du Lac. Place Aristide Briand has a small supermarket (open Mon.-Sat. 8:30am-12:30pm and 2:30-7:30pm) as well as a few bakeries and *crêperies.* Park your keester at **La Chouette Bleue,** 1, rue du Lac, a spacious and upbeat bar/*crêperie*/snack bar/and restaurant by the lake. Try a dozen escargots for 54F. (Entrees 28-52F, *crêpes* 6-31F. Bar open 10:30am-1am. *Crêperie* open daily noon-10pm. Restaurant open noon-2pm and 7-10pm. Open April-Sept.)

Huelgoat is one of the Argoat's more accessible towns; an early morning and an afternoon **SNCF bus** (for info tel. 98 93 06 98) connect it to Morlaix (1hr., 28F) to the north (on the busy Paris-Brest line) and Carhaix to the south (19F). Buses stop in front of the *boulangerie-pâtisserie* in pl. Aristide Briand, across from the church. Schedules are posted in the window. From Morlaix, hitchers and cyclers often take the D769 to Berrien and the D14 to Huelgoat (30km altogether). Unless you have a car or don't mind the bus rides, Huelgoat is not a one-day trip.

Near Huelgoat

To appreciate the whiplash-inducing scenery around Huelgoat, procure a detailed map of the area from the tourist office, rent yourself a sturdy bike, and pack a picnic lunch. Then head 8km past isolated farmhouses and tiny villages on the D764 to **La Feuillée.** The roads become hillier and the landscape more desolate as you approach the Arrée Mountains. **Roc Trévezel** (365m) and 14km from Huelgoat is one of the highest points. It may also be reached from La Feuillée. Eight km south is **Montagne St-Michel,** no relation to the famous religious complex to the north. From the back of the chapel at the summit, you can see the **Yeun Ellez,** a huge peat bog. In winter, the fog becomes so thick and the atmosphere so sinister that Breton tradition calls its center the *"portes aux enfers"* (gates to Hell). An artificial lake at the same spot once supplied a vehemently opposed (and no longer operating) thermonuclear station at Brennilis. Seven km south on the D785 **Brasparts,** a small, typically Breton **parish close,** which includes a church, a fantastically detailed calvary carved in stone, and a charnel house. The D21 to the D14 leads back to Huelgoat via the small parish closes of Lannedern and Loqueffret, and St-Herbot with its *calvaire* dating from 1571.

The town of **Pleyben,** 26km southwest of Huelgoat, is the site of **Eglise St-Germain l'Auxerrois.** With its domed Renaissance bell tower and the magnificently ornate *calvaire,* this is one church in Brittany definitely worth seeing. On the first Sunday of August, a *pardon* takes place here. To reach Pleyben, leave Huelgoat via the road to Quimper, which becomes the D14. After 20km, turn left on the D785.

Southeast of Huelgoat, the small town **Carhaix** has a train station with a train that chugs to Guingamp (5 per day, 1hr., 41F). An **SNCF bus** goes to Rosporden, where you can make an easy connection by train to Quimper (3 buses per day, 52F from Carhaix to Quimper). SNCF (tel. 98 80 50 50 or 98 90 50 50) can give you information on private line schedules, too. **SCETA** (tel. 98 93 06 98) runs buses from Carhaix north to Morlaix via Huelgoat (2 per day, 1 1/2hr., 44F), west to Chateaulin (2-3 per day, 1hr., 44F), and east to Loudéac (3 per day, 1 1/2hr., 44F). **CAT** buses (tel. 99 33 36 60) go directly to St-Brieuc (1 per day, 2hr., 58F). Cheap beds, hot showers, ample kitchen facilities, and a friendly welcome await you at the **gîte d'étape** in **Port de Carhaix**, a 5km hike out of town along the D769. Call the *office des sports* (tel. 98 93 14 40) or M. Kergona (tel. 98 99 54 42); pick up the key at the Café Priol, on the D769 across the road from the *gîte*. The bus to Quimper picks people up and drops them off in Port de Carhaix, near the *gîte*.

Crozon Peninsula

To the north and to the south, the two larger peninsulas of Brittany's *finistère* over-shadow Crozon, a tiny point of land jutting out between the more recognizable profiles of Léon and La Cornouaille. Long dependent upon fishing for economic prosperity, capitalist realities and a lobster shortage have made tourism a more lucrative industry for this little *presqu'île*. While Crozon's floundering-but-picturesque port cities offer scant competition to sprawling Brest or Quimper, its scenery and beaches definitely leave the others flailing in the surf. The rugged, rocky coastline is uniformly stunning. From high, jagged clifftops, lined with convenient hiking paths, you can gaze across the surrounding bays, turquoise and azure pools marred only by the occasional dark swell of a protruding rock formation, offspring of the cliffs underfoot. Descend a path, round a corner, and the knobbed and craggy coast will certainly give way to a shimmering ribbon of sand.

Like much of Brittany, traveling to the area by train or bus requires effort and per-serverance. From Quimper, **SCETA buses** (tel. 99 29 11 15) run three times per day (only once on Sundays in the winter) to Crozon/Morgat and Camaret (48F). From Brest, **Autocars Dougnet** (tel. 98 27 02 02) runs one bus per day to Crozon/Morgat and Camaret (45F). The bus between Camaret and Crozon/Morgat costs 9F. If you're coming from Brest, you might alternatively try **Vedettes Armoricaines** (tel. 98 44 44 04), a ferry service which sails three times daily from April to September from Brest to Le Fret and back. (45F, round-trip 85F. 48F for a one-way ticket that includes the bus from LeFret to Camaret/Crozon/Morgat.) Railpasses are not valid on these buses and ferries.

Camaret

Little Camaret (pop. 2980) is a jewel of a town, its hill-ringed harbor warmly greeting each arriving ship with a string of colorful dockside shops and cafés. Many of the arrivals are pleasure cruisers, but the giant wooden hulls beached at the western edge of the promenade attest to Camaret's past strength as a fishing port. You can swing through its museums in a day, but once you see the beach below the hostel, you may want to stay forever.

Orientation and Practical Information

Camaret lies at the western end of the peninsula, the last stop on the bus lines from Brest and Quimper. In town, follow quai Toudouze and quai Vauban and then take a right onto quai du Styvel. Almost everything listed here is on these two streets, with the **auberge de jeunesse** a noticeable exception.

> **Tourist Office:** quai Toudouze (tel. 98 27 93 60), the beige building with brown trim on the *place* at the bottom of the hill (shared with the *gendarmerie*). Offers walks with historical and natural themes (25F). Open June-Sept. Mon.-Sat. 9am-12:30pm and 2:30-7pm, Sun. 10am-noon. If it's closed, call the *mairie* at 98 27 94 22.

> **Post Office:** 2, rue de Verdun (tel. 98 27 92 51). From pl. St-Thomas, take rue de la Mairie, which becomes rue de Verdun. **Currency exchange.** Open Mon.-Fri. 9am-noon and 2-5pm, Sat. 9am-noon. **Postal Code:** 29570.

Buses: SCETA and **Autocars Donguet** buses stop outside **Café de la Paix**, 30, quai Toudouze (tel. 98 27 93 05). Buy tickets inside. SCETA (tel. 99 29 11 15) buses to Quimper (3 per day, 1 1/ 2hr., 48F). Autocars Donguet (tel. 98 27 02 02) to Brest (1 per day, 1 1/2hr., 45F). Both buses stop in Crozon/Morgat (9F). **Vedettes Armoricaines** (tel. 98 44 44 04) buses stop in pl. Charles de Gaulle to pick up passengers for the boat trip to Brest. The bus stops at Crozon, Morgat, and Le-Fret (3 per day, 48F boat ticket includes bus). **Windsurfer Rental: Club Léo** (tel. 98 27 90 49), at the end of quai du Styvel, next to the beach. 105-125F per 1/2-day 105-125F, 155-175F per day; 1000F deposit.

Laundromat: Way down quai Toudouze. Wash 25F, dry 15F. Open daily 8am-6pm.

Police: tel. 98 27 00 22. **Emergency:** tel. 17.

Accommodations, Camping and Food

The five hotels in Camaret couldn't possibly accommodate the crowd of summer visitors. Either call ahead or cross your fingers and be prepared to spend.

Auberge de Jeunesse de l'Iroise (HI), rte. de Toulinguet (tel. 98 27 98 24). Walk down the quay (along the port), and turn left in front of Hôtel Styvel. Bear right and walk up the hill about 200m. The hostel is on the left. The reception office is the first building on your right, the hostel the second. If no one is at the office, go to the hostel and pay the next day. Minimal facilities are dusty and in want of attention, but showers are hot and the kitchen decent. A spectacular view and beautiful beach await on the far side of the hill. 30F. Open mid-June to Sept.

Hôtel Vauban, 4, quai Styvel (tel. 98 27 91 36). Mostly newly renovated rooms, spacious and sunny with big showers. Friendly proprietors welcome you to the bar downstairs. Singles and doubles 140-170F, with shower 160-190F. Triples 220F. Showers 15F. Breakfast 25F. Open Feb.-Nov.

Hôtel du Styvel (tel. 98 27 92 74), on quai Vauban. Nearly identical to the place next door. Singles and doubles 160F, with shower 200F. Showers 25F. Breakfast 28F. Nice restaurant downstairs posts a 72F *menu.*

Camping: There are 6 other campgrounds in the Crozon-Morgat area; ask at the tourist office. **Camping Municipal de Lannic** (tel. 98 27 91 31), off rue du Gronnach, fairly close to town center. Go to the end of quai Toudouze, take a left at quai Styvel, ascend the hill, and take a right at the sign. Scenic beach nearby. 8F per person, 7F per site, 5F per car. Showers 7F. Open June 15-Sept. 15. **Camping de Lambezen** (tel. 98 27 91 41 or 98 27 93 72), 5km away in Lambezen. Take a left off the road to Crozon just after you've ascended from Camaret. There's a sign at the turn-off, but it faces the other direction. Then follow the signs. 22F per person, 37F per car and tent. Showers included. Open Easter-Sept.

Camaret's top-notch seafood fetches high prices. For a special meal, **La Licorne,** 12, quai Toudouze, has a country-club atmosphere, professional service, and a decent 68F *menu* with mussels or salad, fish or steak, and dessert. (Open daily for lunch and dinner, off-season Tues.-Sun.) For those with smaller appetites and budgets, the town has several good *crêperies.* Try **Crêperie Rocamadour,** 11, pl. Charles de Gaulle, which serves plump dinner *crêpes* (12-32F), an excellent seafood *crêpe* (40F), and a 39F 3-*crêpe menu.* It's diagonally across from the tourist office. (Open April-Sept., Tues.-Sun. noon-11pm.)

Sights

The 17th-century Tour Vauban at the end of the pier houses Camaret's **Musée de la Marine,** a small collection of engravings, paintings, and model ships. (Open June 15-Sept. 15 daily 10am-7pm. Last entry 15min. before closing. Admission 12F.) Nearby **Chapelle de Notre-Dame-de-Rocamadour** continues the marine theme; model boats dangle from the ceiling, lifesavers hang from the walls, and the altar resembles a ship's stern. A *pardon* and a blessing of the sea are held here on the first Sunday in September.

The most spectacular sights lie outside town. Just beyond the edge of town on the D8 is a modest circle of stone *menhirs.* The **Pointe de Penhir,** just 3.5km away on the D8, is one of the finest capes in Brittany. A memorial to the Bretons of the Free French forces stands on the cliff; from there, it's a dizzying 76m drop to the sea. Climb out onto the rocks for a blood-boiling view of the isolated rock masses of the **Tas de Pois.** A grassy plain on the leeward side of the point leads down to a sheltered beach. Farther north, the road passes another stone circle, the **Alignements de Lagatjar,** some 100 *menhirs* arranged in intersecting lines and ending in a Stonehenge-like circle. These prehistoric stones are believed to have been installed in 2500 BC for sun-worshiping rites. The D355 leads to the **Pointe des Espagnols,** another dramatic promontory with a view over Brest and the Plougastel Peninsula. South of Camaret is **Pointe de Dinan,** where you can cross a natural arch and survey the Atlantic.

Morgat and Crozon

These two towns are practically indistinguishable, although for the record, Crozon is the more commercial of the two, with shops and *hypermarchés* around its *place* and on the larger nearby hills, while everything down the hill in Morgat pales before its big, touristy beach. Buses stop fairly regularly in Crozon/Morgat as they meander from Brest, Le Fret, and Quimper toward Camaret, 9km away (9F to Camaret). The *gare routière* is next to the Crozon tourist office on bd. de Pralognan, which becomes the D8 as you head west toward Camaret. The Crozon **tourist office** (tel. 98 26 17 18), has a whole slew of information on both towns and the surrounding area. (Open Mon.-Sat. 9am-7:30pm, Sun. 10am-1pm; Sept.-June Tues.-Sun. 9am-12:30pm and 2-6pm.) Morgat's **tourist office,** across from the beach on bd. de la France Libre (tel. 98 27 07 92), waylays visitors as they enter from Crozon. (Open July-Aug. Mon.-Sat. 9am-7pm, Sun. 9am-noon; Sept. 1-15 Mon.-Sat. 9:30am-noon and 2-6pm, Sun. 9am-noon.) The tourist offices have information on several **bike rental** agencies. The **Peugeot station,** 34, rue de Poulpatre, off the marketplace in Crozon, rents bikes and mountain bikes (60F per day, 250F per week; mountain bikes 90F per day, 480F per week; open Tues.-Sat. 8:30am-noon and 2-7pm). Crozon's **post office** is on rue Alsace-Lorriane (open Mon.-Fri. 9am-noon and 2-5pm, Sat. 9am-noon); the **postal code** is 29160.

If you plan to spend the night, Morgat's pleasant **Hôtel Julia,** 43, rue de Tréflez (tel. 98 27 05 89), is the cheapest place near the beach. (Singles and doubles 110-140F, with shower 180F. Breakfast 27F. Open Feb. 22-Oct.) The elegant dining room downstairs has three-course *menus* from 70F. Make reservations for both the hotel and the restaurant. In Crozon, **Hôtel Moderne,** 61, rue Alsace-Lorraine (tel. 98 27 00 10), has clean, comfortable rooms from 116F. (Singles and doubles with shower 182F. Showers 20F. Breakfast 28F.) There are several **gîtes d'étapes** in this region. **Landévennec**—one of the stops for buses to and from Quimper and Brest—has a beautiful facility on a hill just above the port. Call the *mairie* (tel. 98 27 32 85) to reserve a place (36F per night). At **St-Hernot** a few km outside of Crozon on the Cap de la Chèvre, the *gîte d'étape* is less scrupulously tended. There's no bus to save you from the taxing hike (call Madame le Guillon at the bar/café in front of the *gîte* (tel. 98 27 15 00; 36F). There are also two *gîtes* near the Port du Fret, where the ferry from Brest docks. For the *gîte* Larial-St-Fiacre call Madame Lebreton (tel. 98 27 62 30; 36F); to stay at the *gîte d'étape mer* at Port du Fret call the *mairie* (tel. 98 27 10 28; 36F). The *mairie* (tel. 98 81 90 44) in Le Faou has details about all *gîtes,* or inquire at the **ULAMIR** (Union Locale des Animations de Milien Rural; tel. 98 27 01 68), in the SIVOM building on route du Camaret, for a list of local *gîtes* and maps of hiking trails between them. If you have wheels, look into *chambres d'hôtes* (bed and breakfasts). Rooms range from 100-200F in price. The whole Crozon peninsula is strewn with **campgrounds.** Ask at the Crozon tourist office for a complete listing. **Pen-Ar-Ménez,** on bd. de Pralogan toward Camaret (tel. 98 27 12 36) is closest to this town-and-beach (13F50 per person, 18F per tent and car). **Les Pieds dans l'Eau** (tel. 98 27 62 43), 6km northwest of Crozon in St-Fiacre, lives up to its name with a magnificent view of the sea. (Reception open daily 9am-noon and 2-8pm. 15F50 per person, 16F per site, 6F per car. Showers and light breakfast included. Open June 15-Sept. 15.)

A seafood market takes place at Crozon's pl. de l'Eglise daily from 8am to noon. A number of supermarkets dot the town. An **Intermarché** and **SuperRallye** lie on the rte. de Camaret. Restaurant-goers will enjoy Morgat's **A la Grange de Toul-Bass,** pl. d'Ys, a crooked-roofed restaurant/antique shop with tables in the old farmyard outside. Enormous *crêpes* (13-38F) and seafood dishes (38-71F) are fed to hungry locals seated around the antique plow. (Open April-Sept. daily noon-midnight.) Contrastingly, Crozon's **Restaurant l'Océanic,** 24, rue de Camaret (tel. 98 27 02 70), serves its Italian fare in a thoroughly modern setting—a pseudo-art-deco *salle* filled with the smell of its gorgeous pizzas (33-55F). (Open daily noon-2pm and 6:30pm-midnight; off-season Tues.-Sat. noon-2pm and 7pm-midnight, Mon. 7pm-midnight.)

Two companies offer tours of Morgat's marine grottoes, glittering caverns carved out by seawater. **Les Grottes** (tel. 98 26 26 90) and **Vedettes Sirènes** (tel. 98 27 22 50) both give boat tours in English. Only Vedettes Sirènes offers tours in May, June, and the end of September. From July to Sept. 14, the two companies have practically identical schedules of 45-minute tours departing every 15 minutes. Buy tickets (40F) on quai Kadar in Morgat. Rent windsurfers on the beach at **Point-Passion-Plage** (tel. 98 26 24 90; 75-100F per hr.). If the surf's up, head to **Haleiwa** surf shop on Impasse Dixmude (tel. 98 27 09 28), to the right of the church from the beach. Boogie boards and surfboards rent for 100F and 150F per 1/2-day, respectively, 175F and 200F per day, wet suit included. The store is open from 10am until whenever, dude. There's also waterski and jetski rental available at the beach.

Quimper

Although staunch, half-timbered houses with crooked façades share cobblestoned streets in the *vieille-ville* (old town) with legions of tourists and hordes of fashion-conscious teens, Quimper (KEM-pear; pop. 100,000), capital of La Cornouaille, has managed to retain its Breton flavor. Some women wear *coiffes* to market and to church on Sunday, stores display Celtic books and records prominently, one local high school still conducts its classes in Breton, and for over 300 years, delicate hand-painted *faïencerie* (porcelain) has been crafted here. Each year during the last week of July, Quimper recalls its heritage with the *Festival de Cornouaille,* a cavalcade of mirth and music in Breton costume.

Orientation and Practical Information

Quimper is located at the *kemper* ("confluence" in Breton) of the Steir and the Odet rivers in the heart of La Cornouaille. The center of town is a 10-minute walk from the train station. Turn right onto av. de la Gare and follow it to the Odet river. Cross the bridge, and make a left onto bd. Amiral de Kerguélen. After several blocks, hang a right onto rue du Rois Gradlon which leads to the cathedral and entrance to the old city.

Tourist Office: 7, rue Déese (tel. 98 53 04 05), off pl. de la Résistance. From the train station, turn right and follow av. de la Gare, which turns into bd. Dupleix. Continue 5-10 min. to pl. de la Résistance. Free maps and brochures about everything that ever was, is, or will be in Quimper. May help find accommodations in local homes. Guided French tours June 15-Sept. 15. Call ahead for times of English tours (2 per day, 25F). Also sells bus excursion tickets to nearby sights such as Pointe du Raz. Open Mon.-Sat. 8:30am-8pm, Sun. 9:30 am-12:30pm, all day during the festival; Sept.-June Mon.-Sat. 9am-noon and 1:30-6:30pm.

Post Office: at bd. Amiral de Kerguélen and rue de Juinville (tel. 98 95 65 85). **Currency exchange** open Mon.-Fri. 8:30am-noon and 1:30-6pm, Sat. 8:30am-noon. Post office open Mon.-Fri. 8am-7pm, Sat. 8am-noon.

Flights: Quimper Pluguffan Airport (tel. 98 94 30 30). 8km away on D40, served only by taxi (tel. 98 90 16 45); from train station 55-65F. **Brittany Air International** (tel. 98 62 10 22). To London's Gatwick Airport via Brest (5-6 per day, 1620F, students 570F). **Air Inter** (tel. 98 84 73 73). To Paris (4 per day, 1040F, student fares from 330 to 595F). All prices vary with season.

Trains: av. de la Gare (tel. 98 90 26 21 or 98 90 50 50). To: Paris (2 per day, 3 Sun., 6 1/2hr., 283F); Rennes (8 per day, 3hr., 148F); Nantes (6 per day, 3hr., 153F); Brest (6 per day, 1hr. 20 min., 69F); TGV to Paris (5 per day, 5hr., 283F plus 16-80F reservation). Information office open daily 9:30am-7pm. Baggage check open daily 8am-noon and 1-5pm. If closed, go to the *accueil* on the quai, open until 8pm. 22F for 24 hrs. Also 24-hr. **lockers** (small 5F, large 20F).

Buses: All buses leave from the parking lot to the right of the train station or across the street in front of the **Café Nantais.** Although several companies make stops in town, it's easiest to take buses from the station. Ask at the tourist office for schedules or peruse the ones posted around the parking lot next to the train station. **CAT/TV,** 5, av. Amiral de Kerguélen (tel. 98 95 02 36). Service to Brest (6 per day, 3 Sun, 1hr. 15 min., 62F); Douarnenez (8 per day, 5 Sun., 40 min., 23F);

and Pointe du Raz (4 per day, 2 Sun., 1 hr. 45 min., 40F). Departures from the train station as well as the CAT/TV Agency itself (Sun. departures from agency only). Buy tickets on the bus. This company also guides tours of the region (Pointe du Raz, Crozon Peninsula; 75-115F). **Cars Caoudal** (tel. 98 56 96 72). Service to Quimperlé (7 per day, 4 Sun., 1hr. 40 min., 35F) via Concarneau (40 min., 18F50) and Pont-Aven (1hr., 30F50). Departures in front of Café Nantais. Buy tickets at the bar. **SNCF** (tel. 98 90 26 21) service to Douarnenez (5 per day, 4 Sun., 40 min., 23F) and Camaret (3 per day, 1 Sun., 1 1/2hr., 47F). Departures from the station. Buy tickets at the *guichets* (ticket counters) inside.

Public Transportation: QUB—Quimper's municipal bus company—has 8 lines. All pass through *centre-ville*. The buses run every 15 min. from 6am to 7:30pm. Fare 5F30. Bus #1 serves the hostel and municipal campground. Maps and information available at **Kiosque QUB** (tel. 98 90 72 40), pl. de la Résistance. Open Tues.-Fri. 8am-12:15pm and 1:30-6:30pm, Mon. and Sat. 8am-noon and 2-6pm.

Bike Rental: MBK s.a. Lennez, 13, rue Aristide Briand (tel. 98 90 14 81). Turn right from the train station; on the corner at the end of av. de la Gare. Bikes (60F per day, 200F per week, 1000F deposit); mountain bikes (90F per day, 360F per week, 2000F deposit); mopeds (140F per day, 540F per week, 4000F deposit). Open Tues.-Sat. 9am-noon and 1:45-7pm.

Laundromat: Au Raton Laverie, 4, rue Jacques Cartier. Turn right at the train station and take a right where av. de la Gare forks. Wash 22F, dry 15F. Open daily 8am-10pm. **Lav' Seul,** 9, rue de Locronan, right off rue Douarnenez and just beyond the pl. de Locronan. Wash 20F, dry 2F. Open daily 7am-10pm.

Late-Night Pharmacy: Pharmacie Pernes, 3 ch. des Justices (tel. 98 55 42 05). Near the hostel and campground. From pl. de Samaritaine, take a left onto chemin des Justices. Open daily 9am-10pm. In the evening ring the bell to obtain service. In case of pharmaceutical emergency between 10pm and 9am, go to the main police station, listed below. In case of prophylactic emergency after hours, the **Pharmacie Centrale,** located on pl. Corentin (just across from the cathedral) has a condom dispenser outside. 10F for a *préservatif.*

Hospital: Centre Hospitalier Laennec, 14bis, av. Yves-Thépot (tel. 98 52 60 60).

Police: rue Théodore le Hars (tel. 98 90 15 41). **Emergency:** tel. 17.

Accommodations and Camping

Between July 15 and August 15, written reservations will make life easier. If you don't have reservations, start looking early in the day. The tourist office can direct you to private homes offering B&B (from 150F for 2 people). For accommodations during festival week, make arrangements as early as you can—March, if possible.

Auberge de Jeunesse (HI), 6, av. des Oiseaux (tel. 98 55 41 67). In the Bois de l'Ancien Séminaire. About 2km out of town in a quiet, wooded area. Run by a very friendly woman. Redone in 1991. 40F per person (HI card required). Breakfast 16F. Reception open daily 8-10am and 6-8pm. Kitchen and bathroom areas open during the day, but rooms locked 10am-6pm. Open June-Aug. Take bus #1 to "Chaptal" from the "rue du Parc" stop across from the tourist office.

Hôtel de l'Ouest, 63, rue le Déan (tel. 98 90 28 35), near the train station. Take the small rue Jean-Pierre Calloch next to the Hôtel Le Derby across from the train station. Turn left onto rue le Déan. Energetic owner and her small white dog tend shop. Rooms are clean, mattresses firm, and the neighborhood quiet. Singles 95F, with toilet 130F, with shower 170F. Doubles 130F, with shower 150F. Triples 160F. One four-person room 210F. Showers 15F. Breakfast 22F. Extra bed 30F.

Hôtel Celtic, 13, rue de Douarnenez (tel. 98 55 59 35), on the edge of the old quarter, 1 block up from Eglise St-Mathieu. A little musty but comfortable; firm mattresses. Friendly management speaks English. Reception open daily noon-midnight. Singles 100-165F. Doubles 120F, with shower 170F. Showers 10F. Breakfast 20F. *Menus* from 55F in the restaurant below. From Oct. 15-May. open Mon.-Sat.

Hôtel Le Transvaal, 57, rue Jean-Jaurès (tel. 98 90 09 91). 10 min. from the train station. Turn right onto av. de la Gare. Continue along the Odet river as it becomes bd. Dupleix. Make a left onto rue Ste-Catherine, across the river from the Cathedral, and go to rue Jaurès. Well-maintained, 60s-style rooms make this a place a pretty groovy pad. Singles 104F, with toilet 110F, with shower 140F. Doubles from 168F. Triple 250F. Breakfast 22F. TV room and garage available. Restaurant open noon-3pm and 7-10:30pm, *plat du jour* 40F.

Camping: Camping Municipal, av. des Oiseaux in the Bois du Séminaire, next to the hostel. Take the #1 QUB bus to *Chaptal*. Some pitch their tents in the woods, well away from the legions of campers below. Piping hot water and showers available. Office closed June 15 to July 1. Call the mayor's-office (tel. 98 98 89 89) for additional information. Open Mon.-Sat. 9-11am and 1-7pm. 6F per person, 2F per tent. Showers 5F.

Food

The lively covered **market (Les Halles),** off rue Kéréon, on rue St-François, is the perfect place to taste, smell, or simply stare at food—produce, seafood, meats, and cheeses all abound here. It is also a hot spot for imbibing the local shopping culture, where astute hagglers barrage merchants with vociferous assessments of the products on display. (Open Mon.-Fri. 8am-1pm and 3-8pm, Sat. 6am-8pm, Sun. 9am-1pm). An open market takes place outside of Les Halles twice a week. Merchants come from all over the region for the larger Saturday market; Wednesday's is comprised of locals. (Wed. and Sat. 9am-6pm; Sept.-May 9am-2pm or later).

Le St-Mathieu, 18, rue St-Mathieu in the old town, near the Eglise St-Mathieu. Serves fresh seafood at rock bottom prices. Try the *Salade St-Mathieu* (crawfish, avocado, melon and ham, 40F) or the scrumptious fish soup (30F). Open Mon.-Sat. noon-10:30pm; Sept.-May noon-3pm.

Le Café des Arts, 4, rue Ste-Catherine, across the river from the cathedral. Black-and-white photos of contemporary *artistes* cover the pastel walls in this relaxed and unpretentious people-watching place. Salads 30-40F. *Entrecôte* 48F. Cocktails 30F. Open daily noon-1am.

Le Saint Co., 20, rue Frout, just off pl. St-Corentin. A small but airy restaurant whose specialties are mussels (38F) and oysters (44F). Also serves salads, omelettes, steaks and *crêpes.* Open daily 11am-11pm.

Sights and Entertainment

At the entrance to the old quarter sits the majestic **Cathédrale St-Corentin,** dedicated to Quimper's patron saint, one of many Breton saints unrecognized by the Church in Rome. The spiritual adviser of King Gradlon, this 6th-century bishop is said to have lived off a single fish. After eating his fill, Corentin would throw half the fish back in the river, only to have his scaly friend return regenerated the next day. A statue of the king, erected in 1856, stands between the cathedral's two distinctive spires.

From the small cathedral garden, climb to the **old city ramparts** for views of the cathedral and the Odet River. (Open daily 8am-6pm.) Enter the **Musée Départemental Breton** (tel. 98 95 21 60) from the garden. The history, ethnography and archaeology of Finistère is represented through pottery, furniture, and costumes housed in the former episcopal manor, built between the 16th and 19th centuries. (Open Tues.-Sat. 9am-noon and 2-7pm, Sun. 2-7pm.)

From the cathedral, cross the street onto charming rue Kéréon ("shoemaker" in Breton). In medieval times, each street in this quarter was dedicated to a single trade. Rue des Boucheries (butchers), on the right of rue Kéréon, leads to rue Sallé (salty food), and right again to pl. Beurre (butter).

Across the Odet River is an area of Quimper dedicated to the town's distinctive pottery. The recently opened **Musée de la Faïence Jules Varlingue,** 14, rue Jean-Baptiste Bousquet (tel. 98 90 12 72), along the quai past the Allées de Locamaria, traces Quimper's 300-year history as a center of art. If the 500-plus pieces of pottery—religious icons, elaborately painted plates and pitchers—don't excite you only, the air-conditioning might. (Open May-Oct. Mon.-Sat. 10am-6pm.) Nearby are two *faïenceries* (porcelain studios) where you can watch potters designing Quimper's finest. **Les Faïenceries de Quimper H. B. Henriot,** rue Haute (tel. 98 90 09 36), across from Notre-Dame de Locmaria, guides tours in French (and English if requested in advance). (Open Mon.-Thurs. 9:30-11:30am and 1:30-4:30pm, Fri. 9:30-11:30am and 1:30-3pm. Admission 12F, ages 8-14 6F.) One km out of town on route de Bénodet, the **Faïenceries Keraluc** (tel. 98 53 04 50) leads free tours. (Open Mon.-Fri. 9am-noon and 2-6pm.)

Quimper does have a small art scene, and just to prove it, its museum of contemporary art, **Le Quartier,** 10, Parc du 137*ème* R.I. (tel. 98 55 55 77) has introduced postmodernism to the city. To reach the museum, take a left off rue Douarnenez, across from the St-Mathieu church. (No permanent exhibits. Open Tues.-Fri. 11am-7pm, Sat. 2-6pm, Sun. 2-5pm. Admission 20F, students 15F, ages 12-18 10F.)

Those who missed the Festival de Cornouaille can still catch other celebrations of Breton culture. Every Thursday from late June to early September, festival week excluded, the cathedral gardens fill with traditional **Breton dancers** in costume, accompanied by lively *biniou* and *bombarde* players (9pm, 17F). The first three weeks in August, Quimper holds its **Semaines Musicales.** Some of Europe's finest orchestras, choirs, and soloists perform nightly in the Théâtre Municipal, cathedral, and other churches. (Tickets 80F, students and children 50F, discounts for three or more concerts. Make reservations at the tourist office.)

Popular music in Quimper ensures that Breton hips sway at **Les Naïades** (tel. 98 53 32 22), a disco about 1 km out of town on the route de Bénodet, near the Rallye supermarket (open 10:30pm-5am, cover 70F, one drink included). **L'Escala** (tel. 98 95 32 16) is a popular piano bar, 2km away on the route de Brest. (Open 10:30pm-3:45am. No cover). **The Cavinière** (tel. 98 55 52 86), on rue Saint Marc, off rue Douarnenez, a modern bar brimming with youth, features live rock and folk music on Wednesday and Friday nights. (Open daily 11am-1am. No cover for performances).

Quimper has several cinemas. **Les Studios du Chapeau Rouge,** 1, rue du Paradis (tel. 98 53 43 66 or 98 53 23 11), next to St-Mathieu church, screens mostly art films and revivals. Admission 36F.

Near Quimper

Biking in the area is arduous, but bus connections from Quimper to nearby sights are frequent and reliable. At least seven buses each day go from Quimper to the **Crozon Peninsula** (1-1 1/2hr., about 40F).

Discover the numerous châteaux which line the banks of the gorgeous Odet River with **Vedettes de L'Odet** (tel. 98 57 00 58), whose boats cruise to the resort town of **Bénodet,** 15km away. (July-Aug. 3-4 per day, May-June and Sept. 2-3 per day, 75min., 85F round-trip.)

Halfway between Bénodet and Pont-l'Abbé on the D44 lies the **Jardin Botanique** (tel. 98 56 44 93), 8 1/2 acres of roses, camellias, azaleas, and other exotic flora. (Open Mon.-Sat. 10am-noon and 2-7pm; Oct.-April Sun. and holidays 2-7pm or by appointment. Admission 15F.) Farther along the D44 towards Bénodet is the **Musée de la Musique Mécanique** (tel. 98 56 36 03), a collection of organs, player pianos, and other mechanized musical instruments. (Open daily 2-7pm; Oct.-April Sun. and holidays 2-7pm. Admission 20F, includes guided tour.) Climb the **Phare d'Eckmühl,** the second tallest lighthouse in Europe, for an endless view of the rocky coast and the rough sea, in the town of **St-Pierre Kérity.**

Flatter terrain makes for easier cycling north of Quimper. Lovely but pungent **Douarnenez,** an active fishing port and canning town 22km northwest along the D765, has a 6am fish auction on weekdays — just hours after the fishing boats arrive at 11pm packed with mackerel, sardines, and shellfish. The animated market every Monday, Wednesday, and Friday is quite a sight. Douarnenez is well-connected to Quimper by bus (4 per day). In July and August, a ferry cruises from Douarnenez to Morgat on the Crozon Peninsula.

The **Pointe du Raz,** the westernmost point of all of France, shares a majestic, craggy coastline with the less touristy **Point du Van,** 2km farther north. Nearby lies the tiny village of **Plogoff.** During the late 70s, when construction began on a nuclear power plant at Pointe du Raz, the community rejected all government support and declared itself "independent" for nearly three weeks. The mayor was actually imprisoned and a new leader sworn in. That the plant has been dismantled is proof that you *can* fight city hall. Power to the people. CAT buses serve the Pointe du Raz.

Concarneau

Within its crenellated walls, the round towers and cobblestone streets of Concarneau's *ville close* conceal the city's identity as France's largest tuna fishing port. You'll smell it, however, along the quai Carnot, which is lined by warehouses packing the daily catch. Detracting from this piscine atmosphere are the equally numerous Concarneau souvenir vendors trying to snag a tourist. To avoid the cute crafts shops, head away to the town's beaches.

Concarneau has no railway station, but frequent buses connect it with Quimper and Quimperlé. Buses stop on the quai d'Aiguillon near the harbor, next to the tourist office. From there, the *ville close* is on the right. On the left is the humongous fisherman's warehouse where men and women unload fish. The center of town is behind you.

Concarneau presents its history as a fishing town in the **Musée de la Pêche,** just beyond the entrance to the *ville close.* The museum contains a long line of aquariums, models, and explanations of fishing techniques from all over the world. (Open daily 9:15am-8:30pm; Sept.-June daily 9:30am-12:30pm and 2:30-6pm. Admission 30F, students 25F.) Join locals in their bids for the big one at the *criée* (fish auction) weekdays at 7am on the quai Carnot, inside the huge warehouse.

Smooth sand beaches and startlingly clear water attract swarms of tourists to this summer resort. The **Plage des Sables Blancs** is the town's most popular beach. Take bus #1 from av. Pierre Guéguin across from the quai d'Aiguillon to "Les Sables Blancs." The **Plage du Large** on the other side of town is usually less crowded. Take bus #2 to *Le Cabellou* and walk about 5 minutes from there. During the first week of August, the **Festival International de Folklore** shakes the streets with dancers in ethnic garb, music, and parades. A more local festival, the **Fête des Filets Bleus** (Blue Nets), was first held in 1905 to aid Concarneau's sardine fishers. Now, five days before the second-to-last Sunday in August, the people celebrate their fortunes with folkloric dances, traditional *coiffes* and Breton costumes, and grilled fish.

Finding a place to stay can be difficult in July and August, so call ahead. The superb **Auberge de Jeunesse (HI),** 5-10 min. from the center of town on the Quai de la Croix (tel. 98 97 03 47) looks over the ocean. (Reception open daily 9am-noon and 6-8pm. Midnight curfew. 40F per person. HI card required. Breakfast 16F.) More centrally located, the **Hôtel des Voyageurs,** 9, pl. Jean Jaurès (tel. 98 97 08 06), diagonally across from the bus station, offers spacious, clean rooms. (Singles 125-160F. Doubles from 175F. Breakfast 25F.) The **Camping du Dorlett** (tel. 98 97 16 44) lies about 2km out of town near the Plage des Sables Blancs. Take bus #1 from the bus station to "Le Dorlett." (13 per day, last bus 6:20pm, 4F60.) (Reception open 8:30am-noon and 2-7pm. Camping 11F per person, 19F50 per site. Open late June to mid-Sept.)

The majority of restaurants are concentrated in the *ville close.* **L'Escale,** 19, quai Carnot, caters to a regular clientele of fishermen. (Open Mon.-Sat. 4am-11pm.) Feast on the three-course steak-and-fries 40F *menu.* **La Ville Dorée** 13bis, av. du Docteur P. Nicolas, across from the quai Peneroff, offers a motley selection of the ever-present Breton crêpe as well as seafood. 59F *menu* consists of oysters, fish, and a homemade dessert. (Open daily noon-9pm.)

Near Concarneau: Pont Aven

Before Paul Gauguin left for Tahiti, he spent his last years in France residing in Pont Aven, now home to some of the finest art galleries in Brittany as well as the Trou Mad cookie factory. The school of Pont-Aven was formed here around Gauguin and Emile Bernard. A radically new movement in art during the 1880s, its subscribers emphasized pure color, absence of perspective, and simplification of figures.

The little mossy stream that glides through this tiny town lends a dose of lethargy to Pont-Aven that is absent in Gaugin's work. The **tourist office,** pl. de l'Hôtel de Ville (tel. 98 06 04 70), is a few steps beyond pl. Paul Gauguin where the bus stops. It recommends leisurely walks through the **Bois d'Amour,** one source of inspiration for the impressionists, and further on, the 16th-century **Chapelle de Trémalo,** whose impressive crucifix provoked Gauguin's *Yellow Christ.* (Tourist office open Mon.-Sat. 9am-

12:30pm and 2-6:30pm, Sun. 10:30am-12:30pm and 3-6:30pm; Oct.-April closed
Sun.) The **Musée de L'Ecole de Pont Aven,** in the Hôtel de Ville (tel. 98 06 14 43)
may disappoint Gauguin devotees with its limited collection of drawings, letters, and
sculptures, but it does contain a fine display of works by artists from Gauguin's school
as well as paintings by local masters. (Open April-Sept. daily 10am-12:30pm and 2-
6:30pm. Admission 12F, students 8F.) The calvary next to the 15th-century church at
Nizon, about 1.5km northwest of Pont-Aven, inspired Gauguin's *Green Christ* (now at
the Musées Royaux des Beaux Arts in Brussels).

Despite the number of proverbially starving artists in town, hotel prices are geared to
the wallets of the rich. You can easily make Pont-Aven a daytrip. The cheapest place in
town, **Anjoncs d'Or,** next to the tourist office at 1, pl. de l'Hôtel de Ville (tel. 98 06 02
06), is not cheap enough. (Singles and doubles from 245F. Breakfast 30F.) The closest
campground to Pont-Aven is **Spinnaker** (tel. 98 06 01 77), a luxurious site about 3km
out of town and five minutes from the beach. Take the rue des Abbés Tanguy to the intersection at Kergoz, then a left (direction "Nevez"), and follow the signs (23F per
adult, 26F per site, 11F per car. Electricity 11F). Ask at the tourist office for information on other sites. Cyclists should pedal to the rustic *gîte d'étape* in Riec-sur-Belon,
6km southwest of Pont-Aven (26F per night). Signs for the *gîte* appear on the D783 to
Quimperlé.

Quimperlé

Two rivers, L'Ellé and L'Isole, meet at Quimperlé (pop. 12,000) to form La Laïta,
which winds south some 15km through the Forêt de Carnoët en route to the sea. The
oldest part of the city, the *basse ville,* sits on the island created by this fluvial intersection. Sometimes called the Mont St. Michel of the land because of the large hill on
which it is built, Quimperlé is a sedate Breton town not yet defaced by the tourist onslaught, but slowly eroding under the weight of economic hardship; *à vendre* (for sale)
signs are a common fixture in store windows. Despite its uncertain future, Quimperlé
remains a fine place to visit if only to see a facet of France not always publicized in
glossy brochures.

If arriving by bus from Quimper or Concarneau, stay on past the SNCF station to the
stop on 3, quai Brizeux in the *basse-ville.* To get to the tourist office from there, cross
the Isole river, turn right at pl. de Général de Gaulle, and cross the Ellé river to the rue
de Bourgneuf (2 min.). Otherwise, the walk from the station to the *basse ville* takes
about 15 minutes and serves as a good introduction to the town. From the station, take
a left onto bd. de la Gare, a right onto rue de l'Hôpital Fremeur, go up the hill, straight
across pl. St-Michel, and past the right side of the church (under one of its buttresses).
From here, take the rue Savary to the left (off tiny pl. Gambetta), and turn right onto rue
Jacques Cartier—a cobblestoned staircase that passes for a street. Arriving at the quai,
turn left and cross the bridge to pl. Charles de Gaulle, then turn right for the tourist office.

In the *haute ville* is the Gothic 15th- to 18th-century **Eglise Notre-Dame de L'Assomption.** Inside, along the edge of the nave, note the ghoulish carvings of animals,
horned devils, and grotesque faces. (Open July 1-Aug. 31, free guided tours only.)

The jewel of the *basse ville* is the 11th-century **Eglise Ste-Croix,** which borrows the
cloverleaf shape and all the grandeur of Jerusalem's Holy Sepulchre but none of the
kitschy sectarian clutter. Flick the light switch over your head before descending into
the crypt under the altar. Just outside and to the right of Ste-Croix is the **rue de Bré-
mond d'Ars,** the 17th-century aristocratic center of Quimperlé where several of the
half-timbered gentry houses remain. Up the hill (and it's quite a hill), Quimperlé's
haute ville is the site of 14th- to 15th-century **Eglise Notre-Dame,** so tightly wedged
into its surroundings that the steep streets pass under its arched buttresses. Turn on rue
Dom-Monce to find the **Musée des Archers** (at #7), a repository of local lore in a restored aristocratic residence built without the use of rails or metal. The town's crack
commando squad of *archers* (policemen) used to operate out of this building. (Open
June 15-Sept. 15 Wed.-Mon. 10am-noon and 2:30-7pm. Admission 14F.)

Accommodations in Quimperlé are reasonably priced. **Le Brizeux,** 7, quai Brizeux (tel. 98 96 19 25), centrally located by the river in the *basse ville* and run by a friendly manager, features hilarious shaggy bedspreads and matching chairs. (Singles and doubles 120F, with shower 130F, with bath 170F.) The antique **Hôtel Les Tilleuls,** 25, rue de Bourgneuf (tel. 98 96 07 97), is run by an incredibly energetic 80-year-old couple that swears this workers' hotel rejuvenates them. (Singles 65F. Doubles 70F. Triples 120F. Showers 8F. Breakfast 20F. Open daily. 45F workers' *menu* downstairs.) Two km out of town on the N165 is the **Camping Municipal de Quimperlé** (tel. 98 39 31 30), a comfortable site with showers, swimming, and TV. (11F50 per adult, 9F15 per site, 4F85 per car. Electricity 7F50. Open June 15-Sept. 15.)

For a sense of bovine humor, try **La Vache Enragée,** 5, rue Jacques Cartier (halfway up the crumbling stairway), the ill-natured cousin of *La Vache qui Rit* of cheese fame. The 68F *menu* includes scallops, a chicken brochette, and dessert, all in a cozy grotto. (Open daily noon-2pm and 6:45-10pm.) For something more boisterous, head to **Pizza Rialto,** 2, rue de la Tour d'Auvergne, a Venetian-style joint on a bridge over the Isole, with pastas starting at 40F and a 50F *menu*. (Open daily noon-2pm and 7-10:30pm; Sept.-June. Wed.-Mon.)

Cars Caoudal (tel. 98 56 96 72) sends six buses per day to Pont Aven (45 min., 16F60), Concarneau (1hr., 28F), and Quimper (1hr. 45 min., 35F). All buses stop at the SNCF station (information and tickets at Café de la Gare) and quai Brizeux (same at Café Au Retour de Toulfoën) in the *basse-ville*. Trains (tel. 98 39 24 24) connect Quimperlé with Paris (6 per day, 6 1/2hr., 270F), Lorient (8-10 per day, 20 min., 19F) and Quimper (10-12 per day, 40min., 38F). TGV to Paris (change in Rennes; 5 per day, 5hr., 266F plus 16-80F reservation). You can rent wheels on the quai at **Cycles Peugeot,** 5, rue de la Tour d'Auvergne (tel. 98 96 05 18). Bikes 40F per day, 180F per week, 400F deposit. Mopeds 100F per day, 360F per week, 900F deposit.

Near Quimperlé: Lorient and Ile de Groix

Lorient (pop. 59,000), completely destroyed and rebuilt after WWII, is one of the few cities in France where the central church is a work of modern art. Lorient has an important history as the most powerful port of the French East India Company, the largest military post under Napoleon I and today the second-largest fishing port in France. Past glories aside, Lorient functions for the tourist primarily as a departure point for Ile de Groix.

To get to the **tourist office** and the **ferry port** from the train station (about 20-25 min.), turn right and walk to cours de Chazelles. Turn right down this large boulevard, which becomes rue Maréchal Foch and curves around onto the rue Poissonière; this leads to the quai des Indes. The tourist office is across the bridge in the spaceship-like Musée de la Mer, and the ferries are a bunch of meters farther down the quai. You can also take Bus D from the *gare routière* on cours de Chazelles (direction "Nouvelle Ville") and get off at "Maison de la Mer." (Tourist office open Mon.-Fri. 9am-7pm, Sat. 9am-noon and 2-7pm, Sun. 2-6pm; Sept.-June Mon.-Fri. 9am-12:30pm and 1:30-6pm, Sat. 9am-noon and 2-6pm. Has information about ferry departures.)

A fabulous **Auberge de Jeunesse (HI),** built into the side of a hill and overlooking a lake, sits about 3km out of town. This modern bunker has excellent kitchen trappings and facilities for travelers with disabilities. Take bus C (direction "Kercoman"; 4 per hr. until 8pm, 6F), and get off at the stop marked "Auberge de Jeunesse," then follow the signs for 5-10 minutes. (Reception open daily 8:30am-12:30pm and 5:30-7:30pm. Lockout 10am-5:30pm. 61F. HI card required. Breakfast included. Dinner 45F. Sheets 15F. Open Feb. to mid-Dec.) Lorient sends frequent trains to Paris (4 per day, 1 Sun, 6 1/2hr., 270F), via Nantes (116F) or Rennes (115F). Also to Vannes (10-12 per day, 4 Sun., 45 min., 44F). TGV to Paris (6-7 per day, 2 Sun., 3hr., 270F, plus 16-80F reservation).

Ferries run frequently from Lorient to Port Tudy on the **Ile de Groix** (4-8 per day, 45 min., 75F round-trip), where the hardy weathered population numbers only 2500. Serene, with walking trails along its cliffs, smooth sand beaches, and acres of untouched land, the island entices with a temporary escape from the crowds and streets of the built-up mainland. The **tourist office** (tel. 97 86 54 96 or 97 86 53 08), on the quai at the ferry landing, will equip you with a map and information about the island. (Open for about one hour after each ferry arrival.) Most of the interesting sights can be reached only by foot—the well-marked paths along the coast are generally too narrow and rough for even a mountain bike. The 8km by 4km island is small enough to explore in a day, but you'll probably want to stay longer.

Once a cannery, the **Ecomusée de L'Ile de Groix** (tel. 97 05 84 60), 50m from the port where the ferry docks, provides an interesting introduction to the island. It includes a fascinating discussion of Ile de Groix's unique rock formations, found only two other places in the galaxy. The museum also features a small display on the island's more mundane recent history. (Open daily 9:30am-12:30pm and 3-7pm; Sept. 9-April 27 Tues.-Sun. 10am-12:30pm and 2-5pm). You can walk or bike to the turbulent **Plage des Sables Blancs,** a wide and sandy beach 2km to the left of Port Tudy. Further on is the **Pointe des Chats,** beyond which the wind and sea reach to the edge of the earth. Around the point, the white and stone houses of Locmaria huddle tightly together for protection from the brutal winds. On the other end of the island between **Pointe de Kervédan** and **Pen Mer** point stretches some of the most jagged and beautiful coastline on the island.

On the hill facing the harbor in Port Tudy is a rustic *gîte d'étape* (tel. 97 05 89 81), run by an amiable young local. Walk left from the port and up the hill by the *Douanes* office; the *gîte* is just behind a snack stand. (31F per night, showers and kitchen facilities included.) Two km from Port Tudy is an **Auberge de Jeunesse (HI)** (tel. 99 64 13 14); this former German gun emplacement is now run by a good-humored woman and makes a fine base for exploration. From the ferry dock, turn left, go up the hill, make a left at the first four-way intersection, then turn left again at the auberge entrance. (Reception open 9-11:30am and 7-8pm. 39F per person, showers included. Open May 20-Sept. 20.)

Campers should head for **Camping des Sables Rouge** (tel. 99 64 13 14), an excellent site at Port Coustic, near the Pointe des Chats on the southern tip of the island. (16F per person, 19F50 per site, 6F50 per car. Open June-Sept. 15.) Friendly men in bright orange jump suits rent bikes at **Cycles Martin** (tel. 97 86 84 17) on the harbor in Port Tudy. (Bikes 34F per day, 10F per hr., 6F each additional hr. Mountain bikes 70F per day, 15F per hour.)

Quiberon and Belle-Ile

All roads in Quiberon lead to the smooth, sandy, and wonderfully clean **Grande Plage,** located in the heart of town. Sure, it's crowded with English tourists in July and August. And yes, it has its share of sea resort kitsch. But that is part of Quiberon's charm: everyone hangs out on the boardwalk, enjoying *crêpes* and ice cream, and soaking up the summer sun. To escape the congested port area, head for smaller, rockier **Plage du Goviro** near the campgrounds. From the port, follow bd. Chanard east along the water as it becomes bd. de la Mer and then bd. du Goviro. Back in town, the canneries on quai de l'Océan provide a glimpse of industrial life on Brittany's southern coast.

Spectacular Belle-Ile is just a ferry ride away, and the craggy Côte Sauvage stretches a wild and windy 10km along the western edge of the Quiberon peninsula. Heed the signs marked *Baignades Interdites* (swimming forbidden); many have drowned in these tempting but treacherous waters. Cycling is a popular and convenient means of touring both the island and the coast.

Train service to Quiberon operates only in July and August; in the off-season, buses are frequent and dependable. All buses stop at the train station, Port Maria (the ferry dock) and the central pl. Hoche. **TTO buses** (tel. 97 47 29 64) run to Auray (6-8 per day, 4 Sun., 1hr., 33F) via Carnac (1/2hr., 20F). To find the tourist office from the train station, turn left and walk down rue de la Gare. Veer to the right of the church, down rue de Verdun, and the tourist office is on the right. The professional staff can help you find a B&B for 100-200F, a wise option since hotels are expensive and often full.

Quiberon has a small, centrally located **Auberge de Jeunesse (HI),** 45, rue du Roch-Priol (tel. 97 50 15 54). From the station turn left, take rue de la gare through pl. du Repos, take rue de Lille and turn left on rue Roch-Priol. Continue bearing left for about two blocks until you reach the *auberge.* (44F. Kitchen facilities. Sheets 15F. Open May-Sept. 30.) Only a few hotels meet the needs of the budget traveler. In July and August, reservations are a must. The **Hôtel de L'Océan,** 7, quai de L'Océan (tel. 97 50 07 58) lets clean, color-coordinated rooms on the boardwalk facing the harbor. (Singles and doubles with shower from 190F, with shower and toilet from 220F.) **Le Corsaire,** 24, quai de Belle-Ile (tel. 97 50 15 05), also overlooks the harbor and offers decent, if gaudy, rooms. (Singles and doubles 130F, with shower 145-245F. Triples with shower 250F. Breakfast 21F.) At the **Au Bon Accueil,** 6, quai de L'Houat (tel. 97 50 07 92) the affable boniface rents plain, inexpensive rooms. (Singles and doubles 100F, with shower 130F. Triples with shower 130F. Open late March-Nov. 1.) There are over a dozen campsites on the Quiberon peninsula; the one nearest the city is **Camping du Goviro,** (tel. 97 50 13 54), adjacent to the lovely beach of the same name. (Reception open 8:30am-noon and 2-5:30pm. 8F70 per adult, 6F per tent, 4F70 per car.) Right behind is the slightly more spacious **Camping Bois d'Amour** (tel. 97 50 13 52), whose recent renovation has added a swimming pool and other amenities. (23F per adult, 42F per site, car and shower included. Electricity 16F. Open May to mid-Oct.)

Quiberon specializes in seafood, and most restaurants offer a 69F dinner *menu.* The Quiberon *bon bon* of choice is the *niniche,* a caramel-like hard candy. Try any flavor imaginable at the pink-striped candy store on the boardwalk, just off pl. Hoche. Picnickers will find a **Stoc supermarket** on rue de Verdun (open Mon.-Sat. 8:45am-12:30pm and 3-7:15pm). At **La Criée,** 11, quai de l'Océan, an outgoing, good-humored man serves a terrific seafood *couscous* (70F) from the shellfish table at the entrance. (Open Feb.-Dec. for lunch Tues.-Sun., for dinner Tues.-Sat.) For light Italian food, try **Bella Vita,** 3, place Hoche, which offers salads and pastas (30-60F) and a terrace for people-watching (open daily noon-3pm and 7pm-midnight). Cruise the boardwalk or explore the **Côte Sauvage** on bikes, tandems, 3-seaters, pedal carts, or mopeds from **Cyclomar,** 17, pl. Hoche (tel. 97 50 26 00). (5-speed bikes 30F per 1/2-day, 43F per day; mopeds 78F per 1/2-day, 124F per day. 10% off with ISIC. Open July-Aug. daily 8am-midnight; Oct.-Jan. 5 and Feb. 7-June daily 8:30am-12:30pm and 2-7:30pm.)

Loose your caboose at the **Le Gun** disco, just off the pl. Hoche on rue du Phare. (Open daily 11pm-4am, Oct.-March Fri.-Sat.) Or sample **Le Suroit,** 29, rue de Port-Maria, a disco with a boat for a bar and a striking view. (Open 11pm-4am. Cover 50F, first drink 50F.)

Belle-Ile

At least ten boats depart daily from Quiberon's Port-Maria for Belle-Ile, an island that lives up to its name. More touristy than its smaller sibling, Ile de Groix, Belle Ile's magnificent coast merges high cliffs, narrow creeks, and crashing seas. Farther inland, thick patches of heather, furze, and ferns color the fields. The crossing takes 25-45 minutes; you can take a bike with you (78F per person, 17F per bike round-trip).

Biking is the best way to tour the island. **Didier Banet,** quai de l'Acadie (tel. 97 31 84 74) rents bikes right on the harbor. (40F per day, 35F per 1/2 day; mountain bikes 70F per 1/2 day, 80F per day. 800F deposit. Open April-Sept. 9am-7pm.)

An impressive 15th-century walled citadel protects **Le Palais,** once a strategic port and currently the island's largest town. The museum inside presents the history of the citadel, and reveals gossip on the lives of celebrities who lived on Belle-Ile, including Monet and Sarah Bernhardt. The citadel also affords access to the ramparts (open daily 9:30am-7pm, Sept.-June 9:30am-noon and 2-6pm; 26F).

The tourist office (tel. 97 31 81 93), at the end of the quai in Le Palais, distributes a comprehensive brochure about the island, including suggestions for an ambitious 40km bike ride as well as several 1 1/2- to 2 1/2-hour hikes. (Open July-Sept. 15 8:30am-12:30pm and 2-7:30pm. Oct.-June 9am-noon and 2-6pm.)

Bike 6km to **Sauzon,** a tiny fishing port with picture-book façades. From Sauzon, continue another 4km to the **Pointe des Poulains,** at the northernmost tip of the island.

This storm-battered spot, surrounded by water and rock, suggests impending danger. Four km southwest on the Côte Sauvage lies the impressive **Grotte de L'Apothicaire-rie.** The grotto took its name from the cormorant nests that once lined the rocks like bottles in an apothecary's shop. Heed the signs warning of mortal danger and don't follow other foolish folks into the caves—people have perished in this grotto. On a more pleasant note, the nearby deserted fort was home for many years to actress Sarah Bernhardt. From the grotto, follow D25 south to the rough **Aiguilles de Port-Coton,** which Claude Monet captured in an 1886 painting, and the nearby **Plage de Port-Donnant,** where waves crash onto the sandy beach between high stone cliffs.

Inexpensive accommodations on the island include two campgrounds, three *gîtes d'étape,* and an **HI youth hostel.** The hostel (tel. 97 31 81 33) is located near the citadel, a 20-minute hike from Le Palais port. Turn right from the port and follow the quai to the footbridge leading to the citadel; cross the bridge, walk diagonally left through the parking lot, and enter **Camping Les Glacis.** (Reception open July-Aug. 9am-2:30pm and 3:30-10pm, Sept. to mid-Oct. and April-June 9-11:30am and 4:30-6:30pm. 6F per person, 6F20 per tent. Showers 7F.) To reach the hostel, continue on and turn right at the road by the showers, climb another hill, follow the road through a small residential neighborhood, and look for the sign to the *auberge* on the right. Despite its past as a military barracks and a juvenile prison, the hostel has comfortable two-bed rooms, a decent kitchen and bathroom facilities with wheelchair access. You can also camp on the lawn. (Reception open 8:30-10am and 6-8pm. Members only. 43F. Camping 31F. Breakfast 16F. Sheets 15F.) Besides selling fresh vegetables, the *gîte d'étape* in **Port Guen** (tel. 97 31 55 88), about 3km south of Le Palais, rents beds (31F) in dorm-style rooms in a colorful barn. Reservations are recommended.

A new **Centre d'Accueil** (tel. 97 31 65 39) has just been built in Sauzon, on rue Willaumez. Take rue Lieutenant Riou off the pl. de l'Eglise and turn right. (Reception open 2-4pm and 6:30-8:30pm. 120F per person). Sauzon also has the modest **Hôtel du Phare** at the end of the quai. (Singles and doubles 180F, with shower 240F. Breakfast 35F. Open late March-late Sept.) The tourist office in Le Palais can also help find cheap rooms.

La Chaloupe, 8, av. Carnot in Le Palais, purveys an enormous variety of reasonably priced *crêpes* and *galettes* (10-40F) and is open until midnight from July to August. **Café de la Cale,** quai Guerveur in Sauzon, prepares delicious seafood and salads (40-90F). Two seafood lovers might consider sharing the *grande assiette de fruits de mer* (96F).

Carnac and Auray

Majestic stretches of countryside with great pine forests and open heaths lie northeast of the Quiberon Peninsula. Mesolithic people roamed this area of Brittany as long as 10,000 years ago; their Neolithic heirs settled here between 4800-1700BC, leaving menhirs and dolmens—once thought to be the work of druidic wizardry—scattered throughout the area.

Menhirs are vertical standing stones, ranging from a few centimeters to over 20m in height, arranged either colinearly or in semi-circles called *cromelechs.* Though their purpose has eluded modern scholars, some advance that *menhirs* mark the site of burial grounds, represent divinities, or map out the universe. *Dolmens,* two standing stones with a horizontal slab across the top, are believed to be the skeletons of collective burial chambers. An earthen mass called a *tumulus* once surrounded this stone edifice.

Carnac, a 1/2-hr. bus ride north of Quiberon, has the most formidable series of these ancient monuments at the mysterious **Alignements du Ménec.** Here, more than 1000 menhirs, some over 3m tall, stretch over 2km in a line toward the horizon. Also in Carnac lies the **Tumulus de St-Michel,** an immense burial chamber within an earthen mound. Be prepared for long lines to enter the passageways which have been stripped of most of their original decoration. (Open 10am-noon and 3-6pm. Tour 15 min., 6F, students 3F.) The **Musée de Préhistoire,** 10, pl. de la Chapelle (tel. 97 52 22 04), contains an impressive collection of burial chambers, engraved dolmen stones, jewelry, metal, pottery and other artifacts that shed light on Brittany's history from 450,000 BC to the beginning of the middle ages. (Open daily 10am-noon and 2-6:30pm; Sept.-June Wed.-Mon. 10am-noon and 2-6pm. Admission 28F, students 10F.)

To get to Carnac, take the bus from Quiberon (at least 7 per day, 1/2hr., 17F50) or from Auray (7 per day, 1/2hr., 19F). You can also take the train to Plouharnel and catch a bus from there (7 per day, 5 min., 3F). The bus stop *Carnac-ville* drops you close to the museum, a five-minute walk up rue du Tumulus to the Tumulus de St-Michel. The Alignements du Ménec are 10 to 15 minutes from both the museum and the Tumulus. Head north on rue de Courdriec, rue de Poul Person, or rue des Korrigans until you see the menhirs on route des Alignements.

To get to the **tourist office,** pl. de L'Eglise (tel. 97 52 13 52) from the bus stop in Carnac-ville, walk to town on rue St-Cornely to the church square. The office is in a small building behind and to the left of the church. (Open July-Aug. Mon.-Sat. 9am-1pm and 2-7pm, Sun. 10am-12:30pm and 5-7pm; Sept. Mon.-Sat. 9am-noon and 2-7pm; Easter-June Tues.-Sat. 9am-1pm and 2-6pm.) Another branch is on the beach at 74, av. des Druides (same tel.; open Tues.-Sat. 9am-noon and 2-6pm).

Make Carnac a day trip. The handsome beach understandably attracts many visitors to Carnac and hikes up hotel prices accordingly. B&Bs are the cheapest housing option; ask the tourist office for a list. (Doubles run 100-150F, breakfast included.) A hip young couple who lived in New York for 15 years owns the **Hôtel d'Arvor,** 5, rue St-Cornély (tel. 97 52 96 90) and lets some of the cheapest rooms in town. (Doubles 220F, with shower 260F. About 30F cheaper Sept.-June.) An abundance of campgrounds dots the area around Carnac. The **Alignements de Kermario** (tel. 97 52 16 57) is across the road from the megaliths in a lush, private setting. (Reception open 8:30am-8pm. 14F per person, 26F per tent, 8F per car. Electricity 12F. Open June-Sept.) **Camping Kerabus** (tel. 97 52 24 90) is about three minutes away from the big old rocks on allée des Alouettes off route d'Auray. (Reception open 8:30am-noon and 2-7pm. 10F per person, 13F per tent, 5F per car. Showers 4F50. Electricity 12F. Open June-Sept. 15.)

In Carnac, **Robert Lorcy,** 6, rue de Courdriec (tel. 97 52 09 73), rents **bicycles** for 30F per 1/2-day, 45F per day or 170F per week, with an 800F or passport deposit. (Open Mon.-Sat. 8:30am-12:30pm and 2-7pm, Sun. 8:30am-12:30pm; Sept.-June Tues.-Sat. and sometimes Sun. 8:30am-12:30pm and 2-7pm.) There's no need to rent a bike to get to the beach since it's a short walk from Carnac-*ville*. However, you might want to bike to the nearby village of **Trinité-sur-Mer** which harbors one of the largest pleasure ports in France and affords a phenomenal view across the Bay of Quiberon.

Auray, another base for exploring the area's megaliths, is a picturesque fishing village on the Auray River between the Quiberon peninsula and the Gulf of Morbihan. Its 15th-century fishing port has reeled in a thriving tourist population which throngs to the town's **Festival International d'Auray** each year in the beginning of July. Here you can watch Philippine ballerinas, sing along to old Irish songs, and enjoy exploding fireworks at the Port St-Gouston (tickets at the tourist office, 70-80F).

Auray lies on the Paris-Quimper rail line. (July-Aug., 10 trains per day from Quiberon to Auray, 40 min., 26F.) Frequent buses travel the route the rest of the year. About seven buses per day connect Auray *centre ville* and Quiberon (1hr., 33F). Four to six buses per day run to Vannes (45 min., 17F50) via Ste-Anne d'Auray (15 min., 10F). Finding the centrally located **tourist office,** 20, rue du Lait, means traversing some originally-named streets. Take a diagonal left from the station down rue Jean Jaurès (look for the sign to *centre-ville*), make a right onto av. de Général de Gaulle, bear right onto rue Aristide Briand, then bear right again onto av. Foch which becomes rue Foch and ultimately rue du Lait. The office is in an old chapel on your left. It distributes lists of B&Bs (100-220F) and leads guided tours (in French) in July and August (1-2 per day, 15-20F). (Open July-Aug. Mon.-Sat. 9am-1pm and 2-7pm, Sun. 9am-12:30pm; Sept. and Jan.-June Mon.-Fri. 9am-12:30pm and 2-6:15pm, Sat. 9am-12:30pm.) The train station rents **bikes** (42F per 1/2-day, 50F per day).

Visit the charming museum of fishing and local history, **La Goëlette** (tel. 97 24 07 78 or 97 56 63 38), inside an old schooner on the river. (Walk the decks for free but look inside for 15F, students 10F; open Easter-Sept. 10:30am-12:30pm, 2:30-7pm.)

A selection of inexpensive hotels in Auray welcomes the budget traveler, who should make reservations in July and August. Local geriatrics chat in the cozy bar at

The Hôtel Celtic, 30, rue Clemenceau (tel. 97 24 05 37) with its fresh, quiet doubles. (120F, with shower 150F. Triples with bath 270F. Breakfast 25F.) Got the blues? **Hôtel Le Cadoudal,** 6, pl. Notre Dame (tel 97 24 05 37) has true blue decor and a pleasant bar. (Singles and doubles from 125F, with shower from 205F. Breakfast 30F. All rooms have TV.) For hearty chow, **L'Océan,** 13, rue Clemenceau, provides a 37F50 *menu* in a simple but tasteful joint. (Open Mon.-Sat; Sun. lunch in July and Aug.)

Six km north is the village of **Ste-Anne-d'Auray,** which holds one of the largest *pardons* (see Brittany intro.) in Brittany on July 26 and 27. Smaller, less-touristed *pardons* take place beginning in March.

Vannes

Moving north from Quiberon along the coast, the waters of the Gulf of Morbihan wash into the port of the city of Vannes (pop. 49,000). Most people use Vannes as a base to explore the islands of the Gulf, but the city also features some intriguing museums and a few interesting shops tucked away within the cobblestone *vieille ville*.

Orientation and Practical Information

The train station lies north of the center of town. Turn right out of the station, follow the road to the bottom of the hill, and turn left onto av. Victor Hugo. After several blocks, a right onto rue J. le Brix and a left at the *mairie* onto rue Thiers will bring you to the post office in pl. de la République (15 min.). From there, the *vieille ville* lies to the left and the tourist office 100m ahead on the right. Alternately, take bus #3 or 7 from the train station to pl. de la République. (Service Mon.-Sat. 5F70.)

Tourist Office: 1, rue Thiers (tel. 97 47 24 34), in a 17th-century house. Information on the Gulf of Morbihan, and a booklet about the region and the city itself. In July and Aug., a 1 1/2-hr. guided tours of the city (in French) leave twice per day (22F, under 25 15F). Open Mon.-Sat. 9am-7pm, Sun. 10am-noon, Sept.-June Mon.-Sat. 9am-noon and 2-6pm.

Post Office: pl. de la République, 100m to the right of the tourist office. Offers **currency exchange** Mon.-Fri. 8am-7pm, Sat. 8am-noon. **Postal Code:** 56000.

Trains: (tel. 97 54 11 48 or 97 42 50 50) on av. Favrel et Lincy, north off av. Victor Hugo. To: Paris (4-6 per day, 3 Sun., 6hr., 250F); Rennes (6-8 per day, 4 Sun., 1hr. 15 min., 83F); Quimper (10-12 per day, 8 Sun., 2hr., 80F); Nantes (8-11 per day, 6 Sun., 1 1/2hr., 88F). TGV to Paris (5-8 per day, 2 Sun., 3 1/2hr., 250F, 16-80F reservation). Information office open daily 9am-7pm; Sept.-June 9am-noon and 2-7pm.

Buses: TTO, 4, rue du 116ème R.I. (tel. 97 47 29 64). Line 20 to Nantes (Mon.-Sat. 2 per day, 2 1/2hr., 86F), Line 16 to Rennes (2 per day, 1 Sun., 3hr., 85F50) Line 23 to Quiberon (5 per Mon.-Fri., 2 per day Sat.-Sun., 1hr. 45 min., 50F) via Auray (30 min., 18F) and Carnac (1hr. 10 min., 38F).

Public Transportation: Transports du Pays de Vannes (TPV) (tel. 97 47 21 64) runs city buses. Information and schedules at the Tourisme Verney window (pl. de la Gare, opposite the train station). Connections to *centre ville,* train station, and nearby suburbs. Basic fare 5F70. Central stop at pl. de la République in front of the post office.

Ferries: The most useful is **Vedettes du Golfe/Navix Tourisme** (tel. 97 46 60 00), which leaves from the Parc du Golfe, 10 min. south of the port. It offers tours of the Gulf and stops on Ile d'Arz and Ile Aux Moines. (4 per day; Sept. 15-May 2-3 per day; full-day tour 130F, 1/2-day in the morning with no stops 80F, in the afternoon 105F.) It also goes to Belle-Ile. (July-Aug. 1 per day, 2 hr., leave Vannes at 8:20am and leave Belle-Ile at 5:30pm. 170F round-trip.) Ask at the tourist office for other options.

Laundromat: 5, av. Victor Hugo, opposite the Foyer des Jeunes Travailleuses. Wash 20F, dry 2F per 7 min. 2F and 10F coins. Open daily 7am-9pm.

Hospital: Centre Hospitalier Chubert (tel. 97 01 41 41), on bd. Général Maurice Guillaudot.

Police: 13, bd. de la Paix (tel. 97 47 19 20). **Emergency:** tel. 17.

Accommodations and Camping

Hotels in Vannes fill quickly, and although there's usually room at one of the *foyers*, it's a wise idea to call ahead.

Foyer des Jeunes Travailleuses, 14, av. Victor Hugo (tel. 97 54 33 13). Clean and spacious singles for women, although the hospitable staff usually accepts men too. Register before 10pm. No curfew; ask for keys if you're out past 11pm. 60F, showers included. Breakfast 15F. Lunch and dinner (Mon.-Fri., Sat. lunch only) 33F50. Sheets 24F.

Foyer Mixte des Jeunes Travailleurs, 2, rue Paul Signac (tel. 97 63 47 36), 20 min. from the station. To get there, turn right onto av. Victor Hugo, left onto av. Président Wilson, cross over the highway, make a left onto av. Edgar Dégas, and then a left onto rue Paul Signac. Singles for women and men. Reception open Mon.-Fri. 8am-12:30pm and 2-8pm, Sat. 11am-12:30pm. 70F, breakfast, showers, and sheets included. Dinner 35F.

Hôtel la Chaumière, 12, pl. de la Libération (tel. 97 63 28 51). From the train station, turn right off av. Victor Hugo onto bd. de la Paix and walk 3 blocks. Cheerful, clean rooms but a little noisy. Doubles 95F, with shower 160F. Triples with shower and toilet 210F. Showers 15F. Breakfast 22F50. Lively bar downstairs.

Le Bretagne, 34, rue du Méné (tel. 97 47 20 21). This place offers postered rooms with telephones (a few overlook the old ramparts), an abundance of dried flowers in the hallways, and its own TV room with VCR. Singles 98F, with shower 180F. Doubles 145F, with shower 180F. Breakfast 22F. Call ahead, especially in July.

Camping Municipal de Conleau (tel. 97 63 13 88), a three-star wooded site near the beach about 3km out of town. From pl. de la République, take blue bus #2 (direction "Conleau") and get off at "Camping." Those coming on foot from pl. Gambetta at the head of the port or rue Thiers should follow rue du Port along the harbor for 3km. Reception open April-Sept. 7:30am-8pm. 15F per person, 12F50 per tent, 9F per car. Showers 8F. Electricity 10F.

Travelers with taste buds on a budget will find a **Stoc supermarket** on 19, rue du Mené (open Mon.-Sat. 9am-12:30pm and 2:30-7:15pm) and an enormous **open market** that fills pl. Lucien Laroche, pl. du Poids Public, and pl. des Lices (Wed. and Sat. 8am-noon). But, be warned that Vannes hosts a variety of enticing dens of food that go above and beyond the average *crêperie*. The following might tempt you to forsake the *crêpe* for just one measly night. Then again, they might not.

Le Pavé des Halles, 17, rue des Halles. An almost elegant restaurant, but still easy on the wallet. Serves a 49F lunch *menu*. 69F dinner *menu* includes rabbit pâté, fish in a marjoram sauce, and a sinful dessert. Open for lunch Tues.-Sat., dinner Mon.-Sat.

La Paillote, 8, rue des Halles, off pl. Valencia in the *vieille ville*. A bustling local favorite, glows with quasi-tropical decor. Salads 12-40F, Creole dishes 34-49F, big pizzas 26-50F. The 49F "Super Paillote" pizza groans under the weight of mussels, *coquilles St-Jacques,* and cognac. Open Mon.-Fri. noon-2pm and 7-10pm, Sat. 7-10pm.

Chez Carmen, 17, rue Emile Burgault, near the cathedral in the *vieille ville. Couscous* 50-72F; try the lamb varieties. Good *paella* 72F. Open Tues.-Sat. noon-2pm and 7-10pm

Cafeteria les Arcades, 18, rue francis Decker, across from the *préfecture.* Not as alluring as the other restaurants, this cavernous self-service place offers *plats du jour* (21F50-42F), steak (23F50), desserts (from 12F), a 20F childrens menu, and beer (from 8F90). Open Mon.-Sat. 11:30am-11pm.

Sights and Entertainment

Up from the narrow streets and tall houses in the center of the old town soars the half-Gothic **Cathédrale St-Pierre,** with its remarkable carved portal and magnificent red doors covered with elaborate ironwork. Inside, the dainty stained- glass windows look as though coated with fine jewels. On the other side of the park adjacent to the cathedral, typical half-timbered Breton houses crowd **rue St-Guénahel,** their overhanging second stories braced by diagonal timbers that rest on sculpted heads (look for #17-19). At the bottom of this street, the heavily fortified and still-intimidating 14th- and 15th-century **Porte Prison** gives access to the ramparts (open daily until 7pm), which are illuminated at night in July and August. **Rue St-Vincent** raises eyebrows a wee bit with the 18th- and 19th-century houses that accommodated the members of Parliament and their families after Louis XIV exiled the Parliament of Brittany from Rennes to Vannes in 1675. **Porte St-Vincent,** at the end of the street, replaced the fortified medieval gates at one end of the old city in 1704. Those underwhelmed by these obscurely historical structures will find joy in the pleasant green void of the **Jardin de la Préfecture,** and the neatly manicured gardens outside the ramparts. Back inside the ramparts, the **Musée de Préhistoire,** 2, rue Noé in the 15th-century château Gaillard contains a clever display of artifacts from the megaliths of Carnac and other sites. (Open Mon.-Sat. 9:30am-noon and 2-6pm, Oct.-March Mon.-Fri. 2-5:30pm. Admission 15F, students 10F.) The **Musée de la Cohue,** containing both the **Musée des Beaux Arts** and the **Musée de la Golfe,** is around the corner on rue des Halles, in a restored 16th-century house. The former shows an appealing collection of Rodin sketchings as well as paintings by Gericault, Goya, Corot, and Delacroix. The latter museum discusses the history of the gulf and its fishing techniques, and even explains the lifecycle of those wacky hermaphroditic oysters. (Open daily 10am-noon and 2-6pm; Sept. 16-June 14 Mon. and Wed.-Sat. 10am-noon and 2-6pm. Adults 15F, students 8F.) Each year between August 11 and August 15, Vannes erupts with **Les Fêtes d'Arvor,** a folkloric festival with *biniou* and *bombarde* players, parades and fireworks. At the end of July or the beginning of August, an annual four-day **Jazz Festival** swings in the Jardins de Limur. (Tickets 50-90F, student discounts available.) For more information, call the Palais des Arts at 97 47 47 30 or 97 01 80 00.

Near Vannes: Gulf of Morbihan

Warmed by the Gulf Stream, the waters of the Gulf of Morbihan (Breton for "little sea") nourish 50-odd islands, some no larger than a giant's little toe. **Vedettes du Golfe** (tel. 97 46 60 00) cruises around the gulf (130F) and up the Auray River (170F). Your ticket allows you to get off at any stop and catch a later boat (get a timetable). Boats leave four times per day in late June, July, and August, less often in the off-season. The largest island in the gulf, the **Ile-aux-Moines,** is a 6km sliver of soothing pine groves and pleasant beaches. Palm trees, mimosa, oranges, and lemons all thrive in this near-tropical microclimate. Anywhere on the island, you're never farther than 450m from the sea. Try to get to the other end of the island, where mysterious dolmens, vast heather moors, and deserted little roads compete for attention. Bike rentals on the quay are well worth the price (30F per 1/2-day); pick up a map at the tourist office (tel. 97 26 32 45). The fishing economy and the dearth of cars attest to the endurance of Breton traditions here. The tiny town contains some typical Morbihan thatched-roof cottages and the requisite granite church.

Vedettes du Golfe also passes, but doesn't stop at, the fascinating **Cairn de Gavrinis,** an ancient burial mound 100m in circumference, made of stone and covered with earthworks. Archaeologists continue to explore the mound and its artifacts, estimated to be 7000 years old. To reach the tumulus, take a TTO bus from Vannes to Larmor-Baden (Wed. and Sat. 3 per day, 1/2hr., 16F). From there, **Vedettes Blanches Armors** (tel. 97 57 15 27) runs boats (March-Sept. 25 every 1/2-hr. 9-11:30am and 1:30-5:30pm, 20 min., round-trip 30F). A stop at **Port Navalo** will put you on the less tourist-infested **Presqu'Ile de Rhuys,** which has a fine campground near the tip of the peninsula: **Camping Municipal de Port Navalo,** right up from the ferry stop.

Across from Port Navalo, **Locmariaquer** shines as one of the prettiest villages in Brittany; white houses line the somnolent port, and a lone church steeple breaks the horizon in the distance. Just beyond are the **Grand Menhir** and **Table du Négociant,** the broken remains of a 347-ton menhir and a ritual tomb with remains of rare drawings. The Merchant's Table is composed of three huge "tables" suspended on points to form the imposing galleries. The more modest **Dolmen des Pierres-Plats,** 1km out of town in the opposite direction, is not half as spectacular as the nearby beach—on a good day you'll get a wide view of the coast toward Quiberon and Belle-Ile. Several campgrounds accommodate visitors to this mild and breezy land's end. **Vedettes l'Angelus** (tel. 97 57 30 29) sets sail from Locmariaquer's Port du Guilvin around the gulf on the Auray River (90F), and on to Belle-Ile (you get 6 1/2 hr. on the island, July 1-Aug. 31, round-trip 150F). A whole fleet of ferries leaves regularly from other ports near Vannes (ask at the tourist office). Experienced sailors can obtain an armada of tide, current, and wind information at the tourist office.

Nantes

In Nantes, as in so many of France's respectable *grandes villes,* the stately gray buildings have served as the backdrop for events both gruesome and grand. Under the rule of the great Ducs de Montfort, François I and II, Nantes became firmly established as the administrative center of Brittany. But it was also in this city, in 1532, that Brittany was finally ceded to the French crown. From the 15th-century château at Nantes, Henry IV proclaimed the 1598 Edict of Nantes, establishing religious freedom for Protestants. The château later housed the infamous Maréchal de Retz, who was executed for sacrificing several hundred children in grotesque rituals and who inspired the Bluebeard legends. During the Terror of 1793, Carrier's November *noyades* (drownings) sent hundreds of men and women, bound together in couples, to their deaths in the Loire. Continuing its streak of malevolence, Nantes used the period between the 16th and the 18th centuries to establish an enormously successful slave trade that allowed the city to grow and become, at one point, France's largest port. When the Revolution abolished slavery, Nantes turned instead to an economy supported by canneries, cookie factories, and metal production.

Officially, Nantes is part of the Pays de la Loire. Most *Nantais,* however, feel that their city belongs to Brittany. This geographic and cultural dispute aside, Nantes bears much resemblance to Paris, with public parks and gardens, a large branch of *Galeries Lafayettes,* and wide boulevards marking the boundaries between administrative *arrondissements.* Nantes may ultimately lack the grand scale and uniform beauty of Paris, but it imitates the capital's energy. And, like the capital, Nantes molts in summer when the students leave and the tourists arrive. Stuffed to the gills with historic sights, diverse museums, and nightclubs, Nantes deserves more than a lazy afternoon of sightseeing.

Orientation and Practical Information

50km from the Atlantic and two hours from Paris by TGV, Nantes (pop. 500,000) is split latitudinally by the Loire river and flaunts a 40-story skyscraper, the **Tour Bretagne,** at its center. The city's major axes are **cours John Kennedy,** which becomes **cours Franklin Roosevelt,** running east to west, and **cours des 50 Otages** and **rue de Strasbourg,** running north to south.

To get to the center of town and the tourist office, turn left out of the station onto bd. de Stalingrad, which becomes, interestingly enough, cours John Kennedy. Place du Commerce and the tourist office are 1km ahead. The hostel is a 10-minute walk from the station in the other direction.

Tourist Office: (tel. 40 47 04 51), on pl. du Commerce in the 19th-century commerce building, a stone's throw from McDonald's. A very professional and courteous staff doles out free maps and leads guided tours of different *quartiers* of historic Nantes (1 per day, 35F, students and seniors 25F, reservations recommended). Open Mon.-Fri. 9am-7pm, Sat. 10am-6pm. **Branch office** at pl. Marc Elder, in front of the entrance to the château. Open June 15-Sept. daily 10am-7:30pm.

Post Office: pl. de Bretagne, across from the Tour Bretagne. Currency exchange. Open Mon.-Fri. 8:30am-7pm, Sat. 8:30am-noon. **Postal Code:** 44000.

Flights: 10km south of Nantes. A **Tan Air** shuttle (tel. 40 29 39 39) runs from the pl. du Commerce and the SNCF station, *Accès Nord* (Mon.-Fri. 14 per day, 6 Sat., 3 Sun., 25min., 28F). **Air Inter** (tel. 40 48 09 70) sends 6-8 flights to Paris per day (55 min.,775F, under 25 460F). **Air France** (tel. 40 47 12 33) sends 1 flight per day to London (70min.,1880F, under 25 645F, reserve 7 days before departure).

Trains: 27, bd. Stalingrad (tel. 40 08 50 50). To Paris (4-5 per day, 3-4hr., 216F), Bordeaux (5-8 per day, 4hr., 207F), Rennes (7 per day, 2 Sun., 2hr., 101F). Also a high-speed TGV to Paris (12-14 per day, 2hr., 207F, plus 16-80F reservation).

Buses: TTO (tel. 40 89 27 11). Buses leave from quai Baco at the SNCF station *Accès Sud,* and from 4, allée Duquesne, parallel to and east of cours des 50 Otages. Buy tickets on the bus or at the branch office (tel. 40 20 46 99). To Rennes (3 per day, 1 Sun., 2 hr., 89F), Vannes (2 per day, none Sun., 3 hr.,89F).

Public Transportation: TAN runs an extensive network of buses and one tram line. The hub is at pl. du Commerce. (6F per ticket).

Taxis: tel. 40 69 22 22 or 40 63 66 66. 24 hrs. About 90-100F to airport.

Hitchhiking: Allostop-Provoya, 10, rue Lafayette (tel. 40 89 04 85) at the CRIJ. Give them 3-4 days notice and 60F, and they'll find you a driver entitled to charge you 0.16F per km for gas and tolls. Rides under 300km 30F, above 300km 60F; 6-month subscription 120F. Open Mon. noon-6pm, Tues. 10am-1pm and 2-7pm, Wed-Fri. 10am-7pm.

English Bookstore: Librairie Beaufretow, passage Pommeraye, near the tourist office. Small but respectable collection of classics and light reading from 49F. Open Tues.-Sun. 9:15am-12:30pm and 2-7pm.

Youth Information: Centre Régional d'Information Jeunesse (CRIJ), 28, rue du Calvaire (tel. 40 48 68 25). Youth travel information and a babysitting service. Open Mon. noon-7pm, Tues.-Fri. 10am-7pm.

Laundromat: 56, rue Maréchal Joffre, 5 min. from train station. Wash 17F, dry 2F per 6min., soap 4F. Open 7am-8:30pm.

Women's Center: Centre d'Information Féminin et Familial, for counseling, and **Délégation Régionale aux Droits des Femmes,** for crisis intervention. Both at 5, Maurice Duval (tel. 40 48 13 83). Open Mon. 9:30am-noon, Tues.-Wed. and Fri. 2-5:30pm, Thurs. 9:30am-5:30pm.

Hospital: Centre Hospitalier Régional (tel. 40 08 33 33), on pl. Alexis Ricordeau.

Medical Assistance: SAMU, tel. 40 08 37 77.

Police: (tel. 40 37 21 21), on pl. Waldeck-Rousseau. **Emergency:** tel. 17.

Accommodations and Camping

Nantes has plenty of cheap hotels, and, in summer, lots of student dormitory space opens up. Although the hostel operates only in July and August, the *foyers* welcome travelers all year.

Auberge de Jeunesse (HI), 2, pl. de la Manufacture (tel. 40 20 57 25). From the station, turn right onto bd. de Stalingrad, left onto rue Manille and then left onto pl. de la Manufacture (10 min.). Or take the tram from the train station to "Manufacture" stop (5F50). Lots of space, a few 2-bed rooms, kitchen, and TV. Warm, English-speaking staff. Reception open 7-10am and 6-11pm. Notify the staff if you wish to leave early or stay out late. July-Aug.: 45F. Breakfast 15F. Sheets 15F. Off-season: reception open Mon.-Fri. 5-10pm, Sat.-Sun. 5:45-11pm. 50F. Sheets 17F. Call Cité Universitaire (tel. 40 74 61 86) for more info. on the off-season.

Centre Jean Macé, 90, rue du Préfet Bonnefoy (tel. 40 74 55 74), a 15- to 20-min. walk from the station. Turn left onto cours John Kennedy, then right at pl. de la Duchesse Anne onto rue Henri IV, which becomes rue Sully. The center is on rue Sully at rue du Préfet Bonnefoy. Alternatively, take bus #12 from the SNCF station to pl. Maréchal Foch and continue up rue Sully. Clean but dimly lit 2, 3, or 4-bed rooms. Reception open 7:30am-10pm. 50F. Hallway showers included. With private shower 55F. If you want to be alone, must pay 12F for every unoccupied bed in room. Breakfast 15F. Mon.-Fri. meals 32F.

Foyer des Jeunes Travailleurs, L'Edit de Nantes, 1, rue du Gigant (tel. 40 73 41 46). From the train station, take the tram to pl. du Commerce, walk up cours des 50 Otages either to "St-Nicolas" or "Cathédrale" stops. From there, catch bus #21, 22, or 23, and get off at "Edit de Nantes" stop. The *foyer* is across the street. Men and women welcome. Reception open Mon.-Fir. 9am-6pm, Sat.-Sun. 1-11pm. 55F. Doubles with showers. Dinner from 31F.

Foyer des Jeunes Travailleurs, Beaulieu, 9, bd. Vincent Gâche (tel. 40 12 24 00). From the train station, take the tram to pl. du Commerce and, from there, take bus #24 (direction: "Beaulieu") to "Albert" (5F50). Coed bathrooms and 2-bed rooms. Reception open 8am-5pm. Doors never close. Singles 85F. Doubles 130F. Breakfast included. Kitchen facilities and 39F meals. **Annex,** 1, rue Porte Neuve (tel. 40 20 00 80). From the train station, take the tram to pl. du Commerce and catch bus #40 or #41 from across the street on cours des 50 Otages to "pl. Viarme" stop. Reception open 8am-8pm.

Hôtel Roosevelt, 28, rue des Petites Ecuries (tel. 40 47 17 00), 15min. from the train station. Turn left on cours John Kennedy, right on cours Franklin Roosevelt, and right onto rue des Petites Ecuries. Small rooms but obliging management and firm mattresses. Singles 80-95F, with shower 110-130F. Doubles 130-140F, with shower 150F. Showers 10F. Breakfast 18F.

Hôtel Calypso, 16, rue Strasbourg (tel. 40 47 54 47), off cours John Kennedy on one of the busiest streets. Plain singles 95F, with shower 129F. Doubles 105F, with shower 144F. Showers 15F. Breakfast 18F.

Hôtel Renova, 11, rue Beauregard (tel. 40 47 57 03), off the bottom of cours des 50 Otages. Delightful old couple just loves Americans. Needs renovations, but centrally located and peaceful. Singles and doubles 75-95F, with shower 130F.

Hôtel d'Orléans, 12, rue du Marais (tel. 40 47 69 32), off cours des 50 Otages. Run by a young couple who thinks *Let's Go* travelers are wicked awesome. Bright singles 90-105F. Doubles with shower 115-130F, with 2 beds 150F. Breakfast 20F. Showers 10F.

Camping: Camping du Val de Cens, 21, bd. du Petit Port (tel. 40 74 47 94), 3km from town. Take bus #51 or #53 from pl. du Commerce to "Marhonnière" stop. A superb site with hot water and showers. 15 per person, 20F per site. No telephone reservations accepted, so arrive early in the morning in summer. Reception open 8-11am and 3-8pm.

Food

You won't have trouble finding more than *crêpes* and seafood in Nantes; Lebanese, Italian, Indian, Chinese, and Vietnamese cuisines abound. Try Nantes's delicious seafood, prepared *au beurre blanc* (with butter sauce), and its *Canard Nantais* made with grapes, as well as the white wines, *Muscadet* and *Gros Plant.* **Markets** take place daily except Monday, from 9am to 1pm in pl. du Bouffay and at the **Marché de Talensac,** along rue de Bel Air near pl. St-Similien. A **Decré supermarket** is in the basement of Nouvelles Galeries, rue du Moulin, in the *centre ville.* (Open Mon.-Sat. 9am-7pm.) For dessert, try Nantes's specialties, categorized as *frillandises*—candies, chocolates, and cakes. Home to the Le Petit Beurre cookies we all know and love and eat because we can't afford dinner, Nantes also manufactures *muscadines* (little chocolates filled with grapes and Muscadet wine).

Chez Rémy-La Brasserie des Sportifs, rue de la Bâclerie, off pl. du Bouffay, which is off cours J. Kennedy. Festive atmosphere, outdoor *terrasse.* Try the mountain of delicious *couscous* for 55-95F. Share a single serving with someone else. *Paella* for two 160F. Open Tues.-Sat. noon-2pm and 7-11pm.

Crêperie Jaune, 1, rue des Echevins, off pl. du Bouffay. Students pack it—come early for a seat. The *plat du jour* costs only 38F, but everyone comes for the house specialty, an immense, meaty, double-decker *galette* called *pavé nantais* (37-45F, depending on ingredients). Vegetarian interpretations available. Open Mon.-Sat. noon-3pm and 7pm-2am.

La Mangeoire, 16, rue des Petite Ecuries. Quieter, more elegant place with a 45F *plat du jour.* Beautiful, if not too filling, 58F *menu* of salads, *escargots,* rabbit, chicken, fish, and spiffy desserts. Open Tues.-Sat. noon-2pm and 7-9pm.

L'Arbre de Vie, 8, allée des Tanneurs, parallel to cours des 50 Otages. A small vegetarian restaurant that righteously sits aside the enormous and obnoxious Le Carnivore Brasserie. *L'Aquarelle* salad (50F) is a meal in itself: lettuce, vegetables, seaweed, tofu, raisins, nuts, oats, and wheat germ. Also a 55F *menu* with entree and fresh fruit.

La Cigale, pl. Graslin (tel. 40 69 76 41). Fantastic *belle époque* decor and non-stop animation in this historic monument, open since 1884. Once hosted Sarah Bernhardt and other theater regulars. 69F *menu* offers choice of one entree and a main dish, or a main dish and dessert. Appetizers 25-40F. Entrees 60-150F. Open daily 7am-12:30am. Reservations recommended. Dress appropriately.

Chez Suyen, 7bis, rue Kervégan. Very good Vietnamese food on this "restaurant row." Try the *salade aux crabes* (20F) or the *brochettes de boeuf* (45F). Dinner *menus* 45F, 65F, and 85F. Open Mon.-Sat. noon-3pm and 7-11:30pm.

Sights and Entertainment

Thanks to their lightweight Vendée stone, the Gothic vaults of **Cathédrale St-Pierre** soar 37m into the heavens, even higher than the arches of Notre-Dame in Paris. The original church took more than four centuries to build (1434-1893), and its elaborate façade was finally crowned with plain towers in the 1930s. (Open daily 8:45am-noon and 2-7pm.) Behind the cathedral, on rue Malherbe (off rue Henri IV), **Chapelle de L'Immaculée** has an eerie aerial Virgin for a spire. To the right of the chapel, at 4, rue Malherbe, a smaller iron Virgin prays from a flamboyant perch.

Built by François II, Nantes's heavily fortified 15th-century **château** (tel. 40 47 18 15) once held Gilles de Rais (Bluebeard), who was convicted of sorcery in 1440. Henri IV signed the Edict of Nantes here in 1598, granting religious freedom to Protestants and unleashing a capitalist frenzy. The best of three museums inside the château, the **Musée des Arts Populaires Régionaux,** displays traditional Breton costumes and furniture. The **Musée des Arts Décoratifs** sponsors exhibits of the work of international contemporary artists. The **Musée des Salorges** presents Nantes's commercial history since the 18th century. (Château and museums (tel. 40 41 56 56) open Wed.-Mon. 10am-7pm, Sept.-June Wed.-Mon. 10am-noon and 2-6pm. Entry to the courtyard and ramparts 6F, students 3F. Admission to all three museums 20F, students 10F, Sun. free. Take tram or bus lines #24, 26, 28, or 29 to the "Duchesse Anne" stop.)

Two blocks from the cathedral, at 10, rue Georges Clemenceau, is Nantes's **Musée des Beaux Arts** (tel. 40 41 65 65), which prompted Henry James to reflect on his peculiar fondness for provincial museums: "The pictures may be bad, but the place is often curious; and, indeed, from bad pictures, in certain moods of the mind, there is a degree of entertainment to be derived." James's assessment notwithstanding, the large collection includes fine canvases by Rubens, Courbet, de la Tour, and a gaggle of contemporary artists. (Open Wed.-Mon. 10am-noon and 1-5:45pm, Sun. 11am-5pm. Admission 20F, students 10F, Sun. free. Take bus #11, 12, 21, or 23 to "Trébuchet" stop.) The **Musée Thomas Dobrée,** pl. Jean V (tel. 40 89 34 32), contains a library of rare books and manuscripts, including two rooms chronicling Nantes's rapport with China in the early 1800s. (Open Wed.-Mon. 10am-noon and 2-6pm. Admission 10F, Sun. free.) The **Musée Archéologique,** pl. Jean V (tel. 40 69 76 08), displays Neolithic and Merovingian artifacts as well as interesting temporary exhibits. Take bus #11 or go to "Médiathèque" tram stop. (Open Wed.-Mon. 10am-noon and 2-6pm. Admission 7F.)

The **Musée d'Histoire Naturelle,** 12, rue Voltaire (tel. 40 73 30 03), showcases a mind-boggling array of thousands of stuffed mammals, birds, reptiles, and insects. (Open Tues.-Sat. 10am-noon and 2-6pm, Sun. 2-6pm. Admission 15F, students 7F50. Take bus #1 to "Jean V" stop.) Let your imagination run wild at the innovative **Musée Jules Verne,** 3, rue de l'Hermitage (tel. 40 69 72 52), near the river in pl. M. Schwob, which tries to re-create the world of Captain Nemo and other Verne characters through a collection of the author's novels, letters, and photographs. A *Nantais* born and bred, the 11-year-old Verne made an ill-fated attempt to stow away on a sailing ship before resigning himself to imaginary voyages. Take bus #21 to "Garennes" stop. (Open Mon. and Wed.-Sat. 10am-noon and 2-5pm, Sun. 2-5pm. Admission 8F, students 4F, Sat.-Sun. free.) The nearby **planetarium** at 8, rue des Acadiens (tel. 40 73 99 23), off pl. Moysan, rounds out Nantes's impressive museum armada with galactic vistas and an intricate visual explanation of our rotating solar system. (Showings Tues.-Sat. at 10:30am, 2:15pm and 3:45pm; Sun. at 2:15pm and 3:45pm. 20F, students 10F.) It's possible to buy a global pass to the château museums, the Musée des Beaux Arts, the Musée d'Histoire Naturelle, and the Musée Jules Verne (30F, students 15F).

West of the château, a *quartier* of elegant buildings gives testimony to the city's period of wealth and expansion in the 18th century. Prosperous sea merchants relied on the profits of the slave trade to build lavish houses on the **Ile Feydeau,** between allée Turenne and allée Tuouin. In 1938 the city filled in the water and built streets, but the *Nantais* say Feydeau is "toujours une île" (always an island). Even more stately, 18th-century **place Royale** and **rue Crébillon** lead to **place Graslin.** Locals have so perfected the art of loafing, lounging, and lingering here that the verb "crébilloner" has entered their vocabulary. Off this street, poke around the **Passage Pommeraye,** a 19th-century gallery in iron and glass, executed in marvelous Victorian frill. The **Jardin des Plantes,** across from the train station, nurtures hundreds of species of flora.

Often overlooked, Le Corbusier's **Cité Radieuse** is a place of pilgrimage for architecture and Corbu buffs. Take bus #31 from the "Commerce" stop on cours Franklin Roosevelt.

Although university buildings are scattered throughout the city, the area north of rue Crébillon is most popular in the evening, and rue Scribe has an array of late-night bars and cafés. Every evening at 10, a live jazz ensemble tunes up at **The Tie Break Club,** 1, rue des Petites Ecuries. (Open Mon.-Sat. 10pm-3:30am.) **Le Floride,** 15, rue Michel Columb (tel. 40 47 66 80) on Ile Beaulieu is considered Nantes's alternative nightclub. It hosts occasional concerts by local underground groups. (Open Tues.-Sat. 11:30pm-dawn.) Go with friends, as the walk there is lonely and includes some deserted streets. The intersection of rue Romeau, rue Suffren and rue Grétry is known for its inexpensive, student-filled bars. Rumor has it that the cheapest drinks in town flow at **Le Menure,** on rue Grétry.

During the first two weeks of July, Nantes hosts the annual **Les Fêtes de l'Eté,** a harmonic convergence of more than 1000 dance, music, and theater groups. (Tickets 30-120F, festival pass 250F.) For information and reservations, contact the Office du Tourisme de Nantes, pl. du Commerce, 44000 Nantes (tel. 40 47 04 51).

Near Nantes: La Baule and Pornic

La Baule ("La Belle") boasts that it has the most beautiful beach in Europe; this may well be true. One smooth curve of sand stretches for kilometers along the coast, lapped gently by the warm Atlantic. Unsurprisingly, La Baule is packed with people in summer and always expensive. **Trains** connect Nantes to La Baule (1hr., 61F). There are two train stations: La Baule-les-Pins, east of the center in a quiet area close to camping sites, and La Baule-Escoublac, close to the center. From this station, take av. Serbie to av. Georges Clemenceau, and turn right to reach the **tourist office** (tel. 40 24 34 44), located in a futuristic building on pl. de la Victoire. (Open daily 9am-7:30pm; Sept.-June Mon.-Sat. 9am-12:30pm and 2:15-6:30pm.) From here, av. du Général de Gaulle runs to the beach.

To the west of La Baule, a few km out of town on the road to Batz-sur-Mer, is a vast network of *Marés Salants,* man-made square pools of ocean water which are dried out to make salt. A natural bird sanctuary, the area presents little bumpy roads in between the ponds which make it a peaceful, open area to ride a bike, away from the frenzy of the beach scene. You can **rent bikes** from M. Chaillou, at either 3, pl. de la Victoire (tel. 40 60 07 06) or 213, av. de Lattré-de-Tassigny (tel. 40 60 91 08; 30F per 1/2-day, 40F per day, 1000F deposit. Mountain bikes 50F per 1/2-day, 80F per day. Open 9:15am-7pm; Sept.-June 9:30am-12:15pm and 2-7pm.)

La Baule has few inexpensive hotels, so try to book in advance. The **Hôtel Marini,** right across from the La Baule-Escoublac train station, on 22, av. Georges Clemenceau (tel. 40 60 23 29), lets recently remodeled, plush rooms. (Singles and doubles 155F, with toilet 168F, with shower 186F. Breakfast 27F. Homemade French entrees at all hours downstairs 35-50F. Open April 15-Oct. 15.) A few doors down to the left is the quaint **Violetta,** 44, av. Georges Clemenceau (tel. 40 60 32 16), with flower-painted walls, shutters, and doors, and an affable proprietor. (Singles 190F. Doubles 190F, with shower 220F. Breakfast 22F. Showers 20F.) **Camping Municipal** (tel. 40 60 17 40 or 40 60 11 48) at av. P. Minot, 10 minutes from town, is a three-star site a little too close to the train tracks. (60F per 2 people and tent, 8F per car.) Six km from St-Nazaire and approximately 12km from La Baule, a peaceful *gîte d'étape* occupies a dusty old stone farmhouse with two fireplaces and a complete kitchen. (26F, includes hot showers.) Call 40 22 56 76 or 40 66 05 66 for directions. Hitching from La Baule is reportedly difficult.

A large and lively **market** fills av. Marché at av. des Pétrels in the afternoon. For those hoping to picnic, **Comod Supermarche** is located on pl. de la Victoire, across from the tourist office. (Open Mon.-Sat. 9am-12:30pm and 3-7:45pm.) Down the street from the tourist office, **La Bôle,** 36, av. de Gaulle, is a typical *creperie* with typical *crêpe* prices. Less typical is **Le Premier Pas,** 3, rue du Marché, a charming restaurant decorated with old-fashioned posters. Choose from a small but interesting menu, including crab and avocado salad (39F) or scrambled eggs with smoked salmon (55F). (Open daily.)

The **Côte de Jade,** a sunny crescent of rocky coast curving south from the mouth of the Loire through **Pornic,** boasts the breakers, the beaches, and the *menhirs* you expect from Brittany, all an hour from Nantes. Four to six trains per day run from Nantes to Pornic (49F). Make this a daytrip; after 24 hours, the souvenir shops selling Donald Duck inner tubes provoke violent thoughts. **Cycles Becquet** at 24, rue de la Marine (tel. 40 82 26 80), rents bikes for 35F per day with a 400F deposit. (Open Mon.-Sat. 9am-7pm; Sept.-June Mon.-Sat. 9am-12:30pm and 2:30-6:30pm.)

The **tourist office** in pl. de la Môle (tel. 40 82 04 40) is a five-minute walk from the station in a pavilion on the harbor. From the station, go right, head across the canal, and turn left onto quai Leray. The friendly staff will throw upon you a bouquet of pamphlets and suggest walks. (Open Mon.-Sat. 9am-12:30pm and 2-6pm, Sun 9:30am-12:30pm.) The few moderate hotels are packed for the season. **Relais St-Gilles,** 7, rue Fernand de Mun (tel. 40 82 02 25), has rooms with a double bed, a wash cabinet, and a shower for 156F (breakfast 16F). Ask at the tourist office about bed and breakfasts (85-220F) and nearby campgrounds. Food in Pornic is mostly *crêpes.* **La Sarrasin,** 28, rue des Sables, is better than most and also serves seafood. (Open Mon.-Sat. noon-2pm and 7-9pm.)

If jaded by the not-too-spectacular city of Pornic, head for one of the beaches west of town. Along the way, notice the 9th-century château, restored in 1830, but closed to the public. A promenade on the town side of the new harbor, **Port de Plaisance,** was a favorite of Flaubert and Michelet. Rising on the high ground, the megalithic stones, known as the **Mousseaux,** are disappointing for Brittany but not bad for a stroll within city limits. More magnificent ocean views and less crowded beaches—**Grandes Vallées, Sablons, Porteau,** and **Gordière**—spice the coast toward Ste-Marie.

Pays de la Loire
(Loire Valley)

For years, people have come to the region between Paris and Brittany to see the Loire River and the châteaux, only to find more than one river and more than one type of château. The Loire, France's longest river, shares its fertile valley, its vineyards, its history, and even its châteaux with rivers less well-known, including the Loir, the Indre, the Cher, the Vienne, and the Maine. And the châteaux can be anything from grim, dilapidated medieval fortresses to elegant Renaissance houses, transfixed, like Narcissus, by pools made to reflect their beauty. Rather incongruously, the history of these dignified mansions presents a mixed bag of mischief, genius, promiscuity, and dirty-dealing—rich fodder for the imagination. If the châteaux's true history fails to mesmerize, repair to the world of fairy tales, to Villandry where Rapunzel lets down her hair, or to Ussé, where Sleeping Beauty sleeps for a century until her prince awakens her with a kiss.

Most châteaux were built in the 16th and 17th centuries, when French monarchs forsook Paris and ruled from the countryside around Tours so they could squeeze in hunting excursions between official state decrees. Some structures, however, remain from the days before the region belayed to the French crown. Henry II and Richard the Lionhearted, neither French royalty, mobilized two of the oldest communities, Chinon and Beaugency, to defend the region from the Capetian monarchs of the 12th century. The English and the French played hot potato with the Loire until Joan of Arc helped win it for the French in the Hundred Years War (1337-1453). In the 15th century, under the Valois kings, the French monarchy consolidated the region in a flux of martial and marital activity. The châteaux accumulated works of the finest Italian masters, forging an opulence never before imagined. Some of the finest châteaux, notably Blois and Chambord, were built in the era of scandalous intrigue and multiple mistresses. While the dukes and the counts chased stags with their armies of hounds, their wives hosted bacchanalian orgies.

Moral values decayed, and the valley was scarred by the Wars of Religion (1562-1598), whose terror culminated with the Duke of Guise's bloody murder of Protestants at Amboise. The region finally settled into a political and religious nap in the 17th century, but awoke once again during World War II, when the Loire divided annexed France from Vichy France.

The rich regional specialties served by modern *cuisiniers loirois* would have done justice to the châteaux's ornate dining rooms. Specialties include *rillettes* (a cold minced pork *pâté), fromage de chèvre* (goat cheese), and the sweet, creamy Port Salut cheese. After a long day of sightseeing, sit down to veal *escalope, coq au vin, champignons* (mushrooms) marinated in wine, and *asperges* (asparagus) steeped in butter. The Loire is famous for its light white wines, such as Muscadet, Touraine, Sancerre, Montlouis, and Vouvray, as well as its fragrant reds: Chinon, St-Nicolas-de-Bourgueil, and Saumur.

Unfortunately, the grandeur of the region's attractions inspires poorly proportioned visits. Those who confine their exploration to daytrips from large industrial cities such as Tours and Orléans will leave ill-informed. Those favoring daily three-châteaux blitz bus tours will find tapestries blurring into boredom and fatigue. The excellent hostels in Blois, Chinon, Saumur, Beaugency, and Orléans are comfortable bases, but they pose daunting logistical challenges to those without their own wheels. Public transportation routes fan out of the larger cities, but infrequent service can leave you stranded. Trains don't reach many châteaux, and those that do are scheduled inconveniently. The city of Tours (connected by rail to 12 châteaux) is the best rail hub. Every train station distributes the useful booklets *Les Châteaux de la Loire en Train Eté '93* and *Châteaux pour Train et Vélo* with train schedules, distances, and information on bike and car rental. Ussé, Villandry, and Chambord are reachable only by bicycle, car, tour bus, or

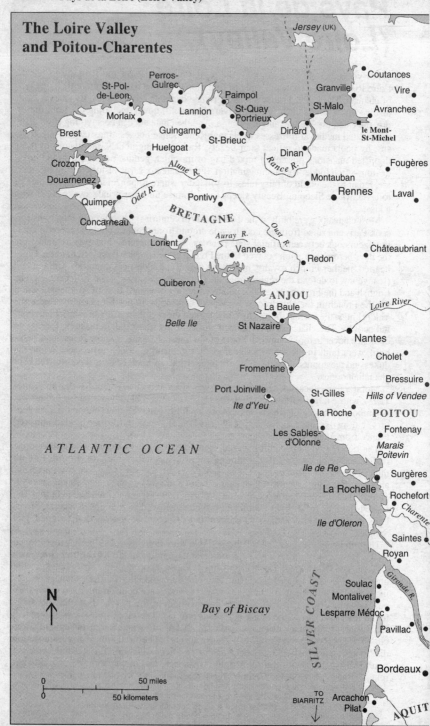

The Loire Valley and Poitou-Charentes

Jersey (UK)

Coutances
Vire
Granville
St-Malo
Avranches
le Mont-
St-Michel

St-Pol-
de-Leon
Perros-
Gulrec
Paimpol
St-Quay
Portrieux
Lannion
Morlaix
Guingamp
Dinard
St-Brieuc
Huelgoat
Dinan
Brest
Alune R.
Fougères
Crozon
Montauban
Douarnenez
Odet R.
Pontivy
Rennes
Laval
Quimper
BRETAGNE
Concarneau
Auray R.
Châteaubriant
Lorient
Vannes
Oust R.
Quiberon
Redon
ANJOU
Loire River
La Baule
Belle Ile
St Nazaire
Nantes
Cholet
Fromentine
Bressuire
Port Joinville
St-Gilles
Hills of Vendee
Ile d'Yeu
la Roche
POITOU
Fontenay
ATLANTIC OCEAN
Les Sables-
d'Olonne
*Marais
Poitevin*
Ile de Re
Surgères
La Rochelle
Rochefort
Charente
Ile d'Oleron
Saintes
Royan
Gironde R.
Soulac
SILVER COAST
Montalivet
Bay of Biscay
Lesparre Médoc
Pavillac
N
Bordeaux
0   50 miles
0   50 kilometers
TO
BIARRITZ
Arcachon
Pilat
AQUIT

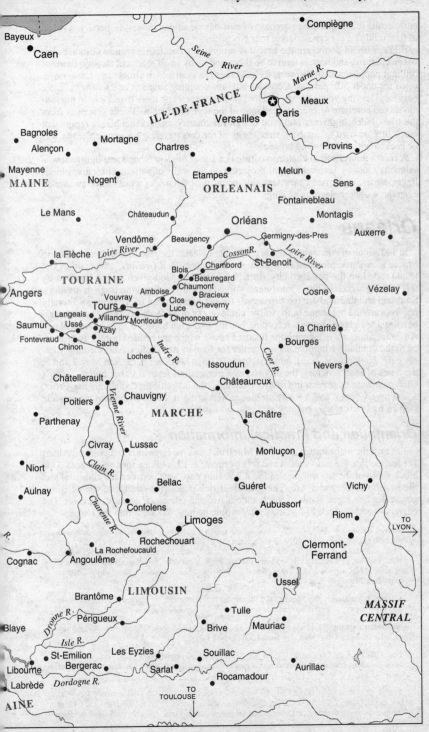

bus circuits that require the purchase of half-day or all-day passes. Generally, a group of four renting a car can undercut tour bus prices.

Bikes, without doubt, are the best way around this flat, fertile region. Distances between châteaux and hostels tend to be short, and many small roads cut through fields of brilliant poppies and sunflowers. Rental bikes are available in almost any Loire town, often for under 50F per day. Consider buying or renting panniers or *sacoches* (saddle bags) and leaving your luggage in a locker. Those spending more than a day in the saddle should purchase *Michelin's* road map of the region, which will steer you away from the truck-laden highways and onto delightful country roads. Hitchhikers report that quick lifts are hard to come by, since many of the cars traveling between châteaux will be packed with families and luggage.

A recent innovation in château-visiting is a *son et lumière* (sound and light) show, a schmaltzy history lesson by night projected on the walls of various châteaux. Floodlights, slides, costumed characters, and occasional fireworks would have awakened even the soundest-sleeping of kings.

Orléans

In 1429 Joan of Arc went to battle to liberate Orléans, then the most important city in France after Paris. Mounted on a white steed, *"la pucelle d'Orléans"* (the maid of Orléans) rode into the besieged city, declaring herself its God-given savior. Inspired by this moving sight, the city's inhabitants surged forward to dispel the English invaders. So proud and thankful are the *orléannais* for her heroism that today the town literally revolves around her statue in the traffic circle on the main pl. de Martroi. The cathedral bears stained-glass windows recording her life and even houses a Joan of Arc chapel. An entire museum, occupying the restored house where she resided briefly, is dedicated to the diminutive heroine, as is a center for Joan of Arc studies. And seemingly every café, *boulangerie,* hotel, and restaurant in town bears her name. On May 7 and 8, the dates of Joan's victory, the city stages a tremendous festival in her honor. Today's Orléans maintains several interesting museums, the magnificent Cathédrale Ste-Croix, a few lovely parks, and a lively ambience, rendering it a convenient and worthwhile stop en route to château country.

Orientation and Practical Information

To reach the main square, **place du Martroi,** cross the large intersection at pl. Albert 1er just outside the train station and follow rue de la République for five minutes. One block south of the square, rue Jeanne d'Arc runs east-west between the cathedral and the Maison de Jeanne d'Arc. The restaurant-rich pedestrian quarter of rue de Bourgogne lies one block south of rue Jeanne d'Arc and one block north of the river. The university and the Parc Floral, easily accessible by bus "S," are across the Loire.

Tourist Office: (tel. 38 53 05 95), on pl. Albert 1er, next to the new shopping center attached to the train station. Energetic staff will book hotel rooms (6F fee, outside of Orléans 22F; 30% deposit) and load you with brochures. A walking tour in French leaves from the office July-Aug. Wed. and Sat. at 2:30pm (33F, students 16F50). English cassettes detailing a walking tour are available (37F, deposit 250F). Open Mon.-Sat. 9am-7pm, Sun. 9:30am-12:30pm and 3-6:30pm; Sept.-June Mon.-Sat. 9am-7pm.

Currency Exchange: most banks have their main branches on pl. du Martroi. **Crédit Agricole** and **BNP** usually offer the best rates.

American Express: 12, pl. du Martroi (tel. 38 53 84 54), 5min. from the train station along rue de la République. Open Mon.-Fri. 9am-12:30pm and 1:45-6pm.

Post Office: pl. du Général de Gaulle (tel. 38 41 35 14). Open Mon.-Fri, 8am-7pm, Sat. 8am-noon. **Branch** office next to the train station open Mon.-Fri. 8am-6:30pm, Sat. 8am-noon. **Postal code:** 45000.

Trains: pl. Albert 1er (tel. 38 53 50 50). To: Paris-Austerlitz (40 per day, 1 1/4hr., 80F); Tours (20 per day, 1 1/4hr., 77F); Blois (22 per day, 40min., 44F); Amboise (12 per day, 1hr., 63F). Most trains require you to change at Orléans-Les Aubrais, a station 5 min. down the tracks. Information office open Mon.-Fri. 8am-8pm, Sat. 8:30am-8pm, Sun. 9am-noon and 2-6:30pm. Ticket booths open 4am-1am.

Buses: Les Rapides du Val de Loire, av. Albert 1er (tel. 38 53 94 75), up the street behind the train station. All buses depart from the *gare routière* downstairs from the office. Buy tickets in the first floor office. Open Mon. 5:45am-12:40pm and 3:30-7:35pm, Tues. and Thurs. 6:30am-12:40pm and 3:30pm-7:35pm, Wed., Fri., and Sat. 6:30am-7:30pm.

Public Transportation: SEMTAO (tel. 38 84 41 11) runs local buses in and around town. Main booth downstairs in the train station. The "S" line goes from pl. Albert 1er to the university and beyond to the Parc Floral and the Loiret; it operates until 12:30am. Bus tickets (good for 1hr.) 7F, *carnet* of 10 55F50 and a one-week pass, 59F.

Taxis: Taxi Radio Orléans (tel. 38 53 11 11), àt pl. Albert 1er. 24 hrs.

Bike Rental: Societé Alexis, 3, rue Grenier à Sel, off rue des Carmes (tel. 38 62 63 50). 50F per day, deposit 300F. Open Tues.-Sat. 8:30am-noon and 2-7pm. Also at the **train station.** 40F per 1/2-day, 50F per day, deposit 500F.

Youth Information: Centre Régional d'Information Jeunesse (CRIJ), 5, bd. de Verdun (tel. 38 54 37 70). Information on jobs, sports, and vacations, as well as tickets for local events, student cards, student bus tickets, and BIJ tickets. Open Mon. and Thurs. 1-6pm, Tues. and Wed. 10am-6pm, Fri. 10am-7pm, and Sat. 2-7pm.

Laundromat: Lav Club, 113, rue faubourg Bannier, around the corner from Hôtel Coligny and 10min. from the station. Wash 6kg for 17F, dry 15min. for 4F. Open daily 7:30am-10pm.

Women's Center: Centre d'Information sur les Droits de la Femme (C.I.D.F.), 2, cloître St-Pierre le Puellier (tel. 38 43 94 36). Open Mon.-Fri. 9am-noon and 2-7pm.

Hospital: Centre Hospitalier Régional, 1, rue Porte Madeleine (tel. 38 51 44 44).

Medical Emergency: SAMU: tel. 15.

Police: 63, rue du faubourg St-Jean (tel. 38 81 63 00). **Emergency:** tel. 17.

Accommodations and Camping

A few superb, inexpensive hotels cluster near rue du faubourg Bannier, north of pl. Gambetta. Other than these, the pickings are slim. The comfortable youth hostel is close to the center of town. Rooms fill by early evening, so arrive early or call ahead.

Auberge de Jeunesse (HI), 14, rue du faubourg Madeleine (tel. 38 62 45 75), on the west side of town. Take bus "B" (direction "Paul-Bert") from in front of the train station (7F, until 8:20pm). On foot, turn right outside the station onto pl. Gambetta. Follow bd. Rocheplate, which becomes bd. Jean Jaurès, and turn right onto rue du faubourg Madeleine. The hostel will be on your right (15min.). Excellent kitchen facilities, 2 single-sex dorms, a large patio and personable *orléannais* managers who give more helpful advice than the tourist office. Reception open daily 7-9:30am and 5:30-10pm; Feb.-March Sun.-Fri. only. Lockout 9:30am-5:30pm. Members only. 34F. Breakfast 13F. Sheets 13F.

CROUS: Résidence Universitaire, Les Hêtres, near the Parc Floral (tel. 38 63 68 57). Take bus "S" from pl. du Martroi or the train station to "La Source Université" (7F). Reception open Mon.-Fri. 9am-noon and 2-4pm. Simple dorm rooms, 57F. Meals 30F. Sheets 15F. Limited space but worth a try. You can stay weekends only if you arrive on Fri. Officially operates July-Aug., but there may be room in June or Sept.

Hôtel de Paris, 29, rue faubourg Bonnier (tel. 38 53 39 58). A 3-min. walk across pl. Gambetta, near the train station. Pretty pastel rooms and new, firm mattresses. Outgoing proprietor speaks English. One single 80F. Wide range of singles and doubles 100-180F. Showers 10F. Breakfast 17F.

Hôtel Cohigny, 80, rue de la Gare (tel. 38 53 61 60), a 10-min. walk from the station. Turn right onto av. de Paris and take a left on rue de la Gare. Bright, white walls, new carpets, and a solicitous owner. Singles and doubles 95-120F, all with shower. Breakfast 17F.

Camping: St-Jean-de-la-Ruelle, rue de la Roche (tel. 38 88 39 39). A wooded site along the Loire, 3km from Orléans. Take bus "D" from pl. Albert 1er to "Roche Aux Fées." 7F per person, 9F per tent. Open April-Sept. **Camping Municipal Olivet** (tel. 38 63 53 94), rue du Pont Bouchet. Take bus "O" or "S" to "Aumône." A 2-star site by the Loire, 5km from Orléans. (10F per person, 10F per tent.) Open April-Oct. 15.

Food

From *pâté d'alouettes* (lark pâté) to *pigeon à la crapaudine* (split and stuffed pigeon), the restaurants of Orléans serve some of the best poultry around. Orléans's cheese is *frimault cendré,* a savory relative of *camembert.* Wash it down with one of the local Gris Meunier or Auvernat wines, available at any shop. Inexpensive Chinese, Lebanese, Greek, Indian, Pakistani, and Moroccan restaurants jockey for customers on rue de Bourgogne. A permanent market roosts at **Les Halles Châtelet,** on the way to the river. (Open Tues.-Sat. 7:30am-7pm, Sun. 7:30am-12:30pm.) Another market changes location daily; check at the tourist office. There is an enormous **Carrefour** supermarket in the mall connected to the train station.

La Nouvelle Orléans, 5, rue de la Cherche, off rue de la République. Pictures of old steamers line the walls of this lively, obliging restaurant. *Plat du jour* with vegetable or fries (38F), copious salads (28-42F), and special Mexican features nightly (fajitas 55F). Open Mon.-Sat. 11:30am-2pm and 7-11pm.

Le Viking, 237, rue de Bourgogne, near the cathedral. Delicious *gratin* (baked cheese dish) entrees, 20-26F. 39F lunch *menu* includes *crudités* (raw vegetables), dinner *crêpe,* drink, and dessert. Open Tues.-Sat. noon-2pm and 7-11pm, Sun. 7-11pm.

Le K. T. Self, 13, rue des Pastoureaux, off rue Jeanne d'Arc before the cathedral. Cafeteria packed with locals at lunchtime. Tasty, generous portions. Steak, sausage, or *plat du jour* 25-30F. Salad 13F. Desserts 10F. Open Mon.-Sat. 11:30am-1:15pm.

Le Pique Feu, 2, pl. du Chatelet. This place knows that meat is where it's at. Real food for real people. 60F *menu* includes salad, meat dish, baked potato, and cheese or dessert. Open. Tues.-Sat. noon-1pm and 8-10pm.

Sights and Entertainment

The **Cathédrale Ste-Croix** is France's unanimous tribute to Joan of Arc, and for a city which exalts everything related to its liberator, Orléans has made sure that the cathedral is worthy of the maid's accomplishments. You don't even have to peer inside this religious fortress to appreciate its jaw-dropping beauty; the marvelous façade, spires, and buttresses would impress even a charging English army. Badly damaged by the Huguenots in 1568, the cavernous cathedral was rebuilt in Gothic style. (Open Mon.-Sat. 8am-noon and 2:15-7pm, Sun. 9am-noon and 2:15-6:45pm.)

The **Musée des Beaux Arts,** just outside of the cathedral, displays French works from the 17th century, including canvases by Watteau and Boucher, as well as some foreign paintings including a spectacular *Saint Thomas* by Velazquez. (Open Wed.-Mon. 10am-noon and 2-6pm. Admission 14F, students 7F.) Around the corner from the museum, the 16th-century **Hôtel Groslot d'Orléans,** now the town hall, opens its sumptuously decorated rooms and romantic garden to the public. This splendid Renaissance structure hosted a long line of kings passing through Orléans, including François II, Charles IX, Henri III, and Henri IV. (Open Sun.-Fri. 10am-noon and 2-5pm. Free.)

The **Maison de Jeanne d'Arc,** 3, pl. de Gaulle, off pl. du Martroi, celebrates the shepherdess's contribution to Orléans and France. This reconstruction of the original house where Joan of Arc stayed in 1429—"profoundly modified" in a 1940 bombing raid—consists of fragments of other 15th-century houses. The period costumes on display and the audio-visual re-creation (in English upon request) of the siege of Orléans are well worth the admission price. (Open Tues.-Sun. 10am-noon and 2-6pm; Nov.-April Tues.-Sun. 2-6pm. Admission 8F, students 4F, under 13 free.)

The **Hôtel Cabu,** pl. Abbé Desnoyers, houses the **Musée Archéologique et Historique de l'Orléannais,** renowned for its beautiful Gallo-Roman bronze animals and figurines. (Open Wed.-Mon. 10am-noon and 2-6pm; Oct.-March Wed.-Mon. 10am-noon and 2-5pm. Admission 9F, students 4F50. Free on Sun.)

Next to the *cité universitaire* and the new high-rise city of Orléans-la-Source, the **Parc Floral** cultivates broad fields of white and purple irises and a few tulip beds in the spring. The park surrounds the source of the Loiret, a tributary of the Loire River, flowing past haughty pink flamingos to the village of Olivet, a few km to the west. Take bus

"S" from pl. Albert 1er in Orléans (7F). (Parc Floral open daily 9am-6pm. Admission 18F, students 9F. Nov.-March daily 2-5pm, admission 9F.)

Every year, during the few days preceding or following the first weekend in July, Orléans sponsors a **jazz festival.** Recent performers at the festival have included Chick Corea, Herbie Hancock, and Dizzy "cheeks" Gillespie. All performances are in the Campo Santo, near the cathedral. (Tickets 90-120F.) Call the tourist office for more information. Or, for a really, really rocking time, let your hair down at the local Scrabble players' club (tel. 38 88 09 95).

Near Orléans

The Middle Ages linger on in **Beaugency,** 30km southwest of Orléans. Because of its strategic importance as the only town between Orléans and Blois with a bridge spanning the Loire, the town has been occupied and bashed repeatedly: four times by the English during the Hundred Years War (1337-1453), and during the Wars of Religion (1562-1598). Despite the pillaging, Beaugency has changed little in the past eight centuries. The 11th-century **bridge** spanning the Loire is still intact, as is the 12th-century **Eglise Notre-Dame,** noteworthy for its gently sloping Romanesque architecture. Next to the church stands the 11th-century **Tour de César,** a dungeon Victor Hugo used as the backdrop for the last act of his play *Marion Delorme.* Though unimpressive compared to most of the Loire's châteaux, **the Château Dunois** houses the appealing **Musée Régional de l'Orléannais,** a jumble of local lace work, costumes, furniture, and children's games. (Open Wed.-Mon. 10am-noon and 2-6:30pm; Oct.-March Wed.-Mon. 10am-noon and 2-5pm. Admission 18F, students 14F.)

The **tourist office,** 28, pl. du Martroi (tel. 38 44 54 42), distributes information on the surrounding region. (Open Mon.-Sat. 9am-12:30pm and 2:30-6:30pm, Sun. 10am-noon.) Finding an inexpensive hotel in Beaugency is about impossible, which is just one more reason to stay at the superlative **HI hostel** (tel. 38 44 61 31), 2km out of town on route de Châteaudun (English directions posted at the train station). Jacques Thomas has spent 20 years improving the hostel, and it shows: new mattresses, rooms for families and couples, excellent kitchen facilities, common rooms with fireplaces, organized bike/canoe tours, and much, much more! Call ahead. (43F per night. Pigout breakfast 16F. Dinner 43F. Sheets 15F.) The hostel is also the best place in town to rent **bikes** (40-50F per day). Campers can pitch their tents on the bank of the river at the **Camping Municipal Le Val de Flux** (tel. 38 44 50 39; 8F50 per adult, 6F50 per site; open March-Sept.). The tiny subterranean **Crêperie de la Tour,** 26, rue Cordonnerie, serves a variety of *crêpes* (10-36F) on a terrace along a cobblestoned street. (Open Tues.-Sun. noon-2pm and 7pm-midnight.) On Saturday mornings, the streets of the town are transformed into a lively **market,** with vendors hawking everything from *paella* to wallpaper to *paella* wallpaper. Try to visit Beaugency on the first weekend in June, when 500 villagers deck themselves out for the **Festival de Beaugency,** a celebration of the town's history. Many of the participants spend up to six months sewing their own delightful period costumes. Frequent **trains** and 11 daily **buses** (26F) connect Beaugency with Blois and Orléans.

About 35km southeast of Orléans, the ancient Benedictine monastery and basilica in **St-Benoît-sur-Loire** constitute one of France's finest examples of pure Romanesque architecture. Columns decorated with scenes from the Book of Revelation support the basilica's belfry and porch, and the luminescent interior features white stone and a Roman floor mosaic imported from Italy in 1531. Vespers are sung in Gregorian chant Monday to Friday at noon, and Sundays at 11am.

The tiny Carolingian church of **Germigny-des-Prés,** founded in 806 by Théodulfe, Bishop of Orléans and friend of Charlemagne, awaits 3km from St-Benoît. The church's Byzantine mosaic, the only one in France, depicts the Ark of the Covenant with dazzling glass cubes brought from Italy by the Emperor himself. The curator will take you on a guided tour through this largely reconstructed church, one of the oldest in Europe. (Tours Mon.-Sat. at 11am and 3pm, Sun. 3:15 and 4:30pm.)

The modest 14th-century château of **Sully-sur-Loire,** reflected in the surrounding moat and presiding over a cobblestone street 8km farther downstream, is known for its chestnut timber work preserved since 1363. (Open daily May-Sept. 9-noon and 2-5:45pm; April and Oct. 10-11:45am and 2-5:45pm; March and Nov. 10am-noon and 2-5pm. Admission 12F, students 6F.)

Germigny, St-Benoît and Sully are all accessible by bus from the *halte routière* in Orléans (5-7 per day to Sully: 1hr., 38F; via Germigny: 45min., 28F; to St-Benoît: 50min., 31F). Bikers may choose to make the challenging 90km round-trip from Orléans. The *levée* route on the south bank of the Loire passes tiny villages and sunflower fields. The wind usually blows west to east.

Blois

Upon gliding into Blois by carriage in 1882, Henry James noted with disappointment that the château did not overhang the river, as he had romantically allowed himself to imagine, but that instead it perched on a hillside above the town. Nevertheless, this most stoic of travelers still found Blois "a sympathetic little town," which "presents a bright, clean face to the sun, and has that aspect of cheerful leisure which belongs to all white towns that reflect themselves in shiny water." Built around steep streets and dozens of old stone staircases, Blois's light façades, blue slate roofs, and pedestrian quarters preserve the flavor of lost centuries. In contrast, intense agricultural activity, including the export of wheat, wine, strawberries, and vegetables has made modern Blois (pop. 50,000) a booming commercial center, whose *vieille ville* streets are often clogged with honking cars.

Orientation and Practical Information

On the north bank of the Loire, Blois is a major stop on the Orléans-Tours rail line. The station is north of the château and the center. Go down av. Jean Laigret to the tourist office (5 min.). Continue in the same direction past the château on your right, and you will reach the *centre ville* almost immediately. The rue Porte-Côte leads to the bustling store- and café-lined pedestrian quarter.

Tourist Office: 3, av. Jean Laigret (tel. 54 74 06 49 or 54 78 23 21). Sightseeing begins here in the lovely Renaissance pavilion of Anne de Bretagne. **Currency exchange** tacks a 22F commission onto its otherwise decent rates. Complete information on châteaux, including tickets for bus circuits and shows at the Blois château. Open April-Sept. Mon.-Sat. 9am-7pm, Sun. 10am-1pm and 4-7pm; Oct.-March Mon.-Sat. 9am-noon and 2-6pm.

Post Office: (tel. 54 44 68 58), on rue Gallois near pl. Victor Hugo, in front of the château. **Currency exchange** and **telephones.** Branch office on rue Ronceraie, across the river, the 3rd left after the bridge. Both open Mon.-Fri. 8am-7pm, Sat. 8am-noon. **Postal code:** 41000.

Trains: (tel. 54 78 50 50), on top of the hill on bd. Daniel Dupris, a 5-min. walk from the tourist office up av. Jean Laigret. To: Paris-Austerlitz via Orléans (18 per day, 1 hr., 111F); Tours (24 per day, 1 hr., 44F); Amboise (15 per day, 20 min., 30F); Angers via Tours (10 per day, 3 hr., 102F). Information office open Mon.-Sat. 9am-7pm. Ticket counters open daily 6am-10pm.

Buses: Point Bus, 2, pl. Victor Hugo (tel. 54 78 15 66), 2 min. from the tourist office. From mid-June to mid-Sept., runs two bus circuits with the **Transports Loir-et-Cher (TLC)** line, allowing you to create your own itinerary of château visits to Chambord, Cheverny, Chaumont, Chenonceau, and Amboise. Circuit #1 (Chambord, Cheverny) 60F, students 45F. Circuit #2 (Chaumont, Chenonceau, Amboise) 100F, students 80F. The passes include reduced admission to the châteaux. Buy tickets at the bus station, tourist office, or on board. Buses leave from the train station. For schedule information, ask at the tourist office or bus office. Open Mon. 1:30-6pm, Tues.-Fri. 8am-12:10pm and 1:30-6pm, Sat. 9am-12:10pm and 1:30-4:30pm.

Bike Rental: Atelier Cycles, 44, levée des Tuileries (tel. 54 74 30 13), across the river from the campground. Close to the "Verdun" bus stop on line #4. Decent 5- and 10-speeds 35-50F per day. Mountain bikes 75F per day. Passport deposit. Open daily 9am-9pm. **Hôtel St. Jacques,** 7, rue Ducoux (tel. 54 78 04 15). New 10-speeds 60F per day. Passport deposit.

Laundromat: 1, rue Jeanne d'Arc, near the river. Wash 20F. Dryer 2F for 7 min. Open Mon.-Sat. 7:30am-8:30pm, Sun. 9am-8:30pm.

Hospital: Centre Hospitalier de Blois, Mall Pierre Charlot (tel. 54 78 00 82).

Medical Assistance: SAMU, tel. 15.

Police: 42, quai St-Jean (tel. 54 55 17 99). Emergency: tel. 17.

Accommodations

The summer droves turn room-finding in Blois into an ordeal; call at least a day in advance to reserve a place. Note that trying to crash on the banks of the Loire is illegal.

Auberge de Jeunesse (HI), 18, rue de l'Hôtel Pasquier (tel. 54 78 27 21), 4.5km outside Blois in Les Grouets. From the tourist office, follow rue Porte Côte, bear right onto rue Denis Papin down to the river, and take bus #4 (direction "Les Grouets") Get off at the "Eglise des Grouets" stop (last bus at 7:30pm, 5F30). A secluded, rambling building with 2 single-sex dorms. Excellent kitchen facilities, hot showers, and a relaxed evening atmosphere. HI card required, but nonmembers can buy a stamp for 19F. Closed 10am-6pm. Office open 6-10:30pm. 39F per person. Sheets 14F. Breakfast 16F. Often full in summer, so call ahead. Open March-Nov. 15.

Foyer des Jeunes Travailleurs, 37, rue Pierre et Marie Curie (tel. 54 43 56 01). Take bus #3 (direction "Sauvageau") from the front of the train station and get off at "Pierre et Marie Curie." 3-night min. stay. Primarily for French workers, although 224 beds in single rooms are rented to anyone aged 16-25. 60F, breakfast and showers included. Monthly rates also available. In summer, call at least a week in advance.

Hôtel St-Jacques, 7, rue Ducoux (tel. 54 78 04 15). Receive a warm welcome to Blois right as you leave the station. Bright, tidy rooms and a TV lounge. Singles and doubles 90F, with toilet 155F, with shower and toilet 165F. One quad 140F. Bath 15F. Delicious breakfast 22F. Owner also rents bikes.

Hôtel St-Nicolas, 33, rue des Trois Marchands (tel. 54 78 05 85), near the Eglise St-Nicolas and the château. Clean and quiet. Singles 90-95F. Doubles 115-125F, with shower 135-145F. Showers 12F. Breakfast 20F. Open Jan. 15-Dec. 15. Reserve two weeks in advance.

Le Pavillon, 2, av. Wilson (tel. 54 74 23 27), just across the bridge and overlooking the Loire. Clean, but a bit noisy. Singles 90F. Doubles 110F, with toilet 130F, with toilet and shower 155F. Triples 160F. Showers 15F. Breakfast 27F.

Etoile d'Or, 7-9, rue Bourg Neuf (tel. 54 78 46 93), up a steep street across the pedestrian quarter from the château. Charming management offers bright rooms and a downstairs café filled with young locals. Singles 115F, with shower 140-160F. Doubles 115F, with shower 170-185. Triples with shower 240F. Showers 10F. Breakfast 20F.

Camping: La Boire (tel. 54 74 22 78), is 2km out of town. (23F per person plus tent. 10F per extra person. Showers included. Electricity 33F. Open March-Nov.) A little farther out is **Lac de Loire** (tel. 54 78 82 05). A campground for the upwardly mobile, this facility offers 2- and 4-star sites. (35F per 2-star camper plus tent, 10F per extra person; 55F per 4-star camper plus tent, 12F per extra person. Showers included. Open June-Oct.) Check at the tourist office for information about the shuttle bus that runs in July and August from the train station to both campgrounds. Both campgrounds are across the river from Blois, in the direction of Orléans.

Food and Entertainment

Pastries in Blois have been fit for kings ever since Catherine de'Medici brought *patissiers* with her from Italy. Indulge on the rue Denis Papin where *patisseries, boulangeries,* fruit stands, and supermarkets abound. Otherwise, fairly pricey restaurants line rue St-Lubin, beneath the château, and less expensive ones line rue Foulérie, in the shadow of the cathedral.

Le Puisatier, 12, rue du Puits Chatel, on a quiet cobbled side street close to the cathedral. 40F lunch *menu* includes pâté, roast chicken, and sorbet. Also 60F *menu* and salads (17-35F). White chocolate fondue, if you dare, 45F. Open Mon.-Sat. noon-2pm and 7-11pm.

La Forge, 18, rue Bourg Neuf. All-you-can-eat buffet with dessert (58F) in a rustic setting. Their specialty is meat cooked over a wooden fire. Steak *au poivre* 50F. Open Mon. noon-2pm., Tues.-Sat. noon-2pm and 7:30-11pm.

La Tosca, 36, rue Foulérie. Delicious fondues and the Swiss potato-and-cheese specialty *raclette* as well as more familiar fare served in a cozy atmosphere. 70F *menu.* Cheese fondue 70-75F. Open daily noon-2pm and 7pm-midnight, closed Oct.-April for Sun. lunch.

Le Maïdi, 42, rue St-Lubin. In the shadow of the château in an old half-timbered house with exposed beams. Traditional 50F and 70F *menus,* plus *couscous* (40-75F). Open Fri.-Wed. 11:30am-2:30pm and 7-10pm.

Sights

Home to French monarchs Louis XII and François I in the late 15th and early 16th centuries, the **château** at Blois housed power during the Renaissance comparable to Versailles in subsequent ages. The octagonal spiral staircase, built by François I's crew, squirms with stone salamanders, his emblem and symbol of immortality. Start with the Aile François I (François's wing), fronted by a grand, ornamental staircase connecting several fine Renaissance rooms. In 1588, Protestant King Henri III hid in a small antechamber while his hired murderers fatally stabbed the Duke of Guise, a Catholic rival for the throne. Henri emerged from his hiding place, surveyed the lacerated Duke, who measured almost seven feet tall, and said coolly, "He looks even bigger dead than alive." The next day, Henri dispatched the Duke's brother, Cardinal de Guise, in similar fashion, but his luck ran out eight months later when he himself was assassinated. The basement of this wing houses the **Musée Archéologique** with its piles of neolithic axe blades and other regional artifacts. Continue into the **Salle des Etats,** the only part of the château surviving from the 13th century. The 15th-century Aile Louis XII next door contains the modest **Musée des Beaux Arts.** Although the exhibits are not particularly important, the bright, warm lighting and elegant decor make these some of the loveliest rooms in the château. (Château and museums open daily 9am-6pm; Oct.-May 9:30am-noon and 2-5pm. Admission to both 27F, students 15F.) The château also presents a *son et lumière,* unveiled every evening at 10:30pm in French and at 11:30pm in English (admission 22F, ages 5-12 and over 65 16F).

South of the château lies the tranquil **Abbaye St-Lomer,** actually called the Eglise St-Nicolas since its transformation into a parish church. A cupola ringed with stained glass caps the broad ambulatory whose chapels typify the late Romanesque style; the Gothic nave was added more than a century later. Blois's **Cathédrale St-Louis** is a 17th-century reconstruction of a Gothic church destroyed in a 1678 hurricane and rebuilt at the pleas of the wife of Colbert, herself a native of Blois. The **Crypt St-Solenne** under the altar crackles with a funny, informative tape (in English) about the church's construction. The cathedral stands just north of the old quarter, a wonderful place to wander among half-timbered houses and ancient archways.

Châteaux Near Blois

Over the river and through the woods south of Blois lie many of the most remarkable châteaux in France. All except Chaumont are inaccessible by train from Blois. Railpassers should go to Tours, connected by rail to several châteaux. The cheapest trips, however, leave from Blois; from mid-June to mid-September, **Point Bus** in Blois sends buses on the Transports du Loir-et-Cher (TLC) line to the châteaux (see Buses, above). The châteaux are within easy bicycling range of town. Because Blois is smaller than Orléans and Tours, cycling in and out of town is a less stressful experience. Ambitious cyclists can pedal over the beautiful, largely flat trails to several châteaux in one day, though beware of turning the excursion into an odyssey that covers more châteaux than can realistically prove enjoyable. The 15km trip to Chambord takes about an hour, while the 9km ride to Cheverny takes half that time. For both châteaux, bikers should start by crossing the Loire in Blois and riding to the roundabout 1km down Av. Wilson. Hitchers who walk past the roundabout report some success with rides to Cheverny; Chambord is supposedly more difficult.

The largest and most extravagant of the Loire châteaux, **Chambord** teems with excess. François I, who loved to hunt on the grounds of the present château when he was a kid, ordered the construction of this royal hunting retreat in 1518. The result, a lavish structure that rivals the architectural magnificence of the great cathedrals, but without any religious or moral aspirations, establishes François I as the Donald Trump (or Alan Bond, if you like) of the Renaissance. Even when his funds dried up, when he couldn't pay the ransom for his sons in Spain, when he had to "borrow" treasures from churches and silver from his subjects, the show went on. The result is mind-boggling: 440 rooms, 700 of François's trademark stone salamanders, and 365 fireplaces (perhaps one for every day of the year). Because of the immodest decision to install all those fireplaces, the hundreds of chimneys, along with sculpted and patterned turrets and spires, create a veritable village on the rooftop terrace. But the château's atmosphere was perhaps a little too decadent: while François and his hounds chased foxes, the ladies of his court threw bacchanalian orgies reminiscent of France's Roman roots.

At the heart of the symmetrical château rises a spectacular double-helix staircase, perhaps designed by Leonardo da Vinci, and constructed so that one person can ascend and another descend while keeping sight of one another through sculpted openings. The château was a favorite *auberge* of Louis XIV, who sponsored the premieres of Molière's *Pourceaugnac* and *Le Bourgeois Gentilhomme* here. To improve the setting, the Sun King diverted the river Cosson and planted the magnificent kilometer-long, tree-lined avenue approaching the château. *Et pourquoi pas?*

Rooms are adequately labeled in English, and a free English pamphlet clarifies the castle's complex layout. A 32km wall defines the periphery of Chambord's grounds, still a wildlife preserve where deer and wild boar hang out even after hours. (Château open daily 9:30am-6:45pm; Sept.-June 9:30am-11:45am and 2-4:45pm. Admission 31F, students 17F.)

Much of the château's appeal lies in its isolation; only a few souvenir shops violate the verdure. Campers may trek to **Camping Huisseau-sur-Cosson,** 6, rue de Châtillon (tel. 54 20 35 26), about 5km southwest of Chambord on D33. (20F per person, tent and showers included. Open Easter-Sept.) The two-star **Camping des Châteaux** in **Bracieux,** on route de Chambord (tel. 54 46 41 84), has a swimming pool, tennis court, and free showers. (8F10 per person, 6F per tent. Open April-Oct. 15 daily 7:30am-11pm.)

Carefully manicured **Cheverny** preserves a rare dignity. Its stately Renaissance façade inspired the Moulinsart mansion belonging to Captain Haddock in the comic-book saga of Tintin. Owned by the same family for 700 years, Cheverny is the only château whose interior fulfills the luxurious promise of its façades. Among the treasures inside are antique furniture, Spanish leather-upholstered walls, ceilings, and chairs, Delft vases, and splendid tapestries, most notably a Gobelin of *The Abduction of Helen.* The current count and his loved ones still live on the third floor. (Note their photos on the ground level). A well-stocked armor room suffices to keep boisterous tourists in line. The **Orangerie** behind the château (closed to the public) sheltered *The Mona Lisa* while German artillery showered Paris during WWII. Seventy mixed English-Poitevin bloodhounds live in the castle's kennels and love to stalk stags. You can see all 70 gulp down entire bins of ground meat in less than 60 seconds. (Mon.-Sat. at 5pm, Sept.-March Mon. and Wed.-Fri. at 3pm. On Tues. and Thurs. in the fall, they're off a-huntin'.) The park around the château has attractive formal gardens, but an electrified fence ensures that plebs see nothing without paying. (Open daily 9:15am-6:45pm; mid-Sept.-May 9:30am-noon and 2:15-5pm. Admission 28F, students 19F.) Cheverny's *son et lumière* explodes with fireworks, fountains and lasers every Thursday and Saturday night in July and August. (Shows at 10:30pm, 1 1/2 hr., 80F. Call the Blois tourist office for information and reservations, tel. 54 74 06 49 or 54 78 23 21.)

If you call far enough in advance, you might get one of the four rooms at the **Hôtel au Pichet,** pl. de l'Eglise (tel. 54 79 97 23), just across from the château entrance and above a bar where the locals congregate. (All rooms with toilet and shower. Two doubles 140F. One triple 170F. One quad 200F. Breakfast 25F.) 2km away on the road to Contres is **Camping Les Saules,** (tel. 54 79 90 01). 35F covers 2 people, tent, and hot showers. (Open June-Sept.) The Cheveney tourist office can help out in a pinch (open July-Aug. Mon.-Sat. 10:30am-12:30pm and 1:30-7:30pm, Sun. 2-6pm.)

Beauregard, a smaller, less crowded château, sits pretty 9km south of Blois. Beauregard is most notable for the upstairs portrait gallery, the largest in Europe, with over 350 portraits dating from 1328 to 1643. The tour guide gives an amusing rundown of European history, pointing out bloodlines between the portrayed royalty. (Open daily July-Aug. 9:30am-6:30pm; Sept. and April-June daily 9:30am-noon and 2-6:30pm; Oct.-Dec. and Feb.-March Thurs.-Tues. 9:30am-noon and 2-5pm. Admission 20F, students 15F. Frequent tours, in French only.) Although difficult to reach by public transportation (the only bus runs infrequently and stops several km away), Beauregard is an easy half-hour bike ride from Blois. The most direct route takes you along a busy four-lane highway; ask at a bike rental shop for touring routes. Hitchhikers headed south on the D956 report that rides are reasonably easy to come by.

Perched high above the Loire river, **Chaumont-sur-Loire** serves as a reminder that castles were first built not to appear in *Brideshead Revisited*, but to really and truly defend kingdoms. A long, steep road leads to this compact feudal fortress whose towers, turrets, moat, and drawbridge pre-date the more lavish Renaissance châteaux. Catherine de'Medici lived here with her astrologer until the death of her husband, Henri II. She then forced Henri's mistress, Diane de Poitiers, to vacate the more desirable Chenonceaux in exchange for Chaumont. The château is best known for its luxurious *écuries* (stables), where the horses were fed from porcelain troughs in richly upholstered stalls with elegant overhanging lamps. (Château open daily 9:15am-5:35pm; April-June and Sept. 9:15-11:35am and 1:45-5:35pm; Oct.-March 9:15-11:35am and 1:45-3:50pm. Admission 24F, students 14F.) The sheltered **Camping Grosse Grève** is just off the bridge on the southern bank of the Loire (tel. 54 20 93 95; 9F per night). Chaumont is accessible by train from Blois (12 per day, 10 min., 15F) and Tours (12 per day, 35 min., 12F). The **train station** (tel. 54 78 50 50) lies in **Onzain**, 2km north of Chaumont.

Amboise

Set on a steep hillside over the Loire, the château d'Amboise was once home to Charles VIII, who began expanding the royal residence when he ascended the throne at age 13. Partly destroyed after the Revolution, the château is neither as ornate as Chambord nor as charming as Chenonceaux, but its view of the Loire and its location on the frequently serviced Blois-Tours train line bring scores of visitors to Amboise during the summer months. Although upstaged by the château, the small town below (pop. 12,000) makes the most of its status as Leonardo da Vinci's adopted hometown. Aside from the hostel and campground, there are few reasonable accommodations here, suggesting it as a convenient daytrip from either Blois or Tours.

Orientation and Practical Information

To reach either the château or the tourist office, walk straight from the station along rue Jules Ferry and cross the first bridge onto the tiny **Ile d'Or**, an island largely devoted to camping facilities. Continue straight and cross the next bridge into the *centre ville*. The château is on your left and the tourist office is down the quay, to the right.

Tourist Office: (tel. 47 57 01 37), quai Général de Gaulle. Friendly staff distributes an invaluable pamphlet containing a map of the town and a list of most hotels and restaurants in Amboise; it also provides bus schedules, advice on château visits, and a free accommodations service. Open mid-June-Sept. Mon.-Sat. 9am-12:30pm and 1:30-8:30pm, Sun. 10am-noon and 4-7pm; Oct. and April-mid-June Mon.-Sat.. 9:30am-12:30pm and 1:30-6:30pm, Sun. 10am-noon; Nov.-March Mon.-Sat. 9am-12:30pm and 3-6pm.

Post Office: On quai Général de Gaulle, down the street from the tourist office. **Currency exchange** with decent rates. Open Mon.-Fri. 8:30am-12:15pm and 1:30-6:15pm, Sat. 8:30-noon. **Postal code:** 37400.

Trains: (tel. 47 23 18 23), on bd. Gambetta, 15 min. from the center of town across the river. On the main Paris-Tours line. To: Tours (12 per day, 20 min., 23F); Blois (20 per day, 10-15 min., 30F); Orléans (20 per day, 1 hr., 66F); Paris (13 per day, 2 1/2 hr., 126F). Station open daily 6:30am-9pm.

Buses: Les Rapides de Touraine (in Tours 47 46 06 60) runs 8 buses daily from Amboise to Tours (20F60) and 1-2 daily to Chenonceau (30F round-trip). Buses leave from the parking lot next to the tourist office. Don't be confused by the Transports du Loir-et-Cher (TLC) schedules posted; these are only for people who have purchased special TLC bus day passes in Blois.

Bike Rental: Cycles Richard, 2, rue de Nazelles (tel. 47 57 01 79), near the station. 50F per day, mountain bikes 90F per day, deposit 500F or passport. Open Tues.-Sat. 9am-noon and 2:30-7pm.

Hospital: Centre Hospitalier Robert-Debré, rue des Ursulines (tel. 47 57 00 62).

Police: Gendarmerie Nationale, rue de Blois (tel. 47 57 26 19), at the bridge across the river from the town. **Emergency:** tel. 17.

Accommodations, Camping, and Food

The possibilities don't dazzle. Amboise's accommodations are expensive and generally rather ordinary. Beware of hotels that require you to eat their overpriced meals. In summer it's a good idea to call at least a week ahead. In July and August the youth hostel is usually booked by groups, but individuals should still give it a try. If you can't get into the youth hostel, your best bet might be to daytrip from Blois or Tours, both just a 15-minute ride away.

Maison des Jeunes—Centre Charles Péguy/Auberge de Jeunesse, Ile d'Or (tel. 47 57 06 36), a 10-min. walk from the train station. Turn right after the first bridge. An animated building where dance classes, bridge club gatherings, and other activities take place year-round. In a peaceful setting by the river. If the office is closed, walk around to the back of the building, ring the bell, and ask for the warden *(directeur)*. Reception open Tues.-Fri. and Sun. 3-9pm, Sat. until 8pm. No lockout or curfew. 74 beds in 2- to 8-berth rooms 46F, Nov.-Feb. 32F. Breakfast 14F. Dinner 45F. Sheets 26F. In summer, arrive early or call ahead. Open Tues.-Sun. Management may let you in on an off-day if you call ahead and arrive 6-8pm.

Hôtel Les Platanes, bd. des Platanes (tel. 47 57 08 60). Turn right from the front of the train station, walk 300m, cross under the tracks and walk straight for 100m. Large, immaculate rooms. Singles 95F. Doubles 120F, with shower 160F. Triples 190F. Hall showers included. Breakfast 25F. Reserve several days in advance in summer.

Hôtel à la Tour, 32, rue Victor Hugo (tel. 47 57 25 04), across from the château. Elderly couple proffers spotless, color-coordinated rooms with firm beds and shiny hardwood floors. Four singles 90F. Three doubles 135F. One triple 210F. Hall showers included. Breakfast 20F. Often full in summer; call at least a week in advance.

Hôtel le Chaptal, 13, rue Chaptal (tel. 47 57 14 46), on a quiet street off rue Nationale. Chirping birds and color TV in the lobby. Laid-back owner lets clean rooms at a modest price (for Amboise). One single with shower 100F; one double with shower 125F. Doubles with bath 170-190F. Triples 155F, with bath 220F. Breakfast 25F. In summer, call 2 weeks in advance.

Hôtel de France et du Cheval Blanc, 6/7, quai Général de Gaulle (tel. 47 57 02 44), across from the tourist office. Comfortable doubles 130-140F, with showers 175-195F.

Camping: The best place to stay in Amboise is at the fine campground on the Ile d'Or (tel. 47 57 23 37), across from the château. 11F per person, 13F20 per tent. In summer, crowded swimming pool 6F25. Showers included. Open Easter-Sept.

Amboise teems with overpriced sidewalk cafés. A few fast food restaurants and sandwich stands that cluster mostly in the pedestrian area around the rue Nationale offer your only hope for a cheap, wholesome meal. Submit to temptation and gorge on *amboisines,* a catch-all name for the sinfully delicious pastries and truffles that beckon from *pâtisserie* windows. **Le Lamparo,** at 17, rue Nationale, serves mussels marinara (38F), duck *foie gras* (70F) and smoked salmon (70F) in an open-front restaurant facing the colorful pedestrian zone. At **L'Epicerie,** 18, rue Victor Hugo, just below the château, the locals rave about the refined French cuisine served in one of the oldest houses in town. Glorious aromas waft through the elegant yet unassuming *maison*. L'Epicerie offers *coq au vin* (38F), veal filet in port wine sauce (78F), and a four-course 99F *menu.* (Open for lunch Wed.-Mon., and dinner Wed.-Sun.)

Sights

Charles VIII, born and raised in the **château d'Amboise,** dreamt of making it larger and more profligate. Though he failed in his bid to conquer Italy in 1495, Charles brought back with him a bevy of Italian artists, architects, sculptors, and landscapers whom he set loose on his humble home. In effect, Charles transported the Italian Renaissance to France, as many of these Italian masters stayed on to embellish Chenonceaux and Chambord. But poor Charles VIII never saw his dream completed. In 1498, the four-foot ruler was rushing out with the queen to watch a suspenseful game of court tennis when he bumped his head on a low door. He died a few hours later. Soon thereafter, the château reached its glorious peak under François I, who adored such distractions as masked balls and leopard and tiger exhibits. Difficulties resumed in 1539, however, when another Charles, the fully adorned Charles V, tripped right smack into a torchbearer leading him into the castle and burned himself alive. The scarred château decayed during the Revolution when its treasures were sold to raise funds for the ailing government. Today, the jewel of the grounds is the flamboyant late 15th-century Gothic **Chapelle St-Hubert,** whose superb relief above the door depicts the legends of St. Christopher and St. Hubert. A plaque inside marks the place where the bones of Leonardo da Vinci are buried, though this claim is questionable.

The interior of the primary part of the château, the **Logis de Roi,** contains extraordinary original Gothic and Renaissance furniture. The **Tour des Minimes,** a giant, spiraling, five-story ramp, sucked carriages into the château. Perched high above the Loire, the château's terraces present a striking view of the river, Blois, and Tours. (Château open daily 9am-6:30pm; April-June 9am-noon and 2-6:30pm, Sept.-March 9am-noon and 2-5pm. Admission 28F, students 18F. Obligatory tour in French, with printed English summary.)

Every Wednesday and Saturday evening from June through August, over 400 locals stage an extravagant Renaissance *son et lumière* entitled *A la Cour du Roy François.* Wandering minstrels, period costumes, fireworks, and 16th-century music are all part of the *spectacle.* Tickets (65F) and mandatory reservations (5F) are available at the ticket and information booth on the ascending ramp (tel. 47 57 14 47).

From the château, follow the cliffs along rue Victor Hugo beside centuries-old *maisons troglodytiques,* hollowed out of the hill and still inhabited today. Just up the road is the **Clos Lucé,** the gracious manor where Leonardo da Vinci, under the patronage of François I, spent the last years of his life. Inside, several models, constructed by IBM from his 15th-century sketches, demonstrate that Lenny knew the principles on which modern hydraulic lifts, cannons, automobiles, and helicopters are built. (Open daily 9am-7pm; Nov.-Dec. and Feb. daily 9am-6pm. Admission 30F, students 22F.)

Just down the street from the exit to the château on 7, rue du Général Foy, **La Maison Enchantée** squirms with over 200 hilarious automated figures who strut in 20 scenes comprising themes ranging from barber shops to *Beauty and the Beast* to Dr. Jekyll in his chemical laboratory. (Open daily 10am-7pm; Nov.-March daily 10am-noon and 2-6pm. Admission 20F.)

The unassuming **Musée de la Poste,** 6, rue Joyeuse (tel. 47 57 00 11), in the Hôtel de Joyeuse, presents the sinister history of mail delivery in France. The eclectic exhibit ranges from the uniforms worn by Napoleonic mail carriers to the first stamp printed in France to more modern postal techniques. (Open Tues.-Sun. 9:30am-noon and 2-6:30pm; Oct.-March Tues.-Sun. 10am-noon and 2-5pm. Through rain, heat and driving snow. Admission 15F, students 7F.)

Tours

In the 15th century, Prince Charles VII's mother sold out the young *dauphin* by conceding the French throne to the English during the Hundred Years War. The rightful heir Charles VII fled from Paris to Tours, one of his domains, and at Joan of Arc's behest took his legitimate place as king. Charles settled permanently in the Touraine, making the region a seat of power and prompting the construction of numerous châteaux. Thanks to this royal relocation, châteaux radiate in every direction from the modern city.

Employed mainly in electronics and metallurgy, the 250,000 *tourangeaux* live and work alongside a large, cosmopolitan student population and a stodgy bourgeoisie, who claim to speak the "purest" French in the country. With its reputation as an educational center dating back to the Middle Ages, Tours also has an old quarter with Renaissance heritage and a glitzy pedestrian zone, thus offering its quota of pretty squares and Renaissance houses.

This all may sound alluring. In fact, it isn't. Tours just isn't wildly attractive or endearing. In an area where buildings are judged by their extravagance, and ancient towns by their preservation, Tours gets left in the dust of its urban sprawl. But, its location 60km from some of the loveliest châteaux in the region and on the doorstep of Vouvray, Montlouis, and other fine wine-growing towns of the Touraine renders it an excellent urban base from which to explore the Loire valley.

Orientation and Practical Information

Tours lies only 56 minutes by TGV from Paris-Montparnasse. The city's focal point is **pl. Jean-Jaurès** (2 min. left of the train station), which is intersected by four large spokes that neatly quarter the town: av. Grammont and rue Nationale (south to north), and bd. Heurteloup and bd. Béranger (east to west). The Loire lies to the north, and the *vieille ville* sits to the left of rue Nationale, stretching along the rue du Commerce and culminating in the **Place Plumereau**. The cathedral and the **Musée des Beaux Arts** stand off rue Colbert about five minutes to the right of rue Nationale. Most of the inexpensive accommodations lie within a ten-minute walking radius of the station.

Tourist Office: (tel. 47 05 58 08), in the Hôtel de Ville on pl. Jean Jaurès. Walk straight out of the station for one block and turn left onto bd. Heurteloup. Staff distributes free maps, books accommodations (for 6F plus deposit equal to one night's stay) and arranges bus tours to the châteaux. A general bus tour covering only the exteriors of sites (May-Oct. 10am, 2 1/2hr., 35F) and a detailed historical tour on foot (June-Sept. 2:30pm, 2hr., 25F) both depart daily from the glass-box office. The Hôtel de Ville **branch** handles tour reservations. A glass box **annex** should be situated next to the new Palais du Congrès in the pl. de la Gare by 1993. Open Mon.-Sat. 8:30am-7:30pm, Sun. 10am-12:30pm and 3-6pm; Sept.-May Mon.-Sat. 8:30am-12:30pm and 2-6pm.

Currency Exchange: Help Hôtels, in the train station, is the best bet if you arrive on the weekend. Changes traveler's checks for 10F commission. Open daily 8:00am-7:30pm. Best deal is at **Crédit Agricole**, diagonally across (to the right) from the train station. Open Mon.-Thurs. 9am-12:30pm and 1:30-5:15pm, Fri. 9am-12:30pm and 1:30-4:15pm.

Post Office: 1, bd. Béranger (tel. 47 60 34 20). Open Mon.-Fri. 8am-7pm, Sat. 8am-noon. **Postal Code:** 37000.

Trains: 3, rue Edouard Vaillant (24-hr. tel. 47 20 50 50). Many long-distance trains require you to change at St-Pierre-des-Corps, an industrial stop 5 min. outside Tours, so check schedules carefully. To: Paris-Austerlitz (22 per day, 2 1/4hr., 149F); Poitiers (17 per day, 30-60min., 72F); Bordeaux (13 per day, 2 1/2hr., 196F); TGV to Paris-Montparnasse, change at St-Pierre des Corps (16 per day, 1hr., 149F plus 32-80F reservation).

Buses: Eurolines, 76, rue Bernard Palissy (tel. 47 66 45 56). Amazing deals on travel throughout Europe, North Africa, and the U.K. Tours-London round-trip 760F. Tours-Casablanca round-trip 1500F. Most buses with video. Information office open Mon.-Sat. 9am-noon and 1:30-6:30pm.

Châteaux Bus Tours: Touraine Evasion (tel. 47 60 30 00 or 47 66 63 81) Mon.-Fri. 9am-6:30pm, Sat. 9am-noon, or 47 66 63 81 Sat. noon-6:30pm, Sun.) leads small, personal van tours, offering a different one for each day of the week. Energetic drivers give colorful commentary in French and English. To: Blois, Chambord, and Cheverny (Tues., all day 180F); Chenonceau, Chaumont, and Amboise (Mon., 1/2-day 110F); Azay-le-Rideau, Ussé and Villandry (Sun., 1/2-day 105F). Groups of 5-7 can create their own itineraries. Entrance fees (21-49F) not included. Reserve 1-2 days ahead. Call for information and reservations, or contact the tourist office at the Hôtel de Ville, from which tours leave. **Service Touristique de la Touraine** (tel. 47 05 46 09). A large outfit run out of the train station. Half-day tours to: Chenonceau, Amboise, and Vouvray; Saché, Azay-le-Rideau, and Villandry; Langeais and Ussé. All 90F (departs at 1:15pm from pl. de la Gare, returns at 7pm). Full-day tours to the same destinations as Touraine Evasion 135-140F (departs 9am from pl. de la Gare). Summer *son et lumière* trips, too; prices include admission. To Azay-le-Rideau (110F), Le Lude (135F), and Amboise (120F). There are daily departures late March-early Oct. with French and English commentary on bus. Office open Mon.-Sat. 8-11am and 3:30-7pm, Sun. 8-11am. Reserve here or at the tourist office (in the Hôtel de Ville) a day in advance.

Bike Rental: Montaubin, 2, rue Nationale (tel. 47 05 62 27). 10-speeds 70F per day, deposit 1000F. Mountain bikes 100F per day, deposit 1800F. **Grammont Cycles,** 93, av. de Grammont (tel. 47 66 62 89). Mountain bikes 80F per day, 150F per weekend (Sat.-Mon.), deposit 400F.

Open Tues.-Sat. 9am-noon and 2-7pm. It may be easier to rent bicycles in smaller towns such as Azay-le-Rideau if rentals in Tours are cleaned out. Phone reservations a week in advance will almost certainly guarantee you a bike even in summer.

English Bookstore: La Boîte à Livres de l'Etranger, 2, rue du Commerce. Large selection of novels and *Let's Go* travel guides. Open Mon. 2-7pm, Tues.-Fri. 9am-7pm, Sat. 9:30am-7pm.

Laundromat: 20, rue Bernard Palissy, 5 min. straight ahead from the station. Wash 8-15F, dryers 2F per 5 min. Soap 2F. Accepts 1F, 2F, and 5F coins. Open daily 7am-9pm.

Services for people with disabilities: (tel. 47 37 60 00). The tourist office provides guides for people in wheelchairs staying in Tours: *Tours en Fauteuil Roulant* and throughout France: *Touristes Quand Même.*

Crisis Line: SOS Amitié, (tel. 47 54 54 54).

Late-Night Pharmacy: Call the police station (tel. 47 05 66 60) and they will point you to the nearest open pharmacy.

Hospital: Hôpital Trousseau, rue de Loches (tel. 47 47 47 47).

Police: 14ter, rue de Clocheville (tel 47 05 66 60). **Emergency:** tel. 17.

Accommodations and Camping

Cheap hotels cluster around the train station. If you arrive before noon and it's not a holiday, reservations are probably unnecessary. The hostel and *foyer* both draw crowds in summer.

Auberge de Jeunesse (HI), av. d'Arsonval, Parc de Grandmont (tel. 47 25 14 45), 4km from the station in a park by the freeway. Take bus #1 (direction "Joue Blotterie," 6F20) or bus #6 (direction "Chambray," 6F20) from the stop on the right side of av. de Grammont, 30m down from pl. Jean Jaurès. The last departure to the hostel is at 8:30pm. Large rooms with 2-12 beds; 2-person rooms cost 10F extra per person. Good kitchen facilities, TV, and phone. Reception open 4-11pm; off-season 4-10pm. Lockout 10am-4pm. Curfew 11pm, but you can get a key (50F deposit). 57F, breakfast included. Dinner 43F, *plat du jour* 26F. Sheets 15F.

Le Foyer, 16, rue Bernard Palissy (tel. 47 05 38 81), across bd. Heurteloup from the tourist office and down rue Bernard Palissy. Good location and big rooms. Accepts both sexes ages 16-25. Office open Mon. afternoon-Sat. morning. Centrally located. Doubles 65F per person. Decent, cheap cafeteria (see Food). Breakfast 8F. Very crowded July-Aug.

Mon Hôtel, 40, rue de la Préfecture, off rue Bernard Palissy (tel. 47 05 67 53). Extraordinarily generous owner offers advice on everything. Fresh, light, newly decorated rooms in a quiet location. Singles 85F, with shower 140F. Doubles 95F, with shower and toilet 160F. Showers 15F. All-you-can-eat breakfast 20F.

Hôtel Vendôme, 24, rue Roger Salengro (tel. 47 64 33 54), 1 block off av. Grammont. Family atmosphere and richly-furnished lobby and breakfast room. Large, immaculate rooms with telephones. Singles 90F, with shower 135F. Doubles 95F, with shower 150F, with two beds 200F. One triple 210F. Showers 15F. Breakfast 15F, with croissant 20F.

Hôtel Regina, 2, rue Pimbert (tel. 47 05 25 36), off rue Voltaire, behind the Grand Théâtre. Helpful English-speaking management. Comfortable rooms with telephones. Singles 93F, with shower 125F. Doubles 115F, with shower 155F. Triples with shower 220F. Showers 15F. Breakfast 20F.

Tour Hotel, 10, rue Edouard Vaillant (tel. 47 05 59 35), immediately to the right when exiting the train station. Not exactly the Ritz, but it feels safe, reasonably clean, and offers the best prices in town. Singles 61-65F. Doubles 70-110F, with shower 120F. Showers 10F.

Camping: Dozens of campgrounds lie within a 30km radius, most near châteaux and the Loire. Pick up a list from the tourist office. **Camping Tours Edouard Peron** (tel. 47 54 11 11 or the mayor's office at 47 66 29 94), a 2-star site on N152, is closest to the city. Take bus #6 (direction "Ste-Radégonde," 6F20). 19F50 per person with tent. Hot showers included. Open May 21-Sept. 11.

Food

Rue Colbert and the area around pl. Plumereau overflow with restaurants serving traditional *cuisine tourganelle*. Local specialities include *terrines* (prepared meats), fish, especially *truite* (trout) and *saumon* (salmon), and anything *aux pruneaux* (with prunes). Be sure to try one of the light white wines from Montlouis, Vouvray, or Touraine. Unfortunately, the culinary excellence associated with the Touraine region has not trickled down to budget-level offerings. Scores of cheap—though not necessarily good—restaurants feed Tours's large student population. There is a small produce **market** at pl. des Halles. (Open Sun.-Tues. and Thurs.-Fri. 8-9:30am.) An **ATAC Supermarket** (open Mon.-Sat. 8:30am-8pm, Sun. 9:30am-12:30pm) is just to the left outside of the train station.

Le Foyer cafeteria, 16, rue Bernard Palissy. Lively, local, and frequented by young French workers. Purchase a membership card at the foyer office (3F). Hearty five-course *menu* 36F50; meat and vegetables 24F50. Open Mon.-Fri. 11:30am-1:45pm and 7-8pm, Sat. 11:30am-1:45pm.

Aux Trois Canards, 16, rue de la Rôtisserie, in the *vieille ville.* This elegant restaurant and bar, run by a single family since it opened in 1934, claims a devoted local clientele. 47F 3-course *menu* and a more delicate 69F *menu* (try the duck mousse with port, veal *à la tourganelle,* salad and dessert. *Coq au vin* 42F. Open Mon.-Fri. noon-2pm and 7:30-10pm, Sat. 7:30-10pm.

Le Bistroquet, 17, rue Blaise Pascal, near the train station. An unassuming place with satiating 49-75F *menus.* Chicken and shrimp *paella* 75F per person (2-person min.). Open Mon.-Thurs. and Sat. noon-1:30pm and 7:30-9:30pm, Fri. noon-1:30pm.

La Bigarade, 122, rue Colbert (tel. 47 05 48 81). Regional specialties, light sauces, and artistic presentation—no Sloppy Joes here. Copious 90F *menu* consists of appetizer (quail pâté with grapes), main course (mackerel in a white wine sauce), and cheese or dessert. A la carte main courses 70-125F. Open Thurs.-Mon. noon-2pm and 7:30-10pm, Wed. 7:30-10pm. Reservations recommended.

Sights

Just south of the Loire and in the eastern sector of the city, the **Cathédrale St-Gatie** is possibly the most compelling sight in Tours. Built from the 13th to the 16th centuries, it demonstrates the evolution of the Gothic style, culminating in the flamboyant façade. Walk around the church to appreciate the exterior details and the flying buttresses, one of which plants itself in the courtyard of the neighboring house that provided a setting for Balzac's novel *Le Curé de Tours.* (Open 7:15am-7pm; Oct.-Easter 7:15am-noon and 2-6:45pm.). Next door, the **Musée des Beaux Arts,** in the former episcopal palace at 18, pl. François Sicard (tel. 47 05 68 73), has assembled works from the Italian Renaissance, including two beautiful Mantegnas, as well as one Rembrandt and several Delacroix paintings. (Open Wed.-Mon. 9am-12:45pm and 2-6pm. Admission 30F, students 15F. Gardens open daily 7am-8:30pm; 7am-6pm in winter.) The **Historial de Touraine,** two blocks down rue Lavoisier in the Château Royale, is a spiffy new museum where 165 wax characters—including Charlemagne, Rabelais, and da Vinci—animate local history. (Open daily 9am-6:30pm; mid-March to mid-June and mid-Sept. to mid-Nov. 9-11:30am and 2-6:30pm; mid-Nov. to mid-March 2-5:30pm. Admission 28F, students 20F. Guide booklets in many languages 3F.)

Although the old quarter suffered serious damage during WWII, several venerable buildings in the area around rue Briconnet and rue du Change survive. At the **Hôtel Goüin,** 25, rue du Commerce (tel. 47 66 22 32), the finest Renaissance façade in Tours conceals a mildly interesting archaeological collection spanning the gamut from Gallo-Roman utensils to Renaissance sculptures to 17th-century scientific instruments. (Open mid-May to Sept. daily 10am-7pm; mid-March to mid-May daily 10am-12:30pm and 2-6:30pm; Feb. to mid-March and Oct.-Dec. Sat.-Thurs. 10am-12:30pm and 2-5:30pm. Admission 17F, students 12F.) Flanking rue des Halles, the **Tour de l'Horloge** and the **Tour de Charlemagne** remain as fragments of the 11th-century Basilique St-Martin, a gargantuan Romanesque masterpiece that collapsed in 1797, several years after looters stole all of its iron reinforcements during the Revolution. The **Nouvelle Basilique St-Martin,** a fin-de-siècle church of Byzantine inspiration, partially overlaps the foundation of the old structure, allowing St-Martin to slumber on undisturbed in his crypt. (Open daily 7:30am-noon and 2-6pm.) Also in the old quarter, the **Musée du Gemmail,** 7, rue du Murier, off rue Bretonneau near pl. Plumereau, takes its name from *gemmes* (gems) and *émail* (enamel). It houses a unique 20th-century art work consisting of illuminated, brightly colored glass shards that blend to yield an unusual "painting of light." (Open April-Oct. 15 Tues.-Sun. 10am-noon and 2-6:30pm. Admission 25F, students 15F.)

The unique **Musée de Compagnonnage,** 8, rue Nationale, (tel. 47 61 07 93), in the Cloître St-Julien, commemorates the forerunner of the trade union and displays a bizarre array of pre-industrial artisanal instruments. (Open mid-June to Sept. daily 9am-6:30pm; April to mid-June Wed.-Mon. 9am-noon and 2-6pm; Admission for bourgeois 20F, students 10F.) Downstairs, the **Musée des Vins de Touraine** (tel. 47 61 07 93) fills an ancient wine cellar. Regrettably, this shrine to wine does not include free samples. (Same hours as the Compagnonnage. Admission 10F, students 5F.) If you're planning to visit several museums, consider buying the 50F **Carte Multivisite** at the tourist office. This global pass will get you in to all museums in Tours, and is also good for the walking tours offered by the tourist office.

Châteaux Near Tours

Many of France's most beautiful châteaux repose on the verdant *campagne* within 60km of Tours. Biking through the small villages along the Loire is an indelible experience, but organized bus tours allow for maximum coverage. Either way, try to make a stop at the many *caves* offering *dégustations* (wine tasting). There are five in **Vouvray,** 9km east of Tours on the N152 and accessible by bus #61 from pl. Jean Jaurès (Mon.-Sat. 14 per day, 20 min.), and several more in **Montlouis,** across the river to the south (11km) and accessible by train from Tours (Mon.-Sat. 5 per day, 20 min., 11F). Weave your way to the castles from there.

Sheltered by an ancient forest 35km east of Tours, the graceful **Chenonceaux** (tel. 47 23 90 07) cultivates an intimacy with its natural surroundings that resists even the most ferocious of crowds. Commissioned and designed by women, the castle arches effortlessly over the Cher River, with tons of white stone suspended in mid-air, capped by slate-grey peaks. While Thomas Bohier, court financier to Charles VIII, Louis XII and François I, was off fighting in Italy (1513-21), his wife Catherine oversaw the plans and assured a dainty yet practical design featuring four rooms radiating from a central chamber, and straight rather than spiraling stairways. Henri II acquired the château in 1547 and gave it to his lover, Diane de Poitiers, who added sublime symmetrical gardens and created the arched bridge over the Cher. Finally, Catherine de'Medici traded the château for Chaumont and built the most spectacular wing of the castle, the two-story gallery spanning the Cher. The gallery served as a military hospital during WWI, and a passageway from annexed France to Vichy France during WWII. Chenonceaux's stunning exterior, viewed from the spacious garden or from a 10F rowboat, will move even the most jaded castle-goer. (Open daily March 16-Sept. 15 9am-7pm; call for closing times at other times of the year. Admission 30F, students and ages 7-15 20F.)

Three **trains** per day (1 on Sun.) link the village of Chenonceaux to Tours (3/4hr., 28F50). The station is 2km from the château. Follow the mob up the road from the station, left onto rue Bretonneau, and then left again onto rue du Château. **Les Rapides de Touraine** (tel. 47 46 06 60 in Tours) runs three buses per day from Tours to Chenonceaux (1hr., 36F) via Amboise (1/2hr., 20F60) and stops at the château gates.

Although your best bet is to make Chenonceaux a daytrip from Tours, you might have a hanker for a night in the *campagne*. If so, the most reasonable prospect in town is the comfortable two-star **Hostel du Roy,** 9, rue Docteur Bretonneau (tel. 47 23 90 17), minutes from the château. (Singles and doubles 110F, with shower 240F. One meal obligatory: breakfast 28F, dinner from 60F. Open Feb.-Nov.) Otherwise, try **La Taverne** (tel. 47 23 92 18), 1km away on the route to Tours (one single 90F; doubles 120F, with shower 150F), or **Chez Madeleine Badier** (tel. 47 23 92 48), 1.5km on the road to Tours (singles and doubles 140F). Chenonceaux's tiny **campground** (tel. 47 23 90 13) is a few blocks left of the entrance to the château. (7F50 per person, 5F10 per tent. Open April 15-Sept.) You can also camp in nearby **Civray** (tel. 47 23 92 13), about 1km away (8F per person, 6F per site. Open June 15-early Sept.), or at a site in **Chisseaux,** about 2km from the château (tel. 47 23 90 75; 10F per person, 10F per tent; open Easter-Sept.).

The château of **Loches**, 40km southeast of Tours, roosts atop a hill over the medieval town of the same name. It consists of two distinct wings at opposite ends of the hill. The 10th-century **donjon** (dungeon) and watchtowers defend the southern end of the hilltop. Built by the Counts of Anjou as protection from their prime enemies, the Counts of Blois, this massive structure was transformed into a state prison under Charles VII in 1450. Ponder the sinister dungeons where Ludovico Sforza, Duke of Milan, covered every inch of his cell from 1500-1508 with mystic messages and symbols. Other prisoners, restrained in dangling cages, were regrettably less creative.

The 13th- to 15th-century **royal residence** on the north end of the hilltop recalls a more familiar history and a much gayer architectural style. A long line of royalty, beginning with Philippe-Auguste in 1205, reposed in the dwelling, and Joan of Arc came here after her 1429 victory in Orléans to implore the *dauphin* Charles to be crowned at Reims.

From June to September, you can visit the apartments and the *donjon* with or without a guide; at other times a tour is required. (Castle open July-Aug. daily 9am-6pm; March 15-June and Sept. daily 9am-noon and 2-6pm; Oct.-March 14 Thurs.-Tues. 9am-noon and 2-5pm. Dungeon opens and closes 30 min. after castle. Admission to both 25F, students 15F.) The castle also stages a *son et lumière* about Joan's adventures. (Every 2nd and 4th Fri. and Sat. in July at 10:30pm, Aug. every Fri. and Sat. at 10pm., 1 1/2hr. Admission 60F. Call the Loches tourist office for information and reservations.)

Fifteen buses per day make the 50-minute trek from Tours to Loches, leaving from the front of the train station. (26F50; purchase ticket from driver.) The **tourist office** (tel. 47 59 07 98), in a pavilion near the station on pl. de la Marne, can help you find one of Loche's few inexpensive rooms. (Open daily 9:30am-7pm, Sept.-June Tues.-Sat. 9:30am-12:30pm and 2:15-7pm.) Two-star **Tour St-Antoine,** 2, rue des Moulins (tel. 47 59 01 06), has four pleasant rooms for 110-130F. (Breakfast 26F. Reserve early in summer.) Aching to see poorly dubbed MacGyver reruns? The **Grill-Motel** on rue des Lézards (tel. 47 91 50 04) has TVs, as well as toilets and showers, in every sterile, relentlessly modern double. Go to pl. de Verdun and follow the signs out of town for 2km. No, you're not lost. Be sure to call ahead. (Doubles 168F, TV 20F extra.) The beautiful **Camping Municipal la Piscine,** rue Guintefol (tel 47 59 05 91) includes a swimming pool. Take the N143 south, and follow route de Châteauroux to Stade Général Leclerc. (41F per 2 people with a tent. Showers included.) For meals, try **La Cordelière,** 31, Grande-Rue for their *crêpes* (22-37F), omelettes (20-23F), or their 48F *menu.* (Open daily noon-2:30pm and 7-10pm.)

Lush **Villandry** maintains fantastic formal gardens with swan pools, vine-covered walkways, and three terraces of sculpted shrubs and flowers. The château pales before its more regal cousins, but the gardens seduce with a gorgeous array of vegetables, roses, box hedges, and 1150 lime trees. Most interesting is the intermediate terrace, where knee-high hedges are arranged in various patterns: a Maltese Cross, a Croix de Lorraine, and a charming reproduction of the *carte du tendre* with symbols of four types of love (tender, courtly, passionate, and flighty). (Gardens open daily 9am-7pm. Castle open May-mid-Sept. daily 9am-6pm; mid-Sept. to Nov. 11 and mid-March to April daily 9am- 5pm. Admission to gardens 23F, students 20F. Admission to the castle an additional 12F, students 11F.)

Villandry is not easily accessible by train, although it is possible to take a train to Savonnières (4 per day, 10 min., 14F) and to walk or bike the several km from there. Both **Touraine Evasion** and **Service Touristique de la Touraine** include it in their full-day and half-day tours. (See Tours, Châteaux Bus Tours for information.) Cyclists coming from Tours should follow the tiny D16, a narrow, paved marvel that winds along the bank of the Loire past Villandry to Ussé.

Ussé's pointed towers, white turrets, and chimneys inspired Charles Perrault's transcription of the *Sleeping Beauty* folktale. Surrounded by the thick forests of the Forêt de Chinon, the 15th-century château rises above terraced gardens and the Indre River. You don't have to take the tour to see models of the *Sleeping Beauty* story in 18th- and 19th-century French costume. If the admission seems steep, you could just relish the view with a picnic outside. (Open March 15-July 13 daily 9am-noon and 2-6pm; July

14-Aug. 31 9am-6:30pm; Sept. 9am-noon and 2-7pm. Admission 44F.) Like Villandry, Ussé is most easily reached by one of the tours offered by **Touraine Evasion** and **Service Touristique de la Touraine.**

Azay-le-Rideau (tel. 47 45 42 04), gazing vainly at its reflection from an island in the Indre river, rivals Chenonceaux in beauty and setting. Built according to the whims of François I's corrupt financier/embezzler, the château embodies the elements of the Renaissance. The interior is well-appointed, although many of the furnishings are restorations or flat-out fakes. (Open daily 9am-6:30pm; Sept. and April-June 9:30am-5:30pm; Oct.-March 10am-noon and 2-4:30pm. Admission 25F, students 14F.) The *son et lumière* performance is spruced up by costumed actors in boats. (Shows May-July at 10:30pm; Aug.-Sept. at 10pm. Admission 45F, children 35F.)

The château is a 2km walk from Azay-le-Rideau's train station (7 trains per day from Tours, 1/2hr., 21F). Turn right from the front of the station and head left on the D57. The **tourist office**, 26, rue Gambetta (tel. 47 45 44 40), 1 km from the train station along ave. de la Gare, can help with accommodations, few of which are cheap. Ask about buses to **Saché** (tel. 47 26 86 50), Balzac's home, located 7km east of Azay. (Open July-Aug. daily 9:30am-6:30pm; Sept. and March 15-June daily 9am-noon and 2-6pm; Oct.-Nov. and Feb.-March 14 Thurs.-Tues. 9am-noon and 2-5pm. Admission 20F.) The **Camping Parc du Sabot** (tel. 47 45 42 72), across from the château on the banks of the Indre, has canoe and kayak rentals and plenty of room (42F per 2 people with tent, showers included; open Easter-Nov. 11). Rent bikes at **Le Provost**, 13, rue Carnot (tel. 47 45 40 94; 25F per 1/2-day, 37F per day; open Tues.-Sat. 8am-noon and 2-7pm).

Between Villandry and Ussé lies the forbiddingly feudal **Langeais** (tel. 47 96 72 60), one of the last medieval fortresses built strictly for defense. Constructed from 1465 to 1469 for Louis XI, Langeais guarded the route from Brittany through the Loire Valley. The 1491 marriage here of France's Charles VIII to Anne de Bretagne consummated Brittany's union with the crown. One room of the castle contains wax figures of the bride and groom at their actual height, or lack thereof. (Recall that this 4-ft. ruler died after somehow managing to hit his head on a door frame.) The tour (in French) includes a walk along the upper fortifications. Note the stone slabs which, when drawn back, reveal slots for hurling boiling oil and stones at attackers. The ruins of the original 11th-century fortress stand in the small château courtyard. (Open daily 9am-noon and 3-6pm. Admission 30F, students 17F. Call 47 96 72 60 for more info.)

Twenty-three trains per day stop in Langeais on their way to Saumur or Tours. The **train station** (tel. 47 96 82 19) is a 1/4-km walk from the château; signs will point you in the right direction. Rent bikes at **Station Glorex,** 24, rue de Tours (tel. 47 96 81 17). Bikes are 40F per day, plus 500F deposit. (Open Mon.-Fri. 8am-8pm.) The 10km bike ride on the D16 from Villandry or Ussé is delightful and hitchhikers find the 10km hitch north from Azay-le-Rideau on the D57 to Langeais fairly easy. The **tourist office** (tel. 47 96 58 22) is across from the châteaux. (Open June-Sept. Tues.-Sat. 9am-noon and 2-6pm, Sun. 10am-noon.) The small town of 4000 has little in the way of indoor accommodations, but there is a **Camping Municipal** (tel. 47 96 85 80) on the N152, 1km from the château. (16F per person, with tent. Open June-Sept. 15.) A 40-bed *gîte d'étape* (tel. 47 96 67 29) awaits in La Rouchouze, 10km out of Langeais and within 20km of Langeais, Azay-le-Rideau, Ussé, and Villandry. (36F per night. Call the Langeais town hall at 47 96 71 62 for information and reservations.)

Chinon

Built into the side of a hill, Chinon's (pop. 9000) cobblestone and rutted-dirt streets twist around the hillside up to ruins of its château. Having parried the thrusts of both heavy tourism and heavy industry, Chinon is not intriguing in its street life. The tree-lined Vienne glides peacefully through the center of town. The *vieille ville,* birthplace of the great 16th-century comic writer François Rabelais (in whose *Gargantua* and *Pantagruel* Chinon's red wine is celebrated), unfolds a delightful maze of alleyways, chimneys, and medieval timber-frame houses, some with fine sculptural detail. A comfortable hostel and bucolic campground make Chinon an ideal spot to rest and plan jaunts to nearby Azay, Ussé, Villandry, and Saumur—all accessible by train or bike.

Orientation and Practical Information

Chinon lies an hour southwest of Tours by train, and 30km southeast of Saumur. To reach the town center, walk straight from the train station along rue du Docteur Labussière, bear left onto rue du 11 Novembre, continue straight along quai Jeanne d'Arc, and bear right before the bridge. Chinon's modest shopping square is pl. Général de Gaulle, from which extends rue Voltaire, which then becomes rue Haute St-Maurice, the main artery of the *vieille ville*.

Tourist Office: 12, rue Voltaire (tel. 47 93 17 85), about 15min. from the station, off pl. Général de Gaulle. Helpful and efficient staff tenders information on excursions to area châteaux and wine caves, books rooms in Chinon for a couple of francs, and changes money when banks are closed (expect to pay the same hefty commission you would at a bank). Open Mon.-Sat. 9am-7pm, Sun. 10am-12:30pm; Sept. 16-June 14 Mon.-Sat. 9am-12:15pm and 2-6:30pm.

Post Office: 10, quai Jeanne-d'Arc (tel. 47 93 12 08). Open Mon.-Fri. 8am-noon and 1:30-5:45pm, Sat. 8am-noon. **Postal Code:** 37500.

Trains: (tel. 47 93 11 04), av. Gambetta at av. du Docteur Labussière. To Tours (3 trains per day, 3 SNCF buses per day; train 1hr., bus 1 1/4hr.; 39F). Open Mon.-Sat. 6am-7:30pm, Sun. 10:15-11:50am and 3:15-8:30pm.

Buses: stop at pl. Jeanne d'Arc. Mon.-Sat. 5 buses per day to the Port-Boulet station for connections to Saumur (20min., 14F). For information, call **Les Bus de Chinonais/Sitravel** at 47 93 18 06, or check at the train station.

Bike Rental: Chris Hôtel, 12, pl. Jeanne d'Arc; **Hôtel Chinon,** Digue St-Jacques; and **Lion d'Or,** 10, pl. Jeanne d'Arc, all rent bikes. Chris Hôtel has the cheapest at 30F per 1/2-day, 50F per day and 280F per week.

Medical Assistance: Clinique Jeanne d'Arc, rue des Quinquenays (tel. 47 93 70 00), off rue de Tours.

Police: 1, rue Voltaire (tel. 47 93 53 62, *poste* 320). **Emergency:** tel. 17.

Accommodations, Camping, and Food

Bargains are scarce so arrive early, call ahead, or plan on staying in the relaxed, un-crowded youth hostel, worth trying even if you don't have an HI card.

Auberge de Jeunesse (HI) (tel. 47 93 10 48), on rue Descartes, about 500m from the center of town and only a 5-min. walk from the train station. A combination youth hostel, *foyer,* and youth cultural center, this large, modern building has an institutional air, with long, barren hallways, and sterile 4- to 9-bed rooms. Work your wrists at the foosball table. Also has kitchen facilities and is across the street from tennis courts, the river, and a shady promenade. Reception open 6-9:30am, 1-2pm, and 6-8pm, although there's almost always someone at the snack bar downstairs. Lockout 10am-6pm. 43F. Sheets 15F. Try to reserve in summer.

Le Jeanne-d'Arc, 11, rue Voltaire (tel. 47 93 02 85), opposite the tourist office. Full of character, with bold *fleur-de-lis* patterned wallpaper and pictures of Rabelais. Some rooms have wood-beam ceilings, some staff speak English. Singles and doubles 120-130F. Triples 150F. Showers included. Breakfast 20F. Reserve.

Hôtel le Point du Jour, 102, quai Jeanne-d'Arc (tel. 47 93 07 20), 5-10min. from the station. Big, clean, and brown rooms are a good value. Run by a nice family. One room without shower 90F. Singles and doubles with shower 125-150F. Triples and quads 250F. Breakfast 20F. Reservations often necessary (July-Aug., 2 weeks in advance).

Camping: Camping de l'Ile Auger (tel. 47 93 08 55), across the river at Ile Auger off the RN749. Crowded, but with pleasant sites and a great view of Chinon. Five minutes from the *centre ville.* 9F per person, 9F20 per tent, 9F20 per car.

If you're not careful, Chinon's cute restaurants will charm you right into debt. Still, a few of the *centre ville*'s cozy spots will wine you and dine you for an acceptable price. The wood-beamed **Les Années 30,** 78, rue Voltaire, has a classy reputation among locals. (Four-course *menus* 80F and 115F, five-course *menu* and *apéritif* for 155F; open for lunch from noon and dinner from 7pm). **Du Grand Carroi,** 30, rue du Grand Carroi, in an old house off rue Voltaire, fries fine *galettes* for 13 to 32F (open Tues.-Sun. noon-2pm and 7-10pm). Save room for the 18F dessert *crêpes* at **Rabelais,** 3, rue Voltaire.

Sights

Let your imagination re-create the decaying **château de Chinon** (tel. 47 93 13 45), now a clifftop ruin overlooking the River Vienne. This hulking rock pile crumbled not under attack but through neglect, under Cardinal Richelieu and, later, Napoleon. Originally constructed during the 10th century by the *seigneur* of Chinon, in the mid-12th century it was passed on to Henri Plantagenet, who was crowned Henry II of England in 1154, but maintained Chinon as one of his principal residences. Before his death placed it in the hands of his son Richard the Lionhearted, Henry made considerable additions to the château, including the Pont de Pierre, the Eglise St-Maurice, and the Fort St-Georges. When the son of Charles VI was chased from Paris in 1418, he made Chinon his chief residence until 1429, when Jeanne d'Arc appeared, "sent by God," to convince the *dauphin* to lead his army to relieve the siege of Orléans by the English. Today, the **Musée Jeanne d'Arc,** housed in the 15th-century Tour de l'Horloge above the entrance to the château, tells the story of the Maid of Orléans, her appearance here, and her quest to restore Charles VII to the French throne. Mulitilingual audiotapes guide you through the exhibit. (Château and museum open July-Aug. daily 9am-7pm; Sept. and May-June daily 9am-6pm; Oct.-Nov. and Feb.-March 14 9am-noon and 2-7pm; March 15-April daily 9am-noon and 2-6pm. Admission 21F, students 17F.)

The 12th-century ruins of the **Chapelle St-Radagonde,** about a 25-minute walk from the center, are attached to a museum explaining the frugal lives of the region's cave dwellers. It presents regional art, tools and utensils. Follow rue Jean-Jacques Rousseau onto a mountain road lined with *maisons troglodytiques,* comfortable caves cut into the chalk, where destitute families live year-round. (Check the tourist office for hours, as caretaker is not always there. 40-min. tour in English. Admission 10F.)

The **Musée du Vieux Chinon et de la Batellerie,** 44, rue Voltaire, housed in the edifice in which Richard the Lionhearted died and where the French Estates General agreed in 1428 to support Joan of Arc in her mission to free Orléans, today contains a model boat collection, local pottery, and a painting of Rabelais by Delacroix. (Open July-Sept. daily 10am-12:30pm and 2:30-7pm. Admission 15F.) The **Cave Plouzeau,** 94, rue Voltaire (tel. 47 93 16 34), conducts free tours and pours out some of their superb white and red Chinon wines. After nipping from the 30 or so bottles, show your appreciation by purchasing a 25-30F bottle. (Open Tues.-Sun. 10am-noon and 2-6pm.) The **Musée Animé du Vin et de la Tonnellerie,** 12, rue Voltaire (tel. 47 93 25 63), provides a refreshing and entertaining break from château history. The museum illustrates the wine-making process with "automatons" who lace their speech with quotations from Rabelais. The 15- to 20-minute tour, which includes a glass of Chinon wine, ends with the exhortation "drink always and never die." (Shows in both English and French. Open April-Sept. Fri.-Wed. 10am-noon and 2-6pm. Admission 20F.) There is a large, all-day **market** every Thursday in pl. Hôtel de Ville. On the first weekend of August, Chinon holds its popular **Marché Médiéval.** Medieval peddlers and artisans crowd the streets, bars serve food and drinks under the trees, and those in vaguely period costume may explore the château and town museums for free (anachronists must pay 40F). The third weekend in August sees a smaller festival, the **Marché à l'Ancienne,** celebrated in a similar manner, with costumed farmers and folk-artists parading their produce and work. You can also take rides along the river in traditional boats. (Embark from the campground, across the bridge. 6 boats per day, 36min., 15F.)

Saumur

Immortalized in Balzac's novel *Eugénie Grandet,* Saumur bears few traces of the provincial idyll from which Eugénie watched life go by. The vines that made old Grandet rich as well as a crop that represents 70% of France's mushroom output still provide the town's main source of income, but the heavy traffic on the cobblestone streets adds a distinctly modern jangle to this city of 30,000. Saumur offers a variety of sights and museums, many of a horsey bent because of the resident *Cadre Noir* equestrian corps, which still stages competitions and public presentations. Once famous for St-Louis's (1226-1270) feasts and parties, events so uniquely extravagant they were known as *Non Pareilles,* Saumur is now, appropriately enough, Europe's largest producer of carnival masks.

Orientation and Practical Information

Frequent trains running between Nantes and Tours stop at Saumur; other destinations often require a change, usually at Tours. The **tourist office** and most of the sights are on the southern bank of the Loire, a 10- to 15-minute walk from the train station on the northern bank. The **auberge de jeunesse** is on an island in the middle. Exit to the right out of the train station, then turn right on the bridge. Cross Pont des Cadets, and turn immediately left to get to the youth hostel, or continue straight on av. de Général de Gaulle to the *centre ville.*

Tourist Office: pl. Bilange (tel. 41 51 03 06), next to pont Cessart. Take local bus A if you want to bypass the walk. Helpful staff will book beds (5F), change money (commission 5%), and suggest tours of châteaux, vineyards, and mushroom caves. Open Mon.-Sat. 9:15am-7pm, Sun. 10:30am-12:30pm and 3-6:30pm; Sept. 16-June 14 Mon.-Sat. 9:15am-12:30pm and 2-6pm.

Post Office: rue Volney (tel. 41 51 22 77). Have your Poste Restante mail addressed to "Saumur Volney," or it will be delivered to the main office on rue des Prés (tel. 41 50 13 00), 1/2hr. out of town. Open Mon.-Fri. 8:30-6:30pm, Sat. 8:30-noon. **Branch office** across from the station open the same hours. **Postal Code:** 49413.

Trains: av. David d'Angers (tel. 41 67 50 50). From pl. Bilange in the *centre ville,* take bus A (direction: "St-Lambert" or "Chernin Vert"). To Tours (11 daily, 3/4hr., 47F), Angers (11 daily, 1/2hr., 37F); Nantes (5 per day, 1hr. 10min., 86F). Get off at Port-Boulet (15F from Saumur) for the bus to Chinon (14F). Call **Les Bus du Chinonais** at 47 93 53 00 in Chinon for information.

Buses: (tel. 41 51 27 29), on pl. St-Nicolas on the southern bank in front of a church. Go 2 blocks west of pont Cessart, then 1 block south. To Angers (4 per day, 1 1/2hr., 39F) and Tours (3-4 per day). **Local buses** depart from pl. Roosevelt (tel. 41 51 11 87). Tickets 7F, *carnet* of 10 44F90.

Bike Rental: Brison, 49, rue Maréchal Leclerc (tel. 41 51 02 09). Best bikes and best deal. 25F per 1/2-day, 40F per day, 163F per week; 300F deposit. Open Tues.-Sat. 8am-noon and 2-7pm. **Cycles Carlos,** 57, quai Mayaud (tel. 41 67 69 32), 45F per 1/2-day, 65F per day, 320F per week; 1200F or passport deposit. Open Tues.-Sat. 9am-noon and 2-7pm.

English Bookstore: The **Maison de la Presse** near the tourist office on pl. Bilange carries a few recent publications. A better option is the **Librairie du Val de Loire,** 46, rue d'Orléans (tel. 41 51 04 66), which has cheaper books and a bigger selection, although most of them are older, "classic" novels. (Open Tues.-Sun. 9am-noon and 2-7pm, Mon. 3-6:30pm. Closed Mon. July-Aug.)

Laundromat: 12, rue Maréchal Leclerc. Cheap, modern, and efficient. Wash 10F, dry 2F per 8min. Takes 2F and 10F coins. Open daily 7am-9:30pm. Also at Camping Ile d'Offard.

Medical Assistance: Centre Hospitalier, rue Seigneur (tel. 41 53 25 00). **SAMU,** tel. 41 48 44 22.

Police: rue Montesquieu (tel. 41 51 04 32). **Emergency:** tel. 17.

Accommodations and Camping

Better visited as a daytrip, sultry Saumur attracts lots of tourists to its cream colored cobblestone, and with a short list of inexpensive accommodations, it's a race to reserve a room. Call ahead.

Auberge de Jeunesse (HI)/Centre International de Séjour, rue de Verden (tel. 41 67 45 00), on Ile d'Offard, between the station and the tourist office. Large, modern hostel next to a 4-star campsite on a delightful island with a superb view of the castle. Helpful multilingual staff and free access to a swimming pool. Ill-kept kitchen facilities. Washing machine. Reception open 8-10am and 5-10pm. Lax lockout 10am-5pm. Curfew 10pm; ask for a key if you'll be out late. Loud 6-berth rooms 39F, nonmembers 41F. Spacious doubles 63F per person. Breakfast 16F. Sheets 21F.

Hôtel de la Croix de Guerre, 9, rue de la Petite Bilange (tel. 41 51 05 88). On a quiet street off pl. Bilange. Rooms are cozy with great, high ceilings. Funny and friendly owner loves to practice speaking English. Singles and doubles 95-150F, with shower 180F. Showers 15F. Breakfast 22F.

Hôtel le Cristal, 10, pl. de la République (tel. 41 51 09 54). Affable proprietor and views of the river and island justify higher prices. Clean and capacious singles and doubles with showers 170-250F. A room with a view 240F. Elegant triples and quads with bath 290F and 300F. All-you-can-eat breakfast 30F.

Camping: Camping Municipal de L'Ile d'Offard (tel. 41 67 45 00), next to the hostel on Ile d'Offard, at the end of rue Verden. 256 places, a pool, washing machines, tennis courts (40F per hr., equipment included), and a snack shop. 21F50 per person, 38F50 per tent and car; in winter 18F50 per person, 31F per tent and car. **Camping Municipal Dampierre** (tel. 41 67 87 99), a 10-min. bus ride southeast along the D947, is considerably cheaper than other area campgrounds. Take bus #16 or D (direction: "Fonteraud") from Saumur's train station. 10F50 per person, 5F25 per tent, 5F25 per car. Open June-Spet. 15. Also **Camping Chantepie** (tel. 41 67 95 34), 6km out of Saumur in St-Hilaire-St-Florent. Four-star site with a pool. 10F50 per person, 50F per tent and car. Showers included. Open May-Sept. 15.

Food

Saumur's proud name graces a fine white, a subtle rosé, and an earthy red wine. The tourist office has extensive information about *dégustations* and *cave* visits. One of the largest *caves,* **Gratien et Meyer,** route de Chinon, founded in 1864, stretches for several km in the limestone caves cut into the hills. Take bus D from pl. Bilange to "La Grue." (Open Sept.-July daily 9am-noon and 2-6pm; Aug. daily 9am-6pm.) Thinly sliced *champignons* (mushrooms) marinated in wine are a locally-grown specialty. The **Champignonnière du Saut-aux-Loups** in Montsoreau offers guided tours. (Open March-Nov. 10 daily 10am-6:30pm. 15F per person, 40 min., tours in English.) Taste the delectable fungi on the terrace or in the cave itself where the cultivators serve a lunch composed entirely of mushrooms (July-Aug. Tues.-Sun. noon-2pm; June and Sept. Sun. noon-2pm. About 60F.) Take the Anjou bus #16 from the train station to Montsoreau. The caves are at the entrance to the town. A small fresh produce **market** fills pl. de la République and av. de Gaulle (Thurs. morning). The larger Saturday **covered market,** Les Halles, pl. St-Pierre, has all a picnicker desires. (Open Tues.-Fri. 8am-6:30pm, Sat. 7am-1pm and 3-7:30pm, Sun. 9am-12:30pm.) The streets around pl. St-Pierre shelter some fine restaurants.

Le Relais, 31, quai Mayaud (tel. 41 67 75 20). A *bar à vin* (wine bar) that serves over 30 regional wines by the glass, accompanied by samples of savory local specialties. The wide stone terrace, with its white stone walls and summer garden, is a delicious setting in which to relish the Loire Valley's delicate flavors. Waiters will highlight the unique features of each wine. Various *assiettes* (plates) include duck *terrine,* salami, *rillettes* cooked over a wood fire (shredded pork cooked in its fat), excellent Bayonne ham, and *foie gras* (34-86F). Open daily 6pm-2am. Reservations a good idea.

La Pierre Chaude, 41, av. du Général de Gaulle, on the island. Catherine and Patrick welcome you with duck, whiskey flambée, a 60F lunch *menu* (Mon.-Fri.), and an exquisite 98F four-course dinner *menu.* Open daily noon-2pm and 7:30-10pm; Oct.-April Mon.-Fri. noon-2pm and 7:30-10pm, Sat. 7:30-10pm.

Auberge St-Pierre, 6, rue Place St-Pierre, next to the church. 45F and 65F *menus* includes various appetizers; steak, roast chicken, or *boeuf bourguignon;* and cheese or dessert. Typical French dishes 30-42F. Listen to next door's organ music if it's Mass time. Open daily noon-1:30pm and 7-9pm.

Sights and Entertainment

The picture-book 14th-century **château** stands aloof above the city's otherwise modest skyline. Charles V's brother, Louis I of Anjou, built this pre-Renaissance edifice as a countryside residence. A couple of centuries later, Protestants studied and prospered at the château, with its large stairwells and crenelated walls, until the revocation of the Edict of Nantes scattered them and left the château to be used as a prison.

The **Musée des Arts Décoratifs** (tel. 41 51 30 46), inside the château, has assembled a fascinating collection of medieval and Renaissance painting and sculpture, 15th- and 16th-century tapestries, and *faïencerie* (porcelain). The **Musée du Cheval** upstairs, with its bridles, bits, horseshoes, and horse skeletons from all over the world, will appeal to even those who aren't Ulmanesque fanatic horse lovers. Climb the wobbly staircase of the **Tour de Guët** for a view of the river and the island far below. (Château and museums open June 15-Sept. 15 9am-7pm; until 10pm Wed. and Sat. in July-Aug.; Sept. 16-Sept. 30 and April-June 14 9am-noon and 2-6pm; Oct.-March Wed.-Mon. 10am-noon and 2-5pm. Admission 28F, students 18F.) Within the château is also the separately run **Musée de la Figurine-Jouet,** a unique collection of 20,000 figurines displayed in the château's old gunpowder storage room. (Open July-Aug. 10am-6pm; April-June and Sept. 10am-noon and 2-6pm. Admission 10F.)

As much as for its château, Saumur is famous for its equestrian associations. One of the most notable, the 18th-century **Ecole de Cavalerie** now houses a **museum** of riding uniforms and paraphernalia (open Sept.-July Tues.-Thurs. and Sun. 9am-noon and 2-5pm, Sat. 2-5pm; free). The spectacular and elaborate *Cadre Noir* riding tradition is taught within the **Ecole Nationale d'Equitation,** whose palatial 19th-century grounds are 15 minutes from the center of town. The tradition demands unwavering obedience from the horses and irreproachable decorum from its riders, who, since 1825, have donned "black dress decorated with gold, and 'lampion' hats worn ready for battle," according to the dictates of M. Cordier, first master-in-chief. From April to September, the school offers 90-minute guided visits on Tuesday through Thursday and Saturday mornings, which include a peek at the *Cadre Noir* drill (visits begin from 9:30-10am; 30F, students 20F). On Monday through Friday afternoons and Friday mornings, one-hour tours of the facilities are given, but there are no performances (visits from 2:30-4pm, 9:30-11am Fri. morning; admission 20F, students 15F). Call the school or the tourist office to confirm this schedule, as it may change in 1993. In late July, the cavalry school shows off in the celebrated annual **Carrousel.** After two hours of jumping, dressage, and stunts, the spectacle degenerates into a three-hour motorcycle show and dusty tank parade. (Admission 50-150F.) Every week in July and August, various performances take place at **pl. de l'Hôtel de Ville.** The tourist office has all the related information.

Near the Ecole d'Equitation, the **Musée du Masque "Jules César"** has a fabulous collection of party and carnival masks from 1870, which it displays in a series of thematic scenes. (Open daily 9am-noon and 2-6pm; Oct. 16-March Sat.-Sun. 9am-noon and 2-6pm. Admission 25F, children 15F.) On a different note, the **Musée des Blindés** (tank museum) gathers 500 tanks, of which it regularly displays 45, accompanied by a video documentary (in French) and a whimsical or warmongering (choose your adjective) show of real French soldiers driving real French tanks like bumper cars. (Open daily 9am-noon and 2-6pm. Admission 20F.) Fifteen minutes southwest of the *centre ville* (direction: "Bagneux," "Cholet," or "Montreuil-Bellay"), the **Dolmen de Bagneux** is a megalithic monument of 15 stone slabs arranged on end and horizontally overhead to form what looks like a giant rectangular hut. (Open March 16-Sept. daily 9am-7pm; Oct.-Dec. 20 and Jan. 4-March 15 daily 9am-6pm. Admission 6F.)

Near Saumur

From its founding in the 12th century until the Revolution, the **Abbaye de Fontevraud** enjoyed fame as a monastic center for royalty and nobility. More than half of the governing abbesses were of royal blood. The guided tour leads through the cupola-capped abbey church past the remains of the tombs of the Plantagenets: Henry II, Eleanor of Aquitaine, Richard the Lion Hearted, and Isabelle of Angoulême, wife of King John of England. The original tombs were destroyed during the Revolution; afterward the British government repeatedly but unsuccessfully sought the transfer of the royal remains to Westminster. The Plantagenets, the French government maintains, were Dukes of Anjou first and Kings of England second. As elaborate as the tombs and church is the enormous octagonal kitchen in the twenty-chimneyed **Tour Evraud.** In July, the abbey also hosts the **Centre Culturel de l'Ouest de la France,** an institute that brings art and architecture exhibits, concerts, and plays to this historic setting. Call 41 51 73 52 for reservations and tickets (40-120F). (Abbey open daily 9am-7pm; Sept.-Oct. 9:30am-12:30pm and 2-6pm; Nov.-Easter 9:30am-12:30pm and 2-5:30pm, Easter-May 9:30am-12:30pm and 2-6:30pm.˙ Admission 25F, students 15F.) Three **buses** per day run from Saumur to Fontevraud. Take bus #16 (30min., 11F50).

Three km west of Saumur along the D751, the **Musée du Champignon** in **St-Hilaire-St-Florent** organizes tours through some of the mushroom *caves*. Originally mined for stone to build the nearby châteaux, the *caves* now grow some 70% of France's mushrooms in about 500km of underground tunnels. (Open mid-Feb. to mid-Nov. daily 10am-7pm. Admission and obligatory tour 28F, students 16F.) Take the local **bus** from pl. Roosevelt to St-Hilaire-St-Florent, and walk the 1km from the last stop.

Angers

From behind the massive, imposing walls of their château in Angers, the Dukes of Anjou ruled over the surrounding territory as well as an insignificant, piddly little island to the northwest of France, home to an odd tea-drinking tribe. The château and its walls remain stunningly well-preserved, but the rest of the Dukes' once verdant valley has been largely supplanted by acres of concrete. Through the concrete *centre ville*, however, forge several white-stone, café- and shop-lined streets, which link a remarkable posse of museums. Two noteworthy tapestries, crafted some 600 years apart, are especially worth seeing, offering a fascinating contrast between old and new that seems strangely appropriate to time-worn Angers.

Orientation and Practical Information

Angers lies roughly halfway between Tours and Nantes; frequent trains run to both cities. To reach the château, go straight out of the station onto rue de la Gare. Turn right at the pl. de la Visitation onto rue Talot. A left onto bd. du Roi-René leads to the château's doorstep (5-10min.). The **tourist office** (tel. 41 88 69 93) is across the street from the château at pl. Kennedy. The unruffled staff organizes trips to châteaux and **changes money** when banks are closed. (Open Mon.-Sat. 9am-7pm, Sun. 10:30am-6:30pm; Oct.-May Mon.-Sat. 9am-12:30pm and 2-6:30pm.) The **train station,** rue de la Gare (tel. 41 88 50 50), is the place to hop a train to Saumur (1/2hr., 37F); Tours (1hr., 72F); Orléans (2 1/4hr., 137F); and Paris-Austerlitz (2 3/4hr., 188F). The station **rents bikes** for 44F per day with a 1000F deposit. (Open daily 8am-7:40pm.) From the **bus station** at pl. de la République (tel. 41 88 59 25; open daily 7am-8pm), buses leave about twice per day Monday to Saturday for Saumur (39F) and Rennes (83F). **Local buses** cost 5F50. The **post office** is in the center of town at 1, rue Franklin-Roosevelt. **Poste Restante** mail should be addressed "Angers-Ralliement." Otherwise it will be carried off to the rue Bamako office, a half-hour walk south of town (open Mon.-Fri. 8am-7pm, Sat. 8am-noon). You can **change money** here, too. Angers's **postal code** is 49052.

Accommodations, Camping, and Food

Well folks, for something completely diffreent: accommodations can be difficult to secure in July and August. You can usually find a place at the *foyer,* though, as it is the largest youth hostel in France and soon to be the largest in Europe.

Foyer des Jeunes Travailleurs (HI), rue Darwin (tel. 41 72 00 20). Take bus #8 (direction: "Beaucouzé") to "CFA." If you miss the last bus at 7:20pm, you can take #1 to "Bull" until about 8pm; consult the bus maps posted at the stop up the stairs and across the street. Green hallways and spartan 2-and 3-bed rooms. The new annex will have more luxurious and more expensive rooms. 320 beds. Kitchen facilities. 44F, nonmembers 62F. Rents **mountain bikes** for 100F per day, 500F per week; 1000F deposit. Has good maps of the city. **Centre d'Accueil du Lac de Maine,** av. du Maine (tel. 41 22 32 10). Take bus #6 to "Accueil Lac de Maine." A lakeside setting and extensive sporting facilities justify the ride. Call ahead to make sure there's space; groups of screaming little kids might deter you in summer. Singles 97F. Doubles 69F per person. Quads 56F per person. Breakfast 16F50.

Hotel des Lices, 25, rue des Lices (tel. 41 87 44 10), near the cathedral and château. Welcoming owners present immaculate, small singles and doubles for 95F, with shower and toilet 155F. Reserve ahead in summer. Bistro downstairs has a home-cooked *plat du jour* for 35F, and sandwiches, salads, and omelettes for 18-38F.

La Coupe d'Or, 5, rue de la Gare (tel. 41 88 45 02). Small, comfy rooms with TV. One single at 85F. Singles and doubles 130F, with shower 150F. Showers 15F. Breakfast 18F.

Camping: Camping du Lac de Maine (tel. 41 73 05 03), next to the Centre d'Accueil, has a sandy lakeside beach. 57F per 3 people, tent and car. 8F50 per extra person. Open Feb.-Dec.

The pleasant pedestrian district around pl. Romain has many enticing sidewalk cafés, *pâtisseries,* and *boucheries,* but Angers's most remarkable inexpensive fare awaits at Les Halles, a covered **market** at rue Plantagenet behind the cathedral. (Open Tues.-Sat. 9am-7:30pm, Sun. 7am-1pm.) **Le Petit Mâchon,** 43, rue Bressigny, serves traditional French fare to a crowd of locals. (59F *menu.* Open Mon.-Fri. noon-1:50pm and 7:15-11pm, Sat. 7:15-11pm.) **Le Spirit Factory,** 14-16, rue Bressigny, attracts a younger crew to its fun, factory-like interior where the owner displays the Dr. Seuss-like machinery in which he brews the house beer, and the black-and-white stools have "udders" underneath. (Mussels any which way but loose, 39-59F. Beers 9F.)

Sights

A deep moat surrounding the thick gray walls of the **château** has been converted to a colorful garden and deer park. Most of the buildings on the inside were constructed during the 15th-century reign of Anjou's last and greatest duke, René le Bon, who not only commanded an empire that included Sicily, Piedmont, and Lorraine, but also found the time to pen several novels and dozens of poems. After René, the château slid into disrepute, eventually becoming a prison. The castle narrowly escaped destruction during the Wars of Religion, when Henry III ordered its demolition. (Fortunately, he died before his nefarious plans were carried out.) Stroll around the ramparts for a view of the gardens, the city, and the Maine River.

Angers's richest attraction, the 90m **Tapisseries de l'Apocalypse,** was woven from wool and gold thread between 1375 and 1380. Louis I, Duke of Anjou, ordered its creation in an effort to prove to his brother, Charles V, that he was his political and economic equal. Recognized as a masterpiece of European medieval art, the tapestry is noted for the consistent flamboyance of its multi-headed lions and serpents, the graphic dialogue attributed to its characters, and its unprecedented size. Renditions of popular fables frame its gory depictions of the plague. (Château open 9am-7pm; Sept. 16-April 9:30am-12:30pm and 2-6pm. Admission 31F, students 17F.)

The next stop on your tapestry tour of Angers is the **Musée Jean Lurçat,** 4, bd. Arago, across the river. Housed in a 12th-century hospital that typifies the Plantagenet style is *Le Chant du Monde* (The Song of the World, 1957-1966), a symbolic, mind-mangling tapestral journey through human destiny. The tapestry's three enormous walls glow with intense mustard yellows, fiery reds, sky blues, and earthy greens, all on a terrifying jet-black background. The museum unrolls a number of other 20th-century tapestries as well. (Open 9:30am-12:30pm and 2-7pm; Sept. 16-June 14 Tues.-Sun. 10am-noon and 2-6pm. Admission 15F.)

Add a new dimension to your museum visits with a stop at the **Musée David d'Angers,** 33bis, rue Toussaint, which displays the sculptor's studio works within a striking 13th-century church. The **Musée Pincé,** 32bis, rue Lenepveu, has gathered an eclectic collection of Greek, Roman, Egyptian, and Chinese artifacts, as well as some important Japanese prints including **The Wave** from Hokusai's Views of Mt. Fuji. The **Musée des Beaux Arts,** 10, rue du Musée, adjacent to the Musée David d'Angers, has a collection of European art dating from the end of the 15th century, including works from Ingres to Watteau and Fragonard to Corot. (All three museums open daily 9:30am-12:30pm and 2-7pm; Sept. 16-June 9 Tues.-Sun. 10am-noon and 2-6pm. Admission 10F each.)

Poitou-Charentes

Recounting images of Monet's impressionism—its stormy seas reflecting sunlight onto chalky white cliffs; its glorious beaches blessed by more sun than any other region of France except the Riviera; and its enigmatic marshland renowned for its unique seductive tranquility—Poitou-Charentes combines the splendor of Romanesque cathedrals with the pretense of summer resorts to produce an area unique for its diversity.

One way to differentiate the characters of this region is to partition it into its four *départements*. **Charente-Maritime** is probably the glitziest, a neon carnival of T-shirts, bumper stickers, and posters flickering with its logo. Tourists fan out from La Rochelle and the islands of Ile de Ré, Ile d'Aix, and Ile d'Oléron for a slice of the beaches. The industrial, architecturally rich city of Niort dominates **Deux-Sèvres** to the northeast, but the area is most renowned for the Marais Poitevin, whose romantic canals have earned the it the nickname "Green Venice." Farther east, **Vienne** is crowned by the jewel of Poitiers, Poitou-Charentes's intellectual and administrative capital, where the student body makes up one-quarter of the population. Nonetheless, the modest town has avoided mass commercialization, and it retains some of the finest Romanesque architecture this side of Burgundy. In contrast to these ancient wonders, Futuroscope, a park devoted to science and technology, looms just 10km from the historic capital. **Charente,** the *département* south of Vienne, is home to one of the region's finest cathedrals, the Cathédrale St-Pierre, in the rampart-fringed capital of Angoulême. But undeniably, this area's greatest renown stems from the thousands of acres of vines that produce grapes used in making cognac, the golden-brown brandy aged in storehouses along the Charente River.

With the acceptance of Christianity in the 4th century, Poitou-Charentes became entangled in modern Western history. In 732, Charles Martel, Duke of the Franks, rebuffed the Moorish attempt to claim the region. Beginning in the 11th century, thousands of reverent pilgrims passed through the region en route to Santiago de Compostela. To accommodate the onslaught, up sprang hundreds of hostels, hospitals, and Romanesque churches.

Possession of medieval Aquitaine was tossed from one side of the English Channel to the other at the behest of the beautiful, powerful, and shrewd Eleanor of Aquitaine. Troubadours' songs, legends, and historical documents record the remarkable life of this heiress, who first married France's St. Louis and then divorced him to marry young Henry Plantagenet, the new King of England. For more than a hundred years the region remained in English hands—long enough for the English to develop a taste for claret (their name for red Bordeaux wine). Aquitaine served as an English outpost during the Hundred Years War, before Joan of Arc indirectly secured it for France. In the 17th century, after the Wars of Religion, the Protestant Huguenots of the port city of La Rochelle sought English help against the machinations of the Catholic Cardinal Richelieu, who, in spite of an English fleet nearby, besieged the city and reduced it to obedience and a century of obscurity. The coastal cities revived only in the 18th century, when trade with Canadian colonies brought unparalleled wealth. Ties with French Canada still remain; the area has actively supported Québecois independence. Though the port industry remains important, tourism is now a major livelihood for the coastal towns and islands, and the beaches and campgrounds are packed all summer long.

Such a diverse region cooks up an equally diverse menu. Poitou-Charentes is probably most noted for its excellent *fruits de mer* (seafood). Its Marennes-Oléron oysters, slightly green from the *navicule bleue* seaweed in which they grow, make up half of France's oyster production. *Moules* (mussels) are often prepared with a wine, cream, and egg sauce known as a *mouclade*. Slightly inland in the Marais Poitevin, the *maraîchins* (inhabitants of the marshlands) prepare a rich *fricassée d'anguilles* (eels cooked in a red wine sauce). *Escargots,* known to the Charentais as *cagouilles* and to the Poitevins as *lumas,* are prepared either with a meat and spice stuffing *à la Saintongeaise* or with a red wine sauce *aux lumas.* One quarter of France's lamb output *(agneau)* comes from the eastern part of Poitou and is usually grilled with herbs. The region's cheese is *chabichou,* a tangy goat cheese often served warm on a bed of lettuce. The Haut-Poitou region produces light red, white, and very young rosés. Charente whites, known as *blanc marine,* are dry, light, and also young. Of course, the most prized nectar of the region is *cognac,* which may age anywhere from two to 180 years. *Pineau des Charentes,* a more affordable mixture of cognac and grape or pear juice, makes a sublimely sweet *apéritif.* Desserts are not acclaimed in Poitou-Charentes though *clafoutis* (a cherry tart) and *marguerites* (chocolate candies) figure among the few.

Trains in Poitou-Charentes run frequently to all major towns, and **bus** transport fills in the few gaps. Hills rise as you head eastward, while western coastal lands and islands are flat and lovely for biking. You may want to renounce terrestrial transport and join a cruise down one of the region's main rivers, the Clain or the Charente.

Poitiers

In the mid-1900s, industrial and commercial institutions interested in establishing a base in Poitiers had to settle for the outskirts of town because the old town's perch on a hill over the Clain and Boivre Rivers could not accommodate large-scale commerce. As a result, Poitiers remains an unusually calm, residential city whose *zone industrielle* sprawls outward from the base of the hill. Inhabited since the Bronze Age, recent excavations have unearthed the remains of a fortress from this era, as well as vestiges of a theater and kilns from Roman times. Built shortly after the end of Roman occupation, the 4th-century Baptitère St-Jean in the *vieille ville* stands as one of the oldest extant Christian edifices in France. From the 10th to the 15th century, the powerful counts of Poitou and Dukes of Aquitaine ruled the expanding city and erected the impressive Palais de Justice and the many remarkable churches that still dot the city. More recently, the arrival of a large Michelin factory in 1972 spurred further economic and cultural growth in this capital of Poitou. Home to one of France's oldest universities, established by Charles VII in 1432, Poitiers today claims that one-quarter of its 80,000 residents are students.

Orientation and Practical Information

Poitiers, 350km southwest of Paris, fits snugly between train tracks to the west and a semi-circular stretch of the River Clain to the east. The city's street life pulses around the stores and cafés near **pl. Maréchal Leclerc** and **pl. Charles de Gaulle,** three blocks north. Buses run frequently from the stop across the street from the train station to the *hôtel de ville* in the center of town; otherwise, it's a ten-minute hike. To get to the tourist office from the train station, climb bd. Solférino straight from the station as it curves uphill to the left. Ascend the long staircase below the ramparts to the right, and take rue Arthur Ranc past the post office. Bear left onto rue H. Petonnet, which becomes rue G. Hulin, turn right onto rue E. Grimaud, and make the second right onto rue des Grandes Ecoles; the tourist office is immediately on the right.

Tourist Office: 8, rue des Grandes Ecoles (tel. 49 41 21 24). Good free maps and lists of hotels and restaurants. Lots of information on the Poitou-Charentes region. Interesting guided tours in July and Aug. vary daily (10am and 3pm; 25F, under 25 15F). Will find rooms in town (10F fee) or in the region (20F). Open Mon.-Sat. 9am-7pm, Sept.-June Mon.-Sat. 9am-noon and 1:30-6pm. **Comité du Département Regional,** 15, rue Carnot (tel. 49 41 58 22), near pl. Maréchal Leclerc. Start at the tourist office above, but this office also stocks excellent regional information. Open Mon.-Fri. 9am-noon and 2-5pm.

Post Office: 16, rue Arthur Ranc (tel. 49 01 83 80). **Telephones** and **currency exchange.** Open Mon.-Fri. 8:30am-7pm, Sat. 8:30am-noon. **Postal Code: 86000.**

Trains: bd. du Grand Cerf (tel. 49 58 50 50; for reservations 49 63 60 60). TGV to Paris (14 per day, 1 1/2hr., 192F plus 32F reservation), and Bordeaux (8 per day, 1 3/4hr., 155F plus 16F reservation). Other trains to: la Rochelle (7 per day, 2hr., 98F); Paris (4 per day, 2 1/2hr., 192F); Bordeaux (6 per day, 2hr., 155F). Information office open Mon.-Sat. 9am-7pm.

Public Transportation: 14 **STP** bus lines crisscross the city; grab the timetable at the tourist office. Few lines operate on Sun. Ticket valid for 1hr. 7F.

Bike Rental: Cyclamen, 49, rue Arsène Orillard (tel. 49 88 13 25). Ten-speeds 45F per day, 165F per week. *Sacoches* (bike bags) 9F per day, 31F per week. Deposit 500F or passport. Open Tues.-Sat. 8:30am-12:30pm and 3-7pm.

Youth Information: Centre d'Information Jeunesse (CIJ), 64, rue Gambetta (tel. 49 88 64 37), near the *hôtel de ville* on a pedestrian street. A gold mine of hints on places to stay, cultural activities, sports, and employment—even a ride board. Free maps. *Carte Jeune* (70F) gives discounts everywhere. Open Mon.-Fri. 10am-7pm, Sat. 10am-noon and 2-6pm.

Laundromat: rue de René Descartes Philosophe, at pl. de la Liberté. I stink, therefore I am (in need of clean clothes). Wash 17F, dry 2F per 4min. Soap 2F. Takes 10F, 5F and 1F coins. Open Mon.-Sat. 8am-6pm. Also at 2bis, rue de la Tranchée. Wash 17F, dry 2F per 5min. Soap 1F. Open daily 9am-7pm.

Hospital: 15, rue Hôtel Dieu (tel. 49 88 02 10).

Medical Assistance: Ambulance Poudat, tel. 49 55 99 66.

Police: 38, rue de la Marne (tel. 49 60 60 00). **Emergency:** tel. 17.

Accommodations and Camping

The hostel and campgrounds are far from the center of town, but it shouldn't be hard to find a reasonable hotel downtown. Those around the train station are fine. It's best to call ahead in July and August.

Auberge de Jeunesse (HI), 17, rue de la Jeunesse (tel. 49 58 03 05), 3km from the station. Take bus #3 from the station (direction "Pierre Loti") to "Cap Sud" (Mon.-Sat. every 1/2hr. until 7:50pm, 7F), or turn right at the station and walk along bd. du Pont Achard to av. de la Libération. Then take the right-hand fork to rue B. Pascal. Rue de la Jeunesse is on the right (35min.). Large building with spotless showers, toilets, and 3-bed rooms with great mattresses. Frequent school groups a slight drawback. Nice lawn out back. Reception open Mon.-Sat. 8-10am, noon-2pm, and 7-11pm; Sun. 8-10am and 7-11pm. Lockout 10am-6pm. Curfew 11pm. 58F, nonmembers 77F. Breakfast 17F. Fantastic lunch or dinner 43F. Sheets included.

Hôtel Jules Ferry, 27, rue Jules Ferry (tel. 49 37 80 14), near Eglise St-Hilaire on a quiet, residential street. From the station, turn right along bd. du pont Achand and climb the stairs to the left, across from the pont. Turn right onto rue Jules Ferry at the top. Kind owners and clean, comfortable rooms. Singles and doubles 120F, with shower 150F. Showers 12F. Breakfast 24F. Closed Sun. 1-7:30pm.

L'Alsace Lorraine, 6, rue du Petit Bonneveau (tel. 49 41 25 83), close to pl. Maréchal Leclerc. Spacious, quiet rooms. Singles and doubles 100-105F, with shower 155-165F. Showers 18F. Breakfast 18F. Occasionally closed on Sun.; call ahead.

Le Printania, 141, bd. du Grand Cerf (tel. 49 58 20 15), across from the station. Large, conveniently located establishment. Slightly dim and noisy, but clean. Singles and doubles 95-110F, with shower 120F, with TV and bathroom 150F. Breakfast 22F, in bed 26F.

Camping: Le Porteau (tel. 49 41 44 88), on a hill 2km out of town. Take bus #7 (direction "Centre de Gros") and ask to be dropped off *"devant le terrain"* (in front of the field). Clean bathrooms, showers, and a patch of grass hungry for a tent. 5F per person, 2F50 per site, 2F50 per car. Electricity 4F. Open July-Aug. **Camping St-Benoît,** rte. de Passelourdin (tel. 49 88 48 55), 5km from Poitiers. Take bus #2 from the train station, transfer to bus #10, and get off at "St-Benoît." 5F15 per adult, 2F45 per site, 2F45 per car. Open April-Sept.

Food

Most hotel bars post good four-course *menus* for around 55F. Avoid the overpriced cafés on pl. Maréchal Leclerc; you need only wander a block or two to find better values. Few places are open on Sunday. There is a **market** at **Les Halles** on pl. Charles de Gaulle (open Mon.-Sat. 7am-6pm, Sun. 7:30-1pm). On Saturday, the market expands beyond your wildest dreams. **Monoprix,** on rue des Cordeliers at rue du Marché Notre Dame, stocks anchovies, underwear, and other staples. (Open Mon.-Sat. 9:15am-7:15pm.) **Santé et Vie,** 68, rue de la Cathédrale, sells life-prolonging legumes and other healthful produce. (Open Tues.-Sun. 9am-12:30pm and 2:45-7pm.)

La Pergola, 71, rue Théophraste Renaudot (tel. 49 41 09 30). 90F buys you a ticket to indulge in this Garden of Eden, where temptation thrives among the roses and ivy-covered walls. Astounding prices include *menus* at 200F, but the ambrosial 90F *menu* includes smoked fish with lime juice, leg of lamb cooked with thyme, and strawberries in Chinon wine. Attentive waiters will help you choose. Attire is relatively casual. Reservations advisable on weekends. Open Mon.-Fri. noon-2pm and 7-10:30pm, Sat. 7-10:30pm.

Le Roy d'Ys, 51, rue de la Cathédrale. A noble *crêperie* with gallant *galettes* (9-40F) and imperial service. If you like fungus, try the *pavé nantais* (32F), filled with egg, ham, cheese, mushrooms, and parsley. Killer peach melba 30F. Open Mon.-Sat. noon-2pm and 7pm-midnight.

Restaurant Claude Lafond, 7-9, rue des Vieilles Boucherie, near the Palais de Justice. Primarily a *patissier* and *traiteur,* but also elegant French lunches. Restrain yourself as you pass the mouth-watering display of pastries and meat dishes to get to the restaurant. Outdoor setting, too. Duck, crab, and other seafood *terrines* 20-30F; salads 24-36F; omelettes 22-30F. Fish and meat entrees 32-58F. Open Tues.-Sat. 11:30am-2pm; Sept.-June Mon.-Sat. 11:30am-2pm. *Patisserie* open 9am-7:30pm.

Le Poitevin, 76, rue Carnot. Regional cuisine worth busting your budget for. Finish the 78F *menu* and the muscular staff will roll you out the door. Open Mon.-Sat. noon-2pm and 7-10pm.

Cafétéria Flunch, 2, rue de Petit Bonneveau at rue Carnot, 1 block south of the *hôtel de ville.* Boulder-sized portions at rock-bottom prices at Cap'n Flunch. Tasty fish or steak with serve-your-self vegetables 20-30F. Salads 6-15F. Open daily 11am-10pm. Only full meals available 11am-2:30pm and 8-10pm.

Sights and Entertainment

Follow rue Gambetta away from the jostling crowds of the *centre ville* and step into eccentric 12th-century **Notre-Dame-la-Grande.** The battered façade is undergoing a much-needed three-year restoration, but the cool interior is supported by attractive columns painted in warm, earthy tones depicting the stories of the Annunciation, the Visitation, the Nativity, and Joseph's meditation. (Open daily 7:15am-7pm.)

Constructed on the orders of Eleanor and Henry Plantagenet, the 12th-century **Cathédral St-Pierre,** a few blocks down rue de la Cathédrale, imposes and impresses with its sheer size and austere horizontal lines. Above the central door, irreverent pigeons hop from heaven to hell and back during the Last Judgment. (Open daily 8am-7pm.)

West of the Cathédrale St-Pierre, parts of the Mediterranean **Baptistère St-Jean** date from the 4th century, making it the oldest existing Christian structure in France. The octagonal font and the floor around it date from this period, and recent excavations have uncovered even older aqueducts. The remarkably sturdy stone-and-brick structure houses carved sarcophagi and friezes from the Roman and early Christian eras. (Open daily 10:30am-12:30pm and 3-6pm; Sept.-Oct. and April-June Wed.-Mon. 10:30am-12:30pm and 3-6pm; Nov-March Wed.-Mon. 2:30-4:30pm. Admission 4F.)

Next to the baptistery, the wonderful **Musée Ste-Croix** contains innumerable relics from Poitiers's Bronze Age and Roman settlements. (Open Mon. and Wed.-Fri. 10am-noon and 1-6pm, Sat.-Sun. 10am-noon and 2-6pm. Free.)

Across the street, the **Devenir Espace Pierre Mendès France,** at 1, pl. de la Cathédrale (tel. 49 41 56 25), leaps through the centuries with its exhibits on scientific, technological, and industrial culture throughout the modern world. Using local companies and businesses as models, the exhibits discuss medicine, environment, communication, sound, and other issues concerning modern culture. The 16 TV screens project broadcasts (in several languages through headsets) addressing history, news, cartoons, and MTV. (Open Tues.-Fri. 10am-7pm, Sat.-Sun. 2-7pm. Admission 20F, students 15F.)

Over the river and back to the past, the **Hypogée Martyrium,** holds the remains of 72 Christian martyrs. Topped by a Gallo-Roman chapel, the 7th-century underground church shelters rare Merovingian sculptures. A peaceful, pine-covered ancient cemetery rests outside. Getting to the Hypogée requires quite a hike. Cross the mossy river, turn left after the Pont Neuf onto bd. Coligny, and follow it to the top toward the golden statue of the Virgin. Turn right at the top of the hill and follow the road as it weaves to the Hypogée. Bus #5 (direction "St-Eloi") to the "Gendarmerie" stop will save you the

15-minute walk. (Hypogée open Wed.-Mon. 10am-noon and 2-6pm; Oct.-March 2-4pm. Free, but expect to tip the guide a few francs.) The **Eglise Montierneuf** and **Eglise St-Hilaire,** on the northern and southern ends of town, respectively, are further examples of Poitiers' many Romanesque churches. While Montierneuf has a light apse floating on tiny flying buttresses, St-Hilaire is lower to the ground and has a wide, flat-domed space.

Throughout July and August, rock, opera, piano, jazz, and fireworks thunder throughout the various squares and courtyards of the town during **Poitiers L'Eté.** Concerts usually begin at 9pm on selected evenings, and most are free. Call the tourist office for more information. During the first two weeks of May, the town hosts **Le Printemps Musical de Poitiers** (tel. 49 41 58 94), a harmonic convergence of concerts, exhibits, and debates (tickets 30-60F). The concert series **Rencontres Musicales de Poitiers** features mostly classical works in biweekly concerts from late October through late April. (Tickets 55F, under 26 38F; available at the kiosk in pl. Maréchal Leclerc.) *L'Affiche Hebdo*, available at the tourist office, lists all local cultural events. Another list includes nightclubs and discotheques.

Near Poitiers

Futuroscope, a science-oriented amusement park with one foot well through the door of the 21st century, looms 10km north of Poitiers. No playground for squealing kiddies, this high-tech Valhalla, Europe's first techno-wonderland boasts "Kinemax" (the largest flat screen in Europe), "Showscan" (which produces a staggeringly realistic image at 60 frames per second, compared to the standard 24), the "Dynamic Simulator" (with moving seats, synchronized with the action on the screen), and the 360-degree Global Image. There is also a park exclusively for children, an animated show, and an amphitheater on the banks of an artificial lake. You can get there on bus #16 (direction: "Rond Point"), or take the Innobus from the Poitiers train station. (Innobus departures 9:15am, 10:15am, and 12:15pm; returns 4:30pm, 6pm, and 7:15pm. 30F round-trip.) (Park open daily July-Aug. 9am-7pm; Sept. and April-June 9:30am-6:30pm; Oct.-Nov. 9am-6pm. Admission 105F, children 80F.)

About 20km east of Poitiers, the ruins of four different fortified castles shape a formidable silhouette above the stone village of **Chauvigny.** Inside the medieval walls that clench the hilltop site, the Romanesque **Eglise St-Pierre** is notable for its intricate sculpture. **Abbaye St-Savin-sur-Gartempe,** 10km to the east, displays the finest Romanesque frescoes in France. Biblical scenes ornament the walls with impressive color and detail. Guided tours are given in July and August; call the tourist office at 49 46 39 01 or the mayor's office at 49 46 30 21 for information. **Les Rapides du Poitou** (tel. 49 46 27 45) launches three or four daily buses to Chauvigny (45min., 25F) and St-Savin (1hr., 36F). Some find the hitch along N151 fairly easy. In Chauvigny, the riverside **Hôtel du Chalet Fleuri** (tel. 49 46 31 12) rents singles from 70F, doubles 90-160F.

Halfway to Angoulême on the D1, the town of **Civray** claims the **Eglise St-Nicholas,** one of the finest Romanesque churches in France. The sculptural work on its classically ordered western façade is remarkable. After seeing the church, there's little to do but fish in the Charente River or camp at **Les Coteaux.** (Call 49 87 17 24 or the mayor's office at 49 87 00 49. Open Easter-Oct. 15.) **Les Rapides du Poitou** sends three buses daily from Poitiers to Civray (1hr., 38F).

Les Sables d'Olonne

Bathing suit boutiques and ice-cream stands outnumber churches and museums ten-to-one, there's not a château in sight, and the alleged local folk tradition survives only in postcards and a few farm houses. But if sun, sport, and surf sound sweet, don't skip Les Sables d'Olonne, where silky smooth sand sweeps along the Vendée coast, and greased-up surfers roll in with the waves. Although the advancing phalanx of high rises and less orderly regiments of sunbathers detract from Les Sables's beauty, the beach in town remains clean and pleasant. **Plage de Tanchet,** farther east near the lake campground, is the first beach in a chain along the east coast. To the northwest lies the **Forêt d'Olonne** reserve, where huge dunes tumble from dry woodlands to the sea.

For ten months of the year, Les Sables rattles along like any other placid, unpretentious town with a brisk fishing port and just enough merchants to sustain the local community. But come July and August, the community explodes into a fab beach resort. If disaster strikes and it rains, spend the day with the cars and motorcycles in the **Musée Automobile de Vendée** (tel. 51 22 05 81), 8km from town on route de Talmont. Old automobile posters line the large hall that displays 140 mechanized vehicles dating from 1885 to the 1960s, all still operational. (Open March 15-Oct. 9:30am-noon and 2-7pm. Admission 30F, children 15F). The **Musée de l'Abbaye Sainte-Croix** (tel. 51 32 01 16), on rue de Verdun, juxtaposes a collection of modern art with a sprinkling of local furniture and painting, all housed in a 17th-century abbey. (Open June 15-Sept. daily 10am-noon and 2:30-6:30pm; Nov. 2-June 14 Tues.-Sun. 2:30-5:30pm. Admission 20F, children 10F. Free Wed.)

Orientation and Practical Information

To get to the center of town from the train station, turn right and walk alongside the station. Turn right onto av. de Gaulle and take this to pl. de la Liberté. Walk past the park on your right to arrive at small pl. du Poilu de France (with a fountain in its center). From here, rue du Général Leclerc, the first street to the right, leads to the tourist office and the port. From the pl. du Poilu de France, you can also take rue de l'Hôtel de Ville, which marks the beginning of the commercial pedestrian district, and then make a left onto rue Bisson to get to **Eglise Notre-Dame de Bon Port,** Les Sables's token church, begun under Richelieu's order in 1622. To get to the beach and the boardwalk (promenade Georges Clemenceau), follow rue Travot from pl. de la Liberté.

Tourist Office: rue du Maréchal Leclerc (tel. 51 32 03 28). Remarkably patient staff will outfit you with a map and list of hotels. Also has a **ride-finding** service and can help find **babysitters** for the young'uns. Open Mon.-Sat. 9am-12:15pm and 2-6:30pm, Sun. 10am-noon and 2-4:30pm; Sept.-June Mon.-Fri. 9am-12:15pm and 2-6:30pm, Sat. 9am-noon and 2-5:30pm, Sun. 10am-noon.

Post Office: rue Nicot, off av. du Général de Gaulle. **Currency Exchange.** Open Mon.-Fri. 8:30am-6pm, Sat. 8:30am-noon. **Postal Code:** 85100.

Trains: av. Général de Gaulle (tel. 40 08 60 60). At least 8 trains per day to La Rochelle (2hr., 91F) via La Roche-sur-Yon (35F). Also to Nantes (6-8 per day, 1 1/2hr., 75F) and Paris (5-7 per day, 5hr., 250F). All trains to Paris except 1 per day connect to TGVs and require a 32F or 80F reservation. Information office open daily 9am-noon and 2-7pm.

Buses: To the left of the train station. **Sovetours** (tel. 51 95 18 71). To La Rochelle (1 per day, 2hr., 73F) and Nantes (2 per day, 2hr., 62F). Office open Mon.-Fri. 8:30am-12:30pm and 2:30-6:30pm, Sat. 9-11:30am. **CTA** (tel. 40 47 62 70). Line #8 to Nantes (4-6 per day, 3 1/2hr., 110F) via all the towns with ferry departures to Ile d'Yeu.

Bike and Moped Rental: Le Cyclotron, 66, promenade Georges Clemenceau (tel. 51 32 64 15). 10-speeds 35F per 1/2-day, 40F per day, 198F per week, deposit 600F. Beat-up mopeds from 90F per 1/2-day, 120F per day, deposit 600F. Helmet included. You can also rent brightly-colored pedecabs that seat 2-8 people for 50-135F per hour. Deposit 50F. Open July-Aug. daily 9am-midnight (bikes due back at 7pm); April-June 10am-noon and 2-7pm. The **train station** has only 6 bikes. 40F per 1/2-day, 50F per day, deposit 500F.

Windsurfer and Sailboat Rental: Océano Sports, 2bis, bd. Franklin Roosevelt, a block from the beach (tel. 51 21 01 67). Rents windsurfers (200F per day, 3000F deposit) and sailboats (1200-2000F for 5 days, 1000 deposit). Open May-Aug. 10am-12:30pm and 2:30-7pm.

Laundromat: 33, bd. Castelnau. Wash 20F, dry 2F per 5 min. Takes 10F and 2F coins. Open 7am-10pm.

Hospital: 75, av. d'Aquitaine (tel. 51 21 85 85).

Medical Assistance: Ambulance, tel. 51 95 32 52 or 51 32 49 09.

Police: rue de Verdun (tel. 51 21 14 43). **Emergency:** tel. 17.

Accommodations, Camping, and Food

Les Sables is swamped with people in July and August. By the beginning of June, most hotels are booked for the summer. If you know when you want to stay, try to reserve a hotel room by February or March. Reserve a bed at the hostel with one night's payment sent well in advance. Finding a room shouldn't be difficult from October through May, and with good reason; there are better ways to spend the off-season.

Auberge de Jeunesse (HI), rue du Sémaphore (tel. 51 95 76 21), in neighboring La Chaume. Take the #1 or #2 bus from pl. de la Liberté (direction: "Côte Sauvage," 1 per hr. until 6:30pm, 6F), get off at "Armandeche," and walk 2min. up rue du Sémaphore. After 6:30pm, take *La Chaumoise,* a puny shuttle boat that leaves from the quai on the port and runs to La Chaume (every 2min. until midnight). From the landing point, make a left onto promenade Georges V and then a right onto rue du Roi Albert 1*er,* which becomes rue du Sémaphore. (15-20min.). The hostel will be on the right. Small and sandy with a fantastic view of the rocky Côte Sauvage and a mellow atmosphere. Great kitchen facilities. Scalding outdoor showers. Reception open 9-11am and 5-10pm. 32 beds outside under a tent 36F. 4- and 10-bunk dorms. Members only. 45F per person. Open April-Sept.

Hôtel le Merle Blanc, 59, av. Aristide Briand (tel. 51 32 00 35). Proximity to beach and supermarket justifies the 25-min. hike from the station. Turn left onto promenade Georges Clemenceau and follow it toward the end of the beach where it becomes promenade G. Godet. Av. Aristide Briand forks to the left of the Utile Supermarket. Bus #4 runs from pl. de la République to the "Ampère" stop just down the street from the hotel (every 1/2-hr., 6F). Spotless, airy rooms, large garden filled with pine trees, and darn cordial owners. Singles 85F. Doubles 145F, with shower 185. Triples with shower 190F. Showers 8F. Breakfast 23F. Open April-Sept.

L'Artimon, 34bis, rue des Corderies (tel. 51 95 12 34), on a small, quiet street between rue Nationale and cours Blossac, about 10min. from the station. Lively and loquacious elderly lady makes your stay as happy as could be. No-nonsense, impeccable rooms. Reception open 8am-8pm. July-Aug: singles 168F, with shower 228F. Doubles 190F, with shower 250F. June and Sept: singles 130F, with shower 160F. Doubles 152F, with shower 182F. Breakfast included. Open June-Sept.

Le Majestic 24, quai Guiné (tel. 51 32 09 71), near the beaches and center of town, facing the fishing port. Reception requires 1/2-pension (breakfast and lunch or dinner) for stays in July and Aug. of more than one night. Light, funky-colored rooms. Doubles 120F, with shower 135F. With 1/2-pension, singles 240F. Doubles 180F per person. Breakfast 23F.

Camping: Dozens of sites in and around Les Sables—camp your heart out. The most convenient are always booked: **Les Dunes** (tel. 51 32 31 21), L'Aubraie-La Chaume, on top of a dune. 45F per 2 people with tent and car; hot showers included. Open June 15-Sept. 15. No reservations accepted. **Les Roses** (tel. 51 95 10 42), centrally located on rue des Roses. Four stars and a long waiting list, so reserve early. 73-81F for the same things at Les Dunes, but here they'll throw in a dip in the pool. Open April-Oct. 15. The tourist office has a list of many more.

The promenades and quais of Les Sables have their catch of seafood restaurants, each as charming and expensive as the next. For lunch, a good plan is to head for **Les Halles,** a picknicker's paradise filled with *charcuteries, crémeries,* and fruit stands. (Open Mon.-Sat. 8am-1pm. Big market days Wed. and Sat. 7am-1pm.) **Monoprix,** 15, rue Hôtel de Ville, will also fill your picnic basket (open Mon.-Sat. 9am-12:30pm and 2:15-7:30pm, Sun. 10am-12:30pm). If it's seeing and being seen that floats your boat, check out **La Salsa: Chez Carmine,** 20, quai Guiné. Even if you can't afford the somewhat elevated prices at this egregiously flamboyant palace of culture, you might just enjoy being near the photos of glam chops like Madonna and Michael Jackson who frequent Carmine. Sit in their seats and inhale their glory! Pizzas 50-65F, *paella* 75F, seafood platter 89F. (Open daily for lunch and dinner.) Next door a young and happily anonymous crowd dines at **L'Attiche,** where you can listen to a selection of jazz and rock-and-roll while savoring a 65F *menu* of mussels *maranière,* followed by a fish or steak dish and a tasty dessert. (Open April-Sept. Wed-Sun. noon-2pm and 7-10:30pm, Tues. 7-10:30pm.) One street inland, and somewhat away from the touristy commotion on the quai, **Le Théâtre,** 20, bd. Roosevelt, offers 52F, 75F, and 100F *menus* that include the daily catch of grilled sardines or salmon. (Open July-Aug. daily noon-2pm and 7-10pm; Feb. 15-June and Sept.-Oct. Thurs.-Mon. noon-2pm and 7-10pm, Tues. noon-2pm.) **Restaurant Rosemonde,** 10, promenade George V in La Chaume (tel. 51 95 25 81), is convenient to the hostel (take the *La Chaumoise* shuttle boat from quai

Guiné). It serves a filling three-course 62F *menu*, huge portions of mussels (36F) and other local platters. (Open 11:30am-2:30pm and 6:30-10:30pm.)

Islands

The islands scattered off the Poitevin coast from Les Sables d'Olonne to Royan make excellent daytrips from the mainland. Although all four islands endure their share of summer visitors, transportation difficulties and scarce accommodations guarantee that fewer sunbathers clog their beaches than those near Les Sables or La Rochelle. Transportation to and among these islands is handled by innumerable ferry lines and three different bus lines: **Océcars** (tel. 46 41 20 40), **CTA** (tel. 51 68 51 98), and **Aunis et Saintonge (AS)** (tel. 46 93 21 41).

Ile d'Yeu

Reclusive monks christened this glorious mound of earth *Ile Dieu* (God's Island) in the 9th century. Although in recent years the seclusion has been commercialized, the beauty that inspired the monks remains. This tiny island of farms and hedges ringed by a splintered coast busies itself with fishing most of the year and endures tourists only in summer. The island even boasts its own microclimate; one coast might be sunny when the opposite is soaked with rain.

The only way to get to the wild, uninhabited, most interesting nooks of the island is on bike or foot. Roads are bumpy, but the hundreds of bikes for rent in **Port-Joinville**, where the ferry docks, are built for the pebbles. Several stores on the quai rent bikes for 35F per half-day and 45F per day. Grab a map at the **tourist office** (tel. 51 59 32 58) on pl. du Marché, just one street inland from the port. (Open Mon.-Sat. 10am-12:30pm and 3-6:30pm.)

Pedal across the island to the **Côte Sauvage.** On the way, zig-zag past the **Grand Phare,** a huge lighthouse that you can climb to revel in the tacitly eloquent view of the turquoise sea. Once at the coast, roll along merrily to the **Pointe du Châtelet,** a tiny peninsula whose crags and enormous, mysterious cross bear the battering winds and the spattering ocean. A bit farther along to the left, the ruined **Vieux Château,** about 3.5km south of Port-Joinville, hangs precariously on rocks in the port. Occupied in turn by Roman, English, and Spanish troops, the château was originally built in the 9th and 10th centuries by monks who must now turn anxiously in their graves at the thought of the **nudist beach** nearby. One km away, **Port de la Meule** is as colorful as a brand-new box of Crayolas with its flamboyant polychromatic shutters and a rainbow of boats bobbing in the harbor. Above the town, the simple white silhouette of 16th-century **Notre Dame de Bonne Nouvelle** lends an austere dignity to the tortuous coast. Heading east from Port de la Meule, the soft sand beaches of **L'Anse des Vieilles,** are in a cove named not after old women but for a local species of fish called *vieilles*. Northwest of Les Vieilles stands **St-Sauveur,** the island's oldest church, whose interior is set aflame by psychedelic stained-glass windows.

Ile d'Yeu remains relatively isolated. Many ferries make the crossing, but problematic bus connections ensure that only the most determined travelers ever reach the island. Ferries to the island leave from Fromentine, St-Gilles-Croix-de-Vie, and Noirmoutier. **Fromentine** is accessible by bus from Nantes and Les Sables d'Olonne (4 per day, 60F). Three or four ferries per day make the trip to Ile d'Yeu. Make reservations and arrive at the port 30 minutes before departure time; call 51 68 52 32 for information. **St-Gilles** is accessible by train from Nantes (5 per day, 57F) or La Roche-Sur-Yon (2 per day, 39F50) and by **CTA** bus (tel. 40 46 14 00. 3-4 per day, 1 3/4hr., 60F). From Les Sables d'Olonne, St-Gilles can also be reached by CTA bus (3-4 per day, 45min., 35F). Ask the driver to drop you at the *embarcadère*. From May through September, **Garcie-Ferrande** (tel. 51 55 45 42) and **Navix Vedettes** (tel. 51 54 15 15) ferries from St-Gilles make 3-14 round-trip sailings per week to Ile d'Yeu. (Garcie-Ferrande 1 1/2hr., 125F, under 12 85F; Navix Vedettes 50min., 175F under 17 125F). St-Gilles's **tourist office**, bd. de l'Egalité (tel. 51 55 03 66), 500m east of the port, can help you with accommodations and iron out the details of your trip. From **Noirmoutier,** accessible by bus from Les Sables (2hr. 15min., 70F), 2 to 4 Navix Vedette ferries make the 45-minute trip between the port and Ile d'Yeu daily (round-trip 175F, under 17 125F). Call 51 39 00 00 for information and reservations.

Hôtel de l'Escale, 14, rue de la Croix du Port (tel. 51 58 50 28), just beyond the harbor in Port-Joinville, rents plain, clean rooms. (Reception open 8am-noon and after 7pm. Doubles with shower 140F. 4-person rooms 240F. Breakfast 20F. Reserve for July-Aug.) A **municipal campground** (tel. 51 58 34 20) is at Pointe de Gilberge, about 1km from the ferry landing and close to the beaches. (6F50 per adult, 9F70 per site, 9F70 per car.) Try the delicious local seafood at **La Burette,** rue du Petit Moulin, just off the rue de la Croix du Port; its three-course 68F *menu* includes the catch of the day. (Salads from 28F. Seafood dishes 40-75F. Mussels 37F.) Otherwise, food is egregiously expensive, so buy supplies on the mainland before departing. Port-Joinville has a **supermarket** on rue de Calypso, five minutes from the port. Take a left from the port and a right onto rue de Calypso (the first light; open Mon.-Sat. 8:45am-12:45pm and 3:30-7:30pm, Sun. 9:30am-12:15pm).

Ile de Ré

Ile de Ré, dubbed *"Ré La Blanche"* for its soft sand beaches and white-washed houses, has long attracted the elegant and opulent elements in French society. Still, Ré is a welcoming rather than exclusive place, which nourishes a diversity of pine forests, golden fields, and Mediterranean vegetation. With small coastal villages connected to each other by scenic roadways and bike paths, the island makes a pleasant daytrip. Although a drive across the toll bridge from La Pallice costs an obscene 110F per car (round-trip), you can hike or bus across the bridge to reach the island's beautiful *marais salants* (salt flats), bird sanctuaries, and charming fishing ports.

Ré is easily accessible by bus from La Rochelle, but you might consider **Citram** (tel. 46 99 01 36) bus tours from Rochefort or **Interîles** (tel. 46 50 51 88) bus and boat service to Sablanceaux. **Rébus** (tel. 46 09 20 15) rolls daily from the train station in La Rochelle to Sablanceaux (15 per day, 25min., 9F), the first town on the island just past the bridge; St-Martin (7 per day, 1hr., 23F), the capital and administrative center; and Les Portes (9 per day, 1 1/2hr., 43F), at the tip of the island. All buses stop in intermediate towns, so once you're on the island, getting around won't be a problem. Flat terrain makes biking an excellent option.

Sun seekers who enjoy beach company should stop at **Sablanceaux,** where colossal beaches curve around the tip of the island. For those who prefer to be left alone with the rays **Plage de la Conche des Baleines,** at the other tip of the island, is less populated with people and more populated with pine-covered dunes on the fringes. Terrific beaches sweep along the entire western coast of the island.

Monument seekers should continue to **St-Martin,** with its fortified port built by Vauban and the citadel still serving as a state prison. The 15th- to 17th-century Renaissance gallery of the **Hôtel Clerjotte,** av. Victor-Bouthilier, houses the **Musée Naval et E-Cognacq,** filled with ship models and paintings tracing the island's maritime history, as well as pottery and furniture depicting the island's folklore. (Open Wed.-Sun. 10am-noon and 3-6pm.) Bikers and hikers find their haven around **Ars** and **Les Portes,** where tiny roads snake through miles of salt flats and a bird sanctuary houses hundreds of live wings-n-things.

Just about every town has its own **tourist office,** but the one in St-Martin, av. Victor-Bouthillier (tel. 46 09 20 06) has the most complete information and is the only one open all day in summer. (Open Mon.-Sat. 10am-7pm, Sun. 10am-noon; Oct.-May Mon.-Sat. 10-noon and 3-5pm.) Definitely consider staying in La Rochelle and making Ile de Ré a daytrip; most hotels start at two stars and 250F. If evening beckons, however, consider **Hôtel Le Sully,** rue Jean Jaurès (tel. 46 09 70 00), a block up from the port in St-Martin. (Singles with shower 140F. Doubles 170F, with shower 200F. Extra bed 50F. Breakfast 25F.) In La Flotte, **L'Hippocampe,** 16, rue Château des Mauléons (tel. 46 09 60 68) rents singles and doubles for 90F, with shower for 167F (showers 10F; breakfast 19F).Campers can choose from over 50 campgrounds (endearingly called hôtels de plein air—open-air hotels) on the island. Try the **Camping Municipal** (tel. 46 09 84 10) in Rivedoux near the bridge (15F for 1 to 3 campers, including site). Restaurants are pricey, so head instead for the pizza and *crêpe* joints. Most towns have morning **markets**—St-Martin's is indoors off rue Jean Jaurès by the port (open daily 9am-12:30pm).

Most towns on the island have bike rentals. One of the bigger outfits is **Cycland** (tel. 46 09 65 27), with its main office at 15, rue du Marché, in La Flotte. It also runs branch offices in Rivedoux and St-Martin. (Bikes 45-75F per day according to quality, deposit 700-1600F or passport or first-born child.) Open 9:30am-12:30pm and 2:30-7pm.) St-Martin's **postal code** is 17400.

Ile d'Aix

South of Ile de Ré, tiny Ile d'Aix is a metaphorical croissant in the gleaming blue Atlantic. Though barely 2km long, it is big enough to have sheltered Napoleon's bruised ego during the Emperor's last days on French soil in July 1815. Low white cottages, bedecked with bright shutters, line dusty streets on this island and while the occasional car draws the same stares of disbelief as a Hyundai in St-Tropez, bikes more than compensate for the lack of motorized vehicles. Despite the island's Hervé Villechaizian size, its vegetation is almost as varied as that on the neighboring islands. One side, sheltered from the wind, is forested by pines and swamped by marshy waters. The other side gives way to a dense oak forest, fine sandy beaches, babbling brooks, and craggy coves. Ramparts and a moat protect **Le Bourg,** the "main" town on the southern tip of the island. Ferries arrive here, teeming with francophiles heading to the **Musée Napoléon,** which presents a fairly substantial collection of the Little Corporal's memorabilia, including some of His clothing. (Open Wed.-Mon. 10am-noon and 2-6pm. Admission 16F, Sun. 8F.) Across the street, the **Musée Africain** displays its menagerie of African animal trophies, tropical birds, weapons, and documents. (Open Thurs.-Tues. 10am-noon and 2-6pm. Admission 14F, Sun. 7F.) You can easily tour the island by foot, but the restaurant/bar **Chez Françoise** on the port rents little bikes with baskets (20F per hr., 35F per 1/2-day, 45F per day; passport deposit) and serves a variety of snacks (12-30F).

Though ferries depart from La Rochelle (May-Sept.) and Ile d'Oléron (July-Sept., 130-170F), the cheapest option is **Fouras Aix Ferries** (tel. 46 84 60 50) from Pointe de la Fumée, 3km west of Fouras and 14km west of Rochefort. (Daily 8am-8pm roughly every 30min., 25min., 49F round-trip; Nov.-April 5-7 per day, 25min., 33F round-trip.) **Citram Buses** (tel. 46 99 01 36) leave Rochefort for La Fumée five to six times per day (1/2hr., 14F50). Two or three buses per day connect La Rochelle and Fouras (45min., 25F).

The island's campground, **Camping Municipal de Fort la Rade** (tel. 46 84 50 64), offers superb sites inside ramparts. (9F per adult, 12F per site. Open year-round.) The island has but one wicked-expensive hotel.

Ile d'Oléron

Ile d'Oléron exults in over 20 fine sand beaches along a 70km coastline, an enormous citadel, some of France's most renowned and extensive oyster beds, and—not to be left out—crowds. In winter, the island's population is 18,000; in summer it reaches 200,000. Affectionately dubbed the "luminous island" by its year-round inhabitants, Oléron is the largest French island after Corsica.

Originally the site of the château of the Dukes of Aquitaine, the mighty but crumbling **citadelle** in the town of **Le Château d'Oléron** was designed in 1630 by Vauban. The eastern coast near the port town of **Boyardville** is one of the island's principal oyster parks, where hundreds of markers bob in the water and locals spend all day collecting those wild and crazy little aphrodisiacs. The beaches around Boyardville are among the island's best because they are sheltered from the wind. **Plage du Vert Bois,** separated from the main road by a thick pine forest, feels almost like an island itself. **St-Pierre d'Oléron** is the island's administrative center and offers a bustling pedestrian sector.

La Cotiniére, with its lively fishing port, is the most picturesque of the island's towns. In **St-Denis,** near the island's tip, climb the 54m lighthouse and peer down at the colorful collage of forest, land, and water below. (Open 10am-noon and 2-7pm; Sept.-June 10am-noon and 2-6pm.)

Two **buses** leave daily for the Ile d'Oléron from the train station in Saintes (tel. 46 93 21 41; 1 1/2hr., 47F) and seven buses leave from the *gare routière* in Rochefort (tel. 46 99 01 36; 1 1/4hr., 34F). On the island, frequent buses shuttle between all the villages (8-27F50, depending on distance). The island's main **tourist office,** pl. Gambetta (tel. 46 47 11 39) in St-Pierre, knows everything. (Open Mon.-Sat. 9am-1pm and 2-7:30pm, Sun. 10am-1pm; Sept.-June Mon.-Sat. 9:30am-12:30pm and 2:30-6pm.) The one in Le Château, pl. de la République (tel. 46 47 60 51), may be more convenient since it is the first town after the mainland. The office here distributes free maps, brochures, and lists of campgrounds and bike rental companies. (Open daily 9am-12:30pm and 3-7pm, Sun. 10am-noon; Sept.-June Tues.-Sat. 10am-noon and 2:30-6pm.)

Lacellerie Cycles, 5, rue Maréchal Foch (tel. 46 47 69 30), just off pl. de la République in le Château, rents bikes for 36F, 47F, or 80F per day, depending on the model. (Open daily 9am-7pm; Sept.-June daily 9am-noon and 2-7pm. Deposit 600F.) Find food at **Supermarché Bravo** on rue des Antioches. (Open Mon.-Sat. 9am-12:30pm and 3-7:30pm.)

The only cheap hotel in Le Château, **Le Mail,** bd. Thiers (tel. 46 47 61 40) rents singles with showers for 170F and doubles for 180F, but you must reserve in January for rooms in July and August. Campers have the luxury of choice, although none of the sites are truly inexpensive. In Le Château, try **Les Ramparts,** bd. Philippe Daste (tel. 46 47 61 93; 55F for 1-3 people, 14F per extra person), or **La Brande,** rue des Huîtres (tel. 46 47 62 37; 78F for two, pool included; open March 1-Nov. 15). Le Château d'Oléron's **postal code** is 17480.

La Rochelle

A more cultured version of Les Sables d'Olonne, La Rochelle adds elegant architecture and a colorful history to the splendid surf of its neighbor to the north. Named after the soft rock on which the earliest settlers built their homes in the 12th century, La Rochelle later became the coastal power of Aquitaine and profited from its position as a port city vital to both France and Britain. In the 17th century, the powerful and unscrupulous Cardinal Richelieu saw in this bastion of French Protestantism an obstacle to unifying France and convinced Louis XIII to besiege the town. After a large portion of the population had starved to death, the city finally surrendered. The city Dumas immortalized in *The Three Musketeers* did not recover its wealth until the 20th century, when vacationers discovered its white sand beaches and refined old buildings.

Orientation and Practical Information

The main seaport of Charentes-Maritimes, La Rochelle lies halfway on the Nantes-Bordeaux railway line. To get from the train station to the center of town and the tourist office, follow av. du Général de Gaulle past pl. de la Motte Rouge to quai Valin. The tourist office is to the left of quai Valin in the quai du Gabut complex, a hub of restaurants and shops. Quai Valin continues over a small bridge, and becomes quai Duperré which leads to the famous towers on the left. The pedestrian shopping district and old town are to the right of quai Duperré.

Tourist Office: Quai de Gabut (tel. 46 41 14 68). Tremendously helpful staff patiently distributes maps and brochures. Accommodations service 10F. **Currency exchange** June-Sept. Mon.-Sat. 10am-1pm and 4-7pm, Sun. 11am-1pm and 3-5pm. Office open July-Aug. Mon.-Sat. 9am-8pm, Sun. 11am-5pm; Sept. and June Mon.-Sat. 9am-7pm, Sun. 11am-5pm; Oct.-May Mon.-Sat. 9am-12:30pm and 2-6pm.

Post Office: Pl. de l'Hôtel de Ville (tel. 46 41 92 88). **Currency exchange** and **telephones.** Open Mon.-Fri. 8:30am-6:30pm, Sat. 8:30am-noon. **Main office** on av. Mulhouse, by the train station. **Poste Restante.** Open Mon.-Fri. 8am-7pm, Sat. 8am-noon. **Postal Code:** 17021.

Trains: Bd. Maréchal Joffre (tel. 46 41 50 50). To: Poitiers (8-10 per day, 1 3/4hr., 94F); Bordeaux (6-8 per day, 2hr., 122F); Paris-Austerlitz (3 per day, 5hr., 236F); Nantes (4-5 per day, 2hr., 113F); TGV to Paris (7-9 per day, 3hr., 236F plus 16F reservation). Information office open Mon.-Sat. 8am-6:20pm, Sun. 9am-noon and 2-6:40pm.

Buses: **Autoplus** local buses (tel. 46 41 32 93) run to campgrounds, the hostel (bus #10 from av. de Colmar off av. du Général de Gaulle), the *centre ville* (bus #1 from the train station), and La Pallice (also bus #1). Fare 7F. Pick up a map at Autoplus in the quai du Gabut complex. To go anywhere else, it's best to start at the small bus station in pl. de Verdun. **Citram** buses (tel. 46 99 01 36) leave from pl. de Verdun. 3 buses per day to Bordeaux (7hr., 175F) via Angoulême (3 1/2 hr., 87F50). You can buy tickets on board. If possible, stick to the trains. Office open Mon.-Fri. 8am-noon and 2-6pm.

Ferries: **Bus de Mer** (tel. 46 34 02 22), near the aquarium, close to the youth hostel. Runs from the old port to port de Plaisance des Minimes (July-Aug. every 1/2-hr. 10am-11:30pm; Sept. and April-June every hr. 10am-7pm, 4min., 9F).

Youth Center: Centre Départemental d'Information Jeunesse (CDIJ), 14, rue des Gentilshommes (tel. 46 41 16 36 or 46 41 16 99). BIJ tickets. *Carte Jeune* 70F. Bulletin boards listing apartments and jobs. Free ride/rider matching service and list of rides. Open Mon.-Fri. 10am-noon and 2-6pm, Sat. 10am-noon.

Bike Rental: Vélos Municipaux Autoplus, off quai Valin in sq. Meyer. With ID as deposit, will lend (for free) 1-speed bikes for 2hr., 6F per hr. thereafter. Open daily May-Sept. 9am-12:30pm and 1:30-7pm. At **train station,** 44F per 1/2-day, 55F per day, deposit 500F. **Locasport,** plage de la Concurrence (tel. 46 41 66 33, Mme. Benard). From the port, walk south past the Tour de la Chaîne and follow the shoreline to the beach. Bikes 45-56F per day, passport deposit. Open daily 9:30am-noon and 1:30-6:30pm; off-season shorter hours. At the **hostel,** first day 40F, additional days 35F, mountain bikes 60F first day, 50F additional days, ID deposit.

Laundromat: Laverie du Gabut, passage du Cotre, in the Gabut complex and near the tourist office. Wash 20F per 7kg. Dry 2F per 5min. Open daily 8am-9pm. Also at 20, rue de la Pépinière (tel. 46 67 56 25), or rue St-Jean du Pérot, near the Tour de la Lanterne. Wash 28F. Dry 9F per 15 min. Open daily 9:30am-7:30pm.

Hospital: rue du Docteur Schweitzer (tel. 46 27 33 33).

Medical Assistance: SAMU, tel. 46 27 15 15.

Police: 2, pl. de Verdun (tel. 46 51 36 36). **Emergency:** tel. 17.

Accommodations and Camping

Hotel prices soar here. Cheaper places line the east side of the harbor, from the train station to just above pl. du Marché. Reservations are almost always required in July and August; La Rochelle's few unreserved rooms usually fill by early afternoon.

Centre International de Séjour, Auberge de Jeunesse (HI), av. des Minimes (tel. 46 44 43 11), 2km south of the station. Take bus #10 (direction: "Port des Minimes") from av. de Colmar a block from the station (Mon.-Sat., every 1/2hr. until 7:15pm, 6F50). Otherwise, walk past the tourist office and the quai du Gabut complex to av. Marillac, which becomes allée des Tamaris and then quai Marillac before intersecting av. des Minimes (20-min. walk). A "state of the art" building with the look of a hospital but the feel of a frat house. Facilities include snack machines, coffee machine, laundry room, and a lively café open until 11pm. The 234 beds occasionally fill up in summer. Reception open daily 8am-noon and 3-11pm. Lockout 10am-12:30pm. Curfew midnight in winter, 1:30am in summer. 6-bed rooms 62F, nonmembers 80F. Singles 92F. Breakfast included. Camping 28F. Lunch or dinner 44F. To reserve, call ahead or write with 1 night's payment.

Hôtel de la Paix, 14, rue Gargoulleau (tel. 46 41 33 44), near pl. de Verdun. An old-fashioned hotel on a quiet street. French-style staircase leads to high-ceilinged rooms. Singles and doubles 130F, with shower 180F. Enormous 5-person suite 360F. Reservations suggested July-Sept. 15.

Hôtel le Bordeaux, 45, rue St-Nicolas (tel. 46 41 31 22), off quai Valin, 5 min. from station. New and improved! New wallpaper and new wall-size posters of horses galloping in the sunset. Singles and doubles 140F, with shower 195F. Reserve for summer.

Hôtel La Marine, 30, quai Duperré (tel. 46 50 51 63), hanging over the harbor in the middle of all the action. Laid back, straight off-the-beach owners remind you you're in a coastal resort. Crisp and clean and no caffeine. Singles and doubles 130F, with shower 160F. Triples with shower 225F. Extra bed 50F. Breakfast in bed 28F. Owner says "reserve in February to be sure."

Hôtel le Florence, 2, rue Marcel-Paul (tel. 46 41 17 24), 10 min. north of the *centre ville.* A bit of a hike, but owners will take you in with glee. Locals carouse in the bar downstairs. Big rooms, calm street. Singles and doubles 120F, with shower 150F. Triples 165F, with shower 195F. Breakfast 22F, obligatory July-Aug. Reservations advised June-Sept.

Camping: Camping Municipal du Soleil (tel. 46 44 42 53), on av. des Minimes. Two-star site only 15 min. from the center of town; take bus #10 which leaves every half-hour until 7:15pm (see Buses). Otherwise, follow directions to the hostel; camping is on the left of av. des Minimes. 38F for two adults, site, and car. 12F per extra adult. Open May-Sept. 15. **Camping Municipal,** bd. A. Rondeau (tel. 46 43 81 20), much farther from town. Take bus #6 from pl. de Verdun to La Grenouillère. Two-star site surrounded by factories. The tourist office has a list of other sites—all more distant.

Food

If you like a seafood diet, this is the town for you. But if you also like your money, you better settle for buying at the outdoor stands near the harbor, which groan under the weight of mussels, oysters, and shrimp, or the **market** in pl. du Marché, which sells fresh fish, fruit, and vegetables daily until 1pm (Fri. until 7pm). Restaurants concentrate in Le Gabut complex off the quai du Gabut. The outdoor restaurants near pl. de la Chaîne will relieve your wallet of at least 90F; better bargains hide on the other side of the harbor and near pl. du Marché. Expect to pay 20-30F extra for a harbor view.

Le Pilote, 18, rue du Port, off quai Duperré. Tiny seafood restaurant on a crowded street near the action. Friendly staff presents a 66F *menu,* a slightly more ambitious 78F *menu,* and an extravagant 98F *menu,* all with seafood or meat. Sample the light pasta/seafood salad (43F50). Open daily noon-3pm and 6:30-11pm; Oct.-June Tues.-Sun. noon-2:30pm and 7-10:30pm.

Café de l'Arsenal, 12, rue Villeneuve. This self-service cafeteria ain't rife with ambience, but with prices like this—who cares? Finger-lickin' chicken or fish dishes 24-35F. Don't leave without some *mousse au chocolat* (7F90) or beer (4F50). Open daily 11:30am-2:30pm and 7-10pm.

Le Cordon Bleu, 20, rue du Cordouan, north of pl. du Marché. Casual place without the portly portside prices. Salads, steaks, sausages, oysters, and desserts. 44F and 54F *menus.* The 35F *plat du jour* comes with wine. Open Tues.-Sat. 11:45am-2pm and 7-9:30pm.

La Rena Blance, 9-11, rue Verdière, off rue du Temple. Classy French cuisine without the classy prices. 38F *plat du jour.* 48F lunch *menu* includes wine, and the 68F *menu* spreads both cheese and dessert. Open Sun.-Fri. noon-2:15pm and 7-11pm, Sat. 7-11pm; Sept.-June Mon.-Sat. only.

Sights

The famous 14th-century towers which guard La Rochelle's port helped the city thrive as a commercial center during the Renaissance. Whenever enemies tried to enter the harbor, guards linked a chain between the forbidding **Tour St-Nicolas** and the **Tour de la Chaîne** thus barring the entrance to the port. The Tour St-Nicolas, most notable for its formidable fortifications, has remained unchanged since its construction. The climb to the top passes several rooms displaying the tower's history and a labyrinth of passageways and spiraling stairways. An award-winning view of boats cruising in and out of the harbor awaits at the top. The **Tour de la Chaîne** presents a miniature reconstruction of the old town from Richelieu's day, accompanied by a hokey, overdramatized *son et lumière.* (Tour de la Chaîne open May-Sept. daily 10am-noon and 2-6:30pm, Oct.-Nov. 11 Sat.-Sun. 2-6:30pm, Easter-April daily 2-6:30pm. Admission 12F.) A low rampart runs from Tour de la Chaîne to the **Tour de la Lanterne.** When fires were lit inside in the 15th century to illuminate the openings, the tower became France's first lighthouse. The tower received its current nickname, **Tour des Quatre Sergents,** after the 1882 imprisonment of four sergeants here for the heinous crime of crying *"Vive la République."* Topped by a flamboyant Gothic steeple, the 45m tower provides a view of the Ile de Ré on clear days. (Tour de la Lanterne and Tour St-Nicolas open June-Aug. daily 9:30am-7pm; Sept. and March 25-May Wed.-Mon. 9:30am-12:30pm and 2-6:30pm; Oct.-March 24 closes at 5pm, Admission 18F, students 10F.)

La Rochelle's graceful arcaded streets, built during the 18th century, stretch beyond the whitewashed townhouses of the harbor. Walk underneath the 14th-century **Grosse Horloge** (clock tower) or visit the mildly interesting archeological exhibit inside; an enthralling view of the town awaits at the top. (Open July-Sept. 15 3-7pm. Free.) Continue through the arcades of rues du Palais and Chaudrier. At 10, rue du Palais, stands the renovated **Palais de Justice,** originally completed in 1789. Step into the *chambre correctionnelle* and watch the lawyers and judges go at it. (Hearings open to the public Mon. and Thurs. at 2pm.) Rumor has it that the ornate Renaissance **Hôtel de Ville** has more chandeliers per square meter than any other building in Europe. (Open Mon.-Fri. 9:30-11am and 2:30-5pm, Sat. 2-5:30pm; Oct.-Easter Mon.-Fri. 2:30-4pm. Guided tours July and Aug. 14F, students 7F.) Back on the port, the **Musée Grévin,** 38, cours des Dames (tel. 46 41 08 71) is home to a happy family of wax people who spend their days re-enacting 16 of La Rochelle's most important historical events. (Open daily 9am-11pm, Oct.-May 9am-7pm. Admission 25F.) The **Musée Maritime de la Rochelle** lets you play captain on a 76m ship equipped for maritime meteorological investigation. The retired vessel harbors the crew's messy bedrooms, a roaring engine room, kitchens, and computer demonstrations. Wash it all down with a drink at the deck bar. (Open daily 10am-6:30pm. Admission 36F. Ouch.)

See our scaly friends at the **aquarium** (tel. 46 44 00 00) in the port des Minimes, the Versailles of French aquariums. Sharks boogie all night long in their 200,000-liter tank, and other marine dwellers roister in their respective homes. The know-it-all staff loves to answer questions. (Open daily June 9am-7pm; July-Aug. 9am-11pm; Sept.-May 10am-noon and 2-7pm. Admission 37F, ages 4-10 20F.)

During the first two weeks of July, La Rochelle holds its **Franco Folies,** an enormous six-day music festival with groups from French-speaking countries all around the world and audiences large enough to move the towers in the port. (Tickets 50-160F. Call 46 50 55 77 or the tourist office for more information.) During the second week of September, hundreds of motor boats and sail boats docked in the Port des Minimes open their immaculately varnished and polished interiors to the public during the **Grand Pavois.** For information call 46 44 46 39. The **Maison de la Culture,** 4, rue St.-Jean-du-Perot (tel. 46 51 54 00) can tell you about other theater, film, and art festivals throughout the year. (Open Mon.-Sat. 1-6:30pm, Sun. 2:30-6:30pm.)

The Marais Poitevin

The paradisical Marais Poitevin stretches 60km northeast of La Rochelle from the Atlantic to the commercial but historically rich town of Niort. A maze of narrow canals, lined by green poplars and weeping willows has earned the region's tranquil, romantic landscape the nickname "Green Venice." The Marais was born in the Middle Ages, when monks dug the canals branching off from the Sèvre River in order to enhance agriculture, control floods, and even help cure certain ailments common to the swampy region.

Discover the charm and serenity of the Marais Poitevin by bike or boat. Dozens of villages within the Marais, cluttered on tiny islets protected from potential floods, make convenient bases to explore the canals. **Coulon,** the closest town to Niort (about 12km) from which you can rent boats, is also one of the prettiest. SNCF buses connect Niort with Coulon (Mon.-Sat., 3-4 per day, 15min., 8F). Although people do report success hitchhiking in the area, a decent alternative is to rent a mountain bike from **J. F. Mainguenaud,** 105, av. de Limoges (tel. 49 28 20 38). (65F per day, deposit 1000F or passport. Open Tues.-Sat. 8:30am-noon and 2-7pm.) The train station also rents rather aged bikes for 44F per 1/2-day or 55F per day (deposit 500F).

Several outfits along Coulon's canals rent boats. One of the largest, **Embarcadère Fichet** (tel. 49 35 90 88) offers both guided and non-guided tours. (Rentals 85F per hr., 180F per 1/2-day. Guided English tours 1hr., 100-175F.) Rent mountain bikes on the quai from **La Libellule,** 58, quai Louis Tardy (tel. 49 35 98 98; 50F per 1/2-day, 80F per day; open daily 9am-10pm; Sept.-June Sat.-Sun. only; call ahead in off-season).

Hotels in tiny Coulon are scarce—only two to be exact—and presently in a state of flux. If it still exists in the summer of 1993, try **Le Central,** 4, rue d'Autremont (tel. 49 35 90 20), which has a grand total of five doubles with showers, each for 195F (breakfast 21F). Otherwise, your best bet is the **Camping Municipal** (tel. 49 35 90 26), which charges 8F per adult, 4F60 per site, and 3F75 per car (open June 15-Sept. 15). Ask at the Coulon **tourist office,** pl. de l'Eglise (tel. 49 35 99 29), for suggestions about biking circuits and accommodations in neighboring towns. (Open April-Oct. 9am-12:30pm and 2-7pm.)

From Coulon, the unofficial gateway to the Marais, explore the region at your own whim. The villages of **La Garette, Damvix Arçais,** and **Maillezais** all have boat rentals along their quais. Maillezais strays from the swampland theme with a Benedictine monastery, the **Abbaye St-Pierre,** whose foundations date from the 11th century. The three Dukes of Aquitaine were buried in this crumbling yet impressive structure. Ask in Coulon for directions. The **Camping Municipal de Maillezais** (tel. 51 00 70 79) charges 8F per adult, 4F75 per site and 4F25 per car (open April-Sept.).

Niort

Although the Marais Poitevin is clearly the region's chief attraction, Niort itself is a worthwhile diversion. Its steep, narrow, twisting streets adorned with low, red tile-covered houses, and its boardwalk along the green **Sèvre-Niortaise River** lend a colorful ensemble to this picturesque city. Commercial rue Ricard and rue Victor Hugo form the city's main axis. The center of town is cradled between two hills, one dominated by the 14th-century **Eglise Notre Dame** and the bold Roman **donjon** (dungeon), the other by the Renaissance **Hôtel de Ville** (also known as **Le Pilori**) and the elegant Gothic **Eglise St-André.** The well-preserved *donjon* provides a remarkable view from atop its battlements. Destroyed during the Wars of Religion, Henry Plantagenet II's 700m ramparts once enclosed a small city within the borders of rues Brisson, Thiers, l'Abreuvoir, and the river. Today, the dungeon maintains a simple collection of local relics, tools, and costumes. (Open Wed.-Mon. 9am-noon and 2-5pm. Admission 15F, students free.)

Despite a small potpourri of museums and monuments, Niort's business is business. The town exports a number of goods such as leather, agricultural machinery, and electrical technology, as well as serving as the insurance capital of France. The **tourist office** (tel. 49 24 18 79), hidden behind some trees on pl. de la Poste, is a short walk from the station up rue de la Gare. It can provide you with more information on the Marais and Niort.

Finding a place to stay in Niort is—surprise, surprise—somewhat problematic. The **Hôtel St-Jean,** 21, av. St-Jean d'Angély (tel. 49 79 20 76), has a cheery owner, shining bathrooms, and clean rooms that are gradually being redecorated. (Singles 80F, with shower 100F. Doubles 85F, with shower 110F. Triples 100F, with shower 130F. Showers 15F. Breakfast 17F.) The two *foyers* are almost always full during July and August and have little space even during the winter. To complicate matters, neither lets rooms on weekend (Fri.-Sun.) nights. Still, try the **Foyer des Jeunes Travailleurs,** 8, rue St-André (tel. 49 24 50 68) or its branch at 147, rue du Clou Bouchet. (Singles 68F. Doubles 124F. Breakfast included.) The main branch's restaurant is open to the public and serves a 30F *menu* (open Sept.-July noon-1pm and 7:30-8:30pm). **Camping Municipal,** bd. S.-Allende (tel. 49 79 05 06), next door to the stadium in Niort charges 28F (14F per extra person). Write during the spring to reserve space for July and August. Take bus #2 from pl. de la Breche (5min. from station) to the "Chabut" stop (6F per person). A covered **market** takes place at Les Halles in a reflective glass and steel structure that doubles as one of Niort's "monuments" (Mon.-Fri. 9am-6pm, Sat. 9am-noon).

Niort is easily accessible by **train** from La Rochelle (6-7 per day, 3/4hr., 49F) or Poitiers (6-8 per day, 1hr., 58F). Call 49 24 50 50 for train information. The **post office,** pl. de la Poste (tel. 49 24 84 03) is open Monday through Friday from 8:30am to 7pm, Saturday 8:30am to noon. Niort's **postal code** is 79000.

Rochefort

Rochefort (pop. 30,000) sits quietly inland, just far enough from the neighboring resorts to avoid the crowds but close enough to allow trips down the coast and excursions to the islands. A young town by French standards, Rochefort was founded in the 17th century when Louis XIV's finance minister, Jean-Baptiste Colbert, sought a sheltered base from which to defend the Atlantic coast. Fifteen km inland but along the banks of the muddy Charente River, the town soon became the nucleus of the greatest naval arsenal in the world, worthy of King Louis XIV himself. The decent youth hostel and frequent bus connections make this animated town an ideal base from which to explore Ile d'Oléron and Ile d'Aix.

Rochefort holds one of the more eclectic mixes of museums in the region. The longest building in France (374m), the **Corderie Royale** (royal ropeworks), opened in 1670 to manufacture ropes for the military fleets. The original building, part of Louis's arsenal, burned down in 1944 but has been beautifully restored. The magnificent structure now houses the Chamber of Commerce and Industry, the municipal library, a bird and animal protection league, and the **Centre International de la Mer.** The last of these contains a permanent exhibit that explains the history of rope-making through models and pictures, as well as occasional temporary maritime exhibits. (Open daily 9am-8pm; Sept.-June 9am-6pm. Admission 25F, under 18 10F.)

Surrounding the Corderie, the **Jardin des Retours** is the only garden in France constructed as a cultural project and sustained by the state. Called the "Garden of Returns" because all its trees and flowers were brought back by sailors from their voyages around the world, the grounds comprise three sections: wild, typical French garden, and exotic. Next to the Corderie, the **Musée de la Marine,** pl. de la Gallissonière, houses France's largest naval collection outside Paris, and includes several impressive ship models. (Open Nov. 15-Oct. 15 Wed.-Mon. 10am-noon and 2-6pm. Admission 25F, students 11F.)

Rochefort's most curious treasure is **La Maison de Pierre Loti,** 141, rue Pierre Loti (tel. 46 99 16 88), the former home of this socialite and writer. The eclectic abode includes a mosque on the top floor, a Spanish banquet hall, and a Turkish smoking room (where Loti wrote and smoked *hashish*) somewhere in between. (Obligatory tours July-Sept. daily at 10am, 11am, 2pm, 3pm, 4pm, and 5pm, Wed. and Fri. also at 5:30pm, but no Sun. morning tours.; Oct.-Dec. 20 and Jan. 20-June Wed.-Mon. at 10am, 11am, 2pm, 3pm, and 4pm; no Sun. morning tours. Admission 30F, under 19 15F.) The **Musée d'Art et d'Histoire,** 63, av. Charles-de-Gaulle (tel. 46 99 83 99) contains a large model of Rochefort's town layout, a notable collection of Asiatic and Oceanic art objects, and the obligatory collection of 16th- to 20th-century paintings. (Open daily 1:30-7pm; Sept.-June Tues.-Sat. 1:30-5:30pm. Admission 10F, under 19 4F.)

Those of you who save old magazines, broken toasters, and spent lighters will find a friend in **Les Métiers de Mercure,** 12, rue Lesson (46 83 91 50). The exhibit arranges all the gadgets a local family has been collecting for years to recreate the interiors of different merchants' shops from the early 1900s. Thousands of various odds and ends come together as an old tavern, a hair salon, a butcher, and a pharmacy. (Open July-Aug. daily 10am-10pm, Sept.-Dec. and Feb.-June Wed.-Mon. 10am-noon and 2-7pm. Admission 30F.)

The welcoming **tourist office,** av. Sadi Carnot (tel. 46 99 08 60), dispenses free maps and complete lists of hotels and restaurants, reserves rooms for 15F, sells excursion tickets, **changes money,** and suggests tours of the surrounding parks, bird sanctuaries, and natural reserves. (Open daily 9am-8pm; Sept. 16-June 14 Mon.-Sat. 9am-12:30pm and 2-6:30pm.) To get to the tourist office from the train station, head down av. Wilson, turn right onto av. Pelletan, left onto rue Denfert-Rochereau, and left again onto av. Sadi Carnot.

Rochefort has a number of cheap accommodations. Nonetheless, the surplus of vacationers from La Rochelle tends to overflow into Rochefort during July and August, so reserve ahead or look early in the day. Rochefort is tranquil in the off-season; finding space should be no problem. The small **Auberge de Jeunesse (HI),** 20, rue de la République (tel. 46 99 74 62), has excellent kitchen facilities, clean four- and eight-bed rooms, a wee garden out back, no curfew, and a short lockout from 10am to 12:30pm. In July and August, reception is at the hostel. (Reception open 8-10am and 1:30-8:30pm.) For the remainder of the year you must go to the Centre Information Jeunesse, 97, rue de la République, to check in. (Open Mon.-Fri. 9am-noon and 2-6:30pm,

Sat. 2:30-5:30pm.) From the train station, head straight out on av. Wilson, which becomes rue Begon; turn right onto rue Pujos and then left onto rue de la République (12 1/2min.). (HI card required. 40F. Camping 22F per person. Breakfast 15F. Sheets 15F. Call a week ahead in July-Aug. Send a 30% deposit if reserving more than a week in advance.) The **Hôtel Colbert,** 23, rue Audry de Puyravault (tel. 46 99 08 28) is in a great central location just off pl. Colbert. An obliging couple rents clean singles and doubles for 115F, with shower for 175F and with two big beds for 165-195F. (Showers 20F. Breakfast 25F.) Call a couple weeks ahead in July and August. A few doors down from the youth hostel, the **Hôtel Roca Fortis,** 14, rue de la République (tel. 46 99 26 32) ensures a peaceful repose with its two lovely gardens, almost luxurious rooms, and way cool managers. (Singles with shower 170F. Doubles with shower 190F. Triples with shower 310F. Breakfast 25F. Reserve 2-3 weeks ahead in July and Aug.) The new **Camping Le Bâteau** (tel. 46 99 41 00) on rue des Pêcheurs d'Islande, 2km from town on the way to La Rochelle, offers a pool, tennis courts, and hot water on a site next to the river. (47F fee covers two adults, tent, and a car. Electricity 11F50.)

The local covered **market** convenes at the intersection of av. Charles-de-Gaulle and rue Jean Jaurès on Tuesday, Thursday, and Saturday mornings. Otherwise, **Prisunic** supermarket is two blocks up on av. Charles-de-Gaulle (open Mon.-Sat. 8:30am-7:30pm). The gardens near the *Corderie* make a good place to chow. Cheap eats abound at the festive **Chez Nous,** 72, rue Jean Jaurès, whose filling 47F *menu* includes soup, oysters (the regional specialty), *plat du jour,* cheese, and dessert. (Open Mon.-Fri. 10:30am-2:45pm and 5:45-10pm, Sat. 10:30am-2:45pm.) **Le Galion,** 38, rue Toufaire, a self-service cafeteria near the entrance to the naval museum, presents filling main courses with veggies for 26-50F. (Open Mon.-Sat. 11:45am-2pm and 6:45-9:30pm, Sun. 11:45am-2pm.) The **Café de la Paix,** pl. Colbert, has tasty French *plats du jour (entrecôte,* sausage skewers, and grilled chicken, all 38F) on the hottest *place* in town. If you don't like cigarette smoke or double-cheek French kisses, scope the scene from a seat next to the gardens in the square. (Open daily 11am-2am.)

Rent bikes from **MBK-Barajas,** 30, rue Gambetta (tel. 46 99 08 56), two blocks from the tourist office, for 20F per half-day, 40F per day (open Tues.-Sat. 8am-noon and 2-7pm; 1000F or passport deposit) or at the **train station** for 44F per half-day, 55F per day (500F deposit). The **train station** sends six trains per day to La Rochelle (20min., 26F), Saintes (1/2hr., 38F), and Royan (change at Saintes, 1hr., 59F). **Océcars** buses at the *gare routière* on pl. de Verdun (tel. 46 99 23 65; open Mon.-Fri. 8:30am-noon and 2-6:30pm, Sat. 8:30am-noon) runs three buses per day to La Rochelle (1 1/4hr., 24F50) and Royan (1 1/2hr., 41F50). The **post office** (tel. 46 99 07 00) is next to the tourist office on rue du Docteur Peltier. (**Currency exchange,** too. Open Mon.-Fri. 8am-7pm, Sat. 8am-noon.) The **postal code** is 17300.

Saintes

35km from the sea, Saintes (pop. 28,000) rests atop a few choice hills banking the green Charente River. The erstwhile Roman capital of southwestern France, Saintes (then known as Medioianum Santonum) adopted Christianity in the 3rd century and spent much of its time thereafter fending off pyromaniacal Gallic invaders, who nonetheless wormed their way in and burnt the city to the ground several times. When things calmed down in the 11th century, the citizens of this provincial town breathed a sigh of relief and set about building churches, many of which survive today. The Revolution of 1789 partially extinguished the town's saintly character when anti-clerical republicans imposed a secular urbanism on the region. Today, the cultural capital of the Saintonge region draws crowds to its music festivals in July and a sizable number of stragglers the rest of the year.

Orientation and Practical Information

Saintes lies halfway along the main La Rochelle-Bordeaux railway line, 25km from Cognac. Activity centers on the **Arc de Triomphe** and the **Pont Palissy.** The center of town is a 15-minute walk from the train station. As you leave the station, take a left, follow av. de la Marne two blocks south, turn right onto av. Gambetta, and follow it to the river. You will see the arch on your left. Cross the bridge and continue straight for about five blocks on cours National; the tourist office is on your right in a villa set back from the street.

Tourist Office: 62, cours National (tel. 46 74 23 82). Helps with accommodations, gives tours of the city, (Mon.-Sat. 2 per day, 2-4hr., 35F), and organizes cruises on the Charente (67F and up). Open Mon.-Sat. 9am-7pm, Sun. 10am-12:30pm and 3-6pm; Oct.-May Mon.-Sat. 9am-noon and 2-6pm.

Post Office: 8, cours National (tel. 46 93 05 84), near the bridge. **Telephones. Currency exchange.** Open Mon.-Fri. 8:30am-7pm, Sat. 8:30am-noon. **Postal Code:** 17100.

Trains: Av. de la Marne (tel. 46 92 04 19). To: La Rochelle (6 per day, 1hr., 49F); Bordeaux (7-8 per day, 1 1/4hr., 79F); Cognac (6 per day, 20min., 25F); Angoulême (6 per day, 1hr., 55F); Paris (2 per day, 5 1/2hr., 252F) via Poitiers (1 3/4hr., 115F). Information office open daily 8:30am-noon and 2-6:30pm.

Buses: Autobus Aunis et Saintonge, 1, cours Reverseaux (tel. 46 93 21 41). To Royan (3 per day, 1hr., 28F50). To Ile d'Oléron: Le Château (3 per day, 1 1/4hr., 47F); St-Pierre d'Oléron (3 per day, 2hr., 56F). Open Mon.-Fri. 8am-noon and 2:15-6:45pm. **Océcars** (tel. 46 99 23 65 in Rochefort). To: La Rochelle (1 per day, 2 1/2hr., 58F) and Rochefort (1-2 per day, 1 1/4hr., 33F). An operator will answer calls Mon.-Fri. 8:30am-noon and 2-7pm. Océcars buses stop at the *gare routière*, 1 cours Reverseaux in Saintes. **Citram** (tel. 46 99 01 36 in Rochefort). To: Cognac (1 per day, 1hr., 27F).

Bike Rental: Héline, 177, av. Gambetta (tel. 46 92 04 38). 40F per day, 140F per week, deposit 400F or passport. Open Tues.-Sat. 8:30am-12:30pm and 2-7:30pm. **Groleau Cycles,** 9, cours Reverseaux (tel. 46 74 19 03). 48F per day, 90F per 2 days, deposit 600F. Open Tues.-Sat. 8:30am-12:15pm and 2-7pm.

Laundromat: Laverie de la Saintonage, 18, quai de la République. Wash 20F per 7kg, dry 2F per 5min. Open daily 8:30am-8:30pm.

Medical Assistance: Hospital, pl. du 11 Novembre (tel. 46 92 76 76). **Ambulance: SAMU,** tel. 46 27 15 15 or simply 15.

Police: Rue du Bastion (tel. 46 93 52 33). **Emergency:** tel. 17.

Accommodations and Camping

Many hotels fill up during the mid-July festivals, but rooms should be easy to find the rest of the year. The youth hostel usually has space.

Auberge de Jeunesse (HI), 6, rue du Pont Amilion (tel. 46 92 14 92), near the center of town next to the Abbaye-aux-Dames. From the train station, take av. de la Marne to av. Gambetta, walk about five blocks, turn left onto rue du Pérat, right onto rue St-Pallais, and left onto rue du Pont Amilion. A big, grassy field out front and a gorgeous view of the illuminated Abbaye-aux-Dames by night. Mellow management ensures a quiet, relaxed atmosphere. Two huge barracks-style single-sex rooms full of bunk beds. Great kitchen. Aging bathrooms (some with Turkish toilets). Reception open 7am-noon and 6-11pm. No lockout, but you must leave a 50F deposit to get the night key. 41F, nonmembers 59F. Camping 25F. Breakfast 16F. Sheets 15F. Open mid-Jan. to mid-Dec.

Hôtel Parisien, 35, rue Frédéric-Mestreau (tel. 46 74 28 92), just left of the train station. Affable management, clean rooms and a little *jardin* out back. Singles and doubles 110F, with shower 150F, with two beds 160F. Triples 165F, with shower 195F. Showers 15F. Breakfast 25F. Call several weeks ahead for July and Aug.

Hôtel St-Palais, 1, pl. St-Palais (tel. 46 92 51 03), overlooking the Abbaye-aux-Dames across the square. Clean, capacious rooms. Manager tends the bar downstairs. Usually full one of the first two weeks in July when musicians from the music festival move in. Singles 95F. Doubles 110F. Triples and quads 175-185F. Showers included. Breakfast 22F.

Camping: Camping Municipal, 6, route de Courbiac (tel. 46 93 08 00). from the train station, follow *auberge* directions to av. Gambetta and turn right onto quai de l'Yser after crossing the bridge (25-30min.). Spread across green fields along the banks of the Charente, next to the municipal swimming pool and a miniature golf course. Only 900m from the *centre ville*. Reception open 8am-1pm and 3-9pm; May 15-June and Sept. 9:30am-noon and 4-8pm. 15F per person, 17F per site, includes car. Open May 15-Sept. 30.

Food

Escargots cooked in garlic and parsley is the local favorite. A boisterous **market** mounts Tuesdays and Fridays on cours Reverseaux, Wednesdays and Saturdays at the base of Cathédrale St-Pierre, and Thursdays and Sundays on av. de la Marne and av. Gambetta near the station (all 8am-12:30pm). The **supermarket E. Leclerc** is east of the hostel, two blocks up rue du Pont St-Amilion (open Mon. 3-7:15pm, Tues.-Thurs. 9am-12:30pm and 3-7:15pm, Fri. 9am-8:15pm, Sat. 9am-7:15pm). Take your goodies to the idyllic riverside **Jardin Public,** near the Arc de Germanicus.

Cafétéria Germanicus, 10, rue Arc de Triomphe. Self-serve buffet with colorful salads (25F) and decent entrees (20-40F), all in a pseudo-Roman villa with columns and ivy. Open Mon.-Sat. 11:30am-2pm and 7-10pm.

Le St-Michel, 28, rue St-Michel. Varied selection in a rustic milieu filled with locals. 55F *menu* includes *pâté,* ray with capers, and cheese or dessert. More refined 75F and 116F *menus.* Salads 38-48F. Open daily noon-3:30pm and 7-10pm.

Le Pistou, 3, pl. du Théâtre. Delectable regional cuisine on a pink-and-green terrace near the theater. The 55F *menu* serves a *plat du jour,* vegetables, and dessert. *Escargots fricassés* with oysters 58F. Open Mon.-Sat. noon-2pm and 7-10pm.

Crêperie Victor Hugo, 20, rue Victor Hugo. Simple, friendly, and in the *centre ville. Galettes* 12-44F, dessert *crêpes* 9-30F. Try the Franco-American "Gourmande," a hamburger *crêpe* (41F). 55F *menu* with salad, *crêpe,* and chocolate mousse. Salads 36-42F. Open Tues.-Sat. noon-2:30pm and 4:30-10pm.

Sights and Entertainment

Rising unexpectedly between street and river in the *centre ville,* the first-century Roman **Arc de Triomphe** (or **Arc Germanicus**) marks the spot where a bridge linked the two sides of town. An inscription still visible along the top dedicates it to Tiberius, Germanicus, and Drusus. From the arch, take rue Arc de Triomphe/rue St-Pallais to the **Abbaye-aux-Dames** (tel. 46 74 23 82), one of the most beautiful of the many Romanesque churches in the region. Built in the 11th century, it was the first convent in the region. The interior was redone with Angevin vaulting in the 12th century. The surrounding white buildings, which housed nuns until the 17th century, now serve as a musical and cultural center. The small museum inside couldn't be any more thorough in explaining the abbey's history. (Open daily 10am-12:30pm and 2-7pm. Admission 15F, under 16 free. Guided tours in French June-Sept. Tues.-Sat. 3 per day. Admission 20F, students 15F.) The original and creative **Musée Archéologique,** on esplanade André Malraux next to the arch, is an intriguing forest of Roman columns, friezes, and cornices, some piled into two buildings, and others scattered across a small square. Most date from the demolition of the town's ramparts during the 3rd century. (Open Wed.-Mon. 10am-noon and 2-6pm; Oct.-May Mon. and Wed.-Sat. 2-5pm, Sun. 10am-noon and 2-6pm. Free.)

Across the river from the arch stands the architectural hodgepodge of **Cathédrale St-Pierre.** Bulky, imposing, and capped by a small dome, it recalls a fortress more than a house of worship. Built in the 12th, 15th and 17th centuries, its nave, transept, and light buttresses seem to belong on separate monuments, not on one cathedral's bell tower. From St-Pierre, walk up rue des Jacobins, climb the stairs, and work your way up to cours Reverseaux. Take a left and then a right on rue St-Eutrope toward **Eglise St-Eutrope,** a split-level Gothic-Romanesque hybrid on a once-important pilgrimage route to Santiago de Compostela in Spain. Descend into the gloomy crypt; illumination will set you back 2F, a small price to pay.

Away from St-Eutrope and the *centre ville,* signs mark the 15-minute walk to the **Arènes Gallo-Romaines,** a crumbling amphitheater overgrown with grass. Built in 40 AD, the tunnel entrance and several of the supporting arches still stand. At one time the structure could seat 20,000 people. (Open 9am-8pm; in winter 9am-6pm, but locals frequent the arena at all hours. Free.)

The **Jeux Santons,** a week-long celebration of folk music from around the world, rocks the town around the second week of July. The opening and closing events take place in the Arènes Gallo-Romaines. Some events are free, but most cost between 45F and 80F. (Call 46 74 47 50, or stop by at 43, rue Gautier for information.) The classical music concerts of The **Fête de Musique Ancienne** take place during 10 days within the first three weeks of July. Tickets sell out fast (60-200F, students 30-100F; call 46 97 48 48 for information and reservations).

Cognac

As one local put it, "If you took away the Cognac distilleries we'd be in the middle of farmlands with cows and ladders." A short ride from Saintes or Angoulême, Cognac rests serenely among cows, ladders, and fields whose strictly regulated soils issue grapes used to produce cognac brandy, a nectar Victor Hugo christened "the drink of the gods." The city itself is strictly small-town, but within its confines stand the megaliths of the trade—Hennessy, Martell, Rémy-Martin, Otard, and every other world-famous exporter of cognac.

Although Cognac's soils historically yielded only mediocre wine, an inspired wine-maker discovered over three centuries ago that by distilling his spirits a second time he obtained a smooth, sweet drink as divine as Jove's nectar. Dubbed *vin brulé* (burnt wine) due to the distillation process, his brandy became a quick success across 17th-century Europe. Nowadays, cognac is made by blending the twice-distilled *eaux de vie* (waters of life), and aging the blends for at least two years in casks crafted exclusively from Limousin oak. Each house has a head taster who chooses the "mixture of the year" after sampling from literally thousands of barrels. The older the cognac is, the smoother, sweeter, and more expensive it becomes. There are five age designations: VS (Very Special), VSOP (Very Superior Old Pale), *Napoléon,* XO, and Extra or *Paradis.* While the youngest may be only two years old, the oldest blends may be between 50 and 180 years old. Remember: cognac does not age in the bottle. A cognac made in 1905 and bottled in 1910 will always be five years old.

The joy of visiting Cognac lies in making your way from one brand name to the next, touring the warehouses, listening to the films about the history of each house, and collecting nip bottles. All have frequent tours in English. **Otard,** 127, bd. Denfert-Rochereau (tel. 45 82 40 00), though not the largest of the houses, is certainly one of the more interesting to visit. Housed in the **Château de Cognac** where François I, future king of France, was born in 1494, this *chais* (aging- and store-house) leads an informative, humorous tour that includes a glimpse of the aging cellars and a stroll through the regal Renaissance-style halls influenced by François himself (he even managed to slip in a few salamanders, his famous emblem). The *dégustation* is free, but nip bottles cost 15F. (Open daily 9:30am-5:30pm; Oct.-March Mon.-Fri. 9:30am-noon and 2-5:30pm; April-May daily 9:30am-noon and 2-5:30pm. Free.) **Hennessy,** 1, rue de la Richonne (tel. 45 82 52 22), is the largest cognac producer in the world, exporting 99% of its three million cases each year. Its tour is slightly less informative but includes a short boat ride across the Charente, a look at the Cooperage museum, which describes the ancient techniques of barrel-making, and a stroll past the assembly-line bottling plant. (Open Mon.-Sat. 9am-5:30pm; Sept. 16-June 14 Mon.-Fri. 9am-noon and 1:45-4:30pm. Free). **Martell,** rue de Gate-Bourse (tel. 45 82 44 44), offers perhaps the most personalized tours; the guides leave plenty of time to answer questions. Their circuit includes a special peek at storage rooms dubbed "Purgatory," which contain special editions dating back to 1927 and "Paradise" which protects the oldest bottles, some dating as far back as 1820. They offer both a complimentary *dégustation* and free nip bottles. (Open Mon.-Sat. 8:30-11am and 2-5pm; June and Sept. Mon.-Fri. 8:30-11am and 2-5pm; Oct.-May Mon.-Thurs. 8:30-11am and 2-5pm, Fri. 8:30-11am. Free.) **Rémy-Martin** (5km), **Polignac** (4km), **Camus** (4km) and several other *chais* are located outside of town. Get a complete list from the tourist office.

The **Musée du Cognac,** located in the *Jardin Public,* elaborates on a familiar theme. Examine the collection of late 19th-century liquor bottles. Logically enough, a gargantuan wooden boat discovered on the banks of the Charente in 1979 and dating back to 2590 BC is also on display. (Open Wed.-Mon. 10am-noon and 2-6pm; Oct.-May Wed.-

Mon. 2-5:30pm. Admission 16F, students 11F.) If you've had enough of Cognac, stumble down for a picnic with the swans in stunning **Jardin de l'Hôtel de Ville,** on bd. Denfert-Rochereau. (Open daily 7am-10pm; in winter 7am-8pm.)

A perfect daytrip from either Angoulême or Saintes, Cognac sees five **trains** chooch daily from Angoulême (1hr., 41F), six from Saintes (20min., 25F). For train information, call 45 82 03 29. To get to the **tourist office,** rue du 14 Juillet (tel. 46 99 08 60), follow av. du Général Leclerc out of the station to rue de Barbezieux. Continue to rue Bayard on your right, across pl. Bayard onto rue du 14 Juillet. The helpful staff will find you a room for the price of a phone call, and **changes money** when the banks are closed (open Mon.-Sat. 8:30am-7pm; Sept. 16-June 14 Mon.-Sat. 9am-12:30pm and 2-6:15pm.)

The **post office** (tel. 45 82 08 99) is on pl. Bayard **(postal code** 16100). You can rent bikes from **J. F. Dupuy,** at Fief du Roi, about 2km out of town past av. Victor Hugo on the road to Angoulême, just to the right after the **Mammouth supermarket.** (Decent 10-speeds 50F per day with a 400F deposit. Open Mon.-Fri. 8:30am-noon and 2-7pm, Sat. 9am-noon).

There are few cheap accommodations in Cognac. The one-star hotels often have room, but call ahead. The **Foyer Ste-Elizabeth,** 12, rue Saulnier (tel. 45 82 04 90), close to the *centre-ville* and the Hennessy plant, is really for workers but travelers are accepted when there is room. Call two weeks ahead in summer. (Clean singles with desk and skylight 40F per night. Breakfast 10F.) The centrally located **Hôtel du Cheval Blanc,** 6-8, pl. Boyard (tel. 45 82 09 55), though slightly worn, rents clean rooms with bouncy mattresses. Ask for rooms that face the back, as those overlooking the *place* are somewhat noisy. (Singles 90F. Doubles 110F, with 2 beds 140F. Showers 12F. Breakfast 25F.) The **Hôtel St-Martin,** 112, av. Paul-Férino-Martell (tel. 45 35 01 29) offers decent rooms over a great restaurant with a 46F lunch *menu* that includes an entree, main course, vegetables, cheese, and dessert. (Singles and doubles 110F, with two beds 150F. Showers 10F. Breakfast 18F. Restaurant open Mon.-Sat. noon-2pm and 7-10pm, Sun. noon-2pm.)

Le Sangria, 35, rue Grande, in the center of town, serves typical French dishes for 40-65F, plus Spanish and Portuguese specialities. (Open Mon.-Fri. and Sun. 10am-3pm and 7:30pm-midnight, Sat. 7:30pm-midnight.) **Le Chantilly,** 146, av. Victor Hugo, is a local spot where you'll eat lots of whatever the boss feels like serving. Soup, appetizer, meat, vegetables, cheese, fruit and wine add up to 60F. (Open Mon.-Fri. noon-2pm and 7-9pm, Sat. noon-2pm.)

Angoulême

The French refer to the inhabitants of Charente as *cagouillards* (from *cagouille,* a type of snail), to convey the phlegmatic pace of life in this region. Angoulême, the capital of Charente, lives up to this reputation. The friendly, soporific inhabitants sit contentedly and watch time slide through the narrow pedestrian *vieille ville,* around the high stone ramparts, and between the 12th-century cathedral and other medieval structures throughout the town—no wonder Balzac came here to gather material for his *Lost Illusions.* The cradle of paper production in France in the 16th century, Angoulême shut its mills in the 1970s, leaving the task to nearby factories in the region. In recent years, the town has emerged as the capital of French comic strip production, as countless *Lucky Luke, Tintin,* and *Astérix* volumes roll off Angoulême's presses each day.

Orientation and Practical Information

Situated in the heart of the Charente Valley, Angoulême lies halfway between Bordeaux and Poitiers. A town with a view, Angoulême's *vieille ville* sits high on a plateau just south of the Charente and southwest of the train station. To get to the main tourist office and the cathedral from the train station (20min.), follow av. Gambetta uphill to the right to pl. G. Perrot. Continue straight up the rampe d'Aguesseau, walk through pl. Marengo, and go straight on rue Marengo one block to the pl. de l'Hôtel de Ville. Veer left around the Hôtel onto pl. Bouillard and take av. Georges Clemenceau to the right to reach the ramparts. Turn right onto rempart Desaix to the cathedral and the tourist office that faces it.

Tourist Office: 2, pl. St-Pierre (tel. 45 95 16 84). Free maps, hotel lists, and self-guided walking tours. Guided tours by foot (1-1 1/2hr., 20F, students 10F). Sells tickets for boat excursions (35-55F), some of which go to a chocolate factory with free tasting. Open Mon.-Sat. 9am-7pm, Sun. 10:30am-12:30pm and 1-3pm; Sept.-June Mon.-Fri. 9am-12:30pm and 1:30-6:30pm, Sat. 10am-noon and 2-5pm. **Information kiosk** (tel. 45 92 27 57), outside the train station. Maps. Open Mon.-Sat. 9am-noon and 2-6pm.

Post Office: Pl. du Champ de Mars (tel. 45 95 23 11). **Currency Exchange** and **telephones.** Open Mon.-Fri. 8am-7pm, Sat. 8am-noon. **Branch office,** on pl. Francis Louvel. Open Mon.-Fri. 8am-6:45pm, Sat. 8am-noon. **Postal Code:** 16000.

Trains: Pl. de la Gare (tel. 45 38 50 50). To: Bordeaux (3 per day, 1 1/2hr., 92F); Poitiers (3-4 per day, 1hr., 78F); Saintes via Cognac (4-5 per day, 1hr., 58F); Paris (3-4 per day, 4 1/2hr., 236F). TGV to Bordeaux (8-10 per day, 55min., 92F plus 16F reservation); Poitiers (10-12 per day, 45min., 78F plus 16F reservation); and Paris (2 1/2hr., 236F plus 16-80F reservation). Information office open Mon.-Fri. 9am-7pm, Sat. 9:30am-noon and 2-6pm.

Buses: Autobus Citram, (tel. 45 25 42 60). To: Cognac (7 per day, 1hr., 38F); La Rochelle (1-2 per day, 3 1/2hr., 90F50); Bordeaux (2 per day, 3hr., 77F). Citram has no office in pl. de Champ de Mars, but its buses stop here. Buy tickets on the bus. For information, you can go to the **Cartans** office in pl. du Champ de Mars. Open Mon.-Fri. 9am-noon and 2:15-6:15pm.

Public Transportation: For public transit, consult **STGA,** pl. du Champs de Mars (tel. 45 91 55 22). Urban bus tickets cost 6F50. Ask for a schedule at the tourist office.

Bike Rental: Ets. Pelton, 5, rue des Arceaux (tel. 45 95 30 91). Rents some decent bikes for 33F per 1/2-day, 41F per day, 1500F deposit. Mountain bikes 60F per 1/2-day, 90F per day, 3000F deposit. Sat. afternoon-Tues. counts as 1 day. Open Tues.-Sat. 9:15am-noon and 2-7pm.

Youth Information: Centre Information Jeunesse, 6, pl. Bouillard (tel. 45 92 86 73), around the corner from the Hôtel de Ville. Offers babysitting, a **ride-finding** service, and information about concerts, festivals, and other events of interest. Open Tues.-Sun. 10am-7pm.

Laundromat: Lavomatique, 3, rue Ludovic Trarieux in Vieil Angoulême. Wash 18F, dry 2F per 6min. Soap 5F. Open daily 7am-8pm. Also at 11, rue St-Roch. Wash 20F, dry 8F per 15min. Open Mon.-Sat. 8am-7pm.

Hospital: Hôpital de Girac, rue de Bordeaux (tel. 45 24 40 40).

Ambulance: SAMU, tel. 45 92 92 92 or tel. 15.

Police: pl. du Champs de Mars, (tel. 45 39 38 37). **Emergency:** tel. 17.

Accommodations and Camping

Finding cheap accommodations in Angoulême shouldn't be a problem. Decent and affordable hotels cluster near the intersection of av. Gambetta and the pedestrian precinct, which leads downhill from the *vieille ville*.

Auberge de Jeunesse (HI), (tel. 45 92 45 80), on Ile de Bourgines, almost 2km from the station next to the campground. Take bus #7 (direction: "Le Treuil") from pl. du Champ de Mars (every 15min. until 9pm, 6F50). Get off at the "St-Antoine" stop, cross the bridge, go down the white staircase, follow the river's edge to the right until you reach the hostel (5-10min.). A gorgeous setting along the Charente on a small, wooded island. About 15 bright 6-bed rooms in a modern building. Excellent management. Free passes to the outdoor, Olympic-sized municipal swimming pool next door. Canoes and kayaks for rent (about 30F). TV and iron. No lockout. No curfew. Members only. 43F. Breakfast 16F. Filling meals 43F. Sheets 15F. Often booked by groups in summer.

Hôtel Le Palma, 4, rampe d'Aguesseau (tel. 45 95 22 89), near the Eglise St-Martial. Kind management lets impeccable rooms. A handful of singles 100F. Doubles (1 or 2 beds) 130F. Hall showers included. Breakfast 22F. Good restaurant downstairs. Sometimes full; call ahead. Open Mon.-Sat.

Hôtel les Messageries, pl. de la Gare (tel. 45 92 07 62), a few steps to the right of the train station. Kind manager treats you like family. Tidy singles and doubles 100F. Rooms with 1 big and 1 small bed (2-3 people) 130F. Showers 15F. Breakfast with croissant 18F. Open Sept.-July Mon.-Fri. and Sat. morning.

Hôtel de Lille, rue de Périgueux (tel. 45 95 03 01), near Eglise St-Martial. Primarily a hotel for pensioners, the "Lille" offers old-fashioned, slightly crusty rooms. Singles and doubles with shower 90-110F. Breakfast 20F. Owner occasionally closes the establishment for a couple of weeks, so call ahead.

Camping: Camping Municipal, on Ile de Bourgines (tel. 45 92 83 22), next to the youth hostel. Reception open 7am-noon and 2-10pm. 25F per site, 12F per adult, 6F per child. Showers included. Open March-Oct.

Food

Angoulême's specialties include *cagouilles à la charentaise,* snails prepared first with garlic and parsley, then with sausage, smoked ham, and spices. A favorite sweet is the flower-shaped *marguerite* chocolate, named for François I's sister, who exerted considerable influence over Angoulême in the 16th century. **Duceau** on pl. de l'Hôtel de Ville sells them. **Les Halles** has the cheapest, freshest produce in town on pl. des Halles Centrales, two blocks down rue de Gaulle from the Hôtel de Ville. (Open Mon.-Sat. 7am-1pm.) Or, try the 20th-century **Prisunic supermarket** on rampe d'Aguesseau (open Mon.-Sat. 8:45am-12:45pm and 2:15-7pm). Excellent but sometimes expensive restaurants crowd the winding streets of Vieil Angoulême west of the market, especially around the Eglise St-André. The best picnic spots are on the ramparts by the streams of the **Jardin Vert** or behind the hostel by the small dam.

Le Chat Noir, rue de Chat, facing Les Halles. Open when you're hungry, this black cat is young, happy, and loud. Meeeow! Crowded at night. Salads 30-32F. Sandwiches 11-23F. More substantial meat dishes 40-58F. Desserts 9-15F. Open Mon.-Sat. 7am-1am.

Marest, 26, rue de Périgueux, near Eglise St-Martial. A classy self-service cafeteria with tasty victuals. Meat and fish entrees 27-42F. Salads 6-14F. Mongo ice creams 6-20F. Restaurant open Sun.-Fri. 11am-2:30pm and 6:30-9:30pm, Sat. until 10pm. Serves tea and pastries between lunch and dinner hours.

Le Palma, 4, rampe d'Aguesseau. Local specialties abound at this pretty restaurant beneath a hotel. 54F *menu* might include soup of the day, spicy meat-filled tomatoes, green salad, and dessert. Bigger and better 78F and 130F *menus. Escargots à la charentaise* 62F. Open Mon.-Fri. 11:45am-2pm and 7:30-10pm, Sat. 11:45am-2pm; Sept.-June Mon.-Sat. 11:45am-2pm and 7:30-10pm.

Le Mektoub, 28, rue des 3 Notre Dames, near Eglise St-André. Good service, friendly folk, and delicious Middle Eastern food. Meat entrees 55-58F. Loads o' *couscous* 58-65F. Open Mon.-Sat. noon-2pm and 7pm-midnight, Sun. 7pm-midnight.

Sights and Entertainment

The word on the street is that on a clear day, you can see Cognac from the ramparts. Follow them far enough and you'll reach the splendid 12th-century **Cathédrale St-Pierre.** Restored once in 1634 after having been destroyed by Calvinists, architect Abadie, who drafted the Sacré Coeur in Paris, gave it its present unity and detail in 1866. Its dome and the square *campanile* may whisper Italy, but the façade's distinctive towers and intricate decoration practically shout Aquitaine. Seventy-five perfectly intact characters on the façade narrate the tales of the Ascension and the Last Judgment.

Behind the cathedral, the **Musée des Beaux Arts (Musée Municipal)** (tel. 45 95 07 69), in the restored 12th-century Bishop's palace, displays French neoclassical, Romantic, and 19th-century landscape paintings. Its prize, however, is the fabulous collection of African art and pottery that makes this the most important provincial museum of African art in France. (Open Wed.-Mon. 10am-noon and 2-6pm. Admission 15F, students 5F, under 18 free.) The small **Musée Archéologique,** 44, rue Montmoreau (tel. 45 38 45 17), displays regional treasures from the Gallo-Roman era to recent centuries. (Open Wed.-Mon. 10am-noon and 2-5pm. Free.)

The 12th-century **Eglise St-André,** sits smack in the center of Vieil Angoulême. The church was redone in a Gothic style but retains its original Romanesque tower and entrance. Nineteenth-century **Eglise St-Martial** rises like a Lego house in the center of town with almost sterile symmetry and a stepped steeple. Set in a 16th-century building with walls nearly a meter thick, the extraordinary **Maison St-Simon,** 15, rue de la Cloche Verte (tel. 45 92 34 10), displays avant-garde, thought-provoking art expositions. (Open Wed.-Fri. noon-7pm, Sat. 2-7pm, Sun. 3-6pm. Free.)

For an explanation of how cloth, plants, and water metamorphose into paper later recycled into the pages of *Let's Go,* visit the fascinating **Atelier Musée du Papier,** 134, rue de Bordeaux (tel. 45 92 73 43), housed in the old paper mill over the Charente which brought renown to Angoulême. Torrents of water that used to power the turbines now rush past the exhibits on the art and history of paper production. Upstairs, the **Association du Centre d'Arts Plastiques d'Angoulême** (tel. 45 92 34 10) presents modern art exhibits, often involving the incomprehensibly twisted works and the postmodern antics of students from Angoulême's Ecole des Beaux Arts. (Open Tues.-Fri. 2-6pm, Sat.-Sun. 10am-noon and 2-6pm. Free.)

If the Sunday funnies jolt you, you'll enjoy the **Centre Nationale de la Bande Dessinée et de l'Image (CNBDI),** 121, rue de Bordeaux (tel. 45 95 87 20), housed in a disconcerting stone and glass complex. A witty presentation of cartoons, slide shows, and television screens traces the history, creation, and politics of comic strips from their origins in the 1800s to the present. (Open Wed.-Sat. noon-7pm, Sun. 2-7pm. Admission 30F, children 20F). Buses #3 and 5 alleviate the long walk to both museums. Both run from pl. du Champ de Mars and pl. de l'Hôtel de Ville to "Nil-CNBDI" stop (6F50).

January brings the world-famous **Salon International de la Bande-Dessinée,** three days of brilliant, free comic strip exhibits and 200,000 visitors. Call 45 95 87 20 for more information. In May, groups from France, South Africa, Jamaica, Nigeria, Italy, Great Britain, and the United States converge for Angoulême's **Festival International de Jazz et Musiques Métisses.** Call 45 95 43 42 for information.

Near Angoulême: La Rochefoucauld

La Rochefoucauld, a serene French village nestled among the trees and farmlands of the Tardoire River Valley, imports a specialty of the Loire Valley to Poitou-Charentes. Balanced on a hilltop above the town, the elegant **Château de la Rochefoucauld** (tel. 45 62 07 42 or 45 63 54 94) looks down upon its modest subjects with grace, prestige, and a touch of arrogance. Foucauld laid the first foundations on a rock in the 10th century. With time, the château came to be known as "Foucauld's rock," and the name de la Rochefoucauld has been used by Dukes and Princes for 10 centuries. Today, the 45th generation of this noble clan not only inhabits the château but occasionally guides tours around the wings they don't live in. The castle contains an 11th-century Roman dungeon, two medieval towers, a soaring yet simple neo-Gothic chapel, a superbly-carved Renaissance façade, and a spiraling staircase. The wife of François II was chummy with Leonardo da Vinci, and the Renaissance man is said to have influenced the château's style. (Open daily May-Sept. 10am-7pm. Tours 35F, or, if no tour, then a free visit.) From early July through mid-August, 550 costumed characters, including members of the Rochefoucauld family and 60 horseback riders, recreate history in the spectacular *son et lumiére.* (Call 45 63 02 33 or 45 63 07 45 for information and reservations. 14 shows on chosen nights, around nightfall. Admission 65F, children 30F.)

To get to the tourist office in the center of town from the train station, follow av. de la Gare on your right to rue Porte Marillac which becomes rue des Halles. The **tourist office** (tel. 45 63 07 45) is at the end of this street, and the château is a bit farther, across the river. (Open June-Sept. 15 daily 10am-noon and 2-6pm. In off-season, go to the library next door for information. Library open Tues.-Thurs. 2-6pm, Fri. 2-5pm, Sat. 8am-noon.) The **Hôtel de France,** 13, Grande Rue (tel. 45 63 02 29), recently taken over by new owners who plan to renovate, has large, clean rooms and a soothing small-town feel. There's a quiet courtyard and a restaurant downstairs. (Singles 90-110F, with shower 140F. Doubles 110-130F, with shower 165F. Breakfast 25F. Hall showers included.) The **municipal campground** (tel. 45 63 10 72) near the château is close to the municipal pool. (10F per adult, 5F per child, 14F per site. Open May 15-Sept. 15.) La Rochefoucauld is accessible by train from Angoulême (5 per day, 1/2hr., 26F).

Guienne

One of the most spectacular areas in the country, it is no wonder that Paleolithic people chose to establish the first of France's human settlements in Guienne. As they wound their ways westward from the Massif Central toward the Atlantic, the Dordogne, Lot, Vézère, and Isle Rivers slashed through the high, porous limestone *causses,* leaving behind towering cliffs and exposing countless caves. These prehistoric grottoes—sheltering 20,000-year-old paintings, carvings, and etchings of stampeding bison, frolicking wild horses, and panicked reindeer fleeing hunters' arrows—are today the life-blood of Guienne's tourist industry. But don't neglect the hundreds of feudal châteaux that cling to the rocky promontories and survey the poplar-lined rivers and valleys carpeted with fields of wheat and sunflowers.

Dubbed the "Capital of Prehistory," Guienne was first settled in the mid-Paleolithic era, 150,000 years ago, in the area around Les-Eyzies-de-Tayac. The region has revealed more artifacts from the Stone Age—tools, bones, weapons, cave paintings, and etchings—than any other place on earth. The painted caves of Lascaux are the most extensive and best-preserved in the world, but floods of tourists brought such drastic deterioration that the caves were closed to the general public in 1963; an exact replica opened 150m away in 1983 at the cave of Lascaux II. Today, the Grotte de Font de Gaume in Les-Eyzies-de-Tayac and the Grotte du Pech-Merle, 25km from Cahors, contain the most extraordinary original cave paintings still accessible to the public.

With the coming of civilization, Guienne found itself a player in the now-familiar story of kings, queens, wars, and châteaux. The French and English began centuries of bickering, fighting, looting, and pillaging in 1152, when Eleanor of Aquitaine, whose dowry contained an enormous portion of southwestern France, divorced Louis VII, King of France, and remarried Henry II, King of England. The Dordogne River formed a natural barrier between the opposing camps, both of which erected châteaux as defensive strongholds. The châteaux of Beynac and Castelnaud remain as evidence of that troubled period. *Bastides,* fortified towns surrounded by ramparts, built to gather scattered populations, began to sprout throughout the region in the 13th century. Domme, Monpazier, and Villeneuve-sur-Lot remain as three of the best-preserved *bastides,* largely unchanged since their founding in the Middle Ages. Since the body of St-Amadour was discovered in Rocamadour in the 12th century, this stunning hill town has been a mecca for both tourists and pilgrims.

After a series of epidemics ravaged crops in the late 19th century, Guienne stagnated as a poor farming region. Only recently, residents of other regions in France have begun to restore dilapidated stone cottages and farmhouses to serve as second homes. The sudden rise in tourism has brought prosperity and even a demand for culinary specialties that were once the region's livelihood. Topping that list is the rich, creamy *foie gras,* made of enlarged goose *(oie)* or duck *(canard)* livers and often thinned out with fat and spices into a *mousse* or *pâté.* Buy *foie gras* directly from farmers, where it's cheaper than in city shops (5-8,000F per kg). The large Boletus mushroom known as *cêpe,* as well as the black, earth *truffe,* found at the base of oak trees, are exported to the greatest restaurants across the world. They are often served in omelettes (50-180F) or in *pâtés.* More affordable are *confit de canard* and *confit d'oie,* the wing or leg of a duck or goose, cooked in its own fat and accompanied by *pommes sarladaise,* potatoes fried in garlic and the grease from the *confit. Noix* (walnuts) are sprinkled on fresh green salads, candied with sugar, dipped in chocolate, or baked into a delicious *gâteau aux noix* (walnut cake). Cahors produces a full-bodied red wine whose quality has only recently been accepted. Sweet Bergerac and Monbazillac whites perfectly accompany *foie gras.*

Unlike other regions of France, Guienne lacks a large cultural center from which to venture to the countryside. Discover your own favorite hamlet somewhere along one of the rivers, and explore the surrounding area from there. There are few enormous cathedrals and even fewer museums. Ask tourist offices for a list of *chambres d'hôtes,* secluded farmhouse accommodations. Bus and train connections in Guienne are neither frequent nor convenient. Unless you have a car, you may have to bike or hike to the loveliest villages. It's also possible to rent a moped in Sarlat, and canoe rentals abound in the region. Many *sentiers de grandes randonnées,* clearly marked long-distance footpaths, pass through remote areas and connect such towns as Les Eyzies, Sarlat, Souillac, and Cahors. Inquire at Dordogne's **Comité Départemental de Tourisme,** 16, rue Wilson (tel. 53 53 44 35) in Périgeux for maps and information on canoeing or kayaking along the Lot, Dordogne, Isle, or Vézère rivers. Although hitching long distances can be very difficult on the small, curving roads, many people make smaller hops to the tourist towns quite easily.

Bordeaux

Like a bottle of the vintage red wines for which it is renowned, Bordeaux has become noticeably darker with age, an apparent victim of its own success. A thin layer of grime blankets the city's resplendent high Gothic churches and cathedrals, grandiose remnants of its prosperous mercantile past. The Garonne River, which has always served as the conduit of trade for France's foremost industrial port, today flows a delicate shade of brown. Yet if history is any indicator, a little adversity (or pollution) has never checked the high spirits of the *bordelais.*

From Barbarian invasions in the 3rd century to the French kings' conquest of Aquitaine in the 15th, Bordeaux has retained a strong sense of identity. Even Eleanor of Aquitaine's marriage to Henry Plantagenet in the 12th century, and the resulting imposition of English sovereignty over Bordeaux, had seemingly little effect on the city's character or economy. Against the backdrop of a 300-year Anglo-French political standoff, *bordelais* merchants quietly profited from their aromatic wines. As Henry James wrote, "Bordeaux is...dedicated to the worship of Bacchus in the most discreet form." Today, the worship is hardly so discreet: the wine industry brings five billion francs a year to the region.

Looking toward the twenty-first century, the *bordelais* are hard at work reviving their city's image. Lackluster monuments are being scrubbed down, and the city planners are in the midst of expanding their acclaimed global wine center to meet the demands of an insatiable market. A multi-faceted population of *bordelais*—including Turks, Spaniards, Northern Africans and, of course, the native French—participates in this frenetic pace of development. Yet to partake of this unique cultural milieu, forgo the showy boutiques of the *centre ville* and explore a city that is at once magnificent and polluted, crowded and diverse, yet never, ever boring.

Orientation and Practical Information

Bordeaux's train station is a healthy half-hour walk from the center of town, and if you arrive late at night, you may want to think twice before venturing off along the sparsely illuminated **cours de La Marne.** Should you decide to make the walk, turn right out of the station onto rue Charles, left onto cours de la Marne and head straight about 12 blocks until you hit pl. de la Victoire. From there, take a right onto cours Pasteur, which leads to the Cathédrale St-André. Go around the cathedral and make a right onto rue des Remparts which leads to rue de la Porte Dijeaux. Make a left and you're just feet away from pl. Gambetta, the center of town. Alternatively, turn left upon exiting the station and walk about 30m to the bus depot. Both buses #7 and #8 make the trip to pl. Gambetta every 10 minutes (7F). Be sure to pick up a map at the information booth in the station. Keep in mind that Bordeaux is a big city: guard your wallet and yourself, especially at night.

Tourist Office: 12, cours du 30 Juillet (tel. 56 44 28 41). Take bus #7 or 8 from the train station, get off at the Grand Théâtre and walk one block toward the Monument des Girondins. Large, well-staffed office. Good maps, extensive hotel listings, information on camping, and more. *Carte Jeune* offers discounts to various restaurants, museums, and events (100F). Arranges bus tours of local wineries year-round. After June 15, tours also organized by the **CDT (Comité Départemental du Tourisme).** Ask about the *Carte Bordeaux Découverte,* allowing unlimited circulation on the city's bus routes (1-day pass 19F; 3-day pass 45F, with *Carte Jeune* 23F). Open Mon.-Sat.

Guienne, Basque Country,
Gascony, Languedoc-Rousillon

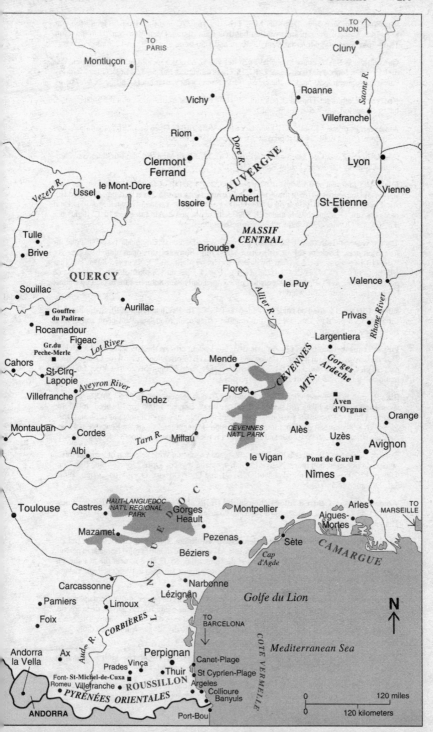

9am-8pm, Sun. 9am-7pm; Oct.-May Mon.-Fri. 9am-7pm. Also at the **airport.** Open Mon.-Sat. 8am-7pm, Sun. 10am-7pm. **Information booth** at train station. Open Mon.-Sat. 9am-7pm, Sun. 10am-7pm; Oct.-May Mon.-Sat. 9am-12:30pm and 1:30-6pm, Sun. 9:30am-12:30pm.

Consulates: U.S., 22, cours Maréchal Foch (tel. 56 52 65 95). Open Mon.-Fri. 9am-5pm. Visa division open Mon.-Fri. 10am-noon. **U.K.,** 15, cours de Verdun (tel. 56 42 34 13). Open Mon.-Fri. 9am-12:30pm and 2:30-5pm. In the case of serious emergency after hours, call 57 22 01 43.

Currency Exchange: Thomas Cook (tel. 56 91 58 80) at the train station. Not the greatest rates, but open on Sun. Open daily 8am-8pm.

American Express: 14, cours de l'Intendance (tel. 56 81 70 02). Open Sun.-Fri. 8:45am-noon and 1:30-6pm. Client mail. 24-hr. refund assistance (tel. 05 90 86 00).

Post Office: 52, rue Georges Bonnac (tel. 56 48 87 48). Open Mon.-Fri. 8am-6:30pm, Sat. 8am-noon. Currency exchange. **Postal Code:** 33000.

Flights: 11 km west of Bordeaux in Mérignac (tel. 56 34 50 00). A shuttle bus connects the train station and the tourist office to the airport (about every 1/2hr. from 5:30am to 10pm, 40min., 32F). **Air France** (tel. 56 00 03 03 or 56 00 03 00) flies once daily to London/Gatwick Mon.-Sat., and twice on Sun. (1 1/2hr., 2425F, under 18 800F with restrictions). **Air Inter** has 10-12 flights per day to Paris (70min., 775F, reduced fares from 205-435F).

Trains: Gare St-Jean (tel. 56 92 50 50), on rue Charles Domercq. City maps available at the information desk. **Lockers** 15F or 20F. Open 5am-11pm. **Showers** 15F, open until 10:30pm. To: Paris (10-14 per day; 4 1/2-5 1/2hr. by day, up to 8hr. by night; 290F); Nantes (5-8 per day, 4hr., 195F); Toulouse (9-11 per day, 2 1/2hr., 163F); Nice (4-5 per day, 9-10hr., 398F); St-Emilion (2 per day, 45min., 41F). Helpful information office open daily 8am-8pm; be sure to pick up a number before lining up at the windows.

Buses: Citram, 14, rue Fondaudège (tel. 56 43 04 04). To: Pauillac (1hr., 39F); St-Emilion via Libourne (3-4 per day, 1hr., 34F50). Information office open Mon.-Sat. 9am-noon and 2-6pm. Buy tickets on board.

Public Transportation: CGTE. An extensive bus system crosses the city and suburbs. Tickets 7F. Maps are available at the train station and at the CGTE information office, 4 rue Georges Bonnac, off pl. Gambetta (tel. 57 57 88 88). Open Mon.-Sat. 8am-7:30pm. See tourist office for information about *Carte Bordeaux Découverte* passes.

Bike Rental: In the *centre ville,* **Cycles Pasteur,** 42, cours Pasteur (tel. 56 92 68 20). Regular 10-speeds and mountain bikes 70F per day, 220F per week. Deposit 1400F for 10-speed, 1600F for mountain bike. Also accepts passports, credit card imprints, or any vital organ as deposit. (Open Mon.-Fri. 8:30am-noon and 2-6:30pm, Sat. 2-6:30pm.) Other rental shops are **Ecocycle** at 47, av. Aristide Briand (tel. 56 96 07 50) and **Delerm,** 211, rue Fondaudège (tel. 56 81 46 21).

English Bookstore: Bradley's Bookshop, 32, place Gambetta. Wide selection of regional travel guides, dictionaries, and more. Native-English-speaking owners. Open Mon. 2-7pm, Tues.-Sat. 9:30am-12:30pm and 2-7pm. Also **Mollat,** 83-91, rue Porte Dijeaux. Open Mon. 2-7pm, Tues.-Sat. 9:15am-7pm.

Women's Center: Centre d'Information sur les Droits des Femmes, 5, rue Jean-Jacques Rousseau (tel. 56 44 30 30). Limited information and counseling. Open Mon. 10am-4pm, Tues. 2-7pm, Thurs. 10am-4pm.

Youth Center: Centre d'Information Jeunesse d'Aquitaine, 5, rue Duffour Dubergier (tel. 56 48 55 50). Information about activities, jobs, etc. All job-related inquiries must be made in person. Open Mon.-Fri. 9am-6pm. **CROUS:** 18, rue du Hamel (tel. 56 33 86 86), near the Marché des Capucins. The office can tell you which university restaurants are open but can't sell you tickets. Open Mon.-Fri. 9:30am-12:30pm and 1:30-4pm.

Laundromat: Take your pick. The most convenient is on cours de Marne, 5min. from the station and hostel. Wash 15 or 16F, dry 5 min for 2F. Open daily 7am-9pm. Also at 27, rue de la Boëtie. Wash 17F, dry 2F for 5min. No 1F coins at either location. Open daily 8am-7:30pm. The one at 107, rue Fondaudège, is near many of the hotels. Wash 16F, dry 2F per 7min. Open daily 7am-10pm.

Medical Assistance: SAMU, tel. 56 96 70 70. Ambulance service. **Hôpital St-André,** 1, rue Jean Burguet (tel. 56 79 56 79). 24-hr. emergency room. **Emergency:** tel. 15.

Police: Headquarters at 87, rue de l'Abbé de l'Epée, also known as rue Castéja. (tel. 56 90 92 75). Smaller precinct at the train station (tel. 56 92 18 90). **Emergency:** tel. 17.

Accommodations and Camping

Bordeaux offers plenty of clean, comfortable lodgings at moderate prices. The main youth hostel, a skip and a jump from the station, is an adequate and convenient place to sleep, but the strict lockout and curfew might limit your carousing. Relatively inexpensive hotels and an elegant student *maison* round out the abundant affordable lodgings in this city. The sidestreets around pl. Gambetta (in particular Huguerie, rue du Palais Gallien and rue La Faurie de Monbadon) and around cours d'Albret are good places to look for cheap rooms. Reserve at least a day in advance during the hectic summer months. Keep in mind, however, that many proprietors will refuse to hold rooms after 7 or 8pm.

Auberge de Jeunesse (HI), 22, cours Barbey (tel. 56 91 59 51), 10min. from the station but 30min. from the station. Bear right out of the station, left onto cours de la Marne, then left again onto cours Barbey. The 250 beds fill quickly in summer. Graffiti mars the exterior walls but inside the hostel remains clean and presentable. The 250 beds fill quickly in summer. Well-equipped kitchen and pristine bathrooms. Single-sex rooms, each with 8 beds. Reception open 8-9:30am and 6-11pm. Strict lockout 9:30am-6pm. Curfew 11pm. Members 39F, passport holders 43F. Breakfast 16F. Sheets 16F. No telephone reservations.

Maison des Etudiantes, 50, rue Ligier (tel. 56 96 48 30). Take bus #7 or 8 from the station to the "Bourse du Travail" stop, and continue in the same direction on cours de la Libération to rue Ligier. If walking from the station, follow cours de la Marne through pl. de la Victoire to cours Aristide Briand and turn right onto rue Ligier. The *maison* is on the right-hand corner (30min.). Singles and doubles. Quiet, clean, and closer to the center of town than the hostel. Ping-pong and TV downstairs. Kitchen lacks pots, pans, and silverware, but you might be able to borrow some. From Oct.-June, the *maison* primarily houses monthly residents, but may have a few beds available for women travelers. In July and August it becomes co-ed and has plenty of space. No lockout or curfew. 57F, 47F with ISIC. Showers and sheets included.

Hôtel la Boétie, 4, rue de la Boétie (tel. 56 81 76 68), a quiet street between pl. Gambetta and the Musée des Beaux Arts. Attentive management lends a personal touch to the spacious, comfortable rooms equipped with a bedside TV, telephone, and fully-stocked mini-bar. Reception open 24hr. VCR (10F) and movie rentals (10F). Singles 120-135F. Doubles 135F, with two beds 160F. Triples 180F. All rooms with shower, toilet, and TV. Breakfast 18F. The same family also runs five other *centre ville* hotels of similar quality and with the same prices: Two are the **Studio Hôtel,** 26, rue Huguerie (tel. 56 48 00 14), where some singles are 98F, and **Hôtel Lafaurie,** 35, rue Lafaurie-de-Monbadon (tel. 56 48 16 33). The reception at La Boétie or Studio can inform you about the other hotels.

Hôtel d'Amboise, 22, rue de la Vieille Tour (tel. 56 81 62 67), in the *centre ville,* off pl. Gambetta. Attractive, clean rooms overlooking pedestrian street below. Washing machine (20F). Singles 65-80F, with shower 100F. Doubles 90F, with shower 110F. Breakfast 18F. Call to reserve at least a day in advance during summer.

Hôtel Bar-Club Les 2 Mondes, 10, rue St-Vincent-de-Paul (tel. 56 91 63 09), a block from the station. Spacious rooms well-maintained by amiable English proprietor. Pretty funky bed covers. Snack bar and daily happy hour (7-8pm) at adjoining bar with 8F beers. Singles 85F, with shower 105F. Doubles 100F, with shower 126-136F. Triples 189F. No hall showers. Breakfast 17F. Reservations held until 6pm.

Camping: There are no campgrounds in the city itself, but in the immediate vicinity is **Camping les Gravières,** Pont-de-la-Maye in Villeneuve d'Ornon (tel. 56 87 00 36). A 3-star campground in a forest by the river. 150 sites. Reception open 8am-11pm; off-season 8am-10pm. 17F per person, 16F per tent, 23F per tent and car. **Camping Beausoleil** (tel. 56 98 17 66) is a 3-star site 10km out of town in Gradignan. Take bus G from pl. de la Victoire. Both sites open all year. Call to make sure there is space before journeying out of the city.

Food

Known in France as *La Région de Bien Manger et de Bien Vivre* (The Region of Fine Eating and Living), Bordeaux offers an extensive array of restaurants to satisfy any palate. Aside from Bordeaux wine, you'll find ambrosial oysters, tender *confits* of duck and goose, and plump, plentiful *champignons* (mushrooms). The city has restaurants in all price ranges. Many of the affordable ones cluster around **place St-Michel,** a multi-ethnic neighborhood located a short walk from downtown madness. Explore St-Michel during the day, as nightfall brings increased crime. The area around place Général Sarrail, especially along rue des Augustins, also has some moderately priced establishments. The restaurants near the **Grosse Cloche** in rue St-James post slightly more expensive *menus,* as do those on **Rue des Faussets,** off pl. St-Pierre. Pizza shops line the sidestreets that converge on place Gambetta. **Markets** are scattered all over town. The newly installed, glittering market at place des Grands Hommes offers regional specialties at upscale prices. The marché des Capucins, off cours de la Marne at the end of rue Clare, and on cours Victor Hugo at pl. de la Ferme de Richemont, is a madhouse and much more fun (open Mon.-Sat. 6am-1pm). There is a cheap **Auchan supermarket** complete with moving sidewalks near the Maison des Etudiantes at the huge Centre Meriadeck on rue Claude Bonnier. (Open Mon.-Sat. 8:30am-10pm.) On Sunday, settle for the grocery stores along cours Victor Hugo.

University Restaurant: If you figure out which branch is open, it's a decent 25F all-you-can-eat meal. Better yet, buy a ticket with your ISIC card or your *Carte Jeune* and eat for 12F. Tickets sold Mon., Wed., and Fri. 11:30am-1pm at the restaurant; otherwise just ask any student. **CROUS** (tel. 56 33 86 86) can tell you which one is open or stop by any location and look for posted schedules. **Lebec,** rue de Cursol (tel. 56 91 79 96), is usually open July-Aug. and Oct.-May. Sun.-Fri. 11:45am-1:30pm and 6:45-8:10pm.

Café des Arts, 138, cours Victor Hugo, at the intersection of rue Ste-Catherine. A jaded but oh-so-busy sidewalk *brasserie* basking in neon. *Salade Niçoise* 24F. *Cassoulet* 35F80. Lamb chops with mustard 49F. House beer 13F. Open daily 9am-1am.

La Perla, 3, rue Gaspard Philippe, facing tour St-Michel in a colorful ethnic neighborhood. Abundant but unspectacular fare includes *couscous* and Spanish specialities. 38F buys soup, hors d'oeuvres, vegetables, meat, dessert, and wine. Open Mon.-Sat. 10:30am-1:45pm and 6:30-8:45pm.

L'Athenée, 44, rue des Trois Conils, 1 block east of the cathedral. Low lighting, dated decor, and good French food in this little ol' nook. 3-course mouth-watering 70 and 80F *menus. Flans* and *profiteroles* for dessert 12-23F. Open Mon.-Fri. noon-2pm and 8-10:30pm; Sat. noon-2pm.

La Crêperie, 23, cours Georges Clemenceau, a block from pl. Gambetta, past the Gaumont cinema. Entire menu consists of *galettes* stuffed with egg, meat and other fillings (30-50F) and over 20 choice *crêpes* for dessert (10-40F). Bustling student crowd; Mother Teresa look-alikes on wall. Open daily noon-1am.

Sights and Entertainment

"Take Versailles," mused Victor Hugo, "add Antwerp to it, and you have Bordeaux." Today's Bordeaux still preserves the blend of extravagance and economy to which Hugo alluded decades ago. Nearly 900 years after its original consecration by Pope Urban II, **Cathédrale St-André** remains the *grande dame* of Bordeaux's Gothic masterpieces. Built between the 11th and 16th centuries, yet sorely neglected in the ensuing decades, the cathedral fell into disrepair and underwent extensive renovation throughout the 19th century. Today, only the exterior wall of the nave survives from the original structure. (Open 8am-noon and 2-5:30pm; free organ recital every other Tues. evening mid-May to mid-Sept. Call 56 81 78 79 for information.) Across town, **Eglise St-Michel** is accompanied by an immense, free-standing 15th-century bell tower. Locals will warn you to exercise caution in exploring the sidestreets around St-Michel after dark (and even in broad daylight). Seedy elements tend to congregate in and around the Turkish game parlors/drinking houses in the area. The flea market held in the square adjacent to the church (Mon.-Fri. 7am-4pm, Sun. 7am-1pm) surveys everything from antiques to farm products. Several blocks up, on cours Victor Hugo, the enticing, duplicitous claims of second-hand clothing peddlers shouting *"A L'oeil!"* reverberate through the street (Sun. morning 7:30am-1pm). One of Bordeaux's showpieces, the recently restored **Grand Théâtre**, pl. de la Comédie, is worth a visit. The spectacular **Grosse Cloche,** on rue Saint James formerly served as an entrance to Bordeaux's old city, as well as a point of departure for pilgrims en route to St-Jacques-de-Compostelle. Today, pigeons nest behind the clock's frozen hands.

The Musée d'Aquitaine, 20, cours Pasteur (tel. 56 90 91 60) houses treasures from Bordeaux's agricultural, maritime, and commercial endeavors through the centuries, and provides an informative history of the Aquitaine region. Of note is the 2000-year-old *Vénus à la Corne.* (Admission 15F, students 8F. Free Wed.)

The **Musée des Beaux Arts** (tel. 50 90 91 60, ext. 1380), on cours d'Albret near the cathedral, houses a modest collection of canvases by Titian, Delacroix, Corot, Renoir, Matisse, and other European painters. (Open Wed.-Mon. 10am-6pm. Admission 15F, students 9F, Wed. free.) Bordeaux's **Entrepôt Laine,** 7, rue Ferrère (tel. 56 44 16 35), two blocks from cours de Maréchal Foch, is a colossal gallery containing the **Musée d'Art Contemporain,** the **Arc en Rêve Centre d'Architecture.** Temporary exhibits of painting, sculpture, and photography complement expositions focusing on specific architects or architectural movements. (Open Tues.-Sun. 11am-7pm, Wed. until 10pm. Admission 30F, students 20F. Free from noon-2pm.) Sip a cappuccino at the neat rooftop café.

The column of the **Monument to the Girondins** with the **Liberty Statue** at its peak has stood in the center of place des Quinconces since the turn of the century. For a respite from *centre ville* fibrillation, wander through the 25 green acres of the **Jardin Public.** (Open daily 7am-8pm; winter 7am-6pm. Free.)

During the year, nightlife centers on the student cafés around pl. de la Victoire. The **Alligator,** 3, pl. du Général Sarrail, is a popular jazz club that hosts a population of chess players as well. Across the square, **The Aviatic Café,** 41, rue des Augustins, serves 15F beers in a cramped bar. And *Bordelais* trend-setters haunt **Le Victoria,** 231, rue Ste-Catherine. The magazine *Confetti* (2F) appears every two weeks and is sold at most kiosks. It offers information about restaurants, entertainment, and *spectacles* around Bordeaux.

Wine and Wineries

> *"God only made water, but man invented wine."*
> —Victor Hugo, Les Contemplations,
> *"La Fête Chez Thérèse."*

Red Bordeaux wines break down into three families, each corresponding to a distinct geographical locale. They include the Médoc and Graves appellations (north and southwest); St-Emilion, Pomerol, and Fronsac from the central Libourne region; and the Bordeaux and Côtes de Bordeaux. Among the whites, especially in the southeastern Sauternes area, a distinction is made between dry and semi-sweet *(liquereux).*

Remember that "wine tasting" is not equivalent to "free beverage service." While many châteaux offer free *dégustations,* they expect visitors to make a purchase. Showing up and demanding a free glass of wine with no inclination to buy does get you a free drink, but it disgusts the attendant and really isn't worth your time.

The most logical approach to Bordeaux wine tasting begins at the **Maison du Vin/ CIVB,** 1, cours du 30 Juillet (tel. 56 00 22 66 or 50 00 22 88). The only house within Bordeaux to offer free tastings, the Maison entitles you to try a red (like a Pomerol or a Fronsac), a dry white (like a Graves or Entre-Deux-Mer), and a sweet white (like a Sauternes or a Loupiac). The attendant is a professional *sommelier* who is paid to evaluate the quality of new wines; feel free to ask questions. Ask at the Maison for a list of châteaux whose wines you think you might like. Visit those with the intent to purchase a bottle, and spend the rest of the day in the beautiful Bordeaux countryside picnicking and enjoying your recent purchase. (Maison du Vin open Mon.-Fri. 8:30am-6pm, Sat. 9am-12:30pm and 1:30-5pm. Ask about showing times for the 15-min. video on Bordeaux wines.)

If you choose to buy wine within Bordeaux, there are two fine establishments within 50m of the tourist office who will gladly sell you a bottle in the 15F-19,000F range. **Vinothèque,** 8, cours du 30 Juillet (tel. 56 52 32 05; open Mon.-Sat. 9am-7:30pm), and **L'Intendant,** 2, allées de Tourny (tel. 56 48 01 29; open daily 10am-7:30pm). Knowledgeable salespeople will offer advice and answer your questions. Don't be overly intimidated by the stuffy atmosphere in these places: feign an air of erudition and limited knowledge about wine, and you'll do just fine. Despite the fact that the store assistants at Vinothèque actually polish their bottles of *Grands Crus,* their prices are lower than those at the châteaux.

A visit to the major wine-producing châteaux requires, at the very least, a preliminary phone call. Many huge houses, such as **Château Haut-Briond** (tel. 56 98 33 73), manage to sell their wines without the help of backpack-laden small fry. Ask them how they may be reached by bus, and they are likely to suggest that you take a cab; hesitate, and it's all over—you've blown your cover. Ask the tourist office to help you make reservations. Depending on your preferences, the Maison du Vin can suggest hundreds of private châteaux for *dégustation* or exploration. If you want to cover a lot of territory in a short time, consider **Lim Tour,** which runs two daily tours within each of the major wine-producing regions. (Daily tours at 2 and 7pm; 150-195F depending on region. Call before 11am for reservations.)

Near Bordeaux

About 38km and a half-hour train ride east of Bordeaux, the medieval market town of **St-Emilion** harbors beautiful cloisters and a glorious hillside view of more than 1000 châteaux and billions of grapes. Although the *bastide* traces its roots to Gallo-Roman times, it wasn't until the 8th century and the arrival of hermit and wine connoisseur St-Emilion that it acquired any hint of its later glory. The subterranean **Eglise Monolithe,** a tribute to Emilion, was painstakingly carved shortly after his death from a single, massive piece of rock. The guided tour of the church passes through the ancient catacombs adorned with open sarcophagi and an occasional bone or two. Tours leave daily from the tourist office about every 45 minutes. (10am-5:45pm; Nov.-March 10am-5pm. 30F, students 19F.)

For an unparalleled panorama of the environs, scale the 198 uneven, stony steps of the 12th-century **Clocher de L'Eglise Monolithe.** (Admission 6F. Buy tickets at the tourist office.) The view from the summit far surpasses that from the deck of the often crowded **Tour du Roy** a stone's throw away.

For a gustatory delight, don't miss the delectable **macaroons** unique to St-Emilion (prices start at about 30F per box of one dozen). Don't plan on wolfing a whole meal in St-Emilion, however, as prices are exorbitant; instead, pack in a picnic from Bordeaux. Free *dégustations* are offered throughout the village; ask to sample the vermilion-hued Pomerols or the semi-sweet Fronsac labels, not to mention the village's own St-Emilion brand. At the far end of town, retreat into the **cloisters** and immerse yourself in their bucolic purity. (Open daily year-round.) The **tourist office,** pl. des Créneaux (tel. 57 24 72 03), sits at the foot of the church tower. (Open daily 9:30am-12:30pm and 1:45-6:30pm; Nov.-March until 6pm.) The tourist office organizes tours (some in English) of the different châteaux (July-Aug. Mon.-Sat., 2 1/2hr., 51F). These include a round-trip bus ride to the winery, a guided tour of the château, and a *dégustation.* If you feel like going out on your own, ask the tourist office for a list of châteaux that offer tours in English. Bring a good pair of sneakers to negotiate the town's sloping cobblestone pathways.

Trains run from Bordeaux to St-Emilion twice per day (1/2hr., 41F). Take a right on the main road from the station and walk the 2km to St-Emilion. **Citram buses** whisk 3-4 times per day from Bordeaux to St-Emilion, with a change of buses in Libourne (1hr., 34F50).

Trains leave Bordeaux about every hour for **Arcachon** (50min., 48F). A popular seaside resort with a beautiful sandy beach, Arcachon itself is not the main attraction. Rather, it is the sublime **Dune du Pilat** at **Pyla-sur-Mer,** 10km south of town, that attracts the most attention. In a never-ending battle of civilization against nature, locals have battled the spread of the dune's 60-million sandy tons; nearby homes have had to relocate and flee the invading sand. In the late afternoon especially, you'll have plenty of room to frolic all over this golden Alp's steep slopes—and to slog painfully back up. Buses leave for Pyla (a short walk from the Dune) from the Arcachon station (about 20 per day, last return at about 7:45pm, 40min., 16F round-trip). Some people report that hitching takes half as long. Take food and water with you. There are average-priced restaurants behind the dune (meaning a climb back over after lunch) and a steeply priced snack bar on the beach.

Surrounded by the ocean to the west and the Landais forests on the east, Arcachon itself attracts squadrons of tourists who appreciate the basin's calm waters. Oysters play a key role in nourishing the town's economy, though most of the region's 750 *ostréiculteurs* (oyster-farmers) operate from the smaller port-village of Gujan-Mestras to the west. Flat-bottomed **boat tours** depart from the Jetée Thiers pier for excursions of the Bassin d'Arcachon (tel. 56 54 83 09 or 56 54 60 32; June and Sept. 9:30-11:30am and 2:30-6pm, July and Aug. 9am-noon and 2-7pm; 45-85F depending on length and destinations). Several restaurants line the beach front, offering the local specialties. **La Fringale,** 12, bd. Marcel Gounouilhou, serves up a refreshing entree of six oysters, bread and a glass of white wine (30F). Opposite the train station in the *centre ville,* **La Coquille,** includes oysters and mussels in its 80F *menu.* For do-it-yourself fare, hit the **Uniprix** supermarket on the corner of cours Tartas and rue du Maréchal de Lattre de Tassigny. (Open Mon.-Thurs. 9am-12:30pm and 2:15-7pm.)

Arcachon's **tourist office** on pl. Roosevelt (tel. 56 83 01 69) is about 3 blocks left of the station. A helpful staff distributes maps, brochures, and lists of hotels (all expensive), camping sites, and B&Bs (some cheap ones from 90-130F). (Open Mon.-Sat. 9am-12:30pm and 2-6pm.) Pyla's **tourist office,** rond-point du Figuier (tel. 56 54 02 22), also provides lists of hotels. You almost certainly won't be able (or willing) to pay for a single one, especially in July and August when prices are inflated 50-80% and the cheapest rooms top the 200F mark. (Open daily 10am-1pm and 3-7pm; Sept.-June 9am-5pm.) Instead, try the three-star **Camping les Abatilles** (tel. 56 83 24 15), on allée de la Galaxie in Arcachon (July-Aug. 37F; Sept.-Oct. 11 and April 6-June 30 34F, tent, car, site, and 1 person included. Extra person 18F; 16F off-season.) Or choose from four campgrounds in Pyla, including a site on the Dune, **Camping de la Dune** (tel. 56 22 72 17; open May-Sept.). Freelance camping is prohibited in the area. Across the bay from Arcachon in Cap-Ferret is an **Auberge de Jeunesse (HI),** 87, av. de Bordeaux (tel. 56 60 64 62; open July-Aug.). Cap-Ferret is accessible by ferry from Arcachon's **Jetée Thiers** (tel. 56 54 83 09, every 1/2hr. July-Aug., every hr. Sept.-June 9am-noon and 2-7pm; 27F, round-trip 40F).

Arcachon's **Ville d'Hiver,** an arboreal, plush district of turn-of-the-century villas and mansions lies across the **Parc Mauresque** north of the beach. The elevated vantage point of the park yields an unobstructed view of the thatched-roof houses of the town below, and the ocean beyond.

Périgueux

Périgueux's Byzantine-Romanesque cathedral, its tangled *vieille ville* streets, and its occasional Roman ruins may offer fleeting glimpses of the past, but this capital of Périgord shows a mostly modern face. For centuries little more than a small market town, Périgueux (pop. 60,000) grew like wildfire with the rise of industrialization shortly after the Revolution. A smattering of sights makes the town a worthwhile stop on the way to the Dordogne, but don't linger. Compared to what awaits beyond, Périgueux is merely a gateway to greater things.

Orientation and Practical Information

Located at the center of the triangle formed by Bordeaux, Limoges, and Brive, Périgueux is a one- to two-hour train ride from any of these cities. The *vieille ville* and tourist office are a 10- to 15-minute walk from the train station. Turn right on rue Denis Papin and bear left on rue des Mobile-de-Coulmiers, which becomes rue du Président Wilson. On your right, you'll pass rue Lafayette, which leads to the Roman ruins clustered around the train tracks. The tourist office is four blocks farther along; take a right just after the Monoprix store and walk a block down to the office, next to the stone Tour Mataguerre. Continuing on rue du Président Wilson leads to the heart of the *vieille ville.*

Tourist Office: 26, pl. Francheville (tel. 53 53 10 63). A mediocre city map, list of hotels and restaurants, and extensive lists of alternative accommodations (farms and *chambres d'hôtes*). Grab the invaluable free brochure *La Fête en Périgord,* loaded with practical information. Guided tours in July and Aug. (Tues.-Fri. 10am and 2:30pm; 18F, students 12F). Open Mon.-Fri. 9am-7pm, Sat. 9am-noon and 2-7pm, Sun. 10am-5pm; Sept.-May Mon.-Sat. 9am-noon and 2-6pm. **Office Départementale du Tourisme,** 16, rue Wilson (tel. 53 53 44 35). Lots of information on all of Périgord. Comprehensive lists of campgrounds, *gîtes,* and *chambres d'hôtes,* and excellent topographic maps (40F). Open Mon.-Fri. 9:30am-noon and 2-4:30pm.

Post Office: rue du 4 Septembre (tel. 53 53 60 82), off pl. André Maurois. **Telephones** and **currency exchange.** Open Mon.-Fri. 8am-7pm, Sat. 8am-noon. **Postal Code:** 24000.

Trains: rue Denis Papin (tel. 53 09 50 50 answered daily 4am-midnight; for reservations 53 08 23 00). To: Paris (6 per day, 6-7hr., 251F); Lyon (4 per day, 7hr., 255F); Bordeaux (10 per day, 2 1/2hr., 87F); Toulouse (7 per day, 4hr., 168F); and Limoges (10 per day, 1 3/4hr., 69F). Information office open Mon.-Thurs. 8:30am-7:45pm, Fri. 9am-7:40pm, Sat. 9am-noon and 2-7:45pm, Sun. 10am-noon and 2-7:45pm.

Buses: pl. Francheville (tel. 53 08 91 06). Regional bus information upstairs; city bus information downstairs. Erratic service to surrounding towns. Schedules are confusing and fluctuate often.

Bike Rental: Au Tour de France, 96, av. du Maréchal Juin (tel. 53 53 41 91). 5- and 10-speeds 40F for first day, 20F per day thereafter. Mountain bikes 70F, 40F per day thereafter. Open Mon.-Sat. 9am-12:15pm and 2-7:15pm. Also **Huot Sports,** 41bis, cours St-Georges (tel. 53 53 31 56). 10-speeds 50F per day. Mountain bikes 80F per day. ID deposit. Open Tues.-Sat. 9:30am-12:30pm and 2-7pm.

Youth Center: Centre d'Information Jeunesse (CIJ), 1, av. d'Aquitaine (tel. 53 53 52 81). Tons of information on concerts, excursions, and other youth activities. Helps find long-term student lodging (free). Open Mon.-Fri. 9am-noon and 2:30-6:30pm.

Laundromat: Laverie Self-Service, 20, rue des Mobile-de-Gulmiers. Wash 20F per 7kg, dry 2F per 5min. Soap 2F.

Hospital: Centre Hospitalier, av. Georges Pompidou (tel. 53 07 70 00).

Medical Assistance: SAMU, tel. 53 08 81 11.

Police: Commissariat, rue A. Gadaud (tel. 53 08 17 67). **Emergency:** tel. 17.

Accommodations and Camping

Several inexpensive hotels cluster around the train station. A few more are scattered on the way into the *vieille ville* and in the pedestrian area. The hostel is not marked at all and can be difficult to find. Use the map in front of the station for orientation before making the trip. **Farms** in the region sometimes let rooms or camping space; ask for a list at the regional tourist office on rue Wilson or use their computer outside. Whether you plan to sleep indoors or out, in the city or on a farm, reserve a few days in advance in summer.

Foyer des Jeunes Travailleurs Résidence Lakanal, off bd. Lakanal (tel. 53 53 52 05). From the tourist office, turn left down cours Fénélon and take a right onto bd. Lakanal. 15m before the dead-end at the train tracks, turn right and walk around the club Périgueux and through the gate out back to get to the front of the *foyer.* The cheapest rooms in town. Comfortable beds in four-bed dorm rooms with peeling paint and intimate insects. Reception open Mon.-Fri. 5-7pm, Sat.-Sun. noon-1pm and 7-8pm. 60F. Sheets, showers, and breakfast (Mon.-Sat.) included. Cafeteria lunch (Mon.-Fri. 35-40F), and dinner (Mon.-Fri. 32F). Call ahead.

Hôtel des Voyageurs, 26, rue Denis-Papin (tel. 53 53 17 44), across from the station. Simple, clean rooms at fantastic prices. Reception open Mon.-Sat. Arrive early morning or late evening on Sun. Singles 68F. Doubles 73F, with 2 beds 88F, with shower 93F. Hall showers included. Breakfast 20F. Closed last three weeks in Aug.

Hôtel du Lion d'Or, 17, cours Fénélon (tel. 53 53 49 03), near the tourist office, with a bright flowery façade. Friendly foreign owners rent small singles (85F) and more spacious doubles (140F). Doubles with shower 180F. Triples 160F. Showers 15F. Breakfast 25F. Open March-Jan.; closed Mon. from Oct. to Easter.

Hôtel du Midi et du Terminus, 18-20, rue Denis-Papin (tel. 53 53 41 06), opposite the train station. Comfortable, modern, and immaculate rooms with telephones. TV lounge. Reception closed

LET'S GO® Travel

1992 CATALOG

When it comes to budget travel we know every trick in the book Discount Air Fares, Eurailpasses, Travel Gear, IDs, and more...

LET'S PACK IT UP

Let's Go Supreme

Innovative hideaway suspension with parallel stay internal frame turns backpack into carry-on suitcase. Includes lumbar support pad, torso and waist adjustment, leather trim, and detachable daypack. Waterproof Cordura nylon, lifetime guarantee, 4400 cu. in Navy, Green or Black.

A • • • • • • • • • • • • • • $165

Let's Go Backcountry

Full size, slim profile expedition pack designed for the serious trekker. Parallel stay suspension system, deluxe shoulder harness, Velcro height adjustment, side compression straps. Detachable hood converts into a fanny pack. Waterproof Cordura nylon, lifetime guarantee, main compartment and hood 6350 cu. in. extends to 7130 cu.

E • • • • • • • • $195

Let's Go Backpack/Suitcase

Hideaway suspension with internal frame turns backpack into carry-on suitcase. Detachable daypack makes it 3 bags in 1. Waterproof Cordura nylon, lifetime guarantee, 3750 cu. in. Navy, Green or Black.

B • • • • • • • • • • • • • • $119

Undercover NeckPouch

Ripstop nylon with soft Cambrelle back. 3 pockets. 6 1/2 x 5". Lifetime guarantee. Black or Tan.

C • • • • • • • • • • • • • • $9.95

Undercover WaistPouch

Ripstop nylon with soft Cambrelle back. 2 pockets. 12 x 5" with 30 x 13cm waistband. Lifetime guarantee. Black or Tan.

D • • • • • • • • • • • • • • $9.95

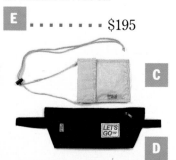

LET'S SEE SOME I.D.

1993 International ID Cards

Provides discounts on accomodations, cultural events, airfares and accident/medical insurance. Valid 9-1-92 to 12-31-93

F1	Teacher (ITIC) ▪ ▪ ▪ ▪ ▪	$16.00
F2	Student (ISIC) ▪ ▪ ▪ ▪ ▪ ▪	$15.00
F3	Youth (IYC) ▪ ▪ ▪ ▪ ▪ ▪ ▪	$15.00

FREE "International Student Travel Guide."

LET'S GO HOSTELING

1993-94 Youth Hostel Card

Required by most international hostels. Must be a U.S. resident.

G1	Adult (ages 18-55) ▪ ▪ ▪ ▪ ▪	$25
G2	Youth (under 18) ▪ ▪ ▪ ▪ ▪ ▪	$10

Sleepsack

Required at all hostels. Washable durable poly/cotton. 18" pillow pocket. Folds into pouch size.

H	▪ ▪ ▪ ▪ ▪ ▪ ▪ ▪ ▪ ▪ $13.95

1992-93 Youth Hostel Guide (IYHG)

Essential information about 3900 hostels in Europe and the Mediterranean.

I	▪ ▪ ▪ ▪ ▪ ▪ ▪ ▪ ▪ ▪ $10.95

Let's Go Travel Guides

Europe; USA; Britain/Ireland; France; Italy; Israel/Egypt; Mexico; California/Hawaii; Spain/Portugal; Pacific Northwest/Alaska; Greece/Turkey; Germany/Austria/Swizerland; NYC; London; Washington D.C.; Rome; Paris.

J1	USA or Europe ▪ ▪ ▪ ▪ ▪ ▪ ▪	$16.95
J2	Country Guide (specify) ▪ ▪ ▪	$15.95
J3	City Guide (specify) ▪ ▪ ▪ ▪ ▪	$10.95

LET'S GO BY TRAIN

Eurail Passes

Convenient way to travel Europe. Save up to 70% over cost of individual tickets. Call for national passes.

First Class

K1	15 days ▪ ▪ ▪ ▪ ▪ ▪ ▪ ▪	$460
K2	21 days ▪ ▪ ▪ ▪ ▪ ▪ ▪ ▪	$598
K3	1 month ▪ ▪ ▪ ▪ ▪ ▪ ▪	$728
K4	2 months ▪ ▪ ▪ ▪ ▪ ▪ ▪	$998
K5	3 months ▪ ▪ ▪ ▪ ▪ ▪ ▪	$1260

First Class Flexipass

L1	5 days in 15 ▪ ▪ ▪ ▪ ▪	$298
L2	9 days in 21 ▪ ▪ ▪ ▪ ▪	$496
L3	14 days in 30 ▪ ▪ ▪ ▪ ▪	$676

Youth Pass (under 20)

M1	1 month ▪ ▪ ▪ ▪ ▪ ▪ ▪	$508
M2	2 months ▪ ▪ ▪ ▪ ▪ ▪	$698
M3	5 days in 2 months ▪ ▪	$220
M4	10 days in 2 months ▪	$348
M5	15 days in 2 months ▪ ▪	$474

LET'S GET STARTED

Please print or type. Incomplete applications will be returned

International Student/Teacher Identity Card (ISIC/ITIC) (ages 12 & up) enclose:

1 Letter from registrar or administration, transcript, or proof of tuition payment. FULL-TIME only.
2 One picture (1 1/2" x 2") signed on the reverse side.

International Youth Card (IYC) (ages 12-25) enclose:

1 Proof of birthdate (copy of passport or birth certificate).
2 One picture (1 1/2" x 2") signed on the reverse side.
3 Passport number _____ **4** Sex: M☐ F☐

Last Name	First Name	Date of Birth

Street — *We do not ship to P.O. Boxes. U.S. addresses only.*

City	State	Zip Code

Phone	Citizenship

School/College	Date Trip Begins

Item Code	Description, Size & Color	Quantity	Unit Price	Total Price

Shipping & Handling	
If order totals: . . . . . . Add	
Up to $30.00 . . . . $4.00	
30.01-100.00 . . . . $6.00	
Over 100.00 . . . . $7.00	

Total Merchandise Price	
Shipping & Handling (See box at left)	
For Rush Handling Add $8 for continental U.S., $10 for AK & HI	
MA Residents (Add 5% sales tax on gear & books)	
Total	

Enclose check or money order payable to: Harvard Student Agencies, Inc.

Allow 2-3 weeks for delivery. Rush orders delivered within one week of our receipt.

LET'S GO® Travel

Harvard Student Agencies, Inc., Harvard University, Thayer B, Cambridge, MA 02138

(617) 495-9649   1-800-5LET'S GO (Credit Card Orders Only)

Prices subject to change

Sun. 3-6pm. Cozy singles 110F. Doubles 120F, with shower 140F. Hall showers included. *Croissant* breakfast 22F; no extra charge for breakfast in bed. Excellent *menus* from 60F include all the local favorites; served daily noon-2pm and 7:30-9:30pm. Call a day ahead. Closed the first 2 weeks of Oct. and 2 weeks around Christmas.

Camping: Barnabé-Plage, 80, rue des Bains (tel. 53 53 41 45), 1.5km from Périgueux in Boulazac. Take the city bus D (direction "Cité Belaire," 12F50) from cours Montaigne and get off at "rue des Bains." A riverside site packed in July and Aug. Open daily 9am-midnight. 12F50 per person, 11F50 per tent, 7F50 per car. Canoe rentals 80F per hr. and 100F per 1/2-day. **Camping de l'Ile,** route de Brive (tel. 53 53 57 75), 3km from town in Boulazac, on the river. 16F50 per person, 11F per tent, 11F50 per car. Open May 15-Sept. daily 9am-11pm.

Food

The most notable of *périgourdin* specialties are truffles and *foie gras. Charcuteries* along rue Limogeanne are palaces of *pâté de foie gras* and other delicacies. Budgetarians (and vegetarians) may have to settle for the fresh produce at the daily morning **market** in pl. du Coderc. There is also a larger market near the cathedral on Wednesdays and Saturdays. The expensive-ish restaurants lie near pl. St-Louis in the *vieille ville,* while the area southwest of the cathedral, toward the tourist office, groups several more wallet-pleasing options. **Monoprix,** on pl. de la République in the *centre ville,* has a mediocre supermarket upstairs. (Open Mon.-Sat. 8:30am-7:30pm.) The gardens surrounding any of the Roman ruins are perfect places to spread your picnic blanket.

L'Amandier, 12, rue Eguillerie, just off pl. St-Louis. Exquisite local cuisine. 50F lunch *menu* and 68F dinner *menu* include chilled cucumber soup, succulent grilled duck, and sensational desserts. Open Mon. and Wed.-Sat. noon-2pm and 7-10pm, Tues. and Sun. noon-2pm. Closed last Sun. of every month.

Le Fromage à Malices, 5, rue Port de Graule, the first right turn when walking up av. Daumesnil from the river. A neat little mousehole of a restaurant with all plates (65-75F) highlighting a type of cheese, and served with meats, salads, vegetables, and wine chosen to complement this omnipresent dairy product. Try the white cheese mousse for dessert (18F).

La Grignotière, 6, rue du Ruy Limogeanne, in a quiet, pleasant courtyard off pl. St-Louis. Fancy place serving fabulous, unusual salads including the *Salade du Périgord,* packed with nuts, duck, *foie gras,* and anything else you may have noticed at the local morning market. Some interesting dinner dishes, too (42-55F). Open Wed.-Sun. noon-2:30pm and 7:30-10:30pm. Closed Aug.

L'Os à Moelle, 9, rue des Places. Rustic, cavernous setting away from the crowds. *Menus* beginning at 50F and a wide choice of salads (32-40F). Open Tues.-Sat. noon-2pm and 8-10:30pm, Sun. noon-2pm.

Sights and Entertainment

All roads lead to the **Cathédrale St-Front,** one of the largest churches in this part of France. Built in the shape of a Greek cross, the cathedral successfully combines Byzantine domes, Romanesque arches, and the stylish turrets of a reformed fortress. A church has stood on this spot since the 6th century, but St-Front's present incarnation only came about in the last century when Abadie (who later took the design one step further to create Paris' Sacré-Coeur) all but dismantled the old church to make way for his more bodacious house of worship. In contrast to the exterior, the inside of the church is largely devoid of ornamentation apart from the gorgeous baroque wooden altarpiece in the apse. (Free tours in summer daily 8am-noon and 2:30-7:30pm, upon request. Admission to the 9th-century cloisters and crypt 10F.)

The **Musée du Périgord,** along cours Tourny, is home to one of France's most important collections of prehistoric artifacts, including several stone carvings and a 15,000-year-old skeleton. When all those pieces of chipped flint start to look pretty similar, admire the impressive Gallo-Roman mosaics that were unearthed near the train tracks, the excellent ethnography collection, or the small painting gallery. (Open Wed.-Mon. 10am-noon and 2-6pm. Admission 10F, students 5F.)

Several Gallo-Roman vestiges crumble amid modern apartments and boutiques, just across the tracks on the west side of town. A tourist office pamphlet suggests a self-guided tour through these ancient monuments. The massive, cut-away cylinder of the

Tour de Vésone remains as evidence of a marble-encased temple that was the center of the important Gallo-Roman city of Vesunna. Legend has it that the break in the tower was made when St-Front shooed away the last demons worshiped by pagans. The excavations at the **Villa de Pompeïus** next door have brought to light a wealth of artifacts that can now be seen in the town museum. Back across the tracks and closer to the train station, fountains swirl and palm trees linger over the overgrown remains of a first-century Gallo-Roman amphitheater in the **Jardin des Arènes.** (Tour de Vésone and gardens open daily 7:30am-9pm; Oct.-March 7:30am-6:30pm.) Up rue de l'Ancien Evêché from the amphitheater, the 12th-century **Eglise St-Etienne-de-la-Cité** was the first Christian edifice to appear in town. With its austere domes and bays, the church is an excellent example of Romanesque architecture with a Périgourdin twist.

Périgeux quiets down every year for about 10 days in August, as the town plays host to the **International Mime Festival.** Many of the most respected mime companies from around the world perform and give free workshops. For more information, contact the Centre Culturel de la Visitation, on rue Littré (tel. 53 53 55 17).

Near Périgueux

Twenty-five km north of Périgueux lies **Brantôme,** a bucolic hamlet built on a tiny island encircled by the Dronne River. Charlemagne founded the **abbaye** in 769 AD next to the enormous grottoes the Christians settled in the 5th century. The abbey's bell tower is one of the oldest in France. Visit on your own with a pamphlet available at the entrance, or take the fascinating tour of the monastic buildings and the caves, from which the earliest inhabitants carved out a chapel and a mill. (Daily tours in French 10-11am and 2-5pm on the hour, 16F.) The monks took refuge in the **Grotte du Jugement Dernier** whenever the abbey was attacked; the eerie apocalyptic reliefs are extraordinary. The rest of the abbey buildings are now the town hall and the **Musée Fernand-Desmoulin,** which exhibits a collection of local prehistoric artifacts and paintings by the museum's obscure namesake, who supposedly drew the portraits in total darkness, guided by a spiritual face. (Tours of the abbey in French on the hour. Abbey open Mon.-Sat. 10am-1pm and 2-7pm, Sun. 2-7pm; Sept. 16-Oct. and April-June Wed.-Mon. 10am-noon and 2-6pm; Nov.-March Wed.-Mon. 10am-noon and 2-5pm. Admission 17F. Museum open same hours. Admission 5F.)

Brantôme's **tourist office** (tel. 53 05 80 52), on av. de Pierre de Bourdeille near the abbey, sells maps with walking circuits of Brantôme and its environs (2F; open Easter-Oct. daily 10:30am-noon and 3-6pm). The **Hôtel de la Poste,** 33, rue Gambetta (tel. 53 05 78 55), has modest but clean rooms. (Singles and doubles 100F, with shower 120F. Triples 140F. Showers included. Breakfast 20F. Closed weekends Oct.-June.) The **Camping Municipal** (tel. 53 05 75 24), near the river on the route de Thiviers, is less than 1km out of town (9F per person, 10F per site; electricity 6F; open June-Sept.). Shaded by beautiful weeping willows, **Au Fil de l'Eau,** 21, quai Bertin, serves delicious quiches and salads (30-65F) on the grassy banks of the river. (Open daily 11am-3pm and 8-10pm.)

Brantôme is accessible by bus from Périgueux (Mon.-Sat. 3 per day, Sun. 1, 40min., 29F). **Delin,** 45-46, rue Gambetta (tel. 53 05 85 78) rents 10-speed bikes for 40F per day (ID deposit; open Tues.-Sat. 8:30am-noon and 2-7pm).

Ten km southwest of Brantôme along the Dronne River and the D78, lies picturesque **Bourdeilles,** site of a medieval fortress and a Renaissance château. You can climb the 13th-century tower inhabited by Philippe le Bel in 1310, or take the guided tour of the incomplete 16th-century wing, now furnished with lavish 15th- to 17th-century furniture. The Salon Doré (gilded salon), an Italian Renaissance chamber with rich tapestries and painted ceilings, was designed for Catherine de'Medici, who never accepted her invitation to visit the château. (Open July-Sept. 7 daily 9am-noon and 2-7pm; Sept. 8-Oct. 15 and April-June Wed.-Mon. 9:30am-noon and 2-6pm; Oct. 16-Dec. 15 and Feb.-March 10am-noon and 2-5pm. Admission 26F.) One bus runs to Bourdeilles from Périgueux every Wednesday at 11:15am, but it won't get you back. The bike ride from Brantôme is probably the most convenient and enjoyable means of transport.

The **Château de Hautefort,** Guienne's tribute to the Loire Valley, towers over a steep hill above a pristine valley east of Périgueux. The chateau's origins date back to the Middle Ages, although the crenelated walls and heavy fortifications were added in the 16th century. Most of what remains today was reconstructed in the mid-17th century in Renaissance style. The perfectly proportioned façade within the three-sided Cours d'Honneur looks over the castle's manicured gardens, while the interior has been lovingly restored after being ravaged by fire in 1968. The château was purchased by the Baron and Baroness de Bastard in 1929. The Bastards still live there. (Open daily July-Sept. 13 9am-noon and 2-7pm; Sept. 14-Oct and March 9:45am-noon and 2-6pm; Nov.-Dec. 13 and Jan. 17-Feb. Sun. only 2-6pm; April-June 9:45am-noon and 2-6:30pm. Admission 24F.) Getting to Hautefort requires time and perseverance. One bus makes the trip from Périgueux in the early evening, but it does not return until the following morning. Four buses (1hr., 28F) per day run from Périgueux to **Excideuil,** a small town with a 12th-century château, set on a hill 26km from Hautefort. Several shops in town rent bikes, on which you could pedal the remaining distance to Hautefort.

South of Périgueux between Bergerac and Agen are the feudal **bastides,** small fortress-towns built by the English and French when both countries claimed sovereignty over the area during the Hundred Years War. The *bastides* share a common design: rows of rectangular blocks, cut at right angles by narrow streets and surrounded by square ramparts. The English fortress of **Monpazier,** the best preserved, retains its church, arcaded town square, and fortifications. It is also quite close to the intimidating medieval castle of **Biron.** Ask the tourist office in Périgueux for suggestions on other daytrips to surrounding medieval towns.

Brive-la-Gaillarde

Situated at the intersection of the Paris-Spain and Bordeaux-Lyon train lines, Brive-la-Gaillarde is a commercial town whose pedestrian quarter is more like a contemporary shopping district than an ancient *vieille ville* of narrow cobblestone streets. Brive received its nickname, "La Gaillarde" (the Bold), when the town's courageous citizens managed to repel English forces stationed outside the thick city walls during the Hundred Years War. Continuing this tradition of brio and gall, Brive became the first town in France to liberate itself from the German Occupation in 1944. These days of peril have passed, however, and modern Brive, surrounded by the countryside of Périgord and Quercy, has embraced its humbler role as regional center and touring base.

The 12th-century **Collégiale St-Martin,** named after the Spaniard who introduced Christianity to Brive in the early 5th century, dominates the center of Brive with its high crossed arches and thin stone columns. Martin interrupted the feast of Saturnus, loudly proclaiming his faith and smashing idols; the shocked worshipers chopped off his head, unknowingly making a martyr of him. The crypt under the nave displays sarcophagi unearthed by recent excavations, as well as reliquaries and polychrome statues. The **Musée Labenche** (tel. 55 24 19 05), housed in the beautiful Renaissance Hôtel Labenche, is one of those little-bit-of-everything-under-the-sun museums common to smaller French towns. In addition to fine prehistoric and numismatic collections, and several brilliantly colored 17th-century tapestries, room upon room is devoted to the subtleties of wool carding, accordion manufacture, and mushroom identification. (Open Wed.-Mon. 10am-6:30pm; Nov.-March Wed.-Mon. 10am-6pm. Admission 24F, students 12F.) Five minutes northwest of the train station, the **Musée Edmond Michelet,** 4, rue Champanatier (tel. 55 74 06 08) has an informative and deeply moving display on the Resistance movement in WWII. There is not a town in France without a street named for Michelet, a native of Brive who was active in the *résistance* and later became a minister under de Gaulle. (Open Mon.-Sat. 10am-noon and 2-6pm. Free.)

One of the biggest in the area, Brive's **market** commands a huge chunk of pl. du 14 Juillet every Tuesday, Thursday, and Saturday. Everything from cheap clothes to gerbils to stereo equipment can be unearthed in the stalls. The prices at the food market are dirt cheap and the shopping is serious—no catering to tourists here. Hold on tight to your purse or wallet (8am-noon).

The **Auberge de Jeunesse (HI),** 56, av. du Maréchal Bugeaud (tel. 55 24 34 00), has comfortable three-bed dorms, a TV room, a common room, and primitive cooking facilities. From the train station, take av. Jean Jaurès to bd. Clemenceau. Turn right and follow it as it becomes bd. Brune, then bd. Amiral Grivel, and finally bd. Voltaire. The hostel is on the left at the intersection of bd. Voltaire and av. Maréchal Bugeaud. The 108 beds rarely fill up, but it's worth calling ahead in July and August. (Reception open 8-11am and 6-11pm. No lockout or curfew. 43F, nonmembers 62F. Breakfast 16F. Dinner 43F—ask for a picnic basket.) The staff at the ivy-covered **Hôtel Champanatier,** 15, rue Dumyrat (tel. 55 74 24 14), around the corner to the left of the train station, does its best to make your stay as comfortable as could be. The trains rumble all too frequently, but the rooms are clean. (Singles 74F. Doubles 100F, with shower 120F, with bathroom 170F. Triples with shower 230F.) The **Hôtel de l'Avenir,** 39, av. Jean Jaurès (tel. 55 74 11 84), down the street from the train station, lets cheery modern rooms five minutes from the train station. (Reception open Mon.-Sat. 7am-11pm. Singles 80F. Doubles 100F, with shower 130F, with bath 150F. Showers 10F. Breakfast 25F. Closed Dec.) The **Camping Municipal des Iles,** bd. Michelet (tel. 55 24 34 74), just beyond the youth hostel, sits by the Corrèze River. (Reception open 7am-noon and 2-10pm. 12F per person, 10F per tent. Showers 5F. Showers 5F.)

Restaurant Ruthène, 2, rue Jean-Maistre, on a tiny street off rue Carnot near bd. Général Koenig, serves a 40F lunch *menu* with a *plat du jour* and dessert, and a fabulous three-course dinner *menu* with *confit de poule* and *spécialités au Roquefort,* such as steak dripping with blue cheese. (Open Mon.-Fri. 11:30am-2:30pm and 7-10pm, Sat. noon-2pm and 7-11pm.) **Le Quercy,** 3, allée des Tilleuls, on pl. du 14 Juillet, has a 62F *menu* that includes *rillettes de canard* (shredded duck), as well as *confit de canard* (65F), and flambéed shrimp (70F; open Tues.-Sun. noon-1:30pm and 7-9pm.)

The **tourist office** (tel. 55 24 08 80), in Immeuble Château d'Eau, towers in a lighthouse on pl. du 14 Juillet. From the train station, follow av. Jean Jaurès to St-Martin, walk around the church and continue on rue Toulzac, which becomes av. de Paris. The office is on the right. (Open Mon.-Sat. 9am-12:30pm and 2:30-7pm, Sun. 10am-1pm; Sept.-June Mon.-Sat. 10am-noon and 2:30-6pm.) The **gare routière,** av. Léon Lagrange (tel. 55 24 29 93), off bd. Voltaire, is far from the center of town, although most buses also stop at the train station and at various points in town. Call the bus station or ask at the tourist office for information. **STUB** (tel. 55 86 07 07) buses groove to Sarlat (1 per day, 1 1/4hr., 34F) and smaller towns in the area. **Trans-Périgord** buses (tel. 55 77 57 65 in Limoges) also make a daily run to Sarlat (1 1/4hr., 43F) via Souillac (35min., 23F). The **train station** (tel. 55 23 50 50) is a major regional hub. Trains roll to: Paris (12 per day, 4hr., 246F); Bordeaux (4 per day, 3hr., 129F); Toulouse (9 per day, 2 1/2hr., 134F); Cahors (8 per day, 1 1/2hr., 69F); Souillac, with connecting buses to Sarlat (4 per day, 1/2hr., 35F); and Rocamadour (4 per day, 45min., 39F). The **post office** is on pl. Winston Churchill (open Mon.-Fri. 8am-6:45pm, Sat. 8am-noon). The **postal code** is 19100. The **Centre Hospitalier,** bd. Docteur Verlhac (tel. 55 92 60 00); the **Commissariat de Police,** 4, bd. Anatole France (tel. 55 74 04 36; emergency tel. 18); and **S.O.S. Médecins** (tel. 55 23 33 33) are all at your service.

Near Brive

With its pointed round roofs, oddly shaped houses, and houses built entirely of red sandstone, enchanting **Collonges-la-Rouge** looks like it just jumped out of a Saturday morning cartoon. Fifteenth- to seventeenth-century houses, replete with fairytale towers and turrets, line the streets, broken only by a 12th-century church and an old wood-covered market. The emerald green vines and trees scattered throughout the *rues* break the crimson monopoly of the village, prosaically named one of the most beautiful in France. Twenty km southeast of Brive, Collonges is accessible by bus from Brive (1 per day, 1/2hr., 14F).

Farther southeast in the Lot region, the crenelated burnt red ramparts of **Castelnau-Bretenoux** have surveyed the valley below since the 11th century. A remarkable example of medieval military architecture, Castelnau was built atop an enormous pedestal in the shape of a triangle, flanked by three corner towers. In the central *cour d'honneur,* the 67m **Tour Sarrazin** commands a view that extends for miles. Partially restored in the early 20th century after suffering heavy damage during the Revolution, the **Château** today displays a splendid series of Aubusson and Beauvais tapestries as well as 15th-century stained-glass windows that miraculously survived the turbulence of five centuries. (Open daily 9:30am-6:30pm; Sept. and April-June 9am-noon and 2-6pm; Oct.-March 10am-noon and 2-5pm. Admission 26F, students 14F.) In contrast to this weighty medieval fortress, the graceful **Château de Montal** teases with a stern Renaissance façade but opens to reveal a charming courtyard on whose white walls mermaids play, idyllic faces grin, and monsters cavort. The interior bursts into a symphony of sculpture; even the underside of each step in the grand stairway is masterfully sculpted. Opulent tapestries, Flemish and Spanish painting, and exquisite furniture adorn this château, still occupied by the current owner. (Open July daily 9:30am-noon and 2:30-6pm; Aug. daily 2:30-7pm; Sept.-Oct. and Easter-June Sun.-Fri. 9:30am-noon and 2:30-6pm. Guided tours in French approximately every 45min. Last tour begins 1hr. before closing. Admission 20F, students 15F.)

Twelve km up the Dordogne from Montal, **Carennac** makes up for its lack of a château with small-town eloquence. Geraniums hang in huge bunches from wooden balconies, themselves attached to lilliputian gray-and-yellow stone houses beneath algae-covered roofs. The town's 10th-century priory was home to famous writer and priest Fénelon, most famous for his *Adventures of Telemachus.* The Romanesque **Eglise St-Pierre** has a lovely intact tympanum with a figure of Christ in the center, surrounded by symbols of the evangelists, apostles, and angels. Inside, off the flamboyant cloister, a 16th-century *Entombment of Christ* features profoundly emotional faces grouped around the body. (Entombment open June-Sept. 9:30am-12:30pm and 2-7:30pm. Admission 8F.)

Halfway between Brive and Aurillac, 10km north of Bretenoux, the Dordogne River village of **Beaulieu** is well known for its 13th-century **Abbaye Benedictine St-Pierre,** one of the region's finest examples of Limousin Romanesque architecture. Down the street along the banks of the river, the 12th-century **Chapelle des Pénitents,** now converted into a religious art and history museum, has been beautifully restored in Spanish style, with golden walls and a rustic wooden balcony. (Open July-Sept. 15 10am-noon and 3-6pm. Call the *mairie,* tel. 55 91 11 31, for tours off-season. Admission 10F.) Just next door, the wonderful **Auberge de Jeunesse (HI),** pl. du Monturu (tel. 55 91 13 82) recalls Swiss chalets with its wooden balconies overflowing with potted geraniums. Should you wish to make the region more than a daytrip from Brive, the hostel makes a perfect base. (Reception open daily 7-10:30am and 6-11pm. No lockout. 12- to 15-bed dorms 39F, nonmembers 58F. Breakfast 16F. Sheets 15F. Kitchen facilities. Open April-Sept.)

Reaching Castelnau, Montal, Carennac, and Beaulieu requires train, bus, bike, time, and planning. For all four, take a train from Brive to **Biars** (4-5 per day, 45min., 37F). A shuttle bus runs through Bretenoux (10min.) and **St-Céré** (15min.) three to four times per day from the Biars train station (15F; call 65 38 08 28 for schedule information). From Bretenoux, it's a flat 4km southwest to Castelnau, 10km southeast to Carennac, and 9km north to Beaulieu. You can rent bikes in Bretenoux from **M Bladier,** rue d'Orlinde (tel. 65 38 41 56; 40F per day, ID deposit; mountain bikes 80F per day, 500F deposit; open Tues.-Sat. 8am-noon and 2-7pm, Sun. 10am-noon; Oct.-June Mon.-Sat. 8am-noon and 2-7pm). From St-Céré, it's a mere 2km to Montal. In St-Céré, you can rent bikes at **Saint-Chaumont,** 45, rue Faidherbe (tel. 65 38 03 23; 3- and 10-speeds 27F per 1/2-day, 35F per day; mountain bikes 60F per 1/2-day, 80F per day; ID deposit; open Mon. 10:30am-noon and 2:30-5:30pm, Tues.-Sat. 9am-12:30pm and 2-7pm; Sept.-June Tues.-Sat. 9am-12:30pm and 2-7pm).

Les-Eyzies-de-Tayac

Some of the world's best-preserved prehistoric cave paintings hide in the limestone cliffs above Les Eyzies-de-Tayac. Sealed in caves for 15,000 years, much of the artwork has been discovered only in the last century—recently enough so that most of the paintings and etchings are still relatively well-preserved, but more than enough time for the word to have gotten around. Every summer, thousands of tourists flock to this "Capital of Prehistory" to gawk at the creations of the Cro-Magnon people (named, incidentally, for the Cro-Magnon cave directly above the town), to take in the beauty of the Vésère and Dordogne valleys, and to inflate hotel and restaurant prices. Despite the overcrowding, though, Les Eyzies (pop. 800) decidedly merits a visit. You will need to start early (most conveniently from Périgueux), and be prepared to kill a few hours between buying your ticket and starting your tour. The caves appear to be least crowded during the weekend, and if you can, try to come outside of July and August, when you'll be better able to appreciate the region as a fascinating account of the past, not merely as a profit-making industry.

Orientation and Practical Information

Les Eyzies is linked by train to Agen, Périgueux, Le Buisson, and Sarlat. There are also weekly tourist buses from Sarlat and Souillac. To get to the center of town from the train station, turn right and walk 1km down the village's only street.

Tourist Office: pl. de la Mairie (tel. 53 06 97 05), 5min. from the train station. Excellent list of nearby caves, advice on getting scarce tickets, **currency exchange,** and, in summer, tours of the museum and outlying area. Also rents bikes (see below). Information on car and canoe rentals, horse trails, and camping. Sells cycling and hiking guides. Open Mon.-Sat. 9am-7pm, Sun. 10am-noon and 2-6pm; March-June and Sept.-Oct. Mon.-Sat. 9am-noon and 2-6pm; Nov.-Feb. Tues. and Sun. 9am-noon and 2-6pm.

Post Office: tel. 53 06 94 11, down the street from the tourist office. **Currency exchange.** Open Mon.-Fri. 9am-noon and 2-5pm, Sat. 9am-noon. **Postal Code:** 24620.

Trains: tel. 53 06 97 22 or 53 09 50 50. To: Périgueux (5 per day, 30-45min., 35F); Sarlat (2-3 per day, change at Le Buisson, 1hr., 42F); Agen (4 per day, 2hr., 75F); Paris (3 per day, 6-8hr., 257F). Open Tues.-Sun. 7:20am-11pm, Mon. 7:20am-5pm and 7:20-11pm.

Laundromat: **Lavérie du Préhisto,** route de Sarlat near the entrance of the town. The world's only prehistoric laundromat. Wash 25F, dry 5F per 5min., 10F per 15min. Soap 5F. Open daily 8:30am-noon and 2-6:30pm.

Bike Rental: At the tourist office. 30F per 1/2-day, 40F per day, 240F per week, deposit 100F. Also at the **Citroën** garage, 500m out of town on the road to Périgueux (tel. 53 06 97 29), near the campsite. Mountain bikes 70F per 1/2-day, 100F per day, ID deposit. Open daily June-Aug. 8am-noon and 2-8pm.

Hospital: tel. 53 31 75 75, in Sarlat.

Police: tel. 53 29 20 17. **Emergency:** tel. 17.

Accommodations, Camping, and Food

Rooms are expensive and the few cheap ones are booked a month in advance during summer. If you want to stay in town, reserve as far ahead as possible. The inexpensive *gîte d'étape*, nestled against the valley wall 4km from town, is paradise regained. Another option is a bed in a private house in town (130-200F), relatively inexpensive if two people share a room. The tourist office has a list of these B&Bs, which often put up signs announcing *chambres*.

Gîte d'Etape: Ferme des Eymaries, rte. de St-Cirq (tel. 53 06 94 73). Cross the tracks at the train station, go over the bridge, and turn left at the Elf gas station. Walk along the road for 2km and turn right 3m before crossing the train tracks. Follow the gravel, then dirt road for 1km (40min.). Easily worth a 40-min. walk. Great owner, friendly dogs, neat dorms built into the cliff, and views that will make you want to settle down here. Call ahead (1 or 2 days in July-Aug.) preferably between 1 and 2pm, or after 6pm. Kitchen facilities and hot showers. 35F. Breakfast 17F.

Hôtel des Falaises (tel. 53 06 97 35), down the street from the tourist office. An oasis of good rooms in a desert of overpriced hotels. Backyard garden overlooks the Dordogne Valley's hills and fields—ideal for budding impressionists. Singles and doubles with shower and toilet 140-190F. Triples with shower and balcony 210-250F. Quads 285F. Breakfast 25F. Open year-round.

Hôtel du Périgord, on D47 near the Grotte de Font-de-Gaume (tel. 53 06 97 26). Quiet rooms. Large lawn. Near the woods. Singles and doubles 115F, with shower and toilet 145F. Hall showers included. Breakfast 20F. Open Easter-Oct.

Camping: Usually plenty of room. The superbly named **La Rivière** (see Title Page), is just out of town on route de Périgueux (tel. 53 06 97 14). Take a left out of the train station and continue just past the river. Reasonable snack bar and restaurant, pool, washing machines, and canoe rental. 20F per person, 29F per site. Electricity 14F. Also has 4 doubles with shower (180F) and 2 quads with shower (240F). Breakfast 25F. Open March 15-Sept. daily 8am-10pm. **Camping Le Pech** (tel. 53 06 95 84), 3km from the train station, mostly uphill. Walk to the end of the main street and follow the signs. Call ahead and the kind managers will come and pick you up. 8F50 per person, 8F per tent and car. Electricity 8F. Hot showers 2F. Open daily 8:30am-midnight; off-season 8:30am-10pm.

Restaurants here serve very expensive, well-prepared meals. Either shell out the dough for the *haute cuisine,* settle for another *croque-monsieur,* or bring a picnic from Périgueux, as even the town's one *épicerie,* across from the tourist office, is overpriced and understocked. The **Halle Paysanne des Eyzies,** on route de Sarlat, brings relief in the form of local produce and cans of *foie gras,* including occasional free tastings. (Open June-Sept. 15 daily 9am-1pm and 2:30-7pm.) A decent-sized market runs the entire length of the town every Monday. The **Resto Mentalo,** just past the Halle Paysanne, serves pizzas (36-42F), salads (18-42F), and *crêpes* (10-32F). For a treat, indulge in the sensational *confit de canard* (50F) or a salad with smoked duck, goat cheese, and walnuts (56F; open July-Aug. 11 daily 11:30am-3pm and 7-10pm; Easter-June and Sept.-Oct. Wed.-Mon. 11:30am-3pm and 7-10pm). The restaurant/snack bar marked **Restauration,** on the left side of pl. de la Mairie, serves omelettes, salads, meat, and fish, with nearly all dishes under 50F (open daily April-Oct. 15 noon-2pm and 7-9pm).

Sights

Les Eyzies itself has two excellent museums, but all the caves lie at least 1km out of town. The **Musée National de Préhistoire** (tel. 53 06 97 03), located in the cliffs with the best views of town right beyond its windows, exhibits a vast collection of weapons, tools, bones, cave drawings, and carvings, including a room of casts of important prehistoric artifacts discovered elsewhere. The museum comments upon the societies that occupied Les Eyzies throughout the millennia. (Open Wed.-Mon. 9:30am-6pm; April-June and Sept.-Nov. Wed.-Mon. 9:30am-noon and 2-6pm; Dec.-March Wed.-Mon. 9:30am-noon and 2-5pm. Admission 17F, ages 18-25, over 60 and Sun. 9F, under 18 free.) A two-minute saunter to the left from the train station, fortified **Eglise de Tayac** impresses with its slate-roofed bell towers and narrow fortress windows. (Open at the discretion of the local priest.)

Opened on April 1, 1990, the **Musée L'Abri Pataud** is the prehistoric version of an open-air folk museum. The site of the museum and adjacent archeological display is on the former property of a local farmer, M. Pataud, who uncovered bones and stone tools practically every time he overturned a shovelful of earth. As it turns out, his farm was built on an *(abri)* (shelter) for several groups of reindeer hunters over a span of 20,000 years. The excavated area exposes layers corresponding to 14 periods of habitation. In the next room, a set of video screens explains prehistory and evolution in rather technical terms. Visitors are supplied with headsets which pick up recordings (in French) corresponding to 16 windows. An excellent English translation is also available. The sculpture on the ceiling of the museum, visible in a mirror, was discovered accidentally, illuminated suddenly one day by the stray flashlight beam of a technician scaling the cliff to lay electrical wire. (Open July-Aug. daily 9am-7pm; Sept.-Dec. and Feb.-June Tues.-Sun 10am-noon and 2-5pm. Last entry 1hr. before closing. Admission 22F.)

Near Les Eyzies

By far the most famous and most remarkable of all the cave paintings in France lie 25km northeast of Les Eyzies, just outside Montignac at Lascaux (see "Near Sarlat" for details). Ever since Lascaux was closed due to significant deterioration, the **Grotte du Pech-Merle** (see "Near Cahors") and the **Grotte de Font-de-Gaume** (tel. 53 06 97 48), 1km outside Les Eyzies on the D47, have become the most important caves still open to tourists. Inside Font-de-Gaume are 15,000-year-old painted friezes of bison, horses, reindeer, and mammoth—faint, but amazing examples of their designers' advanced technique and use of the natural contours of the cave for relief. Modern archeologists and anthropologists have yet to determine accurately whether the paintings were thought to bring good luck or represented a hunt or religious ceremony. Though discovered in the 18th century, locals did not realize the paintings' importance until two centuries later, by which time they had already decayed through neglect and several had been defaced with graffiti. During peak season, 20 people are received at half-hour intervals in closely monitored groups, and only 340 people are admitted per day. Because of these restrictions, and because many of the tickets are bought in advance by tour groups, the road to the famous cave is paved with hard-luck stories. Half the tickets are sold by reservation in blocks of three days (for example, on Fri. tickets may be reserved for Sat.-Mon., etc.). If you did not get a chance to reserve, come as early in the day as possible; the 7:16am train from Périgueux arrives at 7:51am. If you arrive by 8am, you'll probably get a late-morning or afternoon ticket; at the very least, you'll have a few hours to wait. You should return at least 10 minutes before your 45-minute tour begins. (Be aware that it takes 5min. to climb to the mouth of the cave.) The tours are in French, but require little commentary. (Open Wed.-Mon. 9am-noon and 2-6pm; Oct.-March Wed.-Mon. 10am-noon and 2-4pm. Admission 31F, ages 18-25 and over 60 17F, ages 7-18 6F, under 7 and artists or art students free.)

Unlike the Grotte de Font-de-Gaume, whose paintings have been preserved because of the low humidity in the caves, the **Grotte des Combarelles,** 2km farther down the road (tel. 53 06 97 72), has a humid atmosphere, and only etchings remain. While they pale in comparison to Lascaux or Font-de-Gaume, the more than 300 carvings depict dozens of different animals, including rare human figures, in an intimate atmosphere. Visitors are admitted in groups of six for the 45-minute tour. Because the groups are so small and there are only about a dozen tours per day, Combarelles is the toughest ticket in town. Tickets go on sale at 9am for morning tours and 2pm for afternoon tours—get there at least an hour before the window opens. (Open Thurs.-Tues. 9am-noon and 2-6pm; Oct.-March Tues.-Thurs. 10am-noon and 2-4pm. Admission 25F, ages 18-25 and over 60 14F, ages 7-18 6F, under 7 free.)

The hills around Les Eyzies are pock-marked with caves and rock formations. You'll run across a series of roadside attractions northwest of the village along the D47. The tourist office runs weekly tours to those beyond walking distance (see above). Call ahead to reserve and verify the day of the tour. Most interesting is the **Grotte du Grand Roc** (tel. 53 06 92 70), 1.5km from town on the road to Périgueux, which lies halfway up the chalk cliffs and commands a blistering view of the Vézère Valley from its mouth. Decorated by nature rather than by human artists, the cave is filled with a forest of stalactites, stalagmites, and eccentrics—small calcite concretions that grow neither straight down nor straight up. The latter have created dozens of spectacular formations unique to this cave in the shape of crosses, chrysanthemums, and even the Winged Victory of Samothrace. (Open daily June-Sept. 15 9am-7pm; March 15-May and Sept. 16-Nov. 15 9:30am-6pm. Admission 28F.) The **Abri du Cap-Blanc** (tel. 53 59 21 74 or 53 59 05 55) in Marquay, 7km northwest of Eyzies, replaces quantity with quality. There are only a dozen carvings on the cave wall, but the horses and bison have been sculpted in full relief, sometimes as much as 20cm deep. (Open July-Aug. daily 9:30am-7pm; April 10-June and Sept.-Oct. 10am-noon and 2-6pm. Admission 20F.)

Dozens of other prehistoric sites are scattered throughout the area. Unfortunately, regular bus lines do not serve the caves. Ask at the tourist office in Les Eyzies for more information.

Sarlat

Thirty-five years ago, Sarlat (pop. 10,700) was merely the quiet capital of Périgord Noir, a town little different from the rest of the region. But in 1962 the French government targeted it for a massive restoration project that was to clean up virtually every building in the *vieille ville*. Three years later, the new Sarlat emerged—a quaint, handsomely restored and surprisingly medieval town. The old quarter's renovations are so thorough that most of the town looks as if was carved from a single block of glowing sandstone. Such movie-set perfection attracts the gaze of more than a few cameras, but the crowds aren't a good enough reason to skip the narrow streets, hidden corners, and unique doorways of Sarlat's *vieille ville*. In addition, regular bus tours to the surrounding region, moped rentals, and a youth hostel unite to make Sarlat the most convenient base to explore the Dordogne River Valley. To enjoy the town in peace and quiet, wander the streets in early morning or in late evening.

Orientation and Practical Information

Sarlat is off the main rail lines, but several trains per day go to well-connected Brive and Perigueux, each less than two hours away. To get to the center of town from the somewhat distant (1.5 km) train station, follow av. de la Gare to the left and turn right at the junction with av. Thiers, which magically transforms into av. Général Leclerc. After crossing a small square, this becomes rue de la République, the principal thoroughfare, which neatly bisects the *vieille ville*. Bear right on rue Lakanal, past the church, and onto rue de la Liberté, which empties onto pl. de la Liberté, the main square and home to the tourist office.

Tourist Office: pl. de la Liberté (tel. 53 59 27 67). A busy but helpful office housed in the 16th-century Hôtel de Maleville. Free maps of the *vieille ville* with a suggested walking tour. Information on excursions, camping, and bike tours. Accommodations service (10F). **Currency exchange** on days when the banks are closed. Pick up the free booklet, *Guide Pratique*, which includes transport schedules, excursions, and useful practical information on the town. Daily guided tours of the town in French June-Sept., and one English tour per week on Friday. Tours 21F, students 12F. Open daily 9am-7pm; Oct.-May 9am-noon and 2-6pm.

Post Office: pl. du 14 Juillet (tel. 53 59 12 81). **Telephones** and **currency exchange.** Open Mon.-Fri. 8:30am-12:30pm and 1:30-6:30pm, Sat. 8:30am-12:30pm. **Postal Code:** 24200.

Trains: av. de la Gare (tel. 53 59 00 21). Ticket booths open daily 5:45am-9pm. To: Bordeaux (3-4 per day, 2 1/2hr., 106F); Brive (4 per day, 1hr., 46F); Périgueux (3 per day, 1 1/2hr., 63F), via Les Eyzies (3 per day, 1hr., 39F); Le Buisson (4 per day, 1 1/2hr., 27F). The Les Eyzies and Le Buisson connections to Paris are ill-timed and indirect. The route via Souillac, served by SNCF bus, is better. The same buses to Souillac connect with trains to Toulouse (6 per day, 2hr., 116F).

Buses: Most buses stop at the train station and in pl. Pasteur, closer to the center of town. **SCETA** (tel. 55 77 57 65) to Souillac (4 per day, 50min., 24F), where you can hop a train to Paris or Toulouse; and Brive (1 per day, 1 1/2hr., 50F). **STUB** (tel. 53 59 01 48 or 55 86 07 07) to Brive (1 per day, 1 1/2hr., 35F) and Périgueux (2 per day, 1 1/2hr., 39F). Complete schedules are printed in the *Guide Pratique*, free at the tourist office.

Bike and Moped Rental: Maison du Plein Air, 16, rue Fénélon (tel. 53 31 24 18). Ten-speeds 70F per day, 340F per week, 300F deposit. Mountain bikes 110F per day, 540F per week, 300F deposit. Open daily 9am-7pm; Sept.-June 9am-noon and 2-6pm. **Société Sarladaise de Cycles et Cyclomoteurs,** 36, av. Thiers (tel. 53 28 51 87), on the road into town from the train station. Mountain bikes 100F per day, 450F per week, ID deposit. Mopeds 150F per day, 840F per week, ID deposit. Open Mon.-Sat. 9am-7:30pm. The tourist office's **guide pratique** has a list of all bike rental places in town.

Laundromat: 24, av. de Selves. Down the street from the hostel. Wash 24F per 7kg, dry 2F per 5min. Soap 2F. Open daily 6am-10pm.

Hospital: Centre Hospitalier, rue Jean Leclaire (tel. 53 31 75 75).

Police: pl. de la Grand Rigaudie (tel. 53 59 05 17). **Emergency:** tel. 17.

Accommodations and Camping

Sarlat's youth hostel only accepts individuals and small groups from July through October 15. Hotels are very expensive and always fill in summer; reserve a week or more in advance in July and August. There are dozens of campgrounds within a ten km radius of Sarlat.

Auberge de Jeunesse (HI), 15bis, av. de Selves (tel. 53 59 47 59), 30min. from the station but only 5-10min. from the *vieille ville*. From rue de la République, continue straight until it becomes av. Gambetta, follow it for 100m, and bear left at the fork onto av. de Selves. The hostel is 300m up on the right. Friendly, mellow atmosphere with no large groups allowed during the summer. Somewhat run down, with exterior shower and toilets, but excellent kitchen. Reception open 6-8pm—sometimes earlier, sometimes later—but you can always drop off your bags. No lockout. No curfew. 39F. Camping 22F. Sheets 15F. Call ahead, as the 41 beds often fill in summer. Hostel open all year, but groups of 6 or less are only accepted July-Oct. 15.

Hôtel des Récollets, 4, rue Jean Jacques Rousseau (tel. 53 59 00 49), on the western side of town, up the ramp after rue Papucie. Wonderful, flowery hotel 30 seconds from the action yet away from the noise. Super owner loaded with hints for travelers. No parking nearby. Pristine rooms off a new courtyard. Singles and doubles 155-165F, with shower 185F, with shower and toilet 220F. Triples 245-300F. Quads 320F. Breakfast 30F.

Hôtel Marcel, 8, av. de Selves (tel. 53 59 21 98), just down from the youth hostel on a noisy street, but far from the maddening tourist crowds. Spotless, newly renovated rooms, all with shower, toilet, and TV. Singles and doubles 170-180F, with bath 190-220F. Breakfast 28F. Open Feb. 15-Nov. 15.

Camping: there are countless campgroups in the surrounding area, but the ones closest to town usually fill up in summer. Get a full list of campsites from the tourist office. The closest reasonably priced one is **Le Montant** (tel. 53 59 18 50), 2.5km from town on the D57. Bar, washing machines, and hot water. 16F per person, 20F per tent. Open Easter-Sept.

Food

Restaurants in town are all fairly similar—reasonably expensive and extremely good. Most shops purvey every variety of *foie gras* at prices you'll love to hate; do yourself a favor and buy directly from the farmers in the countryside. The Saturday **market** is renowned throughout France; all the live-long day, vendors fill every street in the *vieille ville* offering everything from truffles at 6000F per kg to *espadrilles*. A smaller market takes place Wednesday mornings in pl. de la Liberté. There is a gargantuan **Intermarché Supermarket** 500m up the road from the youth hostel. (Open Mon.-Fri. 9am-12:30pm and 3-7:30pm, Sat. 9am-7:30pm.)

Restaurant du Commerce, 4, rue Albéric Cahuet. In summer, tables overflow into the street and square, and occasional musicians serenade the crowded scene. Many, many choices, including a 50F 4-course *menu* and a 70F 5-course *menu* featuring a crispy *confit de canard*. *Foie gras de canard* 55F. Salads 30-35F. Open April-Nov. daily 8am-5pm and 7-11pm; Jan.-March Tues.-Sun. 8am-5pm and 7-11pm.

Restaurant Criquettamus, 5, rue des Armes, just off rue de la République. The 3-course 60F *menu* offers a taste of local specialties, while the two different 90F *menus* touch all the bases, including regional soups, *foie gras*, and *confit de canard*. Open March-Dec. daily noon-2pm and 7-10pm.

Le Plamon, on rue des Consuls, off rue Victor Hugo. Serves a fine 48F *cassoulet au confit de canard* (duck stew with beans) and hearty 32-48F salads on one of the loveliest streets in the *vieille ville*, right beneath the towering Eglise Ste-Marie. Share a drink or an ice cream on the terrace. Open April 15-Oct. 15 daily 9am-10pm.

Sights and Entertainment

The glowing stone of Sarlat's buildings sheds a golden, smiling light on the *vieille ville*. The joy of discovering the town lies in wandering aimlessly through the twisted streets on your own walking tour. The tourist office's free map points out places that might otherwise evade even the most ardent mavens of architecture. Most of the sights and all of the tourists are east of rue de la République, while the west side tells a quieter story, and some of the picturesque, flower-filled streets might even qualify as deserted.

The **Cathédral St-Sacerdos** stands out for its enormous organ and impressive stained-glass windows. In July and August, the cathedral is often filled with music lovely enough to rouse a gargoyle (tickets 30-80F). A walk behind the cathedral reveals dozens of flying buttresses as well as the **Lanterne des Morts,** a bizarre 12th-century stone beehive of a monument. While it is believed to have served as a lantern for the dead, it is hard to see how the lamp could have been lit, since the second-story chamber is inaccessible.

Next to the cathedral are the **Palais Episcopal** and the **Maison de la Boétie.** Built in the 16th century, the *maison's* pointed gable and ornate windows exemplify Italian Renaissance style. It now serves as the Chambre de Commerce et d'Industrie, and its lower common room frequently houses small exhibitions.

On the other side of the main thoroughfare, the **Musée de la Chapelle des Pénitents Blancs,** on rue de la Charité at rue Jean-Jacques Rousseau, maintains a small but impressive collection of polychrome statuettes and ecclesiastical garments. Of particular interest are the mannequin clothed in a penitent's white robes and pointed hat and the heart-shaped reliquary containing—you guessed it—the heart of the Marquise de Gaubert. (Open Easter-Nov. 15 Wed.-Mon. 10am-noon and 3-6pm. Admission 10F, students 5F.)

The nightlife scene in Sarlat isn't dull, but it is very, very concentrated. All the action happens at the **Pub "Le Card",** just off rue de la République on rue du Minage. Stop by and have a drink, watch a laser disc, or just bust a move.

For two weeks in late July and early August, Sarlat hosts the **Festival des Jeux du Théâtre,** a series of plays held in various venues around town. (Tickets 50-160F. 15% discount with *carte jeune.*) For reservations, write Festival des Jeux du Théâtre de Sarlat, B.P. 53, 24202 Sarlat Cedex. For information, call the Hôtel Plamon (tel. 53 31 10 83).

Near Sarlat

The heart of the Dordogne Valley beats 15km south of Sarlat, as the river winds its slow path by dozens of riveting medieval châteaux perched high on precipitous cliffs. Poplar trees and farmland paint the valley a coat of emerald green, occasionally interrupted by attentive patches of sunflowers. From the peak of one hill town, you can often see several others on the horizon. An armchair monarch's dream come true, the Valley concentrates more châteaux in a single region than the Loire Valley. Although droves of tourists and their screaming children flood the region every summer, it should be possible to find solitude outside of the most prominent towns. The many *chambres d'hôtes* throughout offer farmhouse accommodations and convenient access to the historic sites without the constant bother of whizzing cars. Ask at the Sarlat tourist office for lists of *chambres d'hôtes*, campgrounds, and castles.

Domme, the highest and best-defended of the valley's villages, balances on a hilltop by the Dordogne 11km south of Sarlat. Built in 1281, Domme is a typical example of a mighty *bastide,* a fortified-town design invented ten years earlier at the height of the Hundred Years War. All *bastides* were constructed according to the same plan: a rectangular fortified wall containing narrow, perpendicular streets and a central square with a covered market. Access to the town was only possible through two or three gateways in the wall. More a semi-circle than a square because of its precarious setting on a steep cliff, Domme's fortified archways lead into a spectacular *vieille ville,* whose sunburnt stone houses hover above fields of sunflowers far below. The terrace of the **Belvédère de la Barre** overlooks a breathtaking vista of the poplar-lined river gliding past grazing cows, the châteaux of Montfort and Giverzac, and the villages of Beynac and La Roque-Gageac.

The covered market in the middle of the town square hides the entrance to the network of caves where Domme's inhabitants took refuge during the Hundred Years War. The guided tour winds past gardens of stalactites and stalagmites and a few bison and rhinoceri bones. (Caves open July-Aug. daily 9:30am-7pm; April-June and Sept.-Oct. Mon.-Fri. 9:30am-noon and 2-6pm. Admission 25F, students 20F.) The **tourist office** (tel. 53 28 37 09), just across the square, can help with the difficult task of placing you in one of Domme's three hotels. (Open daily 9:30am-7pm; April-June and Sept.-Oct. 9:30am-noon and 2-6pm; Nov.-March 2-5pm.)

Four km downstream from Domme, tiny **La Roque-Gageac** huddles at the base of a sheer cliff. The imposing Château de la Malartrie at the edge of town was actually built in this century, and is privately owned. The château, the medieval houses, and the tropical plants overflowing into the streets (which flourish because of a microclimate particular to the village) create an ensemble that prompted Henry Miller to exclaim, "If heaven existed on earth, God would surely have chosen this scenery for it!" The **tourist office** (tel. 53 29 52 37) is in a small kiosk in the parking lot.

Between La Roque-Gageac and Beynac, on the south side of the river, the town of **Castelnaud** supports a half-restored, half-ruined 12th- to 16th-century château with a **museum** (tel. 53 29 57 08) more intriguing than most in the area. Displays color the story of the repeated sieges during the Hundred Years War with chivalric armor, frightening spiked torture tools, cannons, models of medieval weapons, and one behemoth of a catapult. The views from the castle terrace are out of this world. (Open March-Nov. 11 daily 10am-7pm. Admission 22F, under 17 11F.) The **Château Les Milandes,** 8km from Castelnaud, built in the 16th century as an aristocratic retreat, has a distinct history in French château lore. After World War II, African-American dancer Josephine Baker, raised in the slums of St. Louis and propelled to fame in the Folies Bergère in Paris, bought the château and constructed in it a *village du monde* (village of the world), where she cared for dozens of children of all races from around the world. The guided tour through the castle shows some of her furniture and gives access to the lovely garden around the château. (Open April-Sept. daily 9:30-11:30am and 2-6:30pm. Admission 28F, under 16 15F.) Castelnaud and Les Milandes are not accessible by bus, but the bike rides from Beynac (6km and 13km, respectively) follow the relatively unchallenging riverbanks.

The restored 13th-century chateau at **Beynac-et-Cazenac,** 12km southwest of Sarlat, commands the Valley from its peak 150m above the Dordogne. One of the best-preserved hill towns in the region, Beynac rises to its summit along tiny cobblestone streets flanked by ancient stone homes decorated with wrought-iron balconies and flowered terraces. Although unfurnished rooms of the still-inhabited castle are the only ones open to visitors, the tour (French only) of this defensive fortress passes by daunting medieval architecture and sensational views of surrounding hill towns from the château terraces. (Château open March-Nov. 15 10am-noon and 2:30-6:30pm. Admission 25F.)

Beynac's **tourist office** (tel. 53 29 43 08) occupies a tiny part of a tiny building by the river. The least expensive room around is at the immaculate **gîte d'étape** (tel. 53 29 40 93 or 53 29 50 75), by the tennis court to the right when entering the town from upstream. You must call before arriving; in July and August, reserve a week in advance. (39F50. Kitchen facilities.)

The delightful **Hôtel de la Poste,** on the road climbing to the château (tel. 53 29 50 22) has been run by the same family for five generations since 1820. The hotel offers small, clean rooms, and spectacular views right from the terrace. Those in the know claim the best hot chocolate in France is served at breakfast. (Singles and doubles 130F, with shower 175F. Showers 6F. Breakfast 25F. Open April-Oct.) One of the least expensive around, this hotel fills up a week in advance during the peak summer season. **Camping Le Capellerou** (tel. 53 29 54 95) is just out of town on the riverbank. (18F per person, 18F per site. Electricity 12F. Open June-Sept.) You can rent bikes at **Le Garage de Beynac** (tel 53 29 42 47), at the entrance to town when coming from Sarlat. (25F per 1/2-day, 50F per day. Mountain bikes 40F per 1/2-day, 80F per day. 15% discount after 3 days. 250F or passport deposit. Open daily 8am-8:30pm; Oct.-June Mon.-Sat. 8am-noon and 2-6pm.)

Beynac, La Roque-Gageac, and Domme are all easily accessible by bus from Sarlat. In July and August, **Trans-Périgord/SCETA** buses (tel. 55 77 57 65) make one run to Beynac in the morning (40min., 22F50) via Domme (20min., 13F50) and La Roque-Gageac (30min., 20F), and back from Beynac in the early evening. **SNCF** also sends regular buses from Sarlat to Beynac (2 per day, 20min., 25F). More expensive but slightly more convenient, **Hep! Excursions** (tel. 53 28 10 04 or 53 28 18 34) runs half-day or full-day tours to all three towns on Tuesday, Saturday, and Sunday (100-135F; ask in the Sarlat tourist office for more information). Similar excursions are run once or twice a week from Souillac and Cahors. Renting a bike in Beynac or a moped in Sarlat gives you more flexibility. One of the best ways to see the Dordogne Valley is to drop that backpack like a ton of bricks and pick up a paddle. Dozens of outfits rent canoes and kayaks by the hour or by the day. A number of places let you rent a boat in Carsac, descend to Beynac at your leisure, and then pick you and the boat up for the drive back upstream, all for 70-80F. The Sarlat tourist office stocks millions of brochures from all the companies.

The most spectacular set of cave paintings yet discovered hide in the caves of **Lascaux,** near the town of **Montignac,** approximately 25km north of Sarlat. Discovered in 1940 by a few teenagers and their dog, Lascaux had to be closed down in 1963 because the humidity which resulted from millions of tourist exhaling fostered algae and microstalactites that ravaged these paintings which nature had preserved intact for 17,000 years. Today, only five archeologists per day, five days per week, are allowed into the original caves. But an abandoned quarry 200m away harbors the 20th century's most elaborate salute to the artistic cave-dwellers: a complete re-creation of the caves of Lascaux, prosaically dubbed **Lascaux II,** which accurately recreates every nook and cranny of the original cave. Painted with the same natural pigments used 17,000 years ago, the new paintings of 5m-tall bulls, horses, and bison look better than the real thing, but at the expense of the sense of awe and mystery that comes with looking at original paintings. Tickets can be bought at the automatic machine near the **tourist office** (tel. 53 52 82 60). Not surprisingly, they go fast; get there early for a tour a few hours later. Weekends tend to be less crowded, although the last tour (at 5pm) is usually sold out by noon. (Open July-Aug. daily 9:30am-7pm; Sept.-Dec. and Feb.-June Tues.-Sun. 10am-noon and 2-5:30pm. Admission 45F.) Montignac's *vieille ville* is a wonderful place to spend an afternoon while waiting for the tour. Catch a great view of the entire yellow-and-red town from the bridge over the Vézère River. The Lascaux twins are about 2km outside town.

Very few buses serve Montignac, and the nearest train station is at LeLardin, 10km away. One bus for Montignac leaves Brive every evening (1 1/2hr., 26F) and another from Périgueux (1 1/2hr., 29F). Two **STUB** buses run every morning from Sarlat to Montignac in July and August (Sept.-June 1 per day, 1/2hr., 19F) and return in the evening. To be guaranteed of tickets, try to catch the 7am bus; the next one is at 12:35pm. The **Camping Municipal** (tel. 53 52 83 95) is just outside town on the D65. (9F per person, 9F per site, 5F per car. Electricity 11F. Open April-Oct. 15.) You can rent bikes at **Ricros,** 27, rue du 4 Septembre (tel. 53 51 87 02) for 70F per day. (Passport deposit. Open Mon.-Sat. 8am-noon and 2-7pm.)

Souillac

Appropriately, "Soulliac" is the *périgourdin* word for doughnut; while there is of little interest aside from a 13th-century abbey in center of town, the caves, castles, hills and valleys which ring it are Périgord and Quercy at their sweetest. Inexpensive hotels, a slew of campsites, good transportation services, and a number of bike rental outfits have combined to make Soulliac one of the most popular bases for exploring the Dordogne region. The twisting, roller-coaster roads radiating out from town all cut through breathtaking scenery, including dense forests, ancient stone farms, and medieval châteaux.

Orientation and Practical Information

Souillac lies along the Paris-Toulouse line, only 45 minutes from Brive. Bus and train departures in all directions are frequent and generally convenient. To reach the *centre ville* from the station go straight down the hill for 200m, turn left onto av. Jean Jaurès, and right after 1km onto av. du Général de Gaulle, which becomes bd. Louis-

Jean Malvy. The tourist office and *vieille ville* are on the right (20min.). To reach the Dordogne, go 1.5km farther along av. de Toulouse.

Tourist Office: bd. Louis-Jean Malvy (tel. 65 37 81 56). Decent maps and plenty of information on hiking circuits, *gîtes d'étapes,* and *chambres d'hôtes* in the region. Organizes excursions (July-Aug.) for a minimum of 5 people to Rocamadour and the Gouffre de Padirac (Wed., 120F) and Sarlat, La Roque Gageac, and Beynac, (Sat., 120F). Also runs a shuttle bus to Rocamadour (July-Aug. Tues. and Fri., 90F round-trip). Open July-Aug. Mon.-Sat. 10am-noon and 2-6pm.

Post Office: 11, bd. Louis-Jean Malvy (tel. 65 37 82 81). **Telephones.** Open Mon.-Fri. 8am-12:30pm and 2-5:30pm, Sat. 8am-noon. **Postal Code:** 46200.

Trains: pl. de la Gare (tel. 65 32 78 21). To: Toulouse (6 per day, 2hr., 116F); Cahors (8 per day, 3/4hr., 49F); Paris (4 per day, 5-6hr., 266F); Brive-la-Gaillarde (6 per day, 30min., 34F); Limoges (5 per day, 1 1/2hr., 92F).

Buses: Information at the train station. **SCETA** buses (tel. 55 77 57 65) to Sarlat (4 per day, 3/4hr., 24F) and Brive (1 per day at 3pm., 50F) from train station; some also stop on av. de Sarlat.

Bike Rental: Evasion Sport, 36, bd. Louis-Jean Malvy (tel. 65 37 03 64). Mountain bikes 70F per 1/2-day, 90F per day; 250F deposit. Open daily 9am-noon and 2-7pm; Sept.-June Tues.-Sat. 9am-noon and 2-7pm. **Carrefour du Cycle,** 23, av. Général de Gaulle (tel. 65 37 07 52). Ten-speeds 50F per 1/2-day, 80F per day; mountain bikes 60F per 1/2-day, 90F per day; ID deposit. Open Mon.-Sat. 8am-12:30pm and 2-7:30pm.

Hospital: tel. 55 92 60 40, in Brive.

Police: rte. de Sarlat (tel. 65 32 78 17). **Emergency:** tel. 17.

Accommodations, Camping, and Food

Hotels are often booked solid in July and August, but if you call a few days ahead or start your search early in the morning, you should be able to snag a room.

Auberge du Puits, 5, pl. du Puits (tel. 65 37 80 32). Attractive ivy-covered hotel with quiet and comfortable doubles from 125F, with shower 153F. Fancy schmancy restaurant downstairs. Showers included. Breakfast 26F. Open Jan.-Oct.

Hôtel L'Escale, 4, av. Gen. de Gaulle (tel. 65 37 03 96), at pl. de Laborie. No-frills rooms in a great location. Inquire about rooms at the Pizzeria Don Camillo across the street or the shoe store next door. Singles and doubles 90F, with showers 150F. Hall showers included. No breakfast.

Hôtel de France, 64, bd. Louis-Jean Malvy (tel. 65 37 81 06). Slightly worn rooms with soft mattresses, but the hotel is big enough that it may have room when other places are full. Singles and doubles 145F, with bath 220F. Breakfast 28F.

Camping: Well-equipped camping sites are ubiquitous in this area. All are crowded in July and August. **Camping Municipal Les Ondines,** av. de Sarlat (tel. 65 37 86 44), on the banks of the Dordogne, makes a fine first choice. Head out of town on av. de Toulouse and turn right onto rue des Ondines. 11F50 per person, 7F50 per tent. Electricity 6F. Open May-Sept. 9am-12:30pm and 2-8pm. **Camping La Paille Basse,** rte. de Borrèze (tel. 65 37 85 48 or 65 32 73 51). A luxurious 4-star site in a wooded area with pool, tennis courts, restaurant, and soccer field. 26F per person, 46F per tent. Open July-Sept. 8:30am-12:30pm and 1:30-9pm, May 15-June and Sept. 1-15 9am-noon and 2-8pm. Ask at the tourist office about other sites.

Souillac's restaurant pool doesn't sparkle. Your best bet might be the hotel restaurants, many of which post satisfactory 50-60F *menus.* One of the better deals in town is at the **Hôtel Beffroi,** pl. St-Martin, known to loyal locals as "Chez Jeanette," where the informal, unhurried service delivers a delicious meaty four-course 60F *menu* that changes daily. (Open Sun.-Fri. noon-2:30pm and 7-9:30pm, Sat. noon-2:30pm; off-season open Mon.-Sat. same hours.) One km out of town on av. de Toulouse, **L'Ajoupa** is undoubtedly the hippest place in town. While the 55F *menu* and the 38-50F pizzas may not be the best value to be found, the meals are served on a beautiful terrace overlooking the Dordogne, and, for an extra 3F, you get a day's use of the pool and jacuzzi; they even rent bathing suits (25F), towels (25F), and deck chairs (10F). July and August bring live music on certain nights. (Open Easter-Nov. Tues. and Thurs.-Sun. noon-3pm and 7-11pm, Wed. noon-3pm.) **La Crêperie,** 33, rue de la Halle, serves *crêpes, galettes,* and salads (9-38F), as well as mounds of *paëlla* (50F) in a quiet atmosphere.

(Open daily noon-midnight; Sept.-June Tues.-Sat. noon-3pm and 7-10:30pm.) There is a small **market** every Monday and Wednesday morning on pl. Doussot from roughly 8am to 12:30pm, while a larger one fills the streets on the first and third Fridays of the month. The **Supermarché E. Leclerc,** at the intersection of av. de Sarlat and av. de Verdun below the train station, has everything you always wanted to eat but were afraid to ask for. (Open Mon.-Sat. 9am-7:30pm; Sept.-June Mon.-Fri. 9am-12:30pm and 2:30-7:30pm, Sat. 9am-7:30pm.)

Sights

The 13th-century **Eglise Abbatiale,** an extravaganza of domes and octagonal chapels, claims three cupolas similar to those of the Byzantine-Romanesque cathedrals of Périgueux and Cahors. Immediately to the left upon entering, the flowing low-relief carving of the prophet Isaiah is rightfully considered one of the jewels of Romanesque artwork. A circus of devils, dragons, monsters and assorted other things that go bump in the night gnaw away at one another on the portal columns. Next door, in the recently opened **Musée de l'Automate,** pl. de l'Abbaye, a New Orleans jazz band bops, and "just-married" seals gambol in this palace of more than 3000 mechanical toys. (Open daily 10am-7pm; Sept. and June daily 10am-noon and 3-6pm; Oct. and April-May Tues.-Sun. 10am-noon and 3-6pm; Nov.-March Wed.-Sun. 2-5pm. Admission 25F, students 20F.) Near the cathedral in pl. St-Martin stands the **beffroi,** a well-ruined 12th-century bell tower.

Souillac's annual **jazz festival,** held the third week of July, is one of the more extravagant Quercy festivals. Tickets for the nightly concerts run 60-120F (270F for 3 nights), but the hoopla in the streets is free. Get dem tix at the tourist office.

Rocamadour

Built into the face of a sheer cliff above the Alzou Canyon, the sanctity and staggering beauty of Rocamadour combine to bring 1.5 million pilgrims and tourists a year to this town of 800, rendering it the second most visited site in France. In 1166, a perfectly preserved body was unearthed near the town's chapel, and subsequently miracles began to occur. It is reputed that St-Amadour was actually Zacchaeus of the gospel, and as the rumor circulated, the town grew into an important Christian pilgrimage site that ranked alongside Rome, Jerusalem, and Santiago de Compostela.

Millions of pilgrims have crawled on their knees up the monumental **Grand Escalier,** which rises steeply beside the town's main street. Henry II climbed it in 1170; Louis XI climbed it twice, in 1443 and in 1463. Even today some pilgrims still kneel in prayer at each of the steps. The 12th-century **Cité Réligieuse** at the summit encompasses seven chapels, only two of which can be visited without a guide. The nucleus of the *Cité* is the **Chapelle Notre-Dame,** which shelters a 12th-century Black Madonna and a 9th-century bell that is said to ring on its own when a miracle is about to occur. (Open daily 9am-6pm and 6:30-10pm; Sept.-June 9am-6pm.) Under Notre Dame lies the **Crypte St-Amadour,** where the saint's body rested until the Wars of Religion when a Protestant tried to set fire to the corpse. Although it would not burn, the body succumbed to the Protestant's ax. The **Basilique St-Sauveur,** home to an evocative gilt wooden altar depicting scenes from Christ's life, and the **Musée d'Art Sacré,** with its bountiful collection of polychromed statues, paintings, and other relics are also open to the public. (St-Sauveur open Easter-Oct. daily 9am-6pm. Free. Museum open July-Aug. daily 9am-6pm; Easter-June and Sept.-Oct. 9am-noon and 2-6pm. Admission 12F.) A guided tour takes visitors to the Crypte St-Amadour, as well as to the Chapelle St-Michel, which has several nice frescoes inside. (6F. Tours in French every hour in French June-Sept. Mon.-Sat. 9am-noon and 2-6pm.) The annual *pèlerinage* to Rocamadour—which draws thousands of pilgrims on their way to Lourdes—takes place during the week of September 8.

On the edge of the plateau above the town, accessible by the zigzagging **Chemin de Croix Blanche,** stands the **château.** Built in the 14th century to defend pilgrims, it is now inhabited by the chaplains of Rocamadour. Only the view from the **ramparts** is accessible to the public. (Ramparts open July-Aug. daily 9am-7pm; April-June and Sept.-Oct. daily 9am-noon and 1:30-8pm. Admission 6F50, students 4F50.) An elevator can whisk you up for 24F, but remember that pilgrims scale these heights on their knees. The nearby **Forêt des Singes** (tel. 65 33 62 72) and **Jardin des Papillons** (tel. 65 33 71 72), 1km along the road from the château, let you cavort freely with *singes* (monkeys) or *papillons* (butterflies). (Forêt des Singes open June 16-Aug. daily 9am-7pm; April-June 15 and Sept.-Oct. daily 10am-noon and 2-6pm. Admission 27F. Jardin des Papillons open July-Aug. daily 9am-6:30pm, April-June and Sept.-Oct. daily 10am-noon and 2-5:30pm. Admission 22F.)

If your wallet has been weighing you down, a night or two in a Rocamadour hotel will work wonders. Expect to pay at least 200F for a single or a double; if trying to reserve less than two weeks in advance in July and August, expect to be laughed at. Be aware that several hotels in town keep one room at about 140F to look good on paper, and then rent the rest for well over 200F. The **Hôtel Panorama** (tel. 65 33 62 13), up in L'Hospitalet, has five nice rooms with showers and TV for 170F. (Breakfast 28F. Open April-Nov. 15). Halfway up the **grand escalier,** a lucky few get 160F doubles with showers at the **Hôtel Ste-Marie** (tel. 65 33 63 07. Open Easter-Oct. 15.) Luckily, there are seven nearby campsites; ask the tourist office for a list. The closest is the **Relais du Campeur** (tel. 65 33 63 28) in L'Hospitalet, which also has a small grocery store. (Reception, in the grocery store, open daily 8am-10pm. 16F per person, 15F per site. Electricity 11F. Free showers and swimming pool. Open Easter-Oct. 15.)

Not surprisingly, all restaurants in town cater to tourists. There are enough *boulangeries* and *épiceries* to get the fixin's for a good picnic in one of the small parks looking down onto the town, but daytrippers will save money by bringing groceries from elsewhere. **Le Château de la Carreta,** just before the **grand escalier,** is definitely the best deal in town. 39F buys an all-you-can-eat buffet with fresh vegetables, salads, and cold cuts. The 50F *menu* includes *pâté de cêpes, cassoulet de canard* (duck stew with beans), and dessert (Open April 10-Oct. daily noon-2pm and 7:30-9pm.)

The main **tourist office** (tel. 65 33 62 59) is in the old *hôtel de ville,* on the main street. The staff distributes maps and a list of hotels and restaurants, finds rooms for free, and operates a **currency exchange.** (Open July-Aug. daily 10am-8pm; Sept.-Oct. and March-June Thurs.-Tues. 10-noon and 3-7pm. Office closed Nov.-Feb., but they still answer the phone.) A smaller office in **L'Hospitalet** (tel. 65 33 62 80) deals primarily with hotel reservations, but can offer other information. (Open July-Aug. daily 11am-1pm and 2-8pm; Easter-June and Sept.-Oct. Sat.-Sun. and bank holidays 2-8pm.) **Trains** run to the Rocamadour-Padirac station (tel. 65 33 63 05) 5km from town. Rocamadour is most easily reached via Brive (5 per day, 45min., 38F). From the south, catch a bus from Sarlat or Souillac for St-Denis-Près-Martel (Mon.-Sat. 3 per day, 45min. from Souillac, 20F), then a train from St-Denis (3-4per day, 15min., 15F). The station is open daily 10:20am-12:50pm and 2-7:30pm.

For 40F each way, a **taxi** (tel 65 33 62 12) will take you between the station and the town; the hour-long walk is nice, though, and many people find hitching surprisingly easy. Rocamadour is accessible by bus only in summer, when tour buses run from Sarlat, Souillac, and Brive. The Souillac tourist office also has a shuttle bus on Tuesday and Friday in July and August, but at 90F for a round-trip, it's little cheaper than a guided tour. Rent **bikes** at the train station (45F per 1/2-day, 55F per day, 1000F deposit) or at Camping Relais du Campeur (mountain bikes 70F per day, ID deposit.) The **post office** (tel. 65 33 62 21), near the main tourist office, is open Mon.-Fri. 9am-noon and 2-5pm, Sat. 9am-noon. Rocamadour's **postal code** is 46500. The **police** can be reached by dialing 65 33 60 17 or, in an emergency, 17.

Near Rocamadour

Twenty km from Rocamadour, 15km from the train station, and 100m underground lurks the astounding **Gouffre de Padirac,** one of the largest natural caves in Europe. At the end of the 19th century, a speleogist (studier of caves) explored Padirac's enormous sinkhole or *gouffre*—held by local superstition to be the site of a bout between St-

Martin and Satan—and discovered enormous underground caverns with over 10km of navigable waterways. A 90-minute tour descends below the *gouffre* to the underground river carved out of the dank passageway. The tour includes a ride on small barges along the river and a walk through a vault with a 100m-high ceiling and past a 80m stalactite that hovers just 20cm off the ground. Bring a waterproof jacket—one of the chambers is appropriately called the *Lac de la Pluie* (Lake of Rain). (Open July-Aug. daily 8am-7pm; April-June and Sept.-Oct. daily 9am-noon and 2-6pm. Admission 34F50.) From July 7 through August, **Arcoutel et Cie** (tel. 65 33 62 12) runs a shuttle bus for a minimum of four people to and from the *gouffre* from the train station in Rocamadour (62F). Call ahead to make arrangements. Daytrippers to the *gouffre* should take the early train to Rocamadour from Brive, which arrives at about 8:45am; then take the excursion, explore the town, and take the train back to Brive at 7:02pm (no evening train on Sat.). An excursion bus also leaves Brive's bus station in pl. du 14 Juillet at 1:30pm (July-Aug. daily) and covers Martel, the *gouffre,* Rocamadour, and Souillac before returning to Brive at 7pm (100F). Contact the Brive tourist office (tel. 55 24 08 80) for reservations. Group excursions to the *gouffre* leave from Souillac once per week from mid-July to August for a minimum of five people (120F); contact the Souillac tourist office (tel. 65 37 81 56). Group excursions also leave from Cahors twice per week; contact the Cahors tourist office (tel. 65 35 09 56).

Cahors

On a tight loop in the Lot River, surrounded by high cliffs, Cahors has been a coveted stronghold since the Gauls settled here in the first century BC. The town reached its zenith of power in the 13th century, when Jean Duèze of Cahors was elected Pope John XXII. While in Rome, he founded a university in Cahors that flourished for several centuries, and the town began to attract financiers who soon made it the premier banking city of Europe. The Hundred Years War and the Reformation brought a reversal of fortune, though, and for the past 400 years the city has been much like the meander of the Lot that flows around it: slow, tranquil, and sublime. Activist and former Prime Minister of France Léon-Michel Gambetta, of street, square, and avenue fame, was born in this sun-baked town in 1838.

Orientation and Practical Information

Situated on the main Paris-Toulouse line, Cahors lies just over one hour north of Brive and south of Toulouse. Clermont-Ferrand is two hours to the east. The center of town is a 15-minute walk from the train station. Leaving the station, cross the street and head down rue Joachim Murat, which bends to the right and then back around to the left. After 10 minutes you arrive at **boulevard Gambetta,** a tree-lined esplanade and the city's main thoroughfare. It separates the *vieille ville* from the rest of Cahors. To get to the tourist office, take a right and walk three blocks.

Tourist Office: pl. Aristide Briand (tel. 65 35 09 56), near rue Wilson at bd. Gambetta. Bring a large, sturdy bag to fill with a multitude of brochures on Cahors and the surrounding region. A free map, camping and canoeing information, a book of suggested routes for hiking and biking, and a guide to regional wines are just the beginning. Ask for the practical information pamphlet, *Sésame pour le Lot* (in English). In July and Aug., daily tours of the *vieille ville* leave at 10am and 3pm (25F). Also, full-day bus excursions to nearby sights (Rocamadour, Pech-Merle, Bonaguil, villages on the Dordogne); there's a different one every day of the week (100-210F). Open daily 9am-12:30pm and 1:30-7pm; Oct.-May Mon.-Sat. 9am-noon and 2-5pm.

Post Office: 257, rue Wilson (tel. 65 35 48 96), between pont Valentré and the tourist office. **Telephones** and **currency exchange.** Open Mon.-Fri. 8am-7pm, Sat. 8am-noon. **Postal Code:** 46000.

Trains: av. Jean Jaurès (tel. 65 22 50 50). To: Paris (7 per day, 5-7hr., 289F); Brive (10 per day, 1 1/2hr., 72F); Souillac (10 per day, 1hr., 49F); Montauban (10 per day, 45min., 49F); Toulouse (9 per day, 1 1/4hr., 78F). Information booth open daily 7am-9:30pm.

Buses: SNCF buses in front of the train station serve mostly nearby villages and vineyards, and go only as far as Figeac (4 per day, 1 1/2hr., 54F). To St-Cirq-Lapopie (4 per day, 1/2hr., 26F).

Bike Rental: Combes, 117, bd. Gambetta (tel. 65 35 06 73). 40F per day, 180F per week; mountain bikes 80F per day, 300F per week, 500F or passport deposit. Open Tues.-Sat. 8:30am-noon and 2-7pm. Also at the **Cycles 7,** 417, quai de Regourd (tel. 65 22 66 60), just upstream from the pont de Cabessut. Ten-speeds 50-80F per day, depending on quality; high-quality mountain bikes 120F per day. 2000F deposit. Open Mon.-Sat. 9am-7pm.

Youth Center: Maison des Jeunes et de la Culture (MJC), 1, pl. Chico Mendès (tel. 65 22 62 62), at the end of Impasse de la Charité, behind and to the right of the cathedral. The latest scoop on canoe trips, occasional concerts and films, and arts and crafts. A friendly hang-out for ping-pong and cards. Open Tues.-Sat. 2-7pm.

Women's Center: Centre Departemental D'Information sur les Droits des Femmes (CIDFF), 50, rue St-Urcisse (tel. 65 30 07 34). Primarily for battered women. Open Mon.-Fri. 9am-noon and 2-5pm.

Laundromat: Laverie Laveco, rue de la Prèfecture at rue Cathala, which becomes rue Coture. Wash 20F per 6kg, dry 1F per 2min. Soap included. Open daily 8am-8pm.

Hospital: Centre Hospitalier, rue Wilson (tel. 65 20 50 50).

Police: rue de l'Ancienne Gendarmerie (tel. 65 35 27 00). **Emergency:** tel. 17.

Accommodations and Camping

There aren't many budget hotels in Cahors, and the few that exist are dispersed among the narrow streets of the *vieille ville*. In summer, try to arrive early or book ahead. Both *foyers* usually have room in July and August, but they sometimes fill up with workers in winter.

Foyer des Jeunes Travailleurs Frédéric Suisse (HI), 20, rue Frédéric Suisse (tel. 65 35 64 71). From the train station bear right onto rue Anatole France and take the 2nd left onto rue F. Suisse. The *foyer* is at the end on the left (10min.). Big on character: worn stone staircases, iron balustrades, and mosquitoes so big they might just carry your pack away. Young and active clientele. TV and ping-pong. The *foyer* functions as a youth hostel in July and August, but accepts travelers year-round. Reception open Mon.-Fri. 9-11:30am and 2-7pm, Sat. 10-11:30am. Always a watch-dog around to let you in. Members pay 47F for singles, doubles, and dorms, 43F in July and Aug. Showers included. Breakfast 13F. Lunch (noon-1pm) or dinner (7:15pm) 41F. Sheets 15F.

Foyer de Jeunes en Quercy, 129, rue Fondue Haute (tel. 65 35 29 32). From the station go straight on rue Murat, cross bd. Gambetta and turn left on rue Fondue Haute, a tiny street parallel to and just behind bd. Gambetta. The *foyer* is on the right. Both sexes and all religions welcome. Peaceful fruit garden and a cozy TV room in a quiet, centrally located neighborhood. Reception open daily 8am-10pm. Large, clean singles, doubles, and triples with comely hardwood floors 55F per person. Showers included. Breakfast 10F, lunch 28F, dinner 32F; order in advance.

Hôtel de la Paix, pl. St-Maurice (tel. 65 35 03 40), overlooking the covered market. Well-kept rooms right on the central *place,* and a lively bar downstairs. Expect early morning noise on market days (Wed. and Sat.). Singles 105F. Doubles 110F, with shower 120F. Showers 10F. Breakfast 25F. Open Mon.-Sat.

Camping: Camping Municipal St-Georges (tel. 65 35 04 64), on the river bank 5min. from the tourist office. Follow bd. Gambetta across pont Louis Philippe. Behind the campground, an alley leads to a path up Mont St-Cyr. 11F per person, 10F per tent. Electricity 10F. Open April-Nov.

Food

Elephantine **markets** romp the city on Wednesdays and Saturdays until 12:30pm in front of the cathedral. On the first and third Saturdays of the month, the circus extends throughout the entire *vieille ville.* The more modest covered market is just off the square (open Tues.-Sat. 7:30am-12:30pm and 3-7pm, Sun. 9am-noon), and a **Prisunic Supermarket** is one block down bd. Gambetta from the tourist office (open Mon.-Fri. 9:15am-12:15pm and 3-7pm, Sat. 9am-12:30pm and 2:30-7pm). Cahors produces a fabulous full-bodied red wine, whose virtues have been extolled by the likes of Julius Caesar, Francis I, Peter the Great, Alexandre Dumas, and Georges Pompidou.

Tartatou, 28, rue Foch. A symphony of quiche. Goat cheese, walnut, endive, poultry, seafood, spinach, and ahuganda quiches as entrees; then proceed to the apricot, raspberry, mint chocolate, and blueberry pies (17-22F). Sit down or carry out. Open Mon.-Thurs. 10am-7pm, Fri.-Sat. 10am-10pm.

Troquet des Halles, tucked away in a corner by the Hôtel de la Paix, next to the covered market. Favorite local hangout with lots of energy. 40F buys 3 courses and wine. *Confit de canard* 35F. Open Mon.-Sat. noon-2pm and 6:30-8:30pm.

Marie Colline, 173, rue Clemenceau. Vegetarian *plat du jour* (34F) rotates daily. Hot soups, crunchy salads, and delicious desserts (18F) in a colorful Indian atmosphere. Personable service. Open Tues.-Sat. noon-2pm.

Le Baladin, 163, rue Clément-Marot. Extravagant *crêperie* and *saladerie* with tremendous selection. *Crêpe flambée* stuffed with salmon and sour cream, and torched in vodka (34F). *Crêpe suprême* packs dried, smoked duck, potatoes, peppers and a *Bleu d'Auvergne* sauce. If salad's your thing, try the *salade pêcheur,* with smoked salmon, shrimp, tomatoes, onions, olives, and hard-boiled eggs (37F). Open Tues.-Sat. noon-2pm and 7-9:30pm, Sun. 7-9:30pm.

Sights and Entertainment

The 14th-century **Pont Valentré** sprouts out of the Lot River more like an intentional monument than an efficient bridge. Although its three towering turrets seem fantastic and impractical, they helped repel invaders during the Hundred Years War and the Siege of Cahors in 1580. A legend holds that the architect, dismayed at how long the construction was taking, bargained with the devil to bring him all the building materials in exchange for his soul. As the work was near completion, the architect told Satan he needed water brought to him in a sieve to finish the bridge. After a futile effort, the frustrated devil ceded defeat, but knocked down the top of the central tower before fleeing back to Hell. When a 19th-century architect replaced it, he added a small carving of the devil struggling to pull it down, visible from the middle of the bridge. You can climb the central tower for an obscene 12F, but don't bother; views from the tower can't compare to views of the tower. Shutterbugs will want to cross the bridge and head up the trail on the other side for the best panoramas.

Like many other churches in Quercy, the 12th-century **Cathédral St-Etienne** is topped by three domed cupolas of Byzantine inspiration. A long term restoration project to clean the frescoes on the cupolas and walls of the church is currently underway. The northern Romanesque portal, formerly the front entrance on the west side, was moved in the 14th century to allow the construction of the fortresslike façade, appropriate to the church's function as a refuge for monks during the religious wars. The northern wall's beautifully sculpted tympanum, dating from 1135, depicts Christ's Ascension. To the right of the choir, a door leads to the **cloître,** built around 1500. The cloister overlooks the cathedral domes and is next to the **Chapelle St-Gausbert,** which contains a remarkable fresco of the Last Judgment. (Cathedral open daily 8:30am-7pm. Chapelle open daily 9:30am-1pm and 3-6pm; Sept. 16-June go next door to l'Agence des Bâtiments de France and ask for the key to the museum.)

For three or four days near the end of July, Cahors's **Festival de Blues** gathers prominent blues artists such as Magic Slim and B. B. King. Tickets are available at the tourist office (100-150F).

Near Cahors

Thirty-six km east of Cahors, the exquisite medieval houses of **St-Cirq-Lapopie** overlook the Lot from their rocky perch 250ft. above the river. The steep, narrow streets of the village overflow with colorful flowers, while the brown tile rooftops look just the way they did eight centuries ago, thanks to a town ordinance forbidding TV antennas. The view from the ruins of **Château Lapopie,** the highest point in town, extends for kilometers over the river, cliffs, and broad plains below. Stop by the **tourist office** in the mairie (tel. 65 31 23 22) if you want to make the town more than a daytrip. (Open daily 9am-7pm.) Four buses a day run past St-Cirq-Lapopie from Cahors' *gare routière* on the way to Figeac. (35min., 26F.) Ask to be let off at "Tour de Faure, Gare SNCF". The town is across the bridge and 2km up the hill.

Thirteen km northwest of St-Cirq-Lapopie and seven km from the nearest bus stop lies the **Grotte du Pech-Merle** (tel. 65 31 27 05). Discovered by teenage boys in 1922, this 3km natural art gallery has 18,000-year-old paintings and engravings of mammoths, bison, horses, and even a big red fish, along with a preserved footprint and several eerie outlined handprints. The one hour tour covers much of the cave and passes dozens of splendid rock formations in addition to all of the artwork. A small museum above the cave houses a decent collection of artifacts and has a 20-minute movie on the prehistory of Quercy. As always, tickets go fast in the summer. (Cave and museum open Easter-Oct. daily 9:30am-noon and 1:30-5:30pm. Admission 42F, under 18 34F.) Ask the Cahors tourist office about Tuesday excursions to Pech-Merle and St-Cirq-Lapopie. (6hr., 130F.) The nearest bus stop, "Bouziès," is on the Cahors-Figeac line. (4 per day, 30min., 23F.) Hitching along the narrow roads takes patience.

Farther from Cahors in the western corner of the Lot Valley, 16th-century **Château de Bonaguil** remains an immense and commanding medieval fortress despite vandalism suffered during the Revolution. The central 35m **Grosse Tour** is one of the largest circular towers in France. Inside, a museum displays a collection of artifacts discovered around the château. (Open March-Sept. daily 10am-noon and 2:30-5pm. Tours in English at 11:30am and 2:45pm. Admission 25F.) Reserve tickets for the castle's concerts and stage productions (July-Aug., 60-90F) at the Fumel tourist office (tel. 53 71 13 70). To get to Bonaguil from Cahors, take the SNCF bus to Fumel (4-6 per day, 1hr., 40F) and follow the D673 for 4.5km and D158 for 3.5km. Inquire at Cahors's tourist office or train station for bus schedules.

Over 70 km of the Lot around Cahors have recently been opened to boaters. For those who can afford the luxury, this is truly the ideal way to experience the region. The Cahors tourist office's pamphlet *Embarquement immédiat* has all the details.

Montauban

The town of Montauban (pop. 55,000) was born of the townspeople's 12th-century struggle against the oppressive abbey at Montauriol ("golden mountain"). Riding a wave of popular discontent, Alphonse Jourdain, the count of Toulouse in 1144, helped the enraged population sack the abbey and use its bricks to build Montauban (originally Montalban, "white mountain"). Although constructed as a *bastide,* complete with a central arcade, the pristine charm of yore has disappeared, overcome by an encroaching urbanism. In spite of local efforts to restore the older *quartiers* and nurture the town's economy, Montauban continues to decay and has little to offer besides an attractive Ingres museum. Either make the town a daytrip from Toulouse (50km to the south), or spend time in the lovely towns nearby.

Montauban's pretty central square, the **Place Nationale,** was redesigned following destructive fires in the first half of the 17th century. From the train station, walk down av. Mayenne and across Pont Vieux; continue uphill on Côte de Bonnetiers past the church and turn right on rue Princesse which runs into pl. Nationale. To reach the tourist office, cross pl. Nationale diagonally to rue Fraîche, which becomes rue Bessières, and turn left onto the narrow rue du Collège. The office is tucked away in the walls of the *ancien collège* on the right. Bus #3, timed for train arrivals, saves you the 15-minute walk; get off at bd. Midi-Pyrénées (4F50). The **tourist office,** 2, rue du Collège (tel. 63 63 60 60) organizes walking tours in French. (July-Aug. Mon.-Sat. at 10am, 1 1/2hr., 12F. Open Mon.-Sat. 9am-noon and 2-7pm, Sun. 10am-noon and 3-6pm; Sept.-June Mon.-Sat. only.)

The belfry of the **Eglise St-Jacques** reveals holes gouged by Louis XIII's cannonballs during an unsuccessful siege of this Protestant stronghold in 1621. When neighboring towns surrendered to royal forces, Montauban, too, was finally conquered. In 1629 Catholicism was reintroduced. After the revocation of the Edict of Nantes (which had guaranteed religious freedom) in 1685, Louis XIV ordered the construction of the **Cathédrale.** To the left of Pont Vieux stand the monasteries where women who refused to convert were imprisoned until they agreed to marry Catholic men.

To the right of the bridge as you face town, the **Musée Ingres** in the Palais Episcopal honors the celebrated *montalbanais* painter with a collection of drawings, preparatory studies, and canvases, such as *Jesus et les Médecins, La Rêve d'Ossian,* and the *Portrait de Madame Gonse.* Many works of the well-known native sculptor, Bourdelle, occupy the ground floor. The museum also includes the **Palais des Evêques** (Bishop's palace), with partially furnished rooms, painted walls, and a basement full of exciting torture instruments. (Open daily 9:30am-noon and 1:30-6pm; Sept.-June Tues.-Sun. 10am-noon and 2-6pm; in winter closed Sun. morning. Admission 15F, students free; Sept.-June free Wed. if no temporary exhibit.) The small **Musée de la Déportation et de la Résistance,** 33, Grand' rue Villenouvelle, presents a collection of documents and photographs concerning the Holocaust, French collaboration with the Nazis, and the resistance movement. All exhibits are in French. (Open Sept.-July Tues.-Sat. 9am-noon and 2-6pm. Free.)

Although some hotels litter the depressed area around the train station, look for rooms closer to pl. Nationale. The **Hôtel du Commerce,** 9, pl. Roosevelt (tel. 63 66 31 32), lets attractive, small rooms with firm mattresses and telephones. (Singles 80-90F, with shower and toilet 149-160F. Doubles 100-125F, with shower and toilet 149-160F. Triples with shower and toilet 160F. Quads 180F, with shower and toilet 220F. Showers 10F. Homey breakfast 15-25F.) The **Hôtel de la Poste,** 17, rue Michelet (tel. 63 63 05 95), off pl. Nationale, offers clean and simple rooms. Some have rather dim lighting. (Singles and doubles 90F, with shower 120-130F, with shower and toilet 140F. Quads with shower 190F. Showers 10F. Breakfast 20F.) The closest **campground** (tel. 63 31 00 44) is just beyond the village of Albias, 10km north of Montauban. The Caussade bus runs to the site from pl. Lalique. (30F per person and tent, 55F per 2 people and tent. Electricity 11F. Showers and pool included.)

A **market** brightens pl. Nationale Tuesdays through Saturdays until 12:30pm. Many inexpensive restaurants line rues d'Elie and d'Auriol, off pl. Nationale. Friendly locals enjoy the robust 55F *menu* and *cassoulet* (21F) at the **Restaurant Toulousian,** 2, rue Gillaque (open Sept.-July Mon.-Sat. noon-1:30pm, until 10pm as a café). **La Clef des Champs,** 3, rue Armand, is a cozy vegetarian restaurant serving up different dishes each day. *Plats du jour* 38F. Entrees 18F. Delicious desserts 16F. A *demi* of "biological" table wine costs 16F. (Open Tues.-Sat. 11:45am-2pm.)

Trains roll from the station on rue Salengro (tel. 63 63 50 50) to Paris (7-9 per day, 5 1/2hr., 344F); Toulouse (every hr., 25min., 43F); Bordeaux (9 per day, 2hr., 129F); Agen (7-9 per day, 1hr., 54F); and Moissac (4-5 per day, 50min., 27F). (Information office open 8am-7pm.) Down av. Mayenne in pl. Lalique, the **bus station** (tel. 63 63 88 88) sends buses to Albi (1 per day, 3hr.), Moissac (4 per day, 1hr.), Toulouse (6 per day, 1hr.), Bruniquel (2 per day, 45min.), and Penne (1 per day). (Information office open Mon.-Fri., Sun. 7am-12:30pm and 2:30-6:30pm; Sat. 2:30-6:30pm.) You can rent **bikes** (40F per day) and mountain bikes (70F per day) from **Gury,** 26, av. Gambetta (tel. 63 63 19 10). (Open Tues.-Sat. 8am-noon and 2-7pm. Deposit 800F.) The **hospital** is at 14, rue du Docteur Alibert (tel. 63 03 91 19); the **police station** is at 30, bd. Alsace-Lorraine (tel. 17) and the **post office** is at 6, bd. Midi-Pyrénées (**postal code: 82000**).

Near Montauban

A strong contender for the prize of world's most beautiful cloister lies a bus or train ride away at the 6th-century **Abbaye de Moissac.** Although anti-clerical revolutionaries hacked off most of their carved faces, the cloister's 76 columns still manage to convey stories from the Old Testament and the lives of the saints. The brightly painted interior of the church is best appreciated from atop the cloister staircase. (Cloister open July-Aug. daily 9am-7pm; Sept.-Oct. and April-May 9am-noon and 2-6pm; Nov.-March 9am-noon and 2-5pm. Admission 9F50, students 4F75.) The **Musée Moissageais,** a former nunnery, now shelters treasures from the cathedral and 19th-century memorabilia. (Open Wed.-Mon. 9am-noon and 2-7pm; Sept.-June Wed.-Mon. 9am-noon and 2-6pm.) From June to August, **Moissac** (pop. 12,000) holds a series of classical concerts in the church and cloister. (Admission around 80F, students 60F. After June 15, call 63 04 06 81 for more information. Otherwise, contact the tourist office.) The **tourist office** (tel. 63 04 01 85) is next to the cloister (open daily 9am-7pm; Sept. 1-Oct. 15 and March 16-June 30 daily 9am-noon and 2-6pm; Oct. 16-March 15 daily 9am-noon and 2-5pm). Moissac is serviced by **bus** and **train** to Montauban, Agen, and Toulouse (see Montauban section above).

Montauban's tourist office distributes a map of the *circuit des bastides,* a route through Bruniquel, Penne, and the other fortified towns in the Tarn region. The tiny hill village of **Bruniquel,** east of Montauban and accessible by bus, has attracted many a troubadour and 19th-century Romantic poet, including Charles Nodier. Its 13th-century **château** overlooks the confluence of the Aveyron and Vere Rivers. (Open July-Aug. daily 10:30am-12:30pm and 2-7pm; June and Sept. Mon.-Fri. 2-6pm and Sun. 10:30-12:30pm and 2-6pm; May and Oct. Sun. only. Admission 6F, with guided tour 12F.) The local chronicler Pierre Malrien, who has penned three books on the village and its neighbor, Penne, always likes to meet visitors interested in learning more about Bruniquel (tel. 63 67 25 18). He does not, however, speak English.

The imposing ruins of the château in **Penne** also lie on the *circuit des bastides.* The tiny **tourist office** (tel. 63 56 36 68) knows about canoeing and kayaking daytrips through the area in July and August (about 60F per person, 100F for 2). **Buses** leave Montauban twice per day for Bruniquel and once per day for Penne but don't return until the following morning. Call the bus station in Montauban (tel. 63 63 88 88) for information.

Agen

Dating back to the first appearance of a Celtic settlement known as "Aginnum" (meaning "height"), Agen has bloomed into the modern capital of the Lot-et-Garonne region. Although the 19th-century poet Jasmin described his hometown as "the pearl of the Midi...with its beautiful Garonne," today the city is less than aesthetically spectacular. Instead, Agen has drawn acclaim for its burgeoning agricultural industry, crowned by the savory *pruneaux d'Agen* (prunes). Agen's other claim to fame is its unbounded passion for rugby: in recent years, the city has won three championship titles. Despite the dubious attention attracted by its prunes and its rugby, Agen warrants a visit, if not for its magnificent art museum and for the treasures hidden along the streets of the old town. then for its convenient location as the gateway to the surrounding region's sensational *bastides* and châteaux.

Housed in four 16th- and 17th-century *hôtels,* **Le Musée des Beaux-Arts** on pl. Esquirol (tel. 53 69 47 23) is the highlight of the *agenais* sights and monuments. Lost artifacts from Agen's Gallo-Roman antiquity, including swords and a bronzed Celtic horse, stand out in the four-level, 30-room exhibit. The jewel of the museum's collection is the exceedingly realistic marble statue of *La Vénus du Mas d'Agenais.* Additionally, several paintings by Goya anchor a collection particularly strong in impressionist landscapes. (Open Wed.-Mon. 11am-6pm, Thurs. until 8pm. Admission 20F. Free for students and children.)

Agen harbors factories employing 15-18,000 *pruniculteurs* who produce about 35,000 tons of prunes annually. For a rollicking good time, watch *pruniculteurs* strut their feathers and sample their products at **La Maison du Pruneau d'Agen** (tel. 53 47 20 68; open Mon.-Sat. 9am-noon and 2-7pm).

The **tourist office** (tel. 53 47 36 09), down bd. Carnot from the train station, distributes a city handbook and guides free tours of the *vieille ville* on summer Mondays at 10am and Thursdays at 9pm. (Open Mon.-Sat. 10am-7pm, Sun. 10am-noon; Sept.-June Mon.-Fri. 10am-noon and 2-6pm. Sat. 10am-noon.) The **Auberge de Jeunesse (HI),** 17, rue Lagrange (tel. 53 66 18 98), 2km outside of town, has kitchen facilities. Take the bus (direction: "Lalande") from the station to "Léon Blum" stop and follow the signs for two minutes. On foot from the station, turn left onto bd. Dumon. Go about five blocks and turn left onto the pont de la Libération, which crosses over the tracks. At the other side, turn right onto the first street, av. Robert Schuman; left onto av. Léon Blum; right onto bd. du Docteur Messines which leads into the housing project, and finally, right onto rue Léo Lagrange. (Curfew 11pm; Sept.-June 10pm. Members only. 39F. Breakfast 16F. Reception open in the morning until 10am and from 6-10pm.) The **Camping Municipal** (tel. 53 68 27 18) has access to hostel facilities (3F50 per person, 7F70 per tent). Down bd. Carnot from the train station, a covered **market** is held every morning at **Les Halles** on pl. des Laitiers. Each weekend a farmers' market fills pl. du

Pin. **Les Mignardes,** 40, rue Camille Desmoulins, about 4 blocks from av. Carnot, offers good food at bargain-basement prices. Waiters scurry around to feed the constant, mostly local crowd. The range of *menus* includes a three-course 48F and a four-course 58F specimen. (Open Tues.-Sat. noon-2:30pm and 7:30-11pm. Mon. noon-2:30pm. Often closed for part of August.)

Agen is accessible from Auch by SNCF **bus** (8-10 per day, 1 1/2hr., 52F). **Trains** run from the station on bd. Sylvain Dumon (tel. 53 66 50 50) to Bordeaux (8-12 per day, 1hr. 20min., 88F; 2-3 are TGV which require a 16F reservation) and to Toulouse (8-12 per day, 1hr. 10min., 80F; 2-3 are TGV with 16F reservation fee).

Near Agen: Villeneuve-sur-Lot

Thirty km north of Agen and girdled by gently sloping green hills and farmland, **Villeneuve-sur-Lot** claims to be the archetype of southwestern French *bastides,* 13th-century medieval towns founded to concentrate scattered populations. Constructed in the mid-13th century by Louis IX's brother, Villeneuve was designed to serve as an administrative center for the various townships throughout the *Haut-Agenais* region. Its idyllic setting on the Lot River has attracted a steady flux of settlers and a new prosperity, yet the charm of the old medieval *bastide,* characterized by a rectangular grid of streets branching out at right angles from a central square, has been perfectly preserved.

The oldest section of town lies around the **Place Lafayette,** once the center of Villeneuve's commerce. The *place* is surrounded by a series of *cornières,* (arcades), which exemplify the architecture of the period. One of the square's more curious sights is the town's oldest surviving structure, a *pigeonnier,* reminiscent of the wooden huts normally found throughout the medieval countryside. Just outside the square, the **Eglise Ste-Catherine,** constructed in the early 13th century, represents an anomaly in the Roman-Byzantine style of architecture, due to its north-south orientation.

Pass through the stone arch of the **Tour de Paris** onto the carless cobblestone **rue St-Catherine,** host to a smorgasbord of boutiques and regional crafts shops. At sunset, the **Vieux Pont,** the region's oldest viable bridge, witnesses a splendid play of light on the grandiose houses lining the banks of the Lot. On the opposite side of town, across from the **Tour de Pujols,** an exhibition devoted to prunes occupies the **Musée Gaston Rapin.** Other rooms include the works of local painters as well as some intriguing archeological artifacts.

Villeneuve reigns as the gastronomic queen of the Lot-et-Garonne region. Despite the deceptive name, *pruneaux d'Agen* are very much a Villeneuve product, for it is here that they are grown and treated. The largest selection of prunes in town is available at **La Boutique des Pruneaux** on bd. George Leygues, to the left of the Tour de Paris (open daily 9am-noon and 2-7:30pm). Sample the delectable *branchettes* (chocolate-covered prunes) in either white or dark varieties. Prunes, prunes, beautiful prunes also run the show at the **market** held Saturday mornings (7am-1pm) in pl. Lafayette. Twice a month (on the first and third Tuesdays), pl. Lafayette sponsors the local **foire,** similar to a flea market, at which vendors hawk clothing and other articles at bargain prices.

Each year for 5 days in the beginning of July, Villeneuve hosts the **Lot-et-Garonne Jazz Festival.** Throughout the town, bands give free concerts in squares and café terraces, while internationally acclaimed musicians (Ray Charles, Fats Domino, and Miles Davis have all played here) play in more enclosed venues. Tickets (90-200F, 50-80F for students) are available from the **tourist office,** located in théâtre Georges Leygues on bd. Leygues (tel. 53 70 31 37). The office offers guided tours of the town in French, with English translation provided on cassette upon request (10F), and also sponsors full-day excursions to the neighboring *bastides* of Monflanquin, Villeréal, and Monpazier (Fri. 9am-7pm, 100F). Canoe and kayak rentals offer an opportunity to strike out along the Lot River, with an option to have transport arranged by the tourist office (30F per hr., 70F per 1/2-day, 120F per day, 150F with transport). (Office open Mon.-Sat. 9:30am-noon and 2-6pm, Sun. 9am-noon; Sept.-June Mon.-Sat. 9:30am-noon and 2-6pm.)

Accommodations in Villeneuve are abundant and relatively affordable. The **Hôtel des Remparts,** 1, rue E. Marcel, has large, high-ceilinged rooms with miniature futons.

(Singles 100F, with shower 145F. Doubles 100F, with shower 155F. Triples with shower 180F. Quads with shower 220F. Showers 18F. Breakfast 20F.) Just outside town, **Camping du Rooy** (tel. 53 70 24 18) offers 66 sites close to a swimming pool. (10F per person, 5F per tent, 10F per caravan. Electricity 8F. Open April 15-Oct. 1, free access to swimming pool.)

Pamper yourself in Villeneuve's exquisite yet inexpensive restaurants. **Le Fin Gourmet,** 46, bd. C. Desmoulins, next to the Tour de Pujols, serves up some of the finest regional specialties. The 68F lunch *menu* includes a *plat du jour,* an entrée, and cheese or dessert. (Open Tues.-Sun. noon-2:30pm and 7pm-midnight.)

Villeneuve is accessible by SNCF **bus** from Agen (7-8 per day, 5 Sun., 45min., 28F). Get off at pl. du 4 Septembre, the stop in the center of town. For bus info in Villeneuve, call 53 40 23 30. Villeneuve's **postal code** is 47300.

Pays Basque
(Basque Country)

An afternoon *pelote* match, a cross shaped like four spiraling teardrops, and the ubiquitous rope-soled espadrilles all at first seem surface tokens of someone else's culture, carried over from the past to stock the shelves of souvenir shops. But the Basque culture is very real, and its survival is extremely important to the Basque people. The Basques hold that the Euzkadi (the Basque Country) is one nation, now unjustly divided between France and Spain. Part of the bond they sense is linguistic, as the Basques share one of only a handful of languages in Europe that did not descend from the monolithic Indo-European family of languages. The region has endured a turbulent development, replete with incessant attacks from successive waves of Romans, Visigoths, and ultimately, Franks. Although these incidents dealt harmful blows to Basque political unity, the culture managed to withstand degradation at the hands of the invader.

Today, the Basque Country is comprised of four highly industrialized provinces in Spain and three agriculturally based provinces in France. The French Basques' relative acquiescence to Parisian central authority has been received by Spanish Basques as complacency. But, in fact, the French Basques have passively supported the aspirations of their more nationalistic Spanish brethren. The militancy of the pro-Basque independence group, *ETA, ("Euzkad, ETA Askatasum,"* meaning "Basque and freedom") has resulted in the group's gradual disenfranchisement from Spain's political mainstream; today its members often seek refuge in the homes of their French neighbors, who shield them from threats of extradition and French police investigations. Notwithstanding sporadic and isolated incidents of violence, most ETA activity is limited to areas remote from tourist pursuits; Basque demonstrations of discontent are confined, for the time being, to graffiti on the market walls of Bayonne and other urban centers.

In *The Sun Also Rises,* Hemingway wrote of the Basque Country with fondness, noting that "the land all looks very rich and green and the houses and villages look well-off and clean." With the Pyrénées soaring to heights of over 1830m in the south and long stretches of forest and valley lounging in the north, this "country full of heather" features some of France's most variegated landscape. Along the coast, resplendent beaches of white and gold sand attract droves of sunseekers. The rip-tides that whip the waters of Biarritz and St-Jean-de-Luz draw the *crème de la crème* of Europe's surfing elite. Farther inland, St-Jean-Pied-de-Port's medieval *vieille ville* has preserved its idyllic allure, and just kilometers from the town lie some of the region's finest hiking and skiing, in the beautiful Forêt d'Iraty.

Although most of the region is poorly served by rail, Bayonne and Biarritz are fairly easy to reach and St-Jean-Pied-de-Port is an easy and beautiful hour's ride through the mountains from Bayonne. Trains run from Bordeaux in the north and Pau in the east. Along the coast from Biarritz to Hendaye, inexpensive buses make up for the scanty rail service. Excursion buses travel to a few towns in the interior, but many people find hitchhiking and cycling the best ways to penetrate the hills.

The regional sport *pelote,* similar to jai alai, is the fastest game played with a ball. Burly players hurl a hard ball at speeds up to 200km per hour at a wall by means of a *chistera* (basket appendage) laced to the wrist. Try to get to a *fronton* (outdoor arena) or a *trinquet* (indoor arena) to appreciate the speed and skill of the local players. Tickets to the world cup matches, played all summer in St-Jean-de-Luz, start at 30F.

Within the Basque villages, a strong tradition of finely choreographed dances accompanied by song has endured. These dances rise to center stage during the diverse Basque summer festivals, such as the **Fête de Bayonne,** which are accompanied by hedonistic bouts of drinking, playing the *ttun ttun* and *txistu,* and whitewashing village farmhouses. These festivals overwhelm Basque cities and villages in July and August, making it an ordeal to find a hotel room amid the revelry. Reserve in advance.

Regional Basque specialties run the gastronomic gamut from Bayonne's densely pressed and cured ham to St-Jean-de-Luz's renowned Basque tuna. The official Basque omelette—known as *pipérade*—served with green peppers, onions, tomatoes, thyme and salt. If a menu lists a dish, especially chicken, as being prepared *à la Basquaise,* expect many of these ingredients to appear. The rich, cream-filled *gâteau Basque* accentuates any meal with a sweet afterthought. The regional *brebis* cheese can be found on all menus. Once a major wine-producing region, the Pays Basque is making a comeback with some vigorous reds, notably *vin d'Irouleguy.* The Basque's home-grown liqueur, *izarra,* is distilled at Bayonne's waterfront factory, established in 1904. A sweeter cousin of *chartreuse,* this after-dinner *digestif* comes in two varieties—yellow and green.

Every year, as the autumn hunting season approaches, Basque mountaineers emerge from their summer lethargy and await the arrival of the migrating ring doves. As the unsuspecting birds are caught in the nets set out for them, joyous celebrations erupt in the villages, marking the successful passage of an eternal ritual.

Bayonne

During the French Revolution, Englishman Arthur Young proclaimed Bayonne "by far the prettiest town" he had seen in France. Hemingway mused that "Bayonne is a nice town. It is like a very clean Spanish town and it is on a big river." With its prominent position on the Gulf of Gascony close to the Spanish border, Bayonne (pop. 43,000) has since retained its grand port status and maintained its small-town appeal. The city that introduced bayonets to the world in the 18th century today engages in less belligerent pursuits. Lively markets crowd the riverbanks of the Nive, and along the backstreets of Petit Bayonne, conversation and laughter stream out of open apartment windows and small bars. After the first Tuesday in August, unrestrained hedonism breaks out as the *Bayonnais* immerse themselves in five days of concerts, fandangos, bullfights, fireworks, and a chaotic race between junk heaps masquerading as boats. A special Red Cross post, the *Château-Margaux,* is set up for the festival to cart off dazed revelers and to recharge them for more partying.

Orientation and Practical Information

Bayonne is linked by bus and train to Bordeaux and the nearby towns of Anglet and Biarritz, both directly to the west. The merging of the Nive and Adour rivers splits Bayonne into three main areas. **St-Esprit,** on the northern side of the Adour, contains the train station and pl. de la République. Pont St-Esprit arches across the Adour to **Petit-Bayonne,** site of Bayonne's two museums, several inexpensive hotels and a wide array of lively bars and restaurants. Five small bridges cross the Nive River and connect Petit-Bayonne to **Grand-Bayonne,** on the west bank of the Nive. The oldest part of town, Grand-Bayonne has a lively pedestrian zone lined by red-shuttered houses *(arceaux)* over charming shops and *pâtisseries.* Less commercialized, Petit-Bayonne feels more like a neighborhood. The center of town is easily manageable on foot and an excellent bus system covers the outskirts and beaches.

Tourist Office: (tel. 59 59 31 31), in Hôtel de Ville, pl. de la Liberté, in Grand-Bayonne under the arcade on the side facing the river. Excellent maps of Bayonne and Anglet. Pick up the *Programme des Fêtes en Pays Basque.* Guided tours of the city (in French) with reservation July-Aug. Tours run Tues. and Fri. 10am, Wed. 3pm (30F). Office can help find rooms but does not offer an official accommodations service. Open Mon.-Sat. 9am-7pm; Oct.-May Mon.-Fri. 9am-12:30pm and 1:30-6:30pm, Sat. 9am-12:30pm.

Post Office: rue Jules Labat, in Grand-Bayonne. **Telephones** and **currency exchange.** Open Mon.-Fri. 8am-6:30pm, Sat. 8am-noon. **Branch office** on bd. Alsace-Lorraine, closer to the train station. **Telephones.** Open same hours. **Postal Code:** 64100.

Trains: (tel. 59 55 50 50), off pl. de la République. To: Paris (6-8 per day, 5 1/2-6 1/2hr., 341F; 2-3 are TGV requiring 16-80F reservation fee); St-Jean-Pied-de-Port (6 per day, 1 1/4hr., 41F); Hendaye (11 per day, 45min., 33F); St-Jean-de-Luz (11 per day, 1/2hr., 21F); Bordeaux (6-7 per day,

2hr., 122F). Information office open 9am-noon and 2-6:30pm. Baggage check open 10am-noon and 2-6pm. **Lockers** on platform 15F.

Buses: STAB, on pl. du Réduit on the riverside in Petit Bayonne (tel. 59 59 04 61). Pick up a bus map here or at the tourist office. STAB kiosk open Mon.-Sat. 8am-noon and 1:30-6pm. Lines #1, 2, 6, and the BAB express go to Biarritz. Line #2 also goes to the hostel in Anglet (direction: "Gare SNCF-La Négresse"); get off at "pl. Leclerc" stop (25min.) and to the Biarritz station (45min.). Hostelers can also take line #4 (direction: "La Barre") to La Barre and switch to #6 (direction: "Arcadie") to be dropped at the hostel's door. Buses leave every 30-40min. The last bus in any direction is usually around 8pm (7pm on Sundays). Tickets are 7F, *carnet* of 5 27F, *carnet* of 10 54F (students 42F).

Bike Rental: Location Vélos, at the train station (tel. 59 46 81 63). 45F per day. Deposit 500F plus ID. Call in advance to reserve. Open daily 9am-6pm; after July 1 8am-9pm.

Laundromat: 16, rue Pointrique, in Petit-Bayonne. Wash 15F per 5kg; 20F per 7kg; 32F per 10kg, dry 2F per 8min. Open daily 7:30am-9:30pm.

Hospital: rue Jacques Loeb, St-Léon (tel. 59 44 35 36). Take bus #3.

Medical Emergency: SAMU: tel. 15.

Police: (tel. 59 25 77 00), on rue Jacques Lafitte in Petit-Bayonne, opposite the Musée Bonnat. **Emergency:** tel. 17.

Accommodations and Camping

Inexpensive hotels abound in Bayonne. The commute to and from the beach will often cost less than a hotel in Biarritz or St-Jean-de-Luz. In the St-Esprit area, decent lodgings dot the train station vicinity. The hotels in Grand-Bayonne are generally more expensive; in Petit-Bayonne browse around **rue Pannecau** and **place Paul Bert.** If possible, call ahead (at least 24 hrs.) for reservations in July and August. During festival days in August, advance notice is imperative. The closest hostel is in Anglet: take bus #2 to "pl. Leclerc" stop or #4 (direction: "La Barre") and change at La Barre for #6 (direction: "Arcadie") to the "auberge de jeunesse" stop.

Hôtel des Arceaux, 26, rue Pont Neuf (tel. 59 59 15 53), 15min. from the station in Grand-Bayonne's pedestrian shopping district. New owners and recently renovated rooms. Bright, airy, and impeccably clean. Singles and doubles 120-220F. Triples 175-250F. Quads 220-290F. Extra bed 35F. Breakfast 22F. Some rooms have shower. Hall showers included for all other rooms. Call ahead especially in July and Aug.

Hôtel Paris-Madrid, pl. de la Gare (tel. 59 55 13 98). A large establishment next to the train station. Fine rooms and helpful English-speaking owner. Reception open 24 hrs. Singles 80F. Doubles 110F, with shower 150F. Triples 180F. Quads with shower 210F. Extra bed 20F. TV in room 20F. Breakfast 20F.

Hôtel des Basques, 4, rue des Lisses (tel. 59 59 08 02), in Petit-Bayonne off pl. Paul Bert. Light and airy rooms overlooking the square. Glossy-tiled bathrooms and newly installed phones. Singles and doubles 80F, with shower 125F. Triples 135F, with shower 170F. Extra bed 52F. Breakfast 20F.

Hôtel du Moulin, 12, rue Ste-Catherine (tel. 59 55 13 29), 2 blocks from the station. A small hotel in a quiet location with a bar downstairs. Simple, somewhat cramped rooms. Singles 75-90F. Doubles 100-110F. Showers 10F. Breakfast 22F.

Camping: Barre de l'Adour, 130, av. de l'Adour (tel. 59 63 16 16) in Anglet. Take bus #4 (direction: "La Barre") from the *Hôtel de Ville* in Bayonne. Two-star site with a view of factories. Reception open 8am-9pm. 10F per person, 12F80 per tent, 4F20 per car. Open June to mid-Sept. **Camping de la Chêneraie** (tel. 59 55 01 31), on RN117 north of town behind St-Esprit. A 4-star facility with everything. 18F per person, 32F per tent or car; 52F with caravan. Open June-Sept. 15 8am-10pm.

Food

The streets of Petit-Bayonne present a number of small restaurants and cafés, most of them with 50-60F *menus*. There are also some decent, inexpensive restaurants on the side streets of St-Esprit. Fresh sardines and anchovies are sold throughout the city, most conspicuously along the waterfront in St-Esprit. Basque fish stew is a popular spicy treat. *Charcuteries* and *traiteurs* display their renowned *confits de canard,* preserved in their own fat. No menu in a Basque restaurant is complete without *jambon de Bayonne* or a *poulet basquaise* served with peppers and onions. Markets are a dime a dozen; the largest, the **Marché Municipal,** on the Quai Roquebert by the Pannecau Bridge (under the parking area) attracts vendors from all corners of the Basque country. (Open Tues.-Sun. 5am-7pm, Mon. 7am-noon.) **Prisunic,** to the right of the Pannecau bridge, offers standard grocery store fare. (Open Mon.-Fri. 8:30am-7pm and Sat. 8am-7pm.) **Open-air markets** are held several days a week. Ask around for the nearest one.

El Mosquito, on teeny rue Gosse, in Grand-Bayonne. South American food in a cozy den decorated with Persian rugs and lit with greenish-blue atmosphere lamps. Chili with mussels and white wine 52F. Beef or cheese enchiladas 50F. 70F vegetarian *menu* from 7:30-8:30pm. Drinks 22-35F. Open daily 7:30-11pm.

Le Moulin à Poivre, pl. de la Gare, in St-Esprit. A la carte offers everything from *riz basquaise* to sheep kebaaahbs (48F) in a relaxed setting. Portraits of local cuisine adorn walls. A little pricey, but well worth it. Dinner daily from 7pm.

Bar des Amis, 13, rue des Cordeliers, in Petit-Bayonne on a street parallel to rue Pannecau. Hearty, plentiful food (three-course *menu* 42F) and unintentionally minimalist decor. Expect some inquisitive stares from patrons at the counter. Menu served daily noon-2pm and 8-9:30pm.

Chez Catal', 14, bd. Alsace-Lorraine, in St-Esprit a block from the river. Delectable pizzas served with a smile. Try the *paysane* pizza. Pizzas run 30-40F, pasta 25-40F, and desserts 10-19F. Open Mon.-Sat. noon-2pm and 7-10pm.

Chocolat Cazenave, 19, rue Pont-Neuf, in the arcades. Dessert only. Taste the divine chocolate Bayonne introduced to France. Not to be missed. Also serves sandwiches and tea. Open daily 9am-7pm.

Sights and Entertainment

The grandiose edifice of the northern-Gothic **Cathédrale Sainte-Marie,** built between the 13th and 16th centuries, greets visitors to Bayonne from afar. The sacristy contains a few paintings and carved stone portals but is usually closed. Ste-Marie—whose stained-glass windows will leave you gaping—made a brief stint as a cemetery in the 16th century, suffered massive destruction during the Revolution, and has endured sporadic fires. (Cathedral open Mon.-Sat. 8am-7:15pm, Sun. 8:30am-7pm.) The **Château Vieux,** a medieval fortress at the end of boulevard Lachepaillet, is believed to stand on the site of the original Roman fortress. Its interior is barred to visitors, but you can climb the steps for a closer view.

Bayonne's recently renovated museum of fine arts, the **Musée Bonnat,** 5, rue Jacques Lafitte (tel. 59 59 08 52) in Petit-Bayonne, bears the name of a celebrated 19th-century *Bayonnais* painter who bequeathed his extensive collection to the city and then directed the construction of the museum. (Open Wed.-Mon. 10am-noon and 3-7pm, Fri. until 9pm; off-season Mon. and Wed.-Thurs. 10am-noon and 2:30-6:30pm. Fri. 3-9pm, Sat.-Sun. 10am-noon and 3-7pm. Admission 15F, students 5F, seniors free.)

The **Izarra Distillery,** 9, quai Bergeret (tel. 59 55 09 45), is in St-Esprit off pl. de la République, enterable on rue de Belfort. Free tours and tastings of *Izarra,* the pungent Basque liqueur. The green herbal-based *Izarra* is slightly more potent than the yellow variety. Temper the liqueur by adding two parts fruit juice for every one part *Izarra.* The sweet *framboise* (raspberry) liqueur runs 75F per bottle, while the yellow (32 herbs used) and green (48-herb) liqueurs cost 93F and 98F, respectively. (Open July 15-Aug. Mon.-Sat. 9-11:30am and 2-6:30pm; Sept.-July 14 Mon.-Thurs. 9-11:30am and 2-4:30pm, Fri. 9-11:30am and 2-3:30pm. 45-min. English tours available.)

Thursdays at 4pm, ferocious *pelote* matches animate the Trinquet St-André. The orchestra **Harmonie Bayonnaise** stages gentler, free shows in the pl. de Gaulle gazebo Thursday at 9:30pm in July and August. In August and early September, Bayonne holds four **corridas** (bullfights) in the large Plaza de Toros. Seats range from 75 to 460F and sell out fast. For ticket information, write or call Bureau des Arènes Municipales, 1, rue Vauban, Bayonne (tel. 59 59 25 98). Tickets also go on sale at the Bureau du Théâtre (tel. 59 59 07 27), next to the tourist office. (Open Mon.-Fri. noon-6pm and Sat. 10am-12:30pm.) The **Jazz aux Remparts** festival lures Dizzy Gillespie and his ilk for five days in mid-July. Tickets (140-170F per night, 120-150F for students) are available at the tourist office.

Anglet

Wedged between Bayonne and Biarritz, Anglet (hard T) is utterly suburban. But excellent beaches, the only hostel within 100km, and access to nearby trails in a 370-acre pine forest make it a suburb worth visiting.

Although there are a number of reasonable hotels in Anglet (singles 80-130F), avoid staying anywhere but the well-equipped, carefree **Auberge de Jeunesse (HI),** 19, route de Vignes (tel. 59 63 86 49), directly uphill from the beach. Bus #6 (direction: "la Barre") runs to the hostel every 40 minutes from the Biarritz *Hôtel de Ville* (Mon.-Sat. 7:13am-7:52pm, Sun. 9am-7:35pm, 6F50). From the Biarritz train station, take bus #2 to the *Hôtel de Ville* and then transfer to #6 (free transfer; direction: "la Barre"). From the Bayonne train station take bus #4 (6:45am-8:20pm, every 20min., 7F) to La Barre and switch to bus #6 (direction: "Arcadie"). This 95-bed hostel is, surprisingly, practically the hub of southwestern France's surfing subculture. (Reception open 8:30-10am and 6-10pm. No lockout. 60F per person. Cot in the circus-style tent 56F. Camping 39F. Showers included. Breakfast included.) Lunch and dinner are served during summer but you must purchase tickets before 10am (44F). Kitchen facilities are available off-season, but cannot be used during summer. Reception rents **surfboards** (75F), boogie boards (65F), and wetsuits (50F) from 8:30-9:30am. All equipment must be returned by 7:30pm (1500F deposit). The hostel is usually packed—so try to arrive at least an hour before opening and make reservations in person at the reception. During the summer, it offers holiday packages, including sporting activities and instruction, meals, and lodging. Prices run from 1990 to 4300F. Write to the hostel in April for information.

Anglet's campgrounds are within walking distance of the beach and boast all of the requisite amenities. **Chambre d'Amour,** route de Bouney (tel. 59 03 71 66), parcels out 220 sites May through September. The closest bus stop is "pl. Leclerc" on the #2 line. Follow signs from pl. Leclerc down route de Bourney. (Reception open 9am-12:30pm and 2-7:30pm. 15F per person, 14F per tent, 7F per car. Showers included and encouraged.) **Barre de l'Adour,** has 200 sites and is open from June through mid-September. Take bus #4 from Bayonne and bus #6 or the Navette-des-Plages bus (July to mid-September) from Biarritz to La Barre. (Reception open 8am-9pm. 10F per person, 12F80 per tent, 4F20 per car.)

The main **tourist office** on pl. du Général Leclerc (tel. 59 03 77 01) has information on accommodations. (Open Mon.-Sat. 9am-12:30pm and 1-7pm, Sun. 10am-noon; Sept.-June Mon.-Fri. 9am-noon and 1-6:30pm, Sat. 9am-noon.) The **post office** is next door (**postal code** is 64600). During the summer months, an additional branch office operates on the beach during the same hours as the main branch.

Anglet's *raison d'être* is its 4km of fine-grained, white sand beaches. Swimmers should be forewarned that despite the beauty of the crashing tides, a strong cross-current undertow accompanies them. Beneath the lighthouse, **Chambre d'Amour** beach looks over a bay surrounded by looming cliffs. Taller waves and more beachfront shops attract the surfing elite to the adjacent **Sables d'Or** beach. Here, the **Waïmea Surf Shop** (tel. 59 03 81 18) rents wetsuits (50F per day, 700F deposit), surfboards (60F for 1/2-day, 100F per day, 550F per week, 2000F deposit), and bodyboards (40F per 1/2-day, 70F per day, 300F per week, 1200 deposit). (Open daily 9:30am-noon and 2-7:30pm.)

Efficient **STAB buses** run to Anglet from Bayonne and Biarritz every half-hour from 7am to 8pm (20min., 7F). Bus #6 follows the coast, stopping at most beaches. From July to mid-September, blue **Navettes-des-Plages** also travel this route, stopping at all beaches. (July to mid-Sept. Mon.-Fri. 12 per day, 7:23am-7:52pm, Sun. 9am-7:35pm, 6F50).

Biarritz

Strolling in Biarritz in the late evening, as Jaguars and Mercedes prowl narrow streets and the sound of crashing waves mixes with music, laughter, and clinking silverware, you may feel as if you've just walked into the pages of *The Sun Also Rises*. You have. Originally a whaling village at the base of the Pyrénées, Biarritz has come to embody all that is quintessentially regal. A stroll up the main avenue on a late summer evening illustrates Victor Hugo's prophetic lament that his one fear was that Biarritz would become "fashionable." Following the first blossoms of pink and blue hortensias, the city emerges from its off-season hibernation and regains its sparkle. Warm waves crash on the "queen of French beaches," and, on higher ground, the town's resplendent hotels, villas, and casinos welcome a flux of tourists in search of the annual sublime marine experience. While Biarritz is not a budget traveler's dream-come-true, a little ingenuity renders it accessible to everyone. The town where Napoleon III, Bismarck, and Queen Victoria summered has now acquired cheap snack bars, reasonable hotels, and California-style surf shops.

Orientation and Practical Information

Getting to Biarritz is not as easy as it was in the grand old days when luxury trains ended their journeys in the now-deserted station. Today, trains cruise through **Biarritz-la-Négresse,** 3km out of town. To get to the *centre ville,* take blue bus #2 (direction: "Bayonne via Biarritz;" 6:30am-7:38pm, every 20-40min.) or bus #9 (direction: "Biarritz HDV," same schedule). Both buses leave directly across from the station. Since many Paris-Hendaye trains don't stop in Biarritz, another option is to get off the train in Bayonne and hop a bus to downtown Biarritz (30min.). Bus #1 runs regularly from Bayonne to the Biarritz *Hôtel de Ville* (daily 6am-11:40pm, Sun. 6am-12:05am; off-season Mon.-Sat. 6:35am-8:45pm). Bus #2 leaves from the Bayonne train station, also rolling to the *Hôtel de Ville* (Mon.-Sat. 6:35am-8pm). All buses cost 7F. *From the Hôtel de Ville,* the tourist office on pl. d'Ixelles is a brief walk up rue Joseph Petit. To get to pl. de Clemenceau, Biarritz's main place, take av. Edouard VII uphill after getting off the bus.

Tourist Office: Javalquinto, pl. d'Ixelles (tel. 59 24 20 24), off av. Edouard VII. The gregarious staff dispenses reams of maps and bouquets of brochures. Be sure to get *Biarritz Service*. They'll also track down a room or a campsite for you. Affordable accommodations go fast. Open daily 8am-8pm; Sept. 16-June 14 Mon.-Fri. 9am-12:30pm and 2:15-6:15pm, Sat. 10am-12:30pm and 3-6pm.

Currency Exchange: The post office and most banks are open Mon.-Sat. **Change Plus,** rue Mazagran, in the heart of town. Posts no commission with lower rates. Open daily 10am-8pm.

Post Office: (tel. 59 24 23 71), on rue de la Poste. **Poste Restante.** Open Mon.-Fri. 8:30am-7pm, Sat. 8:30am-noon. **Postal Code:** 64200.

Trains: Biarritz-la-Négresse station is 3km out of town (tel. 59 23 15 69), but you can ask all of your questions at the office at 13, av. Foch (tel. 59 24 00 94; open Mon.-Sat. 9am-noon and 2-6pm). To: Bayonne (11 per day, 10min., 10F); Hendaye (11 per day, 1/2hr., 24F); St-Jean-de-Luz (11 per day, 15min., 12F). Station office open 24 hrs.

Buses: ATCRB (tel. 59 24 06 99). Buses leave from rue Jospeh Petit, right next to the tourist office. To St-Jean-de-Luz (9 per day, 1/2hr., 13F80); Hendaye (9 per day, 50min., 25F80); St-Sebastian in Spain (2-3 per day, 70min., 33F50). **Les Cars Basques** (tel. 59 24 21 84), 18, pl. Clemenceau, next to the Hôtel le Président. Offers many different excursions, most of which operate only one day per week. La Rhune (Fri., leaves 2:15pm, returns around 8pm, 75F); St-Jean-Pied-de-Port and the Pyrénées (Mon., leaves 2:15pm, returns around 7:45pm, 80F); Pau, Lourdes and the Pyrénées (Wed., leaves 7:20am, returns around 10pm, 125F). Also inquire about their full day excursions into Spain (105-115F).

Bike Rental: SOBILO, 24, rue Peyroloubilh (tel. 59 24 94 47). Bikes 45-70F per day, mountain bikes 90F per day. Deposit 1000F plus ID. Also, the only rentals of motorcycles (350F) in the Basque country. English spoken. Reservations accepted. Open daily 9am-7pm; Oct.-May Mon.-Sat. 9am-noon and 2-6pm.

Surfboard Rental: Freedom Surf Shop (tel. 59 24 38 40), 4, av. Reine Victoria, a block from the Grande Plage. Surfboards 80F per 1/2-day, 100F per day. 200F deposit. Bodyboards 70F per 1/2-day, 80F per day. 500F deposit. Wetsuits 50F. (Open daily 10am-12:30pm and 3-7:30pm.)

Hospital: L'Hôpital de Bayonne, av. Jacques Loëb (tel. 59 44 35 35).

Medical Emergency: SAMU: tel. 59 63 33 33. **Emergency:** tel. 15.

Police: rue Louis-Barthou (tel. 59 24 68 24), opposite the tourist office. **Emergency:** tel. 17.

Accommodations and Camping

Biarritz hotels have more stars than the Milky Way. But fear not, for bargains do exist. Write a month or two ahead for a space in July or August. Otherwise, arrive early and enlist the help of the tourist office to find a room. You might try commuting from Anglet's hostel, 20 minutes by bus from the *centre ville,* or from Bayonne.

Hôtel le Dahu, 6, rue Jean Bart (tel. 59 24 63 36). Take av. Foch from pl. Clemenceau for one block and turn left onto rue Jean Bart. Only 7 rooms, but they're immaculate. Gentle owner doesn't believe in obliging guests to take *pension* because life has "too many obligations already." Superb restaurant downstairs (see Food). Singles and doubles 160-190F. Quads 270F. Shower included. Breakfast 25F. *Demi-pension* 210F per person or 270F per two.

Hôtel Berhouet, 29, rue Gambetta (tel. 59 24 63 36). Recently renovated rooms, some with nice, old wooden furniture. Centrally located. Often full. Singles and doubles 110-180F (July-Aug.), 100-170F (Sept.-June). Showers 20F. Breakfast 20F.

Hôtel du Rocher de la Vierge, 13, rue Port Vieux (tel. 59 24 11 74). Follow signs to "Port Vieux" from pl. Clemenceau. Miniscule elevator is not meant for the claustrophobic. Clean, soothing rooms a few hundred feet from cliff overlooking water. Singles 95F. Doubles with shower 159-176F. Breakfast in bed 21F.

Hôtel Barnetche, 5bis, rue Floquet (tel. 59 24 22 25). Take rue du Helder from pl. Clemenceau, turn right onto rue Maison Suisse, then left onto rue Jean Bart, and walk straight through the small pl. de la Libération to arrive at rue Floquet. Quiet neighborhood and attentive management. Singles and doubles 170F, with shower 230F. Obligatory breakfast 25F. *Demi-pension,* which includes breakfast and one other meal, required in the summer (275F per person) or else arrive early and stay in 12-bed dorm 75F, shower included. Telephone reservations not held after 2pm. Open May-Oct. Restaurant has an excellent 80F *menu.* (Open daily noon-2pm and 7:30-10pm.)

Hôtel Atlantic, 10, rue du Port-Vieux (tel. 59 24 34 08). Clean rooms, but often full. Singles 160F, doubles with shower 210F. Triples and quads with shower and bathroom 250-260F. Showers 20F. Breakfast 22F. *Demi-pension* 380-485F per 2 people. Full *pension* 560-660F per 2 people.

Camping: Municipal (tel. 59 54 59 41), on av. Kennedy, quartier de la Négresse. From the train station, turn left, take av. Kennedy, and go under the overpass. Camping is on the next block (2min.). Far from everything else. 13F50 per person, 15F50 per tent, 6F per car. Open June-Sept. **Biarritz,** 28, rue d'Harcet (tel. 59 23 00 12). Tranquil and close to Milady beach. In July and August, the Navette-des-Plages bus stops right outside the entrance. Other times, take av. Kennedy from the station and follow signs (30-min. walk). 16F per person, 20F per tent, 7F per car. Open April 29-Sept 24.

Food

In Biarritz, dining in style takes precedence over chowing down. Even the ubiquitous pizza, *crêpe,* and snack joints post prices that are at least 10F higher than elsewhere. The **Marché Municipal** on rue des Halles offers an alternative (open daily 7am-1pm). A **Codec supermarket,** 2, rue du Centre, just off rue Gambetta stocks its shelves with plump, fresh regional produce and an extensive selection of local wines. For a picnic à la Hemingway, git yerself some quiche (14F), peppery squares of potato omelette (11F), and cherry- or cream-filled *gâteau Basque* (9F per slice) at the **Epicerie Fauchon,** 41bis, rue Mazagran. (Open Mon.-Sat. 7am-8:30pm.)

Le Dahu, 6, rue Jean Bart. Take av. Foch from pl. Clemenceau and veer left. Come here even if you're not staying at the hotel. Homey atmosphere. 75F *menu* will buy soup or salad, meat or fish, and dessert or cheese. The 40F *plat du jour,* meat or fish with vegetables, is available weekdays. Open daily 12:30-2pm and 7:30-10pm, until 11pm in July and Aug.

Le Majestic, 5, av. Reine Victoria. A hip-hopping combo *crêperie*-pizzeria in a casual atmosphere. Slightly below street level. Pizza 32-42F or *galettes* 24-34F. Pasta 32-45F. Salads 29F. Cup-runneth-over sundaes 10-30F. Open Thurs.-Tues. June-Sept. 7pm-2am; Oct.-May 7pm-midnight.

Hôtel-Restaurant Atlantic, 10, rue du Port-Vieux. Ambience isn't better than *Cats,* but you'll want to eat the food again and again. Mussels 39F. *Poulet basquaise* 44F. 65F menu includes *pâté, filet de poisson, riz basquaise,* and cheese or dessert. Open May-Sept. daily noon-1:30pm and 7-9:30pm.

Sights and Entertainment

While dominated by two casinos, the **Grande Plage** still isn't much of a gamble: you're always sure to find a wealth of surfers and bathers. Just north are **plage Miramar,** nestled against the base of the cliffs, and **Pointe St-Martin,** where bathers escape the crowds and peacefully repose *au naturel.* Protected from the violent surf by jagged rock formations, the old **Port des Pêcheurs** harbors colorful small craft. The scuba diving school, **BAB Subaquatique** (tel. 59 24 80 40), near the steps to the Plateau de l'Atalaye organizes scuba initiation excursions in July and August (100F). Included in the cost is a one-day wetsuit rental. Groups or individuals may also explore the area in and around the Port des Pêcheurs by boat (80F), accompanied by a professional guide.

Jutting out into the sea from the **Plateau de l'Atalaye,** the **Rocher de la Vierge** gazes over spectacular views of the coastline stretching north to the lighthouse and south along the **Plage des Basques,** located at the foot of more stupefying cliffs. Check the tide schedule before venturing onto the rocks. At low tide, this beach boasts the cleanest water and the most open sand in Biarritz. Directly below, iron crosses embedded in the half-sunken rocks commemorate sailors lost at sea. Ask about the one that got away at the **Musée de la Mer,** inland from the crag, which hoists a simple display of North Atlantic marine life and fishing lore. The seals are fed at 10:30am and 5pm. (Open July-Aug. daily 9am-7pm; Sept. 15-July 9am-noon and 2-6pm. Admission 25F, under 16 15F.)

One of Biarritz's lesser-known yet more intriguing attractions is the **Musée de L'Automobile Miniature** perched over the plateau de L'Atalaye. Unique in France, the museum exhibits 7000 matchbox-size vehicles ranging from defunct East German Trabants to the "zil" limousines of Soviet leaders past and present. (Open Mon.-Thurs., and Sat.-Sun. 10am-7pm, Fri. 10am-9pm; Sept.-June Mon., Wed., and Fri. 2-6pm, Sat.-Sun. 10am-12:30pm and 3-6pm. Admission 20F, ages 6-18 15F.)

The *Programme des Fêtes,* published by the tourism and festival committee in Biarritz, lists the flurry of daily activities from July through October. Events range from firework displays, triathlons, and acrobatic water-skiing to conventional cocktail soirées and dancing. A series of frisbee and beach volleyball tournaments justify Biarritz's rather embarrassing nickname: "*la Californie de l'Europe.*"

Basque culture comes home to Biarritz in the guise of animated festivals and electrifying entertainment. In July and August, *pelote* and Basque dancing hit Parc Mazon Mondays at 9pm, matches of *cestapunta* (a complicated traditional game) at the jai alai arena Wednesdays and Saturdays at 9:30pm, and bullfight-parodying *courses de vaches* (cow races) in Parc Mazon Thursdays at 9:15pm. Tickets start at 30F. Hang out at **Le Port des Pêcheurs** until midnight, when the rich and reckless strap on their party boots. The **Brasilia Copacabana,** 24, av. Edouard VII (tel. 59 24 65 39), plays good music, but doesn't admit burblers in beach wear (cover 60F).

Near Biarritz: Bidart

With an ocean view on one side and a Pyrenean panorama on the other, Bidart harbors some of the most spectacular sand and scenery south of Biarritz on the Côte Basque. The town's hard sand promontory, elevated atop a cliff, constitutes one of the highest points in the surrounding region. Unfortunately, an unkindness of cans, bottles, and other refuse litters the beaches at the base of town. **Rue de la Grande Plage** ambles down the cliff towards the **Plage du Centre,** which lures bathers to its cleaner end, beyond a jagged stretch of rocky, soiled beach. Heed the warning flags posted intermittently along the beach: red indicates that swimming is forbidden. **The tourist office,** rue de la Grande Plage (tel. 59 54 93 85), will try to help you find a room in July and August, when most of the hotels are booked solid. (Open Mon.-Sat. 9am-7pm, Sat. 9am-noon and 2-7pm, Sun. 9am-noon; off-season Mon.-Sat. 9am-noon and 2-5pm, Sat. 9am-noon.) **Hôtel Itsas-Mendia,** just past the tourist office, offers soft-carpeted rooms in a comfortable country-home setting. **Campsites** are plentiful and enjoy proximity to the beach. Try **La Plage** (tel. 59 54 92 69), off RN10, near plage de l'Uhabia. (Open June 20-Sept. 33F50 per person with car, 40F70 for two people, electricity 11F). La Côte Basque, located on RN10 a few blocks from the town square, satiates even the most voracious appetites with a steaming pot of paëlla (48F) or its 48F *menu.* Bidart lies on the Bayonne-Hendaye rail line with 6-8 **trains** per day to Biarritz (7F) and 7-10 trains per day to St-Jean-de-Luz (8F). From the train station (open May-Sept. 6am-9:45pm), it's a 15-minute walk to town. Take the small, tree-shaded path to your right, cross a wooden bridge, and walk through the cornfield. After a quick left on the main road, then a right on the street by Camping Ur-Onea, make a right at the top of the hill, turn left onto rue des Ecoles. Cross rue Nationale, and follow rue de l'Eglise (by, uh, the church) up the hill to the central square.

St-Jean-de-Luz

Catapulted to fame on the flukes of its 11th-century whaling industry, St-Jean-de-Luz has since switched to tuna and sardines. Tucked inside the Bay of Biscay and surrounded by a Pyrénéan backdrop, the town shimmers at dusk with the reflection of the sun's final ray off the water onto the whitewashed, red-shuttered houses along the quais. No ugly cousin of glitzier Biarritz, St-Jean-de-Luz also sees some of southwestern France's finest stretches of sand. So stop by charming St-Jean: you just can't Luz.

Orientation and Practical Information

Situated at the mouth of the Nivelle River, St-Jean-de-Luz lies a half-hour from Bayonne by train, 10km south of Biarritz, and only 8km from the Spanish border. **Place Louis XIV,** next to the port, marks the center of town. From the train station, turn left onto bd. du Commandant Passicot, and then bear right around pl. de Verdun to get on av. de Verdun, which leads to the tourist office on pl. Foch. From pl. Foch, rue de la République runs to pl. Louis XIV, two blocks away. The place marks the beginning of **rue Gambetta,** the crowded pedestrian artery.

Tourist Office: (tel. 59 26 03 16), on pl. Foch. Maps and information on events and excursions. Open Mon.-Sat. 9am-12:30pm and 2-7pm, Sun. 10am-12:30pm; Oct.-May Mon.-Sat. 9am-12:30pm and 2:30-6:30pm.

Currency Exchange: Change Plus, 9, rue du 14 Juillet, just off rue Gambetta. Appalling rates but no commission. Open daily 8am-8pm; off season Mon.-Sat. 9:30am-12:30pm and 2-6:30pm. Banks are open Tues.-Sat.

Post Office: on bd. Victor Hugo (tel. 59 26 01 95). **Telephones** and **currency exchange.** Open Mon.-Fri. 9am-6pm, Sat. 9am-noon. Sept.-June 9am-12:15pm and 1:45-5:15pm. **Postal Code:** 64500.

Trains: (tel. 59 26 02 08), on bd. du Commandant Passicot. To: Biarritz (7-12 per day, 13F); Bayonne (7-12 per day, 22F); Paris (5-7 per day, 362F, some are TGV requiring 16-80F reservation fee); Info office open Mon.-Sat. 9:30am-12:30pm and 3-6:40pm. **Baggage check** 15F for 72 hrs.

Buses: pl. Foch, by the tourist office (tel. 59 26 06 99). **ATCRB** sends 9 buses per day to Biarritz (13F80). Also to: Bayonne (17F80); Hendaye (13F80); St-Sebastian, Spain (23F). **Pullman Basque,** 33, rue Gambetta (tel. 59 26 03 37), runs excursions to the Pyrénées and Spain, most of which operate only one or two days per week. Basque Villages (Fri., full day, leaves St-Jean at 8:30am, 105F); La Rhune (Tues. and Fri., 1/2-day, leaves St-Jean at 1:40pm, 75F); Pamplona, St-Sebastian, and Spanish countryside (Fri., full day, leaves St-Jean at 8am, 105F). Le **Basque Bondissant,** 100, rue Gambetta (tel. 59 26 25 87 or 59 26 23 87), runs 3 buses per day to Ascain, Col de St-Ignace, and Sare. (July-Aug. Mon.-Sat., 11am, 2:30pm, and 7pm, June and Sept. Mon.-Fri. same hours, 15F round-trip.) The 11am and 2:30pm buses allow for a connection with the train to

La Rhune. Buses leave from opposite the Hôtel du Commerce, in front of the parking lot by the train station. (Office open Mon.-Fri. 9am-noon and 2:15-6pm, Sat. 9am-noon.)

Bike Rental: Peugeot, 5-7, av. Labrouche (tel. 59 26 14 95), 1 block from the station. Bikes 50F per day, 265F per week, deposit 600F. Mountain bikes 90F per day, 260F per week, deposit 1200F. Also rents mopeds. Open Mon.-Sat. 9am-noon and 2-7pm.

Boat Excursions: Le Tourisme Basque, 100, rue Gambetta (tel. 59 26 25 87) or at the port in front of the Hôtel de Ville. 4-hr. fishing excursion, including equipment (120F). 2-hr. cruises along the Spanish coast (60F). Office hours same as Le Basque Bondissant, above.

Laundromat: Automatique, 1, rue Cheuvin Dragon, at the intersection of bd. Victor Hugo and bd. Thiers. Open daily 8am-9pm. Wash 20F. Dry 2F per 7min. Soap 2F.

Hospital: route de Bayonne (tel. 59 51 45 45). **Polyclinique,** rue Biscarbidéa (tel. 59 51 63 63). 24-hr. emergency service.

Police: rte. de Bayonne (tel. 59 26 08 47). **Emergency:** tel. 17.

Accommodations, Camping, and Food

Hotels fill up rapidly in summer, and it might be tough to reserve since most budget places save their rooms for regular, long-term guests. Arrive early, especially in August. You may have better luck commuting from Bayonne or Biarritz.

Hôtel Toki-Ona, 10, rue Marion Garay (tel. 59 26 11 54), 1 block from the station. Turn left onto bd. du Commandant Passicot, then right onto rue Marion Garay. Formal, immaculate, and usually full—but a worth a try. Bright and airy rooms. Singles 120F. Doubles 145F. Triples 170F. Obligatory breakfast 24F. Showers 10F. Telephone reservations preferred.

Hôtel Bolivar, 18, rue Sopite (tel. 59 26 02 00), off bd. Thiers. Well-equipped rooms on a quiet street in the center of town. Doubles 160-285F. Breakfast 24F. Open June-Sept.

Hôtel Kapa-Gorry, 9, rue Paul Gélos (tel. 59 26 02 00), a short walk out of town. From station, take a right onto bd. du Commandant Passicot. A few blocks up, turn left onto rue Chauvin Dragon, which becomes bd. Thiers, and after about 7 blocks, turn right onto av. Pellot. Follow the signs to the hotel. Spacious rooms are worth the effort. Doubles 160-180F. Large triples 220-250F. Showers 10F. Breakfast 23F.

Hôtel Verdun, 13, bd. du Commandant Passicot (tel. 59 26 02 55), across from the station. Clean, simple rooms and an oddly appealing 70s-style TV lounge. Call early for reservations. Singles and doubles 155-240F, with shower from 190F; off season 130-170F. Showers 10F. Breakfast 20F. Restaurant downstairs serves a 3-course 55F *menu.*

Camping: There are 14 sites in St-Jean-de-Luz proper and 13 more within 13km, most of them 3-star. Incredibly, most fill up; ask the tourist offices in Biarritz or St-Jean-de-Luz to help you find a spot. **Camping Chibaou Berria,** chemin de Chibaou (tel. 59 26 11 94 or 59 26 21 90; 14F50 per person, 21F per tent and car; electricity 11F50; open 7am-10pm), and **Camping de la Ferme** (tel. 59 26 34 26; 16F per person, 19F per tent and car; open June-Sept.) are all in Quartier Erromardie north of downtown. 62F per two people, tent and car; 17F50 per each extra person.

The Basque and Spanish specialties in St-Jean-de-Luz are the best north of the border, and the port town basks in satisfying, affordable cuisine. A true gustatory treat lurks at **Relais de Saint Jacques,** 13, bd. du Commandant Passicot, across from the train station. The three-course, 55F *menu,* includes soup, tuna *basquaise,* and cheese or dessert. (Open daily 7:30am-2pm and 7-9pm.) **Grillerie de Sardines,** overlooking the port off pl. de Verdun, is a simple restaurant popular with everyone but sea creatures. Eat *tuna pipérade* (47F), grilled tuna (43F), or sardines (26F). (Open daily 11:30am-2:30pm and 6-10pm.) **Le Pavillon de Jade,** bd. du Commandant Passicot, across from the station, presents a 55F lunch *menu* and an enormous a la carte selection of Vietnamese, Chinese, and Thai dishes. Try the Thai beef with basil (40F) or the asparagus and crabmeat soup (35F). (Open Thurs.-Tues. noon-2:30pm and 7:15-10:15pm.) Plenty of food shops line bd. Victor Hugo and rue Gambetta; some are even open mid-day. Pick up fresh produce at the **market** on pl. des Halles (open daily 7am-1pm) before picnicking on one of the town's many intimate squares. **Chez Dodin,** av. Gambetta, scoops the best local ice cream in its 1960s-style *salon de thé.* **Chez Etchebaster,** also on rue Gambetta, hails as the purported champion in St-Jean's infamous *gâteaux Basque* bake-off (open Tues.-Sun.).

Sights and Entertainment

The museum in the **Maison Louis XIV** has been redone in 17th-century style, but the 25-minute guided tour is not worth the price. (Open June-Sept. Mon.-Sat. 10:30am-noon and 2:30-5:30pm, Sun. 2:30-5:30pm; July-Aug. until 6pm. Admission 15F, students 12F.) Louis XIV sojourned here in 1660, when the 22-year-old monarch came to St-Jean-de-Luz to sign the Treaty of the Pyrénées. Suitably impressed, the king returned to marry Maria Teresa of Spain. In the nearby **Eglise St-Jean Baptiste,** a portal was ceremoniously sealed for eternity after the royal newlyweds left the church—look to the right of the main entry. Check out the bilingual prayer books in French and Basque and notice the unusual wooden galleries, where men traditionally sat. (The women had the more comfortable seats in the nave.)

The stretch of sand along **promenade Jacques Thibaud** remains festive until about midnight. Protected by dikes, St-Jean-de-Luz's beach and harbor provide some of the best conditions for sailing and windsurfing in the Basque region. For a magnificent glimpse of the bay and dikes, as well as the fort of Sosoa and the Pyrénées, follow boulevard Thiers to the **Pointe Ste-Barbe.** Farther along, the **Plage d'Erromardi,** with its enticing waves, presents the perfect opportunity to hit the surf. The summer season abounds with Basque festivals, bullfights, concerts, and the world cup of *cestapunta* (a version of *pelote*). Ask the tourist office for the free guide, *St-Jean-de-Luz en Fêtes.* Tickets to *pelote* matches cost 35F and up. Matches are usually played Monday, Thursday, and Saturday evenings (at 5:30, 7:30, and 9:30pm) throughout the summer and well into September. Bullfight parodies put on by clowns, cows, and a swimming pool, occur Wednesday at 9:30pm in the Erromardie Arena.

The **Toro del Fuego,** complete with fireworks and manic dancing, ignites at about 10:30pm at pl. Louis XIV on Tuesdays and Sundays during the summer months. The biggest annual festival is the **Fêtes de St-Jean,** which last for three days beginning on the weekend closest to St-Jean's Day (June 21). At the **Fête du Thon** (the Saturday closest to July 6), the whole town gathers around the harbor to eat tuna, toss confetti, and pirouette under fireworks. The **Nuit de la Sardine** takes place on the second Saturday in July at the Campos-Beri jai alai stadium. It features up to 2000 participants, an orchestra, lots of fireworks, Basque singers, and, yes, one giant sardine (20F).

Near St-Jean-de-Luz: La Rhune

Ten km southeast of St-Jean-de-Luz, the miniscule Pyrénéan village **Col de St-Ignace,** serves as a gateway to the Basque country's foremost vantage point. After arriving in Col de St-Ignace, board the wooden, two-car cog-train which labors at a snail's pace up the mountainside to the 1000m summit at **La Rhune.** Along the way, each tortuous turn reveals a postcard-perfect display of dramatic forests glowering over sloping farmland farther below. Don't be surprised if herds of wild Basque ponies *(pottoks)* gaze curiously at the passing train. The slopes teem with sheep who might unexpectedly come bounding down the mountainside. At the peak, chilling air and gusty winds prevail even in the summer.

La Rhune ("Larun" in Spanish) is technically on the Spanish side of the border, and shop-owners chat in French and Spanish. Although the duty-free status of goods in its shops may tempt prospective shoppers, the liquor tends to be expensive. On an elevated podium at the summit of La Rhune, an illustrated panel identifies the geography below. From May through June and October through November 15, two **trains** depart for La Rhune on Saturday, Sunday, and holidays at 10am and 3pm. From July through September, daily scheduled trains depart at 10am and 3pm, while additional trains leave every 35 minutes starting at 9am, if there are enough people to warrant a departure. Purchase tickets from the SHEM office (tel. 59 54 20 26) at the end of the tracks in Col. de St-Ignace (round-trip 35F). In summer, expect an hour's wait. If you decide to walk back down from La Rhune, take the well-marked path to the left of the tracks down to Ascain, and travel the tortuous 3km on D4 back to Col de St-Ignace (1-1 1/2hr.) Descend cautiously, since loose rocks often make for treacherous footing. **Le Basque Bondissant** (tel. 59 26 25 87 or 59 23 23 87) runs three daily buses from St-Jean-de-

Luz to the departure point at Col de St-Ignace, one of which is too late in the evening to ascend to La Rhune (round-trip 15F, see Practical Information for more details).

St-Jean-Pied-de-Port

Nestled in an idyllic niche atop the trout-filled Nive, this Pyrénéan village epitomizes the natural splendor of the Basque country. Narrow, cobblestone **rue de la Citadelle** climbs up through the *haute ville* to the old fortress, while **rue d'Espagne** spans the calm Nive and stretches lazily toward Spain. The village sits at the mouth of the *Col Roncevaux* (Roncevaux pass), where a historically important path squeezes through the Pyrénées to Spain. Through the centuries, this ancient medieval capital of Basse-Navarre has hosted a continual procession of pilgrims en route to Santiago de Compostela. Unspoiled by the advent of modern tourism to the town, St-Jean-Pied-de-Port beckons the curious visitor to the less trodden territory of the inland Pays Basque.

Orientation and Practical Information

St-Jean-Pied-de-Port is 8km from the Spanish border, 55km from Bayonne, and 76km from Pamplona, Navarese capital and home of the running bulls. The only rail access to St-Jean-Pied-de-Port is a wonderful train ride through the mountains from Bayonne (4-6 per day, 1hr., 41F). The picturesque *haute ville* spreads behind the ramparts below the *citadelle*. The modern *basse ville* holds the train station. Twenty-five km from the village lies the Forêt d'Iraty, a hiker's and skier's paradise.

Tourist Office: 14, av. Charles de Gaulle (tel. 59 37 03 57), in the center outside the old city walls. From the station, take av. Renaud and walk 5min. uphill past the post office until you hit av. Charles de Gaulle, the main street running along the base of the ramparts. Turn right onto av. de Gaulle; the tourist office is on the left. Free maps. Walking and hiking itineraries 20F. Hiking information on the nearby Forêt d'Iraty. Grab a free copy of *Programme des Festivités*. Can tell you which hotels have vacancies. Open Mon.-Sat. 9am-12:30pm and 2-7pm, Sun. 10:30am-12:30pm and 3:30-6:30pm; Sept.-June Mon.-Fri. 9am-noon and 2-7pm, Sat. 9am-noon and 2-6pm.

Post Office: (tel. 59 37 04 80) rue de la Poste. **Telephones.** Open Mon.-Fri. 9am-noon and 2-5pm, Sat. 9am-noon. **Postal Code:** 64220.

Trains: av. Renaud (tel. 59 37 02 00). To Bayonne (4-6 per day, 1hr., 41F). The friendly station master may let you leave your pack here free of charge. Station open 5:30am-10pm.

Bike Rental: Chez Steunou, pl. du Marché (tel. 59 37 25 45) next to the tourist office. 50F per day, 90F for two days, deposit 200F or passport. Open daily 8:30am-7pm (until 8pm in July and August). **Garazi Cycles** (tel. 59 37 21 79), in pl. St-Laurent in the *basse ville*. Rugged mountain bikes 90F per day, 450F per week, 150F per weekend. Deposit 500F.

Hospital: Fondation Luro, Ispoure (tel. 59 37 00 55). For taxi-ambulance, call 59 37 05 70 or 59 37 05 00.

Police: (tel. 59 37 00 36), on rue d'Ugagne. **Emergency:** tel. 17.

Accommodations and Food

Don't expect to find a room for under 160F. Consider commuting from Bayonne. **Hôtel des Remparts** (tel. 59 37 13 79), has uninspired but well-appointed rooms, all with a phone and toilet. Take av. de Gaulle over the Nive and turn right onto the next street. (Singles with shower 160F. Doubles with shower 175F. Triples and quads with shower 225F. Breakfast 24F. Open April-Oct. daily; Nov.-March Mon.-Fri.) Recently remodeled, cheerful rooms await you at **Hôtel Itzalpea,** pl. du Trinquet (tel. 59 37 03 66), outside and just opposite the old wall. Ask for rooms 9-11 on the first floor, which enjoy a refreshing mountain view. (One single 120F. One room with two twin beds and shower 180F. Singles and doubles with shower, TV, and telephone 200F. Triples and quads with the same amenities 250F. Breakfast 24F. Great restaurant (see below).) Ask at the tourist office for a list of *chambres d'hôte*, rooms in private homes (90-120F). St-Jean-Pied-de-Port has a decent **Camping Municipal** (tel. 59 37 11 19), on the Nive riverbank, right behind the municipal *fronton;* cross the bridge from the tourist office and follow signs. (10F per person, 5F per tent, 5F50 with caravan, 3F with car.) **Camping Bidegainia** (tel. 59 37 03 75 or 59 37 09 09), 1km away from St-Jean-Pied-de-Port, is a popular site with trout-fishing. (Reception open daily 7am-11pm. 6F50 per person, 6F50 per tent. Showers 4F. Open March-Sept.) **Europ' Camping** (tel. 59 37 12 78), 1.5km from St-Jean on D918 to Bayonne, has a restaurant, pool, and sauna. (26F per person, 36F per tent and car. Electricity 18F. Showers included. Open Easter-Oct. 8am-10pm.) Campgrounds are usually full from July 15 to August 15. Make reservations.

Fresh rainbow trout—often served complete with head, eyes, and tail—star in the superb variety show of Basque specialties prepared in St-Jean. **Hôtel Itzalpea's** restaurant assembles a generous four-course 68F *menu* with hearty vegetable *potage,* trout, a choice of meats, and dessert. (Open daily noon-2pm and 7-9pm.) The **Restaurant Chocolainia,** on pl. du Trinquet at the entrance of the *haute ville* from the train station, cooks a 68F *menu* that includes *jambon pipérade* (an omelette with tomatoes, onions, green peppers, and ham), *poulet Basquiase,* and dessert. It also serves heartier 70F and 95F *menus.* Ask for a glass of the sweet sangria. (Open daily March-Oct. noon-2:30pm and 7:30-10pm.) Farmers bring their *Ardigazna* (tangy, dry cheese made from sheep's milk) and other products to the Monday **market,** which is a day-long affair in place du Marché.

Sights and Entertainment

St-Jean's streets and fairytale location are sights in and of themselves. The ancient *haute ville,* bounded by **Porte d'Espagne** and **Porte St-Jacques,** consists of one narrow street, rue de la Citadelle, bordered by houses made from the crimson stone of the region. As you amble up the street, investigate the small craft shops housed in the *arceaux,* the red-shuttered, whitewashed homes on either side. Along the Nive, at the bottom of rue de la Citadelle, stands **Eglise Notre-Dame-du-Bout-du-Pont,** a church that once doubled as a fortress (open daily 7am-9pm). Vauban fortified the city in 1685, and rue de la Citadelle serves as a ramp up to his fortress (no visitors). From the top of the arch, a postern staircase of 269 steps descends to the Porte de l'Echangette behind the church near the Nive. Farther down rue de la Citadelle at #41, the 13th-century **Prison des Evêques** opens its vaulted underground cells to gawkers. The edifice served as the medieval headquarters of local bishops, and its current name is a misnomer from the 19th century, when the site temporarily served as a detention chamber. Visitors are guided through the dank interior by a recorded narration (in French). (Open 10am-12:30pm and 2-7pm. Admission 6F.) A pleasant, wooded walk leads from the church along the Nive to the **Pont Romain** (about 2km). The area around the Roman bridge on allées d'Eyheraberry is perfect for a late-afternoon promenade or picnic. If you want to venture beyond the Pont Romain, call **Charlotte d'Anjou** (tel. 59 37 22 27), which organizes hiking excursions in the summer and snow frolics in the winter. (Hiking: 50F per 1/2-day, 95F per day; winter·snowshoe excursions 100F.)

The summer months in St-Jean-Pied-de-Port ignite with nocturnal jubilees. *Bals* (street dances) and concerts frequently offer free entertainment. Basque choirs and daily *pelote* matches (Mon. 4pm; Wed, Fri., and Sat. 9pm) add local color. Admission to the *fronton* is 35F, but you can easily watch a match from the fence. For schedule information, check at the tourist office or listen to the loudspeakers. Each weekend one of the region's villages holds a festival that includes public dancing until 3am on Saturday and Sunday. Around August 15, St-Jean-Pied-de-Port celebrates its patron saint, John the Baptist, with fireworks, late-night revelry, and local cuisine.

Near St-Jean-Pied-de-Port: The Forêt d'Iraty

The pilgrim-trodden mountainous trail towards Santiago de Compostela stretches from Paris to the Atlantic coast of Spain. Hitching is difficult and dangerous on the narrow, winding roads. Hiking and biking here are muscle-straining ventures. Pick up the *Ensemble de Circuits de Randonnées dans et autour de St-Jean-Pied-de-Port* from the St-Jean tourist office (20F). It indicates five marked trails that leave from the office and take one to five-and-a-half hours. Superb yet easy hiking awaits in the **Forêt d'Iraty,**

25km southeast of St-Jean-Pied-de-Port along the D18. Unfortunately, no public transportation runs to this forested valley near the Spanish border. Private guides (see Charlotte d'Anjou above) organize excursions into the surrounding mountains and villages.

Serious hikers should buy a *Carte de Randonnées, 1/50,000 Pays Basque Est* (59F), the most complete and detailed hiking map for the Basque Pyrénées. Travel shelters are indicated on the GR10 and GR65, longer paths fanning out from St-Jean-Pied-de-Port. Once in the **Pointe d'Iraty,** consider taking the 9km **Larreluche** trail, which climbs a breathtaking slope of green mountains occasionally crowned by *blondes d'Aquitaine* (cows) or Basque ponies let loose for the summer. The *Randonnées Pyrénées* guide, free at tourist offices, lists the *gîtes d'étape* indicated on the *Carte Randonnée*. If you prefer to see the Pyrénées on four legs, reserve a day ahead for a guided trail ride (70F per hr.) organized by the **Centre Equestre** in the *vieille ville* (tel. 59 28 51 29) from July 6 to September 10. In winter, the trails in the Forêt d'Iraty give way to cross-country skiers. Red signs posted on trees are for skiers only; ignore the warning *access interdit* if you visit in summer.

Gascogne (Gascony)

With some of the most picturesque and physically challenging topography in France, Gascogne offers plunging slopes of forested greenery, the ice-capped Pyrénées, and tiny villages nestled in Pyrenean foothills. The **Parc National des Pyrénées,** south of Pau, offers hikers and skiers an unparalleled commune with nature. As one of five French national parks, it remains the last refuge of *isards* (mountain antelopes), royal eagles, vultures, and the endangered *ours des Pyrénées* (pint-sized brown bears). Elsewhere on the Pyrénéan slopes, Gascon *montagnards* (mountain men) live a precarious existence in the mountains' ferocious alpine climate.

Accommodations at budget prices facilitate travel through the mountains, but you'll need a good map to find them. Four detailed maps of the Parc National (scaled 1:25,000; 15F30) are available in most bookstores. For the serious hiker, these guides are absolutely essential. For simpler excursions, the 1:50,000 scaled maps indicate all the major "refuges" and peaks in the region. The **Grande Randonnée** No. 10 (GR10), passing through some of the most breathtaking Pyrénéan scenery, connects the Atlantic to the Mediterranean. "Grid" guides (available in bookstores; 51F) provide indispensable trail directions and a complete list of accommodations. Although reservations for accommodations are not normally *de rigueur,* consider writing ahead to the offices of the Parc National in Cauterets or Gavarnie. This organization, along with the **Club Alpin Français (CAF)** and the **Comité des Sentiers de Grande Randonnée,** oversees a network of *gîtes d'étapes* (rural lodgings) along the major trails. In wilder areas, shepherds' cabins are available during the summer.

Before tackling the mountains, consider a few preliminary words of caution. Trails may be well-traveled, but you'll still be hours away from emergency services in town. Beware sliding rocks. Wear durable hiking boots on the often-slippery trails, and carry only the bare essentials in your pack: map, compass, army knife, trail food, sweater, matches, and a first-aid kit. Bring a container filled with water, as many sources in the hills can cause*giardia,* a serious parasitic disease. *Never drink the mountain water from its source.* Camping is allowed only when you are more than an hour from a refuge or a road. Travel with somebody, leave a copy of your itinerary with the local CAF or police station, and check the local weather report before leaving. Unexpected storms often whip through the valleys. Once on a trail, stick to it. On a first trip, join a guided hike. Contact the Club Alpin Français office in Pau for details, or a Parc National office in St-Lary, Luz St-Sauveur, Gavarnie, Cauterets, Anens-Marsous, Gabas, or Bedous. Mountain boots, ice picks, and clamps can be rented in Pau, Cauterets, and Gavarnie, all convenient bases.

To most, Gascony also means excellent cuisine. Henri IV, the *bon roi,* who temporarily calmed the Wars of Religion with the Edict of Nantes, glorified the good eating of his native Pau. Gascony still produces the best *foie gras* and goose and duck *pâtés* in the south. Abundant fresh fish and superb rosé wines, the *vins de Béarn,* complete regional feasts. Local farmers use cow and sheep milk to make various *fromages des Pyrénées,* which range in flavor from mild to sadistically strong.

Pau

Three-time winner of France's inspired "Garden-City" Prize, flower child Pau (pop. 85,000) enchants with its urban vitality and rustic realism. Swaths of green and a wide array of exotic flora round every turn, while the boulevard des Pyrénées, on Pau's elevated periphery, offers a stunning view of snowy mountains and nearby villages. Historically, the town, whose famed château served as the birthplace of Henri IV, has both basked in fame as the capital of an independent province, and wallowed in obscurity, annexed to France in 1620 and shirked by royalty who preferred to holiday in Biarritz. Now, it hosts an abundance of concerts and cultural events, rendering it a splendid place to relax, socialize, and stock up on necessities before trekking into the mountains.

Orientation and Practical Information

Pau lies 195km and 2 1/2 hours by train west of Toulouse, and approximately one hour east of the Basque coastal cities. A steep uphill walk separates the train station from the center, but you and your bicycle can take the free funicular across the street, which climbs to bd. des Pyrénées every three minutes (Mon.-Sat. 7am-9:40pm, Sun. 1:30-9pm). Even if it looks closed, it's probably open. Wait a few minutes until someone comes; get on if the gate is open.

Tourist Office: (tel. 59 27 27 08), next to the *Hôtel de Ville* in pl. Royale. Well-equipped office with gregarious staff. Free accommodations service. Pick up a free copy of *Les Fêtes du Béarn*, a calendar of the region's summer activities. Open daily 9am-6:30pm; Sept.-June Mon.-Sat. 9am-noon and 2-6pm. **Service des Gîtes Ruraux**, 124, bd. Tourasse (tel. 59 80 19 13), in the Cité Administrative, gives advice on trails and mountain lodgings. English spoken. Open Mon.-Fri. 9am-12:30pm and 2-5pm.

Post Office: (tel. 59 27 76 89), on cours Bosquet at rue Gambetta. **Currency exchange** and **telephones.** Open Mon.-Fri. 8am-6:30pm, Sat. 8am-noon. **Postal Code:** 64000.

Trains: (tel. 59 30 50 50), on av. Gaston Lacoste at the base of the hill by the château. To: Bayonne (7 per day, 1 1/4hr., 69F); Biarritz (4 per day, 1 1/2hr., 76F); Bordeaux (9 per day, 137F); Lourdes (15 per day, 1/2hr., 34F); Nice (2 per day, 369F); Paris (8 per day, 5hr., 352F). Open daily 5am-11pm. Information desk open in summer Mon.-Sat. 9am-6:25pm. Luggage storage open 8am-8pm.

Buses: CITRAM—Courriers des Basses Pyrénées, 30, rue Gachet, in the Palais des Pyrénées building's ground level (tel. 59 27 22 22). Full-day excursions (July to early Sept.) to Gavarnie (Fri., 150F), Artouste (Sun., 185F), and St-Jean-Pied-de-Port (Sat., 150F). Buses leave at 8am from the Citram office (Artouste bus leaves at 7:45am). Regular service to Agen (1 per day, 3hr. 15min., 144F50). Office open Mon.-Fri. 8:30am-12:15pm and 2-6:15pm. **Société TPR,** 2, pl. Clemenceau (tel. 59 27 45 98). Regularly to Lourdes (5 per day, 30F) and Biarritz (4 per day, 71F). **STAP** (tel. 59 27 69 78), on rue Gachet next to the Citram office. Information on city buses. Free maps. Tickets 6F, *carnet* of 4 23F. All tickets valid for an hour. Open Mon.-Fri. 8:30am-noon and 1:30-6pm.

Bike and Hiking Equipment Rental: Romano Sport, 42, av. Général de Gaulle (tel. 59 80 21 31). They've got it all, from boots to ski gear. Bikes 50F per day. Mountain bikes 120F per day. Hiking boots 27-32F per day. 2000F or passport deposit. Open Mon.-Sat. 9am-noon and 2-7pm; in winter open Sun.

Laundromat: Lavomatique, 14, rue Emile Garet. Wash 12F, dry 2F per 7min. Friendly owner may give you a hand in folding your laundry. Open daily 6am-9pm. **Lavomatique Foirail,** 3, rue de Bordeu. Wash 12F per 4kg. Dry 5F per 10min. Open daily 7am-10pm.

Medical Assistance: Hospital, 4, bd. Hauterive (tel. 59 92 48 48). **SAMU,** tel. 59 27 15 15.

Police: (tel. 59 98 22 22), on rue O'quin. **Emergency:** tel. 17.

Accommodations and Camping

Inexpensive hotels checker the bustling *centre ville.* The clean and fully equipped hostel, a 20-minute walk or bus ride from the station, offers moderately priced single rooms.

Auberge de Jeunesse (HI), 30ter, rue Michel Hounau (tel. 59 30 45 77). A workers' *foyer* that doubles as a hostel. From the station take bus #7 (direction: "Trianon") to the "Fossie" stop (Mon.-Sat. 7:25am-7:10pm, 6F). From the stop, walk 1 block on rue Péré to rue Michel-Hounan and turn right. If walking from the station, take the *funiculaire* and cross pl. Royale to rue St-Louis. Follow rue St-Louis to rue Maréchal Joffre and turn right. Walk 10min. along this main drag, which becomes rue Maréchal Foch and then cours Bosquet. Bear left onto rue E. Garet at the first fork, walk about three blocks and then turn left onto rue Michel Hounau. Hotel-style amenities at *auberge* prices. All single rooms, most with hot showers, clean self-service cafeteria, and game room. 61F, nonmembers and over 24 76F. Breakfast included. Filling 35F meals served Mon.-Fri. 11:45am-1:15pm and 7-8:15pm, Sat. 11:45am-12:45pm. Rooms usually available June-Sept. Call ahead off-season.

University Housing: (tel. 59 02 88 46), at the Cité Universitaire. Take bus #7 from the train station (direction: "Trianon" or "pl. Clemenceau") to pl. Clemenceau and then take bus #4 (direction: "Bocage-Palais-des-Sports") to the "Facultés" stop in the heart of the university complex. Reception open 9am-11:30am and 1:30-4:30pm. 46F with student ID. Available July-Sept.

Hôtel Le Béarn, 5, rue Maréchal Joffre (tel. 59 27 52 50). In the heart of everything. Great rooms. TV room with "Russian" decor (hockey sticks on the wall, etc.). Singles and doubles 85F, with shower 110-130F. Triples with shower 130F. Showers 10F. Breakfast 15F.

Hôtel de la Pomme d'Or, 11, rue Maréchal Foch (tel. 59 27 78 48), between the post office and pl. Clemenceau. Ask for a room facing the courtyard. Welcome proprietor will personally escort you through labyrinthine hallways to "hidden" shower. Singles 85F, with shower 105F, with bath 125F. Doubles 95F, with shower 125F, with bath 150F. Quads 180F, with bath 200F. Breakfast 18F.

Hôtel d'Albert, 11, rue Jeanne d'Albret (tel. 59 27 81 58). Congenial couple offers spacious, usually carpeted rooms on a *rue*-ette near the château. Singles 75F, with shower 105F. Doubles 85F, with shower 115F. Triples 110F, with shower 105F. Shower 10F. Breakfast 16F.

Camping: Camping Municipal de la Plaine des Sports et des Loisirs (tel. 59 02 30 49), a 3km trek from the station alongside an aquatic stadium with 3 pools. Take bus #7 from the gare pl. Clemenceau (direction: "Trianon" or "pl. Clemenceau" and switch to bus #4 (direction: "Bocage Palais des Sports"), which will take you to the final stop. 12F70 per person, 24F80 per 2 people. Open June-Sept. **Camping du Coy** (tel. 59 27 71 38) in Bizanos, a 10-min. walk east of the train station. 9F50 per person, 9F50 per tent. Open daily 8am-10pm.

Food

The region that brought you béarnaise sauce ladels out many other specialties: salmon, pike, *oie* (goose), *canard* (duck), and the *assiette béarnaise,* a platter which usually includes gizzards, duck hearts, and baby asparagus. Elegant regional restaurants are in the château area known as the *quartier du hédas.* Pau's *haute cuisine* justifies a little extravagance, but inexpensive pizzerias and ethnic restaurants can be found on rue Léon Daran and adjoining streets. Try the area around the *cité universitaire* as well. **Epicerie de Nuit,** 21, rue Montpensier, will satisfy late-night grocery cravings. (Open Sun.-Wed. 8pm-3am; Thurs.-Sat. 8pm-4am.) During weekday lunch hours, ravenous *palois* (citizens of Pau) flock to **Flunch,** 2, rue Maréchal Joffe, that self-service cafeteria of the gods. (Open daily 11am-10pm.)

Le Panache, 8, rue Adoue, next to St-Martin. A feast worthy of Henri IV but without the pomp. 72F *menu* including salad or *crêpe,* and *aiguillettes de canard.* Ask for duck heart, a *béarnais* gastronomic favorite. Open daily noon-2pm and 7-11pm.

La Trotte Vieille, 18, rue Henri IV. A cozy restaurant with a fireplace and some of the best chow in Pau. The 3-course, 75F *menu* includes an overflowing serving of *salade béarnaise.* The apple tart is so flaky you'll think Victoria Jackson baked it. Open Mon.-Sat. noon-2pm and 7-10:30pm.

El Mesón, 40, rue Maréchal Joffre. Spicy *bar à tapas* (5-35F) makes a filling meal. Also a lively night spot. Not much English or French spoken. Occasional minstrels. Open Mon.-Fri. noon-2pm and 7-10:30pm, Sat. 7-10:30pm.

La Goulue, 13, rue Henri IV. Small. In the old town. Need you know more? 68F *menu* features the mouth-watering regional specialty, *magret de canard.* Fancier 3-course 85F *menu.* Open Sun.-Fri. noon-2pm and 7:15-11pm, Sat. 7:15-11pm.

Boulangerie "Abert", 4, rue du Mal Joffre. Not a restaurant, but some of the finest pastries in town. Sample the melt-in-your-mouth mocha pastry (8F) or choose from 15 flavors of ice cream (single scoop 8F; double scoop 12F). *Salon de thé* in rear. Open daily 6:30am-8pm.

Sights and Entertainment

Formerly the majestic residence of *béarnais* viscounts and Navarrese kings and now a national museum, the 12th-century **château,** Pau's foremost pride and joy, overlooks the river from the highest point in Pau. Fifty glorious Gobelin tapestries, well-preserved royal chambers, elaborately decorate ceilings, and several ornate chandeliers grace the castle. In Henri IV's bedroom, the guide will show you the tortoise shell that cradled the royal infant. It was believed that the tortoise would endow the toddling *dauphin* with its fabled longevity. (Open daily 9:30-11:45am and 2-5:45pm; off-season daily 9:30-11:45am and 2-4:45pm. Last guided tours 1/2-hr. before closing. Admission 26F, students 14F, under 18 free.) On the third floor, the **Musée Béarnais** offers a comprehensive exhibit of the region's cultural development. The displays include various costumes, crafts, and architectural models as well as stuffed prizes of royal hunting expeditions. (Open daily 9:30am-12:30pm and 2:30-6:25pm; off-season 9:30am-12:25pm and 2:30-5:30pm. Admission 8F.)

Housed in a non-descript 30s Soviet-style building, the **Musée des Beaux-Arts** possesses an overwhelmingly mediocre collection of art. (Open Wed.-Mon. 9am-noon and 2-6pm. Admission 10F, students 5F.) For those interested in Scandinavia and in historical anomalies, the **Musée Bernadotte,** 8, rue Tran, is a fascinating place to spend an afternoon. The birthplace of J.B. Bernadotte, whose brilliant military career catapulted him to the Swedish throne in 1818, has been maintained in its original condition. Though much of the printed material is in Swedish, the knowledgeable curator can respond to any questions. (Open Tues.-Sun. 10am-noon and 2-6pm. Admission 10F.)

From the last week of June to the last week of July, the annual **Festival de Pau** brings plays, concerts, recitals, ballet performances, firework displays, *pelote* tournaments, poetry readings, a leg of the Tour de France, and jazz, rock, ballet, and reggae performances to the château courtyard and other venues. (Admission 90-130F.) Pick up a schedule at the tourist office, which sets up a special table devoted to the festival.

Lourdes

If considering a visit to Lourdes (pop. 16,400) under the sole pretext of tourism, expect to be in a rather conspicuous minority. Ever since the 1858 apparitions of the Virgin Mary to 14-year-old Bernadette Soubirous, a monumental procession of worshippers intent on sharing the miracle of Lourdes has besieged the town. Their numbers have grown astronomically in recent years. With 5 million pilgrims passing through every year, Lourdes has escalated into France's second-most-visited city. Special trains, buses, and charter flights from all over the world bring entire parishes to the sacred site, and the streets are jammed with souvenir stands selling empty Virgin-shaped water bottles, plastic rosary beads, and more statuettes than Europe produced during the entire Renaissance. The **Caverne des Apparitions,** better known as **La Grotte** where Bernadette experienced her successive visitations, has become the focus in Lourdes's pre-packaged spiritual extravaganza. Be prepared for long lines and many elderly and ailing visitors. The concrete echo chamber known as **Basilique Pius X,** designed as an atomic bomb shelter, won an international architecture prize in 1958 despite looking like a hybrid of the new Paris Opera House and a parking garage. Mass is recited daily in four languages on the main esplanade in front of the *Basilique*. On Easter weekend, the **Festival International de Musique Sacrée** fills the local holy buildings with Bach and Mozart. Tickets are available through the tourist office (80-150F).

Orientation and Practical Information

With over 30% of its visitors arriving by train, Lourdes is extraordinarily well-serviced by rail. The train station is located on the northern edge of town; the *centre ville* is 10 minutes away. The grotto, basilica, and souvenir shops all cluster in the northeastern section of town, 15 minutes from the tourist office.

Tourist Office: pl. Champ Commun (tel. 62 94 15 64). Turn right from the train station, then turn left at the chaussée Maransin and walk about 10min. Good maps, free brochure, and a list of Lourdes's 380 hotels. Board with listings of available rooms outside. Staff handles its Herculean task with cheer. Open Mon.-Sat. 9am-7pm, Sun. 10am-noon; Oct. 16-May Mon.-Sat. 9am-noon and 2-6pm; May-June Mon.-Sat. 9am-12:30pm and 2-3:30pm. Information booth **Touristes et Pèlerins Isolés,** in the arcades to the right of the basilica. Provides information on a pilgrimage visit. Open 9am-noon and 2-6pm.

Post Office: At rue de Langelle and chaussée Maransin. **Telephones** and **currency exchange.** Open Mon.-Fri. 8am-7pm, Sat. 8am-noon. **Postal Code:** 65100.

Trains: on av. de la Gare (tel. 62 37 50 50). The terminus of one of the Pyrénées lines. To: Pau (7 per day, 1/2hr., 34F); Paris (5 per day, 7-9hr., 365F); Toulouse (9 per day, 2 1/2hr., 106F); Irun (5 per day, 4-5hr., 106F); Cauterets (change at Pierrefitte, 3-4 per day, 1hr., 34F). SNCF buses to Cauterets accept rail passes. Many other excursion companies post schedules in front of the station. Luggage storage 30F, **lockers** 15F per 72hrs. Open 7:40am-7pm.) Information office (open 8am-1pm and 1:25-7pm) plagued by long lines and harried staff. Hit the tourist office instead.

Buses: (tel. 62 94 31 15), in pl. Capdevieille below the tourist office. Open Mon.-Fri. 8am-noon and 2-6:45pm, Sat. 8am-noon. Local buses run from the train station to the cave every 15min. (Easter-Oct., 9F). SNCF buses run from the station to Cauterets (3-4 per day, 50min., 34F).

Hospital: 2, av. Alexandre Marqui (tel. 62 42 42 42)

Police: 7, rue Baron Duprat (tel. 62 94 02 08). **Emergency:** tel. 17.

Accommodations and Camping

Lourdes is best visited as a daytrip from Pau or Cauterets. For those who choose to linger, over 18,000 rooms await in some 360 hotels; only Paris offers more. Every avenue and sidestreet showcases a miraculous multitude of hotels accessible to budget travelers. Look in the area around **rue Basse** in the center of town. From the train station turn right after you've crossed the bridge. Also try the **route de Pau.** Two lower-priced alternatives, both Christian organizations, serve the pilgrim rather than the tourist. The hostel-like **Centre des Rencontres "Pax Christi,"** 4, rue de la Forêt (tel. 62 94 00 66), is a 10-minute walk up the road behind the basilica. Bed and breakfast cost 40F. Although there is usually space, you can reserve through **Les Amis de Pax Christi,** 18, rue Cousté, B.P. 133, 94234 Cachan (tel. 46 63 10 30). If you're under 25, stay at **Camp des Jeunes, Ferme Milhas,** av. Mgr-Rodhain (tel. 62 42 78 78, ask to be connected to the camp, winter number 62 42 78 38), a 10-minute uphill walk out of town. Dorm accommodations cost 22F per person; camping in your own tent is 15F. You'll need a sleeping bag. Showers are included. You are strongly encouraged to participate in evening services and community activities. Ask for directions and reserve a place at the Service Jeunes booth in the big plaza by the sanctuaries. (Open April-Oct.) For accommodations with a less religious bent, **Hôtel-Restaurant Paix et Continental,** 3, rue de la Paix (tel. 62 94 91 31), provides hospitality and comfort. Two singles at 65F. Singles and doubles 90F, with shower 170F. Showers 15F. Breakfast 20F. Inexpensive restaurants are a dime-a-dozen in a town stuffed to the brink with pizzerias, *crêperies,* and ethnic cuisine. *Menus* from 55-85F abound, especially along the tourist-saturated **rue de la Grotte.**

Cauterets

Set in a breathtaking valley on the edge of the **Parc National des Pyrénées Occidentales,** Cauterets makes a perfect base for exploring the nearby towns and mountains. In winter, some of the best skiing in the region is a gondola, chairlift, or T-bar away. Long, white runs drop hundreds of meters down the slopes, while cross-country ski trails delve into the heart of the national park. In summer, green pastures and an extensive network of hiking paths lure an international crowd of hikers.

Though a gateway to some of the world's most sensational mountain peaks, Cauterets does not offer many home-grown attractions. One exception is its *thermes,* which lure a covey of well-heeled visitors in quest of natural cures and rejuvenation. Thought since Roman times to treat sterility, these sulfuric hot springs inspired the Romantic dalliances of Victor Hugo, George Sand, and Châteaubriand. The headquarters of the Parc National des Pyrénées Occidentales, on Place de la Gare is the foremost authority on mountainous adventures. Their office also contains the **Musée du Parc National,** which leads visitors through a multi-leveled exhibit depicting various stages of elevation in the climb to a mountain summit. (Open mid-Dec. to mid-Oct. 9:30am-12:15pm and 3:30-7pm. Admission 10F.)

Orientation and Practical Information

About 12km from the Spanish border, Cauterets is most easily accessible by SNCF bus from Lourdes (4-5 per day, 1hr., 34F). From the station, turn right and walk up av. Général Leclerc to the tourist office, which is on the right. The city ascends a hillside along the Gave River. A *téléphérique* climbs to the Col d'Ilhéou. Be sure to read the small print on bus schedules, since many departures are limited to certain days of the week.

Tourist Office: (tel. 62 92 50 27), in pl. de la Mairie. List of hotels available, but not the best source of information on the outdoors. Open July-Aug., Christmas, and French winter holidays Mon.-Sat. 9am-7pm, Sun. 9am-noon and 4-7pm; Sept.-June Mon.-Sat. 9am-12:30pm and 2-6pm, Sun. 9am-noon.

Post Office: on rue de Belfort (tel. 62 92 54 00). **Telephones** and **currency exchange.** Open Mon.-Fri. 9am-noon and 3-6:30pm and Sat. 9am-noon. **Postal Code:** 65110.

Buses: (tel. 62 92 53 70), in a chalet-style station on pl. de la Gare. SNCF buses run to Lourdes (6 per day, 34F). **Lourdes-Les Pyrénées** buses (tel. 62 94 22 90) run to Gèdre, Gavarnie, and Luz-St-Sauveur. To Gavarnie via Pierrefitte (2 per day, 53F); to Luz-St-Sauveur (2-3 per day, 35F). Pick up a complete schedule in any regional tourist office, train station, or *gare routière*. Cauterets station open daily 9am-noon and 3-6:30pm. Buy SNCF bus tickets in the station and Lourdes-Les Pyrénées tickets on the bus. **Téléphérique and Ski Information:** The *téléphérique* (cable car) is located a block from the gare, and offers service to Col d'Ilhéou. In summer it operates with departures every 1/2hr. from 9am-12:15pm and 1:45-5:45pm. In winter: school vacations daily 8am-8:30pm, other times 8:45am-7pm. 20F round-trip either season. Ski tickets 98F per day, 105F with insurance. Rates improve the longer you stay. The skiing season runs from Dec.-May 10.

Bike and Mountain Equipment Rental: Skilys, rte. de Pierrefitte at av. de la Gare. Mountain bikes plus guided tour (73-200F, depending on duration). Without tour, 25F per hr., 60F per 1/2-day; 100F per full day. Tours May-Oct. Mountain boots 23-40F per day. Downhill skis 35-270F. Ski boots 27-82F. Cross-country skis and boots 50F per day. Passport deposit. Open daily 9am-7pm; winter 8am-7:30pm.

Hiking Information: Parc National des Pyrénées, Maison du Parc on pl. de la Gare. Hiking trips, nature film "Pyrénéan Reflections" and extensive information on park and its trails, soon to be accessible via newly installed computer system. Open April-Sept., Dec., and Feb. daily 9:30am-12:15pm and 3:30-7pm.

Ski Information: Régie Municipale des Sports de Montagne on av. Docteur Domer (tel. 62 92 51 58).

Weather Update: Météo-Montagne (tel. 36 65 02 65), provides a forecast for the surrounding mountains.

Mountain Rescue Service: tel. 62 92 48 24.

Police: Emergency: tel. 17.

Accommodations and Food

With the arrival of the French summer vacation in early July, hotels in the area fill quickly. Try to make reservations and avoid hotels with a mandatory *pension*. On the immediate outskirts of town, just past the tennis courts, the **Centre UCJG "Cluquet,"** av. Docteur Domer (tel. 62 92 52 95), offers sheets, showers, and clean kitchen facilities as well as a washing machine. Pitch your own tent (18F), or sleep in one of five 14-bed tents for 35F. Bungalows are available for 45F, but should be reserved well in advance. (Open June 15-Sept. 15.) At the far end of town, a *gîte d'étape*, **Le Pas de l'Ours,** 21, rue de la Raillère (tel. 62 92 58 07), welcomes hikers, climbers, and skiers. Situated on a sloping street a few blocks beyond the tourist office, the *gîte* features a well-equipped kitchen and co-ed accommodations with bunk beds (showers included) for 48F (summer) and 53F (winter). (Breakfast 30F. Dinner 70F. Sauna 45F, 70F for 2 people.) **Hôtel du Béarn,** 4, bd. Général Leclerc, directly opposite the covered market (tel. 62 92 53 54), lets large, clean rooms with immense windows. Ask for a quiet room away from the staircase landings. (Singles and doubles 110F. Triples 160F. Showers 10F. Breakfast 20F. Open Dec.-Sept.) **Hôtel-Restaurant Christian,** 10, rue Richelieu boasts friendly management and bright, spotless rooms. Facilities include a bridge salon, bar, ping-pong table and *pétanque* (no additional charge for paddles and balls). (Singles and doubles 120F, with shower 140-180F. Triples 200F. Quads 240F. Open April-Sept.)

The covered **Halles** market in the center of town is a perfect stop for fresh produce. (Open daily 8:30am-12:30pm and 2:30-7:30pm.) Alternatively, an open-air market is held on Fridays (July-Aug.) in pl. de la Gare, before the *téléphérique* terminal. Local producers of honey, wine, and *pâtés* (including occasional free tastings) push their specialties on Thursdays from March to September (9am-1pm), opposite the parking lot in pl. de la Gare. **Supermarket Codec,** on av. Général Leclerc, stocks groceries galore and is open Sundays. (Open daily 8:30am-12:30pm and 4-7:30pm.) **La Flore,** 11, rue Richelieu concocts a delicious 70F *menu* featuring *escalope à la crème* (veal in cream sauce). (Open daily noon-3pm and 7pm-2am.) After a long day of hiking, treat yourself to a four-course, 65F family-style meal at **Hôtel Dulau,** 7, rue du Raillère. (Open Mon.-Sat. 12:15-2pm and 7:25-10pm.)

Near Cauterets

Before venturing off into the mountains, acquaint yourself with the fundamentals of a sensible and enjoyable *randonnée* (hike). Pick up one of the purple 1: 25,000 maps of the Parc National des Pyrénées (57F); for the Cauterets region use *Balaîtous.* The invaluable *Promenades en Montagne* series on the Vallée de Cauterets (available at the tourist office and the Parc National for 32F) details numerous itineraries and lists area refuges. **La Civette,** a bookstore opposite the tourist office in Cauterets, stocks a complete selection of maps. (Open daily 9am-noon and 3-7pm.) In searching for lodgings, keep in mind that a *refuge* is often exactly what its name suggests: a no-frills shelter lacking many amenities, and often merely a roof overhead. By contrast, *gîtes d'étape* (literally, "lying-in-way stations"), normally situated in small villages, provide beds, cooking facilities (or a restaurant), and a resident caretaker. *Gîtes* differ from *auberges* in that they do not belong to an umbrella organization, such as HI. Make sure to call all accommodations first rather than counting on them to be open when you arrive.

The optimal course in hiking around the area is the **GR10** *sentier,* which passes through Cauterets and continues to Luz-St-Sauveur by two separate paths. One ambles gracefully over a plateau, while the other snakes a formidable path past the **Lac de Gaube,** the icy expanses of the **Pic du Vignemale** (3298m) and the villages of Gavarnie and Gèdre. The **Refuge d'Ilhéo** (tel. 62 92 82 38) awaits at the end of the two-hour ascent to the pristine **Col d'Ilhéou** (1198m). Another option is to set out from the **fruitière** (1371m, 10min. by car or an hour on foot from Cauterets) for the **Lac d'Estom** (1804m), which gives way to increasingly more difficult terrain in the vicinity of the **Pic du Vignemale** (3298m).

If you're short on time, consider the four-hour round-trip journey to the **Pont d'Espagne,** graced by sensational scenery. Follow rue de la Raillère to the outskirts of town, and climb a brief flight of stairs to the GR10. Beware of slippery rocks along the way. If you lose the path, simply stick to the left bank of the river. Once at the top, many hitch rides back down with the tourists who congregate at the café alongside the bridge.

Luz St-Sauveur, in the Vallée du Toy, is another excellent launching pad into the Pyrénées. The **Maison du Parc National et de la Vallée** (tel. 62 92 87 05), off the pl. St-Clément, disgorges valuable, precise information for anyone interested. (Open Mon.-Fri. 10am-noon and 2-7pm, Sat.-Sun. 2-7pm.) Lourdes-Les Pyrénées **buses** (tel. 62 94 22 90) run to Luz-St-Sauveur from Cauterets (2-3 per day, 35F).

Postcard-perfect **Gavarnie** is connected by buses to Luz St-Sauveur, though hikers may prefer to cover the route along the GR10. The grandiose, snow-covered **Cirque de Gavarnie** and its mist-wreathed waterfall are also nearby. Hordes of tourists heave themselves onto horses for the hoist to the Cirque (2-3hr., round-trip from the village about 70F). During the last two weeks of July, the **Festival des Pyrénées** animates the foot of the Cirque de Gavarnie. Nightly performances begin as the sun sets over the mountains; afterwards, torches are distributed to light the way back to the village. Past festivals have featured Shakespeare's *Macbeth* and *A Midsummer's Night Dream;* the latter, complete with pyrotechnics and galloping horses, brought its mobile audience to three different settings. Tickets cost 90F (70F for students) at tourist offices, bookstores, banks, and hotels throughout the region.

Auch

A graceful, subdued town with curious streets, a massive cathedral, a crumbling tower, and a somewhat charming dullness, Auch makes a relaxing daytrip from Toulouse. As the historic capital of Gascony, Auch (pop. 25,000) has spent the 20th century as a flourishing urban center built on the shoulders of a glorious medieval past. Narrow sidestreets flanked by wooden-shuttered *arceaux* lead to the flamboyant cathedral, and the peculiarly brownish Gers River flows past a decrepit watchtower-*cum*-prison. The hilly countryside beyond town will test a hiker or biker's worth, while offering a mosaic of sunflower and rose fields, vineyards, windmills, châteaux, and tottering *pigeonniers* (medieval one-story homes supported by a foundation of upright legs). To facilitate your wanderings, try the hiking paths GR65, GR652, and GR653, which pass through the area.

Orientation and Practical Information

Located 77km from Toulouse, 100km from Lourdes and 72km from Tarbes, Auch is easily accessible by SNCF trains and buses. The Gers River fragments the town between its more depressed *basse ville* and the culture-saturated *haute ville*. A bus runs from the train station to the *hôtel de ville* daily from 7am-7pm (6F). The walk to the town center includes a 15-minute uphill climb.

Tourist Office: 1, rue Dessoles (tel. 62 05 22 89), on pl. de la République in front of the cathedral. Free tours of the museum and cathedral. Open Tues.-Sat. 9am-noon and 2-6:30pm, Sun.-Mon. 2-6:30pm; Sept.-June Tues.-Sat. only.

Post Office: rue (what else?) Gambetta. **Telephones. Currency Exchange.** Open Mon.-Fri. 8am-7pm, Sat. 8am-noon. **Postal Code:** 32000.

Trains: (tel. 62 05 00 46), on av. de la Gare in the *ville basse*. To: Toulouse (6 per day, 1 1/2hr., 63F); Montauban (1 SNCF bus per day, 1 1/2hr., 63F); Agen (8-10 SNCF buses per day, 4-5 on Sun., 52F). Information, reservations, and ticket service open Mon.-Sat. 5:15am-9:45pm; Sun. 6:30am-12:30pm, 1:15-7pm, and 8-9:45pm.

Buses: allées Baylac, pl. du Forail (tel. 62 05 76 37). To: Condom (2-3 per day, 1hr., 33F); Bordeaux (1 per day, 4hr., 94F); Toulouse (1-2 per day, 1 1/4hr., 61F). Incoming buses stop at the train and bus stations. Open Tues.-Fri. 7:30-11:30am and 2:30-6:30pm, Mon. and Sat. 7:30am-noon and 2-6:30pm.

Bike Rental: La Boutique du Cycle (tel. 62 05 27 51), 39, bd. Roquelaire. Mountain bikes 50F per 1/2-day, 100F per day. 2000F deposit. May accept passport. Open daily 9am-noon and 2-7pm.

Medical Assistance: (tel. 00 00 00 15), on av. des Pyrénées.

Police: tel. 62 05 24 01. **Emergency:** tel. 17.

Accommodations and Camping

Unless you want to lug your pack uphill, try to find a hotel in the *basse ville*. The youth hostel usually has space. A *gîte d'étape*, 4km from town, sits in the shadow of a château.

Auberge de Jeunesse, Foyer des Jeunes Travailleurs (HI), in the building complex *Cité Grand Garros* (tel. 62 05 34 80). Take bus #2 from the station and get off at the "Grand Garros" stop (last bus 7pm). To walk there, turn left from the station on av. de la Gare (also known as av. Pierre Mendès-France). Turn left at end of street; turn right on the next street just past the train track and follow that street for two blocks to the Grand Garros complex. No kitchen facilities, lockout, or curfew. Bar and self-serve restaurant. Singles 57F. 2- or 3-bed rooms 47F. Breakfast 10F50 (served Mon.-Sat. 7-7:45am). Lunch or dinner *plat du jour* 27F50. Almost always has space, but call before making the trek.

Gîte d'Etape, Château St-Cricq, on the rte. de Toulouse (tel. 62 63 10 17), 4km from Auch. Sleep in the castle annex. Sixteen coed "dorm" beds available to hikers, horseback riders, and cyclists. 40F. Showers included. No breakfast, but kitchen facilities are available. Call before 5pm.

Hôtel de Paris, 38, av. de Marne (tel. 62 63 26 22). From the station, turn right onto av. de la Gare, and then left onto av. de la Marne. An older hotel, home also to a population of stuffed animals. Large but aging rooms. Singles 130F, with shower 160F. Doubles 150F, with shower 190F. Triples 180F, with shower 210F. Showers 15F. Breakfast 23F.

Hôtel-Restaurant Modern, 10bis, av. de la Gare (a.k.a. Pierre-Mendès-France; tel. 62 05 03 47). Right across from the station. Clean rooms with high ceilings in a somewhat dilapidated neighborhood. Singles 120-130F, with shower 160-190F. Doubles 140-170F, with shower 190F. Triples with shower 220F. Breakfast 19F. Shower 10F.

Camping: Camping Municipal (tel. 62 05 00 22), 1.5km from the train station. From the station, turn left onto av. de la Gare, right onto rte. de Pessan which becomes rue du 11 Novembre, left onto rue Augusta which becomes av. Pierre de Montesquieu, and left onto rue du Mauzon (20min.). 12F per person, 10F per tent, 6F per car. Reception open 7am-noon and 2-10pm. Inquire at the tourist office about camping at local farms (around 16F50 per person; you might have to help with some chores).

Food

The Gers *département* holds the distinction of being France's number one producer of *foie gras d'oie* (goose liver), with duck *pâté* coming in a close second. These specialties of the region, along with *tournons à l'ail* or *à l'oignon* (garlic or onion soup), *maigrets* (lean duck), *palombes* (ring doves) and *pastis gascon* (layered apple or plum cake) reappear on menus in local restaurants. The *basse ville* holds an **open market** on av. Hoche every Thursday until 1pm; the *haute ville* holds another near pl. de la Libération in front of the cathedral each Saturday until 6pm. A **Codec supermarket** on rue Bourget in Grand Garros is convenient to the hostel. (Open Mon.-Sat. 8:30am-7pm.) Try the Gascon liqueur of choice, *armagnac.*

Le Corsaire, 9, rue des Grazes, on place Diderot. A delightful family-run affair. 62F *menu* includes chef's salad, *faux-filet grillé,* and dessert. 72F *menu* offers Mexican salad, *entrecôte au poivre vert,* and dessert. Open daily noon-2pm and 7-10pm.

Le Donjon, rue Alsace-Lorraine, a block from the Gers River. A restaurant/*salon de thé/boulangerie* combo with a terrace out front. Small pizza 14F50. Snack dishes 12-18F. Salads 30-45F. Omelettes 19-40F. 55F *menu* serves up *hors d'oeuvres variées, plat du jour,* dessert, and a 1/4-bottle of red or rosé wine. Open Mon.-Sat. noon-2:30pm and 7-10pm.

Les Trois Mousquetaires, 5, rue Espagne, off pl. de la République. Excellent service makes the 65F lunch-only *menu* even better. Situated on an ancient medieval street near the cathedral. Soup, appetizer, meat, and dessert included. Open daily noon-2pm and 7:30-10pm.

Resto Quick Seguin, 6, rue Dessoules, across from the tourist office. Wood-beamed *salon de thé* doubles as a cafeteria. Small pizzas 9F50. Hamburgers 15-20F. Cheeseburgers 15F. Steak with salad or french fries 34F. Chicken with same stuff 23F. Open Tues.-Sat. 7:45am-noon and 2-7:30pm.

Sights and Entertainment

Try to catch the classical west façade of the otherwise Gothic **Cathédrale Ste-Marie** when it basks at sunset. The masterwork of this 15th- and early 16th-century beauty is the ornately carved choir whose assemblage of over 1500 iconographic representations is one of France's most prodigious. (Choir open daily 8:30am-noon and 2-6pm. Admission 5F.) The 16th-century Gascon painter Arnaud-de-Moles created the 14 stained-glass windows in the apsidal chapels. (Cathedral open daily 7:30am-noon and 2-8pm; off-season 8am-noon and 2-6pm.) In July and August, *les lumières du ciel,* held within the cathedral, provide an enlightening perspective on the history of the stained-glass windows. A recorded narration accompanies the light show. (Wed. and Sat. Tickets 35F, students 15F.)

A weathered monolith near the cathedral, the **Tour d'Armagnac** once served as a prison. Leading down to the river from the tower is the **escalier monumental,** a formidable 370-step staircase offering expansive views of the *basse ville* and the countryside beyond. In the middle stands a statue of d'Artagnan, the most famous of Louis XIV's musketeers, who was born near Auch in 1615 and later immortalized by Alexandre Dumas and Hollywood. The road from pl. Salinis leads under medieval **Porte d'Arton** to the steep and narrow *pousterles* (stairways).

The **Maison de Gascogne,** rue Gambetta, is a mall where regional crafts and specialties (largely culinary and alcoholic) are displayed and sold in July and August. Sample baked goods such as the flaky *cronstade* and liquors like the fiery *armagnac,* a drink which ages longer and smoother than cognac. (Open daily 10am-1pm and 2:30-7:30pm.) Set in a former convent, the **Musée des Jacobins,** pl. Louis Blanc, has temporary exhibits of contemporary art, a collection of regional arts and crafts, and a selection of rare furniture from Auch. (Open Tues.-Sun. 10am-noon and 2-6pm; Nov.-April Tues.-Sat. 10am-noon and 2-4pm. Admission 5F, students 2F50.)

At the end of September, Auch stages its ever-popular **Festival de Musique et Danse Contemporain** at the Maison de Gascogne, attracting modern music and an array of national dance troupes. During June and July, **The Festival de Musique Classique** fills the cathedral's acoustic interior. Perhaps the most celebrated of all these music festivals is the annual **Jazz Festival** that swings through **Marciac,** 25km from Auch, in August's second week, rivalling those hosted by much larger cities. Tickets (120-200F) may be purchased by calling 62 09 33 33. If you wish to stay in Marciac, the tourist office there (tel. 62 09 30 55) has information about accommodations.

If you're tempted to visit wine cellars, ask the Auch tourist office for a list of local *caves.* Don't forget to leave a little room at the end for a visit to the small town of **Condom,** north of Auch. The **Musée de l'Armagnac** demonstrates in detail the production of Armagnac, the regional liqueur. Legend has it that the celebrated vineyards of Armagnac once elicited a sword-extended salute from Condé. (Open July-Sept. daily 10am-noon and 2:30-6:30pm. Admission 8F, students 4F50.) During winter, ask the Condom tourist office (tel. 62 28 00 80) if a visit is possible. Erected in the 13th century, the **Château de Cassaigne** once housed the Bishops of Condom. It offers a free Armagnac *dégustation.* (Open summer daily 9am-noon and 2-7pm.)

Andorra

*Great Charlemagne, my father, liberated me from
the Arabs. Alone, I remain the only daughter of Emperor Charlemagne. Faithful and free, eleven centuries, faithful and free I wish to remain between my
two valiant suitors and my two guardian princes.*
                        *—Opening lines from the
                        Andorran national anthem*

Perched high in the Pyrénées between France and Spain, the tiny principality of Andorra (pop. 50,000, area 480 sq. km) remains one of Europe's most intriguing geographical and political anomalies. Although sandwiched by, and dependent on, France
and Spain, Andorra clings fiercely to a distinct culture and an official language—Catalan. But while Andorra offers soaring peaks and lofty culture, it is not the grandeur of
its sights but rather the humility of its sales taxes that draws most visitors. A string of
duty-free shops soaked with the light of neon signs has unfortunately transformed this
dimunitive nation into Europe's largest department store. To best appreciate Andorra,
keep your money in your wallet, break away from the capital, and visit the picturesque
Lilliputian villages cradled within a Brobdignagian mountain range.

According to legend, Charlemagne founded Andorra in 784, in gratitude to the area's
inhabitants for having helped his army against the Arabs. In 839, Charles II, Charlemagne's grandson, transferred sovereignty to the Spanish Counts of Urgell, who gradually ceded their power over the region to the Church of Urgell, which has retained its
hold for over seven centuries. On the secular side, however, a series of complex marriages delivered power to the King of France, who ultimately lost it (and his head) to
the President of the Republic. Thus it is that today French President François Mitterand
and Bishop of Urgell Dr. Joan Martí Alanis share the title "Co-Princes" of Andorra,
with Andorrans still paying a tribute tax called the *Questia* to these men. A popularly
elected "General Council of the Valleys," which consists of 28 members (4 from each
of Andorra's 7 parishes) conducts day-to-day government.

Politically, Andorra appears far less progressive than other industrialized western
European nations. Through 1970, only third-generation Andorran men older than 25
could legally vote. Only in the last twenty years has suffrage been extended to women,
younger voters, and recent immigrants. Andorrans have paid income tax only since
1983. Political parties are illegal, although a *Partit Democràtic d'Andorra (PDA)* does
meet informally. Not until 1990 did Andorra finally vote to create a special commission to draft a constitution. In the same year, the General Council also showed its south
of the border affinity by voting to give Spain all responsibility for representing Andorra
in international organizations.

The hearty Andorran cuisine resembles that of Spanish Catalonia. *Botifarra* (sausage) and *paella* (seafood mixed with rice, sausage and chicken) comprise the staples
of the local diet. *Trinxat,* a mashed potato and green cabbage concoction, is a local specialty more subtly flavored than its ingredients would suggest. Trout is the backbone of
Andorra's fishing industry, and when grilled it provides a respite from the pungent
spices which usually spike local dishes.

Andorra's unabated attachment to its traditional Catalonian culture manifests itself
every summer when each of the seven parishes holds its own festival, a three-day jubilee that is an official public holiday in that parish. These spectacles start the third weekend of July and continue until mid-September.

Most Andorran towns scatter along the principality's three branches of "highways."
Additionally, an extensive network of hiking trails and cabins make the country's beauty accessible to those on foot. Several Gallo-Roman churches, often topped by cylindrical bell-towers, huddle near the Spanish border. North of the capital, clear lakes and
icy mountain peaks shelter tiny villages. Many Andorran towns, notably Canillo, Sol-

deu, and Pas de la Casa, provide a base for skiing from December to April on a wide array of downhill and cross-country terrain. As major towns are separated by mere kilometers, most of the country can be accessed on local buses.

Beware that a strict extradition treaty is in effect between Andorra and the United States; if you have purchased this guide looking for an overseas refuge, we recommend turning to another chapter.

Getting There

With no train tracks in Andorra, two highways—one from France and one from Spain, provide the only access to the principality. All traffic from France must enter Andorra at the town **Pas de la Casa. Sant Julià de Lòria** is the gateway town on the Spanish side. To approach Andorra by **French train**, stop at the SNCF station **l'Hospitalet** (a stop on the Toulouse-Ax-les-Thermes-Barcelona line, 4 per day in each direction) or **La Tour de Carol** (on the same line, and the final stop of the **petit train jaune** from Perpignan, 5 per day, 107F). From l'Hospitalet, **Société Franco-Andorrane de Transports (SFAT),** Carres la Llucuna, 12 Andorra la Vella (tel. 213 72), runs a bus through Pas de la Casa to the capital, Andorra la Vella. (One bus per day leaves l'Hospitalet at 7:40am. Buses leave Andorra la Vella for l'Hospitalet at 5:45am and 4pm. 1 3/4hr., 33F each way.) From La Tour de Carol, **Autos Pujol Huguet** (tel. 410 19) sends a bus to the capital (from La Tour de Carol at 7:30am and 2:30pm; Oct.-June only the morning bus runs, 2 1/2hr., 42F). The same bus also goes to Sant Julià de Lòria on the Spanish border (from Sant Julià to Andorra la Vella at 7:15am and 2pm, from Andorra la Vella to Sant Julià at 1pm and 8:10pm, 20min.).

Several private bus companies run to more distant points beyond the French border towns. **Alsina Graells,** 34, rue Prat de la Creu (tel. 273 79), makes two daily runs (7am and 2pm) to Barcelona, 215km south of Andorra la Vella. (Mon.-Sat. 100F, Sun. 115F. Office open Mon.-Sat. 9:30am-2:30pm and 5-7pm.) For information on international connections to Toulouse or Madrid, contact **Andor-Inter,** 34, rue Prat de la Creu (tel. 262 83).

Getting Around

Andorra la Vella is cradled in a valley at the confluence of Andorra's three principal road networks. An efficient system of **interurban buses** connects villages lying along the major highways; the entire country is navigable via public transportation within an hour or two. The 10-minute ride from Andorra la Vella to **Encamp, Ordino,** or **Sant Julià de Lòria** costs only 4-5F. To reach points farther north than Encamp or Ordino, simply switch to the next line along the route. Bus lines are not indicated by number or color; be attentive to the directional signs posted in the front window. If paying in francs, have exact change, or expect a handful of pesetas in return. Major destinations from Andorra la Vella include: Sant Julià de Lorià (every 15min. 7:30am-9:30pm, 4F); Encamp (every 1/2hr. 7:30am-9:30pm, 5F); and Canillo (every hr. 9am-8pm, 9F). For more information, contact **Cooperative Interurbana Andorrana,** av. Príncep Ben-lloch, 15 (tel. 204 12).

Practical Information

French and Spanish border police require presentation of a valid passport or an identity card (for EC citizens) upon entering the country. Within Andorra, an extensive network of tourist offices (indicated by *Informació* signs) provides information on lodgings and excursions. During the winter, they also distribute information on skiing facilities. The staffs in these offices generally speak fluent Spanish, French, and English. In the capital, the office will provide you with an adequate *plànol* (street plan) of Andorra la Vella, indicating adjoining villages such as Santa Coloma and La Margineda. On the flip side is a listing of emergency telephone numbers and essential services. Ask for the brochure published by the Andorran Ministry of Tourism and Sports, which includes what must be the world's most detailed map of Andorra.

All establishments are legally bound to accept French and Spanish currencies in every transaction, as Andorra does not have its own currency. In practice, however, dominant trading ties with Spain have resulted in a conspicuous preference for pesetas. All prices (except on a few touristy menus) appear in pesetas; you are left to muddle through conversion calculations to francs (about 20 pesetas to a franc). Merchants and bus drivers are so accustomed to receiving payment in pesetas that they almost appear disconcerted if you choose francs. Although establishments will grudgingly accept French currency, they will often give change in pesetas. Bus drivers to the French border towns are, happily, an exception. Moral: Buy pesetas before you buy anything else.

Dual French and Spanish administration of the postal system has resulted in separate post offices, overseen by France and Spain, within a few blocks of one another. Letters and other correspondance forwarded to the **poste restante** in Andorra la Vella will arrive at the French post office. For the Spanish office, address mail to **lista de Correos.**

Phone communications in Andorra are handled exclusively by the **STA** network. You must purchase an STA *teletarja* (telecard) for a minimum of 40F, which provides 50 units of calling time. The cards are available in any post office. French Télécom phone cards do not work in the Andorran payphones. Collect calls are not available, and AT&T does not maintain an access network with Andorra.

Accommodations

Accommodations in Andorra can be dirt cheap. Auberges and hostels don't exist, but there are inexpensive alternatives to hotels, clustering only in and around the capital. The low-cost **residència** is comparable to a pension, with single, double, or larger rooms (50-175F). Most *residèncias* do not have showers or baths in the rooms. Unlike in France, hotel owners tend not to post room prices at the main entrance. Be persistent and be certain of a room's price before committing. Campgrounds abound throughout, and tend to fill quickly in the summer months with French and Spanish vacationers.

Andorra la Vella (Andorre-la-Vieille)

Avinguda Meritxell, Andorra la Vella's main thoroughfare and the Hong Kong of the Pyrénées, does well at disguising that the city is the permanent home of only 16,500 residents. But what Andorrans refer to as a "city" is little more than a narrow stretch of perfumeries, electronics shops, clothing stores, and a host of other boutiques which sprout along this short boulevard overlooking the placid Gran Valira River. Marvel at Europe's largest K-Mart, and move on. Climb the roads leading away from the city, where residents in the tiny mountain villages still practice sheep-husbandry and tobacco cultivation.

Orientation and Practical Information

The official language of Andorra is Catalan, although Spanish is almost as widely spoken and French will get you by in the capital. The city has two strikingly different personalities. Avenguda Meritxell, the city's commercial pipeline, recalls the frenzy of a Parisian shopping district; the tiny streets twisting through the old city recede to medieval tranquility. Geographically, the city is long and narrow, stretched out in an east-west direction in a valley with mountains on either side. To reach the tourist office from the plaça Guillemó, take Carrer Doctor Nequi and make a left onto av. Príncep Benlloch. Signs for the tourist office will appear on the right, after the **Sant Esteve** church.

Tourist Office: av. Docteur Villanova (tel. 202 14). Dispenses information on accommodations and on the surrounding countryside. Pick up the brochures containing practical information and important phone numbers, and a map of the entire country. Also distributes fishing licenses. Open daily 9am-1pm and 3-7pm; Sept.-June Mon.-Sat. 10am-1pm and 3-7pm, Sun. 10-1pm.

Post Office: French Post Office, 57, av. Meritxell (open Mon.-Fri. 9am-noon and 3-6pm, Sat. 9am-noon). **Spanish Post Office,** carrer Joan Maragall, a few blocks away (open Mon.-Fri. 9am-1pm and 4-5pm, Sat. 9am-1pm). Both at the eastern end of town.

Currency Exchange: 10, av. Meritxell, on the street level of the Pyrénées department store. Open Mon.-Sat. 9:30-8pm, Sun. 9am-7pm.

American Express: 12, av. Meritxell. Open Mon.-Fri. 9:30am-1pm and 3:30-7pm, Sat. 9:30am-1pm.

Youth Information: in plaça del Poble (tel. 202 02), down a flight of stairs to the left of a bar. Provides a wide array of information on lodgings and activities in Andorra. Open Mon.-Fri. 9am-1pm and 3-7pm.

24-Hour Pharmacy: Farmàcies de Guardia, as in France, a program in which pharmacies in the city rotate all-night duties. Each pharmacy has the "duty roster" posted on its door, listing which pharmacy is open on a given night.

Hospital: Clinica Verge de Meritxell, Avinguda Fiter I Rossell (tel. 215 21).

Police: rue Prat de la Creu (tel. 212 22.)

Accommodations, Camping, and Food

Pensió La Rosa, Antic Carrer Major, 18 (tel. 218 10), just south of av. Príncep Benlloch, provides immaculate, fresh rooms, all with showers and happy flowered wallpaper. (Doubles 150F. Triples 200F. Quads 250F. Breakfast 15F.) The owner of the **Residència Benazet,** 19, Carrer la Llacuna (tel. 206 98), speaks neither French nor English, but makes a royal effort to bridge any communication gap. The hotel offers simple, no-frills rooms on a quiet street. (Singles 60F. Doubles 120F. Triples 180F.) The **Hôtel les Arcades,** 5, plaça Guillemo, rents clean rooms in a noisy quarter above a large square. (Singles and doubles with shower and toilet Mon.-Thurs. 110-140F, Fri.-Sun. 120-140F. Quads with shower 200F. Breakfast 15F.)

The most convenient campsites are situated about 3km from Andorra la Vella, in Santa Coloma. The **Camping Riberaygua** (tel. 266 99) is a densely packed site about 50m off the main road. Look for signs indicating the campground on the side of the main road from Andorra la Vella. (Reception open daily 7am-9pm. 20F per person, 20F per tent. Hot showers included.) A stone's throw beyond, the **St-Coloma** campground (tel. 288 99) allows breathing room between the tents. (18F per person, 18F per tent. Electricity and showers included.) There are no cooking facilities at either site, but there are cheap restaurants at each and a grocery store nearby.

Moderately priced restaurants rule in Andorra la Vella; the highest concentration is along the busy Avinguda Meritxell. The restaurants on the quieter streets around Cap del Carrer tend to have more authentic cuisine, but no six-language tourist menus. The Parisian owner of **Les Tortorès,** 4, place Guillemo, serves delightful French cuisine with a delicious *crème Catalane* for dessert (58F *menu;* open daily 12:30pm-1am). The **Restaurant Marti,** 44, Avinguda Meritxell, offers some of the cheapest Catalan fare in town with its 41F and 60F four-course *menus.* (Open daily 10am-4pm and 7:30-10pm.) Bedecked in photos and memorabilia pertaining to the life and times of Charlie Chaplin, **Charlot,** 2, Avinguda Riberaygua, serves a 56F *menu* featuring delicious Andorran-style trout. (Open daily 1-3:30pm and 8-10:30pm.) Hearty Catalan cuisine and no French speakers await at **El Meson,** on Prada Guillemo. Two 47F *menus* include gazpacho, meat or poultry, and dessert. (Open daily noon-2pm and 7-10pm.) **El Grill,** a cafeteria in the **Pyrénées** department store on Avinguda Meritxell with a panoramic terrace, offers a cheap 48F *menu.* Other choices, however, have prices as steep as the mountains surrounding Europe's highest capital city. (Open daily 12:30-4:30pm.)

Sights

Although most visitors get too caught up in the shopping vortex to notice anything else, Andorra la Vella has more to offer than cheap liquor and cigarettes. Removed from the delirium of contemporary consumerism, the city has managed to preserve its *Barri Antic* (old city). The centerpiece of this ancient neighborhood, the 16th-century **Casa de la Vall** (House of the Valleys), which resembles a medieval fortification, doubles as Andorra's official parliament house and courthouse. The ornate interior contains the chapel of Sant Ermengol and the principality's "Room of Seven Keys"—one for each Andorran parish. The "Very Illustrious General Council" holds its sessions in the historic structure, which retained the status of a private residence until 1580. (Open Mon.-Fri. 10am-1pm and 3-7pm, Sat. 10am-1pm. Free.) Like its counterparts in Luxembourg and Liechtenstein, the **Museu Filatelic** (tel. 291 29), inside the Casa de la Vall, an impressive array of stamps and related postal paraphernalia will deliver a parcel of excitement to any philatelist (same hours as Casa de la Vall). Bordering on the *Barri Antic,* the charming square **Plaça del Bisbe Benlloch** centers on the narrow twisting streets behind the main avenue. During the summer, the **Festival Major** brightens the adjacent neighborhood of **Cap del Carrer** with Catalan bands and free cups of a tasty hot chocolate paste distributed by the local restaurants.

Avinguda Meritxell, Andorra's central thoroughfare, is flanked by a slew of glitzy hotels and shops. The country's largest department store, cleverly named **Pyrénées,** 10, Avinguda Meritxell, looms over the madcap activity of the avenue below. More like a self-contained city than a mere store, Pyrénées features street-level information booths and exchange desks, and stretches for several city blocks. (Open Mon.-Sat. 9:30am-8pm, Sun. 9am-7pm.)

The tourist office sells tickets for the Andorra la Vella's annual **Festival Internacional de Música i Dansa,** highlighting an international array of ballet and classical concerts during the first half of October. Most events take place in the auditorium of the centrally situated plaça del Poble's or in the Sant-Esteve Church. (Tickets 275F.) For information on this and other festivals in Andorra, contact the Collectiu d'Activitats Culturals, plaça del Poble S/N. (tel. 202 02). Andorra la Vella's annual festival colors the capital on the first Saturday, Sunday, and Monday in August.

Near Andorra la Vella

Andorra's countryside is a veritable Wallyworld of alpine delights: high peaks, mountain lakes, pristine hamlets, and some of the best ski slopes in Europe. **Santa Coloma,** five minutes from Andorra la Vella by bus, features a solitary 12th-century church notable for its unique cylindrical Romanesque bell tower. The curious stone bridge of the Margineda arches gracefully over the diminutive **Gran Valira River** in **Sant Juliá de Lorià,** just north of the Spanish border. **La Massana,** lying on the route toward **Ordino** in the Valira del Nord nestles idyllically under an imposing Pyrénéan backdrop, climaxing in the **Pic de Coma Pedrosa,** Andorra's highest at 2946m. The approach to La Massana follows a formidable series of tunnels carved through the mountain rock. A reconstructed Romanesque church with an impressive baroque altar stands across from the Comú de la Massana (town hall; open for information Mon.-Fri. 9am-1pm and 3-6pm) in La Massana. On the outskirts of the village, situated on a small riverbank in the valley, the **Camping STA Catarina** offers a bucolic setting in which to pitch your tent.

Ordino rests comfortably in a valley in the shadow of the imposing Pic de Casamanya. Although the least populated of Andorra's seven parishes, Ordino is distinguished by its former status as home to the principality's **seigniorial mansions** *(pairals).* The nobility of the town built a small fortune in the regional iron industry; the home of Don Guillem, a prominent Andorran iron magnate and author of the 1866 new reform, stands near the church. The colossal **Palau de Gel D'Andorra** (Andorran ice palace; tel. 515 15), an eclectic recreational facility, dominates the tiny town of **Canillo.** The facilities of the "palace," including an overflowing swimming pool, ice-skating rink, squash courts, and cinema, are accessible by individual admission tickets. (20F for pool, 20-24F for skating, 25F per 1/2hr. squash plus 8F for racket rental. Under 21 entitled to a 40% reduction. Palace open Mon.-Fri. 8:30am-11pm, Sat.-Sun. 11am-midnight. Schedule changes; ask for times.) During the winter, the area around Canillo attracts droves of alpine and cross-country skiers. Three principal stations at **Soldeu-El Tarter, Incles,** and **Envalira** embrace over 35km of well-maintained trails. Artificial snow makers ensure a white winter even in the absence of much snow. On the French border, **Pas de la Casa,** is a glorified shopping center by summer, but a world-class ski resort by winter.

Two **walking routes** traverse much of the country and access parts of Andorra invisible to cars. Along each path, Andorra maintains **mountain refuges,** simple cabins that give the backpacker a fireplace and roof overhead at no charge. All tourist offices can provide detailed maps and information on the refuges.

Languedoc-Roussillon

Languedoc and Roussillon have never been comfortable with Parisian authority, and it's easy to see why. This is a rugged southern land, and its people are as much Spanish as French in origins, accent, and architecture. The Moorish Palais des Rois de Majorque in Perpignan, the Catalonian ecclesiastical stronghold at St-Michel de Luxa, and a landscape peppered with crumbling *châteaux cathars* (the final bastion of an heretical sect near Carcassonne) are badges of the multicultural identity that has shaped this region. Languedoc-Roussillon still harbors the ramparts and *donjons* which sheltered and shielded the chivalric defenders of an endangered heritage. The sweeping hills yield sweet and fruity wines, and a strong Mediterranean influence throughout the Middle Ages influenced styles of art and architecture altogether different from those in the North. In smaller villages, such as Cordes, a former refuge on the Cathar frontier, the medieval character has been preserved down to the last cobblestone.

The name Languedoc-Roussillon indicates the two cultures that have maintained the strongest influence in the area. Languedoc dominated most of southern France from the 9th to the 13th centuries. The region stretched from the Rhône all the way to the foothills of the Pyrénées, including the Catalan coastal region of Roussillon in the south, and Toulouse to the west. The people spoke the *langue d'oc* (named for its word for "yes," "oc,") as opposed to the northern *langue d'oïl,* the language of northern France, which evolved into modern French. Their courts enjoyed a literary blossoming with tales of adventure and courtly love recounted by wandering troubadours. Heretical sects seemed to sprout more easily here than in other regions of France, and they, along with the erotic aesthetics of the troubadours, aroused the wrath of a Catholic Church at the height of its power. Accustomed to war and frustrated by unsuccessful crusades, the northern French nobility needed little prodding to turn on its rival to the south as a land ripe for conquest. King Philippe August allowed Pope Innocent III to preach a crusade against the area's Cathar or Albigensian heretics, and dispatched Simon de Montfort, an opportunistic baron from the Ile-de-France, on the Albigensian crusade, a campaign of conquest against all of Languedoc. After his armies crushed the province in 1213, the *langue d'oc* faded, and in 1539 the Edict of Villiers-Cotterets imposed the northern *langue d'oïl.*

In ensuing years, localized manifestations of discontent against Parisian rule were gradually suppressed, and the 1659 Treaty of the Pyrénées legally incorporated Cerdagne and the southern part of Languedoc, Roussillon, into the French domain. With the discovery of thermal springs in the Pyrénées in the early 19th century, the bubbly of the remedial waters purged much of the simmering resentment as rising prosperity in the region washed away lingering political differences.

In recent times, French law has often stood in conflict with local tradition, fueling economic difficulties and a distinct leftist political ideology. While much of France has lurched to the right, victim to an endemic xenophobia, Languedoc has remained faithful to its socialist tradition. The newspapers on the stands today, such as *L'Humanité* and *La Dépêche du Midi,* are direct descendants of the 19th-century journals founded by Jean Jaurès and other leftist politicians. Though Jaurès was assassinated in 1914, his ideal has lived on. Today, one of Castres's principal museums commemorates his work. As for the linguistic fate of the region, the *langue d'oc*—commonly referred to as *occitan*—has ceded in most areas to standardized French. Students can learn the language at school, however, and count it as a foreign language on the *bac,* the national university qualifying exam. The *occitan* banner, with its yellow and red vertical stripes and a black cross, still flies throughout the region. A formidable medieval power, Catalonia is the region around Perpignan extending into Spain, with Barcelona as its capital. *Catalan* is also offered as a subject in school and a large Catalonian literary center thrives in Perpignan.

Tourist offices throughout the region distribute itineraries which follow *Les Traces des Cathares* (tracks of the Cathars) and ancient Roman roads. Along the Mediterranean coast, clean, sprawling beaches washed by the ocean's calm blue waves lie at the foot of the eastern Pyrénées chain. In addition to an intricate web of **hiking** trails, the Pyrénées attract skiers to fine resorts such as Bonascre (near Ax-les-Thermes) and Font Romeu (near Perpignan). Frequent **trains** to both the mountains and the Mediterranean run from the hubs of Toulouse and Montpellier. Its locks visible in the centers of Toulouse and Perpignan, the Canal du Midi, connecting the Atlantic to the Mediterranean, also links some towns in the region. Unfortunately, however, drought has greatly reduced the canal's navigability. The hilly countryside makes **cycling** a bit difficult, and the sparse traffic reduces hitching possibilities.

Few regions can claim beaches as unspoiled and unpretentious as the **Côte Vermeille.** Nestled within its rugged coastline lie such jewels as Collioure, where the Pyrénées nearly spill directly into the beautiful waterfront. Europe's largest *quartier naturiste* (nudist colony) is a short ride from Montpellier on the Cap d'Agde. One of the most popular regional dishes is *cassoulet,* a hearty stew of white beans, sausage, pork, mutton, and goose. Along the coast, chefs have been known to toss octopus into the pot. In Roussillon, refined diners prefer *cargolade* (snails stuffed with bacon) to the many other seafood offerings. The tangy fermented Roquefort and St-Nectaire cheeses complement the assortment of luscious fruits grown in the Garonne Valley. Accompany your meals with a glass of one of the region's full-bodied red wines such as Minervois or Corbières. For dessert or as an aperitif, try the sweet white wines of Lunel, Mireval, and St-Jean-de-Minervois.

Toulouse

One of the fastest-growing cities in France, Toulouse (pop. 380,000) has spent much of the 20th century establishing itself as the technopolis of the future. During World War I, the French Air Force chose this city, far from the raging front, as its construction center. In the 1920s, Antoine de St-Exupéry (known to most students as author of *The Little Prince)* and other pilots launched mail service from Toulouse to Africa and South America. More recently, these pioneers of aviation have been supplanted by **Aérospatiale,** the nerve center of European aeronautic research. *Ariane* rocket systems (responsible for launching most of the world's satellites) and the *Airbus* (the most technologically advanced jumbo jet) are both brainchildren of *toulousain* expertise.

Unlike many high-tech centers, Toulouse is a city with a grand if unfortunate past to match its present. Once the capital of southern Aquitaine, Toulouse now enjoys a role as the capital of historic Languedoc. The city came of age in the 16th and 17th centuries when many merchants who had amassed large fortunes through the pastel (a plant used to dye fabrics blue) trade gained appointments as consuls or *capitouls* and built extravagant townhouses to symbolize their new power and status. But religious intolerance plagued the town through these years. Thousands of Huguenots perished here in the mid 16th century; in 1619, Lucilio Vanini, a free-thinking philosopher, was burned alive in the center of town, after having his tongue cut out. Nonetheless, novelist and travel writer Henry James, while he found this history "detestable, saturated with blood and perfidy," did find ample cause for admiration in Toulouse's splendid churches, especially St-Sernin. Youthful and energetic, France's second student capital succesfully combines technology with history, art, and erudition.

Orientation and Practical Information

Toulouse sprawls on both sides of the Garonne River, but the museums, interesting churches, and sights are located within a compact section east of the river, bounded by the rue de Metz in the south and the boulevards Strasbourg and Carnot to the west and north. To reach the tourist office, turn left from the station and then right onto the broad allées Jean Jaurès. Bear right at pl. Wilson, and then take a right onto rue Lafayette. The tourist office is in a small park on the left of the intersection with rue d'Alsace-Lorraine. The tourist office map verges on useless; try to get the *Plan Guide Blay* (available in many hotels and stores, 35F), including detailed maps of Toulouse and outlying areas.

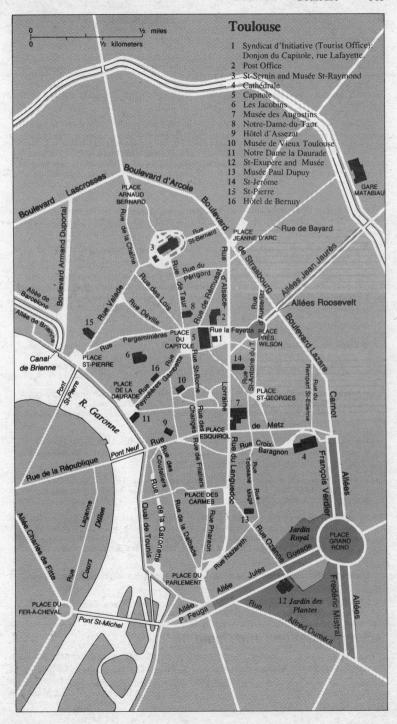

Toulouse

1 Syndicat d'Initiative (Tourist Office);
  Donjon du Capitole, rue Lafayette
2 Post Office
3 St-Sernin and Musée St-Raymond
4 Cathédrale
5 Capitole
6 Les Jacobins
7 Musée des Augustins
8 Notre-Dame-du-Taur
9 Hôtel d'Assezat
10 Musée de Vieux Toulouse
11 Notre Dame la Daurade
12 St-Exupère and Musée
13 Musée Paul Dupuy
14 St-Jérôme
15 St-Pierre
16 Hôtel de Bernuy

Tourist Office: Donjon du Capitôle, rue Lafayette (tel. 61 11 02 22), in the little park behind the Capitôle. Don't expect lavish attention. Efficient staff makes accommodations reservations here and in other cities. Walking tours of the old city (42-54F) and bus excursions to nearby sights (130F). Most tours leave daily July-Sept. **Currency exchange** open May-Sept. Sat.-Sun. and holidays 11am-1pm and 2-4:30pm. Office open daily 9am-7pm; Oct.-April Mon.-Sat. 9am-6pm.

Post Office: 9, rue Lafayette (tel. 61 22 33 11), opposite the tourist office. **Poste Restante, currency exchange,** and **telephones.** Open Mon.-Fri. 8am-7pm, Sat. 8am-noon. **Postal Code: 31000.**

Flights: Blagnac (tel. 61 42 44 64 or 61 42 44 65), 10km northwest of Toulouse. **Air Inter,** 76, allées Jean-Jaurès (tel. 61 30 68 68) flies to Paris 10-13 times per day (70min., 845F, reduced fares 295-490F). **Air France,** 2, bd. de Strasbourg (tel. 61 10 01 01) flaps to London's Heathrow once per day from Mon.-Sat. (2hr., 2425F, reduced fare 800F). **British Airways** (tel. 61 71 10 00) also flies to London once per day. **Navettes Aérocar** (tel. 61 30 04 89) shuttle from the *gare routière* (next to the train station) and allées Jean Jaurès to the airport (every 20min. from 5:20am to 11:30pm, 20-25min., 20F one-way, 25F after 9pm, 16F for students with *carte jeunes,* 20F after 9pm.)

Trains: (tel. 61 62 50 50; reservations 61 62 85 44), on bd. Pierre Sémard. To: Paris (9 per day, 8hr., 326F); Bordeaux (10 per day, 2 3/4hr., 158F); Lyon (6 per day, 6hr., 278F); Marseille (11 per day, 4 1/2hr., 226F). Station open 24 hrs.

Buses: 68, bd. Pierre Sémard (tel. 61 48 71 84), next to the train station. SNCF buses accept Eurailpasses. Buy tickets in train station.

Public Transportation: SEMVAT buses (tel. 61 41 70 70). Information office on 7, pl. Esquirol. (Open Mon.-Fri. 8:30am-6:30pm, Sat. 8:30am-noon.) Tickets can be bought on the bus, at ticket booths, or at many *tabacs.* Tickets 6F50 (1 zone), 9F (2 zones), 47F (*carnet* of 10 1 zone), and 70F (*carnet* of 10 2 zone). Bus route maps are available at the bus station's ticket booths and at the tourist office. Toulouse is currently building a metro system, part of which should be operational in 1993. **Taxis:** tel. 61 80 36 36 (24-hr. service) or 61 62 37 34.

Hitchhiking: Those choosing to hitch take bus #2 to RN113 for Carcassonne. For Paris, they take bus #10 to start. For Auch and Bayonne, bus #64 to RN124. For Albi, bus #16 or 19. For a small fee, **Allostop-Provoya,** 9, pl. du Capitale (tel. 61 23 25 29), can match riders with drivers (57F per 500km). Open Mon.-Fri. 10am-noon and 1:30-5pm.

English Bookstore: The Bookshop, 17, rue Lakanal (tel. 61 22 99 92), down from Les Jacobins. *Let's Go* guides available. Large selection of novels, non-fiction, comic books, and dictionaries. Trade in used paperbacks. Open Tues.-Sat. 10am-noon and 3-7pm; Sept.-July 13 Mon.-Sat. 9:30am-1pm and 2-7pm.

Youth Center: Centre d'Information Jeunesse, 17, rue de Metz (tel. 61 21 20 20). Information on sports, leisure, travel, and education. Foreigners welcome. Open Mon.-Fri. 10am-noon and 2-6pm; Sept.-June Mon.-Fri. 10am-noon and 2-6pm, Sat. 10am-noon.

Women's Center: CIDF—Centre d'Information sur les Droits des Femmes, 95, rue Grande St-Michel (tel. 61 52 83 59). Provides legal information and assistance in finding counseling services. Open Mon.-Fri. 9am-12:30pm and 1:30-5pm.

Laundromat: Toulouse has a shocking number of laundromats. Ask at the hostel or your hotel for the one nearest you. Otherwise...**Laverie Self-Service,** 20, rue Cujas, off the pl. de la Bourse. Wash 15F per 7kg, dry 2F per 6min. Soap 2F. Open daily 7am-9pm. Also **Laundromatique,** 20, rue Arnaud Bernard, a few blocks north of St-Sernin. Wash 18F per 7kg, dry 2F per 6min. Open daily 7am-9pm.

Late-Night Pharmacy: 13, rue de Sénéchal (tel. 61 21 81 20). Open 8pm-8am, only for emergencies.

Hospital: C.H.R. de Rangueil, chemin de Vallon (tel. 61 53 11 33). **Medical Emergency,** tel. 61 49 33 33 or tel. 15. **Police:** (tel. 61 29 70 00), on Rempart St-Etienne. **Emergency:** tel. 17.

Accommodations and Camping

Finding a room in Toulouse should never be a problem, even during the summer. Plenty of inexpensive hotels surround the train station, especially on rue Caffarelli, off allées Jean Jaurès. Lodging in this unpleasant and unsafe neighborhood, however, is no cheaper than at budget hotels scattered beyond pl. Wilson in the *centre ville.* Many hotels in Toulouse (including those on the budget end) are indicated by street signs pointing in the direction of the establishment.

Auberge de Jeunesse (HI), Villa des Rosiers, 125, rue Jean Rieux (tel. 61 80 49 93). Call ahead before making the trek. From the station, take bus #14 (direction: "Purpan") to pl. Dupuy and change to bus #22 (direction: "Gonin-La Terrasse"). Get off at Leygues. If walking, turn left out of the station and follow bd. de la Gare (which undergoes myriad name transformations) for about 7 very long blocks along the canal, then turn left onto rue Jean Rieux and walk for another 8 blocks. The hostel is on your left in front of the housing development. Small, and somewhat rundown, but very friendly. Reception open 8-10am and 4:30-11pm. Lockout 10am-4:30pm. Pay a 50F deposit to get the front door key if you want to "come home" after 11pm. Members only. 39F per person. Breakfast 15F. Sheets 14F. Kitchen available. Open Feb.-Dec.

Hôtel du Grand Balcon, 8, rue Romiguières (tel. 61 21 48 08), on a corner of pl. du Capitole. Roll out of bed and into the hub of Toulouse. St-Exupéry stayed here in in 1920; ask the obliging proprietor to show you the author's room (no. 32) and the intriguing photos in the main floor foyer. Singles 105F, with shower 146F. Doubles 125F, with shower 146-195F. Triples and quads 146F, with shower 195F. Showers 11F. Breakfast 21F. Closed Christmas and last 3 weeks in Aug.

Hôtel des Arts, 1bis, rue Cantegril (tel. 61 23 36 21), at rue des Arts off pl. St-Georges. Take bus #14 from the station to "Musée des Augustins" and walk one block up rue des Arts. The hotel is to the right on rue Cantegril. Lively and central. Rooms with "artsy" posters. Run by a delightful, young English-speaking couple. Singles 80F. Doubles 90-130F, with shower 125-170F. Breakfast 22F. Showers 15F.

Hôtel de l'Université, 26, rue Emile Cartailhac (tel. 61 21 35 69), near pl. St-Sernin. Attractive rooms in a quiet neighborhood. For extra tranquility, ask for a room overlooking the little courtyard. Singles and doubles 90-100F, with shower 110-120F. Triples with shower 160F. Showers 10F.

Nouvel Hôtel, 13, rue du Taur (tel. 61 21 13 93), off pl. du Capitôle. Ideal location and decent rooms. Doubles 135F, with shower 145F. Triples with shower 210F. Breakfast 20F. Showers 8F.

Hôtel St-Antoine, 21, rue St-Antoine (tel. 61 21 40 66), one block off pl. Wilson. Pastel rooms and a bizarre mélange of furniture in the sitting area. Two rooms at 105F. Singles and doubles with shower and TV 150F, with shower, TV, and toilet 180F. One quad with shower and TV 200F, plus toilet, 220F. Breakfast 20F. No showers on the floor.

Camping: There are several excellent sites outside the city. You need a car or a lot of energy to get to the last two. **Pont de Rupé** (tel. 61 70 07 35) on av. des Etats-Unis (N20 north), at ch. du Pont de Rupé. Take bus 40 or 74 from the station (direction: "pl. Jeanne d'Arc") to pl. Jeanne d'Arc and then change to bus P (direction: "Lespinasse"). Get off at Rupé. Free swimming pool. 14F per person, 6F50 per site; 53F50 for 2 people, site, and vehicle. **La Bouriette,** 201, ch. de Tournefeuille (tel. 61 49 64 46), along N124 in St-Martin-du-Touch. Call for directions. 14F50 per person, 14F50 per site. Car included. Open all year. **Les Violettes** (tel. 61 81 72 07), on N113 after Castanet. 25F per person or site. Showers included.

Food

Inexpensive eateries scattered throughout Toulouse represent dozens of ethnic cuisines. **Markets** take place Tuesday through Sunday mornings at pl. des Carmes and on bd. Victor Hugo. In addition, a sprawling market is held daily (9am-1pm) on bd. de Strasbourg. Retreat with your purchases to the Jardin Royal or the Jardin des Plantes. On Wednesdays, the Place du Capitôle transforms into an open-air department store, and on Saturday mornings it stages a bazaar of macrobiotic products. Restaurants thrive on the tiny streets on either side of rue St-Rome, but the most economical eateries lie along the rue du Taur on the way to the university. **Les Halles,** on the ground floor of the Parking Victor Hugo, has a truly frightening number of food stands, all open daily. A **grocery store** occupies the basement of the **Nouvelles Galeries,** 6, rue Lapeyrouse. (Open Mon.-Sat. 8:30am-7pm.) **Le Moulin,** 40, rue Peyrolières, has fava bean toothpaste, goat's milk coffee creamer, and other life-prolonging products. (Open Mon. 3-7:30pm, Tues.-Fri. 9:30am-12:30pm and 3-7:30pm, Sat. 9:30am-12:30pm and 4-7:30pm.)

CROUS, 7, rue des Salenques (61 21 13 61). Provides information on the city's university cafeterias and restaurants. Meal tickets may be purchased from the *agence comtable* of CROUS (open Mon.-Fri. 2-4pm) or at the university *guichet* (11:30am-12:45pm). Tickets cost 10F50.

Les Caves de la Maréchale, 3, rue Jules-Chalande, off rue St-Rome on a narrow pedestrian street. Sophisticated restaurant in an old wine cellar. Pamper yourself with some of Toulouse's most refined food. The 65F lunch *menu,* which resembles their dinner menu at nearly half the price, includes an hors d'oeuvre buffet, *plat du jour,* dessert, wine, and coffee. Open Mon. 8-11pm, Tues.-Sat. noon-2pm and 8-11pm.

Auberge Louis XIII, 1bis, rue Tripière. Tucked away in a quiet street off rue St-Rome. An old restaurant with dark wood walls, a graceful bar, and chandeliers. Interesting student crowd. 45F and 58F *menus.* Open Sept.-July Mon.-Fri. noon-2pm and 7-9:45pm.

La Tantina de Burgos, 27, av. de la Garonette. A bit of a walk from the center, but well worth it. Hearty Spanish specialties include a burgeoning portion of *paella* (60F) and a *bar à tapas.* Relaxed and carefree atmosphere. 48F lunch *menu.* Open Tues.-Sat. noon-1:30pm and 7:30pm-midnight.

Place du May, 4, rue du May, off rue St-Rome next to the Auberge Louis XIII. Stylish terrace, soft background music, and tasteful interior. 51F lunch *menu* (without dessert 41F). 86F dinner *menu.* Open Mon.-Sat. noon-2pm and 8-11pm.

Mille et Une Pâtes, 3, place du Peyron. Two blocks from St-Sernin in a student-studded area. Creatively prepared healthy salads (30-42F). Not quite 1001 versions of pasta, but close to it (39-58F). Open Mon.-Fri. 11:30am-2pm and 7:30-10pm, Sat. 11:30am-2pm and 7pm-midnight (10pm in summer).

Salade Gasconne, 75, rue du Taur. Taste-bud-tantalizing regional specialties. Students love it, platonically, of course. Salads 29-44F. 49F *menu* includes a 1/4-carafe of wine. *Plat du jour* 49F. Open Mon.-Fri. noon-2pm and 7:30-10pm, Sat. noon-2pm and 7:30pm-midnight.

Au Coq Hardi, 6, rue Jules-Chalande, off rue St-Rome. This hardy cock crows with traditional family-style meals. Two-course, 55F lunch *menu.* 89F dinner *menu.* Otherwise, it's a little pricey. Open Mon.-Sat. noon-2pm and 7-10pm.

Au Chat Digne, 40bis, rue Peyrolières. Petit and elegant, with a sleek 60F lunch *menu.* The dinner *menu,* at 130F, might prove too expensive. Open Mon.-Sat. noon-2pm and 8-11pm.

Le Ciel de Toulouse, Nouvelles Galeries, 6, rue Lapeyrouse (tel. 61 23 11 52). Not terribly French, but fun. On the 6th floor of a department store, this place serves hundreds of people in 5 bar-like units. Pizza 18F, big *plats du jour* 24-40F. Snack food 11-18F. Open Mon.-Sat. 11am-3:30pm; only a *salon de thé* 2-6:30pm.

Cafétéria Casino, on pl. Wilson. Uh oh, Café Flunch meets its fiercest budget-generic-cheap-I-have-no-money-or-job-spare-a-dime?-food rival. Main courses 27F50-45F. Ice cream 7F90. Cheap beer and wine. It's a *salon de thé* in the afternoon. Open daily 11am-11pm.

Sights

An unwavering Catholic stronghold in a region torn by wars of religion, Toulouse shelters some of France's most architecturally distinctive and historically important religious monuments. Start your ecclesiastical tour by heading up rue du Taur from pl. du Capitôle. The magnificent **Basilique St-Sernin,** the largest Romanesque structure in the world, was built on the site of the basilica containing the tomb of St-Saturnin. The oldest part of the church, the brick west façade, is modest, even dull next to the solemn grandeur that lurks inside. St-Dominique, most vigilant of Cathar-hunters, preached his inquisition from this church. (Tours leave in summer at 2:15 and 3:30pm. 35F. Open Mon.-Sat. 8-11:45am and 2-5:45pm, Sun. 2-5:45pm. Subterranean crypt with St-Saturnin's remains open 10-11:30am and 2:30-5pm. Admission 8F.)

Down rue du Taur is **Eglise Notre-Dame-du-Taur,** originally known as St-Sernin-du-Taur after Saturninus, the first Toulousain priest, martyred in 250 AD. Legend has it that he was tied to the tail of a wild bull that dragged him to his death; the building marks the alleged spot where his corpse finally rested. His name was corrupted over the years to St-Sernin, and his remains were long ago moved to the crypt of the cathedral.

While Basilique St-Sernin is one of the finest southern Romanesque churches, **Les Jacobins,** rue Lakanal, holds the honor for southern Gothic, or *gothique du Midi.* (The name of the church derives from a monastic order founded some eight centuries earlier, whence came the designation for the radical French Revolutionaries, who first met in a Jacobin monastery.) The extraordinary stained glass and the calm cloister, site of weekly summer piano concerts, complement the elegant proportions of the church. A modest crypt inside contains the ashes of philosopher and theologian St. Thomas Aquinas. (Church open Mon.-Sat. 10am-noon and 2-6pm, Sun. 2:30-6pm. Admission to the cloister 7F. Concert tickets from 60F available at the tourist office.)

Sporadic attempts to transform 11th-century Romanesque churches into grandiose cathedrals based on northern models resulted in **Cathédrale St-Etienne.** Constructed haphazardly over five centuries, the church eventually acquired a rose window whose design is based on that of Notre-Dame in Paris, and an enormous Gothic choir. (Open 7:30am-7:30pm; Oct.-May 2-7pm.)

Although many of Toulouse's museums tend to be somewhat dull, several deserve a visit. You can buy a pass allowing you to visit any three museums for 15F, any 6 for 25F. The **Musée des Augustins,** 21, rue de Metz, (tel. 61 22 21 82), off rue Alsace-Lorraine, displays an unsurpassed assemblage of Romanesque and Gothic sculpture and a superb collection of Romanesque capitals. Especially noteworthy are the 15 sniggering gargoyles from Les Cordeliers, an abbey that was pillaged mercilessly after burning to the ground in the 19th century. (Open Thurs.-Mon. 10am-6pm, Wed. 10am-10pm; Oct.-May Thurs.-Mon. 10am-5pm, Wed. 10am-9pm. Admission 8F.) Next to St-Sernin, the **Musée St-Raymond** boasts an extraordinary array of archeological finds dating from prehistory to 1000 AD, many uncovered right in Toulouse. Its pride is the first floor sculpture gallery of Roman emperors, including the busts of Caesar, Augustus, and Tiberius. A rich collection of antique coins, dating back to Greek, Gallic, and Roman times occupies the upper level of the museum. (Open Wed.-Mon. 10am-6pm; off-season, Wed.-Mon. 10am-5pm. Admission 8F, students free.) Cozy **Musée de Vieux Toulouse,** rue de May, contains several exhibits on Toulouse's history and popular culture. (Open June-Sept. Mon.-Sat. 3-6pm; May and Oct. Thurs. 2:30-5:30pm. Admission 10F, students 5F.) The **Galerie du Château d'Eau,** pl. Laganne, just across from *centre-ville* on the Pont Neuf, is devoted exclusively to photography. Three exhibit spaces, two of which are in the old turret, display new expositions each month. (Open Wed.-Mon. 1-7pm. Admission 10F, students 5F, Sun. 5F.) Housed in an old refectory, the Réfectoire des Jacobins, the **Musée d'Art Moderne et Contemporain,** 69, rue Pargaminières, presents regular exhibitions of both well-known artists and younger talents. (Open Wed.-Mon. 10am-6pm. Admission 10F.)

Over 50 *hôtels particuliers,* built for counts, dukes, and rich merchants during Toulouse's "golden age" (1500-1700) still adorn the city's skyline. The **Hôtel D'Assezat,** pl. D'Assezat, on rue de Metz currently houses the ancient literary society, *L'Académie des Jeux Floraux;* the **Hôtel Bernuy** on rue Gambetta now serves as a high school.

The **Jardin Royal** and the less formal **Jardin des Plantes,** across the street, offer plenty of benches, a few drinking fountains, and lots of shade. For bicyclists seeking a bit of greenery, the **Grand Rond** unfurls into allées Paul Sabatier, which just keeps rolling to the Canal du Midi. On Sunday mornings, the **marché aux puces** (flea market) surrounds the Basilique St-Sernin.

Entertainment

Although Paris it ain't, Toulouse is a fine host for those looking to go foot-loose and fancy-free, as well as for the more mellow "let's see a movie and talk about it over a cappuccino" crowd. The least expensive and most eccentric places lie along **rue des Blanchers. Place St-Georges** is the heart of *toulousain* student life. Gay bars concentrate on **rue de Colombette.** The weekly journal of entertainment, *Flash,* gives complete club listings (7F at newsstands).

Le Broadway, 11, rue des Puits-Clos (tel. 61 21 10 11), tucked away on a tiny side street in the center of town. Popular with both gay and heterosexual people. Regarded as the city's leading nightclub by *les branchés* (the hip). Open Tues.-Sun. 11pm-whenever. Cover charge 40F.

L'Ubu, 16, rue St-Rome (tel. 61 23 26 75). Sit Ubu, sit. The jet-set landing pad for over 20 years. The doorman will let you in if you have *le look.* With 80-90F drinks and a certain stuffiness, it might not even be worth it. Open Tues.-Sun.

L'Artlor, rue de Colombette, just off bd. Lazare Carnot, is a good stylish bar with Keith Haring-esque painted walls. Popular with gay men. Open Tues.-Sun. from 9pm; winter from 6pm.

Le Florida, 12, pl. du Capitôle (tel. 61 21 87 59). The best-looking café on the square. Come for a drink before hitting the club scene. Open daily 7am-2am.

Le Van Gogh, 21, pl. St-Georges (tel. 61 21 03 15), on the ever-lively pl. St-Georges. A café with live piano music on weekends. Open daily 7am-2am.

Café des Allées, 64, allées Charles-de-Fitte (tel. 61 42 81 87). Though technically a restaurant, after dark this humble niche becomes a popular gathering spot for the student set. Nightly billiard tournaments attract as many spectators as competitors. (Open daily 7:30pm-roughly 3am).

The free *Regard* magazine, available in newsstands and *tabacs,* lists concerts and theater events in the area. Pick up a copy of *50 festivals de musique en Midi-Pyrénées* from the tourist office. From July to September, **Musique d'Eté** brings classical concerts, jazz, and ballet to a variety of outdoor settings, concert halls, and churches. (Tickets 50-70F sold at the tourist office and on location before the performance.) The **Fête de la Musique,** nationally celebrated on June 21, is especially riotous in Toulouse. Several movie theatres in pl. Wilson occasionally show American films in English. Look for "V.O." *(version originale).*

Near Toulouse: Pays de Foix and Ax-les-Thermes

Nestled in the eastern Pyrénées 85km south of Toulouse, the tiny town of **Foix** (pop. 10,000) was home to Gaston Phébus, the great 14th-century warrior who gave Foix its motto—*Toco y se gausos* (Don't you dare meddle). On first view of the intimidating **château** (tel. 61 65 56 05), it's not hard to reason why Simon de Montfort, the powerful count of Toulouse, never mustered the force to vanquish Foix. Inside this extraordinarily well-preserved medieval fort, the **Musée d'Ariège** displays artifacts from Roman through medieval times. (Château and museum open daily 9:45am-6:30pm; Oct.-April 10am-noon and 2:30-6:30pm. Guided tours every hr. when it is open, plus one at 5:30pm. Admission 10F, students 5F.) Don't you dare fail to appreciate the charm of the top-heavy medieval houses on place Parmentier, the fowl of a fountain on pl. de l'Oie, and the other surprises tucked away in the tiny streets.

In July and August, Foix relives its medieval glory with the **Médiévales Gaston-Phébus.** Parades, mounted jousts, medieval concerts and feasts, and a fantastic *son et lumière* (80-100F) animate the city for two weeks. The **tourist office** on av. Gabriel Fauré (tel. 61 65 12 12) has complete information on the festival and sends English-speaking guides to the château. (Office open Mon.-Sat. 9am-noon and 2:30-7pm; Sept.-June Mon.-Fri. only.) To reach the office, turn right out of the train station and then right onto the main road RN20. Follow the highway to the second bridge, cross it, and follow av. Gabriel Fauré for about three blocks to the tourist office on your right.

To appreciate the prehistoric caves and almost shameless beauty of the surrounding countryside, you'll have to stay overnight. A modern hostel, the **Foyer Leo Lagrange,** 16, rue Peyrevidal (tel. 61 65 09 04), provides clean, attractive rooms and plenty of vacation ideas and packages. To get there, follow the previous directions to av. Gabriel Fauré, and make the first right just after the steel "marketplace" structure. (Reception open 24 hrs.; Sept.-June 8am-7pm. 50F. Showers included. Breakfast 10F. Lunch 38F. Dinner 50F. Showers included. Call ahead to reserve.) The friendly **Hôtel Eychenne,** right across the street at 11, rue Peyrevidal (tel. 61 65 00 04), with its elegant wooden interior and firm beds, assures a soothing stay. (Doubles from 80F, with shower from 120F. Triples and quads 130F, with shower 200F. Showers 15F. Breakfast 22F.) The **Hôtel Echauguette,** rue Paul Laffont (tel. 61 02 88 88), just off av. Gabriel Fauré and across from the post office, lets quiet rooms. (Singles and doubles 150-160F, with shower 180F, with toilet and shower 210-280F, with toilet and bath 240-290F. Breakfast 20F.) **Camping La Barre** (tel. 61 65 11 58), 3km on foot up N20 toward Toulouse, sprawls across a large riverside site. (8F20 per person, 7F20 per tent. Car included. 5F showers. Open Dec.-Feb.)

The capital of the ancient duchy and the modern *département* of Ariège, Foix is an excellent place to sample some *ariégeois* specialties. *Truite à l'ariégeoise* (trout) and *écrevisses* (crayfish), the highlights of the hearty local cuisine, make fantastic (if messy) finger food. Try Gaston Phébus's drink, the stiff, herbal *hypocras*—make sure it's served cold. A jolly prize-winning pastry chef runs the attractive **Le Médiéval,** 42, rue des Chapeliers (tel. 61 02 81 50). Despite his affection for *chantilly,* (whipped cream), the 65F *menu* includes a few low-calorie options; the 90F *menu* includes rich *ariégeois* specialties. (Open Mon.-Tues. and Thurs.-Fri. noon-2pm and 7:30-10pm, Sat. 7:30-10pm, Sun. noon-2pm.) The **Auberge Miranda,** 36, rue Labistour fixes a copious 45F *menu* (55F on Sundays) of Spanish specialties, with wine included. (Open Mon.-Sat. for lunch only, Sept. 16-Oct. 15 daily for lunch and dinner, Oct. 16-July 10 Mon.-Sat. for lunch and dinner.) An **open-air market** fills pl. St-Volusien on Friday mornings.

The Ariège boasts some of the most spectacular caves in France. To explore them, rent a mountain bike from **Itineraire VTT,** 8, allées de Villote (tel. 64 02 66 44). The rental fee includes accessories. (55F for 1/2-day, 80F per day, 100F per person with transport into the mountains included. Guided tours 130F. Open daily 8:30-9:30am and 6-7pm.) An hour-long boat ride takes visitors through the caves at **Labouiche** (tel. 61 65 04 11), 6km from Foix. (Open July-Aug. 9:30am-5pm; April-June and Sept. to mid-Nov. 10-11:15am and 2-5pm. 35F, students in the morning 28F.) The **Grotte de Niaux,** 16km south of Foix, contains 20,000-year-old paintings of leaping herds of bison, deer, and horses. Ask the Foix tourist office about visiting this and other prehistoric caves.

Rising high above the plain 35km southeast of Foix along the D9, the **Château de Montségur** served as the funeral pyre for Cathar *parfaits* ("perfect ones") who chose death by fire over allegiance to the Pope in 1244. A ticket to the château entrance to the museum in the village below, which displays artifacts found in the castle. (Open daily 10am-7pm; Oct.-Feb. Sat.-Sun. 10am-1pm and 2-7pm.)

Trains connect Foix with Toulouse (6 per day, 1hr., 71F); La Tour de Carol (5 per day, 1 1/2hr., 58F); and Ax-les-Thermes (45min., 35F). The **train station** (tel. 61 65 27 00) is north of town off N20. The **post office** and the **hospital** (tel. 61 05 40 40) are both on av. Gabriel Fauré; Foix's **postal code** is 09000. Contact the **police** at 61 65 52 55. In an emergency, call 61 65 00 17.

Formerly referred to as the *Pays des Eaux,* **Ax-Les Thermes,** a small resort town 50km southeast of Foix and 130km south of Toulouse, owes its appeal partly to the remedial powers of its bubbly sulfuric waters. Under the reign of St-Louis in the mid-13th century, the count of Foix dispatched his leprosy-stricken soldiers to cleanse their feet in the town's **Bassin des Ledres.** Several centuries would pass before the "cures" of Ax gained the sanction of the medical community, as a result of Abraham Sicre's 1758 study on the salubrious properties of Ax's thermal waters. Since then, a steady flow of mostly sedentary visitors have partaken of the water's beneficent effects. Many others have based themselves in the town while exploring the hilly hinterland of the *Pyrénées Ariégois.* The **tourist office** (tel. 61 64 20 64) on pl. du Breilh has information on local spas and nearby ski areas. (Open Mon.-Sat. 10am-noon and 2-7pm, Sun. 9am-noon and 2-6pm.) To reach the office, turn left out of the train station and follow the street to the pl. du Breilh. The **Office du Tourisme de la Vallée d'Ax** (tel. 61 64 60 60) in **Luzenac,** 3km from Ax on the road to Toulouse, has information on hiking trips and cave visits. In Ax, **Oxygène,** av. du Docteur Gomma (tel. 61 64 35 72), **rents mountain bikes** for 60F per half-day, 90F per day, 160F per weekend, and 550F per week.

Several paths passing near Ax offer easy, year-round rambles and hikes which might pass through snow even in July. The **Grandes Randonnées** 10 and 7 are rather difficult. The easier *sentier Cathar* and the *Tour des Vallées d'Ax* accommodate year-round hikers of all levels. A guide based out of the tourist office (tel. 61 64 20 64) offers a range of half-day or full-day tours. (ranging from 30-50F.) Otherwise, the *Topoguide d'un Village à l'Autre* (55F) or *100 Randonnées en Ariège* (89F) published by Editions Randonnées Pyrénéennes will help you go it alone. Call 61 66 40 10 or write to **CI-MES Pyrénées,** BP 88, 09200 St-Girons; ask for information on the Ariège.

Eight km above Ax, **Bonascre** (tel. 61 64 21 81) offers excellent, challenging, and relatively warm skiing with excellent moguls. (Lift pass 70F per 1/2-day, 100F per day.) Rent skis and boots in front of the lifts for 58F per day. Agence Ferrer (tel. 61 64

20 53) runs four shuttles per day between Ax and Bonascre from December through April when there is snow. (July-Aug. 3 per day, 27F round-trip.)

Ax has a number of comfortable places to rest after a day of soaking, skiing, or bush-whacking. Kind Spanish owners keep the **Hôtel la Terrasse,** 7, rue Marcaillou (tel. 61 64 20 33), a clean place with a river view. Large rooms make up for a somber entrance filled with scary hunting trophies. (Singles 110F, with shower 160F. Doubles 140F, with shower 190F. Triples with shower 247F. Quads with bunks and showers 304F. Showers 10F. Breakfast 20F.) The **Hôtel le Breilh,** pl. du Breilh (tel. 61 64 24 29) of-fers simple, pretty rooms with balconies (doubles 200F, with shower and toilet 230F; triples with shower 335F; breakfast 29F). The snack bar on the ground floor serves cheap pizzas (24-35F) from 8am to 10pm. (Hotel and bar open Dec.-Oct.) The **Hôtel de la Paix,** pl. Breilh (tel. 61 64 22 61), has two singles/doubles at 90F and two at 105F. Other singles and doubles start from 198F with shower, 215F with shower and toilet. Breakfast costs 30F, and the restaurant downstairs posts filling 62F and 79F *menus.* (Open Thurs.-Tues. noon-2pm and 7-10pm.) Great home-style cooking awaits at the semi-tropical **Martudo,** 6, rue Rigal, one block off pl. Breich. 59F *menu* includes a creative salad and roast lamb. 79F *menu* offers *tarte à l'oignon* and steak with rum. Also offers a 100F *fondue* for two. (Open daily noon-3pm and 6-11pm.)

The local rendition of nightlife centers around the **Casino,** on allée de Couloubret, which doubles as a cinema (tickets 35F) and concert hall on some weekend evenings. Check the bulletin board at the tourist office for upcoming events.

Trains connect Ax with Toulouse (83F), Pamiers (41F), La Tour de Carol (37F), and Foix. Train service also connects Ax to **Hospitalet** (17F), a small town near the Andor-ran border. Buses await the train's arrival for a final leg to the tiny principality. You can check your packs and skis at the station between 5am and 8:30pm for 5F. **Agence Fer-rer,** pl. du Breilh (tel. 61 64 20 53), runs daily afternoon **buses** to Pas de la Case in An-dorra (30F). **Exchange currency** is at the **post office** on pl. Roussel (tel. 61 69 22 71); Ax's **postal code** is 09110.

Albi

Albi's claim to fame—and the source of its name—derives from a fleeting brush with destiny during the ill-fated 13th-century Albigensian Crusade. Orchestrated by Pope Innocent III, the Crusade's bloody campaigns were intended to purge Languedoc-Roussillon of the heretical Cathars (or *albigeois)* who had gathered in Albi. As viewed by the ecclesiastical elite, Catharistic asceticism, with its complete rejection of material pleasure in favor of the spiritual, posed a threat to mainstream religious practice. This unorthodox doctrine enraged the church by the thought of lost souls and lost mass at-tendees. Though the Treaty of Meaux in 1229 apparently marked the crusade's conclu-sion, it wasn't until after the restoration of the inquisition in 1294 that the heresy was decisively squelched. Its aura of belligerency having long since dissipated, today's Albi is an energetic city of 48,500 that attracts admirers of the work of native son Henri de Toulouse-Lautrec. An extraordinary assemblage of his art fills the local museum, and the magnificent cathedral stands right next door. The cultural floodgates open wide during the summer months, when exuberant music and theater festivals descend on the *vieille ville.*

Orientation and Practical Information

The capital of the *département du Tarn,* Albi makes an easy daytrip from Toulouse, which lies 76km southwest. To make the 10-minute walk to the tourist office and the center of town, turn left in front of the station onto av. Maréchal Joffre. Make another left onto av. Général de Gaulle, and then bear left over pl. Laperouse to the cobblestone pedestrian streets of the *vieille ville.* Rue Ste-Cécile will lead you to pl. Ste-Cécile, where signs point to the tourist office. The hostel is a 10-minute walk from the center, in a more residential part of town.

Tourist Office: pl. Ste-Cécile (tel. 63 54 22 30). Accommodations service 10F. Detailed map of the city 15F. **Currency exchange** (commission 25F, 1200F max.) Sun. and Mon., when banks are closed. Open Mon.-Sat. 9am-7pm, Sun. 10:30am-12:30pm and 4:30-6:30pm; Sept.-June Mon.-Sat. 9am-noon and 2-6pm.

Post Office: pl. du Vigan (tel. 63 45 76 02). **Telephones** and **currency exchange.** Open Mon.-Fri. 8am-7pm, Sat. 8am-noon. **Postal Code:** 81000.

Trains: (tel. 63 53 31 64), at the end of av. Maréchal Joffre. To Toulouse (14 per day, 1hr., 55F). Open daily 5:30am-9:30pm. To Castres, via St-Sulpice (5 per day, 1 1/2hr., 66F). **Automatic lock- ers** 5F.

Buses: Gare Routière Halte des Autobus (tel. 63 54 58 61), on pl. Jean Jaurès, inside a bar/ newsstand. To Toulouse (7 per day, 44F), and Castres (5 per day, 28F). Open Mon.-Sat. 6am-7pm. **Cars Bécardit** (tel. 63 45 03 03). Excursion to Castres and Cordes once per day in July and Aug.

Taxis: Albi Taxi Radio, tel. 63 54 85 03. 24hrs.

Youth Center: Le Bureau de Jeunesse de l'Albigeois, 19, pl. Ste-Cécile, opposite the tourist of- fice. Information on employment opportunities, lodgings, and special events. Helpful staff wel- comes foreigners. Open Mon.-Fri. 9am-noon and 2-6pm, Sat. 2-5pm.

Bike Rental: Cycles Andouard, 7, rue Séré-de-Rivières (tel. 63 38 44 77). Rents mountain bikes at 90F per day; 1000F or passport deposit. Open Mon.-Sat. 9am-noon and 2-6pm.

Laundromat: 8, rue Emile Grand. A few blocks from the *auberge,* off rue Lices Georges Pompi- dou. Wash 16F, 20F for large load, dry 2F per 7 1/2min. Bring 10F and 2F coins. Open daily 7am- 9pm.

Medical Assistance: Centre Hospitalier, rue de la Berchere (tel. 63 47 47 47).

Police: 23, rue Pompidou (tel. 63 54 12 95). **Emergency:** tel. 17.

Accommodations and Camping

Tourists pour into Albi in the summer on their pilgrimage to the Toulouse-Lautrec museum. Arrive early or call ahead for best results.

Maison des Jeunes et de la Culture, 13, rue de la République (tel. 63 54 53 65), off Lices Georg- es Pompidou. Clean, mostly 16-bed rooms. Information on events and activities prominently dis- played on bulletin boards. Coed bathrooms (but usually single-sex dorm rooms). No kitchen. Reception open 6-7pm; answering machine at other times. No lockout or curfew. Dorm bunks 24F. Breakfast 12F. Filling home-cooked meals 38F. Sheets 15F.

Hôtel Le Vieil Alby, 25, rue de Toulouse-Lautrec (tel. 63 54 14 69), in the *vieille ville.* Very proper rooms. Friendly owner requires that you eat in his excellent restaurant in summer (70F *menu).* Singles and doubles 130F, with shower 150F. Quads with shower 270F. Showers 15F. Breakfast 25F. Hotel and restaurant open Tues.-Sun. afternoon.

Hôtel Régence, 27, av. Maréchal Joffre (tel. 63 54 01 42). From the train station, turn left and walk 1 block. Owner collects antique furniture, and the tastefully decorated rooms profit from his ef- forts. Wind down your evenings with *Canal +* (France's premier movie channel), free in every room. Singles and doubles 100-110F, with shower 150F. Triples with shower 210F. Hall showers 15F, but often in disrepair. Breakfast 24F.

Hôtel du Parc, 3, av. du Parc (tel. 63 54 12 80). From the train station follow av. Maréchal Joffre as it becomes bd. Carnot. On the left across from a park. Exceptionally clean, quiet rooms, all with TV. Singles and doubles 140F, with shower and toilet 170F. Triples with shower 230F. Quads with shower/bath 270F. Breakfast 25F.

Camping: Parc de Caussels (tel. 63 60 37 06), 2km east of Albi on D99 (rte. de Millau). Take bus #5 from pl. Jean Jaurès (every 1/2hr. until 7pm). Ask the driver for the stop near the camp- ground, next to the **L'Univers** store. If walking, go out on rue de la République and follow the signs (30min.). Swimming pool nearby. 40F per 2 people. Hot showers included.

Food

Treat yourself to *cassoulet* and *tripes,* two of the region's typically hearty dishes. The latter specialty consists entirely of sheep intestines—unappetizing, some would say— but you should wolf some down at least once. Just to say you have. Albigensian stew should be washed down with a local red, *Gaillac* or *Cunac.* You'll find good deals at the large indoor **market** on pl. du Marché (open Tues.-Sun. 8am-12:30pm) or at the supermarket/cafeteria **Casino,** 39, rue Lices Georges Pompidou. (Store open Mon.-Thurs. 8:30am-12:30pm and 2:30-7:30pm Fri.-Sat. 8:30am-7:30pm. Cafeteria open daily 11am-10pm.) A large, open-air market fills pl. Ste-Cécile on Saturday morning. A *marché organique* sells organically grown products every Tuesday from 5 to 7pm at pl. du Jardin National. **La Vie Claire,** 23, rue Séré-de-Rivières, serves fairly expensive health food (open Tues.-Sun. 9am-12:30pm and 2:30-7pm).

Auberge St-Loup, 26, rue de Castelviel, behind the cathedral. Local specialties served in an intimate medieval tavern. Real men and women eat the *gras double* (a dish featuring sheep tripe). 70F and 80F *menus*. Open Tues.-Sun. noon-2pm and 7:30-10pm.

Le Petit Bouchon, 77, rue Croix Verte, just off rue Lice Georges Pompidou. 55F *menu* features a choice of several *plats du jour,* including a juicy roast beef or rabbit, and vegetables *au choix*. Includes wine. Ask the champion bartender/owner to show you his awards. Don't mind the French poodle lounging on the bar. Open Mon.-Fri. 8am-10pm, Sat. 8am-4pm.

Le Jardin Secret, 1, rue Timbal. Elegant outdoor dining in a secluded courtyard surrounded by ivy-covered brick walls. Filling 65F three-course *menu* includes a sumptuous *crépinotte de volaille* (thinly sliced stuffed chicken). Open Tues.-Sat. noon-2pm and 6-11pm.

La Kahïna, 3, rue Caminade. Immerse yourself in Algerian ambience in a small, brick interior. Walls bedecked with black and white photos of Algerian village scenes. Feast on *couscous* (45-70F) or the more traditional 51F *menu* of *spaghetti bolognaise* or chicken (salad, dessert and 1/4-carafe of wine included). A four-course 68F *menu* will also please. Heavenly pastry selection. Open daily 10am-3pm and 7pm-2am.

Sights and Entertainment

Born in 1864 to an aristocratic family, Henri de Toulouse-Lautrec led a brash life that some would call extravagant and debaucherous. To characterize it thus, however, belies a legacy in innovative artistic production. Toulouse-Lautrec single-handedly bred and nurtured the art of lithography (poster printing) and raised controversy with his bold interpretations of French society. His portraiture captured people and objects off-guard, engaged in their natural occupations. Until his death in 1901 at the age of 37, he stayed clear from both the impressionist circle and academic taste. The collection of works assembled by the artist's mother and ferreted away in the **Musée Toulouse-Lautrec** in the Palais de la Berbie is the best anywhere. The museum contains not only all 31 of the famous posters of Montmartre nightclubs, but also dozens of oils and pastels and rooms full of sketches and drawings. Upstairs is a fine collection of contemporary art, including sculpture and painting by Degas, Dufy, Matisse, and Rodin. (Open daily 9am-noon and 2-6pm; Oct.-Easter Wed.-Mon. 10am-noon and 2-5pm. Admission 18F, students 9F. Guided tours in 4 languages upon sufficient interest 10F.)

Still owned by the original family, the artist's birthplace, the **Maison Natale de Toulouse-Lautrec,** otherwise known as the *Hôtel du Bosq,* at 14, rue Toulouse-Lautrec in Vieil Albi, normally opens its doors in July and August. A childhood accident, which left his legs in an atrophied state and drew him to painting, occurred in the inner salon. (Open daily 9am-noon and 3-7pm.)

The **Basilique Ste-Cécile,** built in 1282 after papal crusaders vanquished Albi's heretics, was designed to serve as a fortress as well as a church. Carved entirely out of soft stone, the choir depicts thirty Old Testament figures in astounding detail. Bright 16th-century frescoes cover the interior. Just below the organ, an immense mural depicts *Le Jugement Dernier* (The Last Judgment), in which Jesus presides over the condemnation of seven sinners, dispatched to the fiery depths of hell for their vices. Only one element of the fresco is missing: the central segment of Jesus himself, which vanished in 1693 following the piercing of the fresco wall to provide an opening into Chapelle St-Clair. (Open daily 8:30am-7pm; Sept.-May 9-11:30am and 2-5:30pm. Admission 2F.) Guided tours leave between 8:45am and 10:30pm (17F, students 12F). The largest in France, the church's 18th-century organ bursts into song on Wednesday afternoons in July and August (concerts free).

In intimate **Eglise St-Salvy,** the radiant violet light of the stained-glass windows pervades the humble pews. While the fragrant garden of the cloister is usually accessible, the church is only open from 8:30am to 12:15pm and from 2:30 to 6pm. A pathway next to the entrance to the church leads to the narrow pedestrian streets of **Vieil Albi,** where artisans make and sell wares in a somewhat artificial atmosphere.

Albi entertains visitors with an abundance of summertime festivals and celebrations. The **Feu de la St-Jean,** celebrated throughout Languedoc-Rousillon, flickers on a Saturday night around June 24, kicking off the season with nimble Jacques jumping over a giant log fire. The **Festival Théâtral** takes place during the last week of June and the first week of July (tickets 88F). The six-day **Festival International du Film 9.5mm** features a full agenda of screenings and banquets during the last few days of July and the first few of August (tickets free at the tourist office). The **Festival de Musique,** a series of concerts, opera, ballet, and flamenco guitar recitals, resounds from July 25 through the first week in August featuring heavy doses of Mozart and a sprinkling of Glenn Miller. The **Bureau de Festival** (tel. 63 54 26 64), opposite the tourist office, sells tickets (80-140F); buy them in advance. The **Centre Culturel de l'Albigeois** (tel. 63 54 27 17), on the felicitously named pl. de l'Amitié Entre les Peuples, off bd. Carnot and opposite **Parc Rochegude,** shows foreign films in their original languages throughout the year. Pick up a schedule at the center (center open Tues.-Fri. 2-7pm, Sat. 10am-noon and 2-7pm; 35F, students and seniors 22F).

Near Albi

Set on a hillside 24km north of Albi, **Cordes-sur-Ciel** beckons to approaching visitors much as it has since serving as a sentinel on the Cathar frontier during the 13th-century Albigensian crusades. Jutting high above the fertile valley of the Cerou River, the walled city has been extensively renovated in recent years, thanks largely to artist Yves Brayer, who arrived in 1940. To his credit, the double-walled, seemingly impregnable *vieille ville,* distinguished by its steeply inclined cobblestone streets, has entirely retained its medieval character.

The world's only museum devoted wholly to the delicious art of sucrology, Cordes's **Musée de l'Art du Sucre,** to the left of the tourist office, will leave you drooling over the potential applications of granulated sugar. Three rooms present a medley of sculptures confected entirely from sugar, and in a few anomalous cases, chocolate. The museum is the single-handed effort of Yves Thuriès, a two-time French champion *patissier* who has at long last realized his sweet-toothed ambitions. (Open Feb.-Dec. daily 10am-noon and 2:30-6:30pm. Admission 5F.)

Eglise St-Michel, with a 19th-century organ from Notre Dame in Paris, rests at Cordes's summit. The **Musée Yves Brayer** is worth visiting for its colorful and fanciful renditions of the town. (Open Mon.-Sat. 10am-noon and 2-6pm, Sun. 2-6pm; Sept.-June Mon.-Fri. 8:30am-noon and 1:30-6pm. Off-season, call ahead to the tourist office. Admission 5F). The **Musée Charles Portal** has interesting exhibits on local traditions and archeology and a reconstructed farmhouse interior. The first-floor photo exhibit describes the town's architectural and historical evolution. (Open July-Aug. Mon.-Sat. 2-6pm; April-June and Sept.-Oct. Sun. and holidays 2-5pm. Admission 10F.) The **tourist office** (tel. 63 56 00 52) is on pl. de Halle. (Open daily 10am-12:30pm and 2:30-6:30pm; Nov.-Easter Sat.-Sun. 2:30-6pm.) While everyone else in France is celebrating the liberation of the Bastille on July 14, Cordes's **Fête du Grand Fauconnier** (July 12-14) sends the town back 300 years further. Denizens wrap their homes in garlands and medieval bunting and cavort as queens, princes, knights, and fair damsels, celebrating with a banquet and a torchlit procession in a festival unrelated to the French national holiday. (Entrance 45F; free if you're in costume.)

Hotels in Cordes tend toward the prohibitively expensive. For information on *chambres d'hôte* ask at the tourist office or write to ATTER, Maison des Agriculteurs, B.P. 89, 81003 Albi Cedex (tel. 63 54 39 81). With doubles from 105-165F, these B&B farmhouses make seeing the countryside a breeze. Avoid the overpriced **restaurants** near the Halle and in the old city. An affordable compromise with a light musical ambience is **La Canaille,** a *saladerie/crêperie* on place de la Bride. To the left is a magnificent panorama of the patchwork fields of the sprawling Crédo Valley. (Salads 30-42F. Open mid-June to mid-Sept. 9am-11pm.)

Getting to Cordes can be a logistical nightmare. **SNCF mini-vans** (35F) leave pl. Jean Jaurès in Albi. (Mon. and Wed.-Fri. at 7:40am, Tues. and Sat. at 11:45am; 35F; normally, a bus returns each day at 4:50pm.) An easier route involves two **trains** and a bike or a hike. Take the train from Albi to Gaillac and change there for Vindrac-Cordes (33F). Once at the station rent a bike (35F per 1/2-day, 50F per day) and ascend 5km to Cordes. If you prefer, **Minicar** (tel. 63 56 14 80) can pick you up at the station for 18F, 26F at night. The station (open 5:30am-10:30pm) also sends six trains per day to Toulouse (52F).

Albi cradles in the western tip of the Tarn Valley, an expansive stretch of cliffs, forests, and bucolic villages. The 12th-century **Château du Bosc** (tel. 65 69 20 83), where Toulouse-Lautrec spent a happy childhood, hides in a forest 45km northeast from Albi. (Open Easter-Dec. 9am-noon and 2-7pm. Off-season, call for reservations.) The **Gorges du Tarn**, with high limestone cliffs, grottoes, and caves, snake eastward from Albi. The **tourist office**, av. Alfred Merle (tel. 65 60 02 42), in **Milau**, has extensive information on the region and will direct you to **Le Rozier**, the best place to begin your descent. Pick up *Le Guide Millau-Grands Causses Rocquefore-Gorges du Tarn-Lézevou* (25F).

Castres

Situated on both sides of the diminutive Agoût River, Castres (pop. 46,300) has managed to keep itself in the historical spotlight. The town's prosaic development around the St-Benoît abbey in the 11th century took on new importance with the acquisition of the remains of the revered St-Vincent. Subsequently, Castres became an intriguing stopover on the acclaimed pilgrimage route towards Santiago de Compostela. As the town's reputation swelled, a burgeoning textile industry took root along the banks of the Agoût.

More recently, Castres caught attention as the hometown of celebrated French socialist and journalist, Jean Jaurès. Jaurès leapt into prominence as leader of the striking glass-workers of Carmaux in 1896 and later joined other socialists, notably Emile Zola, in vehement defense of Captain Richard Dreyfus, the Jewish officer framed as a traitor by French generals. As an ardent defender of a nascent political ideology, Jaurès had to wage a continuous battle with adversity. In 1914, his fate as a martyr was sealed when he was assassinated in a Paris café. Perhaps more out of lack of imagination than true respect, his name is given to a prominent street in every city in France; in Castres, he is also the central theme of one of the city's main museums. Despite a propensity for the politically volatile, Castres boasts an artistic side as well. The Musée Goya maintains the largest collection of Spanish art in France, including several canvases by the Aragonese master himself. Magnificently pruned gardens add a touch of grandeur to the *centre ville* of this relaxed and slower-paced city.

Orientation and Practical Information

Castres lies 72km due east of Toulouse and 65km north of Carcassonne on the direct Toulouse-Mazamet rail line. To reach the center of the town from the train station, turn left onto av. Albert 1er and then bear right onto bd. Henri Sizaire. At pl. Alsace-Lorraine, turn left onto the rue de l'Evêché. The tourist office is on the left in the Théâtre Municipal, a 10-minute walk. Along with the tourist office and the Hôtel de Ville, museums, shops, and banks cluster on the west side of the river (especially around pl. Jean Jaurès), connected by the pedestrian streets of the *vieille ville*. Rue Alquier Bouffard and its continuation, rue Villegoudou, cross the pont Neuf and lead to the central **place Soult.**

Tourist Office: (tel. 63 71 56 58), on pl. de la République in the Théâtre Municipal. Information on the national park nearby. Staff suggests walks and car excursions in the Tarn region. Open Mon.-Sat. 9:15am-12:30pm and 2-7pm, Sun. 10:30am-12:30pm; Sept.-June Mon.-Sat. 9:15am-12:30pm and 2-6:30pm.

Post Office: (tel. 63 59 28 54), on allée Alphonse Juin near the tourist office. **Telephones** and **currency exchange.** Open Mon.-Fri. 8am-7pm, Sat. 8am-noon. **Postal Code:** 81100.

Trains: av. Albert 1er (tel. 63 59 22 00). To: Toulouse (8 per day, 1hr., 64F); Carcassonne via Toulouse (8 per day, 2 1/2 hr., 116F); Albi via St-Sulpice (7 per day, 2hr., 66F). Information office open daily 5:20am-12:45pm, 1-7:30pm, and 8:30-9pm. **Automatic lockers** 5F.

Buses: pl. Soult (tel. 63 35 37 31). To: Carcassonne (Mon.-Tues. and Thurs.-Sat. 1 per day at 3:50pm, 2hr., 68F); Toulouse (Mon.-Sat. 4 per day, 2 Sun.; 46F); Albi (Mon.-Sat. 4 per day, 50min., 28F).

Taxis: tel. 63 59 99 25. 24 hrs.

Bike Rental: Tabarly, 38, pl. Soult (tel. 63 35 38 09). Rents mountain bikes for 80F per day; 500F or credit card deposit. Open Tues.-Sat. 8:30am-noon and 2-7pm.

Laundromat: Lavomatic, 13, rue Consulat (tel. 63 72 03 97). Wash 18F per 5.5kg, dry 2F per 6min. Open daily 8am-9pm.

Women's Information: Centre d'Information sur les droits des femmes et de la familles (C.I.-D.F.F.) 9, rue Henri IV (tel. 63 72 15 00). Advises and counsels women on their legal and professional rights. Open Mon. and Tues. 9am-noon and 2-6pm, Fri. 9am-noon. Other services, including those for the young, the old, and people with disabilities, are listed in **Social Castres,** a booklet distributed by the tourist office.

Crisis Hotline: S.O.S. Amitié (tel. 63 54 20 20).

Hospital: 20, bd. Maréchal Foch (tel. 63 71 63 71).

Police: tel. 63 35 40 10. **Emergency:** tel. 17.

Accommodations and Camping

The lonely neighborhood near the train station offers nothing of interest. Try to make the 15-minute hike to the center of town. The tourist office can direct you to a number of *chambres d'hôtes* (B&Bs) in the surrounding area.

Hôtel du Périgord, 22, rue Emile Zola (tel. 63 59 04 74), in the *centre ville.* Large rooms with high ceilings and attractive furniture. Singles and doubles 85F, with shower 110F. Breakfast 22F. Restaurant downstairs posts a 60F *menu,* wine included. Open Sept.-July Sun.-Fri.

Hôtel de France, 8, rue des Trois Rois (tel. 63 59 04 89), off quai Tourcadière. Clean rooms, all with shower (no curtain), toilet, and telephone. Rooms with a TV cost 30F more. Singles and doubles 120-130F. Triples and quads 170F. Breakfast 18F.

Hôtel Carcassés, 3, rue d'Augue (tel. 63 35 37 72), off pl. Soult. Family establishment has gigantic rooms with sloping floorboards. Double beds 80F each. Showers 10F. Breakfast 20F.

Camping: Camping Municipal (tel. 63 59 56 49), on av. de Roquecourbe in the "domaine de Gourjade," 20min. from the *centre ville.* Cross the canal and turn left onto av. Luicien-Coudert. On the riverbank. 22F per 2 people. Showers included. Electricity 10F.

Food

A large **market** convenes on pl. Jean Jaurès (Tues. and Thurs.-Sat. 7am-1pm). Bring a *baguette* and the local *roquefort* and *bleu* cheeses to the shady Jardin de l'Evêché, beside the Hôtel de Ville. Restaurants cluster off pl. Jean Jaurès and near rue Villegoudou. For a quick and filling meal on the run, **Cafétéria du Mail,** on pl. Soult, offers a wide selection of self-service pickings. (Open Mon.-Thurs. 11:30am-2pm and 6:30-9:30pm, Fri.-Sun. 11:30am-2:30pm and 6:30-10pm.)

Les Sarrasines, 34, rue Villegoudou. Lavender and lace decor, and art exhibitions on the wall. *Crêpes* 14-38F, salads 13-35F. 40F lunch *menu.* Open Tues.-Sat. noon-5pm and 7pm-midnight.

La Piazzetta, 23, rue M. Ducommun, across the river from pl. Jean Jaurès. Italian specialities in a quiet place with polished wood. Pizzas baked before your eyes in a wood-fired oven, 45-55F. Gargantuan *salade tomate* (28F). Filling, rich *spaghetti carbonara* (42F). Open Fri.-Wed. noon-2pm and 7-11pm.

Restaurant Carcassés, 3, rue d'Auque, same place as the hotel. Workers' restaurant with filling, no-frills 60F *menu,* wine included. Lively back-street ambience. Open daily noon-3pm and 7-10pm.

L'Eau à la Bouche, 6, rue Malpas. Turn left at pl. Jean Jaurès before the Banque Nationale Populaire. White wicker furniture and lots of baby blue. Refined 68F *menu* with lamb kebabs, wine included. Open Tues.-Sat. noon-2pm and 7-10pm, Sun. noon-2pm.

Sights and Entertainment

Situated in front of the impeccably sculpted arabesques and shrubs of the **Jardin de L'Evêché,** the **Musée Goya** houses a terrific sampling of Spanish painting dating back to the 14th century. The museum's treasured Goya collection (spanning 50 years) reigns supreme among the sprinkling of Catalanese and Aragonese masters. The three-work Goya assemblage includes a self-portrait, a portrait of Francisco del Mayo, and the celebrated *Assemblée de la Compagnie des Philippines.* (Open daily 9am-noon and 2-6pm; Sept.-June Tues.-Sat. 9am-noon and 2-6pm, Sun. 10am-noon and 2-6pm. Admission 10F, students 5F, under 14 free, Nov.-March Wed. and Sun. free.)

Castres's other bauble, the **Musée Jaurès,** pl. Pélisson (tel. 63 72 01 01), is packed with pamphlets, trenchant political cartoons, photographs, and faded newspaper articles that recount Jean Jaurès's spirited, often bitter rhetoric. Organized chronologically, the displays detail Jaurès's diverse accomplishments while placing them in clear historical contexts. A slide show, narrated in French, traces the activist's life. The upper floors of the museum contain projection rooms which screen films on Jaurès's activities, and a small library. (Museum open same hours as the Musée Goya.)

The **Centre d'Art Contemporain,** marooned in a lovely 18th-century *hôtel particulier,* features exhibits often assembled by the artists themselves. Recent exhibitions have featured household chairs jutting out from a wall and indecipherable canvases of geometric shapes resembling oversized capital letters. (Open Mon.-Sat. 9am-noon and 2-6pm; Sun. 10am-noon and 2-6pm. Admission 5F, students free.) Sick of merely gazing at canvases? Then become one yourself at the **tattoo shop,** 8, pl. Jean Bouffard. The shop proudly displays newspaper articles that attest to the safety record and talent of the artists within. (Open Fri.-Sat. 2-8pm; Sept.-June Mon.-Tues. and Thurs.-Sat. 2-8pm.) The **quai des Jacobines** presents a fine view of the medieval textile merchants' houses flanking the Agoût River. The wooden galleries were used for drying, while the arched entryways opening onto the river facilitated shipment. Today little of the industry remains; the dilapidated houses have been renovated by the government to provide rent-controlled housing.

During the final two weeks of July, the **Festival Goya** celebrates Spanish music, dance, art, and theater; tickets (30-150F) are available at the tourist office (tel. 63 71 56 58). On the first weekend in July, the **Festival Occitan** reenacts "The tragedy of Occitanie," from Simon de Montfort to the 19th century. Fireworks provide comic relief. The tourist office has tickets (80F).

Near Castres

Accessible by train from Castres (10 per day, 18F), **Mazamet** makes an excellent base for the **Montagnes Noires** in the Parc Natural Régional du Haut Languedoc. For information on hiking routes and *gîtes,* write to the Parc Naturel Régional du Haut Languedoc, 13, rue du Cloître, 34220 Saint-Pons (tel. 67 97 02 10), or buy the brochure *Sidobre, Monts de Lacaune, Montagne Noire* at the Mazamet tourist office (tel. 63 61 27 07). The area of the **Sidobre,** 28km from Castres in the northwest corner of the park (tourist office tel. 63 50 64 25), has supplied southern France with granite since the 11th century. Explore the area on bike or with the Castres-based **Tourisme Vert** (tel. 63 35 54 67). Call three days ahead to book tours.

Carcassonne

*Even by day it has the air of a vignette of Gustave
Doré, a couplet of Victor Hugo. It is almost too perfect...as if it were an enormous model, placed on a
big green table at a museum.*

—Henry James

The *Cité de Carcassonne* is a life-sized toy castle, a 13th-century Disneyland: a double-walled, fortified city with towers and turrets rising from a precipitous plateau in the
Garonne Valley. Beginning with the first-century arrival of Roman invaders, subsequently supplanted by Visigoths, Invisigoths, and Arabs, Europe's largest fortress came
to exemplify stalwart opposition in the face of attack. When Charlemagne's troops besieged the Cité over a five-year period in the 8th century, the wife of the murdered
Moorish king rushed to its defense. Dame Carcas moved mannequin soldiers around
the ramparts to fool the enemy into overestimating the size of her defensive corps. To
complete the illusion of continuing prosperity, she forced the last pig to eat the last bag
of wheat and then tossed the star-crossed porker over the outer wall. When Charlemagne saw the exploded pig, he called off the attack. If, after five years, the besieged
population still had enough food to feed their pigs, thought he, his army had clearly
failed. But in medieval folklore, Charlemagne can't lose. As his troops retreated, the
Grande Dame rang the bell to signal her acquiescence to drawing up a treaty. The tin-
tinnabulation drew the attention of the king's men, who called to their lord: "Carcas
sonne!" (Carcas summons). To rectify the egregious state of disrepair into which the
city had fallen following the 13th-century Wars of Religion, the revered architect Viollet-le-Duc was commissioned in 1844 to restore the ancient fortress.

The allure of the Cité however, is no secret. Even before providing the backdrop for
the 1991 movie *Robin Hood: Prince of Theives,* the Cité had attracted droves of tourists and the inevitable, overpriced gift shops. At night, however, the crowds disperse
and the fortress, bathed with floodlights and filled with music from frequent concerts,
regains its elusive charm.

Orientation and Practical Information

The Cité nicknamed *La Pucelle du Languedoc* (The Maiden of Languedoc), perches
imperiously above its ugly stepsister, the modern *basse ville* (pop. 45,000). Most shops,
offices, and hotels—as well as the train station—are down below. To reach the Cité,
catch the #4 bus, the black line, from the train station (every 1/2hr. until 6:53pm, 4F80)
or from pl. Gambetta (every 1/2hr. until 7:02pm, 5min.). Otherwise, it's a 30-minute
hike.

Tourist Office: 15, bd. Camille Pelletan, pl. Gambetta (tel. 68 25 07 04). A 10-min. walk from
the train station. Walk straight from the station over the canal on rue G. Clemenceau. Turn left
onto rue de la Liberté and then right onto bd. Jean Jaurès. The office is on the right, on a corner
of pl. Gambetta. **Currency exchange** on weekends when the banks are closed (10F commission).
Accommodations service (5F). Open Mon.-Sat. 9am-7pm, Sun. 10am-noon; Sept. and April-June
Mon.-Sat. 9am-noon and 2-7pm; Oct.-March Mon.-Sat. 9am-noon and 2-6:30pm. **Annex** in the
porte Narbonnaise (tel. 68 25 68 81), to your right as you enter the Cité. Open July-Aug. daily
9am-7pm; Sept.-Oct. and April-June 9am-12:30pm.

Post Office: rue Jean Bringer (tel. 68 25 03 53). **Currency exchange, telephones, photocopiers**
and **Poste Restante.** Open Mon.-Fri. 8am-7pm, Sat. 8am-noon. Branch office, rue Vicomte Trencavel, in the Cité. Open Mon.-Fri. 9am-noon and 2-5pm, Sat. 8:45-11:45am. **Postal Code:** 11000.

Trains: (tel. 68 47 50 50), behind Jardin St-Chenier. Carcassonne is a major stop between Toulouse (11 per day, 50min., 66F) and points south and east, such as Montpellier (10 per day, 2hr.,
104F); Nîmes (7 per day, 2 1/2hr., 129F); Lyon (3 direct per day, 5 1/2hr., 241F); Marseille (every
2hr., 3hr., 192F); Toulon (5 per day, 4hr., 220F); Nice (5 per day, 6hr., 267F); and Narbonne (10
per day, 1hr., 46F). Information office open Mon.-Sat. 9am-6:20pm.

Buses: bd. de Varsovie (tel. 68 25 12 74). Check complete schedule posted at the station or ask the tourist office. To: Toulouse (3 per day, 2 1/2hr., 52F); Narbonne (2 per day, 1hr., 33F); Foix (1 per day, 3hr., 43F50). Information office open Mon.-Fri. 8am-noon and 2-6pm. **Cars Teissier** (tel. 68 25 85 45), across from the Café Bristol in front of the station. Service to Lourdes (43F), and other nearby towns. Office open Mon.-Sat. 8am-noon and 2-6pm.

Taxis: tel. 68 71 50 50.

Bike Rental: At the train station (tel. 68 71 79 63). 50F per 1/2-day, 50F per day, 350F per week, 500F deposit. Open 8am-8pm.

Laundromat: LAV2000, 68, rue Jean Bringer. Wash 20F, 40F per 16kg, dry 2F per 8min. No 5F coins. Open 8am-9pm.

24-Hour Pharmacy: Pharmacie de Garde program. After 8pm call 68 77 49 00 to find out which local pharmacy is on duty.

Medical Assistance: SAMU, tel. 15; **Centre Hospitalier,** rte. de St-Hilaire D342 (tel. 68 25 60 30).

Police: 40, bd. Barbès (tel. 68 77 49 00). **Emergency:** tel. 17.

Accommodations and Camping

The large, comfortable youth hostel will put you smack in the middle of the Cité. When the hostel is full, find a hotel in the *ville basse*—those in the Cité are ferociously expensive. Try to arrive before 10am. The **M.J.C. Centre Internationale de Séjour,** 91, rue Aimé Ramon (tel. 68 25 86 68), is for groups, but may accept desperate individuals.

Auberge de Jeunesse (HI), rue de Vicomte Trencavel (tel. 68 25 23 16). Friendly and immaculate dorm accommodations. Amiable proprietor will safeguard valuables at front desk. Small kitchen facility. Reception open July-Aug. daily 8-11am and 6pm-midnight; June and Sept. until 11pm; April until 10:30pm; Feb., March, and Nov. until 10pm. 59F, nonmembers with no sleepsack 77F. Showers and breakfast included. Call a few days in advance.

Hôtel Astoria, at the intersection of rue Montpellier and rue Tourtel (tel. 68 25 31 38). After crossing the bridge in front of the station. Pristine rooms, many with oriental rugs. Quiet location. Singles 75F. Doubles 100F, with shower 150F. Quads with shower and toilet 185F. Showers 10F. Breakfast 20F. TV 20F.

Le Cathare, 53, rue Jean Bringer (tel. 68 25 65 92), near the post office. Cozy and very bright rooms. Singles and doubles 100F, with shower 130F. Quads and quints with shower 265F. Hall showers included. Breakfast 22F. Restaurant downstairs posts a 65F *menu.*

Hôtel Bonnafoux, 40, rue de la Liberté (tel. 68 25 01 45). From the station, follow rue G. Clemenceau and turn at the second right, rue de la Liberté. Simple rooms with a warm owner. Doubles 70F, with shower 118F. Triples with shower 153F. Quads with shower 166F. Showers 15F. Breakfast 18F.

Hôtel de la Poste, 21, rue de Verdun (tel. 68 25 12 18), near the post office. Worn, slightly stale rooms above a bar. Singles and doubles 95-115F, with shower 125F. Quads with shower and toilet 230F. Showers 18F. Breakfast 20F.

Camping: Camping de la Cité (tel. 68 25 11 77), across the Aude 2km from the modern town. Currency exchange and swimming pool. July-Aug. 60F per 2 people; Easter-June and Sept.-Oct. 42F per 2 people.

Food

Most of the surprisingly inexpensive restaurants in the *Cité* serve the regional specialty *cassoulet,* a greasy stew of white beans, herbs, and meat (usually lamb or pork). On **rue du Plo,** 60 to 70F *menus* abound. For produce, visit the **market** in pl. Carnot (also known as pl. aux Herbes; open Tues., Thurs., and Sat. until 1pm), or the **covered market** in pl. d'Eggenfelden, off rue Aimé Ramon (Mon.-Sat. mornings). In the *basse ville,* simple but affordable restaurants line bd. Omer Sarraut. Restaurants in the Cité tend to shut down in winter.

L'Ostal des Troubadours, 5, rue Viollet-le-Duc, in a 15th-century building. A fun place for coffee or drinks. Musicians play Provençal songs, Irish ballads, blues, and rock beginning at 8pm. The restaurant serves some of the cheapest *menus* around (39F and 59F, plus service). Drinks 10-15F. Open noon to midnight. *Menus* served noon-2pm and 6-10pm.

L'Hippocame, 38, rue du 4 Septembre. Relaxed countertop restaurant with tables in rear. Chef whips up salads and local favorites while you watch. Miraculously low prices. Pizza *Royale* 26F. Four-course and five-course *menus,* with wine, for 50F and 75F respectively. Open Mon.-Sat. 11:30am-2pm and 6:45-10pm.

Au Bon Pasteur, 29, rue Armagnac, in the *ville basse* near Eglise St-Vincent. A friendly, English-speaking owner, and a 60F *menu, vin compris.* Excellent *cassoulet* and *confit de canard* (conserves of duck). Open Feb.-Dec. 23 Tues.-Sat. noon-2pm and 7-9pm.

La Rotonde, 13, bd. Omer Sarraut, in the *ville basse* across from the train station. A late-night *brasserie* and café, with a quick 60F *menu* of veal and pork dishes. Also an all-you-can-eat hors-d'oeuvre bar with vegetables, *pâtés,* and a limited dessert bar. Open daily 6:30am-2am.

Sights and Entertainment

Occupying a strategic position on the road between Toulouse and the Mediterranean, Carcassonne's original fortifications date back to the Roman Empire in the first century and the Visigoths in the 5th century. An early fortress here repelled Clovis, King of the Franks, in 506 AD, and subsequent invaders, but Carcassonne fell with Languedoc during the Albigensian crusade in 1209. When the Cité passed to the control of the French King Louis IX (St-Louis), the monarch ordered the construction of the second outer wall, copying the double-walled fortress design the French crusaders had seen in Palestine. The city lapsed into neglect until Viollet-le-Duc reconceived it, rather controversially, in 1844. The blue slate roofs used for the towers of the inner ring of fortresses are so out of place among the red-tiled roofs of the Midi that local authorities here recently embarked on a scheme to reroof them using local materials.

Originally constructed as a palace in the 12th century, the **Château Comtal** transformed into a citadel following Carcassonne's submission to royal control in 1226. While entrance to the grounds and outer walls is free, admission to the château requires a guided tour. Included in the visit, the **Cours du Midi** contains the remains of a Gallo-Roman villa, former home to Occitan troubadours who entertained their viscounts with song and verse. The **Tour de la Justice's** treacherous staircase leading to nowhere served as a final judgment stand for the ill-fated heretics who penetrated the fortress and instinctively rushed upstairs; they were trapped and easily vanquished. Tours in French run continuously; two English tours run daily in July and August. All begin inside the château's gates. (Open daily July-Aug. 9:30am-7:30pm; Sept. 1-15 and May-June 9:30am-12:30pm and 2-6:30pm; Sept. 16-April 9:30am-12:30pm and 2-5pm. French tours begin at 9am. Admission 25F, ages 18-25 and over 60 14F, under 18 6F.)

At the other end of the Cité, the apse of **Basilique St-Nazaire,** with its radiant stained-glass windows and delicate Gothic ribbed vaulting, is generally considered the finest in southern France and the coolest place in Carcassonne on a sultry summer afternoon. The nave is done in a simple, pure Romanesque style enhanced by the lightness of the choir and windows. The tower represents another Viollet blunder—he restored it with crenellations in a Visigoth style which clashes with the charm of the rest of the structure. (Open daily 9am-noon and 2-6pm. Free.) Despite their tourist shops, the narrow streets outside radiate a medieval atmosphere. About a thousand people live here year-round in a sort of 13th-century time warp.

Though unsightly by day, the *ville basse* brightens by night, especially between September and June. With its octagonal bell tower and rose windows, the **Cathédrale St-Michel,** rue Voltaire, exemplifies 14th- and 15th-century *gothique languedocien.* **Eglise St-Vincent,** rue Tomey at rue du 4 Septembre features only one lonely nave and a 54m tower. Pilgrims flocked to **Notre Dame de Santé,** a tiny 16th-century chapel to the right of pont Vieux, on the way to the Cité.

During July, the eclectic, month-long **Festival de Carcassonne** graces the Château Comtal with a vibrant selection of dance, opera, theater and concerts. (Admission 80-240F, slight reductions for students.) For information, contact Festival de la Cité,

Théâtre Municipal, 11005 Carcassonne (tel. 68 25 33 13). In August, the entire Cité returns to the Middle Ages for the **Mediévales.** People dressed in medieval garb talk to visitors, display their crafts, and pretend nothing has changed in eight centuries. Jousts clang daily at 6pm. Contact the tourist office for ticket information (30F). On summer nights, the Cité stages an elaborate sound and light show (80F).

Collioure

With the foothills of the *Pyrénées Orientales* providing a magnificent backdrop and the aquamarine waters of the Mediterranean lapping the beach in the foreground, Collioure's innocent beauty has enchanted civilization ever since the Greeks and Phoenicians visited these shores over 2000 years ago. The resort drew an inspired, then-unknown Matisse in 1905, and Dérain, Gris, Dufy, Dali, and Picasso soon followed. In summer, painters still line the *quais* with their easels, to capture the decorated *barques* (little wooden fishing boats) beached on the **plage Boramar.** For the price of a drink (try the local *Banyuls,* a sweet *apéritif),* you can marvel at the canvases covering every iota of wall space in the **Hôtel des Templiers,** quai de l'Amirauté (tel. 68 82 05 58). Matisse, Picasso, Dalí and lesser-known artists donated their work in exchange for meals and unlimited lodging privileges. Concerned more with local tradition than with making a profit, the proprietors have held on to these works in the face of an increasingly bullish art market.

The 13th-century **Château Royal** (tel. 68 82 06 43) underwent a 14th-century expansion coordinated by Pierre IV of Aragon and subsequent fortification by Louis XIV's strategist Vauban in 1679. The palace now houses a hodgepodge of regional history and modern art exhibits. Scale the winding stone staircase of the château for a salubrious view of town, sea, and mountain. (Open June 20-Sept. Wed.-Mon. 10:30am-6:30pm, Oct.-Nov. and March-June 19 Wed.-Mon. 2-6pm. Admission 20F, students 14F.) The 17th-century **Notre Dame des Anges,** rising majestically at the northern tip of the croissant-shaped village, replaced an earlier church in the upper city which had been razed by Vauban. A gilded altar crafted by Catalonian sculptor Joseph Sunyer in 1698 brightens the dark interior. (Open 8am-noon and 2-5:30pm.)

The **Centre International de Plongé,** 2, rue du Puits-St-Dominique, in the *basse ville* (tel. 68 82 07 16), rents **windsurfers** (60F per hr., 250F per 5hr., 480F per 10hr.). The CIP also offers training in scuba-diving and windsurfing from April through early November. The one-week courses include room and board at the center's clubhouse (1100-1490F). Write ahead to: CIP Collioure, B.P. 38, 66190 Collioure. **Subchandlers Location,** 13, rue de La Tour (tel. 68 82 06 34), rents scuba equipment (50F per 1/2-day, 80F per day, 390F per week); mountain-bikes (VTT) (60F per 1/2-day, 100F per day, 360F per week; 1500F or ID deposit); and surfboards (100F per 1/2-day, 180F per day, 800F per week; 3000F or ID deposit). Ask the staff about other rentals. (Open Mon.-Sat. 9am-8pm, Sun. 9am-noon and 5-8pm.)

Small motorboats dock at the Bay of Collioure. Consider joining the *Saint-Laurent* for one of its daily **promenades en mer** south along the coast to the **Criée de Port Vendres** (where it makes a brief stop) and on to **Cap Béar.** All excursions depart from the port just beyond the quai de l'Amirauté. (Only sails under favorable weather conditions. 5 trips per day beginning at 11:30am, 70min., 35F, children 20F.) Consider taking an early *promenade* and getting off at Port Vendres, a lively village with terrific seafood restaurants, before returning to Collioure on a late-afternoon run. Longer excursions (2hr.) sail on Tuesdays and Fridays southward along the Côte Vermeille to the Spanish border port of Cerbère.

The **féria de Collioure** kicks off August 14-18. Portuguese-style bullfights (the bull isn't killed) and fireworks make braving the crowds worthwhile. During July and August, join the *sardanes,* traditional Catalonian dances which sprout spontaneously in village squares. Make hotel reservations early for these festival months.

A very popular retreat for vacationing French, German, and Spanish families, Collioure is a town of inflated hotel prices and precious little available space. The pristine **Hôtel des Templiers** (tel. 68 98 31 10), beautifully decorated with hundreds of oil paintings, rents doubles for 160 to 365F. **Hôtel Le Majorque,** 16, av. Général de Gaulle (tel. 68 82 29 22), offers simple, clean rooms. (Doubles 140F, with shower and toilet 180F. Quads 200F, with shower and toilet 250F.) **Hôtel Triton,** 1, rue Jean Bart (tel. 68 82 06 52), sits on the waterfront and is newly renovated, with sparkly fresh rooms and mermaid-tiled bathrooms. (Doubles with shower 110F, with full bathroom 270F.) **Camping Les Amandiers** (tel. 68 81 14 69), a 20-minute walk north of town, but only 150m from the beach, includes hot showers and shaded tent sites. (18F per person, 14F per tent. Open April-Sept.)

A fantastic **market** on the pl. de Général Leclerc offers inexpensive, locally grown fruit and *charcuteries.* (Open Wed. and Sun. 8am-1pm.) Somewhat less expensive than the hotels, Collioure's restaurants serve *sardines à la braise,* as well as other locally caught fish. **L'Albatros,** 48, rue de la Démocratie, in the *basse ville* facing the port, has a small, bright interior decorated like a Matisse paper collage. (Mussels 40F, pizza 32F. Open daily noon-3pm and 7pm-midnight.) **Le Chiberta,** 18, av. du Général de Gaulle, also in the *basse ville,* offers a 68F *menu* of Catalonian specialties. (Open daily noon-2pm and 7-10pm; Sept.-June daily noon-2pm and 7-9pm.) Off av. Général de Gaulle, **Le Welsh,** 5, rue Edgar Quinet, serves 56F and 79F *menus* that feature traditional Catalonian fare. (Open daily 11am-1pm and 6-10pm.)

The **train station** (tel. 68 82 05 89), at the end of av. Aristide Maillol, sends trains north to Perpignan (24F) and Narbonne (8 per day, 62F) and south to Port Bou in Spain (6 per day, 14F) and Barcelona (5 per day, 58F). For information on the coastal bus routes, call **Cars Inter 66** (tel. 68 82 15 47) or inquire at the **tourist office,** pl. du 18 Juin (tel. 68 82 15 47). The tourist office's brochure, *Collioure, Joyau de la Côte Vermeille,* helps in planning short hikes from the village. (Open daily 9am-8pm; Sept. and June. Mon.-Sat. 9:30am-noon and 3:30-7pm, Sun. 10am-noon and 3-6pm; Oct.-May Mon.-Tues. and Thurs.-Sat. 9:30am-noon and 2-5pm.) The **post office,** rue de la République, has **telephones.** (Open Mon.-Fri. 9am-noon and 2-5 pm, Sat. 8:30-11:30am.) Collioure's **postal code** is 66190.

Perpignan

Comfortably nestled between the Mediterranean and the Pyrénées, Perpignan (pop. 120,000) has bounced between French and Spanish ownership as former capital of the Counts of Roussillon and the Kings of Majorque and later as the northern capital of the *catalogne française* (French Catalan). Beginning with the 1344 incorporation of Roussillon and Cerdagne into the principality of Catalonia, a powerful bond tightened between growing Perpignan and its Catalonian counterparts to the south, nurtured by pride and strengthened by a common linguistic heritage. In their centuries-long efforts to annex Roussillon to the state, French kings found themselves repeatedly pitted against a stalwart population of *perpignannais*—wherein the resistors derived their name of *mangeurs des rats* (rat eaters) from the desperate method used in their struggle for survival. Louis XIII finally won Perpignan in 1642, an act which was made legitimate by the signing of the Treaty of the Pyrénées 17 years later. Today, friendlier, less pretentious, and less expensive than the vacation resorts along the Côte d'Azur, Perpignan is only minutes from the wide and spacious beaches of the Côte Vermeille. The city's train station, once referred to as "the center of the world" by a rather off-center Salvador Dalí, also provides convenient connections to the surrounding Catalan region, Spain 50km south, picturesque fishing villages 25km south, and the Pyrénées, whose foothills begin rolling 30km west.

Orientation and Practical Information

To reach the regional tourist office from the train station, walk straight up av. Général de Gaulle and turn right at **place Catalogne** onto cours Lazara Escarguel. Immediately after crossing the canal, turn left onto quai de Barcelone, which becomes quai de Lattre de Tassigny. The office is on the right, 15 minutes from the station. The bulk of the sights, restaurants, cafés, and shops lie inside the triangle formed by this tourist office, place de la Victoire (farther up the canal) and the Palais des Rois de Majorque. The municipal tourist office is inconveniently situated at the opposite end of town from the train station; if you can reach it, you will already know your way around the city.

Tourist Office: in the Palais des Congrès, pl. Armand Lanoux (tel. 68 66 30 30). Unhelpful, crowded, and on the other side of Dalí's world (a solid 1/2-hr. walk from the train station). Follow the canal to bd. Wilson, and walk along the Promenade des Platanes to the Palais des Congrès. Walking tours of the city leave daily June-Sept. at 3:30pm (20F, under 12 10F). Open Mon.-Sat. 9am-7pm, Sun. 9am-1pm and 3-7pm; Oct.-May Mon.-Sat. 8:30am-noon and 2-6:30pm. **Regional Tourist Office,** 7, quai de Lattre de Tassigny (tel. 68 34 29 94). Better prepared to distribute information on the city and the Roussillon region. Information on hotels, camping, *gîtes d'étape,* restaurants, walks, train and bus schedules, festivals, and more. City maps. Open Mon.-Sat. 9am-8pm, Sun. 9am-1pm; Sept. 16-June 14 Mon.-Sat. 9am-noon and 2-7pm, Sun. 9am-noon.

Currency Exchange: Eurochange, 35, av. du Général de Gaulle (tel. 68 34 44 34). Good rates and no commission. Open Mon.-Sat. 9am-noon and 2-7pm, Sun. 9am-noon. High commission at **train station.** Open daily 8-11am and 5-7pm.

Post Office: quai de Barcelone. **Currency exchange** with decent rates. **Telephones.** Open Mon.-Tues. and Thurs.-Fri. 8am-7pm, Wed. 9am-7pm, Sat. 8am-noon. **Postal Code:** 66020.

Trains: tel. 68 35 73 1. On rue Courteline. To: Narbonne (30 per day, 1/2hr., 43F); Paris (6 per day, 10hr., 394F); Marseille (12 per day, 4hr., 180F); Nice (5 per day, 7hr., 262F); Lyon (233F). Office open Mon.-Sat. 8am-6:30pm. **Automatic lockers** 5F.

Buses: 17, av. Général Leclerc (tel. 68 35 29 02), near pl. de la Résistance. To: Narbonne (Mon.-Sat. 1 per day, 1 1/2hr.); Béziers (Mon.-Sat. 1 per day, 2hr. 20min.); airport (Mon.-Sat. 3 per day, 15min., 25F). **Car Inter 66,** 17, av. Général Leclerc (tel. 68 35 29 02). Four buses per day to all the beaches from Le Barcarès (to the north) to Cerbère (to the south). Ten buses connect individual beaches. Schedules available at both tourist offices. Car Inter 66 offers a **tourist pass** good for 8 days within the *département* (150F). Office for all buses open Mon.-Sat. 8am-noon and 2-6pm.

Public Transportation: CTP (Compagnie de Transport Public), pl. Gabriel-Péri (tel. 68 61 01 13). City bus #1 goes to Canet-Plage every 20min. (last bus at 8:30pm, last return from Canet-Plage at 9pm; 25min.). Buses leave from pl. des Platanes (11F). Intra-city bus tickets 6F; *carnet* of 6 28F.

Taxis: tel. 68 34 59 49 or 68 51 11 84. 24hrs.

Laundromat: Laverie Automatique, off av. Dalbiez, near corner of rue Renaudel. Wash 20F, dry 2F per 5min. Soap 2F. Open daily 7am-9pm.

Youth Center: Bureau Information Jeunesse, 16bis, cours Lazare Escarguel (tel. 68 34 56 56). Employment listings, accommodations options and information on local events and activities. Close to youth hostel. Open Mon.-Tues. and Thurs.-Fri. 10am-12:30pm and 1:30-6pm, Wed. 10am-6pm.

Hospital: av. du Maréchal Joffre (tel. 68 61 66 33). **Emergency: SAMU,** tel. 68 61 06 66 or 68 61 66 66.

Police: Emergency: tel. 17.

Accommodations, Camping, and Food

With the youth hostel close to the train station and numerous inexpensive hotels throughout the city, affordable lodgings should be in ample supply. Many budget-friendly hotels lie on av. Gén. de Gaulle, only steps from the station. Other options lie in the heart of the old city, near the sights and the action. At all hotels, expect an additional 4-5F daily tax per person.

Auberge de Jeunesse (HI), La Pépinière (tel. 68 34 63 32), off av. de la Grande Bretagne, next to the police station. From the train station, turn left onto bd. du Conflent. Turn right onto av. de Grande Bretagne; the hostel is behind the park on the left (10min.). Somewhat archaic facilities (Turkish toilets), but plenty of hot water for the showers. 8- to 10-bed single-sex dorm rooms. Small, adequately supplied kitchen. Strictly enforced 10am checkout. Lockout 10am-6pm. No curfew with building key. 57F. Breakfast included. Sheets 13F. Call ahead or arrive early in July and Aug.

Hôtel le Bristol, 5, rue Grande des Fabriques (tel. 68 34 32 68), off pl. de Verdun. Spacious rooms, jovial manager in central but quiet location. Request one of the 5 recently renovated rooms. Singles 80F, with showers 110F. Doubles 100F, with shower and TV 140F. Triples with shower and TV 170F. Quads with shower and TV 190F. Showers 15F. Breakfast 22F. Call ahead in July and Aug.

Hôtel Métropole, 3, rue des Cardeurs (tel. 68 34 43 34), off pl. de la Loge. Calm and convenient location in the *vieille ville*. Large, fresh rooms and checker-tiled bathrooms. Phones in all rooms. Singles and doubles 90F, with shower 110F, with shower and toilet 135F. Triples with shower and toilet 175F. Breakfast 19F.

Hôtel le Berry, 6, av. de Gaulle (tel. 68 34 59 02), in front of the train station. Barebones, but cheap and clean. Funky bathrooms wouldn't mind a little renovat-o-rama. Large doubles 90F, with shower 110F. Triples with shower 150F. Extra bed 30F. Showers 15F. Breakfast 16F.

Express Hôtel, 3, av. de Gaulle (tel. 68 34 89 96). The cheapest within reasonable geographic proximity to the center of Dalí's world. Filled with pictures of horses, Van Goghs and Gauguins, all snipped from magazines. Singles and doubles 70-90F, with shower 110F. Triples with shower and toilet 160F. Quads with shower 180F. Breakfast 18F.

Camping Le Catalan, route de Bompas (tel. 68 63 16 92). Take the "Bompas" bus from the train station. Pools and hot showers. 64F per 2 people; Sept.-June 48F per 2 people.

Place de la Loge and pl. de Verdun in the *vieille ville* are filled with cafés and restaurants that stay lively at night. Pricier options line quai Vauban along the canal. Try av. de Gaulle, directly in front of the train station for cheaper alternatives. An **open-air market** fills pl. de la République (open Tues.-Sun. 8am-12:30pm and 4:30-7pm). The grocery store in the basement of **Nouvelles Galeries,** pl. de la Résistance, provides all the fixings for a picnic on the nearby beaches. (Open Mon.-Sat. 9am-7:30pm.) The **Cafeteria Royaldine,** 3-5, rue du Marché de Gros offers all the usual self-service fare in a dull setting near the bus station. (Open daily 7am-10pm.)

Le Perroquet, 1, av. Général de Gaulle, a stone's throw from the train station, serves surprisingly cheap and tasty cuisine. Their 65F *menu* features *escargots* and *lapin* (rabbit), prepared with Catalan pizzazz. (Open Sat.-Wed. noon-1:45pm and 7-9:30pm, Thurs. noon-1:45pm.) **L'Assiette de Boeuf,** 16, av. de Gaulle offers chicken stuffed with crab meat and other tantalizing choices on its 57F *menu.* (Open Mon.-Fri. noon-2pm and 7-10pm; Sat.-Sun 7-10pm.) The atmospheric self-service cafeteria **Le Palmarium,** pl. Argo, attracts the entire town to its outdoor terrace overlooking the canal. Watch the overhead TV, or admire the interior decor, featuring a poster-sized photo of old-time Perpignan. *Plats du jour* run 25-42F. (Open daily 11:30am-2:30pm and 7-9:30pm.) Tucked away on a small street near the Palais des Rois de Majorques, **La Mesa,** 3, rue de la Petite Monnaie thrives in its family-style French ambience. The selection features excellent seafood and a 55F *menu* of Spanish specialties (65F with wine and coffee). (Open Mon. and Wed.-Sat. noon-1:30pm and 7:30-9:30pm, Tues. noon-1:30pm.)

Sights and Entertainment

With its immense arcaded courtyard and two curiously superimposed chapels, the 13th-century **Palais des Rois de Majorque** (tel. 63 34 48 29) is the city's most impressive sight and one of the best examples of medieval civil and military architecture in southern France. The **citadelle,** whose formidable walls still surround the palace, was used as an arsenal in the 19th century, and is just now being restored. (Open daily 10am-6pm; Oct.-May. Wed.-Mon. 9am-5pm. Admission 10F, students 5F, under 7 free.) Guided tours in French leave from the entrance of the palace at 10am, 11am, 3pm, 4pm, and 5pm. Ask the tourist office for a list of summer concerts held in the palace courtyards.

Built in the late 14th century and redesigned by Louis XI almost a century later, **Le Castillet** is a remarkably well-preserved red-brick castle that has served Perpignan as a gate, a prison, and later a fortress. The tower's terrace, just beneath the unique pink belfry, commands a view of the sea, the Pyrénées and the Rousillon plain in between. Currently, the castle houses a museum, **La Casa Païsal,** pl. de Verdun (tel. 68 66 30 66), which displays several floors of exhibits devoted to Catalonian culture and folklore.

(Open Wed.-Mon. 9:30-11:30am and 2:30-6:30pm; Sept. 16-May Wed.-Mon. 9am-noon and 2-6pm. Free.) Stop off on the second floor for free *dégustations* (tastings) of the local Roussillon wines. (Daily at 4pm when museum is open.) The **Musée Numismatique Joseph Puig,** 42, av. de Grande Bretagne (tel. 68 34 11 70), boasts a collection of numismatic rarities from all corners of the earth, but specializes in extremely rare Catalan and Rousillon coins. (Open Wed.-Sat. and Mon. 9:15am-noon and 2:15-7pm, Sun. 2:15-7pm; Sept. 16-June 14 Wed.-Sat. and Mon. 8:45am-noon and 1:45-6pm, Sun. 1:45-6pm. Free.) The **Musée Hyacinthe Rigaud** contains works dating from the 13th century by Spanish and Catalan masters, and paintings by Rigaud, the court artist for Louis XIV and one of the great portrait artists of the 17th century. The museum also contains works by Ingres, Picasso, and Dufy.

The **Fête de St-Jean** occurs every June 23, when the sacred fire is brought from the Canigou, a nearby mountain. According to popular legend, jumping over a bonfire lit by the *feu de St-Jean* cleanses the spirit. The ritual **Procéssion de la Sanch** at the end of March ushers in the Easter holiday with traditional songs and several concerts. By night, traditional Catalonian dancing in front of **Le Castillet** makes for a lively café scene around **place de Verdun,** especially in summer. Later on, live bands, cheap beers, and a spirited twenty-something crowd at **Le Centre Ville Bar,** on cours Escarvel, animate an otherwise subdued town. For the most hedonistic night-life in the area, head to the clubs that line the beaches at nearby **Canet-Plage.** Be aware, however, that public bus service stops long before all the fun starts, and returning to Perpignan can pose quite a challenge.

Near Perpignan

Stretching 50km from Port-le-Barcares in the north to Cerbère near the Spanish border, the **Côte Vermeille** attracts more French vacationers than any other region in the whole wide world except the glitzy Côte d'Azur. Although beaches are most crowded in July or August, ample patches of sand evade the spread of blankets and bodies. In many of these seaside towns, the awe-inspiring edifices of Rousillon's past merit visits—if only for a brief interlude in between applications of tanning lotion. Since hotels and campgrounds fill quickly in the peak season, consider commuting by bus from Perpignan.

Shuttles run to **Canet-Plage** from the promenade des Platanes in Perpignan (2-3 per hr., 25min, 10F). The **tourist office,** pl. de la Méditerranée (tel. 68 73 25 20), will direct you to a campground.

Cars Inter 66, 17, av. Général Leclerc (tel. 68 35 29 02), links Perpignan to the resorts of **St-Cyprien-Plage** (5 per day, 3 Sun., 1/2hr., 20F), **Argelès-sur-Mer** (8 per day, 4 Sun., 1/2hr., 25F), and **Banyuls-sur-Mer** (4 per day, 70min., 34F). These buses depart from the *gare routière* on av. Général Leclerc. The **Inter Plages** line connects all the coastal resorts from **Bacarés** to **Cerbère.** Pick up schedules in the Perpignan tourist offices or at the Cars Inter 66 office at the bus station. Cars Inter 66 is an umbrella organization that administers two private operators: **F. Ponsaty (FP)** and **Les Courriers Catalans (LCC).** The SNCF yellow-line between Narbonne and Port-Bou also stops at many of the central coastal towns every 45 minutes. For more information on the Côte Vermeille, contact the regional tourist office in Perpignan or the **Association Catalane des Communes du Littoral Rousillon** (A.C.C.L.R.), quai de Lattre de Tassigny, Perpignan (tel. 68 35 43 00).

West of Perpignan, a local train (20min., 22F) ascends into the Pyrénées to **Prades** (pop. 6000), which presides over the mountainous agricultural area called the **Conflent.** Until the beginning of the 20th century, the town reaped the rewards of a lucrative iron-forging industry spearheaded by the region's Catalan mining organizations. Today, however, Prades's renown is linked to the fate of celebrated Catalonian cellist Pablo Casals (1876-1973), who spent 23 years in the town as a political exile from Franco's Spain. Following a three-year self-imposed isolation from the musical world (in protest of the world's recognition of Franco's Spain), Casals chose **Eglise St-Pierre** (in the central square) as the site of his return concert in 1950. The 1000-year-old **Abbaye de St-Michel de Cuxa,** an easy and beautiful 2.5km walk from the center of town, hosts the annual **Festival Pablo Casals** from July 25 to August 13. As the key-note event in Prades's cultural calendar, the festival attracts an array of international musicians for three weeks of classical and chamber music concerts and workshops. Tickets (110-150F, 25% reduction for students) are available after May 15 from the Association Pablo Casals, rue Victor Hugo (tel. 68 96 33 07). During the fifty weeks of the year when the festival is not in town, the abbey still merits a visit. Consecrated in 974, the abbey existed peacefully until the the French Revolution torched and pillaged it. Today a small community of Benedictine monks resides in the since-restored edifice. (Open Mon.-Sat. 9:30am-11:50am and 2-6pm; Oct.-April 2-5pm. Last admission 45min. before closing. Admission 10F, students 6F.)

The **tourist office,** next to the Casals academy at 4, rue Victor Hugo (tel. 68 96 27 58), distributes reams of brochures and pamphlets. Ask for the booklet on the hiking trails around Prades, which includes directions to the abbey and other day hikes. (Open Mon-.Sat. 9am-noon and 2-6pm.) Located directly above the tourist office and housed in a single room, the **Musée Pablo Casals** displays one of the master's cellos and correspondence between Casals and his buddy, Albert Schweitzer. Also upstairs, the **Musée d'Archéologie** contains prehistoric artifacts discovered in the environs of Prades. (All museums open Mon.-Sat. 9am-noon and 2-6pm. Free.) The **Festival du Cinéma,** from July 16 to 24, features retrospectives on a particular individual or theme (tickets 32F). Every Tuesday, an **open-air market** colors the square in front of Eglise St-Pierre (8am-1pm). Seven daily **trains** head for Prades from Perpignan (40min., 36F) Seven daily **tours** head to Prades from Perpignan. (40min., 36F). Alternatively, explore the Conflent on two wheels with **mountain bikes** from **Flanent Cycles,** 8, rue Arago (tel. 68 96 07 62). (Open Tues.-Sun. 8am-noon and 2-7pm. Mountain bikes 90F per day, 200F per 3 days; 1200F deposit.)

Although hotels are few and expensive, **Hostalrich**, 156, av. Général de Gaulle (tel. 68 96 05 38), offers 150F singles with shower and doubles for 160-240F. **Camping Municipal** (tel. 68 96 29 83), in a valley 5 minutes downhill from the tourist office, charges 10F50 per site and 9F50 per adult, and vaunts shady spots, hot showers and laundry facilities. (Open May-Oct.)

Deeper in the mountains of the Conflent and honored by the national tourist office as "*un des plus beaux villages de France*" (one of the most beautiful towns in France), **Villefranche-de-Conflent** occupies a prized location at the confluence of the Cady and Têt Rivers and at the base of three mountains. The 11th-century military ramparts completely enclose the town and its equally well-preserved 13th- and 14th-century façades. Built into the mountainside high above the town, 17th-century **Fort Liberia** was designed by chief French military architect Vauban to protect Villefranche after the 1659 Treaty of the Pyrénées established the nearby French-Spanish border. Although never attacked, the three levels of fortification formed an elaborate defense system that guarded Villefranche from all angles. To reach the fortified heights of Liberia, take the 22F *Navette,* a bus that departs every half-hour from the Porte de France. The subterranean staircase of "1000 steps" (thankfully an overstatement), the only link between Liberia and the town below, descends from the fort. (Fort open daily 10am-6pm. Admission 28F, children 14F.) On June 23, the Catalonian **Fête des Feux de St-Jean** burns brightly in Villefranche. As in Perpignan, torches lit on nearby Canigou mountain bring the sacred fire back to the village, where locals dance the traditional *sardane,* drink wine, and hop over bonfires. The **tourist office,** pl. de l'Eglise (tel. 68 96 22 96), can help with lodging and hiking information. (Open daily 9am-7pm; Oct.-May Mon.-Fri. 9am-5pm.) Guided tours of Villefranche and its ramparts leave pl. de l'Eglise at 10am (Tues. and Thurs.-Fri., 1 1/2hr., 25F). The **Association Culturelle,** 38, rue St-Jean (tel. 68 96 25 64), has a remarkably dedicated staff that offers information on historical hiking tours of the area. (Open Mon.-Fri. 8:30am-noon and 2:30-7:30pm.) During July and August, the *Association* also leads tours of the town (25F). For exhaustive maps (53F) and information about hiking locally and throughout the Pyrénées, contact **Editions et Diffusions Randonnées Pyrénéennes,** B.P. 88, 09200 St-Girons (tel. 61 66 71 87).

Just outside the walls of Villefranche the **Grotte des Canalettes,** discovered in 1951, is remarkable for the forest of sprouting stalagmites in its vast caverns. The *Grotte* actually comprises a complex of three proximate caves. (Open Mon.-Sat. 10am-6:30pm, Sun. 2-6pm; Sept.-June daily 10am-noon and 2-6:30pm. Admission 28F, under 12 14F.)

Hotels fill quickly in summer. **Hôtel Le Terminus,** (tel. 68 05 20 24), outside the village next to the train station rents attractive doubles for 80F. (Doubles with shower 120F. Breakfast 20F.) The attached restaurant offers 55F and 65F *menus* starring trout. The town hall (tel. 68 96 10 78) on pl. de l'Eglise operates **gîtes communaux** where you can stay for up to one week if you have a sleeping bag. (Doubles 675F per week. Quads 900F per week. Town hall open Mon.-Fri. 9am-noon and 3-6pm.)

The same **train** that stops in Prades continues to Villefranche (7 per day, 45min., 37F). Buses also run the same route from Perpignan. Schedules are available at **Cars Inter 66** 17, av. Général Leclerc in Perpignan (tel. 68 35 29 02).

From Villefranche, catch the charming, open-air *petit train jaune* through the Pyrénées to **La Tour-de-Carol** (2 1/2hr., 78F), where trains connect to Toulouse and Barcelona, and buses ply on to Andorra. Six trains daily make the climb through the mountains, stopping at small villages along the way. The 63km stretch of track once transported iron and marble produced in the region. The Association Culturelle can suggest hikes from any of the villages where the train stops. The paths are well-marked and dotted with *gîtes,* which facilitate longer stays in these spectacular mountains. In winter, the fashionable ski area at **Font Romeu,** accessible by the *petit train jaune,* is fully equipped with snow machines and ski lifts and offers first-rate **skiing.** Contact the **tourist office,** av. E. Brousse (tel. 68 30 02 74), for information.

Narbonne

Faced with the memories of a glorious historical heritage, the 45,000 contemporary *narbonnais* are trying to ward off the lingering lethargy that has plagued the city in recent times. Founded by a decree of the Roman senate in 118 BC, *Narbo Martius* became Rome's first colony outside of Italy. Back in those good ol' days, the city flourished with a lucrative export of cheese, meat, butter, and other produce. The installation of archbishops and viscounts in medieval Narbonne marked the height of the port city's commerce, which thrived with the fortunes brought by its vineyards. With the *dégringolage* (downward tumbling) of its grape, Narbonne has set out in search of renewal. Today, many of the town's summer visitors are would-be sunbathers, responding to the bewitching siren song of the nearby beach developments at **Narbonne-Plage** and **Gruisson-Plage.**

Before hitting the waves, make a (brief) round of Narbonne's attractive monuments, which congregate in the *vieille ville.* The **Cathédrale St-Just et St-Pasteur,** an imposing Gothic structure, is only half as large as its architects intended it to be. Construction began in 1272 but stopped in 1340 during a long, bitter zoning dispute (the church wanted to dismantle the city's surrounding walls and use the materials to build the cathedral) between the archbishops and city hall. Fortunately, the church lost—although further construction would have given Narbonne France's largest cathedral. The walls saved the city when the English Black Prince attacked in 1355. Scale the 251 steps of the cathedral's **Tour Nord** (10F). At the summit awaits a dizzying 360° view of the *vieille ville's* thatched-roof houses below, and the hilly countryside beyond. (Cathedral open Mon.-Sat. 9:30am-5:45pm.)

All museums sell a 10F global ticket, good for entrance to four museums over two days. The opulent **Palais des Archevêques,** next to the cathedral, testifies to the wealth and power of the former archbishops of Narbonne. Within its walls, the **Musée Archéologique** displays a collection of artifacts stretching from hunting-and-gathering societies to the relatively recent Gallo-Roman civilization. (Open daily 10-11:50am and 2-6pm.) Across the atrium, the **Musée d'Art et d'Histoire** hangs an assemblage of French, Flemish, and Italian 17th-century paintings formerly in the apartments of the archbishops. An uncovered Roman grain warehouse, **L'Horreum,** rue Rouget de l'Isle, off rue Droite, is Narbonne's only remaining ancient monument and is not yet completely excavated. The **Maison Vigneronne,** rue l'Ancienne Porte Neuve, is a restored

17th-century powderhouse containing displays of maps, photographs, and traditional winemaking tools. The church of **Notre-Dame de La Mourguier** has a lapidary museum with Roman stones, inscriptions, sculptures, and sarcophagi found in the area. (All museums open Tues.-Sun. 9:30am-12:30pm and 3-7pm; Sept. 16-June Tues.-Sun. 10am-noon and 2-5pm.)

The large and clean **Foyer des Jeunes Travailleurs "Le Capitole,"** 45, av. de Provence (tel. 68 32 07 15), rents spacious singles and doubles, both with private bathrooms and showers, for 90F and 150F, respectively, including breakfast. The *foyer* serves 35F dinners from Monday to Friday and unlocks a kitchen on the weekend. From the train station, expect a 10- to 15-minute walk: go left down av. Carnot, turn right onto bd. de 1848, and left onto av. de Provence. **Hôtel de la Gare,** 7, av. Pierre Semard (tel. 68 32 10 54), only inches from the station, is apparently unfamiliar with the concept of inflation and plies fresh rooms with soft, clean carpeting. Zowie! (Singles and doubles with shower 95F, with shower and toilet 98F. Quads with shower 145F, with shower and toilet 148F. Breakfast 20F.) The owner of **Hôtel Novelty,** 33, av. des Pyrénées (tel. 68 42 24 28), will eagerly show dozens of postcards from satisfied customers and now-faithful correspondents. (Singles 70F, with shower 80F. Doubles with shower 100-110F. Triples 110F. Quads 150F, with shower 170F. Breakfast 16F.) **Chez Felix,** 20, bd. Général de Gaulle (tel. 68 32 10 67), has simple cabin-like rooms, which cost 95F for two people and 125F for three; breakfast costs 17F. The restaurant below serves 46F and 65F *menus* with wine. (Open daily noon-2pm and 7:30-9pm; Sept.-June Mon.-Sat. noon-2pm and 7:30-9pm.) Several campgrounds sprinkle the Narbonne area. Those on the coast are usually full and always crowded. **Camping le Languedoc** (tel. 68 65 24 65), 1km southeast, has washing machines and a currency exchange.

A number of inexpensive restaurants, including some ethnic choices, cluster off rue Droite, branching off to the left of the Palais des Archevêques. Grab a quick bite at one of the food stalls lining the promenade des Barques, along the canal, or pick up picnic items at the **vegetable market** on plan (not place) St-Paul on Thursday mornings. On Sunday mornings, a *brocante* (flea market) with antiques and furniture descends on pl. des Pyrénées. The giant **covered market** at the **Halles** on the canal on cours Mirabeau is open daily 7am-1pm. **L'Escargot,** 9, rue Corneille, on a small street off rue de l'Ancien Courrier near Monoprix, serves trout or chicken (each 38F), salads (12-15F), and a four-course 48F *menu.* (Open daily Oct.-Aug. noon-2pm and 7-9:30pm.) **La Paillote,** passage de l'Ancien Courrier, has a pleasant outdoor terrace. Try the scrumptious *escargots* (33F; open daily noon-2:30pm and 7-10pm).

Narbonne's **tourist office,** pl. Salengro (tel. 68 65 17 52 or 68 65 15 60), is a 10-minute walk from the train station. Turn right onto bd. Frédéric Mistral; after 5-10 minutes, turn left onto rue Chennebier, which leads to pl. Salengro; the tourist office will be on your left. The staff **exchanges currency** and offers the usual information. (Open daily 8am-7pm; Sept. 15-June 15 Mon.-Sat. 8:30am-noon and 2-6pm, Sun. 9:30am-12:30pm.) Ask about the guided walking tours of the city (July-Sept. 15 Mon.-Sat. at 10am and 4pm, Sun. 10am, 1 1/2hr., 20F). The **post office,** 25, bd. Gambetta, has **poste restante, telephones,** and a **currency exchange.** (Open Mon.-Fri. 8am-7pm, Sat. 8am-noon.) **Postal code:** 11000. A **butter croissant tattoo** on your left buttock might be the perfect souvenir of your visit to France. **Rose Tattoo,** 78, rue Droite, a tiny shop with lovely people performing a necessary civic service. Does 'em for a decent price. (Large selection starts at 100F. Open Tues.-Sat. 2:30-7:30pm.) Take your clothes for a spin next door at **Salon Lavoir,** 80, rue Droite, a bigger shop with ordinary people performing a mundane service. (Wash 5.5kg for 16F, dry 7F per 2min. Open daily 7am-9pm.) The **train station** (tel. 67 62 50 50) lies close to the main sights and the downtown area. (Open Mon.-Fri. 7:30am-12:30pm and 2-7:30pm, Sat. 3-7:30pm.) Trains go to Perpignan (14 per day, 3/4hr., 44F), Toulouse (13 per day, 1 1/2hr., 93F), and Montpellier (12 per day, 55min., 64F). The *gare routière* (tel. 68 32 07 60), normally at the end of quai Victor Hugo, is indefinitely without a home. In the meantime, catch buses from the train station to Perpignan, Carcassonne, and local beaches.

Beaches near Narbonne

Jean-Jacques Beneix's steamy *37°2 le matin (Betty Blue)* was filmed in **Gruisson,** an old fishing village 15km from Narbonne. Although you must bring your own loony lover, you may be able to rent a windsurfer on the beach.

Five kilometers from Narbonne, **Narbonne Plage's** huge beach attracts families all summer long. Three fine beach-side campgrounds obviate the commute from Narbonne. **Camping des Côtes des Roses** (tel. 68 49 83 65) has a Gothic mini-golf course (53F per 2 people) and food store. (Open Easter-Oct.) **Camping Soleil d'Oc** (tel. 68 49 86 21) rents tents (64F per 2 people; open Easter-Oct. 15). **Camping la Falaise** (tel. 68 49 80 77) has washing machines (60F per 2 people; open April-early Oct.). Six daily buses leave for both beaches from Narbonne's train station (20min., 30F).

Béziers

The swarms of peacefully tanning tourists found near Béziers today belie the town's early history. For 2000 years Phoenicians, Greeks, Romans, Arabs, and Franks have plagued the *biterrois,* the inhabitants of Beziers. When Béziers gave refuge to the outlawed Cathars and refused to cooperate with Pope Innocent III's anti-heretical campaign in 1209, the town was sacked and its inhabitants uniformly slaughtered. Not until wine production revitalized the local economy did the town begin to rebuild itself. In 1907, the *phylloxéra,* a disease which attacks grapevines, laid waste to the town's lifeblood. Recently, this hapless city of 90,000 began to revive itself through tourism, and once again, wine. Though Béziers has traditionally been known for its simple table wine, the few remaining vineyards pride themselves on quality. For a taste of this new prosperity, try the Minervois or Fitou labels. Despite its graceful parks and a scattering of monuments and cultural opportunities, Béziers today lacks the vitality that elicited the wrath of crusaders in its medieval past. Indeed, much of its modern appeal derives from attractions away from the urban fulcrum, with beaches to the east and vineyards to the west leading the recreational list.

Any of the nearby private vineyards or *caves coöperatives,* central outlets for local wines, give tours ending with samples of the St-Chignon, Bourlou, and St-Saturnin wines. **Le Club des Grands Vins des Chateaux du Languedoc** will provide information on *dégustations* of the region's acclaimed *appellations d'Origine Controlée* (A.O.C.): Minervois, Saint-Chinian, Fauceres, and a spicy red, Cabrières. Contact the club's offices at the château de Raissac (tel. 67 28 15 61), 2km west of Béziers on the A9. The cellars of the château itself are open to visitors year-round (Mon.-Sat. 9am-noon and 3-7pm).

The **tourist office,** 27, rue du 4 Septembre (tel. 67 49 24 19), directs you to the local producers as well as the nearby beaches. (Open Mon.-Sat. 9am-7pm, Sun. 10am-noon; Sept.-June Mon.-Fri. 9am-noon and 2-6:30pm, Sat. 9am-noon and 3-6pm.) From 1667 to 1681, native Paul Riquet planned and built (with a little help from his friends) the 245km **Canal du Midi,** which connects the Atlantic to the Mediterranean. Full-day cruises pass through the system of nine locks in Béziers and on to local vineyards and a fish hatchery. For information, call 67 37 13 96 between 8am and 8pm. Cruises leave at 8:45am and return about 5pm (220F, lunch included).

The **Cathédrale St-Nazaire,** a Roman church built on the ruins of a pagan temple, was destroyed with the rest of the city in 1209 but rebuilt and expanded by the 14th century. Climb to the top for an unobstructed view of the surrounding countryside. (Open Mon.-Sat. 9am-noon and 2:30-7pm.) The **Fabrégat des Beaux Arts,** pl. de la Révolution, and its annex, **Hôtel Fayet,** 9, rue de Capuces, house a small but important collection of late 18th-, 19th-, and 20th-century paintings including works by Dufy, Delacroix, and Corot. (Open Tues.-Sat. 10am-noon and 2-6pm, Sun. 2-6pm; Sept.-June for Hôtel Fayet Tues. and Thurs. 10am-noon and 2-5pm. The Fabrégat's hours do not change off-season. Admission 10F, students 5F.) Béziers's public garden, the **Plateau des Poètes,** in front of the train station, is a pleasant spot for picnicking or hiding from the sweltering sun (open 7am-10pm).

At the end of August, a local **féria** that has earned Béziers the nickname the "French Seville," fills the evenings with *corridas* and traditional dancing. Traditional stampeding is all the rage in Béziers's **running of the bulls.** Tickets are available at the *arènes,* av. Emile Claparède (tel. 67 76 13 45). A less frenetic festival at the end of July features classical music and operas in local churches. Buy tickets at the Théâtre Municipale, allées Paul Riquet (tel. 67 28 40 75). (60F, under 18 or over 60 30F.) The third Sunday in October brings the **Fête du vin nouveau** and much drunkenness.

Béziers has no youth hostel, but there are a handful of simple, inexpensive hotels. The **Hôtel Angleterre,** 22, pl. Jean Jaurès (tel. 67 28 48 42), in the city center, rents quiet, clean, and cozy rooms with soft carpeting. (Singles 85F. Doubles 110F, with shower 150F. Quads with shower and toilet 260F. Breakfast 25F.) Up the street from the train station, the **Hôtel de Paris,** 70, av. Gambetta (tel. 67 28 43 80), has crisp-n-clean rooms, some of them cozy attic chambers. (Doubles 95-105F, with shower 140F, with shower and toilet 170F. Triples with shower 190F. Quads with shower 210F. Showers 15F. Breakfast 20F.) **La Dorade,** 10, rue André Nougaret (tel. 67 49 35 39), off pl. du Général de Gaulle, run by a kind Spanish couple, fills quickly in summer. (Singles and doubles 90F, with shower 105F. Quads with shower 140F. Breakfast 24F.) The restaurant downstairs serves a 45F *menu.* The **Hôtel Paul Riquet,** 45bis, allées Paul Riquet (tel. 67 76 44 37), lets airy rooms with track lighting, carpeting, and a color TV. Reservations are advisable in July and August. (Singles and doubles 100F, with shower 130F. Quads with shower 210F. Showers 10F. Breakfast 20F, in bed 25F.) If price is everything, try **Hôtel Métropole,** 16, rue des Balances (tel. 67 28 45 50), in the center of the *vieille ville.* From allées Paul Riquet, take rue du 4 Septembre—the hotel is on the second small street on your left. Call ahead; many of their incredibly cheap rooms are rented by the month. (Singles and doubles 70-75F. Quads with shower 150F. Showers 10F.)

Mykonos, 5, rue Bagatelle, near the top of plateau des Poètes, serves economical Greek favorites (55-65F). Moussaka is 40F a la carte, baklava 22F. (Open Tues.-Sun. 7:30pm-midnight.) Down from the cathedral on rue Viennet, **Le Thé Retrouvé** serves salads (15-40F), pastries (20F), and a light 45F lunch *menu.* (Open Tues.-Sat. noon-2pm and 7:30-10:30pm; Sept.-June noon-6:30pm.) **L'Hacienda,** 14bis, rue des Balances, posts a traditional 57F *menu.* (Open daily 2pm-midnight.) The indoor **market** at Les Halles, rue Paul Riquet, is open daily 7am to 1pm. Another market fills allées Paul Riquet Monday through Saturday. The **Monoprix supermarket,** also on the allées is open Monday to Saturday from 8:30am to 7pm.

The bus station, at pl. Jean Jaurès (tel. 67 28 23 85), sends four-wheeled behemoths to local beaches. Buses run to Narbonne (5 per day, last bus 7:05pm, 40min., 23F20), and Montpellier (15 per day, 1hr. 35min., 43F60). Frequent **trains** connect Béziers to Narbonne (20 per day, 20min., 22F) and Montpellier (28 per day, 40min., 51F). The station (tel. 67 62 50 50) is open from 6am to midnight. (Information Office open Mon.-Sat. 8am-7pm.)

City buses (tel. 67 76 90 10) leave pl. du Général de Gaulle for **Valras** beach (11 per day, last return 8pm, round-trip 22F). Fifteen km from Béziers, this one-time fishing village has developed into an all-purpose family beach resort complete with water slide and ferris wheel. In the evening, join a game of *boules* or indulge in fresh seafood caught by the returning fishing boats.

Near Béziers

On the coast between Béziers and Sète, lie the condominia, pine groves, and long beaches of **Cap d'Agde,** which claims the noble distinction of being Europe's largest nudist colony. Although only a few hundred people inhabit the colony during the chilly clothes-mandating winter months, 50-60,000 free-body culturists (including many English and Germans) bare all during the summer. The *quartier naturiste* is renowned for its clothes-optional character, and in most of its beachside restaurants, grocery stores, souvenir shops and photo labs, many soul-seeker non-materialists will be pursuing their daily activities without superfluous rags covering the epidermis. Prepare to do the same, lest you feel like an inhibited ninny in a crowd of to-hell-with-convention bathers. The 10F entrance fee to the *quartier privé* includes access to a **Baskin Robbins,** where the nude staff coolly dishes out scoops of heavenly hash. Take one of the frequent trains to the town of **Agde** (1/2hr., 25F), then catch the hourly shuttle bus to Cap d'Agde, 7km away (10F).

Sète

Spread along a narrow strip of land cordoning the Bassin Thau from the Mediterranean, and crisscrossed by gray streets and blue canals, Sète (pop. 40,000) has been unofficially dubbed *"la Venise Languedocienne"* (the Venice of Languedoc). Sparsely settled since 1000 BC, modern Sète sprang to life in 1666, when Louis XIV's finance minister, Colbert, pointed to the "cap de Cette" as the site for a new port. The choice was auspicious; Sète is currently France's largest Mediterranean fishing port, pulling some 14,000 tons of fish from the sea each year. Indeed, with canals and docks dissecting its *centre ville,* Sète has sea water coursing through its very veins.

Most *setois* revel in their aquatic playground. On **Mole St-Louis,** a dock at the southern end of town, lounges the **Société Nautique de Sète,** one of France's oldest yacht clubs. Farther out on the Mole lies the home slip of 1992 America's Cup challenger, *French Kiss,* which is now on display in drydock. Throughout the summer, numerous yacht races—including the prestigious Tour de France at the end of July—set sail from the Mole. Sun-n-swim along the twelve km of powdery yellow sand that begins with the Plage de la Corniche in the southwestern corner of town. The **beaches,** which have earned the town an unfortunate, but self-given, nickname as "capitale de la Floride française," can be reached on bus #6.

For those with land legs, Sète offers a unique assortment of museums. **Le Vignerai,** bd. Camille Blanc, occupies 1400m of passages in the Grottes des Pierres Blanches, a network of caves beneath Mont St-Clair. The museum traces the history of wine-making with the aid of humorous exhibits, wild sculptures, and entertaining music. The final cavern rewards visitors with a free *dégustation* (tasting) of this revered libation. (Open March-Nov. Tues.-Sun. 10am-7pm; June-Aug. open daily. Admission 28F, students 10F.) Afterward, walk straight—if that's still possible—down the road to the **Espace Brassens,** 67, bd. Camille Blanc, a high-tech museum devoted to the life and works of the poet, singer, and musician Georges Brassens, one of Sète's favorite sons. The self-guided tour here involves wireless remote control earphones that narrate the visit, with miraculous topic changes as you move from zone to zone. (Open daily 10am-noon and 3-7pm; Oct.-May. Tues.-Sun. 10am-noon and 2-6pm. Admission 30F, students 10F.) Bus #2 accesses both sites from the *centre ville* (5F); otherwise, it's a 30-minute walk around Mont St-Clair. Closer to town is the **maritime cemetery** that inspired the Paul Valéry's poem *"Cimetière Marin."* Valéry, a tremendously influential 20th-century poet, began his life here in 1871; upon his death in 1945 he was interred in his cherished cemetery. Just a few steps from the tombstones, the **Musée Paul Valéry** is another attractive, modern facility with exhibits on local archeology, history, Sète's nautical jousts, Georges Brassens, and, of course, Valéry. (Open June-Sept. 10am-noon and 2-6pm; Oct.-May Wed.-Mon. same hours. Admission 10F, students 5F. Free Wed.) If your legs have it in them, climb to the summit of Mont St-Clair (183m) for a ravishing vista of Sète, its canals and docks, and the sea beyond.

Every year from August 23 to 25, Sète cuts loose for its **Fête Locale de la St-Louis,** which it celebrates with traditional music and dancing, fireworks, balls, and nautical competitions. On the final weekend in August, Sète holds its animated **tournois de Joutes Nautiques,** in which participants joust from ramps extending from oversized rowboats.

Like any good alternative to the Côte d'Azur, Sète is stuffed to the gills with cheap accommodations. The **Auberge de Jeunesse (HI),** "Villa Salis," rue du Général Revest (tel. 67 53 46 68), peers down on the town from the sides of Mont St-Clair. From the station, walk straight onto Pont de Gare, go over the canal and turn right onto quai Vauban. Continue around the corner and cross the first bridge on the right. Go left on the other side and walk down quai Général de Lattre de Tassigny. Turn right onto rue

Général de Gaulle and follow the friendly *auberge* signs. If you can scale the final hill, it should be a 15-minute walk. Appropriate to Sète's fishing heritage, the single-sex dormitories are better suited for sardines than for people. Great view compensates somewhat. (Reception open 8am-noon and 6pm-midnight. No lockout or curfew. Members only. 104F with obligatory dinner and breakfast. Sheets 15F. Safe-box for valuables.) At **Hôtel Tramontane,** 5, rue Frédéric-Mistral (tel. 67 74 37 92), only 50m off the canals, expect a friendly manager, a mellow basset hound, clean rooms and beds, and sparkling bathrooms. Doubles run 110F, with shower and toilet 155-175F. Triples are 130F, with shower 175F, with shower and toiet 195F. Quads go for 175F, with the works 235F (breakfast in bed 24F). **Hôtel le Valéry,** 20, rue Denfert Rochere-au (tel. 67 74 77 51), is just minutes from the train station and offers doubles for 110F, with shower 150F, and triples with showers from 160F. (Showers 5F. Breakfast 20F.) Feel right at home in the **Hôtel Family,** 20, quai Lattre de Tassigny (tel. 67 74 05 03), with its immaculate and spacious rooms. Singles and doubles start at 100F (without shower) and run to 175F (all-dressed up). Triples and quads, both with shower, will set you back 185F and 195F, repectively. (Breakfast 20F. Open all year.)

Inexpensive eateries line the heart of the *centre ville*, just behind quai Général Lattre de Tassigny. **Promenade J. B. Marty,** just one block from the water near the mole St-Louis, has waves of affordable seafood restaurants. **Restaurant Le Skipper,** 24, prom-enade J. B. Marty, serves up a four-course 55F *bouillabaisse menu* that Ginger would do anything for. On rue Frédéric-Mistral, **La Lampiote** offers homemade pastas for 38-42F and pizzas for 30-38F. (Open Tues.-Sat. noon-2pm and 7-10:30, Sun. 7-10:30pm.) Alternatively, head to the **Casino supermarket** on the corner of rue Général de Gaulle and rue Alsace-Lorraine (open Mon.-Sat. 8am-noon and 4-8pm, or the **daily market** at the **Halles,** just off rue Alsace-Lorraine (open 7am-1pm).

Sète's **tourist office,** 60, Grand rue Mario-Roustan (tel. 67 74 71 71), which lies be-hind the quai Général Durand, bubbles with information and will **change money** (up to 500F) or your baby (not really) with no commission. A 15-minute walk from the train station, continue along quai Général Lattre de Tassigny (see directions for the youth hostel) and follow the signs. (Open daily 9am-8pm; Sept.-June Mon.-Sat. 9am-noon and 2-6pm.)

Sète's **train station,** quai M. Joffre (tel. 67 46 51 00 or 67 58 00 00) receives fre-quent trains from both Montpellier (20 per day, 20min., 25F) and Beziers (18 per day, 25min., 39F). The **bus station,** 13, quai de la République (tel. 67 74 66 90), rolls 11 buses daily to Montpellier (1hr., 29F50) and three to Pezenas (1 1/4hr., 35F). To get anywhere else entails a transfer at one of these sites. The **post office,** bd. Danièle Casanova (tel. 67 74 70 60) has Poste Restante and **photocopying** services. (Open Mon.-Fri. 8:30am-6:30pm, Sat. 8:30am-noon.) **Postal code**: 34200.

Montpellier

In his *Mémoires d'Un Touriste,* Stendhal called Montpellier "la seule ville française de l'intérieur qui n'a pas l'air stupide" (the only French city of the interior that doesn't look stupid). Claiming to admire Stendhal's memoir despite his "often singularly false" taste and "perversely colourless" style, rival 19th-century literary traveler Henry James called Montpellier "one of those places that please, without your being able to say wherefore." Despite the city's history of damningly faint praise, the charm and vitality of Montpellier (pop. 211,000) is infectious. First mentioned in a deed in 985, Montpel-lier quickly became an important commercial center and, thanks to Jewish and Arab scholars, boasted Europe's most prestigious medical school in the 12th century. Al-though devastated by the Hundred Years War and, at the turn of this century, the wine industry's disease crisis, Montpellier has recently regained its economic and cultural footing. Touting itself as the "Mediterranean Eurocity," Montpellier has attracted a number of high-tech industries, including IBM. Attracted by the opportunity in this technopolis, 55,000 students have given rise to a prestigious higher educational net-work including schools of medicine and law. Yet this booming cultural mecca remains close enough to the beach to torture its students during final exams.

During the day, narrow and surprisingly quiet streets entice visitors into the *vieille ville,* which harbors many 17th- and 18th-century *hôtels particuliers.* Cafés on pl. de la Comédie, fondly known to *montpellierains* as *l'Oeuf* (the egg), offer expensive coffee and hours of four-star people-watching. Come sundown, the student population casts off its daytime reticence and bursts into nocturnal revelry; the lively bars clustered in pl. Jean Jaurès are always buzzing. Though many students leave during the summer, an international modern dance festival and numerous theatrical productions keep the town animated year-round.

Orientation and Practical Information

A major stop in the rail system, the *gare SNCF* lies just south of the shield-shaped *vieille ville,* with rue de la République, on the left, and rue Maguelone, on the right, radiating away from the station to form the V-shape. The modern town center, on the southwest corner of the *vieille ville,* is the fountain-filled pl. de la Comédie, a combination of slick office buildings, 19th-century *hôtels,* and a large open space that springs to life at night. To reach the main tourist office from the train station, walk up rue Maguelone and turn right onto the pl. de la Comédie. Continue until **Le Triangle,** the modern building that houses the tourist office, appears on the left.

Tourist Office: passage du Tourisme (tel. 67 58 67 58), in Le Triangle. Excellent maps and information on Montpellier and Languedoc-Roussillon. Hotel reservation service and **currency exchange** with vile rates and a satanic 3% commission. Guided tours of the city in French (1-2 per day, 34F, students 21F) and English (Tues., 41F, students 27F). Open Mon.-Sat. 9am-1pm and 2-7pm; Sept.-June Mon.-Sat. 9am-1pm and 2-6pm. **Branch offices** at the train station (tel. 67 92 70 03; open Mon.-Fri. 9am-noon and 2-6pm) and south of the station at Rond Point des Prés d'Arènes (tel. 67 22 08 80; open Mon.-Sat. 10am-8pm, Sun. 4-8pm).

Budget Travel: Council Travel, 20, rue de l'Université (tel. 67 60 89 29). Books domestic and international flights on French and US carriers at low, low, student rates. Open Mon.-Fri. 9:30am-12:30pm and 2-6pm.

Post Office: pl. Rondelet (tel. 67 34 50 00). **Poste Restante, currency exchange** and **telephones.** Open Mon.-Fri. 8am-7pm, Sat. 8am-noon. **Branch office** at pl. des Martyrs de la Résistance. **Postal Code:** 34000 (main branch).

Trains: pl. Auguste Gilbert (tel. 67 58 50 50). **Exchange** desk with excellent rates open daily 8am-9pm. To: Avignon (20 per day, 1hr., 65F); Marseille (8 per day, 2hr. 10min., 102F); Nice (8 per day, 4 1/2hr., 206F); Toulouse (every hr., 3 1/4hr., 142F); Perpignan (10 per day, 1hr. 50min., 95F); Paris (9 per day, with change in Lyon, 5hr., 362F plus 16F TGV reservation). Information office open Mon.-Fri. 8am-7pm, Sat. 9am-6pm. **Automatic lockers** 15F.

Buses: rue Jules Ferry (tel. 67 92 01 43), on the second floor of the parking garage next to the train station. Béziers (every hr., 1hr. 40min., 43F60); Carnon (2 per hr., 20min., 15F10); Nîmes (2 per day, 1 3/4hr., 41F50); Alès (4 per day, 1 3/4hr., 58F10). Information office open Mon.-Sat. 9am-noon and 2-7pm. **Local buses: SMTU,** 23bis, rue Maguelone (tel. 67 22 87 00). Lines 1-14 leave from the front of the train station (6F).

Taxis: tel. 67 41 37 87 or 67 04 99 02 (English).

Bike Rental: Vélos Pour Tous, esplanade Charles de Gaulle, next to pl. de la Comédie (tel. 67 58 56 44). A unique place: bikes are **free** with a deposit of 800F and ID. Sponsors who advertise on the bikes cover most costs; the city forks over the rest. Open May-Aug. daily 9am-9pm.; Sept.-Oct. and March-April daily 9am-5pm.

Laundromat: Lav'Club Miele, 6, rue des Ecoles Laïques. Right near the hostel. Wash 17F per 6kg, dry 4F per 7 1/2min. Soap 1F. Open daily 7:30am-9pm.

English Bookstore: Bookshop, 4, rue de l'Université (tel. 67 66 09 08). Large selection includes newspapers, periodicals, and video rental. English-speaking workers during academic year. Carries the complete line of *Let's Go.* Open Tues.-Sat. 9:30am-1pm and 2:30-7pm; Sept.-June Mon.-Sat. 9:30am-1pm and 2:30-7pm.

Library: American Library, 11, rue St-Louis (tel. 67 58 13 44). Huge collection of current periodicals and large selection of books. Membership (150F per year, students 100F per year) required to check out materials. Open Mon. 2-6:30pm, Tues. and Fri. 10am-6:30pm, Wed.-Thurs. 10am-noon and 2-6:30pm, Sat. 10am-noon.

French-American Center: 4, rue St-Louis (tel. 67 92 30 66). Has a small bookstore (tel. 67 58 13 44). All anglophones welcome. Center organizes Franco-American soirées. Open Mon.-Fri. 9am-noon and 2-6:30pm.

Women's Center: Union Femme Civique et Sociale, 1, rue Embouque d'Or (tel. 67 60 57 93). A headquarters for almost all issues pertinent to women. **Centre d'Information Feminine** (tel. 67 60 59 65) at the same address, and **Droit des Femmes et des Familles,** 38, rue Proudhon (tel. 67 72 00 24), both advise women on their social, legal, and professional rights.

Services for People with Disabilities: Centre Communal d'Action Sociale, 9, rue Montpellieret (tel. 67 60 58 44).

Crisis Lines: SOS Amitié: tel. 67 63 00 63. 24-hr. crisis line.

Hospital: St-Eloi, 2, av. Bertin Sans (tel. 67 33 90 50).

Medical Assistance: SAMU: tel. 15.

Police: 22, av. Georges Clemenceau (tel. 67 22 78 22). **Emergency:** tel. 17.

Accommodations and Camping

In addition to the youth hostel and *foyers,* Montpellier has many inexpensive hotels. During the summer, find a room in the morning; it may be booked by afternoon. Expect a 4F city tax per person at most hotels.

Auberge de Jeunesse (HI), 2, impasse de la Petite Corraterie (tel. 67 60 32 22). Take bus #3, 5, 6, 9, or 16 from the train station and get off at bd. Louis-Blanc and walk up rue des Ecoles Laïques. The hostel will be on the left after only one block. Otherwise, head away from the station on rue Maguelone, cross the pl. de la Comédie, and continue on rue de la Loge. Take the first right onto rue Jacques Coeur, which becomes rue de la Monnaie. After a few blocks, go left up rue Glaise and right onto rue de l'Aiguillerie, which becomes rue des Ecoles Laïques. Impasse de la Petite Corraterie will be on the right. Modern facility in the heart of the *vieille ville.* 8- to 10-bed, single-sex dormitories. Coed bathrooms with temperamental showers. A safe for valuables. Reception open 8-10am and 6pm-1am. No lockout. Members only. 56F plus 15F required sheet rental on first night. Breakfast included.

Foyer des Jeunes Travailleurs, 3, rue de la Vieille (tel. 67 52 83 11), off of rue de l'Argenterie. In a renovated 14th-century mansion 10min. from the train station. Clean, modern facilities include a washing machine (wash 7F, dry 10F). Reception open daily until 10pm. Singles 80F. Doubles 120F. Sleeping bag required. Breakfast included. Lunch and dinner 35F. Call ahead. Rooms, and then only a handful, available June 15-Sept. 15.

Foyer des Jeunes Travailleurs Fontcarrade, 543, rue Fontcarrade (tel. 67 92 15 52). Take bus #1 to "Cité Astruc" or #4 to "Cité Gely." One-week min. stay, although desperate individuals might be accepted for shorter periods. Singles 460F per week, one meal per day included.

Hôtel Plantade, 10, rue Plantade (tel. 67 92 61 45). From the train station, bear left on av. de la République, which becomes bd. du Jeu de Paume. Turn left onto rue du Faubourg du Courreau, then take the first right. Friendly, English-speaking proprietor. Shabby outside, nice inside. Singles 80F, with shower 102F. Doubles 95F, with shower 125F. Showers 12F. Breakfast 18F. Usually full in June and Sept.

Hôtel Majestic, 4, rue du Cheval Blanc (tel. 67 66 26 85), 3 blocks down rue des Etuves from pl. de la Comédie. Centrally located. Rooms facing inner courtyard have small windows and will get hot in summer; try to get the rooms facing the street. Singles 90F. Doubles 110F, with shower 130-150F. Triples with shower 200F. Showers 20F. Breakfast 18F.

Nova Hôtel, 8, rue Richelieu (tel. 67 60 79 85), down the street from the Majestic. Delightful family-run affair housed in an *ancien hôtel particulier.* 86-year-old matriarch founded hotel 60 years ago, and has hosted a diverse clientele of artists and rock musicians, including Bruce Springsteen. Bright rooms in central location. Doubles 140F, with bath 170-210F. Triples and quads with bath 240-300F. Showers 25F. Breakfast 25F. 10% discount with *Let's Go.*

Hôtel Fauvettes, 8, rue Bonnard (tel. 67 63 17 60). Near the Jardin des Plantes, 25-min. walk from the station. Take rue de la République until it becomes bd. Prof. Louis Valleton. Left onto rue Faubourg St-James, right onto rue Bonnard. The hotel has its own garden. Very cozy rooms. Singles 90F. Doubles 105F, with shower 140F. Triples and quads with shower 220-230F. Showers 10F. Breakfast 17F.

Hotel France, 3/4, rue de la République (tel. 67 92 68 14), down the street from the station. Huge hotel with spacious rooms. Doubles with shower 150F, with bathroom 180F. Extra person 80F. Breakfast 35F.

Camping: The closest is about 8km away in Lattes, a coastal town. **L'Eden** (tel. 67 68 29 68) offers four-star camping with amenities including hot showers, a pool, electricity and ping-pong (site for 2 people 120F). **L'Oasis** offers 2-person sites for 86F50 with showers and electricity. Both sites are open April-Oct. To reach either take the #17 bus (direction: "Palavas") from the train station and get off at "Lattes."

Food

Rue des Ecoles Laïques in the old city offers a variety of ethnic choices, including Greek, Egyptian, Italian, and Lebanese. Inexpensive *saladeries* and *crêperies* abound on rue Jules Latreille, off pl. St-Côme. The **university restaurants** are **Arceaux,** rue Gustave; **Boutonnet,** rue Emile Duployé; **Triolet,** rue Prof. Joseph Anglada; and **Vert-Bois,** 209, rue de la Chênaie. In summer, check at **CROUS,** 2, rue Monteil (tel. 67 63 53 93), to see which are open; you must show an ISIC card to buy a meal ticket. Morning **markets** are held daily at pl. Cabane, and pl. Jean Jaurès. Inexpensive groceries leap off the shelves of **Monoprix,** pl. de la Comédie. (Open Mon.-Sat. 8:30am-7:30pm.) On Sundays, when all other grocery stores are closed, **Alimentation/Corbeille de Fruits,** 8, rue des Balances, comes to the rescue with doors open from 10am to 9pm.

La Tomate, at the corner of rue Rocher and rue Four des Flammes. 45F three-course lunch *menu* and 50F three-course, 62F four-course, and 80F five-course dinner *menus* offering veal, duck, chicken, and lamb, all with veggies. Savory *cassoulet maison* (house stew) is a good choice. Open Tues.-Sat. noon-1:45pm and 7-10pm.

Tripti-Kulai, 20, rue Jacques Coeur. Vegetarian restaurant serving salads, omelettes, grains, vegetables, and cheese. 42F *plat du jour*. 60F *menu* with soup, main course, and dessert. Open Mon. noon-5pm, Tues.-Fri. noon-5pm and 6-9pm, Sat. 6-9pm.

La Stromboli, rue du Faubourg St-Jaumes, at corner of bd. Prof. Louis Valleton (tel. 67 63 58 62). Pizzas 29-35F. Pasta dishes 28-36F. Three-course *menu* with wine and coffee 60F. Call ahead. Open Mon.-Sat. noon-2pm and 7-11pm.

Ramses, 26, rue des Ecoles Laïques. Exquisitely presented and delicious Egyptian specialties. Faux pharaohs adorn walls. Vegetarian plate 38F. 70F *menu*. Try the mint tea after dinner. Open daily 7-11pm.

Le St-Côme, 7, pl. St-Côme. Terrace seating. Try the *boeuf camarguaise*. Copious 50F *menu*. Open daily 7:30am-7:30pm.

Sights and Entertainment

The *vieille ville* is bounded by bd. Pasteur and bd. Louis Blanc to the north, the Esplanade Charles de Gaulle and the bd. Victor Hugo to the east, and bd. Jeu de Paume to the west. The old city's pedestrian streets, bookstores, and the sprawling pl. de la Comédie offer some of the best entertainment in Montpellier, all of it free. The tourist office distributes a walking guide and will indicate which of the 100-odd *hôtels particuliers*—built in the 17th and 18th centuries by the emerging bourgeoisie—open their doors to the public.

The **Musée Fabre,** 39, bd. Bonne Nouvelle, near the tree-lined esplanade, displays an important and widely heralded collection of works by Courbet, Géricault, Delacroix, and 17th-century Dutch and Flemish painters. The top floor exhibits contemporary and local art. (Open Tues.-Fri. 9am-5:30pm, Sat.-Sun. 9:30am-5pm. Admission 16F, students and Wed. free.) The **Collection Xavier-Atger** (tel. 67 66 27 77), next to the cathedral at the Faculté de Médecine, rue de l'Ecole-de-Médecine, contains drawings and preliminary sketches by Fragonard, Watteau, Caravaggio, and others. (Open Oct.-May Mon.-Fri. 1:30-4:30pm. Free.)

In the northwestern corner of old city, the **promenade du Peyrou** links a large **Arc de Triomphe,** erected in 1691 to honor Louis XIV, to the **Château d'Eau,** the arched terminal of a beautifully preserved aqueduct. Both the arch and the pool are illuminated in the evening. Midway along the promenade stands the imposing equestrian statue of Louis XIV, resurrected in 1839 after being destroyed during the Revolution. Follow bd. Henri IV to the **Jardin des Plantes,** France's first botanical garden. Designed in 1593 for local botany students to study medicinal herbs, the garden is now a historical monument. (Open April-Oct. Mon.-Sat. 8:30am-noon and 2-6pm; Nov. 16-March 8:30am-noon and 2-5pm. Free.)

The lower side of pl. la Comédie leads to the most recent architectural additions to the city. **Antigone** is an exceptional neoclassical housing complex conceived by Catalonian architect Ricard Boffil. The pride of Montpellier, these buildings were designed as shops, offices, and housing for people of low income. Montpellier is currently constructing **Port Marianne,** a project to regain access to the sea. (The port had filled up with sand by the end of the Middle Ages.)

From late June through early July, the **Festival International Montpellier Danse** brings performances, workshops, and films to local stages and screens (admission 50-150F). Call 67 61 11 20 for information and 67 61 41 10 for reservations. The festival office at 7, bd. Henri IV, is open Friday 9am-2pm and 3-7pm. The **Festival de Radio France et de Montpellier** sponsors performances of opera, jazz, and classical music during the final weeks of July (admission 50-150F). Call 67 61 66 81 for information, 67 02 02 01 for tickets (150-210F, discounts for those under 25 and seniors). Early June brings an array of theatrical presentations; contact the **Printemps des Comédiens,** av. des Moulins (tel. 67 61 06 30). For year-round information on plays and concerts, contact the **Opéra Comédie,** pl. de la Comédie (tel. 67 66 31 11; ticket window open Mon 2-6pm, Tues.-Sat. noon-6pm; tickets 70-165F, 55-135F for students). The **Centre Culturel Celtic,** 10, rue du Berger (tel. 67 66 22 66), off rue des Ecoles Laïques, sponsors classical guitar concerts and Irish singing.

Clubs keep hopping to satisfy even the most hedonistic appetites for *la vie nocturne*. The back half of a 1955 red Cadillac, complete with tail fins and a Tennessee "Elvis 1" license plate, protudes precariously from above the entrance to **Rockstore,** on rue de Verdun (tel. 67 58 70 10), off pl. de la Comédie. Bands of varying fame and talent perform thrice weekly. On nights *sans* band, arrive before 11:30pm and avoid the 50F cover (including one drink). Imbibe 12F draft beers amid an American and French student crowd at **Kennedy's Irish-American Pub,** 13, faubourg de Nîmes (tel. 67 02 09 87). (Open nightly 10pm-2am.) A more strictly French crowd frequents **Bar du Musée,** at the corner of rues Montpelleirent and du Collège (beers 10F; open Mon.-Sat. 10pm-whenever).

Near Montpellier

Northwest of Montpellier, the spectacular **Gorges de l'Herault** stretch for 50km along the Herault River, which runs parallel to the D4. **St-Guilhem-le-Desert,** founded during Charlemagne's reign, is only 20km from Montpellier and has ruins of castles, fortifications, and an abbey whose cloisters now reside in the Cloisters Museum in New York City. To reach the gorges, take a bus from Montpellier to Gignac or Ganges. To reach New York, take a plane from Toulouse. The **tourist office** in Gignac, pl. Général-Claparède (tel. 65 57 58 83 or 67 57 62 87) can help map out hiking tours. The Montpellier tourist office also can pump you up with information on driving tours to visit the villages along the Gorges. To reach the beaches only 10k from Montpellier, take buses #17 or #18 from the *gare SNCF* to **Palavas,** on the Mediterranean shores.

Nîmes

In 1860, an Austrian named Lévi-Strauss began exporting a heavy fabric from Nîmes to California to serve as tent cloth for gold diggers. Produced here since the 17th century, this cloth *de Nîmes* still indicates its origins in its name—denim. But two thousand years before *Guess?* and *Jordache* ever dropped a stitch, toga was all the rage in this city that still competes with Arles for the title of *la Rome française*.

Nîmes, like Rome, was built with Roman labor on seven hills. A crocodile, shackled to a palm tree and visible throughout the city, commemorates Roman Emperor Augustus's victory over Antony and Cleopatra in Egypt and symbolizes Egypt's demise. Firmly in control of the empire, Augustus sent his auxiliary soldiers to colonize Nîmes as a Rome away from Rome. Although the products of much of the ancient labor have succumbed to time, Nîmes still possesses a remarkably well-preserved *arènes* (Roman arena) and a temple, the *maison* Carrée, as well as remains of the ramparts that once encircled the city.

In addition to such classical influence, Spanish culture also colors modern Nîmes (pop. 132,000), which lies on the frontier between Languedoc and Provence. France's primary school of bullfighting, l'Ecole Française de Tauromachie, resides in Nîmes, while *corrida* (bullfights) at the *arènes* and flamenco music enliven the city with the passion of the south. A multitude of other cultural offerings, from rock concerts at the *arènes* to Greek drama amid the Roman ruins, spice up the city's alluring cosmopolitan flavor.

Orientation and Practical Information

Most of Nîmes's restaurants, shops, and museums cluster in the *vieille ville* between bd. Victor Hugo and bd. Admiral Courbet. Pick up a map of the city in the tourist bureau's branch office at the train station. To get to the main tourist office from the station, go straight up av. Feuchères, veer left around the small park, and scoot clockwise around the arena; continue straight on bd. Victor Hugo for five blocks until you reach the Maison Carrée. The Maison Carrée's façade faces rue Auguste.

Tourist Office: 6, rue Auguste (tel. 66 67 29 11). Free accommodations service. Information on bus and train excursions to Pont du Gard, the Camargue, and nearby towns. Guided tours of the city July-Aug. daily at 2:30pm (20F, students 15F). Exhaustive festival information. **Currency exchange** (1% commission). Open Mon.-Sat. 8am-7pm, Sun. 10am-5pm; Oct.-May Mon.-Sat. 9:30am-12:30pm and 2-6pm, Sun. 10am-noon. **Branch office** in the train station distributes a map with important telephone numbers. Open Mon.-Sat. 9:30am-12:30pm and 2-6pm, Sun. 10am-noon and 1-3pm. **Regional Tourist Office,** 3, pl. des Arènes (tel. 66 21 02 51). More information on Nîmes and the surrounding area. Open Mon.-Sat. 8:45am-7:30pm, Sun. 9am-noon.

Post Office: bd. de Bruxelles (tel. 66 76 67 06), across from the park at the end of av. Feuchères. **Telephones** and **currency exchange.** Branch office on bd. Gambetta (tel. 66 96 67 64). Open Mon.-Fri. 8am-7pm, Sat. 8am-noon. **Postal codes:** 30000 and 30900, respectively.

Trains: av. Feuchères (tel. 66 23 50 50). Nîmes is a stop on the major line between Bordeaux and Marseille. Direct to: Toulouse (16 per day, 3hr., 164F); Arles (38F); Montpellier (1 or 2 per hr., 1/2hr., 42F); Paris (6 per day, 4 1/2hr., 390F plus obligatory 16F TGV reservation); Orange (6 per day, 1 3/4hr., 64F); Marseille (82F). **Information office** open Mon.-Sat. 8am-6:30pm. Automatic **lockers** 15F.

Buses: (tel. 66 29 52 00) on rue Ste-Félicité, behind the train station. Timetable posted in the station. Information office open Mon.-Fri. 8am-noon and 2-6pm. **Société des Transports Départementaux du Gard (STDG)** (tel. 66 29 27 29 or 66 84 51 25). To: Uzès (Mon.-Sat. 7 per day, Sun. 3 per day, 55min., 28F); Pont-du-Gard (5 per day, 1/2hr., 30F); Avignon (7 per day, 1 1/4hr., 31F50). **Cevennes Cars** (tel. 66 29 11 11). To: Aigues-Mortes (6 per day, 55min., 35F); Alès (5 per day, 1 1/2hr., 45F). **Les Courriers du Midi** (tel. 66 92 05 00) goes to Montpellier (every hr., 1 1/2hr., 41F).

Bike Rental: Vespa, 6, bd. Alphonse Daudet (tel. 66 67 67 46). 50F per day, 250F per week, deposit 400F. Open Mon.-Sat. 9am-noon and 2-7pm. **Cruz José,** 23, bd. Talabot (tel. 66 24 91 03). 50F per day. 450F deposit. Open Mon.-Sat. 9am-noon and 2-6pm.

Laundromat: Lavomatique, 26, rue Porte de France. 15F per 2kg, dry 2F per 8min. Open 7am-8pm. Also **Washmatique,** 47, rue de la République. 17F per wash, dry 2F per 6min. Open 9am-8pm.

Hospital: Gaston Doumergue, 5, rue Hoche (tel. 66 27 41 11). Or take bus #7 to **Hôpital Carremeau** (tel. 66 27 34 09).

Medical Emergency: tel. 66 21 60 01. **SAMU:** tel. 15.

Police: 16, av. Feuchères (tel. 66 62 82 82). **Emergency:** tel. 17.

Accommodations and Camping

Finding accommodations in Nîmes is only difficult when you most want to be there—during the festival in early June and for the biggest summer concerts. Book ahead.

Auberge de Jeunesse (HI), chemin de l'Auberge de la Jeunesse (tel. 66 23 25 04), off chemin de la Cigale, 3.5km from the station. Take bus #20 from the station to the "Auberge de Jeunesse" stop, or the more frequent #8 to the "Cigale" stop, and walk 500m uphill. If walking from the station, pass the Masion Carrée (see directions for tourist office) on bd. Victor Hugo and continue straight on bd. A. Daudet. Go right at sq. Antonin onto quai de la Fontaine. Pass the Jardins de la Fontaine and continue straight on av. Roosevelt. Go right onto rte. d'Alès and bear left onto ch. de la Cigale. Follow the signs. Relaxed, hospitable hostel set in a recently completed botanical park. 78 beds in 8- to 10-bed, single-sex dormitories. Camping space available. Snack bar. Reception open 7-10am and 6pm-midnight, but generally staffed all day. HI card not required. 56F. Breakfast included. Sheets 13F. Often filled by school groups April-June; call ahead or arrive early.

Hôtel de France, 4, bd. des Arènes (tel. 66 67 47 72). Excellent location with a view of the arena. Small singles 90F. Larger doubles with shower and private toilet 130F. Triples and quads with shower, toilet, and TV 170-200F. Breakfast 18F.

Le Lisita, 2, bd. des Arènes (tel. 66 67 66 20). Wild matadorian decor. Alphonse, the mockingbird, greets you sarcastically. Elevator. Singles and doubles with shower and toilet 180F. Quads with shower and toilet 400F. Oct.-Easter 20F lower per room. Breakfast 20F.

Hôtel Concorde, 3, rue des Chapeliers (tel. 66 67 91 03), off of rue Couronne. Prime location with simple but well-kept rooms, all with telephone. Singles 95-100F, with shower 130-150F. Doubles 105F, with shower 160F. Triples with shower 200F. Showers 20F. Breakfast 20F.

Hôtel Majestic, 10, rue Pradier (tel. 66 29 24 14), off av. Feuchères near the train station. Bright rooms; some sport nifty bathrooms that swivel back into the wall when not in use. All rooms have a shower and toilet. Some rooms have TV, but save your money and use the TV lounge near the lobby. Singles 190F. Doubles 200-220F. Triples 255F. Breakfast 30F.

Nouvel Hôtel, 6, bd. Amiral Courbet (tel. 66 67 62 48). Spotless and carpeted rooms right in the heart of town. All have telephones. Singles and doubles 147F, with shower 185F. Triples with shower 228F. Quads with shower 249F. Breakfast 28F.

Camping: Domaine de La Bastide (tel. 66 38 09 21), on rte. de Générac, 5km south of the train station. Until 8pm, take bus #4 (direction: "Generac") from av. Feuchères, near the train station (6F). A 3-star site with a grocery store, laundry, electricity, and recreational facilities. 30F per person, including tent., 50F per 2 people.

Food

Nîmois specialties are often seasoned with *herbes de Provence* (a mixture of herbs and olive oil). But the city's most tempting treats are *caladons,* honey cookies sprinkled with almonds. The greatest concentration of restaurants lie along the *rues piétonnes* (pedestrian streets) between bd. Victor Hugo and the Grand'Rue. In the same area, **place aux Herbes** and the **Place de Marché,** with its single palm tree and crocodile fountain, are prime territory for late afternoon café relaxing. The terraced herb gardens and goldfish ponds on the back slopes of **Jardins de la Fontaine** make for equally unforgettable picnicking. Stock up at the open-air market near the Maison Carrée (Wed. and Mon. 8am-1pm), or at **Prisunic,** on the corner of bd. de la Libération and rue Couronne. (Open Mon.-Sat. 8:30am-7pm.)

Pizzerie Cerrutti, 25, rue de l'Horloge, behind the Maison Carrée. Portions will make your wallet smile and your stomach sing. Great homemade pasta dishes 42-50F, with wine and coffee 65F. Pizzas 42F. Open daily noon-2:30pm and 7pm-1am.

Les Persiennes, 5, pl. de l'Oratoire. Casual restaurant in an elegant setting, a 55F unlimited hors d'oeuvre bar, and a 70F *menu.* Try the curried chicken kebab or any of the fish *pâtés.* Open Sept.-July Tues.-Sat. noon-2pm and 8-10pm.

Les Hirondelles, 13, rue Bigot, at rue Porte de France. Popular with locals, this small bistro posts a 49F 4-course *menu* of traditional specialties such as *brochette d'agneau aux herbes de Provence* (lamb kebabs with local herbs) and *ratatouille niçoise* (mixed vegetables in garlic and olive oil). Wine included. Open Mon.-Fri. noon-3pm and 7:30-10pm.

L'Oeuf à la Côte, 29, rue de la Madeleine, in the *vieille ville.* Sit inside where it's cool and quiet. The 70F *menu* features *gigot de fruits de mer* (a platter of seafood specialties), and a 50F three-course *menu.* Open daily noon-midnight.

La Perle d'Orient, 26, rue de l'Etoile. Chinese and Taiwanese specialties include *canard aux champignons de chine* (duck in a Chinese mushroom sauce, 42F), and *provençal* specialties such as *langoustines avec bamboo* (lobster with bamboo, 26F). Open Mon.-Sat. noon-2pm and 7-10pm.

Cafétéria Flunch, 11, av. Admiral Courbet. Oh Cap'n, my Cap'n Flunch, delight us with your roast chicken and potatoes for 19F; bless us with your macaroni and ham *au gratin* at 23F. Open your portals to us from 1am-2:30pm and 6-10pm.

Sights

Most of Nîmes museums and Roman monuments line up between the **jardins** to the north and the *arènes* to the south, and all are within walking distance of each other. As an added bonus, admission to all sights save the Musée des Beaux-Arts and the *arènes* is free.

Nîmes's magnificent **Amphithéâtre Romain,** one of the best preserved Roman monuments in the world, has been the focus of the city's theater district for 2000 years. In summer, bullfights and concerts draw crowds who either roar for blood or wave cigarette lighters, depending on the occasion. A removable covering, installed in 1988, makes the space usable year-round; astro-turf, thankfully, has not yet followed. (Open 9am-6:30pm.) Nîmes's **Maison Carrée** (Square House) is actually rectangular; its length (26.5m) is almost exactly twice its width (13.5m). Built in the first century BC and dedicated to Lucius and Caius Caesar, grandsons of the Emperor Augustus, the Roman temple is ornamented by fluted Corinthian columns and exquisite decorations. Used as stables in the 17th century, the building now houses modern art exhibits. Archeologists currently excavating around the base of the *maison* expect to uncover even more ancient treasures. (Open daily 8am-6pm.)

The **Musée des Beaux-Arts,** in a recently renovated neoclassical building accented with marble pillars and mosaic floors, contains paintings of the French, Italian, Flemish, and Dutch schools from the 15th to 19th centuries, as well as important temporary exhibits. (Open daily 9:30am-6:30pm; Sept. 16-June 14 Mon.-Sat. 9:30am-12:30pm and 2-6pm, Sun. 2-6pm. Admission 20F, students 10F.) The **Musée du Vieux Nîmes,** pl. aux Herbes, resides in the palace of a 17th-century bishop and boasts a remarkable collection of regional arts, furniture, and looms, including a meticulously detailed 18th-century billiards table. (Open June-Sept. daily 10am-6:30, Nov.-May 10am-6pm. Free.)

While away the afternoon amid marble sculptures and vases in the **Jardins de la Fontaine,** to the left along the canals from the Maison Carrée. Maréschal, the military engineer who designed the park in the mid-18th century, drew criticism from contemporaries who thought his masterpiece looked more like a soldiers' parade field than a retreat for the city. Nonetheless, slumber peacefully around the ponds here, which are illuminated on summer evenings. Atop the hillside rear of the park, the **Tour Magne,** built by Augustus in 15 BC, was originally part of the ramparts that encircled the city. One of the few remnants of that fortification, the frayed tower now gazes over the entire city and the verdant countryside. Also in the park, the misnamed Roman **Temple of Diana,** where plays and chamber concerts take place throughout the summer, was never a temple at all, but rather the remains of two adjacent secular buildings (check with the tourist office for concert and play schedules). (Park, temple, and tower open 9am-7pm; Sept. 16-Oct. and March-June 15 9am-noon and 2-6pm; Nov.-Feb. 9am-noon and 2-5pm.)

Nîmes's younger "children" include the **Cathédrale St-Castor.** This Romanesque site, originally consecrated in 1096 and rebuilt in present form in 1646, contains a well-preserved frieze depicting famous Biblical scenes. On bd. Victor Hugo, the 18th-century **Eglise St-Paul** merits a visit.

Entertainment

From June to September, the nightlife in Nîmes centers around the *arènes*. Concerts, movies, plays, and opera are staged throughout the year and run 65-180F. The 1992 calendar featured Elton John, Dire Straits, and Joe Cocker. Ask the tourist office for a schedule of events. For more information or reservations, contact the **Bureau de Location des Arènes,** 1, rue Alexandre Ducros, 30000 Nîmes (tel. 66 67 28 02).

In the spirit of Roman gladiatorial entertainment, Nîmes sponsors three important *corridas.* In February, June, and September, the streets resound with clattering hooves as the bulls are herded to their deaths in the *arènes*. The largest of these festivals is the **Ferria de Pentecôte,** held annually around the first week of June. The **courses camarguaises** offer more humane entertainment; the aim of the fighters is to strip the bull of the decoration on his horns and forehead: to humiliate rather than to kill him. For more information, contact the Bureau de Location des Arènes.

In addition to Nîmes's festival activities, several theaters, clubs, and cinemas keep legions of visitors entertained. **Café-Théâtre le Titoit de Titus,** 7, rue Pierre Simard (tel. 66 67 64 73), off rue de Baudelaire, sponsors drama, comedy, and concerts. Pick up a current calendar at the theater; shows usually take place on weekend nights (75F, students 60F). **La Comédie,** 28, rue Jean Reboul (tel. 66 21 73 73), offers junkyard decor and live bands (Thurs.-Sat. nights). The excellent cinema **Le Sémaphore,** 25a, rue Porte de France (tel. 66 67 88 04), one block over from bd. Victor Hugo, mounts a great summer film festival during July and August. Foreign films play in their original language year-round (Tues.-Sun. 30F, Mon. 24F), and the theater also hosts occasional concerts and lectures by directors. Pick up a schedule in front of the box office. Several active bars also inhabit the streets around the *Porte de France*. **Queen's Beer** specializes in beers from, you guessed it, England, but offers a world-wide array of the malted brew. (Open daily 4pm-1am. Beers 10-20F.)

Near Nîmes

Pont du Gard and Uzès

A legend recorded by Frédéric Mistral claims that the devil built the **Pont du Gard** in return for the soul of the first creature to cross the bridge. A hare was first to make the trip, and the devil, infuriated by his poor catch, flung himself into the river. Today, bronzed bathers hurl themselves into the crystal-clear waters of the Gard River for far less than a bunny soul. Spanning the tree-lined gorge out by the river is this first-century Roman aqueduct 20km from Nîmes. One of the biggest and best-preserved of all Roman aqueducts, the Pont du Gard stretches 50km and once brought water from the Eure spring into Nîmes. The bridge itself consists of three levels of 52 arches spanning 275m and is a testament to the skill of Roman architects and engineers. Unfortunately, repairs (until 1994) have closed the narrow top of the structure, which lacks even guard-rails to separate you from the rock-filled river below, to those hoping to imitate the devil's stunt. A more mundane bridge next to the aqueduct is now the only crossing.

The Pont du Gard's **tourist office** (tel. 66 37 00 02), located 200m to the left after crossing the bridge, provides information on campgrounds and hiking as well as a **currency exchange.** (Open daily 9am-7pm; Sept.-June 10am-6pm.) The staff will also direct you to **Collias,** 4km away toward Uzès, where **Kayak Vert** (tel. 66 22 84 83) rents canoes (50F per hr., 140F per day). For 170F, you can paddle downstream from Collias to the Pont du Gard and then shuttle back to Collias. The **Camping le Barralet,** rue des Aires in Collias (tel. 66 22 84 52), offers a pool in addition to river bathing (30F per person; open Easter-Sept.).

The **Société des Transports Départementaux du Gard (STDG)** (tel. 66 29 27 29) runs daily buses from Nîmes to the Pont du Gard (8 per day, 3/4hr., 41F). Buses also leave for the Pont du Gard from Avignon (6 per day, 1/2hr., 26F). During July and August, a 64F ticket allows you one full day of unlimited travel between the Pont du Gard, Nîmes, Uzès, and Avignon; buy it before boarding the bus. Thirty-five km from Nîmes is the small city of **Uzès,** the childhood home of André Gide, surrealist poet and Nobel Prize winner. The **Duché,** a medieval fortress, stands formidably in the center of the *vieille ville.* This complex, begun in the 11th century by the noble family of the Crussol d'Uzès, who had the sole rights to mint money in the region, was renovated by each subsequent generation until the 18th century. A flag flying over the castle tower means that the Uzès are home. Inside the Duché are paintings, tapestries, Louis XIII and Louis XIV furniture, a 15th-century Gothic chapel, and a brand-new wax museum exhibit in the castle's cellars. More than 50 wax mannequins act out the marriage of Simone de Crussol d'Uzès in 1486 in something akin to a medieval Disneyland exhibit. But the fun doesn't end here. Beware the **Salle de Fantôme** (Room of the Ghost), which uses lasers and holograms to conjure an assortment of ghouls and spooks. (Open daily 9:30am-noon and 2:30-6:30pm; Sept.-May Tues.-Sun. 9am-noon and 2:30-5pm. Admission 35F, students 20F.)

The six-story **Tour Fenestrelle** has a (non-leaning) Pisa-style bell tower uncommon in France. **Place aux Herbes,** next to the castle, is the site of a lively **market** on Saturdays. Bulls stampede through the streets, and cascades of *pastis,* Uzès's anise-based liqueur, flow freely during the **féria,** or **fête votive** (patron saint's day) during the first week of August. An international music festival, the **Nuits Musicales d'Uzès,** brightens the second half of July. Tickets (50-150F) are available from the **tourist office,** av. de la Libération (tel. 66 22 68 88). The friendly office distributes transportation information, **changes money,** and helps with lodging. It also has a list of nearby farms that accept campers. (Open Mon.-Fri. 9am-6pm, Sat. 10am-noon and 3-5pm, Sun. 10am-5pm; Sept.-June Mon.-Fri. 9am-noon and 3-5pm, Sat. 10am-noon.)

The **Hostellerie Provençale,** on rue Grande Borgade (tel. 66 22 11 06), rents singles and doubles with shower for 125F, with shower and toilet for 155F. (Breakfast 25F.) **La Taverne,** 4, rue Sigalon (tel. 66 22 13 10), has doubles for 150F, with shower 210F; breakfast is 25F. The hotel's restaurant, down the street toward the cinema, posts a 65F *menu.* **Camping Municipal Vallée de l'Eure** (tel. 66 22 11 79) has sites near Uzès (10F per person, 5F per tent; open June 15-Sept. 15).

Uzès is easily reached by **bus** from Nîmes (8 per day, 2 Sun., 55min., 28F), or from Avignon (3 per day, 1hr., 36F).

Alès and the Gorge de l'Ardèche

Between the Rivière du Gard to the north and the Lazère River to the south lie 32,000 square km of rugged mountain range called the **Cévennes.** In the heart of the territory's *zone centrale,* an expansive national park, stands the former mining town of **Alès.** The unique mining museum **Mine Témoin,** chemin de la Cité Ste-Marie (tel. 66 30 45 15), takes visitors back to Zola's *Germinal.* Don a hard hat before descending 650m into the human mole hole. A one-hour guided tour and 20-minute video complete the visit. (Open July-Aug. daily 10am-12:30pm and 2-6:30pm; Sept.-Nov. 11 and April-June 9am-12:30pm and 2-5:30pm. Admission 30F, students 14F.) The mining museum testifies that the Cévennes is serious rock country, a hiker's and geologist's dream. Because of its location inside the western border of the **Parc National des Cévennes,** Alès also makes an excellent base for forays into this region of densely packed mountains. *Sentiers de grandes randonnées* (hiking trails) lace through the park. The **tourist office,** Alès's Chambre de Commerce, rue Michelet (tel. 66 78 49 10) has information on both the town and park. For more information, write Chambre de Commerce B.P. 49, 30101 Alès Cedex (open Mon.-Fri. 8am-noon and 1:30-5:30pm). **Hôtel de Flore,** 23, bd. Victor Hugo (tel. 66 30 09 84), rents doubles for 88F (with shower 130F) 30m from the station. **Hôtel Durand,** 3, bd. Anatole France (tel. 66 86 28 94) has cheap singles, nice rooms, and a friendly manager. (Singles with shower, toilet, and TV 150F. Doubles with shower, toilet, and TV 170F.) **Camping Les Châtaigniers,** chemin des Sports (tel. 66 52 53 57), maintains a pool and organizes horseback excursions. (14F per person, 8F per tent. Open June-Sept.) **Cévennes Cars,** 530, av. Robert-Bompard in Nîmes sends three buses from Monday to Saturday to Alès (1 1/4hr., 32F50).

North of Nîmes in the **Gorges de l'Ardèche,** the sparkling Ardèche River winds between precipitous white cliffs. Scrub pine blankets the spectacular, rugged canyon, Cévennes's answer to the Grand. Start the tour of the Gorges de l'Ardèche at **Vallon Pont d'Arc,** itself an unpleasant tourist trap. Accessible by bus from Alès, the town lies a few km from the natural bridge that spans the gorge. The **tourist office** (tel. 75 88 04 01; open Mon.-Sat. 9am-6pm) provides useful trail maps and lists of boat rental agencies. Rental prices of two-person **canoes** (300F per day) include the paddle from Vallon to Sauze and the taxi service back. Try **Ardèche Bateaux,** Camping la Rouvière, on the river at Vallon Pont d'Arc (tel. 75 30 10 07). If you allow only one day for a descent into the gorge, be sure to leave before 9am. Novice canoers should consider a mini-descent of 6km. All boat trips start from the riverhead at Vallon Pont d'Arc. June is the best month for more experienced paddlers.

There are plenty of places to pitch your tent near Vallon; ask the tourist office for a complete list. Two municipal sites on the river at **Gaud** and **Gournier** have no amenities (5F per night). **Monsdial Camping,** route touristique (tel. 75 88 00 48), maintains a store and a tennis court (60F per 2 people). **Ardèche Bateaux,** also on the route touristique (tel. 75 37 10 07), runs a site and rents boats (48F per 2 people).

Aigues-Mortes

Because of its location in the Camargue *marais* (swamp), Aigues-Mortes bears the morbid name "Dead Waters." And yet, despite being populated as much by swamp-bred insects as by humans, the town has survived since the 13th century. Louis IX launched two crusades from Aigues-Mortes in 1248 and 1270. For two days beginning August 23, the **Fête de St-Louis** commemorates the king with historical reenactments, jousting, and a medieval market. Though never attacked, the remarkable fortress **Tour de Constance** remains equipped with the latest in medieval Strategic Defense Initiative. Its 6m-thick walls also prevented dozens of Huguenots from escaping in the 17th and 18th centuries; one woman languished in the 10m-diameter tower for 35 years. (Open June-Sept. daily 9am-6pm; Sept.-March 9:30-noon and 2-4:30pm; April-May 9am-noon and 2-5pm. Admission 25F, students and over 60 15F.) The **tourist office,** Porte de la Gardette, pl. St-Louis (tel. 66 53 73 00), has information on walking, cycling, and horseback-riding (60F per hr.) in the Camargue region. (Open daily 9am-8pm; Oct.-June 19 9am-noon and 2-6pm.)

The **Théâtre Populaire des Cévennes** sponsors the annual **Theater Festival** in the last week of July and the first week of August. Performances include a blend of French classical and contemporary theater, a pinch of Molière, and a dash of Jean-Paul Sartre. (Tickets 70F and 90F, available at the tourist office. For information, call 66 53 91 96 or 66 53 76 95.) Held during the second week of October, the **Fête Votive** involves "harmless" bullfighting games that only citizens of the most civilized nation on earth could concoct. One of these gracefully named games, the **Toro Piscine,** involves convincing a bull to hop into a small swimming pool at the center of the stadium.

Aigues-Mortes has only a few budget hotels; call ahead. The **Hôtel l'Escale,** 3, av. Tour de Constance (tel. 66 53 71 14), just outside the town walls, provides spacious rooms. (Doubles with shower 223F. Breakfast included. Open March-Oct.) **La Petite Camargue,** quartier le Môle (tel. 66 53 84 77), has camping in a luxurious four-star setting. Prepare to do battle with a savage army of elephantine mosquitoes. (100F per 2 people. Open April-Sept.) Fresh citrus fruit stocks the **market** along the outer walls on Wednesday and Sunday mornings. The **place St-Louis** has many restaurants with terraces, but you'll find affordable places elsewhere. Try the regional specialties presented by the staff at **La Duende,** 16, rue Amiral Courbet (78F *menu).* **Le Carré d'Art,** 4, rue du 4 Septembre (tel. 66 53 77 56) serves regional specialties for 45-65F. The **cave cooperative "Les Remparts"** has free *dégustations* of the *vin de sable,* an extremely sweet wine made from grapes planted in sandy soil. (Open Mon.-Sat. 8am-8pm, Sun. 8am-12:30pm; Sept.-May Mon.-Sat. 8am-noon and 2-6pm.)

Buses for Aigues-Mortes leave from Nîmes (4 per day, 55min., 30F) and Montpellier (4 per day, 32F). Five daily **trains** also connect Aigues-Mortes and Nîmes (40min., 35F).

Provence: Rhône Valley

Visitors may safely suspect they are in the region the Romans named Provincia (literally, "the province") when carpets of olive groves and vineyards begin to unroll between hills dusted with lavender and mimosa, and the fierce winds of the *mistral* carry the scent of sage, rosemary, and thyme—the *herbes de Provence.* The enchanting qualities of the region inspired medieval troubadours in their fanciful verses of courtly love, later attracting artists such as Cézanne and Picasso. Van Gogh, too, came to Provence searching for "another light...a more limpid sky," and spent years struggling to capture the too-blue light.

Ever since Roman times, writers have rhapsodized about Provence's fragrant and varied landscape, undulating mountains to the east, haunting rock formations in the Delta, the flat marshland of the Camargue, and the rocky cliffs of the Vaucluse. Provence's apex is the white limestone peak of Mont Ventoux, which looms about 30km east of Orange. Soon after Petrarch recorded his climb to the summit in 1327, a small chapel at the top began to lure intrepid pilgrims. Petrarch also haunts the region's low point, the Fontaine de Vaucluse, a natural spring that gurgles about 25km east of Avignon. The poet composed many of his sonnets to Laura next to the seemingly bottomless pool that, six centuries later, nearly swallowed Jacques Cousteau for good. With their impressive Roman remains and cobblestone grace, Orange and Arles recline near the Rhône as it flows toward the Mediterranean. Briefly home to the medieval papacy, Avignon still possesses the formidable Palais des Papes, and today hosts an arts festival that unites masses in varied celebration. Revel in the elegant nightlife of Aix-en-Provence, or relax in the tranquility of Vaison-la-Romaine in the idyllic Vaucluse. Life plays itself out gently along the shaded promenades, next to fountains, in endless games of *pétanque* and glasses of *pastis* at sidewalk cafés.

Provence is famous throughout France for its festivals; in the summer, even the smallest hamlets revel with music, dance, theater, and outdoor antique markets. In Avignon, you'll find theater and music (July to mid-Aug.); in Arles, photography (July); in Aix, music (mid-July to Aug.); in Orange, opera (mid-July to early Aug.); and in Vaison-la-Romaine, ballet and classical music (July-early Aug.).

Ever since Julius Caesar exalted the Provençal wines in his *Commentaires,* the region has been exporting its sun-soaked nectar. Vintage wines include Châteauneuf-du-Pape, Gigondas, and Côtes du Rhône. In certain areas of Provence you can follow the *route du vin* and stop in at the local *caves* for tastings. The area's temperate climate yields a cornucopia of fruits and vegetables—dozens of varieties of melons, olives, cherries, sweet figs, asparagus, and herbs. Local cuisine includes *ratatouille* (a rich blend of eggplant, zucchini, and tomatoes); *bouillabaisse* (a spicy fish stew), served with toasted bread and *rouille* (a saffron-flavored mayonnaise); and *soupe au pistou* (soup made with *pistou,* a fragrant basil-garlic sauce). *Aïoli,* a mayonnaise sauce made from olive oil and garlic, goes with hors d'oeuvres, vegetables, and fish soup. Honey here is made from lavender and other flowers.

Provence, geographically defined as the region stretching from the Rhône River to the Alps, including the Côte d'Azur, draws a climate that ranges from unpredictable to highly pampered. Rail and bus service in the region is excellent, with frequent direct connections to most of France as well as Italy and Spain. Many people hitch along the country roads but report long waits for rides out of cities like Aix and Avignon. To see the region properly, rent a car and take only the smallest roads or, better yet, bike along them. During festivals, make hotel reservations or arrive early in the day.

Vaison-la-Romaine

Surrounded by miles of sun-drenched vineyards in the Rhône River Valley, Vaison-la-Romaine (pop. 5500) recalls a long history of international tourism. The Romans arrived in 118 BC to build the city of Vasio, which thrived until 70 AD. The Christians visited in the 12th century and built the **château** there, which became a country home for the Pope in nearby Avignon during the 13th century. Contemporary visitors no longer build, of course, but they do come in masses to admire the work of their touristic predecessors. Although the town is a manageable daytrip, do as the Romans did and stay a while. The youth hostel in nearby Séguret makes a fantastic base from which to explore the surrounding area.

Orientation and Practical Information

Be forewarned that there is no luggage storage in, or train service to, Vaison. A good bus service runs frequently to and from the SNCF *gare routière* on av. des Choralles. To reach the tourist office from the bus station, cross the parking lot of the adjoining Codec supermarket and make a right onto av. Victor Hugo to pl. Monfort. Continue past the *place* for one block and take a right onto the Grand'Rue. Walk two short blocks to the tourist office on your right (10min.).

Tourist Office: pl. du Chanoine Sautel (tel. 90 36 02 11). Delightful staff doles out free maps and historical information. Ask about guided tours, in French and English, of the Roman ruins and amphitheater, the *haute ville* and château, and the cloister and cathedral. Tours 30F, students 16F, ages 12-18 10F (tickets valid 5 days and include admission to all sites). Tourist office also offers **currency exchange** and coin-operated **telephones.** Open daily 9am-noon and 2-7pm; Sept.-June Mon.-Sat. 9:30am-noon and 2-6pm.

Post Office: pl. du 11 Novembre (tel. 90 36 06 40). **Currency exchange, telephones,** and **Poste Restante.** Open Mon.-Fri. 8:30am-noon and 2-5pm, Sat. 8:30am-noon. **Postal Code:** 84110.

Buses: Cars Lieutaud, (tel. 90 36 05 22, in Avignon 90 86 36 75), av. des Choralles. To Avignon (Mon.-Sat. 3 per day, Sun. 2 per day, 1hr. 20min., 37F); Orange (5 per day, 3/4hr., 23F); and Séguret (Mon.-Sat. 5 per day, Sun. 2 per day, 15min., 11F50). Buses double as school buses in the afternoon and drivers might refuse to go to Séguret. If so, walk 2km from nearby Sablet.

Bike Rental: Mag 2 Roues, cours Taulignan (tel. 90 28 80 46), near av. Victor Hugo. Mountain bikes 60F per 1/2-day, 100F per day, 540F per week, deposit 1200F. Open Tues.-Sat. 8am-noon and 2-7pm, Mon. 8am-noon.

Laundromat: La Lavandière, cours Taulignan. Wash and dry 25F per 5kg. Soap 5F50. Open Mon.-Sat. 9am-noon and 3-7pm.

Medical Assistance: Centre Hospitalier de Vaison-la-Romaine, Grand'Rue (tel. 90 36 04 58). **Ambulance. Emergency:** tel. 18.

Police: (tel. 90 36 04 17), quai de Verdun and rue Gevandau. **Emergency:** tel. 17.

Accommodations and Camping

Vaison's hotels fill quickly in summer. Call ahead to make reservations. The hostel at Séguret will generally have space, but beware the flocks of French school children who materialize here in May and June. Several slightly pricier B&Bs sprinkle the *ville medievale.*

Auberge de Jeunesse (HI) (tel. 90 46 93 31), 8km south of Vaison on D977 (last bus leaves Vaison at 4pm). Surrounded by vineyards and nestled at the base of a small mountain, this hostel, in a rambling old farmhouse, enjoys unrivaled scenery. Henri, the manager, has written a handful of books on hiking in the region. Pool in back. 63F. Doubles 165F, with shower 190F. Breakfast included. Dinner with local wine 66F (58F for HI members).

Centre Culturel à Coeur Joie (tel. 90 36 00 78), on av. César Geoffroy, next to the campgrounds. Spartan but spotless singles 111F, with shower 135F. Doubles 155F, with shower 175F. Breakfast included. Dinner 63F. Office open 8am-9pm. Open March-Dec.

Hôtel du Théâtre Romain (tel. 90 36 05 87), on pl. de l'Abbé-Jautel near the tourist office. Large, clean rooms with happy sunflower wallpaper. A few small doubles 120F, with shower 185F. Triples with shower 225F. One quint with shower and private toilet 340F. Hall showers included. Breakfast 25F. TV in room 20F.

Les Voconces (tel. 90 36 00 94), on pl. de Montfort across from the bus stop. Small hotel; large rooms. Singles and doubles 110-120F, with shower 150-160F. Triples and quads with shower 210F. Breakfast 25F.

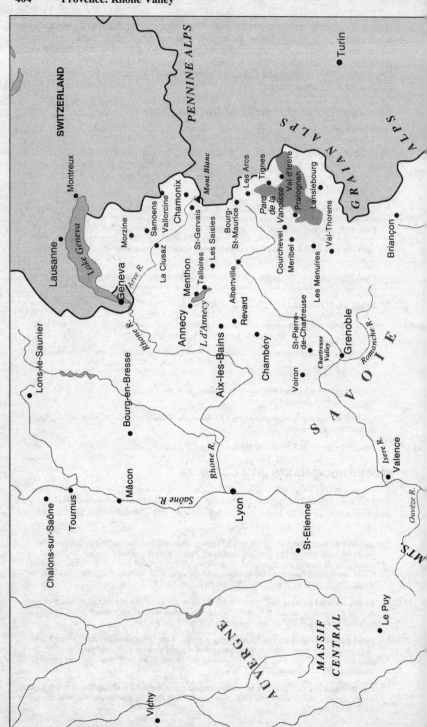

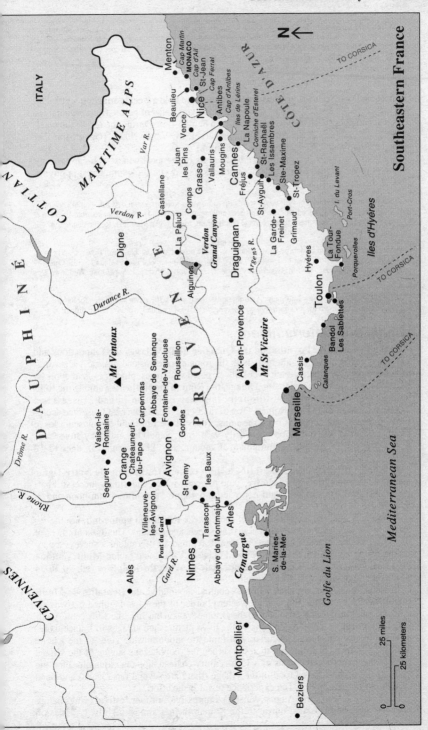

Southeastern France

Camping: Le Moulin de César, av. César Geoffrey (tel. 90 36 06 91), next to the Centre Culturel. 260 large, wooded, attractive sites. Hot showers, laundromat, grocery store, volleyball courts, and bike rentals (80F per day). 17F50 per person, 9F per child under 11, 11-13F per tent. Electricity 9F. Open mid-March to Nov.

Food

In 1483, Pope Sixtus II granted Vaison the right to hold a weekly **market,** a privilege Vaison exercises every Tuesday morning. This lively salad of herbs, fruits, vegetables, clothes, and pottery fills the town center from 8am to 1pm. During the rest of the week, squeeze the melons at the **SuperU** supermarket, av. Victor Hugo. (Open Mon.-Fri. 9am-12:30pm and 2:30-7:30pm, Sat. 9am-7pm.)

Many of the *caves* in town offer *dégustations* of the local wines. You can taste the Ventoux rosés and the strong reds of Gigondas free, if you show an interest in buying. Ask at the tourist office for a list of *caves.*

Muscade, Grand'Rue. The 68F *menu* serves up *salade au roquefort, émince de poulet à la crème et aux herbes* (thinly sliced chicken in an herb and cream sauce), and *mousse au chocolat.* Excellent *couscous.* Elegant piano playing in the small dining room. Open Mon.-Fri. for lunch and dinner, closed for lunch Sat.-Sun.

La Grasihado, pl. du Chanoine Santel, across from the post office. Oak bar, fresh flowers, and an eclectic fan collection. Four-course (84F) and 3-course (67F) *menus.* Filling salads 15-38F. Omelettes 26-28F. Pizza 33-49F. Open daily noon-2:15pm and 7:15-11pm; Sept.-June Wed.-Sun. only.

La Merinjano, 45, cours Taulignau. An Italian restaurant with a 70F *menu* and pizzas for 35-40F. Also famous in town for its *bouillabaisse provençale* (65F). Open daily for lunch and dinner.

Sights and Entertainment

In the **Quartier de Puymin** and the **Quartier de la Villasse,** the foundations and columns of Roman houses alternate with the remains of baths and mosaics. The ruins, which are precisely that, stretch over hills carpeted with roses, pine trees, and cypresses. Although not as large as that in Orange, the **Roman amphitheater** among the ruins in the Puymin excavation is still pretty impressive. The un-ruined **Musée Theo Desplans,** a veritable Gallo-Roman "Top of the Pops," boasts the best preserved sculptures, mosaics, and ceramics from the ruins. Tours of the ruins and the museum leave from the tourist office. (Ruins open daily 9am-7pm; Sept.-Oct. and May-June 9am-6pm; Nov.-April 9am-5pm. Admission to all monuments 30F, students 15F, ages 12-18 10F.)

Near the Quartier Villasse, the 11th- to 13th-century **Cathédrale de Notre Dame** and its adjoining 12th-century **cloître** stand perfectly intact, enduring a successful battle against time. (Open daily 9am-noon and 2-6:45pm; Sept.-May. 10am-noon and 2-4:45pm.)

Across the small Roman bridge over the Ouvèze River, and up the hill, are the remains of the medieval town with its twisting streets and gardens. The lookout tower of the 12th-century **fortress,** built under Count Raymond VI of Toulouse, surveys a panorama of the new town, the vine-covered Ouvèze Valley, and fabled **Mont Ventoux** (1912m). Unwind at the **Centre Internationale d'Art et de Sculpture** (tel. 90 36 34 85), a terrific outdoor sculpture museum.

Just east of Vaison stretches a line of conical mountains, the **Dentelles de Montmirail,** which constitute the waning western border of the Alps. Perched halfway up one of them, 8km from Vaison and on the Orange-Vaison bus line, the 14th-century village of **Séguret,** recently named one of the most picturesque villages in France, is renowned for its vineyards, lavender, and fantastic mountainside view of the Rhône Valley. Even more breathtaking than the serpentine, cobblestone streets of the village itself is the vista from the ruins of a 15th-century château atop the mountain. Find the path off the highest paved road in the village (there are several false leads) and head straight up for 20 minutes. The experience rewards the effort.

From early July to early August, Vaison's impressive **summer festival** brings ballet, opera, drama, and classical music to the Roman theater almost nightly. (Admission

100-200F.) Contact the tourist office. The second week of November brings **Les Journées Gourmandes** to Vaison, a festival celebrating the food of Provence. Call the tourist office for details.

Orange

In 46 BC, Julius Caesar presented his triumphant seventh legion with Aurision, a new town built over the remains of a Celtic market. The Roman homes, arena, baths, and city walls have disappeared, but the ancient theater and the triumphal arch endure among the 12th-century houses that dot modern Orange (pop. 29,000). The *Choregies,* a prestigious opera and choral festival, resuscitates the theater each July. Ironically, this ancient town is known not for its citrine namesake, but for the infinitely nobler grape. The view from St-Eutrope hill, which looms in the middle of the city, exposes acres of vineyards and sunflowers carpeting the neighboring valley of the Vaucluse beyond the city's appropriately orange rooftops. *Caves* scattered throughout the region produce red and rosé Côtes du Rhône wines.

Orientation and Practical Information

From the train station at the eastern edge of town, turn right onto av. Frédéric Mistral, which becomes rue de la République. Follow rue de la République to pl. de la République, where it feeds into rue St-Martin, and follow rue St-Martin to the intersection of cours Aristide Briand. The tourist office is on the right. The Roman theatre is two blocks to the left from pl. de la République.

Tourist Office: cours Aristide Briand (tel. 90 34 70 88). Helpful staff provides free maps and an exhaustive information booklet on Orange's sights and history. Will organize guided tours, but no longer performs spontaneous renditions of Berlioz's *Symphonie Fantastique.* **Telephones. Currency exchange.** Open Mon.-Sat. 9am-7pm, Sun. 10am-6pm; Oct.-March Mon.-Sat. 9am-6pm. **Annex,** pl. de Frère Mounets, across from the Roman theater. Maps and loads of information on the surrounding region. Open June 15-Aug. daily 10am-6pm.

Post Office: bd. E. Daladier on cours Pourtoules (tel. 90 34 08 70). **Poste Restante** and **telephones**. Open Mon.-Fri. 8:30am-7pm, Sat. 8am-noon. **Postal Code:** 84100.

Trains: (tel. 90 82 50 50), on av. Frédéric Mistral. Direct to: Avignon (20 per day, 17min., 24F); Marseille (14 per day, 1 1/2hr., 96F); Lyon (16 per day, 2hr. 10min., 118F); Paris (14 per day, 4 1/2hr., 330F plus 16F TGV reservation). Information desk open Mon.-Sat. 8am-noon, 2-5pm, and 5:30-6:45pm.

Buses: (tel. 90 34 15 59), on cours Pourtoules across the street from the post office. To: Avignon (Mon.-Sat. 5:50am-6:45pm about every hr., 5 on Sun., 3/4hr., 21F); Vaison-la-Romaine (3 per day, 70min., 24F); Séguret (2 per day, 65min., 17F50). Office open Mon.-Fri. 8am-noon and 2-6pm, Sat. 8am-noon.

Bike Rental: Cycles Lurion, 48, cours Aristide Briand (tel. 90 34 08 77), across from the tourist office. 45F per day, deposit 500F. Mountain bikes 80F per day, same deposit. Credit cards accepted. Open Tues.-Sat. 8am-noon and 2-7pm.

Laundromat: Lavomatique, 5, rue St-Florent (tel. 90 34 74 04), off bd. Edouard Daladier. Wash 20F per 5kg, dry 2F per 7min. Soap 4F. Open daily 7am-8pm.

Hospital: Hôpital Maternité, quartier Cagnan (tel. 90 34 46 33). **Clinique Mistral,** 75, av. Frédéric Mistral (tel. 90 51 23 00). **Medical Emergency: SAMU,** tel. 15

Police: Parc de la Brunette (tel. 90 51 71 04). **Emergency:** tel. 17.

Accommodations and Camping

Good rooms cheap is what you get at the hotels of Orange. During weekends in late July and early August, however, hotels are booked solid well in advance. The region's youth hostel, set amid acres of vineyards, is 20km away in Séguret (see Vaison-la-Romaine for info). Buses roll from Orange to Séguret at 1 and 6pm (17F50).

Arcotel, 8, pl. aux Herbes (tel. 90 34 09 23), between the Roman theater and rue St-Martin. Although the name sounds like a service station, this recently renovated hotel is anything but. The rooms are big, with carpets and modern, sparkling bathrooms. Singles and doubles 95-125F, with shower and toilet 150-190F. Triples 150F, with shower 210F. Quads with shower and toilet 220F. Discounts for *Let's Go*-toters. Breakfast 20F.

Hôtel St-Florent, 4, rue du Mazeau (tel. 90 34 18 53), near pl. aux Herbes. Another gem. Handsomely furnished with bright rooms and brown-tiled floors. Singles with shower 120F, with shower and toilet 160F. Doubles with shower 140F, with shower and toilet 180-250F. Telephones in all rooms. Breakfast 20F.

Hôtel Freau, 3, rue Ancien-College (tel. 90 34 06 26), off rue St-Martine. In an old converted house. Kind management, spacious rooms, and comfortable old furniture. Likely to have rooms during the week. Singles and doubles 95F, with shower 120F. Triples 140F. No hall showers. Breakfast 20F. Open Sept.-July.

Hôtel le Français, 34, rue des Lilles (tel. 90 34 67 65), next to the train station, so no lugging heavy bags across towns. All rooms with carpets and telephones. Pool and private parking. Singles and doubles with shower 150F, with shower, toilet, and TV 230-250F. Breakfast 30F.

Camping: Le Jonquier (tel. 90 34 19 83). 15min. walk from tourist office. Head north on av. des Etudiants, pass rue du Limousin, go left onto rue du Bourbonnais, then right onto rue Carrel. Le Jonquier is on the left. Four-star site with pool, snack bar, hot showers and mini-mart. Miniature golf, tennis, and pony rides extra. Reception open 8am-10pm. 25F per adult, 28F per tent. Open March-Oct.

Food

The cafés in pl. aux Herbes and pl. de la République serve *pain bagna,* the traditional salad-filled sandwich of the Midi. Avoid the overpriced bars in pl. des Mounets in front of the Roman theater. Order some local wine from the Côte du Rhône with your meal or buy some at the **Codec Supermarché,** pl. de la Mairie, off pl. de la République. (Open Mon.-Sat. 8:30am-7:15pm.) Open air **markets,** on cours A. Briand on Thursdays and on rue du Pont Neuf daily, teem with shoppers and vendors who hawk everything from fresh produce to men's leopard print micro-briefs.

La Fringale, 10, rue de Tourre at cours A. Briand. Fast food (steak and fries 25F, sandwiches 10-17F) or slow food *(plat du jour* 45F, lasagna 39F; 45F and 75F *menus).* Either way, it's cheap food. Proud owner points to his stomach as a testament to the value, quality, and generosity of his servings. Open Mon.-Tues. and Thurs.-Sat. 11:30am-2:30pm and 6-10:30pm, Wed. and Sun. 6-10:30pm.

La Roselière, 4, rue du Renoyer, off pl. Clemenceau. Great French food served indoors or out. The affable and innovative chef varies his menu with different provençal dishes. The 65F *menu* features specialties such as *gigot d'agneau à la crème d'ail* (lamb roast in a garlic cream) and *salade méditerranné.* Open daily noon-2pm and 7-11pm.

Restaurant Le Gaulois, 3-5, pl. Sylvain (tel. 90 34 32 51), next to the theater. 76F 4-course *menu* includes *escargots de mer.* Open Mon.-Sat. noon-3pm and 7-11pm.

Le Viet Nam, 51, av. de l'Arc de Triomphe, near the end of av. Victor Hugo. Affordable Vietnamese food. Duck with mushrooms (38F). Chicken with almonds (35F). 3-course 50F *menu.* Open Wed.-Mon. 12:30-2pm and 7-11pm.

Le Bosphore, 53, av. Charles de Gaulle, just past the tourist office on the left hand side. Compensates lack of atmosphere with gargantuan portions. 45F *menu* of filling French specialties. Open daily 5:30am-10:30pm.

Sights and Entertainment

Orange's striking **Théâtre Antique,** is the best-preserved Roman theater in France. A 3m statue of the Emperor Augustus, discovered in the orchestra pit and reconstructed in 1931, presides over the scene from above the portal. (Open daily 9am-6:30pm; Oct.-March daily 9am-noon and 1:30-5pm. Admission 22F, students 17F.) The ticket to the theater also admits to the **Musée Lapidaire** (tel. 90 51 80 06, *poste* 319) across the street, which houses stonework unearthed from the theater site as well as 17th- and 18th-century artwork from the region. (Open Mon.-Sat. 9am-6:30pm, Sun. 9am-noon and 2-6:30pm; Oct.-March daily 9am-noon and 2-5pm.)

Orange's other Roman monument, the gripping **Arc de Triomphe,** stands on the ancient via Agrippa, which once connected Arles to Lyon. Completed in 26 AD, this monument to Roman vanity and power—its northern façade depicts Caesar's gory victory over the Gauls—provided the model for Napoleon's monument to his own vanity and power, the Arc de Triomphe in Paris.

From late July to early August, the theater returns to its original function when the **Choregies,** a series of opera and choral productions, come to town. Information is available from the Maison des Choregies, 18, pl. Sylvain, 84100 Orange (tel. 90 34 15 52 or 90 34 24 24), next to the theater. (Open Mon.-Fri. 9am-noon and 2-5pm; after June 10 Mon.-Sat. 9am-noon and 2-6pm.) Tickets range between 40F and 750F. Special discounts of up to 50% are avaliable for those under 25, or those with disabilities.

Avignon

Nestled among the lush vineyards of the Rhône Valley, the walled city of Avignon (pop. 92,000) has shone with cultural and artistic brilliance since it snatched the papacy away from Rome some 700 years ago. Writes Lawrence Durell, "The past embalmed it, the present could not alter it."

In 1309, Pope Clement V shifted the papacy to Avignon, in his native France, partly to escape the regional warfare and corruption of feudal Italy, and partly to oblige the more powerful French king Philippe le Bel. This "Babylonian Captivity," as it was dubbed by the stunned Romans, lasted almost three-quarters of a century, during which seven popes erected and expanded the **Palais des Papes,** a sprawling Gothic fortress of white stone. Innocent VI raised the town's ramparts, which also endure today, to encircle and protect the town's population. With the death of Gregory XI in 1378, the papacy returned to Rome, leaving behind only an industry of papal aggrandizement—a legion of artists and artisans.

Papal legates continued to rule Avignon until the French government took possession of the city after 1790, dispersing its large Jewish community, expelling all religious orders, and shackling the thriving publishing houses with strict censorship laws. Still, by 1854, Avignon had regained cultural prominence as the center of the *Félibrige,* Frédéric Mistral's Provençal nationalist literary group.

It is for the celebrated Festival d'Avignon that the city is culturally heralded today. From early July to early August, people from all over the world descend on Avignon to enjoy both the official performances and the general bacchanalia in the streets. Hotel prices and restaurant prices soar, accommodations become scarce, and authorities crack down on festival-induced vagrancy. Throughout the year, a combination of sights, festivals, street performers, and plenty of French- and English-speaking students make Avignon an excellent base for exploring the Rhône Valley and the surrounding Vaucluse.

Orientation and Practical Information

Avignon lies on a bend in the Rhône River and is a stop on the TGV line between Paris (4hr.) and Marseille (1hr.). The 14th-century ramparts enclose a labyrinthine city of endless alleyways, cramped streets, and sudden squares. To reach the tourist office from the train station, walk straight through porte de la République onto cours Jean Jaurès. The tourist office is about 150m up, on the right. Cours J. Jaurès becomes rue de la République and leads directly to the pl. de l'Horloge, Avignon's central square. At night, lone travelers should avoid the area around rue Thiers and rue Philonarde. In addition, Avignon harbors many car thieves and pickpockets.

Tourist Office: 41, cours Jean Jaurès (tel. 90 82 65 11), 3 blocks from the station. Free brochure *A Comme Avignon* lists hotels, restaurants, museums, and other useful addresses. Guided tours (in French) of town June-Sept. Mon.-Sat. (25-40F, students 20-30F). Office open Mon.-Fri. 9am-6pm, Sat. 9am-noon and 2-6pm. During the Festival, the tourist office remains open daily 9am-7pm. The **branch office** in the train station (tel. 90 82 05 81, for reservations 90 82 05 81) will book hotel rooms for the same day (20F). Open daily 9am-8pm; Aug. 16-June Mon.-Fri. 9am-

6pm, Sat. 10am-6pm. **Festival Information,** Bureau du Festival, 8bis, rue de Mons (tel. 90 82 67 08).

Post Office: av. du Président Kennedy (tel. 90 86 78 00), inside the walls across from the train station. **Currency exchange, Poste Restante,** and **telephones.** Open Mon.-Fri. 8am-7pm, Sat. 8am-noon. **Branch office,** pl. Pie. (tel. 90 86 40 30). **Poste Restante:** specify which branch on letters by indicating either Poste Restante-Place Pie, or Poste Restante-Avignon (for the main branch). **Telephones.** Open Mon.-Fri. 8am-6:30pm, Sat. 8am-noon. **Postal code:** 84000.

Trains: porte de la République (tel. 90 82 50 50, for reservations 90 82 56 29). TGV to Paris (13 per day, 4hr., 340F plus obligatory 16F reservation). Marseille (17 per day, 1 1/4hr., 80F); Nice (9 per day, 4hr., 190F); Montpellier (24 per day, 1hr., 65F); Dijon (11 per day, 4 1/4hr., 220F); Toulouse (7-8 per day, 4hr., 190F). Lockers 15F. Information desk open daily 8am-7pm.

Buses: bd. St-Roch, east of the train station. Departure times for buses are synchronized with train arrivals. Information desk (tel. 90 82 07 35) open Mon.-Fri. 8am-noon and 2-6pm. **Cars Lieutaud** (tel. 90 86 36 75). To Vaison-la-Romaine (3 per day, 1 1/4hr., 32F) and Orange (3 per day, 40min., 23F). **Rapides Sud-Est** (tel. 90 82 48 50). To Châteauneuf-du-Pape (5 per day, 1/2hr., 16F). **Cars Contadins** (tel. 90 67 20 25). To Carpentras (every hour until 7pm, 17F50).

Taxis: Radio Taxi, pl. Pie (tel. 90 82 20 20). 24 hrs.

Bike Rental: Cycles Peugeot/Dopieralski, 80, rue Guillaume Puy (tel. 90 86 32 49). 50F per day, 230F per week, 1300F deposit plus a photocopy of your passport (make photocopies at the post office). Open Tues.-Sat. 9am-noon and 2-6pm, Sun. 9am-noon. **Transhumance** (tel. 90 82 05 81), at the train station. (tel. 90 82 05 81). 65F per 1/2-day, 95F per day, 530F per week. Deposit 1200F.

Lost Property: Police Municipale, *gare routière* (tel. 90 82 94 26). Yeah, right.

French-American Center: Centre Franco Américain de Provence, 10, montée de la Tour, Villeneuve (tel. 90 25 93 23; across Pont Daladier, or take bus #10). Organizes various cultural exchanges, *au pair* stays, language courses, and the well-publicized French-American Film Workshop. Open to all nationalities. **The English Bookstore** (tel. 90 25 93 23), at the same address, has an excellent collection of books. Open Mon.-Sat. 9:30am-noon and 2-7pm.

American Institute: Institute for American Universities, 5, rue Figuière (tel. 90 82 58 50), off rue de la République. Independent of the French-American Center, the American Institute sponsors language classes and cultural activities for young Americans abroad. Open Mon-Fri. 9am-noon and 2-6pm.

Women's Center: Vaucluse Information Femmes, 9, rue Carnot (tel. 90 86 41 00). Information on professional, social, legal, and familial rights. Open Mon.-Wed. 9am-noon and 2-6pm, Thurs. 9am-6pm.

Disabled Services: La Commission Départementale des Handicapés, 70, rue Montfavet (tel. 90 89 26 21).

Laundromat: Laverie, 19, rue des Lices. Wash 13F per 5kg, dry 2F per 7min. Dryers require 2F coins. Open daily 7am-9pm. **Lavomatique,** 9, rue du Chapeau Rouge, off pl. Pie. Wash 16F per 5kg, dry 2F per 5min. Open daily 7am-8pm.

Hospital: Hôpital de la Durance, 305, rue Raoul Follereau (tel. 90 89 91 31).

Medical Emergency: SOS Médecins, tel. 90 82 65 00. **SAMU:** tel. 15.

Police: tel. 90 85 17 17. **Emergency:** tel. 17.

Accommodations

Although there are no "official" youth hostels, Avignon's four *foyers* usually have room; during the festival, however, even they may be booked. Reasonable hotel rooms are reserved long in advance; expect to pay at least 110F for a single. The tourist office has a list of organizations that set up inexpensive dormitory accommodations during the festival. If you are sleeping outside, buy insect repellent and use it generously; the Rhône breeds bloodthirsty bugs. Consider staying in Nîmes, Orange, or Arles and commuting by the frequent trains (30F, 26F, and 33F, respectively).

Foyer Bagatelle, Ile de la Barthelasse (tel. 90 86 30 39), across the river, just over Pont Daladier. (20min. walk from train station.) 250-bed *foyer* in the middle of a campground. All the essentials—hot showers, clean bathrooms, spacious dorm rooms (6-8 beds per room), snack bar, cafe-

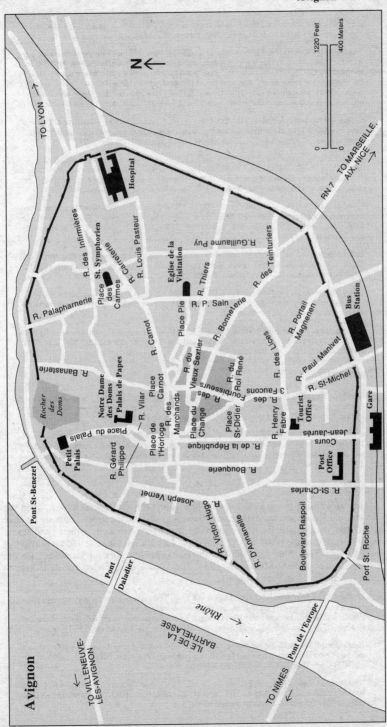

Avignon

teria, and mini-market—and the cheapest prices in town. No curfew or lockout. 49F. Sheets 15F. *Demi-pension* 118F. Often occupied by large groups; call ahead.

The Squash Club, 32, bd. Limbert (tel. 90 85 27 78). Walk 30min. along the walls to the right from the train station, or ride bus #1 from the station to "Hôpital" stop. In a simple building next to a warehouse. Chummy managers will give you a 10% discount if you can beat them at squash. Bring your own racquet, and don't count on it unless you're Mark Talbott. Spacious 16-bed rooms. Reception open 8-11am and 5-11pm. Lockout 11am-5pm. Curfew 11pm. 45F. Breakfast on the squash courts (mandatory) 14F. Sheets 14F. Call ahead during festival and off-season.

Centre Pierre Louis Loisil (tel. 90 25 07 92), on av. Pierre Sémard in Villeneuve *centre ville*. Take bus #10 in front of the post office across from the train station. Dorm-style quarters with 3-4 beds per room. No curfew. 55F. Breakfast 16F. *Demi-pension* 112F. Sheets 21F.

Foyer YMCA, 7bis, ch. de la Justice (tel. 90 25 90 20), in Villeneuve, across Pont Daladier. A 1/2-hr. walk from the train station: cross Pont Daladier, continue straight, take a left onto ch. de la Justice after 200m. By bus, take #10 (6F30) to "Monteau" stop. Swimming pool. Reception open daily at 5pm. Curfew midnight. 90F. Breakfast 20F. *Demi-pension* 155F. Open April-Sept.

Hôtel le Parc, 18, rue Perdiguier (tel. 90 82 71 55), off cours J. Jaurès, near the tourist office. Manager, in a perpetual cleaning-frenzy, keeps impeccable, bright rooms. Singles and doubles 110F, with shower 140F. Triples with shower 180-200F. Quads with shower 200F. Showers 12F. Breakfast 16F.

Hôtel Mignon, 12, rue Joseph Vernet (tel. 90 82 17 30). Carpeted rooms with telephone and TV. Small "library" stocks English books. Trade read for unread books. Singles with shower 130F. Doubles with shower 165F. Triples with shower and toilet 220F. Breakfast 20F.

Hôtel Splendid, 17, rue Perdiguier (tel. 90 86 14 46), off cours J. Jaurès near the tourist office. Spacious rooms right near *centre ville*. Singles with shower 140F. Triples with shower 200F. Quads with shower 250F. Breakfast 20F.

Hôtel Innara, 100, rue Joseph Vernet (tel. 90 82 54 10), near rue de la République. Friendly manager with 2 cats and a narcoleptic dog. Singles and doubles 130F, with shower 150F. Triples with shower 220F. Quads 250F. Breakfast 22F.

Camping

Camping Bagatelle (tel. 90 86 30 39), Ile de la Barthelasse. Walk 20min. from station over Pont Daladier. Immense campground with cafeteria, 2 bars, supermarket, and laundromat next to the Piscine Municipale (pool, 18F per day). 15F per person, 7F per tent.

Camping Municipale St-Bénezet (tel. 90 82 63 50), Ile de la Barthélasse, 10min. past Bagatelle. Hot showers, laundry, restaurant, supermarket, and tennis and volleyball courts. Grassy, shady tent sites. Reception open 8:30am-10:00pm. 16F per person, children 9F, 13F per tent. Electricity 13F. Open March-Oct.

Food

The cafés filling pl. de l'Horloge are best suited for after-dinner drinks, when the clowns, musicians, and annoying mimes have appeared on the streets. **Parc de Rocher des Doms,** overlooking the Rhône, provides many scenic spots for a picnic and has an outdoor café near the pond. Buy provisions in **Les Halles,** the large indoor **market** in pl. Pie (open Tues.-Sun. 8am-1pm), at the less expensive open-air market outside the city walls near porte St-Michel (Sat.-Sun. 7am-10pm), or at **Codec,** rue de la République (open Mon.-Sat. 9am-7:15pm).

Le Pain Bis, 6, rue Armand-de-Pontmartin, off a small *place* with some outdoor seating, pastel colors, and contemporary art. All the ingredients are *biologique* (organic), and most dishes are vegetarian. Sandwiches and cold plates for lunch, and 54F (lunch only) and 67F *menus*. Open daily noon-2:30pm and 7pm-midnight, Sept.-June Mon.-Sat. noon-2:30pm and 7:30-11pm.

Restaurant l'Arlequin, 84, rue Bonneterie. Jolly multicolored dining room and wonderful local cuisine. *Curry d'Agneau* (lamb curry), 85F and *Feuilleté d'escargots,* 122F. 2-course lunch special 47F. Open Mon.-Sat. noon-3pm and 7-10pm.

Restaurant Oanh, 31bis, rue Bonneterie. Small, family-run Vietnamese restaurant with great food at great prices. Curry chicken 31F. *Crevettes Xao Lang* (shrimp in red curry noodles and vegetables) 35F. Open daily 11am-2pm and 6-11pm.

Cafétéria Flunch, 11, bd. Raspail, off rue de la République. Goodbye atmosphere, hello Cap'n Flunch. Yup, he's back and he wants you to eat cheap(ly). Roast chicken with 2 veggies for a low 19F. Fish, rice, and veggies at an unbeatable 25F. Open Mon.-Sat. 11am-10pm, Sun. 1-10pm.

Tapas Dobega, 10, rue Galante. Tasty small dishes best for a light lunch or snack. Wide variety of hot and cold foods and salads, including fried mushrooms, squid, pork, gazpacho, and other Spanish flavors served amid matadorian decor. 10F per serving. Open Mon.-Sat. noon-1:30am, Sun. 7pm-1:30am.

Tache d'Encre, 22, rue des Teinturiers. A pleasant *café-théâtre* with live jazz and blues music on most weeknights and excellent French cuisine. 49F (3-course, lunch only), 74F, and 89F *menus* featuring pork, chicken, or veal in mushroom sauce, vegetables, and dessert. *Plat du jour* 38F. Open Tues.-Sat. noon-2pm and 7:30-midnight, Sun.-Mon. 7:30-midnight.

Le Magnanen, 19, rue St-Michel, off pl. des Corps Saints. Tiny and popular with locals. Talented Canadian chef explores his French roots, preparing a 3-course 50F *menu*, and a 5-course 90F *menu*, wine included. Open Mon.-Fri. 11:45am-2pm and 6:45-8:30pm, Sat. 11:45am-2pm.

Sights

The **Palais des Papes** (tel. 90 86 03 32) stands in white-granite majesty at the highest point in Avignon. Benoît XII, the third of the *avignonnais* popes, ordered the construction of the palace in the 14th century. Expanded by Clement VI and other popes, the palace became a residence for papal legates and vice-legates during the 17th and 18th centuries, and was converted to military barracks in 1906. Take the self-guided tour through the interior of the palace. (Open daily 9am-7pm; Oct. and April-June daily 9am-12:15pm and 2-6pm; Nov.-March 9am-noon and 2-5pm. Admission 38F, students and over 65 29F. English guided tours daily 10am and 3pm. 46F, students 37F.)

On a hillside next to the palace, **Le Rocher des Doms,** a lovely park with a duck-and-goldfish pond, enjoys sightlines to Mont Ventoux, the fortifications of Villeneuve-les-Avignon, and 12th-century **Pont St-Bénezet,** which was the "Pont d'Avignon" immortalized in a French nursery rhyme. Today, this fabled bridge ends disillusioningly halfway across the Rhône, only four of its original 22 arches intact. It is said that, in 1177, angels instructed a shepherd boy, St-Bénezet, to begin the 11-year task of erecting the bridge. Enjoy the bridge from where you are; it costs 10F to walk on the bridge, and, alas, 'tis not really worth it. (Open daily 7:30am-9pm.) Newer **Pont Daladier,** which makes it all the way across the river to the campgrounds, is a good vantage point from which to see both the broken bridge and the towering Palais des Papes—and it costs nary a centime.

Adjacent to the Palais sits 12th-century **Cathédrale Notre-Dame-des Doms,** a Romanesque church with a richly decorated interior. Popes Benoît XII and Jean XXII lie ornately entombed within. Traces of a Simone Martini fresco, *The Virgin Surrounded by Angels,* remain above the porch. (Open daily 11am-6pm. Free.) At the far end of pl. du Palais, is the **Petit Palais** (tel. 90 86 44 58), once home to cardinals, holds fine Italian primitive, Gothic, and Renaissance paintings and sculpture. (Open Wed.-Mon. 9:30-11:50am and 2-6pm. Admission 16F, students 8F; Oct.-March free on Sun.)

Entertainment

Dubbed *"la ville sonnante"* ("the ringing city") by Rabelais because of its plethora of bells, Avignon still peals every year from early July through early August, when the riotous **Festival d'Avignon** spurts an effusion of drama, dance, mime, and everything else from Gregorian chants to an all-night reading of the *Odyssey.* (Admission varies with event.) Hardly a cloister, church, or basement stands without a play in its gut. The official festival, the most prestigious theatrical gathering in Europe, has at least 12 different venues, the courtyard of the Palais des Papes and the municipal theater being the most impressive. (Events start 9:30-11pm. Tickets 90-165F per event; other venues are cheaper; some are free.) The festival has at least 65 official locations, but every street resounds with the euphony. The cinemas in town show an average of five movies each day; afternoon and midnight showings are usually cheaper. During and after the festival, there are jazz beats nightly around pl. Grillon and theater around pl. de l'Horloge.

On Bastille Day, Avignon ignites an impressive fireworks display. For information, contact the Bureau de Festival, 8bis, rue de Mons (tel. 90 82 67 08).

Although it calms down the rest of the year, Avignon hardly hibernates. The **Théâtre du Balcon**, 38, rue Guillaume Puy (tel. 90 85 00 80), stages dramatic performances almost every weekend (tickets 40-80F). Regular performances of opera, drama, and classical music take place in the **Opéra d'Avignon**, pl. de l'Horloge (tel. 90 82 23 44). The **Centre d'Action Culturelle**, 8bis, rue de Mons (tel. 90 82 67 08), provides information on jazz clubs and theater groups. Rue des Teinturiers is lined with theaters, including the **Théâtre du Chien qui Fume** at #75 (tel. 90 85 25 87) and **La Tache d'Encre** at #22 (tel. 90 85 46 03). Avignon's cinemas throw film festivals during the summer months. The **Utopia Cinéma,** 15, rue Galante (tel. 90 82 65 36), off rue de la République, screens a wide variety of avant-garde flicks throughout the year, including an annual American film festival sponsored by the Institut Américain in late June. (Admission 30F, card for 10 showings 220F). Not to be outdone, the **French-American Film Workshop,** in conjunction with the French-American Center, unwinds its own reels at a festival the first week in July to recognize young American and French directors. (Admission 30F, pass for 10 showings 150F.) The **Maison Jean Vilar,** 8, rue de Mons (tel. 90 85 59 64), plays free videos; the schedule varies, and it may be necessary to make a reservation. The **Palace Cinéma,** 38, cours Jean Jaurès (tel. 90 86 13 94), rolls five films per day in French only. (Admission 40F, students, under 18 or over 65 30F.)

If you'd rather deliver your own lines, join the raucous French and American student crowd at **Pub Z,** pl. Pie. Lively bars color pl. des Corps Saints (Holy Bodies). Heavenly bodies or not—be careful whom you "get to know" as Avignon's prostitutes have taken a liking to this street. Cheap suds and an expensive sound system draw a boisterous Australian and backpacker crowd to the **Koala Bar,** 2, pl. des Corps Saints (tel. 90 86 80 87). (Happy hour Wed. and Fri.-Sat. 9-10pm). According to hip locals, the best and most hedonistic clubs lie well outside city limits. **Le Sholmès,** 20km away in Rochefort de Gard (tel. 90 31 73 43), offers wild dancing around its indoor swimming pool. In town, **Le Top,** 27, rue Bancasse (tel. 90 86 31 55), is the best to bust a move.

Near Avignon: The Vaucluse

The Vaucluse, affectionately called "the crossroads of Southern Europe" because of its central location between Spain and Italy, is one of France's smallest *départements*. But parked within its 2200 square miles in southeastern France are the foothills of the Alps (to the east), the Rhône Valley (to the west) and the Vaucluse mountain range. All the region's villages celebrate their existences with lavish annual festivals. In the most extravagant of these, thousands converge on the Vaucluse for Avignon's annual summer festival, Orange's *Choregies,* and Vaison's tri-annual *Choralies.*

Carpentras (pop. 26,000), Petrarch's boyhood home, dwells at the base of Mt. Ventoux (1820m), the Vaucluse's highest peak. The town, 25km southeast of Avignon, retains a Roman arch, a 14th-century synagogue (the oldest in France, and the second-oldest in all of Europe (open Mon.-Fri. 10am-noon and 3-5pm; free), and the **Cathédrale St-Siffrein,** a flamboyant Gothic hybrid.

Carpentras stands up to the Vaucluse's festival tradition with its annual **Passion Festival.** From mid-July to mid-August, 19th-century operettas, ballet, drama, and classical music animate the open-air theater. (Admission 80-300F, students from 30F.) For information, contact Festival, B.P. 113, 84200 Carpentras (tel. 90 63 46 35). After July 1, the festival office operates at pl. d'Inguimbert (tel. 90 63 05 72). The Carpentras **tourist office,** 170, allées Jean Jaurès (tel. 90 63 00 78 or 90 63 57 88), distributes a list of hotels but won't make reservations. (Open Mon.-Sat. 9am-7pm, Sun. 9:30am-12:30pm; Sept.-June Mon.-Sat. 9am-12:30 and 2-6:30pm.) Try **Hôtel La Lavande** on bd. Alfred Roger (tel. 90 63 13 49). Doubles are 100F. Hourly **buses** run from Avignon to Carpentras (45min., 17F50). For more information, call **Cars Contadins,** 38, av. Wilson (tel. 90 67 20 25).

The largest natural spring in Europe courses through the tiny village of **Fontaine-de-Vaucluse.** Even Jacques Cousteau has yet to explore the 400m-deep pool at the spring's source just below the cliffs. Unfortunately, this idyllic natural setting loses a certain *je ne sais quoi* during summer when you-know-what-loads of visitors descend upon the village. A moss-covered waterwheel and stone bridge now share the town center with gift stands, overpriced restaurants, and snack bars. This hyper-development is well-contained, however, and around the scenic **auberge de jeunesse (HI),** chemin de la Vignasse (tel. 90 20 31 65), on a hill 11km out of town, the valley exalts in un-spoiled splendor. From town, cross the bridge heading away from Avignon and follow the signs. The helpful manager has extensive information on hiking, and bike rides of varying lengths throughout the region. These excursions will reveal the Vaucluse's nat-ural beauty, perhaps convincing you, as they did Henry James, that "Vaucluse is indeed cockneyfied, but...I should have been a fool, all the same, not to come." (Lockout 10am-5:30pm. Curfew 11:30pm. Members only. 7- to 8-bed dorms 40F. Breakfast 15F. Kitchen facilities. Limited camping available.)

Contrary to popular belief, the picturesque village of **Châteauneuf-du-Pape** (pop. 2070) was not named after the world-famous wine. Nay, it was named after the castle built between 1316 and 1333 for Pope John XXII, and destroyed by four escaping Ger-man soldiers in August 1944. One wall remains visible on the outskirts of town. Luck-ily, however, the then-famous pope's vineyards continue to produce the divine elixir known the world over.

The **Musée des Vieux Outils de Vignerons,** av. Pierre de Luxembourg (tel. 90 83 70 07), a small museum of winemaking in the Père Anselme *cave,* displays the equipment and techniques used in making the famous wine. You might even get lessons on the pretentious art of wine-tasting. (Open daily 8am-noon and 2-6pm. Free.) The **tourist office,** pl. du Portail (tel. 90 83 71 08), in the center of town, provides a long list of *caves* accepting visitors. (Open Tues.-Sat. 9am-8pm; Sept.-Oct. and Dec.-June Tues.-Sat. 9am-12:30 and 2-6pm.) Tasting the grape derivative is free at all of these as long as you appear to be a serious buyer. Small *caves* will give you more personal attention. One such place is **Domaine Perges,** 8, av. St-Joseph (tel. 90 83 71 34), which sells both white and red wine at 35-45F a bottle. (Open Mon.-Sat. 11am-6pm; April-June Sat.-Sun. 2-6pm.) For more information on area *caves,* contact the Fédération des Syndicats de Producteurs de Châteauneuf-du-Pape, route d'Avignon (tel. 90 83 72 21). Five bus-es per day leave Avignon for Châteauneuf-du-Pape (16F). Contact **Les Rapides du Sud-Est** (tel. 90 82 51 75) for more information.

Châteauneuf is a great day trip but an expensive overnight trip. If you choose to sleep in the valley of the grape, **La Mère Germaine,** pl. de la Fontaine (tel. 90 83 70 72), next to the tourist office offers comfortable doubles for 150F, with shower 200F. Two km away by foot lies the two-star campground **Islon St-Luc,** ch. des Grands Serres (tel. 90 83 76 77; 16F per person, 12F per site; open April-Sept.). All of Châteauneuf's restaurants consider their cuisine *haute* and charge accordingly.

During WWII, the Germans scorched the tiny mountain hamlet of **Gordes,** 35km from Avignon, in a disaster that left much of Gordes in rubble. Luckily, some of the vil-lage's medieval stone buildings survived with rock-hard resilience, as has its sense of jubilee. A fashionable retreat for Avignon festival directors and actors, the village wel-comes its own music and theater **festival** during the last weekend of July and the first of August (tel. 90 72 08 14; admission 140F). During the rest of the year, the town's most notable attraction is the exhibit of Vasarely's vibrant geometric paintings in the **Château de Gordes** (tel. 90 72 02 89), a medieval castle restored during the Renais-sance. (Open daily 10am-noon and 2-6pm; Sept.-June Wed.-Mon. 10am-noon and 2-6pm. Admission 20F, students 14F.)

Hotels in Gordes are expensive, so consider making the visit a daytrip from Avignon. The **tourist office,** pl. du Château (tel. 90 72 02 75), has information on Gordes, the Village des Bories, the Moulin de Bouillons, and the Abbaye de Sénanque, as well as on camping and lodging in the Vaucluse region. (Open daily 9:30am-12:30pm and 2-6pm; Sept.-April closed Sun.) The only semi-affordable hotel is luxurious **Le Provençal,** pl. du Château (tel. 90 72 01 07), where doubles with bath go for 200F, tri-ples for 280F. The closest campground, the no-frills **Camping Municipal des Chal-ottes** (tel. 90 72 05 38), is 9km away in Murs. (Hot showers. Open Jan.-April and June 16-Sept. 15.) Getting to Gordes requires a little perseverance. From Avignon, bus to

Cavaillon (5-10 per day, 35-40min.), and then catch one of the inconveniently timed buses to Gordes. (Mon.-Sat. 3 per day, last bus from Cavaillon to Avignon 5:45pm, Avignon-Gordes 34F.) For more information, call **Rapides Sud-Est** (tel. 90 82 48 50).

Arles

Located just south of the Rhône's split into its Grand and Petit branches, Arles (pop. 50,000) embraces a little of everything for which Provence is famous. The sturdy arches of its *arènes Romaines* have survived the centuries beautifully and now preside over summer bullfights, just as the Roman *théâtre antique* approximates its original function as a stage for concerts and dance performances. Arles inspired the likes of Van Gogh, who spent his final years (and an ear) here, and Picasso, who loved Arles so much that he donated his collection of drawings, now on exhibit. The city preserves its artistic heritage by maintaining several first-rate museums and by hosting an international photography festival in early June. Additionally, Arles boasts excellent (and affordable) restaurants and spirited summer festivals, both *de rigeur* in Provence. With the wildlife of the Camargue and the beaches of Les Saintes-Maries-de-la-Mer and Piemanson less than an hour away by bus, Arles' millenia-old appeal lives on.

Orientation and Practical Information

Arles is a 30-minute train ride from both Nîmes and Avignon; lower prices make it a superior base for exploring the adjacent towns and natural attractions. The most interesting section of town lies between the Rhône and bd. des Lices. To make the 15-minute trek from the station to bd. des Lices and the tourist office, turn right out of the station and walk to pl. Lamartine (the first large square after the station). Enter the medieval gate, onto rue la Cavalerie. At pl. Voltaire, take a right onto rue du 4 Septembre and then a left onto rue de l'Hôtel de Ville. Continue until you intersect bd. des Lices. The tourist office is straight ahead.

Tourist Office: (tel. 90 96 29 35), in esplanade Charles de Gaulle at bd. des Lices and across from the Jardin d'Eté. Guided tours of the city (every Tues. and Fri. at 5pm, 2hr., 20F, students 10F). Accommodations service 4F. Open Mon.-Sat. 9am-8pm, Sun. 9am-1pm; Oct.-March Mon.-Sat. 9am-6pm. **Currency exchange** with evil rates operates same hours. **Branch office** in the train station (tel. 90 49 36 90).

Post Office: 5, bd. des Lices (tel. 90 96 07 80). **Currency exchange, telephones,** photocopiers, and **Poste Restante.** Open Mon.-Fri. 8:30am-7pm, Sat. 8:30am-noon. **Postal Code:** 13200.

Trains: av. P. Talabot (tel. 90 96 43 94). Arles is on the Paris-Marseille and Bordeaux-St-Raphaël lines, with frequent service to Avignon (about every hr., 20min., 33F); Nîmes (15 per day, 25min., 38F); Montpellier (15 per day, 70min., 65F); Toulouse (9 per day, 3 1/2hr., 200F); Marseille (16 per day, 1hr., 68F); and Aix-en-Provence (10 per day, 1 3/4hr., 82F). **Luggage lockers** 10F per day. Tourist information booth open Mon.-Sat. 9am-noon and 2-6pm.

Buses: Walk straight out of the train station to a place so modern, you'll think you've died and gone to the *gare routière* (tel. 90 49 38 01). Schedules posted outside. Information desk open Mon.-Sat. 8am-12:30pm and 2:30-6pm. **Les Carts Verts de Provence,** 5, chemin de Brissy (tel. 90 93 74 90 or 90 93 76 75). To: Aix-en-Provence (5 per day, weekends 2 per day, 1hr. 50min., 60F); Marseille (5 per day, weekends 2 per day, 2hr. 25min., 76F). **Les Cars de Camargue,** 4, rue Jean-Mathieu (tel. 90 96 36 25). To: Stes-Maries-de-la-Mer (8 per day, 1hr., 32F); Nîmes (5 per day, 50min., 34F). **Cars Ceyte et Fils,** 5, chemin de Brissy (tel. 90 93 74 90). To: Avignon (5 per day, 45min., 32F50).

Bike Rental: L'Arène du Cycle/Dall'Oppio, 10, rue Portaguel (tel. 90 96 46 83). 50F per day, 300F per week, 500F deposit. Mountain bikes 100F per day, 1000F deposit. Open Tues.-Sat. 8am-noon and 2-6pm. Also at the **train station** (tel. 90 49 92 18). 50F per day, 500F deposit.

Laundromat: Washmatic, 16, av. de Stalingrad (tel. 90 96 26 37), just past the Monoprix. Wash 12F per 5kg. Dry 1F per 7min. Soap 5F (1/2F pieces only). Open Mon.-Sat. 8:30am-noon and 2:30-7pm.

Medical Assistance: Centre Hospitalier J. Imbert, quartier Fourchon (tel. 90 49 29 29).

Police: bd. des Lices (tel. 90 96 02 04). **Emergency:** tel. 17.

Accommodations and Camping

Arles abounds with inexpensive hotels, especially around rue de l'Hôtel de Ville and pl. Voltaire. Don't count on finding an unreserved room during the first two weeks of July, when the photography festival exposes itself to townspeople and tourists alike; call ahead.

Auberge de Jeunesse (HI) (tel. 90 96 18 25), on av. Maréchal Foch, 5min. from the center and 20min. from the station. Take bus #4 from the station (4F50) and transfer to bus #3 at bd. des Lices. Get off at "Fournier" stop. Last bus at 7pm. If walking from the tourist office, take bd. des Lices to av. des Alyscamps and follow the signs (10min.). Near the municipal swimming pool. Clean and modern. Personal lockers. Bar open until 2am. 8-bed dorms. Reception open 7-10am and 5pm-midnight. Curfew 2am. 75F for first night, 65F thereafter. Showers and breakfast included. Dinner 45F. No kitchen facilities. Often clogged with groups, so call ahead and arrive early.

La Gallia Hôtel, 22, rue de l'Hôtel de Ville (tel. 90 96 00 63). A real gem. Spacious, spotless rooms in an excellent location. Super-friendly managers. Singles or doubles with shower 110F. Doubles with shower and toilet 130F. Breakfast 25F.

Hôtel Gauguin, 5, pl. Voltaire (tel. 90 96 14 35). Carpeted and well-kept rooms. Convenient location. Managers proficient in English. Singles 130F, with shower 150F. Doubles 140F, with shower 160F. Triples 200F. Open March-Dec.

Hôtel-Pizzeria de Studio, 6, rue Réattu (tel. 90 96 33 25), by the Musée Réattu. Don't let the generic name dissuade you. The hotel has bright, flowery rooms, friendly management, and an inexpensive restaurant. Glass-lovers enjoy! Singles 80F. Doubles with shower 120F. Triples with shower 150F. Breakfast 20F.

Hôtel de Provence, 12, rue Chiavary (tel. 90 96 03 29), off rue du 4 Septembre, on a straight line into town from the train station. Oil still lifes hang everywhere, but alas, none by Van Gogh. Rooms with soft beds and a view of the arena. Small but clean singles 90F, with shower 120F. Doubles 100F, with shower 130F. Showers 15F. Breakfast 18F.

Hôtel Lamartine, 1, rue Marius-Jouveau (tel. 90 96 13 83), right inside the medieval gate near pl. Lamartine. Caring management; simple, clean rooms. Singles and doubles 120F, with shower 160F. Triples 160F. Breakfast 20F.

Terminus Van Gogh, 5, pl. Lamartine (tel. 90 96 12 32), 1 block from the train station. Charming M. and Mme. Garrigues offer small, well-decorated rooms. Singles 100F, with shower 130F. Doubles 130F, with shower 160F. Hall bath 20F. Breakfast 24F.

Camping: The closest is **Camping-City**, 67, route de Crau (tel. 90 93 08 86), a terrific two-star site with pool, snack bar, washing machine, and hot showers. Take the #2 bus toward "Pont de Crau" from bd. des Lices (6F50) and get off at the "Greauxeaux" stop. 15F per person, 15F per tent. Open March-Oct.

Food

Unique in the pantheon of Provençal cities, the restaurants of Arles feature high quality and low prices. Three-course meals with wine average only 60F. *Arlésien* specialties are seasoned with thyme and rosemary, both of which grow wild in the region. Other regional produce fills the **open markets** on bd. Emile Courbes (Wed. 7am-1pm) or on bd. des Lices (Sat. 7am-1pm).

The best lookouts for people-watching are the cafés on **pl. du Forum,** where, come nightfall, everyone knows or wants to know everyone else. Alternatively, the cafés on **pl. Voltaire** by the arena are strung merrily with colored lights and animated by rock and jazz music on Wednesday nights in summer. The cafés on bd. des Lices tend to be noisy, crowded, and overpriced.

Le Criquet, 21, rue Porte-de-Lauve, on the hill behind the Jardin d'Eté. Four-course 60F *menu* includes wine and the *specialité de la maison,* veal in white wine sauce with herbs *provençales.* Seats only 23, so you get lots of personal attention in an intimate setting. Open Sat.-Thurs. noon-2pm and 7-10pm.

Lou Gardian, 70, rue du 4 Septembre, at the end of rue de l'Hôtel de Ville. Family-run place serving provençal specialties. Great food and large portions will stuff even the most accomplished eaters. 59F (4-course), 73F (5-course), and 95F (6-course) *menus.* Specialities include *La gardiane au toro sauvage,* a hearty bull stew. Open Mon.-Sat. noon-2pm and 7-9:30pm.

La Gueule du Loup, 39, rue Arènes. Run by a gregarious Australian woman and her French husband who is the chef. Elegant tile floors, patterned tablecloths, and an ivy-covered entrance. Try the delicious *magret de canard* (breast of duck) and warm *chèvre* (goat cheese salad). 85F and 120F *menus.* Open Tues.-Sun. 7-10pm.

Magali, 2, rue Chiavary, just off rue du 4 Septembre. Run by same management as Hôtel de Provence. 65F *menu* includes *salade niçoise* or *pâtés,* choice of steak, pork, or chicken, and dessert. Wine included for hotel patrons. Outdoor seating, or candlelit dining indoors. Open daily noon-2pm and 7-11pm.

Le Galoubet, 22, rue du Doctor Fanton, near pl. du Forum. Eat on a terrace shaded by a vine-covered trellis. Geraniums everywhere. 4-course *menu* including *vin* and *café* (65F). Open daily 11:30am-2pm and 7-11pm.

Le Restaurant du Méjan, quai Marx Dormoy. Appetizer: leaf through books. Main course: local specialties. Dessert: watch a movie. Nightcap: browse through photography. You can spend an entire evening at this movie theater-bookstore-gallery-restaurant. Films in original language (33F, students 25F). Try the *formule rapide:* salad, dessert, wine, and coffee (55F) or the filling *lapin à la couscous de poivre* (rabbit in pepper *couscous*), 90F. 90F *menu.* Open daily noon-2pm and 7-11pm.

Sights and Entertainment

The tourist offers three flavors of passes allowing access to different sight categories within Arles. The **Forfait 3** accesses all of the town's major sights (44F, students 31F). The **Forfait 2** accesses only the Roman monuments (30F, students 20F), and the **Forfait 1** admits you to the town's museums (25F, students 19F).

The elliptical **arènes** (tel. 90 96 03 70), measuring 136m by 107m and one of the largest and best preserved Roman amphitheaters in France (seating approximately 12,000 people), dates from the first century AD. In the 8th century, it was converted into a fortified stronghold; three of the four towers still exist, as do the pits that once contained gladiators and lions (separately, of course). Sporadic bullfights staged here from Easter through September (tickets 60-190F, children 30F) are as bloody and carnally satisfying as anything the Romans staged. The top of the structure commands a fine view of the Rhône, the Camargue, and surrounding plains. (Open daily 8:30am-7pm; Oct. and March 9am-12:30pm and 2-6pm; Nov.-Feb. 9am-noon and 2-4:30pm; April 9am-12:30pm and 2-6:30pm; May 9am-12:30pm and 2-7pm. Admission 17F, students 8F50.)

The **Musée Réattu,** rue du Grand Prieuré (tel. 90 49 37 58), once a stronghold of the knights of Malta, now houses a collection of contemporary art, watercolors, and oils of the Camargue by Henri Rousseau, and two rooms of canvases by the neoclassical artist Réattu. The museum takes most pride, however, in the 57 drawings with which Picasso honored the town in 1971, not long before his death. Upstairs, prominent modern European photographers and artists stage temporary exhibitions. (Open June-Sept. daily 9am-12:30pm and 2-7pm; Oct.-Jan. daily 10am-12:30pm and 2-5pm; Feb.-May daily 10am-12:30pm and 2-7pm. Admission 15F, students 8F50.) The **Musée Arlaten,** rue de la République (tel. 90 96 08 23), is a superb folk museum founded in 1896 by author Frédéric Mistral. Mistral used the money he received from his Nobel Prize in literature to buy the 16th-century townhouse the museum now occupies. The attendants wear regional dress, and the signs are in the local dialect. (Open daily 9am-noon and 2-7pm; winter Tues.-Sun. 9am-noon and 2-5pm. Admission 12F, students 6F50.)

The nearby **Théâtre Antique** (tel. 90 96 93 30) retains the plan, if little of the elevation, of the original Augustan construction. Only two marble columns remain of the original stage wall, contributing an eerie effect to summertime drama and dance spectacles. (Hours same as the arena. Admission 12F, students 6F50.) The **Jardin d'Eté,** behind the theater on bd. des Lices, is a pleasant picnic spot, but don't even think of sitting on the manicured lawns. The beautiful capitals of 12th- to 14th-century **Cloître St-Trophime** (tel. 90 49 36 36) merit a visit. (Admission 17F, students 8F50.) The **Thermes Constantin,** now in ruins, once served as public baths for the Romans. (Hours same as the arena. Admission 12F, students 6F50.) The **Musée d'Art Chrétien** (tel. 90 49 36 36) owns one of the world's richest collections of early Christian sarcophagi, second only to that of the Vatican Museum. Many of the more interesting ones come from the Alyscamps, an ancient Roman burial ground later consecrated for Christian use by St-Trophime. Mentioned by Dante in his *Inferno,* this cemetery enjoyed such Middle Age fame that pilgrims flocked to it from great distances. Beneath the museum lie the **crypto-portiques,** four extensive, forbidding galleries dating from the Roman era. (Museum open daily 8:30am-7pm; Oct.-April daily 9am-noon and 2-5pm. Admission 12F, students 6F50.)

During the second week in July, the festival **Rencontres Internationales de la Photographie** is the major development in town. Undiscovered photographers, from as far as Australia, try to court agents by roaming around town with portfolios under their arms. More established photographers present their work in some 15 locations (including parked train cars and a salt warehouse), conduct nightly slide shows (50F each, 200F for all 6), participate in debates, and offer pricey workshops. When the festival crowd departs, you can still see the remarkable exhibits the photographers leave behind (10-20F per exhibit; global ticket 120F, students 100F). For more information, visit the tourist office or contact **Rencontres,** 10, Rond-Point des Arènes (tel. 90 96 76 06).

Arles also has plenty of colorful local and regional festivals. On May 1, the ancient *Confrèrie des Gardians* (the people who herd the Camargue's wild horses) parade through town and then gather in the arena for the **Fête des Gardians,** a traditional but tame version of a rodeo. On the last weekend in June and the first in July, bonfires blaze in the streets and locals wear traditional provençal costume to the beautiful **Fête de la Tradition.** At the end, the city crowns the *Reine d'Arles* (Queen of Arles), a young woman chosen to represent the region's language, customs, and history. For the bloodthirsty, the arena holds bullfights on the festival's final weekend (admission 70F).

Near Arles

"There is nothing terrible and savage belonging to feudal history of which an example may not be found in the annals of Les Baux," wrote 19th-century historian John Addington Symonds. Eighteen km from Arles, **Les Baux de Provence** (pop. 484; 5000 with tourists) is a magnificent site of feudal ruins, a demolished castle, and gracefully restored Renaissance homes. The **Cité Morte,** the decomposing remains of the lords of Baux's 13th- and 14th-century citadel, commands a diabolic view of the **Val d'Enfer** (the Valley of Hell) and of patch-worked vineyards and olive fields. (Open daily 9am-7pm; Sept.-May daily 9am-6pm.) Once the site of a regional court frequented by the finest troubadours, the *centre ville* has surrendered to souvenir shops, expensive ice cream stands, overpriced cafés, and more than enough tourists to support them. A few legitimately starving artists populate the galleries scattered throughout the town. To avoid the clutter and the crowds, walk through **Porte Eyguières** ("water door" in Provençal), once the town's only entrance, to the Cité Morte above.

The **tourist office** in the *Hôtel de Ville* (tel. 90 97 34 39 or 90 54 34 39), about halfway up the hill between the parking lot and the Cité Morte, has maps, information on the surrounding region, advice on budget restaurants, and a **currency exchange** without commission. (Open April-Nov. 10 daily 9:30am-12:30pm and 2:30-6:30pm.) Don't make plans to stay here, however. The hotels, with a single exception, are all beyond the budget range. **Le Mas de la Fontaine** (tel. 90 54 34 13), at the foot of the village, has old furniture, a garden, and a pool. (Doubles with shower 180F, with shower and toilet 220F.) Most backpackers bring picnics to the Cité Morte; buy supplies at the small *épicerie* in the parking lot (open daily 7am-7pm). Better yet, stop at the **Monoprix** in Arles before you leave. For an inexpensive sit-down meal, try one of Les Baux's many *crêperies*. **La Voute** (tel. 90 54 45 65), near the *mairie,* offers 58F and 68F *menus* that include salad, *crêpes de la région,* and dessert.

Buses to Les Baux run regularly from Arles (Mon.-Sat. 4 per day, 1/2hr., 24F50), and Avignon (June-Aug. 3 per day, 55min., 38F). Contact **Cars Verts de Provence,** 5, chemin de Brissy (tel. 90 93 74 90), for information.

St-Rémy (pop. 9400), 21km from Arles, and the birthplace of doomsaying Nostradamus, has two predictably well-preserved Roman monuments. One km south of town on av. Pasteur, the **Mausolée,** virtually intact and decorated with bas-reliefs of battles, contains statues of Caius and Lucius Caesar, grandsons of the Emperor Augustus. The

Arc de Triomphe, ornamented with fine sculpture, is the oldest in the region. If these Roman relics aren't old enough for you, head for the **Ruines de Glanum** (tel. 90 92 23 72) across the road. Founded in the 6th century BC by Phocaean traders from Asia Minor, the city was destroyed in the 2nd century BC, restored by the Romans around the turn of the century, and sacked once and for all in the 3rd century. Only ruins of old houses, temples, and baths remain. (Open daily 9am-noon and 2-6pm; Oct.-March daily 9am-noon and 2-5pm. Admission 28F, ages 18-24 and over 60 16F). Van Gogh devotees can flock to the **Monastère de St-Paul-de-Mausole,** the tranquil 12th-century monastery where mad Vincent was treated from May 1889 to May 1890. (Open daily 9am-noon and 2-6pm, 12F). Six km from St-Rémy, in **Tarascon,** the behemoth, sprawling **castle of Tarascon** dominates the banks of the Rhône as a monument to a bygone age. To get there, take the bus from St-Rémy (3 per day, 20F) or Avignon (3 per day, 42F); or take the train from Arles (6 per day, 20min., 15F) or Avignon (10 per day, 10min., 20F).

Accommodations are cheaper in St-Rémy than in Les Baux, but singles are often expensive. The **Hôtel Ville Verte** on av. Fauconnet (tel. 90 92 06 14) has singles (70F), doubles with shower and toilet (165F), parking, and a pool. The **Grand Hôtel de Provence,** 36, bd. Victor Hugo (tel. 90 92 06 27), is an old hotel with small rooms overlooking a garden. (Doubles with showers 150F. Triples and quads with showers 280F.) **Camping Monplaisir** (tel. 90 92 22 70) squats just outside of town on chemin de Monplaisir. (10F per person, 14F per tent. Open March-Oct.) The **tourist office** (tel. 90 92 05 22), on pl. Jean Jaurès, provides a free brochure on bicycle tours of the region, including a three-hour haul to Les Baux. (Open Mon.-Sat. 9am-noon and 2-7pm, Sun. 9am-noon.) To get to St-Rémy, take the bus from Les Baux (2 per day, 7F); Avignon (9 per day, 40min., 25F); or Tarascon (3 per day, 1/2hr., 20F).

The Camargue

Between Arles and the Mediterranean coast stretches a wedge-shaped region, bounded by the Grand-Rhône and Petit-Rhône rivers, known as the Camargue. Although starkly contradicting the rolling hills of Provence to the north, this vast delta, with its tall marsh grasses and bounty of wildlife, is music to the eyes. Pink flamingos, black bulls, and the famous white Camargue horses roam freely across the flat expanse of wild marshland, protected by the confines of the natural park. The area's human inhabitants include *gardians,* rugged herders with wide-brimmed hats, and large numbers of gypsies who wander through intermittently. The rice fields in the northern sections of the marshland supply Provence tables with *riz de Camargue.* A small zone is accessible to tourists without a permit, but entry into the **Réserve Naturelle Zoologique et Botanique de la Camargue,** one of Europe's most celebrated natural sanctuaries, is limited to keepers, scientists, and researchers. Fortunately, much wildlife wanders outside the preserve, whose borders are lined by biking and hiking paths. The **Parc Ornithologique de Pont de Gau** (tel. 90 97 82 62), conveniently on the bus line from Arles to Les Stes-Maries-de-la-Mer, provides pathways through acres of marsh and offers views of a bounty of bird species and grazing bulls. Watch for snakes (non-dangerous), although your greatest foe will be mosquitoes. (Open Feb.-Nov. 9am-sunset. Admission 25F, students 15F.)

The best way to see the Camargue is on horseback. Organized rides are geared mostly towards beginners and follow somewhat limited routes. Advanced riders are allowed more freedom. The tourist office in Les Stes-Maries-de-la-Mer has a list of all the horse rental agencies in the area (80F per hr., 200F for 3 hr., 350F per day, meal included). Rates remain constant from one establishment to another.

Although most of the trails are open only to horseback riders, bicycle touring is another way to see much of the area. Keep in mind that the bike trails may be sandy and difficult to ride on, making the more expensive mountain bikes a wise choice at Les Stes-Maries's rental shop. Trail maps are available from the tourist office at Les Stes-Maries-de-la-Mer. Bring an ample supply of fresh water—it gets hotter than Hades and there aren't *any* Coke machines. A two-hour pedal will reveal some of the area, but you'll need a whole day if you plan to stop along the miles of wide, deserted white-sand beaches lining the bike trail. **Camargue Safaris** (tel. 90 97 86 93) offers jeep tours of the Camargue—or at least the limited portion accessible to cars (55F per hour, 1/2-day 200F, full day 320F, meal included). One-hour **cruises** ply the interior waters of the Camargue (60F, under 7 30F). Schedules vary throughout the year; call Le Tiki III (tel. 90 97 81 68 or 90 97 81 22) for more information.

Les Saintes-Maries-de-la-Mer

Unofficial capital of the Camargue, Les Saintes-Maries-de-la-Mer harbors a rich maritime and Biblical history. It is here that Mary Magdalen, Mary, mother of the Apostles John and James, and Mary, sister of the Virgin, are said to have landed in 40 AD, after fleeing persecution in Palestine, giving their names to the town. Today, Les Saintes caters primarily to tourists and sun-worshipers lured not by the natural wealth of the Camargue but by the din of temperate, crashing Mediterranean waves. Consequently, the town effervesces with snack trailers and honky-tonk stores rife with cheap sunglasses and tacky flip-flops. Avoid this and go instead to the squares and restaurants with lulling flamenco music and dancing, enjoyed also by the large gypsy population in these areas; many, in fact, claim relation to Chico, lead singer of the *Gypsy Kings* (the Camargue's #1 export). If you must do it, outside of town stretches some of the finest, least crowded sand in all of France.

Orientation and Practical Information

There is no train service to Les Stes-Maries, but regular buses make the trip from Arles in under an hour. To get to the tourist office from the bus stop, walk down av. de la République (just next to pl. Mireille) to the beach. The tourist office is ahead on the right.

Tourist Office: 5, av. van Gogh (tel. 90 97 82 55), next to the arena. Information on horseback riding and camping. Maps for walking tours. **Currency exchange.** Open daily 9am-8pm; Sept.-June daily 9am-12:30pm and 1:30-7pm.

Currency Exchange: Rates across town insult all economies but the French. **Bureau de Change,** 3, av. van Gogh, next to the tourist office. Open June-Sept. daily 9am-1pm and 3-6pm. Also at the **tourist office** Oct.-May daily 9:30am-noon and 2:30-6pm.

Post Office: av. Gambetta. **Poste Restante** and **telephones.** Open Mon.-Fri. 9am-noon and 2-5pm, Sat. 8:30-11:30am. **Postal Code:** 13460.

Buses: Regularly from Arles (11 per day, 10 on weekends, 55min., 32F). Buses leave from the area opposite the Station Bar on bd. des Lices in Arles and from the *gare routière*. In Les Stes-Maries, the buses stop just north of pl. Mireille. Call **Les Cars de Camargue,** 4, rue Artaud (tel. 90 96 36 25) in Arles for more information.

Bike Rental: Le Vélociste (tel. 90 97 83 26 or 90 97 86 44), next to the church on pl. des Remparts. The friendly folks here rent the best bikes and will point out great rides. 60F per day. Mountain bikes 80F. Open daily 9am-midnight, Sept.-June daily 9am-7pm. Passport deposit. **Camargue Vélo,** 27, rue Frédéric Mistral (tel. 90 97 94 55 or 90 47 94 55). Mountain bikes 80F per day. Passport and 200F deposit. Open Feb.-Nov. daily 8:30am-8:30pm.

Hospital: tel. 90 97 83 07. **Emergency:** tel. 18.

Police: (tel. 90 97 89 50), av. van Gogh, near the tourist office. **Emergency:** tel. 17.

Accommodations, Camping, and Food

Although sleeping on beaches is illegal, rows of cocooned tourists invariably decorate the sand at night. Hotels fill quickly in summer, and rooms for under 100F are scarce. You can always base yourself in Arles and make the town a daytrip.

Auberge de Jeunesse (HI), hameau de Pioch Badet (tel. 90 97 51 72), a regular bus stop between Les Stes-Maries and Arles (6 per day; from Ste-Maries, 15min., 10F; from Arles, 40min., 25F). Get off at "Pioch Badet" stop. Fills early in summer, so take the 8am bus from Arles. Reception open daily 7:30-11am and 5-11pm; Oct.-June daily 7:30-11am and 5-11pm. Members only. 56F, under 15 42F. Breakfast included. Dinner 44F. Sheets 13F. Bike rental 35F per 1/2-day, 70F per day.

Hôtel Le Delta, pl. Mireille (tel. 90 97 81 12), just south of the bus stop. Very clean rooms with loud flowery wallpaper. Doubles with shower and toilet 215F. Triples with shower and toilet 275F. Quads 330F. Breakfast 25F.

La Roulotte, 5, rue Joseph Roumanille (tel. 90 97 71 70). Swedish owner, fluent in five languages, lets clean and simple rooms. Singles 135F. Doubles 155F. Triples 210F. Quads 265F. Hall showers included. Breakfast 15F. By 1993 will offer vegetarian dinners, salads, and swordfish. Open Easter-Oct. 15.

Hôtel Méditerranée, 4, bd. Frédéric Mistral (tel. 90 97 82 09), off rue Victor Hugo. Plush, spotless, comfortable rooms. Doubles 160F, with shower 200F, with shower and toilet 260F. Breakfast 24F. Open Jan.-Nov. 15.

Camping: La Brise (tel. 90 47 84 67), an oceanside site 5min. from the center of town. 22F per person, ages 5-12 9F30, 24F per tent. **Le Clos du Rhône** (tel. 90 97 85 99), 2km on the other side of town on the banks of the Petit Rhône. Close to the beach and the center of town. Quieter 4-star site with pool and open-air theater. 25F per person, ages 5-12 15F, 28F per tent or caravan. Open April 15-Sept.

Rice is the Camargue's main resource; you will find it in gelatinous cakes sold at *pâtisseries,* as side dishes in local restaurants, and on the shelves of supermarkets such as the **Casino** on av. Victor Hugo (open daily 8am-8pm; Aug. 16-July 14 8am-12:30pm and 4-7:30pm) and **Co-op supermarket,** 12, route de Cacharel (open Mon.-Sat. 8:30am-12:30pm and 3:30-7:30pm, Sun. 9am-12:30pm). A **market** fills pl. des Gitanes Monday and Wednesday mornings (7am-2:30pm). A posse of restaurants lurk away from the waterfront around av. Victor Hugo and serve up French and Spanish specialities, such as *paella* (60-70F). A generic meal of burger, fries, and drink adds up to 30F at the **Snack Restaurant,** 4, rue du Capitaine Fouque. Their 60F *menu* features French classics. They also serve a 60F *paella royal.* (Open daily 11am-midnight.) Le **Jardin des Délices,** 36, av. T. Aubanel (tel. 90 97 91 83) posts a 69F four-course *menu* of seafood and salads (30-45F). **Les Flamants Roses,** 49, av. F. Mistral, radiates an eccentric bright pink interior and a cooler terrace. Local specialties such as *soupe de poisson, moules marinières,* and melon grace its four-course 65F *menu.* The *specialité de la maison* is a creamy *bouillabaisse* (110F).

Sights

Local legend recalls that the three Marys who landed here were accompanied by the risen Lazarus and their Egyptian servant Sarah, patron saint of the gypsies. In the 19th century, gypsies began attending the annual **Pèlerinage des Gitans,** held on May 24 and 25. On these days and during a smaller version in mid-October, nomadic people assemble from all over Europe and, amid flowers and fanfare, bear Sarah's statue from the crypt of the fortified church down to the sea. (For *flamenco* aficionados, this is an unequaled time to enjoy the artform.) The church tower affords an encompassing view of town, sea, and Camargue. (Open daily 10am-noon and 2-7pm. Admission 10F, students 7F.)

During the second week in July, the **Feria du Cheval** attracts horses from around the world for shows, competitions, and rodeo events. (Tickets range from 60-300F, depending on event. Call the **Comite des Fêtes** at 90 97 85 86 for more details.) During July and August, bullfights and horse-shows occur regularly at the modern **arènes** (tickets 80-200F, tel. 90 97 85 86). Aspiring botanists and zoologists should stop at the **Centre d'Information de Ginès** (tel. 90 97 86 32) along the D570, which distributes information on the region's unusual flora and fauna. (Open daily 9am-noon and 2-6pm, Oct.-March Sat.-Thurs.) Next door, the **Pont de Gau** bird park cages several rare local species in its aviaries and marks out ornithological trails in the marsh nearby (see The Camargue). In town, **Musée Baroncelli,** av. Victor Hugo, presents exhibits on the region's zoology, as well as on the history of Les Stes-Maries-de-la-Mer. (Open Mon.-Sat. 9:30am-noon and 2-6pm, Sun. 10am-noon and 2-6pm. Admission 10F, students 7F.)

Aix-en-Provence

Blessed with plentiful restaurants, elegant cafés, spellbinding museums and exuberant festivals, Aix (pronounced Ex) truly marks the spot as the gastronomic and cultural core of Provence. Even when the city swells with the summer tourist-invasion, and English rivals French for airspace, Aix exudes a *joie de vivre* that is uniquely and endearingly *provençale*. While the birthplace of Paul Cézanne takes pride in its pedigree as the oldest Roman settlement in Gaul, this stylish university city retains no monuments from that era. The rows of sand-colored townhouses with iron grillwork that flank the town's streets housed wealthy magistrates from the *Parlement,* the supreme court of justice that operated in Aix between 1487 and the Revolution. The carved dolphins and cherubs, which seem to spew water in every square, sprouted after the Plague of 1721, which made it necessary for the city to renew its water supply. The morning flower market in the pl. Hôtel de Ville injects the *vieille ville* with a most redolent brilliance.

Every summer in July and early August, Aix bursts into a symphony of revelry. While Avignon's events are more informal, concerts in Aix are refined and expensive, complete with ushers in tuxedos. Thankfully, the festival assumes a more bohemian air in the streets, particularly around cours Mirabeau; electric guitars rock through cranked amplifiers, open-air painters hawk their watercolors, and Aztec pipes cut through the din of clinking glass and pealing laughter rising from the cafés.

Orientation and Practical Information

Shaded under an arched canopy of trees and rightly hailed in Peter Mayle's *A Year in Provence* as "the most handsome street in France," the glorious **cours Mirabeau** sweeps through the center of town, linking the tourist office at the west end with roads connecting to the Catholic college at the east end. **La Rotonde,** at the west end of cours Mirabeau and accented by magnificent fountains, is the central terminus for city buses. To get it from the train station, go straight onto av. Victor Hugo and bear left at the fork, staying on av. Victor Hugo (5min.) until it feeds into La Rotonde. The tourist office will be to the left.

Tourist Office: 2, pl. du Général de Gaulle (tel. 42 26 02 93). A busy office with the customary services: hotel reservations, **currency exchange** (open May-Sept. daily Mon.-Sat. 9am-noon and 2-6pm), and guided tours of the city (daily at 10am, 3:30pm, and 9pm; tours in English Wed. at 10am; 45F, students 25F). Pick up a map of Aix with suggested walking tours. The monthly guide to events in Aix, *Le Mois à Aix* (free), is particularly useful during the festival. Open Mon.-Sat. 8am-10pm, Sun. 6-10pm; Sept. 16-June Mon.-Sat. 8am-7pm, Sun. 8:30am-12:30pm.

Festival Information: For the music festival, the Palais de l'Ancien Archevêché (tel. 42 17 34 34 or 42 21 14 40). Reserve tickets by mail or call before July 1. Open Feb.-June Mon.-Sat. 9am-1pm and 3-7pm; July-Jan. 10am-1pm and 3-6pm.

Budget Travel: Council Travel, 12, rue Victor Leydet (tel. 42 38 58 82), off pl. des Augustins. Books international and domestic flights at reduced student prices. Check Air Inter prices for domestic flights, as some are as cheap (if not cheaper) than 2nd-class train tickets. London 500F, Paris 420F. Special prices on flights within Europe for Americans and Canadians under 25. Open Sun.-Fri. 9:30am-12:30pm and 2-6:30pm.

Currency Exchange: L'Agence Voyages-Change, 15, cours Mirabeau (tel. 42 68 84 77). No commission and good rates. Open Mon.-Sat. 9am-7pm, Sun. 9:30am-12:30pm; off-season Mon.-Sat. 9am-5:30pm. Another **bureau de change** at the post office, 2, rue Lapierre. Commission 1%. Open Mon.-Fri. 8am-7pm, Sat. 8am-noon. The large banks on cours Mirabeau keep short hours and slap on a steep commission.

Post Office: 2, rue Lapierre (tel. 42 27 68 00), across La Rotonde from the tourist office. **Poste Restante, telephones,** and **photocopiers.** Open Mon.-Fri. 8:30am-7pm, Sat. 8:30am-noon. The less crowded postal **annex** (tel. 42 23 44 17), 1, pl. de l'Hôtel de Ville, provides the same services until 6:30pm daily in Aug. **Postal Codes:** 13100 and 13090, respectively.

Trains: (tel. 91 08 50 50 in Marseille) at the end of av. Victor Hugo, off rue Gustavo Desplace. To get just about anywhere from Aix, you must pass through Marseille via the hourly trains (23 per day, last train 9:40pm, 40min., 35F). To Nice (10 per day, 3hr., 150F) and Cannes (12 per day, 2 1/2hr., 142F). Station open daily 6am-10pm.

Buses: rue Lapierre (tel. 42 27 17 19), behind the post office. A confusing place. About 20 different companies operate independently. Ask for help at the information desk inside. **SATAP** (tel. 42 26 23 78) goes to Avignon (6 per day, 1 1/2hr., 75F). **SCAL** (tel. 42 26 29 13) travels to Nice (3 per day, 2 1/4hr., 130F) and Cannes (3 per day, 1 3/4hr., 140F). Other companies go to Arles (5 per day, 1 1/2hr., 64F) and Marseille (every 15min., 45min., 20F, round-trip 23F). **City buses** 6F, 10 tickets 33F. Information office open Mon.-Sat. 6am-7pm, Sun. 8am-noon and 2-6pm.

Taxis: From 6am-9pm, call 42 27 71 11. From 9pm-6am, call 42 26 29 30 9pm-6am.

Bike Rental: Cycles Naddéo, 54, av. de Lattre de Tassigny (tel. 42 21 06 93), 15min. from La Rotonde by bd. de la République. Mountain bikes 80-100F per day, 3000F or passport deposit. Also a well-stocked bike store and workshop. Open Tues.-Sat. 9am-noon and 2-7pm.

English Bookstore: Paradox Bookstore, 2, rue Reine-Jeanne (tel. 42 26 47 99), at the northern end of Parc Jourdan, off bd. Roi René. Claims to be the largest English bookstore south of Paris. 15,000 titles, including the entire line of everybody's favorite travel guide (181-220F). Open Mon.-Sat. 9:30am-12:30pm and 2-6:30pm.

French-American Center: Centre Franco-Américain de Provence, 9, bd. Jean Jarès (tel. 42 23 23 36). Organizes exchanges, *au pair* stays, and 3- to 4-week crash language courses. Unofficial apartment-finding service for members only. Membership (150F) and services open to all nationalities. Also runs a bookstore where you can exchange or buy American novels for 20-50F. Open Mon.-Sat. 9am-noon and 2-7pm.

American Center: Centre Américain, 409, rue Jean Paul Coste (tel. 42 38 42 38), near the university. Sponsors cultural events, stocks a wide selection of American publications and organizes study-abroad programs. Open Mon.-Fri. 9am-noon and 2-7pm.

Women's Center: Centre d'Information sur les Droits des Femmes (C.I.D.F.), 24 rue Mignet (tel. 42 63 18 92). Provides free information and advice on women's familial, social, legal, and professional rights. Publishes *Femmes à Aix,* full of useful phone numbers, addresses, and hours of useful services for women (available at the tourist office). Open Mon.-Tues. and Thurs.-Fri. 9am-4pm.

Laundromat: Lots of 'em. A sampling includes **Lavomatique,** off La Rotonde on the corner of rue Bernadines and rue de la Fontaine. Wash 16F per 4.5kg, dry 2F per 6min. Open daily 7am-8pm. Also **Inter-Laverie,** bd. Carnot, opposite the Ecole d'Arts et Métiers. Wash 16F per 5kg, dry 2F per 6min. Open daily 7am-8pm. The hostel has its own laundry facilities (soap, wash, and dry 20F).

Medical Emergency: Hôpital Pasteur Général, av. Tamaris (tel. 42 33 50 00), north of La Rotonde. **SOS Médecins:** tel. 42 26 24 00. Available 24 hrs. **SOS Amitié:** tel. 91 76 10 10. 24-hr. crisis hotline.

Police: 8, pl. Jeanne d'Arc (tel. 42 26 04 81). **Emergency:** tel. 17.

Accommodations and Camping

There are few inexpensive hotels near the center, and during the festival they are all booked in advance. Do likewise, or arrive early and hope for cancellations.

Auberge de Jeunesse (HI), 3, av. Marcel Pagnol (tel. 42 20 15 99), quartier du Jas de Bouffan, next to the Fondation Vasarely. A 25-min. walk from the center of town. Bus #12 makes the trip from La Rotonde (every 1/2hr. until 5:30pm, 6F) to "Vasarely" stop. From La Rotonde, walk down av. des Belges to pl. Anouar El Sadate. Take a right onto the av. de l'Europe. At the 1st rotary after the highway overpass, bear left and climb the hill. The hostel will be on your left in a private wooded area. A big, modern but impersonal hostel with TV room, bar, tennis courts, volleyball net and clean bedrooms and bathrooms. 9-bed rooms. Reception open 7:30-10am and 5:30-10pm. Lockout 10am-5:30pm. Curfew 11pm. 63F. Breakfast included. Meals 43F. Laundry facilities (25F wash and dry). No kitchen facilities. Sheets 10F. No sleeping bags. Call ahead or make reservations in advance (20F deposit required).

CROUS: Cité des Gazelles, 38, av. Jules Ferry (tel. 42 26 33 75), 20-min. walk from La Rotonde. The university occasionally offers 55F singles with a 2-day min. stay July-Aug. Call ahead or ask at the tourist office about availability.

Hôtel Vigouroux, 27, rue Cardinale (tel. 42 38 26 42), between pl. des Dauphins and the Musée Granet. University boarding house in winter. Spacious and well-scrubbed rooms with high ceilings, hardwood floors, and decorative moldings. Polished antique furniture and marble fireplaces. Peaceful location, yet near all the action. Singles and doubles 140-160F, with shower 200-260F.

Splendid Hotel, 69, cours Mirabeau (tel. in day 42 27 68 89, at night 42 38 19 53), at the eastern end of town. True to its name, with bright murals depicting *la vie provençale* adorning the walls. All rooms are carpeted and have shiny bathrooms. Unparalleled location. Singles with shower 137-157F. Doubles with shower 184F. Triples with shower 306F. Breakfast included.

Hôtel du Casino, 38, rue Victor Leydet (tel. 42 26 06 88), off cours Mirabeau. Way cool location. Clean rooms, fluffy pillows, and outgoing managers who love students. TV lounge. Singles 130F, with shower 150F. Doubles 180F, with shower 175F, with bathroom and TV 230F. Breakfast 25F.

Hôtel des Arts, 69, bd. Carnot (tel. 42 38 11 77), near la Rotonde. Small, modern, art-deco hotel under friendly new management. Rooms are extremely modern, bright, and clean. Doubles with shower 175F, with TV 195F. Breakfast 195F.

Hôtel le Moulin, 1, av. Robert-Schuman (tel. 42 59 41 68), only minutes from the train station. Take a right out of the station and bear right at the first traffic circle. Modern, spacious rooms with gargantuan beds and plush carpets. Clean as a whistle. Singles 150F, with shower 190F. Doubles 195F, with shower, toilet, and TV 260-275F. Breakfast 36F.

Camping: Although all the local campgrounds lie outside of town, these two are accessible by bus #3 from La Rotonde at the "Trois Sautets" and "Val St-André" stops, respectively. **Arc-en-Ciel** (tel. 42 26 14 28), Pont des Trois Sautets, rte de Nice, 3km from the center of town. A 4-star site with a pool and hot showers. 25F per person, 30F per tent. **Chantecler** (tel. 42 26 12 98), av. St-André, by rte de Nice, 3km from the center. Swimming pool and hot showers, telephones, restaurant, and bar. 55F for 1 person with tent, 2 people with tent 105F. Open all year.

Food

Although restaurants in Aix serve delicious regional specialties often seasoned with the garlic *aïoli* sauce, the city's culinary reputation rests on its *confisseries* (candy). Most almonds used in French cakes and cookies originate in Aix; its most famous *bonbon* is the *calisson d'Aix,* a small iced-almond cookie. Other regional specialties include soft nougat and hard praline candies. Pass by the *pâtisseries* on rue d'Italie or rue Espariat for a lip-smacking exhibit.

Rue d'Italie also has *boulangeries, charcuteries,* and a fruit market to arrange a hearty picnic lunch. For fresher produce, shop at the **open air market** at pl. de Verdun on Tuesdays, Thursdays, and Saturdays from 7am to 1pm. Otherwise, check out the **Supermarché Casino** on 1, av. de Lattre de Tassigny, near bd. de la République (open Mon.-Sat. 9am-8pm) or the **Monoprix supermarket** on cours Mirabeau (open Mon.-Sat. 8:45am-7:30pm).

The streets north of cours Mirabeau are packed with restaurants for all palates and wallets. The cafés on cours Mirabeau might be expensive, but they provide unrivaled seats for viewing Aix's *chic* university crowd. An *espresso* at the famed **Café des Deux Garçons,** once a favorite watering hole of Paul Cézanne, costs 8F and buys about three hours of viewing time.

Hacienda, 7, rue Mérindol, in the pl. des Fontêtes. Outdoor seating around a cherubed fountain. Quick service and an excellent value. The 57F *menu* includes *gigot rôti d'agneau* (roast leg of lamb)*, tomates à la provençale,* wine, and dessert. Great salads 30-40F. Open Sept.-Aug. Mon.-Sat. noon-2pm and 7-10:30pm.

L'Arbre à Pain, 4, rue Emeric David, near the *Palais de Justice.* Offers a *bio-végétarian* fare, including a 3-course vegetarian *menu* for 42F. Open Thurs.-Sat. 11am-2:30pm and 6-11pm, Mon.-Wed. 11am-2:30pm.

Bistrot Aixois, 37, cours Sextius (tel. 42 27 50 10). Popular restaurant with regional specialties such as *salade Aixois* (green salad with tomatoes, asparagus, salmon, and crab, 47F), *maigret de canard aux poivres* (roast duck in a pepper sauce, 60F) and *escalope de saumon* (salmon, 43F). Open daily noon-2pm and 7-10pm.

La Cigale, 48, rue Espariat, off pl. des Augustines, just off La Rotonde. 57F (3-course) and 68F (4-course) *menus* with French and Italian specialties. Lasagne and ravioli both 45F. House specialties include *Raviolis frais à la Napolitaine,* 45F. Super salads 36-42F. Open Thurs.-Tues. noon-2:30pm and 7-11pm.

La Table Provençale, 13, rue Maréchal Joffre (tel. 42 27 36 99), at the far end of the cours Mirabeau. 62F *menu* features salad, chicken, wine, dessert, and coffee. Fantastic *filet aux herbes de Provence* (40F) and *gratin de fruits de mer* (50F). Open Mon.-Sat. noon-2pm.

Cafétéria Flunch, 2, av. des Belges, next to the tourist office. Ah oui! Mon amour! Mon argent t'embrace! Et mon estomac te donne un bec mouillé. The price is right. Roast chicken with vegetables 19F. Open daily 11am-10pm.

Sights

Cultured Aix sports several terrific museums. The most unusual of these is the **Chemin de Cézanne,** a walking tour that transforms the entire city into an open-air museum of Paul Cézanne's life and works. Pick up the tourist office's English brochure "In the Footsteps of Paul Cézanne," and follow the bronze markers embedded in the sidewalks of Aix's streets. The two-hour walk covers Cézanne's birthplace, the cathedral where he worshipped, and his studio, frozen as the **Musée d'Atelier Paul Cézanne,** 9, av. Paul Cézanne (tel. 42 21 06 53). It remains much as he left it in 1906, with easel, smock, and an unfinished canvas. (Open Wed.-Mon. 10am-noon and 2:30-6pm. Admission 12F; students, children, and seniors 6F.)

The **Musée Granet,** pl. Saint-Jean-Marie-de-Malte (tel. 42 38 14 70) contains several Cézannes, as well as paintings by Dutch and French painters and an exhibit of contemporary art. (Open Wed.-Mon. 10am-noon and 2-6pm. Admission 13F, students 7F.)

For a larger collection of contemporary art, stunning and defiant **Fondation Vasarely,** 1, av. Marcel Pagnol (tel. 42 20 01 09), Jas de Bouffan, lies outside town next to the youth hostel. Take bus #12 (5F60) from La Rotonde to "Vasarely." The black and white museum houses 42 of mad Hungarian Victor Vasarely's enormous, vibrant experiments with color, known as "mural integrations." The paintings—all in hexagonal rooms— trick the viewer into believing that they are three-dimensional. (Open daily 9:30am-12:30pm and 2-5:30pm; off-season Wed.-Sun. Admission 30F, ages 7-18 15F.) After this visual tomfoolery, the placid park outside provides a welcome respite.

A fine collection of Beauvais tapestries from the 17th and 18th centuries hangs in the **Musée des Tapisseries,** pl. des Martyrs de la Résistance (tel. 42 21 05 78), at ancienne pl. de l'Archevêché. (Open Wed.-Mon. 10am-noon and 2-6pm. Admission 11F, students 5F.) **Cathédrale St-Sauveur** is an architectural melange of additions and carvings from 11th-century Romanesque to late Flamboyant Gothic. The main attraction, the 16th-century carved panels of the main portal, remain in perfect condition, thanks to their protective wooden shutters. The interior's bread and butter is its *Triptych du Buisson Ardent,* which depicts King René and his queen oddly juxtaposed with the Virgin and Child and the burning bush of Moses. This work is usually closed away, but for a small tip, the affable guard may show it and the front panels to you. Adjoining the church, the delicate 13th-century **Cloître St-Sauveur** has a wooden roof over the galleries instead of the usual heavy arches. During the festival, mass is held Sundays at 10:30am. (Church open Wed.-Mon. 8am-noon and 2-6pm. Free.)

The **Bibliothèque Méjanes,** 8-10, rue des Allumettes (tel. 42 25 95 95), near the *gare routière,* was formerly one of France's largest match factories and has since been renovated into a widely used public space. (Open Tues.-Wed. and Fri. noon-6pm, Sat. 10am-6pm. Free.) Guarded by giant replicas of Sartre's *L'Etranger* and Antoine de St-Exupéry's *Le Petit Prince,* this bright and modern library stocks current issues of *Newsweek* and a small collection of British and American literature. The library also boasts an impressive collection of illuminated manuscripts, but you'll need special permission from the curator before viewing them. The **Fondation St-John Perse,** in the same building (tel. 42 25 98 85), stores materials and manuscripts related to the 1960 Nobel Prize-winning poet. (Open Tues.-Wed. and Fri. noon-6pm. Free.)

Entertainment

Aix's **International Music Festival,** held from mid-July to early August, attracts first-rate musicians and orchestras from around the world. Unfortunately, most of these musical delights exceed tight budgets and outclass the wrinkled wardrobes that stuff most backpacks. The program features opera in the **Théâtre de l'Archevêché** (tickets 240-880F); concerts in **Cathédrale** and **Cloître St-Louis,** 60, bd. Carnot (tickets 120-380F); and recitals by advanced music students at **Cloître St-Sauveur** (tickets 75F).

Beginning with the second week of June, all of Aix celebrates with **Aix en Musique,** a realistically casual two-week jamboree of big-band jazz, classical quartets, and wind ensembles. Most concerts are free, and each evening the streets of the *vieille ville* resound with conservatory students performing everything from rock to classical music. The tourist office lists concerts and locations; call 42 63 06 75 or 42 21 69 69 for more information. During the first two weeks of July, Aix holds an international **Dance Festival,** with acts that range from classical ballet to modern and jazz. (Tickets 80-130F, students 60-110F.) Contact the Comité Officiel des Fêtes on cours Gambetta (tel. 42 63 06 75), at the corner of bd. du Roi René, for information on the Music and Dance Festivals.

During spring and winter months, cheap student theater and concerts abound at the university. Students and professionals share the stages at the **Théâtre Jacques-Prévert,** 23, bd. de la République (tel. 42 26 36 50), the **Théâtre 108,** 37, bd. A. Briand (tel. 42 21 06 20), and the **Théâtre de Verdure,** parc Paysage du Jas de Bouffan (tel. 42 59 38 30).

Aix's vaguely anarchistic student population gives rise to extraordinary after-dark opportunities year-round. Rock around the clock to 50s and 60s music at **La Palette Club 60,** 21, rue Lisse des Cordeliers (tel. 42 26 44 05), a small street just before the intersection of rue Cordeliers and cours Sextius. (Open Wed. and Fri.-Sat. 10:30pm-dawn.) **Le Mistral,** 3, rue Frédéric Mistral (tel. 42 38 16 49), next to the restaurant Gu et Fils, just simmers with students. (Open nightly 11pm-dawn. Admission 80F.) **Le Scat,** 11, rue Verrerie (tel. 42 23 00 23), is a terrific club with live jazz and blues every night from 10:30pm. (Open Mon.-Sat. 10pm-whenever.) **La Chimère,** montée d'Avignon (tel. 42 23 36 28), quartier des Plâtrières, outside of town, attracts a sizeable gay crowd to its bar and disco. (Open Tues.-Sun. 10pm-6am.)

Chic cafés and bars, some lit by candlelight after dark, line the Forum des Cardeurs, behind the *Hôtel de Ville.* Try the **Croquet Bar** or the **Royal Bar,** both open daily from 7:30pm until everyone's gone.

The **Blue Note** club, 10, rue de la Fonderie (tel. 42 38 06 23), brings a little of New York to Aix. Live jazz piano on Wednesdays and Fridays, a "happy hour" between 7 and 8:30pm, and milkshakes from 16F make this a great home away from The Village. (Open Mon.-Sat. 7pm-midnight.) The **Cézanne Cinema,** 21, rue Goyraud (tel. 42 26 04 06), rolls ten films every night, some in the original language (39F). **Le Mazarin,** 6, rue Laroque (tel. 42 26 99 85), also shows decent *version originale* films (admission 37F, under 13 26F).

Near Aix

Retrace Cézanne's easel stops along the D17, now known imaginatively as the **route de Cézanne,** to the small village of **Le Tholonet,** 5km from Aix. Le Tholonet's **Châteaunoir** and the Cézanne family's private residence, the **Jas de Bouffan,** both stand in Le Tholonet. The stunning landscapes along the way provided inspiration for many of Cézanne's canvases. The tourist office in Aix also sponsors minibus tours to Le Tholonet (April-Sept. at 1:30pm, 140F, call **Les Autocars de Provence** at 42 23 14 26 for more information).

Picasso devotees, stop your sulking; you can seek out your master's grave in **Vauvenargues,** 16km east of Aix. Three or four buses per day run from Aix. For more info call **RDT 13** (tel. 42 26 01 50). Although visitors are not allowed entrance to the 19th-century château where Picasso lived, some of the artist's sculptures are on display in the park.

Provence: Côte d'Azur

> *Why cross the sea to Algiers, why go to semi-barba-*
> *rous Spain, when we have but to come to the South*
> *of France to change dark November into smiling*
> *June?*
>
> —Lord Brogham

Paradises are made to be lost. Sparkling between Marseille and the Italian border, the sun-drenched beaches and waters of the Mediterranean form the mythical backdrop for this fabled playground of the rich and famous. But its seductive loneliness has almost been its undoing, as shrewd developers have turned its beauty to profit and its pleasures into big business. Today, the area is as crammed with low-budget tourists as with high-handed millionaires, and many French condemn the coast as a shameless Fort Lauderdale, a mere shadow of its former self. But despite the fact that only a desire to tan unites the masses here, the *Côte* remains alluring, an uncommonly beautiful garden of delights, distinguished by its vibrant colors. Dazzling pastel Belle Epoque villas rim a remarkably blue sea, while silvery olive trees shelter roses and mimosas. By day, beaches invite swimming and sunning *au naturel;* by night, clubs and casinos tender pleasures of a more sophisticated sort.

The Riviera's reputation developed in the 18th and 19th centuries, when the English and Russian aristocracy came to the Riviera's unspoiled fishing villages to cure winter ailments, from consumption to hangnails, and maybe catch a glimpse of Queen Victoria or Tsar Nicolas II on holiday. Historically a winter resort, the *Côte* became a favorite destination of French sunseekers only after World War II, when new highways and railroads and a government-mandated increase in vacation time made the area accessible to millions of average working people with a few weeks on their hands.

Some of the past century's greatest artists have found a niche on the *Côte.* Images linger of F. Scott Fitzgerald and Cole Porter at Cap d'Antibes, and of Picasso, Renoir, and Matisse sketching in the luminous foothills of Nice. Nearly every town along the eastern stretch of the *Côte* lays claim to a chapel, room, or wall decorated by Matisse or Chagall, and there are superb museums everywhere. Look for the Fauves at St-Tropez's Musée de l'Annonciade, the excellent temporary exhibits at the Maeght Foundation in Vence, the Matisse and Chagall museums in Cimiez (near Nice), the Picasso preserve in Antibes, the Cocteau cache in Menton, and the dozens of other collections scattered throughout the region. Jazz festivals mount throughout the summer; the Cannes Film Festival is held in May, Nice's *Carnaval* in February, the Monte-Carlo Grand Prix in May, and Monaco's Fireworks Festival in August. If you feel like creating your own *fête,* order a steaming cauldron of *bouillabaisse* (a hearty fish soup), *soupe au pistou* (a brew of pine nuts, fresh basil, and the ubiquitous garlic), *aïoli* (a garlic dip to accompany fresh vegetables), or fresh seafood. Whatever your feast, wash it down with the flavorful whites or reds of the Côte du Rhône, the fruity rosés of the Côte de Provence, or one of the region's other respectable vintages.

The coast from Marseille to Italy is well-served by frequent, inexpensive trains and buses. Most of the famous attractions lie along the coastal two-hour stretch from St-Raphaël to Menton. Trains for the coast leave Paris's Gare de Lyon every hour in summer; the trip takes five hours on the TGV to Marseille and seven to eight hours to Nice. While hitchhiking is said to be difficult along the coastal highway, and is as risky as elsewhere, hitchers reportedly have better luck on the inland country roads. You might want to base yourself in some of the less expensive coastal towns (St-Raphaël and Grasse, for example) and take daytrips to the purse-emptying cities and inviting beaches. Like western Provence, the Riviera is best visited during early June and in September when crowds are low and hotel vacancies are high. In July and August, seemingly all of France tries to squeeze onto the *Côte's* beaches. Make reservations in advance or start looking in the early morning.

Beaches

Life's a beach and so's the Riviera, so familiarize yourself with the *Côte* before you lie down and bake. In general, the largest towns have the worst beaches. Marseille has an artificial beach, the Nice beaches are rocky, Cannes is private, St-Tropez and Monte-Carlo are remote. Seek out the quieter alcoves between towns: Cap Martin (between Monaco and Menton), Cap d'Ail (between Monaco and Nice), and St-Raphaël (between Cannes and St-Tropez) are all lovely and much less crowded. West of Nice, Antibes and Juan-les-Pins both have long, white-sanded beaches with clear water and fine swimming. St-Raphaël shelters smooth, public, and fairly crowded stretches of sand right off the train line and many other fine but less crowded beaches nearby. Some of the finest sandy expanses stretch between St-Raphaël and St-Tropez.

If you've come just for the sun, try to arrive in early June or in September, when the air and water are warm but the beaches aren't replete with basking, bathing, glorious bodies. In summer, optimal swimming tends to be during the two-hour period before the 9pm sunset. Bring a towel and a woven reed mat (10F at the supermarkets in Nice and Cannes); even the sand beaches are a bit rocky. Nearly all beaches are topless, and many are now bottomless, too. Nude bathers will find a wealth of secluded beaches where they can bare it all. Two of the most famous are Héliopolis, one of Europe's largest nudist colonies, on the Ile du Levant, and in the *calanques* between Eze-sur-Mer and Cap d'Ail. Just be careful of the merciless rays. Since almost all the towns on the *Côte* lie along one local rail line, just hop off and on at small stations to see what you can find. Do not neglect the less-frequented coastal islands. The Porquerolles and Ile du Levant off Toulon and the Iles de Lerins off Cannes all have fine rock ledges and secluded coves.

Accommodations are extremely tight in high season; youth hostels and hotels are often booked months in advance. Although sleeping on the beach is illegal, many travelers just end up where they put their towels during the day. A number of beaches provide showers, toilets, and even towels for a small fee (10-15F). Those who spend the night on the beaches at Nice, Cannes, and Juan-les-Pins may run afoul of more than the law. You may find yourself bedding down next to groups of often "respectable" looking youths whose summer jobs consist of relieving tourists of their mopeds, jewelry, and spare cash. Daytrippers can make use of the lockers (15F-20F) available at most train stations—always hide the key. Even in stations where lockers have been closed because of vandalism, you can always check your luggage for 12F.

Marseille

France's third city, Marseille is sort of like the *bouillabaisse* for which it is famous. It's steaming hot, full of spice, and has a little bit of everything mixed in it. But unlike *bouillabaisse,* the everything is hardly delectable. Marseille is a spoonful of Detroit, a dash of Bogota, a slice of Tripoli, and a pinch of Miami. Although Nice may actually harbor more of the French mafia these days, it is grimy Marseille (pop. 1.1 million) which enjoys a universal reputation for roguishness and danger. Ever since Hellenic civilization penetrated Gaul here in 600 BC, the city Dumas called "the meeting place of the entire world" has seen black, white, and brown, rich and poor live in uneasy proximity.

Although racial tensions pervade the city, Marseille remains strangely alluring, charged throughout with color and commotion. Its daily fish market, nearby beaches, wild nightclubs, and big-city adventure merits a (brief) stop-over on the way to Nice or Avignon.

Orientation and Practical Information

The heart of Marseille is the humming **vieux port** (old port) and the adjacent streets of the *vieille ville*. At night, these areas can be dangerous for travelers of either sex. Extending straight out of the port is Marseille's main artery, **La Canebière,** affectionately known to English sailors as "Can o' beer." Jammed in the day but empty after 10pm,

La Canebière can also be dangerous. Avoid the streets adjoining La Canebière, especially cours Belsunce and bd. d'Athènes. The **North African quarter** twists through the narrow, dusty streets between the train station and La Canebière, roughly bounded by bd. Nedelec, bd. d'Athens, rue d'Aix and La Canebière. In the day, the stores and restaurants are intriguing and inexpensive, but at night, muggers replace beggars. In addition, the area in front of the opera (near the port) is often the meeting ground for prostitutes and their clients; exercise caution in this corner of Marseille after dark. When in doubt, stay in a group or call a cab; they operate 24 hrs. It is virtually impossible to make a phone call without a phone card in Marseille except in the train station and at the post office.

The tourist office is a 15-minute walk from the station. Turn left as you leave the train station and descend the majestic steps. Continue straight down bd. d'Athènes until you arrive at McDonald's and La Canebière. Take a right on La Canebière and walk all the way to the port. The tourist office will be on your left, in front of the metro entrance.

Tourist Office: 4, La Canebière (tel. 91 54 91 11), near the *vieux port*. Well-staffed office with information on boats, festivals, and youth activities. Free accommodations service. SNCF information and reservations. Daily tours of the city leave June-Sept. at 10am (90F). The free brochure, *A Tout Marseille*, has loads of helpful information on sights and upcoming events. Open daily 8am-8pm; Oct.-June Mon.-Sat. 9am-7:30pm, Sun. 10am-5:30pm. **Annex** at the train station (tel. 91 50 59 18) performs the same services. Open Mon.-Sat. 9am-7pm; Sept.-June Mon.-Fri. 9am-12:30pm and 2-6:30pm.

Youth Information: Centre d'Information Jeunesse: 4, rue de la Visitation (tel. 91 49 91 55), off bd. Françoise Duparc, just north of the Palais Longchamp. Information on sports, short-term employment, and activities, including climbing excursions to the *calanques*. They also have a *Guide des Loisirs* for people with disabilities (12F). Open Mon. 2-7pm, Tues.-Fri. 9am-7pm. **CROUS**, 38, rue du 141*ème* R.I.A. (tel. 91 95 90 06) has information on housing, work, and travel for students.

Consulates: U.S., 12, bd. Paul Peytral (tel. 91 54 92 00). Open Mon.-Fri. 8:30am-noon and 1-5:30pm. **U.K.,** 24, av. du Prado (tel. 91 53 43 32). Open Mon.-Fri. 9am-noon and 2-5pm. All other consulates reached through the **Secretariat du Corps Consulaire,** 56, La Canebière (tel. 91 54 24 34). Open Mon.-Fri. 2-3pm only.

Currency Exchange: La Bourse, pl. Général de Gaulle (tel. 91 84 68 88). Competitive rates and no commission. Open Mon.-Fri. 8:30am-noon and 2-6:30pm; Sept.-May Mon.-Fri.. 9am-7pm. **Comptoir de Change Méditerranéen** (tel. 91 84 68 89), at the train station, charges a 10F minimum commission (1% if over 100F). Open daily 6am-9pm; Oct.-June 8am-6pm.

American Express: 39, La Canebière (tel. 91 90 18 33). Changes money only. Open Mon.-Fri. 8am-6pm, Sat. 8am-noon and 2-5pm.

Post Office: 1, pl. Hôtel des Postes (tel. 91 90 31 33), at the intersection of rue Colbert and rue Barbusse. **Poste Restante** and **currency exchange** at this branch only. Open Mon.-Fri. 8am-7pm, Sat. 8am-noon. **Branch offices** at 11, rue Honnorat (tel. 91 50 89 25), near the train station (open Mon.-Fri. 8:30am-6:30pm, Sat. 8:30am-noon); and pl. de Stalingrad, at the end of La Canebière (open Mon.-Fri. 8am-6:30pm, Sat. 8am-noon). **Postal Code:** 13001.

Flights: Aéroport Marseille-Provence (tel. 42 89 09 74 or 42 78 21 00). Cheap student flights to Corsica (Ajaccio, 294F), Paris (370F), and Lyon (420F). Shuttle buses connect the airport with the Gare St-Charles (every 20min. 5:30am-9:50pm, 36F).

Trains: Gare St-Charles (tel. 91 08 50 50). Nearby *bureau d'accueil* (reception desk) open daily 4am-1am. Information and reservation desk open Mon.-Sat. 8am-8pm. Marseille is a major rail center with connections to all major towns in the south. Paris (4 TGV per day, 4 3/4hr., 382F plus 16F required reservation); Lyon (about every 2hr., 3 1/2hr., 182F); Toulon (every 20min., 1hr., 51F). **SOS Voyageurs** (tel. 91 64 71 00), in the train station. Cheery senior citizens will help you get oriented and find lodgings. Open Mon.-Sat. 8am-8pm. Baggage lockers open 6am-midnight, 15F.

Buses: Gare des Autobus de Marseille (tel. 91 08 16 40), on pl. Victor Hugo behind the train station. Open Mon.-Sat. 8am-6:30pm, Sun. 9am-noon and 2-6pm. **Cars Phocéens** (tel. 91 50 57 68). To: Cannes (3 per day; 1 3/4hr., 103F, students 75F) and Nice (3 per day; 2 3/4hr.; 114F, students 80F). **Société Cars et Autobus de Cassis** (tel. 42 73 18 00). To Cassis (17 per day, 50min., 22F). **Autocars SATAP** (tel. 91 62 32 98). To Avignon (4 per day, 2hr., 84F). **Société des Transports Régionaux** (tel. 42 23 14 26). To Aix-en-Provence (6 per day, 45min., 28F). **Les Cars Verts**

de Provence (tel. 90 93 74 90). To Arles (Mon.-Fri. 4 per day, Sat.-Sun. 2 per day, 2hr.; 65F). **Société Varoise de Transport (SVT)** (tel. 42 70 28 00). To Toulon (Mon.-Fri. 2 per day, 1 3/4 hr., 45F).

Public Transportation: A practical network of subways and buses is run by **RTM,** 6-8, rue des Fabres (tel. 91 91 92 10). Open Mon.-Fri. 7:30am-6:30pm. Exact change or tickets (7F50, 30F for *carnet* of 6; sold at metro and bus stops). Ticket good on metro or bus for 70min. Metro lines #1 and 2 both stop at the train station. The former will take you to the *vieux port* (direction: "Castéllane"). The tourist office distributes the free *RTM Plan-Guide du Réseau.*

Ferries: SNCM, 61, bd. des Dames (tel. 91 56 62 05, for reservations 91 56 80 20). Information and tickets to Corsica (200F, students 180F), Sardinia, and North Africa. Open Mon.-Fri. 9am-5pm, Sat. 8am-noon.

Taxis: Available 24 hrs. Phone requests taken. Prices are based on zone and time of day, and drivers have been known to overcharge. **Taxi Plus** (tel. 91 03 60 03). **Maison du Taxi** (tel. 91 95 92 50). **Marseille Taxi** (tel. 91 49 91 00).

Laundromat: Point Laverie, 56, bd. de la Libération. Wash 20F for 7kg. Dry 2F for 6min. Open daily 7am-9pm. Another outlet at 8, rue de l'Academie. Same prices. Open daily 8am-9pm.

Special Services: SOS Amitié (tel. 91 76 10 10). 24-hr. crisis line. **CORPS** 48, rue de Bruys (tel. 91 94 19 91). A gay center. Open in summer at 8pm. **CODIF,** 81, rue Sénac (tel. 91 47 17 05). Information for women. **Office Municipal pour Handicapés et Inadaptés,** 128, av. du Prado (tel. 91 81 58 80). An excellent center for people with disabilities. Open Mon.-Fri. 9am-noon and 2-6pm. For transportation service, call 91 78 21 67 a day ahead (8am-noon and 1-6pm). Service operates daily 6am-midnight. **Association d'Aide aux Victimes de la Déliquence (AVAD),** 56, rue Montgrand (tel. 91 54 81 00). Will aid victims of crime. The sympathetic staff can even help you replace stolen train tickets and provide emergency accommodations. Open Mon.-Fri. 9am-noon and 2-5pm.

Hospital: Hôpital Timone, bd. Jean Moulin (tel. 91 38 60 00). Take metro line #1 to "Castéllane," then bus #91. Ask the driver to drop you off.

Medical Emergency: For a home visit call 91 52 84 85. **SAMU ambulances:** tel. 91 49 91 91. **SOS Médecins:** tel. 91 52 91 52.

Police: 2, rue Antoinne Becker (tel. 91 91 90 40). Also in the train station on Esplanade St-Charles (same tel., ask for *poste* 4017). **Emergency:** tel. 17.

Accommodations and Camping

Inexpensive hotels abound in Marseille, especially on rue Breteuil and rue Aubagne. A herd of one and two star hotels sits on allé L. Gambetta. Resist the temptation of cheap accommodations in the North African quarter; the area is dangerous after dark and some of the hotels front prostitution. Both hostels are far from the center of town, but are easily accessible by bus and usually have space, even in summer. Nevertheless, call ahead to be sure before making the trip.

Auberge de Jeunesse de Bois-Luzy (HI), 76, av. de Bois-Luzy (tel. 91 49 06 18). Take bus #6 from pl. de la Libération, #8 from La Canebière by day, or bus K after 8:20pm (until 10pm) from La Canebière (7F50). Exit at "Bois-Luzy" stop. Head to the dead end of av. Bois-Luzy. Walk to the left, clockwise on a path, to reach the hostel. Former château overlooking the city and the sea has clean, well-kept rooms and hot showers but is pretty isolated. Dorm rooms of 8-12, doubles also available for couples. There are neither meals nor nearby markets or restaurants, so eat or shop before boarding the bus. Reception open 7:30-10am and 5-10:30pm. Curfew 11pm. 40F. Breakfast 15F. Basic cooking facilities.

Auberge de Jeunesse Bonneveine (HI), 47, av. J. Vidal (tel. 91 73 21 81). From the station, take the metro to "pl. Castéllane" (7F50), then bus #19 to "Les Gatons Place" or bus #44 to pl. Bonnefon (same ticket for metro and bus). Often filled though very large. Probably not worth the extra dough. Reception open 7-10am and 5-11pm. No curfew. 70F. Breakfast included. Other meals 43F. Cooking facilities.

Hôtel Azur, 24, cours Franklin Roosevelt (tel. 91 42 74 38), about 15min. from the train station. Take allée Gambetta from bd. d'Athènes. Immaculate, spacious rooms overlook a small garden. Many rooms with color TV, telephone, and carpeting. So warm and homey that you might forget you're in Marseille. Singles 165F, with shower and TV 185F. Doubles with shower 220F, with shower and toilet 250F. Quads 390F. Showers 15F. Breakfast 27F.

Hôtel Moderne, 11, bd. de la Libération (tel. 91 62 28 66). Follow La Canebière to rue du Mont-sabert, which becomes bd. de la Libération. A great bargain. M Reynaud keeps very clean rooms and has a seasonal following. A popular place, so call ahead. Singles 70F, with shower and TV 130F. Doubles 130F, with shower 150F. Triples with shower 190F. Showers 15F. Breakfast 20F.

Hôtel Moderne, 30, rue Breteuil (tel. 91 53 29 93). From the train or bus station, take bd. d'Athènes (which becomes bd. Dugommier), turn right on La Canebière to the *vieux port,* and look for rue Breteuil. This diamond in the rough has sparkly clean rooms, winding staircases, and funky murals. Singles 85F, with showers 100F. Doubles with shower, toilet, TV, and radio 170-220F. Breakfast 22F.

Hôtel Montegrand, 50, rue Montegrand (tel. 91 33 33 81), off rue Paradis. Charming owner keeps the place squeaky clean. Soft pillows and a great location. Singles 110F, with shower 120-140F, and toilet 150F. Doubles with bath and toilet 160-180F. Triples with bathroom 160-220F. Breakfast 20F.

Hôtel Gambetta, 49, allée Léon Gambetta (tel. 91 62 07 88), centrally located and near the train station. Spacious, spotless modern rooms. Singles 82F, with shower 120F. Doubles with shower 150F, and toilet 200F. Showers 15F. TV in room 20F. Breakfast 23F.

Camping: The **Auberge de Jeunesse de Bois-Luzy** (tel. 91 49 06 18) is cheapest and closest to town. (27F per person, breakfast 15F).

Food

Marseille is the home of *bouillabaisse,* a fish stew cooked with wine, saffron, and a touch of cayenne pepper. Mussels, eel, lobster, and anything that swims may be thrown in. Expect to pay 70-170F, depending on quality and location. The slightly more expensive restaurants on quai du Port serve fine *bouillabaisse* and include a view of Notre Dame de la Garde. Every morning until 1pm, *marseillais* stock for their stews at the **fish market** on quai des Belges. Because of its large immigrant population, Marseille also supports a bevy of superb North African restaurants. The greatest variety of *couscous* on the Côte lurks in the area between La Canebière and bd. Charles Nedelec. Plan to eat out at lunch; after nightfall, tourists become the prey as the muggers come out of hiding. Before heading to the youth hostels, stock up at the **Timy** supermarket, 14-16, rue de la République, near the *vieux port.* (Open Mon.-Sat. 7:30am-1:30pm and 3-7pm.)

Racasse-Dauphin, 6, quai de Rive-neuve, in the *vieux port.* Great *marseillais* favorites include a creamy *bouillabaisse* (75F) and a 5-course *menu* of *fruits de mer* (seafood; 75F). Open Fri.-Wed. noon-2pm and 7-11pm.

Le Vaccares, 64, rue de La République, west of quai des Belges. Fun-loving staff and unforgettable portions. Delicious *escargots de Bourgogne* 35F. Pizza 20-40F. 60F *menu* with terrific lamb or pizza, fries, and wine. Open Mon.-Sat. noon-2pm and 7-11pm.

La Sirène, 2, quai de Rive-Neuve. Offers seafood specialities in 4-course (59F) and 5-course (75F) *menus.* Open daily 11am-1pm and 6-11pm.

Cafétéria Flunch, on rue St-Féréol, off La Canabière near the tourist office. A budget traveler's dream come true with large portions at small prices. Roast chicken and potatoes, 21F. Open daily 11am-10pm.

Le Jardin d'à Côté, 65, cours Julien. A chic café. Large outdoor parasols and appetizing salads. The blue and white interior provides a cool, air-conditioned refuge from the Marseille heat. *Plat du jour* with wine 45F. Specialties include *salade niçoise* and *coquillages* (shellfish). Large salads 45F. Open daily noon-2:30pm and 8pm-1am.

La Flamiche, 16, rue de la Paix (tel. 91 33 00 74), on the *vieux port.* Outstanding selections include *soupe de poisson* and a decadent *saumon fumé maison* (house smoked salmon, 65F). 50F and 78F *menus* feature local dishes, salad and dessert. Open Mon.-Fri. noon-2pm and 7-10pm, Sat. 7-10pm.

Le Mondial, 68, rue Tilsit, off rue de Lodi near cours Julien. Cheap hole in the wall which locals love to crawl into. 4-course 40F *menu* incorporates French classics such as *steak frites* and *brochette d'agneau.* Open Sept.-July Mon.-Fri. noon-2pm and 7-10pm.

Country Life, 14, rue Venture, off rue Paradis. Vegetarian *menu* of salad, pasta, and dessert (50F). Scrumptious pastries 7-15F. Open Mon.-Fri. 11:30am-2:30pm.

Sights

The majestic 19th-century **Basilique de Notre Dame de la Garde** balances high on a hill above Marseille. Even in the summer haze of the Marseille skyline, the basilica's gold-gilded Virgin sparkles over the Mediterranean Sea 700m below. To see things from the Virgin's point of view—the harbor islands, the Château d'If, and the surrounding mountains, that is—take bus #60, or follow rue Breteuil, turn right on bd. Vauban, and then turn on rue Fort du Sanctuaire. (No shorts. Free.) Also dating from the 19th century, the **Cathédrale Nouvelle Major** houses a 15th-century altar dedicated to Lazarus. Ironically, the cathedral, which seats 3000, was built just before a major decline in France's practicing Catholic population (open Wed.-Mon. 9am-noon and 2-6pm). The **Abbaye St-Victor** (tel. 91 33 25 86), perched at the end of quai de Rive Neuve, evokes the ascetic beginnings of Christianity. The 5th-century catacombs and basilica contain an extensive array of both pagan and Christian relics, including the 3rd-century remains of two martyrs. (Open daily 8am-6:30pm.)

Marseille supports a flotilla of fine museums. The gaudy 19th-century **Palais Longchamp** at the eastern end of bd. Longchamp, contains the eclectic **Musée des Beaux-Arts** (tel. 91 62 21 17). Particularly strong in Provençal painting, the museum also exhibits paintings of Marseille's early history and devotes one room to Honoré Daumier (1808-1879), the satirical caricaturist from Marseille. Works by Ingres, David, and Rubens, as well as some early Dufy landscapes round out the collections. (Open daily 10am-5pm. Admission 12F, students 6F, over 65 free.)

Spend an afternoon at Marseille's colossal **Aquarium del Prado,** pl. Amiral Muselier (tel. 91 71 00 46), at Promenade de la Plage by the Plage du Prado. Over 8000 exotic fish of 350 different species swim in 400 tons of water—now *that's bouillabaisse.* (Open Sun.-Thurs. 10am-7pm, Fri.-Sat. 10am-midnight. Admission 44F; students, seniors, and children 38F.) Take bus #19, 83, or 72 (7F50). The **Musée Cantini,** 19, rue Grignan (tel. 91 54 77 75) features modern art from Fauvism to the present in constantly changing exhibitions. The house alone, a 17th-century mansion with an elegant courtyard, merits a visit. (Admission 17F, students 10F, over 65 or under 10 free.) The rest of Marseille's museums—including the **Musée d'Histoire Naturelle, Musée Grobet Labadié,** and **Musée du Vieux Marseille**—don't justify their admission fees.

A short boat-ride away, the **Château d'If** (tel. 91 59 02 30) perches precariously on one of Marseille's small harbor islands. The château's dungeon, immortalized by Alexandre Dumas in *The Count of Monte Cristo,* held Mirabeau and a number of Huguenots. Although originally built as a fortress to defend Marseille from naval intruders, foreign ships have never threatened Marseille; the cannon inside the chateau's three stark turrets have been fired only in salute. Frequent boats depart from the quai des Belges. Call the **Groupement des Armateurs Côtiers** (tel. 91 55 50 09) for information (20min., round-trip 40F, office open daily 9am-7pm).

Along bd. Michelet (en route to the *calanques),* Le Corbusier's 1950s **Cité Radieuse** is a nifty 17-story concrete box standing on an army of short, curved legs. Those wacky 50s.

Entertainment

France's oldest city is far from tired; don't let Marseille's seedy reputation send you to bed early. But do take some basic precautions. Neither men nor women should cruise the streets alone after dark. Even groups should be careful, especially around the *vieux port.* Steer clear of the North African quarter, cours Belsunce, and bd. d'Athènes altogether after 10pm.

Le Couvent, 13, rue Leca (tel. 91 56 66 78) projects live jazz and dancing in a 17th-century convent (open Wed.-Sat. 10:30pm-1am). **Le Club,** 14, rue Sénac and **Le Golf,** up the street at 3, rue Sénac, blast rock, jazz, and new age to a young and trendy crowd. (Open Mon.-Sat. 11pm-2am. Cover 30F.) The **London Club,** corniche John Kennedy (tel. 91 52 64 64), plays similar music for a mostly French crowd. (Open nightly 11pm-2am. Cover 60F, including first drink.)

Cours Julien and the adjacent **rue Vian** were made for evening promenades and people-watching. The popular **Il Caffe,** 63, cours Julien (tel. 91 42 02 19), is an ideal spot for a cold drink (13F) on a hot summer evening (open Mon.-Sat. 9am-10pm). **Chez Ludo et Sergio,** 13, rue Beauvau (tel. 91 33 69 69), is a terrific piano bar right on the *vieux port.* Everyone from Sid Vicious to Bob Marley haunts the **Maison Hantée,** 10, rue Vian (tel. 91 92 09 40), which blares everything from punk to reggae. (Open nightly 7pm-1am. Live bands from 10pm.)

Recover from last night's festivities at the beaches 3km east of the city, near the aquarium. Both the **Plage du Prado** and the **Plage de la Corniche** offer wide beaches, good surf, and surprisingly scenic views of the grayish-white cliffs surrounding Marseille.

Marseille Decembers bring the international **Festival de Musique,** a week-long jubilee of jazz, classical, and pop music at l'Abbaye de Saint-Victoire; call the tourist office for ticket information. Theater buffs can check out the program at the **Théâtre National de Marseille,** quai de Rive Neuve (tel. 91 54 70 54). (Tickets 75-120F. Box office open Tues.-Sat. 11am-6pm.) The latest English and French films unwind at the **Cinéma Capitole,** 134, La Canebière (tel. 91 48 27 64) and the **Cinéma Breteuil** 120, bd. Notre Dame (tel. 91 37 71 36).

Near Marseille

The **Calanques** are inlets of azure blue water surrounded by walls of jagged rock. They extend from Marseille to Toulon, blending the sort of precipitous cliffs found on the Norwegian coast and the brilliantly translucent sea that surrounds the Greek Isles. Bleached white houses skirt the hills, looking down on the swarms of scuba divers, mountain climbers, and cliff divers who invade the area every summer. The most impressive *calanques* are at **En Vau.** At **Port Miou,** the craggy rocks vogue a fashionable five o'clock shadow of blooming heather. A small, tree-studded beach lies between the angular walls of **Port Pin.** During July and August, the **Société des Excursionnistes Marseillais,** 16, rue de la Rotonde (tel. 91 84 75 52), conducts free walking tours of the *calanques* twice per week. Their boat trips leave daily in summer from the quai des Belges (round-trip 100F). You can also take bus #21 (direction: "Luminy," 7F50) to the end of the line—near the **Morgiou** and **Sormiou.**

Twenty-three km from Marseille, the charming resort town of **Cassis** clings to a hillside overlooking the deep greens and blues of the Mediterranean. Immaculate white villas clump around the slopes above Cassis, while the town itself—a network of winding staircases, slender alleyways, and thick gardens—rests beside a devilishly bright port. Swimmers should follow the signs to the **Calanque de Port-Pin,** about 20 minutes east of town along a footpath. From there, it's another half hour of difficult hiking to **En Vau** and more magnificent *calanques.* Since the **train station** is 3km outside of town, it's simplest to take a bus to Cassis. The **Société Cars Autobus de Cassis (SCAC** (tel. 42 73 18 00) runs almost 20 buses daily (50min., 20F) from Marseille to Cassis's **transit office,** pl. Baraguon. Cassis makes a terrific daytrip, since hotels in town soar beyond the budget traveler's means. The only reasonable option, the **Auberge de Jeunesse La Fantasse (HI)** (tel. 42 01 02 72), 10km from Marseille on the B559, has no hot water and is a 4km walk from the nearest bus stop. Take the bus from the tourist office (direction: "Les Calanques") before 6pm. (40F, nonmembers 59F.) You might prefer the **Camping Les Cigales** (tel. 42 01 07 34), a 10-minute walk on av. de la Marne. (45F for 1 person with tent, 22F for each additional person or tent.)

Toulon

Though smaller than Marseille, the salty, sassy city of Toulon (pop. 185,000) is hardly tame. In this, France's leading naval base and second-largest port, uniformed sailors wander the streets like children on a school outing. Toulon's harborside bars and cafés escape the tourist frenzy that plagues much of the Riviera and course instead with the spirit of an active maritime city. Because Toulon is small, however, a good neighborhood rapidly passes into an unsafe one; solo travelers should exercise care after dark on the streets between rue Jean Jaurès and the port.

Orientation and Practical Information

Toulon is connected by frequent trains to Marseille, St-Raphaël, and Nice. The center of the city lies between the train station and the shore. Between bd. Strasbourg and rue Jean Jaurès around pl. Victor Hugo and pl. Dauphius there is a pleasant pedestrian zone of shops and cafés. The enigmatic **North African quarter,** with its narrow streets and colorful shops, spreads from rue Jean Jaurès south to the port. Although the North African quarter is dangerous at night, this area invites some of the most enjoyable daytime strolling in Toulon. To get to the main tourist office and the center of town, walk left out of the train station for three blocks and turn right on av. Colbert; the office is on the left. Alternatively, visit the branch office in the station.

Tourist Office: 8, av. Colbert (tel. 94 22 08 22), at rue Victor Clapier. Welcoming staff makes free hotel reservations and provides tons of advice on sights, accommodations, and restaurants. Open Mon.-Sat. 8am-7pm; Sept.-June Mon.-Sat. 8:30am-6:30pm. **Annex** in the train station (tel. 94 62 73 87). Same services as above. Open Mon.-Sat. 7:30am-8pm; Sept.-June Mon.-Sat. 8:30am-noon and 2-8:30pm.

Currency Exchange: Bureau de Change, 15, quai Stalingrad, at the port. Charges 10F commission for exchanges less than 500F and 20F for those from 500-1000F. Open July-Aug. daily 9am-7pm. Also in the **train station.** Open daily 9am-noon and 2-6pm.

Post Office: rue Prosper Ferrero (tel. 94 92 36 04), at the western end of the pedestrian zone. **Poste Restante** and **telephones.** Open Mon.-Tues. and Thurs.-Fri. 8am-7pm, Wed. 8am-6pm, Sat. 8am-noon. The *recette principale* (main receiving office) in Toulon is 15min. east of the city on rue Raymond Poincaré; **Poste Restante** for the downtown office should be marked "rue Prosper Ferrero." **Postal Code:** 83000.

Trains: bd. Toesca (tel. 94 91 50 50). Information office open Mon.-Sat. 8am-7pm. Tickets sold daily 5am-midnight. About every 30min. to: Marseille (1hr., 49F); St-Raphaël (1hr., 68F); Nice (2hr., 102F); Cannes (80min., 80F). Baggage storage open daily 7:30am-8:30pm. Lockers (25F) open 6am-10pm.

Buses: (tel. 94 93 11 39), across from the train station in an office labeled with a "Sodetrav" sign. Open daily 8:30am-7pm. Buses depart in front of the train station. **Francelignes** (tel. 91 98 32 05). To Aix-en-Provence (3 per day, 75min., 70F, students 42F). **Sodetrav** (tel. 94 92 26 41). To: St-Tropez (7 per day, 2 1/2hr., 80F), with many stops including Hyères (6:30am-9:25pm, 1 per hr., 35min., 32F).

Public Transportation: Local buses gather in the traffic circle in front of the station. Marked with the initials "RMTT" (tel. 94 27 20 30), they run throughout Toulon and adjoining areas. Fare 7F.

Ferries: SNCM, 21, and 49, av. de l'Infanterie-de-Marine (tel. 94 41 25 76 or 94 41 01 76), at the far eastern end of the port. To Corsica (2 per day, 10hr., round-trip 490F). In the "blue" period (most of Oct.-April): reductions for married couples on cabin tickets; ages 12-25 30% off; over 60 50% off. **Transmed 2000,** quai Stalingrad (tel. 94 92 96 82), sends 4 boats per day mid-July to Aug. 2 to Porquerolles (50F, round-trip 80F), Port Cros (80F, round-trip 130F), and Ile du Levant (90F, round-trip 160F).

Taxis: Near the train station (tel. 94 93 51 51 or 94 93 51 84). 24 hrs.

Bike/Moped Rental: Sun Bikes Location, 748, bd. de la Marine (tel. 94 57 39 11), near the Toulon airport. Rent bikes for 60F per day, 800F deposit; mountain bikes 70F, 1000F deposit; mopeds 90F, 1900F deposit. Also motorcycles, waterskis, and jet skis available. Open daily 9:30am-noon and 1-6pm.

Laundromat: Laverie, 25, rue Baudin and rue Pèreisc. Wash 16F per 7kg. Dry 2F per 6min. Open daily 8am-9pm.

Special Services: Cercle Amical Feminin de Toulon et Environs (C.A.F.T.E.), Foyers de la Jeunesse, pl. d'Armes (tel. 94 41 41 33). Sponsors conferences, debates, films, and houses a library—all dedicated to women's issues. Meetings every Thurs. 2-5pm. **SOS Racisme** (tel. 94 60 90 00 or 94 60 92 00) works to combat racism and offers support for those experiencing it.

Medical Emergency: SAMU, tel. 94 27 07 07. **SOS Médecins,** tel. 94 31 33 33.

Hospital: Ste-Anne, bd. Ste-Anne (tel. 94 09 90 00), off av. Victoire de 8 Mai 1945, just behind the train station.

Police: rue Commandant Morandin (tel. 94 09 80 00). **Emergency:** tel. 17.

Accommodations and Camping

Although Toulon has no official youth hostel, the Centre International de Séjour (set up in a school building every July and Aug.) provides inexpensive accommodations. Toulon is also chock full of small, affordable hotels. Even in July and August, inexpensive lodging should be easy to find. Head for the areas of the upper *vieille ville,* and near the SNCF station, both safer than the neighborhoods near the port. A number of cheap hotels huddle on and around rue Jean Jaurès in the middle of the pedestrian zone.

Centre International de Séjour, rue Philippe Rameau (tel. 94 31 16 35). From the train station, follow bd. de Tesse which becomes rue F. Fabie. At pl. Noël Blanche, take av. Clemenceau until you reach the busy rotary at Rond Point Bir Hakeim. Rue Poincaré (on the opposite side of the Rond Point) will lead you to the post office. The *centre* is just beyond the post office on the left. Set up in the classrooms of an active secondary school, the *foyer* has dorm-style rooms and showers and toilets that plead for renovation. But the staff is most hospitable, and it's the cheapest place in town. Pillows and toilet paper not guaranteed. Reception open July-Aug. daily 8am-1am. 40F. Breakfast 15F.

Hôtel Molière, 12, rue Molière (tel. 94 92 78 35), on pl. Victor Hugo. An ideally situated gem with management as bright and cheerful as the daily display of flowers. TV lounge. Telephones in all rooms. Singles 85F. Doubles 95F, with shower 135F, with 2 beds 155F. Triples with shower 210F. Showers 10F. Breakfast 22F.

Hôtel La Résidence, 18, rue Gimelli (tel. 94 92 92 81), off av. Vauban, near the train station. Well-kept rooms, some carpeted. Great location. Singles 100F, with shower 110F. Doubles 120F, with shower 160F. Showers 15F. Breakfast 22F. Beer 10F.

Hôtel de Provence, 53, rue Jean Jaurès (tel. 94 93 19 00), also in the pedestrian zone and across from the post office. Clean, simple, and centrally located. Friendly managers. Singles 90F, with shower 125F. Doubles 100F, with shower 135F. Triples with shower 170F. Quads with shower 160F. Breakfast 20F.

Hôtel des Trois Dauphins, 9, pl. des Trois Dauphins (tel. 94 92 65 79), near pl. Puget. Spacious rooms, each with carpet, desk, and dresser. Renovated in 1992. Singles 75-90F, with hall shower 85-95F, with shower 120F. Quads 180F. Breakfast 20F.

Hôtel Little Palace, 6-8, rue Berthelot (tel. 94 92 26 62), across from Hôtel des Trois Dauphins, just off pl. Puget in the middle of the pedestrian zone. Kind and jovial manager keeps the small, dimly lit rooms immaculate. Singles 75F. Doubles 120F. Triples and quads with shower 200F.

Camping: Camping Beauregard (tel. 94 20 56 35), in La Garde, *quartier* Ste-Marguerite, 6km from Toulon and 400m from the sea. Take bus #7 from the station to the Promised Land ("La Terre Promise" stop). 15F per person, 13F per tent. **Camping des Mimosas,** av. Marcel Paul (tel. 94 94 73 15), 4km away in La Seyne sur Mer. Take the bus from the *gare routière.* 14F per person, 12F per tent. Open daily 9am-9pm.

Food

Restaurants bunch around the pedestrian zone. Look out for them. For seafood, try around the *vieux port,* but remember that the places on the waterfront might rip you off, so establish prices clearly at the start of the meal. Try rue du Pomet and rue Poncy near the opera, but be careful at night, when prostitutes stalk the streets nearby. Fruit and vegetable **markets** attract throngs of shoppers on cours Lafayette and rue Paul Landrin every morning from 6am to noon. The nearest supermarket is **Carrefour,** in the **centre Mayol** mall, next to the stadium (open Mon.-Sat. 8:30am-9pm). Stock-up here before beaching it or else pay dearly at overpriced snack stands by the water.

Piano Crêperie, 45, rue Victor Clappier (tel. 94 91 93 04), near the tourist office. Over 50 *crêpes* (31-66F) and as many jazz styles. 71F *menu.* Huge video screen to boot. Better than *Cats.* Open Tues.-Sun. 7pm-1am. Nightly concert 9pm-midnight. 15F cover. Call for reservations.

Au Sourd, 10, rue Molière. Great seafood place specializing in bouillabaisse (30-50F), *coquillages* (shellfish) (32-64F), and other fresh seafood. Open Tues.-Sat. 11:30am-2pm and 5-10pm.

Chez Mimi-Pascal, 83, av. de la République. Tunisian delights served daily from the kitchen's wood-burning stove. *Couscous* dishes with pork, chicken, or beef (74-89F). Salads (30-40F). Tunisian pastry (22F). Open Tues.-Sun. noon-2:30pm and 7-10:30pm.

Le Murat, 52, rue Jean Jaurès. Great French classics on a 75F *menu*. *Plat du jour* 45F, *pêche du jour* (catch of the day) 50F. Open Mon.-Wed. and Fri.-Sat. noon-1:30pm and 7-10pm, Sun. noon-1:30pm.

Al Dente, 30, rue Gimeli, a few blocks from the tourist office at rue Dumont d'Urville. Eight varieties of fresh homemade pasta in a slick atmosphere. Ravioli Roman-style (heavy on the cheese and herbs) 38F. *Spaghetti au pistou* 32F. Weekday lunch *menu* 46F. Open daily noon-2pm and 7:15-11pm; Sept.-June Mon.-Sat. noon-2pm and 7:15-11pm, Sun. 7:15-11pm.

Cafétéria du Centre, rue Chavannes, at rue Gimelli. Open daily 11am-2:30pm and 5:30-10pm. **Cafétéria Casino,** 1, rue Françaïs Fablé. Open daily 11am-10pm. Both serve huge portions at low prices. Roast chicken and vegetables 21F.

Sights and Entertainment

During the day, Toulon's **North African quarter** (between rue Jean Jaurès and the port) is a colorful cornucopia of merchants, tea-rooms, and local gossip. Vendors hawk Persian rugs, tapestries, T-shirts, and spices at low prices. At night, stay away from this crime-ridden area.

Toulon's waterfront harbors France's second-largest port. The nearby **Plage du Marillon** consists of small, uncrowded, and relatively isolated beaches where you can tan the day away. Walk to the *vieux port,* and follow av. de la République and av. de Tassigny for 20 minutes. Buses make the trip from the train station (10 per day, 7F). The **Musée Naval,** pl. Ingénieur Général Monsenergue (tel. 94 02 02 01), displays relics of Toulon's naval history, including enormous ship models (up to 3m) and an actual torpedo (be good!). (Open daily 10am-noon and 2:30-7pm. Admission 22F, students 11F.)

For a trance-inducing view of Toulon reflecting off the Mediterranean, take the *téléphérique* (cable car) (tel. 94 92 68 25) to the top of **Mont Faron** from bd. Perrichi, several blocks behind the station. (Open Tues.-Sun. 9am-noon and 2:15-6:15pm. Round-trip 28F, students and children 20F.) At the top, the **Musée du Débarquement** (tel. 94 88 08 09) contains exhibits on the 1944 Allied landing. Eight different galleries, each devoted to one of the allied nations, commemorate the historic landing that General de Gaulle called "an event of primordial importance" for the liberation of France during WWII. (Open July-Aug. Tues.-Sun. 9:30-11:30am and 2-5:30pm. Admission 20F, under 13 8F.) Also at the top is an excellent **zoo** (tel. 94 88 07 89; open daily 10am-noon and 2-7pm; admission 30F, ages 4-10 20F).

Tours of the harbor and the surrounding islands depart daily from quai Stalingrad. Visit the rocky isthmus of **St-Mandrier** or the 16th-century fortress on the isthmus of **Tamaris** (ferry 10F; admission to fort 20F, students 15F). For more information, call 94 62 41 14 or 94 36 01 32, or contact the tourist office.

From late May to mid-July, Toulon throws an **international music festival,** which attracts renowned ensembles and a wide range of non-classical performers from as far away as Moscow. Tickets to the first few shows in May are free. After that, tickets run 50-180F and are sold at the tourist office (tel. 94 93 52 84). The Centre Culturel Châteauvallon, 5km from Toulon, hosts the **Festival de la Danse et de l'Image** throughout July (tickets 80-160F). Call 94 24 11 76 for information.

Toulon rocks on through the night, but avoid the areas around rue Jean Jaurès, rue Pierre Sémard, and rue des Riaux, well-known for their drug and flesh trades. Stay in groups and consider taking taxis.

The **Piano Crêperie,** 45, rue Victor Clappier (tel. 94 91 93 04) swings with live jazz every night. (See Food.) **Le Hi-fi Club,** 44, bd. de Strasbourg (tel. 94 92 31 14), near the tourist office, is a popular dance club with great rock, jazz, and pop. (Open nightly 11pm-4am. Cover and first drink 80F, 2nd drink 50F.) The **Femina Cinéma,** 20, rue Victor Clappier (tel. 94 92 39 31), near the tourist office, plays 10 films (original version with French subtitles) each night from 2-10pm (40F, students 32F, Mon. 27F).

Near Toulon

The islands off the coast of Toulon are known as the **Iles d'Hyères,** or the Golden Isles, for the color of the sun's reflection off the mica rock. Reaching these treasured isles can be expensive, but few regret the trip. **Porquerolles** (pop. 350), the largest island, was home to a religious order until François I declared it an asylum for criminals who had agreed to defend the mainland against pirates. The convicts, however, soon transformed the island into a base for their own piratical forays. Decades later, Louis XIV finally ended their raiding. Today, travelers visit the island for its wealth of natural treasures. Rugged cliffs separate small, hidden coves splashed by clear turquoise sea. Pick your favorite crag and swim all day without seeing a soul.

The Côte d'Azur as it was meant to be awaits you at the **Calanque de l'Oustaou de Dieu,** across the island from the village. Rising from the island's refreshingly unspoiled south side, a giant nite-lite of a lighthouse looks out over rocky cliffs plunging into blue waves. To get there, walk straight through town from the port and continue through the island's dry interior. Both the *calanques* and the lighthouse are easily accessible by bicycle or foot. To reach the yacht-filled cove at **Plage d'Argent,** turn right just outside the port and look for signs. The beaches are thinner on the other side of the village, but so are the crowds. A shop 100m left of the port rents bikes for 50-80F per day with a 500F deposit. Try to get a sturdy mountain bike. The **tourist office** (tel. 94 58 33 76) at the port lists yacht accommodations (100-300F per night). For more information, call 94 58 34 15.

The neighboring **Ile du Levant,** originally settled by monks, now harbors one of Europe's most famous nudist colonies, **Héliopolis.** Except for the western tip where ferries land, the entire island goes *au naturel.* Visitors are welcome—if they're willing to bare it all. The island has many small and quiet beaches but the most popular one lies just east of the boat-landing. The two one-star hotels, **H. Gaëtan** (tel. 94 05 91 78) and **La Brise Marine** (tel. 94 05 91 15) are booked solid well in advance throughout the summer. Rough it in the buff at the island's three campgrounds: **Le Colombéro** (tel. 94 05 90 29; open Easter-Oct.), **Les Eucalyptes** (tel. 94 05 91 32), or **La Pinède** (tel. 94 05 90 47; open April-Oct.).

Boats for the islands (tel. 94 92 96 82) depart from quai Stalingrad in Toulon. Boats go to Porquerolles (45F, round-trip 80F) and Ile du Levant (90F, round-trip 160F) twice per day, once off-season. The trips take 1 1/2 to 2 hours. Boats also depart for the islands from Port d'Hyères, accessible from Toulon by train (3 per day, 5min., 21F).

Back on the mainland, the old resort town of **Hyères** sits overlooking the Mediterranean like the *grande dame* of the Riviera. Agatha Christie's fictitious sleuth Hercule Poirot fancied the resorts and adventure of Hyères in *Mystery of the Blue Train.* The **bus,** however, is the best way to get here from Toulon (every hour from 6:30am to 9:30pm, 35min., 32F). Most of the town's accommodations exceed tight budgets, but the **tourist office** in Hyères, at Roton de Jean Salusse, av. de Belgique (tel. 94 65 18 55), has lists of campgrounds and affordable hotels. (Open daily 9am-8pm; Sept. 16-June 14 Mon.-Sat. 9am-noon and 2-6pm.) International talents overtake the town in mid-July for the week-long **Jazz Festival.** Tickets (60-120F) are available at the Théâtre Denis, cours Strasbourg (tel. 94 65 22 72) or in Toulon at the Phonothèque, pl. de la Liberté (tel. 94 32 27 30).

Two excellent wine-growing regions, Bandol and Côtes de Provence, lie respectively west and east of Toulon. They produce mostly rosés, but also some light whites and reds. Once a refuge for Bertolt Brecht and Thomas Mann, **Bandol** (pop. 6700) is now popular with less luminous Germans, and even more so with the French. Its white, snaking streets surround a delightful town square, which doubles as marketplace and a nighttime dance floor. Bandol's **tourist office** (tel. 94 29 41 35), on allées Vivien near the bus station, **changes money** in summer. (Open Mon.-Fri. 9am-12:30pm and 2-8pm, Sat.-Sun. 9am-noon; Sept.-June Mon.-Fri. 9am-noon and 2-6pm, Sat.-Sun. 9am-noon.) Bandol is best known for its gentle rosés and its intense sailing competitions. Regional regattas take place off the port in May and June.

Rent a **windsurfer** at Hookipa Beach (tel. 94 29 53 15) for 70F per hour (discounts for longer rentals). Many folks inconspicuously cut between private condominiums to reach the perfect public beaches west of town. **Buses** to Bandol leave the Toulon train station twice every hour from July to September. Call **S.A.R.C.V. Littoral Cars** at 94 74 01 35 for a schedule. Ten daily **trains** stop in Bandol on the way to Marseille in summer (25min., 17F).

St-Tropez

Hollywood and *Lifestyles of the Rich and Famous* have popularized an image of St-Tropez as a veritable modern day *El Dorado*. One expects a city in which Hermès goes to bathe with Yves St-Laurent, Lamborghinis prowl streets paved with gold, celebrities pay for drinks from a string of pearls and *everybody's* had a difficult day at the beach. Surely, Robin Leach's nasal voice, venerating the beautiful and ogling the mansions in a town that even the French have nicknamed *Saint Trop d'Aise* (St. Too-much-luxury), serves as the primary introduction to St- Tropez for most budget travelers.

Yet while swanky Cannes to the east might fit this image, the St-Tropez of reality bears mercifully little resemblance to that of myth. Instead, an intimate coastal village embraces the glitter of modern life while clinging to centuries-old architecture and traditions. *Mais,* don't misunderstand: there's no shortage of wealth on display, and enough exclusive restaurants and boutiques exist to challenge even the mightiest of platinum credit cards. Nonetheless, all of this occurs in a tasteful and understated ambience where the humble budget traveler can exist comfortably alongside the exquisite and wealthy "natives."

St-Tropez consists roughly of two parts: the town itself and the famous beaches that stretch out in the sun 4-10km to the southeast Either can be thoroughly enjoyed as a daytrip but be forewarned that there is no place to store luggage. To appreciate St-Tropez thoroughly, plan on spending at least one night. The town is quite compact and easily explored on foot. To reach the beaches, catch the **Sodetrav buses** (tel. 94 97 41 21) at the *gare routière* (which doubles as the tourist office) on av. du Général de Gaulle, near the *nouveau port*. The "St-Tropez-Ramatuelle" line runs thrice daily Monday to Saturday and passes **Plage Tahiti** (10min, 7F), which has the most wealth, **Plage des Salins** (10min, 7F), the most public space, and **Plage de Pampelonne** (10min, 8F), the most sand. Better yet, rent a pair of wheels from **Louis Mas**, 3 and 5, rue Quarenta (tel. 94 97 00 60), where **bicycles** go for 40F per day (deposit 500F), mountain bikes for 70F (deposit 1500F), and mopeds for 80-135F (deposit 2000-4000F, gas 25F, helmets 6F). (Open Easter-Oct. 15 Mon.-Sat. 9am-7:30pm, Sun. 9am-12:45pm and 5:30-7:30pm). Great swimming and good climbing rocks await at **Plage de l'Escalet**, 15km away; the Sodetrav bus goes twice daily to the village of Escalet (25min, 10F). By the way, while considering your beach excursion, keep in mind author Peter Mayle's observation that "at any given moment during any day in the month of August there are five thousand people making *pipi* in the sea."

In town, the **tourist office** between avs. du Général de Gaulle and Général LeClerc is well-staffed and stocked with French and English information on hotels, restaurants, sights, buses and boats. They also offer a free accommodations service, invaluable in July and August. (Open Mon.-Sat. 9am-8pm, Sun. 10am-1pm and 3-7pm; Oct.-March. Mon.-Sat. 9am-12:30pm and 2-6:30pm; April-June 15 Mon.-Sat. 9am-7pm, Sun. 10am-1pm and 3-7pm.) The **branch office,** on quai Jean Jaurès, performs the same functions and holds the same hours. Although the American Express office has up and left town, a **Thomas Cook** office (tel. 94 97 88 00; open daily May-Sept. 9am-11pm.), and many banks cluster on quai G.-Péri, by the *vieux port* to sate your financial hungers.

If Daddy's been arrested for junk-bond fraud or the stock-market crashed, don't despair; there *are* some semi-affordable hotels in St-Tropez, and no one has to know. But by mid-June, they're booked nearly solid. Call ahead or hope for the best at **Hôtel le Méditerranée,** bd. Louis Blanc (tel. 94 97 00 44), across from the Hôtel de Paris. (Singles and doubles 250F, with shower 280F, with toilet 380-410F. Quads with shower and toilet 530F. Breakfast 30F.) **Lou Cagnard,** 18, av. Paul Roussel (tel. 94 97 04 24 or 94 97 09 44), has spacious rooms with carpeting and telephones. (Doubles with bath 230F, with shower and toilet from 380F. Obligatory breakfast 34F.) **La Roman,** ch. des Conquettes (tel. 94 97 15 50), has palatial, modern rooms, each with a full bathroom, TV and private, walled-in garden. (Doubles 410F, Breakfast 40F.) Camping is by far the cheapest option, but again, make reservations. The tourist office will tell you which sites have space, but few will in July and August. Try four-star **La Croix du Sud,** route de Pampelonne (tel. 94 79 80 84), (25F per person, 36F per tent; open Easter-Sept.), or **Kon Tiki** (tel. 94 79 80 17; 67F per tent). Both lie just behind the Pampelonne beach. Toward l'Escalet is **Les Tournels,** route du Phare de Camarat (tel. 94 79 81 38; 28F50 per person). Camping on the beach is strictly prohibited; this law is enforced. The closest **HI youth hostel** (tel. 94 52 18 75) is in Fréjus. Take the ferry (3 per day, 50min., 47F) or the bus (6 per day, 80min., 41F) to St-Raphaël and then the direct shuttle bus to the hostel (daily at 6pm, 5F). The hostel has terrific facilities and wonderful management. (Reception open 7:30-10am and 6-11pm. 59F. Breakfast included. See Fréjus Accommodations.)

The *vieux port* and the narrow, cobbled streets of the hillside *vieille ville* behind the waterfront is the hub of St-Tropez's restaurant and café activity. Sit at **Café Senequier,** quai Jean Jaurès, next to the tourist office,and watch the portside spectacle of yachts, artists, wealth, and of course, gaping tourists. For dinner, inexpensive restaurants hang out up on the hill. **Mario,** 9, rue Aire du Chemin offers a 65F French-Italian *menu* on a pink and lavender terrace (open daily 7-11pm). **Le Cigalon,** 12, rue Cd. Guichard, next to the **Eglise Paroissiale,** serves pizza and traditional French fare in a 49F three-course and a 69F four-course *menu* (open daily noon-6:30pm). **La Petite Tante Marie,** at the corner of rue Bergère and rue de la Miséricorde, also lets you escape into the old city and fill-up on an 80F *menu.* (Open daily 6-11pm.) If you prefer to create your own ambience, head to the picnic pick-up spot, **Prisonic Supermarché,** 7, av. du Général Le Clerc (open Mon.-Sat. 8am-8pm) or the outdoor *grand marché* in pl. des Lices (open Tues. and Sat. 6:30am-1pm). Great picnic spots lounge along the water only ten minutes from the *vieux port.* Follow ch. des Graniers past the brilliantly flowered **Cimetière Marin** to the small but uncrowded **Plage des Graniers.** On the beach basks the **Les Graniers** restaurant and bar, where barefoot servers wait tables planted in the sand. If you choose to arrive by boat, just drop anchor and wait for the restaurant's complimentary motorboat to whisk you ashore. Of course, this ambience will cost you; stick to the 10F espresso (open daily 11am-9pm). A small, public path continues past the beach, snaking between the shore and posh villas. Choose a cove and bask *au naturel*—in St-Tropez, tan-lines are a distinct *faux-pas.*

The **Citadelle,** perched on a hill at the eastern end of town, offers an encompassing view of the entire gulf. This 16th-century fortress, with a moat now brimming with peacocks, houses the **Musée Naval,** which displays maritime articles from the waterfront's less ostentatious days. (Both open Wed.-Mon. 10am-6pm. Admission 18F, students and groups 9F.) In the serene confines of an ancient chapel, the **Musée de l'Annociade,** pl. Grammont (tel. 94 97 04 01), exhibits a wild collection of Fauvist and neo-impressionist paintings (open 10am-noon and 3-6pm; admission 24F, students 10F).

Each year between May 16 and 18, St-Tropez goes all out for its defiant *bravade* in honor of its patron saint, who was beheaded by Nero and then set adrift on a raft with a cock and a dog. To commemorate his eventual and certainly malodorous arrival here, locals don religious costumes and race through the streets firing guns for two days. Cultural relativism insists that you accept this practice unquestioningly.

Reaching this self-proclaimed "jewel of the Riviera" requires some extra effort, as the town lies well off the rail line. Take the bus (but don't admit it) from St-Raphaël (8 per day, 1 1/2-3hr., 41F); Toulon (8 per day, 2 1/2-4hr., 70F); or Hyères (6 per day, 2-3hr., 60F). Call **Sodetrav buses** (tel. 94 97 62 77), or ask the tourist office for more information. The faster and more scenic boat ride from St-Raphaël is much more suave, and not much more expensive (mid-June to mid-Sept. 3-4 per day, April-June and Sept.-Oct. 4 per day, 50min., one-way 47F, round-trip 80F, but only 68F if you stay at the Fréjus hostel). Contact **Gare Maritime de St-Raphaël** (tel. 94 95 17 46) for more information (open daily 9am-noon and 2-6pm). Hitching is poor; you'd soil the upholstery, darling.

Near St-Tropez

Known to the French as the "land of blue, green, and gold," the rocky coastline and sapphire *calanques* between St-Tropez and Cannes shelter several charming towns. In the early 1960s, hoping to recreate a typical Mediterranean fishing village, the people of **Port Grimaud** let the sea flow into canals dug throughout town. Boats have completely replaced cars, which must be left outside the town limits. As a result, the beaches are long and uninterrupted—the most beautiful (and most popular) running along the length of rue Grande. But that chic piscene ambience sought by the wealthy locals is emphatically absent.

Most hotels are quite expensive, but there are large campgrounds just outside town, including the out-of-control, 1400-site **Les Prairies de la Mer** (tel. 94 56 25 29) at St-Pons les Mûres, equipped with a minimarket, restaurant, bar, tennis courts, hot showers, and a TV room (60F per 1-2 people in a tent; open April-Oct.). Port Grimaud is accessible from St-Tropez by **ferry** (tel. 94 96 51 00; 24F) and by a bus which stops at nearby St-Pons (8F). Another ferry (tel. 94 95 17 46) cruises from St-Raphaël Tuesday and Saturday at 2:30pm (40min., one-way 90F).

Two km inland, **Grimaud** hangs quietly on a hill overlooking the Mediterranean. The town's shady lotus trees, old fortress, and 11th-century barrel-vaulted church offer a respite from the beaches of the port. The town is on the St-Raphaël-Toulon bus line, with a connection at La Foux (from St-Raphaël 6:30am-8pm, 8 per day, 50min.-3hr. in summer traffic; 42F from Toulon, 2 1/2-4hr., 82F). The bus from Toulon goes on to the less frequented, more picturesque village of **La Garde-Freinet,** 15 minutes from Grimaud. The **Camping Municipal St-Eloi** (tel. 94 43 62 40) includes hot showers, a swimming pool, and a snack bar. (20F per person, 10F per tent. Open June 15-Sept. 15.) The friendly **tourist office** (tel. 94 43 67 41); open Wed.-Mon. 9:30am-12:30pm and 5:30-7:30pm) has the usual information.

Across the gulf from St-Tropez, **Ste-Maxime** sports a great beach, tennis courts, and an 18-hole golf-course at the **Salle Omnisports,** route du Plan de la Tour (tel. 94 96 31 32). For more information, contact the **tourist office,** promenade S. Lorière (tel. 94 96 19 24). **Buses** run daily to Ste-Maxime from St-Raphaël (4 per day, 1 1/2hr., 24F). From Fréjus, Ste-Maxime is an easy 18km bike ride.

St-Raphaël and Fréjus

Sandwiched between St-Tropez and Cannes, the twin cities of St-Raphaël and Fréjus twinkle with a slightly dimmer, and eminently more affordable Riviera brilliance than their exclusive neighbors. The towns boast all the wide, sandy beaches, seafood restaurants and coastal charm of their swanky Côte d'Azur cousins at half the cost. Add relatively inexpensive accommodations, Roman monuments and unique museums, and St-Raphaël and Fréjus become the towns of choice for anyone tied to a budget.

Orientation and Practical Information

In a nutshell, St-Raphaël has the restaurants and the hotels, while Fréjus has the sights. St-Raphaël is a major stop on the Marseille-Nice train line, with frequent **trains** to Toulon (20 per day, 50min., 68F); Cannes (25 per day, 25min., 30F); and Nice (25 per day, 1hr., 42F). The **information office** at the **train station,** pl. de la Gare (tel. 93 99 50 50) has a full list of schedules. **Sodetrav buses** connect St-Raphaël to St-Tropez (8 per day, 2hr., 41F) and **Forum Cars** (tel. 94 95 16 71) makes the scenic trip to St-Raphaël from Cannes (with a fantastic view of the *calanques;* 8 per day, 70min., 23F). The **gare routière,** located across the train tracks from the train station, is a hub for both local and inter-city travel (open daily 8am-noon and 2-6:15pm). Buses run between St-Raphaël and Fréjus every half hour from quai #7 (Mon.-Sat. 7am-7pm, Sun. 7am-6pm; fare 5F).

A prominent resort even in Roman times, St-Raphaël had its two days in the sun when Napoleon landed here on his return from Egypt in 1799 and set sail for exile in Elba from here in 1814. You can set sail for St-Raphaël from the *Nouveau Port* in St-Tropez (4 per day, 50min., 47F). Contact the **gare maritime** at the *vieux port* in St-Raphaël (tel. 94 95 17 46) for more information (open daily 9am-noon and 2-6pm). The staff in the **tourist office** in St-Raphaël (tel. 94 95 16 87 or 94 95 19 70), across the street from the train station, has the scoop on transportation and room availability and also distributes reams of brochures on the Var, the region of Provence extending from St-Raphaël to Toulon. (Open Mon.-Sat. 8:15am-12:30pm and 1:30-7:30pm, Sun. 8:15am-noon; Oct.-June Mon.-Sat. 8:15-noon and 1:30-6pm.) The smaller **tourist office** in Fréjus, 325, rue Jean Jaurès (tel. 94 51 54 14), in front of the fountain in pl. Paul Vernet, stocks piles of information on Fréjus's attractions (open Mon.-Sat. 9am-7pm). To reach it, take the bus from St-Raphaël to the "Pl. Paul Vernet" stop in Fréjus (5F). The **post office** in St-Raphaël, av. Victor Hugo (tel. 94 95 12 03) is behind the train station (open Mon.-Fri. 8:30am-7pm, Sat. 8:30am-noon). **Postal code:** 83700. A **laundromat** (wash 18F for 5kg; open Mon.-Sat. 8:30am-12:30pm and 2:30-7:30pm) is in the **Intermarché** supermarket, av. André Léotard, near the Fréjus hostel.

Accommodations, Camping, and Food

Affordable accommodations make the two towns a favorite base for budget travelers, so be sure to book ahead. Most of the inexpensive options are in St-Raphaël, although the youth hostel in Fréjus is a notable exception.

Auberge de Jeunesse de St-Raphaël-Fréjus (HI), chemin du Counillier (tel. 94 52 18 75), 4km from the St-Raphaël train station. A direct shuttle bus runs from quai #6 of the *gare routière* to the hostel daily at 6pm (5F); a return shuttle leaves at 9:15am. If you miss the direct shuttle, take the regular buses (direction "Fréjus-pl. Paul Vernet," at quai #7, every 30min. from 7am-7pm, 5F) to "les Chênes" stop. Walk up av. Jean Callies to the chemin du Counillier; the hostel is at the top of the path. Superb hostel with comfortable beds (10-20 per room), a view of the inland wine valley, kind managers, and a great crowd of backpackers who hang out every night on the terrace out front. Lockout 10am-6pm. Curfew 11pm. 59F. Breakfast included. Delicious dinners 45F, also sells spaghetti and sauce 10F. Kitchen facilities.

Centre International du Manoir (tel. 94 95 20 58), in Boulouris. Plush oceanside site 5km from St-Raphaël. A bus from the *gare routière* makes the trip approximately every 30min. until 6:30pm (5F). Comfortable dorms in the annex. Lively bar and a disco. Lockout 4-5pm. 100F. Rooms with 1-6 beds 142F per person. Breakfast included. Meals 55F.

La Bonne Auberge, 54, rue de la Garonne (tel. 94 95 69 72) in St-Raphaël. Simple but pretty rooms in an excellent location. Doubles 130F, with shower 180F. Breakfast 26F. Open March-Oct.

Hôtel des Pyramides, 77, av. Paul Doumer (tel. 94 95 05 95) in St-Raphaël. Clean, comfortable rooms just off the beach, but near train tracks, which begin to grumble in the wee morning hours. Singles 85F. Doubles 160F, with showers 205F. Breakfast 25F.

Hôtel Bellevue, pl. Paul Vernet (tel. 94 51 42 41) in Fréjus, next to rue Reynaude. Great location in the center of town. Pinball machine and pool table downstairs. Compact but clean rooms. Singles 110F. Doubles 140F, with shower 180F. Breakfast 25F.

Les Templiers, pl. de la République (tel. 94 95 38 93), behind the train station. Jolly hotel with bright rooms. Tavern downstairs. Singles 130F. Doubles 160F. Breakfast and showers included.

Camping: At the youth hostel, in an attractive wooded area. 27F per person with tent. Hot showers included. Also **Royal Camping,** on camp-Long (tel. 94 82 00 20), along bus route to Cannes from St-Raphaël. Perks include hot showers, supermarket, and restaurant. 1-3 people and car 90F. Open April-Oct.

Affordable restaurants center around the *vieux port* and bd. de la Libération. If you're planning a picnic, try the **Intermarché Supermarket** on chemin du Counillier, beside the youth hostel in Fréjus, or the **Monoprix** on bd. de Félix Martin, off av. Alphonse Karr near the train station (open Mon.-Sat. 8:30am-7:15pm). A daily morning **market** brings color to pl. de la République, just behind the train station (8am-12:30pm). **Restaurant La Grillade,** 32, rue Boëtman, serves delicious *brochette d'agneau* (lamb skewers, 62F) and a 78F seafood *menu.* Pizzas run 36-55F. (Open Mon.-Fri. and Sun. noon-2:30pm and 7-10:30pm, Sat. 7-10:30pm.) **Le mistral,** 80, rue de la Garonne, offers a 55F and a 70F *menu,* both featuring *paella* and *couscous* (open daily 6-10pm). At **Le Nantic,** chow down on *chile con carne* and BBQ ribs (both 60F) amid Tex-Mex decor enhanced by 50s-style neon signs. (Open daily 11am-1:30pm and 4-11pm.)

Sights and Entertainment

While St-Raphaël supports a larger number of affordable hotels and restaurants, Fréjus claims the monopoly on sightseeing. Founded by Julius Caesar in 49 BC, Fréjus preens with several monuments from its heyday as an important Roman stronghold. Built at the end of the first century, the **Roman amphitheater,** rue Henri Vadar (tel. 94 51 34 31), is one of the oldest in Gaul. Since the place is a bit shabby—not having been reupholstered for nearly 2000 years—it is undergoing renovations in 1992. Remnants of Fréjus's ancient **Roman aqueduct** are scattered throughout town. One conspicuous fragment lines the walk to the youth hostel along the chemin du Counillier.

Fréjus also bears an unusually eclectic assemblage of religious architecture, with Christian, Buddhist, and Muslim houses of worship all functioning within walking distance of each other. Fréjus's **Cathédrale,** pl. J. C. Formige (tel. 94 51 26 30), off rue Bretagne in the northwest corner of the *centre ville,* has a 4th-century baptistery that marks it one of the oldest buildings in France; the original mosaics merit a visit. (Open daily 9am-7pm; Oct.-March daily 9am-noon and 2-5:30pm. Admission 20F, students or seniors 12F, ages 7-17 6F.) In 1918, the **Pagode Hong-Hiên,** across av. Jean Callies from the hostel, was built in Fréjus to accommodate the large number of colonial refugees from Asia. The Buddhist temple, built in Tibetan style, still functions as a spiritual center (open Mon.-Sat. 9am-noon and 2-6pm). The **Mosquée Soudanaise,** modeled after the grand mosque in Djenne, Mali, stands 2km from the town center as a sign of the area's active Muslim heritage.

Fréjus's most modern (and avant-garde) religious edifice is a round chapel designed by the famous "Prince des Poètes," Jean Cocteau. The **Cocteau Chapel** (tel. 94 53 56 45), the artist's last, was built in 1965 and provides a sort of neo-spiritual artistic inspiration. (Open Wed.-Mon. 4-6pm. For more information, call 94 53 56 45.) The elegant 19th-century **Villa Aurelienne,** av. du XV*ème* Corps (tel. 94 51 01 89), and the 20th-century **Villa Marie,** rue Aristide Briand (same tel., now the public library), testify to Fréjus's long-lost status as a luxury resort. Although the town is currently recovering its former glory, these two posh, pillared, palm-treed mansions with elegant public gardens hint at the decadence of the 19th-century lifestyle that first gave the Riviera its fabled reputation. (Both open Mon.-Fri. 9am-noon and 2-6pm.)

Bake in the sun along the long and sandy **Plage Fréjus,** just a ten-minute walk along the waterfront from the St-Raphaël train station, or make a splash at Fréjus's water park, **Aquatica,** RN98, just beyond the Géant Casino supermarket (tel. 94 52 01 01). A measly 15-minute walk from the beach, this watery wonderland features three pools, four water slides and four daily diving shows—tons of fun and a great break from the sand and salt water at the beach. (Open Mon.-Sat. 9am-7pm. Admission 91F.) Outside the *centre ville,* but still in Fréjus, is the **Parc Zoologique Safari de Fréjus** (tel. 94 40 70 65), a huge animal safari park that you can visit by car or—if you're brave—by foot. Take the Fayence-St-Raphaël bus line from St-Raphaël to the "Le Camps le Coq" stop. Go right at the fort and continue for about 10 minutes. (Open daily 10am-5:30pm. Admission 50F, ages 3-10 28F.) To take in all the sights or to daytrip in the area, rent wheels at **Cycles Patrick Beraud,** 337, rue de Triberg, near the Fréjus beach. (Bikes 50F per day, 500F deposit. Open Mon.-Sat. 9am-noon and 1-6pm.) Kill the night at the popular **L'Odyssée Disco,** bd. de la Libération (tel. 94 53 52 63). This dance club, right on the beach and only a ten-minute walk from the center of St-Raphaël along the water, attracts a hoppin' young crowd every night. (Open nightly 11pm-the wee hours. Cover and first drink 80F.) Take Lady Fortuna as your partner and head for the roulette wheels, backgammon tables, and slot-machines at the **Grand Casino** in St-Raphaël. (Open daily 11am-4am. No shorts.)

Near St-Raphaël and Fréjus

The nearby town of **Mandelieu-La Napoule** prides itself on being the "home of one-hundred sports." Mandelieu boasts over 30 different *associations sportives* where you can play tennis, golf, soccer, basketball, volleyball, *boules,* water ski, wind surf, sail, canoe, cycle, hike, ride horseback, or toss lawn darts. Wow! Call the **Centre d'Athlétisme** (tel. 92 97 30 60) or the **tourist office** (tel. 93 49 14 39 or 93 49 95 31) for more information. The town lies on the train line between St-Raphaël and Cannes and also receives daily buses from the two cities.

About 80km northwest of Cannes, the **Grand Canyon de Verdon**, 630m deep and 20km long, reigns as the deepest canyon in Europe. Here, massive cliffs streaked with yellow and pink wildflowers plunge to swift rivers and forested valleys. Seek out the vertiginous views at Point Sublimes and at the Balcons de la Mescla. The tourist offices in St-Raphaël and Fréjus have hiking maps and sundry information on the canyon. The cheapest and easiest way to see the canyon by public transport is by bus tour. **Havas Voyage,** av. Karr (tel. 94 95 33 43), at the bus station by the port in St-Raphaël, runs tours every Thursday (June-Sept. departure 8am, return around 7pm, 110F). Reservations are advised. (Office open Mon. 9:30am-noon and 2-6pm, Tues.-Fri. 9am-noon and 2-6pm, Sat. 9:30am-noon.) Similar tours leave twice per week (April-Sept.) from Antibes and Cannes (both 120F).

Although the canyon is easily seen on a daytrip, you might want to watch the sunset and then bed down in the nearby **Auberge de Jeunesse (HI)** at La-Palud-sur-Verdon (tel. 92 74 68 72), accessible by bus from Castéllane at the eastern end of the canyon. (40F. Camping 27F. Open March-Nov.) Pleasant lodging is also available at the **Auberge du Point Sublime,** 17km from Castéllane (tel. 92 83 60 35). Call to make sure there's room before taking a taxi. Some hitch. (Doubles with shower 100F. Breakfast 20F.)

Cannes

All preconceived notions of the French Riviera materialize in Cannes (pop. 69,000). Sister city to Beverly Hills, Cannes is one of the favorite stops of the international jet-set. The city's relationship with the rich and famous began in the middle of the 19th-century, when Lord Brougham came to the then-small village to flee a cholera epidemic in northern Europe. His rave reviews attracted more and more royalty to the town and helped make Cannes the "pearl of the Riviera" that it is today. These days, hundreds of millionaires lighten their purses in Cannes's swank cafés, plush hotels, wallet-walloping boutiques, and palm-lined boardwalk every summer. Less reclusive than St-Tropez, Cannes allows even the unshaven budget traveler to tan on the beach with Matt Dillon or browse in boutiques with Madonna without ever spending a dime. You'll still be terribly underdressed, but Armani and Hermès will forgive you.

Cannes reaches its zenith in the month of May, when the **Festival International du Film** brings the cream of Hollywood across the ocean. Executives will sign deals for $50 million flops on cocktail napkins; heartthrobs and starlets will stare glassily at bodies on the beach, waiting to be taken seriously; and Spike Lee wanna-bes will leave in a huff, proclaiming they've been robbed. None of the festival's 350 screenings is open to the public, but the sidewalk circus is absolutely free. And so are the pyrotechnics at Cannes's annual **Fête Americaine** and **Fête Nationale.** Fireworks, parades, and dancing in the streets occur every July 4 and July 14, Bastille Day.

Orientation and Practical Information

Cannes lies on the Côte d'Azur train line, with frequent connections to both Nice and Marseille. The station is located on rue Jean-Jaurès, which runs parallel to the sea. After exiting the station, follow rue des Serbes (across from and perpendicular to the station.) This leads to **bd. de la Croisette,** Cannes's long and lavish promenade that sweeps alongside the coast. The tourist office is located in the huge Palais des Festivals to the right.

Most of Cannes's daytime activity (and spending) pulses between rue Félix-Faure and the waterfront. Cafés, shops, *grandes dames,* and poodles line this oh-so-chic quarter of town. Stroll down lovely rue Meynardier—one of Cannes's few pedestrian streets—or down the boardwalk between **bd. de la Croisette** and the beach. Sandy public beaches are sandwiched between parasol-studded private ones, both of which are occasionally interrupted by docks securing multi-million dollar yachts.

Tourist Office, 1, bd. de la Croisette (tel. 93 39 01 01 or 93 39 24 53), in the Palais des Festivals next to the *vieux port.* Expert staff speaks excellent English. Loads of information on Cannes and the surrounding area. Free accommodations service. Open daily 9am-8pm; Sept.-June Mon.-Sat. 9am-6:30pm. Extended hours during festivals. **Branch office,** 1, rue Jean-Jaurès (tel. 93 99 19 77), upstairs in the train station. Another helpful office with accommodations service. Open Mon.-Sat. 9am-12:30pm and 2-6:30pm.

Currency Exchange: Office Provençal, 17, rue Maréchal-Foch (tel. 93 39 34 37), across from the train station. No commission, good location, and mediocre rates. Open daily 8am-8pm. **Agence du Casino,** 7, square Merimeé (tel. 93 39 11 96). Great rates but a 1% commission. Open daily 8am-noon and 1-7pm.

American Express: 8, rue des Belges (tel. 93 38 15 87), on the corner of rue Notre Dame and not far from rue Bivouac Napoléon. Open Mon.-Fri. 9am-noon and 2-6pm, Sat. 9am-noon.

Post Office: 22, rue Bivouac Napoléon (tel. 93 39 14 11), off rue Jean de Riouffe and near the Palais des Festivals. Open Mon.-Fri. 8am-7pm, Sat. 8am-noon. **Branch office** at 37, rue Mimont (tel. 93 39 33 15), behind the train station. Open Mon.-Fri. 8am-6:30pm, Sat. 8am-noon. Both have **telephones** and **Poste Restante. Postal Code:** 06400.

Trains: 1, rue Jean-Jaurès (tel. 93 99 50 50). Cannes lies on the major coastal line, with connections approximately every 30min. (6:11am-11:59pm) to: St-Raphaël (25min., 31F); Juan-les-Pins (10min., 8F); Antibes (15min., 9F); Nice (35min., 28F); Monaco (50min., 39F); Menton (1hr., 40F). Also hourly (6:30am-11:05pm) to Toulon (1 1/4hr., 80F) and Marseille (2hr., 112F). TGV to Paris via Marseille (449F). Station open 6am-midnight. Information desk open 8:30-11:30am and 2-6pm. Ticket sales 6am-11pm. Baggage service open daily 6am-1:30pm and 2-9:30pm.

Buses: *Gare routière* (tel. 93 64 50 17), next to the Hôtel de Ville, on the *Vieux Port.* Information office open Mon.-Tues. and Thurs.-Sat. 9am-noon and 2-6:30pm. Nice Airport (every 40min. 6am-7:40pm, 45min., 70F). Every 20min. to Antibes (30min., 13F), Nice (1 1/2hr., 28F). Also to St-Raphaël (8 per day, 70min., 23F) and Grasse (21 per day, 45min., 17F50). **Local buses** 6F; *carnet* of 6, 22F.

Taxis: Tel. 93 38 30 79, in front of the train station, and tel. 93 39 60 80 in front of the *Hôtel de Ville.*

Bike Rental: Cannes Location Rent, 5, rue Allieis (tel. 93 39 46 15), off pl. Gambetta in front of the train station. Bicycles 50F per day, deposit 1000F. Credit cards accepted. **SNCF Train Vélo** (tel. 93 90 33 50), in train station. Bicycles 50F per day, deposit 500F. Open daily 7am-1pm and 2-8pm. **Palm Beach Surfing,** 102, av. de Lérin. (tel. 93 43 16 31), off Palm Beach. Bicycles 55F per day, deposit 550F.

English Bookstore: Cannes English Bookshop, 11, rue Bivouac-Napoléon (tel. 93 99 40 08), two blocks inland from Palais des Festivals. Sells *Let's Go* books, as well as other (lesser) travel guides. Friendly, English-speaking staff. Open Mon.-Sat. 9:30am-1pm and 2-7pm.

Youth Center: Cannes Information Jeunesse, 5, quai St-Pierre (tel. 93 68 50 50), facing the port. Information on long-term housing, activities, and part-time jobs. Open Mon.-Fri. 9am-12:30pm and 2-6pm.

Laundromat: Lav'Azur, 9, av. de Grasse. 10min. west of train station. Wash 24F for 6kg; dry 2F per 4 min. Open daily 7am-9pm. **Lavarie,** 9, rue Hélène Vagliano, conveniently located between the station and the waterfront. Same prices. Open daily 8am-8pm.

Hospital: Pierre Nouveau, 13, av. des Broussailles (tel. 93 69 91 33). **Sunny Bank Anglo-American Hospital,** 133, av. du Petit Juas (tel. 93 68 26 96).

Medical Emergency, tel. 93 38 39 38 or 93 99 12 12. English spoken. **Emergency:** tel. 15.

Police: 15, av. de Grasse (tel. 93 39 10 78), 10min. west of the train station. **Emergency:** tel. 17.

Accommodations and Camping

Although Cannes's hotels have enough stars to start a galaxy, a few bargains lurk just off rue d'Antibes and close to the beach. Single prices may melt the lenses in your sunglasses. Double and triple prices are less apocalyptic. Try to book ahead—an absolute must in July and August. If you arrive early in the day, the tourist office can usually find you a room. Most hotels in Cannes charge a 2F lodging tax, and be warned that prices vary as much as 60F from off-season to summer (May-Aug.).

Although there is no youth hostel in Cannes, the **Auberge de Jeunesse Fréjus-St-Raphaël** (tel. 94 52 18 75; 31F) is just 20 minutes away by train and the **Relais International de la Jeunesse** (tel. 93 61 34 40) is only 15 minutes away in sunny Antibes (11F).

Hôtel Chanteclair, 12, rue Forville (tel. 93 39 68 88), a few streets from the western end of rue Félix-Faure. Follow the signs to the sheltered courtyard. Clean, comfortable rooms with bright flowery wallpaper. Singles 160F. Doubles 240F, with shower 275F. Quad with shower 360F. Breakfast 20F.

Le Florian Hôtel, 8, rue du Commandant André (tel. 93 39 24 82), off rue d'Antibes only 2 blocks from the beach. Manager keeps immaculate rooms, all with showers and telephones, and is helpful to backpackers. TV room. Singles 130-160F. Doubles 150-240F. Breakfast 20F.

Hôtel de Bourgogne, 13, rue du 24 Août (tel. 93 38 36 73), on a small street 1 block to the right off rue des Serbes as you leave the station. Central location. Spotless rooms with carpeting and telephones, some with TV. Kitchen available. TV room. Singles 122-202F. Doubles 160-255F. Triples with shower 300F. Shower 20F. Prices increase by 60F July-Aug. Breakfast 22F. Open Dec.-Oct.

Hôtel du Nord, 6, rue Jean-Jaurès (tel. 93 38 48 79), across from the train station. Owner loves the U.S., speaks English, and readily gives advice on how to do Cannes right. Eat breakfast among pictures of the Grand Canyon. Singles 132F. Doubles 184F, with showers 2244F. Quads with shower 368F. May-Aug. prices rise 30-80F. Hall showers included. Breakfast 25F. Open Dec.-Oct.

Chalet de L'Isere, 42, av. de Grasse (tel. 93 38 50 80). Go right out of the station, up the hill to a major intersection. Cross the intersection and find av. de Grasse. Hotel is near the top of the hill (10min.) Nice shady garden in front. Singles and doubles with shower 180F. Triples with shower 260F. Breakfast 20F. Dinner 70F.

Hôtel Les Charmettes, 47, av. de Grasse (tel. 92 23 17 13). In same quiet neighborhood as preceding hotel. Two-star place with sizable rooms. TV in every room. Singles and doubles with shower 210F-350F. Less off-season. Breakfast 27F.

Camping: Le Grand Saule, 24, bd. Jean Moulin (tel. 93 47 07 50), in nearby Ranguin. Take bus #610 from pl. de l'Hôtel de Ville toward Grasse. Three-star site with pool, hot shower, and laundry facilities. 50F per person, 81F per 2, tent included. Open April-Oct. **Caravaning Bellevue,** 67, av. M. Chevalier (tel. 93 47 28 97), in Cannes-La Bocca. Take the SNCF train to Cannes-La Bocca. 211 spaces. 70F per person, tent included. Weekdays 60F per 2 people with tent, weekends 70F. Open Jan.-Oct. **Le Ranch Camping,** chemin St-Joseph (tel. 93 46 00 11), in Rochville, 2km from town. Take bus #10 from the station and ask driver for the "camping" stop. Weekdays 60F per 2 people with tent, weekends 70F.

Food

The elegant sidewalk cafés on bd. de la Croisette, Cannes's center of conspicuous consumption, attract violinists and accordion players but cost an arm and a leg, and a bit of money too. The smaller cafés and restaurants on rue Meynardier are just as lovely and much less expensive. The cool shade and sea breeze in the palm-tree-filled **Jardin de la Croisette** render it the perfect spot for a picnic. Buy your supplies at **Monoprix Supermarket,** 9, rue Maréchal Foch across from the train station (open daily 9am-7:30pm). The **Casino Supermarket,** 55, bd. d'Alsace, has a better selection but higher prices. The cafeteria upstairs is good for a quick bite. (Entrees 15-50F; open daily 11am-10pm.) The Cannes **outdoor markets** find happy homes in pl. Gambetta and rue Forville (Tues.-Sun. 7am-1pm).

Chez Mamichette, 1, rue St-Antoine, off the western end of rue Félix-Faure. A tiny, delightful *savoyard* restaurant on a hill near the vieux port. Reasonable prices in a ritzy area. Try the *fondue savoyarde* (50F), the 65F *menu,* the *plat du jour* (40F), or if you're really hungry, the rib-sticking *raclette.* Open Mon.-Sat. noon-3pm and 7-11pm.

Restaurant le Pacific, 14, rue Venizélos, across from the train station on the right. Excellent pizzas (32-50F), a 54F 4-course *menu,* and an 85F 6-course *menu.* Open Sun.-Thurs. 11am-2:30pm and 6:30-9:30pm, Fri. 11am-2pm.

La Sangria, 76, rue Meynadier (tel. 93 68 35 39). This small *restau-café* serves a filling *paella gitane* (95F) and delicious seafood *crêpes* (32-45F). Open Mon.-Sat. 11am-2pm and 7-11pm.

Au P'tit Creux, 82, rue Meynadier, at the corner of rue Docteur Gazagnaire next to La Sangria. Four hearty varieties of Tunisian *couscous* (52-76F) and a 65F *menu* with French classics like *brochette d'agneau* and *crêpes salés*. Outdoor seating. Open Tues.-Sat. noon-2:30pm and 7-10pm, Sun. noon-2:30pm.

Le Bouchon, 10, bd. de Constantine, off rue d'Antibes. A 10-min. walk left of the train station. Dine among seagulls. Varied 70F and 95F *menus* feature *canard à l'orange* (duck with orange sauce) and *aïoli* (Provençal garlic mayonnaise dip with raw vegetables). Open Jan.-Nov. Tues.-Sun. noon-2pm and 7-10pm.

Entertainment

Should you tire of indulging in the French national pastime of eyeing passersby, head over to a more expensive option—one of Cannes's three casinos. The most accessible, **Le Casino Croisette,** 1, jetée Albert Edouard (tel. 93 38 12 11), next to the Palais des Festivals, has slots, blackjack, roulette, and French roulette. (Gambling daily 5pm-4am, open for slots at 11am. No shorts. Must be 18. Free.) If your luck has soured, take to the clubs. Unless your wardrobe-designer's name ends in a vowel, however, be prepared to feel underdressed. From 11pm until dawn, dance at **Jane's,** 38, rue des Serbes (tel. 93 99 04 94), in the Hôtel Gray d'Albion (cover and first drink 120F), or at the **Mogambo Palm Beach** (tel. 93 43 91 12), at point de la Croisette, which rocks from 11pm to 7am (cover 50F). If you're losing sleep and breaking into a cold sweat over the prices at the clubs, you'd enjoy the less expensive and more informal entertainment at the many pubs and piano bars that lie within blocks of the waterfront.

Cannes has about as many gay nightspots as straight ones. **Les 3 Cloches** (tel. 93 68 32 92) rings with jazz, rock, and blues every night. (Open 11pm-dawn. Cover 50F.) The **Club 7 Disco,** 7, rue Rouguière, near the port, is newer and equally popular. (Open nightly 11pm-morning. Cover 90F. Drinks 25-35F.) **Zanzi-Bar,** 85, rue Félix-Faure (tel. 93 39 30 75), attracts a mixed crowd. (Open daily 2pm-4am. No cover.)

Near Cannes

Both the **Iles de Lérins** provide a welcome respite from fast-paced Cannes. The smaller island, **St-Honorat,** harbors pine forests and an active monastery, the **Abbaye de Lerins,** where Cistercian monks live in silence, piety, and chastity. (Open daily 10am-2:30pm. Free.) More tranquil and more densely forested, **Ile Ste-Marguerite** is famous for the fort Cardinal Richelieu built here in 1712. Both islands, particularly Ste-Marguerite, offer beautiful beaches, with much less wind and far fewer people than the mainland beaches. Eighteen boats leave daily between 7:30am and 6pm from the *gare maritime des îles* (tel. 93 39 11 82), across from the Cannes tourist office on bd. de la Croisette. (St-Honorat 30min., round-trip 45F; Ste-Marguerite 15min., round-trip 40F. Both islands round-trip 55F. Ages 4-10, 1/2-price.) Boats to both islands also leave from Golfe-Juan and Juan-les-Pins. (Round-trip to both islands 55F, ages 4-10 28F.)

On a hill 8km from Cannes, **Mougins** hides peaceful streets behind its old fortified walls. Picasso came here in 1924 to find inspiration. Walk through the streets of this old fortified town and climb to the top of the monastery tower for an unrivaled view of the coast and a glimpse of the snowy Alps to the northeast. The Cannes-Grasse bus stops at Val du Mougins (every 30min., 20min., 9F); from there it's a pleasant one-hour climb past gracious villas to the old town.

Vallauris, a few km inland and east of Cannes, has long been known as the pottery capital of France. Picasso was fascinated by the town's ceramics and came here to work shortly after WWII. Most of the stores sell mass-produced, low-quality ware. The **Galerie Madoura** (tel. 93 64 66 39) stocks high-quality reproductions, but at 1500F per plate, you might opt just to look. (Open Mon.-Fri. 9:30am-12:30pm and 2:30-7pm.) The fascinating **Musée Lefoll,** bd. F. Durbec., displays colorful modern works by French cubists Titi, Valérie de Paris, and Yann Monk. (Open Mon.-Sat. 10am-noon and 2-6pm. Free.) Also, meander over to the **Musée National de Picasso,** pl. de la Libération (tel. 93 64 18 05), which resides in the 13th-century chapel of a castle and features Picasso's *War and Peace*. (Open Wed.-Mon. 2-6pm. Admission 8F, students 4F.) To reach Vallauris, take a bus from Cannes (near the train station or the pl. de l'Hôtel de Ville; every hr. 8am-7:30pm, 40min., 12F) or from Antibes (5 per day). Ask at the **tourist office,** 84, av. de la Liberté (tel. 93 63 73 12), for information about Vallauris's biannual exhibition of ceramics and modern art from over 30 countries. (Open Mon.-Sat. 9am-noon and 3:30-6:30pm.)

Grasse

Only 15km inland from Cannes, Grasse (pop. 45,000) is galaxies away from its star-studded neighbor on the sea. Regarded as the perfume capital of the world and boasting three of France's largest, oldest, and most distinguished *parfumeries,* Grasse intoxicates more than olfactory senses. The town's 13th-century buildings and walls cling to the side of a hill, affording spectacular views. At the top of this pre-Alps town is a panorama of the Provençal interior, fields of jasmine, roses, and other flowers used in perfume production, and finally, the Mediterranean Sea. Day and night, the cobblestone streets in the *vieille ville* hum with the din of open-air markets and restaurants. Without the droves of sun-worshiping tourists who stick to the coast, Grasse offers a relaxed pace of life as well as a good base from which to make daytrips to Nice and Cannes. If splendid sights and smells don't tickle your fancy, however, follow your nose to a more vigorous town.

Although Grasse spreads well into the valley below, most sights, hotels and restaurants are concentrated on the southward-facing hillside where the town originated in the Middle Ages. Because of its proximity to Cannes, Grasse can be enjoyed as a daytrip, but store your luggage in Cannes, as Grasse lacks automatic lockers. The *gare routière,* pl. de la Boucherie (tel. 93 36 96 63), is the transportation hub of the city, receiving both regional and local buses (from Cannes's *gare routière* or SNCF station: 21 per day, 45min., 17F50; from Nice: 15 per day, 90min., 28F; local buses run Mon.-Sat. 6:30am-7pm, 5F). Across the *place* is an **SNCF information office** to attend to all of your rail needs. (Open Mon.-Sat. 8:30am-12:15pm and 1:30-5:55pm.) The **tourist office,** pl. de la Foux, is also only a hop, skip, and a jump away: cross the *place* from the bus station, cross bd. du Jeu de Ballon, and the office is straight ahead. (Open. Mon.-Sat. 9:30am-noon and 2-6:30pm.) If the narrow, walled *traversées* (stairways cut into the hill) and the welcoming aroma of the *parfumeries* have induced you to spend the night, Grasse provides several low-cost options, almost all of which offer luxurious vistas onto the valley below. **Le Napoléon,** 6, av. Thiers (tel. 93 36 05 87), is only meters from the bus station and has some of the best digs in town for the money. (Singles 103F. Doubles 130F, with shower 149F. Triples 184F, with shower and toilet 237F. Quads 248F, with shower and toilet 292F. Breakfast 21F. Open. Feb.-Christmas.) **Pension Ste-Thérèse,** 39, bd. Y.E. Baudoin (tel. 93 36 10 29), ten minutes up the hill from the bus station, sits in a pristine white stucco church perched delicately on the cliff. The interior is bright and modern with large and immaculate rooms. (Singles 135F, with shower and toilet 195F. Doubles 160F, with shower and toilet 200-210F. Open Nov. 13-Sept.) **Pension Michèle,** 6, rue du Palais de Justice (tel. 93 36 06 37), just above bd. de Jeu de Ballon, is surrounded by a garden of grapevines and jasmine. Rooms are large, with comfy beds. (3-night min. stay. Singles 90-105F. Doubles 183F, with shower 220F. Breakfast 20F. Other meals 58F. Open. Dec.-Oct. Call ahead.) Finally, **Les Palmiers,** 17, bd. Y.E. Baudoin (tel. 93 36 07 24) is neat and tidy with a peaceful breakfast garden. (Doubles 150F, with shower 150-180F. Triples with shower and toilet 190-275F. Quads 190-305F.)

For a town of its size, Grasse contains a surprising wealth of restaurants, markets, and speciality shops (*boulangeries, fromageries,* and all the other *-ries*). Stay away from the main streets and plunge into the labyrinth of serpentine passages in the *vieille ville.* Most culinary action centers around the cobblestone **Place aux Aires,** which jostles with an open-air market every morning from 7am-noon. Check out the *cuisine traditionelle* at **Le Vieux Bistrot,** 5, rue des Moulnets, near the Place aux Aires. (3-course *menu* 67F. Open daily 5-10pm.) **Le Trappa,** pl. Georges Norel, serves 30-45F pizzas and a filling 55F *menu* that features French and Italian specialties. (Open daily 11am-

1pm and 5-10:30pm.) Also in the vicinity is a **Monoprix** supermarket, rue Paul Goby, when cost is the overriding factor. (Open Mon.-Sat. 8:45am-7pm.)

The *parfumeries* of **Fragonard, Molinard, and Galimard,** three of France's most fragrant sights, are Grasse's main attractions. At Fragonard's original 1873 factory, **Usine de Fragonard,** 20, bd. Fragonard (tel. 93 36 44 65), catch a glimpse and take a whiff of a perfume design and manufacturing process. (Open daily 9am-6pm; free tours in French, English, German, Italian, and Spanish.) The nearby Molinard *usine,* 60, bd. Victor Hugo (tel. 93 36 01 62) offers similar free, multi-lingual tours. (Open Mon.-Sat. 9am-6:30pm, Sun. 9am-noon and 2-6pm.) All three companies operate their modern facilities outside of Grasse, in the direction of Cannes. Ask at the tourist office for more information. Appropriately, Grasse is the home of the **Musée International de la Parfumerie,** 8, pl. du Cours (tel. 93 36 80 20). The museum traces 4000 years of perfume-making and brims with brass distilling cauldrons as well as Marie Antoinete's jeweled travel case. (Open daily 10am-7pm; Oct. and Dec. 8-May Wed.-Sun. 10am-noon and 2-5pm. Admission 12F, students 6F.) Grasse also contains the **Musée d'art et d'Histoire de Provence** and the **Musée de la Marine.** Ask at the tourist office for more information. **Le Petit Train,** a small trolley, leaves **Cours Honoré Cresp** for a narrated tour (in French) of the entire town. Even if you can't understand the guide, the tour offers a view of the sea from **parc Princesses Pauline** which speaks volumes. (Daily every hr. from 10am-3pm and at 9pm; 25F, under 12 15F.) The enticing essences of Grasse become positively effervescent every May and August during the town's two annual flower festivals. In May, **Exporose** attracts rose growers from around the world for the largest exhibition of its kind. In August, **La Jasminade** commemorates the jasmine flower, one of the traditional staples of perfume-making. This festival wafts into Grasse's streets with parades, dances, and regional music.

Antibes

Like its *nouveau chic* neighbor to the west, St-Raphaël, Antibes has become one of *the* new hotspots on the Riviera. Located between Cannes and Nice, Antibes's beautiful beaches and the Picasso museum have actually been drawing crowds for years. But the new theater and music festivals, a seaside youth hostel, and a pack of inexpensive restaurants have made it an increasingly popular destination on the budget itinerary. Avoid the crowds and prices of the big cities, and unload your pack here for a few days of music, sun, and R&R.

Once home to celebrated English writer Graham Greene and a host of other writers and artists, Antibes takes great pride in its **Musée Picasso** (tel. 93 34 91 91) in the Château Grimaldi on pl. Mariejol. Hanging onto a seaside cliff for dear life, this château housed Picasso for a productive six months in 1946. Several small rooms display drawings, ceramics, and a sampling of the canvases Picasso painted here. The top floor features his *atelier* (studio) and paintings by young contemporaries, such as de Staël, Hartung, and Mathieu. (Open June 15-Aug. Wed.-Mon. 10am-noon and 2-7pm; Sept.-Oct. and Dec.-June 14 Wed.-Mon. 10am-noon and 2-6pm. Admission 20F, students 10F.) The **Musée Archéologique** (tel. 93 34 48 01), along the waterfront in the Bastion St-Andrée sur les Remparts, discusses archeological digs of the area and the history of Antipolis, the ancient Greek city on the site. (Same hours. Admission 10F, students 5F.) The **Musée Peynet,** pl. Nationale (tel. 93 34 36 64), presents over 200 creative masterpieces by local artist Raymond Peynet. (Same hours. Admission 22F, students and ages 12-18 12F, under 12 free.)

Some of the most beautiful beaches east of Nice lie along Antibes's bd. Leclerc and bd. de la Garoupe. If you've gotten your share of the sun, retreat to the charming *vieille ville.* Old Antibes, which stretches between bd. Maréchal Foch and the port d'Antibes, is crowded with pricey boutiques but inexpensive restaurants. The **Cathédrale d'Antibes,** next to the Château Grimaldi, has a 17th-century nave and an altar from 1515. The impressive 16th-century **Fort Carré** stands guard over the blue Mediterranean waters of the *vieux port.* (Open July-Aug. 9am-noon and 2-4pm. Admission 20F, students 10F.)

At the end of July, Antibes holds its annual **Eté Musicale** in front of the château. For this musical mélange of jazz, classical music, and opera, tickets (50-150F) are available at the Antibes and Juan-les Pins tourist offices. Also at the end of July is Antibes's **Festival de Théâtre.** Six plays are produced every year and run the gamut from Euripides to Albert Camus. Pick up tickets at the tourist office (80F, students 50F). Antibes's annual **Festival d'Art Lyrique,** held every July-August, brings world-class opera soloists such as Montserrat, Cabale, and Marilyn Horne to the *vieux port.* For information, call 93 34 56 64. (Tickets 50-150F.)

The best deal in town is the Antibes **Relais International de la Jeunesse,** at the intersection of bd. de la Garoupe and av. l'Antiquité (tel. 93 61 34 40). Coed bathrooms, cheap rooms, and a fun backpacking crowd make this a good option—just don't expect the Ritz. Take bus #2A from the *gare routière* to the "L'Antiquité" stop on bd. de la Garoupe (5F). (Lockout 9:30am-6pm. Curfew midnight. 55F. Breakfast included. Dinner 45F. Sheets 10F. Open June-Sept.) Surprise, surprise—hotels in Antibes aren't cheap. Try **La petite Reserve Hôtel,** 20, bd. James-Wylie (tel. 93 61 55 86). Located directly across from Cannes's public beach, the hotel offers the same view that hotels three times its price provide and has comfortable rooms. (Singles 160F. Doubles 200F, with shower 230F. Shower 10F. Breakfast 30F.) Less cozy but more centrally located is the Novel Hôtel, 1, bd. du 24 Août (tel. 93 34 44 07), next to pl. Guynemer and the bus station. Clean doubles for 180F, breakfast included, with shower and breakfast 244F. (Office closed Sun. afternoon.) The **Hôtel Jabotte,** av. Max Maurey (tel. 93 61 45 89), is a small establishment just two minutes from the sea. (Singles 180F. Doubles 220F. Breakfast 20F.)

Place Nationale, in the heart of the *vieille ville,* holds a great selection of cheap restaurants. Try the *crêpes salés* (50-80F) at **Adieu Berthe,** 26, rue Vauban. Or enjoy the filling homemade ravioli (42F) and pasta (60-80F) at **La Famiglia,** 34 av. Thiers. **La Palmeraie,** 6, rue Rostan, off rue de la République and near pl. Nationale, serves regional and North African dishes; five types of *couscous,* including vegetarian, will run 50F and up. (Open daily noon-2pm and 7pm-midnight.) For some real Tex-Mex food, head for **Taco's Grille,** 41, rue James Close, right off pl. Nationale. (Tacos 30-42F. Chili *con carne* 75F. Open daily noon-2pm and 7-11pm.) If the restaurants are out of range, resign yourself to the **Codec Supermarket,** 8, av. Niqué, near pl. de Gaulle (open Mon.-Sat. 8am-7:30pm), or the morning **open market** at cours Masséna, near the Picasso Museum and the beach (open daily early morning-early afternoon).

Antibes lies on the main Marseille-Nice rail line and enjoys frequent connections to Cannes (9 per day, 16min., 9F); Marseille (9 per day, 2 1/2hr., 120F); and Nice (9 per day, 18min., 19F). The information office at the **train station,** av. Robert Soleau (tel. 93 99 50 50), is open Monday through Saturday, 9am to 6pm. To reach the **tourist office,** 11, pl. de Gaulle (tel. 93 33 95 64), exit the station, turn right onto av. R Soleau, and follow signs for the *Maison du Tourisme.* The helpful staff has information on accommodations, camping, and the frequent festivals. (Open Mon.-Sat. 8:30am-8pm, Sun. 10am-1pm; Oct.-June Mon.-Sat. 9am-noon and 2-6pm.) The **gare routière** is at pl. Guynemer, a two-minute walk to the left of the tourist office. Buses run to Nice, Cannes, and Juan-les-Pins, as well as provide local coverage for 5F per ride (daily 7am-11pm). The **hospital** (tel. 93 33 91 00) is on rue de la Fontaine; the **police station** (tel. 93 34 78 05) is at bd. Albert 1er; and the **post office** (tel. 93 34 09 00) is on pl. Daumier (open Mon.-Fri. 8am-7pm, Sat. 8am-noon).

Near Antibes

Most towns on the Riviera stay up late, but no place burns the midnight oil like **Juan-les-Pins.** Boutiques remain open until midnight, cafés until 2am, and nightclubs until 4 or 5am. Most clubs charge a cover of 60-100F. If you have any money left after clubbing, you may want to gamble the rest of the night away at the **Eden Beach Casino.** (Open nightly 8pm-4am. Minimum age 21. No shorts or sneakers. Free.) Famous for its antediluvian pine trees, the *Pinède* of Juan-les-Pins is the site of the **Festival International de Jazz (Jazz à Juan),** an outstanding annual musical program which runs the second week in July and attracts such greats as Dizzy Gillespie, Ray Charles, Tracy

Chapman, and The Manhattan Transfer. (Tickets 150-180F, available at the Juan-les-Pins and Antibes tourist offices.) During the day, take advantage of the uncrowded, sandy beaches at Juan-les-Pins.

Juan-les-Pins is accessible by train from Nice (27min., 26F), Cannes (12min., 8F) and Antibes (5F). The English-speaking staff at the **tourist office,** 51, bd. Guillaumont (tel. 93 61 04 98), distributes maps and makes hotel reservations. To reach the tourist office from the station, turn right and go to the end of the street by the beach; take a left on Guillaumont and look to your left. (Open Mon.-Sat. 9am-8pm, Sun. 9am-1pm; Sept.-June Mon.-Fri. 9am-noon and 2-6pm, Sat. 9am-noon.)

The ancient, walled town of **Biot,** one train stop east of Antibes, is known for its fine glassware; many glass-blowing shops are open to the public. Peek into one of France's most prestigious glass-blowing factories, **La Verrerie de Val de Pome** (tel. 93 65 03 78; open Mon.-Sat. 10am-12:30pm and 2-7pm, Sun. 2-7pm; free). From the Biot train station, it's a pleasant, sign-posted hike along the route de Biot (2km). Along route de Biot, you'll also find **Marineland** (tel. 93 33 49 49), a giant aquarium with one of the best water shows in Europe. Divers from across Europe and the United States perform daily. (Open daily from 11am. Shows at 2:30, 4:30, and 6pm. Admission 80F.)

Biot has a handful of campgrounds, none of which rents tents. The best bargain is the monstrous three-star **Le Logis des la Brague** (tel. 93 33 54 72), right across from the train stop. Facilities include hot showers, washing machines, a supermarket, and a snack bar. (1-2 people on foot 45F; 1-3 people by car or caravan 75F. Electricity 15F. Open May-Sept. 8am-noon and 2-8pm.) Wallow in luxury at four-star **Les Embruns,** 7, route de Biot (tel. 93 33 33 35), which has hot showers, washing machines, mini-market, tennis courts, and the all-important TV room. (2-3 people on foot 60F. 2 people in a caravan 100F each. Electricity 10F. Reception open May-Sept. daily 9am-12:30pm and 2-8pm.)

Two train stops from Biot is the bustling town of **Cagnes-sur-Mer.** Filling nine rooms of the house Auguste Renoir occupied from 1908-1919, the **Musée Renoir,** av. des Collettes (tel. 93 20 61 07) off av. des Tuilières, contains works from the artist's "Cagnes period" and is surrounded by beautiful gardens of olive and palm trees on a hill overlooking the town. (Open May-Oct. 15 Wed.-Mon. 10am-noon and 2-6pm; Nov-May Wed.-Mon. 2-5pm. Admission 20F, children 10F.) Cagnes's other attraction is the **Château-Musée des Cagnes,** montée de la Bourgade (tel. 93 20 85 57), a 14th-century stronghold built after the Crusades to keep watch over both the sea and its own prisoners. At the top of the tower, the expansive view ranges from the Alps to the coast from Cap d'Antibes to Cap Ferrat. Cagnes's **tourist office** (tel. 93 73 66 66) is at 6, bd. Maréchal Juin. From the station, take a right and then another right under the autoroute. Continue to bd. Maréchal Juin and take a left. (Open in summer and fall Mon.-Sat. 9am-12:30pm and 2-6pm, in winter and spring 9am-noon and 3-5pm.)

Nice

Blessed with a beautiful beach and all the nightlife, arts, and entertainment of a big city, Nice is unofficially known as the capital of the French Riviera. Come on, Nice *is* the Riviera. It has all the accoutrements of a Riviera town—casual affluence, an ample beach, top-notch museums, flowery avenues—but without the affected aloofness of its neighbors. Furthermore, Nice is blessed with reasonably priced hotels, excellent local and regional transport, a population accustomed to visitors, and all the other conveniences of an authentic metropolis. Every summer, thousands of sun worshipers descend upon Nice to set up house for a vacation of sunbathing, dancing, concert-going, and (if they can find the time) relaxation. But don't let Nice's popularity and crowds scare you away. It's a big place and there's room for everyone with a sense of carnival. Every spring on Fat Tuesday, Nice erupts into song and dance during the annual *Carnaval,* the grandmother of New Orleans's *Mardi Gras.* Floats decorated with orchids, spices, and roses wind down the boulevards during the annual parade to the beat of reggae, jazz, and blues bands. The entire city feasts in costumed jollity. But even if you can't make it to Nice for the carnival, you'll find plenty of revelry in the streets of

Vieux Nice. Tucked into the southeastern pocket of the city and limited to pedestrians, Vieux Nice twists through a labyrinth of tiny streets, hiding the boisterous bars, clubs, and restaurants which more poised Riviera towns lack. Vibrant flower, fish, and vegetable markets color **cours Saleya** (Tues.-Sun. dawn-noon.)

Orientation and Practical Information

The SNCF train station (Gare "Nice-Ville") is in the center of town, next to the tourist office on **avenue Thiers.** The area around the station is fairly seedy and packed with cheap restaurants and hotels. To the left, **avenue Jean-Médecin** runs toward the water to **place Masséna.** Vieux Nice lies just south of pl. Masséna. Heading right from the train station, you'll run into **boulevard Gambetta,** the other main street running directly to the water. Sweeping along the coast, the majestic and festive **promenade des Anglais** is rock-covered, crowded, and noisy.

Dotted with cafés, boutiques, and overpriced restaurants, the pedestrian zone west of pl. Masséna is an ideal place to plant yourself and watch the world go by. Port Lympia, a warren of alleyways, boulevards, *brasseries,* and *tabacs,* lies on the opposite side of the château and below Vieux Nice. Unfortunately, Nice's big-city appeal is coupled increasingly with big-city crime. Women should avoid walking alone after sundown, and both sexes should exercise caution at night near the train station and Vieux Nice. If you're leaving a club late at night, be especially careful as teams of pickpocketers have been known to do what they do best in these areas.

Tourist office: Av. Thiers (tel. 93 87 07 07), beside the train station. Books a limited number of rooms after 10am. Stake out a place in line early. 12F for a reservation in a 1-star hotel and 21F for 2-star hotels, of which 12F will be deducted from your hotel bill. Crowded and slightly impersonal, but information on absolutely everything. Because of the office's close proximity to the train station, be especially mindful of your bags once inside. Ask for the detailed map, extremely helpful in Vieux Nice. Open daily Mon.-Sat. 8:45am-7pm, Sun. 8:45am-12:30pm and 2-6pm; Oct.-May Mon.-Sat. 8:45am-12:30pm and 2-6pm. Another office at 5, av. Gustave V (tel. 93 87 60 60), near the intersection of av. de Verdun and promenade des Anglais. Open same hours as av. Thiers office, except closed 12-2pm July-Sept. A 3rd office at the airport (tel. 93 83 32 64), near the Ferber parking area. Open Mon.-Sat. 8am-6pm.

Budget Travel Office: Council Travel, 37bis, rue d'Angleterre (tel. 93 83 23 23), near the SNCF station. Branch of New York-based office. Competitive prices on airfare to U.S. Open Mon-Sat. 9:30am-noon and 2-6pm.

Consulate: United States Consulate, 31, rue Maréchal Joffre (tel. 93 88 89 55). Open Mon.-Sat. 9-11:30am and 1:30-4:30pm.

Currency Exchange: Cambio, 17, av. Thiers (tel. 93 88 56 80), across from the train station. No commission; good rates. Open daily 7am-midnight. **Banque Populaire de la Côte d'Azur,** 457, promenade des Anglais (tel. 93 21 52 00). Great location. Open Mon.-Sat. 9am-6pm.

American Express: 11, promenade des Anglais (tel. 93 87 29 82), at the corner of rue des Congrès. Expect long lines in summer. Open Mon.-Fri. 9am-noon and 2-6pm.

Post Office: 23, av. Thiers (tel. 93 88 52 52), near the train station. Open Mon.-Fri. 8am-7pm, Sat. 8am-noon. **Branch offices** at 18, rue Hôtel des Postes (tel. 93 85 98 63) at pl. Wilson (open Mon.-Fri. 8am-7pm, Sat. 8am-noon) and at 2, rue Clemenceau (tel. 93 88 72 88), off bd. Jean Médecin (open Sun.-Wed. and Fri. 8am-6pm, Thurs. 8:30am-6pm, and Sat. 8am-noon). Another office at the airport (open Mon.-Fri. 9am-5pm, Sat. 9am-noon). All offices have **Poste Restante** and **telephones. Postal code:** 06000.

Flights: Aéroport Nice-Côte d'Azur (tel. 93 21 30 30). Take the airport bus (every 20min., 14F) from the bus staion by pl. Le Clerc, or the slower #9 from pl. Masséna or the port (45min., 8F). An SNCF minibus runs between the train station and the airport 7:30am-7:15pm (14 per day, 15min., 32F). **Air France,** 10, av. Félix-Faure (for reservations 93 83 91 00, for information 93 80 66 11), near pl. Masséna. To Paris (515F). Open Mon.-Sat. 9am-6pm. **Air Inter,** 4, av. de Suède (tel. 93 14 94 84), at the corner of av. de Verdun, the continuation of av. Félix Faure after pl. Masséna. Domestic flights only. To Ajaccio (255F). Open Mon.-Sat. 9am-6pm.

Trains: Gare SNCF Nice-Ville, av. Thiers (tel. 93 87 50 50). Information office open Mon.-Sat. 8am-7pm, Sun. 8am-noon and 2-6pm. Trains about every 20min. (5:40am-midnight) to Cannes (35min., 28F) and Antibes (18min., 14F); about every 15min. (6:30am-11:30pm) to Monaco (25min., 13F) and Menton (35min., 18F). Also to other coastal towns, northern France, Italy, and

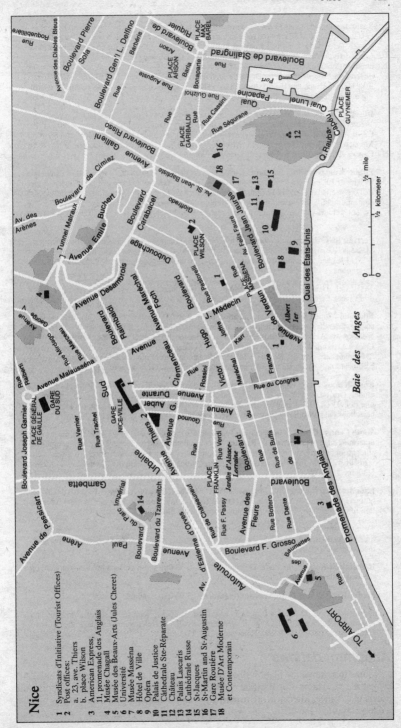

Nice   453

Nice

1 Syndicats d'Initiative (Tourist Offices)
2 Post offices:
   a. 21, ave. Thiers
   b. place Wilson
3 American Express,
   11, promenade des Anglais
4 Musée Chagall
5 Musée des Beaux-Arts (Jules Cheret)
6 Université
7 Musée Masséna
8 Hôtel de Ville
9 Opéra
10 Palais de Justice
11 Cathédrale Ste-Réparate
12 Château
13 Palais Lascaris
14 Cathédrale Russe
15 St-Jacques
16 St-Martin and St-Augustin
17 Gare Routière
18 Musée D'Art Moderne
   et Contemporain

Baie des Anges

Spain. In summer, about 11 per day connect with the TGV express from Marseille to Paris (71/2hr., 465F plus 18F required reservation). Showers at the station 12F, towels 3F, soap 1F. Toilets 2F. Open daily 7am-7pm. **Lockers** 11F for 72hrs. Luggage stored for 15F per day per piece (open daily 5:30pm-midnight). **Gare du Sud,** 33, av. Malausséna (tel. 93 84 89 71), on the upper continuation of av. Jean-Médecin, 800m from the Nice-Ville station. Special trains, the *chemins de fer de la Provence,* leave for Digne through the southern Alps (5 per day, 3 1/4hr., 94F). There's little to do in Digne, but the ride through the valleys is spectacular, and you can stop in the charming mountain towns along the way. Open Mon.-Fri. 8am-12:30pm and 2-6pm, Sat. 8am-12:30pm.

Buses: *Gare routière,* promenade du Paillon (tel. 93 85 61 81), off av. Jean Jaurès, across from Vieux Nice. Open Mon.-Sat. 9am-6:30pm. Buses every 20min. (6:30am-7:30pm) to: Eze (12F); Cap d'Ail (16F); Monaco (19F); Menton (45min., 27F); last return bus leaves Menton at 8pm and Monaco at 8:30pm. Every 15min. (6:15am-7:30pm) to: Antibes (24F); Juan-les-Pins (28F); Cannes (90min., 29F). To Grasse: 15 per day (90min., 28F).

Public Transportation: Station Centrale, the TN (Transports Urbains de Nice) bus system has its base at 10, av. Félix Faure (tel. 93 62 08 08), near pl. Général Leclerc and pl. Masséna. Information on city buses. Bus #12 from the train station goes to pl. Masséna and the beach (Mon.-Sat. 6am-midnight, Sun. 7:45am-midnight). All buses 8F per person. Buy *carnets* of 5 (27F40) at the av. Thiers tourist office, or at kiosks and *tabacs.* Buy 20F day passes or a 107F week passes on board.

Ferries: SNCM, quai du Commerce (tel. 93 13 66 66), at the port. Take bus #1 or #2 from pl. Masséna. Passage to and from Corsican cities: Bastia (4-5hr., one way 255F, students 190F, ages 4-12 145F) and Ajaccio (6-7hr., same prices). Open Mon.-Fri. 8am-noon and 1:30-6:30pm, Sat. 8am-noon.

Taxis: (tel. 93 80 70 70). Very expensive (about 40F to go around the block, even more if you don't speak French).

Bike and Moped Rental: Nicea Location Rent, 9, av. Thiers (tel. 93 82 42 71), near the train station. Friendly owners will help you with directions. Bikes 120F per day, deposit 2000F (accepts credit cards). Also rents mopeds and motorcycles for mucho francs. Open Mon.-Sat. 9am-7:30pm. **Cycles Arnaud,** 4, pl. Grimaldi (tel. 93 87 88 55), near the pedestrian zone and the beach. Bikes 85F, credit card deposit. Mopeds 130F, including enough gas for a round-trip to Monaco, deposit credit card only. Reductions for longer periods. Open Mon.-Fri. 8am-noon and 2-7pm.

English Bookstores: Home de la Presse, 27, av, Jean-Médecin (tel. 93 88 84 16). Sells *Let's Go* guides. Open daily 9:30am-11pm; Oct.-June 14 9am-8pm. The **Cat's Whiskers,** 26, rue Lamartine (tel. 93 80 02 66), near av. Jean-Médecin. Good selection of new and used books. Will buy back books at half-price when you're done. Open Mon.-Sat. 9am-12:30pm and 2-7pm.

Youth Center: Centre d'Information Jeunesse, 19, rue Gioffredo (tel. 93 80 93 93), close to the outermost edge of promenade du Paillon. Posts a bulletin board (in French) with summer jobs for students of any nationality. Jobs are tough to find (takes about 1-2 weeks); priority is given to citizens of the EEC. Jobs include babysitting, bartending, and landscaping. Open Mon.-Fri. 9am-6:30pm.

Laundromats: Lavomatique, 11, rue du Pont Vieux near the *gare routière.* Wash 20F, dry 5F per 6min. Open Mon.-Sat. 8am-8pm. Also **Quick Lav',** 4, rue Gioffredo, near the Centre d'Information Jeunesse. Wash 9F, dry 5F per 6min. Open daily 8am-10pm.

Twenty-Four Hour Store: 7j, at the Shell station in the promenade du Paillon, near Vieux Nice. Snacks, hot dogs, and soft drinks. Perfect for late night munchies after the clubs close. Some pharmaceuticals. Open daily.

Hospital: St-Roch, 5, rue Pierre Devoluy (tel. 93 13 33 00). From av. Jean Médecin, turn left on rue Pastorelli, which turns into rue P. Devoluy.

Medical Services: SOS Medical Service (tel. 93 53 03 03). Available 24 hrs.

Police: tel. 93 92 62 22, at the opposite end of bd. Maréchal Foch from bd. Jean Médecin, and scattered throughout the city. English interpreter on call. For stolen items, call the **Police Bureau Châteauneuf** (tel. 93 96 90 02). **Emergency:** tel. 17.

Accommodations

Rooms in summer are like Marlboros in Russia: gone as soon as they're on sale. Arrive at the av. Thiers tourist office early for help in finding a room, or call individual hotels in advance. Managers are usually reluctant to accept phone reservations without a deposit through the mail.

Arrive in Nice in the morning during the summer, or you'll almost certainly be forced to join the legion of visitors who camp outside the train station. Because of its fabled reputation, Nice endures an annual student invasion; the station moonlights as one of the largest and most dangerous bedrooms in France. Although police do sporadically enforce a law that prohibits sleeping on the beach, groups of young people often check their baggage at the *concièrge* and head for the rocky waterfront.

The largest concentrations of decent, affordable hotels cluster around Notre Dame, on rue d'Angleterre, rue de la Suisse, and rue de Russie. Nice's two youth hostels and two *résidences* (temporary youth hostels set up in university dorms) are great, but often full. Arrive in the wee hours, book ahead, and you should avoid the fate that befalls many innocents: sleeping on one's luggage at the station. Be sure to guard your luggage well.

Auberge de Jeunesse (HI), route Forestière du Mont-Alban (tel. 93 89 23 64), 4km away from it all—but worth the commute. Take bus #5 from the train station or walk to pl. Masséna, then take bus #14 from bd. Jean-Jaurès (every 25-40min. until 7:30pm). Otherwise, it's a 45-min. walk. 62 beds in 8- to 10-bed dorms. Friendly place, usually bursting with a bustling, bronzed crowd. Opens at 5pm. Lockout 10am-5pm. Curfew midnight. 65F. Showers and breakfast included. Required sheet rental 15F. Kitchen and fridge available. Laundry service 30F.

Relais International de la Jeunesse "Clairvallon," 26, av. Scudéri (tel. 93 81 27 63), in Cimiez, 10km out of town. Take bus #15 from pl. Masséna (every 10min., 20min.). A large, luxurious hostel in an old villa with a free swimming pool, tennis courts, and basketball courts. Luggage must be kept in a common storage room. 6 bunks per room. Check-in 6pm. Curfew midnight. Bed and breakfast 65F.

Résidence Les Collinettes, 3, av. Robert Schumann (tel. 94 21 11 86, after June 6: 93 97 10 33), near the train station, off pl. St-Philippe. Temporary summer hostel set up in a university *résidence* (dorm). Great location and a lively backpacking crowd. Curfew midnight. Open for reservations all day but lockout 10am-6pm. 90F, 80F per night if you stay over 2 weeks. Open July 7-Aug. 31.

Espace Magnan, 31, rue de Coppet (tel. 93 86 28 75), near the promenade des Anglais and the beach. From the train station, take bus #23 (8F) and ask the driver to drop you off. Clean and efficient, somewhat impersonal hostel similar to Résidence Les Colinettes. 6-bed dorms. 50F per person. Baggage rooms 10F per day. Café and restaurant inside the complex. **Piscine J. Medecin** (public pool, 12F) and a **Casino Supermarket** nearby. Open for reservations 8:30am-12:30pm and 2pm-midnight. Lockout 10am-6pm. Open June 15-Sept. 22.

Hôtel Belle Meunière, 21, av. Durante (tel. 93 88 66 15), near the station. This quasi-villa with a large garden was a gift from one of Napoleon's generals to his mistress. The friendly managers keep the place immaculate. In summer, expect the atmosphere of a school dorm. 80F per person in 3- to 5-bed rooms. Singles 90F. Doubles 140F, with shower 170F. Triples 225F, with shower 310F. Showers 15F. Breakfast included. Baggage room 5F. Open Feb.-Dec.

Hôtel Les Orangers, 10bis, av. Durante (tel. 93 87 51 41) across the street from Hôtel Belle Meuniere. Newly renovated rooms and exterior. New, firm mattresses and attractive wood paneling in all rooms. Balconies in most. Dorms 80F per person. Singles 80-100F. Doubles 150F, with shower 180-190F. Triples with shower 270F. All rooms with kitchenette and fridge. Breakfast 18F. Open Dec.-Oct.

Hôtel Central, 10, rue de Suisse (tel. 93 88 85 08), off rue d'Angleterre. Clean and airy rooms, most renovated recently with modern bathrooms. Singles with shower 80F. Doubles with shower 120F. Breakfast 20F. Depending on the size of the group, they will fit students into dorms, singles, doubles, or triples. Call ahead.

Hôtel Clair Meuble, 6, rue d'Italie (tel. 93 87 87 61), near the station. Rooms renovated recently, with kitchenettes and refrigerators. Clean and spacious. Singles with shower 100-120F. Doubles with shower 160-180F. Triples with shower 210-240F. Quads with shower 300F. Call for reservations.

Hôtel Idéal Bristol, 22, rue Paganini (tel. 93 88 60 72), off of rue Alsace-Lorraine. Ideal hotel in an ideal spot within earshot of the peals of Notre Dame. M. and Mme Salen keep spacious and spotless rooms. Beautiful TV room. Dorm-style rooms (4-5 in room) with kitchenette and refrigerator 82F. Singles 112F. Doubles 139F, with shower 174F. Triples 201F, with shower 246F.

Hôtel Notre Dame, 22, rue de Russie (tel. 93 88 70 44), at the corner of rue d'Italie. Rooms are a bit small, but clean, quiet, and carpeted; all have telephones. Charming managers. Singles 100F, with private bathroom 120F. Doubles 140F, with shower 200F. Showers 10F. Breakfast 15-20F.

Hôtel Lyonnais, 20, rue de Russie (tel. 93 88 70 74), near rue d'Italie with a view of the windows of Notre Dame just across the street. Fairly spacious and clean rooms with telephones. Elevator for the weary. Singles 100-140F, with showers 155-175F. Breakfast 18F.

Hôtel St-François, 3, rue St-François (tel. 93 85 88 69 or 93 13 40 18), in Vieux Nice near the morning fish market and *gare routière*. Cramped rooms, and dark hallways, but location and view add a little flavor. Singles 75-80F. Doubles 120F. Triples 210-225F. Showers 15F. Breakfast 15F.

Hôtel Novelty, 26, rue d'Angleterre (tel. 93 87 51 73), near the train station. Modern foyer with glass and polished brass. Clean rooms with firm, comfy beds. Manager speaks English. Dorm rooms 70F, with shower 80F. Singles 130F. Doubles 200F, with shower and T.V. 280F. Triples with shower 390F. Breakfast 30F. Safe for valuables available.

Hôtel St. Jacques, 27, rue d'Angleterre (tel. 93 88 80 96). Rooms spacious, many recently renovated. All with stove and fridge. Singles 85-105F. Doubles 150F, with shower 170F. Triples 195F, with shower 225F. Quads with shower 275F. Call ahead.

Hôtel de la Mer, 4, pl. Masséna (tel. 93 92 09 10). Two-star hotel facing the grand fountain of pl. Masséna. Friendly, English-speaking owner welcomes foreign tourists. Spacious and clean rooms, all with shower, toilet, mini-bar, TV. Singles 250-320F. Doubles 280-350F. Triples 350-450F. Quads 500F. 40-50F less per person during off-season. Breakfast 25F.

Food

Conveniently located just across the Mediterranean from North Africa and an hour's train ride from Italy, Nice offers a smorgasbord of seafood, North African, and Italian gastronomic delights. Boulevard Jean Jaurès, opposite the fountain, and cours Saleya in Vieux Nice, are wellsprings of savory *bouillabaisse*. Many North African restaurants serve sensational *couscous* and lamb-and-rice feasts. *Pissaladière,* an onion, olive, and anchovy pizza, is a *niçois* specialty. And, of course, Nice is the home of the *salade niçoise;* with tuna, eggs, tomatoes, and a spicy mustard dressing, it's the French answer to chef's salad.

Many fine restaurants cluster around the *vieux port.* Avoid the cheap, touristy places near the train station. Nice's restaurants offer a great excuse to splurge. But if you find your stomach and your wallet simultaneously empty, head for one of Nice's many university cafeterias, which serve filling meals for about 36F. The convenient **Restaurant Université,** 3, av. Robert Schumann (tel. 93 97 10 20) is open from September through June. The cafeteria at **Montebello,** 96, av. Valrose (tel. 93 52 56 59), near the Musée Matisse, is open until mid-August. All student cafeterias are open daily 11:30am-1:30pm and 6-8pm.

Cafés and food stands along the beach are expensive, so shop for lunch before you hit the waves. The **fruit market** east of pl. Masséna bustles each morning, as does the **fish market** in pl. St-François. You'll find everything else at **Prisunic,** 42, av. Jean Médecin (open Mon.-Thurs. and Sat. 8:30am-7pm, Fri. 8:30am-8pm) or **Supermarché Casino** on rue Deudor, behind the Nice Etoile on av. Jean Médecin, off rue Biscarra (open Mon.-Sat. 8:30am-8pm). At both supermarkets, mineral water costs one quarter of what street vendors charge.

Le Säetone, 8, rue d'Alsace Lorraine, off rue d'Angleterre near the train station. A comfortable restaurant serving regional dishes. Fills up quickly. Try the *soupe au pistou* (26F) and the special dessert, *mousse au café.* 50F, 65F, and 80F *menus* include local favorites like *salade niçoise* and *salade aux fruits de mer. Plat du jour* 40F. Open Tues.-Sat. 11:30am-2pm and 6-10pm.

Chez Annie, 6, rue Delille, near the pedestrian rue Masséna. Wonderful bistro serves traditional *niçois* specialties such as *aîoli* (raw vegetables with a garlic mayonnaise dip, 32F) and home-made *raviolis à la niçoise* 45F). Open Mon.-Sat. 11:30am-2pm and 7-11pm. Closed Aug.10-24.

Le Faubourg Montmartre, 32, rue Pertinax, off av. Jean Médecin. Fantastic beef, chicken, and pork *couscous* (55-70F). Excellent *bouillabaisse* (60F, 110F for two). *Menu* 65F. Manager loves students. Open daily 1-3pm and 5pm-midnight.

Restaurant de Paris, 28, rue d'Angleterre, near the train station. Offers a variety of specialties at affordable prices, including beef fondue (with fries or salad 45F) and *tarte aux pommes chantilly* (apple tart with whipped cream, 22F). *Menus* 40F, 50F, 65F. Open Dec.-Oct. daily 11:30am-2:30pm and 7:30pm-midnight.

Chez Davia, 11bis, rue Grimaldi, a short walk from pl. Masséna off bd. Victor Hugo. Excellent French and Italian food at great prices. Run by a charming Italian woman whose family has owned the establishment for 30 years. Wide selection. Four-course 55F *menu* and 5-course 75F *menu*. Sun. specialty is duck or rabbit. *Plat du jour* with dessert 38-44F. Ravioli and pasta dishes 28-30F. Open Thurs.-Tues. noon-2:30pm and 7-10:30pm.

Le Pacific Pizzeria, 18, rue Miron, 5min. from the station and the Chagall Museum. Savor the largest pizzas (35-55F) in Nice amid 50s and 60s American decor. *Plat du jour* 35F. Casual, fun-loving management. Open daily noon-2pm and 7-11pm.

La Gitane, intersection of rue Rossetti and rue Droite (tel. 93 62 06 77), in Vieux Nice. 58F 4-course menu offers *salade niçoise* and broiled trout. Entrées served with ample helpings of rice. Tasty and filling. Open daily 11:30am-2pm and 6-10pm.

Cafétéria Flunch, av. Thiers, next door to the train station. A budget traveler's best friend. Good food, large portions, and the cheapest prices in town. Half a roast chicken or sausages with 2 vegetables 20F. Open daily 11am-10pm.

Sights

Nice's **Promenade des Anglais** is a sight unto itself. A cross between a *grand boulevard* and the Malibu boardwalk, this promenade stretches the length of Nice's waterfront and rocky white beach. Bikini-clad youth on roller blades zip past shuttling retirees, while monokinis rule the show down below. Private beaches cramp the water between bd. Gambetta and the Opéra, but lots of public spaces compensate, especially west of bd. Gambetta. Bring a beach mat.

The most confirmed museum-hater will have a hard time resisting Nice's varied collections. Since most of the city's museums are hidden among attractive houses in quiet suburbs, visiting them gives you a respite from the beach and pl. Masséna as well as a glimpse of the luxurious residential areas. Furthermore, virtually all the museums are free. The tourist office's leaflet *Museums of Nice* provides more detailed information. The pride of Nice's museum collection, the **Musée Matisse,** 164, av. des Arènes de Cimiez, is closed for renovations until December 1992.

Despite the temporary loss of its captain, Nice's fleet of museums is one of France's strongest. The elegant **Musée National Marc Chagall,** av. du Docteur Ménard (tel. 93 81 75 75), is a 15-minute walk north of the station. Or take bus #15 (every 20min., 8F) to "Docteur Moriez" stop. Like many museums on the *Côte,* this building incorporates radiant uses for glass, space, and light. The 17 oil paintings devoted to Old Testament themes, including the vivid *Song of Songs,* exemplify Chagall's colorful whimsy. The collection contains mosaics, sculptures, tapestries, lithographs, and engravings—works into which Chagall said he injected all his sadness and happiness. (Open Wed.-Mon. 10am-7pm; Oct.-June. Wed.-Mon. 10am-12:30pm and 2-5:30pm. Admission 17F; students, seniors, and Sun. 8F. Library on history of art and religion open Tues.-Thurs. 10am-12:30pm.)

Housed in the former villa of Ukrainian princess Kotschoubey, the **Musée des Beaux-Arts,** 33, av. Baumettes (tel. 93 44 50 72), is a must-see for fans of the surreal. Take bus #38 from the train station to "Chéret," or #12 to "François Gross" (both 8F). Among the artists whose works are displayed here is Gustave Albert Mossa (1883-1971), a shamefully under-appreciated *niçois* painter whose surrealist works are steeped in those crazy existential themes of love, sex, and death. The collection also highlights the work of Degas, Monet, Sisley, Renoir, Bonnard, and Dufy. The sculpture garden blooms with the work of Rodin and Carpeaux. (Open Tues.-Sun. 10am-noon and 3-6pm; Oct.-April Tues.-Sun. 10am-noon and 2-5pm. Free. Guided tours 25F, but you can probably get by without one.)

The new **Musée d'Art Moderne et d'Art Contemporain,** promenade des Arts (tel. 93 62 61 62), is at the intersection of av. St-Jean Baptiste and Traverse Garibaldi; take bus #5 from the station. The museum occupies an open space (which serves as a theater during *carnaval* and festival times) and four marble towers joined by transparent foot bridges. The museum's holdings feature over 400 French and American avant-garde pieces from 1960 to the present, including works by Roy Lichtenstein, Andy Warhol,

Kenneth Noland, and Yves Klein. (Open Sat.-Mon. and Wed.-Thurs. 11am-6pm, Fri. 11am-10pm. Free.)

The inner and outer decor alone of the **Musée Masséna,** 65, rue de France (tel. 93 88 11 34 or 93 88 06 22), at the corner of the promenade des Anglais, make it worth a visit. Housed in an opulent villa, the museum is completely decorated in the style of the First Empire. Furnishings in the villa originate from Italian royal residences, and paintings by Renoir and watercolors by *niçois* artists Mossa and Costa embellish the walls. (Open May-Sept. Tues.-Sun. 10am-noon and 3-6pm; Oct. and Dec-April 10am-noon and 2-5pm. Free.)

Nice's aquatic heritage shifts inland from the beach to the town's aquarium and shell collections at the **Musée International de Malacologie,** 3, cours Saleya (tel. 93 85 18 44) in Vieux Nice. (Open Dec.-Oct. Tues.-Sat. 10:30am-1pm and 2-6pm. Free.) Other museums include a **Musée Archéologique,** 160, av. des Arènes de Cimiez (tel. 93 81 59 57). Take bus #15, 17, 20, or 22 to "Arènes" (8F), where you can visit the Gallo-Roman baths for 5F, 2F50 for students and seniors. (Guided visits every Sat. and Sun. at 3pm 20F, students 10F. Open May-Sept. Tues.-Sat. 10am-noon and 2-6pm, Sun. 2-6pm; Oct. and Dec.-April Tues.-Sat. 10am-noon and 2-5pm, Sun. 2-5pm.) On the other end of the spectrum, the **Musée Aléxis et Gustav-Adolf Mossa,** 59, quai des Etats-Unis (tel. 93 62 37 11), exhibits works from the 1960s to the present and always has room for new talent. (Open Tues.-Sat. 10:30am-noon and 2-6pm, Sun. 2-6pm. Free.)

After you've had your fill of Nice's art treasures, take a look at the **Cathédrale Orthodoxe Russe St-Nicolas,** 17, bd. du Tsarévitch, off bd. Gambetta, a five-minute walk east of the train station, and a welcome departure from the Gothic and Romanesque heritage that rules the rest of the country. Built in 1912 under the patronage of Tsar Nicholas II, this gorgeous church points to the pre-Revolution importance of the Côte d'Azur as a getaway for wealthy Russians. Its design borrows from the 17th-century Yaroslav style seen in the Kremlin. Every Sunday, Nice's Russian Orthodox community still worships under the six onion domes roofed with typical *niçois* tiles. (Open 9am-noon and 2:30-6pm, Sept.-May 9:30am-noon and 2:30-5pm. Admission 12F. No shorts or sleeveless shirts allowed.)

Once the spiritual center of another of Nice's religious communities, the **Monastère Cimiez,** pl. du Monastère (tel. 93 81 55 41), housed Nice's Franciscan brethren from the 13th to the 18th centuries. The monastery's cloister, the Eglise Gothique, and 350 works of religious art, are open to the public. (Open Mon.-Sat. 10am-noon and 3-6pm. Take bus #15 or 17 from the station. Free.)

Nice maintains many beautiful parks and public gardens, the most central of which is the sprawling **Jardin Albert 1er.** Located at promenade des Anglais and quai des Etats-Unis, this quiet refuge has benches, fountains, plenty of shade, and the ornate 18th-century Triton fountain. The garden also contains the **Théâtre de Verdure** (tel. 93 82 38 68), a small amphitheater that hosts a variety of summer events including jazz concerts and outdoor theater. (Box office open daily 10:30am-noon and 3:30-6:30pm.) The fragrant, equally sprawling **Esplanade du Paillon,** near pl. Masséna, surrounds a spectacular central fountain and serves as an ideal setting for a picnic.

Like many centers on the *Côte,* Nice has a colorful, convoluted old section, known to residents as **Vieux Nice.** Sprawling out southeast from bd. Jean Jaurès, this *quartier* is a perilous mix of tourist trap cafés and shops and homes of the *vrai niçois* ("real" *niçois.)* To experience the authentic old city, stick to the tiniest of the already tiny streets. Avoid the Galeries des Ponchettes and the area around the Cathédrale Ste-Réparate where most establishments display American Express decals in the windows. Just east of Vieux Nice lies **Le château,** a hillside public park rising above the city. Enter the park via rue Rossetti and climb upward through a forest of exotic pines and cacti, or give your lungs a break and take the elevator up to the top. Once there, you'll surely enjoy the spectacular view of the city, its beaches, the port, and the Baie des Anges (Bay of Angels).

Entertainment

Nice guys do finish last. Nice's party crowd swings long after the folks in St-Tropez and Antibes have called it a night. The bars and nightclubs around rue Massena and Vieux Nice are constantly frolicking and rollicking with jazz, snazz, and rock and roll. The area around the clubs in Vieux Nice can be dangerous at night and should not be visited alone.

Nice's nightclubs are relentlessly expensive. The **Jok Club,** 1, promenade des Anglais (tel. 93 87 95 87) is Nice's latest hotspot. Bust a move 'til you drop, and then cool off with the sea breeze on the promenade. (Open daily 10pm-3am. Cover 60F.) **Ruby's,** 8, descente Croh (tel. 93 62 59 60), along bd. Jean Jaurès opposite the promenade de Paillon, plays reggae and calypso music to a diverse crowd. (Cover 60F, 75F on Sat. Drinks 50F. Open nightly 11:30pm-6am.) At **Le Centre Ville Discothèque,** 1, pl. Masséna (tel. 93 88 88 47), a young crowd (ages 17-25) moves to pop, funk, rap, and new wave. Women dance free on Wednesday, Thursday, and Sunday. (Cover and first drink 75F, Sat. 100F. Open July daily 11pm-6am, Aug.-June Wed.-Sun. 11pm-6am.) **The Quartz Discothèque,** 18, rue Congrès (tel. 93 88 88 87), attracts a mixed gay and straight crowd to its long bar, comfy chairs, and small dance floor; doors open at 11pm (cover 70F).

Nice's bar and pub scene can also be lots of fun, but again, be careful; don't venture out alone. **The Hole in the Wall,** 3, rue de l'Abbaye (tel. 93 80 40 16), about a block from rue de la Préfecture in Vieux Nice, has a lively pub atmosphere with live pop and rock nightly at 9pm. (Open Tues.-Sun. 8pm-midnight). **Jonathan's,** 1, rue de la Loge (tel. 93 62 57 62), in Vieux Nice off rue Centrale, close to the bus stop at av. Jean Jaurès, draws a slightly older (21-27) and less touristy crowd with live folk music and soft rock every evening in a candle-lit cellar. (Open nightly 8:30pm-12:30am.) **Scarlet O'Hara's,** 22, rue Droite (tel. 93 80 43 22), off rue Rossetti in Vieux Nice, is a pub that attracts a predominantly French crowd. (Open Mon.-Sat. 7pm-12:30am.) **Chez Wayne,** 15, rue de la Préfecture (tel. 93 13 46 99) attracts an English-speaking crowd with its mellow blues and jazz. Call ahead for reservations. (Cover 20F, beers 20-30F. Open nightly 9pm-1am.)

The **Théâtre du Cours,** 2, rue Poissonnerie in Vieux Nice, stages traditional dramatic performances Thursday through Saturday at 9pm and Sunday at 7pm (75F). The more experimental **Central Dramatique National,** Promenade des Arts (tel. 93 80 52 60 or 93 13 90 90), at the corner of av. St-Jean Baptiste and Traverse Garibaldi, offers a show almost every weekend (50-160F). The grand **Théâtre de Nice** on the promenade des Arts (tel. 93 80 52 60) hosts concerts and theater performances (50-200F), and the **Nice Opéra,** 4, rue St-François de Paule (tel. 93 85 67 31) has an annual performance series of visiting symphony orchestras and soloists (75-250F).

Nice's **La Grande Parade du Jazz** in mid-July at the Parc et Arènes de Cimiez (tel. 93 80 59 83), near the Musée Matisse, attracts world-famous European and American jazz musicians to its three stages. In 1992 alone, performers included Wynton Marsalis, Bobby McFerrin, Roberta Flack, and Fishbone. Past performers have included B. B. King and Miles Davis. The **Festival de Folklore International** and the **Batailles des Fleurs,** pageants of music and flowers along promenade des Anglais, bloom every year on the last weekend of July. (Reserved seats in the stands 60F.) Fireworks fan across the city's skies every February as parades roll through the crowds celebrating Nice's **Carnaval.** *Semaine des Spectacles,* published every Wednesday, carries entertainment listings for the entire Côte and is available at newsstands (8F). The **Comité des Fêtes,** 5, promenade des Anglais (tel. 93 87 16 28), has information about all the above events (open Mon.-Fri. 10am-noon and 2-5pm). The **FNAC** in the Nice Etoile shopping center on 24, av. Jean Médecin, sells tickets for virtually every musical or theatrical event in town. Call the tourist office for more information.

Nice to Monaco

Uncrowded beaches, secluded, small-town charm, and a slower pace make the sequestered towns between Nice and Monaco the real hidden treasures of the Riviera. The narrow streets and pastel houses of **Villefranche-sur-Mer,** only two stops from Nice, enchanted Aldous Huxley, Katherine Mansfield, and a bevy of other writers. Trains run from Nice every half-hour (8F). **Rue Obscure,** the oldest street in Villefranche and perhaps one of the least understood in France, was built in the 13th century. Its small, cramped houses huddle with their backs to the sailboats floating in the crescent-shaped bay. Jean Cocteau decorated the 14th-century **Chapelle St-Pierre,** quai Courbet, with boldly executed scenes from the life of St. Peter and the Camargue gypsies of Stes-Maries-de-la-Mer. (Open July-Sept. Sat.-Thurs. 9am-noon and 2-7pm; Oct.-Nov. 15 Sat.-Thurs. 9:30am-noon and 2-4:30pm; Dec. 15-June Sat.-Thurs. 9:30am-noon and 2:30-6pm. Admission 15F.) The **tourist office** on Jardin François Binon (tel. 93 01 73 68) suggests excursions by foot, bus, or train to the small villages around the region. They do not make hotel reservations but know which hotels have space. (Open daily 9am-7pm; Sept. 16-June 14 Mon.-Sat. 9am-noon and 2-6pm.) Both of the town's excellent museums are located in the 16th-century **Citadelle,** near the waterfront. The **Musée Volti** (tel. 93 76 61 00) displays the contemporary art and sculpture of Villefranche resident Antoniucci Volti, while the **Musée Goetz-Boumeester** (tel. 93 76 61 00) traces the work of Villefranche painter and sometime Surrealist Henri Goetz and his wife, Christine Boumeester. (Both open Wed.-Mon. 10am-noon and 2-5pm; June-Sept. Wed.-Mon. 10am-noon and 3-7pm. Free.)

Peaceful **Beaulieu-sur-Mer,** three stops east of Nice on the coastal rail line, enjoys relatively uncrowded gravel beaches. **Kérylos,** a seaside Greek villa, has been reconstructed with ivory-and-marble mosaics and frescoes. (Open July-Aug. Tues.-Sun. 2:30-6:30pm; Sept.-Oct. and Dec.-June Tues.-Sun. 2-6pm. Admission 30F, students and children 15F.) The **tourist office,** pl. de la Gare (tel. 93 01 02 21), makes hotel reservations for free (open Mon.-Fri. 9am-noon and 2-6pm, Sat.-Sun. 9am-noon). The secluded hamlet of **St-Jean-Cap-Ferrat** snuggles inside a tiny peninsula that juts out into the Mediterranean. From Beaulieu, walk 2km south along a seaside path full of secluded beaches, and then uphill to get to St-Jean. On the way stands the **Fondation Ephrussi de Rothschild** (tel. 93 01 33 09), a pink Italian villa built at the turn of the century to house the superb furniture and art collection of the Baroness de Rothschild. Canvases by Monet and Fragonard, Chinese vases, and Beauvais tapestries accompany the spectacular gardens surrounding the villa. Recent renovations have uncovered a new wing of the villa decorated almost entirely with Louis XIV furniture and 18th-century artwork, making Chez Rothschild the Versailles of the Côte. The inspiring view from the backside of the villa of cliffs descending to the sea is unrivaled anywhere in the Riviera. (Open July-Aug. Tues.-Sat. 10am-noon and 2-6pm, Sun. 2-6pm; Sept.-Oct. and Dec.-June Tues.-Sat. 10am-noon and 2-6pm, Sun. 2-6pm. Admission to museum and garden 30F, students 20F; garden only 12F.)

The finest beach east of Antibes is at **Cap d'Ail,** 20 minutes by train from Nice. From the station, walk down the stairs, under the tracks, and turn right. You'll find small, rocky coves to the east that are perfect for sunning or fishing but dangerous for swimming. A 500m walk west leads to the pebbly, better-for-swimming **Plage de la Mala,** sheltered by cliffs. Princess Stéphanie of Monaco is said to tan on this secluded beach, far from the crowds (and cameras) of her country's coast. On the way to the beach is the **Relais International de la Jeunesse** on bd. de la Mer (tel. 93 78 18 58), a glorious seaside youth hostel in an old villa. Men and women are housed in separate villas, but can stay together if they sleep in the 12-person tents perched directly above crashing waves. Breakfast is always included. As there's a midnight curfew (Fri.-Sat. 1am), don't stay here if you plan to gamble the night away at Monaco's casino. (3-night max. stay. Lockout 10am-5pm. 65F first night, 55F each subsequent night. Dinner 45F. Beer 6F. Snack bar.)

Several km inland from Nice, **St-Paul-de-Vence** is among the best-preserved hill towns in France. For a panoramic view of the hills and valleys of the Alpes-Maritimes, walk along the ramparts, virtually unchanged since the 16th century. Studios, galleries, and expensive boutiques fill the lower floors of the houses in this artists' colony. The St-Paul-de-Vence **tourist office** (tel. 93 32 86 95) is near the entrance of the village at the beginning of rue Grande. (Open Mon.-Tues. and Thurs.-Sat. 10am-6pm, Sun. 2-6pm; Oct.-June Mon.-Tues. and Thurs.-Sat. 10am-noon and 2-6pm, Sun. 2-6pm.) Buses roll regularly to St-Paul-de-Vence from Nice's *gare routière* (20 per day, 55min., 26F).

The pride of careless St-Paul-de-Vence is the **Fondation Maeght** (tel. 93 32 81 63), a 1km walk from the center of town. Get off at the second St-Paul-de-Vence bus stop, just outside the center of town on the way to Vence, and follow the signs up a steep, winding hill, chemin des Gardettes. If you can go to only one museum in the whole Riviera, make this the one. Designed by Josep Louis Sert, the Fondation is actually part museum and part park, with fountains, wading pools, and split-level terraces. Works by Miró, Calder, Arp, and Zadkine are arranged with such care that, despite their innate abstractness, they fit elegantly into their garden setting. Stained-glass windows by Braque and Ubac are set in the garden chapel. Inside is an excellent permanent collection, as well as rotating exhibits usually devoted to a single artist. (Open daily 10am-7pm; Oct.-June 10am-noon and 3-6pm. Admission 45F, students 30F, but worth every centime.)

Moving right along on Mr. Bus-to-Vence, the **Chapelle du Rosaire,** yet another shrine to French impressionism and the avant-garde, lies 1.5km from the last bus stop on av. Henri Matisse. The chapel's tiny interior was designed by Matisse, who considered the green, yellow, and blue stained glass his masterpiece. (Open Dec. 15-Oct. Wed., Fri., and Sat. 10-11:30am and 2-5:30pm. Free. Photographs forbidden.) Vence's well-stocked **tourist office** (tel. 93 58 06 38) is in a booth on pl. du Grand Jardin beside the bus stop. (Open Mon.-Sat. 9am-noon and 2-7pm; Sept.-June Mon.-Sat. 9am-noon and 2-6pm.) This former Roman market town is also known for its elegantly crafted pottery. Browse through the earthenware shops on av. Jean Jaurès, but beware of street vendors selling "Matisse originals." Vence can be reached by bus from Nice's *gare routière* (20 per day, 55min., 26F).

Monaco/Monte-Carlo

The Monaco Grand Prix, the Casino, Princess Grace, and the young brunette Stephanie—the myth of Monaco seems larger than life, fast and furious, rich and risky. The legend, in fact, seems to have outgrown the reality of this tiny principality. While the casino still bubbles with furious excitement, those who arrive in Monaco seeking to waltz with fame and make their fortunes amidst the already fortunate will leave bitter, broke, and broken. Those who resist the myth's powerful pull, however, will leave with memories of a place pretentious and comical, yet subtly beautiful.

In its time, tiny Monaco has changed status from independent country to autonomous principality to its current role as a principality independent in name only. Prince Rainier III is the sovereign ruler, but there's not much to reign over. The *monégasques* number only 4500, and the entire principality occupies only 2 square km. Their electricity, tap water, and money are all French, with stamps and tobacco about the only things that Monaco does not sponge off France. Such freeloading, however, does not mean that state functions are not performed with comic self-importance. Whether through the zeal of its street cleaners or the pomp of the changing of its palace guards, Monaco is eager to prove and practice its statedom.

Orientation and Practical Information

Picture Monaco as a U-shape opening to the sea with the train station at the curved end. When you exit the station, go right onto av. Prince Pierre for two blocks, left onto av. du Port, and then left onto quai Albert overlooking the harbor. Above you on the right sits the *quartier* of Monaco-Ville with its *vieille ville* and the Prince's palace. To the left of the port rises the fabled *quartier* of Monte-Carlo and its grand casino. Some people confuse Monte-Carlo with Monaco. Monte-Carlo is, in some ways, a city within the state of Monaco. But since Monaco itself is only 2 square km, Monte-Carlo is actually more like a *quartier* of the grander city of Monaco.

Tourist Office: 2a, bd. des Moulins (tel. 93 50 60 88), near the casino. Very helpful staff speaks English and makes room reservations. An avalanche of maps and information. Ask for the helpful map of the city and the steamy brochures *Monte-Carlo: A Dream Come True* and *Monte-Carlo: Places of Interest.* You can also call hotels from a special phone at the train station. **Annexes** are set up in the train station and in the port in summer. Open Mon.-Sat. 9am-7pm, Sun. 10am-noon.

Currency Exchange: Compagnie Monégasque de Change, parking des Pêcheurs (tel. 93 25 02 50), in the parking complex next to the Musée de l'Océanographie. Commission only on French traveler's checks. Open daily 9am-7pm. Closed in Dec. Also in the **train station.** Open daily 8:30am-noon and 2-4:30pm.

American Express: 35, bd. Princesse Charlotte (tel. 93 25 74 45). Open Mon.-Sat. 9am-6pm.

Post Office: pl. Beaumarchais. Monaco issues its own stamps, but unless you mail your postcards here, you'll have to start a stamp collection. **Telephones.** For **Poste Restante,** specify Palais de la Scala, Monte-Carlo. **Branch office** across from the train station, with **telephones.** Both offices open Mon.-Fri. 8am-6pm, Sat. 8am-noon. **Postal Code:** MC 98000 Monaco.

Public Transportation: tel. 93 50 62 41. Five routes connect the entire hilly town every 10min. from 7am-9pm. Bus #4 links the train station to the Casino in Monte-Carlo. Tickets 8F each, *carnet* of 8 29F.

Trains: av. Prince Pierre (tel. 93 87 50 50). Monaco lies on the St-Raphaël-Ventimiglia line with direct connections 5:30am-11pm to: Nice (every 30min., 25min., 15F); Antibes (every 30min., 45min., 30F); Cannes (every 30min., 70min., 45F); Menton (every 30min., 10min., 7F). Information desk open daily 9am-7pm. **Lockers** 20F for 72 hrs.

Buses: Buses to other cities leave from several locations. Buses to Nice (20F), with stops at Cap d'Ail (4F), Eze-sur-Mer (6F), Beaulieu-sur-Mer (10F), and Villefranche-sur-Mer (13F), leave every hr. Mon.-Sat. 6:30am-8:30pm, Sun. 7:30am-8:30pm from av. de la Costa, near bd. des Moulins and the tourist office. Buses to Menton (11F) leave from pl. des Moulins. For information on above buses, call 93 85 61 81 or ask the tourist office.

Bike Rental: Auto-Moto Garage, 7, rue de la Colle (tel. 93 30 24 61), near the station. Five-speed bikes 66F per day, mountain bikes 100F per day, deposit 1900F. Open Mon.-Fri. 8am-noon and 2-7pm, Sat. 8am-noon.

Hospital: Centre Hospitalier Princesse Grace, av. Pasteur (tel. 93 25 99 00).

Police: 3, rue Louis Notari (tel. 93 30 42 46). **Emergency:** tel. 17. **Lost and Found:** tel. 93 15 30 15.

Accommodations and Camping

Monaco is a nice place to visit, but you wouldn't want (and can't afford) to sleep here. Most of the principality's lavish appeal can be soaked up in a day. And because Monaco is so close to the hostels of Antibes, Cap d'Ail and Nice, it makes a convenient daytrip. But if you plan to gamble the night away at the casino, try making an early reservation at the lovely Centre de Jeunesse Princesse Stéphanie. There are also a few bargains near the train station and in **Beausoleil,** a five-minute walk from Monte-Carlo, in nearby France.

Hôtel de Paris, pl. du Casino (tel. 93 50 80 80), in Monte-Carlo. No lockers for ze backpack and no kitchen facilities, but Mmmmm comfy beds and room service at no extra charge. Book ahead and avoid the lines of European royalty at the reception desk. Singles and doubles 2800F. Showers included.

Centre de Jeunesse Princesse Stéphanie, 24, av. Prince Pierre (tel. 93 50 83 20), 100m up the hill from the train station. This excellent facility is perennially packed. In the summer, arrive before 7:30am if you want a bed—reservations are accepted off-season only. Only foreign students ages 16-26 (ID required) will be allowed to stay. 3-day max. in summer, 5 days in winter, but first-day arrivals have priority. Reception open 7am-12:45am; off-season 7am-11:45pm. 60F. Breakfast and sheets included.

Hôtel Cosmopolite, 4, rue de la Turbie (tel. 93 30 16 95), very near the train station. Homey and clean. Singles 146F, with shower 230F. Doubles 160-200F, with shower 246F. Showers 15F. Breakfast 28F.

Hôtel Helvetia, 1, rue Grimaldi (tel. 93 30 21 71), on the way to Monte-Carlo from the station. A lovely hotel over a bookstore and a perfume shop. Rooms are spotless and the pillows are elephantine. Singles 150F, with shower 200F. Doubles 200F, with shower 250F. Breakfast included.

Hôtel Villa Boeri, 29, bd. du Général Leclerc (tel. 93 78 38 10), in Beausoleil. Some rooms have balconies overlooking the sea, others have wall-to-wall mirrors. All are clean and boast TVs (including CNN and an English movie channel). Singles and doubles 180-240F, triples 300-500F. Showers included. Breakfast 30F.

Although there are no **campgrounds** in Monaco, Nice's and Menton's five excellent sites are just minutes away by rail. The closest campground is a five-minute walk from Monaco, in Beausoleil. **Point Accueil Jeunes de Beausoleil,** Quartier Fondivine (tel. 93 78 63 63), by rue Moyenne Corniche in Beausoleil, is open June 15 to September 30, and has only 20 spots. You *must* call in advance for reservations (5-night max. stay. 12F per person, 10F per tent.)

Food

Monégasque specialties include *barbaginan,* a crispy fried dough cake, and *stofaci,* a delicious fish casserole cooked with white wine, cognac, tomatoes, and olive oil. Most of Monaco's restaurants aren't designed for budget travelers, but there are a few exceptions. **Le Calypso,** av. Princesse Grace, is the first café you'll hit on the *plages du Larvotto* when walking from the Casino. They offer cheap and tasty beachfront meals. Savor especially the *escalope de veau* (veal cutlet, 65F) or the lasagna (51F). **Le Cavagnetu,** 14, rue Compte Félix Bastaldi (tel. 93 30 35 80) serves a 65F and an 85F *menu* of *monégasque* delights. (Open daily 6-11pm.) Or else, hit **Le Périgordin,** 4, rue de la Turbie (tel. 93 30 06 02), a high-class operation (don't wear shorts) with surprisingly pedestrian prices. Go for lunch and sample French duck specialties on the 55F *menu*; dinner has similarly priced a la carte delicacies. (Open Mon.-Sat. noon-2pm and 7:30-10:30pm.)

Picnickers should stop by the fruit and flower **market** on pl. d'Armes (open daily 6am-1pm), at the end of av. Prince Pierre or the **Codec Supermarket,** 30, bd. Princesse Charlotte, near the corner of bd. des Moulins by the tourist office. (Open Mon.-Fri. 8:30am-noon and 3-7pm, Sat. 8:30am-7pm.)

Sights and Entertainment

All the wealth, mystery, and intrigue of Monte-Carlo revolves around the famed **Casino.** Here Mata Hari once shot a Russian spy; here in 1891 the Englishman Charles Deville Wells broke the bank repeatedly and turned 10,000 gold francs into a million; and here Richard regaled Liz with an obscenely huge diamond. Mata, Charles, and Richard have long since cashed in their chips, but the grandeur of yesteryear lives on within the Victorian walls of the casino. Surrounded by gardens overlooking the coast, the old casino building was designed by Charles Garnier and resembles his Paris opera house. The interior, a shining paragon of 19th-century extravagance with red velvet curtains, gilded ceilings, and gold and crystal chandeliers, is worth visiting, even if you're not a gambler. The slot machines open at noon, and the *salle américaine* (where blackjack, craps, and roulette require a 30F minimum bet) at 4pm; hardcore veterans don't arrive until after 10pm. Admission to the main room—or "kitchen"—is free (you must be over 21 and cannot wear shorts), but it costs 50F to enter the *salons privés,* where French games such as *chemin de fer* and *trente et quarante* begin daily at 3pm.

The casino also houses the sumptuous **Théâtre** (tel. 93 50 76 54), occasional stage to Sandra Bernhardt's smash-hit one-woman show and long-time venue of Diaghilev's Ballets-Russes. You can visit only by attending a ballet or opera performance; tickets cost 130-200F (students 75F), but here you are at least guaranteed a return for your money. Outside the theater, across the main lobby from the casino rooms, is an extensive display of costumes from the theater's opera productions.

Even if you've lost your shirt at the casino, you can still admire the royal robes at the **Palais Princier.** Perched on a cliff high above Monte-Carlo, the palace is the some-time home of Prince Rainier and the one-time home of his bride, Princess Grace. Daily at 11:55am, you can see the changing of the guard outside the palace, a ritual which, given the size of the principality, recalls a Marx Brothers routine. In their lily-white uniforms, the soldiers look about as functional as the palace cannon, strategically posi-tioned to bombard the shopping district. Take a tour of the small but lavishly decorated palace and see Princess Grace's stunning official state portrait, Prince Rainier's throne, and—of special interest to American patriots—the chamber where England's King George III died.

Next door is the stately **Cathédrale de Monaco,** 4, rue Colonel Bellando de Castro (tel. 93 30 88 13). Each of the former Princes of Monaco is buried within this Ro-manesque-Byzantine church. Prince Rainier and Grace Kelly were wed here in 1956; her grave, behind the altar, is marked simply with her latinized name, "Patritia Gracia." (Open Mon.-Sat. 10am-6pm, Sun. 2-6pm.)

Once directed by Jacques Cousteau, the tremendous **Musée de l'Océanographie,** av. St-Martin (tel. 93 15 36 00), houses thousands of species of fish and marine animals from every sea on earth. (Open daily 9am-9pm; Sept.-June 9am-7pm. Admission 50F, ages 6-18 and students 25F.) The **Jardin Exotique** (tel. 93 30 33 65), with its devastat-ing cactus collection, is privy to exquisite coastal views and grottos with stalagmites and stalactites. (Open 9am-7pm; Oct.-May 9am-noon and 2-6pm. Admission 40F, stu-dents 28F.)

The **Orchestre Philharmonique de Monte-Carlo** performs evening concerts in July and August at the Cours d'Honneur of the Palais Princier. (Admission 100-300F. Tickets available in the Atrium of the Casino de Monte-Carlo.) The royal family usual-ly attends these concerts (program information available at the tourist office). The **Open Air Cinema,** av. Princesse Grace (tel. 93 25 86 80), plays a different film (in En-glish with French subtitles) each night at 9:30pm (admission 45F).

Just like its French Provençal neighbors, Monaco cannot resist an opportunity for a festival. One of the highlights of the summer season is the **Fireworks Festival,** an ex-plosive international competition that lights up the sky in late July and early August. If you're in the area in winter, go to a night of **Festival International du Cirque,** which features the world's best circuses, including the renowned Moscow Circus. A gala per-formance on the last night features the best acts from all the circuses (Jan. 28-Feb. 4, 1993). For more information on Monaco's festivals, call the tourist office or the **Co-mité des Fêtes** (tel. 93 30 80 04).

Menton

Bought by France in the 19th century, Menton (pop. 30,000) has prospered nicely in the shadow of its neighbor and former owner, Monaco. It is in this town, known for its tart lemons and Belle Epoque gentility, that those proverbial old gamblers who never die just fade away in sherbet-colored deck chairs. The snug embrace of green moun-tains and the intense heat (which residents claim is the most relentless in France) seems to have lulled this community of affluent retirees and their coiffed poodles into a per-manent siesta. On the way to Italy or before returning to hectic Nice, join the nappers in this town of beautiful stone beaches and orange stucco Italian architecture.

Orientation and Practical Information

Lying on the St-Raphaël-Ventimiglia rail line, Menton is 8 stops (35min.) from Nice and 2 stops (10min.) from Monaco. The main drag of the town, extending from the wa-terfront Casino to the mountains beyond Menton, is av. Boyer, where the tourist office, numerous streetside cafés, and a colorful flower garden lie.

Tourist Office: 8, av. Boyer (tel. 93 57 57 00). Follow rue de la Gare from the train station and turn right on av. Boyer until you reach the grandiose Palais d'Europe. The office is inside. A refreshingly friendly staff will make reservations or direct you to available rooms. Open Mon.-Sat. 8am-7:30pm, Sun. 8am-noon; Oct.-June 14 Mon.-Sat. 9am-12:30pm and 2-6pm.

Post Office: cours Georges V (tel. 93 35 45 00). Directly across av. Boyer from the tourist office. Phones, **currency exchange,** and lines. Open Mon.-Fri. 8am-6:30pm, Sat. 8am-noon. **Postal Code:** 06503.

Trains: rue de la Gare (tel. 93 35 87 89). To: Nice (2 per hr., 35min., 21F); Cannes (2 per hr., 80min., 49F); and Monte Carlo (2 per hr., 10min., 6F). Luggage storage 15F per day, lockers 6F per day. Connections available from Nice.

Buses: *gare routière,* promenade Maréchal Leclerc (tel. 93 28 43 27). Cheaper than the train for round-trips only. **Autocars Broch** sends buses almost every hour to Nice (24F round-trip) and Monte Carlo (11F round-trip). Prices are the same for one-way excursions. **TAM** also runs excursions into the Alps (Valberg 74F).

Taxis: tel. 93 35 72 37. The youth hostel is 35F away.

Hospital: tel. 93 28 15 15.

Police: tel. 93 35 81 32. **Emergency:** tel. 17.

Accommodations, Camping, and Food

Hotels in Menton are expensive; consider staying in nearby Cap d'Ail (at its wonderful Relais Youth Hostel). A 24-hour electronic board outside the tourist office lists availability of hotel rooms.

Auberge de Jeunesse (HI), plateau St-Michel (tel. 93 35 93 14). Nothing your mother did, o young Sisyphus, can prepare you for the hike to the hostel. Follow rue de la Gare and cross under the train tracks at the bridge. Take the immediate first right up the hill, the second left onto rue des Terres Chaudes, and brace yourself for 390 grueling steps. Non-sado-masochists may prefer the bus during the day (6F from the *gare routière*), or a taxi (35F) at night. Strict management runs a clean, modern hostel with a breathtaking view of Menton and its bay. Call ahead before making the trek. Reception open 7-9am and 5pm-midnight. Lockout 9am-5pm. Curfew 11pm or midnight depending on the season—be sure to ask. 60F, nonmembers 80F. 45F in 8-person tents with pillows, beds, and lights. Showers and breakfast included. Required sheet rental 14F. Delicious three-course dinners 43F. No reservations. Open Feb.-Nov.

Hôtel Belgique, 1, av. de la Gare (tel. 93 35 72 66), near the train station. Small but clean rooms. Welcoming manager and a lively local café downstairs. Singles 140-165F. Doubles 197-330F. Breakfast 25F.

Hôtel Beauregard, 10, rue Albert 1er (tel. 93 35 74 08), behind and below the train station. A peach-painted wonder with a pretty garden in front. Sprightly owner keeps squeaky-clean rooms. Comfortable TV room. Singles and doubles 150F, with shower 199F. Breakfast 26F.

Le Terminus, pl. de la Gare (tel. 93 35 77 00), opposite the train station. Genial family welcomes you into their comfortable rooms near the station. Singles and doubles 135F, with shower 199F. Extra beds 40F. Showers included. Breakfast 26F.

Camping: Campground Municipal du Plateau St-Michel, by the hostel on route des Ciappes de Castellar (tel. 93 35 81 23). Hot showers, a small grocery store, snack bar, and a lovely view of Menton and the Italian Riviera. 12F per person, 11F per tent. Refrigerators 19F. Open Mon.-Fri. 8am-noon and 3-8pm, Sat.-Sun. 8am-noon and 5-8pm.

The pedestrian street of rue St-Michel in the *vieille ville* overflows with lively shops and interesting restaurants as well as plenty of supermarkets. The municipal market, across from the Hôtel de Ville, sells quail, rabbit, goat, horse, cheese, fruits, and *pâtés.* (Open Tues.-Sun. 5am-1pm.) **Le Calypso,** 3, av. Boyer, is an excellent sidewalk café with delectably fresh fish (from 68F) and pasta dishes (35-70F). It posts an 85F *menu.* (Open daily noon-2:30pm and 6-11pm.) Otherwise, sate your hunger at **Le Merle Blanc,** 24, rue St-Michel, where a friendly, fun-filled atmosphere permeates the wooden dining area. The cook makes a fine fresh fish dish for 48-68F. Meat dishes cost the same. (Open daily 12:30-2:30pm and 6pm-midnight.) Finally, **La Régence Cafétéria,** 23, rue Parouneaux slakes the human thirst for cheap food with 40F *steak-frites,* 25-45F salads, and 20-35F sandwiches. (Open Mon.-Sat. 7am-9pm.)

Sights and Entertainment

The expansive **Plage des Sablettes** next to the *vieille ville* fronts an assortment of orange stucco restaurants and quaint cafés. Menton's prized possession is the **Musée Jean Cocteau,** quai Napoléon III (tel. 93 57 72 30), next to Vieux Port 18 and the *vieille ville* on promenade du Soleil. Though best-known for his brilliant work in film and drama, Cocteau was also skilled in the plastic arts. Menton's 17th-century stronghold houses a representative collection of his work, rarely displayed elsewhere. (Open Wed.-Sun. 10am-noon and 3-6pm; Sept. 16-June 14 Wed.-Sun. 10am-noon and 2-6pm. Free.) Devoted Cocteau fans can also visit **La Salle des Mariages** in the Hôtel de Ville (tel. 93 57 87 87), a room the artist decorated after a Greek temple. (Open Mon.-Fri. 8:30am-12:30pm and 1:30-5pm. Admission 10F.) Rising above the *marché* is the bell tower of **Eglise St-Michel** (tel. 93 35 73 73), a fine 17th-century baroque church with side chapels decorated by local artists. The cobblestone square in front of the church affords a glorious view of the **plages des Sablettes** below and the Italian coastline beyond.

Menton has a lively festival schedule. To usher in the Mardi Gras, the citizens devote Sundays in early February to the tart **Fête Internationale du Citron.** This exaltation of the lemon includes a *Corso des Fruits d'Or,* in which floats of various shape and form made from lemons, oranges, and orchids parade through town. Fruit juice runs freely and there is dancing in the streets. This year's gala takes place from February 20 to March 7, 1993.

In August, the **Festival de Musique** takes over the square in front of the church (concerts cost 40-250F). In July, the **Soirées de Musique Chorale** features such choral groups as the King's Singers and the Red Army Chorus (admission 70-150F). September brings **piano recitals** to the **Théâtre du Palais de l'Europe.** (Tickets for all events are available at the Palais de l'Europe, av. Boyer, tel. 93 35 82 22, or at the tourist office.)

In June and July, Menton hosts its annual festival of French and American film, **Le Cinéma d'Eté en Plain Air** at the parc de la Madonne. (Contact the tourist office for schedules and times. Admission 40F.)

Corse (Corsica)

For travelers who've finally cracked after too many impressionist paintings and provincial Parisian ways, isolated Corsica provides a welcome and breathtaking respite. Appropriately called Kallysté, "the most beautiful," by the Greeks, the island combines the mountainous splendor of the Alps with the sandy beaches and crystal-blue Mediterranean water of the Riviera while vineyards, twisting creeks, and sweet-smelling *maquis* (scrub) cover the steep, craggy mountains of the interior. Culturally and historically, Corsica cross-breeds its French and Italian heritage, but Corsicans themselves frequently prefer to recall their own, independent history.

While officially a part of France, Corsica shrugs off its connection to the mainland. Although all Corsicans speak French, they much prefer their own language, an Italian dialect whose closest mainland relative is Tuscan. In the past, the French government has prohibited Corsicans from speaking the language or even from using Corsican names, in an attempt to integrate the island into French society. But more recently, Corsican was reinstituted in the public school system, a sign of the island's growing cultural autonomy. Some groups, notably the outlawed Front de Libération National de la Corse (whose initials adorn every graffiti-marked surface), continue to bomb their way toward independence.

Despite this fierce streak of nationalism that pervades the island, Corsica has only known independence for a brief 14 years (during the 18th century). Prized property throughout the ages, the island has suffered Greek, Roman, Pisan, Genoese, Saracen, and French invasions. Even today, strategic 16th-century Genoese *citadelles* dominate the hilly landscape, seemingly surveying the Mediterranean for signs of attack. Genoa gained control of the island in 1347, when internal clan rivalry hobbled Corsican unification, for nearly four centuries. Corsica's contribution to the international vocabulary—*vendetta*—refers to the bloody family feuds that supplanted any Genoan justice system. A series of uprisings in 1729 initiated the Corsican War of Independence, otherwise known as the Forty Years War. In 1755, the revered Pasquale Paoli proclaimed the island an autonomous republic, created a university, and drafted a new constitution. The retreating Genoese ceded their protectorate to the French, who humiliated Paoli's army at Ponte Nuovo on May 8, 1769. Among the Corsican officers who quickly swore their allegiance to France was a certain Charles Bonaparte. On August 15, 1769, his second son Napoleon was born in Ajaccio.

With a total population of less than 250,000, and with the protected haven of the **Parc Naturel Régional** blanketing a quarter of the island, it is always possible to escape from the crowds on the coast by sneaking to the wilderness or retreating to one of the tiny villages of the heartland. Try to visit Corsica in the off-season; although ferries and other tourist services multiply between June 15 and the end of September, prices soar by as much as 50%. Half the island's one million annual tourists (mostly French, Italian, and German) visit in July and August, and the beaches and hotels in the coastal resorts are packed. The summer climaxes in a double-barreled blast of holiday mirth on August 15 as all of France celebrates the **Fête de l'Assomption;** Corsicans get to observe **Napoleon's birthday** too. Every town on the island erupts with fireworks in honor of their diminutive native son. Most of the tourists depart by September, ignorantly leaving the weather at its best and the Mediterranean waters at their warmest. Additionally, winter visitors can stay on coastal towns, where balmy winter temperatures await them, or head inland to the snow capped mountains for downhill or cross-country skiing.

The indispensable quadrilingual *Informations Pratiques* booklet contains the addresses and phone numbers of all of the island's tourist offices, plus information on transportation, sports (including equipment rental), museums, and emergency numbers. Most tourist offices also stock the guide *Circuits Archéologiques en Corse,* which has eight driving itineraries to the principal prehistoric and archeological sites.

Getting There

Air France and **Air Inter** fly to Bastia, Ajaccio, and Calvi from Paris (810F, with discounts 630F), Nice (390F, with discounts 282F), and Marseille (424F, with discounts 300F). Discounted fares apply to everyone under 25 or over 60, and to students under 27, on off-peak "blue flights" (several per week, boxed in blue on the schedule). Air France maintains offices at 3, bd. du Roi-Jérome in Ajaccio (tel. 95 29 45 45) and at 6, av. Emile Sari in Bastia (tel. 95 54 54 95). Air Inter's offices are at the airports in Ajaccio (tel. 95 29 45 45), Bastia (tel. 95 54 54 95), and Calvi (tel. 95 65 20 09). Reservations are advisable; telephone lines are open daily between 8am and 6pm.

The **Société National Maritime Corse Méditerranée (SNCM)** sends car ferries from Marseille, Toulon, and Nice on the continent to Bastia, Calvi, Ile Rousse, Ajaccio, and Propriano on Corsica. The passages, many of which are overnight, take six to twelve hours. About two boats per day travel between Corsica and the mainland in the off-season, a few more per day during summer. The schedule fluctuates, sometimes wildly; call ahead to confirm times, and always arrive at least a half-hour before departure. The trip from Marseille or Toulon costs 285F (255F off-season); from Nice, 255F (230F off-season). From October to April, SNCM boasts a "blue period," when people under 25 receive a 25% discount, and those over 60 a 50% discount. Additionally, people under 25 traveling to and from Nice get a 30% reduction all year. If you plan to bring a car, it'll cost from 395F to 735F (185-320F off-season). Prices fluctuate according to exact day of departure, size of car, and return departure point, if applicable. SNCM has offices in Ajaccio, quai l'Herminier, (tel. 95 29 66 99 or 95 26 66 88), Bastia, Nouveau Port (tel. 95 54 66 99 or 95 54 66 88), Calvi, quai Landry (tel. 95 65 01 38), and Ile Rousse, av. J-Calizi (tel. 95 60 09 56). On the mainland, SNCM offices are in Nice, quai du Commerce (tel. 93 13 66 99), Marseille, 61, bd. des Dames (tel. 91 56 80 20), Toulon, 21, av. de l'Infanterie de Marine (tel. 94 41 25 76) and Paris, 12, rue Godot-de-Mauroy, *9ème,* (tel. 49 24 24 24). **Corsica Ferries** crosses from the Italian ports of Livorno, Genoa, and La Spezia to Bastia (145-175F). From mid-May to mid-September, extra service plows from Genoa to Ajaccio and Calvi (150-200F). Corsica Ferries has a central reservation office in Bastia, 5bis, rue Chanoine Leschi (tel. 95 51 06 39). In addition, **NAVARMA** sends ferries to Bastia from La Spezia, Livorno, Piombino, and Porto San Stefano on the Italian mainland (135-155F); it also links Bonifacio, on Corsica, to Sardinia (60F). Call the office in Bonifacio, port de Bonifacio (tel. 95 73 00 29) for reservations to Sardinia, or the office in Bastia, 4, rue Commandant-Luce-de-Casablanca (tel. 95 31 46 29 or 95 31 62 47), for all others.

Getting Around

While all forms of transportation in Corsica are slow, both rail lines and roadways compensate with stunning scenery. **Train** service in Corsica is slow and limited; it doesn't serve all the major towns (no rail to Bonifacio or Porto-Vecchio); and it accepts no passes. **Buses** mire in a seemingly endless maze of carriers, connections, and times (many before 8am). Bus services connect major towns but are neither cheaper nor more frequent than trains. **Hitchhiking** on the island is reportedly near impossible. Some exceptionally patient people manage to hitch short rides. Those with a sign saying "Je vous offre l'essence" (I will pay for gas) have had better luck. Ten liters (about 55F) usually covers 100km on flat roads, but buses are safer and about as cheap.

Renting a **car** is convenient but costs 120-250F per day for the least expensive models, plus 1F37-3F30 per km. Weekly rentals (from 1700F) usually include unlimited free mileage. **Bicycle** rental is rare and relatively expensive (about 70-100F per day with 1500F deposit). **Mopeds** *(mobylettes)* run about 150F per day (with a 2500F deposit). Note that narrow, curving mountain roads make biking difficult and dangerous. Even drivers should be careful; remember to honk before rounding mountain curves. Summer crowds can make all types of road travel painfully slow. (The bus from Ajaccio to Bonifacio, for example, takes 4hr. to cover 145km.) Gas stations are few and far between; if you run out, call the local **Brigade de Gendarmerie.**

Hiking is the best way to explore the island's mountainous interior. The longest marked trail, the **Grande Randonnée-20,** is a difficult 160km 15- to 21-day trail,

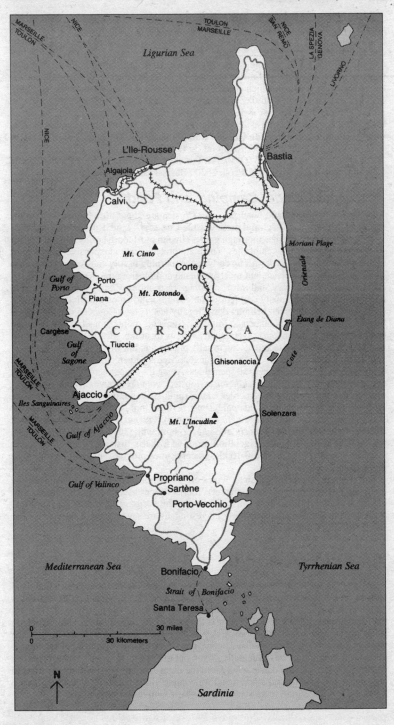

Ligurian Sea

MARSEILLE
TOULON

NICE

TOULON
MARSEILLE

SAN REMO

NICE

LA SPEZIA
GENOVA

LIVORNO

NICE

L'Ile-Rousse

Bastia

Algajola

Calvi

Mt. Cinto

Corte

Moriani Plage

Gulf of
Porto

Porto

Piana

Mt. Rotondo

Orientale

Étang de Diana

Cargèse

C O R S I C A

Gulf
of
Sagone

Tiuccia

Ghisonaccia

Tavignano

MARSEILLE
TOULON

Ajaccio

Iles Sanguinaires

Mt. L'Incudine

Solenzara

MARSEILLE

Gulf of Ajaccio

Gulf of Valinco

Propriano

Sartène

Porto-Vecchio

Mediterranean Sea

Tyrrhenian Sea

Bonifacio

Strait of Bonifacio

Santa Teresa

30 miles

30 kilometers

N

Sardinia

which takes hikers across the island from Calenzana (southeast of Calvi) to Conca (northeast of Porto-Vecchio). About 10,000 people each year follow the trail from one end of the island to the other, and many hike shorter segments. Do not tackle this trail alone, and be prepared for cold, snowy weather, even in early summer. Two other popular routes are the **Mare e Monti,** a seven-day trail from Calenzana to Cargèse and the easier **Da Mare a Mare,** which crosses the southern part of the island between Porto-Vecchio and Propriano (4-6 days). All are well-marked, and it is possible to stay in *gîtes d'étapes* (about 50F per night) every night. From January through May, additional trails are available for cross-country skiing. For further information, contact the **Comité National des Sentiers de Grande Randonnée,** 8, av. Marceau, 75008 Paris (tel. 47 23 62 32), or **Parc Naturel Régional de la Corse,** rue Général Fiorella, BP 417, 20184 Ajaccio Cedex (tel. 95 21 56 54). For skiing information, contact the **Comité Régional Corse de Ski,** 34, bd. Paoli, 20200 Bastia (tel. 95 32 01 94).

Accommodations, Camping, and Food

In the summer, food and hotel prices in Corsica are about 30% higher than on the mainland. The **Comité Régional du Tourisme Corse,** at 17, bd. Roi Jérôme (tel. 95 21 56 56) in Ajaccio, publishes thorough guides (free in most tourist offices) to all of Corsica's hotels, hostels, and campsites. There are precious few inexpensive hotels; most accommodations of all types fill up early in the morning in July and August. There are about 25 hostels on Corsica, but most are inland and far from the major towns. Hostel cards are rarely necessary, and most set no age restrictions. Campgrounds lie close to most major cities, and many rent tents. The government ban on unofficial camping is strictly enforced, and even bedding down legally has its own Corsican dangers: bushfires are frequent and spontaneous. Mind the frequent, spontaneous brushfires before bedding down in the *maquis,* even legally. The beds at the *gîtes* fill on a first-come, first-served basis, but latecomers can usually pitch a tent unofficially.

Corsican cuisine is hearty, fresh, and pungent. Herbs gathered in the *maquis* impart a distinct flavor to many of the local specialties. Along the coast, seafood is excellent but expensive; try *calamar* (squid), *langouste* (lobster), *gambas* (prawns), or *moules* (mussels). In fall and winter you can order *nacres* (pink-shelled mollusks) and *oursins* (sea urchins). Other delicacies include *pâté de merle* (blackbird *pâté), saucisson* (pork sausages), *truite* (river trout), and *sanglier* (wild boar). *Pulenta* is made of chestnut flour. Excellent cheeses include *brocciu* and *chèvre,* both white cheeses made from goat's milk which keep without refrigeration; *niolo* is a sharp, dry, goat cheese. Corsican *menus* are usually expensive (90-100F); grocery stores provide a more affordable taste of the island.

The fragrant, flavorful Corsican wines are as inexpensive as their cousins on the mainland (10-15F per bottle in a market). Tourist offices usually have leaflets describing local vineyards open to visitors. The sweet white *Muscat* from the Cap Corse and the reds from *Sartène* are particularly interesting, as are several potent *eaux de vie* flavored with Corsican berries.

Ajaccio (Aiacciu)

Striking the perfect balance between the large, hectic resorts of the French mainland and the small, isolated ones which dot Corsica's coastline, Ajaccio (pop. 60,000) is both a picturesque beachside resort and a bustling industrial center. Every August 15, the town springs to life to celebrate the birthday of its most famous son, Napoleon Bonaparte, whose name still adorns many of the town's streets, cafés, and hotels. The irony of celebrating, in nationalist Corsica, the birth of a man who symbolizes French imperial conquest and was eventually driven out of their town, apparently escapes the citizens of Ajaccio, who dance wildly into the night. Yet one need not invade Ajaccio on August 15 alone to find a warm and welcoming village: the city's beaches, leisure facilities, and museums create an appealing year-round resort atmosphere.

Orientation and Practical Information

Ten hours by boat from the mainland, Ajaccio lies on Corsica's western coast, about 80km north of Bonifacio. Relatively frequent bus and train connections make the city an ideal place to begin exploring the island.

Cours Napoléon, which runs from pl. de Gaulle past the train station, is the city's main drag. The pedestrian **rue Cardinal Fesch** starts at pl. Maréchal Foch and runs parallel to cours Napoléon. A livelier street, it packs smaller, more interesting stores and some restaurants. The *vieille ville* is bounded by pl. Foch, pl. de Gaulle, and the citadel.

From the ferry dock on quai l'Herminier, bear left and walk toward the citadel to pl. Foch and the tourist office. To reach cours Napoléon, walk through the *place* and up av. du 1*er* Consul.

Tourist Office: (tel. 95 21 40 87 or 95 21 53 39), Hôtel de Ville, pl. Maréchal Foch. Makes no hotel reservations, but knows where there's room. Well-stocked with pamphlets listing all of the island's hostels, campsites, and hotels, as well as bus and boat excursion schedules. Pick up their free map and practical information brochure. Open daily 8am-8pm; Sept. 16-June 14 Mon.-Sat. 9am-6:30pm.

Currency Exchange: Decent rates at the **bus station** (tel. 95 51 23 43) and the **airport** (tel. 95 20 13 48). Open daily 7am-8pm; Sept.-June 9am-noon and 3-5pm.

Post Office: (tel. 95 21 41 78), on cours Napoléon at rue Ottavy. **Telephones** downstairs. Open Mon.-Fri. 8am-6:30pm, Sat. 8am-noon. **Postal Code:** 20000.

Flights: Campo dell'Oro (tel. 95 21 03 64), 7km away. Take bus #1 ("Ricanto") from cours Napoléon (every hour 7am-7pm; 13F50). To: Nice (2-3 per day); Marseille (2-3 per day); and Paris (5-6 per day). See Getting There above for prices and information numbers.

Trains: rue Jean-Jérôme Levie (tel. 95 23 11 03), between cours Napoléon and bd. Sampiero. To: Corte (4 per day, 2 1/2hr., 56F); Calvi (2 per day, 5hr., change in Ponte Leccia, 122F); Bastia (4 per day, 4hr., 106F). Open daily 6am-8pm.

Buses: *Gare routière,* quai Herminier (tel. 95 21 28 01), part of the Gare Maritime. The station is open daily 7am-8pm; Sept. 16-June 14 Mon.-Sat. 9am-noon and 3-5pm. The information kiosk will help you sift through the motley assortment of companies, fares, and times; services and companies change seasonally. **Eurocorse Voyages** (tel. 95 21 06 30) sends 2 buses per day to Bonifacio (8am and 4pm, 3 1/2hr., 105F) via Porto-Vecchio (3hr., 90F); and to Bastia (7:45am and 3pm, 3 1/2hr., 105F) via Corte (2hr., 55F). **Autocars S.A.I.B.** (tel. 95 21 02 07) runs two buses Mon.-Sat. to Calvi (7:30am and 3:30pm, 10hr., 130F) via Porto (2 1/2hr., 65F), from July 1 to Sept. 15, an additional bus runs daily at 8:30am.

Public Transportation: TCA buses (tel. 95 50 04 30) run daily on the hour from 7am-7pm. Take bus #1 from pl. de Gaulle to the train station and airport (13F50) or down cours Napoléon (6F80). Bus #5 from av. Dr. Ramaroni stops at Marinella and the beaches on the way to the Iles Sanguinaires (9F50).

Ferries: (SNCM), quai l'Herminier (tel. 95 29 66 99 or 95 29 66 88), across from the bus station. Two boats usually leave each day for one of several mainland cities. See Getting There above for more information.

Taxis: pl. de Gaulle (tel. 95 21 00 87). 24 hrs. 3F per km daytime, 5F50 per km at night, 10F luggage charge. At night, after the buses stop running, a cab from the airport will cost you about 110F.

Car Rental: Locafab, at the airport (tel. 95 22 76 11). 150F per day plus 1F50 per km. 1800F per week (unlimited mileage). Deposit 1500-2000F. Drivers must be 23.

Bike Rental: Corsica Loisirs, 3, montée St- Jean (tel. 95 20 22 42), 6 blocks past the train station and left off cours Napoléon. Mountain bikes 80F per day, 400F per week, with 1700F deposit. Mopeds 150F per day, 750F per week, with 2500F deposit.

Hiking Information: Parc Naturel Régional, rue Général Fiorella (tel. 95 21 56 54). Maps for the Grande Randonnée-20 and other mountain trails. Stocks information on shelters and trail conditions. Open Mon.-Fri. 9am-noon and 2-6:30pm.

Laundromat: rue Maréchal Ornano. Wash 36F, dry 6 min. for 2F. Soap 2F. Open daily 7am-9pm.

Hospital: av. Napoléon III (tel. 95 21 90 90).

Medical Emergency: tel. 95 21 50 50.

Police: tel. 95 23 20 36. **Emergency:** tel. 17.

Accommodations and Camping

Ajaccio has more hotels than most Corsican towns, but you can still expect to pay as much for mediocre lodgings here as you would for luxury on the mainland. Call ahead to make reservations for July and August, when prices are also highest. Most hotels are open year-round.

Hôtel Colomba, 8, av. de Paris (tel. 95 21 12 66). A small hotel in the center of town, near pl. de Gaulle. Three flights up, but pleasant rooms—some with a view of the gulf. Singles 130F, with shower 150F. Doubles and triples with shower 160F.

Hôtel Kallysté, 51, cours Napoléon (tel. 95 51 34 45). Luxury rooms (TV, A/C, double beds) at vaguely affordable prices. Quadrilingual managers have oodles of tourist information, including arrangements for inexpensive car rentals. Singles 250F. Doubles 300F. Triples 350F. Breakfast 30F. Nov. 15-June 30: singles 235F. Doubles 260F. Triples 300F.

Hôtel le Dauphin, 11, bd. Sampiero (tel. 95 21 12 94), halfway between the train station and the *gare maritime.* Clean, renovated rooms all have showers and toilet. Lively bar and restaurant downstairs. Singles 214F. Doubles 274F. Triples 362F. Oct.-May: singles 202F. Doubles 238F. Triples 292F. Breakfast included.

Hôtel Bonaparte, 1-2, rue Etienne-Conti (tel. 95 21 44 19). Neat, small rooms with a view of the port. Singles with shower 230F. Doubles with shower 270F. Breakfast 25F. March-June and Oct. to mid-Nov.: singles with shower 220F. Doubles with shower 260F.

Camping: Barbicaja (tel. 95 52 01 17), 3km away, but the closest to town. Take bus #5 from av. Docteur Ramaroni just past pl. de Gaulle (last bus at 7pm). 30F per person, 12F per tent. **U Prunelli** (tel. 95 25 19 23), near the bridge of Pisciatello—next to Porticcio—which is accessible by ferries from Ajaccio (every 1/2hr., round-trip 40F) and by bus (tel. 95 25 40 37). Friendly and cheerful. 22F per person, 10F per tent. Other campgrounds are more than 10km away. Ask the tourist office for a list.

Food

The morning **market** on bd. Roi Jérôme and in pl. César Campinchi behind the tourist office will tempt you to fill your picnic basket (8am-noon). Pizzerias congregate in the *rues piétonnes* off pl. Foch towards the citadel (35-50F). There is a **Monoprix supermarket** at 31, cours Napoléon (open Mon.-Sat. 8:45am-12:15pm and 2-7pm).

L'Artisanat, rue de la Porte, in a cobbled alley off pl. Foch. Spanish owner offers *menus* with Corsican fish specialties from 65F. Eat in the garden. Open noon-2pm and 7-11pm.

Restaurant A Cantina, 3, bd. Roi Jérôme, right next to the morning market. Cheap and tasty pasta (40-50F), sandwiches (20-25) and omelettes (20-25F) in a streetside café. Open May-Oct. daily 11am-3pm and 6-11pm.

Chez Paulo, 7, rue Roi-de-Rome. Three different 85F *menus* strewn with Corsican specialties, including *sanglier* (wild boar). Pizza (38-48F) and pasta (32-58F) too. Open noon-2:30pm and 7:30pm-5am.

La Serre, 91, cours Napoléon, past the train station. Cheery, stylish cafeteria. Hot entrees from 31F. Salads 20F. Open 11:30am-2:30pm and 7-11pm.

Sights and Entertainment

Modestly tucked away in the *vieille ville* between rue Bonaparte and rue Roi-de-Rome, the **Musée National de la Maison Bonaparte,** birthplace and childhood home of Napoléon, contains portraits of the Bonaparte family, documents concerning their life in Ajaccio, and lovely period furniture. Ironically, this 18th-century house briefly sheltered Hudson Lowe, Napoléon's jailer on St-Helena. (Open Mon. 2-6pm, Tues.-Sat. 9am-noon and 2-6pm, Sun. 9am-noon; Oct.-May Mon. 2-5pm, Tues.-Fri. 10am-noon and 2-5pm, Sat. 10am-noon. Admission 17F, under 26 and over 60 9F.) On the second floor of the *hôtel de ville,* next to the tourist office, the **Salon Napoléonien** (tel. 95 21 90 15) consists of a large entrance hall decorated with portraits of the Bonaparte family, a beautifully painted ceiling tracing Napoleon's life, and a smallish room that offers a quick summary of Napoléon's accomplishments through a collection of commemorative coins. (Open Mon.-Fri. 9am-noon and 2-5pm. Admission 2F.)

The recently renovated **Chapelle Impériale,** rue Fesch, is the final resting place of most of the Bonaparte family. Next to the Chapelle stands the **Palais Fesch,** which houses works by 15th- and 16th-century Italian masters. (Museum and chapel open Tues.-Sat. 9:30am-noon and 3-6:30pm; Oct.-June Tues.-Sat. 9:30am-noon and 2:30-6pm.) The newest addition to Ajaccio's collection of museums is the **Musée à Bandera,** 1, av. Général Levie (tel. 95 51 07 34), which contains five rooms of mostly military memorabilia tracing Corsican history from 6000BC. (Open Mon.-Sat. 10am-noon and 3-7pm; Sept.-May. Wed.-Fri. 10am-noon and 2-6pm. Admission 15F, students 8F.) The **Musée du Capitellu,** opposite the citadel at 18, bd. Danielle Casanova (tel. 95 21 50 57), covers the history of Ajaccio through paintings and sculptures. (Open Tues.-Sat. 10am-noon and 2-6pm; Sun. 10am-noon, Mon. 2-6pm. Admission 20F, under 18 10F.)

Southwest of Ajaccio at the mouth of the gulf, the **Iles Sanguinaires** (Bloody Islands) bathe in a scarlet glow at sunset. **Bateau des Iles** (tel. 95 25 51 52) runs daily excursions from quai de la Citadelle (late May to mid-Sept., 75F). Call for reservations. Visible from the excursion boats, the Genoese **Tour de la Parata** can be reached by bus #5 from av. Dr. Ramaroni (hourly 7am-7pm, 9F50), which also stops at numerous beaches along the way. The closest beach to the town center is the **plage St-François,** beyond the citadel. You can rent **windsurfers** (40F per hr.) **sailboats** (40-70F per hr.) or **kayaks** (30F per hr.) from the **Société Nautique d'Ajaccio** (tel. 95 21 07 79) on port de la Citadelle.

Most of Ajaccio's clubs and discos are on the route des Sanguinaires; the tourist office has a complete list. Unfortunately, there is no public transportation after 7pm. If you do go, remember that during the off-season most of these clubs open only on weekend nights and are usually full of lonely men nursing martinis. Lively late-night cafés along the quai de la Citadelle provide a more comfortable option, especially for single women.

In July, Ajaccio hosts an **International Music Festival** (tel. 95 21 50 90) and, as mentioned, August 15 and the days surrounding it bring the **Fêtes Napoléoniennes** (tel. 95 21 50 90) to town.

Ajaccio to Calvi

Corsica's most heart-stopping road snakes from Ajaccio to Calvi, clinging to the tortuous mountainside above fabulous beaches. Blind hairpin turns without guard rails may strike fear into even the most intrepid drivers. Yet the scenery is awesome, and the beaches along the coast by the **Golfe de Sagone** are among the island's finest. If riding the bus, ask the driver to let you out 3km before **Tiuccia** at the shade-endowed **Camping Le Calcatoggia** (tel. 95 52 28 31; 20F per person, 8F per tent; open May-Aug.). **Cargèse,** at the end of the Golfe de Sagone, is a small community built into the cliffs with Greek and Roman churches facing one another. The **tourist office** (tel. 95 26 41 31) can provide a map and a list of hotels. (Open daily 8:30am-noon and 4-7pm; Oct.-May Mon.-Sat. 3-5pm.) You can spend the night at the **Hôtel de France** (tel. 95 26 41 07; doubles from 160F; shower and toilet in all rooms; open May-Oct.). There is a pizzeria next door and a supermarket across the street. Down the road (20min.) lies the beautiful Plage de Pero with its Genoese tower.

Halfway to Calvi (3hr., 65F), **Porto (Portu)** is a larger, livelier town renowned for its colorful, watery sunsets. The Ajaccio-Calvi bus stops here for three and a half hours, just long enough for the driver to steady her or his nerves and for riders to relax on the beach beneath the cliffs. The Porto **tourist office,** up the main road leaving the port (tel. 95 26 10 55), can help with camping and transportation and provide a list of area *gîtes d'étape* (about 50F per night). Before mid-July, hotels are reasonable and easy to come by. The ones near the pharmacy bus stop, about 1km from the beach, are more affordable than those near the marina. **Hôtel Beau Séjour's** small, clean rooms are the least expensive (tel. 95 26 12 15; singles 120-220F; doubles 150-250F, shower included). In addition, a 26-bed **hostel** (tel. 95 26 16 41) remains open all year in **Ota,** 3km from Porto (50F). **Autocars S.A.I.B.** runs two buses per day from Porto to Ota. **Camping Les Oliviers** (tel. 95 26 14 49) is a two-minute walk outside of town along the road to Ajaccio. (27-30F per person, 10F per tent. Open Easter-Oct. 31.) Make reservations if you plan to arrive at the end of July or August. The camping office rents **bikes** (70F per day) and mountain bikes (80F per day).

The Hôtel Monte Russo in Porto (tel. 95 26 17 10) sells tickets for **Alpana Revellata** excursions to the tranquil Gulf of Girolata (May-Sept. 2 per day, 5hr., 150F). Accessible only by boat or on foot, this sheltered part of the bay enjoys a ban on hunting, fishing, and building. Early morning visitors may glimpse the rare African fish-eagle; this area is its only known European habitat.

The slow buses that run between Ajaccio and Calvi daily in summer don't leave time for quick stops at the beaches and villages along the way. Hitchhiking is reportedly very slow, and often impossible. Those in the hitching know recommend leaving plenty of time, and taking a bus schedule along just in case.

Calvi

While retaining the Genoese heritage and oceanic splendor of Corsica's other major ports, Calvi noticeably lacks their industrial character. With its well-preserved Genoan citadel, mountainous backdrop, and stretches of white-sand beaches, the town is an ideal place to bask in the sun and the beauty of the island. Ideal, that is, until July and August, when the small (pop. 5500) seaside resort balloons into a massive mecca of some 25,000 Samsonite-wielding outsiders. Founded in the 13th century by Genoese creditors, Calvi won't throw you into debt; it offers affordable hotels and eateries.

Orientation and Practical Information

About 120km north of Ajaccio, Calvi is the closest Corsican city to France. **Avenue de la République,** which becomes **boulevard Wilson,** runs parallel to the port, leading from the train station to the citadel. The **tourist office** is two minutes to the left of the train station.

Tourist Office: Port de Plaisance (tel. 95 65 16 67). Next to the train station; look for the sign directing you to the office. Distributes the indispensable *Guide Calvi,* which includes a map and a list of hotels. Won't make hotel reservations, but keeps abreast of vacancies. Provides info on a vast array of local excursions and services. Open daily 10-6pm; Sept.-June Mon.-Fri. 10am-6pm, Sat. 10am-noon.

Currency Exchange: Change Wilson, 3, bd. Wilson, a block up from the station on the left. Surprisingly good rates. Open daily 9:30am-noon and 4-7pm.

Post Office: bd. Wilson (tel. 95 65 00 61), just across from the train station. Phone, currency exchange. Open Mon.-Fri. 8:30am-5pm, Sat. 8:30am-noon. **Postal Code:** 20260.

Flights: Aéroport de Calvi Ste-Catherine is 7km southeast of town, ignored by public transportation. **Air Inter** (tel. 95 65 20 21) flies to Paris, Nice, Marseille, Lyon, and Lille. See Getting There above for more details.

Trains: pl. de la Gare (tel. 95 65 06 74), between the Port de Plaisance and Quai Landry. To: Bastia (3 per day, 3hr., 80F); Corte (3 per day, 3hr., change at Ponte-Leccia, 67F); Ajaccio (3 per day, 5hr., 122F); Ile Rousse (5 per day Sept.-June, every hr. July-Aug., 50 min., 24F). Open 6am-8pm.

Buses: Call ahead, since services and rates change seasonally. **Eurocorse Voyages** (tel. 95 31 03 79) runs one bus per day to Ajaccio (4 1/2hr., 100F). **Agence Beaux Voyages,** on av. Wilson across from the post office (tel. 95 65 11 35), runs a daily bus to Bastia (8am, 2hr., 63F) with connections to Ajaccio. **Autocars S.A.I.B.** sends one afternoon bus to Porto (3:20pm, 2 3/4hr.). They have no office in Calvi; call the one in Porto (tel. 95 26 13 70) and buy your ticket when you get on the bus at the Monument aux Morts, at the end of bd. Wilson, by the citadel's foot.

Ferries: SNCM tickets may be purchased at **Agence Tramar** (tel. 95 65 10 84), quai Adolphe Landry. Open Mon.-Fri. 9-11:30am and 2-5:30pm, Sat. 9-11:30am. **Corsica Ferries** (tel. 95 65 10 84) has an office at the Porte de Commerce. Open Mon.-Fri. 9am-noon and 2-6pm. For rates and scheduling info, see Getting There above.

Taxis: (tel. 95 65 03 10), next to the train station on av. de la République. Open 24 hrs., but rates go up after 8pm. Fare to airport depends on time of day, number of passengers, and luggage, but shouldn't exceed 100F.

Bike and Moped Rental: Garage Ambrosini, 4, Villas St-Antoine (tel. 95 65 02 13) near the pl. Bel Ombra. Bikes 95F per day, deposit 1500F; mopeds 120F per 1/2-day, 170F per day, deposit 2000F. Ages 18 and over only. The tourist office lists other rental places.

Laundromat, av. C. Colomb, behind the Super U. Wash 30F, dry 20 min. for 10F. Soap 2F. Open daily 8am-9pm.

Emergency Medical Unit: route du Stade (tel. 95 65 11 22).

Emergency: tel. 17.

Accommodations and Camping

Although the hostel and campgrounds are the best options for budget travelers, hotels become more affordable for groups of three. Prices rise from June through September, but even in peak season you should have no problem finding a room. Weekly rentals are often cheaper; the tourist office can help you find one.

BVJ Corsotel, av. de la République (tel. 95 65 14 15). Enthusiastic owners turn this 130-bed hostel into a bustling "youth center." Rooms with 2-8 beds, 2-bedders reserved for couples. No curfew or lockout. 100F. Huge breakfast included. Open late March-Oct. Reservations only accepted for week-long stays. Arrive early in high season, and if you value your blood supply bring insect repellent and close the windows: the mosquitoes on Corsica are mean and hungry.

Hôtel Laeticia, 5, rue Joffre (tel. 95 65 05 55). A bit hard to find; on a small sidestreet between rue Joffre and bd. Wilson. Comfortable, tastefully decorated rooms. Doubles with shower 180F. Open June-Sept. Call ahead.

Hôtel du Centre, 14, rue d'Alsace (tel. 95 65 02 01). Friendly manager keeps plain but pleasant rooms. Doubles 180-240F, with shower 200-280F. Triples 220-300F, with shower 240-340F. Hall showers included. Price varies seasonally. Open June-Oct. 10.

Hôtel Belvedere, av. de l'Urugay (tel. 95 65 01 25). Superb location near the foot of the citadel. Clean, comfortable rooms, all with toilet and shower; some overlook the port. Singles 180F. Doubles 200-350F. Triples 450F. Open year-round.

Camping: La Clé des Champs, (tel. 95 65 00 86). Follow the road from the train station to Ile Rousse and watch for the sign on your right (15-min. walk). Clean with lots of shade. 20F per person, 12F per tent. Tent rental 25F. Open May-Oct. Nine other campgrounds at the entrance to town and along the coast. All are listed in the tourist office brochure.

Food

Pick up supplies at the **market** near the church (Tues.-Sat. 8am-noon). There are huge **Super U** and **Prisunic supermarkets** on av. Christophe Colomb (the continuation of av. de la République towards Ile Rousse) and a smaller **Codec** on rue Clemenceau, near the center. While the restaurants along the port are expensive, the old pedestrian streets above it teem with moderately priced establishments with outdoor seating. At **Le Corsaire,** av. de la République (tel. 95 65 37 31), right next door to the hostel, a wooden bar and interior provide the backdrop for a righteously filling meal. Sample the 65 and 80F *menus,* pastries from 40F, and excellent desserts. (Open daily 9am-3pm and 6pm-1am.) **U Fornu,** at the impasse bd. Wilson (one block up on the left), serves moderately priced Corsican specialities (65-75F) on a pleasant terrace overlooking the port. (Open daily noon-2pm and 5-10pm.) **Cappucino,** quai Landry (tel. 95 65 11 19) is undoubtedly the cheapest place on the waterfront (though that's not saying much), with pizza from 35-50F. (Open daily 11am-2pm and 6:30-9pm.)

Sights and Entertainment

The inscription *"civitas Calvi semper fidelis"* (the city of Calvi is always faithful), at the entrance to the **citadelle** (tel. 95 65 36 74), recalls Calvi's loyalty to Genoa during the 16th century. (Open daily 11am-2pm and 6:30-9pm.) Just beyond the entrance, a mini information center sells the *Guide of the Fort* (in English, 5F), which includes a map and information about the sights. Wandering through the cobblestone streets, you'll enjoy splendid panoramas of the yacht-filled port, and the mountains which rise above the town's tangerine roofs. Along with several other Mediterranean towns, Calvi claims to be the birthplace of Christopher Columbus; a small plaque marks the house where he may have been born. Calvi's "other" famous house tells a more likely story: Napoleon and his family sojourned here in 1793 when fleeing from their political opponents in Ajaccio. The 16th-century **Cathédrale St-Jean-Baptiste,** at the top of the citadel, contains several ecclesiastical works of art, as does the museum in the **Oratoire St-Antoine.**

Calvi is a beach-goer's paradise, its 6km of sand fronting clear, blue waters. The prices, though, will make your heart sink. On the beach, **Nautic Club,** port de Plaisance (tel. 95 65 10 65), offers windsurfing and sailing lessons year-round (3 2-hr. lessons 500F). You can also rent **kayaks** (60F per hr., 150F per 1/2-day), **windsurfers** (70F per hr., 180F per 1/2-day), or **sailboats** (110-160F per hr., 280-380F per 1/2-day) from the club. (Open daily 8am-8pm; Sept. 16-May 9am-noon and 2-6pm.)

Ask at the BVJ *foyer* for information about organized day-hikes in the region. **Autocars Mariani,** Quai Landry (tel. 95 46 00 35) runs bus excursions to the Calanches de Piana, Porto and Evisa (145F), Cap Corse (145F), Ajaccio (180F), Bonifacio (220F), and along a half-day circuit of traditional Corsican villages (75F). Several different companies also pilot boat excursions to the spectacular rock formations (inaccessible by road) in the regional park (200F); contact **Revellata** on quai Landry (tel. 95 65 28 16).

At the foot of the citadel on bd. Wilson, **Café Rex,** shakes with Corsican song and guitar every night at 9pm. (No cover.) The most famous and chic club in town is **Chez Tao,** in the citadel. Calvi hosts an annual **jazz festival** during the third week in June, with a 40F cover gaining you week-long admission to all of the concerts (tel. 95 65 16 67). In August, the citadel comes alive with the **Citadella in Festa** celebration (tel. 95 62 02 57).

Near Calvi

In 1758, Pasquale Paoli, leader of independent Corsica, built the **Ile Rousse** (Isula) to compete with Calvi, which he resented for its allegiance to Genoa. The stretch of coastline between the two famous rivals is among the most beautiful on the island, luring crowds with its powdery white sand and calm, translucent water. Look for the trains called **Tramways de la Balagne,** which travel the coast between Calvi and Ile Rousse (every hr., Sept.-June 5 per day, 50 min.) The line is divided into three sections; each costs 8F, a *carnet* of six tickets 36F. Several beaches and campgrounds lie along the route—hop off the train when you see one you like. In Ile Rousse, shop for picnic supplies at the morning market off pl. Paoli (8am-noon). **La Cave** is the least expensive restaurant on pl. Paoli, serving a traditional French *menu* for 75F. Ile Rousse's **tourist office,** at the foot of pl. Paoli (tel. 95 60 04 35) can brief you on local camping and hiking. (Open Mon.-Fri. 10am-noon and 3-6pm.) Most of the town's hotels cost more than 300F a night, so it's better to stay in Calvi and take the train in. SNCM sends two ferries per week from Ile Rousse to Nice, with less frequent service to Marseille or Toulon (220-255F one way). Two stops and 16F from Calvi is the village **Algajola** (Algaghjola), which has grown up inside and around the walls of a 17th-century stone fortress. **Hôtel l'Esquinade** (tel. 95 60 70 19), the most affordable in town, has comfortable rooms overlooking the sea. (Singles 110-200F. Doubles 220-300F. Triples 400F. Showers included. Breakfast 20F.)

Both Calvi and Ile Rousse are located in the **Balagne** region of Corsica, dotted with olive trees and pristine mountain villages, many accessible by foot. Ask at the Ile Rousse tourist office for the map *Sentiers en Balagne,* which marks footpaths and gives approximate hiking times. The most interesting hikes include: **Sant' Antonino,** a well-preserved 9th-century hamlet; **Pigna,** which contains many artisans' boutiques, the 12th-century church at **Aregno,** and **Corbara,** known for its pottery and 15th-century convent. All of these inland towns are also accessible by car. **Autocars Mariani** (above) runs half-day bus excursions to the villages from Calvi and Ile Rousse (75F).

The **vineyards** surrounding Calvi often give tours of their *caves.* Many are within a few km of town; all are listed in the tourist office's brochure on Corsican wines. Visiting hours lengthen in September, when much of the wine is actually made. **Domaine Orsini** (tel. 95 62 81 01) in Calenzana (open daily 2-7pm), and **Clos Landry** (tel. 95 65 04 25), 2km from Calvi on the road to the airport (open daily 8am-7:30pm), both offer free tastings.

Corte (Corti)

Halfway between Ajaccio and Bastia, Corte's history, character, and mountainous location in Corsica's geographical center, distinguish it from its coastal friends. Rather than being a relic of Genoese dominance over the island, the town's remarkable citadel, towering 100m over the town, was built by a 15th-century Corsican feudal lord. And it was from Corte that Pasquale Paoli ran the island during its brief independence (1755-69). Known as the *"capitale sentimentale de l'Ile"* (sentimental capital of the island), Corte (pop. 5400) is home to Corsica's only university, where over 2600 students have the option of taking courses in the island's native tongue.

Orientation and Practical Information

Corte is a small and easily navigated town. To reach the *centre-ville* from the train station 1km out of town, turn right, cross the bridge, and climb up av. Jean Nicoli past the university. The shops, banks, and hotels on **Cours Paoli,** which runs through the center of town, will sate every traveler's needs.

Tourist Office: Commission Muncipale du Tourisme. Follow the signs to the citadel's entrance (tel. 95 46 24 20). Basic info on food, lodging, and excursions. Open daily 9am-8pm; Oct.-May 9am-noon and 1:30-5pm.

Currency Exchange: Any number of banks along Cours Paoli, the post office (cash only), and the Hôtel Résidence (see Accommodations) all change money.

Post Office: 3, av. du Baron Mariani. Open Mon.-Fri. 8am-noon and 2-5pm, Sat. 8am-noon. **Postal Code:** 20250.

Trains: At the roundabout where av. Jean Nicoli and N193 meet (tel. 95 46 00 97). Trains to: Bastia (4 per day, 2hr., 50F); Calvi (2 per day, 2 1/2hr., change at Ponte-Leccia, 67F); and Ajaccio (4 per day, 2 1/2hr., 56F).

Buses: Eurocorse Voyages (tel. 95 21 06 30). Call to find out fares and pickup locations; there's no actual office in Corte. To: Bastia (2 per day, 1 1/4hr.), Calvi (1 per day, change at Ponte-Leccia, 2hr.); Ajaccio (2 per day, 1 3/4 hr).

Car Rental: Europcar, Cours Paoli (tel. 95 46 02 79).

Bike Rental: Tomasi Location (tel. 95 46 07 13).

Laundry: At the Hôtel-Porette. 35F per load. 6 min dry for 2F.

Hospital: Hôpital civil (tel. 95 46 05 36).

Police: tel. 17.

Accommodations and Camping

There are only nine hotels in Corte, and only three of them contain more than 12 bedrooms, so call ahead in July and August. There are also eight campgrounds near the town. From July to September students with ID can stay in University dorms. Contact **CROUS** (tel. 95 46 02 61), av Jean Nicoli, for info (open Mon.-Fri. 9am-noon and 2-

5pm). The least expensive hotel in town is the **Hôtel-Résidence Porette**, 6, av. du 9 Septembre (tel. 95 61 01 21). While hauntingly similar to a Motel 6, it offers clean, sparse rooms with sink and hall shower. The hotel also holds a sauna, weight room, TV rooms, laundry service, and restaurant, with a swimming pool and tennis courts nearby. (Singles 135F. Doubles 150F. Breakfast 19F.) The **Hôtel de la Poste**, 2, pl. du Padoue (tel. 95 46 02 61) off Cours Paoli and near the (you guessed it) post office boasts comfortable rooms in a nice, old-fashioned building. (Doubles 135-175F. Triples 195-210F. Breakfast 22F. Open May-Oct.)

For a night under the stars, **U Sognu** (tel. 95 46 09 07) is the closest campground. From pl. Paoli, go down av. Xavier Luciani and then turn right onto av. du Président Perucci. A five-minute walk downhill brings you to the campground and its clean, pleasant facilities. (20F per person, 12F per tent. Open March-Oct.) Alternatively, continuing past U Sognu, turn left on chemin de Baliri. Ten minutes down the path, **U Tavignanu** (tel. 95 46 16 85) is the only campground open all year. (13F per person, 10F per tent. Call for reservations.) The tourist office has a complete list of hotels and campgrounds.

Food

Most of the restaurants in Corte are either generic pizzerias or glitzy tourist traps. An exception, **Restaurant Le Bips**, 14, Cours Paoli (tel. 95 46 06 26) is a crowded and ebullient streetside café with 65F *menus* and less expensive dishes. (Open Mon.-Sat. 10am-8pm.) The romantic and dimly lit **U Spanu**, 1, av. Xavier Luciani (tel. 95 46 02 96), just off Cours Paoli, offers 55F *menus*, 95F *menus Corses*, and 35F pizzas. (Open daily 10am-2:30pm and 7pm-midnight.) Or try the less romantic but better lit **Ecomarché** supermarket next to the Hôtel Porette. (Open Mon.-Sat. 9am-12:15pm and 3-7:30pm.) **CROUS** (tel. 85 46 02 61) is scheduled to open both a cafeteria and restaurant at the university by 1993.

Sights and Entertainment

Corte's **citadel** dominates the landscape of the small town, and a visit not only gives you an excellent view of the town and valley beyond, but also allows you to peer into Corte's fascinating past. Excellent, multilingual tours leave every hour from 9am to 8pm in July and August (May-June and Sept. every hr. 9-11am and 2-7pm; admission 10F, students 5F). At the highest point of the fortress, the *nid d'aigle* (eagle's nest) presides over the town, the Restonica valley, and the surrounding mountains.

Nightlife in Corte is, well, subdued. The citadel (tel. 95 46 24 20) often has nightly *spectacles*. Call ahead for info. Corte hosts a **folk music festival** in July; the tourist office can tell you all about it. Fêtes and spectacles aside, sit in a café on Cours Paoli and absorb the laid-back *esprit* that makes the town a welcome stop on any itinerary.

Near Corte

Southwest of Corte, a tiny road stretches 16km through the **Gorges de la Restonica,** one of Corsica's loveliest and least populated areas. A crystal-clear, trout-filled stream glides through the fig, poplar, and chestnut trees covering the mountainside. Gnarled pines crowd the road as it climbs above 1600m, and the peaks stay snowy until early summer. Lakes and rivers offer chilly summer swimming. Follow the road in the direction of the river to the orange-marked one-hour trail leading to the **Lac de Melo,** a snow-fed beauty that lies at 1700m, near the foot of Mt. Rotondo (2622m) and ringed by peaks including Mt. Cinto (2700m), Corsica's highest. You can continue to the **Lac de Capitellu** (1930m) and join the red-and-white-marked **Grande Randonnée-20,** the challenging trail that winds its way across the entire breadth of Corsica (accessible mid-June to Oct.). In winter, cross-country ski trails replace many of the summer hiking paths. Be prepared for cold, even snowy weather as late as June. For more information, and for help mapping out trails, contact the **Parc Naturel Régional** office at the citadel in Corte (tel. 95 46 27 44; open late June-Sept. daily 10am-1pm and 3:30-7pm). Alternatively, write to Parc Naturel Régional de Corse, rue Général Fiorella, BP 417,

20184 Ajaccio Cedex, for trail guides and general information year-round. Topographic maps, essential for all longer hikes, are available from local bookstores.

For **horseback riding,** l'Albadu (tel. 95 46 24 55) on ancienne route d'Ajaccio in Corte, offers guided excursions (90F per hr., 400F for a full-day trip including 2 meals; longer trips for experienced riders 450F per day including food and lodging).

Bastia

Once a Genoese stronghold, Bastia's name derives from the Italian *bastiglia,* meaning dungeon. Yet given the region's beauty, the town's namers must have spent time in some pretty luxurious dungeons. Although the warehouses and apartment blocks which ring the old village have earned the town the dubious moniker of "the Corsican Marseille," venture past this metal circus into the cobblestone streets and arcades around the old port. The students and crowds that meander in the streets—perhaps the most pictueresque *rues* on the island—bestow upon the city (pop. 45,000) a colorful and vibrant character. Sit down, relax, and take it easy here in France's most delightful dungeon.

Orientation and Practical Information

Corsica's economic center, Bastia is at the southeast corner of the Cap Corse. From the train station, **avenue Maréchal Sebastiani** heads to **pl. St-Nicolas** and the tourist office. The commercial bd. Charles de Gaulle, bd. Paoli, and rue César Campinchi run parallel to pl. St-Nicolas and lead to the old port and old town.

Tourist Office: pl. St-Nicolas (tel. 95 31 00 89). From the train station, take a right and walk down av. Maréchal Sebastiani 5 min. to pl. St-Nicolas. Information on Bastia and Cap Corse, hotels, camping, and transportation. Open daily 7am-11pm; March-June daily 8am-noon and 2-7pm; Oct.-Feb. Mon.-Sat. 8:30am-noon and 2-6pm.

Currency Exchange: Banque de France, 2, cours Henri Pierangeli, at the far end of pl. St. Nicolas. Open Mon.-Fri. 8:45am-12:10pm and 1:35-3:30pm. Or, try the post office (1% commission). Other agencies cluster along av. Maréchal Sebastiani.

Post Office: (tel. 95 31 00 60) av. Maréchal-Sebastiani. **Telephones** and **currency exchange** too. Open Mon.-Fri. 8am-7pm, Sat. 8am-noon. **Postal Code:** 20200.

Flights: Bastia-Poretta (tel. 95 36 02 03), 23km away. A bus timed for airplane departures leaves from pl. de la Gare, in front of the Préfecture (1/2hr., 35F). To: Marseille (2-3 per day, 50min.); Nice (2-3 per day, 40min.); Paris (5-6 per day, 1 1/2hr.). See Getting There above for fare information and office locations. Both Air Inter and Air France also have booths in the SNCM office off pl. St-Nicolas. Open Mon.-Fri. 8-11:30am and 2-5:30pm.

Trains: pl. de la Gare (tel. 95 32 60 06), just off av. Maréchal Sebastiani. To: Calvi (2 per day, 3 1/2hr., 80F); Corte (4 per day, 2hr., 50F); Ajaccio (4 per day, 4hr., 106F). Leave your **luggage** at the *consigne* for 14F per day, but the station is only open Mon.-Sat. 6am-8pm, Sun. 8am-12:15pm and 1:15-6:45pm.

Buses: Rapides Bleus, 1, av. Maréchal Sebastiani (tel. 95 31 03 79). Open Mon.-Fri. 8:45am-noon and 2:30-6:30pm, Sat. 9am-noon. To: Ajaccio (Mon-Sat.. 7:45am and 3pm, 3 1/2hr., 100F) and Porto-Vecchio along the Côte Orientale (Mon.-Sat. 8:30am and 4pm, Sun. 8:30am; 3hr.; 105F). Mon.-Sat., you can take the 8:30am bus to Porto-Vecchio and change to the Trinitours noon bus to Bonifacio—the only connection from Sept.-June. The Rapide Bleus office in Porto-Vecchio will point you to the Trinitours office. Additionally, you may get off the Ajaccio bus in Corte (1 1/4hr., 50F); a bus leaves Corte at 5:35 pm Mon.-Sat. for Calvi.

Ferries: SNCM, Hôtel de la Chambre de Commerce (tel. 95 31 03 79). Open Mon.-Fri. 8-11:30am and 2-5:30pm. See Getting There above for information. **Corsica Ferries,** 5bis, rue Chanoine Leschi (tel. 95 31 18 09) floats to Livorno and La Spezia (4-5hr., 150F) and Genova (8hr., 190F) in Italy. All ferries arrive and depart at the Quai de Fangs, next to pl. St-Nicolas. See Getting There above.

Car Rental: ADA Location, 35, rue César Campinchi (tel. 95 31 09 02). 285F per day, 450F per weekend, 1129F per week, unlimited mileage. Drivers must be over 21 and have held a license for 2 years. Open Mon.-Fri. 8am-noon and 2-6pm; Sat. 8am-noon.

Bike and Moped Rental: Locacycles, 40, rue César Campinchi (tel. 95 31 02 43). 10-speeds 110F per day, 660F per week, deposit 1000F. Mopeds 190F per day, 967F per week, deposit 2000F. Prices may rise in Aug. Open Mon.-Fri. 8am-noon and 2-6pm; Sat. 8am-noon.

Taxis: tel. 95 34 07 00. About 150F to airport.

Youth Information: Centre Information Jeunesse, 3, bd. Auguste Gaudin (tel. 95 32 12 13). Information on jobs, excursions, and limited travel information. Open Mon.-Fri. 10am-noon and 1-5:30pm.

Hospital: Falconaja, route Impériale (tel. 95 55 11 11). **SAMU:** tel. 15.

Police: tel. 95 33 99 33, on rue Commandant Luce de Casabianca. **Emergency:** tel. 17.

Accommodations and Camping

Hotels in Bastia tend to be less comfortable than those in the resort towns, but it's a cinch to find rooms, even in summer. Prices drop in winter to around 100F for a double. The tourist office does not reserve hotels, but has a complete accommodations list.

Hôtel de l'Univers, 3, av. Maréchal Sebastiani (tel. 95 31 03 38), down the street from the train station. Clean rooms in the middle of town. Singles 120F, with shower 180F. Doubles 150F, with shower 200F. Triples 180F, with shower 250F. Breakfast 30F.

Central Hôtel, 3, rue Miot (tel. 95 31 03 08), great location betwen bd. Paoli and rue Campinchi. Doubles with shower 160F, with shower and toilet 180-250F. Prices go down the longer you stay.

Hôtel San Carlu, 10, bd. Auguste Gaudin (tel. 95 31 70 65). Fine young rooms in the charming *vieille ville.* Manager brims with recommendations of places to eat and sights to see. Singles 150F. Doubles 160F. Oct.-May: singles 120F. Doubles 140F. Triples 180F all year. Breakfast 18F.

Camping: Camping Casanova, route du Tennis (tel. 95 33 91 42). Clean, pleasant location 5km north of Bastia. Take the bus marked **Erblanca** across from the tourist office kiosk (every 1/2hr. 7:30am-7pm, 8F). 20F per person, 8F per tent. **Camping San Damiano** (tel. 95 33 68 02), on route de la Lagune de Pinette, 15km south of Bastia. Closer to the airport. 22F per person, 10F per tent. Open June-Oct.

Food

Restaurants ring the *vieux port,* many with terraces from which you can watch the boats. Bd. Général de Gaulle is full of cheap, filling sandwich shops, while bd. Paoli is lined with well-stocked Corsican specialty markets.

Le Dépot, 22, rue César Campinchi. An intimate place with a winding wooden staircase and brick walls. Fire-cooked pizza 28-48F, *plats du jour* 50-90F, pasta 42-50F. Open Tues.-Sat. noon-3pm and 7-11pm, Mon. noon-3pm.

Nanny, 28, rue César Campinchi. A chic *salon de thé;* great for lunch. *Crêpes* and *tartes salées* (savory tarts, 1550F), as well as sundaes and ice cream delights (18-30F). Open daily 7am-8pm.

Crêperie les Zéphyrs, quai des Martyrs in the *vieux port.* The best deal on the waterfront. Tasty *crêpes* 12-32F, pasta 25-35F, pizza 28-48F, and fish specialities 23-45F. Open Mon.-Sat. noon-3pm and 7-10pm.

Chez Gino, 11, av. Emile Sari, 5 min. from the ferry terminal. A lively neighborhood eatery, ideal for a pre- or post-ferry snack. Pizzas 22-48F. Open Tues.-Sun. noon-9pm.

Sights

The tourist office distributes a free leaflet (in English) outlining an excellent two-hour walking tour of Bastia. The route covers several beautiful churches, the charming *vieux port,* and the narrow streets and stone staircases that meander up to the citadel through the refreshing shade and bright flowers of the **jardin de Romieu.** In the 15th-century **Palais des Gouverneurs Génois,** overlooking the port, the **Musée d'Ethnographie** depicts traditional Corsican life in different regions. (Open daily 9am-8pm; August 16-June 14 9am-noon and 3-6pm. Admission 10F.) For the best view of the citadel and the port, walk to the lighthouse at the end of the **Jetée du Dragon.**

Near Bastia: Cap Corse

North of Bastia, a string of fishing villages and quiet inlets rim Cap Corse, a 48km peninsula pointing toward France. The 113km road around the Cap passes sheltered coves and forest-covered mountains; sprinkled amidst hills of chestnut, lime, and olive trees are fortified Genoese towns like **Cagnano,** 5 1/2km inland from the port of **Porticciolo.** On the coast are several Genoese towers, including the restored **Tour de Losse,** part of an elaborate system that once could spread word of impending barbarian and pirate raids to every Corsican town within two hours.

Getting to and traveling around the Cap is difficult. Hitchhiking is reportedly a non-option, due to the preponderance of tourists among the already small numbers of cars heading toward the cap. Renting a moped or a car is the best way to see the Cap, but is rarely economical: gas alone will run you about 5F per litre. Some travel agencies in Calvi (**Autocars Mariani,** tel. 95 65 05 32, 145F) and Bastia (**Autocars Olladini,** cours Paoli, tel. 95 31 44 04, July and Aug. only, 100F) run infrequent and hurried (6-8hr. long) excursions to the Cap.

Macinaggio, 40km from Bastia, is one of the few port towns where you can find services and supplies (including gas and a supermarket). The **tourist office** (tel. 95 35 42 60) is open daily from 9am to noon and 3pm to 7pm. The **post office** exchanges money (open Mon.-Fri. 9am-noon and 2-4:30pm, Sat. 9-11:30am). **Hôtel des Iles** (tel. 95 35 43 02) has clean rooms with a view of the port. (Doubles 180-240F, with shower 260F.) From July to September 15, **Camping de la Plage** (tel. 95 35 43 76) offers beach-side camping (20F per person, 15F per tent). Guided horseback tours leave from the campground; call Jean Albertini (tel. 95 35 43 76) for information. **Domaine de Gioielli** (tel. 95 35 42 05) opens its caves to the public. Their vineyard, on the left, 500m toward Rogliano from Macinaggio, is most interesting in September.

Rogliano, Macinaggio's sister village 2.5km inland, is solemn and undisturbed. Shaped like an amphitheater, it contains the ruins of a Genoan castle, **Château de San Colombano,** and a large 16th-century church, **San' Agnello.** Walk from Macinaggio to Rogliano, or take the free shuttle bus (April-Oct. 7-8:30pm) run by the **Restaurant u Sant Agnellu** (tel. 95 35 40 59), which has a 75F *menu* and spacious doubles with shower for 220F. The **tourist office** (tel. 95 35 40 40) has more information.

In the port of **Centuri,** on the other side of the peninsula, 57km from Bastia, boats bring in their daily haul of lobsters, mussels, and fish. Sublimely picturesque, Centuri is often photographed as an example of the prototypical fishing village. **Camping l'Isulottu** (tel. 95 35 62 81) is near the beach. (20F per person, 12F per tent, 10F per car. Open April-Oct.) In town, three one-star hotels all have high prices. **Le Centuri** (tel. 95 35 61 70) is a modern hotel with large rooms, all equipped with shower and private bath or toilet. (Doubles 290F, breakfast included. Open April-Oct.) Look for *rapo,* a wonderful but seldom-produced dessert wine.

Bastia to Bonifacio: Côte Orientale

One of the island's few flat roads stretches 170km from Bastia to Bonifacio, hugging the coast of the Island's far southern tip. Nothing remarkable except lower prices awaits visitors to **Moriani** and **Solenzara,** the two main beach resorts on the island's east coast, and indeed the waterfront of the Côte Orientale has relatively little to recommend it. Inland the **Plaine Orientale** includes orderly vineyards, lush orange groves, and even kiwi farms, as well as the coarse *maquis* whose blooms are used to make an unusual-tasting honey. **Castagniccia,** a low, hilly region filled with chestnut trees, lies east of Corte. You'll need a car to explore the virtually untouched back roads of this area.

A possible exception-to-the-rule on the Côte Orientale is the nicey-but-pricey **Porto-Vecchio,** 143km south of Bastia and a scant 27km from Bonifacio. On an inlet of the Tyrrhenian Sea, the town (pop. 12,000) sits tight in its 16th-century Genoese walls. The *vieille ville* gazes over the port and the salterns surrounding the town. The **tourist office,** pl. de l'Hôtel de Ville (tel. 95 70 09 58), will help you find a hotel or campground.

Its English-speaking staff also provides information on transportation and hiking. (Open Mon.-Sat. 9am-1pm and 4-8pm, Sun. 10am-noon and 5-7pm; Sept. 16-June 14 Mon.-Fri. 9am-noon and 3-6pm.)

A mediocre beach lies at the edge of town; continue 7km further south to reach the gorgeous **Plage de Palombaggia,** where turquoise water laps onto fine white sand, surrounded by jagged red cliffs and fragrant pine trees. **Trinitours** (tel. 95 70 13 83) runs shuttles to the beach in July and August. (Mon.-Sat. at 10am, returning at 6pm. Roundtrip 25F.) **Rapides Bleus,** 7, rue Jean Jaurès (tel. 95 70 10 36), runs two buses per day (1 on Sun.) between Bastia and Porto-Vecchio (3hr., 100F). Trinitours sends buses from Porto-Vecchio to Bonifacio (4 per day, 29F; Sept.-June Mon.-Sat. noon, 1/2hr., 29F) and Ajaccio (Mon.-Sat. 6:30am and 2pm, 105F).

Hotels in Porto Vecchio are terribly overpriced, with the wonderful exception of the **Hôtel Panorama,** 12, rue Jean-Nicoli (tel. 95 70 07 96), which has spacious doubles with wooden ceilings, showers, and views of the port for 190F (Nov.-May 160F) You can get off the bus at the port, just outside the city, and camp at **La Matonara** (tel. 95 70 37 05) for 8F per person, 10F per tent). Finding something to eat in town should be no problem. The streets surrounding the church and the tourist office are jammed with cheap sandwich shops. Head to **La Vigie,** on the south side of the old town on rue Bougo, for more substantial fare and excellent pizza (42-60F) and pasta (45-65F). (Open daily noon-3pm and 7am-10pm.) Pack for a picnic at **Super U,** across from the post office on av. Général Leclerc. (Open Mon.-Sat. 9am-noon and 4-7:45pm.) **Cave Corsica,** on rue Jean Antoine Nau, has inexpensive Corsican specialties such as local wine (only 4F90 per liter), honey, cheese, and *charcuteries.*

For hiking information, including advice on the six-day **da mare a mare** trail that crosses the southern part of the island between Porto-Vecchio and Propriano, visit **Parc Naturel Regional's** office on rue Col. Quenza. (Open Mon.-Sat. 9:15am-12:15pm and 4-7:30pm.) Porto Vecchio also screens a **film festival** in July; for times and information call 95 70 35 02.

Bonifacio (Bonifaziu)

Try as they might, no other Corsican towns can match the sea-side grace and splendor of tiny Bonifacio (pop. 2500). Nestled on the extreme southern tip of the island, the postcard-perfect *haute ville* perches atop stunning limestone cliffs 90m above the water, while the town itself, a former fortress, commands a magnificent view of the emerald Mediterranean and the nearby island of Sardinia. Neither the cheapest nor easiest to reach of Corsican towns, Bonifacio and its *haute ville* encircled with heavy stone walls will reward your perseverance (and expenditures).

Orientation and Practical Information

Wonder twin powers activated Bonifacio into the shape of a letter U, and the form of a port. On each of the arms of the U are the quays—the quai du Nord and quai Jérôme Comparetti. To the west of the quai Comparetti lies the *haute ville,* the old, fortified city.

Tourist Office: Syndicat d'Initiative, rue des Deux Moulins (tel. 95 73 11 88), in the Hôtel de Ville at the western end of the *haute ville.* Has information on B&Bs, hotels, and distributes the very useful *Guide Officiel de Bonifacio* (10F). Open daily 9am-8pm; Sept.-June 9am-noon and 3-6pm.

Currency Exchange: The best rates are at the post office (see below) and in the port at the **Société Centrale** bank (tel. 95 73 02 49) at the far end of the quai Comparetti (open Mon.-Fri. 9am-noon and 2-5pm). After-hours and on weekends, try your luck at the less competitive exchanges which line quai Comparetti.

Post Office: pl. Carrega in the *haute ville* (tel. 95 73 00 15). Currency exchange, telephones. Open Mon.-Fri. 9am-noon and 2-5pm, Sat. 9am-noon. **Postal Code:** 20169.

Buses: catch 'em at the **Agence de Voyages Ollandini,** 77, quai Comparetti (tel. 95 73 01 28). Although it runs no buses itself, Ollandini is the only place in town that knows who runs them, when, and for how much. To: Ajaccio (Mon.-Sat. 6:30am and 2pm, 4hr., 105F); Porto-Vecchio (4 per day, 29F; Sept.-June Mon.-Sat. 1 per day at 2pm); and Bastia (Mon.-Sat. at 2pm, change in Porto-Vecchio, 129F).

Ferries: The only ferry destination from Bonifacio is Santa Theresa in Sardinia. Two companies, **Siremar** (tel. 95 73 00 96) and **NAVARMA** (tel. 95 73 00 29) sail there several times each day. You can buy tickets for both lines, as well as for SNCM, Corsica Ferries, and Air Inter, at the Ollandini office (see Buses). All boats leave from the **Gare Maritime** at the end of quai Comparetti, beneath the walls of the upper city. Buy tickets shortly before departure time. If you plan to bring a car, reservations are essential in July and August.

Taxis: Cantara Antoine (tel. 95 73 02 06). Some may need a taxi to avoid the grueling hike to the *haute ville;* the fares vary wildly, but shouldn't be more than 50F. You can catch a cab at the cab stop at the end of Quai Comparetti.

Car Rental: None are cheap. **Avis** (tel. 95 73 01 28) rents for 276F per day plus 4F50 per km, or 3290F per week.

Moped Rental: Corse Moto Services, Quai du Nord (tel. 95 73 15 16). 160F per day, or 900F per week. 2000F deposit. Open daily 10am-12:30pm and 4:30-7:30pm.

Bike Rental: Location VTT, av. Sylver Bohn (tel. 95 73 18 98), next door to the Hôtel des Etrangers. Mountain bikes 90F per day, 160F per weekend, 500F per week. 1500F deposit. Open daily 10am-noon and 2-5pm.

Laundromat: Laverie Automatique, quai du Nord. Wash and dry 50F. Open Mon.-Sat. 8am-noon and 2-6pm, Sun. 8-11am.

Pharmacy: Pharmacie Guverle, 87, quai Comparetti (tel. 95 73 00 02). Open Mon.-Sat. 9am-noon and 3-7pm.

Hospital: tel. 95 73 95 73.

Police: tel. 95 73 00 17. **Emergency:** tel. 17.

Accommodations, Camping and Food

"Budget Accommodations" is an oxymoron, a paradox, a contradiction in terms, in Bonifacio: hell, even the campgrounds are overpriced. Nonetheless, there are a few options for the shallow-pocketed *voyageur.* If traveling in July and August, definitely call ahead.

Perhaps the best value is at **Hôtel les Voyageurs,** quai Comparetti (tel. 95 73 00 46), which offers sparse but spacious rooms in a perfect portside location. (July-Sept.: doubles 300F. Triples and Quads 500F. Breakfast included. March-June: doubles 160F, with shower 200F. Triples and Quads 320F.) Also consider the **Hôtel des Etrangers,** av. Sylvère Bohn (tel. 95 73 01 09) at the entrance to the lower town, 300m from the port. (Doubles 240-340F. Quads 370-440F. Shower and breakfast included. Open April-Oct.) Camping provides the most affordable opportunity to see the town. Pitch your tent at **L'Arguina,** av. Sylvère Bohn (tel. 95 73 02 96), at the entrance to the port—the closest campground to the town, and priced accordingly. (60F for 1-2 people, 50F Sept.-June.) **Cavallo Morto,** rte. de Porto-Vecchio (tel. 95 73 04 66), 2km out of town, is more affordable. (24F per person, 10F per tent. Open April 15-Oct. 15.)

Every *boulangerie* in Bonifacio sells its own version of *pain des morts* (bread of the dead), a non-lethal raisin-and-walnut concoction that's the town's self-declared contribution to Corsican cuisine. For groceries, at the port head to **Supermarché Simoni,** on quai Comparetti (open daily 8am-noon and 3-6pm) and in the *haute ville* try the supermarché at 16 rue Doria (open Mon.-Sat. 9am-noon and 4-7pm). Though seaside eateries line the port, most are overpriced and generic, an exception being **L'Ancura,** on quai Camparetti. Modestly priced, it allows you to select your own fish from the catch-of-the-day showcase. Try the 70F *menu* with its tempting and tasty *soupe du poisson* (fish soup). (Open May-Oct. noon-2:30pm and 7:30-11pm.) For *haute ville* cuisine, descend into **A Cantina,** 16 rue Ste-Dominique, a subterranean restaurant with Corsican specialities and a bustling atmosphere. Delve into the *pâté à sanglier* (boar paté) on the 55F and 70F *menus,* or sip the fine Corsican wine at 6F per glass. (Open Mon.-Sat. noon-9pm.) Finally, sway to some lovely Corsican guitar tunes at **Cliper's Restaurant**

and Pizzeria, 10, rue Cardinal Zigliara, in the *haute ville.* It proffers excellent *menus* from 50-85F, pizza (35-50F) and seafood specialities. (Open daily noon-3pm and 7-11pm.)

Sights

Founded in 833 by Boniface of Tuscany, rulership of Bonifacio has been bounced from Pisa to Genoa and finally to Paris: the *haute ville* contains relics from all three periods. The best way to explore Bonifacio after wandering through its fortress is to follow the cliffs to the **Phare Pertusato,** the lighthouse at the southern tip of the island. The 40-minute walk will inspire you to paint a picture, compose a poem, or just pull out a Polaroid. The end of the path looks out over the craggy narrow islands of **Lavezzi** and **Cavallo. Thalassa** (tel. 95 73 05 43 or 95 73 01 17) sends frequent boats on excursions to the islands (2 1/2hr.) and explorations of the grottoes and impressive natural rock formations nearby (50 min). Prices vary depending on season and demand. Call ahead for details. Descend the stairway next to **Chapelle St-Roch** to reach Bonifacio's narrow, rocky beach below the cliffs. The tourist office distributes a worthwhile self-guided tour of the old town. To discover the countryside and the luxurious beaches nearby, rent a moped and follow route du Phare, which runs west out of town to **Piantarella,** or take D58 to **Gurgazo** (6km). At night, if you've got the francs, **L'Agora,** in the *haute ville* on av. Carotella (tel. 95 73 00 44) stakes a claim as the town's only hot spot. (Open until 5am, cover 100F.) In September, Bonifacio entertains with a festival of Mediterranean music, **Les Voix de la Méditéranée** (tel. 95 73 10 72 or 95 73 03 48).

Bonifacio to Ajaccio

The road from Bonifacio northwest to Ajaccio crawls through mountains with intermittent glimpses of the sea in the distance. Try to leave the main route and explore some of the isolated coastal villages. A stunning example of the unusual rock formations whipped out of the cliffs along the entire western coast, the lion-shaped **Rocher du Lion** crouches 55km from Bonifacio at **Roccapina.**

Megalithic stones and fantastically-shaped rock faces surround *"la plus corse des villes corses"* (the most Corsican of Corsican towns), **Sartène,** built on granite and practically hidden in the mountains. On Good Friday, Sartène sponsors **La Catenacciu,** a procession imported from Seville, Spain. A red-hooded Christ bearing a wooden cross and dragging a long chain walks through the candlelit streets of the old town in a re-enactment of the Calvary drama. Although most of the local vineyards are now only terraces on the mountainsides, **La Cave Sartenèse,** in pl. Porta (tel. 95 77 01 05), continues to pour the potent *vin Sartène* (3F50 per glass, bottles from 15F30). Local specialties include peach and orange wines in a muscat base (open Mon.-Fri. 7:30am-noon and 1-5pm). **Camping Olva** (tel. 95 77 11 58), 5km from Sartène on the mountain road D69, has its own pool (10F per tent, 26F per person; open April-Sept.). The **tourist office** (tel. 95 77 15 40) is on rue Borgo. (Open Mon.-Fri. 9am-noon.) Sartène is a stop on the Ajaccio-Bonifacio bus line (2 per day, 2hr., 38F).

To understand the popularity of **Propriano,** between Ajaccio and Sartène, follow the beach path which extends several km south of this fishing village-turned-resort, or simply plop down on the sand right in town. The **tourist office,** 17, rue Général de Gaulle (tel. 95 76 01 49), stores baggage for 3F per day and **exchanges currency.** Although it does not make reservations, it can help with hotels and transportation. (Open Mon.-Sat. 9am-noon and 3-7pm; Sun. 9am-noon.) Buses to Ajaccio leave twice per day (2hr., 45F); others run twice per day to Bonifacio (2hr., 50F), Sartène (1/2hr., 15F), and Porto-Vecchio (2hr. 20 min., 55F). Buy tickets at the **Ollandini** agency at 22, rue Général de Gaulle (tel. 95 76 00 76). **Hôtel Le Bellevue,** 9, av. Napoléon (tel. 95 76 01 86), on the port, has big, clean rooms with an ocean view. (Doubles and triples 150-320F. Open March-Nov. Make reservations for July and Aug.) Two km from Propriano at the **Centre Equestre de Barachi,** an **auberge de jeunesse** (tel. 95 76 19 48) has slightly cramped dorm rooms, kitchen facilities, a restaurant, and a washing machine (50F per person, shower included). Don your spurs, because the stable next door offers **horse-**

back riding. (Tel. 95 76 08 02. 1-hr. trail ride 100F, 2hr. 180F; trips of several days also available. Open Mon.-Sat. 9am-noon and 4-7pm.) **Camping Colomba** (tel. 95 76 06 42), next to the youth hostel, also has a restaurant. (24F per person, 10F per tent. Open Easter to Sept.) There are other camping facilities nearby. The restaurants on the port serve overpriced seafood. For more affordable meals, try the places on rue du 9 septembre. **Le Diana,** at the corner of rue de la Misericorde, serves a fine three-course seafood *menu* (open daily noon-2pm and 7-10pm).

From June to September, a second **Ollandini** agency, 2, rue Général de Gaulle (tel. 95 76 05 36), makes weekly excursions to **Filitosa** (60F), where recently uncovered faces carved into stone monoliths silently watch the ebb and flow of the tide. (Office open Mon.-Sat. 8am-noon and 3-7pm, Sun. 8am-noon and 6-8pm.) **Valinco Accessoires** on Porte de Plaisance (tel. 95 76 11 84) rents **bikes** for 90F per day with an 800F deposit, and mopeds for 170F per day with a 2500F deposit. (Open June-Oct. Mon.-Sat. 9am-noon and 3-7:30pm.) From May through September, the good ship **Valinco** runs four snorkeling tours per day through the **Golfe du Valinco.** (100F, children 70F. Mask and snorkel included.)

Savoie-Dauphiné
(The Alps)

After museum corridors and exhausting urban centers, the majestic Alps and the glassy rivers that carved their valleys here turn city smog into a distant memory. Commercialized resorts and occasional undisturbed hamlets here may entertain or enchant visitors, but the natural architecture is the Alps' real attraction. The curves of the Chartreuse Valley grow to rugged crags in the Vercors range, and climax in Europe's highest peak, Mont Blanc. Magnificent but hardly unspoiled, this spectacular region drew international attention in February 1992, when it hosted the Winter Olympics for the third time. Though construction altered the face of the region for years prior to the games, it hasn't laid waste to the area's charm: decades of development have alerted the government to the need to protect the natural beauty that has earned the French Alps their popularity.

The Alps are shared by two historical provinces, Savoie and Dauphiné. Dauphiné, the lower region, consists of the Chartreuse Valley, the lovely Vercors regional park, the smaller Ecrins national park in the east, and the Belledonne and Oisans mountain ranges. The university center of Grenoble has been the capital of the region since the 14th century, when Louis XI designated the town the permanent parliamentary seat. Numerous late medieval châteaux, scattered to the northwest of Grenoble, are listed in the tourist offices' brochure, *La Route Historique des Dauphins*.

Savoie, which includes the magnificent peaks of Haute Savoie, the Olympic resorts in the expansive Tarentaise valley, and the awesome Vanoise national park, bears the name of the oldest royal house in Europe. After 1000 BC, this region of the Alps became the possession of Humbert aux Blanches Mains, founder of the House of Savoie and a vassal of the German Emperor. Humbert established his capital at Chambéry and began extracting exorbitant tolls from neighboring kings who wanted to march through the mountain passes. By the 14th century, this powerful kingdom included Nice, the Jura, Piemonte, and Geneva, a choice expanse of territory that attracted the military attention of generations of French monarchs. In 1860, weary from centuries of invasion, a vote showed an overwhelming number of *savoyards* in favor of becoming French, and the region was incorporated into the Republic.

Train lines efficiently link the Alps's main cities to those in France, Italy, and Switzerland, while a thorough bus system serves the higher altitudes and more remote villages. This is fortunate, since distances are considerable and the roads arduous. Hitching on back roads can leave travelers stranded far from urban centers.

Once you're off the train, down from the bus, or out of the car, head in the most logical direction—up. After the spring thaw, flowery meadows, icy mountain lakes, and staggering panoramic views reward experienced and amateur hikers alike. Most towns have sports shops that rent appropriate footwear for about 40F per day, even on Sunday; local tourist offices will often provide free trail guides. Trails are clearly marked, but serious climbers should invest in a *Topo-Guide* (hiking map). Talk with experts at the hiking information offices listed for updated information on trail and weather conditions and suggested hikes.

Skiing in the Alps has always been expensive, and the Olympics drove prices even higher. Begin making arrangements six to eight weeks in advance or, better yet, in late summer. The least crowded and cheapest months to go are January, March, and April. Most resorts close in October and November, between the hiking and skiing seasons. **FUAJ,** the French Youth Hostel Federation, offers affordable week-long winter skiing and summer sports packages. For more information, contact local FUAJ offices, youth hostels, or the central office at 27, rue Pajol, 75018 Paris (tel. 46 07 00 01).

Food here takes a Swiss twist. Regional specialties include *fondue savoyarde*—a blend of three Alpine cheeses, white wine, and kirsch, served with cubed bread for dunking. Other cheesy dishes include *raclette* (scrapings from a strong Swiss cheese melted and served with boiled potatoes, pickled onions, and gherkins) and *gratin dauphinois* (potatoes baked in a cream and cheese sauce). *Savoyards* and *dauphinois* also cure excellent ham and salami and net superb trout from the icy mountain streams, which end up in a buttery preparation called *truite meunière*. The renowned *montagne* cheeses are mild and creamy: try Tomme, the oldest of Savoie cheeses, St-Marcellin (half goat's milk), Beaufort, and Reblochon. Fine regional wines include the whites of Apremont, Marignan, and Chignin and the rich reds produced in Montmélian and St-Jean-de-la-Porte. If there's room left for dessert, try the *roseaux d'Annecy* (liqueur-filled chocolates), *St-Genux* (a *brioche* topped with pink praline), or the *gâteau de Savoie* (a light sponge cake). *Eaux de vie,* strong liqueurs distilled from fruits, are popular here, especially when made from local *framboises* (raspberries).

Grenoble

The historic capital of Dauphiné, Grenoble (pop. 392,000) has emerged in modern times as its academic and sporting capital as well. The immaculately clean city is home to the science-oriented University of Grenoble, one of the largest in France. Its 36,000 students and the town's large immigrant population help explain Grenoble's many cafés, shaggy radicals, dusty bookshops, and serious politics. But even the most bookish cannot ignore the splendor of the city's surroundings, exploited by *téléphériques* (cable cars), hikers, and skiers. Stendhal, Grenoble's most famous bookworm, said of the town "at the end of every street, there is a mountain." The truth of his words was not lost upon the Olympic committee, which chose Grenoble as the site of the 1968 Winter Olympics. And because Grenoble's proximity to Albertville, site of the 1992 Winter Games, earned the city an improved road system, jaunts to the Chartreuse, Vercors, and Oisans ranges are easier than ever. Whether you're here to hike the hills or puff cigarettes in a café, Grenoble will impress with its floating peaks and soaring discussions.

Orientation and Practical Information

Although public transportation in Grenoble is extremely efficient, both the downtown and the *vieille ville* are easily accessible on foot, and the train station is ten minutes from the center. The **Guide DAHU,** (15F), a guide to restaurants, shopping, sports, and nightlife written in a hip and breezy style by Grenoble students with razor-sharp wit is available in French at some *tabacs.*

Tourist Office: 14, rue de la République (tel. 76 54 34 36), in the center of town. From the station, trek up rue Alsace-Lorraine and bear left along pl. Victor Hugo. Continue up rue Molière and rue Félix Poulat and turn right onto rue Raoul Blanchard. The tourist office will be on your left (15min.). Alternatively, take the tram (direction: "Grand Place") to the "Maison du Tourisme" stop, take your first left and then your first right. Information on public transportation, trains, hiking, horseback riding, and guided tours. Decent map (2F). For a steep 25F, you can buy a better one at most *tabacs* and stationery stores. Reserves hotel rooms in Grenoble and other cities (20F). Open Mon.-Fri. 9am-6:30pm, Sat. 9am-12:30pm and 1:30-6:30pm; off-season Mon.-Sat. 9am-6pm. Also, **Grenoble Spectacles,** a cultural center. Open Tues.-Sat. 10:30am-12:30pm and 1:30-6pm. **Annex** at train station (tel. 76 56 90 94). Open Mon.-Sat. 9am-noon and 2-6pm.

Hiking Information: CIMES (Centre Informations Montagnes et Sentiers), Maison de la Randonnée, 7, rue Voltaire (tel. 76 51 76 00). Organizes hiking trips. Stocks detailed guides of hiking, mountaineering, and cross-country skiing trails in alpine areas. *Topo-Guides* (57-75F). Open Mon.-Fri. 9am-6pm, Sat. 10am-noon and 2-6pm. **Club Alpin Français,** 32, av. Félix Viallet (tel. 76 87 03 73). Advice on all mountain activities. Organizes group hiking, mountaineering, ice-climbing, and parachuting trips. Map library. Club membership (mainly an insurance policy) 300F, ages 18-25 200F. Open Tues.-Wed. 3-7pm, Thurs.-Fri. 3-8pm, Sat. 9am-noon.

Budget Travel: Jeunes Sans Frontière-Wasteels, 50, av. Alsace-Lorraine (tel. 76 47 34 54), near the train station, and 20, av. Félix-Viallet (tel. 76 46 36 39). BIJ tickets and cheap excursion packages. Both offices open Mon.-Fri. 9am-noon and 2-7pm, Sat. 9am-noon and 2-6pm.

Currency Exchange: Comptoir de Change, rue Philis de la Charce, near the tourist office. Open Sat. and Sun. noon-5pm. During the week, the post office posts fair rates with no commission.

Post Office: bd. Maréchal-Lyautey (tel. 76 76 14 14). **Currency exchange** and **telephones.** Open Mon.-Fri. 8am-6:45pm, Sat. 8am-noon. **Branch office** attached to the tourist office. Open Mon.-Fri. 8am-6:30pm, Sat. 8am-noon. **Postal Code:** 38000.

Flights: Aéroport de Grenoble St-Geoirs, St-Etienne de St-Geoirs (tel. 76 65 48 48). Eight buses per day leave from the *gare routière* (15F). **Air Inter,** 42, cours Jean Jaurès. Flights to Paris from 501F round-trip, 400F with discounts. **Air France,** pl. Victor Hugo. Both offices open Mon.-Fri. 9am-noon and 1:45-6pm, Sat. 9am-noon.

Trains: pl. de la Gare (tel. 76 47 50 50; for reservations 76 47 54 27). Trains almost every hr. to: Chambéry (1hr., 49F); Avignon (3hr., 140F); and Lyon (2hr., 83F). Paris (5-7 per day, 3-8hr., 296F plus 16-40F reservation). Information office open Mon.-Fri. 8:30am-7:30pm, Sat. 9am-6pm. Also has a desk at tourist office.

Buses: *Gare routière,* to the left of the train station. Four companies offer summer excursions as well as service to ski resorts and surrounding towns. **VFD** (tel. 76 47 77 77) is the largest. Office open daily 7:40-11:30am and 2:30-6pm. For other companies, call 76 87 90 31.

Public Transportation: TAG, has a desk in the tourist office. The modern tram and bus system costs 8F a ride, 47F for a *carnet* of 10 tickets. Tram runs roughly every 10min. from 5am to 10pm; buses run from 6am to 9pm. The central city is conveniently dotted with "you-are-here" maps, and each TAG stop posts a complete transit map.

Taxis: tel. 76 54 42 54. 24 hrs.

Bike Rental and Climbing Equipment: Borel Sport, 42, rue Alsace-Lorraine (tel. 76 46 47 46). Bicycles 90F per day, deposit 1000F. Also rents mountain climbing equipment. Shoes 25-40F per day. Open Tues.-Sat. 9am-noon and 2:30-7pm.

English Bookstore: Just Books, 1, rue de la Paix (tel. 76 44 78 81). Sizable, entirely English collection of paperbacks, including the full line of *everybody's* favorite budget travel guide. Open Tues.-Sat. 10am-noon and 2-7pm.

Women's Center: Centre d'Information Féminin, 9, rue Raoul Blanchard (tel. 76 54 08 19). Free advice and pamphlets. Open Mon.-Wed. and Fri. 1-6pm.

Youth Center: Centre Régional d'Information Jeunesse, 8, rue Voltaire (tel. 76 54 70 38), near the tourist office across from CIMES. Information on housing, sports, and cultural events. BIJ train tickets. *Carte Jeune* 75F. Open Mon.-Fri. 1-6pm.

Laundromat: rue Alphand, behind the tourist office. Wash 15F. Soap 2F. Open daily 7am-10pm.

Snowfall Information Service: tel. 76 51 19 29. **Weather:** tel. 76 51 11 11.

Mountain Rescue: Secours en Montagne, tel. 76 21 44 44.

Hospital: Centre Hospitalier Régional de Grenoble, La Tronche (tel. 76 42 81 21).

Medical Emergency: SAMU, tel. 76 42 42 42.

Police: bd. Marèchal Leclerc (tel. 76 60 40 40). **Emergency:** tel. 17.

Accommodations and Camping

Plenty of budget hotels scatter throughout the pedestrian zone. Grenoble's *foyers* are especially suitable for longer stays. For rentals, see the tourist office's board marked *Locations Meubles.*

Auberge de Jeunesse (HI), 18, av. du Grésivaudan (tel. 76 09 33 52), about 4km from Grenoble, in Echirolles. Take bus #8 from cours Jean Jaurès (1 block straight ahead from the train station) or from the tourist office to "La Quinzaine." The hostel is on the right, a block behind the Casino supermarket. If walking, follow cours Jean Jaurès and turn right just before the Casino. Modern building with garden, bar, game room, cooking facilities, and TV. Open daily 7:30am-11pm. Ask for the door combination if out late. 4- to 6-bed rooms 60F, nonmembers 80F. Sheets 15F. Showers included. Breakfast included.

Le Foyer de L'Etudiante, 4, rue Ste-Ursule (tel. 76 42 00 84), near pl. Notre Dame, on a quiet street close to the center. From the tourist office, follow pl. Ste-Claire to pl. Notre Dame and take rue du Vieux Temple. Ordinary rooms in a friendly atmosphere. Kitchen facilities, TV, and a piano. 70F per person, doubles available. Showers 10F. Sheets included. Make reservations a week in advance. Accepts male and female travelers mid-June to mid-Sept. Only women at all other times.

Hôtel de la Poste, 25, rue de la Poste (tel. 76 46 67 25), in the center of the pedestrian zone. Nice family management, purple petunias, and barking dog welcome you to spacious, clean rooms. Singles 112F. Doubles 134F. Triples 166F. Showers included.

Hôtel Victoria, 17, rue Thiers (tel. 76 46 06 36), midway between the train station and the tourist office. Elegant lobby with simple, clean rooms. Singles and doubles 116F, with shower 150F, with bathroom 175F. Breakfast 25F.

Hôtel Acacia, 13, rue Belgrade (tel. 76 87 29 90), near the Jardin de Ville. Modern hotel with spotless green and white, recently renovated rooms. All rooms with shower. Singles 170F, with toilet 190F. Doubles 220F, with toilet 240F. Breakfast 23F.

Camping: Les 3 Pucelles, in Seyssins (tel. 76 96 45 73) just on the southwest corner of Grenoble. The closest to town and the only one open all year. 60 sites. 10F per person, 10F per tent. Call ahead in the summer.

Food

Inexpensive North African restaurants congregate around rue Chenoise and rue St-Laurent, on the right bank of the river *(menus* around 45F). Several affordable regional restaurants cater to locals at pl. de Gordes, between pl. St-André and the Jardin de Ville. **Prisunic,** across from the tourist office (open Mon.-Sat. 8:30am-7pm) or **Casino,** near the youth hostel (open Mon.-Sat. 8:30am-9pm) will supply your *al fresco* feasts. Alternatively, try the big **markets** at pl. St-Bruno, near the station west of the tracks; and at rue Joseph Rey, where cours Jean Jaurès meets the tracks. (Both open Mon.-Sat. 8am-1pm.) The covered market in pl. Ste-Claire, near the tourist office, features fruit, meats, and regional cheeses every morning.

Bleu Nuit, 9, pl. de Metz, 1 block south of pl. de Verdun. Cozy blue and white interior. Service with a smile. Try the *croûte bornandine* (potato with dried meat and melted cheese, 50F) or, for a lighter meal, the *salade bleu nuit* (salad with delectable *pâté* and smoked duck, 38F). *Fondue savoyard,* 70F. *Plat du jour* 39F. Open Tues.-Sat. 11:30am-2pm and 7:30-10:30pm, Mon. 11:30-2pm. Closed first half of Aug.

Le Tonneau de Diogène, 6, pl. Notre-Dame. Simple, tasty food served at outdoor tables. Breakfast with fresh OJ and eggs (34F), salads (14-29F), and a variety of omelettes (18-21F). Open daily 11:30am-midnight.

Brasserie Bavaroise, 2, rue Vicat, near the tourist office. Delicious meals in an unpretentious setting full of locals. *Choucroute* 60-100F, 75F lunch *menu.* Open Mon.-Sat. 11:30am-2pm and 7-10:30pm.

Le Cantilène, 11, rue Beyle-Stendhal, near pl. de Verdun. Small and crowded with shiny, happy locals. 65F *menu.* Mostly seafood menu, including *moules-frites* (mussels with fries) 42F. Open Mon.-Thurs. 11:30am-2pm and 7-10pm, Fri.-Sat. 11:30am-2pm and 7-10:30pm.

La Tarte Flambée, 16, rue de Strasbourg, off pl. de Metz. As the address might suggest, this small, wooden restaurant serves savory Alsatian specialities. *Tarte Flambée* 30F, *choucroute* 48F. Open Mon.-Sat. 7:30pm-midnight. Arrive early or late or you will stand in line.

University Restaurants: Scattered around town. One at 5, rue Arsonval. Call **CROUS** at 76 87 07 62 to find out what's open. Buy a ticket from a student waiting in line (10F). Open Sept.-May.

Sights

A futuristic bubble of a cable car (the *téléphérique de la Bastille)* pops out of the city every three minutes from quai Stéphane-Jay and whisks visitors up to the imposing **Bastille** dungeon, with its jarring view of Grenoble, and, on a clear day, Mont Blanc. *(Téléphérique* open Mon. 10am-12:30am, Tues.-Sun. 9am-12:30am; Sept. 16-Oct. and April-June 15 Sun. 9am-7:30pm, Mon. 10am-7:30pm, Tues.-Sat. 9am-12:30am; Nov.-March daily 10am-6pm. 18F, round-trip 29F; students 10F, round-trip 15F50. Wheelchair access.) From the top, the ambitious can follow well-marked trails of varying difficulty. Walk—don't ride—down through the **Jardin des Dauphins** and **Parc Guy Pape.** (Open, weather permitting, daily 9am-7:30pm; Sept.-Oct. and April-May 9am-7pm; Nov.-Feb. 9am-4pm; March 9am-5:30pm.) For general information on the *téléphérique,* call 76 44 33 65 or 76 51 00 00.

Halfway down the hill from the Bastille, the **Musée Dauphinois,** 30, rue Maurice-Gignoux (tel. 76 87 66 77), stands out in France's collection of regional museums. Formerly the convent of Ste-Marie-d'en-Haut, the 17th-century building has a fine collection of *dauphinois* folk art. (Open Wed.-Mon. 9am-noon and 2-6pm. Admission 15F, students and seniors 10F, Wed. afternoon free.)

Students and recent immigrants now occupy most of the 18th-century houses on the river bank, Grenoble's most attractive neighborhood. Victorian **Pont St-Laurent,** an early suspension bridge, takes the place of a former Gallo-Roman bridge. Overlooking the manicured **Jardin de Ville,** the elaborate Renaissance **Palais de Justice** has a set of intricately carved ceilings. The only organized visits depart from pl. St-André at 10am on the first Saturday of each month (10F, students 5F), but you can try to sneak a look.

The *Guide DAHU* and the tourist office have complete lists of Grenoble's museums. The **Musée de Peinture et de Sculpture,** pl. Verdun (tel. 76 54 09 82), displays a well-organized assortment of Egyptian art, Renaissance and baroque paintings (including a few beautiful Tintorettos), and a notable modern collection (Chagall, Picasso, Matisse) in a flashy room with geometric designs by Calder. (Open Wed.-Mon. 10am-noon and 2-6pm. Admission 15F, students 10F, Wed. free. Tours on request.) The **Musée de la Résistance et de la Déportation,** 14, rue J.J. Rousseau (tel. 76 44 51 81), located in the apartment where Stendhal was born, contains an interesting and disturbing set of documents and objects from the occupation, regional and foreign resistance, and deportation during World War II. (Open Mon. and Wed.-Sat. 2-5:30pm; Sept.-June Wed.-Sat. 2-5:30pm. Free.) A renovated warehouse at 155, cours Berriat, houses **MAGASIN** (Center National d'Art Contemporain; tel. 76 21 95 84), an exhibition center for temporary displays of modern art. Take tram A to "Berriat" or walk 5 minutes from the train station (open Tues.-Sun. noon-7pm; admission 15F, under 25 10F). The **Musée Stendhal,** 1, rue Hector Berlioz (tel. 76 54 44 14), next to the Jardin de Ville, displays an interesting exhibit on the life of the 19th-century realist author from Grenoble. (Open Tues.-Sun. 2-6pm. Free.) Guided tours of the *vieille ville* leave from the tourist office at 5pm Monday through Saturday from July 1 to September 15 (2hr., 50F).

Entertainment

Hot nightspots in Grenoble come and go like nobody's business, so if you're about to warm it up, consult the *Guide DAHU*. Bars and cafés are usually less pretentious than the clubs, but still active and vibrant. Traditional international bars include **Le Saxo,** 5, rue d'Aiger (tel. 76 51 06 01; open Mon.-Sat. until 1am) and **King Charly,** 12, rue de Sault (tel. 76 47 29 72; open Mon.-Sat. noon-1am); young people, native and foreign alike, flock to these places. Both are less expensive than your average nightclub, where cover runs between 50 and 100F and drinks nearly as much. **Le George V,** 124, cours Benriot (tel. 76 73 64 47) is a popular gay club (cover 70F, open Wed.-Sun. 11pm-4am).

Grenoble suffers a shortage of neither the banal nor the bizarre. Annual offerings include February ice car racing, an August 15 outdoor Summer Feast of the Assumption, and the spectacular Bastille Day (July 14) fireworks over its Bastille. The **Festival du Court Métrage** (short films) takes place July 5-9. (Contact the Cinémathèque Française, 21, rue Génissieu (tel. 76 24 13 83), for details.) The European Theatre Festival, with shows ranging from 0-100F, hams it up in July (call the Bureau du Festival at 76 44 60 92 for further information). The famous **Festival International du Roman et du Film Noir** comes to town during the second week of October. Over 100 authors from around the world converge on Grenoble to sign, display, and sell their books. For more information, contact Association Grenoble-Polar, 21, rue Génissieu (tel. 76 24 13 83) or Le Cargo, Maison de la Culture de Grenoble (tel. 76 54 34 36), at the tourist office. (Open Mon.-Fri. 1-5:45pm, Sat. 10am-7pm). For more information on cultural events including concerts and theater, pick up a free copy of *Lumières sur la Ville* at the tourist office.

Near Grenoble

In 1605, the monks of the **Monastère de la Grande Chartreuse** tried to manufacture the elixir of long life; they came up with the celebrated Chartreuse liqueur. Today, only three monks know the secret recipe of 130 ingredients. Of course, this does not stop local stores from selling "the real thing" in plastic bottles for around 70F. The design of the actual monastery is the prototype for the "charter-house style" that has influenced communal institutions and hermitages around the world. You cannot visit the monastery (the monks live there in silence and seclusion) but there is an excellent view of it from **Correrie**, about 1km from the main road. The **museum** in Correrie (tel. 76 88 60 45) faithfully depicts the monks' daily routine. (Open April-Sept. Mon.-Sat. 9am-noon and 2-6:30pm. Admission 12F.) From Grenoble's *gare routière,* buses run to **Voiron**, from which it's a short trek to Correrie. (5 per day, 45min., 18F). While in Voiron, take a free tour of the **Caves de la Grande Chartreuse,** 10, bd. Edgar Kofler (tel. 76 05 81 77). It ends with a free tasting of the colorful spirits. (Open July-Aug. daily 8am-6:30pm; Oct. 1-8 and Easter-June daily 8-11:30am and 2-6:30pm; Oct. 9-Easter Mon.-Fri. 8-11:30am and 2-5:30pm.)

Swimming, sailing and camping await 10km north of Voiron at **Lac de Paladru,** the largest in Dauphiné. Four buses per day run to the lake from Voiron (45min., 30F). Free beaches and more camping can be found at Charavines, Paladru, Bilieu, Le Pin, and Montferrat. The local **tourist office** is in Charavines-Paladru (tel. 76 06 60 31). The Grenoble tourist office also has a list of all the lakes in Dauphiné.

Directly north of Grenoble, in the Chartreuse Valley, the scenic resort town of **St-Pierre-de-Chartreuse** offers swimming, tennis, golf, and hiking during the summer. The 15km route near **St-Laurent-du-Pont** passes through some of the most picturesque countryside in the Alps; locals consider this road a national monument. The tourist office in St-Laurent-du-Pont can be reached at 76 88 62 08. **Camping La Martinière** (tel. 76 88 60 36) is in nearby **Martinière** (36F per 2 people).

Site of the 1968 Winter Olympics, in which native son Jean-Claude Killy swept all three downhill events, Grenoble is the gateway to some of the Alps' most renowned ski resorts. Weekly passes run 500-800F; weekend passes average 90-150F. Ski equipment in most areas rents for 100-160F per day. In summer, weekly passes (120F-150F) provide access to pools, tennis courts, golf courses, and other sporting facilities.

Alpe d'Huez lies at the heart of the Oisans, only 63km from Grenoble (tourist office tel. 76 80 35 41). There is an **auberge de jeunesse** on chemin de la Goutte (tel. 76 80 37 37). For **snow conditions,** call 76 80 34 32; for general information, call 78 58 33 33. Buses run to Alpe d'Huez from Grenoble (4 per day, 2hr., 62F).

Named for the union of two villages on Mont de Lans and Venosc, **Les Deux Alpes** (75km from Grenoble) is also served by bus from Grenoble (3 per day, 2 1/2 hr., 75F). Call the tourist office (tel. 76 79 22 00) for more information. Closer to Grenoble (30km), **Chamrousse** (tourist office tel. 76 89 92 65) in the Belledome mountains is also a major resort. The two **auberges de jeunesse (HI)** (tel. 76 89 91 14 and 76 89 91 31) are both 1.5km away in St-Martin d'Uriage (both open June 15-Aug. 15 and Oct. 14-March 5). **Autrans,** in the Vercors is called the cross-country ski capital of France. The tourist office can be reached at 76 95 30 70.

A less glittery but somewhat more affordable resort is **Villard-de-Lans** (tourist office tel. 76 95 70 38; open Dec.) in the Vercors mountains, accessible by bus from Grenoble.

Chamonix

Just as Nice *is* the Riviera, Chamonix *is* the Alps. Hidden in the valley of the river Arne, the town is propped between the bookend peaks of Le Brévent (2525m) to the west and L'Aiguille du Midi (3842m) to the east. Yet both shrink before the majesty of nearby Mont Blanc, which at 4807m is Europe's highest peak. The town itself (pop. 10,000) seems to exist solely for the exploitation of the mountains—the French national ski team and mountain-climbing school set base here, the first Olympic Winter

Games were held here in 1924, and many of the streets are named after climbers and guides.

Non-Olympians, the aphysical, and the antisocial needn't fear: the slopes yield to the novice as well as to the expert; some 62 lifts and *téléphériques* (cable cars) will fight gravity, taking you to hiking trails that wag their way up the mountain to icy lakes, creeping glaciers, and treacherous snow-covered ridges; and while Chamonix's splendor draws the obligatory buses of tourists, there's plenty of under-populated mountain for everyone.

Orientation and Practical Information

Chamonix consists of both the central town and the complex of nearby villages, scattered between forests and mountains. Les Bossons, Les Pélerins, Les Praz, Les Bois, Les Tines, Lavancher, Les Chosalets, Argentière, Montroc, and Le Tour all spread along the narrow valley. The center of town is the intersection of the three main commercial streets: av. Michel Croz, rue du Docteur Paccard, and rue Joseph Vallot, each named for a past cònqueror of Mont Blanc's summit. The Arve River splits the town in half, with the train station and the most prominent peak, L'Aiguille du Midi, on one side and the tourist office and Le Brévent on the other. From the train station, follow av. Michel Croz straight through town, take a left onto rue du Dr. Paccard, and then follow your first right to the pl. de l'Eglise and the tourist office.

Tourist Office: on pl. du Triangle (tel. 50 53 00 24). Efficient, modern center with lists of hotels and dormitories and a map of campgrounds. Everything in English. Free hotel-finding service. Hotel reservations (tel. 50 53 23 33) require a 30% deposit. Sells the *Carte des Sentiers d'Eté* (hiking map, 22F) and *Chamonix Magazine*. List of the area's *téléphériques* (cable cars) has hours, telephone numbers, and prices. A user-friendly computer system (in French and English) provides on-line telephone numbers and weather conditions. **Currency exchange** on weekends. Open daily 8:30am-7:30pm; Sept.-June 8:30am-12:30pm and 2-7pm.

Currency Exchange: 252, av. de l'Aiguille du Midi, near the *téléphérique*. No commission. Cashes personal checks with American Express card. Open daily 9am-12:30pm and 1-6pm.

Post Office: (tel. 50 53 15 90), on pl. Jacques-Balmat. Wheelchair access. **Telephones,** telex, and **Poste Restante.** Open Mon.-Fri. 8am-7pm, Sat. 8am-noon; Sept.-June Mon.-Fri. 8am-noon and 2-6pm, Sat. 8am-noon. **Postal Code:** 74400.

Trains: av. de la Gare (tel. 50 53 00 44). To Annecy (5 per day, 2hr., 80F); Lyon (6 per day, 4-5hr., 185F); and Paris (5 per day, 7hr., 365F). Information office open daily 9am-noon and 2-6:30pm.

Buses: Société Alpes Transports, at the train station (tel. 50 53 01 15). To: Annecy (2 per day, 2 3/4hr., 90F); Grenoble (1 per day, 3 1/2hr., 142F); Geneva (2 per day, 2hr., 130F to bus station, 165F to airport); Courmayeur, Italy (8 per day, 40min., 48F). Also runs summer excursions.

Public Transportation: Chamonix Bus (tel. 50 53 05 55), on pl. de l'Eglise. Buses go up and down the entire valley to Les Pèlerins, Les Praz, Les Houches, Argentière every 30min. in summer, every 15min. in winter, and every hr. off-season. Tickets 6F. *Carnet* of 6 tickets 33F, *carnet* of 10 50F. Summer excursions to Interlaken and Grindelwald (Tues., 195F), Venice (Fri., 380F), and Zermatt (Sat., 195F). Tours of Lac Leman (Thurs., 160F) and Mont Blanc (Tues. and Fri., 160F).

Taxis: tel. 50 53 13 94. A general dispatch number; ask for **Dick Taxis,** whose drivers speak English and have cars for up to 7 people. Not cheap.

Bike Rental: Le Grand Bi, 240, av. du Bois du Bouchet (tel. 50 53 14 16). 10-speeds 50F per 1/2-day, 60F per day, 350F per week. Mountain bikes 75F per 1/2-day, 100F per day, 600F per week. Open Mon.-Sat. 9am-noon and 2-7pm. **Mountain Bike,** 138, rue des Moulins (tel. 50 53 54 76). High-quality mountain bikes 70F per 1/2-day, 95F per day, 450F per week. Open May-Nov. 9am-7pm.

Hiking Equipment and Ski Rental: Sanglard Sports, 31, rue Michel Croz (tel. 50 53 24 70), in the center of town. One of almost 20 choices. Staff speaks English. Hiking boots 45F per day, mountain climbing boots 70F per day. Ski equipment 100-180F per day. Open daily 9am-12:30pm and 2:30-7:30pm.

Hiking Information: Maison de la Montagne, pl. de l'Eglise next to the church. The **Office de Haute Montagne,** tel. 50 53 22 08, stocks topographic maps (53F), a weather monitor, and a library of hiking and mountaineering guides. Open daily 8:30am-12:30pm and 2:30-6:30pm; Sept.

16-June 14 Mon.-Fri. 8:30am-12:30pm and 2-6pm, Sat. 8:30am-noon. **Compagnie des Guides** (tel. 50 53 00 88), organizes skiing and climbing lessons and leads guided hikes in summer and guided ski trips in winter. Call for prices. **Club Alpin Français,** 136, av. Michel-Croz (tel. 50 53 16 03). Information on mountain refuges and road conditions. Their bulletin board matches drivers, riders, and hiking partners. If you're considering a long stay, membership gets you 50% off all Alpine refuges, insurance, and participation in their skiing and hiking expeditions. Annual membership fees: 420F, ages 18-24 290F, under 18 265F. Open Mon.-Sat. 9am-noon and 3:30-7:30pm; Sept.-June Mon.-Tues. and Thurs.-Fri. 3:30-7pm, Sat. 9am-noon.

English Bookstore: Librairie V.O., 24, av. Ravanel-le-Rouge. Massive English selection (50-90F), including your-and-my favorites, *les guides de Let's Go.* Open Mon.-Sat. 10am-noon and 3-7pm.

Laundromat: Lav'matic, 40, impasse Primevère, left of rue Vallot a few blocks up from the supermarket. Wash 27F, dry 10F per 20min. Soap 2F. Takes 5F and 1F coins. Open daily 8am-8:30pm.

Weather Conditions: Issued 3 times per day by the meteorological office in the Maison de la Montagne. Bulletins in the window of the Pharmacie Mont Blanc at the intersection of av. Croz and rue Vallot and the Club Alpin Français. Call 36 65 02 74 for a recording (in French) of weather and road conditions. Also check tourist office computer. English recording in July and Aug. tel. 50 53 17 11.

Mountain Rescue: PGHM Secours en Montagne, 69, rte. de la Mollard (tel. 50 53 16 89). Accident victims are responsible for all expenses. Register any serious hiking itinerary here. Open 8am-noon and 2-6pm; 24 hr. for emergencies.

Pharmacy: Pharmacie Ferrari, 262, av. de l'Aiguille du Midi (tel. 50 53 40 93), next to the currency exchange. Condom machine outside. Open daily 9am-12:15pm and 2:30-7:15pm.

Medical Assistance: Hôpital de Chamonix (tel. 50 53 04 74), on rue Vallot. **Emergency,** tel. 50 53 02 10. **Ambulance,** tel. 50 54 40 36.

Police: 109, rte. de la Mollard (tel. 50 53 10 97). **Emergency:** tel. 17.

Accommodations and Camping

Mountain chalets with dormitory accommodations combine affordability with splendid settings, but many of them close off-season (Oct.-Nov. and May). All hotels and many dormitories require reservations (preferably 6 weeks in advance) for the hectic school vacations (Dec. and Feb.) but usually have some space January, March, and April. The crowds start coming again in July and early August. If you camp, be prepared for chilly nights, even in summer.

Auberge de Jeunesse (HI), 127, montée Jacques Balmat (tel. 50 53 14 52), in Les Pélerins. Take the bus from pl. de l'Eglise (direction: "Les Houches"), get off at "Pélerins Ecole" (6F), and follow the signs uphill to the hostel. By train, get off at "Les Pélerins" and follow signs. You can also walk—follow rte. des Pélerins until you see signs (25min.). Simple and comfortable. Discounts on all *téléphériques.* Reception open Dec.-Sept. daily 8-10am and 5-10pm, but you can drop your bags off anytime. No curfew. 66F, nonmembers 85F. Breakfast included. Meals 44F. Sheets 16F. Often full in winter; reservations accepted with deposit.

Les Grands Charmoz, 468, chemin de Cristalliers (tel. 50 53 45 57). Comfortable lodgings in a large house. Beautiful People and a 90210-*ish* crowd. Close to town; from the train station, take a right and go under the bridge to the dead end, take a right across the tracks, then a left and walk about 100m to the house. Phone ahead to reserve, then confirm one day before arrival. Nice kitchen and occasional garden barbecue. Dorms 57F per person. Doubles 150F. Triples 205F. Showers and sheets included.

Chamoniard Volant (Chalet le Chamoniard), 45, rte. de la Frasse (tel. 50 53 14 09), 15min. from the town center; follow av. du Bouchet to La Frasse. Run by a young English-speaking French couple. Clientele a veritable global salad bowl. Kitchen facilities. Reception open daily 10am-10pm. No curfew. Chummy co-ed dorms (4-6 per room). 60F per person. Sheets 15F. Continental breakfast 27F.

Gîtes d'Etape: Chalet Ski Station, 6, rte. des Moussoux (tel. 50 53 20 25). Friendly atmosphere. No kitchen but space for cooking if you have a camp stove. Discount on Brévent *téléphérique.* Reception open 8am-11pm. No curfew. 45F per person in crowded dorm. Showers 5F. Sheets 30F. Open June 21-Sept. 19 and Dec. 21-May 14.

La Valaisanne, 454, av. Ravenel-le-Rouge (tel. 50 53 17 98). Follow rue du Dr. Paccard until it becomes av. Ravenel-le-Rouge. Simple, clean singles and doubles 122-136F, with bathroom 230-265F. Showers 15F. Breakfast 25F.

Le Lion d'Or, 255, rue du Dr. Paccard (tel. 50 53 15 09), in the center of town. Large, tastefully decorated rooms. Singles and doubles 170F. Showers included. Breakfast 25F. Restaurant downstairs serves 65F and 95F *menus.*

The tourist office distributes a map and descriptions of the 20 campgrounds in the area. Most have hot showers and refreshingly few trailers. Several lie near the foot of the Aiguille du Midi *téléphérique.* **L'Ile des Barrats,** route des Pélerins (tel. 50 53 51 44), is one of the nicest. From the *téléphérique,* turn left and look to your right (37F per tent; reception open June-Sept. 8am-9pm). **Les Rosières,** 121, clos des Rosières (tel. 50 53 10 42), off route de Praz, is the closest on the other side of Chamonix and often has space (open Dec. 15-Nov. 10). Follow rue Vallot for 2km or take a bus to Les Nants (39F per tent; reception open 8am-9pm). *It is illegal to pitch tents in the Bois du Bouchet.*

The tourist office dispenses a list of more secluded chalets and hotels in smaller, neighboring villages.

Food

Stick to the basics in Chamonix. Anything but fondue will probably break the bank. Luckily, most chalets have kitchens. The well-stocked **Supermarché Payot Pertin,** 117, rue Joseph Vallot, is by far the cheapest place to buy groceries (open Mon.-Sat. 8:15am-7:30pm, Sun. 8:30am-12:15pm). **Markets** take place Saturday mornings at pl. du Mont Blanc and Tuesday mornings in Chamonix Sud, near the foot of the Aiguille du Midi *téléphérique.*

Poco Loco, 45, rue du Dr. Paccard. This self-touted "bar of 101 sandwiches" serves nearly that many (12-38F) and a 59F *menu.* An oasis in the budget desert. Open daily noon-4am. **Brasserie des Sports,** 82, rue Joseph Vallot. Simple food. Simpler prices. Locals like it. *Fondue savoyarde* 48F. *Menus* 57F and 75F. Open Wed.-Mon. noon-2pm and 6:30-9pm; off-season Mon. and Wed.-Sat. noon-2pm and 6:30-9pm.

Le Sabot, 254, rue du Dr. Paccard. Good selection of cuisine in a wooden chalet-type place. Meat 60-69F. Pasta 40F. *Crêpes* 15-40F. Salads 16-40F. 68F *menu.* Open daily noon-2pm and 7-10pm.

Caféteria Grillande, rue Joseph Vallot at the Impasse Primevères. CROUS-esque outfit with a wide variety of salads (8F50) and main courses (beef 42F, veal 38F, spaghetti 26F) at great prices. Open daily 11am-10pm.

Sights and Entertainment

For **hikers,** an intricate web of trails wraps around the town, each clearly marked by lines painted on trees indicating degree of difficulty. The 20F hiking map of this network available at the tourist office, is well worth the investment. Serious climbers should buy the IGN topographic map (53F), available at the Office de Haute Montagne and at local bookstores. The best trail guide is the pricey *Guide Vallot* (55F). The helpful staff in the Office de Haute Montagne can help you plan a day-hike or longer trek. The Compagnie des Guides has daily group hikes. Register the day before between 5:30 and 7:30pm (70F per 1/2-day, 105F per day).

Whatever your skill, a few precautions are in order: bring layers of warm, waterproof clothing and wear sturdy shoes, preferably hiking boots. Be aware that the weather can change extremely quickly. Do not underestimate the length of your hike. The tourist office hiking map gives an estimate of hiking times for most trails. Discuss any serious plans with the Office de Haute Montagne and register the hike with the PGHM Secours en Montagne (see Practical Information), in case a medical emergency should arise. Many beautiful trails begin at the edge of town. *Téléphériques* give you access to the higher trails, but wreak havoc on your budget. A large board in the pl. de l'Eglise reports daily on which *téléphériques* and lifts are open.

One of the more spectacular trails leads up to **Lac Blanc,** a small, turquoise mountain lake dominated by snow-covered peaks. Take a bus (6F) or walk (25min.) along rue Vallot/route de Praz to the town of Les Praz and ride the La Flegère téléphérique (tel. 50 53 18 58; 35F, round-trip 45F; open in summer 8am-5:30pm, last ascent 5pm). From the top of the téléphérique, turn right and climb the steep, well-marked trail for about 90 minutes. The more energetic can begin the hike in Chamonix—take the téléphérique of Le Brévent (tel. 50 53 13 18) up the hill from the tourist office (38F, round-trip 45F), then follow the **Grand Balcon Sud** trail for two hours to the La Flegère téléphérique, and continue up from there.

Still, such puny cable cars pale before the towering **Téléphérique de l'Aiguille du Midi,** which climbs higher than any other in the world. Those with acrophobia (fear of heights) or argentophobia (fear of shelling out big bucks) might avoid the pricey and often frightening ride, which ascends above towering forests and rocky, snow-covered cliffs to the needlepoint peak at the top; as for the brave and well-to-do, however, few are disappointed by the ride. Go early, as clouds and crowds usually gather by mid-morning. Cars leave regularly from the station in South Chamonix. The simplest trip takes you to Plan de l'Aiguille (50F, round-trip 65F), but most people continue through the clouds to the next stage, the Aiguille du Midi, to glimpse a stupendous Alpine panorama. (120F, round-trip 160F from Chamonix; elevator to the summit for a slightly better view 12F.) The round-trip to the summit takes at least one and a half hours. Be aware that the air thins out considerably at the top, and that many people begin to feel faint after several minutes. From the Midi, you can continue to a third stage, Gare Helbronner in Italy (170F, round-trip 240F from Chamonix; take your passport), and if you've got money to burn, you can continue on to the Italian town of Courmayeur. No matter how far up the mountain you go, take warm clothes and expect a wait for the car back down. The Helbronner station is also an approach to rather limited summer skiing. Inquire at the tourist office before you go; most sports stores in Chamonix rent skis. If you aren't yet experiencing the agony of da feet, consider hiking back down to Chamonix from the first level (Plan de l'Aiguille). The strenuous two-hour descent passes through several microclimes; species of flora change from only mosses at the top to evergreens to sparse mountain flowers to deciduous vegetation as you near the town. (Téléphérique open 6am-5pm; Sept.-June 8am-5pm.)

A cheaper but less dazzling alternative is the two-part téléphérique **Brévent** at the north end of town, near La Mollard. The télécabine to Planpraz costs 40F, round-trip 50F, and the téléphérique to Brévent is 50F, round-trip 70F. The walk down from Planpraz is not too strenuous (1 1/2hr.).

One of the more arresting phenomena in Chamonix is the **Mer de Glace,** a glacier which slides 30m per year. Special trains run from a small station next to the main train station (May-Sept. 8am-6pm; 38F, round-trip 50F), but you might prefer the two-hour hike. Accessible via téléphérique (10F) or a short hike, nearby tourist-laden **La Grotte de Glace** is a kitschy cave in which the ice has been carved into a grand piano, a sofa set, and other imaginative shapes. (Admission 11F.)

For a longer excursion, try the celebrated **Tour du Mont Blanc,** a six-day trail that passes through France, Italy, and Switzerland. Refuges are conveniently located about six hours apart. Available for anything from the shortest hike to the most difficult climb, guides are advisable for all but the most expert climbers. The Maison de la Montagne, Compagnie des Guides, and Club Alpin Français (see above) all have information. Many of their guides speak English.

Summertime Chamonix may seem to be a hiker's domain, but the resort has extensive facilities and opportunities for many other activities. **Biking** is an excellent way to see the mountains surrounding Chamonix (see Practical Information for details). There are numerous sports shops around town which lead parachuting and river rafting excursions. For the renaissance athlete, the **Ecole Parapente de Chamonix,** 79, rue Whymper (tel. 50 55 99 49), offers the Multi-Baptême package. For a mere 820F, you can get a parachute jump, a river rafting trip, a half-day of biking, and a river trip on a body board. For 1090F, a bungee jump is added to the package. (Package available May-Aug.; bungee jump July-Aug. only.) There is also an Olympic-size indoor **ice-skating** rink. (Open Thurs.-Tues. 3-6pm, Wed. 3-6pm and 9-11pm. Admission 20F. Skate rental 15F.) Chamonix has its own 18-hole golf course, tennis club, and hydroglisse school for shooting down the Arve on canoe or raft. Rent at **Centre Sportif,** promenade du Fori (tel. 50 53 55 70; open May 15-Oct. 15.). Fulfill your Olympic fantasies on **La Luge d'Eté** (tel. 50 53 08 97), which sends flattened human cannonballs down two concrete *pistes* behind the gare du Montenoers. (Open July-Aug. daily 10am-7:30pm; June and Sept. daily 10am-noon and 1:30-6pm; May and Oct.-Nov. Sat.-Sun. 1:30-6pm. Admission 27F50 or 110F for five.)

Add a dash (but just a dash) of culture to your athletic potpourri. The **Musée Alpin,** off av. Michel Croz (tel. 50 53 25 93), displays paintings and photographs of Mont Blanc from every conceivable angle. (Open June-Sept. daily 2-7pm; Christmas-Easter daily 3-7pm. Admission 15F.)

Winter in Chamonix challenges even the best skiers, but novices won't feel out of place. You can buy a day pass on one *téléphérique* (in La Flegère 100F per day) or a ski pass, which allows you access to *téléphériques* up and down the valley (2-day ski pass 310F, 3-day 455F, 1-week 930F). Unfortunately, you often have to take the shuttle bus from one *téléphérique* to another. Over 20 shops in Chamonix rent skis.

Indulge in a little *après-ski* at **La Choucas,** 206, rue Docteur Paccard (tel. 50 53 03 23), a popular place with a bistro-café club atmosphere and a large video screen usually showing mountaineering and ski movies. (No cover. Open daily 5pm-1am.) There are also four discos in town. **Le Refuge,** 269, rue Paccard (tel. 50 53 00 94) is closest to town. (Open nightly 10:30pm-dawn; cover 60F, women free on Thurs.)

Annecy

With its winding cobblestone streets, overstuffed flower boxes, turreted castle, and clear mountain lake, relentlessly photogenic Annecy recalls those high school homecoming queens whom everyone resented for their perfection but fell in love with anyway. Despite the efforts of envious rivals, Annecy (pop. 50,000) always comes in first. This capital of the Haute Savoie won the 1989 prize for the cleanest city in France, consistently claimed the title in the National Flower City contest (now out of competition), and carefully guards its reputation for having the purest lake in Europe. This beauty even had a sitting with Cézanne, whose *Le Lac d'Annecy* may provide admirers with their only daytime glimpse of the lake free of the dense flotilla of sailboats and windsurfers that now flit over its crystalline waters.

Orientation and Practical Information

Frequent trains link Annecy to Chambéry, Lyon, Grenoble, and Paris. Most activity centers on the lake, southeast of the train station. The canal runs east to west through the old town, leaving the elevated château on one side and the main shopping area on the other, closer to the *centre ville*. To reach the tourist office, follow rue Sommeiller from the station for one block, turn right and then left onto rue Vaugelas. The tourist office will be on your left, inside the greenhouse-style *Bonlieu* shopping mall.

Tourist Office: 1, rue Jean Jaurès (tel. 50 45 00 33), at pl. de la Libération on the ground floor of the *bonlieu.* Free, detailed maps. Information on hiking, hotels, campgrounds, rural lodgings, excursions to nearby towns, and mountain climbing. Guided tours (30F) daily at 10am and 3pm in summer (in English on Tues. at 2:30pm). Ask for the helpful *Le Guide Pratique d'Annecy.* Open daily 9am-6:30pm; Oct.-May 9am-noon and 1:45-6:30pm.

Currency Exchange: Bureau de Change, 2, pl. Ste-Claire (tel. 50 45 59 97), in the *vieille ville.* Open daily 10am-noon and 2-7pm.

Post Office: 4, rue des Glières (tel. 50 45 10 19), around the corner from rue de la Poste, down the street from the train station. **Currency exchange** on the ground floor and **telephones** in the basement. Open Mon.-Fri. 8am-7pm, Sat. 8am-noon. **Postal Code:** 74000.

Trains: (tel. 50 66 50 50), on pl. de la Gare. To: Grenoble (9 per day, 2hr., 73F); Aix-les-Bains (every hr., 15min., 34F); Chambéry (10 per day, 45min., 41F); Chamonix (8 per day, 2-2 1/2hr., 80F); Lyon (8 per day, 2hr., 102F); Paris (by TGV 8 per day, 4 1/2hr., 287F with required reservation; 1 night train per day, 6-8hr.); and Nice (4 per day, 6hr., 308F). Information office open Mon.-Sat. 8:15am-7:15pm, Sun. 9am-7:15pm. Station open daily 5am-11:30pm.

Buses: Adjacent to the train station. **Voyages Crolard,** tel. 50 45 08 12. To: La Clusaz (4-7 per day, 1 1/4hr., 31F); Chamonix (1 per day, none Sun., 2 1/2hr., 75F). Also runs several summer excursions.

Public Transportation: SIBRA, tel. 50 51 70 33. Tickets 6F20, *carnet* of 8 31F20, students 23F20. Get a bus map and schedule from the tourist office or the kiosk on rue de la Préfecture. Open Mon.-Sat. 8:30am-7pm.

Bike Rental: Loca Sports, 37, av. de Loverchy (tel. 50 45 44 33), 10min. from the *centre ville.* 10-speeds 50F per day, mountain bikes 100F per day; lower rates for longer rentals. Also at the **train station.** 42F per 1/2-day, 50F per day; 500F deposit.

Hiking Information: Club Alpin Français, 38, av. du Parmelan (tel. 50 45 52 76), at rue de Mortillet. Information on mountain activities and organized group trips. Open Wed. 3-7pm, Fri. 5:30-7pm, Sat. 10am-noon.

Laundromat: Lav Plus, 10, av. de Chambéry. Wash 25F, dry 2F per 6min. Soap 2F. Open daily 8am-8pm.

Women's Center: Centre d'Information Féminine et Familial de Haute-Savoie, 4, Passage de la Cathédrale (tel. 50 45 61 25). English spoken. Open Mon.-Fri. 9am-noon and 2-4pm.

Hospital: av. des Trésums (tel. 50 88 33 33).

Medical Assistance: SAMU, tel. 50 51 21 21.

Police: 15, rue des Marquisats (tel. 50 45 21 61). **Emergency:** tel. 17.

Accommodations and Camping

Annecy's prices confirm its popularity. Try the Maison des Jeunes, the hostel, or one of the many small campgrounds. Reservations are highly recommended; call far in advance for high season and festival weekends.

Maison des Jeunes et de la Culture (MJC), 52, rue des Marquisats (tel. 50 45 08 80), on the lake, a 10-min. walk from *centre ville.* A modern building among the pines. Gorgeous view. Comfortable rooms. TV and recreation areas. No curfew. 6-bed dorm rooms 54F per person. Singles 110F. Doubles with shower and toilet 80F per person. Showers and sheets included. Breakfast 18F. Cafeteria meals 55F. Call Mon.-Fri. 9am-3pm for reservations as far in advance as possible.

Auberge de Jeunesse "La Grande Jeanne" (HI), 16, rte. de Semnoz (tel. 50 45 33 19). Take the bus marked "Semnoz" across the street from the *hôtel de ville* (6F20). A quiet chalet in the woods with basic dorm accommodations (4-6 per room). Reception open 5-10pm. No curfew. Members only. 56F. Breakfast included. Off-season: 30F. Breakfast 16F. Sheets 16F all year.

Hôtel Savoyard, 41, av. de Cran (tel. 50 57 08 08), in a residential neighborhood behind the train station. The managers define hospitality. Clean, comfortable rooms. Large singles and doubles 100F, with luxurious bathroom 170F. Triples 140F. Showers 10F. Breakfast 20F. Open May.-Nov.

Hôtel du Château, 16, rampe du Château (tel. 50 45 27 66), up a winding ramp, near the castle in a secluded part of the old town. Perfect location. Old-fashioned stone building with flowers and spectacular views. Singles and doubles 150F, with shower 180F. Triples 170F, with shower 250F. Showers 10F. Breakfast 24F. Reserve early. Closed Oct. 16-Dec. 14.

Rive du Lac, 6, rue des Marquisats (tel. 50 51 32 85). A fine location near the lake and *centre ville.* Large, sunny singles 120F. Doubles and triples from 162F, some with fancy French windows and small balconies. Showers 15F. Breakfast 21F. You can never reserve too early.

Hôtel des Alpes, 12, rue de la Poste (tel. 50 45 04 56). Centrally located near the train station. Small and comfortable, though some rooms are noisy. Singles 105-160F. Doubles from 200-250F. Showers 15F. Breakfast 25F.

Dozens of small **campgrounds** border the lake in the town of **Albigny,** which can be reached by Voyages Crolard buses or by following av. d'Albigny from the tourist office. The larger **Belvedere,** route de Semnoz (tel. 50 45 48 30), on the same road as the hostel, is closer and usually packed. The adjacent food store sells basics at reasonable prices. (Closed Oct. 16-Dec. 14.)

Food

Annecy has few inexpensive restaurants; lakeside picnics are probably the only budget options. Fill your basket at the **markets** on Tuesday, Friday, and Sunday mornings around pl. Ste-Claire, and Saturday morning on bd. Taine. The town has lots of small grocery stores, and a **Prisunic supermarket** fills the better part of the pl. de Notre Dame. (Open Mon.-Sat. 8:30am-12:15pm and 2:15-7pm.)

Taverne du Freti, 12, rue Ste-Claire. A find for those fond of fondue. *Fondue savoyarde* and many other varieties 52-92F. *Raclette* 57F. Salads 18-34F. Open Tues.-Sat. 7-11:30pm, Sun. 7-10:30pm.

Au Lilas Rose, passage de l'Evêché. Prize location in *vieille ville.* Everything from *fondue savoyarde* (61F per person) to lamb cutlets with fries (69F) to pizza (38-49F). A unique "do-it-yourself" meat dish which you cook on hot stones and eat with vegetables and lettuce (95F per person). Open daily 11:45am-2:30pm and 6:45-11pm.

Au Bord du Thiou, 4, pl. St-François-de-Sales. Scenic location on the canal near the Palais de l'Ile. Terrific choice for salads (16-38F), *crêpes* (from 18F50), and ice cream. The unusual "*crêpe* Rock" includes Roquefort cheese, nuts, raisins, and cognac (28F). Open daily noon-2pm and 5pm-midnight.

Le Cellier, 7, rue Perrière, in the heart of the old town. Less expensive than its neighbors. Pizza 35-52F. *Plat du jour* 40F. Open daily noon-2pm and 6:30-11pm.

La Matalan, quai de l'Evêque. Join the lively crowd sitting outside, along the canal. Numerous tasty *savoyarde* specialities (65-85F); plate of *savoyarde* cheeses 18F. *Fondue savoyarde* 65F.

Sights and Entertainment

To capture the awesome beauty and tranquility of Annecy at its most sublime, awake at dawn and watch the motionless fishermen in their rowboats scattered throughout the mist-covered lake. By mid-morning, the lake surrenders to sailboats, windsurfers, and swimmers. Along the public garden of the **Champs de Mars,** you can rent windsurfers (90F per hr.), canoes and kayaks (60F per 2hr.), sailboats, pedal boats, motor-launches, and small outboard boats (105-180F per hr.). You have to pay 15F to swim at the glamorous **Impérial plage,** but there is a free beach, the **plage des Marquisats,** across from the MJC. Continue past the *centre ville* to escape the crowds. **La Compagnie des Bateaux,** 6, pl. aux Bois (tel. 50 51 08 40), at the quai Napoléon III, conducts various cruises which all dock frequently for photo breaks. (1-hr. cruise: 5-6 per day, 50F, ages 5-14 40F. 1 1/2-hr. cruise 61F, ages 5-14 50F. Mealtime cruises 168F.)

In the *vieille ville,* follow the swans along the canal du Thiou and past the baroque locks, to the formidable **Palais de l'Ile,** a 12th-century prison rising out of a tiny island. For a panorama of the old town's aquatic labyrinth, climb up to the **Château d'Annecy** (tel. 50 45 29 66). In addition to a folklore collection, the château houses an ongoing series of expositions. (Open daily 10am-noon and 2-6pm; Sept.-June Wed.-Mon. 10am-noon and 2-6pm. Admission 15F, students 10F. Free Wed. Sept.-May.)

The **Fête du Lac** enlivens the first Saturday in August with fireworks and water shows (admission 45-190F). Each year the floats on the lake take on different themes; "Monsters and Legends," "Adventures in the Far West," and "Beyond the Planet Earth" have featured in the past. The **Festival de la Vieille Ville** in mid-July features free concerts, street and church performances, and a few big-time musical events.

Near Annecy

Ten km from Annecy, waterfalls roar over the scarred cliffs of the **Gorges du Fier,** a canyon carved by prehistoric glaciers. (Open March 15-Oct. 15 daily 9am-6pm. Admission a steep 22F for the 40-min. walk. Call 50 46 23 07 for more information.) The medieval **Château de Montrottier** (tel. 50 46 23 02) lies five minutes up the hill from the entrance to the gorges. The castle contains centuries-old East Asian costumes, armor, and pottery. (Open Easter-Oct. 15 daily 9-11:30am and 2-5:30pm. Obligatory, informative tour 25F; students 20F.) To get to the gorges and the château, take the Voyages Crolard (tel. 50 45 09 12) excursion bus (Wed., 2:45pm, 87F). Alternatively, take the train to **Lovagny** and then walk the 800m to the gorges (3 per day stop at Lovagny at odd hours, 10min., 10F); or take bus A to the end of the line at Poisy and walk the 4km to Lovagny and the château.

Ask at the Annecy tourist office for a guide to hikes around the lake. **La Forêt du Cret du Maure,** next to the Parc Regional du Semnoz (near the youth hostel), is peaceful, flowery, and fragrant. **Talloires,** 13km from Annecy, makes a good starting point for hikes to **La Cascade d'Angon** (1hr.) and to the beautiful gardens of the **Ermitage de St-Germain** (45min.). Ask at the tourist office about the spectacular boat ride from Annecy to Talloires.

The lakeside towns of **St-Jorioz, Dousard, Menthon-St-Bernard** (birthplace of St-Bernard, founder of the famed Hospices), and **Duingt** (beloved of Cézanne), are all within 20km of Annecy and accessible by bus. (Check with **Voyages Crolard** excursions; 2-3 per day in high seasons, 50-72F.) The tourist office in Annecy distributes brochures describing their main attractions. All offer a smorgasbord of swimming, hiking, tennis, and nightlife.

In winter, hotel prices drop and the skiers pour in. The nearest ski resort is **La Clusaz** (accessible by bus). Contact the **tourist office** in La Clusaz (tel. 50 02 60 92; **postal code** 74220) for information. The **Auberge de Jeunesse Chalet "Marcoret" (HI)** (tel. 50 02 41 73), has dorm rooms for 45F. (Reception open 7-10am and 6-10pm. No curfew. Ask for key after 10pm. Showers included. Breakfast 16F.) Voyages Crolard goes to La Clusaz for 32F50.

Aix-les-Bains

Unlike the rest of inland France, water, and not wine, is the lifeblood of Aix-les-Bains, a small (pop. 25,000) town in a fertile Alpine valley. Aix's precious fluid gathers in two places. The first is the expansive **Lac du Bourget,** France's largest natural lake, which is scenic enough to have inspired La Martine, yet rugged enough to attract scores of waterskiers, windsurfers, and sailors. The second comprises the warm thermal baths which give the town its name, first enjoyed by the Romans, and now the mecca of an older, monied crowd, who flock here like so many Ponce de Léons, searching out personal fountains of youth. If nothing else, the baths will cure a bulging pocketbook. Fortunately, you don't have to be ill (or wealthy) to visit Aix-les-Bains.

Orientation and Practical Information

Aix-les-Bains lies 10 minutes north of Chambéry on the Lyon-St-Gervais train line. The center of town is up the hill from the train station; the **lake** and **beach** are a 20-minute walk in the opposite direction. From the station, take bus #2 to the beach (every 15min., last bus 8pm, 7F). To reach the tourist office and the center of town, follow av. Général de Gaulle (directly in front of the train station) and turn left before the Thermes Nationaux. The **tourist office,** pl. Maurice Mollard (tel. 79 35 05 92) distributes free maps and flaunts an automated city map *(robhotel)* which gives information about hotel locations and vacancy. It also leads occasional tours of the town in French; ask for times and prices. (Open Mon.-Sat. 8:30am-12:30pm and 1:30-7pm, Sun. 9am-12:30pm and 3-6:30pm; Oct.-April Mon.-Sat. 8:30am-noon and 1:30-6:30pm, Sun. 9am-noon and 3-6pm.) The **post office** is on av. Victoria at av. Maris de Solms (tel. 79 33 15 15) and houses a **currency exchange;** the **postal code** is 73100. (Open Mon.-Fri. 8am-7pm, Sat. 8am-noon.) **Trains** leave almost hourly for Chambéry (10min., 14F); Annecy (45min., 34F); Grenoble (1 1/4hr., 52F); and Geneva (every 2-3hr., 1 3/4hr., 86F). The **hospital** is on bd. Pierpont-Morgan (tel. 79 88 61 61); **police** can be reached at 79 35 61 98.

Accommodations, Camping, and Food

Securing information on hotel prices and vacancy is easy in Aix-Les-Bains. Simply pick up a copy of the large blue *Guide Aix-Les-Bains* at the tourist office, which lists all the hotels in town, including their prices. Then go outside the tourist office, or outside the train station on your right, and look at the automatic, 24-hour *Robhotel* electronic map. Two streets—**Bd. Wilson,** where the station is, and **av. du Tresserve,** 3 blocks to the right of the station, pack cheap one- and two-star hotels (singles 90-110; doubles 150-200F). Make reservations for all hotels in July and August.

Auberge de Jeunesse (HI), promenade de Sierroz (tel. 79 88 32 88). Take bus #2 to the left of the station and get off at the "Camping" stop. The 30-min. walk from the *centre ville* is enjoyable if you take a short-cut along the stream *(le Sierroz).* Comfortable, modern hostel; façade looks a lot like an orange Batman mask. Volleyball out back. Large TV room and pool table. Four minutes from the lake. Reception open 7-10am and 6-10pm. No curfew; key available for those out after 10pm. Members only. Spacious 6-bed dorm rooms 44F per person. Showers included. Breakfast 16F. Dinner 43F. Sheets 16F. Open all year. Rents mountain bikes at 70F per 1/2-day, 100F per day.

Hôtel Angleterre, 22, av. Victoria (tel. 79 35 03 59), 2 blocks up from the train station. Caw blimey! Clean, comfy rooms. Affable owners. Singles 90F, with shower 100F. Doubles 120F, with shower 180F. Showers 10F. Breakfast 23F. Open March 15-Nov. 30.

Avenue Hôtel, 16, av. du Grand Port (tel. 79 35 24 63). Just outside the center on the continuation of rue de Genève. Small, clean rooms. Singles 100F, with shower 125F, with shower and toilet 135F. Breakfast 20F.

Touring Hôtel, 17, av. de Tresserve (tel. 79 88 99 18). From the station turn right on bd. Wilson and left on av. de Tresserve (5min.). Simple, quiet singles 110F. Doubles 150F. Showers 10F. Breakfast 15F. Open May-Oct.

Camping: Camping Municipal Sierroz (tel. 79 61 21 43), conveniently located across from the lake about 2km from the station and just down the street from the youth hostel. Large. Showers, grocery store, and volleyball. Reception open daily 8am-noon and 3-7pm. 13F per person, 25F per tent. Electricity 12F. Prices slightly lower Oct.-Nov. 15 and March 15-May. Reservations required in advance July-Aug. Open March 15-Nov. 15.

The *centre ville* abounds with restaurants and sandwich shops. **Restaurant La Régence,** 33, bd. Wilson, has numerous *menus* from 52F to 115F, as well as a tasty *plat du jour* (rotates between fish, chicken, and meat) for a mere 40F. (Open daily noon-11pm; full meals not served 2-6pm.) On the road to the lake and the hostel is **Le Sporting,** 58, rue de Genève, which has a vast array of culinary delights including the requisite *fondue savoyard* (60F). (Open Tues.-Sun. noon-2pm and 6-10:30pm). For picnic supplies, a large **market** fills pl. Clemenceau on Wednesdays and Saturdays. There is a **Prisunic** supermarket at 17, rue de Genève. (Open Mon.-Fri. 8:30am-12:15pm and 2:30-7pm.)

Sights and Entertainment

The **Thermes Nationaux,** Aix-les-Bains's *raison d'être,* give tours of the modern baths followed by a descent underground to see the remains of the ancient Roman ones. Outside, visit the grottoes and the sinus-clearing sulphur springs. Tours leave from opposite the tourist office on pl. Maurice-Mollard. (Mon.-Sat. at 3pm; Oct.-April Wed. and Sat. at 3pm, or call 79 35 38 50 for an appointment. Admission 10F.) Treatments in the baths involve mud, mineral water, massages, and money. An underwater massage runs 60-100F. (Reservations recommended July-Aug.) The **Musée Faure,** bd. des Côtes (tel. 76 61 06 57), atop a hill overlooking the town and the lake beyond, diverts spirits sodden by bath water with works by Sisley, Pissarro, Renoir, Cézanne, and Rodin. (Open Wed.-Mon. 10am-noon and 2-6pm. Admission 15F.) Check out and outcheck the locals at the oversize **chess** board on the corner of rue Davat and rue des Bains, across from the Thermes and next to the Hôtel de Ville; it measures 2m x 2m, with 1/2m-high pieces. (Free.)

Aix has three free beaches in addition to its **Centre Nautique,** which has a swimming pool right on the beach (20F, under 18 13F). Rent boats and windsurfers from several agencies along the shore. Weather permitting, the Centre Nautique also makes waterskiing available (70F per 5min. ride, *carnet* of 10 rides 500F).

One of the best excuses to stay overnight in Aix-les-Bains is the morning excursion to the **Abbaye d'Hautecombe.** Gregorian chants emanate from this Benedictine abbey, completely restored in the 19th century and now sheltering the tombs of the Princes of Savoie. (Free. Donations appreciated.) A boat for the abbey plies twice daily from

Aix's Grand Port (4hr., 45F). A special Sunday trip to attend mass at the abbey leaves at 8:30am. Call 79 88 92 09 for more information. Other water excursions include a two-hour trip to the southern end of the lake (July-Aug., 45F).

The village of **Le Revard,** a 20-minute bus ride from Aix, is surrounded by an extensive network of trails for hiking and cross-country skiing, flanked by Lac du Bourget on one side and Mont Blanc on the other. Buses leave from the kiosk in the Parc de Verdure. For information call **Gonnet Excursions** (tel. 79 35 21 74). You can also make the two-hour hike up to Le Revard. The well-marked trail starts at the base of the Les Mentens *téléphérique* in **Mouxy,** 4km east of Aix-les-Bains.

Aix hosts a variety of (mostly free) summer concerts in the **Théâtre de Verdure.** Larger concerts take place at the Palais du Congrès and the Esplanade du Lac. For two or three days in the last week of August, Aix mounts a lakeside **Fête des Fleurs** (Flower Festival), with fireworks, singing, and the proverbial good, clean fun. The town also presents a three-opera **Opera Festival** (tel. 79 88 09 99) in July.

At night, activity centers around the brash, pink art-deco **Casino,** just west of the Thermes Nationales. Or putter away the night at the **miniature golf** course next door (open daily 4pm-midnight, 20F). The rue du Casino is full of overpriced nightclubs, but **Pub 31,** 31, rue du Casino, has a friendly ambience and 80 different types of beer.

Chambéry

Chambéry presents an excellent opportunity to see Savoie in an atmosphere relatively untainted by the bunches of tourists attracted to the lakes of Annecy and Aix-Les-Bains or the mountains of Val d'Isère and Chamonix. The magnificent château of the dukes of Savoie, which was the region's capital for centuries, stands watch over a pleasant and picturesque *vieille ville* whose parks and fountains add to the subtle splendor of the town. Chambéry's charms were sung by Rousseau in his *Confessions,* and a house where he frolicked with Mme. de Warens remains, along with an impressive art museum, one of the town's main attractions. A short 10 minutes from Aix-Les Bains and only an hour from Grenoble, Chambéry makes an excellent daytrip from either, as well as a good starting point for forays into the Alps.

Orientation and Practical Information

All east-west trains between Bourg St. Maurice and Lyon, as well as all North-South trains from Grenoble to Aix-les-Bains, pass through Chambéry. The *centre ville* is concentrated in an area south of the train station, with the château and *vieille ville* in the southwest corner. To reach the tourist office from the station, walk left for one long block, then cross pl. du Centenaire to bd. de la Colonne.

Tourist Office: 24, bd. de la Colonne (tel. 79 33 42 47). Wheelchair access from the other side at 19, av. des Ducs de Savoie. English-speaking staff dispenses reams of pamphlets on the city and region. Bi-monthly *15 jours à Chambéry* (free) lists activities. Open Mon.-Sat. 9am-noon and 2-6pm. **Association Départementale de Tourisme de la Savoie** 24, bd. de la Colonne (tel. 79 85 12 45), in the same building. Information on Savoie, including hotels, campgrounds, and ski resorts. Open Mon.-Sat. 9am-noon and 2-6pm.

Post Office: (tel. 79 69 10 69), on pl. Paul Vidal. **Telephones** and **currency exchange.** Open Mon.-Fri. 8am-7pm, Sat. 8am-noon. **Postal Code:** 73000.

Trains: (tel. 79 85 50 50; reservations 79 62 35 26), on pl. de la R. Sommeiller. Trains at least every hour to: Lyon (1 1/2-2hr., 75F) and Grenoble (1-2hr., 49F). To: Annecy (12 per day, 45min., 43F); Geneva (8 per day, 1 1/2hr., 72F); Paris via Lyon (5 1/2hr., 300F). Information office open Mon.-Sat. 8am-12:20pm and 1:30-6:20pm.

Buses: pl. de la R. Sommeiller, across from the train station. Many companies share this central depot. **VFD,** tel. 79 69 28 78. All other companies, call 79 69 11 88. Annecy (8 per day, 1hr., 40F); Grenoble (6 per day, 1hr., 44F).

Public Transportation: STAC, bd. de la Colonne (tel. 79 69 61 12). Efficient bus service run daily 7:30am-7pm and covers the entire town. Has buses to Les Charmettes (Mon., Thurs., Fri., Sat., 2:25pm) and the Lac du Bourget (Mon.-Sat. 2:20pm and 4:05pm) from the train station. All rides 6F20, *carnet* of 10 32F20, 22F90 for students.

Taxi: tel. 79 33 39 14. 24 hrs.

Bike Rental: Cycles Peugeot, 20, rue Jean-Pierre Veyrat, on the edge of the *centre ville.* Mountain bikes 80F per day, 450F per week. Open Tues.-Sat. 8am-noon and 2-7pm.

Hiking Information: Club Alpin Français, 70, rue Croix d'Or (tel. 79 33 05 52). Advice on hiking and mountaineering in the area. Open Tues.-Fri. 5:30-7:30pm, Sat. 10am-noon.

English Bookstore: Librairie Garin, bd. du Théâtre (tel. 79 33 53 64), a block east of the tourist office. Limited English books in the high-school section; *Let's Go: France* available—the perfect gift for that special someone. Open Mon. 2-7pm, Tues.-Sat. 9am-noon and 2-7pm.

Youth Information Center: Centre d'Information et de Documentation Jeunesse (CIDJ), 4, pl. de la Gare (tel. 79 62 66 87), across from the train station. Information on sports, hostels, and *foyers.* Bulletin board posts rides, jobs, baby-sitting, and housing information. BIJ/Transalpino tickets. Open Mon.-Fri. 9am-noon and 2-6pm.

Laundromat: 1, rue Doppet, next to the Musée des Beaux Arts. Wash 18F, dry 2F per 5min. Soap 2F. Open daily 7:30am-8pm.

Pharmacy: Pharmacie Dufour, 4, rue Sommeiller (tel. 79 33 64 16), 100m to the left of the train station. Condom machine outside (10F). As elsewhere, the list of all-night pharmacies is posted on pharmacy doors. Open Mon.-Sat. 8am-noon and 2-7pm.

Hospital: Centre Hospitalier, pl. François-Chiron (tel. 79 62 93 70).

Medical Emergency: SAMU, tel. 79 69 25 25.

Police: 585, av. de la Boisse (tel. 79 96 17 17). **Emergency:** tel. 17.

Accommodations and Camping

Budget hotels in Chambéry are as cheap as hostels in other towns, and always nice, clean, and centrally located. There are no campgrounds in the immediate vincinity; the closest is in Aix-les-Bains.

Hôtel le Maurennais, 2, rue Ste-Barbe (tel. 79 69 42 78), in the shadow of the château. The cheapest hotel in town. Simple, clean rooms with sink and brown-flower wallpaper. Ever seen a brown flower? One more reason to stay here. Singles 65F. Doubles 95-130F.

Hôtel du Château, 37, rue Jean-Pierre-Veyrat (tel. 79 69 48 78). It's near the castle. Duh. And you know what else: it's clean and simple. Singles 80F. Doubles 100F. Triples 150F. Quads 170F. Showers included. Breakfast 22F.

Hôtel Home Savoyard, 15, pl. St-Léger (tel. 79 33 47 80). Sparingly spacious set-up with sinks, sheets, and showers. All rooms with telephones, some with TV. Singles 135-200F. Doubles 160-270F. Breakfast 25F. Extra bed 70F.

Hôtel de la Banche, 10, pl. de l'Hôtel de Ville (tel. 79 33 15 62). Small, half-timbered house which will have you singing "Edelweiss" in no time. Singles 130F. Doubles 220F. Triples 300F. Showers included. Breakfast 25F.

Food

Cheap pizzerias, *crêperies,* and sandwich shops are scattered throughout the *vieille ville,* making budget meals rather easy to find. For more refined cuisine at low prices, try **Grill aux Piétons,** 30, pl. Monge, whose excellent steaks (60-70F) and *menus* (65-100F) are far from pedestrian. (Open Tues.-Sun. noon-2pm and 6-10:30pm). Alternately, try **La Bodega,** 18, rue Jean-Pierre Veyrat, for excellent fish (5 varieties, 70F) and pasta dishes (37-45F). (Open daily 7pm-midnight.) To mingle with the locals over a great meal and freindly service, head to **La Poterne,** 3, pl. Maché, at the entrance to the château. *Menus* at 52F (lunch only) and 68F; *fondue savoyarde* 70F. (Open Mon. 11:30am-2pm, Tues.-Sat. 11:30am-2pm and 7pm-midnight.) **Les Halles** on pl. de Genève house a covered market on Tuesday, Thursday, and Saturday (6am-noon). A

Prisunic supermarket lays in wait on the corner of rue de Boigne and pl. du 8 mai (open Mon.-Sat. 8:15am-12:10pm and 2:15-7pm).

Sights and Entertainment

For six centuries, independent Savoie's power emanated from the imposing **Château des Ducs de Savoie,** built on an artificial hill in the 13th century. The château's last prominent master was King Vittorio Emmanuele II, who presided over Italy's unification. Enter through the majestic 15th-century Porte de l'Eglise St-Dominique. Repainted in *trompe l'oeil* in the 19th century, **Ste-Chapelle** had been partially destroyed in a 16th-century fire. The frequent invasions by French kings eventually convinced the Duke of Savoie to transfer the capital, and Jesus' alleged burial cloth (housed in the chapel in the 16th century) to Turin, Italy, where the Holy Shroud remains today. (Obligatory 1-hr. tours July-Aug. 5 per day; June and Sept. 2 per day; March-May and Oct.-Nov. Sat. at 2:15pm, Sun. at 3:30pm. Admission 20F, students 10F.) From July 25 to August 19 the château presents a short play, *Confessions d'un Chambérien,* complete with authentic 18th-century costumes and dialogue from Rousseau's *Confessions* (Sat. at 9pm, 40F, reserve at tourist office).

Stroll through Vieux Chambéry and admire the Italian-influenced *hôtels particuliers* on rue Croix-d'Or and pl. St-Léger. The tourist office has a list of the city's most interesting mansions. (Tours of the old city leave from pl. du Château June-Sept. daily at 4pm; March-May and Oct.-Nov. Sat. only at 4pm. Admission 25F, students 15F.) The **Fontaine des Eléphants**—the best-known monument in Chambéry—serves as a good compass for discovering the city's other sites. Erected in 1838 to honor Count de Boigne, the elephants' trunks still spout occasional showers. North of this aquatic stampede in place du Palais de Justice is the **Musée des Beaux Arts** (tel. 79 33 44 48), home to the second-largest collection of Italian paintings in France (after the Louvre). Alongside such Italian masters as Titian, Tintoretto, and Lorenzo Lutto hangs a not insignificant French collection, including works by Watteau and Fragonard, and a smaller Dutch collection. The gallery is on the building's third floor. (Open Wed.-Mon. 10am-noon and 2-6pm. Free.) The **Musée Savoisien** (tel. 79 33 44 48), south of the pachyderms on bd. du Théâtre in an old Franciscan convent contains an extensive archeological collection, including pottery and jewelry, exhibits on Chambéry's history, and fragments of the beautiful 13th-century mural painting of Cruet. (Open Wed.-Mon. 10am-noon and 2-6pm. Free.)

Garden spots in the center of town include the **Jardins du Verney;** the **Clos Savoiroux,** with its famous statue of Rousseau; and the **Parc des Loisirs de Buisson Rond,** with its fine rose garden and swimming pool. For ten days in September, the **Foire de Savoie** raises local spirits, and in early October, a series of small festivals brightens the town.

Two km out of town on the uphill chemin des Charmettes stands the **Musée des Charmettes** (tel. 79 33 39 44), the house where Jean-Jacques Rousseau cohabited in vice and debauchery with Mme. de Warrens. The interior has been reconstructed and now displays Rousseau memorabilia; the pretty, vine-covered garden looks out onto a splendid view of Chambéry and the surrounding mountains. From pl. Monge, take av. de la République to rue J.J. Rousseau to chemin des Charmettes; follow the mountain stream (uphill of course) until you run out of breath. The museum is just a little further. (Open Wed.-Mon. 10am-noon and 2-6pm; Oct.-March Wed.-Mon. 10am-noon and 2-4:30pm. Admission 10F.)

Near Chambery: Albertville and Bourg St-Maurice

The snow on the slopes has settled, the crowds in the rink have quieted, and the locals have timidly taken back their city. The 1992 Winter Olympics have passed, and Albertville is a town destined to live in the past. While the town offered the Olympic athletes easy access to surrounding sports facilities, it offers the average tourist very little. Perhaps its only attractions are across the river in the town of **Conflans,** a charming medieval village with twisting cobblestone streets and tiny arched passages. Ask the tourist office for a copy of an English guide to the town, which points out the major attractions. Especially worth seeing are the **Château de Manuel de Locatel** (daily tours July-Aug. at 3pm and 4:30pm, 7F; at other times call 79 32 04 22 to arrange a visit), and the vine-covered park next to the **Tour Sarrasine,** which enjoys a decent view of the surrounding mountains and the not-so-picturesque valley. The **Musée Municipal de Conflans** displays a collection of archeological findings, pottery, and regional furniture. Most interesting is the room of wooden skis and cannonballs used in the 1600 siege of Conflans by Henry IV.

Similarly bland **Bourg St-Maurice** has pristine mountain scenery and little else. Unless, of course, you've been staying up nights wondering how Beaufort cheese is made; the **Cooperative Latière,** pl. de Castex (tel. 79 07 04 47), next to the tourist office, will have you dozing soundly in no time. (Open daily 9:30am-noon to visit *caves,* guided tours Wed. 9:30am. Store open Mon.-Fri. 8:30am-12:15pm and 3-7:15pm, Sat. 8am-7:15pm, Sun. 9am-noon.)

Bourg St-Maurice has the added attraction of the **Auberge de Jeunesse Seez-les-Arcs (HI)** (tel. 79 41 01 93; fax 79 41 03 36), in a secluded forest 5km from Bourg-St-Maurice. Take the bus toward Val d'Isère from Bourg-St-Maurice (las bus at 4:30pm in summer, 7F); ask to get off at the "Longefoy" stop, 2km past Seez. It is stuffed to the brim December to April and July-August. Call far in advance. Friendly atmosphere and minuscule 6-bed dorms. (Members only. 62F. Sheets 19F. Breakfast included. Meals 41F.) In summer months, ask about rafting, kayaking, and hiking excursions.

The eastern terminus of a train line from Lyon, Bourg St-Maurice is the place to catch a bus for Val d'Isère (56F). The **tourist office** is outside the train station to your left (tel. 79 07 04 92), the **post office** is on av. du Centenaire (tel. 79 07 19 11). The **postal code** for Bourg St-Maurice is 73700.

Val d'Isère

Aaah, yes. It seems like only yesterday that Alberto Tomba was swooshing toward Olympic gold and a date with Katarina Witt here at "Val Dezair," as it was known among English-speaking sportscasters. Still, save for the ultramodern commercial center erected for 1992's Winter Games and the numerous unbought "Albertville '92" lighters that still litter its shops, you would never know that the Olympics once gusted through town. It remains a pristine Alpine hamlet, seemingly always at play in its spectacular mountain locale. Indeed, for skiers and hikers, this town is still as close to heaven as you can get in France; it makes no secret of its superb winter skiing conditions and its better-than-average summer conditions. Luckily, the *formidable* skiing mitigates Val d'Isère's high prices and zealous crowds.

Orientation and Practical Information

Val d'Isère lies tucked away in the Isère River valley, east of Chambéry and a few km from the Italian border. The nearest train station is in Bourg-St-Maurice, 30km north, from which a bus leaves for Val d'Isère three times per day (56F). Take the bus to **Les Boisses** (50F) if you are going to the hostel. In summer, the last bus is at 4:30pm. **L'Espace Killy,** named for Jean-Claude, the Frenchman who swept all the men's skiing events in the 1968 Grenoble games, comprises Val d'Isère and its younger neighbor, **Tignes,** site of the youth hostel.

There are no street names in Val d'Isère; fortunately there is only one main street. From the bus stop, walk up for about 100m and the tourist office will be on your left.

Tourist Office: (tel. 79 06 06 60), Boîte Postale 28. Free maps and glossy brochures, many in English. **Val Hôtel** (tel. 79 06 18 90), for hotel reservations, is upstairs. Open daily Dec. to mid-May and June 25-Aug. 30 8:30am-7:30pm; Sept.-Nov. and mid-May to June 24 9am-noon and 2:30-7pm.

Currency Exchange: On Sun., go to the **Galerie du Solaise,** 50m down and to the left of the tourist office. Open Dec.-April daily 9am-12:30pm and 3-8pm; July-Aug. 9:30am-12:30pm and 3:30-7:30pm.

Post Office: (tel. 79 06 06 99), across from the tourist office. Open Mon.-Fri. 8:30am-7:15pm; Sat. 8:30am-noon, Sun. 4-7pm. **Postal Code:** 73150.

Buses: Autocars Martin (tel. 79 06 00 42), 100m down the main street from the tourist office. Main office at pl. de la Gare (tel. 79 07 04 49), in Bourg-St-Maurice. Open Wed.-Mon. 9:30am-noon and 2:30-7pm. Buses coordinate with trains. In winter, buses to Geneva airport (3 per day, Sat.-Sun. 5 per day, 4hr., 270F). Buses to and from Les Boisses and the youth hostel (5 per day, in summer 2-3 per day, 10min., 15F). Daily excursions to nearby ski resorts (60-165F) usually leave around 10:45am.

Bike and Ski Rental: Jean Sports (tel. 79 06 04 44), 100m up from tourist office. Mountain bikes 50F per 1/2-day, 80F per day, 450F per week. Skis and boots 50-70F per day in summer; 120F per day in winter. Open daily 8am-7:30pm.

Ski Conditions: Call tourist office at 79 06 06 60, or listen to 96.10FM on the radio for ski, lift, road, and weather conditions. **Ski lifts,** tel. 79 06 00 35. **Ski Patrol,** tel. 79 06 02 10.

Police: tel. 79 06 10 96. **Emergency:** tel. 17.

Accommodations, Camping, and Food

Hotel rooms in Val d'Isère cost a bundle—reserve early at the hostel or the refuge. To rent an apartment for a week or more, contact the tourist office for a list of agencies. For reservations in Tignes, call 79 06 35 60.

Auberge de Jeunesse "Les Clarines" (HI) (tel. 79 06 35 07 or 79 41 01 93), 10km out of town in Tignes. Take the bus marked "Tignes/Val Claret" from Bourg-St-Maurice or Val d'Isère and get off at "Les Boisses." Spotless rooms and a friendly atmosphere. Reserve in Sept. for Dec. and Feb.; 6 weeks ahead for Jan., March, and April. Reception open 5-10pm but you can drop off bags all day (the bus from Bourg-St-Maurice gives you about 10min. before heading to Val d'Isère). Ask for entry code if out past 10pm. Requires *demi-pension*, which includes dinner, room, and board. 105F per person, still a bargain in this town. Showers included. Breakfast 19F. Open mid-Nov. to mid-May and mid-June to mid-Sept., depending on ski season dates.

Le Relais du Ski (tel. 79 06 02 06), past the tourist office on the left. One of the best deals in town, but not exactly cheap. Small singles 150F. Doubles and triples 300F. Breakfast 32F. In winter *demi-pension* required (room, breakfast, and dinner; 245F per person).

Hôtel Bivouac (tel. 79 06 05 48), past the tourist office on the right. Comfortable singles from 155F. Doubles from 220F. Triples from 300F. Breakfast and showers included.

Gîte d'Etape: Refuge le Prarion (tel. 79 06 06 02). Head up from town for about 1hr. to the National Park parking lot. (The shuttle to Le Fornet takes you about halfway.) From there it's an exhilarating, well-marked hike up to a mountain valley (45min.). Cozy. Ski to and from lifts. Popular base for cross-country skiing. 58F. Breakfast 30F. Meals 70F. Kitchen facilities available. Call ahead to reserve. Open all year.

Camping: Camping les Richardes (tel. 79 06 00 60), 500m up from tourist office. Plain campground in a beautiful setting with few trailers. Crowded in Aug. Reception open daily 7:50am-12:50pm and 2-8pm. 7F per person, 7F per tent. Showers (5min.) 5F. Open June 15-Sept. 15.

Val d'Isère has yet to discover affordable dining. The well-stocked supermarkets, **Prety** and **Unico,** are the budgetarian's only hope. The town's most popular pizzeria, **La Perdrix Blanche,** serves a 68F *plat du jour* and pizza from 42F. The **Bar/Restaurant L'Olympique,** 200m up and across the street from the tourist office, has a hearty 80F *menu* and a pricey *fondue savoyarde* with green salad (75F) in a relaxing ambience. Next door, the **Pub Alphonse** serves up a cheap pizza at 18F, quiche at 19F, and Lasagna at 41F.

Sights

See? See? Nay, friends, one does not "see" in Val d'Isère; one does. With over 100 lifts and *téléphériques* giving access to 400km of trails, no skier will ever be bored. Lift tickets cost 130F per half-day, 190F per day, and get progressively cheaper per day over longer periods. Tickets are valid in Tignes and Val d'Isère. A new *téléphérique* and seven ski lifts serve a few decent ski runs on the **Glacier Pissaillas** in July and August. A summer ski lift ticket (good 7:30am-1pm) costs 110F.

Hikers should buy the detailed *Guide des Promenades de Val d'Isère* (11F) and a hiking map (20F) from the tourist office. The 40 routes described include hikes to the **Rocher de Bellevarde** and **Tête du Solaise,** the most popular hikes from Val d'Isère. A *téléphérique* can whisk you part way to the Rocher or to the Tête; unrelentingly spectacular mountain vistas reward the next hour or so of legwork. The hike alongside a steep gorge up to the refuge raises spirits as well.

Ask at the tourist office for information on horseback riding. If you'd like to try paragliding but don't have the time, money, or courage to take a week-long course, try twin paragliding with an instructor (320F) or a one-day course that ends with a solo flight (750F). For information, contact **G.R. Sports** (tel. 79 06 11 37) or the tourist office.

Central France

Industry and tourism have only recently made inroads into Central France, a rugged farming region long ignored by Parisian authority. Parts of Central France, partially isolated by difficult overland routes, seem barely touched by modernization. Tiny villages dot the hills, lorded over by solid cathedrals and churches built of local volcanic stone. Numerous feudal châteaux retain their original character, virtually untouched by Renaissance embellishment, while Central France's characteristic mountains—extinct volcanoes—trade the severe crags of the Alps and the Pyrénées for a lush lining of thick forests and clear blue lakes. This rugged geographical heartland of France, this region that has traditionally provided the waft and weft of the defiant French character, is enjoying a resurgence due in part to the renewed French quest for an unequivocal national identity.

During the Middle Ages, pilgrims treaded the foothills of the region en route to Spain, while popes, troubadours, and Bourbon kings added color and diversity to the intricate social tapestry. Sensing an undercurrent of support, Pope Urban II chose Clermont-Ferrand as the launching pad for the first crusade in 1095. "Each must renounce his own self-interest and take up the cross," the Pope incited his loyal subjects. During the Hundred Years War, this region was held initially by the Duke of Berry and in ensuing years by the *dauphin* Charles VII. Residing in his capital at Bourges, the *dauphin* took advantage of Berry's proximity to northern France to recapture the area from the English.

The Massif Central has, in its modern incarnation, encountered turmoil. The region's farmers struggle in a poverty unknown to most of France. The population has declined as inhabitants migrate to more prosperous urban centers. River valleys, forests, and volcanic mountains are the trademark of the Massif, yet their pristine beauty is threatened by industrialization and urbanization. To avert the plundering of their environment, locals have banded together to create autonomous national parks that contain some of France's most spectacular natural scenery. Clermont-Ferrand, headquarters of the Michelin tire empire, sits in a haze of noxious industrial pollution. Farther north, the reigning queen of thermalism, Vichy, struggles to cure itself of the remnants of a tainting historical legacy as seat to Maréchal Pétain's Nazi-collaborationist government from 1940 to 1944. While Vichy boastfully encouraged its German occupiers, neighboring locales played host to an active *Résistance,* centered in Lyon.

In the countryside, folk traditions have retained their ancestral character. *Auvergnais* villages hold traditional *Fêtes Patronales* in the late summer, culminating in an exuberant *bourrée,* a dance to the strains of the *cabrette* (a type of bagpipe). *Auvergnats* frequently recall the heroic exploits of native-son Vercingétorix (of *Astérix* comic-book fame) who led his Gallic troops to victory against a daunted Caesar at the battle of Gergovia near Clermont-Ferrand. In Limousin, periodic *ostensions* celebrate patron saints with processions and displays of holy relics, while each of the cities of Central France enjoys its own local gastronomic specialties. Among these, the acclaimed *cantal* cheese (known as *fourme* in the region) has contributed its name—*fromage*—to describe an entire institution in France.

Train lines run to the major cities and make some small villages accessible, but more remote areas are served only by private bus companies with limited schedules timed for workers and local students rather than tourists. The steep, winding country roads are made for the *Tour de France,* not a leisurely afternoon pedal. Many people who choose to hitch do so along the main roads where locals appreciate a cordial chat with a foreigner.

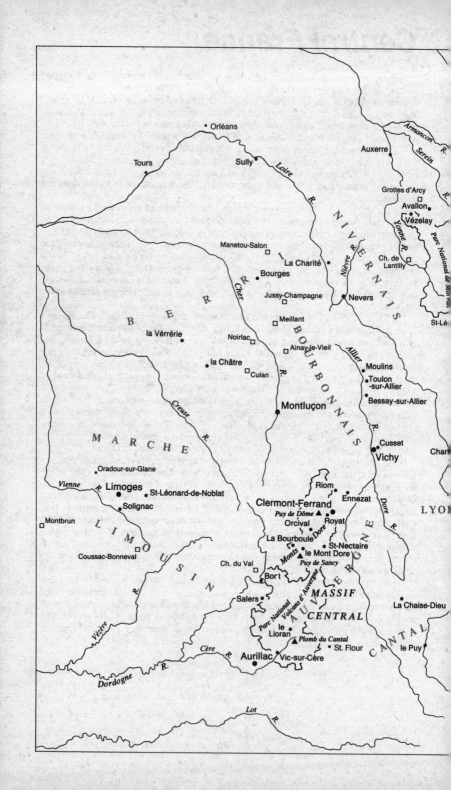

Lyon

One would expect France's second largest city (pop. 1,500,000) to quiver in the gargantuan shadow cast by Paris, but Lyon has established itself as a cultural and economic alternative to, rather than subordinate of, the capital. While millions of visitors to Paris each year salivate over the Eiffel Tower and Notre-Dame, visitors to Lyon do so over a much more tactile attraction: the city's world-renowned cuisine. Some of the greatest chefs in the world—Paul Bocuse, Georges Blanc, Jean-Paul Lacombe—all call Lyon home, initiating a trickle-down effect whereby even the cheapest restaurants seem always to delight the palate.

The other flavors of Lyon's culture stem from its historical position as an economic and transportation hub. Scattered throughout the *vieille ville* are numerous Roman amphitheaters and ruins, relics of the empire that founded the city as Lugdunum over 2000 years ago. The martyrdom of a band of Christians, led by Blandine, in the amphithéâtre des Trois Gaules (177AD), marked the beginning of the decline of the Roman power here and the rise of Christendom.

Despite the Bronze Age trade and religious fervor which passed through the town, it was not until the Renaissance that Lyon truly began to gain prominence. Medieval fairs, the silk trade, banking, and printing brought wealth and commercial power to the city, while Rabelais (many of whose works were first published here) and the Petrarchian poets Louise Labé and Pierre Ronsard gave the city newfound status as a cultural force as well. The legacy of Lyon's power and prosperity during these years lies in the *vieille ville's* vast and well-preserved display of Renaissance architecture.

Twentieth-century Lyon has continued the tradition of economic dominance and political and cultural significance. The city's epithet: "The Chicago of France" (a comparision perhaps unduly flattering of Lyon's American counterpart) underlines the metropolis's current state as a rich, industrial capital; witness also the miles of factories and industrial complexes surrounding the town. Such diverse personalities as the Lumière brothers, inventors of the film projector; the opinionated marionette Guignol, who has parodied political figures here since 1808; and Ampère, the electrodynamics pioneer, have kept the city in the world's eye. And Lyon played perhaps the most significant role of any French city during World War II, due at least in part to its sudden political ascendancy before Hitler's invasion. Indeed, from its tastefully restored *vieille ville* to its modern commercial centers, today's Lyon offers excellent museums, marathon nightlife, a friendly student population, world-renowned cuisine, and affordable accommodations. This attractive, cultured city merits an extended visit.

Orientation and Practical Information

The Saône and the Rhône cleave Lyon into three parts. Vieux Lyon (the old city) unfolds on the west bank of the Saône. East of the Rhône spreads a quieter residential neighborhood, an extensive shopping district, and the mammoth Part-Dieu commercial center and train station. Between the Saône and the Rhône, the pedestrian zone runs from the Perrache train station north to pl. Carnot, up rue Victor Hugo to pl. Bellecour, and along rue de la République to pl. des Terreaux. Like Paris, Lyon is divided into nine *arrondissements,* but there is no simple way to decipher this system. Note, however, that the 2ème *arrondissement* comprises the pedestrian zone between the Saône and the Rhône, including Perrache and Place Bellecour; all of the restaurants we list in the 2ème are between pl. Bellecour and pl. des Terraux, while all the hotels we list in the 2ème are southwest of the restaurants, between pl. Bellecour and Perrache.

To get to the main tourist office from Perrache, walk straight out onto rue Victor Hugo and follow it all the way up to pl. Bellecour. The tourist office is on the right (15min.). From the Part-Dieu station, go left out of the station and turn right onto av. Félix Faure. Follow this down and turn right on cours Gambetta. Continue over the bridge (Pont de la Guillotière) until you hit pl. Bellecour (a 30-min. walk). The tourist office is on your left. Alternatively, ride the *métro* from either station to the "Bellecour" stop.

Lyon is a reasonably safe city. Solitary travelers should feel comfortable almost anywhere in the city during the day, but at night be especially careful inside Perrache and at pl. des Terreaux.

Tourist Office: pl. Bellecour (tel. 78 42 25 75). An incredibly efficient office with a smorgasbord of information. Excellent introduction to Lyon *Lyon Vous Aimerez...* (free). Ask also for *Lyon Spectacles Evènements,* a comprehensive list of the year's shows and events, and *Guide de Lyon,* a list of hotels, restaurants and nightlife (both free). Accommodations service 5F (1-star), 10F (2-star), 30F (outside Lyon). Open Mon.-Fri. 9am-6pm, Sat. 9am-6pm, Sun. 10am-6pm; Sept. 16-June 14 Mon.-Fri. 9am-7pm, Sat. 9am-5pm, Sun. 10am-5pm. **Annex** in the Centre d'Echange (tel. 78 42 22 07), attached to the **Perrache** train station. Same services as the Bellecour office, but not quite as efficient. Open Mon.-Sat. 9am-12:30pm and 2-6pm. Another **annex** in **Villeurbanne,** 3, rue Aristide Briand (tel. 78 68 13 20), east of the Rhône. Open Mon.-Fri. 9am-6pm, Sat. 9am-5pm.

Budget Travel: La Bigerie, in the **Galerie Marchand** of Perrache (2nd floor). BIJ and Transalpino tickets. Long lines. Open Mon.-Fri. 9am-7pm, Sat. 9am-6pm.

Consulates: U.S., 7, quai Général Sarrail, 6*ème* (tel. 78 24 68 49), near Pont Morand. Open Mon.-Fri. 9am-12:30pm and 1:30-5pm. In a real emergency, however, there is *always* someone available; call. **U.K.,** 24, rue Childebert, 2*ème* (tel. 78 37 59 67), off rue de la République. Open Mon.-Fri. 10am-12:30pm and 2:30-5pm.

Currency Exchange: AOC, in the tourist offices on pl. Bellecour and Perrache. **Thomas Cook** (tel. 78 33 48 55), in the Part-Dieu train station. Open daily 9:30-7:30pm.

American Express: 6, rue Childebert (tel. 78 37 40 69), up rue de la République from pl. Bellecour. Open Mon.-Fri. 9am-noon and 2-5:30pm, Sat. 9am-noon; Oct.-April Mon.-Fri. 9am-noon and 2-5:30pm.

Post Office: pl. Antonin Poncet (tel. 78 42 60 50), next to pl. Bellecour. Regular service and **Poste Restante** open Mon.-Fri. 8am-7pm, Sat. 8am-noon. **Telephone** and telegraph services open Mon.-Sat. 8am-midnight, Sun. 8am-2pm. **Branch office,** rue Henri IV, near Perrache train station. **Postal Codes:** 69000-69009. (Main post office and *centre ville* are 69002.) Last digit is the *arrondissement.*

Flights: Aéroport Lyon-Satolas (tel. 72 22 72 21), 30km east of Lyon. Direct flights to Paris, London, Berlin, and Casablanca. **Satobuses** leave from Perrache via Part-Dieu (Mon.-Fri. every 20min. 5am-9pm, Sat. every 20min. 5am-1pm and every 30min. 1-9pm, Sun. every 30min. 5am-9pm, 45min., 43F). **Air France,** 69, rue de la République, 2*ème* (tel. 78 42 79 00). **Air Inter,** 100, rue Garibaldi, 6*ème* (tel. 78 52 84 30). Both open Mon.-Fri. 8:30am-12:30pm and 1:30-6pm, Sat. 8:30am-12:30pm.

Trains: Lyon has two train stations, but there is no telling which station sends trains where. TGV trains to Paris pass through both stations. Check the schedule posters at either station to find out about other destinations; the stations post the same schedules, listing departure and arrival times for both stations. Like Paris's stations, Lyon's are communities unto themselves, with malls, food stands, and thieves. **Perrache** (tel. 78 92 50 50), between the Saône and Rhône rivers. More central of the 2 stations. Sprawling mall with shops, bars, and **currency exchange** (open daily 5:15am-12:30pm and 1:15-8:30pm). **SOS Voyageurs** provides wheelchairs, baby-changing facilities, and sick beds. **Le Mail** offers similar services as well as hot drinks, language translation, and a place to leave bags. SNCF information and reservation desk open Mon.-Sat. 8am-7:30pm. **Part-Dieu** (tel. 78 92 50 50), in the middle of the business district on the east bank of the Rhône. Blissfully understanding **SOS Voyageurs** staff. SNCF information desk open Mon.-Sat. 8am-7:30pm, Sun. 9am-noon and 2-6:30pm. **Trains To:** TGV to Paris (every hr. 6am-9pm, 2hr., 258F plus 14-48F mandatory reservation). Dijon (8 per day, 2 1/2hr., 126F); Grenoble (15-20 per day, 2hr., 86F); Strasbourg (6 per day, 5-7hr., 245F); Geneva (11 per day, 2hr., 109F); Marseille (13 per day, 3-4hr., 198F); Nice (14 per day, 7hr., 279F).

Buses: (tel. 78 71 70 00), on the bottom floor of the Perrache train station. Open Mon.-Sat. 7:30am-6:30pm; Sept.-June Mon.-Sat. 6:30am-5pm. Frequent service to Vienne. Daily service to Annecy and Grenoble. **Philibert** (tel. 78 23 10 56). **CDL** (tel. 78 70 21 01). **Cars Grery** (tel. 78 96 11 44).

Public Transportation: TCL (tel. 78 71 80 80), outside the Part-Dieu train station. Open Mon.-Sat. 9am-6:30pm. **Métro** operates 5am-midnight. Tickets good for 1hr. in 1 direction, bus and trolley connections included. 7F per ticket, 38F for a *carnet* of 6, students 30F50. **Trolleys** *(funiculaires)* operate until 8pm and go from pl. St-Jean to the Théâtre Romain and the Musée Gallo-Romain. **TCL** network's Samedi Bleu tickets available on board the buses grant unlimited travel on Saturday. *Plan Guide Blay* (35F) gives the complete low-down on the public transport system (available at any *tabac).*

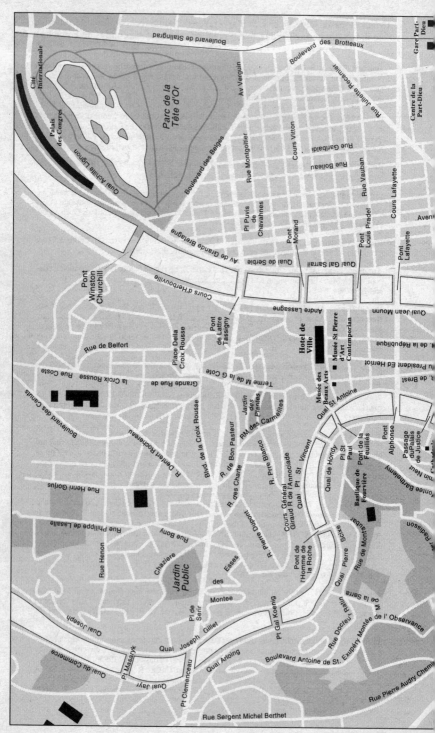

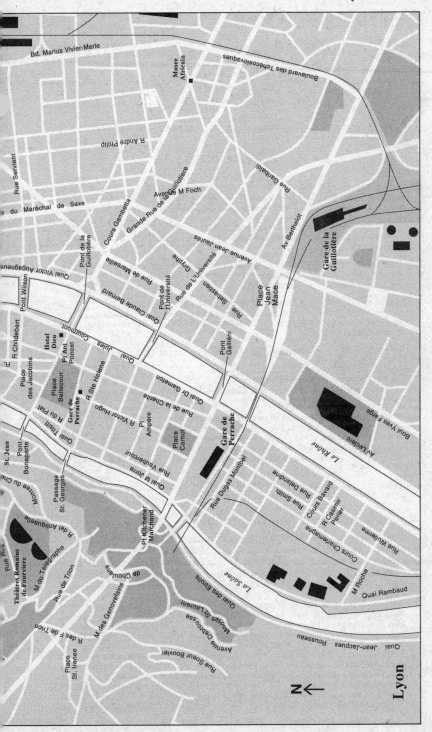

Lyon

Taxis: Allô Taxi (tel. 78 28 23 23). **Taxi Radio de Lyon** (tel. 78 30 86 86). 24 hrs. Expensive.

Hitchhiking: Those choosing to hitchhike are aware that for Paris, the *autoroute* approaches are difficult places on which to hitch; taking bus #2, 5, 19, 21, 22, or 31, and standing past pont Monton at the intersection with the N6 is reputedly easier. Those heading to Grenoble usually take bus #39 as far as the rotary at bd. Pinel. Believe the tales of 3-day waits.

English Bookstore: Eton, 1, rue du Plat (tel. 78 92 92 36), one street west of pl. Bellecour toward the Saône. The only all-English bookshop in Lyon. Open Mon. 2-7pm, Tues.-Sat. 10am-12:30pm and 1:30-7pm.

Assistance for People with Disabilities: L'Association des Paralysés de France, 73, rue Francis de Préssené (tel. 72 43 01 01). Publishes *Guide d'Accessibilité pour Personnes Handicapées,* an excellent guide with tons of pertinent information and listing access for all of Lyon. Available at the pl. Bellecour tourist office. Open Mon.-Fri. 8:30am-5pm.

Youth Center: CROUS, 59, rue de la Madeleine (tel. 78 72 55 47). Information on university housing and cafeterias. Open Mon.-Fri. 1:30-4:30pm; Sept.-July 14 Mon.-Fri. 8:30am-12:15pm and 1:30-4:30pm. **Hostelling International,** 5, pl. Bellecour (tel. 78 42 21 88). Sells membership cards to those who can prove French residence (100F) and student ID cards (47F). Information on all of France's hostels and HI-sponsored summer trips. Open Mon.-Fri. 10am-noon and 2-6pm. **Centre Régional d'Information pour Jeunes, (CRIJ),** 9, quai des Célestins (tel. 78 37 15 28). Lists of jobs, *au pair* opportunities, and sports. Open Mon. 1-7pm, Tues.-Fri. 10am-7pm, Sat. 10am-1pm and 2-7pm.

Laundromat: Salon Lavoir GTI, 38, rue Jean Jaurès. Wash 15F per 5kg, dry 2F per 7min. Open daily 7am-9pm. **LavPlus,** 28, rue Condé, near Perrache. Turn right from pl. Carnot. Wash 20F, dry 2F per 5min. Soap 2F. Open daily 7am-9pm.

Special Services and Crisis Lines: CISL (tel. 78 76 14 22), an international center for visitors to Lyon. **SOS Friendship** (tel. 78 29 88 88). For the lonely traveler. **SOS Depression** (tel. 78 65 98 92). **SOS Racism** (tel. 78 39 24 44). **Rhône Accueil** (tel. 78 42 50 03). Regional service for those unfamiliar with Lyon.

Women's Center: Centre d'Information Féminin, 18, pl. Tolozan, 1*er* (tel. 78 39 32 25). Open Mon.-Fri. 9am-noon and 2-5pm.

All-Night Pharmacy: Pharmacie Blanchet, 5, pl. des Cordeliers (tel. 78 42 12 42), in the *centre ville* between pont Lafayette and rue de la République. If you need something from 12:30-7am, call ahead.

Medical Emergency: Hôpital Edouard Herriot, 5, pl. Arsonval (tel. 78 53 81 11). Best-equipped to handle serious emergencies, but far from center of town. For non-emergencies, go to **Hôpital Hôtel-Dieu,** 1, pl. de l'Hôpital (tel. 78 92 20 00), near quai du Rhône. Call **SOS Médecin** (tel. 78 83 51 51), for home visits. In a dire emergency, **SAMU** (tel. 15 or 78 33 15 15) is on the scene in 10min. by ambulance or helicopter. **Combat Against AIDS Association** (tel. 78 27 80 80).

Police: pl. Antonin Poncet (tel. 78 28 92 93), next to pl. Bellecour and the post office. **Emergency:** tel. 17.

Accommodations and Camping

France's second financial center, Lyon fills with businesspeople during the week. The centrally located hotels are often packed Monday to Thursday nights and then empty over the weekend. Even if the hotels near Perrache are full, cheap accommodations should be available near pl. des Terreaux, which is less popular with business travelers. Of course, your best bet is to plan ahead; a few days should suffice.

Auberge de Jeunesse (HI), 51, rue Roger Salengro, Vénissieux (tel. 78 01 04 35, after 5pm 78 76 39 23), just outside the city limits. Take bus #35 from pl. Bellecour to "George Lévy" (30min.); after 9pm, take bus #53 from Perrache to "Etats-Unis-Viviani" and walk 500m along the abandoned train tracks. From Part-Dieu, take bus #36 to "Vivani Joliot-Curie" (last bus at 11:15pm, but call ahead if you'll be late). If walking from Perrache, turn right outside the station, and cross Pont Galliéni to av. Berthelot. Make a right on bd. des Etats-Unis, and another right when you get to the aforementioned abandoned tracks. From Part-Dieu, make a left on bd. Marius and continue as it becomes rue des Tchécoslovaques. Turn left on av. Berthelot and follow the directions from Perrache. Friendly cinder-block hostel with 130 beds, excellent kitchen facilities, a TV room, and a bar (food and drinks 10-20F until 11pm). Almost always room, but check in early in summer. Grape-picking jobs listed at the hostel, especially in Sept. Lockout 11:30am-5pm, but you can leave bags all day. Curfew 11:30pm. 6-bed dorms 43F per person. Nonmembers 62F, but 2nd and 3rd night at regular price. Breakfast 16F. Sheets 15F. Phone reservations accepted.

Résidence Benjamin Delessert, 145, av. Jean Jaurès, *7ème* (tel. 78 61 41 41). From Perrache, take any bus that goes to "J. Macé," walk under the train tracks (5-10min.), and look to your left. From Part-Dieu, take the metro to "Macé." Large, plain dorm rooms, all with telephones and comfortable beds. TV room. Singles 70F. Doubles 58F per person. Hall shower and sheets included. Open July-Aug.

Hôtel Croix-Pâquet, 11, pl. Croix-Pâquet, *1er* (tel. 78 28 51 49), in Terreaux. From either station take the subway to the "Croix-Pâquet" stop, or walk up rue Romarin from pl. des Terreaux to pl. Croix-Pâquet. Enter from the 4th floor off the courtyard. The LeClercqs keep these spacious rooms absolutely spotless. Singles 90-130F. Doubles 110-120F, with shower 130-150F. Showers 15F. Breakfast 18F.

Centre International de Séjour, 46, rue du Commandant Pegoud, *8ème* (tel. 78 01 23 45), near the youth hostel. From Perrache, take bus #53 to "Etats-Unis-Beauvisage" (15min., last bus at 11:30pm). From Part-Dieu, take bus #36 (every 20min., last bus 11:15pm). A hopping polyglot place with 24-hr. reception. Modern rooms with showers. Singles 111F. Doubles 176F. Triples 220F. Quads 275F. Breakfast included. Self-service meals from 30F.

Hôtel Vaubecour, 28, rue Vaubecour, *2ème* (tel. 78 37 44 91), about halfway between Perrache and Bellecour. Some of the cheapest and nicest rooms in town. Cozy, but not cramped. Singles 83F, with shower 154F. Doubles 116F, with shower 165-258F. Breakfast 19F. Showers 13F.

Hôtel Alexandra, 49, rue Victor Hugo, *2ème* (tel. 78 37 75 79). A large, old hotel in an ideal location. Large rooms with TV and phone. No hall showers. Often close-to-full during the week. Singles 110F, with shower 186F, with shower and toilet 199F. Doubles 128F, with shower 204F, with shower and toilet 217F. Breakfast 22F.

Hôtel Le Terme, 7, rue Ste-Catherine, *1er* (tel. 78 28 30 45), in Terreaux. Fairly small rooms (all with TV and phone) in an otherwise expensive area. Singles 120-130F. Doubles 165-185F, with shower 210F. Hall showers included. Breakfast 20F.

Hôtel de la Loire, 19, cours Verdun-Gensoul, *2ème* (tel. 78 37 44 29), off pl. Carnot. Small, pleasant rooms with carpeting, desks, and telephones. Singles 128F, with shower 163F, and toilet 190F. Doubles 156F, with shower 190F, and toilet 230F. Breakfast 25F. TV 20F.

Camping: Dardilly (tel. 78 35 64 55). From the Hôtel de Ville, take bus #19 (direction: "Ecully-Dardilly") to the "Parc d'Affaires" stop. One of the most beautiful campgrounds in the Rhône Valley. Hot showers, swimming pool, grocery store, bar, and restaurant. 50F per tent and car, 15F per extra person. Electricity 12F. Open March-Oct.

Food

Lyon's galaxy of *Michelin* stars proclaims this city as the gastronomic capital of western civilization, but there are plenty of affordable options for budget travelers. Head for one of the city's *bouchons,* descendants of the inns where travelers would stop to dine and to have their tired horses *bouchonné* (rubbed down) with straw. Today, the 20 or so remaining *bouchons* serve *cochonailles* (hot pork dishes), *tripes à la lyonnaise* (heavy on the onions and vinegar), and *andouillette* (sausage made of chitterlings). The original *bouchons* concentrate around pl. des Terreaux (the oldest is **Le Soleil,** 2, rue St-Georges). The most pleasant (and tourist-laden) places in Vieux Lyon will seat you outdoors on narrow, cobblestone streets. The variety of ethnic restaurants on rue St-Jean provides another affordable alternative.

The **university restaurants** in Villeurbanne serve cheap but unappetizing food. Ask at the CRIJ for names and locations. The market at **La Halle,** 102, cours Lafayette, *3ème,* sells celery, *escargots,* and truffles to His Majesty Paul Bocuse, the King of French dining (open Tues.-Sat. 7am-noon and 3-7pm. Sun. 7am-noon). If you hanker for a hunk o', canker for a chunk o' cheese, head to **Richard,** which exports to some of the world's finest restaurants. Open **markets** are held at quai St-Antoine (Tues.-Sun. 7:30am-12:30pm), and on bd. de la Croix Rousse (on the Rhône, Tues.-Sat. 8am-12:30pm). The **Carrefour Supermarché,** one of the largest in France, looms across the highway from the hostel. (Open Mon.-Fri. 8:45am-10pm, Sat. 8:45am-8pm.)

Chocolate lovers swoon at Lyon's grandest and most famous *pâtisserie,* **Bernachon,** 42, cours Franklin Roosevelt, *6ème.* To get there, cross Pont Morand to the east bank of the Rhône and continue straight through the park to cours Franklin Roosevelt. The showcase sparkles with heavenly pastries and the ambrosial *Palets d'Or*, probably the best chocolate in France (open Tues.-Sat. 8am-7pm, Sun. 8am-1pm; Sept. 16-June 14 Tues.-Sat. 8am-7pm, Sun. 8am-5pm).

Paul Bocuse, 50, quai de la Plage (tel. 78 22 01 40) in Collonges-au-Mont-d'Or, 9km north along the D433. Inhale the luxuriance, the euphoria. And why not? You're in the sanctuary of the greatest of French chefs, a true gastronomic mecca for the most refined of cosmopolitan gourmands. Dinner will set you back 390F, 580F, or 650F—yes, those are zeros—but you get what you pay for. Dress appropriately. Open daily noon-2pm and 7-10pm. All credit cards accepted.

Café de Jura, 25, rue Tupin, *2ème,* the 6th block north on your left from Hôtel-Dieu. An authentic *bouchon* run by Henri, a charmer with a classic handlebar mustache. New selection of entrees daily (46-75F). Open Mon.-Fri. at 7:30am; lunch noon-2pm, dinner 7:30-10:30pm.

Chez Mounier, 3, rue des Marroniers, *2ème,* just north of pl. Antonin Poncet and the post office. Another *bouchon,* whose *Gnafron* (sausage in fresh cream sauce) alone justifies the visit. 57F, 80F, and 90F *menus* change daily. Open Tues. and Thurs.-Sun. noon-2pm and 7-10pm, Wed. noon-2pm.

Garioud, 14, rue du Palais-Grillet, *2ème* (tel. 78 37 04 71). From rue de la République, take a left onto rue Ferrandère; rue du Palais-Grillet is the first street on the right. Great *cuisine lyonnaise* by Paul Griard, a Bocuse acolyte. 118F, 134F, 159F, 188F, 218F, 269F *menus.* Dress appropriately (no shorts). Open Mon.-Fri. noon-2pm and 7:30-10pm, Sat. 7:30-10pm. Reservations recommended.

Chez Carlo, 22, rue du Palais Grillet, *2ème,* near Restaurant Garioud. Recommended by locals for the greatest pasta and pizza (40-42F) in Lyon. *Hyper-populaire.* Open Tues.-Sat. noon-1:30pm and 7-11pm, Sun. noon-1:30pm.

L'Etoile de l'Orient, 31, rue des Ramparts d'Ainay, *2ème.* Small, cozy restaurant full of regulars who flock here for the best North African cuisine in town. Fresh *couscous* 52-92F. 65F *menu.* Open Thurs.-Tues. noon-2pm and 7-11pm.

Titi Lyonnais, 2, rue Chaponnay, *3ème,* off cours de la Liberté on the east bank of the Rhône by pont Wilson. 59F lunch *menu* includes entree, dessert, and coffee. Classic *cuisine lyonnaise* on 75F, 85F, and 118F *menus.* Open Tues.-Sat. noon-2pm and 7:30-10:30pm, Sun. noon-2pm.

Le Confort Impérial, 10, rue Confort, *2ème* (tel. 78 42 41 88), off rue de la République. 3-course 41F lunch *menu* and 62F dinner *menu.* Winner of the "Golden Chopsticks Award" for gourmet Chinese cookery. Frequented by both the Mayor of Lyon and the ex-emperor of Vietnam. Open Tues.-Sun. noon-11pm.

Sights

Those who find Lyon a dull place have not yet cultivated a taste for *la flânerie* (strolling). Start at **place Bellecour,** fringed by shops and flower stalls and dominated by an equestrian statue of Louis XIV in the center. If you've been traveling through small towns and seek big-city commotion, head out of the square along rue de la République (or its parallel, rue du Président Edouard Herriot) to **Terreaux.** At pl. des Terreaux, the ornate Renaissance **Hôtel de Ville** stands guard opposite the **Musée des Beaux Arts,** in the Palais St-Pierre. The museum houses an extensive collection of painting and sculpture that includes works by Spanish and Dutch masters, two rooms of impressionism, and several rooms of excellent early 20th-century canvases. (Open Wed.-Sun. 10:30am-6pm. Admission 20F, students 15F, under 18 free.) The courtyard has a beautiful sculpture garden. The **Musée d'Art Contemporain,** located in the same building but with an entrance at 16, rue Edouard-Herriot, displays some excellent temporary exhibitions of works from the past three decades. (Open Wed.-Mon. noon-6pm. Admission 20F, students 15F, under 18 free.) A few blocks north of the museums on rue Burdeau, 1*er* are the ruins of the Roman **Amphitéâtre des Trois Gaulles,** built in 19 AD and the site of the martyrdom of a band of Christians in 177. (Open dawn-dusk. Free.)

Lyon revels in its long-standing dominance of the European **silk** industry. At the turn of the 18th century, 28,000 looms operated in Lyon. The *canuts* (silk workers), who toiled in basement sweatshops, were driven to riot against the profiteers who controlled the business. Familiar story, *non?* Although silk manufacturing is based elsewhere today, an extraordinary collection of silk and embroidery ranging from the Coptic to the Oriental remains at the **Musée Historique des Tissus,** 34, rue de la Charité. (Open Tues.-Sun. 10am-5:30pm. Admission 20F, students 10F. Free Wed.) Weave through the **Musée Lyonnais des Arts Decoratifs,** down the street at 30, rue de la Charité, which displays furniture, porcelain, silver, and tapestries from the 17th and 18th centuries. (Open Tues.-Sun. 10am-noon and 2-5:30pm. Free with ticket from Musée des Tissues.) **La Maison des Canuts,** 10-12, rue d'Ivry (tel. 78 28 62 04), demonstrates the actual weaving techniques of the *canuts lyonnais.* (Open Mon.-Fri. 8:30am-noon and 2-6:30pm, Sat. 9am-noon and 2-6pm. Admission 6F.)

A brief walk across the Saône leads to the most intriguing part of town, **Vieux Lyon.** The renovated Renaissance buildings in the St-Paul, St-Georges, and St-Jean quarters are the most costly residences in Lyon. The intriguing *traboules* (from the Latin *trans ambulare,* to walk across) were built under and around the buildings to compensate for the lack of crosswalks. Connecting the neighborhood widthwise, these passages helped protect the city's precious silk as it was transported through the city in stormy weather. They also protected members of the Résistance (of which Lyon was the center) from Nazi search parties—the entrances are difficult to find. (Obtain a *Liste des Traboules* from the tourist office. The passages are closed after dark.) A particularly interesting church in the St-Jean quarter is the *bourguignon*-style **Cathédrale St-Jean.** Its northern transept holds a 14th-century astronomical clock that shows the feast days from 600 years ago all the way to the year 2000. (Open Mon.-Fri. 7:30am-noon and 2-7:30pm, Sat.-Sun. 2-5pm. Free.)

From the **Fourvière Esplanade,** high above the old city, gaze down at Lyon's urban sprawl. The most scenic route follows rue de la Bombarde to rue du Boeuf. Take the montée des Chazeaux staircase and turn left on montée St- Barthélémy. On the right lie the *Jardins du Rosaire,* from which a beautiful uphill path climbs to the extravagant 19th-century **Basilique de Fourvière.** (Open daily 8am-noon and 2-6pm.) This hillside was the site where Lugdunum, Julius Ceasar's commercial and military center of Gaul, was founded in 43 BC. The **Musée Gallo-Romain,** 17, rue Cléberg, on the Fourvière hill, displays a collection of mosaics, swords, rings, statues, and money from Lyon's Roman past. (Open Wed.-Sun. 9:30am-noon and 2-6pm. Admission 20F, students 15F, under 18 free.) On the descent, go past the **Théâtre Romain,** still a stage for everything from opera to rock concerts. (Open daily 9am-dark. Free.)

Back in the lower section of Vieux Lyon, the **Musée de la Marionette,** pl. du Petit Collège in the Hôtel Gadagne, exhibits the famous *lyonnais* puppets, including their proud mascot Guignol himself, as well as international specimens. (Open Tues.-Sun. 10am-5:30pm, Fri. until 8:30pm. Admission 20F, students 15F.) Your ticket will also admit you to the **Musée Historique de Lyon** in the same building, where you can gawk at the beds on which Napoléon and Joséphine slumbered when they visited Lyon in 1805. Bonus. (Open Wed.-Thurs. and Sat.-Mon. 10:45am-6pm, Fri. 10:45am-8:30pm. Admission 20F, students 15F.)

In shocking contrast to Vieux Lyon, modern Lyon on the east bank of the Rhône is made up of sleek buildings and space-age conveniences. The **Part-Dieu District** is worth a visit just to see its modern train station. The **Tour Crédit Lyonnais,** on the other side of the mall, symbolizes commercial Lyon. Next to it, the shell-shaped **Auditorium Maurice Ravel,** hosts some of Europe's major cultural events.

The **Musée de la Résistance,** 5, rue Boileau, has assembled documents and photos of the Résistance, which was centered in Lyon. (Open Wed.-Sun. 10:30am-noon and 1-6pm. Free.) The **Musée Africain,** 150, cours Gambetta, addresses the culture of West Africa and its integral part in France's colonial history and current economy. (Open Wed.-Sun. 2-6pm. Admission 10F, students 5F.) Film and photography buffs will want to see the **Institut Lumière,** 25, rue du Premier-Film, 8*ème* (tel. 78 00 86 68), a museum which examines the lives of the brothers who invented the first film projector. (Admission 10F. Open Tues.-Sun. 2-6pm.) The **Fondation de la Photographie,** in the same building has posters and photography exhibits (free).

Those overwhelmed by the size and variety of Lyon might take one of the tourist office's three theme tours. In the language of your choice, a guide will show you old Lyon, the *traboules,* or Bellecour. (July-Aug. 45F, ages 8-18 50F. For info call 78 42 25

75.) Those with a passion for museum-going might consider the tourist office's 30F one-day ticket that covers all the city's museums.

When urban fatigue sets in, leave city noise behind for the roses of the **Parc de la Tête d'Or,** Lyon's botanical garden, so called because it is believed that a golden bust of Christ is buried somewhere within. Here you can bounce about on a pony or tour around the park in a go-cart or a mini-train, but don't dig; it might vex the city authorities. (Open daily 6am-10pm; off-season 8am-8pm.) **Boat trips** along the Saône and Rhône leave from quai des Célestins (April-Oct. daily 2, 3, 5, and 6pm for a 1-1 1/2-hr. trip; 50F, under 10 30F). The boats also make a long, leisurely trip to Vienne. For more information, contact **Navig'Inter,** 13bis, quai Rambaud (tel. 78 42 96 81).

Entertainment

To find out what's up in Lyon each week, pick up a copy of *Lyon Poche* (9F) at a newsstand. Lyon supports a variety of resident theaters as well as an opera company, but the highlight of its cultural activities arrives in June, with one of two annually alternating music and dance festivals. (Schedules available from the tourist office.) In May, **Festival des Musiques Européennes** draws musicians from all across Europe (Contact the Centre Charlie Chaplin-Vaulx-en-Velin, tel. 72 04 37 03) and the **Festival de Théâtre Amateur** gives aspiring thespians a chance to show their stuff. (Call 78 25 00 58 for information.)

On each December 8 since 1852, candles have lit the city's windows and parades have flooded the streets for the **Fête de la Vierge,** honoring the Virgin Mary on the Feast of the Immaculate Conception for having protected Lyon from the Black Plague. On a different note, July 1 starts off the **Festival du Jazz à Vienne,** a festival that lasts nearly two weeks and we lcomes international jazz celebrities to **Vienne,** a town just outside Lyon. It is accessible by bus or train. For information, call 74 85 00 05 or the Vienne tourist office (tel. 74 85 12 62) on 11, quai Reonded.

Lyon is a terrific place to see silver screen classics. The **Cinéma Opéra,** 6, rue J. Serlin (tel. 78 28 80 08), and **Le Cinéma,** 18, impasse St-Polycarpe (tel. 78 39 09 72), specialize in black-and-white oldies, all in the original language (30-40F). You'll find avant-garde flicks and more classics at the **CNP Terreaux Cinéma,** 40, rue Président Edouard Herriot (37F).

Lyon may well have more pubs per capita than any other French city. For the twenty-something crowd, **Eddie and Domino,** 6, quai Gailleton, 2*ème* (tel. 78 37 20 29), off Pont de l'Université, is a British-style pub with a huge selection of whiskeys and a bartender who allows you to create your own cocktails. (Open Mon.-Sat. 6pm until dawn.) Local students kill the night at **Albion,** 12, rue Ste-Cathérine, 1*er* (tel. 78 28 33 00; open Sun-Thurs. 6pm-1am, Fri.-Sat. 6pm-2am.) For a wide variety of music (rock, blues, Brazilian, African) in a more refined atmosphere, try **Mozart,** 53, rue Mercière, 2*ème* (tel. 78 92 89 16). (Open Mon.-Sat. 6pm-5am; concerts at 6pm May-Sept. 10 pm Oct.-April. Cover varies from 25-75F.)

Nightclubs swarm on rue Therme, off rue d'Algérie and near pl. des Terreaux. Classy discos include **Comoedia,** 30, rue Neuve, 2*ème* (tel. 78 30 82 86; open Mon.-Sat. 7:30am-11pm), and **Quartier Latin,** 7, quai Saint-Vincent, 1*er* (tel. 78 28 14 87). **Le Club des Iles,** 1, grande rue des Feuillants (tel. 78 39 16 35; open 10:30pm-dawn), off petite rue des Feuillants by quai A. Lassagne, plays a big West Indian beat in a pseudo-island setting. Popular gay bars include the **Broadway,** 9, rue Terraille, 1*er* (tel. 78 39 50 54; open Wed.-Mon. 6pm-late), **Bar du Centre,** 3, rue Simon-Maupin, 2*ème* (tel. 78 37 40 18; open daily 10am-3am), and **Le Mylord,** 112, quai Pierre Seize, 5*ème,* a more dance-oriented place than the others. (Open Mon.-Thurs. 10:30pm-4am, Fri.-Sat. 10:30pm-dawn.)

Moulins

Moulins, so-named because of the *moulins à eau* (water mills) that once lined the nearby Allier River, is the ancient Bourbon capital. According to legend, a Bourbon noble named Archambault built the **Château des Ducs de Bourbon** for his mistress, the daughter of Bréchimbault. Though the castle has since fallen into disrepair, Moulins itself seems to have discovered the fountain of youth. The courtyards and half-timbered houses of Moulins's *vieille ville,* as well as the entire pedestrian zone, are wired for sound, and everything from Europop to the Village People blares from inconspicuous speakers all summer long.

The tourist office's self-guided walking tour of the town provides a good introduction to the beautiful but disorienting *vieille ville.* Should you lose your bearings, the 16th-century **Jacquemart clock tower** will direct you back to the pl. de l'Hôtel de Ville, as the mechanical couple Jacques and Jacquette, along with their children, Jacquelin and Jacqueline, make a noisy appearance every 15 minutes. Nearby, the striking **Cathédrale Notre Dame** houses several noteworthy treasures: a 12th-century Black Virgin, said to have miraculous powers, a 16th-century entombment scene in polychromed stone, and the spectacular **Triptyque du Maître de Moulins,** a 15th-century work by an unknown artist. (Cathedral open daily 8am-noon and 2-7pm. Admission to Triptyque 10F, students 5F.)

Connected to the château, the **Pavillon Anne de Beaujeu** is reputed to be the oldest building in France constructed in the style of the Italian Renaissance. It now houses the **Musée d'Art et d'Archéologie,** whose ten rooms run the artistic gamut from Gallo-Roman bronzes to 19th-century French painting. (Open Wed.-Mon. 10am-noon and 2-6pm. Admission 10F, students 5F, under 19 free.) Moulins's other museum, the **Musée de Folklore et des Moulins** on pl. de l'Ancien Palais, is a never-ending assortment of cooking utensils, clothing irons, dolls, and dusty religious statues. (Open Wed.-Fri. 10am-noon and 3-6:30pm. Admission 12F, students 6F.)

The **tourist office,** pl. de l'Hôtel de Ville (tel. 70 44 14 14), across from the Jacquemart, is about 15 min. from the train station. Turn right onto rue M. Desboutin, bear left onto rue du Cerf Volant, left again onto rue de Bourgogne, and veer right onto rue Epargne. The staff distributes free maps and a hotel and restaurant list. Every afternoon in July and August they offer guided tours of the *vieille ville.* (Open Mon.-Sat. 9am-noon and 2-7pm, Sun. 9am-noon; mid-Sept. to mid-June Tues.-Sat. 9am-noon and 2-6:30pm. Admission 16F, students 8F.) The **post office,** pl. Jean Moulin (tel. 70 20 13 86), has a **currency exchange** (open Mon.-Fri. 8am-7pm, Sat. 8am-noon); Moulins's **postal code** is 03000. About six **trains** per day run to Lyon (2 1/4hr., 126F), Paris (2 1/2hr., 176F), and Nevers (30min., 47F). More than 10 per day run to Clermont-Ferrand (90min., 75F). (Information office (tel. 70 46 50 50) open Mon.-Sat. 9am-6pm, Sun. 9am-noon and 2-6:45pm.)

Although the **Foyer des Jeunes Travailleurs,** 60, rue de Bourgogne houses a number of pensioners, there is usually room for travelers. The *foyer* occupies an old townhouse with a central courtyard, bar, TV room, washing machines (10F wash, 5F dry), and dining room. Be forewarned that temporary guests are often put on the ground floor in rooms facing onto a noisy street. (Reception open Mon.-Fri. 8am-midnight, Sat.-Sun. 9am-midnight. Dorm-style accommodations 40F, without hostel card 50F. Breakfast 12F50, lunch or dinner 29F. Sheets 30F.) To get there from the train station, follow the directions to the tourist office, but turn right onto rue Bourgogne. **La Taverne de France,** 8, rue des Bouchers (tel. 70 44 04 82), offers newly renovated doubles with great views of the château (70F, with shower 90F. Breakfast 20F). The **Hôtel le Français,** 8, pl. de la Liberté (tel. 70 44 32 19), on rue Gambetta, has adequate singles and doubles for 80-100F, with shower 140F. The bar downstairs attracts a young and lively crowd. The **Camping Municipal** (tel. 70 44 19 29) is on the river, about 2km from the station and just south of Moulins's one-car bridge. (10F per person, 7F per site, 5F per car. Electricity 9F. Open June-Sept.)

Most restaurants in the *vieille ville* tend to be overpriced. The **Crêperie le Vieux Moulin,** 2, rue de l'Ancien Palais, just under the clock tower, serves mounds of *crêpes* and *galettes,* with none costing more than 40F. In the lower city, the **Restaurant l'Or-angerie,** on pl. Jean Moulin near the post office offers a filling 65F *menu* featuring *brochette d'agneau* (lamb skewers) with salad, cheese, and *tarte aux pommes* (apple tart) for dessert (open daily for dinner). There is a **Uniprix** supermarket on rue D'Englien, just below the château. (Open Mon.-Sat. 9am-12:30pm and 2-7:30pm.)

Bourges

Bourges (pop. 76,000) lies at the very *coeur* (heart) of France, the geographical center of the mythical *hexagone.* Although inhabited for nearly 2500 years, Bourges did not gain prominence until 1433, when Charles VII's corrupt finance minister, Jacques Coeur, chose Bourges as the site of his magnificent residence. In addition to the house that Jacques built, Bourges lures visitors with its labyrinthine *vieille ville* of cobblestone streets and half-timbered houses, and its monumental hilltop cathedral towering over the town below. Also home to a national conservatory and two annual music festivals, Bourges's pulse quickens during the festival season in late April and June. Unfortunately, it's a bit of a flat-liner the rest of the year.

Orientation and Practical Information

Bourges, 221km from Paris, sits on the major train route between Orléans (105km) and the Loire Valley to the north, and Montluçon (93km) and the Massif Central to the south. *Berruyers* (as the inhabitants of Bourges are called; no, they're not "Bourgeois") live in a jumble of narrow cobblestone streets that add charm to the city but may confuse newcomers. Avenue H. Laudrier and its continuation, av. Jean Jaurès, lead directly from the train station to rue Moyenne, the principal north-south artery, and home of the tourist office.

Tourist Office: 21, rue Victor Hugo (tel. 48 24 75 33), facing rue Moyenne near the cathedral, 20 min. from the train station. Efficient staff hands out maps and lists of hotels and restaurants. 90-min. walking tours (French only) leave July-Sept. daily (23F, students 18F); night tours July-Aug. Fri.-Sat. at 8:15pm (28F, students 24F). Open Mon.-Sat. 9am-7pm, Sun. 9am-1pm and 2:30-7pm; Sept. 15-June Mon.-Sat. 9am-noon and 2-6pm.

Post Office: 1, rue Michel de Bourges, on the corner of rue Moyenne (tel. 48 24 21 01). **Currency exchange** and **telephones.** Open Mon.-Fri. 8am-7pm, Sat. 8am-noon. **Postal Code:** 18000.

Trains: pl. Général Leclerc (tel. 48 65 50 50). Bourges is just off the main north-south train line. Many destinations, including Paris, require a transfer at nearby Vierzon. To: Paris (13 per day, 2 1/2hr., 148F); Tours (4 per day, 90min., 97F); Lyon (5 per day, 3 1/4hr., 185F); Clermont-Ferrand (4 per day, 2 1/2hr., 218F).

Bike Rental: The **youth hostel** is the only reasonable deal in town. Members only, but it might be cheaper to buy a membership than to rent somewhere else. Great new bikes at 25F per 1/2-day, 50F per day, deposit 250F.

Laundromat: Lavomatiques are at 117, rue Edouard Valliant, 15, bd. Juranville, and 79, av. Marcel Haegelan. Wash 7kg for 22F. Dry 12 min. for 5F. Open daily 7am-8pm.

Hospital: Centre Hospitalier, 34, rue Gambon (tel. 48 68 40 00).

Medical Emergency: SAMU Ambulance, tel. 15.

Police: 6, av. d'Orléans (tel. 48 24 42 46). **Emergency:** tel. 17.

Accommodations and Camping

Hotels in Bourges are scattered, rather expensive, and often closed in August. Call a day or two in advance, especially during the festival season.

Auberge de Jeunesse (HI), 22, rue Henri Sellier (tel. 48 24 58 09), in a wooded site overlooking a stream. A 10-min. walk from the center of town and 25 min. from the train station. From the station, take av. H. Laudier onto av. Jean Jaurès to pl. Planchat. Follow rue des Arènes, which becomes rue Fernault and then rue Messire Jacques before making a sharp left onto rue Henri Sellier. The hostel is set back slightly from the street. If your bags are getting you down, take bus #1 (direction "Chancellerie") from the station. Get off at "Château-d'Eau," turn right onto rue du Château d'Eau, then right onto rue Charles Cochet, and right again onto rue Henri Sellier. Fine hostel with kitchen, TV room, washing machines, and clean bathrooms. Members only. Reception open 8-10am and 5-11pm, but you can drop your bags off at any time. Curfew 11pm. Members only. 40F. Breakfast 16F. Dinner and wine 50F. Sheets 15F.

Centre International de Séjour, 17, rue Félix-Chédin (tel. 48 70 25 59). Cross the bridge over the tracks at the train station and head up rue Félix-Chédin for 5 min. The only lodgings in France to advertise a "good assortment of street obstacles," this lively youth center—half hostel, half *foyer*—is *the* skateboard mecca of Europe, with the bowls, ramps, and half-pipes to prove it. In summer you can sleep under the same roof as many of the best skaters in the world, who teach week-long skating camps. For non-skaters, the friendly management organizes everything from French classes to rock concerts. 78F per person, breakfast and skateboard facilities included. 4-course lunch or dinner 45F. Thrash on!

Hôtel de la Nation, 24, pl. de la Nation (tel. 48 24 11 96). Good rooms in a good location. Singles 95F, with shower 130F. Doubles 110F, with shower 145F. Showers 15F. Breakfast 20F. Open Mon.-Sat. Closed last 2-3 weeks in Aug. and at end of December.

Hôtel L'Etape, 4, rue Raphael Cassanova (tel. 48 70 59 47), just off rue Juranville. Tucked into a quiet street close to downtown. Kind managers. Clean singles and doubles 100F, with shower 130F. TV 20F extra. Breakfast 16F.

Camping: Camping Municipal, 26, bd. de l'Industrie (tel. 48 20 16 85). Follow directions to the hostel, but continue on rue Henri Sellier away from the *centre ville,* and turn right on bd. de l'Industrie. 12F per person, 13F per tent. Open March 15-Nov. 15.

Food

The cobblestone streets off rue d'Auron, rue Bourbonnoux, rue Corsarlon, and rue Mirabeau form a network of *rues pietonnes* (pedestrian streets) lined with shops, cafés, and restaurants. Look for bargains on local specialties such as *poulet en barbouille* (chicken roasted in a local aromatic red wine) and *oeufs en meurette.* Bourges has a number of produce **markets,** the largest of which fills pl. de la Nation on Saturday mornings. The other notable market rocks pl. des Marronniers on Thursdays until 1pm, while there is a smaller permanent market from Tues.-Sun. at pl. St-Bonnet.

D'Antan Sancerrois, 50, rue Bourbonnoux. Popular with *berruyers* who linger over filling lunches of Berry specialties. Delicious *Veau au vin* (veal in wine sauce) 60F, and *oeufs en meurette* 32F. Open Wed.-Sun. noon-2pm and 7-10pm, Tues. 7-10pm.

La Main à la Pat, 108, rue Bourbonnoux, behind the cathedral. Loud chattering and pizzas baked over a wood fire (25-45F). *Main à la Pat* salad with chicken and avocado 28F. Take-out available. Open Mon. 7pm-midnight, Tues.-Sat. noon-2pm and 7pm-midnight.

Chez Charles, 19, rue des Ecoles, off rue Juranville. Small place, big meal. The 36F *menu* is satisfying; the monumental 70F *menu* includes omelette or *escargots*, pizza, choice of meat, vegetable, cheese, and sensational dessert. Open Mon.-Sat. for dinner.

Sights and Entertainment

One of the largest and most magnificent cathedrals in France, Bourges's **Cathédrale St-Etienne** presides over the town. The cathedral's massive 13th-century façade features a central portal representation of the Last Judgment. Light streams gracefully through the cathedral's awe-inspiring stained-glass windows. The main windows (located behind the main altar) have recently undergone extensive restoration and are brilliantly clean. Throughout the summer, prominent international organists play the cathedral's tremendous *grande orgue.* The schedule of free concerts is posted below the organ. (Open daily 7am-6pm.) The crypt contains little more than a white marble figure of the Duke of Berry and a few polychromed statues; it certainly isn't worth the steep 20F admission fee.

The intricate late medieval architecture of the **Palais Jacques-Coeur** is a testimony to the man's own motto: *A vaillant Coeur, riens impossible.* ("To the bold Heart, nothing is impossible."). The obligatory 45-minute tour winds past storerooms, reception halls, and bedrooms, none of which are alike. The tours are in French, but a printed English translation is available from the front desk. (Tours at 9:15am, 10:15am, 11:10am, 2:15pm, 3:15pm, 4:15pm, and 5:10pm. Admission 20F, ages 18-24 and over 60 12F.)

Each of Bourges's three museums sells a 28F global museum ticket (students 14F). The **Musée du Berry** (tel. 48 57 81 15) gathers prehistoric, Gallo-Roman, and medieval artifacts in an elegant 16th-century *hôtel* on rue des Arènes. (Open Mon. and Wed.-Sat 10am-noon and 2-6pm, Sun. 2-6pm. Admission 12F, students 6F.) Built by a rich 15th-century merchant, the luxurious **Hôtel Lallemant,** 6, rue Bourbonnoux (tel. 48 57 81 17), is embellished with furniture, tapestries, and other decorative works from the 17th and 18th centuries. (Open Tues.-Sat., 10am-noon and 2-6pm, Sun. 2-6pm. Admission 14F, students 7F.) The **Musée Estève**, 13, rue Edouard-Branly (tel. 48 24 75 38), houses works of modern art, including paintings by Buranlure and local hero Maurice Estève. (Open Mon. and Wed.-Sat. 10am-noon and 2-6pm, Sun. 2-6pm. Admission 14F, students 7F.)

Well over 200,000 ears crowd Bourges to enjoy performances by internationally renowned artists at the **Festival Printemps de Bourges** (April 20-25, 1993). Although most tickets cost 60-150F, some of the informal folk, jazz, classical, and rock concerts are free. For information, contact l'Association Printemps de Bourges, 5, rue Samson, 18000 Bourges (tel. 48 24 30 50). The **Fête de Jacques-Coeur,** a celebration of traditional Berry music and dance, crescendos from the last two weeks in June to Bastille Day. From mid-July through August the tourist office sponsors **Ballades à Bourges,** yet another conflagration of classical concerts, rock, theater, and folk dancing. Tickets go on sale one hour before showtime at the concert spot (often a church or park) or one week in advance at the tourist office. Most cost 30-80F.

Near Bourges: Châteaux on Route Jacques-Coeur

Jacques may have left his *coeur* in Bourges, but his ego spilled far into the surrounding countryside. The Route Jacques-Coeur is a string of 18 châteaux, many once owned by Jacques, that stretches from La Buissière in the north, through Bourges and south to Culan. While lacking some of the grandeur and ostentation of the more famous Loire châteaux, those on route Jacques-Coeur provide a welcome respite from long lines and tour groups and present a fascinating variety of architectural styles. Bourges's tourist office provides helpful pamphlets with detailed maps, photographs, and English descriptions of each château. Though none lie more than 90km from Bourges, virtually all are accessible only by car or bike. Buses run only once per day and return the following morning. For more information on travel connections and occasional bus excursions, contact the Bourges tourist office.

Culan (tel. 48 56 64 18), 69km south of Bourges on the Châteauroux-Montluçon train line, perches gracefully atop a steep crag. Joan of Arc was once a house guest in this 11th-century château, now lavishly furnished with 15th- and 16th-century pieces. (Open daily 9:30am-7pm; mid-Sept. to Nov. and Feb to mid-June 9:30am-noon and 2-6:30pm. Admission 25F, students 12F.) A few miles north of Culan is the fortress-like **Ainay-le-Vieil** (tel. 48 63 50 67), where a moat and guard towers steadfastly protect the inner courtyard. (Open daily 10am-noon and 2-6:30pm; Sept.-Nov. and Feb.-March Wed.-Mon. 10am-noon and 2-5pm. Admission 23F, students 10F.) Ainay is also a stop on the train line between Bourges and Montluçon.

Set in a lovely park with a pond 35km south of Bourges, **Château Meillant** (tel. 48 63 30 58) incorporates elements of both medieval and flamboyant Gothic style. (Open Feb.-Dec. 15 daily 9-11:45am and 2-6:45pm. Admission 23F, students 12F.) Close to Meillant, the 12th-century Cistercian abbey of **Noirlac** (tel. 48 96 23 64), shares its lovely symmetry with the surrounding gardens. (Open daily 10am-noon and 2-6pm; Nov.-March daily 10am-noon and 2-5pm; Oct. Wed.-Mon. 10am-noon. Admission 20F, students free.) Other worthwhile châteaux in the area include **Menetou-Salon** (tel. 48 64 80 54), an ornate mansion from the end of the Renaissance (open mid-April-Oct. Wed.-Mon. 10-11:30am and 2-6pm; admission 30F, students 20F), and **Jussy-Champagne** (tel. 48 25 00 61), a small 17th-century brick and stone construction with a large garden (open daily 9-11:30am and 2-6pm; Oct. to mid-Nov. and March-April 2-6pm; admission 23F, students 10F). Forty km north of Bourges stands **La Verrerie,** a 15th-century Renaissance château by a small lake in the middle of a forest. (Open daily mid-Feb. to mid-Nov. 10am-noon and 2-6:30pm; admission 23F, students 10F.)

Limoges

Someone's gotta do the dirty work. Limoges (pop. 200,000) is a busy industrial center that holds little allure for tourists apart from the museums and boutiques displaying the city's acclaimed porcelain. For a comparative study of the local porcelain and its foreign competition, check out the **Musée National Adrien-Dubouché,** av. St-Surin (tel. 55 77 45 58), which houses the largest porcelain collection in Europe. (Open Wed.-Mon. 10am-noon and 1:30-5:15pm. Admission 17F, ages 18-25 and over 60 9F. You break it, you buy it.) The **Pavillon de la Porcelaine,** in an industrial zone out of town on av. John Kennedy, has videos and live demonstrations of porcelain craftsmanship, as well as a busy sales floor. (Open daily 8:30am-7:30pm.) Avoid the long walk by taking bus #15 (direction "Magré") from pl. de Jacobins near the *hôtel de ville.* Closer to the center of town, the **Pavillon de Verdurier** mounts an exhibit of porcelain and enamel from July to September. (Open daily 10am-12:30pm and 2-7pm. Admission 10F, under 19 5F.) If you're enameled out, head for the **Musée Municipale de l'Evêché,** pl. de l'Evêché. In addition to their fine enamel collection, which includes works dating back to the 12th century, the museum displays a large collection of Egyptian artifacts and several lesser canvases by hometown hero Renoir. (Open July-Aug. daily 10-11:45am and 2-6pm; Oct.-June Wed.-Mon. 10-11:45am and 2-5pm. Free.)

Nearby, the **Cathédrale St-Etienne** boasts a formidable number of gargoyles, as well as a flamboyant Gothic façade on the north end of the transept. The best views of the cathedral can be had from the well-kept **Jardins de l'Evêché** and the adjacent **Jardin Botanique. La Boucherie,** a district of narrow streets and medieval houses, has been home to the town's butchers since the 10th century. In mid-October, La Boucherie reverts to the 13th century for the **Feast of the Butchers' Brotherhood.**

You will have little trouble finding a room in Limoges. The **Foyer des Jeunes Travailleuses,** 20, rue Encombe Vineuse (tel. 55 77 63 97), 15 minutes from the station, has sparkling-clean singles with a sink and a desk; walk around the right side of the station and take rue Théodore Bac to pl. Carnot, turn left onto av. Adrien Tarrade, and make the first left onto rue Encombe Vineuse. There is almost always room (this being Limoges), but it's probably worth it to call ahead. (There is always someone at the front desk. 60F, sheets and showers included. Breakfast included.) The **Hôtel de France,** 23, cours Bugeaud (tel. 55 77 78 92), two minutes from the station (up the left side of the park), rents large, clean singles and doubles for 90-100F (with shower and TV 145-160F; showers 12F; breakfast 20F). The closest campground is the **Camping de la Vallée de l'Aurence** (tel. 55 38 49 43), 5km east of Limoges. Take bus #20. (12F per person, 12F per site. Electricity 2F50.)

Le Paris, at 7, pl. Denis Dussoubs, is *the* place to hang out in Limoges. All of the 40-55F entrees are served with one of the restaurant's four delicious home-brewed beers. With less atmosphere than the moon, **Caféteria Flunch,** 5, rue Dalesme, is one small step for cuisine, one giant leap for cheap food; a meat dish and two veggies cost less than if you bought all your ingredients at the supermarket. (Meals from 20F. Open daily 11am-2:30pm and 6-10pm.) Several **university restaurants** are scattered throughout Limoges. Call **CROUS** (tel. 55 01 46 12) for information. There is a permanent indoor market at **Les Halles,** off pl. de la Motte, while a larger market brightens pl. Carnot on Saturday mornings. A well-stocked **Monoprix Supermarket** sits on pl. de la République. (Open Mon.-Sat. 8:30am-7:15pm.) The **Champ de Juillet** near the train station is a brilliant place for a picnic.

To get to the **tourist office,** bd. de Fleurus (tel. 55 34 46 87), from the train station, head straight down av. du Général de Gaulle to pl. Jordan and cut diagonally across to bd. Flerus. The tourist office is on the left. The staff gives out maps and *beaucoup de* brochures, offers two-hour guided theme tours of the city in July and August, and **changes money** with a painful 4% commission. The **train station** (tel. 55 01 50 50) is a major transport hub, and has the shady characters to prove it. Trains run to: Paris (11 per day, 3 1/2hr., 220F); Lyon (4 per day, 6hr., 224F); Bordeaux (5 per day, 2hr., 143F); Toulouse (7 per day, 3 1/2hr., 184F); and Brive (12 per day, 1hr., 69F). The Limousin region is blanketed by an extensive and efficient **bus system;** if you don't mind lugging around 140 pages, you can get the full timetable at the tourist office or at the station on pl. des Charentes (tel. 55 77 39 04). The **post office** is on rue de la Préfecture near pl. Stalingrad. (Open Mon.-Fri. 8am-7pm, Sat. 8am-noon.) Have a Certs encounter at the **laundromat,** 28, rue Delesculze. (Open daily 7am-9pm. Wash 15F per 4.5kg, dry 2F per 7min. Soap 2F. The **police,** 2, rue des Vénitiens, can be reached at 55 77 58 91; the number for the **hospital** is 55 05 61 23.

Near Limoges

On June 10, 1944, Nazi SS troops massacred all 642 inhabitants of **Oradour-sur-Glane.** Since that day, this martyred village has been left untouched. Obsolete electrical wires dangle from slanting poles and 1944 automobiles rust on the road. The women and children were slaughtered in the town church; fingernail imprints are still visible on the walls. One of France's most vivid testimonies to the devastation of World War II, this town is not a place to take children. Seven buses per day make the trip from the Limoges bus station, stopping at Limoges's train station on the way (14F50). The hitching along the N141, then the D9, is reportedly not difficult.

In **Aubusson,** 50km east of Limoges, tapestry-weaving has been an art since the 8th century. The town is full of private galleries displaying local handiwork. Get more information, on the hiking trails skirting the nearby cliffs as well as on the tapestries, from the **tourist office** on rue Vieille (tel. 55 66 32 12) in the pedestrian zone (open daily 9:30am-6:30pm; Sept.-June Mon.-Fri. 8am-1pm and 2-6pm). Two trains per day run from Limoges to Aubusson via Busseau-sur-Creuze (2hr., 66F).

From Arbusson, it's a 20km trek south to **Lac de Vassivière,** where dozens of campgrounds accommodate swimmers, canoers, sailors, and windsurfers. In the summer, free shuttle buses circle the lake and transport passengers 10km to the nearest train station in Eymontier. The **Camping Châteaucourt** (tel. 55 69 22 40) is in nearby Beaumont-du-Lac. (14F50 per person, 11F50 per site. Electricty 8F50. Open July-Aug.)

Ask the tourist office in Limoges about excursions to surrounding châteaux as well as historic towns that were once on the pilgrimage route to Santiago de Compostela.

Le Puy

Situated at the confluence of the Borne and Loire Rivers and surrounded by the fertile slopes of extinct volcanoes, Le Puy (pop. 46,000) embodies the rugged beauty of the French interior. In stark contrast to the gentle green hills around them, three jutting crags of volcanic rock pierce Le Puy's skyline above a humble spread of red-tiled houses. Balancing atop these rocky pinnacles, an assortment of statues and churches demonstrates the determination of their builders to conquer nature with human will. As for God's will, Le Puy's glorious Romanesque cathedral is part of a larger ecclesiastical complex which guards many masterpieces within its walls. Beyond the holy city, in the back streets of the cobblestone *vieille ville, dentellières* (lace-makers) continue a centuries-old tradition as they meticulously attend to their craft.

Orientation and Practical Information

Le Puy is 132km southeast of Clermont-Ferrand and 134km southwest of Lyon, in the southeastern corner of Auvergne. A few direct trains per day connect Le Puy with both cities, but most trains arriving from southern France or Clermont-Ferrand require a change at St-Georges d'Aurac, while trains from Lyon or Paris require a change at St-Etienne (Châteaucreux). From the train station, walk left along av. Charles Dupuy and turn left onto bd. Maréchal Fayolle. After five minutes you will reach two adjacent squares, pl. Michelet and pl. de Breuil. The tourist office and most of the hotels are here and on the adjacent bd. St-Louis; the cathedral and *vieille ville* are just up the hill to the right.

Tourist Office: pl. du Breuil (tel. 71 09 38 41). Free hotel reservations and a good map of the city with hotels and restaurants marked on it. Helpful staff also offers hiking suggestions and guided tours of the city in French (July daily at 3pm, Aug. daily at 9:30am and 3pm, 2hr., 25F). Nocturnal guided visits of the city mid-July to mid-Aug. (Tues. and Fri.). Open daily 8:30am-7pm; May-June and Sept. 8:30am-noon and 1:30-6pm; Oct.-April Mon.-Sat. 8am-noon and 1:30-6pm. **Annex** operates in July and Aug. at 23 rue des Tables, off av. de la Cathédrale. Open Tues.-Sat. 9am-noon and 2-7pm.

Post Office: 8, av. de la Dentelle (tel. 71 07 02 00), on the corner of av. Charles Dupuy, 2min. from the train station. **Telephones** and **currency exchange.** Open Mon.-Fri. 8am-7pm, Sat. 8am-noon. **Branch office,** 49, bd. St-Louis. Open Mon.-Fri. 9am-noon and 2:30-5:30pm, Sat. 9am-noon. **Postal Code:** 43000.

Trains: pl. Maréchal-Leclerc (tel. 71 02 50 50). To Lyon (9 per day, 2 1/2 hr., 95F). To St-Etienne (Châteaucreux), where you can take a train to Paris (9 per day, 1hr. 20min., 62F). To Clermont-Ferrand via St-Georges d'Aurac (4 per day, 2-3hr., 95F). Lockers 5F and 10F. Information office open daily 9am-1pm and 2:30-6pm.

Buses: (tel. 71 09 25 60), next to the train station. Useful free *Horaire Air-Rail-Route* has times for all transportation in the area. To St-Etienne (4 per day, 2 1/4hr., 67F). Open Mon.-Fri. 8:30am-12:30pm and 2:30-7pm, Sat. 8:30am-12:30pm and 2:30-6pm; Sept.-June Mon. 7:30am-noon and 2:30-7pm, Tues.-Fri. 8:30am-12:30pm and 2:30-7pm, Sat. 8am-12:30pm and 2-7pm.

Taxis: Radio-Taxis, pl. du Breuil (tel. 71 05 42 43). 24 hrs.

Youth Center: Bureau d'Information Jeunesse (BIJ), rue Jean-Baptiste Fabre (tel. 71 02 25 14). Provides information on activities and opportunities in and around Le Puy. Open Mon.-Fri. 2-5pm.

Laundromat: 12, rue Chèvrerie, at rue Boucherie Basse, off pl. Michelet. The place to take your lace. Wash 14F per 5kg, dry 8F per 20min. Soap 2F. Open Mon.-Sat. 7:30am-noon and 1-8pm.

Bike Rental: Squash Tonic, place du Breuil (tel. 71 02 22 97). Street-corner outfit rents 16 shiny *vélo tout terrain* (mountain bikes). 30F per hr., 70F per 1/2-day, 120F per day. 2500F or ID deposit. Open July-Aug. daily 9am-3pm and 5-6:30pm. At other times of the year, go to any bike store and ask for pamphlets on bike rentals in nearby towns.

Medical Emergency: Centre Hospitalier Emile Roux, bd. Dr. Chantemesse (tel. 71 05 66 77). **Clinique Bon Secours,** 67bis, av. Maréchal Foch (tel. 71 09 05 84). **SAMU,** tel. 15 or 71 02 02 02.

Police: rue de la Passerelle (tel. 71 04 04 22). **Emergency:** tel. 17.

Accommodations and Camping

Cheap hotels cluster around pl. du Breuil, especially on busy bd. Maréchal Fayolle. Even in July and August, rooms are usually available in the morning. Reserve by phone if you plan to arrive late in the day. The tourist office has a list of the three *foyers* in town, one of which is for women only.

Centre Pierre Cardinal (HI), 9, Jules Vallés (tel. 71 05 52 40). From pl. Michelet, take rue Porteil d'Avignon north to the dead end, and turn right on rue Général Lafayette, walking past the zigzag in the road. The hostel is on the left, 50m past the HI sign, in a beautiful building overlooking the city (10min.). Two hundred years ago, this building was a barracks for Revolutionary troops. Great hostel with a friendly atmosphere and excellent kitchen facilities. If closed during the day, check after 8pm or use telephone by entrance to call the *accueil.* (Dial 5) Reception open daily 8am-noon, 1:30-7pm, and 8-11pm. Curfew 11pm. 33F. Breakfast 8F50. Lunch or dinner served if there are enough people 30F, with wine 36F; order a day in advance. Sheets 17F.

Hôtel des Cordeliers, 17, rue des Cordelières (tel. 71 09 01 12), off rue Crozatier, which is off bd. Maréchal Fayolle. Wow. A one-star hotel with two-star rooms and three-star originality. Each room is unique, ranging from good to regal. Room 23 has to be seen to be believed. Singles and doubles 100F, with brand-new shower, bath, and toilet 155F. Triples and quads with shower, bath, and toilet 165-215F. Huge hall showers and baths included. Breakfast 23F. Restaurant downstairs (see Food). Call ahead in summer. Open Dec.-Oct.

Hôtel le Régional, 36, bd. Maréchal Fayolle (tel. 71 09 37 74), a short walk from pl. Michelet, on the noisy corner of av. Dupuy. Reasonable, well-kept rooms and a lively bar downstairs. Singles and doubles 85F, with shower 120F. Triples and quads 200F, with bath 210F. Hall showers included. Breakfast 22F. No shower in winter.

Hôtel le Veau d'Or, 7, place Cadelade (tel. 71 09 07 74), near the intersection of bd. Maréchal Foyolle and av. Dupuy. Small, clean, and simple, and run by a friendly couple. Singles and doubles 80F. No showers. Breakfast 22F. Arrive early, since phone reservations are not accepted.

Camping: Camping Municipal Bouthezard, chemin de Roderie (tel. 71 09 55 09), in the northwest corner of town. Walk up bd. St-Louis, continue on bd. Carnot, turn right at the dead end on av. d'Aiguille, and look to your left. Bus #7 makes the 2km trip (only 7 per day, 10min., 5F). Hot showers and a restaurant. 20F per person with tent, 8F per additional person.

Food

Look for inexpensive restaurants on the sidestreets off pl. du Breuil. There is a **Supermarché Casino** on the corner of av. de la Dentelle and rue P. Farigoule which stocks a wide range of regional specialties and has a surprisingly good cafeteria above it. (Supermarket open Mon.-Sat. 8:30am-8pm. Cafeteria open daily 11am-10pm. Meals 25F50-46F50.) Every bar and many stores (which often give free samples) serve the algae-hued after-dinner liqueur *verveine,* made from a collection of indigenous herbs (55-70F a bottle).

Restaurant des Cordeliers, 17, rue des Cordelièrs, at the end of a small alley, under the hotel (see Accommodations). Chummy neighborhood joint with a huge variety of tasty dishes. 48F lunch *menu* with tomato and onion salad, choice of pork or chicken, lentils, and the *dessert du jour.* 5-course 69F *menu* has tons of choices. Open Tues.-Sat. noon-2pm and 7:30-10pm, Sun. noon-2pm.

Pizzeria Pépino, 9, rue Vibert. Tranquil side-street restaurant, off pl. du Breuil. Pizzas 28-49F. Those who shrink from the challenge of the full-size pizzas may opt for the 55F *menu*, which offers salad, *tortellini*, and dessert or cheese. Open Mon. and Wed.-Sat. noon-2pm and 7:30-11pm, Sun. 7:30-11pm.

Café Le Palais, 27, pl du Breuil. Stylish café with 38F *plats du jour. Quiche lorraine* 22F. Salads 16-40F. Open daily noon-2pm and 7-10pm.

Le Nom de la Rose, 48, rue Raphaël. Eclectic blend of local and Mexican dishes. 69F *menu* offers *terrine de la maison, chile con carne* or leg of lamb, and cheese or dessert. Open daily noon-2pm and 7-9:30pm.

Sights

A long procession of streets and steps climbs dramatically to the façade of **Cathédrale Notre-Dame,** one of the largest and most striking Romanesque churches in Auvergne. Though established as the seat of a local bishopric by the 6th century, the cathedral only rose to prominence half a millennium later as a transit point for Bourguignon and Teutonic pilgrims on the sacred road to Santiago de Compostela. A dark-skinned rendition of the Virgin Mary, dressed in the regional white lace, graces the main altar. The origins of the Black Virgins, commonly encountered throughout central France, have been at the center of an ongoing theological debate. One of the more likely theories proposes that the statuettes were brought by crusaders from the Middle East, where artists endowed them with the dark complexion the Virgin most likely had. The original Black Virgin, which dated from the 12th century, went up in flames during the Revolution, but its replacement is still paraded reverently through the streets on August 14, the evening before Assumption Day. (Cathedral open daily 8:30am-7pm. Free tours leave from the nave July-Sept. at 3:30pm.)

The 12th-century **Roman cloister** next to the cathedral suggests an Islamic influence with its alternating black-and-white-stoned arcades. A 13th-century fresco on the Byzantine arches depicts the crucifixion amid vivid red tiling and black volcanic rock. The intricate frieze of grinning faces and mythical beasts is barely visible under the edge of the roof. The admission fee includes entry to the **Trésor d'Art Religieux** and the **Chapelle des Reliques.** Tucked in the *trésor* are walnut statues, jeweled capes, and paintings, while the celebrated Renaissance mural *Les Arts Libéraux* hangs in the Chapelle. Thought to be unfinished, the painting represents only four of the seven liberal arts: Grammar, Logic, Rhetoric, and Music. (*Cloître, chapelle,* and *trésor* all open daily 9:30am-7:30pm; April-June 9:30am-12:30pm and 2-6pm; Oct.-March 9:30am-noon and 2-4:30pm. Admission 20F, students 12F, under 17 6F.)

From the Holy City, you can climb the **Rocher Corneille,** which is actually the eroded core of an ancient volcano. The summit looks out over a sensational countryside of jagged crags spoiling an otherwise uniformly green terrain. Insatiable thrill-seekers can climb the cramped 24m red statue of the Notre Dame de France for a view from Mary's neck; her halo has been sealed from the public for security reasons. At the base of the Rocher lies a pile of cannons, military bounty from Sebastopol, 213 of which were melted in 1860 to cast the Virgin statue. (Open daily 9am-7pm; Oct.-March 15 Wed.-Mon. 10am-5pm; March 16-April daily 9am-6pm. Admission 9F.) Nearby, 10th-century **Chapelle St-Michel d'Aiguilhe** crowns a narrow, 80m spike of volcanic rock. The view from the top is unreal. (Open daily June 15-Sept. 15 9am-7pm; Sept. 16-Nov. 12 9:30am-noon and 2-5:30pm; Nov. 13-March 14 2-4pm; March 15-31 10am-noon and 2-5pm; April-June 14 10am-noon and 2-5pm; April-June 15 10am-noon and 2-6pm. Admission 8F, under 14 5F.)

The **Musée Crozatier,** (tel. 71 09 38 90) at the back of the lovely Jardin Henri Vinay, houses a small collection of archeological items and artwork, including a display of Le Puy's needlework lace from the 16th to the 20th century. (Open Wed.-Mon. 10am-noon and 2-6pm; Oct.-April Mon. and Wed.-Sat. 10am-noon and 2-6pm, Sun. 2-6pm. Admission 11F, students 5F50.) Le Puy's ornate lacework traces back to rather modest origins as a family industry, though by the 16th century almost the entire female population of the Velay region was employed in its creation. With its bloody attack on bourgeois culture, the French Revolution removed a major source of funding for the lace industry. The emergence of mechanical lace production at the turn of the century dealt yet another painful blow to the purity of the lacemakers' art. If the history of Le Puy's lace industry intrigues you, head to **L'Atelier Conservatoire National de la Dentelle,** 2, rue Duguesclin (tel. 71 02 01 68), founded in 1976 to safeguard the techniques of a profession long in decline and to encourage its resurgence. Through the unmarked door on the street and up a flight of stairs is a small museum, which exhibits lace samples from around the world and also includes a demonstration of lacemaking techniques. (Open Mon.-Sat. 9-11:30am and 2-5:30pm; Oct.-May Mon.-Fri. 9-11:30am and 2-5:30pm. Admission 10F.)

Saturday *is* market day in Le Puy, and practically every square in town puts on its own show. From 6am to 12:30pm, farmers bring what they've grown (fruits, vegetables) and made (cheeses, breads, jams, honey). The one in **place du Plot** throws in a few live chickens, rabbits, and puppies. The adjacent **place du Clauzel** hosts an **antique market** (7:30am-1pm). Bargaining for the items on sale, which include World War II medals, pipe paraphernalia, and old silverware, is *de rigueur.* In **place du Breuil,** the biggest spread of all includes new and used clothing, hardware, toiletries, and footwear.

In the third week of September, all of Le Puy goes Renaissance for the week-long **Fête du Roi de l'Oiseau,** derived from the title bestowed annually on the town's champion *tireur* (archer) of the *papagaï* (parrot, in old French). Locals dress in period costume, jugglers and minstrels ramble the streets, food and drink in the *vieille ville* can be purchased only with the currency minted for the festival, and a different theatrical performance takes the stage each day. In addition, an elaborate system of tunnels carved centuries ago into the rock below the Holy City is opened up and turned into one great party hall, with beer and wine flowing freely. (Admission to nightly shows at 9pm 60F, but you'll be expected to be in costume.) A limited number of Renaissance outfit rentals is usually available. In early Spring, the **Festival Carnivalesque de Musique de Rues** brings over 400 street musicians from around Europe to town for a two-day celebration. Le Puy hosts its annual **Festival International de Folklore** during the third week of July. More than 15 countries send musicians and dancers in traditional attire to roam the streets and show their stuff. (For more information, call 71 09 20 91.)

The **Forteresse de Polignac,** 5km from Le Puy, once housed the most powerful family in the area. To reach the ruins, follow bd. St-Louis past the bridge to the N102, or take the bus from the *gare routière.* (Open May-Sept. daily 9:30am-noon and 2:30-7pm; off-season call 71 05 70 74.) Forty-five km north is the ancient mountain town of

La Chaise-Dieu, best known for its Gothic **Abbaye St-Robert** (tel. 71 00 06 06), which contains a chilling *danse macabre* fresco. (Open daily 9am-noon and 2-7pm; Sept.-June Wed.-Mon. 10am-noon and 2-5pm. Admission 12F.) In late August and early September, the abbey holds an enormously popular festival of French and classical music. (Admission 60-420F.) La Chaise-Dieu's **tourist office** (tel. 71 00 01 16) is in pl. de la Mairie. (Open in summer Tues.-Sun. 10:30am-noon and 2-6pm; winter Tues.-Sat. same hours.)

Clermont-Ferrand

Once a thriving cultural center, Clermont-Ferrand's (pop. 140,000) socially flirtatious character expired with the arrival of industrialization at the beginning of the 20th century. Industry descended on Clermont quite by accident, when, in the mid-19th century, one Madame Daubrée serendipitously discovered that rubber dissolves in benzene, and she proceeded to make little rubber balls for her children's amusement. Ultimately, the idea caught on, and Edouard Michelin capitalized on the discovery, founding Clermont's major industry. Today, Clermont-Ferrand remains the headquarters of the lucrative Michelin tire empire, which has recently influenced further industrialization. Yet despite the massive housing project and smoke-spitting factories that ring the city, don't roll right on past this centrally located city; Clermont-Ferrand merits a visit, if only for a day. The *vieille ville* contains a number of elegant old buildings and a strikingly beautiful cathedral, all constructed from jet black volcanic stone culled from the surrounding area. The town's three museums are all free, and together they present a comprehensive history of Clermont-Ferrand and of the nearby Parc Naturel des Volcans d'Auvergne. Finally Clermont-Ferrand's several universities annually draw some 30,000 students who inspire the factory-laden city with a breath of fresh air.

Orientation and Practical Information

Some believe that Clermont-Ferrand occupies the site of ancient Gergovia, where Vercingétorix defeated Julius Caesar. If, like Caesar, you are stuck in Clermont-Ferrand, take bus #2, #4, or #14 from the station (6F) to lively **place de Jaude.** Bounded on either end by statues of local hero General Desaix and the valiant Vercingétorix, the *Place* is an expansive, tree-lined esplanade with cafés, a theater, and the modern **Centre Jaude,** a vast, slightly upscale shopping center. If you'd rather make the 20-minute walk, go left from the station onto av. de l'Union Soviétique, left again onto bd. Fleury, and take a quick right onto av. Carnot. The street bends to the left and turns into rue Maréchal Juin for 2 blocks, and then bends to the right, turning into bd. Desaix before it dumps you onto pl. de Jaude.

Tourist Office: 69, bd. Gergovia (tel. 73 93 30 20). From pl. de Jaude, head down rue Gonod, which becomes bd. Charles de Gaulle, and bear left onto bd. Gergovia. Buses #2 and #4 also continue this way (get off at "Salins/Gare Routière"). Excellent city map, list of hotels and restaurants, and bus timetables. Open Mon.-Sat. 8:30am-7pm, Sun. 9am-noon and 2-6pm; Oct-May Mon.-Fri. 8:45am-6:30pm, Sat. 9am-noon and 2-6pm. There is a **branch office** at the train station (tel. 73 91 87 89). Open Mon.-Sat. 9:15-11:30am and 12:15-5pm; Oct.-May Mon.-Fri. 9:15am-11:30am and 12:15-5pm.

Post Office: 1, rue Louis Renon (tel.. 73 30 63 00). In two buildings. The building up the hill handles mail while the other handles finances and has a **currency exchange.** Both open Mon.-Fri. 8am-7pm, Sat. 8am-noon. **Postal Code:** 63000.

Trains: av. de l'Union Soviétique (tel. 73 92 50 50). To: Paris (8 per day, 3 1/2hr., 219F); Lyon (7 per day, 3hr., 137F); Bordeaux (3 per day, 6hr., 211F). **Lockers** 15F for 72 hr. Information office open Mon.-Sat. 8am-7:30 pm.

Buses: The *gare routière* (tel. 73 93 13 61) is just behind the main tourist office. Buses run throughout the Massif Central, including to Le Puy (1 per day at 4pm, 3 1/4hr., 57F).

Public Transportation: 15/17, bd. Robert Schuman (tel. 73 26 44 90). T2C blankets the city with frequent, efficient buses (6F). From the station to Montferrand take #17 (direction "Cebazet" or "Montel"); from pl. de Jaude to Montferrand take bus #1, 9 10M, 13, or 16.

Taxis: Taxi Radio (tel. 73 92 57 58) or **Allo Taxi** (73 90 75 75).

English Bookstore: Via l'Europe, 15, pl. du Terrail (tel. 73 92 39 60). Decent selection of novels, with a few *Let's Go* guides waiting to be perused. Open Mon. 2-7pm, Tues.-Sat. 10am-12:30pm and 1:30-7pm.

Laundromat: Laverie Automatique, pl. Renoux. Wash 16kg for 5F, dry 6 min. for 2F. Open daily 7am-8pm. Other laundromats at 62, av. Charras and 10, rue St-Antoine.

Late-Night Pharmacy: Pharmacie Ducher, 1, pl. Delille (tel. 73 91 31 77). Open 24 hrs.

Hospital: Hôpital St-Jacques, 30, pl. Henri Dunant (73 62 57 00).

Medical Emergency: SAMU, tel. 15.

Police: 2, rue Pélissier (tel. 73 92 10 70). **Emergency:** tel. 17.

Accommodations and Camping

Plenty of decent, inexpensive hotels gather near the train station. Finding a cheap room in the center of town can be more challenging.

Auberge de Jeunesse (HI), 55, av. de l'Union Soviétique (tel. 73 92 26 39), just to the right of the train station. Basic dorm accommodations with no hot water. Open March-Oct. 7-9:30am and 5-10:30pm. 39F. Breakfast 16F. Sheets 15F. HI card required, but they will accept you for one night without a card.

Foyer St-Jean/Auberge de Jeunesse, 17, rue Gauthier de Béauzat (tel. 73 37 14 31), just off pl. Gaillard. From the station, take bus #2, 4, or 14 to "Gaillard." Friendly place with bar, pool table, tennis courts, and washing machines. Singles, doubles, or triples 70F per person, nonmembers 80F. Sheets and breakfast included. Meals 35F. Call ahead.

Hôtel d'Aigueperse, 4, rue Aigueperse (tel. 73 91 30 62), near the train station off av. Albert et Elizabeth. Spacious, flowery rooms and an affable proprietor. Singles and doubles 78-88F, with shower 114F. Doubles with 2 beds 178F. Shower 10F. Breakfast 16F50.

Hôtel Foch, 22, rue Maréchal Foch (tel. 73 93 48 40), off pl. de Jaude. Recently renovated. Excellent mattresses in quiet rooms, most overlooking a courtyard. Singles and doubles 120-130F, with shower 145-155F. Triples and quads 240-250F. Showers 15F. Breakfast with homemade jam 24F.

Camping: Le Chanset, av. Jean-Baptiste Marrou (tel. 73 61 30 73). From the station, take bus #4 to "Préguille." 10F per person, 7F per tent. Open all year.

Food

Finding a good, inexpensive meal in Clermont-Ferrand should be no problem. The area around rue St-Dominique, off Av. des Etats-Unis, has dozens of ethnic restaurants, while the narrow streets behind the cathedral shelter many restaurants specializing in local cuisine. There is a **Casino Supermarché** on av. Marx Dormay, with an inexpensive **cafeteria** next door (supermarket open Mon.-Sat. 8:30am-8pm; cafeteria open daily 11am-10pm), but you'd have to be crazy to get your groceries anywhere other than the **Marché St-Pierre,** off pl. Gaillard, a huge covered market with hundreds of *auvergnat* specialities. (Open Mon.-Sat. 6am-7pm.)

Cafétéria Flunch, 8, av. des Etats-Unis. Roast chicken with 2 vegetables for just 18F90, *steak frites* for 30F. Whoever started this cafeteria chain deserves the slobbering affection of all starving backpackers. Open daily 11am-10pm.

Le Stramboli, 18, rue du Cheval Blanc. Great selection of pizzas (30-50F) and pasta (25-45F), and the *salade stramboli* (30F), with its palm hearts and other exotica. Open Mon.-Sat. noon-2pm and 7-11pm, Sun. 7-11pm.

La Tonkinoise, 23-25, rue des Chaussiers. If French fare and Flunch flare are not in the stars tonight, treat yourself to copious portions of Vietnamese specialities. Try *my sao,* a yellow vermicelli with vegetables, stir-fried with chicken (42F), beef (44F), or crab (45F). Open Mon.-Sat. 7-11pm.

Le Relais Pascal, 15, rue Pascal. Dozens of *auvergnat* specialities, and a selection of more than 100 wines. 75F *menu* includes *terrine de campagne, tripaux* (tripe), cheese, and dessert. Open Tues.-Sat. noon-2pm and 7-10pm.

Sights and Entertainment

The **Ville Noire,** which derives its name from the somber black volcanic stone used in its construction, harbors an impressive array of religious and secular edifices. Follow rue du Port to the **Basilique de Notre-Dame-du-Port,** whose elegant austerity exemplifies its 12th-century *auvergnat* Romanesque style. (Open daily 9am-noon and 2-6pm.) Constructed only a quarter of a century after the basilica, the Gothic **Cathédrale Notre Dame de l'Assomption** is remarkable for the radical departure in style from the former structure. Modeled after the flamboyant cathedrals of the north, Notre Dame commands attention with the majestic jet black of its volcanic stone brought from Volvic during construction. The strength of this lava-based material allowed the cathedral's architects to elongate the spires to a height of 100m, rendering them more slender and graceful. Step inside to admire the three beautiful rose windows and the magnificent 13th-century windows in the chapels behind the altar. A free guided tour of the windows (in French) is given Wednesday, Thursday, and Saturday at 3pm.

The **Musée Bargoin,** 45, rue Ballainvilliers (tel. 73 91 37 31), is undoubtedly the most interesting museum in town. Devoted to prehistoric and Gallo-Roman archeology, the museum displays artifacts recovered from the Temple of Mercury on the Puy de Dôme, as well as Pompeiian wall paintings (some desecrated with ancient Roman graffiti), 2000-year-old braids of hair, mummified infants, and some of the 10,000 Gallo-Roman wooden votive offerings discovered in 1968 at the Source des Roches in nearby Chamalières. (Open Tues.-Sat. 10am-noon and 2-6pm, Sun. 2-6pm; Oct.-April Tues.-Sat. 10am-noon and 2-5pm, Sun. 2-5pm. Free.) One block away, the **Musée Lecoq,** 15, rue Bardoux (tel. 73 91 93 78), is devoted to the botany, zoology, and geology of Auvergne. The museum has an exceptionally strong collection of locally-found minerals. (Same hours as Musée Bargoin. Free.) The **Musée du Ranquet,** 34, rue des Gras (tel. 73 37 38 63), records the last two centuries of Clermont-Ferrand's existence, but, perhaps predictably, does not thrill. It is free however, and merits a quick stop, if only to see the two adding machines invented by local son Blaise Pascal at the ripe old age of 18. (Same hours as Musée Bargoin. Free.)

Clermont-Ferrand was once two distinct cities: the Episcopal city of Clermont and the 12th-century Montferrand, built by the dukes of Auvergne to rival their competitor's power. The two merged in the 18th century. **Vieux Montferrand** is sedate and sparsely populated compared to its industrial neighbor. Buses #1, 9, 10M, 13, and 16 take you from the northeast corner of pl. de Jaude to pl. de la Fontaine, at the foot of picturesque **rue Guesde.** From the train station, bus #17 will whisk you on the short ride to Montferrand. Continue up the hill to the 13th-century **Notre-Dame-de-Prosperité.** Built out of volcanic stone, it stands on the site of the long-demolished château of the *auvergnat* dukes. For a more secular sight, take a look at the 15th-century carvings on the **Maison de l'Aphotécaire,** at the intersection of rue des Cordeliers and rue Séminaire. On the right be sure to note the doctor and his unfortunate patient, who is caught forever, in stone, with his pants down. Bummer.

Every year in late January and/or early February, filmmakers from all over Europe gather for Clermont-Ferrand's **Festival International du Court Métrage** (International Festival of Short Films). With up to 75 films in competition, the festival is an effort to publicize and reward the often-underappreciated short film industry. Ticket prices range from 26F to 40F for closing night. For information, contact Sauve Qui Peut le Court Métrage, 26, rue des Jacobins, 63000 Clermont-Ferrand (tel. 73 91 65 73). On June 21, everyone in town floods the *vieille ville* to usher in sumer with the **Fête de la Musique.** Dozens of local bands, playing everything from jazz to speed metal, station temselves at hundred foot intervals throughout the pedestrian zone and peddle their sonorous wares. There's dancing in the streets and the beer flows freely, but at 10F a can, you'd do best to bring your own supply.

A large student population does its best to brighten Clermont throughout the year. **Thoren's,** 16, pl. de Jaude (tel. 73 93 32 55), is a plush bar with a powerful sound system on a prominent location on the square. (Open daily 10am-1am. Beer 14F.) Fooze while you booze at **Le Clown,** 65bis, rue Anatole France (tel. 73 92 17 75), a small bar behind the train station that sometimes attracts local musicians. (Open Mon.-Thurs. 8am-1am, Fri.-Sun. 8am-2am. Beer 8-14F.) The **Horn Pub,** 31, rue Anatole France, behind the train station, is a lively British pub that lures students with live music nearly every weekend during the academic year. (Open Tues.-Sun. 7:30pm-late; Sept.-June Tues.-Sun. 6pm-late. Admission to better shows 35F.) One of the happiest—and most exclusive—nightclubs is **Club l'Arlequin,** 2, rue d'Etoile (tel. 73 37 33 88), off av. des Etats-Unis. (Open Tues.-Sun. 11:30pm-late. Cover Sun. and Tues.-Thurs. 50F, Fri.-Sat. 60F. No sneakers.)

Near Clermont-Ferrand

When Clermont-Ferrand begins to wear a little thin, head for the surrounding region's extinct volcanic hinterland and its pristine mountain villages. Although difficult to reach, the **Parc Naturel Régional des Volcans d'Auvergne** (Auvergne Natural Volcano Park; tel. 73 65 67 19) west of Clermont-Ferrand rewards hikers and skiers with France's longest stretches of unspoiled and strictly protected terrain. The park was founded in 1967 to save the local scenery from industrial development and to preserve cottage industry and agriculture. Historical monuments in the park, including medieval castles built from volcanic stone and churches in the local Romanesque style, have been restored. Hiking paths through the most picturesque parts are marked and catalogued in a booklet available at the Clermont-Ferrand tourist office. The protected area includes three main sections—the **Monts Dore,** the **Monts du Cantal,** and the **Monts Dômes**—last of which is the best place to explore the many extinct volcanoes.

A climb to the top of the massive, flat-topped **Puy de Dôme** (1465m) rewards with a view across the Chaîne des Puys that encompasses over an eighth of France (that's 6,000 *boulangeries).* If you scale the Dôme in the fall—especially in November—you may behold the wondrous *mer des nuages* (sea of clouds) phenomenon, in which a blanket of clouds obscures the plains below, and only the solitary mountain peaks protrude into the clear blue sky. For those who like to take a little history with their nature, there is a Roman Temple of Mercury on the summit.

Although it lies only 12km from Clermont-Ferrand, reaching Puy de Dôme takes some planning. In the summer, town buses leave every Monday morning from the Clermont-Ferrand train station and from pl. de Jaude. Otherwise , head out of town on av. du Puy de Dôme and follow the signs for about 8km to the base of the mountain. In July and August, frequent shuttle buses run from the base to the summit (12F one-way, 18F round-trip). For the other 10 months, head up the road until you're halfway around the mountain, and then follow the *sentier des muletiers,* a Roman footpath that leads to the top in about 40 minutes. If you do decide to walk, get a good weather forecast for the whole day, as conditions can change rapidly; even in June, hailstorms on the summit are not uncommon. Hitching from the town to the base of the Dôme is reported to be easy.

Two small towns set among the most beautiful of the Monts Dores are **Orcival** and **St-Nectaire,** both with intriguing Romanesque churches, and the latter with a delicious, mild cheese of the same name. Each is served by occasional buses from Clermont and excursion buses from nearby Mont Dore.

The **Comité Départemental de Tourisme du Puy du Dôme,** 26, rue St-Esprit (tel. 73 42 21 21) in Clermont-Ferrand, has reams of information on the surrounding area. The office also sells copies of its colorful *Puy-de-Dôme* brochure, with detailed historical and cultural information on the area's towns (50F). (Open Mon.-Thurs. 8:30am-12:15pm and 1:45-5:30pm, Fri. 8:30am-12:15pm and 1:45-5pm.) **Chamina,** 5, rue Pierre-le-Vénérable (tel. 73 90 94 82), also in Clermont, sells maps and suggests hiking and mountain climbing excursions through the Massif. (Open Mon.-Fri. 2-6pm.) The **Comité Régional du Tourisme de l'Auvergne** on the top floor of an office building at 43, av. Julien (tel. 73 93 04 03), provides information on the region, but you may want to lose your backpack before entering their swanky offices.

Riom

In the 17th century, Riom and Clermont were great commercial and cultural rivals. Riom soon yielded its status as a great metropolis, but this ancient city seems to be winning the cultural race. Although a wide boulevard has replaced the old city ramparts, many ornate *hôtels particuliers* (bourgeois mansions) and half-timbered houses have been restored and transformed into museums; others house doctors' and lawyers' offices, as well as the occasional *masseur.* The old town of Riom, the only attraction worth seeing, is coverable in an afternoon, even allowing for a leisurely browse through the two main museums.

Dozens of trains each day connect Riom with Clermont-Ferrand (10min., 13F) and Vichy (25min., 35F). To get to the old town from the station, head straight down av. Virlogeux, bear right onto rue Jeanne d'Arc, and turn right on rue du Commerce. The **tourist office,** 16, rue du Commerce (tel. 73 38 59 45), distributes an annotated walking tour of Riom's 16th-century *hôtels particuliers* and a decent free map. (Open Mon.-Fri. 9am-noon and 2-6:30pm, Sat. 9am-noon and 2-6pm.)

The most impressive among the *hôtels particuliers,* the **Maison des Consuls,** rue de l'Hôtel de Ville, sports five arcades and a row of busts of women and Roman Emperors glaring down from above the first-story windows. The nearby **Hôtel Guimoneau,** 12, rue de l'Horloge, hides a beautiful courtyard and an ornately sculpted stairway. An interior gallery displays four small statues representing strength, justice, prudence, and temperance. Across the street, the **Tour de l'Horloge** lords over a dazzling panorama of red Riom rooftops melting into the greenery of nearby Monts Dômes. (Open Mon.-Sat. 9am-6:30 pm; off-season Mon.-Sat. 10am-4:30pm. Free.) The austere Eglise Notre Dame du Marthuret, 44, rue du Commerce shelters the moving 14th-century statue **la Vierge à l'Oiseau,** rightfully recognized as one of the Middle Ages' most beautiful statues. The **Ste-Chapelle,** the only remaining vestige of the **Palais de Justice,** built in the 14th century by Jean de Berry, holds exquisite stained-glass windows. (Obligatory tour given Mon.-Fri. every 1/2 hr. 3-6pm; May-June Wed. 3-5pm; Sept. Wed. and Fri. 3-6pm. Admission 15F.)

The two museums in Riom are beautiful and certainly merit a visit. The handsomely renovated **Musée Mandet,** 4, rue de l'Hôtel de Ville (tel. 73 38 18 53), housed in adjacent 16th- and 18th-century *hôtels particuliers,* preserves a delightful collection of Gallo-Roman bronzes, pottery, and jewelry, early French and Flemish paintings and sculpture, and an extensive if prosaic collection of paintings from the 17th to the 19th centuries. (Open. Wed.-Mon. 10am-noon and 2-6:30pm; Oct.-May Wed.-Sun. 10am-noon and 2-5:30pm. Admission 16F, students 8F, free Wed.) The well-organized **Musée Régionale Folklorique d'Auvergne,** 10bis, rue Delille (tel. 73 38 17 31), near the Palais de Justice, shelters a truly fascinating collection of local arts and crafts, costumes, and musical instruments particular to Auvergne. (Same hours and admission as the Musée Mandet. Admission to both museums 21F.) Every year in June (and sometimes spilling over into July), ivory-ticklers descend on Riom, which hosts the week-long **Piano à Riom,** an international piano festival. (Admission 50-150F per concert, under 25 35-50% reduction. For information, call the tourist office.) The **Festival de Jazz** bops though town at the beginning of September (tickets 60F).

Vichy

While made out by some to be literal modern-day fountains of youth, Vichy's *sources* remain tainted by the city's nefarious role as the seat of Nazi-sympathizer Maréchal Philippe Pétain's collaborationist government during WWII. Forced to leave Paris in 1940 due to German occupation, the French government settled in Vichy because of its extensive rail linkages and telephone network. It was in Vichy's famed opera house that the parliament convened on July 9 and 10 to decide the fate of the Third Republic: 569 of the 649 members voted to abolish it, and the new *Etat Français* was formed. The approval of Pétain's policies buttressed the German occupiers' position for four wretched years, until peace was restored in 1944.

Today Vichy's main preoccupation is with restoring health—especially the wine-sodden livers of the silver-haired from *le tout Paris* (i.e. wealthy Parisians) who flood the town every summer to take the waters and stroll around parks and gardens. Thus, for its somewhat festive summer atmosphere, its pricey athletic complexes, and its lovely boutiques vending marvelous sweats, quichey Vichy is a treasure, but be forewarned that the town lacks vigor.

The **tourist office,** 19, rue du Parc (tel. 70 98 71 94), as well as the most popular *sources,* lie in the **Parc des Sources,** about 10 minutes from the train station. Leaving the station, walk straight on rue de Paris; at the fork take a left onto rue Georges Clemenceau and then a quick right onto rue Sarnin. The tourist office is staight ahead across the park, in the former *Hôtel du Parc* that housed the nucleus of the Pétain leadership. They distribute a decent free map and a list of Vichy's countless hotels and restaurants, as well as help find rooms for no charge. In addition, they sell a comprehensive booklet of suggested walking and car tours in Vichy and the region (5F) and the *Carte Loisir* (50F), which provides discounts to operas, concerts, and cultural activities for the summer season. (Open Mon.-Sat. 9am-7pm, Sun. 9:30am-12:30pm and 3-7pm; Sept.-June Mon.-Sat. 9am-12:30pm and 1:30-7pm, Sun. 9:30am-12:30pm and 3-7pm.)

The glass and white cast-iron **Halle des Sources** (tel. 70 98 95 37) at the edge of the Parc des Sources is where most of the *curistes* go each morning to take their daily dose of the lukewarm carbonate-laden water. *Chomel* and *Grande Grille,* the strongest, and consequently, the most popular of the city's six *sources* have their outlets in the *halle.* Before marching in, make a trip to the **source des Celestins** on bd. Kennedy, where you can fill your Evian bottles with a kinder, gentler version of this *aqua vitae* for free. Have a sip and then decide if you really want to pay 9F for something twice as hot and twice as disgusting as this.

A wide array of flora and fauna romp within the verdant confines of the English-style gardens in the elegant riverside **Parcs de l'Allier,** commissioned by Napoleon III. Across the river, and a brisk 20- to 25-minute walk along the promenade to the right of the Point de Bellerive lies the sprawling complex of the **Centre Omnisport** (tel. 70 32 04 68), Vichy's ultimate recreational facility. The center coordinates tennis courts, gymnasia, and kayaking on the river. You can rent windsurfers along the river. An **information office** within the Maison des Jeunes provides pamphlets on lodgings, as well as sporting and cultural activities in the area. (Open Mon.-Sat. 8:30am-10pm, Sun. 8:30am-8pm; Sept.-June Mon.-Sat. 8:30am-10pm, Sun. 8:30am-7pm.) An outdoor **swimming pool** (tel. 70 32 27 20) and a sunbathing beach (no swimming allowed) lie across the river by the campground and youth hostel. (Open June-Aug. Mon., Wed., and Fri.-Sat. 10am-7:30pm, Tues. and Thurs. 10am-9:30pm, Sun. 10am-7pm. Admission 11F50, under 18 7F50.)

Throughout the summer, the tremendous organ in the **Eglise St-Louis** attracts prominent organists from around the world. Concerts take place every few weeks, and tickets are 80F (students 60F). Ask the tourist office for a schedule. Also in summer, six operas ring in the beautiful **Opera House.** The ticket office (tel. 70 59 90 50) is on the side of the opera house, on rue du Parc.

The **Auberge de Jeunesse (HI)**, 19, rue du Stade, Bellerive (tel. 70 32 30 11), stands across the river on the left after crossing pont de Bellerive. The rooms are clean, the kitchen facilities are available 24 hrs., and the place is rarely full, but the hostel is situated in the middle of nowhere about 20 minutes from the heart of the town. Each of the rooms has 12 beds, and the Turkish toilets are in a shack outside. For the hostel or for any of the campgrounds (see below), take bus #4 (direction "Chantemerle") from the train station (2 per hr. 6:13am-7:45pm, 5F) and get out after the bridge; cross the street and head straight toward the "Le Bellerive" sign atop the high-rise apartment. Keep going along the lamp-lined pavement onto rue du Stade and the hostel. (Reception open daily 8am-10pm. No curfew. No lockout. 40F. No breakfast. Sheets 15F. Open April-Oct.) With over 120 hotels, finding a decent, inexpensive room in Vichy is wonderfully simple. It's easiest to confine your search to the small streets off rue de Paris, as many of the hotels farther along cater to long-term tenants. The **Hôtel Antilles,** 16, rue Desbrest (tel. 70 98 27 01), offers well-kept singles and doubles with squishy mattresses (85-95F, with shower 120-130F; breakfast 20F). The **Camping Municipal** (tel. 70 32 03 00), behind the hostel, is the nearest of several campgrounds along the river bank. (6F per person, 3F per tent. Electricity 10F. Open April-Oct.)

Although Vichy is known as a health center, don't expect granola for breakfast and tofu burgers for dinner. Many of the one- and two-star hotels scattered throughout town post large, appetizing lunch and dinner *menus* in the 50F range. At **Le Trocadero,** 3, av. Aristide Briand, near pont de Bellerive, they don't just serve meals; their 45F lunch *menu* with *couscous 3 viandes* does no less than "democratize couscous and disarm the semolina crisis." For 14-30F, you can get a hearty salad with no political obligations attached. (Open daily for lunch and dinner.) The **Caféteria Casino,** 13, rue de Paris, is a welcome standby with a potpourri of *plats du jour* (30-40F) and sundaes for dessert (open daily 11am-10pm). **Restaurant de la Nièvre,** 17-19, av. de Gramont (tel. 70 31 82 77), just right of the train station, posts a 60F *menu* with a choice of salad, sausage, or *pâté en croûte;* chicken *cordon bleu* or *steak garni;* and dessert (open daily 7am-11pm). The large covered **market** is in pl. du Grand Marché (Tues.-Sun. until 12:30pm).

The **post office,** pl. Charles de Gaulle (tel. 70 59 90 90), has a **currency exchange** with competitive rates. (Open Mon.-Fri. 8am-7pm, Sat. 8am-noon.) Vichy's **postal code** is 03200. The **train station,** pl. de la Gare (tel. 70 46 50 50), is on the heavily used Clermont-Ferrand-Paris line. Trains run to Clermont-Ferrand (20 per day, 36min., 44F); to Riom (20 per day, 25min., 35F); and to Paris (8 per day, 3 1/2hr., 195F). (Information office open Mon.-Sat. 9am-6:30pm, Sun. noon-2pm.) Buses for the surrounding region leave from the *gare routière,* pl. Charles de Gaulle (tel. 70 98 41 33; office open Mon.-Fri. 8am-noon and 2-6pm). In a **medical emergency,** dial 15 for an ambulance. The **Centre Hospitalier** (tel. 70 97 33 33) is on bd. Denière. The **police** are at 35, av. Victoria (tel. 70 98 60 03).

Le Mont Dore

Situated amid a long-dormant chain of volcanoes in the heart of the Massif Central, Le Mont Dore (pop. 2400) suffers from a split personality. Each summer, more than 14,000 variously afflicted *curistes* invade the *Etablissement Thermale* in quest of a panacea to their aches, pains, and blues; they sit in long rows inhaling the carbonated gas that allegedly purges rheumatism and respiratory ailments. Meanwhile, a more vigorous and intrepid clientele besieges the resort town's neighboring white slopes during the winter ski season. Jagged volcanic peaks, culminating in the Massif Central's highest peak at Le Puy de Sancy (1886m), don't quite match the altitude or the glitz of the Alps, but they offer an excellent alternative at significantly lower prices. Unfortunately, if you don't ski, hike, or wheeze, Le Mont Dore holds little allure.

An introduction to the town's *curiste* tradition begins with a tour of the **Etablissement Thermal** on pl. du Panthéon (tel. 73 65 05 10). Five of the springs used today were first channeled by the Romans, and the center, built between 1810 and 1817, has grand arcades and granite Roman-style columns. The tour (30min.) passes the sanitized quarters of patients undergoing treatments; visitors are barred from entering. (Tours May-Sept. Mon.-Sat. 11:15am, 11:30am, 3pm, 3:30pm, 4pm, and 4:30pm; 5F). Elsewhere in the richly decorated complex, Le Mont Dore's most ancient thermal waters, the bubbly **Source-César,** resembles a giant high-school science project awaiting final judgment. Down the hill on av. Michel-Bertrand, the **Musée Joseph Foret** opened its doors in September 1992. The highlight of the collection is the **Livre de L'Apocalypse,** a 460-pound monstrosity of a book designed by Foret and illustrated with original drawings by Salvador Dalí and other artists. (Ask the tourist office for more information.)

Although the town is crowded during the winter and summer seasons, you can usually find a room in one of the dozens of one-star hotels. The **Auberge de Jeunesse (HI),** route du Sancy (tel. 73 65 03 53), 3km uphill from the station, is a fantastic hostel with two to eight beds per room, a mini-tennis court, mini-golf course, mini-TV bar, and mini-game room. Less than 1km from its source, the Dordogne River (miniature sized, of course) flows through the back yard. Buses leave from across from the train station (1 per hr. 9am-6pm; summer 2-6pm, 9F40, round-trip 14F20). Ask to be dropped off at the *auberge de jeunesse,* which is a chalet on a ski slope. Hitching from town to the hostel is reportedly quite easy. The hostel is filled with families during the winter (reserve 2 weeks ahead) and popular with school groups all year round, but there is usually some space during the summer. Be sure to call before you arrive. (No lockout. No curfew. 43F. Breakfast 16F. Meals 43F. Sheets 12F.) The **Hôtel du Centre,** 8, rue Jean Moulin (tel. 73 65 01 77), above the Café de Paris, rents good rooms at great prices overlooking the center of town. (Singles 65F. Doubles 70F. Triples 85F. Hall showers included. Large breakfast 25F. Open Dec. 15-Nov. 15.) **Hôtel Helvetia,** 5, rue de la Saigne (tel. 73 65 01 67), is cozy, clean, and keeps a fine restaurant downstairs. (Singles and doubles 90-100F, with shower 140F. Hall showers included. Breakfast 20F.) If the smaller hotels are full, try the 36-room **Royal Hôtel,** 7, rue Rigny (tel. 73 65 01 26). Most of the large, bright quarters overlook a busy street adjacent to the *établissement thermal;* an elevator is available for those who refuse to climb any more heights by foot. (Singles 85F, with shower 100-175F. Doubles 100-135F, with shower 165-215F. Triples and quads 155-175F, with shower 165-215F. Prices increase by 10-30% in Feb., July, and Aug. No hall showers. Breakfast 15F. Call ahead in summer.) There are four **campgrounds** in and around Le Mont Dore, of which the most convenient is **Les Crouzets,** av. des Crouzets (tel. 73 65 21 60), across from the train station. (Reception open Mon.-Sat. 8:30-9:30am, 10:30-11:45am, 2-2:30pm, and 5-6:30pm, Sun. 9-11:30am and 5-6:30pm. 9F70 per person, 5F40 per site, 3F80 per car. Open all year.) One km behind the train station is **L'Esquiladou,** route des Cascades (tel. 73 65 23 74; 11F per person, 10F per tent; open May 15-Sept.). The tourist office can provide information about all campgrounds.

Le Mont Dore's restaurants post *menus* in the 55-60F range for a three- or four-course meal. If you can stand the incessant buzz of the overhead insect zapper at **A Tout Va Bien,** rue Marie Thérèse, on the corner of av. Général Leclerc, you will be rewarded with a bouquet of regional specialties. In addition to a 55F *menu,* their *fondue gauloise* (70F) and *fondue arverne* (90F) allow you to grill your own meat without oil or grease in their *pierre chaude.* (Open daily noon-2pm and 7-10pm.) A covered **market** does its thing in pl. de la République (open 8am-6pm), except when it is supplanted by an open-air market on Friday (8am-4pm). There is a **Supermarché Atac** 10 minutes behind the train station in the zone Artisanale du Queureuille (open Mon.-Sat. 9am-12:15pm and 2:30-7pm), but the selection is not significantly better than those of the smaller markets in town.

From the train station, scale av. Michel Bertrand and follow the signs to the **tourist office,** av. de la Libération (tel. 73 65 20 21), which distributes free maps and organizes hikes. It **exchanges currency** without commission on Saturdays and Sundays, when banks are closed. (Open Dec.-Sept. Mon.-Sat. 9am-12:30pm and 2-6:30pm, Sun. and holidays 10am-noon and 4-6pm; Oct.-Nov. Mon.-Sat. 9am-12:30pm and 2-6:30pm.) The **post office,** pl. Charles de Gaulle (tel. 73 65 05 48), has **telephones.** (Open Mon.-Fri. 8am-7pm, Sat. 8am-noon.) Le Mont Dore's **postal code** is 63240. The **train station** (tel. 73 65 00 02) is at pl. de la Garé. (Information desk open daily 9:30am-12:30pm and 2-6pm.) Nine trains per day run to Laqueuille (18min., 12F) with transfers to Clermont-Ferrand (1 1/2hr., 55F). Five trains per day run to Paris (8hr., 245F). In a **medical emergency** call **Centre Médico Thermal,** 2, rue du Cap-Chazotte (tel. 73 65 22 22). The **police station** (tel. 73 65 01 70) is on av. Michel Bertrand.

Near Le Mont Dore

With 40km of runs, a 600m vertical drop, and a season that only runs from December to April, the slopes at Le Mont Dore are geared toward families rather than hot-dogs. The base of the slopes is at **Le Sancy,** 3km out of town on route du Sancy and right next to the hostel. Buses leave on the hour from the train station and in front of the tourist office. (9am-6pm in winter, 2-6pm in summer, 9F40, round-trip 14F20.) Le Mont Dore and the surrounding area have recently been connected to the **Super Besse** area, nearly doubling the total trail length. You can buy lift tickets for just Le Mont Dore (72F per 1/2-day, 95F per day, 170F per 2 days) or for both (82F per 1/2-day, 105F per day, 225F per 3 days, 450F per week). The price of multi-day lift tickets is somewhat lower off-season (Jan. 18-Feb. 16 and March 14-May 10). In addition, 300km of cross-country trails run circles around Mont Dore.

During summer, don't miss the opportunity to get to the mountains via the Grande Randonnée and other terrific hiking trails. Any of Le Mont Dore's eleven sporting goods stores will happily outfit you. **Jacky Sport,** 17, pl. Charles de Gaulle (tel. 73 65 06 79), offers complete ski rental packages for both alpine (49F per day, 310F per week) and cross-country enthusiasts (30F per day, 190F per week). (Open daily 9am-1pm and 2-7pm.) **Bessac Sports,** rue du Maréchal Juin (tel. 93 65 02 25), rents mountain bikes (50F per morning, 70F per afternoon, 100F per day, 250F for 6 mornings, 350F for 6 afternoons, 500F for 6 days; open daily 9am-noon and 2-7pm).

The tourist office can recommend a hike suited to your endurance. For a stunning overview of the region, start at the **Salon de Capucin,** accessible by funicular (one-way 16F) or by climbing the **Chemin des Mille Gouttes.** Then hike the 8km to the top of the **Puy du Sancy** (1886m), the highest peak in Central France. The three-hour walk takes you past extinct volcanoes, along a narrow ridge on the rim of the **vallée de Sancy,** and past the source of the Dordogne River. Study or buy a map before you take off; the first few km below the tree line are confusing and poorly marked. Those short on time or lung capacity can also reach Puy du Sancy by the *téléphérique* at the end of the road up the valley (every 15-20min. 9am-noon, 1:30-5:30pm, 22F, return 28F); the summit is only a hop, skip, and a few hundred stairs away.

Before setting off on a serious trek, pick up the tourist office's detailed map (45F). Contact the police station at the base of the Puy de Sancy (tel. 73 65 05 03), and have them approve your route. You may want to invest in the *Massif du Sancy et Artense* guide (66F), which elaborates in detail 38 *randonnées* (hikes) originating from all areas of Le Sancy. The pocket-sized guide *Sancy Haute Dordogne* (38F) includes a plethora of topographical information and meticulously prepared maps of the areas surrounding Le Mont Dore.

East of Puy de Sancy, wildflowers carpet the cloistered **Vallée de Chaude-Four.** Many endangered species of flora exist here; tread lightly. Volcanic lakes along the trail, including **Lac Servieré** (20km northeast of Le Mont Dore), and **Lac de Guery** (7km north), are suitable for windsurfing, sailing, and fishing, and (when warm enough) swimming. An alternate 25-minute walk from the southern end of town leads to the **Grande Cascade,** where the more adventurous and clueful can stand under the projecting rocks behind falling water. The rocks near the base of the waterfall are extremely slippery. The tourist office books excursions, run by **Tourisme Verney** (tel. 73 37 31 06), of the region's lakes, volcanoes, châteaux, cheese and honey farms, and more (45-90F). Reserve through the Le Mont Dore tourist office. **Volcatours** offers bus outings to surrounding volcanic peaks. Tickets (40-100F) are available at the tourist office.

Five km away lies the mountain resort of **La Bourboule,** another *station thermale* and cross-country ski center. The town's natural setting rivals that of Le Mont Dore. The **tourist office,** av. Agis Ledru (tel. 73 81 07 99), can help you organize your stay.

Aurillac

An agricultural center 110km southwest of Clermont-Ferrand, Aurillac (pop. 33,000) lies on the banks of the River Jordanne, in a basin of steep green hills encircled by high volcanic ranges. If not for the fortune bestowed on the town by the founding of an abbey in the 9th century, Aurillac might have have remained immersed in the obscurity of its Gallo-Roman origins. In the apocalyptic year 999, the abbey produced Christianity's first French pope, Sylvester II, formerly known by the name of Gerbert. A man of great talent, young Gerbert studied medicine and mathematics at Arabic universities and was subsequently credited with incorporating the system of Arabic numbers into western society. Despite such promising beginnings, Aurillac soon fell victim to internecine religious warfare. In 1552, amid the reprisals of the Wars of Religion, the abbey and much of the town was razed by Protestants. Today, Aurillac holds little of interest besides a nice *vieille ville,* but its location in the center of the Cantal *départe-ment* makes it a good base for excursions into the gorgeous surrounding countryside.

All that remains of the original 13th-century **Château St-Etienne** is a small, boxy tower overlooking the city. The renovated château next door houses the **Maison des Volcans/Musée des Sciences,** which has a mildly interesting exhibit on the hydrology, geology, and paleontology of the surrounding region, as well as a room on vulcanology. (Open June-Sept. Tues.-Sat. 10am-noon and 2-6pm, Sun. 2-6pm. Free.) The **Maison Consulaire,** also known as the **Musée du Vieil Aurillac,** 2, rue de la Coste, traces the development of Aurillac's religious art and customs. (Open April-Sept. Wed.-Sat. 2-6pm. Admission 5F.) On pl. Gerbert, off cours Monthyon, the **Historial de Haute Auvergne** presents wax figures of Charlemagne, Mitterrand, and assorted other luminaries who came in between. (Open Mon.-Sat. 10am-noon and 2-6:30pm, Sun. 2-6:30pm; Oct.-May Mon.-Sat. 10am-noon and 2-6pm. Admission 18F, students 10F.) The **Museé d'Art et d'Archéologie,** in the Jardin des Carmes, is home to a jumble of artifacts, 17th- to 20th-century paintings, and old umbrellas. (Open Tues.-Sun. 1:30-6:30pm; Oct.-May Tues.-Sat. 10am-noon and 2-6pm. Free.) Across the garden, **La Sellerie** is a converted stable devoted to contemporary photography. (Open June-Sept. Mon.-Sat. 1:30-6:30pm. Free.)

In recent years, the town has developed a surprising reputation as a center for avant-garde visual and performing arts. The **Eclat d'Aurillac,** an international street-theater festival in the last week of August, includes plays in outdoor tents, store windows, and moving trains (most shows free, others 15-80F). Aurillac's giant **Festival International du Cinéma et du Monde Rural,** held in late October, allows only films dealing with rural life to compete (tickets 20F). Throughout the summer, **Café Musique,** held on the terraces of local cafés, brings jazz, funk, rock, blues, and reggae bands to the streets. For more information on all festivals, contact the Bureau des Festivals, 8, pl. de la Paix (tel. 71 64 34 32; open Mon.-Fri. 9am-noon and 2-6pm).

To reach the center of town and the **tourist office** (tel. 71 48 46 58) from the train station, turn right, bear left onto rue de la Gare, and continue straight to pl. du Square. The office is diagonally across the square. The staff will give you a free map and information on the area, and can help you find a room. They also hand out annotated walking tours and operate a **currency exchange** in July and August when banks are closed. (Open Mon.-Sat. 9am-12:30pm and 1:30-7pm, Sun. 10am-noon and 1:30-3:30pm; Sept.-June Mon.-Sat. 9am-noon and 2-6:30pm.) The staff of the **Comité Départemental du Tourisme,** av. Gambetta (tel. 71 46 22 00), on the first floor of the Hôtel du Département building, can answer questions regarding the Cantal region. They stock reams of brochures on cheap lodging, camping, hiking, and food in the surrounding countryside. (Open Mon.-Thurs. 8:30am-noon and 1:30-5:30pm, Fri. 8am-noon and 1:30-5pm.)

Aurillac hotels are generally only full when there's a festival in town. The **Foyer des Jeunes Travailleurs,** 25, rue Robert-Garrie (tel. 71 63 56 94), offers somewhat dilapidated singles for 55F or studios for 80F. (Reception open daily 8:30am-9pm. Studios for two people, 140F; for three 230F. Showers included. Breakfast 15F.) Take bus #1 from the station or pl. du Square (direction: "Arpajon") and ask to be dropped off at the *foyer* (2 per hr., last bus at 7:39pm, 5F80). Otherwise, make the 25-minute walk. From the station, take a right on av. Milhaud and another right at the end on av. des Pupilles de la Nation. Bear right at the fork on av. des Prades and turn left on av. de Tivoli just before the church. The *foyer* is 200m down on the left. **Hôtel Le Club,** 4, rue du Salut (tel. 71 48 10 49) has basic rooms above a bar in the center of the *vieille ville* (Singles and doubles 70F. Triples and quads 120F. No showers.) The **camping municipal** (tel. 71 48 28 87) is 1km east of the *vieille ville* along the banks of the Jordanne, near pl. du Cap Blanc. (8F per person, 12F per site. Open May-Sept.)

By far the best meal bargain in Aurillac is the cafeteria at the *foyer* (guests welcome). A mere 40F buys a surprisingly enjoyable, appallingly large five-course meal, drinks included. (Open Mon.-Fri. noon-1pm and 7-8pm, Sat. noon-1pm. Call the *foyer* to confirm hours.) In the *centre ville,* off pl. du Square, local and ethnic restaurants sprinkle the area around rues des Frères and Baldayrou. **Don Camillo,** 17, rue Baldayrou, attracts locals who gorge themselves on the hearty pizzas (29-38F) and wide salad selection. Treat yourself to an overflowing sundae brimming with whipped cream for dessert. (Open Mon.-Sat. noon-2pm and 7pm-midnight.) A covered **market** holds forth at pl. de l'Hôtel de Ville on Wednesday and Saturday mornings (7am-noon). A **Supermarket Topco** is just across the street from the *foyer.* (Open Mon.-Fri. 8:30am-12:30pm and 3-7:30pm, Sat. 8:30am-12:30pm and 2:30-7:15pm.) Don't leave Aurillac without stopping by the **Marché aux Fromages,** 7, rue du Buis, for a taste of some of the local cheeses: the sharp Bleu d'Auvergne, the delicate, hazelnut-tinged St-Nectaire, and the hard, tangy Cantal.

The **train station** (tel. 71 48 50 50) is on pl. Pierre Sémard (information office open Mon.-Sat. 5:30am-1pm and 2-7pm). **Trains** run to Toulouse (4 per day, 3 1/2hr., 137F); Brive (6 per day, 1 3/4hr., 69F); Clermont-Ferrand (5 per day, 3hr., 105F); and Paris (via Brive or Nevers; 6 per day, 6 1/2hr., 274F). The station has 5F and 10F **lockers.** You can rent a **bicycle** at **Magasin Cycles Pouget,** 13, av. Gambetta (tel. 71 48 32 25) for 80F per day or 300F per week, with an 800F deposit. (Open Tues.-Sat. 8:30am-noon and 1:30-7pm.) **Urban buses,** 8, rue Denis Papin (tel. 71 64 54 55), cost 5F80 a ride, 40F for a 10-ticket *carnet.* **Regional buses** to the surrounding Cantal region all stop at the *gare routière* in the parking lot to the left of the station. A schedule is posted in the train station. The main **post office** on rue Salvador Allende (tel. 71 45 62 00) has a **currency exchange** and **telephones.** (Open Mon.-Fri. 8am-7pm, Sat. 8am-noon.) The more convenient **branch office** (tel. 71 48 14 04) is at 3, rue Rieu. (Open Mon.-Fri. 8:30am-noon and 1:30-6pm, Sat. 8:30am-noon.) The **postal code** is 15000. **Poste Restante** letters must be marked "Préfecture" to arrive at the branch office. In a **medical emergency,** call **Centre Hospitalier,** 83, av. Charles de Gaulle (tel. 71 45 45 45). The **police** can be reached by dialing 17.

Cantal Countryside

A series of tremendous earthquakes and volcanic eruptions 13 million years ago ushered in the geological splendor of the Cantal region. Older and greener than the Monts Dôme and the Monts Dore to the northeast, the volcanic mountains of the Cantal are dotted with feudal *châteaux,* ancient *burons* (farmhouses), and bell-bearing bovines genuinely surprised to see people trotting down the country roads. Mercifully, the beauty of the Cantal has not been overrun by tourism: foreign tourists are rare, and even visitors from other parts of France are the exception rather than the rule. Locals, on the other hand, regard their backyard as a national treasure, and every weekend the roads are filled with villagers out for a drive in the country.

Don't plan on getting anywhere in the Cantal fast without a car. Train and bus service is spotty at best, and the hilly terrain that challenges *Tour de France* veterans can torture the amateur cyclist. Masochists unfazed by steep hills can rent bikes at the **Magasin Cycles Pouget** (tel. 71 48 32 25) in Aurillac, or in several small towns in the Cantal. Word has it that hitching is fairly esy; while drivers can be few and far between, they are often willing to offer a lift when they do appear.

Before you wander too far out into the countryside, pick up maps, guides, and accommodations listings at the **Comité Départemental du Tourisme,** av. Gambetta (tel. 71 46 22 00), in Aurillac. Although generally less comprehensive, the Aurillac tourist office dispenses descriptions of towns, lists of campgrounds and hotels, and a free regional accommodations service. *La Montagne,* a local newspaper, often lists events and festivals in the region (4F).

Only two **train** lines pass through the Cantal: one runs from Clermont-Ferrand to Aurillac (6 per day, 128F), and the other runs between Aurillac and Bort-les-Orgues (3 per day, 69F). Double check whether your intended destinations are subject to an *arrêt facultatif,* for which the train stops only upon prior request. There is also an SNCF **bus** that runs from Neussargues to Bort-les-Orgues and back twice a day (52F). In addition, 30 (yes, three-zero) different private bus companies serve the region. Most run only one or two lines, and there is no single office which coordinates them all. Check the schedules posted at the train station, or ask for complete schedules at the tourist office. **STAC Transports,** 9, pl. du Square in Aurillac (tel. 71 48 48 33), covers Le Lioran (3 per day, 70min., 29F), St-Flour (3 per day, 2hr., 52F), and Vic-sur-Cère (3 per day, 1/ 2hr., 18F). Most buses leave from the *gare routière,* to the left of the train station.

The train line between Aurillac and Neussargues (on the way to Clermont-Ferrand) covers a beautiful stretch of the Cantal countryside. The first stop on the line is the tiny village of **Polminhac** (13F from Aurillac), which cowers in the shadows of the **Château de Pesteils.** From 13th-century towers to the imposing dungeon, the fortress exudes the strength which rebuffed several invasions. Perched in the lofty deck of the 40m tower, château guards were able to track the movements of their enemies in the Cère Valley below. Inside the tower are some beautiful 14th-century frescoes. The 17th-century wing contains finely painted ceilings and furniture and Aubusson tapestries. The riveting spectacle of the castle, set against a Cantal backdrop, has attracted the attention of several filmmakers; it most recently appeared in *L'Eternel Retour,* starring Jean Marais. (Open July-Aug. 10am-noon and 2:30-6pm; May-June and Sept. 2:30-6pm. Admission 17F, students 13F, under 10 free.) The **tourist office** (tel. 71 47 40 07) will help you find a place to stay. (Open July-Aug. Mon.-Sat. 3-7pm.) The **Camping Val de Cère** (tel. 71 47 41 03) is open June to September 15. Prepare for chilly evenings (8F per person, 12F per site. Electricity 10-14F).

The next train stop on the Aurillac-Neussargues line (19F from Aurillac) is **Vic-sur-Cère** (pop. 2048), home to a sprightly goose named Archimède. A popular summer resort in a gorgeous valley by the Cère River, the town derives its terse and lively name ("Vic") from the supposedly curative qualities of its mineral water. A town legend maintains that this very water revitalized Anne d'Autriche, who subsequently gave birth to Louis XIV. Nestled within the town's compact *vieille ville* are the diverse remainders of a long-gone prosperity, including the 15th-century **Maison des Princes de Monaco** and the attractive Romanesque **Eglise St-Pierre.** After exploring the old city, several walking paths guide you into the surrounding mountains. Walk toward **Thiézac** to the **Pas de Cère, Rocher de Muret,** or the **Grotte des Huguenots,** where the Huguenots held cabals during the Wars of Religion. The **tourist office,** pavillion du Parc (tel. 71 47 50 68), has ideas for walking, cycling, and hiking routes. If in town for more than a day, invest in their 13F map that details a number of local walks. Open daily 9:30am-noon and 2:30-7pm; Sept.-June daily 9:30am-noon and 2:30-6pm). **Hôtel de Terrasse,** 47, av. du Docteur Jean Lambert (tel. 71 47 50 24), has clean and comfortable doubles for 100F (with shower, 120F. Quads 140F.) If it's full, start digging into those pockets or head for the **Camping Municipal,** av. des Tilleuls (tel. 71 47 51 04), opposite a supermarket. (Reception open daily 9am-noon and 3-8pm. 12F50 per person, 5F50 per tent. Hot showers included. Open April-Sept. Reserve ahead in July and Aug.)

Also on the Aurillac-Neussargues line, **Le Lioran** (33F from Aurillac) is the Cantal's only ski resort. In summer its ski runs become hiking trails. On one side of the valley, a *téléphérique* whisks hikers and skiers up nearly to the summit of the **Plomb du Cantal,** the Cantal's highest peak of 1855m. The **Puy Griou** (1694m) lies on the other side of the valley and is just a few km from town on the **Grande Randonnée 4** hiking trail. With its perfectly symmetrical core culminating in a needle-sharp point, the Puy Griou offers staggering views of the Cantal countryside, while itself looking like a third-grader's drawing of a volcano. From the train station, turn left, take the first right, and climb the 1km up to the ski area and hiking trails. The **tourist office** (tel. 71 49 50 08), at the foot of the *téléphérique,* distributes information on skiing and hiking. (Open April-Nov. daily 9am-noon and 1:30-6:30pm; Dec.-March daily 9am-6:30pm.) There are no cheap hotels in Le Lioran. **Vallagnot Camping** (tel. 71 20 11 34 or 71 20 04 42) lies 5km outside town. (Reception open 8-11am and 4-7pm. 9F50 per person, 4F per tent. Open June-Sept.)

The old village of **Murat** (pop. 2813) is the last town of interest on the Aurillac-Neussargues train line. The **tourist office** is on pl. de la Mairie (tel. 71 20 09 47 or 71 20 03 80; open Mon. and Wed.-Sat. 10am-noon and 2-5pm). Facing one another, two soaring *rochers* preside over the town, their peaks supporting the **Statue de Notre Dame de la Haute Auvergne** and a 13th-century Benedictine chapel. A stroll through the narrow *ruelles* of the old quarter passes the former **Maison Consulaire** and a marvelous panorama of the town. Murat's most compelling attraction is the **Maison de la**

Faune, pl. Balat, in the *centre ville* (tel. 71 20 00 52). Housed within a 17th-century *hôtel particulier,* this natural history museum has assembled a seemingly exhaustive collection of over 600 birds, 6000 insects and butterflies, and a motley crew of other *auvergnat* fauna. (Open Mon.-Sat. 10am-noon and 3-6pm; Sun. 3-6pm. Admission 15F, ages 6-12 12F, students 12F.)

East of the Aurillac-Neussargues train line, accessible by bus from Murat or Aurillac, **St-Flour** sits pretty on a high plateau. To get to the *centre ville* from the station, turn right onto av. de la République and make a left onto rue du Pont Vieux when you hit pl. de la Liberté. Take a right onto chemin des Chèvres and then start climbing like a mountain goat. When you reach the top, you'll stumble upon the severe Gothic **Cathédrale St-Pierre,** the graceful interior of which shelters a beautiful 15th-century wooden crucifix called *Le Bon Dieu Noir.* (Open daily 9am-6pm. Guided tours in English daily 9am-noon and 2-6pm.) The **Musée de la Haute Auvergne** (tel. 71 60 22 32) next to the Cathedral in the Hôtel de Ville, contains several displays of *auvergnat* folklore and a few rooms devoted entirely to a traditional *auvergnat* instrument, the *cabrette* (similar to a bagpipe). (Open daily 10am-noon and 2-7pm; Sept.-June daily 10am-noon and 2-6pm. Admission 17F, students 8F50.) **The Musée Douet,** in the **Ancienne Maison Consulaire** on pl. d'Armes, contains several richly furnished rooms, ancient arms, and various paintings and sculptures. (Open daily 9am-noon and 2-7pm; Oct.-June Mon.-Sat. 9am-noon and 2-6pm. Admission 17F, students 8F50.) The **Musée de la Poste,** pl. des Jacobins, reveals its well-endowed postcard and stamp collection to the public every summer. (Open June-Sept. daily 10am-noon and 2-7pm. Admission 20F, students 10F.) The **tourist office,** 2, pl. d'Armes (tel. 71 60 22 50), next to the cathedral, offers guided tours of the city every Wednesday in summer (18F; open July-Aug. daily 9am-noon and 2-7:30pm; June and Sept. Mon.-Sat. 9am-noon and 2-7pm; Oct.-May Mon.-Sat. 9am-noon and 2-6pm). In July and August, an **annex** (tel. 71 60 26 29) operates down below at pl. de la Liberté. (Open July-Aug. Mon.-Sat. 10am-noon and 3-7pm.) The cheapest hotel is **Les Orgues,** av. des Orgues (tel. 71 60 06 41), where adequate singles and doubles cost 95F, 170F with shower (breakfast 18F). **Camping de l'Ander,** rue de Massales (tel. 71 60 29 27) is next to the covered market (8F per person, 6F per tent, 5F per shower). **Camping les Orgues,** off av. du Dr. Mallet (tel. 71 60 44 01), has a restaurant and grocery store. (10F per person, 6F per tent, showers included; open May 15-Oct. 15.)

Two hours north by train from Aurillac (3 per day, 69F) is **Bort-les-Orgues** (pop. 4500). Itself unattractive, the town is a good place to start hikes in the beautiful valley of the Dordogne River and the nearby **Lac du Barrage de Bort.** Bort-les-Orgues is actually closer to Le Mont Dore (40km south on N89) than Aurillac but there is no train line in that direction. **SNCF buses** connect Bort-les-Orgues to Neussargues (52F) and also run between Bort-les-Orgues and Ussel (40F). Get a list of the many campgrounds in the area from the **tourist office,** pl. Marmontel (tel. 55 96 02 49; open daily 9am-noon and 2-7pm; Sept.-June 2-6pm.)

The 15th-century **Château du Val** (tel. 71 40 30 20) lies 6km from Bort in the tiny village of **Lanobre.** The six fortified round towers with pepper-pot roofs and a Gothic chapel once overlooked the sleepy Dordogne until construction of the dam at Bort enclosed the castle with a lake. Although the castle tends to look more impressive on postcards, the rustic interior makes for an interesting visit. To get there, follow the N122 north for 5km out of Bort, and turn left on the well-marked road to the lake (2km). The busy roads are unpleasant to walk along. (Open July-Aug. daily 10am-noon and 2-5:30pm; Sept.-Oct. 15 and Dec. 15-June Wed.-Mon. same hours. Courtyard admission 3F. Admission with obligatory tour 20F, students 12F.)

About midway between Bort and Aurillac, **Salers** (pop. 450) is possibly the most beautiful town in Cantal, and everybody knows it. The one village in this region where tourism is a full-fledged industry, Salers is nonetheless worth visiting for its uniformly gorgeous old houses and cobblestone streets, and for the fantastic panoramas it gives of the surrounding countryside. The somber **Eglise St-Mathieu** contains a renowned *mise au tombeau* (entombment) sculpture and five Aubusson tapestries. On the edge of town, the **esplanade de Barouze** provides picnickers with a delectable view of the peaceful Maronne Valley a thousand feet below. Highlighting Salers's cultural agenda,

Le Festival Renaissance is held annually for three days near the end of July. The festival features exuberant spectacles, expositions, ancient music concerts, and film screenings. Brilliant fireworks close the event. During the Festival, it costs 40F just to enter the town. Salers is inaccessible by public transportation; hitching a ride from Mauriac (on the Bort-Aurillac train line) is one possibility. Hitching out of Salers to Aurillac on the D680 is supposed to be generally easy, as well. The **tourist office,** pl. Tissandier d'Escous (tel. 71 40 70 68 or 71 40 72 33), will direct you to hotels and campgrounds. (Open daily 10am-12:30pm and 2-7pm.)

The villages along the main road from Mauriac to Aurillac (D922) offer plenty of rustic charm, and, well, rustic charm. **St-Martin Valmeroux, St-Chamant,** and **St-Cernin** also contain enchanting 15th- and 16th-century churches. The stately **Château d'Anjony** (tel. 71 47 61 67) languishes 5km from St-Cernin in the village of **Tournemire.** (Open Easter-Oct. 2-7pm. Admission 25F, students 15F.)

Bourgogne (Burgundy)

Encompassing the upper valley of the Saône and its surrounding hills—the Côte d'Or, the Plateau de Langres, and the wild, forested Morvan—Burgundy is best known for its Romanesque architecture and the 40 million bottles of wine it produces annually. Today, small vineyards splash the hills that gave feudal lords control over important passes leading toward Paris and the northern provinces. Each of the four distinct *départements* that make up Burgundy—Côte d'Or, in the east, Saône-et-Loire in the south, Yonne in the north, and Nièvre in the west—makes a contribution to the collection of renowned wines. Fine whites—notably the dry Pouilly-sur-Loire from Nièvre and Chablis from L'Yonne—as well as full-bodied reds including Vougeot, Gevrey-Chambertin, Nuits-St-George, and Corton from the Côte d'Or, and Givry from Saône-et-Loire, can be sampled at other châteaux. Signs advertising *dégustations* (free tastings) at local *caves* flank the roads throughout wine-producing areas, and tourist offices distribute complete lists or brochures.

While wine may be Burgundy's best ambassador, the area's non-alcoholic sites and surroundings make fine diplomats. The Roman conquest of Gaul began in the area around Autun, and the impressive Gallo-Roman ruins of that city, combined with the thousands of Roman objects displayed in regional museums, constitute a fascinating historical legacy. The pamphlet *Bourgogne Archéologique,* free at most tourist offices, lists excavation sites and noteworthy museums throughout the region. With their Romanesque and Gothic architecture, the area's churches lend each town a distinct flavor. The unharnessed beauty of nearby woodlands indulges hikers, and the flat countryside facilitates bike rides between towns. Two pamphlets, *Romanesque Burgundy* and *La Route des Ducs de Bourgogne* list churches and châteaux in the region and suggest excursions.

Making the most of its cream-and-wine-based sauces, Burgundy's renowned cuisine includes such specialties as *boeuf bourguignon, coq au vin,* Dijon *moutardes* (mustard made with white wine instead of vinegar), and *kir* (a beverage concocted with white wine and black currant liqueur). Other culinary delights include *gougère* (a soft bread made with cabbage and cheese), *escargots,* and *quenelles* (little dumplings). Luckily, these gastronomic masterpieces are usually affordable, and if the restaurants are too expensive, you can always sample Burgundian specialties at a *charcuterie.* The pamphlet *Bourgogne Gourmande* describes the regional cuisine, mentions food festivals, and throws in several recipes.

Summer brings a flurry of cultural festivals. From mid-July to mid-August, under the auspices of **Musique en Bourgogne,** classical and early music fills the cathedrals and churches of Sens, Beaune, Vézelay, Tournus, and other towns. Many of these events, and particularly those in Dijon, attract prestigious international groups. Ask any tourist office for the *Petit Guide des Manifestations Musicales en Bourgogne.*

Hotels are relatively expensive, but *foyers* and hostels are common throughout the region. For a list of campgrounds, ask at the tourist office for *Camping en Bourgogne, 1992.* Burgundy is fairly well served by rail, less so by bus. Famous wine routes and many of the most idyllic villages are most easily reached (or, in some cases, can only be reached) by car or bike; inexpensive rentals are available in most towns. Over 1200km of rivers and canals course through Burgundy and support numerous boat tours. For more information, pick up a copy of *Bateaux de Bourgogne* at one of the tourist offices.

Opportunities to participate in the annual grape *vendange* (harvest) abound during September and October; be aware that the work is physically taxing. For information, contact the **Agence Nationale pour les Emplois,** 6, bd. St-Jacques, 21200 Beaune (tel. 80 24 60 00). You can also go directly to the local vineyards, where employers may not ask for a work permit. Youth centers also stock information on grape and cherry harvest jobs; if your French is shaky, the staff might be persuaded to make some phone calls for you.

Dijon

Dijon's prospects looked bleak in 1513 when 30,000 Swiss gripped the city in a vise-like siege. Negotiations faltered until, in a stroke of Burgundian brilliance, the *dijonnais* sent wine casks across enemy lines. The Swiss, with an inebriation-induced generosity, acquiesced and retreated, sparing Dijon.

While Dijon is universally synonymous with the spicy, wine-based mustards it produces, the town does not survive on Grey Poupon alone. Dijon (pop. 157,000) is an important industrial center and home to a respected university. Burgundy's animated capital stands at the tip of one of the world's finest wine producing regions: the Côte d'Or. As well, it encompasses a colorful and tastefully restored *vieille ville,* myriad churches, museums, festivals, and a prestigious university replete with students who keep this ancient city fresh. Any way you consider it, Dijon cuts the touristic mustard.

Orientation and Practical Information

Dijon is two-and-a-half hours southeast of Paris and one-and-a-half hours north of Lyon. The city is relatively small and compact. The main east-west axis, the pedestrian zone of **rue de la Liberté,** runs roughly from **place Darcy,** where the tourist office is located, to **place St-Michel.** From the train station, follow av. Maréchal Foch straight to pl. Darcy, a few minutes away. The *vieille ville* and most of Dijon's other attractions are on the small streets radiating from rue de la Liberté to the north and south. The **place de la République,** northeast of pl. Darcy, is the central roundabout for roads leading out of the city.

Tourist Office: pl. Darcy (tel. 80 43 42 12). Accommodations service 15F. **Currency exchange** without commission. The pamphlet, *Châteaux en Côte d'Or,* lists things to see and do in the region. Ask for the extremely useful guide *Divio 1992.* Open daily 8am-9pm; April 15-June and Sept.-Nov. 15 9am-noon and 2-9pm; Nov. 16-April 14 9am-noon and 2-7pm. **Branch office** at 34, rue des Forges (tel. 80 30 35 39). Distributes the same brochures. Open Mon.-Fri. 8-11am and 2-6pm.

Post Office: pl. Grangier, close to pl. Darcy. Open Mon.-Fri. 8am-7pm, Sat. 8am-noon. **Poste Restante, telephones. Postal code:** 21000.

Trains: SNCF (tel. 80 41 50 50; reservations 80 43 52 56), at the end of av. Maréchal Foch. Station and ticket office open 24 hrs. Reservation and information desk open Mon.-Sat. 8:30am-7pm, Sun. 9am-noon and 2-6pm. **SOS Voyageurs** (tel. 80 43 16 34) is open Mon.-Fri. 8am-7pm, Sat. 8am-6pm. To Paris by TGV (5 per day, 1 1/2hr., 176F plus 13F reservation). To: Lyon (every hr., 2hr., 114F); Strasbourg (1 per day, 4hr., 181F); Nice (6 per day, 7 1/2hr., 349F).

Buses: av. Maréchal Foch (tel. 80 42 11 00), connected to the train station. Information and ticket office open Mon.-Fri. 8:30am-12:30pm and 2:30-6:30pm, Sat. 8:30am-12:30pm. You can also buy tickets aboard. The most convenient and scenic way to travel the *route de vin* is on the 8 daily buses to Beaune (1hr., 32F50); Nuits St-George (40min., 20F50); and other towns.

Public Transportation: Buses (STRD), (tel. 80 30 60 90), booth in pl. Grangier. Covers greater Dijon Mon.-Sat. 6:30am-8:30pm, Sun. 1-8:30pm. Tickets 4F90, available on bus. Five-trip pass 15F50. 12-trip pass 36F. Map available from tourist office. **Taxis: Taxi Radio Dijon cour Gare,** tel. 80 41 41 12.

Hitchhiking: Those choosing to hitchhike to Paris via Sens usually take av. Albert 1er. Southbounders take av. Jean Jaurès (N74 for Chalon). Rides posted at CIJB when available.

English Bookstore: Librairie de l'Université, 17, rue de la Liberté. An extensive collection of new (42-127F) English paperbacks on 2nd floor. Open Mon. 10:15am-7pm, Tues.-Sat. 9:15am-7pm.

Youth Information: Centre d'Information Jeunesse de Bourgogne (CIJB), 22, rue Audra (tel. 80 30 35 56). Information on accommodations, French classes for foreigners, festivals, cheap restaurants, wine harvesting, sports, and travel throughout France. Open Mon. noon-6pm, Tues.-Fri. 10am-6pm. **CROUS,** 3, rue du Docteur Maret (tel. 80 30 76 33). Information on university housing and cafeterias. Open Mon.-Fri. 9-11:30am and 2-4:30pm.

Laundromat: 36, rue Guillaume Tell, above the train station. Wash 15F, dry 2F per 5min. Open daily 6am-9pm.

Women's Centers: SOS Amitié, tel. 80 67 15 15. Open 24 hrs. **SOS Femmes Battues** (tel. 80 46 21 66). For battered women. **Solidarité Femmes,** 4, rue Choncelier de l'Hôpital (tel. 80 67 17 89).

Medical Assistance: Hôpital Général, 3, rue Faubourg Raines (tel. 80 41 81 41). **SAMU,** tel. 80 41 12 12.

Police: 2, pl. Suquet (tel. 80 41 81 05). **Emergency:** tel. 17.

Accommodations and Camping

From mid-June to mid-August and during the first week of September, the profusion of reasonably-priced hotels fill quickly. Reserve a place early or use the accommodations service at the tourist office. The *foyers* are a good 45min. walk from the station, and buses stop running at 8:30pm. Plan ahead, take a cab, or lace up your walking shoes.

Auberge de Jeunesse (HI), Centre de Rencontres Internationales, 1, bd. Champollion (tel. 80 71 32 12), a 4km ride from the station. Take bus #5 from the "Bar Bleu" in pl. Grangier (direction: "Epirey"), or bus #6 from pl. Darcy (last bus 8:30pm). A classic concrete "mega-hostel," complete with electronic surveillance, bar, and shrieking school groups. Hosts language programs in summer. Reception open all day until 12:30am. Lockout 9am-5pm. 5- to 8-bed dorms 60F. Singles 120F. Doubles 160F. Breakfast and showers included. Self-service dinner 42F. Fills quickly July-Aug., so call ahead and pick up keys early in the day.

Foyer International d'Etudiants, av. Maréchal Leclerc (tel. 80 71 51 01). Take bus #4 (direction: "St-Apollinaire"), and get off at "Vélodrome." From av. Paul Doumer, turn right onto rue du Stade, then take the first left. A sleek, noisy place with 300 beds. One of the best deals in town. 55F. Breakfast 12F. Cafeteria lunch 25F. Showers included. Normally long-term residents, but travelers admitted year-round if there's room.

University Dorm Rooms: Residence Universitaire (R.U.) Mansart, bd. Mansart (tel. 80 66 18 22) and **Residence Universitaire Montmuzard,** bd. Gabriel (tel. 80 39 68 01). Two stops away from each other on bus #9. Take the bus from the train station or pl. Darcy to "Mansart" (for R.U. Mansart) or to "Faculté des Sciences" (for R.U. Montmuzard). Clean, comfortable singles available July-Sept. 78F, students 57F. Often full in Aug., so call ahead. Cafeterias at Mansart (tel. 80 66 18 22) open in Aug. only, at Montmuzard (tel. 80 39 69 50) in July only. Breakfast 16F. Lunch or dinner 30F, with student ID 12F.

Hôtel du Sauvage, 64, rue Monge (tel. 80 41 31 21), near Eglise St-Jean and not far from pl. Darcy. The closest modern travelers can get to Astérix's Gaul. Rugged, wood-beamed building overlooks a quiet, arboreal courtyard. Singles and doubles 130F, with shower 180F. Triples and quads with shower 250-260F. Showers 16F. Breakfast 25F.

Hôtel Confort, 12, rue Jules Mercier (tel. 80 30 37 47), on an alley off rue de la Liberté. Delightful chambers and a breakfast room mural that'll make you feel like royalty. Neat singles and doubles 80-115F; with shower 145F, and TV 170F. Triples with shower 180F. Baths 23F. Breakfast 22F.

Hôtel du Théâtre, 3, rue des Bons Enfants (tel. 80 67 15 41), ideal location on a quiet sidestreet off pl. de la Libération. Comfortable rooms, no hall showers. Especially full weeknights. Singles and doubles 85F, with shower 95F. Breakfast 22F.

Hôtel Monge, 20, rue Monge (tel. 80 30 55 41), up the street from Hôtel du Sauvage. Set away from the street and overlooking a courtyard. Clean and cozy rooms. Singles 115F, with shower 150F. Doubles 125F, with shower 150-160F. Triples and quads 180-250F. Showers 20F. Breakfast 23F.

Hôtel Montchapet, 26-28, rue Jacques Cellerier (tel. 80 55 33 31). On a quiet street in a residential neighborhood 10min. from the train station. Family atmosphere and spotless rooms with air-conditioning. Reception always open. Singles 120-140F, with shower 160-190F. Doubles 170F, with shower 190-210F. Triples and qauds 260-290F. Showers 20F. Breakfast 25F.

Hôtel L'Etendard, 4, rue des Perrières (tel. 80 41 51 32). One block from the train station. Plaid hallways and decent rooms with showers. Singles 130F. Doubles 150F. Triples 190F. Quads 250F. Breakfast 20F.

Camping: Camping Municipal du Lac (tel. 80 43 54 72), at bd. Kir and av. Albert 1er. On a beautiful lake about 1km behind the train station; follow the signs for Paris. Take bus #12 to "Chartreux." Spacious, with good facilities. 12F per night. Open April-Nov. 15.

Food

Sadly, Dijon's reputation for noble cuisine, dating from Gallo-Roman times, has inflated restaurant prices. *Charcuteries* provide a reasonably priced option for sampling different *dijonnais* specialties. Bring 100g of *jambon persillé* (a ham *pâté* with parsley), *tarte bourguignon* (a pie with meat and mushrooms in a creamy sauce), or *quiche aux champignons* (mushroom quiche) to the **Jardin de l'Arquebuse** behind the train station. *Dijonnais* chefs take every possible opportunity to garnish their delicacies with heavy portions of their vinegars, wines, and mustards. University cafeterias stay open all summer; R.U. Maret, 3, rue Docteur-Maret (tel. 80 66 39 85), has an all-you-can-eat dinner for only 12F with student ID. (Open 11:45am-1:15pm and 6:40-7:45pm.) There is a large **supermarket** in the basement of the Nouvelles Galeries on rue de la Liberté, and a superb **Géant Casino** on bd. Clemenceau, in the direction of the *foyers* (open Mon.-Sat. 8:30am-9pm).

Au Moulin à Vent, 8, pl. Françoise Rudé, near the ducal palace. Rustic ambience, with white wrought-iron tables and chairs outside. Generous 80F and 120F *menus.* Excellent *boeuf bourguignon* (50F). Open Tues.-Sat. noon-2pm and 7-10pm.

Le Vinarium, 23, pl. Bossuet, (tel. 80 30 36 23). By Eglise St-Jean in a 13th-century crypt. Four *menus,* 110-175F, from different parts of Burgundy. *Boeuf bourguignon, confit de canard,* and *charlotte* (a cake made with ladyfingers). Expensive, but worth it. Open Mon. 7:30pm-late, Tues.-Sat. noon-2pm and 7:30-10pm. Reservations recommended.

Au Bec Fin, 47, rue Jeannin. Rue Jeannin starts behind Notre Dame, about 1 block north of rue de la Liberté. 52F (lunch only), 72F, and 92F *menus.* Try the *Filet de Canard* (duck) in a port wine sauce (75F). Open Mon.-Fri. noon-1:30pm and 7:30-10:30pm, Sat. 7:30-10:30pm.

Restaurant La Soupière, 15-17, av. Maréchal Foch, in the Hôtel Climat de France, across from station. A large buffet with a delectable array of to-die-for *dijonnais* desserts (26-33). *Menus* from 85F. Open daily 11:45-9:45pm.

La Théière, 6, rue Verrerie, behind Notre Dame. Cozy tea salon with light lunches. 45F *menu* includes salad, *tarte salée* (vegetable tart) and your choice of mouth-watering desserts. Open Mon.-Sat. noon-3pm. Tea served until 7pm.

La Vie Saine, 27-29, rue Musette, off pl. Grangier. A vegetarian outpost in *boeuf* country. Attached to a health-food store. *Menus* with vegetarian sausage or ravioli 55F. Open Mon.-Sat. noon-2pm.

Brasserie Foch, 1, rue Foch, near the train station. Pleasant café with superlative meals. *Plat du jour* 38F. Most excellent *escalope de veau* 50F. Open daily 9am-10pm.

Sights

In their hundred-year heyday (1364-1477), the Dukes of Burgundy were fearless (Jean sans Peur), fair (Philippe le Bon), and bold (Philippe le Hardi). Wielding as much power as French kings, these leaders built the colossal **Palais des Ducs de Bourgogne** on the pl. de la Libération at the center of the *vieille ville.* Most of the buildings currently house administrative offices, but the elegant **Musée des Beaux Arts,** pl. de la Sainte Chapelle, fills the palace's east wing. First, wander through the enormous ducal kitchens on the ground floor. Then head up to the first floor where Italian, Dutch, Flemish, German, Swiss, and French works from the 14th through 18th centuries fill more than 20 rooms. The most famous gallery in the museum is the **Salle des Gardes,** dominated by the huge sarcophagi of Philippe le Hardi and Jean sans Peur. Note the 39-statuette funeral procession at the base of Philippe's tomb, sculpted by the 14th-century master Claus Sluter. Save time for the notable 19th- and 20th-century French works—including drawings by Géricault and Delacroix, paintings by Monet and Manet, sculptures by Rodin and Pompon, and Victor Hugo's small canvases—displayed on the second floor. (Open Mon. and Wed.-Sat. 10am-6pm, Sun. 10am-12:30pm and 2-6pm. Admission 10F, students free, Sun. free. A 14F card will admit you to all of Dijon's museums.) The **Tour Philippe Bon** is closed for renovations until 1993.

Three-hundred-year-old *hôtel* façades and hidden courtyards flank the ancient streets behind the palace. The demure exterior of the **Hôtel Chambellan,** 34, rue des Forges, gives no indication of the extravagant Gothic courtyard within. Farther down rue des Forges, at #38, the **Maison Milsand** flaunts a lavishly decorated Renaissance front by Hugues Sambin. Compare the 13th-century façade of the **Hôtel Aubriot** at #40 with its classical doorway. The owl is the bird of Dijon, and **rue de la Chouette** (street of the owl) boasts several wizened residences. Gawk at the sumptuous Renaissance portico of 17th-century **Hôtel de Vogüé,** at #8. Next door, at #10, notice the elaborately carved wooden beams of the half-timbered **Maison Millière.** The grooved center of the pavement on rue Verrerie was a sewage conduit in the 17th century.

Its façade a morass of gargoyles, 13th-century **Eglise de Notre Dame** exemplifies the Burgundian Gothic style. To the right of the choir sits the 11th-century *Vierge Noire* (Black Virgin). The colorful tapestry to her right celebrates Dijon's two liberations—from the Swiss in 1513 and from German occupation in 1944. Outside, the **Horloge à Jacquemart,** which Philippe le Hardi commissioned in 1382 after his victory over the Flemish, continues to tick above the right tower. In 1610, the lonely male statue who sounded the hour was given a spouse, then a son to strike the half hour, and finally, in 1881, a daughter to announce the quarter hour.

At the end of rue de la Liberté, the **Eglise Saint-Michel** is a mélange of Gothic and Renaissance artistry. In a fit of fancy, one stone worker superimposed mythological and biblical themes from Leda and the Swan to St. John the Baptist—behold the result over the central portal. Across from the pl. de la Libération, the recently renovated **Musée Magnin,** 4, rue des Bons Enfants houses an extensive private collection of paintings in the elegant 17th-century **Hôtel Lantin.** Though most of the artists are relatively obscure, the mansion itself is worth a visit. Look for Allesandro Allori's 1561 painting, *Suzanne et les vieillards,* which depicts a beautiful nude woman being ravaged by two salacious old men. The highlights of the collection are the period furnishings, which include a spectacular orange, black, and gold table made of tortoise shell. (Open Tues.-Sun. 10am-6pm; Oct.-May Tues.-Sun. 10am-noon and 2-6pm. Admission 11F, students and over 60 6F.)

The elegant 93m apse and spire in the **Cathédrale St-Bénigne,** rue Docteur Maret, memorialize a 2nd-century missionary priest whose martyred remains were unearthed near Dijon in the 6th century. Rebuilt four times since the 6th century, the abbey houses a unique circular crypt dating from 1007 (open Easter-Oct. 9am-6pm; admission 5F). Next door to the Cathédrale St-Bénigne, the **Musée Archéologique,** 5, rue Docteur Maret, depicts the history of the Côte d'Or. (Open Wed.-Sun. 9:30am-6pm; Sept.-May Wed.-Sun. 9am-noon and 2-6pm. Admission 9F, students free.)

The tombs of Philippe le Hardi and kin, now in the Musée des Beaux Arts, once stood in Claus Sluter's **Chartreuse de Champmol** on the western edge of town. Partially destroyed in 1793, the sculpture group includes the **Puits de Moïse** (Wells of Moses) and three portals depicting the prophets. To reach the Chartreuse (now on the grounds of a psychiatric hospital) from pl. Darcy, follow bd. de Sevigne, go under the train overpass, and continue on av. Albert 1er. The entrance is on bd. Chanoine Kir. (Open to the public 9am-6pm.)

No culinary pilgrimage is complete without a stop at the **Grey Poupon** store, 32, rue de la Liberté, named for its founders, Messrs. Grey and Poupon. This establishment has been making *moutarde au vin* since 1777 and sells a vast array of decorated mustard pots.

Entertainment

Throughout June, Dijon's **Eté Musical** stages many of the world's best symphony orchestras and chamber groups. From mid-June to mid-August, **Estivade** brings dance, music, and theater to the streets. Dijon devotes a week in the first half of September to the **Fête de la Vigne,** a well-attended celebration of the grape with various folklore ensembles. Call the tourist office ahead for tickets—they go fast.

The best source (aside from *Divio 92*) of information on films, festivals, and Dijon's numerous amateur and professional dramatic productions is *Dijon Nuit et Jour,* available free from the tourist office. Opera, classical music concerts, and operettas are performed in season (mid-Oct. to late April) at the **Théâtre de Dijon,** pl. du Théâtre (tel.

80 67 20 21), a beautiful 18th-century opera house. (Tickets 150F, students 75F.) Investigate the shows at **Nouveau Théâtre de Bourgogne,** located at Théâtre du Parvis St-Jean, pl. Bossuet. The box office of this church-turned-theater opens at 5pm. Since 1989, a comedy group from Aix-en-Provence has entertained young and old *dijonnais* at **Le Bistrot de la Scène,** 203, rue d'Anxonne (tel. 80 67 87 39), about 3km from *centre-ville*. Food, drink, and lighthearted *bavardage* (chat) with the actors is included with each hysterical performance. (30-50F, Thurs.-Sat. at 8pm.)

La Cathédrale, 4, pl. St-Bénigne (tel. 80 30 42 10), is a popular student bar (open daily 9am-1am). **Le Messire Bar,** 3, rue Jules Mercier (tel. 80 30 16 40), is a dark bar with flashing lights and an obstreperous clientele. (Open until 2am.) On the quieter side, **Hunky Dory,** 5, av. Maréchal Foch (tel. 80 43 40 07), is a pool bar with a classy interior and cheap (10-14F) draft beer (open daily 3pm-3am; pool 40F per hr.). For a complete list of bars, nightclubs, and restaurants, as well as shops and services of interest to the young twentysomething crowd, get a free copy of *Divio 92* from the tourist office.

Beaune

> *I think if I could take any town, and hold it up, and*
> *say "This, this is France in a nutshell," well I think*
> *it would have to be Beaune.*
> —*Tired English hosteler*

This man's words are perhaps more profound than he realized. Situated in the heart of Burgundy, Beaune displays two quintessentially French treasures—fine architecture and even finer wine—with a ferocious intensity found in precious few spots. Surrounded by the famous *Côtes de Beaune* vineyards, the town itself is packed with wineries offering free *dégustations*, hoping to transform tasters into buyers. Beneath the town's streets a labyrinth of *caves* (wine cellars) protects most of the bottles from the tipsy throngs above. Sampling one's way into a stupor, however, is ill-advised—there's too much else to see. Between the wine boutiques are some unique architectural gems, from the 12th-century Romanesque austerity of Basilique Notre-Dame to the Burgundian Gothic flamboyance of the Hôtel Dieu. Surrounded by 15th-century ramparts, the cobblestone streets of the *vieille ville* contain enough free drink and unusual sights to keep even the weariest tourist delighted. Indeed, while Paris may be the heart and mind of France, cities like Beaune are its soul.

Orientation and Practical Information

Rue Carnot leads directly south from Dijon to the Hôtel Dieu on pl. Carnot in Beaune's *centre ville*. From the train station, follow av. du 8 Septembre, which becomes rue du Château. Turn left onto rempart St-Jean, and cross rue d'Alsace onto rempart Madeleine. Turn right onto rue de l'Hôtel-Dieu, which leads to the impressive **Hôtel Dieu** and the tourist office (15min.). Note that the streets of the *centre-ville* run in more or less concentric rings around the Basilique Notre-Dame; without a map or a good sense of direction, you may literally end up walking in circles (especially after a few *dégustations).*

Tourist Office: rue de l'Hôtel-Dieu (tel. 80 22 24 51). Well-equipped. Free maps. **Currency exchange** when banks are closed. Free accommodations service. Lists of *caves* in the region offering tours. Free guided tours of the town in French July-Aug. daily at 3pm. Open 9am-midnight; March-May and Oct.-Nov. 9am-10pm; Dec.-Feb. 9am-7:15pm.

Post Office: bd. St-Jacques (tel. 80 22 22 32), near the tourist office. **Telephones** and **currency exchange** with 1% commission. Open Mon.-Fri. 8am-7pm, Sat. 8am-noon. **Postal Code:** 21200.

Trains: av. du 8 Septembre (tel. 80 44 50 50). Beaune is on the Dijon-Lyon train line. To: Chalon-sur-Saône (8 per day, 20min., 28F); Lyon (6 per day, 2 1/2hr., 102F); Dijon (12 per day, 1/2hr., 33F). The TGV to Paris stops in Beaune twice daily (2hr., 192F plus 16F reservation fee).

Buses: Transco (tel. 80 42 11 00). To: Chalon-sur-Saône (3 per day, 45min., 36F); Dijon (8 per day, 1hr., 32F50). Stops at all the important wine centers along the Côte d'Or. A schedule is available at the tourist office. Transco does not have an office in Beaune (the phone number listed is for Dijon). Buses depart from several locations, most of which are outside the *centre-ville;* ask for the one most convenient to you. Also be aware, that while the buses will drop you off at any of the wineries, you may have to wait 2-3hr. to catch one going back.

Bike rental: at the station (tel. 80 22 80 56). 39F per 1/2-day, 50F per day, 1000F deposit.

Laundromat: next to the supermarket, off pl. Madeleine. Wash 20F, dry 5F per 8min. Soap 5F. Open daily 7am-8pm.

Hospital: Centre Hospitalier, av. Guigone de Salins (tel. 80 24 44 44).

Medical Emergency: tel. 80 26 60 46. **Ambulance,** tel. 80 22 23 09.

Police: av. du Général de Gaulle (tel. 80 24 64 00). **Emergency:** tel. 17.

Accommodations, Camping, and Food

Beaune welcomes hordes of "house guests" between April and November. It's wise to make reservations far in advance as most hotels fill by afternoon. You can always base yourself in Dijon or at the youth hostel in Chalon-sur-Saône, each only a 20-minute train ride away.

Hôtel Rousseau, 11, pl. Madeleine (tel. 80 22 13 59), in the far left-hand corner of the square. From the station, follow rue des Lyonnais and rue Celer, and then turn right onto rue Faubourg Madeleine. Beautiful wooden beds in clean rooms off a secluded courtyard. Proprietors keep a large garden and cages of white doves out back. Strict 11:30pm curfew, but Beaune shouldn't keep you out late. Singles from 95F. Doubles from 140F. Showers 20F. Breakfast included.

Hôtel le Foch, 24, bd. Foch (tel. 80 24 05 65). Take av. de la République from the tourist office and turn right. Simple and clean rooms. Singles 140F, with shower 170F. Doubles 155F, with shower 175F.

Hôtel de France, 35, av. du 8 Septembre (tel. 80 22 19 99), facing the train station and all its noise. Comfortable rooms. May have space when others don't. Singles and doubles 180F, with shower 220F, with toilet 240F.

Camping: Les Cent-Vignes, 10, rue Dubois (tel. 80 22 03 91), 500m from the town center off rue du Faubourg St-Nicolas. Head north on rue Lorraine from pl. Monge. Often overrun by trailers. Restaurant and grocery store. Always has some space in the morning, but full by mid-afternoon in summer. 11F50 per person, 17F per tent or car. Hot showers included. Restaurant and grocery store. Reservations accepted by mail before May 30. Open March 15-Oct.

Beaune's restaurants are predictably expensive. You'll probably find yourself at the **Supermarché Casino,** through the arches at 28, rue du Faubourg Madeleine (open Mon.-Sat. 8:30am-7:30pm), or the large **market** that takes place Saturday mornings at pl. Carnot. The **Brasserie de la Gare,** 33, rue du 8 Septembre, next to the **Hôtel de France,** serves a 55F meal with wine included. (Open daily 11am-2pm and 7-10pm.)

For excellent local cuisine, try **L'Auberge Bourguignonne** (78F and 87F *menus)* or **Le Maxime** (70F and 88F *menus)* both on place Madeleine. For pizza (38-47F) or salad (30-42F), head to **Véry Table,** 16, rue Véry, near Hôtel-Dieu.

Sights and Entertainment

A trip to Beaune demands a descent into one of the many *caves.* The tourist office has information on those open to public *dégustation.* A fulfilling (and filling) visit to a *cave* demands a little tact, lest you give the impression that you are little more than a boorish mooch in quest of some cheap wine (which you may well be). The *dégustations* are inexpensive given the amount of wine available, but the wineries expect that they will yield many sales. While you are not required or expected to purchase a bottle, at least try to show *some* interest in the wines themselves, and not merely their effects. In the end, consider buying a bottle—most are less expensive here than anywhere else.

The **Marché aux Vins,** rue Nicolas-Rollin (tel. 80 22 27 69), housed in a 15th-century church near the Hôtel Dieu, is the most popular of the *caves.* For 40F, you can descend into a candle-lit cellar and follow a trail of 37 wine kegs, each with a different Burgundian vintage atop it for your sampling delight. The requisite souvenir imitation-silver tasting cup (more like a spoon) costs an extra 10F. Don't drink your limit too quickly—the best wines *(les grands crus)* always come near the end. Relish the Corton, the only *grand cru* of the Côte De Beaune. (Open daily 9:30am-noon and 2:30-6:30pm; Nov.-March daily 9:30am-noon and 2:30-4:30pm.)

Among the oldest *caves* are the **Halles aux Vins,** 28, rue Sylvestre Chauvelot (tel. 80 22 18 34), in the 13th-century crypt of the former Eglise St-Martin. The 35F *dégustation* of 18 wines includes a slide show. (Open daily 10am-noon and 2-7pm; Oct.-March Mon.-Sat. 10am-noon and 2-6pm.) **Maison Calvet,** 6, bd. Perpreuil, ends its tour of the three cobwebbed km of *caves* with tastings and a slide show. (Open Tues.-Sun. 9-11:30am and 2-5pm.) The elegant tour offered by **Maison Patriarche Père et Fils,** 7, rue du Collège, leads past millions of dusty, aging bottles heaped along 9km of tunnels in a former convent. The tour omits most of the tunnels and culminates in an energetic, though brief, tasting session of 21 of Burgundy's most extensive collection of labels. (Open March 5-Dec. 18 9:30-11:30am and 2-5:30pm. Admission 40F; proceeds go to charity.) The **Caves des Cordeliers,** next to the Hôtel Dieu, features a mediocre tour but satisfactory sampling *du tonneau* (from the keg). (Open daily 9am-noon and 2:30-7pm.) When you emerge from subterranean Beaune, dock your liver in beautiful **Parc de la Bouzaise** beyond the city ramparts or **place des Lions** just within the ramparts.

Nicholas Rollin, Chancellor of Burgundy and a most effective tax collector, founded the splendid **Hôtel Dieu** as a charity hospital in 1433. The colorful courtyard roof tiles and Roger Van der Weyden's paneled mural *The Last Judgment* both demonstrate the political and cultural ties this region once maintained with Flanders. The informative free brochure explains the daily operation of the infirmary, chapel, kitchen, and pharmacy. (Open daily 9am-6:30pm; Nov. 18-March daily 9-11:30am and 2-5:30pm. Admission 25F, students 20F.) In the center of town, the Romanesque **Basilique Collégiale Nôtre-Dame** merits a visit for its venerated 12th-century carved wooden Virgin and 15th-century Flemish tapestries (tapestries being restored until Jan. 1993).

The **Musée du Vin** lures oenophiles inside the **Hôtel des Ducs de Bourgogne,** in the picturesque pedestrian zone. The museum contains an informative series of exhibits on the history of wine, the geology of Burgundy, and the process of wine-making. Displays of wine-tasting cups, bottles and pitchers, and two Aubusson tapestries round out the collections. (Open 9:30am-6pm. Admission 25F, students 17F. Free pamphlet in English.) The ticket also admits you to the **Musée des Beaux Arts** and the **Musée Etienne-Jules Marey,** both on rue de l'Hôtel de Ville next to the police station (ticket for just these two museums 20F, students 7F). The former has a mediocre collection of Gallo-Roman funerary monuments and a small but impressive collection of paintings, by 15th- and 16th-century Dutch and Flemish artists, and later French artists and architects such as Corot, Léger, and Le Corbusier. The latter museum is superb, especially if you're interested in the history of photography. Marey, also a *Beaunois,* invented a camera that supposedly took 2000 pictures per second, and is considered the inventor of motion photography (chronophotography). (Open June-Sept. daily 9:30am-1pm and 2-6pm; Oct.-Nov. and April-May 2-6pm.)

Côte d'Or: The Wine Route

La Côte d'Or is a 60km strip of land that runs from Dijon to Cheilly Les Maranges, 20km south of Beaune. (Note that it lies in and takes its name from the larger *département,* the *Côte d'Or.)* Ever since the Romans brought wine-making to Burgundy, this "golden hillside" has produced some of the world's greatest reds in vineyards covering some 17,000 acres. The Côte's location on a sloping hillside and valley with heavy exposure to the morning sun and fertile limestone soil lends an exquisite taste to the wines of the region.

The Côte is divided into two distinct regions. Stretching from Dijon to Corgoloin is the **Côte de Nuits,** the region where such robust wines as Musigny, Clos de Vougeot, and Chambertin are produced. The more delicate Meursault and Montrachet whites and Corton, Beaune, and Pommard reds come from the **Côte de Beaune,** which extends from south of Corgoloin to the Southern tip of the Côte.

Your options for seeing the vineyards of the region are car, bike, or thumb. Take the **Route des Grands Crus,** through the rolling hills covered with vines and punctuated by wine châteaux. *Circuits en Côte d'Or,* a booklet available in English from tourist offices in the region, contains ten suggested itineraries. It's also possible to travel by bus, but be aware that the roundtrip excursions are generally aimed at the more solvent traveler; fares run between 300 and 500F. Both the Dijon and Beaune tourist offices can provide you with information on bus services, fares, and schedules.

While many *caves* offer free *dégustations,* a few gulps of wine are hardly worth the long rides between *caves.* And while the bigger growers expect many tasters and few buyers, the smaller growers hope that tasters are at least seriously considering buying. Buy something you like and imbibe it at lunch when the *caves* (and buses) are taking a break. All tourist offices stock an outstanding series of free brochures designed to help you relax in the countryside. Ask for *Châteaux en Côte d'Or* (detailed information on all sites, not just castles), and *Destination Côte d'Or,* which includes information on sports, concerts, class, and more. Pick up the Dijon tourist office's colorful map *Le Vignoble de Bourgogne* (15F) and the Beaune office's even more useful (and free) *Liste des Viticulteurs et Négociants-Eleveurs de la Côte d'Or et de l'Yonne.*

Since most of the wines of the region may be sampled in town at one of Beaune's numerous *caves de dégustations,* it will be worth your while to seek out those locations on the *Côte* that offer something more than a free taste. The **Château du Clos de Vougeot,** about 16km south of Dijon, is an interesting restored château, parts of which date back to the 13th century. The château is also home to the **Confrérie des Chevaliers du Tastevin,** a ritualized fraternity founded in 1934 to defend the honor of Burgundian wines. (Open daily 9am-7pm; Oct.-April Mon.-Sat. 9-11:30am and 2-5:30pm. Admission 13F.)

One of the most fascinating wineries to visit is the 10th-century **Château de Gevre-Chambertin,** just south of Dijon (tel. 80 34 36 13), which combines a smidgen of history with a visit to its extensive *caves.* (Open Fri.-Wed. 10am-noon and 2-6pm, Sun. 2-6pm. 30-min. tour 20F.) Also stop at the ruins of 9th-century **Monastère de St-Vivant** and the 15th-century polychrome wood reliquaries in 12th-century **Eglise St-Saturnin.** The **Château de Rochepot,** remarkable for its seductive hilltop setting and interiors, and a nearby 12th-century Roman church lie about 10km southwest of Beaune, accessible only by car.

Semur-en-Auxois

In 606, the monks of the Abbaye de Flavigny signed their charter in a village they called *Sene muros,* the "old walls." Though legend attributes the town's founding to Hercules, this is the earliest written record of Semur-en-Auxois, today a tiny, provincial town of cobblestones and archways overlooking a bend in the sluggish Armançon River. From the tourist office, venture under the arch and down rue Buffon to the towering Gothic **Eglise Notre-Dame.** Many of the chapels, decorated with 14th-century stained-glass windows, are dedicated to the patron saints of various professions. Check out the windows in the chapel of St. Claude, patron saint of butchers. Leaving the church, head down rue du Rempart to the huge granite **Tour de l'Orle d'Or,** the dungeon of the dismantled château, which, in spite of 5m-thick walls, is cracked from base to summit. (Open mid-June to Aug. daily 10am-noon and 2-6pm. Guided tour in French, 30min., 10F.) Semur's **Musée Municipal,** rue J. J. Colenot, contains the original plaster sculptures for several of Augustin Dumont's famous monuments, including a statue of Napoleon for the place Vendôme column in Paris. (Open Wed.-Sun. 2-5:45pm; Oct. to mid-June Wed. and Fri. 2-5:45pm. Admission 10F, students 5F.) The stroll from pont Joly to pont Pinard, around the bend of the Armançon River, affords lovely views of the town and surrounding countryside. For yet more loveliness, admire the *vieille ville* when it is illuminated (mid-June to Sept. nightly about 10pm-midnight). Every May 31st since 1369, Semur has hosted the **Fête de la Bague,** France's oldest horse race. Circuses, outdoor concerts, expositions, gallery exhibits, and general good cheer raise Semur's spirits the week before and after the races.

The **Foyer des Jeunes Travailleurs (HI),** 1, rue du Champ de Foire (tel. 80 97 10 22), is at the end of rue de la Liberté. If there's no room at this comfortable inn, there will be at the annex. Ring the doorbell to enter after 10pm; the reception is open all day. (Members only. Singles 37F50. Breakfast 8F60. Self-service lunch and dinner 36F50. Sheets 14F.) **Hotel-Bar du Commerce** offers comfortable rooms with bath and TV off a courtyard at 19, rue de la Liberté (tel. 80 96 64 40), in the center of town. (Singles and doubles with shower and toilet 150F. Buffet breakfast 25F.) A **campground** lies 3km south of Semur on scenic Lac du Pont. (Open May-Sept. 8F50 per person, 6F50 per tent.)

For affordable meals and an exceptionally welcomimg atmosphere, try **Entr'act,** 4, rue Fevret (tel. 80 96 60 10), down the street from the church. (Fresh pasta from 30F. Pizza from 28F. Open Wed.-Mon. noon-2pm and 7:30pm-midnight.) On Thursday and Saturday mornings, sample local produce at the small **market** on rue de la Liberté.

TRANSCO (tel. 80 42 11 00), runs buses throughout the entire Côte d'Or, connecting Semur directly with Dijon (3 per day, 1 Sun., 11/2hr., 46F); Avallon (3 per day, 1 Sun., 1hr., 35F); Saulieu (3 per day, 1 Sun., 50min., 16F). Semur's **tourist office,** pl. Gustave Gaveau (tel. 80 97 05 96), at the head of rue de la Liberté, distributes bus schedules, maps, and a list of hotels. (Open daily 8:30am-noon and 2-6:30pm; Oct.-May Mon. 2-6:30pm, Tues.-Fri. 8:30am-noon and 2-6:30pm, Sat. 8:30am-noon.)

Chalon-sur-Saône

During the Roman campaigns in Gaul, Julius Caesar coveted Chalon-sur-Saône (pop. 63,000) for its strategic position on the navigable Saône river. In the Middle Ages, Chalon claimed fame with its sponsorship of one of the most bodacious pelt fairs in Europe. Today, this small industrial city, still a crossroads, remains ever bodacious, throwing some of the most popular parties in Burgundy. These include a hedonistic week-long **Carnaval** celebration in the spring, the world off-shore powerboat championship in late June, *Chalon dans la Rue*—the national street artists' festival—in mid-July, and a film festival in October.

Chalon's most celebrated resident was Joseph Nicéphore-Nièpce, who invented photography in 1816. The fascinating **Musée Nicéphore-Nièpce,** 28, quai des Messageries, housed in a large 18th-century *hôtel* overlooking the river, contains an exceptional collection of cameras, from the first ever made to the one used on the Apollo mission, as well as occasional temporary exhibits of photographs. (Open Wed.-Mon. 10am-6pm; Sept.-June Wed.-Mon. 9:30-11:30am and 2:30-5:30pm. Admission 10F, students 5F. Free Wed.)

The **Musée Denon,** on pl. de l'Hôtel de Ville, showcases Bronze Age implements and other archeological discoveries. The highlight of the 19th-century exhibition halls is Gericault's *Tête de Nègre.* (Open Wed.-Mon. 9:30am-noon and 2-5:30pm. Admission 10F, students 5F. Free Wed.) The handsome 12th-century **Cathédrale St-Vincent** displays unique stone latticework in the chapels of the south (right) aisle and a 15th-century cloister houses several lovely and saintly statues. For a view of the city and the Saône Valley, cross pont St-Laurent to the small island in the middle of the Saône and climb the red brick **Tour du Doyenné,** at the southern end near the ancient hospital. (Open April-Sept. Mon.-Sat. 2-4:30pm. Free.)

Finding a room in Chalon is not difficult. The basic **Auberge de Jeunesse,** rue d'Amsterdam (tel. 85 46 62 77), has a spacious kitchen and dining area, a large patio, a river view, and a swimming pool and sailing club next door. As elsewhere, the mosquitoes can be annoying. Take bus #11 from the train station and get off at "Piscine," or walk down av. Jean Jaurès and continue under the highway (past the tourist office) as it changes to bd. de la République. At pl. de l'Obélisque, turn right onto rue du Général Leclerc. Turn left at the river and follow it to the hostel (30min.). Notice the weird, carved Manon elm tree on your right before you reach the hostel. (Reception open daily 7-10am and 5:30-10:30pm; Sept. 15-Dec. 15 and Jan. 15-March 15 Tues.-Sun. 7-10am and 5:30-10:30pm. Lockout 9:30am-5:30pm. 40F. Sheets 15F.) The town's cheapest, **Hôtel Gloriette**, 27, rue Gloriette (tel. 85 48 23 35), has clean, simple rooms at the top of a wildly tilted staircase. (Singles from 75F. Doubles 98F, with shower 110F. Showers 25F. Breakfast 22F. Closed Sun. noon-8pm.) **Camping Municipal de la Butte** (tel. 85 48 26 86) is a riverside site in nearby St-Marcel. (10F50 per person, 15F per site.) Follow the directions to the hostel but cross the bridge when you come to it, continue straight across two islands, and turn left along the river on rue Julien Lenevu. Past the campground is the gorgeous **Roseraie St-Nicolas** which blooms over 600 different species of roses.

Plenty of restaurants in Chalon serve affordable regional cuisine. Rue de Strasbourg, on the island across Pont St-Laurent, offers a huge array of choices, from the 52F vegetarian lunch *menu* at **La Pierre Vive** (open Tues.-Sat. 11am-3pm), to good ol' artery-clogging red meat at **L'Eau à la Bouche.** Their 75F four-course *menu* is worth shortening your life for. For a memorable feast, try **La Réale,** 8, pl. Gen. de Gaulle (tel. 85 48 07 21), which serves a delicious 120F *menu.* There is a **Supermarché Casino** on av. Nicéphore-Nièpce, just off av. Jean Jaurès, two blocks from the train station. (Open Mon.-Sat. 8:30am-8pm.)

Trains (tel. 85 93 50 50) run frequently to Beaune (20min., 25F); Dijon (3/4hr., 46F); and Lyon (2hr., 80F). **Bus information** (tel. 85 48 79 04) is available from the *gare routière,* across from the train station (open Tues.-Fri. 8:15am-noon and 2:15-6:15pm. Sat. 8:15am-noon and 2:15-4:30pm). Buses run several times a day to Autun (1 1/2hr., 40F50) and Cluny (1 1/4hr., 39F). The **tourist office** (tel. 85 48 37 97) is in pl. Chabas on bd. de la République. (Open Mon.-Sat. 9am-12:30pm and 1:30-7pm.) The **post office** is on pl. de l'Obélisque at bd. de la République. (Open Mon.-Fri. 8:30am-7pm, Sat. 8:30am-noon.) Chalon's **postal code** is 71100.

Cluny

One of the most influential religious institutions of Western civilization, the **Abbaye** at Cluny (pop. 48,000) was founded in 910 as part of an effort to purify monasticism. To halt creeping secularization, the Cluniacs demanded that the abbot exercise supreme control over the abbey and answer only to the Pope. For hundreds of years afterward, Cluny stood at the center of a vast ecclesiastical empire that reached from Poland to Portugal. Until the construction of St. Peter's in Rome, the abbey's church was the largest in all of Christendom. With power and opulence, however, came a relaxation of discipline. When the abbey fell under control of the French state, Cluny's influence began to wane. The anti-clerical fervor of the French Revolution touched off 25 years of uninterrupted destruction of the abbey. The French government continued to sanction the pillage of Cluny and eventually sold it to enterprising masons who dismembered the buildings and sold the stones. The only remains of the once-proud abbey are the south transept of the church, a handful of storage buildings, and a collection of finely carved capitals. Appreciate the enormous size of this Romanesque structure and its influence by joining one of the excellent guided tours that leave from the **Musée Ochier.** (Open daily 9am-6pm, tours every 1/2hr.; April-June and Oct. 9:30am-noon and 2-6pm, tours every hr.; Nov.-March 10am-noon and 2-4pm, tours every hr. Admission 25F, students 14F. English tours in July and Aug. only, but free written translation available year-round.) Enjoy a magnificent overview of the abbey and the surrounding valley from the top of **Tour des Fromages;** enter through the tourist office. (Same hours as tourist office. Admission 5F, students 3F.) Ponder the mystery of **Le Cellier de l'Abbaye** on rue Lamartine, which now houses a wine shop. The top floor dates from the 12th century, the middle from the 14th, and the bottom from the 16th.

To imagine the long-gone splendor of Cluny's abbey, drive, bike, or ride the bus to the **Basilique de Paray-le-Monial,** a well-proportioned if smaller replica of the abbey at Cluny. St. Margaret Mary Alacoque, then a humble nun, had her vision of the Sacred Heart of Jesus here in the 19th century. Today the site draws pilgrims from all over the world. (Open May-Sept. 9am-noon and 1-7pm; April and Oct. 1-7pm. Free.) The beautiful 12th-century murals at **Berzé-le-Ville's Chapelle Monacale** are almost identical to those that decorated Cluny's church.

The least expensive place to stay in Cluny is the large, clean, and comfortable hostel-like **Cluny Séjour** (tel. 85 59 08 83), on rue Porte de Pans behind the bus stop. (Singles 115F. Doubles, triples, and quads 66F per person. Breakfast and showers included. Reception open 7-11am and 5:30-10pm.) Be sure to reserve in advance at the hotels in town. **Hôtel du Commerce,** 8, pl. du Commerce (tel. 85 59 03 09), lets comfortable, nicely decorated rooms. (Singles from 100F. Doubles from 120F.) The campground **Camping Municipal St-Vital** (tel. 85 59 08 34), rue des Griottins, is across the river to the right (11F per person, 6F50 per tent or car; open June-Sept. 8am-10pm).

Most restaurants in town can drain tight budgets with a single meal, so you may be better off at the **Maximarché supermarket** on av. Charles de Gaulle or the smaller **Casino** on rue Lamartine. For regional specialties, try the 49F *menu* at **Les Marron-niers,** 20, av. Charles de Gaulle or the fancier 80F or 120F *menus* at the **Auberge du Cheval Blanc,** 1, rue Porte de Mâcon, both off pl. des Fossés.

To reach Cluny, take the SNCF **bus** from Mâcon or Chalon-sur-Saône (tel. 85 93 50 50; 3 per day, 1 1/2hr., 44F). From the bus stop to the tourist office, turn left onto rue Porte de Paris, then right onto rue des Tanneries to rue Filaterie, which becomes rue Lamartine and then rue Mercière. The **tourist office,** 6, rue Mercière (tel. 85 59 05 34), distributes maps of the town and region and runs a **currency exchange.** (Open daily 10am-7pm; April-June and Oct. 10am-noon and 2-6pm; Jan.-March 2-4:30pm.) Cluny's **post office** (postal code: 71250) is on route D-980, adjacent to the Cluny Séjour and bus stop. (Open Mon.-Fri. 8am-noon and 2-7pm, Sat. 8am-noon.)

Tournus

Situated on the Saône River, midway between Chalon-sur-Saône and Mâcon, Tour-nus bridges the border of two distinct Burgundian regions. To the east lie the flat plains of Bresse, sliced by undulating rivers. To the west rise the hills of the *Mâconnais* region, covered with vineyards and Romanesque churches. In between, Tournus itself (pop. 7000) is a relaxed town of ivy-covered houses, lone fishers, and cordial local bars and cafés filled with farmers and metalworkers. Crenelated battlements crown the exposed red brick and unadorned columns of the **Abbaye St-Philibert.** Inside, the 12th-century wooden statue of Notre-Dame-la-Brune embraces a baby Jesus and the adjacent chapel guards Saint-Philibert's bones. The crypt and its 12th-century frescoes are worth a look as well. When the abbey was secularized in the 17th century, its refectory metamorphosed into a tennis court.

On the other side of the cloister, behind the abbey, is the excellent **Musée Bourgui-gnon,** rue Perrin de Puycousin. The somewhat dilapidated exterior conceals 18th-century Burgundian rooms filled with life-sized figures in period costumes, utensils, textiles, and ironwork. (Open April-Oct. Wed.-Mon. 9am-noon and 2-6pm, Sun. 2-6:30pm. Admission 6F, students free.) In the old town, somber façades give way to ornate Renaissance courtyards, the most interesting of which are at #13, 21, and 63, rue de la République.

Several affordable hotels populate the town. The **Hôtel-Gras,** 2, rue Fénélon (tel. 85 51 07 25), to the right of the abbey, has plain rooms for 92-116F. (Reception open Mon.-Sat. 7am-10pm.) Downstairs is a restaurant where you can try the regional specialty, *quenelles au brochet*—dumplings made with *pâté aux choux* and fish drenched in a creamy sauce—on the 58F and 92F *menus*. At the **Hôtel de Bourgogne,** 37, rue Docteur Privey (tel. 85 51 12 23), beautiless purple hallways will lead you to comfortable singles and doubles for 100-190F. The simple restaurant downstairs posts 69F and 102F *menus*. To get to the **Municipal Campground** (tel. 85 51 16 58), follow av.

Général-Leclerc or av. du 23 Janvier out of town to N6 (direction: "Lyon"), and turn left. It lies at the river's edge, behind the soccer field. (6F per person, 3F50 per tent or car. Hot showers 4F50. Open April-Sept.)

The outdoor **market** (Sat. mornings on rue de la République) stretches from one end of town to the other and sells just about everything, but is more expensive than the **Supermarché Champion,** av. de la Résistance, off av. Gambetta. (Open Tues.-Thurs. 8:30am-12:30pm and 2:30-7pm, Fri. 8:30am-12:30pm and 2:30-7:30pm, Sat. 8:30am-7pm, Sun. 8:30am-noon.) **Le Voleur du Temps,** 32, rue Docteur Privey (tel. 85 40 71 93), features a 60F *menu* with delicious dishes from North and West Africa, including *couscous* (60F). (Open Tues.-Sun. noon-2pm amd 7-10pm.)

Trains leave from the station on av. Gambetta (tel. 85 51 07 30) for: Dijon (6 per day, 1 1/2hr., 66F); Chalon-sur-Saône (4 per day, 15min., 23F); Mâcon (3 per day, 25min., 32F); and Lyon (6 per day, 1 1/2hr., 75F). For information about buses to the same places, call the *gare routière* in Chalon (tel. 85 48 79 04).

The **tourist office** (tel. 85 51 13 10), on pl. Carnot is managed by a knowledgeable staff. From the station, walk right on av. Gambetta then left on rue Docteur Privey. Grab one of their excellent free city maps and some brochures on châteaux and Romanesque churches in the surrounding villages. (Open daily 9am-noon and 3-7pm; March-June and Sept.-Oct. 9am-noon and 2-6pm; Nov.-Feb. open at manager's whim.) The **post office** is on rue du Puits des Sept Fontaines. (Open Mon.-Fri. 8am-noon and 2-6pm, Sat. 8am-noon.) The **postal code** is 71700. It's hard to **exchange currency** when banks are closed (neither the tourist office nor the post office changes money); plan ahead if you are considering a weekend trip to Tournus.

Autun

In 15 BC, Emperor Augustus founded the city of Augustodunum in the lush green valley that cradles modern Autun. The prosperity of this "sister and rival of Rome," as it was called by its inhabitants, did not survive the decline of the Roman Empire. Thought to have been the home of Queen Brunhild and her Niebelung kin whose internecine struggles fill the medieval German epic *Niebelungenlied,* the beleaguered city eventually splintered into separate religious and economic settlements. In 1120, the ground-breaking for the cathedral and the arrival of the relics of Saint-Lazare drew pilgrims who brought in enough wealth to invigorate the two cities, but it wasn't until the 16th century that a single fortified wall reunited the upper and lower cities. Autun has flourished ever since, and, in recent years has outgrown the boundaries of old Augustodunum. A well-preserved *vieille ville,* a fine cathedral and museum, and the impressive theater, temple, and other remains of one of the largest Roman cities in Gaul brighten this upbeat town of 30,000. Encircled by dense forests and adjacent to the Parc Natural Regional du Morvan, Autun makes a convenient base for forays into the surrounding wilderness.

Orientation and Practical Information

The main street, **avenue Charles de Gaulle,** connects the train station to the central pl. du Champ de Mars. Rue St-Saulge and rue aux Cordiers both run from pl. du Champ de Mars into rue Chauchien, which changes name twice before reaching the cathedral in the heart of the old city.

Tourist Office: 3, av. Charles de Gaulle (tel. 85 52 20 34 or 85 86 30 00), off pl. du Champ de Mars. Map, brochure, and list of hotels and restaurants. Accommodations service (1-5F). From July-Sept. 15. Daily guided tours at 10am and 3pm (18F, students 13F). Open Mon.-Sat. 9am-noon and 2-7pm; Oct.-March Mon.-Fri. 9am-noon and 2-6pm, Sat. 2-6pm. From June-Sept. a small information booth next to the cathedral is open daily 10am-7pm.

Post Office: rue Pernette, up rue de la Grille from the train station. **Telephones.** Open Mon.-Fri. 8:30am-6:30pm, Sat. 8:30am-noon. **Postal code:** 71400.

Trains: pl. de la Gare (tel. 85 52 28 01), on av. de la République. To: Paris (3 per day, 5hr., 176F); Chalon-sur-Saône (6 per day, 2hr., 47F). TGV trains between Paris and Lyon stop at Le Creusot, where buses depart for Autun (Mon.-Fri. 5 per day, 2 Sat., 1 Sun., 40min., 33F).

Buses: 13, av. de la République (tel. 85 52 30 02). The office is up the street to the left of the station, but buses leave from the station and stop at pl. de Champ de Mars. To Dijon daily at 5:10pm (2 1/2hr., 58F). To Chalon-sur-Saône (4 per day, 1 1/2hr., 42F50).

Medical Emergency: Clinique du Parc (tel. 85 52 18 34.)

Hospital: 9, bd. Fr. Latouche (tel. 85 86 65 66).

Police: rue de la Jambe-de-Bois (tel. 85 52 14 22). Also 26bis, av. Charles de Gaulle. **Emergency:** tel. 17.

Accommodations and Camping

The cheapest lodgings are near the train station. Make reservations in advance during July and August.

Hôtel de France (tel. 85 52 14 00), across from the train station on pl. de la Gare. Magnificent stairways adorned with neat photographs from the cathedral. Cheery, wallpapered rooms on a busy street. Open Mon.-Sat., Sun. only after 5:30pm. Singles from 75F. Doubles from 80F, with shower 136F. Breakfast 22F.

Hôtel le Grand Café, 19, rue de Lattre de Tassigny (tel. 85 52 27 66), on pl. du Champ de Mars. One of the livelier spots in Autun. Central location. Fairly luxurious rooms with showers. Singles and doubles 150F, with toilet 215F. Breakfast 20F. Open Mon.-Sat.

Tête Noire, 1-3 rue Arabesque (tel. 85 52 25 39), 1 block from pl. du Champs de Mars. Nice two-star hotel. Has a few rooms within the reach of the budget traveler. Four doubles 110-125F; the rest are 170F and up. Call ahead. Breakfast 27F. Restaurant downstairs with *menus* from 67F.

Camping: Camping Municipal de la Porte d'Arroux (tel. 85 52 10 82), 1.5km from town, past the Porte d'Arroux. Swimming, fishing, and other water sports. Restaurant and grocery store nearby. 9F50 per person, 9F50 per tent. Open Easter-Oct.

Food

Several decent, inexpensive pizzerias line the cobblestone streets of the *haute ville,* near the cathedral. Buy groceries at the **Prisunic** on pl. Champ de Mars or at the **Casino** opposite the tourist office. A **market** enlivens pl. du Champ de Mars Wednesday and Friday morning. If you must sit, lounge at **the** cozy **Restaurant Lardreau,** 58, av. Charles de Gaulle, near the train station. Sample a *menu* (66F and 80F), or try the *fondue de volaille au porto* (chicken fondue with port, 54F), or the *poulet rôti avec frites* (chicken 'n' fries, 28F). (Open daily noon-2pm and 7-9pm.) Run by an award-winning chef, the **Chalet Bleu,** 3, rue Jeannin (tel. 85 86 27 30), near pl. du Champ de Mars, serves 80F, 115F, 145F, and 185F *menus.* (Open Wed.-Mon.) Finally, the dough flies at the **Au Relais des Hauts-Quartiers,** 2, rue des Bancs, near the cathedral, specializing in pizza and pasta. Virtually every dish weighs in under 40F. (Open Wed.-Mon.)

Sights and Entertainment

In its heyday, Autun was not only the largest city in Roman Gaul, with a population of about 70,000 but it was also the only city in Gaul to boast a circus, a theater, and an amphitheater. Today, only ruins of Roman monuments remain as testimony to the prosperity of the past. Standing behind the train station, across the river Arroux, is the huge brick **Temple de Janus,** dedicated in the first century AD to an unknown Roman deity (it wasn't Janus, however—go figure). This square tower is a rare example of a temple built in Gallic form using Roman construction techniques. A pleasant footpath off rue Faubourg d'Arroux starting just past one of the city's two remaining Roman gates, the **Porte d'Arroux,** passes the crumbling temple and returns to town via rue Faubourg St-Andoche. Two of the city's four Roman gates still stand: **Porte d'Arroux** on rue de Paris and **Porte de St-André** on rue Faubourg St-André. The **Théâtre Antique** was the largest amphitheater in Gaul. Once capable of seating 15,000 enthralled spectators, it now entertains only picnickers for most of the year. Occasionally, however, the thousands throng once again, when 600 locals re-enact the early days of Augustodunum in a majestic sound and light performance. The spectacle takes place during the first three weekends of August. (Tickets available at the tourist office, 65F.) From the top of the amphitheater, you can see the bizarre 30m jumble of bricks known as the **Pierre de Couhard,** 1km away on the hillside. Its purpose remained unknown until excavations unearthed a 1900-year-old plaque cursing anyone who dared disturb the eternal slumber of the man buried inside.

The intricately carved capitals of the **Cathédrale St-Lazare** recall those at the basilica in Vézelay, also constructed between 1120 and 1140. The magnificent tympanum of the Last Judgment over the central portal, a phantasmagoric vision in fresco, is the work of Autun native Gislebertus. In the center sits Jesus in majesty, surrounded by four angels. Notice, below him, the difference between the thankful blessed on the left and the terrified damned on the right.

Inside, the intricately carved capitals portray various Biblical scenes. Try not to get all capital-ed out in the main part of the church, however, because the best capitals await in the *salle capitulaire,* above the sacristy. Many of the grotesque figures leering out from the 800-year-old carvings resemble slightly satanic muppets. The 1834 painting by Ingres in the second chapel on the left depicts the martyrdom of St-Symphorian at the Porte St-André. Lightning destroyed the original lead-covered **beffroi** in 1469; the current stone belfry was built at the end of the 15th century. Climb the 230 steps for a view of Autun rooftops and Morvan hills (admission 3F).

On the same square as the cathedral, the **Musée Rollin** occupies a 15th-century hotel which belonged to Chancellor Nicolas Rolin. Even if you don't have time to inspect the well-arranged Gallo-Roman exhibit, examine the three delicate statues from the tomb of Saint-Lazare and Gislebertus's *Eve,* which poignantly capture the moment of The Fall. (Open Wed.-Mon. 9:30am-noon and 1:30-6pm; Oct.-March 10am-noon and 2-4pm. Admission 10F, students 5F.) Larger Gallo-Roman architectural fragments occupy the courtyard of the **Musée Lapidaire,** 10, rue St-Nicolas. (Open Wed.-Mon. 10am-noon and 2-6pm; Oct.-Jan. and March to mid-April 10am-noon and 2-4pm. Free.)

Every year in late July, the festival **Musique en Morvan** brings an international sampling of young people's choirs to Autun. Throughout the summer, concerts take place at the Château of Arnay-le-Duc and at the Eglise Saulieu, two nearby sites accessible by car. Tickets are available from the Lycée Bonaparte (tel. 85 52 04 76).

Near Autun

Twenty-eight km along D978, on the bus route to Chalon-sur-Saône, the impressive 15th-century **Château de Couches** (tel. 85 49 68 02) has been restored but retains its original fortifications, chapel and dungeon. (50-min. tour July-Aug. daily 10am-noon and 2-6pm; Sept. and June daily 2-6pm. Admission 23F.) Fifteen km northeast of Autun along the D326, **Château de Sully** (tel. 85 82 10 27) was aptly dubbed the "Fontainebleau of Burgundy" by Paris socialite Mme de Sévigné. Birthplace of Maréchal MacMahon, 19th-century president of France, and brief home to Voltaire, this 16th-century palace now houses the current Duke. (Gardens open Palm Sunday-Oct. 9am-7pm. 30-min. château tour 10F. Open Easter-Oct. daily 9am-6pm.)

Nevers

Canals, forests, fields, and the Loire and Nièver rivers all converge on Nevers. Although this small city on the western edge of Burgundy brushed with fame in Marguerite Duras's novel and screenplay, *Hiroshima Mon Amour,* its real claim to fame is as the final resting place of Ste-Bernadette de Lourdes. Bernadette Soubirous, the young girl who reported conversing with the Virgin Mary in Lourdes, came to Nevers in 1866 to enter the **Couvent Saint-Gildard.** She is still there, preserved in the convent's chapel.

Beyond the bustle of a modern industrial city, Nevers sequesters carefully-tended parks, modest squares, and a long tradition of excruciatingly detailed ceramics. If at first you aren't impressed by this reticent city, remember Duras's words, "To speak badly of Nevers would be an error of both the spirit and the heart."

The **Cathédrale St-Cyr et Ste-Juliette** was rebuilt five times between 502 and 1945, allowing a rich mix of Romanesque, Gothic, and even modern styles. *Malheureusement,* the builders never got it quite right—if you stand in the center and gaze at the ceiling, you can see that the nave is crooked. Opposite the cathedral, the Renaissance **Palais Ducal** sits under fairytale turrets with a view of the Loire. On pl. Charte, to the east of the cathedral and beyond the major pedestrian streets, the 11th-century **Eglise St-Etienne** consists of a series of circular chapels radiating from one circular nave.

A walk among the pleasant gardens lining the **Promenade des Remparts** which runs from the Loire to av. Général de Gaulle, shows the crumbled remains of Never's 12th-century ramparts. Also on the Promenade des Remparts is the **Musée Municipal Frédéric Blandin,** which houses a fine collection of the ceramics for which Nevers is famous. (Open Wed.-Mon. 10am-12:30pm and 2-6:30pm. Admission 10F, students 5F.) At the end of the street lies the **Porte du Croux,** a 14th-century fortified tower harboring the uninspiring **Musée Archéologique du Nievernais.** (Open Wed.-Sun. 10am-noon and 2-7pm; Mon. 2-7pm. Admission 10F, students 5F.) Nevers's fortifications along the av. Général de Gaulle have crumbled to leave only the **Porte du Croux,** a fortified tower harboring a dull Romanesque sculpture museum in the former guards' rooms. (Open Wed. and Sat. 2-4pm.) The lively **Parc Municipal,** off pl. Carnot, occasionally hosts summer concerts in its elaborate central grandstand. Some of Nevers' fine ceramics languish in the **Musée Municipal Frédéric Blandin,** 16, rue St-Genest. (Open Wed.-Mon. 10am-12:30pm and 2-6:30pm. Free.) The **Couvent St-Gildard,** on the corner of rue Jeanne d'Arc and rue St-Gildard (tel. 86 57 79 99), houses the Congregation of the *Soeurs* (sisters) of Nevers and the corpse of Sainte-Bernadette. The body of this saint who lies preserved under a thin layer of wax, reposes in a glass case in the chapel. (Open daily 6:30am-7:30pm. Free.) A small museum in the convent gives a thorough overview of Bernadette's life, and displays many relics, including an original letter describing one of her visions. (Open daily 7am-7pm. Free.)

Nevers revolves around the pl. Carnot. From the train station, head straight up av. Général de Gaulle for four blocks. The **tourist office,** 31, rue du Rempart (tel. 86 54 07 03), is on the right, across the square. Ask for the brochure *Nevers et sa région,* which has a map of the town and describes architectural landmarks in the area. (Open Mon.-Sat. 9am-noon and 2-6pm.) The **post office,** 25bis, rue Rempart, has a **currency exchange.** (Open Mon.-Fri. 8am-6:30pm, Sat. 8am-noon.) Nevers's **postal code** is 58000. The **Centre d'Accueil Universitaire,** 57, faubourg du Grand Mouësse (tel. 86 30 00 02), helps travelers find cheap housing in universities and hostels. **Trains** pass through Nevers to: Dijon (7 per day, 3hr., 137F); Lyon (4 per day, 3hr., 164F); Paris (16 per day, 2 1/2hr., 160F); and Bourges (4 per day, 1hr., 51F).

Finding a decent inexpensive room in Nevers is no problem. The two-star **Hôtel Villa du Parc,** 16-18, rue de Lourdes (tel. 86 61 09 48), across the park from pl. Carnot and near the **Couvent St-Gildard** occupies the best location in town. (Singles and doubles 95-110F, with shower 140-180F. Breakfast 25F.) The **Hôtel de l'Avenue,** 38, av. Colbert (tel. 86 61 01 97), is a bit distant (15min. walk) but a good bargain. (Ask for a key if out past 11pm. Singles 80F. Doubles 90F. Breakfast 15-20F.) From pl. Carnot, walk down rue des Remparts to the Porte de Paris and turn left onto av. Colbert. The **Camping Municipal** (tel. 86 37 56 52), across the river, is near a swimming pool. From the cathedral, follow rue de la Cathédrale to the river, cross the bridge, and turn left. (7F per person, 5F50 per tent. Open March-Oct.)

Nevers's *vieille ville* is studded with rather pricey *brasseries,* but there are inexpensive spots scattered in all directions from pl. Carnot. Rue du 14 Juillet, between pl. Carnot and the cathedral, boasts a bevy of inexpensive ethnic restaurants, serving everything from Moroccan delights like *couscous* and *tahini* at **L'Alhambra** (open Tues.-Sat. 6-10pm), to down-home-style cooking like grandma probably didn't used to make at **L'Apple Pie.** For more traditional French fare, try the great 54F *menu* featuring *quiche lorraine* and *brochette de dinde* (turkey skewers) at **Au Petit Caveau,** 55, av. Général de Gaulle, near the train station. The baguette-hunk-of-cheese-and-an-apple crowd can stock up on staples at the **Supermarché Major,** on av. Général de Gaulle halfway between the train station and pl. Carnot. (Open Mon.-Fri. 9am-7:30pm.)

Near Nevers: La Charité-sur-Loire

Twenty-three km north of Nevers (4 trains per day, 25min., 32F), the red roofs, church spire, and ramparts of La Charité-sur-Loire make the tiny town-on-the-banks-of-the-Loire an idyllic daytrip destination. Founded in the 8th century and appropriated by Cluniac monks, La Charité grew in power and wealth until it was known as "the older sister" of Cluny, with 400 dependent monasteries throughout Europe. Virtually annihilated by a 1559 fire and the Wars of Religion, La Charité continued to decline under eventual Protestant control. Only 12 monks remained by the time of the Revolution, and the monastery still has not quite recovered from a three-day fire in the 19th century that destroyed most of the buildings. A Romanesque monastery and fine stained-glass windows recommend the 12th-century **Eglise Notre-Dame.** The **tourist office,** 49, Grande Rue (tel. 86 70 16 12), opposite the Hôtel de Ville, will give you information on all of the sights in town, and will help you find a room, if you decide to spend the night. (Open Mon.-Fri. 8am-noon and 1:30-5:30pm, Sat. 8am-noon.) If the great outdoors is your room of choice, there is a **camping de la Saulaie** (tel. 86 70 00 83) near a swimming pool, the Loire, and a beach. (Open June 15-Sept. 15.)

Avallon and Vézelay

The untarnished *vieille ville* of Avallon (pop. 10,000) peaks above medieval ramparts high on a granite mountain. The two most prominent remnants of bygone days stand adjacent to one another at the southern end of the *vieille ville.* Once the principal portal to the city, the **Tour de l'Horloge** now straddles rue Aristide Briand and keeps the *avallonais* running on schedule. Just down the street stands the **Eglise Collégiale St-Lazare,** which gained its present name in the year 1000 when the philanthropic Duke of Burgundy, Henry LeGrand, donated a part of St-Lazare's skull to the church. The 11th-century origins of the church appear most prominently in its two ornately carved Romanesque portals. (Open daily 6:45am-noon and 2-7pm.) Also in the southern part of town is the **Musée de l'Avallonais,** which contains a lovely Gallo-Roman mosaic, the *Mercure de Ste-Vertut,* and an important statuette of a god from Charancy. (Open Easter-Oct. Wed.-Mon. 10am-noon and 2-6pm. Admission 15F, students 7F50.) A walk along the nearby western and southern ramparts yields an excellent view of the dense forests and verdant pastures of the Vallée du Cousin and several small châteaux.

The **tourist office,** 4, rue Bocquillot (tel. 86 34 14 19), is next to St-Lazare but a 15-minute walk from the station. Head down av. du Président Doumer, and make a right onto rue Carnot. At the large intersection make a left onto rue de Paris, which passes a large parking lot, becomes Grand Rue Aristide Briand, passes through the Tour de l'Horloge, and lands you at the foot of the tourist office. The staff will give you a map and help you find a hotel room (5F). (Open daily 9:30am-7:30pm; Sept. and Easter-June daily 9am-12:30pm and 2-6:30pm; Oct.-Easter Tues.-Sat. 9am-12:30pm and 2-6:30pm.) When the tourist office is closed, call the **mairie,** 37-39, Grande Rue (tel. 86 34 13 50). The **post office** is at 29, rue de Lyon, near rue Carnot. (Open Mon.-Fri. 8am-noon and 2-6:30pm, Sat. 8am-noon.) Avallon's **postal code** is 89200. **Bikes** are available from the station (55F per day, ID and 1000F deposit required). Vézelay is only 15km away, and except for a steep climb at the end, the route via Vallée du Cousin is relatively flat.

Located 30 minutes from the train station and 20 minutes from the *vieille ville,* the **Foyer des Jeunes Travailleurs,** 10, av. de Victor Hugo (tel. 86 34 01 88), has singles in a modern high-rise. From the station, walk down av. du Président Doumer, turn right onto rue Carnot, which becomes route de Paris after the intersection, then go left onto av. de Pepinster after the Casino supermarket. Stay on Pepinster when it becomes av. du Morvan and, finally, go left onto av. Victor Hugo. One block down from there, the *foyer* is often full; call before you make the trek (66F; breakfast 13F50, lunch or dinner

36F50). **Au Bon Accueil,** 4, rue de l'Hôpital (tel. 86 34 09 33), at the bottom of the parking lot at the entrance to the *vieille ville,* rents large rooms with TV. (Reception open Mon.-Sat. Singles 100F. Doubles and triples with shower 175-215F.) The popular restaurant below has 44F, 56F, and 67F *menus*—possibly the most affordable meals in town. Another candidate is the **Pizzeria de la Tour** (tel. 86 34 24 84), at the base of the clock tower. (Pizza 30-45F, pasta 32-42F, dessert *crêpes* 10-24F. Open Tues.-Sat. 12:15-3pm and 7:15-10pm, Sun. 7:15-10pm.) Picturesque **Camping Municipal de Sous-Roche** (tel. 86 34 10 39) lies 2km away; walk along route de Lourmes and then climb to the riverside (fishing allowed) campground. There's a restaurant nearby. (10F per person, 5F per tent or car. Open March 15-Oct. 15.)

Eight **trains** per day run from Avallon to Laroche-Migennes, which connects to Paris (3hr., 144F) and Auxerre (1hr., 46F). Six trains per day run to Autun (2hr., 53F). **TRANSCO buses** (tel. 80 42 11 00) roll from the train station to Dijon (3 per day, 2 1/2hr., 70F), with a stop in Semur-en-Auxois (45min., 21F).

Perched high on a hill 15km from Avallon, the village of Vézelay (pop. 600) towers over a valley and offers postcard-esque views of the surrounding fertile pastures and dense forests. Yet most people don't visit Vézelay to admire the scenery; they flock, pilgrims and tourists alike, to visit the stunning 12th-century **Basilique de la Madeleine** and its crypt, still believed by some to contain the remnants of Mary Magdalen. The multitude is at its thickest on July 22, the official day of homage to *la Madeleine.* Carved in 1125 and subsequently restored, the **tympanum** above the narthex's main portal portrays a risen Christ welcoming worshipers to the inner nave of the church. (Open daily 7am-6pm, Sept.-June sunrise-sunset. Basilica illuminated Tues. and Fri. 9:30-10:30pm.) In July and August, a small **museum** above the chapter room opens its doors to display sculptures removed from the church as well as to detail the 19th-century restoration work. (Open Mon.-Sat. 10am-noon and 2:30-5:30pm. Admission 5F.) Adjoining the church is the rebuilt Franciscan abbey (the original was destroyed in the Revolution), the first brotherhood of St. Francis of Assisi established in France.

Run by Pax Christi, a Catholic peace movement, the **Centre de Rencontres Internationales,** rue des Ecoles (tel. 86 33 26 73), provides simple and inexpensive accommodations just below the Basilica. (36F for first night, 26F for subsequent nights.) Located on a peaceful, rural site 700m from town, the **Auberge de Jeunesse (HI),** route de l'Etang (tel. 86 33 24 18 or 86 33 25 57), has slightly more luxurious accommodations with only four people per room. Follow the signs toward the *gendarmerie* from the base of the hill to the left. (Lockout 10am-5:30pm, but you can leave bags all day. Members only. 40F. Kitchen facilities. Open June-Sept.) Camping is available behind the hostel (10F per person, 3F per tent or car; includes showers, bathrooms and access to hostel kitchen facilities). Stock up on food at the **Casino** near the bottom of rue St-Etienne (Open Mon.-Tues. and Thurs.-Sat. 8:30am-12:30pm, and 3-7:30pm, Wed. and Sun. 8:30am-12:30pm.) Or sit down for a meal at the earthy **A la Fortune du Pot,** below the parking lot on rue St-Etienne. (Lunch *menus* from 46F. Open Mon.-Fri. noon-2pm and 6-9pm, Sat. noon-2pm.)

Vézelay's **tourist office,** rue St-Pierre (tel. 86 33 23 69), just down the street from the church, offers a free map and an accommodations service (10F) and will **exchange currency.** (Open daily 10am-1pm and 2-6pm; Sept.-Oct. and April-June Mon.-Tues. and Thurs.-Sat. 10am-1pm and 2-6pm; closed Nov.-March, but will respond to mailed inquiries.) **Trains** run from Auxerre to Sermizelles (7 per day, 3/4hr.); a bus then shuttles passengers to Vézelay once at 10am and once at 3pm. **Cars de la Madeleine** (tel. 86 33 25 67) serves the route between Avallon and Vézelay. The schedule stays roughly the same: a bus departs for Vézelay from Avallon's Café de l'Europe (on pl. Vauban) at about 8am, and then returns at about 6:30pm (15min., 32F round-trip). Many travelers report hitchhiking in the area is easy.

Avallon and Vézélay are on the northern edge of the huge **Parc Naturel du Morvan.** Located atop a huge bed of granite, the park will regale you with *plein air* (fresh air), and a gaggle of activities such as hiking, horseback riding, fishing, and canoeing. For more information on the park, contact the **Maison du Parc Naturel Régional du Morvan**, St-Brisson, 58230 Monbtesuache (tel. 86 78 70 16).

Auxerre

Once soaked with grape vines, Auxerre suffered from a phylloxera epidemic in the late 19th century. The cause of massive vineyard destruction, the outbreak forced the city to change its livelihood from wine to industry. Nonetheless, today's Auxerre (pop. 42,000) retains much of its historical and architectural charm; maintains a superb location on the Yonne River, making it an excellent port for the litter of leisure boats which cruise Burgundy's waterways; and provides those traveling by boat, car, bike, or foot with a superb base from which to venture into northern Burgundy.

Orientation and Practical Information

Fifty-two km north of Vézelay and Avallon, and midway between Paris and Dijon, Auxerre is well-connected to both major cities. The *vieille ville* and most of the action lie on the west bank of the river. From the train station, follow the signs for the *centre ville* along rue Ferry, hang a right onto av. Gambetta, and cross the river on pont Bert. The tourist office lies to the right, three blocks down quai de la République.

Tourist Office: 1-2, quai de la République (tel. 86 52 06 19), below the cathedral on the bank of the Yonne. City map. Accommodations service (10F). Open daily 9am-7pm; Sept. 16-June 14 daily 9am-12:30pm and 2-6:30pm. **Branch office** at 16, pl. des Cordeliers (tel. 86 51 10 27), adjacent to the pedestrian streets. Open Mon. 9am-12:30pm, Tues.-Sun. 9am-12:30pm and 2-6:30pm.

Post Office: (tel. 86 48 57 21) on pl. Charles-Surugue, in the town center. **Telephones.** Open Mon.-Fri. 8am-7pm, Sat. 8am-noon. **Postal code:** 89000.

Trains: (tel. 86 46 50 50), on rue Paul Doumer, east of the Yonne. To: Paris (13 per day, 2hr., 112F); Lyon (9 per day, 4 1/2hr., 206F); Avallon (9 per day, 1hr., 46F); Autun (6 per day, 3hr., 87F).

Hospital: Hôpital Général, bd. de Verdun (tel. 86 48 48 48).

Medical Emergency: SMUR, tel. 86 46 45 67.

Police: bd. Vaulabelle (tel. 86 51 42 44). **Emergency:** tel. 17.

Accommodations, Camping, and Food

There should be no problem finding clean, inexpensive places to stay all the year round. July and August weekends can, however, reel in the crowds; reserve if arriving mid- to late Saturday. The tourist office has a BIJY guide of local farmers who welcome campers.

Foyer des Jeunes Travailleuses (HI), 16, bd. Vaulabelle (tel. 86 52 45 38). Follow the signs from the train station to *centre ville*, cross the bridge, and turn left; the first right is rue Vaulabelle. The *foyer* is in an inconspicuous apartment building to the left, set back from the street and past a gas station. Singles 72F. Breakfast included. Meals 31-36F.

Foyer des Jeunes Travailleurs (HI), 16, av. de la Résistance (tel. 86 46 95 11). From the train station, walk south along the tracks to the end of the platform. After crossing the tracks on the little footbridge, continue straight to the high-rise on the right (5min.). Members only. 62F per person, including breakfast and sheets. Accepts travelers May-Aug. Lunch and dinner served at other *foyer.*

Hôtel de la Renomée, 27, rue d'Egleny (tel. 86 52 03 53), in the *vieille ville.* Open Mon.-Sat. Quiet rooms off a courtyard. Singles 95F, with shower 110F. Doubles 125F, with shower 140F. Hall showers included. Restaurant downstairs has *menus* from 46F. Closed last 3 weeks in Aug.

Hôtel de la Porte de Paris, 5, rue St-Germain (tel. 86 46 90 09), on the edge of the *vieille ville,* near the *abbaye.* A pleasant, clean hotel-bar. Often full by evening, but has a high turnover rate. Singles and doubles with shower 125F. Triples with shower 150F. Quads with shower and toilet 180F. Breakfast 22F.

Camping: (tel. 86 52 11 15), on route de Vaux, south of town on D163. A shady spot along the Yonne, with TV, laundry facilities, and a pool nearby. 10F per person. Open April-Sept.

Bourguignon cuisine is expensive everywhere, and Auxerre is no exception. For fresh seafood, try **La Marée,** 55, rue Joubert, near the pedestrian zone. A 78F *menu* includes mussels and trout or salmon (open Mon.-Sat. noon-2pm and 7-9:30pm). **Le Repaire du Cadet Roussel,** 6, rue Fourier, serves tasty *crêpes* and *galettes* from 24F (open daily noon-2pm and 7:30-9:30pm). **INNO supermarket,** 9-10, place Charles Surugue, provides everything for a picnic, while the cafeteria upstairs is packed with locals at lunchtime. A **market** fills pl. de l'Arquelouse from Tuesday through Friday. The Sunday market keeps the same hours in pl. Degas.

Sights and Entertainment

Thirteenth-century **Cathédrale St-Etienne** masks its elegant Gothic structure with a flamboyant façade. Bas-reliefs on the left portal depict Biblical accounts of the Creation, the Garden of Eden, Noah's Ark, and Abel's murder, while those on the right portal show David and Bethlehem. The small **treasury** contains enamel work, illustrated manuscripts, and 5th-century tunic of St-Germain. You'll find the ochre fresco *Christ on Horseback,* the only representation of its sort in existence, in the 11th-century **crypt.** (Open Mon.-Sat. 9am-noon and 2-6pm, Sun. 2-6pm. Admission 10F, students 5F.)

The **Abbaye St-Germain,** which attracted several medieval pilgrimages in honor of St-Germain, still draws crowds to its exceptional Carolingian crypts. The frescoes of St. Stephen getting stoned (with rocks, that is) are the oldest in France. (Open Wed.-Mon. Obligatory tours every 1/2hr. 9am-12:30pm and 2-6:30pm; Sept. 16-June 14 9am-noon and 2-6:30pm. Admission 16F, students free. All free Wed.) The ticket includes admission to the adjacent **Musée d'Art et d'Histoire,** a new museum with artifacts from four centuries of Roman occupation.

Stroll around the pedestrian zone near pl. des Cordeliers to see old Auxerre and the **Tour de l'Horloge,** a two-faced 15th-century clock tower. The **Musée Leblanc-Duvernoy,** 9bis, rue d'Egleny, in the western part of town, contains five 18th-century Beauvais tapestries, as well as painting and pottery collections. (Open Wed.-Mon. 2-6:30pm; Sept. 16-June 14 Wed.-Mon. 2-6pm. Closed Nov. 1-15. Admission included in ticket to the Abbaye.)

Auxerre hosts a week-long **jazz festival** every year in mid-June. Several of the concerts are free. Contact the tourist office for more information.

Sens

In 390 BC the powerful Senoni tribe, centered in the region which now envelops Sens, seized a small Italian town named Rome. While the tribe eventually relinquished control of the imperial capital, Sens remained prominent for several centuries, becoming the capital of one of the Lyonnaise provinces during the Roman occupation. The *Sénonais* one-upped the Romans again in 1163, when Alexander III's papacy made Sens the center of world Christianity for one brilliant year. Today, Sens remains a peaceful town of 30,000, quietly proud of its glorious past.

"It is art and history combined," Victor Hugo said of the magnificent **Cathédrale St-Etienne,** France's first authentic Gothic cathedral. (Though St-Denis in Paris was built five years earlier, it was officially an abbey church until consecrated a cathedral in 1960.) Construction began in 1140, but changes and additions continued into the 16th century. Of particular interest are the four blue-toned stained-glass windows in the north ambulatory, the aisle by the chancel. In July, hourly tours of the cathedral are given in French or English (1hr., 10F). Heretics were imprisoned in the downstairs courtroom of the **Palais Synodal** next door. Ask the custodians to show you the 13th-century system of cells off the vaulted passageway, untouched since their construction. The **cathedral treasury,** which contains relics and liturgical vestments that belonged to Canterbury's renowned archbishop, St. Thomas à Becket, and the **painting gallery** (which also contains the hat that Napoleon wore at Waterloo), are housed in the Henry II wing of the former archbishopric. Neolithic and Gallo-Roman collections are next door in the François I wing. (Open 10am-noon and 2-6pm; Oct.-May Wed. and Sat.-Sun. 10am-noon and 2-6pm; Mon. and Thurs.-Fri. 2-6pm. One ticket for all exhibits. Admission 12F, students 9F50. Free Wed.)

Amble through the town's narrow back streets in search of the Renaissance and neo-classical *hôtels particuliers,* whose beams and posts are occasionally adorned with decorative or religious figures. The tourist office's guide mentions almost all of them, including the exquisite carved wooden beams of the **Maison d'Abraham,** on rue de la République at rue Jean Cousin.

Reservations are advisable if you plan to spend the night in Sens. The hotels around the train station all offer reasonable rooms in the 90-120F range. Consider spending an extra 20-30F to stay at the **Hôtel Esplanade,** 2, bd. du Mail (tel. 86 65 20 95), just off pl. Jean Jaurès, which offers nicer rooms, TV, and a choicer location. (Reception open Mon.-Sat. Singles and doubles 95-220F. Hall shower included. Breakfast 21F, in bed 25F.) **Camping Municipal Entre-deux-Vannes** (tel. 86 65 64 71) is outside town on route de Lyon (10F50 per night; open June-Nov. 15). Affordable meals are scarce; decent pasta and pizza (34-65F) await you at **La Rosa,** 162, rue des Deportes et de la Résistance, next to the cathedral. For a more Burgundian flavor, sample the 85F *menu* at **Le Soleil Levant,** 51, rue Emile Zola, on the main road to town from the train station.

Frequent service links Sens to Paris (1 1/2hr., 75F) and Dijon (2hr., 118F). The **tourist office,** pl. Jean Jaurès (tel. 86 65 19 49), has maps, historical commentaries, an accommodations service (5F), and a **currency exchange** in summer. (Open daily 9am-noon and 1:30-7:30pm; Sept.-June Mon.-Fri. 9am-noon and 1:30-6:15pm, Sat. 9am-noon and 1:30-5:15pm.) From the station, walk down av. Vauban, cross the river, and follow the signs left on the curving road (20min.). The cathedral looms two blocks away.

Franche-Comté

Franche-Comté ascends like an enormous stairway from the plains of central France to the mountains of Switzerland. Loosely translated, the province's name means "Free Country," a testimony to 700 years of struggle to maintain the region's independence. Grim military fortifications occupy the highest ground in most towns, where streets bear the names of generals and soldiers. First inhabited by the Celts in 58 BC, Franche-Comté came under German rule in 1032 but was ceded to Philippe le Bel of France in 1295. In 1447, the Habsburgs annexed the region, only to lose it to Spain in 1556. Finally, in 1604, the French seized control of the war-torn area once and for all. When King Louis XIV annexed Franche-Comté, he sent the famous military architect Vauban to fortify the area with his ingenious constructions.

Composed of three *départements* (Doubs in the center, Haute-Saône in the northwest, and Jura in the south), Franche-Comté welcomes visitors. Among other things, it features serene, cordial towns, handfuls of grottoes and caves, the Jura and Vosges mountain ranges, and an overall natural grace. With rushing torrents, meandering streams, and placid lakes, Franche-Comté is a paradise for canoe and kayak enthusiasts. Local tourist offices provide publications with information on hiking, hang-gliding, camping, skiing, and other outdoor activities. They also distribute a series of brochures *Itinéraires Franc-Comtois,* which include information on châteaux, regional gastronomy, and Jura wine routes.

Franche-Comté's rapid climb to world renown and prosperity began in the early 18th century, when Daniel Jean-Richard, a Geneva artisan, established a small watchmaking shop in the Jura. His willingness to pay higher wages than available in agriculture or textiles attracted numerous apprentices. Before long, Jean-Richard's success with his industry enticed Geneva watchmakers, frustrated with the fierce competition in Switzerland, to move to the Jura and establish their own shops. When Frédéric Japy developed a way to mechanize the production of watches, the price of local timepieces dropped through the floor, forced Geneva to cater to the upper end of the market by focusing on watches as ornamentation, and established Franche-Comté as the leader in watchmaking for the common consumer. By the 1830's, the region had even surpassed Paris as the watch capital of the world, a distinction which it still proudly claims.

Scientist Louis Pasteur was born in Dole and raised in Arbois. Today, just about everyone but the region's 300,000 milk cows seems bent on perpetuating Pasteurmania. The fresh, foamy, country milk may just as well be the local beer. It is also the main ingredient in most of the area's delicacies: 600 liters go into every 50kg of *Comté,* the regional cheese. Fruity Arbois wines (including *Arbois, L'Etoile, Château-Chalon,* and *Côtes de Jura)* and cherry-flavored *kirsch* complement these mild flavors, as do the pungent smoked hams, sausages, and *eaux-de-vie* cheeses of Fougerolles. Trout thrive in local rivers, and heaps of wild mushrooms fill locals' baskets.

Trains run frequently between all cities in the region, and the Monts Jura bus company operates decent service to smaller towns and excursions into the mountains. Besançon is an excellent base for trips into the Jura or surrounding country, as most other towns are less than an hour away by train. As elsewhere in France, hitchhiking is not always safe or easy here.

Besançon

Capital of Franche-Comté and twice voted the greenest city in France, Besançon (pop. 120,000) delights both cultural connoisseurs and nature lovers. Home to a major university, an international language school, and several important museums, Besançon has a diverse and vibrant cultural flavor, while its ubiquitous flower beds and parks and mountain backdrop offer serene respite from the bustle of the *vieille ville.* Indeed, Besançon strikes a perfect balance between urban vigor and rural beauty, making it a most suitable gateway between Burgundian vineyards and Alpine ski slopes.

Orientation and Practical Information

A horseshoe bend in the calm Doubs River cradles the old town of Besançon, while the expanded, modern city spreads out in the valley below. Besançon's *vieille ville, citadelle,* and cultural centers all lie within the Doubs horseshoe, a 10-minute walk from the station. Follow av. Foch across the pont Denfert-Rochereau. To reach the tourist office from the train station, follow rue de Belfort, turn right onto av. Carnot, and walk through the pl. Flore. Turn right and walk to the pont de la République. The tourist office is next to the bridge.

Tourist Office: 2, pl. de l'Armée Française (tel. 81 80 92 55). Friendly facility stocks information on regional excursions and festivals and will supply a list of hotels and restaurants or book a room for 6F. **Currency exchange** when the banks are closed. Open July-Aug. Mon.-Fri. 9am-noon and 1:30-7pm, Sat. 9am-noon and 1:45-6pm, Sun. 9am-noon; Sept.-Oct. and Easter-June Mon.-Fri. 9am-noon and 1:30-6:30pm, Sat. 9am-noon and 1:45-5pm; Nov.-Easter Mon.-Fri. 9am-noon and 1:30-6pm, Sat. 9am-noon and 1:45-5pm. **Annex,** pl. du 8 Septembre, aide de l'Hôtel de Ville (tel. 81 61 51 41). Small supply of useful local brochures. Open July-Aug. Mon.-Fri. 2-6pm. **Centre d'Information et d'Accueil Municipal:** 2, rue Megevand (tel. 81 83 08 24). Further information on sports, wheelchair facilities, health care, lodging, etc. Open Mon.-Fri. 8am-noon and 1:30-6pm; Sept.-June Mon.-Fri. 8am-noon and 1:30-6pm, Sat. 9am-noon.

Post Office: 19, rue Proudhon (tel. 81 82 23 12), off rue de la République. **Telephones, Poste Restante,** and **currency exchange.** Open Mon.-Fri. 8am-7pm, Sat. 8am-noon. The **main office** 4, rue Demangel (tel. 81 53 81 12), is way out in the new town. **Postal Code:** 25000.

Trains: (tel. 81 53 50 50), on av. de la Paix. Besançon is about 4hr. from Paris's Gare de Lyon via Dole and Dijon (6 per day, 217F). Local connections run to: Lyon (8 per day, 2 1/2hr., 135F); Belfort (12 per day, 1hr., 68F); Strasbourg (8 per day, 2 1/4hr., 157F); Dijon (12 per day, 1hr., 65F). Office open Mon.-Sat. 8:30am-6:30pm, Sun. 9:30am-12:30pm and 2-6:30pm.

Buses: Monts-Jura, 9, rue Proudhon (tel. 81 81 20 67). From the tourist office, turn left off rue de la République. To Pontarlier (4 per day, 1 1/2-2hr., 39F). **City Buses: CTB,** 46, rue de Trey (tel. 81 50 28 55). Efficient city bus system. Tickets 5F per hr., *carnet* of 10 38F. "Bus-info" trailer/caravan in pl. 8 Septembre most summer afternoons.

Taxi: tel. 81 80 17 76 or 81 88 80 80. 24 hrs.

Bike Rental: At the train station. 40F per 1/2-day, 50F per day, 500F deposit.

Youth Information: Centre Information Jeunesse (CIJ), 27, rue de la République (tel. 81 83 20 40). Complete library has regional, national, and international information on lodging, travel, excursions, sports, concerts, tickets, employment. BIJ/Transalpino tickets. Ride board. Open Mon. 1:30-6pm, Tues.-Fri. 10am-noon and 1:30-6pm, Sat. 1:30-6pm.

Laundromat: 54, rue Bersot, near the bus station. Wash 18F, dry 5F per 20min. Soap 5F. Open 7am-8pm.

Gay Hotline: Collectif Homosexuel de Franche-Comté, tel. 81 83 58 50. A gay hotline (in French) for regional services, events, and advice.

Hiking Information: Club Alpin Français, 14, rue Luc Breton (tel. 81 81 02 77), in the *vieille ville.* Topo-guides 37F. Open Tues.-Fri. 5-7pm.

Hospital: Centre Hospitalier Régional, 2, pl. St-Jacques (tel. 81 52 33 22). Emergency, tel. 81 66 81 66.

Medical Assistance: SAMU, tel. 15.

Ambulance: AUMB Urgence Médicale et Médecine de nuit, tel. 81 52 11 11 or 81 83 11 11.

Police: av. de la Gare d'Eau (tel. 81 82 03 67). **Emergency:** tel. 17.

Accommodations

Hotels in Besançon are generally pleasant and rarely full. Fortunately, finding a room in one of the inexpensive *foyers* isn't tough, and the CROUS service can find you space in university buildings in summer.

Centre International de Séjour, 19, rue Martin-du-Gard (tel. 81 50 07 54), near the university. Take bus #8 from the station to the "Intermarché" stop. Reception open 7am-1am. Singles 84F.

Doubles with 2 beds 57F per person. Triples or quads 50F per person. Hall showers included. Breakfast 16F. Meals 48F. Rarely full. Reservations for up to 1-week stays accepted up to 1 week in advance.

Foyer des Jeunes Filles, 18, rue de la Cassotte (tel. 81 80 90 01). Women only. Friendly, quiet place maintained by nuns and long-term boarders. Reception open daily 8am-10pm. Comfortable singles 60F. Showers and breakfast included. Meals 31-38F. Sheets 15F.

University Housing: CROUS, Service d'Accueil d'Etudiants Etrangers, 38, av. Observatoire, bldg. B (tel. 81 50 26 88), is the administrative office. To get a room July-Sept., go to the **Cité Universitaire.** From the tourist office, cross the bridge and take bus #7 (direction: "Campus") to the "Université" stop. Head to bldg. A-B, to the right of the Resto U. From Mon.-Fri. 10-11:45am and 1-4:15pm go to the *secrétariat,* where you pay and get a room. At other times go directly to the concierge in the lobby of the same building. Ordinary dorm singles 70F, with student ID 45F. Call as far in advance as possible. CROUS offices can also arrange longer stays in university housing.

Hôtel Florel, 6, rue de la Viotte (tel. 81 80 41 08), left of the train station and 1min. away. Comfortable, spotless singles and doubles with TV 130F, with shower 187F. Triples with shower 250F. Breakfast 24F, in bed 30F.

Hôtel Regina, 91, Grande Rue (tel. 81 81 50 22), smack in the middle of town. "Very nice. Very very nice. Very," notes hotel critic Keven McAlester. All rooms are recently renovated and have toilet, shower, TV, and telephones. Singles and doubles 185-225F. Breakfast 24F.

Hôtel le Levant, 9, rue des Boucheries (tel. 81 81 07 88), on pl. de la Révolution. Good location in the *vieille ville* near the river. Some rooms without windows. Plain singles 96F, with shower 130F. Doubles 140F, with shower 160F. Triples with shower 240F. Breakfast 20F. Lively restaurant downstairs.

Camping: Camping de la Plage (tel. 81 88 04 26), rte. de Belfort in Chalezeule northeast of the city. Take bus #1 (direction: "Palente") and ask for the *camping.* A superb municipal campground, with access to a nearby pool. 17F per adult and tent, 9F50 per additional adult, 5F20 per child, 5F per car. Open March-Oct.

Food

An eclectic selection of restaurants caters to Besançon's cosmopolitan student population; look along rue des Boucheries and the rue Claude-Pouillet. Young *bisontins* pack the cafés on pl. de la Révolution. Inexpensive pizzerias line rue Bersot. Tuesday through Saturday afternoon, visit the outdoor **market** in pl. de la Révolution. The sharp *Comté* cheese is abundant here; among the famous Arbois wines is expensive *vin jaune* (yellow wine), which tastes like sherry and goes well with *Comté*. Many excellent *charcuteries* along rue des Granges sell *jambon de Haut Doubs,* a regional smoked ham.

University Restaurants: The best food deals in Besançon. Mediocre but filling cafeteria meals 26F. People sometimes buy tickets from students in line (12F). A la carte options are slightly more expensive. Three locations: **Restaurant Canot,** 73, quai Veil-Picard, entrance on rue A. Janvier, across the river from the old town; **Restaurant La Bouloie,** at the *cité universitaire;* and **Restaurant Megavand,** rue Megavand, near rue de la Préfecture. In July and Aug., the restaurants rotate service—call CROUS (tel. 81 50 26 88) to find out which is dishin'. Open Mon.-Fri. 11:30am-1:15pm and 6:30-7:50pm, Sat. 11:45am-1:15pm and 6:45-7:50pm, Sun noon-1:15pm. From Sept.-June all three are open Mon.-Sat. 11:30am-1:15pm, with Canot and Bouloie serving dinner from 6:30-7:50pm and Megavand serving breakfast from 8:30am-10:30am. Expect huge lines, even in summer.

La Boîte à Sandwiches, 21, rue du Lycée, the next street to your right after Grande Rue from rue de la République. A sandwich oasis in the desert of 3-course, sleep-inducing French lunches. Over 50 types of sandwiches, including seaweed (13-25F). Salad selection allows every possible concoction (15-35F). Due to renovations, prices may rise in 1993. Open Mon.-Fri. 11:15am-2pm and 6:45-10pm, Sat. 11am-2pm.

Le Poker d'As, 14, square St-Amour, off rue d'Alsace (tel. 81 81 42 49). For the best of Franche-Comté cuisine, treat yourself to Chef R. Ferreux's *bûche forézienne* (made with local mushrooms and Arbois wine, 78F) or *dos de Sandre au vin jaune* (Doubs River fish with local yellow wine, 138F). Four *menus* 118-220F. Open Tues.-Sat. noon-2pm and 7-10 pm; Sun. lunch only. Reservations a good idea.

Le Levant, 9, rue des Boucheries. Shady place always crowded both inside and out. *Couscous* 42F. Good 49F *menu* and 70F regional *menu*. Open Sun.-Fri. noon-1:45pm and 7-9:45pm.

Au Petit Polonais, 81, rue des Granges, in the *vieille ville*. Several different *menus* with regional specialties (58-90F). Open Mon.-Fri. 11:45am-2pm and 7-10pm. Sat. lunch only.

Sights and Entertainment

Built in 1674 by Vauban on the site of an ancient Gallo-Roman acropolis, the impressive **citadelle** rises from sheer rock over the green mountains and the winding Doubs. Vauban's works, intended to thwart the Swiss, are described in the brochure *A la recherche de Vauban et de ses successeurs en Franche-Comté,* available from tourist offices. The series of buildings within the 20m-thick walls houses a variety of museums, an aquarium, and a zoo. The **Musée de la Résistance et de la Déportation** (tel. 81 83 37 14) contains thought-provoking photographs, texts and original documents from World War II. Ask the guards to open a room on the third floor that displays a unique collection of sculpture and painting crafted by survivors of Nazi concentration camps. Endless rows of butterflies are impaled on the walls of the **Musée d'Histoire Naturelle.** Other rooms contain African masks and yummy stuffed mammals and birds. To relieve stress, do a primate scream back to screaming monkeys and then gallop merrily with the ponies at Besançon's wonderful zoo. (Museums, zoo, and aquarium open Wed.-Mon. 9am-6:15pm; Oct.-March 25 9:30am-6pm. Admission Wed.-Mon. 23F, students and ages 10-18 16F, under 10 free. Admission to citadel, aquarium, and zoo on Tues. 16F.) To reach the citadel, take the steep Grande Rue to rue des Fusillés de la Résistance.

At the foot of the citadel stands the **Porte Noire,** a stern 2nd-century Roman triumphal arch, and the marvelously ornate 18th-century **Cathédrale St-Jean.** Inside, the unique circular altar *Rose de St-Jean* and wooden Renaissance masterpiece *La Vierge aux Saints* deserve a look. (Tours July-Sept. Wed.-Mon. at 10:30am and 3:30pm, 1/2hr., 10F.) Behind the church ticks the locally crafted **Horloge Astronomique,** the sum of 30,000 parts. Daily at noon, Jesus leaps from his tomb as Hope blesses Faith and Charity, and two soldiers doze at their posts despite the ringing bells; another thrilling presentation occurs at 3pm, and less flamboyant mechanical theatrics occur every hour. Arrive at 11:45am or 2:45pm for a tour. (Admission 18F, students 10F.)

Past Porte Noire and along Grande Rue, the elegant **Renaissance Palais Granvelle** will contain the new **Musée du Temps** in 1995. Appropriately, the museum will be located in this, the city that replaced Paris as the watch capital of the world. A preview exhibit, with antique watches and elegant grandfather clocks, is on display at the **Musée des Beaux Arts,** pl. de la Révolution (tel. 81 81 44 47). The exceptional permanent collection also includes works by Tintoretto, David, Ingres, Constable, Courbet, Matisse, Picasso, and Renoir. (Open Wed.-Mon. 9:30-11:50am, 2-5:50pm. Admission 17F, students and Wed. free.)

Les Vedettes Bisontines (tel. 81 68 13 25) runs daily *bateau-mouche* cruises on the Doubs and inside the citadel canals from Pont de la République, near the tourist office. (July-Sept. 14 Mon.-Fri. at 10:30am, 2:30pm, and 4:30pm, Sat.-Sun. at 10:30am, 2:30pm, 4:30pm, and 6:30pm; fewer run April-June and Sept. 15-Oct. 5, 1 1/4hr., 40F, under 18 30F.) The **Piscine du Sport Nautique Bisontine,** av. de Chardonnet (tel. 81 80 56 01), on the same side of the river as the tourist office near pont de Bregille, gives instruction in sculling, canoeing, and kayaking (introductory course 300F per week; open May 15-Sept. 15 daily 10:30am-7pm). They also have a pleasant outdoor swimming pool with the same hours. (Admission 20F, students 13F.)

The tourist office publishes a comprehensive list of all cultural events. In late June, Besançon has a week-long **Festival des Idées,** with concerts, art exhibits, and plays. The only remaining competition for young orchestra conductors in the world, the **Festival de Musique de Besançon** (tel. 81 80 73 26) features world-famous classical musicians under nascent batons in the first two weeks of September. (Admission 60-270F, students 20% off.) **Jazz en Franche-Comté** brings a flurry of free concerts in June and July. Most of Besançon's *boîtes de nuit* (nightclubs) have a 60F cover. **Le Show Bizz,**

42, chemin de Mazagran (tel. 81 80 73 26), features French Top 40 in one room, and anything else (from the tango to Jacques Brel) in the other.

Near Besançon

Besançon is a good base for excursions into the **Jura Mountains.** The prehistoric glaciers of Franche-Comté have created a natural underground amusement park of grottoes and rivers. The closest (15km from Besançon), **Grotte d'Osselle,** is home to 3000 cave-bear skeletons. To cool off, head 525m underground to the **Grotte de la Glacière,** a subterranean safe deposit box for a sparkling collection of minerals and crystals. Both are easily accessible by car on N83 or D30. (Osselle open June-Aug. 8am-7pm; April-May and Sept.-Oct. 9am-6pm. Glacière open June-Aug. 8am-7pm; March-May 9am-noon and 2-6pm; Sept.-Nov. 9am-noon and 2-5pm.) Call the central Jura tourist office at 84 24 19 64, or pick up a copy of *Welcome to Jura,* which contains information on kayaking and hiking through the Jura massif.

Pontarlier, near the border of Switzerland, produces a variety of liqueurs, chocolates, honey, and smoked hams in addition to proclaiming itself the capital of mountain *gruyère.* Eight footpaths take you away from the 17th- and 18th-century town center and into the forest. The first week in August, Pontarlier hosts a colorful international dance festival. In winter, locals ski at the nearby **Super-Pontarlier** on the Montagne du Larmont. In town, stay at the **Auberge de Jeunesse** on rue Marpaud (tel. 81 39 06 57; 42F per person; breakfast 14F; sheets 16F), or try **Les Gentianes** (tel. 81 39 19 73), a three-star campground near the Paul Robbe municipal stadium. The **tourist office** is in the Hôtel de Ville (tel. 81 46 48 33). To get to Pontarlier, take a *Monts Jura* bus from the Besançon bus station (4 per day, 1 3/4hr., 39F) or a train from Mouchard. **Ornans,** accessible by the Pontarlier bus from Besançon, is home to the **Musée Gustave Courbet,** the artist's onetime residence, now filled with his works. It was here that Courbet painted the monumental but controversial *Burial at Ornans* (now at the Musée d'Orsay in Paris), which angered the bourgeoisie for candidly depicting a group of aristocrats looking incredibly bored at an occasion so solemn as a funeral.

Belfort

At the crossroads of four regions (Franche-Comté, Burgundy, Alsace and Lorraine) and three countries (only 15min. from Switzerland and 30min. from Germany), Belfort's (pop. 50,000) strategic placement has ensured its importance as a military site for centuries. Only recently has it begun to offer something to the tourist, with newly renovated monuments, museums, and a charming *vieille ville.* First fortified in 1226, Belfort became a key defense city only after 1675, when military architect Vauban began enlarging and strengthening the fortress following the Treaty of Westphalia returned it to France after three centuries of Austrian rule. Today, **la Porte de Brisach** is the only remaining gate from the old fortifications.

The rest of the fortress, however, is well-preserved and most of the city's attractions lie in this northern section. Follow the signs uphill to the 24m **Lion,** Belfort's mascot, which stares fiercely toward the town from the northern face of the citadel. Sculpted from pink sandstone by Frédéric Auguste Bartholdi (Mr. Statue of Liberty himself), the lion honors those who defended Belfort during the Franco-Prussian War. (Open daily 8am-11:45am and 2-6:45pm. Admission 3F.) Continue up past the fearsome feline to the **Château de Belfort.** (Open daily 8am-noon and 2-7pm; Nov.-March Wed.-Fri. and Mon. 10am-noon and 2-5pm, Sat.-Sun. 8am-noon and 2-5pm; April and Oct. Wed.-Mon. 8am-noon and 2-6pm.) The 10F charge (free Wed.) admits you to the ramparts and tunnels and to the **Musée d'Art et d'Histoire,** which has several rooms with a variety of exhibits. Look for the 18th-century tarot cards in the basement and the André Villers photographs of Picasso and other artists scattered across the courtyard. Climb the final set of stairs to the viewing deck; a clear day brings a vision-quenching view of Belfort and the Jura Mountains across the Savoreuse River. For an even tastier view of the Vosges Mountains in the north, climb avenue de la Miotte to **La Tour de la Miotte,** a small turret built on the ruins of Château de Montfort.

Back in town, wander around the *vieille ville,* a roughly pentagonal area at the base of the château, where the pink buildings match the color of the fortress. Pay homage to the patron saint of travelers at **Cathédrale Saint-Christophe,** on place d'Armes, an 18th-century classical sandstone structure that houses intricate carvings and a grand organ.

The **tourist office,** at pl. de la Commune (tel. 84 28 12 23), in the pedestrian zone, distributes several useful brochures, including the free student-published *Le Petit Guide,* a practical guide to Belfort's restaurants, lodgings, and sights. (Open Mon.-Sat. 9am-12:15pm and 1:45-7pm, Sun. 10am-12:30pm; Sept. 16-May Mon.-Sat. 9am-12:15pm and 1:45-6pm.) Ask for pamphlets suggesting hikes through Belfort, and a for list of festivals. Every Wednesday in July and August, free outdoor musical entertainment enlivens various locations throughout the town. Belfort has a **train station** (tel. 84 28 50 50) with direct trains to Paris (236F), Strasbourg (104F), Colmar (66F), Dijon (121F) and Besançon (69F), and a **bus station** at pl. Corbis (tel. 84 28 59 02).

Accommodations, Camping, and Food

Belfort has plenty of cheap, clean rooms. University housing is only available during the school year; contact the **CROUS** office in Belfort (tel. 84 21 06 01) or Besançon (tel. 81 50 26 88). The attractive **Foyer des Jeunes Travailleurs,** 6, rue de Madrid (tel. 84 21 39 16), has comfortable singles, doubles, and triples for 57F per person. (Showers and sheets included. Breakfast 10F.) From the station, go left under the underground passage, continue up rue Parisot and av. Le Clerc to rue de Madrid (10min.). The **Hotel Vauban,** 4, rue du Magasin (tel. 84 21 59 37), rents singles and doubles for 90-180F. (Breakfast 23F.) The **Nouvel Hôtel,** 56, rue Faubourg de France (tel. 84 28 28 78), has simple, clean rooms. (Singles 95F. Doubles 100F. Showers 12F. Breakfast 24F.) The **Camping Municipal,** promenade d'Essert (tel. 84 21 03 30), before the *foyer,* occupies a grassy knoll in a shady park. (5F50 per person, 5F50 per tent, 4F per car. Open May-Sept.)

Join local students and families for a meal at **L'Ancêtre,** 4, faubourg des Ancêtres, which serves formidable pizzas (30-50F) in a plush, pink setting. For regional specialties, sample the selection of *charcuteries* on bd. Carnot, or for a real treat try the *feuilleté de saumon* (salmon in flaky pastry, 65F) and *confit de lapin à l'ancienne* (rabbit, 38F) at **Le Rond de Serviette,** 2, rue de la Grande Fontaine (72F lunch *menu,* 82F and 102F dinner *menu).* For the gourmet on the go, there are **Casino supermarkets** next door to the *foyer* and on rue Faubourg de France. Wednesday, Friday and Saturday mornings, a **market** occupies rue Docteur Fréry on the old-town bank of the river; Tuesday, Thursday, and Sunday morning it moves to the Marché des Vosges, on av. Jean Jaurès, 20 minutes from the *centre ville.* Take bus #1 (direction: "Valdoie") to "Marché Vosges."

Arbois

Sedate Arbois (pop. 4000), home of the unique *vin jaune* (yellow wine), dozes at the heart of the *jurassien* vineyards. While the town itself may excite only die-hard Louis Pasteur fans, the seemingly endless numbers of nearby *caves* provide an interesting alternative to the more crowded wineries in Burgundy, and a walk through the surrounding countryside testifies to the serene majesty of the Jura region.

Orientation and Practical Information

Less than 50km from Besançon, Arbois is served frequently by trains and buses. The central square, **place de la Liberté,** is one block up from the bus terminus and a 15-minute walk from the *gare.* From av. de la Gare, turn left onto av. Pasteur, which becomes rue de Courcelles and then Grande Rue before it reaches pl. de la Liberté. Everything in this compact town is near this square or on the multi-named main street.

Tourist Office: 10, rue de l'Hôtel de Ville (tel. 84 37 47 37), in the Hôtel de Ville, off pl. de la Liberté. Dispenses train and bus schedules, a map, and a list of hotels and restaurants. The friendly staff will tell you of hotel vacancies and *caves* open to the public. Open Wed.-Sat. and Mon. 9am-6pm, Tues. 9am-12:30pm and 2:30-6pm, Sun. 10am-noon and 2-4pm; Sept.-June Tues.-Sat. 9:30am-noon and 2-6pm, Mon. 3-6pm.

Post Office: av. Général-Delort (tel. 84 66 01 21), off pl. de la Liberté. **Telephones.** Open Mon.-Fri. 8am-noon and 2:30-5:30pm, Sat. 8am-noon. **Postal Code:** 39600.

Trains: (tel. 84 47 50 50), on rte. de Dole. To: Dijon (4-5 per day, 1hr., 61F); Besançon (6 per day, 1/2hr., 39F); Lyon (6 per day, 2hr., 105F). Station open Mon. 5:30am-8:30pm, Tues.-Fri. and Sun. 6:40am-8:30pm, Sat. 5:30am-8pm.

Buses: SNCF buses (free with railpasses) stop at pl. Notre-Dame across from the Hôtel des Messageries. Schedules posted at the stops; ask at the train station or the tourist office.

Bike Rental: Patrick Aviet, 1, rue de Bourgogne (tel. 84 66 03 13). Decent 10-speeds 40F per 1/2-day, 80F per day. Mountain bikes (VTT) 30F per hr., 80F per 1/2-day, 100F per day. Open Mon.-Sat. 9am-noon and 2-5pm.

Police: 17, av. Général-Delort (tel. 84 66 14 25). **Emergency:** tel. 17.

Accommodations, Camping, and Food

Although tourists crowd Arbois in summer, you shouldn't have trouble finding a room. Many hotels close one day per week in winter; call ahead.

Hôtel le Memphisto, 33, pl. de Faramand (tel. 84 66 06 49), near the church. Comfortable, spacious rooms. Singles 70F. Doubles 110F. Breakfast 22F. Pizzeria below has a 50F *menu*.

La Poste, 71, Grande Rue (tel. 84 66 13 22), above a bar. Basic and clean with easygoing management. Singles 90F. Doubles 125F. Showers 20F. Breakfast 25F. The restaurant downstairs serves *steak-frites* for 38F.

La Cuisance, 62, pl. Faramand (tel. 84 66 19 99), across from the Memphisto. Simple rooms with showers. Singles and doubles 100F. Triples with 2-3 beds 130F. Open Feb.-Dec.

Camping: Camping des Vignes (tel. 84 66 14 12), on av. Général-Leclerc, about 1km outside town next to an Olympic-size swimming pool. Follow the signs from pl. de la Liberté. 12F per person, 12F per tent or car. Grocery store in July and Aug. Open April-Sept.

A number of cafés around pl. de Faramand serve basic 40F *menus* (appetizer, *steak-frites,* and dessert). **La Finette, Taverne d'Arbois,** 22, av. Pasteur, serves a hearty 73F *menu* on tables made from wooden barrels. Their *mâchons* (snacks) can be a meal in themselves—try the *fondue des trois cantons* (3 cheese fondue, 33F). (Open daily 9am-midnight.) On the other side of town, choose the main courses cooked in Arbois wine, such as *Poularde au Vin Jaune,* at **La Cuisance,** 62, place Faramand (meals 40-100F). A regional **market** fills pl. du Champs de Mars Tuesday and Friday until 1pm. **Casino Supermarket,** on Grande Rue, is a good bet. A smaller one on pl. de la Liberté is open on Sunday.

Sights and Entertainment

Come to Arbois to savor *jurassien* wines and learn about different wine-making techniques. The best deal in town is at **Les Deux Tonneaux,** at pl. de la Liberté, where **Henri Maire,** the biggest wine-producer in the region, shows an excellent free 20-minute film about wine cultivation in English and French. The comparison between a wine cellar and a cathedral borders on the pretentious, but you can taste the wine, accompanied by bread, cheese, and salami (all free!) in the shop. (Shop open daily 8:30am-7pm; Nov.-April 9am-noon and 2-6pm.) Free bus tours—which are followed by a traditional *dégustation*—leave frequently from the shop to the vineyards. The visit takes you to *caves* where red, white, and the expensive yellow wines are produced. *Vin jaune* takes six years to make; 20% of it turns to vinegar. An *apéritif* is included in the tour: try *Montagnard,* a sweet rose-colored wine. Henri Maire also makes *vin de paille* (straw wine), a sweet white made by pressing grapes dried on straw. *Vin fou,* another local product, is Arbois's answer to champagne. From July to mid-September,

Fruitière Vinicole d'Arbois, 2, rue des Fosses, also gives frequent *cave* tours which include free tastings. Go only if you can't make a tour at Maire—these *caves* usually cater to bus tours. The tourist office distributes a list of smaller wine-making operations, but only the large businesses give tastings. At smaller houses, at least offer to pay for the tasting *(payer la dégustation)* if you don't buy a bottle. For a further dose of local oenology, visit the **Musée de la Vigne et du Vin** on rue du Vieux Château (Open July-Aug. Wed-Mon. 10am-noon and 3-7pm; June and Sept-Oct. 15 Sat.-Sun. 3-7pm. Admission 8F.)

Arbois was Louis Pasteur's childhood home and later his vacation retreat from the university where he taught. The ivy-covered **Maison Pasteur,** 83, rue de Courcelles (tel. 84 66 11 72), still contains his original furniture and the laboratory where he did his experiments on fermentation. (Open for 1/2-hr. guided visits in French Wed.-Mon. 10-11:30am and 2-5:30pm, Sun. 10-11:30am and 2-4:30pm. Ring the bell to summon the guide. Admission 14F, students 7F.) Pasteur's small vineyard is now privately cultivated by Henri Maire; a film on Pasteur's life is shown several times per day in Henri Maire's shop.

For a view of Arbois dwarfed by vast fields of grapes, climb to the top of the bell tower of the odd **Eglise St-Just** (visits 3 times per day at 11am, 4pm, and 5:30 or 6pm). A 15-minute *circuit pédestre* begins outside the church and passes an old waterwheel, a babbling brook, vegetable gardens, and herds of sheep.

The largest of Arbois's annual festivals is the **Les Bacchanales du Verres** (first weekend after July 14), when wine and dancers in traditional garb flow freely down the main street (20F to see parade). First prize in the raffle is the winner's weight in wine. The September and October harvests bring a flurry of smaller wine festivals.

Near Arbois

About 5km from Arbois and and 250m underground are the **Grottes des Planches,** the eerie handiwork of a subterranean river. (45-min. tours 9:30am-6:30pm; Sept. and April-June daily 10am-noon and 2-6pm; Oct.-March Sun. by appointment only. Admission 20F, under 12 10F.) You can't get to the caves by public transportation—walk or try to get a ride on one of the many tour buses passing through Arbois (they often have extra seats). Worth the trip for the beautiful scenery alone, the grottoes adjoin a crystal-clear lake in the shadow of the highest cliff in the Jura Mountains.

Dole

If you're looking for the perfect "out" from the bustling student populations of Besançon and Dijon or the foggy stupor of winetasting in Beaune and Arbois, you have found it in Dole's beautiful canal, flower-covered gardens and soporific tranquility. Established as a monastic village in the 14th century, Dole reached its cultural and political peak as the capital of the Comté de Bourgogne in 1479. The town's stubborn resistance to annexation by France spurred an enraged Louis XI to raze the town to its foundations. Two centuries later, Dole finally surrendered to Louis XIV. Showing no signs of past destruction, today's Dole presents a pleasant, if insignificant, stop between Dijon and Besançon.

Orientation and Practical Information

Dole lies along the Doubs River, halfway between Dijon and Besançon. **Place Grévy,** a few blocks north of the river, marks the center of town. From the train station, turn left and follow av. Aristide Briand to rue de la Sous-Préfecture, the second left after the post office. Follow the street as it turns into rue du Gouvernement. When it dead-ends into pl. Grévy, the tourist office is on your left (15min.).

Tourist Office: 6, pl. Grévy (tel. 84 72 11 22). Small office distributes a free map and list of hotels. Ask for a copy of *Jura été,* which lists cultural events. Open Mon.-Fri. 9am-noon and 2-6:30pm, Sat. 9am-noon and 2-5:30pm.

Post Office: 3, av. Aristide Briand (tel. 84 82 15 71). **Telephones, currency exchange.** Open Mon.-Fri. 8am-6:30pm, Sat. 8am-noon. **Postal Code:** 39100.

Trains: (tel. 84 47 50 50), on pl. de la Gare, 5min. from the center of town. To: Dijon (10 per day, 30min., 40F); Besançon (10 per day, 30min., 39F); Strasbourg (10 per day, 3 1/2hr., 175F); and Belfort (5 per day, 1 1/2hr., 95F).

Buses: Monts Jura, 17, av. Aristide Briand (tel. 84 82 00 03). Excursions to towns in the Jura mountains and beyond.

Hospital: Centre Hospitalier, av. L. Jouhaux (tel. 84 72 81 21).

Police: Commissariat de Police, 1, rue du 21 Janvier (tel. 84 72 01 68). **Emergency:** tel. 17.

Accommodations, Camping, and Food

Comfortable student *foyers* welcome budget travelers throughout the year. Dole's several reasonably priced hotels usually have space.

Foyer L'Accueil Dolois, 8, rue Charles Sauria (tel. 84 82 15 21) in the center of town. From the train station, take av. Aristide Briand; take your 2nd right after the post office onto rue Raguet-Lépine. The *foyer* is at the end. Men and women accepted. In a beautiful old convent with large, clean rooms. Reception open daily 8am-7pm. No lockout. Curfew midnight. Singles 90F, under 25 85F. Doubles 80F per person, under 25 75F. Prices go down if you stay longer than one night. Showers, breakfast, and sheets included. Contains the **Restaurant Associative,** where you can eat five-course meals amid a crowd of locals. Lunch and dinner 38F. Open daily noon-2pm and 7-8pm.

Foyer des Jeunes Travailleurs: Foyer St-Jean (HI) (tel. 84 82 36 74), on pl. Jean XXIII, a 15-min. walk from the station. Walk straight ahead, turn right on bd. Président Wilson (the main street that becomes av. L. Jouhaux), turn left at the 3rd light (rue des Paters), right onto rue Lachiche, and head toward the hideous modern St-Jean church. The hostel is in a parking lot. Reception open Mon.-Fri. 9am-6pm, Sat.-Sun. noon-1pm and 7-11pm. No curfew. Members only. Clean singles 58F. Sheets and showers included. Croissants (3F) and coffee (3F) for breakfast. Lunch (noon-12:45pm) or dinner (7-7:45pm) 34F. You should have no problem getting a room here, even July-Aug. Wash 20F, dry 10F. **Bike Rental** free with 400F deposit.

Auberge du Grand Cerf, 6, rue Arney (tel. 84 72 11 68), off pl. Grévy. Lots of regulars. Clean and comfortable. Singles 120F. Doubles 160F. Showers and toilets included. Breakfast 15F. Open Sept.-July.

Hôtel Le Petit-Parc, pl. de la Gare (tel. 84 72 13 82), across from the station. Simple, clean rooms with views of a pretty garden. Singles from 100F. Doubles from 125F. Showers 10F. Breakfast 20F. Open Mon.-Sat.

Camping: Camping du Pasquier (tel. 84 72 02 61), a 10-min. walk from pl. Grévy and on the river. One of the best views of the town and Eglise Notre-Dame. Hot showers. 12F per person, 21F per tent. Electricity 13F. Open March 15-Oct.

Skip the expensive cafés and *salons de thé* around pl. Grévy and rue de Besançon. Put together your own meal in the nearby food shops and eat along the canals. Tuesday, Thursday, and Saturday mornings, the **market** in pl. du Marché, opposite the church, does its thing. There is an **Intermarché supermarket** on av. L. Jouhaux. (Open Mon.-Fri. 8am-noon and 2-7pm, Sat. 8am-7pm.) **La Demi-Lune,** 39, rue Pasteur, serves good salads and *crêpes* (14-50F) in a canalside vaulted cellar. (Open March-Sept. and Nov.-Jan. noon-2pm and 7pm-midnight.) **La Bucherie,** 14, rue de la Sous-Préfecture, serves excellent pizza (25-45F) in an underground restaurant with fresh roses on every table. Try the unusual pizza *Franc-Comtoise* with artichokes, *escargots,* and bacon (43F). (Open Tues.-Sat. noon-2pm and 7-10pm, Sun. 7-10pm.) For a change of pace, try the 49F lunch menu with rice, chicken, or vegetable curry and fruit salad at **Taj-Mahal,** 73, rue Pasteur. (Open daily 11:45am-2:30pm and 7-11pm.)

Sights

To put it delicately, Dole isn't Paris or Rome or London or even Providence, RI, for that matter. Nonetheless, wander over to the 16th-century **Eglise Notre-Dame,** whose 74m steeple dominates the downtown district. Notice the intricately carved marble sculptures of the organ tribune and the grand façade of the main chapel. The eclectic courtyard of **Hôtel Terrier de Santans,** 44, rue de Besançon, preserves three staircases from the 16th, 17th, and 18th centuries. From rue de Besançon, take a right onto rue de la Bière as you approach pl. Grévy. This narrow street leads down the hill to rue Pasteur; the **Maison Natale de Louis Pasteur** stands at #43. The town has made this a veritable shrine full of anything remotely associated with Pasteur, from old clothing to flasks of liquid used in his fermentation experiments. (Open July-Aug. Wed.-Sat. and Mon. 10am-6pm, Sun. 10am-5pm; Sept.-Oct. Wed.-Sat. and Mon. 10am-noon and 2-6pm. Admission 14F, students 7F, disabled free.)

A small arch to the right of the house leads to the **Canal des Tanneurs,** where Pasteur's father cured hides. The **Musée Municipal,** 85, rue des Arènes, contains works by Vouet, Le Brun, Courbet, and others, as well as an archeological section with Celtic, Gallo-Roman, and Merovingian displays. (Open Mon. and Wed.-Sat. 10am-noon and 2-6pm, Sun. 2-5pm. Free.) Tours of Dole, the Basilica, and the Hôtel-Dieu run from the tourist office July and August (20-25F).

Dole's most interesting "sights" are not found inside its churches and museums, but along the network of canals, paths, and gardens in the southern part of the *vieille ville.* Barges pass frequently through the locks; check out the slow process of changing water levels and opening gates. The particularly friendly *dolois* often invite strangers to join the endless games of *boules* in the **Cours St-Marius,** across from the pl. Jules Grévy.

Alsace-Lorraine

Alsace and Lorraine have served France and Germany as political pawns since the 3rd and 4th centuries, when barbarian tribes first swept westward through these regions. They have been ravaged repeatedly ever since, most recently after the Franco-Prussian War of 1870-71 and during both World Wars. The result is an unusual combination of Frankish and Germanic influences, coupled with an often fervent loyalty to France. Having jointly endured almost two millennia of shifting political fortunes, Alsace and Lorraine maintain a fascinating blend of local *patois* (lingo), cuisine, architecture, and customs. Thus, the unique cultural hybrid they represent is not so much a case of cultural confusion as it is a case of cultural Darwinism: only the strongest elements of each culture has survived. Culture in the region is not the bastard child of Franco-German conflict, but a resilient offspring that transcends national sovereignty. Indeed, one gets the impression that, regardless of which country's flag flies over the region, the unique flavor of Alsace and Lorraine would scarcely notice a change.

Set amid a carpet of vineyards and fields unrolling east from the forested Vosges, the well-preserved cities of Alsace offer geranium-draped half-timbered Bavarian houses flanking the many waterways. Strasbourg, a stone's throw across the Rhine from Germany, was the birthplace of both Gutenberg's printing press and of "La Marseillaise," a Rhine Army marching song that became the French national anthem after revolutionaries from Marseille sang it in Paris. Strasbourg has retained its patriotic fervor and today serves as the base of the ecumenical European Parliament and the Council of Europe. Along the *route du vin,* a string of vineyards and picturesque villages runs about 140km from Marlenheim to Thann. Wooded hills slope down to sunlit valleys and deep blue lakes in the Vosges Mountains, where hiking, camping, and cross-country skiing flourish in an unspoiled setting. Hundreds of kilometers of trails dotted with *fermes auberges* (overnight refuges) have been marked on maps and guides available from tourist offices and from the Club Vosgien, 4, rue de la Douane, Strasbourg (tel. 88 32 57 96; open Mon.-Fri. 9am-noon and 2-5pm).

Although many Alsatians are proudly, loyally French, Alsace did spend much of the last century under German rule. It doesn't attempt to disguise its German flavor, recognizable in the architecture, the bilingual swearing, and in cuisine, where *baguettes* complement sauerkraut and sausage. Among the traditional dishes are *tarte à l'oignon, pâté de foie gras, choucroute garnie* (sauerkraut cooked in white wine sauce and topped with sausages and ham), *coq au Riesling* (chicken in a white wine sauce), and *baeckaoffe* (a casserole of marinated beef, pork, lamb, and potatoes that must sometimes be ordered a day in advance). *Tarte flambée,* another popular specialty, is a bacon tart traditionally cooked in a wood stove. Alsatian cheeses include the Germanic *Münster* and *Emmenthal.* Local vineyards produce six white wines and the dry rosé *Pinot Noir. Riesling,* dry but fruity, is the king of the local wines, while the sharper *Gewurtztraminer* is extraordinarily fragrant. Cheese and wine often come together in the many *caves* along the *route du vin,* which offer combined *dégustations.*

West of Alsace, Lorraine unfolds among similar hills and wheat fields, but its cities find a serene elegance in their Renaissance and baroque architecture. This alternately wooded and industrial region derives its name from the Frankish Emperor Lothair, who received the so-called "Middle Kingdom" between France and Germany when the 843 Treaty of Verdun split Charlemagne's empire. It was annexed to France in 1766, when Duke Stanislas of Lorraine (former king of Poland and father-in-law to Louis XV) burned to death in his own fireplace. Devastated by two world wars, Lorraine has rebuilt its cathedrals and cultural centers. The energy of Nancy pulsates around its splendidly gilded place Stanislas. Tiny Bar-le-Duc, former capital of the powerful duchy of Bar, was one of the few towns to avoid the World Wars' destruction. Metz, a former fortress town and cultural center, boasts the resplendent Cathédrale St-Etienne and Basilique St-Pierre-aux-Nonnais, one of the oldest churches in France. In chilling contrast, however, is Verdun. Reduced to rubble in World War I, the city and its surroundings are haunted by dozens of military cemeteries and echoing crypts.

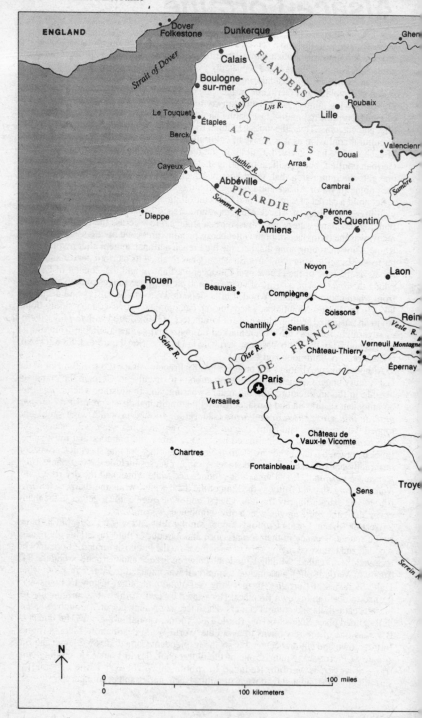

What Lorraine's culinary specialties lack in delicacy, they make up in heartiness: the bread is heavier than French breads, and potatoes or cabbage normally complement meals. Bacon, butter, and cream are key ingredients in artery-hardening dishes such as *quiche Lorraine,* the region's claim to gastronomic fame. In original versions of this much-maligned peasant dish, a hollowed-out loaf of stale bread was filled with egg custard and a few bits of meat. The hearty *pâtés* of Lorraine often contain marinated veal and beef. Desserts include *madeleines* (little flower cakes in the shape of a shell called a *raméquin)* from Commercy, *macarons* from Nancy, and *dragées* from Verdun. The fantastically rich chocolate/cherry *gâteau Forêt Noire* (Black Forest cake) is a specialty burgled from Bavaria.

Trains are undoubtedly the best means of transport in both regions. Buses usually take twice as long and cost nearly the same as trains. Steep hills and frequent storms discourage all but the most determined bikers. Many hitchers take advantage of the heavy industrial traffic, especially in Lorraine.

Be forewarned that Alsace and Lorraine share a Germanic tendency to enforce regulations to an extent unthinkable elsewhere in France. Expect regular and brusque examinations by *contrôleurs* (conductors) aboard buses and trains; losing your bus ticket before the end of the ride or forgetting to validate your train ticket on the platform could cost you 100F—no exceptions or excuses.

Strasbourg

Strasbourg impressed both Goethe and Rousseau—quite possibly a feat never duplicated. Straddling the German-French border, Strasbourg seems to belong to both cultures. Gothic churches, covered bridges, and half-timbered houses hanging over cobblestone streets seem imported from Germany; wide boulevards and spacious squares are all France. Part of the Holy Roman Empire in the Middle Ages, Strasbourg nonetheless leaned toward Paris. First annexed to France in 1681, Strasbourg did not shift its allegiance under the more recent German presence in the city (1870-1918 and 1940-1944). In part, however, the city has eschewed cultural allegiance to any particular ruling power by developing a distinctly international flavor. The elite Université de Strasbourg boasts a diverse student body and draws thinkers from across France and around the world. Strasbourg remains the seat of numerous European Community governing agencies, including the European Parliament, the Council of Europe, and the European Commission for the Rights of Man. From the medieval Cathedral to the ultra-modern European parliament building, this city—perhaps more than any other French city—evokes a vision of Europe's past, present, and future.

Orientation and Practical Information

Poised just beside the German border, Strasbourg lies four and a half hours by train from Paris and two hours from Zürich. The *vieille ville* is virtually an island in the center of Strasbourg, bounded on all sides by a large canal. From the station, go straight down rue du Maire-Kuss and cross the bridge to Grand'Rue, which leads directly to the cathedral via rue Gutenberg and rue Hallebardes. If you turn right after crossing the quay from the train station, you will arrive in **La Petite France,** a lovely traditional neighborhood of old Alsatian houses, narrow canals, and restaurants.

Tourist Office: pl. de la Gare (tel. 88 32 51 49), opposite the train station. Another office at pl. de la Cathédrale (next to the cathedral, *natürlich),* with the same phone number. 2F leaflet (in English) has an adequate map with a street index. Also stocks bus routes, festival pamphlets, the monthly booklet *Strasbourg actualités* (which covers various events, including the sessions of the European Parliament), and *Saison d'été à Strasbourg* (which lists summer events). Station office open daily 8am-7pm; Oct. and April-May daily 9am-12:30pm and 1:45-6pm; Nov.-March Mon.-Fri. 9am-12:30pm and 1:45-6pm. Cathédrale office open daily 8am-7pm; Oct. and April-May daily 9am-6pm; Nov.-March Mon.-Sat. 9am-12:30pm and 1:45-6pm.

Consulates: U.S., 15, av. d'Alsace (tel. 88 35 31 04), next to pont John F. Kennedy. Open daily 9:30am-noon and 2-5pm. **Canada,** rue du Ried (tel. 88 96 25 00). Open Mon.-Fri. 11am-noon.

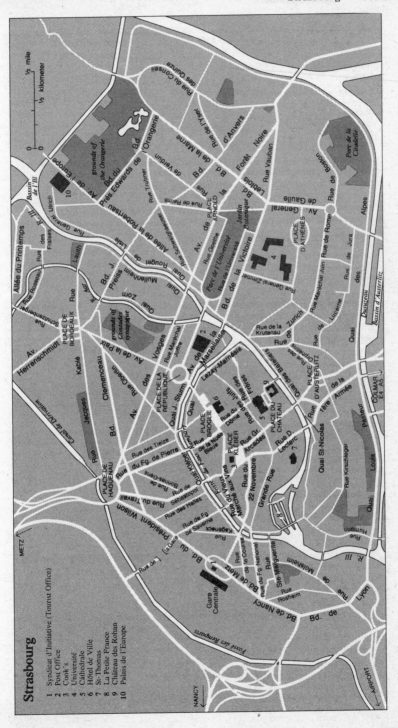

Strasbourg

1 Syndicat d'Initiative (Tourist Office)
2 Post Office
3 Cook's
4 Université
5 Cathédrale
6 Hôtel de Ville
7 St-Thomas
8 La Petite France
9 Château des Rohan
10 Palais de l'Europe

Currency Exchange: Change Cathédrale, 7, pl. du Marché-aux-Cochons-de-Lait (tel. 88 23 26 46), behind the cathedral. Decent rates with no commission on a square riotously named for a market of milk pigs. Open daily 9am-6pm.

American Express: 31, pl. Kléber (tel. 88 75 78 75). Open Mon.-Fri. 8:45am-noon and 1:30-6pm.

Post Office: 5, av. de la Marseillaise (tel. 88 23 44 00). **Currency exchange** and **Poste Restante.** Open Mon.-Fri. 8am-7pm, Sat. 8am-noon. **Branches** at the train station and pl. de la Cathédrale. **Postal code:** 67000.

Flights: Strasbourg-Entzheim (tel. 88 64 67 67), 10km from Strasbourg center, served by Air France and Air Inter. To: Paris (720F, ages 12-25 231-436F); London (2165F, ages 18-25 with one-day advance reservation 800F). **Navette** (tel. 88 64 67 67) runs white shuttle buses from pl. de la Gare and from pl. Kléber in front of the AmEx office (Mon.-Fri. every 1/2hr. 5:30am-8pm, Sat.-Sun. every 1-2hr., 35min., 35F).

Trains: pl. de la Gare (tel. 88 22 50 50). Strasbourg is a major European rail junction. To: Paris (every 2hr., 4 1/2hr., 253F); Luxembourg (4 per day, 2 1/2hr., 140F); Frankfurt (every hr., 2 1/2hr., 201F); Zurich (6 per day, 3hr., 203F); Vienna (2 per day, 11hr., 662F); Rome (3 per day, 15hr., 625F). Information office open Mon.-Fri. 7:30am-8pm, Sat.-Sun. 7:30am-7pm. **Lockers:** 15-30F.

Taxis: pl. de la République (tel. 88 36 13 13). 24 hrs.

Buses: Compagnie des Transports Strasbourgeois, pl. des Halles (tel. 88 32 36 97). Office open daily 6am-7pm. For local buses, purchase tickets (7F) from driver. *Carnet* of 5 (23F50) available from tourist office, banks, vending machines, and *tabacs* within sight of a bus stop. Buses go to a few larger towns along the *route du vin*, such as Obernai (every 2hr., 50min., 21F).

Hitchhiking: Those hitching to Paris take bus #2, 12, or 22 to rte. des Romains. Those going to Colmar take bus #3, 13, or 23 to bd. de Lyon and then follow the signs for Colmar to the highway ramp. **Allostop-Provoya** (tel. (1) 47 70 02 01) in Paris can set you up with a driver for a small fee.

Bike Rental: At the train station. 12-speeds 44F per 1/2-day, 55F per day, 1000F deposit. Check at *bagages consigné.* Open daily 6:30am-9:15pm.

Bookstores: Librairie Internationale Kléber, 1, rue des Francs-Bourgeois (tel. 88 32 03 83) sells expensive new books in English, as well as those tomes of the gods, *Let's Go: France* and *Let's Go: Europe.* Open Mon.-Sat. 9am-noon and 2-7pm. **La Librocase,** 2, quai des Pêcheurs (tel. 88 25 50 31). Eight shelves of cheap, used English paperbacks. Open Mon.-Fri. 2-7pm; Sept.-June 9am-7pm.

Youth Center: CROUS, 1, quai du Maire-Dietrich (tel. 88 36 16 91). Will try to set you up in a dorm for 55F per night (July-Aug. only; student ID required). Meal vouchers 11F50. BIJ/Eurotrain tickets, BritRail passes, French railpasses, and ISICs. Lists hours and locations of student dining halls. Open Mon.-Fri. 9-11:30am and 1:30-4pm.

Centre d'Information Jeunesse d'Alsace, 7, rue des Ecrivains (tel. 88 37 33 33). Mainly for locals but provides information on occasional organized excursions to the surrounding area. Open Mon.-Fri. 1-6pm.

Public Baths and Swimming Pool: 10, bd. de la Victoire (tel. 88 35 51 56). Laneless heated pool open Sept.-June Mon. noon-7:30pm, Tues. 11:45am-2pm and 4-9:30pm, Wed.-Sat. 8:15am-7:30pm. Admission 10F, students 6F. Admission to the sauna or *bain romain* 50F. Massage 90F (8:15am-noon and 2-6:30pm). Call before you go, as times vary for men and women. To catch some rays, try the outdoor **Piscine du Wacken,** rue Pierre du Coubertin (tel. 88 31 49 10). 12F. Open June-Aug. daily 10am-7pm.

Laundromat: 2, rue Deserte, near the train station. Wash 16F, dry 2F per 7min., 10F per 20min. Soap 2F. Open daily 8am-8pm.

Pharmacy: Pharmacie Internationale de la Gare, 8, pl. de la Gare (tel. 88 32 02 59). Open Mon.-Fri. 8:30am-12:30pm and 1:30-7:15pm, Sat. 9:30am-12:30pm and 2:30-7pm. **Late-night:** Late-night pharmacy duty rotates. After 7pm, call the police to find out which two are on duty.

Rape Crisis Line: SOS Femmes, tel. 05 05 95 95. Toll-free. 24 hrs.

Hospital: Hospices Civils de Strasbourg, 1, pl. de l'Hôpital (tel. 88 16 17 18). **Hôpital Hautepierre,** tel. 88 28 90 00. **Ambulance: SAMU,** tel. 88 33 33 33.

Police: 11, rue de la Nuée-Bleue (tel. 88 32 99 08). **Emergency:** tel. 17.

Accommodations and Camping

Strasbourg is *très populaire:* everyone stays the night here. Bargain hotels certainly exist, but the centrally located places fill quickly in summer. Student dormitories open their doors to travelers from June through September (singles 55F), but availability may be limited. Call CROUS (tel. 88 36 16 91) at least a week in advance. None of the three hostels, all brimming with groups and all immaculate and modern, accepts phone reservations in summer, but you can make written reservations. CIARUS claims by far the best location. Call hotels a minimum of two days in advance, or else arrive early in the day and expect to make many calls.

CIARUS (Centre International d'Accueil de Strasbourg), 7, rue Finkmatt (tel. 88 32 12 12). From the train station, take rue de Maire-Kuss to the canal, turn left, and after 500m along the canal, take a left onto rue Finkmatt (15min.). A sparkling new hostel affiliated with the YMCA. Excellent facilities and central location, but a harried, impersonal atmosphere. No lockout. Curfew 1am. 6- to 8-bunk dorms 75F per person. 12-bunk dorms 70F. Triples and quads 90F. Singles 170F. Breakfast included. Lunch or dinner 45F.

Auberge de Jeunesse René Cassin (HI), 9, rue de l'Auberge de Jeunesse (tel. 88 30 26 46), 2km from station. Take bus #3, 13, or 23 from rue du Vieux-Marché-aux-Vins (7F, every 20min.). To get to the bus stop from the train station, go up rue du Maire-Kuss, cross the canal, and take the 2nd left. To walk (it's a ways), take a right from the train station onto bd. de Metz and follow it as it becomes bd. Nancy and then bd. de Lyon. Turn right onto rue de Molsheim and go under the underpass. Follow rte. de Schirmeck 1km to rue de l'Auberge de Jeunesse (on the right). Try to stay in the modern half with views of the canal. Friendly and fun young staff. Game room. Bar open until 1am. Reception open 7am-12:30pm and 2pm-midnight. Curfew 1am. No lockout. Members only. 6-berth dorms 62F. Doubles, triples, and quads 88F. Singles 136F. Breakfast, sheets, and shower included. Hearty lunch or dinner 43F per person. Camping 36F per person, including breakfast.

Auberge de Jeunesse, Centre International de Rencontres du Parc du Rhin (tel. 88 60 10 20), on rue des Cavaliers on the Rhine across from Germany, but 7km away from the Strasbourg train station. Take bus #1, 11, or 21 from the train station to Parc-du-Rhin. Then turn right onto rue des Cavaliers and walk 5min. Sparkling new rooms all with toilet and shower. Peaceful riverside location in a park. Open daily 7am-1am. No lockout. Curfew 1am. Singles 171F. Doubles 106F. Triples and quads 91F. Breakfast, sheets, and showers included. Lunch and dinner 49F.

Hôtel de la Cruche d'Or, 6, rue des Tonneliers (tel. 88 32 11 23), off pl. Gutenberg. Scrubbed-down, capacious rooms 3 blocks from the cathedral. Friendly owners post *menus* from 85F in the elegant restaurant downstairs. Singles and doubles 110F, with shower 150-170F. Extra bed 40F. Breakfast 25F.

Hôtel de l'Ill, 8, rue des Bateliers (tel. 88 36 20 01), near Eglise Ste-Madeleine, but 30min. from station. Modern and luxurious. Recently renovated. Quiet location near the river. Singles from 125F, with shower 180F. Doubles from 170F, with shower 210F. Breakfast 25F.

Hôtel Patricia, 1a, rue du Puits (tel. 88 32 14 60), in the *vieille ville* between rue de l'Ail and rue de Serruriers, behind Eglise St-Thomas. Tranquility and comfort in clean, simple quarters. Singles 105-125F. Doubles 125-220F. Showers 15F. Breakfast 20F.

Hôtel du Jura, 5, rue du Marché (tel. 88 32 12 72), on a pedestrian street near the station inside the old city off rue du Vieux-Marché-aux-Vins. Clean and comfortable. Lockout 11am-2pm. Curfew midnight. Singles and doubles 120-180F, with shower 180-200F. Showers 10F. Breakfast 20F.

Hôtel Weber, 22, bd. de Nancy (tel. 88 32 36 47), near the train station. Turn right out of the station and follow bd. de Metz as it becomes bd. de Nancy (5min.). Large nondescript rooms, but boy, the sparkly new bathrooms will twinkle while you tinkle. Delightful owner. Near the station. Singles 95-105F, with shower 160F. Doubles 105-130F, with shower 140F. Showers 12F. Breakfast 21F.

Camping: La Montagne Verte (tel. 88 30 25 46), on rue du Schnokeloch near the René Cassin youth hostel. Take bus #3, 13, or 23 to "Nid de Cigogne." Perks include showers, tennis courts and a bar. 22F per adult and tent, 15F for under 10. Open March-Oct. 7am-10pm.

Food

Although restaurants around the cathedral and La Petite France are predictably expensive, you'll also find many small *winstubs*—informal restaurants that were traditionally affiliated with individual wineries—in these areas; they usually bear an

Alsatian timber exterior and red-and-white checkered tableclothed interiors. *Strasbourgeois* restaurants are best known for their delicious *choucroute garnie,* sauerkraut spiced with regional secrets and served with meats. Bread and pastry shops display shelves stocked with *Kougelhopf,* a light cylindrical raisin bread, and *tartes* made with *foutin* (egg pastry) and locally-grown cherries. Ask the tourist office about Strasbourg's numerous markets, held every day but Sunday. The largest fills pl. de Bordeaux with fruit and vegetables (Tues. and Sat. 9am-1pm). **Suma Supermarket,** rue des Grandes Arcades, off pl. Kléber, grabs highest honors for its eminently fresh produce. (Open Mon.-Sat. 8:30am-8pm.)

Maison Kammerzell, pl. de la Cathédrale (tel. 88 32 42 14). Probably the most famous restaurant in Strasbourg for its unique 15th-century architecture and its extraordinary cuisine (150-260F *menus*), centered around Alsatian seafood and *choucroute.* Try to put aside visions of impending financial ruin and a lifetime of dining on bread and Nutella, while you enjoy these pricey works of art in a sumptuous dining room. Open daily 8pm-1am. Reservations required.

Pizzaria Aldo, 8, rue du Faisan (tel. 88 36 00 49). Packed by students during the school year. Design your own pizza (40F), salad (39F), or pasta (29-48F) with a huge selection of toppings. Lively and energetic. Make reservations for weekend evenings. Open daily noon-2pm and 6:30pm-1:30am. Delivers.

Au Pont St-Martin, 13-15, rue des Moulins. You can't miss this enormous triple-decker restaurant by the river in the La Petite France area. Huge servings of seafood, salads, and *choucroute.* Ask to sit downstairs overlooking the canal locks. 3-course 52F lunch *menu* served Mon.-Fri. *A la carte* 46-90F. Open daily noon-3pm and 7-11pm.

La Plouzinette, 9, pl. St-Etienne, east of the cathedral. Small, pleasant *traiteur* with dozens of *crêpes* for under 30F and picnic tables facing the square. Kirsch and Grand-Marnier *flambées* 25F. Open Tues.-Sat. 11:30am-11pm, Mon. 6-11pm.

Restaurant au Petit Tonneliers, 16, rue des Tonneliers, off rue de la Douane. Small, homey, and relaxed. *Quiche Lorraine* (35F), and other French favorites. 4-course dinner *menu* 85F. Open Tues.-Sun. noon-2pm and 7-11pm.

FEC, pl. St-Etienne. The best of the student restaurants. Tickets 24F, from local students 12F. Other student restaurants are **Paul Appel,** 10, rue de Palerme (tel. 88 35 66 00); **Esplanade,** 32, bd. de la Victoire (tel. 88 61 32 57); **Gallia,** 1, pl. de l'Université; and **Le Minotaure,** next door to Gallia. First 4 are open in summer. CROUS knows what's open when.

Sights

Constructed between the 11th and 15th centuries from rose-colored Vosges sandstone, the ornate Gothic **Cathédrale de Strasbourg** thrusts its heaven-tickling tower 142m into the sky, making it the tallest monument in Christendom until the last century. If you climb for a view, you'll be following in the footsteps of Victor Hugo, who had particular affection for "perpendicular travel," as well as the young Goethe, who scaled the tower regularly as an antidote for his acrophobia. The slightly corny yet eerie *son et lumière* within presents a history of the city and cathedral. Inside the south transept of the cathedral, the **Horloge Astronomique** demonstrates the technical wizardry of 16th-century Swiss clockmakers. Each day at 12:30pm, the apostles troop out of the face while a cock crows to greet Saint Peter. Get there at least a half-hour early in July and August to beat the crowds. (Admission 4F; tickets sold at the tourist office or cathedral.) In front of the clock, the cathedral's central **Pilier des Anges** (Angels' Pillar), decorated by an anonymous 13th-century master from Chartres, depicts the Last Judgment with its seraphic jury. The same artist also crafted the statues flanking the south portal, which portray the church and the synagogue as two women. (Tower open daily 8:30am-7pm. Admission 8F. *Son et lumière* late April-Sept. daily at 8:15pm in German; at 9:15pm in French.) Admission 25F, students 14F50. Cathedral open daily 7-11:40am and 12:45-7pm.)

The museums all crowd around the cathedral. The **Musée Alsacien,** 23, quai St-Nicolas, displays a showcase of handicrafts, costumes, furniture, and regional art. The 14th- to 16th-century mansion opposite the cathedral, the **Maison de l'Oeuvre Notre-Dame,** is more interesting for its interior architecture than for its collection of sculpture, stained glass, and other period artifacts. The palatial **Château des Rohan,** a magnificent 18th-century building commissioned by the first Cardinal de Rohan-Soubise, houses a trio of small, noteworthy museums that focus on archeology, fine arts, and objets d'art. The superb **Musée d'Art Moderne,** 5, pl. du Château, also across from the cathedral, has painting and sculpture by Klimt, Chagall, Klee, and Arp (a *strasbourgeois*) as well as some impressionist works. Many of the famous works are (rather prematurely) in storage while the museum prepares for its 1994 relocation to a larger building for which the ground has yet to be broken. (All museums open Wed.-Mon. 10am-noon and 2-6pm; Oct.-March Mon. and Wed.-Sat. 2-6pm, Sun. 10am-noon and 2-6pm. Admission to Château des Rohan and its collections 15F, students 8F. All other museums 10F, students 5F. For information on all museums, call 88 52 50 00.) Excellent temporary exhibits on different themes prepared by Strasbourg museums fill the **Ancienne-Douane,** 1, rue du Vieux-Marché-aux-Poissons (tel. 88 32 48 95; open daily 11am-7pm; admission 30F, students 15F).

La Petite France, the old tanners' district, remains Strasbourg's prettiest neighborhood. Slender Alsatian houses with steep roofs and carved wooden façades overlook narrow canals and locks. Swans gliding beneath the **Pont du Couverts** ignore the pedestrians who ogle them from the cobblestone canal sidewalks. **Place de la République** (next to the 19th-century imperial Palais du Rhin) and the extensive **Parc de l'Orangerie** farther north share the prize for the loveliest flower beds in the town. Residents routinely escape to the park's shaded walks, peaceful fountains, and wide lawns, designed in 1692 by Le Nôtre, planner of Versailles's gardens. A small **zoo** lurks inside the park.

Composed of Vosges sandstone and oxidized aluminum, the modern **Palais de l'Europe,** seat of Council of Europe and the European Parliament, lies at the northwest edge of the Orangerie, on av. de l'Europe. When either organization is in session (at least one week every month), you may register at the desk for a look from the visitor's gallery, where headsets translating the debates into several languages are available. (Bring your passport. Guided visits by advance request only. Call 88 41 20 29 several days in advance.)

Goethe, Napoleon, and Metternich all graduated from the **Université de Strasbourg,** founded in the 17th century. Follow bd. de la Victoire or rue de Zurich out to the new university quarters at the esplanade. The seven faculties are located in the area known as Palais de l'Université, which extends across bd. de la Victoire to the beautiful botanical gardens around rue Goethe and rue de l'Université.

Entertainment

Those without tuxedos and spare cash may find themselves whiling summer evenings away in **place de la Cathédrale,** where musicians, mimes, comedians, caricaturists, and acrobats perform for huge crowds. Wet'n'wild **water-jousting** competitions occur Tuesday and Thursday evenings on the Ill River outside the Palais de Rohan (July-Aug. 8:30pm).

For information on all kinds of free entertainment in summer, pick up *Saison d'été à Strasbourg* or the more complete *Strasbourg actualités* at the tourist office (both free). In the courtyard of the **Château des Rohan,** a series of folk dancing demonstrations takes place in June, July, and August (Sun. 10:30am and various evenings 8:30pm). From June to mid-September, free concerts animate the **Pavilion Joséphine** in the Parc de l'Orangerie three to four times per week. June brings the celebrated **Festival International de Musique;** for information, contact Wolf Musique, 24, rue de la Mésange (tel. 88 32 43 10). Jazz and classical artists vie for invitations; past participants include Jessye Norman, Herbie Hancock, and Dizzie Gillespie. Some concerts are free, but most start at 150F. **Musica,** a contemporary music festival which arrives each September or October, has featured such exotica as music played underwater in the public swimming pool. Call 88 35 32 34 or 88 75 19 88 for schedules. From October through June, the **Orchestre Philharmonique de Strasbourg** (tel. 88 37 67 77) performs at the Palais de la Musique et des Congrès, behind pl. de Bordeaux. Productions of the **Théâtre National de Strasbourg** are staged in the resident theater at 7, pl. de la République (tel. 88 35 63 60; admission to most plays 70-120F, students 50-85F). The

Opéra du Rhin features opera, operetta, and ballet in the hall at 19, pl. Broglie (tel. 88 36 43 41; admission 40-220F). The annual **Festival Européen du Cinéma d'Art et d'Essai,** 32, rue du Vieux-Marché-aux-Vins (tel. 88 32 12 30) unreels each November and December.

Get a taste (literally) of the German influence on Strasbourg, at the **Kronenburg Brewery,** 68, route d'Oberhausbergen, which features a guided tour of the brewery, a look at different stages of brewing, a film, and a free tasting session at the end, at which you may indulge to your heart's (and liver's) delight. Nightlife in Strasbourg picks up from September to May, when the tourists leave and the students arrive. **Café Brant,** 11, rue Goethe, at quai du maire Dietrich, across from the university, packs with students chomping sandwiches (14F) or gulping beers (12F) at its numerous sidestreet tables. (Open daily 9am-8:30pm.) Those wanting to see and be seen should head to the perenially hip **Les Aviateurs,** 12, rue des Soeurs, an upscale bar with a young, vibrant clientele. (Cocktails 25-50F, wine 20F, port 25F, beer 18-28F, Dom Perignon 700F. Open Tues.-Sun. 9pm-2am. Dress nicely.) For a wide variety of music in a smoky, bohemian atmosphere, try **Café des Anges,** 5, rue Ste-Catherine (tel. 88 37 12 67 or 88 35 29 54). The bar hosts concerts nightly featuring jazz, blues, rock, or reggae bands; call ahead for times and cover charges, which vary nightly. **L'Appollo,** 1, rue du Miroir (tel. 88 32 63 74), is a popular gay and lesbian disco.

From Strasbourg to Colmar: The Route du Vin

The back roads connecting the many small towns and extensive vineyards, known collectively as the *route du vin,* offer a rich sampling of Alsace's varied bouquets. Medieval ruins and small villages, whose immense popularity hardly diminishes their charms, scatter throughout the vineyards. During the autumn grape harvests, the towns host bacchanalian fests; residents don traditional Alsatian red capes and black hoods, wine and beer flow, and *choucroute* is doled out *en masse* amid dancing and cavorting.

The vineyards are most easily visited by car. Hitchhiking is slow, and many of the smaller towns are served either infrequently or not at all by buses from Strasbourg and Colmar. **Hertz,** 6, bd. de Metz (tel. 88 32 57 62) in Strasbourg, offers the cheapest rates, a Ford Fiesta for about 400F per day, plus kilometrage. (Open Mon.-Fri. 8am-noon and 2-7pm; Sun. open until 6pm.) **Budget,** 31, bd. de Nancy (tel. 88 75 68 29), and **Avis,** pl. de la Gare (tel. 88 32 30 44), are worth a try, too. Biking is another popular alternative, especially from Colmar, but keep in mind that the gentle but persistent hills may challenge novices. Look for vine wreaths hung outside establishments where *vin nouveau* is available. You'll want plenty of time to stop for *dégustations* in various *caves.* The most prolific source of information on the region and specific routes is the **departmental tourist office** in Strasbourg, 9, rue du Dôme (tel. 88 22 01 02; open Mon.-Fri. 9am-12:30pm and 1:30-6pm, Sat.-Sun. 10am-12:30pm and 1:30-5pm; Oct.-June Mon.-Fri. 8am-noon and 2-6pm.) The city tourist offices of both Strasbourg (tel. 88 32 51 49) and Colmar (tel. 89 41 02 29) provide information and maps as well. Cyclists can pick up detailed trail maps with indicated distances and suggested routes.

Several of the larger towns are accessible by local trains. At the foot of the Vosges, **Molsheim** is the largest and quite popular. The town hall, the **Metzig,** retains its tower, clock, and moondial from the 16th century. Pick up information near the center at the small **Musée Régional,** which displays wine equipment and other local curiosities. (Open Mon.-Fri. 2-6pm. Free.) There is no tourist office; call 88 38 76 95 for information on *cave* tours and wine tastings. Guided tours of the surrounding vineyards leave from the town hall (June-Aug. Mon. and Thurs. at 10am). Hourly trains run from Strasbourg to Molsheim (30min., 18F).

Kintzheim, near Sélestat on the edge of the *route du vin,* possesses a remarkable library of priceless Merovingian documents descended from the 9th-century Carolingian kings. The **tourist office,** pl. de la Fontaine (tel. 88 82 09 90) stocks brochures of local sights. (Open in summer daily 10am-12:30pm and 2:30-6:30pm. In winter, call 88 82 09 88.) The ruined **Château de Kintzheim** (tel. 88 92 84 33) now claims Europe's best-known aviary of predatory birds; eagles, vultures, and falcons fly only a few meters above your head. (Open April-Sept. daily from 2pm; Oct.-Nov. 11 Wed. and

Sat.-Sun. only. Visits at 2:30, 3:30, 4:30, and 5:30pm. Admission 14F.) At **La Montagne des Singes** (tel. 88 92 11 09), in the mountains fringing the town, 300 Moroccan macaques roister freely in 20 hectares of enclosed Vosgian forest. (Open April-Sept. daily 10am-noon and 1:30-6pm. Admission, including a handful of popcorn to feed the simians, 35F.) Ascend to the 755m peak of the mountain, where hundreds of tourists photograph the view from the **Château du Haut Koenigsbourg.** Constructed in the 12th century and burned by the Swedish in 1618 during the Thirty Years War, it was occupied and rebuilt by Emperor William II of Germany in the late 19th century. (Open March 16-Sept. daily 9am-noon and 1-6pm; Oct.-Jan. 5 and Feb. 5-March 15 9am-noon and 1-4pm. Admission 31F, students 17F.) No accommodations exist at the top of the mountain, and those in the valley are expensive. The closest you can get to Kintzheim by train is charming St-Hippolyte; from there you'll have to walk the remaining 4km. (2 trains per day from Strasbourg, 1hr., 44F.)

Riquewihr, 60km south of Strasbourg but not connected to it by bus or train, is widely considered the most beautiful town on the route. The 16th-century walled village lures thousands of tourists in summer, and prices for food and lodging are correspondingly high. Built in 1291, the **Musée du Dolder** in the Tour du Dolder houses a collection of 15th-century firearms (open May-Oct. 5 daily 9am-noon and 1:30-6pm; admission 5F), while the beautiful **Tour des Voleurs** (Thieves' Tower) contains a bloodcurdling torture chamber stocked with a collection of evil-looking devices that could have aroused the Marquis de Sade. (Open Easter-Oct. daily 9:15am-noon and 1:30-6:30pm. Admission 5F.) The **tourist office,** 2, rue de la 1ère Armée (tel. 89 47 80 80; open daily July-Aug. 10am-7pm; June and Sept. 10am-noon and 2-7pm), distributes a list of rooms in private houses. Prices vary; the cheapest run from 90F. Otherwise, try the **Camping International** (tel. 89 47 90 08), 1km from the town center, with a restaurant and grocery store. (15F per person, 18F per tent. Open April-Oct.)

A few km south of Riquewihr at the entrance to the Weiss valley, the ancient, flower-filled village of **Kaysersberg** attracts its share of visitors to its lovely streets. The 13th-century fortress is just a ruin, but some graceful half-timbered 15th-century houses cluster around the fortified bridge. The 13th-century **Eglise Ste-Croix** is home to Jean Bogartz's outstanding *retable,* completed in 1518. Set off a medieval courtyard at 62, rue du Général de Gaulle, the town's **musée** displays some blinding polychrome statues and a prized 14th-century statue of the Virgin. (Open July-Aug. daily 10am-noon and 2-6pm; June and Sept.-Oct. Sat.-Sun. 10am-noon and 2-6pm. Admission 6F, students 4F.) Kaysersberg was the birthplace of Nobel Prize-winning physician Albert Schweitzer; visit the **Centre Culturel Albert Schweitzer,** 126, rue du Général de Gaulle (open May-Oct. daily 9am-noon and 2-6pm; admission 10F, students 5F). Farther along the street near the entrance to the village, the **tourist office** (tel. 89 78 22 78), occupies the ground floor of the town hall. (Open Mon.-Fri. 9am-noon and 2-6pm, Sat.-Sun. 9am-noon and 3-5pm; Nov.-May Mon.-Fri. 9am-noon and 2-6pm.) With its nearby tennis courts and swimming pool, the **municipal campground,** outside of town on rue des Acacias (tel. 89 47 14 47), opens from April through September (26F50 per person and tent). Kaysersberg is accessible by bus from Colmar (3-5 per day, 25min., 12F20).

If you're heading back to Strasbourg, try to pass through **Obernai, Dambach-la-Ville,** and nearby **Scherwiller,** quaint villages hidden among vineyards. Several local *caves* offer *dégustations.*

Colmar

If you prefer small town serenity over big city bustle, Colmar allows you to experience the beauty of Alsace without the ubiquitous students and requisite tourists of Strasbourg. Surrounded by vineyards and the craggy Vosges Mountains, the city derives its name from the *colombes* (doves) Charlemagne kept at his estate along the Lauch river. While the town proper (pop. 65,000) is extensive, most of the museums and churches have lined themselves conveniently along the cobblestone streets of the pedestrian zone and the scenic 15th- and 16th-century alleys of *Petite Venise.* Housed in two of the city's former churches are two superlative works of Renaissance religious art—Grünewald's *Issenheim Altarpiece* and Schongauer's *Virgin in the Rosebush*—which themselves justify a visit to Colmar.

Orientation and Practical Information

Colmar lies 75km south of Strasbourg. The pedestrian zone and its sights lie between the tourist office and the train station. To get to the tourist office from the station, turn left onto rue de la Gare and follow it as it becomes rue de Lattre de Tassigny and rue Roesselmann. Turn right onto rue des Unterlinden, and the tourist office will be on your left.

Tourist Office: 4, rue des Unterlinden (tel. 89 20 68 92), across from the Unterlinden Museum. Fine city map. Hotel reservations with first night's deposit. Guided tours of city in July and Aug (in French only; 3 per week, 1hr., 20F, students 10F). **Currency exchange** (cash only). Open Mon.-Fri. 9am-7pm, Sat. 9am-5pm, Sun. 9:30am-1pm; Sept. and May-June Mon.-Fri. 9am-12:30pm and 1:30-7pm, Sat. 9am-noon and 2-5pm, Sun. 9:30am-12:30pm; Oct.-April Mon.-Sat. 9am-12:30pm and 2-7pm.

Post Office: 36-38, av. de la République, (tel. 89 41 19 19), across from a park. **Currency exchange** and **Poste Restante.** Open Mon.-Fri. 8am-7pm, Sat. 8am-noon. **Postal code:** 68000.

Trains: pl. de la Gare (tel. 89 41 66 80). To: Paris (6 per day, 5hr., 278F); Basel (Bâle), Switzerland (15 per day, 1hr., 58F); Nancy (3 per day, 2hr., 137F); and Lyon (4 per day, 4 1/2hr., 220F). Countless runs to Strasbourg (1/2hr., 51F) and Mulhouse (1/2hr., 37F). Lockers 15-30F. Information office open Mon. 7:30am-8pm, Tues.-Thurs. 7:40am-7:30pm, Fri.-Sat. 8am-10:30pm, Sun. 9:10am-8pm.

Buses: pl. de la Gare (tel. 89 41 40 27) To Kaysersberg (3-5 per day, 25min., 12F20) and other small towns such as Riquewihr, St-Hippolyte, Ribeauville, and Eguisheim on the *route du vin.* The tourist office's *Actualités de Colmar* lists schedules and destinations.

Bike Rental: tel. 89 23 17 17, at the train station. 3-speeds 49F per 1/2-day (5am-1pm or 1-9pm), 50F per day. 10-speeds 55F per 1/2-day, 75F per day. 1000F or credit card deposit. Open daily 5:15am-9:15pm.

Laundromat: 8, rue Turenne, through La Petite Venise off the main canal. Wash 15F, dry 2F per 7 1/2min. Soap 4F. Bring 10F and 5F coins. Open daily 8am-9pm.

Hospital: Hôpital Pasteur, 39, av. de la Liberté (tel. 89 80 40 00).

Ambulance: SAMU, tel. 15.

Police: 6, rue du Chasseur (tel. 89 41 08 00). **Emergency:** tel. 17.

Accommodations and Camping

The possibilities don't dazzle. Try to stay in one of the hostels; hotels in Colmar are expensive and usually full in summer.

Maison des Jeunes (Centre International de Séjour), 17, rue Camille-Schlumberger (tel. 89 41 26 87), 3 blocks from the station in a pleasant residential neighborhood, 10min. from the center of town. Walk straight out of the station and take the third right. The best deal in Colmar. TV room, beer, and soda in the evening. Registration 8am-noon and 2-11pm. Curfew 11pm. 39F. Showers included. Sheets 16F.

Auberge de Jeunesse (HI), 2, rue Pasteur (tel. 89 80 57 39). A 25-min. walk from the station alongside the tracks. Take the underground passage in the station to rue du Tir and follow it as it curves and becomes rue du Florimont. Cross pl. St-Joseph on your right, and take rue de la Bagatelle 1 block. Turn left onto rte. d'Ingersheim, then right onto rue Pasteur. Alternatively, take bus #7 from the station to "Pont-Rouge." Way away, but clean and modern with 14-bunk dorms and a TV room. Lockout 9am-5pm. Curfew midnight. 56F. Breakfast and showers included. Sheets 18F.

La Chaumière, 74, av. de la République (tel. 89 41 08 99), near the station. Most of the clean, simple rooms face a courtyard. Bar downstairs is a local hangout, and the owner is exceptionally friendly. Singles and doubles 150F, with shower 220F. Showers 20F. Breakfast 25F.

Camping: Municipale (tel. 89 41 15 94), about 3km out of town. Take rte. de Neuf Brisach (RN415) out of town and across the Ill River. Alternatively, take bus #1 (direction "Wihr") to plage d'Ill. Immaculate bathrooms and expensive restaurant (90F *menu,* 60F entrees) alongside the river. Fills quickly in summer. 12F per person, 14F per tent and car. Open Feb.-Nov.

Food

Inexpensive restaurants have forsaken Colmar; do yourself a favor and head to **Monoprix,** across from the Musée d'Unterlinden and the tourist office (open Mon.-Sat. 8:30am-7:30pm). Several concessions on **rue des Clefs** serve piping hot *tartes flambées* and pizza during the day. Fresh produce goes on sale in **pl. de l'Ancienne Douane** (Thurs. 7am-noon) and in **pl. St-Joseph** (Sat. 7am-1pm).

Villa Romana, 8, rue de l'Ill (tel. 89 24 25 66), 2km northeast of town on rte. de Neuf Brisach (RN415). Two blocks beyond the canal, near the campground. Take bus #1 (direction "Horbourg") and stop at "Dornig." A real trek from the center, but definitely worth the effort; some of the largest portions since Louis XIV. Where locals go for a special night out. Main courses 50-90F. Salads and spaghetti from 40F. Open Thurs.-Tues. noon-2pm and 7-10pm. Call ahead or prepare to wait.

Le Petit Gourmand, 9, quai des Poissonneries, alongside the canal. Small and cozy. Enjoy the *veau à la crème rocquefort* (veal in roquefort sauce, 68F) or the delicious 4-course *menu* (84F). Main dishes 60-85F. Open Tues.-Sun. noon-2:30pm and 7-10pm.

La Pergola, 24, rue des Marchands, on a terrace. Sets down a 79F dinner *menu* on fruity tablecloths. *Tarte flambée* (40F). Open daily noon-2:30pm and 6:30-10pm.

L'Ami Frit, av. de la République, on the edge of the park, across from Flunch. The "fried friend" rustles up cheap burgers (15-25F) and cheaper sandwiches (8-20F). Eat in the park beyond the parking lot. Open daily 8am-midnight.

Sights and Entertainment

Colmar's restored Alsatian houses epitomize the regional architecture and the local penchant for painting plaster with various pastel shades. For the finest specimens, visit the **Quartier des Tanneurs,** then follow rue des Tanneurs over a small canal to the delightful area called **La Petite Venise.** Carved wooden doors and a rainbow of muted colors accentuate the houses that line the canals, and geraniums hang from the window boxes above cobblestone streets. Polychrome roofs, amber-colored stone, and the peal of noon-day bells of the **Collégiale St-Martin** preside over this charming neighborhood. Hidden among the ancient homes around rue des Marchands, a beautiful 14th-century home with Gothic windows faces the church, and the old **Maison des Douanes** (customs house) at the end of rue des Marchands supports the region's ubiquitous yellow-, green-, and red-tiled roofs. Two blocks to the west on pl. des Dominicains, **Eglise des Dominicains,** illuminated by resplendent 14th-century stained-glass windows, displays Martin Schongauer's intricate *Virgin in the Rosebush* in its choir. Alongside the painting, newspaper clippings recount how the painting was stolen in 1972 and recovered the following year in an antique shop in Lyon. (Altar open for viewing April-Oct. daily 10am-6pm. Admission 10F, students 5F.)

The extraordinary **Musée Unterlinden,** pl. Unterlinden (tel. 89 41 89 23), has assembled a respectable showcase of medieval religious art in a former Dominican convent that surrounds a gracious fountain at the center of its green cloister. Do not miss the magnificent gem of the collection, Mathias Grünewald's *Issenheim Altarpiece.* An ambitious and expansive polyptych (multi-paneled painting), the 16th-century work juxtaposes realistic scenes of Christ's crucifixion with more fantastic Biblical depictions. Additionally, two rooms in the basement display modern art, including several typically haunting works by the French master Rouault. (Open daily 9am-6pm; Nov.-March Wed.-Mon. 9am-noon and 2-5pm. Admission 25F, students 15F.) At 30, rue des Marchands, across from the 16th-century Maison Pfister, the **Musée Bartholdi** (tel. 89 41 90 60) houses Colmar memorabilia from the 11th through the 19th centuries as well as the personal trinkets of Auguste Bartholdi, a native *colmarien* and sculptor of the Statue of Liberty. (Open daily 10am-noon and 2-6pm; Nov.-March Sat.-Sun. 10am-noon and 2-5pm. Admission 15F, students 5F.)

Every Tuesday evening at 9pm from June to September, a folk art exhibition fills pl. de l'Ancienne-Douane. **Eglise St-Pierre** stages evening concerts on Thursdays in July and August. (45F, under 21 25F; the tourist office has a schedule.) The annual **Alsatian Wine Festival,** held in early August, spouts wine, beer, and agricultural equipment for all. In early September, the overwhelmingly popular **Jours Choucroute** (Sauerkraut Days), mean feasting, dancing, Alsatian costumes, and—you guessed it—*choucroute.*

Nancy

According to the history books, Nancy dates from the 11th century, when Gérard d'Alsace, founder of the hereditary duchy of Lorraine, built a fortified castle on a tract of land between two marshes of the Meurthe River. But if eyes don't lie, Nancy dates from the 17th century, when Poland's King Stanislas Lesczynski mounted gilded gates around pl. Stanislas and designed the intricate façades seen throughout the city before he burned to death in his own fireplace. Bustling, modern Nancy (pop. 100,000) merges heavy industry and concrete commercial high rises with serene parks and a fine baroque *vieille ville.* With a resident symphony, ballet and opera companies, and numerous museums, this rather aloof city is the cultural focus of Lorraine. Nancy's 30,000 students fuel the city's passion for jazz, evident in the live bands at many bars and restaurants as well as in the city's festivals.

Orientation and Practical Information

The major transportation hub in Lorraine, Nancy is accessible by direct trains from Paris, Strasbourg, and Germany. Although the town center lies close to the train station, Nancy's sights are scattered across a huge valley. Learn the bus system or wear sturdy shoes. As you leave the station to the left, take a right at the Hôtel Agora on rue Raymond-Poincaré, which turns into rue Stanislas, and opens onto the main square, pl. Stanislas and the tourist office.

Tourist Office: 14, pl. Stanislas (tel. 83 35 22 41), to the right of the triumphal arch. The eager staff will help find you a room free and court you with dozens of brochures and maps. Daily French tours of the city at 3pm and 9pm (July-Sept., 1/2hr., 20F). Open Mon.-Sat. 9am-7pm, Sun. 10am-1pm; Nov.-March Mon.-Sat. 9am-6pm, Sun. 10am-1pm.

Post Office: rue Pierre-Fourier, (tel. 83 36 51 47), behind the Hôtel de Ville, 1 block from pl. Stanislas. **Poste Restante** and **currency exchange.** Open Mon.-Fri. 8am-7pm, Sat. 8am-noon. **Postal code:** 54000.

Trains: pl. Thiers (tel. 83 56 50 50). Frequent connections to Strasbourg (every 1-2hr. 1 1/2hr., 104F), Metz (every 2hr., 40min., 46F), and Paris (every hr., 2 1/2hr., 197F). **Lockers** 15-30F. Information office open Mon.-Sat. 5:30am-7:30pm, Sun. 6:30am-8:30pm.

Buses: Rapides de Lorraine, pl. de la Cathédrale (tel. 83 32 34 20). To: Verdun (2 per day, 2 1/2hr., 82F), Lunéville (1 per day, 1hr., 26F), and Vittel (1 per day, 2hr., 60F). Also **Transcars: Les Courriers Mosellans,** pl. Colonel-Driant (tel. 83 32 23 58). To Metz (2 per day, 1 1/2hr., 45F). Information office open Mon.-Sat. 6am-8pm. Buy local bus tickets here.

Public Transportation: Municipal buses (tel. 83 35 54 54). All lines cross at *point central* on rue St-Jean near the cathedral. The tourist office gives out free schedules and maps. Buy tickets from driver, at the train station, or at the information office on pl. de la Cathédrale. 6F, *carnet* of 10 36F20.

Taxis: 1, rue Crampel (tel. 83 37 65 37). 24 hrs.

Laundromat: Lavomatique, rue Palton at rue Raymond Poincaré. Wash 12F, dry 2F per 10min. Soap 2F.

Hospital: C.H.U. Brabois (tel. 83 55 81 20), on the RN74. **Emergency: SAMU,** tel. 83 32 85 79.

Police: Commissariat Central, 38, bd. Lobau (tel. 83 32 34 20). **Emergency:** tel. 17.

Accommodations and Camping

Seldom a problem, even in summer. The less expensive hotels lie far from the sights but close to the shops and residential sections of the city. To get to the cheaper hotels near the train station, take a left on rue Raymond-Poincaré and cross the bridge across the tracks. Rue Jeanne d'Arc, home to many budget establishments, is two blocks up.

Hôtel Pasteur, 47, rue Pasteur (tel. 83 40 29 85). From rue Jeanne d'Arc, turn right onto rue de Mon-Désert and left onto rue Graffigny to rue Pasteur. Attractive rooms in an upscale neighborhood. Management puts all others to shame. Singles and doubles 95-110F, with shower 120-135F. Showers 10F. Breakfast 20F.

Centre d'Accueil de Remicourt, 19, rue de Vandoeuvre (tel. 83 27 73 67), in Villiers-lès-Nancy, 4km southwest of town in the Château de Remicourt. Buy a bus ticket at the *consigne-bagages* desk in the train station. Take bus #4 from the station to "Basch" and walk left past 3 lights along the uphill bd. des Aiguillettes (25min.). Bus #26 stops uphill from the hostel ("St-Fiacre" stop) but runs only Mon.-Sat. 7am-7:45pm. To your left, across a park, you will see the castle. Spectacularly inconvenient location, but it sure is peaceful. Kitchen facilities. Curfew 10:30pm. Singles, doubles, and quads 45F per person. Showers and sheets included. Breakfast 12F.

Hôtel Le Jean Jaurès, 14, bd. Jean-Jaurès (tel. 83 27 74 14), on a continuation of rue Patton and rue Kennedy. Luxurious flowered rooms, some overlooking the private garden. Fun young owners. Singles 110F, with shower from 175F. Doubles 130F, with shower from 200F. Breakfast 23F.

Hôtel Moderne, 73, rue Jeanne d'Arc (tel. 83 40 14 26). Sprightly, elderly proprietor manages the weary but fairly decent rooms. Frayed carpet. Peeling paint. Singles 44-47F. Doubles 55-67F, with shower 80-100F. Breakfast and shower 13F50 each.

Camping: Camping de Brabrois (tel. 83 27 18 28), on the RN74 towards Dijon. A grassy site with telephones and showers. 12F50 per person, 6F per tent or car. Open April-Oct.

Food

Nancy's restaurants exude vibrancy and variety. The highest concentration of eateries radiates from the Basilique St-Epvre and the Grande-Rue. You can buy produce at the **market** held in front of Eglise St-Sébastien. (Open Mon.-Sat. 9am-noon and 2-5pm.)

L'Elephante Sous la Tonnelle, 47, Grande-Rue. Wicker and linen act as unusual complements to ivory elephant statues. The tropical *tabouli* (26F) is mixed with corn, mint, and cucumber, and the 65F lunch *menu* comes with a surprise *"entrée du moment."* Dinner *menu* 85F. Open Mon. 7-11pm, Tues.-Sat. noon-2pm and 7-11pm.

La Miltonne, 2, rue St-Michel, near St-Epvre. Enjoy a selection of *fondues* (54-65F) beneath wooden beams and stone walls. Open Tues.-Sat. noon-2:30pm and 7-10pm.

Taverne des Dominicains, 47, rue des Dominicains. Authentic *choucroute* (45-60F) and live bands on Sun. in winter. Open daily 8:30am-late.

Le Bosphore, 5, Grande-Rue. Turkish *and* Greek specialties such as *kebab voleur:* lamb, eggplant, mushrooms, and *gruyère* on a skewer (60F). Salads (28-35F). Open Tues.-Sat. noon-2:30pm and 6-10:30pm.

Sights and Entertainment

Designed by 18th-century architect Emmanuel Héré, the regal showpiece of the **Place Stanislas** provides a magnificent setting for the façades, balustrades, gilt-tipped wrought iron railings, and fountains of the 17th-century Hôtel de Ville. The square is most spectacular around 10pm, when the *son et lumière* (free) arrives. The Bastille Day celebration here is fabulous, supposedly rivaled only by the festivities in Paris.

The **Musée des Beaux-Arts,** 3, pl. Stanislas, sequesters an impressive collection of 17th-century paintings and a decent selection of modern works by Matisse, Modigliani, and Dufy. (Open Wed.-Sun. 10:30am-6pm. Admission 15F, students 8F, students free on Wed.) The **Porte Royale,** finest of Nancy's seven triumphal arches, was built in 1742. The lovely **Parc de la Pépinière,** a blend of English and French garden styles, is also the site of frequent summer concerts. Peacocks strut proudly in the free **zoo,** while tourists and *nancéiens* pose in the outdoor café. Irked by a continuous barrage of dry bread crumbs and stale celery stalks, the bears and chimpanzees stage fierce debates over which side of the fence contains the more dignified species. In the far corner of the gardens, a large playing field sees equally competitive *boules* games. Cross the deliciously aromatic **rose garden** to the **Palais Ducal** and the **Musée Lorraine** (tel. 83 32 18 74), which contains an eclectic collection of paintings, sculpture, Roman artifacts, costumes, tapestries from the ducal palace, and Henry II's standard, reputedly the oldest extant French flag. (Open Wed.-Mon. 10am-6pm; Sept. 15-April Wed.-Mon. 10am-noon and 2-7pm. Admission 20F, students 15F.)

A walk through the **Arc de Triomphe** from pl. Stanislas carries you to the 18th-century **Place de la Carrière.** At the end of this courtyard, twisting streets lead to the **Porte de la Craffe;** the impressive guard towers are all that remain of this 14th-century fortification. The **Musée de l'Ecole de Nancy,** 36, rue du Sergent-Blandan (tel. 83 40 14 86), is on the periphery of the city, opposite the train station. Nancy's contribution to *art nouveau,* the museum holds rooms with carved wood paneling, furniture, and glasswork, notably that of Emile Gallé. (Open Wed.-Mon. 10am-noon and 2-6pm; Oct.-March Wed.-Mon. 10am-noon and 2-5pm. Admission 13F, students 9F.) Walk 20 minutes from the town center, or take bus #5 (6F) from *point-central.* The **Musée des Arts et Traditions Populaires** in the Couvent des Cordeliers, 66, Grande-Rue, depicts life in Lorraine before the industrial era. (Open Wed.-Mon. 10am-6pm; Sept. 15-April 10am-noon and 2-5pm. Admission 20F, students 15F.) Other museums include the **Musée des Sciences de la Terre** (geology), **Musée de Zoologie et Aquarium Tropical** (zoology), and the **Musée du Fer,** which traces the history of iron production through three millennia.

In mid-October, the **Festival de Jazz** brings an international convoy of musicians who swing from dusk to dawn in a tent in Parc de la Pepinière. Call the tourist office (tel. 83 35 22 41) for information. In winter, **La Comédie de Lorraine** produces excellent contemporary plays. Every two months, the tourist office publishes the free pamphlet *Spectacles à Nancy,* which prints complete listings of current expositions and free concerts, theater productions, and movies. **Le Téméraire,** 17, Grand-Rue (tel. 83 32 52 62), presents live jazz weekly; call ahead for reservations. (Open noon-2pm and 6pm-2am.) University students shake to trendy top-40 beats at popular **La Scala,** 22, rue St-Dizier (tel. 83 32 83 42) and **Les Caves du Roy,** 9, pl. Stanislas (tel. 83 35 24 14). Both charge a 55F cover and are open from 10pm.

Near Nancy: Vittel

The charming town of **Vittel** (pop. 6000) nestles peacefully in a valley of the **Vosges** mountains, 75km south of Nancy. Internationally known for its bottled mineral water, locals recognize Vittel primarily as a fashionable resort. Although Club Med has monopolized many of the hot springs, the public still enjoys access to the large **Parc des Thermes** with water sports of all varieties. The expansive forest surrounding Vittel invites a pleasant sojourn. The **tourist office,** av. Bouloumié (tel. 29 08 37 37) will equip you with trail maps and a list of the (very few) non-budget accommodations. The **campground** (tel. 29 08 02 71) may be the best option in this popular town. It lies 5km from the train station on rue Claude Bassot. (33F40 per car, tent, and 2 people. Open April-Oct.)

Trains to Vittel run on the Nancy-St-Die line (2-3 per day, 2hr. from Nancy, 60F). **Buses** from Nancy run once per day in the evenings (2hr., 60F), leaving from pl. de la Cathédrale. Call Buses Rapides de Lorraine at 83 32 34 20 in Nancy for information.

Lunéville

Lunéville's fifteen minutes of fame came and went in the early 18th century, when Duke Leopold of Lorraine fled from French-occupied Nancy to this negligible town. Here, he and Duchess Elizabeth-Charlotte relished peeled grapes at an elegant court, the so-called "Versailles of the last dukes of Lorraine and Bar." Leopold laid out wide boulevards and elegant public squares based on formal conceptions of 18th-century urban planning and began building Eglise St-Jacques. In 1766, Lunéville passed into the hands of the dethroned adventurer-king of Poland, Stanislas Leszczynski, builder of the flamboyant pl. Stanislas in Nancy, who completed Eglise St-Jacques in effusive Eastern European baroque style, and transformed his court into an important intellectual center, drawing Voltaire and other glowing literati. But after a glorious half-century in the limelight, Lunéville receded into tranquil obscurity. Upon Stanislas's accidental death in his own fireplace, Lunéville (and the rest of Lorraine) shifted into French hands, where, despite a few stints as a German *burg*, it remains today. The town's marvelous château and gardens, set among verdant gardens and lakes and recalling the splendor of a bygone era, make an enjoyable a daytrip from Nancy or Metz.

Orientation and Practical Information

Lunéville is 30km east of Nancy and 70km southeast of Metz. To reach the center of town from the station, walk straight ahead and bear left. Everything of interest is within a small radius of the old town.

Tourist Office, pl. de la 2*ème* D.C. (tel. 83 74 06 55), in the château's left wing (to your right as you face the building). Maps and a walking guide, *Un jour à Lunéville* (French only). *Lunéville programme* outlines the month's events. Gregarious staff. Open daily 9am-noon and 2-6pm.

Post Office, rue de Sarrebourg (tel. 83 73 19 32). Open Mon.-Fri. 8am-7pm, Sat. 8am-noon. **Postal Code:** 54300.

Trains: 2, pl. Pierre Sémard (tel. 83 56 50 50 or 83 73 60 70). To: Paris (4 per day, 4hr., 203F), Strasbourg (5 per day, 1/2hr., 77F), and Nancy (every 2hr., 30min., 30F). Information office open Mon.-Sat. 8am-7pm.

Buses: pl. Monseigneur Ruch in Nancy (tel. 83 32 34 20). Call for schedules of buses to Nancy and surrounding villages. To: Nancy (1 per day, 1hr., 26F).

Laundromat: 8, rue de la Charité, between pl. Léopold and Eglise St-Jacques. Wash 14-20F, dry 2F per 5min. Soap 2F. Open daily 8am-9pm.

Hospital: Centre Hospitalier St-Jacques, 1, rue Level (tel. 83 73 17 49).

Ambulance: Ambulances Pierre, 52, rue d'Alsace (tel. 83 73 48 66).

Police: Château Stanislas (tel. 83 73 02 40). **Emergency:** tel. 17.

Accommodations, Camping, and Food

Several inexpensive hotels flank rue d'Alsace, off rue Carnot. Reservations are recommended for this popular destination. The solicitous owners of **Hôtel Saint-Nicolas,** 1, rue Chanzy (tel. 83 73 20 12), across from the château in a beautiful setting along the canal, offer small rooms. (Singles 90F. Doubles 100F, with shower 115F. Showers 15F. Breakfast 22F.) The restaurant downstairs serves *menus* from 55F (open daily noon-2pm and 7-9pm). Close to the station, the spacious but dark rooms of **Le Cheval Gris,** 65, rue d'Alsace (tel. 83 73 21 91), are maintained by a welcoming staff. (Reception open Tues.-Sun. Singles and doubles 90F, with shower 115F. Showers 15F. Breakfast 22F.) **The Camping Municipal de Lunéville,** 69, quai des Petits Bosquets (tel. 83 73 37 58), along the foot of the château's extensive park, includes hot showers and clean bathrooms (4F75 per person, 8F40 per tent or car; open April-Oct.).

Pack a picnic lunch and head for the château gardens on a sunny day. **Bravo Supermarket** at 41, rue Basset, off pl. Léopold, will fill your basket (open Mon.-Thurs. 8:30am-12:30pm and 2-7pm, Fri.-Sat. 8:30am-7pm). Most of Lunéville's restaurants cluster near the château; rue de Lorraine is lined with *salons de thé, brasseries,* and a few ethnic restaurants. **Le Lunéville,** 43, rue de la République, suggests appetizing 55F and 65F *menus* featuring typical Lorraine specialties, such as the *truite comme en Lorraine,* served with mussels, shrimp, and cream sauce, served in a cozy low-ceilinged dining room. (Open Tues.-Sun. noon-3pm and 7pm-late.) **Les Bosquets,** 2, rue des Bosquets, evokes rural manorial living with its huge fireplace in the upstairs dining room. Main courses fit to satisfy a king. (Open Mon.-Tues. and Thurs.-Sat. noon-2pm and 7-9:15pm, Wed. noon-2pm.)

Sights

Designed by French architect Boffrand, the **Château de Lunéville's** pristine flower gardens, huge artificial lakes, shaded walkways, Greek and Roman statues, and fountains emulate the style and grandeur of Versailles. Dignified black and white swans floating effortlessly on the canal alongside the gardens seem to recall the erstwhile elegance of this stately mansion. July, August, and September bring a *son et lumière* to the south gate. (Fri.-Sat. 9:30pm, Sept. 8:30pm; off-season by appointment only. In foul weather and off-season held in the chapel.) The château houses the **Musée Municipal,** where you'll find an Egyptian mummy with shreds of skin and hair still clinging to it, marooned among unexceptional military exhibits. The museum also contains an interesting collection of Lunéville *faïencerie,* enameled ceramics renowned since the 18th century for their floral patterns, bucolic pageants, and *chinoiseries*—18th-century interpretations of Asian designs. (Open Wed.-Mon. 10am-noon and 2-6pm. Admission 10F, students 5F.)

Leopold also began the construction of the pink sandstone **Eglise St-Jacques,** completed under Stanislas according to the baroque-modeled plans of Boffrand and Héré, designer of Nancy's pl. Stanislas. The interior shines with a startling yellow paint and brightly decorated capitals atop the large columns, also influenced by Versailles. The **Maison du Marchand,** 15, rue de Lorraine, near the church, shares the same baroque architecture and beautiful pink-hued sandstone. Also in the *vieille ville,* in the courtyard at 45, rue de la République, a twisting 17th-century stairway rises among stone medallions. Across from the tourist office, the small, private **Musée du Cycle et de la Moto** (tel. 83 74 07 20) chronicles the development of the bicycle and the motorcycle with actual models. (Open Tues.-Sun. 8am-noon and 2-6pm. Admission 18F.)

Only 15km away in **Baccarat,** the **Musée de la Crystalline** traces the history of the famous glasswork. Gawk at the Shah of Persia's candelabra and a glass set specially commissioned in 1896 by Nicholas II, Tsar of Russia. (Open daily 2-6:30pm; July 16-Sept. 15 daily 10am-noon and 2-6:30pm; Sept. 16-June 14 Sat.-Sun. 2-6:30pm. Admission 9F.) Contact the **tourist office,** Résidence Centre, rue Division-LeClerc (tel. 83 75 13 37), for details. **Trains** run from Lunéville to Baccarat every two hours (30min., 22F).

Metz

When the French rolled out of then-German Metz after World War I, city administrators voted to preserve the vast denuded tracts of land in the center of town as green parks. Today, Metz boasts 25 square meters of green land for each of its 123,000 residents, making it one of France's three official "green cities." Thought to be the oldest city in eastern France, Metz guards traces of a settlement dating from 1000 BC. Recognized as French by the Treaty of Westphalia, then German again by the Treaty of Frankfurt, Metz was one of the principal strongholds of Germany's western front in World War II. Today, low taxes and a laudable social security system make Metz a great place to live, while its golden cobblestone streets and seductive canals make it a great place to visit. Nonetheless, refreshingly few tourists course through this beautiful and spirited town, whose 3000 years of existence have given rise to intriguing museums, architecture, and monuments, all in a delightful setting of rivers, parks, and a well-preserved *centre ville.*

Orientation and Practical Information

Metz sits in the northeast corner of Lorraine, at the confluence of the Moselle and Seille Rivers. The train station is located in a fashionable neighborhood designed by the Germans. From the station, turn right and follow the contour of the gardens, making a left onto rue Haute-Seille. Take another left onto En Fourinirue and follow it to the cathedral and the tourist office. You can also take a bus from the pl. Charles de Gaulle, directly across from the station; #11 takes you right into the pl. d'Armes.

Tourist Office: pl. d'Armes (tel. 87 75 65 21), across from the cathedral. Staff will book you a room for a deposit of half the first night's price. 2-hr. city tours leave from here Mon.-Sat. at 10am and 3:00pm; call a day ahead to request an English-speaking guide (25F, in French 20F). Maps of cycling and hiking routes in the region. Open Mon.-Sat. 9am-9pm, Sun. 10am-noon and 2-5pm; Oct.-May Mon.-Sat. 10am-6:30pm, Sun. 10am-1pm and 3-5pm. **Annex** at the train station (tel. 87 65 76 69) open Mon.-Fri. 11am-12:30pm and 1:45-8pm. Avoid the rotten rates and 3.5% commission of the cash-only **currency exchange** in both offices.

Post Office: 1, pl. Général de Gaulle (tel. 87 63 13 55), across from the train station. **Poste Restante** and **currency exchange. Postal code:** 57007. Open Mon.-Fri. 8am-7pm and Sat. 8am-noon.

Trains: pl. Général de Gaulle (tel. 85 56 50 50; for reservations 87 63 50 50). To: Nancy (every 2hr., 1hr., 44F); Strasbourg (every 2hr., 1 1/2hr., 104F); Luxembourg (every 2hr., 1 1/2hr., 45F); Basel, Switzerland (3 per day, 3hr., 168F); Lyon (6 per day, 5hr., 222F). Open Mon.-Sat. 8am-7:30pm, Sun. 9:30am-noon and 2-6:30pm.

Buses: Pl. Coislin (tel. 87 75 73 73). Mostly local routes. To Verdun (4 per day, 1 3/4hr., 58F) and Nancy (2 per day, 1 1/2hr., 47F50). Municipal buses and minibuses are frequent and thorough. Route information at the tourist office. Local buses leave from pl. de la République. 4F80 per ticket, *carnet* of 6 18F20.

Hitchhiking: Hitching, though not recommended, is common here. The only legal place from which to hitch a ride in *any* direction lies just west of the train station under the ramp of av. Joffre, before the entrances to the main highways.

Laundromat: 7, rue de la Fontaine. Wash 15F, dry 5F per 12min. Open daily 7am-7pm. Bring lots of 5F and 10F coins.

Women's Center: A.I.E.M., tel. 87 76 07 55.

Late-Night Pharmacy: 24, rue du Commandant-Biosseur, tel. 87 37 91 91.

Hospital: Hôpital Notre Dame-de-Bon-Secours, 1, pl. Phillipe de Vignuelles (tel. 87 34 51 00).

Ambulance: Croix Bleue, tel. 87 75 69 00. **Emergency:** tel. 15.

Police: 6, rue Belle Isle (tel. 87 37 91 11). **Emergency:** tel. 17.

Accommodations, Camping, and Food

The range of options is limited, but there are two excellent hostels and a few reasonable establishments in the center of town.

Auberge de Jeunesse (HI), 1, allée de Metz Plage (tel. 87 30 44 02), on the far side of town from the train station. Take bus #3 or 11 (last bus 8:50pm) from the station to "Pontiffroy." On the Moselle River. Clean, simple hostel with jolly management and terrific perks. Free bike storage. Storage for valuables. Game room and TV room. Give them your laundry at night, and for 30F they'll return it clean and folded the next morning. Lockout 10am-5pm. No curfew. 56F. Breakfast included. Singles 85F. Doubles 150F. Sheets 15F. Dinner 25-41F. Reservations accepted.

Foyer Carrefour (HI), 6, rue Marchant (tel. 87 75 07 26). Turn right from the tourist office, then again on rue St-Georges, and finally a left on rue Marchant. A fine 2nd choice, but not as fun as the *auberge*. Members only. Impersonal dormitories 50F. Singles and doubles 62F50 per person. Cold showers and breakfast included. Lunch or dinner 30F. Kitchen facilities. Sheets 16F50. Reservations accepted.

Métropole, 5, pl. Général de Gaulle (tel. 87 66 26 22), across from the train station. Luxurious hotel and agreeable management with straightforward, modern rooms. Small singles 100-120F, with shower 150F. Doubles with shower 250F. Breakfast 22F.

Hôtel de France, 25, pl. de Chambre (tel. 87 75 00 02), behind the cathedral. Energetic and friendly young owner lets worn rooms in a great location. Singles and doubles100F, with shower 140-160F. Showers 15F. Breakfast 20F.

Foyer de la Jeune Fille, 16, rue Mozart (tel. 87 66 67 01). Somewhat sterile, but certainly clean and liveable. Only women 18-25 accepted. Dooubles 80F per person, including shower.

Camping: Metz-Plage (tel. 87 32 05 58). Enter behind the hospital on rue Belle Isle. Beautiful tree-shaded spot next to the Moselle River and the youth hostel. Telephones, showers, and a nearby indoor swimming pool. 16F per person with tent, 11F per extra person, 6F per car. Open June-Aug. only.

Several unabashedly touristy restaurants line av. Robert Schumann off pl. de la République. For cheaper, though probably not French, cuisine, look around pl. St-Louis. **Albion,** 8, rue de Père-Potot (tel. 87 36 55 56), off rue de la Fontaine, serves delicious and elegant traditional 70F *menus.* Reserve for weekend evenings. (Open daily noon-2:30pm and 7-11pm.) Bright turquoise stucco walls, dioramas of Mexican village life, and Aztec masks adorn **Le Toucan,** 46, pl. St-Louis. Try the *mariachi* salad with shrimp and guacamole (45F) and the side order of grilled corn (18F; open Tues.-Sat. 10am-2pm and 6-11pm). And yes folks, to your delight and mine, **Cafétéria Flunch,** 17, rue des Clercs, is back and more supremely mediocre than ever. Decent food for decenter prices (main dishes from 25F; open daily 11am-10:30pm). **Markets** glorify pl. St-Jacques Tuesday and Thursday mornings and pl. du Marché and pl. de la Cathédrale on Saturday mornings.

Sights and Entertainment

The unique warm mustard color of Metz's principal buildings is, at first glance, striking. This *pierre de jaumont* (yellowish stone) is now quite rare and conserved specially for the restoration of Metz's churches and public buildings. Ironically, the delightful uniformity of more recent constructions with 14- to 16th-century homes is typically the result of clever paint jobs. Take in the lovely urban sprawl by walking or biking the verdant gardens and canals around the *centre ville.* The cathedral and museum huddle near **place d'Armes,** an 18th-century square designed by Blondel, where a cloister and four churches once stood.

Only the naves of St-Pierre in Beauvais and Notre-Dame in Amiens soar higher than that of the **Cathédrale St-Etienne,** erected between the 13th and 16th centuries. The 6500 square meters of sensational stained-glass windows have earned it the moniker "Lantern to God." On the west side of the nave, opposite Chapelle du Sacré-Coeur, Hermann de Münster's 14th-century rose window sucks in enough light to bleach a priest's cassock. The gallery of stained glass continues with Chagall's colorful specimens on the left as you face the northern transept and farther along where the ambulatory envelops the choir. (Open daily 7:15am-6:45pm; Oct.-June 7:30am-noon and 2-6pm.)

Outside pl. d'Armes and to the right of the Hôtel de Ville, the fascinating **Musée d'Art et d'Histoire,** 2, rue du Haut-Poirier (tel. 87 75 10 18) preserves a wealth of Gallo-Roman sculpture from Metz's days as a Roman frontier town. Downstairs, the ruins of the Roman public baths were excavated during the 1935 construction of a new wing for the museum. The exhibit exposes the meticulous methods the Romans used to assess the quality of their water. Upstairs, the interiors of entire medieval and Renaissance homes, artfully mounted in order to re-create their original appearances, are arranged by themes, such as "daily life" and "religious architecture." The plain rooms of the art museum house works by Corot, Zurbarán, and others. (Open Wed.-Mon. 10am-noon and 2-6pm; Oct.-May Wed.-Mon. 10am-noon and 2-5pm. Admission 15F, students 7F50.) Rue des Clercs leads from pl. d'Armes to pl. de la République and the **esplanade,** a French garden with a balustrade overlooking the Moselle Valley. The oldest church in France and currently under renovation, **Basilique St-Pierre-aux-Nonnais** is to the left along the esplanade. Built on 4th- and 7th-century foundations, it underwent alterations until the 15th century. In July and August, a *son et lumière* lights up the interior of the basilica. (Fri.-Sun. evenings. Admission 10F.)

The octagonal **Chapelle des Templiers** stands behind the esplanade and next to the similarly styled Ecole des Beaux-Arts. The 13th-century chapel, resembling a witch's hat but modeled after Charlemagne's original Aix-la-Chapelle in Germany, is one of the only remaining structures of the powerful and mysterious Knights of the Temple, an order of Catholic warrior monks whose roots originate in their shrewd Wall Street-esque banking role during the crusades of the 11-13th centuries. Rumors and legends abound about whether the Templars still exist. (Chapel open Tues.-Sun. 2-6:30pm.)

Below the esplanade, the largest of Metz's parks borders on the Moselle River; pleasant shaded walks run alongside small lakes and canals. Built by the Chevaliers Teutonique, a German-based order of militaristic monks and rivals of the Templars, the

Porte des Allemands has commanded its defensive position on the other side of town, beside the Seille River, since the 13th century.

Many street musicians and vivacious crowds support Metz's claim to be a city of "living art." The city's entire population takes its afternoon coffee in the cafés on pl. St-Jacques. For evening outings, consult the tourist office's monthly *Calendrier des manifestations* (calendar of events, free). Its slicker magazine, *Spectacles à Metz* (free), lists sports and cultural events. For three weeks in late June and early July, the **Festival Etonnante Musique** (tel. 87 36 16 70 for information) delivers just what the title promises: contemporary and jazz musical productions with such novel production techniques such as mimed animation. The **Fête de la Mirabelle** on the last weekend in August and the first weekend in September features a hot-air balloon exhibition, fireworks, bands, and a parade led by the cherry-plum queen as the aromas of the local specialty, crusty mirabelle plum tarts, waft through the streets. November brings a contemporary music festival, **Rencontres Internationales de Musique Contemporaine**, with many free choral and classical concerts.

Bar-le-Duc

Refreshing in its openness, small size, and noticeable deficit of tourists, Bar-le-Duc cushions its population of 33,000 in the valley and two hills that comprise its domain. Capital of the ancient duchy of Bar, Bar-le-Duc's name derives from the barriers built by the Celts to repel invading Huns in the 5th century. After a 13th-century era of economic prosperity and flourishing court life, the town was ravaged by plague and the Thirty Years War. Just a century later, Bar-le-Duc and the surrounding region were obliged to give away the better part of 50,000 jars of the area's famous *confiture de groseilles épépinnées* (seedless currant jam) in exchange for protection on the eve of the French Revolution. The jam, locally produced since the beginning of the 15th century, is widely exported, and the traditional method of hand-plucking the seeds out of currants with a goose feather endures today.

During World War I, Bar was an important transport and relief base to the Verdun battlefields but escaped the heavy bombardments suffered by other cities. The steep cobblestone streets, the esplanade of the citadel, and the Renaissance façades on rue du Bourg all recall the former prominence of the town, which today wallows in tranquil obscurity.

Orientation and Practical Information

The hilltop *haute ville* comprises the older part of the city, including the Eglise St-Etienne and what remains of the castle. The train station and commercial center are below in the *basse ville*. Walk straight out of the station onto rue de la Gare for three blocks and you'll reach bd. de la Rochelle, the *basse ville's* main thoroughfare. To reach the *haute ville,* continue on rue de la Gare until it becomes rue Lapique, which becomes av. du Château as it wriggles through the old city. To reach the neighborhood behind the train station, where the pool, Hôtel Bertrand, and the Parc Varin Bernier are, make a left from the station onto rue de Sébastopol, and make the next left onto rue St-Mihiel. To cross the tracks, take the stairs or the underpass one block farther on.

Tourist Office: 5, rue Jeanne d'Arc (tel. 29 79 11 13), in the old hospital. Turn right onto rue Allende from the train station, and follow it as it becomes rue Jeanne d'Arc. Open Mon.-Fri. 9am-noon and 2-6pm, Sat. 9am-noon; Oct.-April. Mon.-Fri. 9am-noon and 2-6pm. Guided tours (Sat., 20F) of the city leave from the **branch office,** pl. St-Pierre in the *haute ville.* Open July-Aug. Sat.-Sun. 3:15-7pm.

Post Office: 32, bd. de la Rochelle (tel. 29 79 70 11). **Currency exchange. Poste Restante.** Open Mon.-Fri. 8am-7pm, Sat. 8am-noon. **Postal code:** 55000.

Trains: pl. de la République (tel. 29 45 50 50). To Paris (13 per day, 2hr., 160F); Strasbourg (3 per day, 3hr., 160F); and Nancy (7 per day, 1hr., 69F). Information office open Mon.-Sat. 8am-12:15pm and 2-6:40pm, Sun. 9:30am-12:15pm and 2-6:40pm.

Buses: Rue du Four (tel. 29 79 60 00), across from pl. Exelmans. To Verdun (4 per day, 1-1 1/2hr., 46F); St-Dizier (5 per day, 1hr., 32F50), and other wee towns. Information office open Mon.-Sat. 7am-8pm.

Laundromat: 10, rue du Bourg. Wash 10F, dry 1F. Soap 3F. Accepts 10F and 1F coins. Open 7am-8pm.

Hospital, 1 bd. d'Argonne, tel. 29 79 48 26. **Emergency:** tel. 15.

Police: 19, rue Louis Joblot (tel. 29 79 02 80). **Emergency:** tel. 17.

Accommodations, Camping, and Food

Intimate Bar-le-Duc accommodates its guests in a few very reasonable hotels. Reservations are advisable, since workers from neighboring towns often fill many cheaper rooms during the winter. Conveniently located in the center of town, the **Grand Hôtel de Metz et du Commerce** (tel. 29 79 02 56) peddles clean and large, if somewhat worn, rooms, all with TV. (Singles and doubles 100F, with shower or bath 180F. Breakfast 25F.) On the other side of the station, the warm proprietor of the **Hôtel Bertrand,** 19, rue de l'Etoile (tel. 29 79 02 97) offers down comforters and spotless bathrooms. (Singles and doubles 85F, with shower 125-165F. Breakfast 19F.) The restaurant downstairs posts 65F *menus.* A small lake and an 18th-century château just behind the train station in the Parc Varin Bernier constitute the **camping municipal** (tel. 29 79 17 33), where showers are the only real comforts. (5F per person, 2F per tent or car. Gates close 10pm. Open April-Sept.)

Occupying an old guard tower in the *haute ville,* the **Grill de la Tour,** 15, rue du Baile, has a crackling fire, low wooden beams, and 52F and 75F *menus* of grilled trout or *andouillette* (open Mon.-Sat. noon-1:15pm and 7-8:15pm). The **Restaurant la Chaumière,** 44, rue St-Jean, resembles an alpine ski lodge with its dark wood and cuckoo clock. The four-course *menu* runs 55F; try the delicious fruit pastries for dessert. (Open Mon. noon-1:15pm, Tues.-Sun. noon-1:15pm and 7:30-9pm.) For cheaper fare, head for the enormous **Monoprix,** bd. de la Rochelle (open Mon.-Sat. 8:30am-7:30pm). On Tuesdays and Thursdays, a **market** re-defines the area left of rue André Theuriet, up from pl. Exelmans (9am-noon). The **student cafeteria,** at the Accueil des Jeunes, 2, pl. Exelmans, fills locals with abundant if somewhat greasy food. Meal tickets cost 25F for students under 25, 33F for students over 25. (Ticket office open Mon.-Fri. 11:30am-12:30pm. Cafeteria open Mon.-Fri. 11:30am-1pm and 7-7:45pm, Sat. 11:30am-12:45pm.)

Sights

Alsatian timbered houses stand alongside sophisticated 16th- and 17th-century stone residences in the charming, uncrowded *haute ville.* From the commercial center, take rue de l'Horloge left off av. du Château and plow uphill. The **Eglise St-Etienne,** Gothic in structure but Renaissance in proportion, commands the skyline. The church was built over several centuries, beginning in the 14th, and features lower arches and a wider deambulatory. In 1793, the church suffered tremendous damage at the hands of violently anticlerical Revolutionary forces, who pulverized windows, statues, and tombstones. It continued decaying until the 19th century, when sweeping renovations began. Today, its white limestone interior sequesters the astounding **Tombe de René de Chalon** in the transept. *Le Squelette,* which alone would merit a visit to Bar-le-Duc, is Ligier Richier's rendition of de Chalon three years after his death, commissioned by de Chalon's loving, if somewhat macabre, widow. The triumphant stance of the emaciated corpse symbolizes the Christian hope of resurrection. (Church and tomb open daily 9am-noon and 2-7pm.) Outside, well-preserved 14th- to 17th-century stone buildings fringe the **place St-Pierre.** The 16th-century *hôtel* of the Florainville family, which bears French and *barrois* coats of arms, stands out among these.

Between pl. St-Pierre and rue des Ducs lies **La Halle,** a tiny Roman marketplace. In the other direction lies the entrance to what remains of the **château.** A map near where rue François de Guise forks off to the right shows the château's original plan. The only remaining structures are the **esplanade** (with an excellent view of the city), **Porte Ro-**

maine (a relic of the original Roman settlement dating from the first century AD), and the 16th-century **Neufchâtel,** which now houses the **Musée de Bar-le-Duc's** exhibits on local archeology, popular traditions, military history, and fine arts. (Open Mon. and Wed.-Fri. 2-6pm, Sat.-Sun. 3-6pm; Oct.-May Wed. 2-6pm and Sat.-Sun. 3-6pm. Admission 5F, students and Wed. free.) Avenue du Château roughly traces the outline of the ancient fort. Once lined with shops, the rebuilt 14th-century **Pont Notre Dame** in the *basse ville* leads to the 13th-century **Eglise de Notre Dame,** with its 18th-century façade. Notre Dame eclipsed St-Pierre when the nobility shifted the town's center from the *haute ville* to the *basse ville,* a fortunate displacement which allowed the preservation of the *haute ville.* Bar-le-Duc's most peaceful green preserve, the **Clinique du Parc** on rue Lapique, hides a tiny zoo, lovely streams, and shady gazebos. **Parc Varin Bernier,** off rue St-Mihiel behind the train station, lures picnickers with its fragrant flower beds, shaded benches, and an 18th-century château (closed to the public).

Verdun

Verdun and its war memorials, such as the 15,000 marble crosses in the National Cemetery, and the Trench of Bayonets, where most of the French 137th Regiment perished, testify to the horror of the battles fought in the area during the First World War. Despite the long shadow cast by wartime devastation, Verdun (pop. 25,000) has been painstakingly rebuilt into an attractive, pleasant city popular with the French and foreigners alike. Much of Verdun is modern and commercial, built to blend with the remnants of the original town. The restored twin peaks of the cathedral suggest a less tumultuous past, and the frequent fishing boats and rowers cruising up and down the Meuse River add a somber note of tranquility to the pedestrian district. But the grain fields carpeting the valleys surrounding Verdun were once blood-soaked battlefields, and Verdun will not soon forget the million casualities sustained during the battles fought here during World War I.

Orientation and Practical Information

Be sure to coordinate your travel schedule in advance, or plan to stay the night. Trains run infrequently from Nancy and Châlons-sur-Marne, and buses from Metz and Bar-le-Duc run only a few times per day to Verdun. The bus and train stations stare at each other from opposite ends of av. Garibaldi. The *centre ville* is to the west, snugly tied up in a loop of the Meuse. To get to the tourist office from the train station, follow av. Garibaldi straight ahead. Take a right through the Porte St-Paul (the Rodin sculpture) and then a left onto rue Chausée. The office will be directly across the bridge.

Tourist Office: on pl. de la Nation opposite Porte Chaussée (tel. 29 86 14 18 or 29 84 18 85). Maps of Verdun and the battlefields nearby. Four-hr. bus tour to the principal sights (April-Sept. only; 135F, includes museum entrance fees). Open June-Sept. Mon.-Sat. 8:30am-7pm, Sun. 10am-noon and 1:30-4:30pm; Oct.-Dec. and March-May Mon.-Sat. 9am-noon and 2-5:30pm, Sun. 10am-1pm; Jan.-Feb. Mon.-Sat. 9am-noon and 2-5:30pm.

Post Office: av. de la Victoire. (tel. 29 86 09 11). **Poste Restante** and **currency exchange.** Open Mon.-Fri. 8am-7pm, Sat. 8am-noon. **Postal Code:** 55100.

Trains: pl. Maurice Genevoix (tel. 29 86 25 65). To: Paris (change at Châlons-sur-Marne; 4 per day, 3hr., 165F); Châlons-sur-Marne (4 per day, 1 1/2hr., 73F); Nancy (change at Conflans-Jarny; 2 per day, 2hr., 77F); Metz (2 per day, 1 1/2hr., 57F). Information office open daily 6am-7pm.

Buses: Pl. Vauban (tel. 29 86 02 71). To Metz (4 per day, 1 3/4hr., 60F) and Bar-le-Duc (4 per day, 1-1 1/2hr., 46F).

Bike Rental: Flavenot, 12, rue de la Marne (tel. 29 86 12 43), off rue Louis Maury. Mountain bikes 85F per day, 1000F or ID deposit. Open Tues.-Sat. 8:30am-noon and 2-7pm.

Hospital: Centre Hospitalier St-Nicholas, 2, rue Anthourd (tel. 29 83 84 65). **Emergency:** tel. 15.

Police: 2, rue Chaussée (tel. 29 86 00 17). **Emergency:** tel. 17.

Accommodations, Camping, and Food

Verdun is extremely *populaire* during the summer. Your best bet is to reserve ahead, or to ask the tourist office to help you find bargain accommodations. There are a number of budget establishments, but no hostel.

Hôtel de la Porte Chaussée, overlooking the river to the right of Porte Chaussée (tel. 29 86 00 78). Spacious, clean rooms in a superb location. Singles and doubles from 115F, with shower 160F. Showers 12F. Breakfast 20F.

Hôtel de France, 21, rue Général de Gaulle (tel. 29 86 09 85), near the train station, but far from everything else. Hardwood floors and immaculate rooms kept by a proud owner. Singles and doubles from 90F, with shower 130-180F. Showers 10F. Breakfast 19F.

Camping: Les Breuils, allée des Breuils (tel. 29 86 15 31), 1km from town. Winsome but crowded riverside site with grocery store, bar, swimming pool, and spotless hot showers and bathrooms. 15F per person, 12F per tent or car. Open April-Nov.

Stock up on groceries in front of the train station at the huge **Match,** av. de Gaulle (Open Mon.-Sat. 9am-12:15pm and 3-7:15pm.) Or, if you're in town on Wednesday or Friday morning, the open air **market** on vexatiously named rue du Rû provides fresh fruits and vegetables (8am-noon). Cafés and fast food joints line quai de Londres by the River. **Des Deux Gares,** 23, av. Garibaldi, is a *brasserie* serving a delicious *menu* for 52F (open daily 11:30am-2:30pm and 6:30-10pm). **Le Liberty's,** 40, rue Poincaré, specializes in Algerian cuisine. Try the take-out *couscous* (40-55F) or the 52F and 72F *menus* among colorful hanging gourds and stuffed iguanas. (Open daily noon-3pm and 6:30-11pm.)

Sights

Fifteen thousand marble crosses. A trench of bayonets. War memorials. And Verdun's chosen symbol, a dove floating above two hands clasped in peace. If the future of peace rests in memories of past turbulence and savage wholesale destruction, then Verdun certainly stands as a powerful symbol for future tranquility. Up to 420,000 French and Germans lost their lives here during the Battle of Verdun, which raged from February 21, 1916, until October of that year. Because of the length of the battle and the French system of troop rotations, seven-tenths of the French Army had a taste of what military historian Alistair Horne calls "the worst battle in history." The battle left a permanent scar on the French psyche, and the town and its surroundings bear ample evidence of this devastating bloodbath.

Rodin's bronze *Victory* in front of the **Porte Châtel** drawbridge on pl. St-Paul, symbolizes the agony and the triumph of war. The drawbridge itself remains from the 12th century, when ramparts protected Verdun from northern invaders. Built in 1350, **Porte Chaussée,** on the quai des Londres, served as a prison and a guard tower before ultimately providing passage into the city for troops during the Great War. Past the gateway stretches the **Monument à la Victoire,** a flight of 72 granite steps surmounted by a resolute warrior figure and cannons aimed at the German front. Its crypt encloses gravestones with war decorations. (Open daily 9am-noon and 2-6pm. Free.)

The massive cement and stone **Citadelle Souterraine** (tel. 29 86 62 02), constructed on the site of the ancient Abbaye de St-Vanne, sheltered 10,000 soldiers on their way to the front during the war. The 7km of underground galleries were equipped with everything necessary to support an army, including nine huge ovens that could cook almost 29,000 rations of bread in 24 hours. (Open daily 9am-12:30pm and 2-6:30pm; Sept.-June 9:30-noon and 2-5:30pm. Admission 17F, students 13F.) Battlefields envelop the city in a 25km circumference, a swath encompassing entire villages annihilated during the battles waged here. The gold and green fields of grain and meandering canals seem ironically serene 75 years after the War. The two best-preserved forts are **Fort Vaux** and **Fort Douaumont.** On February 25, 1916, Douaumont fell to the Germans almost without a shot, after a breakdown in communications reduced its garrison to 57 men. It was not retaken until October, at a cost of thousands of lives. Vaux was lost in June, after several days of hellish fighting in which the Germans held the superstructure while the French defended the underground caverns. (Both open 9am-6:30pm; Oct. to mid-

March 10am-noon and 1:30-5pm. Admission 13F.) Along the road to Douaumont, the stark concrete **Mémorial-Musée de Fleury** (tel. 29 84 35 34), displays models, uniforms, artillery, and reconstructed battlefields. (Open daily 9am-6pm; mid-Sept. to mid-March 9am-noon and 2-6pm. Admission 18F.) Near the fort, the rocket-shaped **Ossuaire de Douaumont** contains the bones of 100,000 soldiers. (Open daily 9am-6:30pm; Oct.-April 9am-noon and 2-5pm. Admission 16F.) The **Tranchée des Baïonnettes** nearby marks the spot where an entire company of infantry perished in a trench, only to be discovered three years later when someone noticed bayonet ends poking through the earth. (Always open. Free.) The immense stone statues of World War I military leaders stare down at the entrance to Verdun from the walls of the citadel. The two choirs and transepts of **Cathédrale Notre Dame,** begun in 1048, rest on the highest point in the city. Once the most powerful in Lorraine, the cathedral's organ was warped during the drought of 1976. (Open daily 7am-noon and 2-7pm.) Above the Monument de la Victoire, the **Musée de la Princerie** (tel. 29 86 10 62) holds an intriguing 12th-century ivory comb engraved with scenes of the resurrection and an apparition of Mary Magdalene. Housed in a restored 16th-century mansion, the otherwise unimpressive museum also contains earthenware, arms, armor, and local archeological finds. (Open April-Oct. Wed.-Mon. 9:30am-12:30pm and 2-6pm. Admission 6F, students 2F.)

Champagne

> *Brothers, brothers, come quickly! I am drinking stars!*
>
> —*Dom Perignon*

Grapevines have existed in the Champagne region since the Tertiary Period, but the Romans were the first to undertake a systematic program of wine production. The natural effervescence of champagne enchanted everyone who tasted it; the key to consistent production, however, remained a mystery. Not until the 17th century did a few individuals (among them the blind cellarer of the Benedictine abbey of Hautvillers, Dom Perignon) hit upon the idea of tying down the cork to bottle up the effervescent sparkle. From that moment on, the wine's popularity expanded incredibly; it became known as the "wine of kings and the king of wines." Even Voltaire rhapsodized that "of this fresh wine the sparkling froth is the brilliant image of our French people."

The name "champagne" is selfishly guarded by the region's vintners. If you have tasted the real stuff outside France, you have paid dearly for the privilege. According to French law, the champagne name can only be used for wines vinted from grapes of the region and produced according to the rigorous and time-honored *méthode champenoise,* which involves the blending of three different varieties of grape, two stages of fermentation, and frequent realignment of bottles by *remueurs* (highly trained bottle turners) to facilitate removal of sediment. If they are scrupulously faithful to the procedure, foreign impostors may use the word "champagne" with its place of origin ("California champagne," for example) on their bottles. Sparkling wines made by a different process are called *"mousseux;" "crémant"* refers to a less effervescent variety. You can see the *méthode* in action at the region's numerous wine cellars *(caves)*. The master wine makers carefully scrutinize and control each stage of the long process. From the two stages of fermentation to the tricky *dégorgement* of sediment and the final addition of an old vintage to ensure quality, all the precious bottles are painstakingly monitored to assure the centuries-old standards that revelers across the world have come to expect. John Maynard Keynes once remarked that his major regret in life was not having consumed enough champagne. Make up for lost time and ensure this does not happen to you. As each producer will remind you, it's the region's unique combination of altitude, climate, chalky soil, and cellars carved from limestone that makes champagne production possible. Originally carved by Roman chalk exporters, the fascinating *caves* all smell of penicillin mold, which thrives in the damp, cool air. Some *caves* have operated as wineries since Roman times. Epernay may have the most kilometers of *caves,* but the most impressive of Champagne's 640km of *crayères* (chalk quarries turned *caves)* lie beneath Reims.

Many champagne houses in both Epernay and Reims offer free samples to polish off their tours. You can also enjoy regional gastronomical specialties (essentially, anything cooked *in* champagne) such as *volaille au champagne* (poultry) or *civet d'oie* (goose stew). Buying by the bottle can be expensive, even if you purchase directly from a *cave.* Monoprix supermarkets have the best deals, but do not offer the personal advice you will find in small wine stores.

There is much more to La Champagne than *le champagne.* French civilization is, so to speak, deeply rooted in the chalky soil of the *campagne* (country). In 451 at the mysterious Champs Catalauniques, Romans, Visigoths, and Franks turned back the pillaging forces of Attila the Hun. Newly Christian Clovis received the first royal coronation in Reims in 498, inaugurating the city's symbolic association with the French monarchy. Every king from Henri I to Charles X (except Henri IV and Louis XVIII) was consecrated here. Charles VII helped turn back the tides of the Hundred Years War by receiving the *sacre* at the cathedral in 1429, at the insistence of Jeanne d'Arc. Thousands died here during the Wars of Religion, the Franco-Prussian War, and the slaughter of World Wars I and II.

Champagne is a great place for excursions into the countryside by car, bike, or foot. Drivers would do well to follow any of the *routes de champagne* through the Montagne de Reims, the Marne Valley, or the *Côtes des Blancs*. Tourist offices distribute road maps; ask for the free pamphlet *The Champagne Road*. Wander off to visit the small villages and lakes dotting the region south and west of Epernay. Champagne's two national parks are ideal for hiking. The tourist office in Troyes has information on the Forêt d'Orient, while the office in Reims sells a booklet of trails through the Parc Naturel de la Montagne de Reims (15F). The Forêt de Verzy, a curious forest of twisted, umbrella-shaped dwarf beeches *(tortillards)*, and the vast Forêt de Germaine are also worth visiting. Campgrounds here are often crowded. Frequent trains connect the major towns, but you will have to rely on slow and infrequent buses to reach the smaller villages off the tourist route.

Reims

A city some 2000 years old, Reims (pop. 182,000) is probably best known for coronations and champagne. Since the year 496, when the Frankish king Clovis was baptized here, coronation at Reims has been the *sine qua non* of legitimacy for French monarchs. Joan of Arc's mission was to deliver the indecisive Charles VII to Reims so the French could unite behind a strong monarch and drive "Les Goddams"—as the English were called because of their penchant for the expression—back across the channel. In 1814, the city had the somewhat dubious honor of being the site of Napoleon's last victory, causing General Marmont to declare Reims "the last smile of Fortune." Fortune frowned on another would-be conqueror of Europe on May 8, 1945, when the Germans surrendered in the small schoolroom Eisenhower used as his headquarters.

Orientation and Practical Information

Unlike many French cities its size, Reims was built on ancient land trade routes rather than on a river. Trains from Paris's Gare de l'Est roll a scenic and flat 154km to Reims (1 1/2hr.). Because the city is on a secondary rail line, connections to other cities often involve changing trains. The tourist office and most of the sights are within easy walking distance east of the train station.

Tourist Office: 2, rue de Machault (tel. 26 47 25 69), next to the cathedral, in the ruins of the old charterhouse. About 15min. from the station. Head straight onto pl. Drouet d'Erlon (actually a road). After the church St-Jacques, hang a left onto rue Carnot and then a right after the theater. The tourist office is on the right. Efficient staff distributes well-indexed town map. The more detailed *Plan Blay* shows all bus routes (25F). Distributes lists of *caves* and day hikes around Reims *(Promenades autour de Reims)*. List of hotels and restaurants includes museum hours and local festival dates. Poor rates and a 20F commission at the **currency exchange.** Open Mon.-Sat. 9am-7:30pm, Sun. and holidays 9:30am-6:30pm; Oct.-March Mon.-Sat. 9am-6:30pm, Sun. 9:30am-5:30pm.

Post Office: rue Olivier-Métra (tel. 26 88 44 22), at pl. de Boulingrin, near the Porte Mars. **Currency exchange** and **Poste Restante.** Branch office at 1, rue Cérès (pl. Royale), closer to the tourist office. Both open Mon.-Fri. 8am-7pm, Sat. 8:30am-noon. **Postal Code:** 51100.

Trains: bd. Joffre (tel. 26 88 50 50), across the park from the town center and pl. Drouet d'Erlon. To: Paris (12 per day, 1 1/2hr., 100F); Metz (4 per day, 3 3/4hr., 148F); Strasbourg (4 per day, 6hr., 207F); Luxembourg (2 per day, 3hr., 136F). Luggage storage open daily 5:45am-8:30pm. **Lockers** 15-30F. Information desk open Mon.-Fri. 8:30am-7:30pm, Sat. 9am-6:15pm.

Public Transportation: Transport Urbains de Reims (TUR) buses stop in front of the train station. Information office, 6, rue Chanzy (tel. 26 88 25 38), open Mon.-Sat. 8:30am-12:30pm and 2-6pm. 5F50 per ticket. 30F for *carnet* of 10. Tourist ticket allows rides *ad infinitum* for one day (20F) or three (43F)—on sale in most *tabacs* or from automatic distributor in front of the theater near the tourist office.

Taxis: Taxi de Reims (tel. 26 47 05 05 or 26 02 15 02). 24 hrs.

Bike Rental: Daniel Dubar, 26, av. de Paris-Tinquieux (tel. 26 08 53 12). Mountain bikes 80F per day, 150F per weekend. Open Tues.-Sat. 8:30am-noon and 2-7pm. **Boulanger,** 5, bd. Lundy (tel. 26 47 47 59), rents mountain bikes for weekends only. 35F. Open Tues.-Sat. 8:45am-noon and 2-7pm.

Hitchhiking: Those headed to Paris follow the N31 via Soissons; they take bus B or #2 (direction: "Tinquieux"). Hitchers who choose Luxembourg often try the N380; they take bus B (direction: "Point de Witry"), and get off at the terminus. Hitching is not recommended, but it is not uncommon.

Women's Center: SOS Femmes (tel. 26 40 13 45). Provides moral support and abortion information.

Gay and Lesbian Services: Francine à Reims (tel. 26 88 40 01). **Oméga** (tel. 29 86 23 72). Anonymity guaranteed.

Laundromat: 59, rue de Chanzy. Wash 15F. Dry 5F per 10min. Open daily 7am-9pm.

Pharmacy: Pharmacie d'Erlon, 70, pl. d'Erlon (tel. 26 47 26 08). Open Mon.-Sat. 9:30am-10pm.

Hospital: Maison Blanche, 45, rue Cognacq Jay (tel. 26 40 70 70).

Ambulance: Descarrega, 29, rue Cognacq Jay (tel. 26 06 10 46). **Emergency:** tel. 15.

Police: 3, rue Rockefeller (tel. 26 61 44 00). **Emergency:** tel. 17.

Accommodations and Camping

You must make reservations two or three days ahead of arrival in this popular city, especially at the youth hostel. Inexpensive hotels cluster around rue de Thillois and pl. Drouet d'Erlon. The tourist office has information on Reims's numerous *foyers,* which usually start at about 60F and may accept travelers for one or two nights, although they prefer longer stays.

Auberge de Jeunesse (HI)/Centre International de Séjour, 1, chaussée Bocquaine (tel. 26 40 52 60), across from Parc Leo Lagrange, beside Espace André Malraux. A 15-min. walk from the station. Continue straight from the train station, turn right at the far side of the gardens, follow bd. Général Leclerc, and cross the bridge. Take your first left on chaussée Bocquaine; the hostel is on the left. TV room with satellite reception of British and German channels. Kitchen facilities. Reception open daily 7am-11pm. Members only. Singles 70F. Showers included. Doubles and triples 61F per person. Breakfast 11F. **EF Ecole Internationale de Français** (tel. 26 40 61 09) shares the same building and offers 2-week intensive French courses.

University Housing: CROUS, 34, bd. Henry Vasnier (tel. 26 85 50 16). Take bus D from the train station to "Yser" (2-3km). 40F. May have room for travelers in July and Aug. Call at least three weeks ahead.

Hôtel d'Alsace, 6, rue Général Sarrail (tel. 26 47 44 08), near the station. Proprietor offers brochures and helpful advice. Funky flowered stained glass in halls and large, simple rooms. TV and phones in most rooms. Relaxed bar downstairs. Singles 110-120F. Doubles 130F, with shower from 145F. Showers 12F. Breakfast 20F.

Hôtel Linguet, 14, rue Linguet (tel. 26 47 31 89), on a residential street off bd. Lundy. Clean rooms, some with fireplaces and stained-glass windows. Amiable management. Bonsai trees in the courtyard and fish tanks in the dining room. Singles and doubles 75-100F, with shower 115-125F. Showers 15F. Breakfast 19F. Closed Sun. 10am-8pm.

Au Bon Accueil, 31, rue Thillois (tel. 26 88 55 74), off pl. d'Erlon, only 10min. from the station in the center of town. Modern and large rooms with squishy beds. Singles from 75F. Doubles from 95F, with shower 140F. Showers 10F. Breakfast 20F.

Hôtel Thillois, 17, rue Thillois (tel. 26 40 65 65), down the street from Au Bon Accueil. Somber rooms. Singles from 85F, with shower 110-120F. Doubles from 95F, with shower 105-150F. No hall showers. Breakfast 18F.

Camping: Camping-Airotel de Champagne, av. Hoche, route de Châlons (tel. 26 85 41 22), 9km from downtown. Take bus F from the theater. Three-star site with 3-day max. stay. 20F per adult, 9F per child, 7F per tent, 4F per car. Open Easter-Sept.

Food

Place Drouet-Erlon spills over with fast food joints, cafés, and bars. Along its side-streets, a few small restaurants serve diverse and reasonably priced *menus.* Students often gather at the pizzerias and *brasseries* on rue Gambetta.

Shop around before you buy champagne. There are occasional sales on local brands at shops around the cathedral. Check first at **Monoprix,** one block south of the cathedral. If you missed the free taste that caps off the tour at Mumm, order a *coupe de champagne* in any bar (about 25-30F). The even smaller *coupette de Champagne* (15-20F) is barely worth the money but will at least tease you with a tidbit of the bubbly stuff.

Le Flamm' Steak, 17, rue Libergier, 2 blocks from the cathedral. Delectable regional dishes and *crêpes* cooked before your eyes. Elegant candlelit setting upstairs; cozy wood and stucco interior down below. 60-85F *menus.* Dinner *crêpes* 15-30F, main dishes 30-60F, dessert 10-30F. Try the *truite meunière.* Open daily 11am-3pm and 6-11pm.

Le Colibri and **Le Notre Dame,** 12, rue de Chanzy (tel. 26 88 45 46), facing the cathedral. Touristy restaurant and bar, but at night you can reserve a table with a touristy view of the illuminated cathedral. *Menus* from 60F. *Plat du jour* 36F. Filling take-out quiche and sandwiches 12-16F. Open daily 11am-10:30pm.

Les Brisants, 13, rue de Chativesle (tel. 26 40 60 41), off pl. Drouet d'Erlon. Sit inside the refreshing pastel green room or in the courtyard during summer. *Galettes* 29-58F, main dishes 46-89F, Four-course *menu* 69F. Open Mon.-Fri. noon-2pm and 7-10:30pm, Sat. 7-11pm. Reservations recommended on weekends.

La Forêt Noire, 2, bd. Jules César, off pl. de la République; take a left from the station. Small place with wood ceiling beams and carved furniture. Dinner *menus* from 60F feature traditional *campagnard* dishes. Specialties include kidney *flambée* (30F). Open Tues.-Sun. noon-2:30pm and 7-10pm.

L'Os et l'Arête, 15, rue du Colonel Fabien, near the youth hostel. Filling basic 48F *menu* served on an outdoor terrace or in the comfy indoor dining room. Open Mon.-Sat. noon-2pm and 6:30-10:30pm.

La Station Sandwich, 11, pl. d'Erlon. A sandwich bar with large selection of both hot and cold species (15-30F). Open daily 9:30am-1am.

La Boule d'Or, 39, rue Thiers. Excellent value, homey atmosphere, fresh food. *Menus* 44F and 60F. The traditional favorites, like *pâté champenois* (10F) or *plat du jour* (30F). Open Tues.-Sun. 9am-10pm.

Drink

Four hundred kilometers of *les crayères,* Roman chalk quarries, wind underground through the countryside around Reims. Today, they shelter bottles emblazoned with the great names of Champagne—Pommery, Piper Heidsieck, Mumm, Taittinger. Some of the smaller *caves* were built from chapels; others contain illuminated shrines to St-Jean, the patron saint of *cavistes.* (Dom Perignon, who spent 50 years of his life perfecting the *méthode champenoise,* was himself a monk.) The tourist office stocks a map with a list of the *caves* that are open to the public. Most of them are open Monday through Saturday from 9am to noon and 2 to 5pm, and sometimes on Sunday afternoons. Individuals should call in advance, as many establishments give tours by appointment only. In some cases, it may be possible to join a scheduled tour leaving the same day. Tours last from a half-hour to an hour and are offered in both French and English.

Mumm, 34, rue du Champ de Mars (tel. 26 49 59 70), endears itself as the only house to offer free samples on its tour. (Open daily 9-11am and 2-5pm; Nov.-March Mon.-Fri. 9-11am and 2-5pm.) **Taittinger,** 9, pl. St-Nicaise (tel. 26 85 45 35), in a former crypt, has some of the oldest and eeriest *caves;* its tour is a solid history lesson, beginning with a slide show. (Open Mon.-Fri. 9:30am-1pm and 2-5:30pm, Sat.-Sun. 9am-noon and 2-6pm; Dec.-Feb. weekends only. Admission 15F.) **Piper-Heidsieck,** 51, bd. Henry Vasnier (tel. 26 85 01 94), bumps you around its cellars on a little electric train. (Open daily 9-11:45am and 2-5:15pm; Dec.-Feb. Mon.-Fri. 9-11:45am and 2-

5:15pm.) **Pommery** 5, pl. du Général Gouraud (tel. 26 05 71 61), probably gives the most elegant tours, while **Veuve Clicquot-Ponsardin,** 1, pl. des Droits-de-l'Homme (tel. 26 85 24 08), leads mediocre tours, but screens a fine film about Madame Clicquot, the *grande dame* of champagne history. Both are only open for visits by appointment; call ahead.

Sights and Entertainment

The main sights of Reims stick to the *centre ville* like glue and are easily toured on foot. The **Cathédrale de Notre Dame** presided over a long line of royal coronations, which began when St-Remi converted and baptized Clovis here in 498. The coronation of Charles VII, whom Joan of Arc led to Reims through the English lines in 1429, may be the most famous. The present cathedral, the third to occupy the site, is built with blocks of golden limestone quarried in the Champagne *caves* beginning in 1211; with the current restoration, the figures over the elaborate eastern façade radiate a warm, pink, tinted glow. Inside, elaborately detailed figurines of saints and apostles stand with their backs to the wall and stare down disconcertingly. The west façade contains a spectacular rose window, with deep blue glass made from lapis lazuli. WWI mortar shattered many of the building's other original windows, but all have been replaced. Chagall filled one of the gaps in the apse with a stained glass window depicting the tale of Jesus's infancy as well as scenes from the *Song of Songs.* The tapestries that formerly hung here, now on display next door at the Palais du Tau, portray the same events. (Cathedral open daily 9:30am-7:30pm.) Tours in French depart daily at 10:30am from the tourist office (15F). For tours in English, ask at the tourist office or buy the 30F *guide de visite* in the cathedral.

Next to the cathedral stands the former archbishop's palace, the **Palais du Tau** (tel. 26 47 74 39), so named because the original floor plan resembled a "T." A museum here displays exquisite tapestries, statuary from the cathedral (including a Goliath-sized Goliath), and the extravagant gold and velvet coronation vestments of Charles X. The cathedral's dazzling treasure, housed in two exhibition halls, includes Charlemagne's 9th-century talisman and the 12th-century chalice from which 20 kings received communion. (Open daily 9:30am-6:30pm; mid-March to June and Sept. to mid-Nov. 9:30am-12:30pm and 2-6pm; mid-Nov. to mid-March Mon.-Fri. 10am-noon and 2-5pm, Sat.-Sun. 10am-noon and 2-6pm. Admission 25F, students 14F, children 6F.)

To the east lies the less-visited but equally interesting **Basilique St-Remi,** a Gothic renovation of a Carolingian Romanesque church reputed to contain the tombs of many of France's earliest kings. Behind the altar lies the tomb of St-Remi himself, whose baptism is credited with bringing Catholicism to the French people. The interior of the basilica is 122m long but only 28m wide, giving it the appearance of a huge, dark vault. Adjacent to the church is the **Abbaye St-Remi,** 53, rue St-Simon (tel. 26 85 23 36), the city's archeological museum. (Open Mon.-Fri. 2-6:30pm, Sat.-Sun. 2-7pm. Admission 10F, students free.)

By the cathedral and near rues Colbert and Carnot, the **Place Royale** has been restored to look as it did during the reign of Louis XV. (The original *place* by Pigalle was destroyed during the Revolution.) A Cartellier statue of the smirking monarch stands in the center.

The **Salle de Reddition,** 12, rue Franklin Roosevelt, is the simple schoolroom where the Germans surrendered to the Allies on May 8, 1945. It has recently been modernized and now shows maps, period newspapers, photos, and an excellent film. (Open Wed.-Mon. 10am-noon and 2-6pm. Admission 8F, students free.)

Formerly an abbey, the **Musée des Beaux-Arts,** 8, rue Chanzy (tel. 26 47 28 44), has assembled an eclectic collection of paintings and tapestries, including a noteworthy display of ceramics and enamel, an extensive Corot cache, and two rooms of impressionist canvases. (Open Mon. and Wed.-Fri. 10:30am-noon and 2-6pm, Sat.-Sun. opens at 10am. Admission 10F, students free.)

For a glimpse of Reims's august Roman past, walk around the **Porte Mars,** a Corinthian-style triumphal arch erected by pl. de la République in honor of Augustus two centuries after his death. The enormous three-arched monument preserves several bas-reliefs depicting Jupiter and Leda and Romulus and Remus.

The world capital of alcohol production may seem like an unusual place to establish an automobile museum, but Reims dares. Take a bus from the theater at 6, rue de Chanzy, to the **Musée de l'Automobile Française** (tel. 26 82 83 84), which displays French cars dating from 1891. (Open daily 10am-noon and 2-6pm, Dec.-March Sat.-Sun. 10am-noon and 2-5pm. Admission 30F, students 20F, under 10 free.)

Throughout July and August, Reims hosts the fantastic **Flâneries Musicales d'Eté,** with almost-daily classical concerts, many of which are free. The best concerts take place in front of the cathedral on Friday and Saturday nights before the immense **Nuit des Sacres Royaux** sound and light show. At 60F a pop you may be reduced to a *baguette* budget for the next few days, but this is one show that's worth the fee. It all starts with a high-tech light performance in the Palais du Tau, crescendos with a laser-beam reenactment of various coronations in the cathedral, and climaxes with yet another light show outside, tracing the construction of the cathedral and the ongoing restoration process. (July-Sept. Fri. and Sat. evenings. 60F, children 20F.)

A university town, Reims has more jazz clubs, wine bars, and discos than the average reveler would care to navigate in a month of Saturdays. The trendy set sips *espresso* at **Café Gaulois,** on the corner of rue Condoret and pl. d'Erlon, examining the laminated hairdos of punkers and poodles alike as they saunter past. After hours, the same set goes out dancing. Ever fickle, the disco set seems to presently enjoy **L'Echiquier,** 110, av. Jean-Jaurès (tel. 26 89 12 38; open Fri.-Sun.), and **Club St-Pierre,** 43, bd. Général Leclerc. **Le Palace,** 114, rue du Barbatre, features jazz bands in a luxurious bar decorated with works by local artists. (Cover Sun.-Thurs. 60-70F, Thurs.-Sat. up to 80F; one drink included.) Reims is understandably proud of its **Théâtre de la Comédie,** 1, rue Eugene-Wiet (tel. 26 85 60 00), whose doors open to present a wide repertoire of operas and plays. Ticket prices vary according to event. Call or stop by the office around the corner at 9, rue du Chanzy for more information (open Tues.-Sat. 10am-noon and 2:30-6pm).

Epernay

If Reims is the jewel of champagne country, Epernay is its 24-carat setting, solidly upholding the region's fame and wealth with the countless bottles of bubbly it turns out each year. Some of the world's most distinguished champagne producers call Epernay home; the palatial mansions on avenue de Champagne emblazoned with Moët & Chandon, Perrier-Jouet, Mercier, de Castellane, and other labels further testify to the wealth that springs from the region's chalky soil. Miles of subterranean cellars contain 700 million bottles of "the king of wines." Each year, visitors eagerly guzzle more than 30,000 bottles—roughly one for every local citizen. Situated at the crossroads of three different grape-growing regions (the Montagne de Reims, the Côte des Blancs and the Marne valley), above-ground Epernay sparkles with the opulence of the surrounding mansions. The town hall, public gardens, and museums are grand 19th-century symbols—all bequeathed to the town by former champagne merchants. If it all seems a little too effervescent, it probably is; don't come to Epernay seeking profundity. Rather, tour a *cave,* raise a glass, toast your health, and sip a few stars.

Orientation and Practical Information

Epernay straddles the Marne in the heart of Champagne. By train, the town is a half-hour south of Reims and one hour east of Paris's Gare de l'Est. From the station, cross the square to rue Gambetta and follow it to pl. de la République. The tourist office and the *caves* lie to the left on av. de Champagne (a 10-min. walk).

Tourist Office: 7, av. de Champagne (tel. 26 55 33 00). Information on Epernay's bubbly makers and suggestions for 3 different *routes de Champagne* to towns within 30km. Ask for the pamphlet *Epernay and its Surroundings,* a brief guide to the town's history and architecture. Open Mon.-

Sat. 9:30am-12:30pm and 1:30-7pm, Sun. and holidays 11am-4pm; mid-Oct. to mid-April Mon.-Sat. 9:30am-12:30pm and 1:30-5:30pm.

Post Office: pl. Hughes Plomb, (tel. 26 55 59 31). **Poste Restante.** Open Mon.-Fri. 8am-7pm, Sat. 8am-noon. **Postal Code:** 51200.

Trains: tel. 26 88 50 50. Epernay is on the main rail line between Paris and points east. To: Paris (12 per day, 1 1/4hr., 81F); Reims (frequent service, 1/2hr., 29F); Strasbourg (4 per day, 3 1/2hr., 196F); Metz via Bar-le-Duc (2 per day, 2hr., 131F). Information office open Mon.-Sat. 9am-noon and 2-6pm.

Buses: Rue Rousseau (tel. 26 55 22 22), off pl. Notre-Dame. Service to Châlons-sur-Marne (Mon.-Sat. 3 per day, 1hr., 30F), Bergères (Mon.-Sat. 2 per day, 40min., 24F), and loads of puny villages along the way. Information telephone answered Mon.-Fri. 9:30am-noon and 2-5pm.

Bike Rental: Claude Jeannel, 49, rue Cuissotte (tel. 26 55 22 90), off pl. de la République. 50F per day. Deposit 500F. Open Tues.-Sat. 9am-noon and 2-7pm.

Laundromat: 18, av. Jean Jaurès. Wash 15F, dry 2F per 5min. Open daily 7am-9pm.

Hospital: Hôpital Auban-Moët, 137, rue de l'Hôpital (tel. 26 58 70 70). **Emergency:** tel. 15.

Police: 7, rue Jean Chandon Moët (tel. 26 54 11 17). **Emergency:** tel. 17.

Accommodations, Camping, and Food

Epernay has only a few affordable hotels; reserve a few days in advance or make Epernay a daytrip from Reims or Paris.

Foyer des Jeunes Travailleurs, 8, rue de Reims (tel. 26 51 62 51), a 3-min. walk from the station. Bear left along the square and turn left onto rue de Reims; the *foyer* is one block up on your right. A friendly workers' residence with lots of travelers. Reception open daily 9am-7pm; Sept.-June 8:30am-8:30pm. Ages 18-25 only. Singles and dorms 62F. Breakfast, sheets, lockers, and showers included. Laundry facilities. Cafeteria meals 38F. Reserve ahead, as rooms fill quickly in summer.

Hôtel St-Pierre, 1, rue Jeanne d'Arc (tel. 26 54 40 80), off av. Paul Chandon, about 10min. from the station. Elegant rooms and kind management. TV in all rooms. Singles from 93F. Doubles 105F, with shower 150F. Showers 15F. Breakfast 23F.

Hôtel le Progrès, 6, rue des Berceaux (tel. 26 55 24 75), conveniently located right off the pl. de la République. Comfortable, renovated singles and doubles 140-180F, with shower 180-225F. Breakfast served in a pretty, skylit room (25F). Check in at **Bar le Progrès,** a lively hangout on pl. de la République, around the corner from the hotel.

Camping: Camping Municipale, allée de Cumieères (tel. 26 55 32 14). Three-star site about 4km from the train station. 15F per person. Tent and car 18F. Open April-Sept.

Restaurants in Epernay tend to be expensive and inconveniently located. For something light (sandwich, salad, etc.) try any of the *tabacs* or cafés betweeen the train station and the pl. de la République. The cheapest option is the huge supermarket, **Intermarché,** on rue Henri Dunant at the other end of town from the *foyer.* (Open Mon.-Fri. 9am-12:30pm and 2-7:15pm, Sat. 9am-7:15pm.) Inside the *foyer,* the **MJC Caféteria,** 8, rue de Reims, serves complete meals for 38F. (Open daily 11:30am-1:30pm; Sept.-June 11:30am-1:30pm and 6:45-8pm.) Join the townies enjoying *raie aux pommes* and other local specialties at **L'Ancêtre,** 20, rue de la Fauvette, near pl. Hugues Plomb, in a half-timbered house with a profusion of geraniums partially obscuring the sign. (Salads 29-49F. *Menus* from 58F. Open Thurs.-Tues. noon-2pm and 7-9:30pm.) Across the river from the train station, **La Terrasse,** 7, quai de Marne, is one of Epernay's more pleasant affordable restaurants; try the simple 75F *menu* or spiffier 110F and 155F *menus.* (Open Tues.-Sun. noon-2pm and 7-9:30pm; closed last 2 weeks in July.) Also across the river, **Mme Préjent,** 13, rue J. J. Rousseau, serves a 50F *menu* that includes drinks (open Mon.-Sat. afternoon; check ahead for exact hours).

Sights and Entertainment

Epernay compensates for its lack of pre-19th-century monuments with the tastes and smells which emanate from sweeping **avenue de Champagne,** distinguished by its mansions, gardens, and monumental champagne firms. The best known is **Moët &**

Chandon, 20, av. de Champagne (tel. 26 54 71 11), producers of the grandfather of the breed, Dom Perignon. The highly technical and informative 45-minute tours (often in English) end with a free tasting. Napoleon was a close buddy of Jean-Rémy-Moët and usually picked up a few thousand bottles of champagne on his way to the front. Unfortunately for the Emperor, Epernay was not on the way to Belgium in 1815; tour guides like to joke that the dearth of Moët & Chandon caused his crushing defeat at Waterloo. (Open Mon.-Sat. 9:30-11:30am and 2-4:45pm, Sun. and holidays 9:30am-noon and 2-4pm; mid-Oct. to mid-March Mon.-Fri. 9:30-11:30am and 2-4:45pm. Free.) A ten-minute walk down the avenue, at #73, is **Mercier** (tel. 26 54 75 26 or 26 51 71 11), whose tour includes transport by electric train and a free sample. (Open April-Oct. Mon.-Sat. 9:30-11:30am and 2-5pm, Sun. and holidays 9am-5pm; Nov. and March daily 9:30-11:30am and 2-5pm; Dec.-Feb. Sat. and Sun. only 9:30-11:30am and 2-4pm. Free.) The great Parisian restaurant Maxim's orders its bottles from **De Castellane,** 57, rue de Verdun (tel. 26 55 15 33), across the street from Mercier. The highlight of the visit is the comprehensive museum of champagne production. Tours (in English) culminate in tastings (tour 15F, students 10F).

Between De Castellane and Mercier, the rainbows of thousands of butterflies flutter inside the **Jardin des Papillons** (tel. 26 55 15 33). Species indigenous to both the Andes and Appalachians fly freely around the visitors. (Open May-Oct. 10am-6pm. Admission 20F, students 15F.) At the **Musée du Champagne et de Préhistoire,** 13, av. de Champagne (tel. 26 51 90 31), ascend to the top floor to view a collection of archeological finds from Champagne, as well as various bottles and dishes from the region's history. (Open March-Nov. Mon. and Wed.-Sat. 10am-noon and 2-6pm, Sun. 10am-noon and 2-5pm. Admission 10F, students 8F.)

Despite Epernay's preoccupation with things that go on in dark, moldy caves, conventional nightlife enjoys its own ferment here. **Le Miami,** 160, av. Foch (tel. 26 54 17 72) combines fast food with an eclectic mix of music (open Mon.-Sat. 10pm-4am). **Le Tap-Too,** 5, rue des Près Dimanche (tel. 26 51 56 10), presents a bizarre new experiment in intergenerational disco: one half of the club blares top-40 while the other half spins 70s disco. Groovy. (Open Thurs.-Sun. 9:30pm-4am.)

Châlons-sur-Marne

Lacking the monumental majesty of Reims and the effervescence of Epernay, Châlons (pop. 65,000) appears to be a mere *petit village* stuck in a region of alcoholic preeminence. But enter the churches and see Châlons awake from its apparent lethargy with the most astonishingly beautiful stained glass this side of Chartres. The **tourist office,** 3, quai des Arts (tel. 26 65 17 89), in the center of town across the Marne River from the station, guides excellent introductory tours to the city. Your hard-earned 19F (students 8F) buys two to three hours of churches, parks, museums, *hôtels particuliers,* and many corners otherwise locked or obscure. Each day's tour emphasizes a different church or area of Châlons; call for schedules. There are also night tours (7pm) on Wednesdays and Fridays. (Tours from the tourist office July-Sept. Tues.-Sat. at 2:30pm. Office open Mon.-Sat. 8:30am-12:30pm and 1:30-6:30pm, Sun. 10am-1pm; Sept.-June Tues.-Fri. 8:30am-noon and 1:30-6pm. Mon. and Sat. 2:30-6pm.)

Near the tourist office and the *Hôtel de Ville,* 12th-century **Eglise de Notre-Dame en Vaux** glows with light filtered through 13th- and 16th-century rose windows set in the same pattern as those at Chartres. On Wednesdays and Saturdays, the church's 56 bells sound a mellifluous peal over the nearby market. (Open Mon.-Sat. 9am-noon and 2-6pm.) From the side street to the north, enter the **Musée du Cloître** (tel. 26 64 03 87), where medieval cathedral relics decapitated during the Revolution have been happily reunited with their heads. (Open Wed.-Mon. 10am-noon and 2-6pm. Admission 18F, children 5F.) **Eglise St-Alpin,** off pl. Foch, features striking Renaissance windows in *grisaille,* gray and white glass with delicate yellows. To visit, call the tourist office—it will give you the key if you leave your passport; otherwise, catch mass here at 6pm on Sundays.

Brilliantly evocative windows summon visitors to the 12th- to 16th-century **Cathédrale St-Etienne,** where Saint Stephen's death by stoning is commemorated in glass and stone. Note the pervasive dark green tint—a hallmark of Châlons, just as the blue of Chartres. Renovations require you to enter at the less-than-stunning southern side of the church (open daily 7am-7pm). Nearby, Châlons's deepest shade of green carpets **Le Petit Jard** and the adjacent **Grand Jard,** where pleasant canal-side paths lead past rare trees and a Henri IV-style turret and bridge. Enter the gardens at the corner of bd. Victor Hugo and av. du Leclerc. (Open 6:45am-11pm; Oct.-April 7:30am-6:30pm.) Châlons's municipal library, housed in the 17th-century **Hôtel des Dubois de Crancé,** proudly guards what is supposedly Marie Antoinette's prayer book, in which she wrote at 4:30am on the day of her execution, "My God, have pity on me! My eyes no longer have tears to cry on you, my poor children, Adieu, Adieu! Marie-Antoinette." Call two to three days ahead to see the actual autograph; the attendants at the circulation counter can give you a booklet with photographs which argue (in French) for and against the document's authenticity. (Open Tues.-Sun. 9am-noon and 1:30-6pm.)

The **Musée Municipal,** on pl. Godart by the library, displays a collection of statues representing Hindu deities, a reconstruction of a traditional *champenois* interior, local medieval sculptures, and a small collection of paintings. (Open Mon. and Wed.-Sat. 2-6pm, Sun. 2:30-6:30pm. Free.) The **Musée Garinet,** 13, rue Pasteur, preserves the atmosphere of a wealthy *châlonnais* townhouse of the 19th century, with period furniture and a typical 19th-century clutter of international objets d'art. (Open Wed.-Mon. 2-6pm. Free.)

The dormitory-style **Auberge de Jeunesse (HI),** rue Kellerman (tel. 26 68 13 56), is located on the other side of town from the train station on rue Chevalier as it runs through the park into a gate on your right. Caters mostly to groups—individuals are accepted in July and August only. (Reception open 7-10am and 5:30-10:30pm. Members only. 54F. Breakfast included.) Alternatively, the **Foyer de Jeune Travailleur Châlonnais,** 1, rue faubourg St-Antoine (tel. 26 68 31 79), often has space for travelers ages 18-15 only. Bear left upon exiting the station and walk 15 minutes along the quai or take bus B to "pl. aux Chevaux." Clean, well-located, and overwhelmingly friendly, this *foyer* serves filling three-course *menus* in its downstairs restaurant (33F). (Reception open daily 7am-10:30pm. No lockout. No curfew. Singles 52F. Breakfast 8-10F. Reserve in advance.) Near the hostel, a friendly owner manages the **Hôtel de la Cité,** 12, rue de la Charrière (tel. 26 64 31 20). (Singles 100F. Doubles 150F, with shower 150-180F.) There is an excellent **campground** (tel. 26 68 38 00) just south of town on av. des Alliés, with a restaurant and hot showers. (15F per person. Tent 15F. Car 9F. Open April-Oct.)

Traiteurs (similar to *charcuteries*) sell the cheapest lunches in town. At 32, rue de Jaurès, near the station, **A Marion** has a tempting selection of salads. Cucumber salad and various Greek and Moroccan dishes run 40-50F per kg. Young *châlonnais* relish the delicious if smallish pizzas (36-45F) at **Il Fluvio,** 18, rue Pasteur, a lively place decorated with plastic grapes and wagon wheels. (Open Mon.-Sat. noon-2pm and 7:30-11pm.) A fruit and meat **market** on Wednesday and Saturday mornings (8am-noon) gives new meaning to pl. d'Art. After dark, forget you're in Champagne and sample a few of the 100 whiskeys at **La Cocktaillerie,** 26, pl. de la République (tel. 26 65 10 27); the ice cream *coupes* are nearly as potent. (Open Tues.-Sat. 5pm-2am.)

From the **train station,** pl. de la Gare (tel. 26 88 50 50), across the Marne from the *centre ville,* trains depart for Reims via Epernay (7-8 per day, 35min., 44F), Paris's Gare de l'Est (8 per day, 1 1/2hr., 108F), Strasbourg (2 per day, 3 1/2hr., 184F), and Metz (7-8 per day, 1 1/2hr., 113F; information office open Mon.-Sat. 8am-noon and 2-7pm.) **STDM Buses** (tel. 26 65 17 07) also run from here to Reims (3 per day, 2 hr., 84F) and Troyes (3 per day, 1 1/4hr., 65F.) The **post office,** 36, rue Jaurès, is around the corner from the station; the town's **postal code** is 51000.

Troyes

With its enormous medieval *foires* (fairs), Troyes made Champagne the hub of European commerce in the later Middle Ages. Two factors, however, forced Troyes into early retirement: bubbly production in the north overshadowed the town's importance, and a 1524 fire destroyed it for the third time. After this fire, the town's artists and architects applied their efforts to make a masterpiece of the town itself, and designed the churches, gabled houses, tiny streets, and secret passages you can still explore today. Modern Troyes (pop. 65,000) bears little resemblance to its grape-crazy northern neighbors. It has no *caves,* and while its downtown area has been nicknamed *"bouchon de champagne"* (champagne cork), this stems from its shape, not its industry. Rather, the charming town proffers gripping museums, picturesque Renaissance houses, a dazzling Gothic cathedral, and graceful pedestrian cobblestone streets, although neon sometimes obscures the half-timber.

Orientation and Practical Information

Troyes is about 130km south of Reims. If you're traveling by train, you'll have to go through Paris—and spend about four hours doing it. The station at Troyes is only a block from the tourist office and two blocks from the rectangular old city, where almost all the shops, restaurants, and hotels are located. From the station, cross over bd. Carnot and continue straight onto rue Général de Gaulle. The pedestrian district occupies the side streets on the right, just after Eglise Ste-Madeleine.

Tourist Office: 16, bd. Carnot (tel. 25 73 00 36), across from the train station on the right. Free city guide and accommodations list. From June to Sept. 15, guided walking tours of the city leave daily at 3pm from the front of St-Jean's church (in English by appointment, 2 1/2hr., 15F). Open Mon.-Sat. 9am-8:30pm, Sun. 10am-noon and 3-6pm; Sept. 16-May Mon.-Sat. 9am-12:30pm and 2-6:30pm. **Annex** at 24, quai Dampierre (tel. 25 73 36 88), in an old house opposite the Musée de la Pharmacie. Open June-Sept. 16 Tues.-Sat. 9am-12:30pm and 2-6:30pm. Beware of low **currency exchange** rates at both offices.

Post Office: rue Louis Ulbach (tel. 25 73 49 22). **Currency exchange.** Open Mon.-Fri. 8am-7pm, Sat. 8am-noon. **Postal Code:** 10000.

Trains: tel. 25 73 50 50. Ridiculously few destinations are directly linked to Troyes. Most involve a trip to Paris-Est (6 per day, 1 1/2hr., 102F). The main eastern line serves Chaumont (8 per day, 1hr., 64F) and Mulhouse (5 per day, 3hr., 180F). **Lockers** 12-20F. Information office open Mon.-Sat. 8:30am-noon and 2-6:45pm.

Buses: STDM (tel. 25 82 23 43). Buses depart next to the train station, which can help you with schedules but does not provide prices. Regional schedules are also available at the tourist office for 5F. To: Sens (7 per day, 1 1/2hr., 50F); Châlons-sur-Marne (2 per day, 1 1/4hr., 62F50); and Reims (3 per day, 3hr., 87F).

Taxis: Taxis Troyens (tel. 25 78 30 30), in the circle outside the station. Open Mon.-Thurs. 5am-2am, Fri.-Sun. 24 hrs. **Taxi Mestre,** 168, rue Général de Gaulle (tel. 25 73 07 40).

Laundromat: Salon Lavoir GTI, 15, rue Turenne, in the pedestrian district. Wash 20F, dry 6F per 15min. Soap 2F. 10F and 2F coins only. Open daily 8am-9pm.

Hospital: Centre Hospitalier, rue Auxerre (tel. 25 49 49 49). **Emergency: SAMU:** tel. 15.

Police: tel. 25 73 44 88. **Emergency:** tel. 17.

Accommodations and Camping

Troyes has many inexpensive hotels, but they often fill; make reservations. The several inexpensive *foyers* only accept tourists on a one-day basis and often do not have room. Ask the tourist office for a complete list.

Auberge de Jeunesse (HI), 2, rue Jules Ferry (tel. 25 82 00 65), 7km from Troyes in Rosières. Take bus #6B (direction: "Chartreux") from the tourist office to the last stop (last bus 10pm). From there, take bus #11 to the hostel, or walk 2.2km down a country road. In an old farmhouse complete with fireplace, garden, and gardener. Well worth the trek. Kitchen facilities. Reception open from 6pm. Members only. 58F in new building, 48F in older building. Breakfast 15F.

Hôtel du Théâtre, 35, rue Lebocey (tel. 25 73 18 47), one block from the train station on a street parallel to rue Gén. de Gaulle. Large but plain rooms. Warm and engaging proprietor. Singles 80F, with shower 103F. Doubles 98F, with shower 113F. Breakfast 15F. Open Sept.-July Tues.-Sun. evening. *Menus* starting at 52F downstairs. Restaurant open Tues.-Sat. noon-2pm and 7-9:30pm, Sun. noon-2pm.

Hôtel Butat, 50, rue Turennes (tel. 25 73 77 39), off rue Emile Zola. Spacious rooms with Oriental rugs. Singles from 100F, with shower 140F. Doubles from 120F, with shower 160F. Breakfast 20F. Reservations recommended a week in advance.

Hôtel de Paris, 54, rue Roger Salengro (tel. 25 73 11 70). Stylish 2-star hotel with a garden terrace. Housed in a beautifully restored 12th-century building that once served as the mint for the counts of France. Singles 100-135F, doubles with shower 120-175F. Breakfast 18F. Restaurant downstairs serves a 50F dinner *menu* and a 29F *plat du jour.* Restaurant open Mon.-Fri. 7-11pm.

Hôtel Le Marigny, 3, rue Charbonnet (tel. 25 73 10 67). A rickety, half-timbered hotel close to the center of town. Freshly renovated rooms. Singles from 100F, with shower 150F. Doubles 110F, with shower 185F. Showers 15F. Breakfast 20F.

Camping: Camping Municipal (tel. 25 81 02 64), on RN60, 2km from town. Take bus #1 (direction: "Pont St-Marie.") Two-star site with showers, shops, and restaurant. 8F per person, 12F per tent and car. Open April-Oct. 15.

Food

The Quartier St-Jean is full of *crêperies* and inviting restaurants, especially on rue Paillot de Montabert and rue Champeaux. **Les Halles,** near the *hôtel de ville,* unites modern shops and traditional farmers from the Aube region. (Open Mon.-Thurs. 8am-12:45pm and 3:30-7pm, Fri.-Sat. 7am-7pm, Sun. 9am-12:30pm.) Take your picnic to place de la Libération, a wonderful park with fountains, flowers, and ice cream vendors. Try *andouillette à la mode de Troyes,* a small chitterling sausage served throughout France.

L'Accroche Coeur, 24, rue de la Trinité, off rue Emile Zola. Serves traditional dishes (including *andouillettes)* and a lip-smacking *steak au poivre* (42F). 53F *menus,* entrees 25-65F. Open Mon.-Sat. noon-3pm and 7-11pm.

Crêperie la Tourelle, 9, rue Champeaux, just east of Eglise St-Jean. Pocket-sized *crêperie* right in the middle of things. Tables trail out onto the sidewalk, and plates pass through the windows. *Crêpes* 12-38F. Open Tues.-Sat. noon-midnight.

La Botticelli, 39, rue de la Cité. Pizza and delicious pasta (39-48F) served under a skylit indoor terrace. For dessert, try the ice cream flavored with plum *armagnac* (35F). Open Tues.-Sat. 11:45am-2:30pm and 7-10:30pm.

Le Tricasse, 2, rue Charbonnet. Shake your booty to a *troyen* beat at this popular bar. Beers from 10F. Standard café food, 12-18F. Open Mon.-Sat. 1pm-3am.

Le Grand Café, 4, rue Champeaux, in the pedestrian district. You pay for the central location. Sandwiches 15-25F. 54F *menu.* Try the *flan froid d'aubergines à la tomate fraîche* (cold eggplant soufflé with tomato sauce). Café open daily 7:30am-12:30am. Fancier restaurant upstairs open daily 12:30-2pm and 7-10pm.

Sights and Entertainment

Perhaps the best way to explore Troyes is to wander through the streets around its handicraft museum (see below). In contrast to the commercial Quartier St-Jean, this residential area exemplifies Troyes's commitment to the preservation of its past in the beautifully restored 16th-century *hôtels particuliers* and narrow wood-framed passageways. The balance of the *bouchon de champagne* boasts eight museums and nine churches dating from the 12th to the 17th centuries.

The most impressive of the churches, **Cathédrale St-Pierre et St-Paul** was begun in the 13th century, expanded in the 16th, and like many others, never finished. Inside, 112 stained-glass windows light the nave and choir, among the longest in France. (Open daily 8am-6pm; Sept. 16-June 9am-noon and 2-5pm.) The adjacent **trésorerie** contains the jewels of the counts of Champagne. (Open June-Aug. Tues.-Sun. 2-6pm. Admission 6F.) Built in 1150, **Ste-Madeleine,** the city's oldest church, is distinguished by its delicate stone latticework. **Eglise St-Urbain,** illuminated by 13th-century stained-glass windows, was founded by Pope Urban IV in 1261. The **Eglise St-Jean** witnessed the marriage of Catherine de France to Henry V in 1420. The groom's signature on the Treaty of Troyes in 1420 opened the door to an English invasion—a misfortune only rectified on July 9, 1429, when Jeanne d'Arc liberated the town from the English as she led Charles VII toward his coronation in Reims. (Churches open daily 10am-noon and 3-6pm.) Troyes couples history and theater in **Cathédrale de Lumière,** a sound and light show focusing on the stained-glass windows outside the cathedral (July-Aug., free).

Troyes's museums are expensive unless you buy the 25F **pass** that admits you to all the museums except the Maison de l'Outil and the Musée Marguerite Bourgeoys. In the ancient Episcopal Palace next to the cathedral on pl. St-Pierre, the **Musée d'Art Moderne—Collection Pierre et Denise Levy** (tel. 25 80 57 30) displays modern masterpieces in an old stone mansion. The Levys' cache includes 350 paintings and over 1300 drawings and sketches by the likes of Braque, Cézanne, Degas, Dufy, Matisse, Modigliani, and Picasso. (Open Wed.-Mon. 11am-6pm. Admission 15F. Guided tours Sun. at 11am and 4pm. 25F.) On the other side of the cathedral at 21, rue Chrétien-de-Troyes, the eclectic **Musée St-Loup** (tel. 25 73 49 49), housed in the old Abbaye St-Loup, presents a fascinating if somewhat disorganized collection of Merovingian weaponry, Gallo-Roman statuettes, medieval sculpture, and 15th- through 20th-century paintings. A locked glass door on the second floor allows you to admire from afar the largest library hall in France, once the dormitory of the abbey's monks in the 17th and 18th centuries. The room contains 85,000 volumes, with over 4000 precious manuscripts from the 7th to 18th centuries and 46,000 volumes from the 16th century alone. (Admission 15F, students free.) The French Revolution helped augment the collection with works confiscated from the libraries of other abbeys and monasteries. The **Musée Historique de Troyes** (tel. 25 42 33 33), in the 16th-century Hôtel de Vauluisant on rue de Vauluisant, exhibits religious articles, documents, and pieces of Renaissance *troyen* sculpture. In the same complex is France's only **Musée de la Bonneterie** (tel. 25 42 33 33), a collection of gloves, hats, and hosiery, for which Troyes is, amazingly, famous. The **Pharmacie de l'Hôtel-Dieu** (tel. 25 49 49 49), quai des Comtes de Champagne, houses a rare 16th-century apothecary with 320 painted wood boxes and 2140 *faïence* receptacles; the adjoining **Musée des Hôpitaux** contains old documents and a collection of ancient bust reliquaries. (Museums open Wed.-Mon. 10am-noon and 2-6pm. Admission 15F each.)

The **Maison de l'Outil et de la Pensée Ouvrière,** 7, rue de la Trinité (tel. 25 73 28 26), is a marvelously restored 16th-century *hôtel* turned into a giant regional toolshed. Although the collection is poorly documented, the beautiful 18th-century tools are artfully displayed in polished wood-paneled rooms and glass cases. (Open daily 9am-noon and 2-6pm. Admission 20F, students 10F.) The **Musée Marguerite Bourgeoys,** 8, rue de l'Isle (tel. 25 80 54 96), is worth a visit for those interested in hagiography. (You know who you are.) The displays trace the life and works of Marguerite Bourgeoys, a 17th-century *troyenne* who founded the Congrégation Notre Dame in Montréal and was canonized by Pope John Paul II in 1982. (Open April 15-Sept. Mon.-Sat. 2-5pm. Free.)

Movie theaters jostle shops on rue Emile Zola. The young and the trendy head for the newly-opened **Le Scoop** (tel. 25 74 26 27), just outside the *centre ville* in the Parc des Activitiés Savipol, in St-Servine. You're on your own for transport—buses run only until 8pm. (Open Thurs.-Sat. 10pm-4am. Cover 65F.) Inside the town limits, the popular pub **Le Tricasse** (tel. 25 73 14 80), at the corner of rue Paillot de Montabert and rue Charbonnet, attracts live musicians, a mellow atmosphere, and many young locals. (Open Mon.-Sat. 1pm-3am.)

The North

Even after nearly fifty years of peace, the memory of two world wars is never far from the towns and villages of northern France. The world's battlefronts have moved back and forth across the region four times in this century alone. Nearly every town bears scars from the wanton bombing of World War II, and German-built concrete observation towers still peer over the land. Regiments of tombstones stand as reminders of the massacres at Arras in Flanders, at the Somme in Picardie, and at Cambrai in Artois.

In spite of the numerous memorials to the soldiers who left their lives here and some of the most magnificent Gothic cathedrals in the world, the North remains the final frontier of tourist-free France. Although thousands traveling to and from Britain pass through Calais, Boulogne, and Dunkerque every day, surprisingly few take the time to explore the ancient towns between the ports and Paris.

The best course for a tourist here is to bypass the overpriced major ports and make a pilgrimage to the great cathedrals, especially in Laon, Noyon, and Amiens, all built during the 12th and 13th centuries. Some of the North's unfavorable reputation stems from its role as an early 20th-century industrial center. In recent years, however, the major cities have been cleaned up and offer excellent museums, cultural opportunities, and residents who will actually be delighted to meet a foreigner. In Picardie, undulating fields of wheat extend in all directions, broken by the occasional clump of trees or a wooden windmill. Along the rugged coast, chalk cliffs loom over the beaches, and cultivation gives way to cows and sheep that graze near collapsed bunkers and coils of rusty barbed wire. If you're coming from Paris, this countryside will purge you of urban residue.

Once a possession of Flanders, the region has retained much of its Flemish influence. The architecture of many town halls (such as that of Dunkerque, Calais, and Lille) is entirely Flemish, and Flemish cuisine remains the regional specialty. Mussels, bathed in myriad different sauces, are especially popular, as are *pâté de canard* (duck *pâté*), *galettes* (salty *crêpes*), and *ficelle picarde* (a cheese, ham, and mushroom *crêpe*).

Calais

As the closest French port to England, Calais's touristic appeal is solely a matter of convenience. This year some 15 million voyagers will de-ferry in Calais from as many as 160 daily channel crossings. And the tourist mobs will only get denser after May of 1993, when the long-awaited tunnel connecting Calais with Dover, England, is scheduled to be completed. Completely rebuilt after World War II, the town is little more than a homely commercial crossroads, full of chintzy shops and flashing neon. With the mildly interesting Hôtel de Ville, the famed Rodin sculpture *Burghers of Calais,* and the attractive beach as the town's only redeeming features, move on from here once you have made the necessary ferry or train connection

Orientation and Practical Information

Calais is two and a half hours from Paris's Gare du Nord and has two train stations: **Gare Calais-Ville** and **Gare Calais-Maritime,** the latter near the ferry and hovercraft ports. Free buses connect the hoverport and ferry terminal with Gare Calais-Ville, in the center of town. Taking a hovercraft is the fastest way to cross the channel for foot passengers (35min. by hovercraft, 75min. by ferry) and costs the same as or less than a trip by ferry.

Tourist Office: 12, bd. Clemenceau (tel. 21 96 62 40), 1 block from the Calais-Ville station. Ferry information, a free accommodations list, accommodations service (10F), and a perplexing city map. For 12F, buy a better map. **Currency exchange.** Open Mon.-Sat. 9am-12:30pm and 2:30-6:30pm.

Currency Exchange: Open 24 hrs. at ferry terminal and hoverport, but rates are obscene.

Post Office: 174, rue Mollien (tel. 21 96 55 30), on pl. d'Alsace. **Telephones.** Open Mon.-Fri. 8:30am-6:30pm, Sat. 8:30am-noon. **Postal Code:** 62100.

Trains: Gare Calais-Ville, bd. Jacquard (tel. 21 80 50 50). To: Paris (14 per day, 2 1/2hr., 161F); Lille (15 per day, 1 1/2hr., 69F); Boulogne (14 per day, 30min., 36F); Dunkerque (4 per day, 50min., 39F). Information office open Mon.-Sat. 9:30am-12:30pm, 1:30-7pm (Sat. 1:30-6pm). **Gare Calais Maritime,** Car Ferry Terminal. To Paris only in the afternoon. Open daily 8am-9pm. Helpful information office with free city maps. Lockers 5F. Open daily 9-10:45am and 2-7:40pm.

Ferries: Hoverspeed, Hoverport (tel. 21 96 67 10). To Dover (every 1/2-1hr., 35min., one-way 230F, 120-hr. return 350F). **Sealink,** Car Ferry Terminal (tel. 21 96 70 70). To Dover (every 2hr., 75min., one-way or 60-hr. return 220F, 120-hr. return 335F; 15% student discount). Information office open Mon.-Fri. 9am-5:45pm, Sat. 8:30am-noon. **P&O Ferries,** Car Ferry Terminal (tel. 21 97 21 21). To Dover (every 90min., 75min., one-way 215F, 120-hr. return 320F; 15% student discount). Bicycles cross for free on all 3 lines. Usually enough room, even in peak season.

Hitchhiking: Those going to Paris try bd. Gambetta (which leads to the N1) or bd. Victor Hugo (to the A26). Those heading for Lille take bd. de l'Egalité to the A25.

Laundromat: rue des Thermes at rue des Prêtres. Dry clean 40F per 4kg, wash and dry 12-18F. Takes 10F and 2F coins. Open 7am-10pm.

Medical Assistance: SAMU (tel. 21 96 72 19). 24-hr. emergency service or tel. 15.

Police: pl. de Lorraine (tel. 21 34 37 00). **Emergency:** tel. 17.

Hospital: L'Hôpital du Calais, quai du Commerce (tel. 21 46 33 33).

Accommodations and Food

Should you decide to spend the night here (why?), reserving one or two days in advance in July and August isn't a bad idea. Try the large and modern **Point Accueil Jeunes/Maison Pour Tous (HI),** 81, bd. Jacquard (tel. 21 34 69 53), past the town hall away from the station. (Reception open 5-10pm. Lockout 11am-5pm. Curfew midnight. 30F, nonmembers 40F. Open July-Aug.) The friendly owner at **Hôtel le Littoral,** 71, rue Aristide Briand (tel. 21 34 47 28) lets huge rooms with comfortable beds. (Singles 100F. Doubles 120F, with shower 140F. Showers 10F. Breakfast 20F.) And directly across from Gare de Ville on bd. Jacquard, **Hôtel Liberté** (tel. 21 96 10 10) has clean, modern rooms, with private bathroom and TV (155F for 1, 2, or 3 people). The **Camping Municipale,** 26, av. Raymond Poincaré (tel. 21 97 89 79), off rue Royale packs 'em in like sardines, but has good beach view. (Reception open 8am-noon and 2-5pm. 8F per adult, 10F per site. Showers 4F80.)

Like sleeping, dining in Calais is generally an unremarkable experience. Generic cafés with 55-80F *menus* line **rue Royale** and **bd. Jacquard.** Try **Taverne Kronenbourg,** 46, rue Royale, a large, friendly establishment with a three-course, 75F *menu* (open daily 9am-10pm). At **Aux 3 Suisses,** 14, bd. Jacquard, a sometimes excruciatingly long wait culminates in a delicious, well-presented meal (75F *menu;* open daily 9am-9pm). Both the hoverport and the ferry terminal maintain mediocre, expensive self-service cafeterias (open 8:30am-3pm). The **Supermarket Prisunic,** 17, bd. Jacquard, stocks all the usual picnic supplies (open Mon.-Sat. 8:45am-7pm, Sun. 9:30am-7pm).

Sights

If you have some spare time between arrival and departure in Calais, check out the flamboyant **Hôtel de Ville,** a 20th-century reconstruction in Flemish Renaissance style. In front, Rodin's *Burghers of Calais* recalls a near-tragic moment in the final year of the Hundred Years War. England's King Edward III had agreed to hang the mayor and several prominent citizens rather than slaughter all the city's inhabitants; the burghers decided to sacrifice their lives for the city's townsfolk, and their heroism prompted the impassioned and successful eleventh-hour intervention of Edward's French wife, Philippine. Calais remained British until François de Guise reclaimed it for the French in 1558. Pick up a copy of the tourist office's free booklet, *Calais and Its History,* much more interesting than the town proper. Directly across from the town hall in **Parc St-Pierre,** a camouflaged bunker served as the German navy's principal telephone exchange from 1941 to 1944. The building now houses the **War Museum,** a fine collection of military artillery and uniforms. (Open March-Nov. daily 10am-5pm. Admission 12F, students 8F, children 6F.)

Boulogne

According to legend, in 636 a boat carrying only a statue of the Virgin Mary washed up on the beach of Boulogne, which subsequently became a famous pilgrimage site. Today, Boulogne (pop. 44,000) is Mecca for no one, but stopover for many. Like Calais, Boulogne ushers thousands of passengers through its port every day, but hasn't succumbed to the kitsch level of its northern neighbor. In this, the largest fishing port in France, French remains the first language in shop windows, and cafés still outnumber fast food joints. On July 12-28, the **Fête du Poisson** (Festival of the Fish) brings 20,000 seafood lovers to the Casino to partake in the fruits of the city's most important industry.

Orientation and Practical Information

Like Calais, Boulogne lies two and a half hours northwest of Paris and is served by two train stations: Gare Boulogne-Ville (from which most trains leave) and Gare Maritime. To reach central pl. Frédéric Sauvage from Gare Boulogne-Ville, cross bd. Voltaire and follow bd. Daunou to the canal. The post office, on your right, is at the southern end of the square, the tourist office at the northern. Pont Marquet, the bridge adjacent to the tourist office, leads to the ferry booking offices.

Tourist Office: pl. Frédéric Sauvage (tel. 21 31 68 38). Crowds of ferry travelers make for a harried staff. Free accommodations service, map, and ferry brochures. Open Sun.-Thurs. 10am-7pm, Fri.-Sat. 10am-9pm; Oct.-May Tues.-Sat. 9am-noon and 2-6pm.

Currency Exchange: Wretched rates at the ferry terminals (open daily). Try **Le Persan,** 19, rue de Faidherbe (tel. 21 87 23 50). A *tabac,* bar, and exchange. (Open daily 7am-2am.)

Post Office: pl. Frédéric Sauvage (tel. 21 31 65 40). **Telephones.** Open Mon.-Fri. 8:30am-5:30pm, Sat. 8:30am-noon. **Postal code:** 62200.

Trains: Gare Boulogne-Ville, bd. Voltaire (tel. 21 80 50 50). To: Paris (12 per day, 3hr., 147F); and Lille (13 per day, 1 1/2hr., 90F). **Lockers** 15F. Information office open Mon.-Sat. 9am-12:15pm and 1:45-6:45pm. **Gare Maritime,** Car Ferry Terminal. Service only to Paris, connecting with ferry arrivals.

Ferries: Hoverspeed (tel. 21 30 27 26). To Dover (every 2hr., one-way 215F). **Sealink** (tel. 21 30 25 11). To Folkestone (every 3hr.; one-way 220F, 60-hr. return 220F, 120-hr. return 320F, 15% student reduction). **P&O Ferries** (tel. 21 31 78 00). To Dover (every 3hr., one-way 230F, 120-hr. return 335F, 15% student discount). Booking offices for all three lines are located on Pont Marquet. Bicycles sail for free on each.

Laundromat: Lavomatique, 62, rue de Lille, across the street from the cathedral. Wash 14F, dry 2F per 5min. Takes 2F pieces only. Open 7am-10pm.

Police: rue Perrochel (tel. 21 83 12 34). **Emergency:** tel. 17.

Hôpital Duchenne, allée Jacques Monad, (tel. 21 99 33 33).

Accommodations and Food

During the peak season, Boulogne's hotels fill quickly, so make reservations 2-3 days in advance or show up early in the morning.

Auberge de Jeunesse (HI), 36, rue de la Port Gayole (tel. 21 31 48 22), just outside the *vieille ville* and a 10-min. walk from Gare-Ville. Take a right on bd. Voltaire, walk 1 block, turn right onto bd. Daunoy to rue de Brequerecque, turn left, and go up the hill. Crowded but clean dormitories with 8-10 beds per room. Kitchen facilities. Reception open 8-10am and 5-11pm. Curfew 11pm. 58F, nonmembers 76F. Breakfast included. Sheets 14F. Camping amid overgrown shrubs

20F. In July and Aug., make reservations a week in advance. **Bike rental** 35F per day; 300F deposit.

Hôtel Hamiot, 1, rue Faidherbe (tel. 21 31 44 20), facing the beach. Large, plain rooms. Cheerful owner runs the fine restaurant downstairs (main courses 40-90F). Singles 110F. Doubles 120-130F. Breakfast 20F.

Hôtel le Mirador, 2, rue de la Lampe (tel. 21 31 38 08), off bd. Daunou. Efficient, personable management. Large, airy rooms. TV and private bathroom in each room. Singles 93F. Doubles 110F. Breakfast 20F.

Camping: Moulin Wibert, bd. Ste-Beuve (tel. 21 31 40 29), 2km west of the tourist office (quai Gambetta turns into bd. Ste-Beuve). 18F30 per adult, 10F per child, 8F per car. Hot showers and pool included. Open April-Oct. 15.

Restaurants in Boulogne range from self-service cafeterias to *haute cuisine,* and almost all specialize in seafood. In the *vieille ville,* several attractive restaurants and *crêperies* line rue de Lille. **Au Bascaille-la,** on rue de Lille across from the Hôtel de Ville, serves 60F, 90F, and 130F *menus* on a sunny terrace; try the *crabe farcis* (stuffed crab). **La Petite Bouffe,** 90, quai Gambetta, is a *super chouette* little place specializing in seafood and pizza. (45-60F; open Tues.-Sat. noon-2:30pm and 7-11pm). **Le Nabucco,** 78, bd. Gambetta, overlooking the port, serves excellent fish and grilled meat dishes. *Menus* run 59F and 99F; the *plat du jour* is 50F. (Open Mon.-Tues. and Thurs.-Sat. noon-2:30pm and 7-10pm, Sun. noon-2:30pm.) On Wednesdays and Saturdays from 7:30am to 1:30pm, pl. Dalton boils over with an excellent **open-air market.**

Sights

Boulogne's *vieille ville* inhabits the same hill that the Romans settled to watch over their domains some two millennia ago. The original 13th-century wall, one of only three complete ramparts in France, surrounds the maze of charming tortuous streets. Scale the wall for a fine view of Boulogne's harbor. The 19th-century **Basilique de Notre Dame** sits atop the labyrinthine **crypts** of a 12th-century edifice. One of the 14 chambers contains the vestiges of a 3rd-century Roman temple; another exhibits jeweled religious artifacts. (Crypt and treasury open Tues.-Sun. 2-5pm. Admission 12F, children 6F.) Next to the cathedral, the 13th-century **beffroi** (belfry), sends acrophobes into a swoon with its dizzying view of the port. (Open Mon.-Sat. 8am-noon and 2:30-6pm, Sun. 8am-noon. Free.) The recently opened aquarium, **Nausica,** bd. Sainte-Beuve, pipes atmospheric underwater music to its aquatic denizens. (Open daily 10am-8pm; off-season 10am-6pm. Admission 45F, under 12 35F.)

Dunkerque

From its tiled sidewalks in the town center to its beautiful beach at the other end, Dunkerque (pop. 75,000) seems wholly oblivious to visitors. Few restaurants display multilingual menus, and even the staff at the tourist office betrays a conspicuous delight in watching each visitor step through the door. A fishing village and small port since the 10th century, Dunkerque has survived Flemish, Burgundian, Spanish, and English rule before becoming French in 1662, when Louis XIV wrote Charles II a bad check. The city's darkest hour came in June, 1940, when battleships, private yachts, humble rowboats, and anything else British that could float, gathered here to evacuate troops fleeing the monolithic power of the advancing German army. Four years passed before the Allied troops returned to France, on the beaches of Normandy.

Orientation and Practical Information

Dunkerque lies on the RN1 40km from Calais and 20km from the Belgian border, three hours by train from Paris. The city consists of two main sections: the town center, spreading east from the train station, and the area by the beach. To reach the tourist office from the station, follow av. Guynemer, which turns into rue Thiers and rue du Sud. Turn left onto rue Nationale from rue du Sud, and continue to the belfry (3 blocks).

Tourist Office: 4, pl. du Beffroi (tel. 28 66 79 21), on the ground floor of the belfry. Provides excellent map (2F), a free list of hotels and restaurants, and, only if you're desperate, a free accommodations service. Cash only **currency exchange.** Open Mon.-Sat. 9am-6:30pm; Sept.-June Mon.-Sat. 9am-noon and 2-6:30pm. Late-night arrivals can try the 24-hr. information line (tel. 28 63 00 00).

Post Office: rue Pres. Poincaré, at pl. du Général de Gaulle. Open Mon.-Fri. 8:30am-6pm, Sat. 8:30am-noon. **Postal Code:** 59140.

Trains: pl. de la Gare (tel. 20 78 50 50). To: Paris (5 per day, 3hr., 180F); Arras (7 per day, 1 1/2hr., 74F); Lille (9 per day, 1hr., 63F). Information center open daily 8am-7pm.

Ferries: Sallyline, pl. Emile Bollaert (tel. 28 21 43 44), entrance on rue des Fusilliers Marins. To Ramsgate (every 2hr.; one-way 146F, 60-hr. return 146F, 120-hr. return 300F). Information office open Mon.-Sat. 2-8pm.

Laundromat: 43-45, rue Terquem. Wash 20F, dry 2F per 5min. Takes 10F and 2F coins only. Open Mon.-Sat. 7am-7:30pm, Sun. 7am-1pm.

Hospital: Hôpital de Dunkerque, av. Louis Herbaux (tel. 28 29 59 00). **Emergency:** tel. 15.

Police: quai des Hollandais (tel. 28 66 30 05). **Emergency:** tel. 17.

Accommodations and Camping

Dunkerque is filled with inexpensive hotels, which usually have room even in high season. Ask the tourist office for a comprehensive list.

Auberge de Jeunesse (HI), pl. Paul Asseman (tel. 28 63 36 34). 15min. from the train station. Dorm rooms cramped, but clean. No lockout. Curfew 10:30pm. Members only. 43F. Showers included. Breakfast 15F.

Hôtel du Tigre, 8, rue Clemenceau (tel. 28 66 75 17). Sleek 2-star hotel, in prime location, deserves the name. Singles from 90F. Doubles from 120F. Breakfast 20F.

Hôtel le Lion d'Or, 4, rue de Chemin de Fer, (tel. 28 66 08 24). Right down the street leading from the train station. King of the Jungle it ain't, but attentive management keeps it clean. Singles 95F. Doubles 110-120F. Showers included. Breakfast 19F.

Camping: Dunkerque-Malo-les-bains, bd. de l'Europe (tel. 28 69 26 68). Take bus #3 (every 20min. from 6am-9pm) to the "Malo CES Camping" stop or follow av. des Bains east for 4km. Comfortable campground with swimming pool. 12F per person, 5F per tent, 7F per car. Showers included. Open March-Nov.

Food

Inexpensive restaurants and cafés flank the boardwalk along the beach. The local specialty is *moules* (mussels), which come swathed in various wine sauces. If all else fails, try the **Cabri Supermarket,** 89, av. de la Mer (open Mon.-Sat. 8am-7:30pm).

Tête d'Ail, 26, rue Terquem. Intimate family-run restaurant serving traditional French and seafood dishes. The 89F 3-course *menu* is *formidable,* as is the 49F lunch *menu.* Open Mon.-Fri. noon-1:30pm and 7pm-2am, Sat. 7pm-2am, Sun. noon-1:30pm and 7-11pm.

L'Iguane, 15, digue des Alliés, overlooking the ocean. Huge but always crowded. Serves excellent mussels (45F) and other seafood (35-65F) under the envious gaze of large iguanas. Open daily 10am-10pm.

Pavois, 175, digue de Mer. Cavernous restaurant on the waterfront specializing in seafood. Always busy and always delicious. *Saumon à la Parisienne* 40F, *soupe de poisson* 30F. Open March-Oct. daily 11:30am-midnight.

La Torcia, 16, rue de Flandre, off digue des Alliés (tel. 28 59 15 08). Microscopically thin-crusted pizza (30-50F) baked before your eyes in a wood-burning oven. Open Wed.-Mon. noon-3pm and 7-10:30pm.

Sights and Entertainment

Directly opposite the tourist office on rue Clemenceau, the 15th-century **Eglise St-Eloi** shelters Flemish paintings and Jean Bart's body inside its impressive Gothic walls.

The church's 500-year-old **belfry,** across the street, houses 58 bells including the enormous seven-ton "Jean Bart" bell named after the famous pirate who became lieutenant of the *Marine Royale* under Louis XIV. In July and August, the viewing deck surveys the city (free). Continue along rue Clemenceau to reach the town's Flemish **Hôtel de Ville,** a twin to Calais's flamboyant city hall.

The **Musée des Beaux-Arts** (tel. 28 66 21 57), near the theater on pl. du Général de Gaulle, houses an impressive collection of 16th- to 18th-century paintings by salient albeit relatively unknown French and Flemish artists. The ground floor presents a large display modeling major naval advances throughout the centuries. (Open Wed.-Mon. 10am-noon and 2-6pm. Admission 6F, students 3F, Sun. free.) The **Sculpture Garden** across the bridge from the youth hostel surrounds the fantastic **Musée d'Art Contemporain,** rue des Bains (tel. 28 59 21 65), itself shaped like a folded paper sailor's hat. (Open Wed.-Mon. 10am-7pm. Admission 6F, students 3F.) The **Musée Aquariophile** (aquarium), 35, av. du Casino, swims with 1000 fish of various exotic origins. (Open Wed.-Mon. 10am-noon and 2-6pm. Admission 6F, students 3F.)

Between the aquarium and the beach lies the picturesque neighborhood of **Malo-les-Bains.** Built in the late 19th century as an independent commune for wealthy literati, this commercial and residential district contains an eclectic mix of brick, tile, and half-timbered structures.

From May to September, the **Maison des Jeunes pour la Culture,** 43, rue Docteur Louis Lemaire (tel. 28 66 47 89), shows popular movies in English with French subtitles (28F). The Dunkerque **carnival,** the biggest festival in Northern France, unleashes a tide of drunken salaciousness every February. Between July and September, the **Contemporary Art Festival** indulges Dunkerque's sun-loving cultural connoisseurs by bringing culture to the beach. In the first week of September, the **Fête des Moissons** (harvest celebration) spurs dancing, drinking, and good, clean fun. Call the Mairie de Dunkerque (tel. 28 26 26 26) for details on these and other events.

Lille

Founded in the 11th century to serve as a transit station for trade boats passing on the Deûle River, Lille has grown into the largest city in the north, and the fifth-largest in France. Since being presented as dowry to Burgundy in Margaret of Flanders's marriage to Philip the Bold in 1363, Lille has become a center for French textile production. The town has retained much of its bustling Flemish character—especially in the townhouses lining rue Esquermoise off pl. de Gaulle, and in the inhabitants' gargantuan consumption of mussels, a habitual Flemish favorite. To be sure, Lille's location on the Pas-de-Calais, the main route connecting Paris with the ports of Boulogne and Calais, brings flourishing commerce, and with it a tendency to eschew the aesthetic in favor of the practical. Still, if Lille is not beautiful or particularly interesting, at least the throngs of students here (they comprise a quarter of the population) ensure a lively atmosphere all night long.

Orientation and Practical Information

Lille is two hours by train from Paris's Gare du Nord and one hour from Calais. From the centrally located train station, head straight down rue Faidherbe to pl. de Gaulle; pl. Rihour is just a bit beyond to the south. Lille's residents are proud of their fully automated *Métro,* which they claim is "the most modern in the world." Although distances are short, it is worth taking at least one trip just to ride in a train without a conductor (the entire system is computerized) and to see the stations, each designed in a contemporary style by a different local architect. (Tickets 7F10 per ride; *carnet* of 10, 50F.) The areas around the train station and the Wazemmes Market may be dangerous at night.

Tourist Office: pl. Rihour (tel. 20 30 81 00), in the remaining fragment of a 15th-century castle. Group tours Mon.-Sat. in English and French 30F. Free accommodations service. Open Mon. 1-6pm, Tues.-Sat. 10am-6pm. The **information center** (tel. 20 06 40 65) at the train station can give you a list of accommodations and a map. They also perform a cash-only **currency exchange,** although the rates verge on highway robbery. Open Mon.-Sat. 9am-12:45pm and 4-8:30pm. Diagonally across pl. Rihour is the **Comité Régional de Tourisme Nord-Pas de Calais,** 26, pl. Rihour (tel. 20 60 69 62). Maps and regional information. Open Mon. 2-6:45pm, Tues.-Sat. 10am-6:30pm.

Budget Travel: Centre Régional d'Information de la Jeunesse, 2, rue Nicolas Leblanc (tel. 20 57 86 04), at pl. de la République next to the post office. Information on flights, temporary jobs, and housing. They match riders with drivers through a Paris-based network. Open Mon.-Tues. and Thurs.-Fri. 1-6pm, Wed. 10am-6pm and Sat. 10am-12:30pm. **Wasteels,** 25, pl. des Reignaux (tel. 20 06 24 24). Student rates for rail and air travel.

Post Office: 7, pl. de la République (tel. 20 54 70 13). **Currency exchange** and **telephones.** Open Mon.-Fri. 8am-7pm, Sat. 8am-noon. Branch office, behind the Vieille Bourse and pl. de Gaulle, on bd. Carnotard at pl. du Théâtre. **Poste Restante** address: Lille Bourse, 59001. Both open Mon.-Fri. 8am-6:30pm, Sat. 8am-noon. **Postal Code:** 59000.

Flights: Aéroport de Lille-Lesquin (tel. 20 49 68 68). Fairly extensive service. Shuttles depart for the airport from the train station every 2-3hr. (30F). Contact the tourist office for schedules.

Trains: pl. de Gare (tel. 20 74 50 50; reservations 20 06 26 99). To Paris (every 1-2hr. 2-2 1/2hr., 160F); Brussels (76F); Amsterdam (213F); Nice (3 per day, 10hr., 553F); Lyon (3 per day, 5hr., 355F). Information office open Mon.-Fri. 7:45am-8pm, Sat. 8:30am-7:30pm, Sun. and holidays 8am-8pm.

Public Transportation: Buses, rue le Corbusier, next to the train station. **Metro Information Office,** pl. des Buisses, also next to the train station. Information for both, tel. 20 98 50 50.

Bookstore: Le Furet du Nord, 11, pl. du Général de Gaulle (tel. 20 78 43 43). A 4-story mammoth that claims to be the largest bookstore in Europe. 5% discount with student ID. Open Mon. 2-7pm, Tues.-Sat. 10am-7pm. **Book 'n Broc,** 17, rue Henri Kolb (tel. 20 40 10 02), off rue Léon Gambetta near pl. de la République. Buys and sells English books.

Women's Center: Centre d'Information des Droits de la Femme, 155, rue du Molinet (tel. 20 54 27 66). Sexual harassment information. Open Mon.-Fri. 9am-12:30pm.

Laundromat: Lavorama, 72, rue Pierre Legrand. TV and stereo while you wash. About 16F per 5kg. Open daily 6am-9pm. Also at 175, rue des Stations; open daily 7am-9pm. Another at 148, rue de la Louvière; open daily 6:30am-8pm.

Hospital: Cité Hospitalière, 2, av. Oscar Lambret (tel. 20 44 59 62).

Police: 16, bd. du Maréchal Vaillant (tel. 20 62 47 47). **Emergency:** tel. 17.

Accommodations

Pleasant hotels in Lille are not cheap. If you choose to stay in a budget hotel in the seedy area around the train station, be careful of pick-pockets. If you are planning to stay in town a while, ask about summer university housing at **CROUS,** 70, rue de Cambrai (tel. 20 52 84 00), or **Fédération des Etudiants,** 125, rue Meurein (tel. 20 30 60 26). (Open Mon.-Fri. 9am-noon and 2-4pm; Sept.-June Mon.-Fri. 9am-noon and 1-4pm.)

Auberge de Jeunesse (HI), 1, av. Julien Destrée (tel. 20 52 98 94), next to the Foire Internationale. From the train station, turn left onto rue de Tournai. Take the pedestrian underpass beneath the highway, cross the parking lot, and go under the overpass. A newly renovated place with spacious, dorm-type accommodations. Reception open daily 7-9am and 5-11pm. Curfew 11pm; strictly enforced. 55F. Nonmembers 75F 1st night, 65F thereafter. Showers, sheets, and breakfast included. Camping in back 30F, nonmembers 40F.

Relais Européen de la Jeunesse (UCRIF), 40, rue de Thumesnil (tel. 20 52 69 75), in a run-down neighborhood. At night, go in a group. From the station, take the metro (direction: "St-Philibert") and get off at "Porte d'Arras" stop. Take rue d'Alsace for 2 blocks to rue de Thomesnil (30min.). Large, comfortable, dorm-style doubles. No curfew or lockout. Photo ID needed. 70F. Breakfast included.

Hôtel Faidherbe, 42, pl. de la Gare (tel. 20 06 27 93). Clean, dark, and padded with brown shag on the floors and walls. Personable management. Singles 100F, with shower 130F. Doubles 120F, with shower 150F. Showers 20F. Breakfast 20F.

Hôtel Chopin, 4, rue de Tournai (tel. 20 06 35 80). Small but decent. Affable proprietor. Singles 100F, with shower 130F. Doubles 120F, with shower 150F.

Hôtel Paris-Nord, 14, rue du Molinel (tel. 20 06 27 54). Across the street from the station. A Black and red doors. Sufficient, if uninspired, rooms will be totally revamped by 1993. Singles and doubles 70-140F.

Camping: Les Ramiers, 52, rue César Loriden (tel. 20 23 13 42), in Bondues. Take the bus from Lille to Bondues Centre (last bus 11:30pm). Open April-Oct. For more information about camping in the area, call **Camping Club de Lille,** 13, rue Baggio (tel. 20 53 77 40). 15F per person, 5F per tent, 5F per car.

Food

Inexpensive restaurants and cafés pepper the fashionable pedestrian area around **rue de Béthune,** a neighborhood also filled with *patisseries, boulangeries,* pizzerias, and ice cream stands. Long under the influence of Flemish traditions, Lille is known for mussels, fish, cheese, and *genièvre* (juniper berry liqueur). Pick up edibles and wearables every Sunday, Tuesday, and Thursday at the **Marché de Wazemmes,** at pl. de la Nouvelle (8am-1pm). **Supermarkets** are located on rue Léon Gambetta and on rue de Paris at av. Pres. Kennedy. (Open Mon. 3-7pm, Tues.-Sat. 8:30am-12:30pm and 3-7pm.) With Lille's substantial student population, the cafés in the pedestrian section jangle through the early morning hours.

Aux Moules, 34, rue de Béthune. Mussels, mussels, and more mussels (40-60F). Open daily 11:30am-11:30pm.

La Crêperie de Beaurepaire, 1, rue St-Etienne, in an alley-like street parallel to rue Nationale, 2 blocks from pl. de Gaulle. Sit in the cobblestone courtyard or join the students indoors under the beautiful vaulted ceilings. *Galettes* 11-45F, dessert *crêpes* 11-30F, and delicious cider. Open Mon.-Sat. 11:45am-2pm and 7-10:45pm. Also **Beaurepaire II,** 6 pl. du Lion d'Or. Same food, prices and ambience, but open until midnight.

Grillop's, 18, rue Anatole-France, behind the theater. Delicious pizza (35-47F) and pasta (35-44F) among marble statues and mirrored pipes. Open Sept.-July Mon.-Sat. noon-2:30pm and 7:30pm-midnight.

Les Brasseurs, 22, pl. de la Gare, (tel. 20 06 46 25). A Lille institution, renowned for its Welsh rarebit and heady, globe-dotting beers. 60F *menu.* Open daily noon-midnight.

Grand Café, 1, pl. Rihour. Two mirror- and brass-accented floors packed with the in crowd. Typical café fare (10-30F) and beers from around the world, including Leffe, the monarch of Belgian beers and the local favorite.

Sights and Entertainment

Acknowledged as one of France's finest museums, Lille's **Musée des Beaux Arts** (tel. 20 57 01 84) confines works by Rubens, Goya, El Greco, David, Delacroix, and Renoir in a majestic 19th-century building on pl. de la République. Sucks for you, however, that the museum will be closed for restoration until May 1993. The **Musée de l'Hospice Comtesse,** 32, rue de la Monnaie, founded in 1237 by the Comtesse de Flandre and used as a hospital in the 15th century, displays antique furniture and art works but is most notable for the beautiful Flemish tile work on its walls. Additionally, it houses some works from the closed Musée des Beaux Arts. (Open Wed.-Mon. 10am-12:30pm and 2-6pm. Admission 5F, Wed. and Sat. afternoon free.) Just off rue de la Monnaie (entrance off rue du Cirque), **Cathédrale de Notre-Dame-de-la-Treille** is an unfinished neo-Gothic church begun in the 19th century. Despite the unappealing brick of the west façade, the church contains some fine chapels and interesting choir masonry, and, in the crypt, the **Musée Diocésain d'Art Réligieux.** (Open Sat. 4-5pm, 1st Sun. of each month 11am-noon. Free.)

The **Museum of Natural History and of Geology,** 19, rue de Bruxelles (tel. 20 85 28 60) features Egyptian mummies, two-headed **mutant cows,** and more conventional stuffed animals from around Europe. (Open Mon. and Wed.-Fri. 9am-noon and 2-5pm, Sun. 10am-5pm, 6F.) **Charles de Gaulle's birthplace** at 9, rue Princesse, now marred by graffiti, has a vast collection of photographs and newspaper clippings on the leader of the *Résistance* and two-time French president, whose name decorates street signs across the country. (Open daily 10am-noon and 2-5pm. Admission 7F, children 2F.)

The **Vieille Bourse** (Old Stock Exchange), on pl. du Général Charles de Gaulle between rue des Sept Acaches and rue Manneliers, is a masterpiece of the Flemish Renaissance. Built in 1650 by Julien Destrée, its four buildings border on a courtyard that once served as the only stock exchange in France. It has since eschewed greed and avarice for love and erudition—today's courtyard houses flower and book markets.

The ancient, star-shaped **citadelle** on the north side of Lille was restored in the 17th century by the Marquis de Vauban, as were many other fortresses in northern France. To enter this active army base, you must sign up for a group tour at the tourist office (Sun. 3-5pm only, 35F). Otherwise, settle for a view from the lovely **Jardin Vauban** across the street. The triumphal **Paris Gate,** on bd. Louis XIV, used to open onto the Roman road connecting Lille to Paris. **Eglise St-Maurice,** a 14th-century blackened Gothic church near the station will initiate you to the peculiarities of the Flemish *hallerkirk* style.

Although the modern university lies several km outside the city, most of its students partée in Lille. A few specimens philosophize at **Le Why-Not,** 9, rue Maracci, with its vaulted ceilings and 15F beers. (Open Tues.-Sat. 7pm-2am, Sun. 5pm-2am.) The resounding **Bar de l'Echo,** 20 pl. C. de Gaulle (tel. 20 57 36 28), is a typical crowded English pub pub pub pub (beers 12-14F; open Mon.-Sat. 5pm-2am). **L'Angle-Saxo,** 36, rue d'Angleterre (tel. 20 06 15 06), is a fantastic live jazz bar with a charming basement lounge and delicious drinks (around 45F; open daily 9pm-2am). **Le Chalet,** 33, rue Colbert, is a refined and quiet bar primarily for gay men. Drink in a movie at one of Lille's several movie theatres showing mostly French and American films. **Gaumant,** 25, rue de Béthune (tel. 20 54 72 55), and down the street, **Les Arcades,** 53, rue de Béthune (tel. 20 57 15 48) both roll films nightly for about 40F (students 30F).

The first weekend of September, Lille hosts *La Braderie,* a terrific festival which clears cars off the streets and replaces them with a gargantuan city-wide flea market. *Lillois* peddle junk by day and munch on mussels by night. For the past several years, **Aux Moules** (see "Food") has captured the prestigious prize of being the city's most popular restaurant: its pyramid of empty mussel shells has towered above those of all other restaurants.

Arras

Historians argue stodgily that the name Arras derives from *"arras,"* the hanging tapestries produced here during the 16th century. Legend, however, maintains that the name commemorates a gang of rats that stalked the star-crossed city in the Middle Ages, thus enabling the King of France to conquer the territory. Every year on Whit Sunday, the **Fête des Rats** pays homage to the rodents. Although badly damaged during the Revolution and again during the bitter trench warfare of 1914-1915, Arras has retained many of its medieval buildings. Its finest Flemish treasures, the Grande Place and the Place des Héros (Petite Place) display reconstructed Flemish façades identical to those on the Grande Place in Brussels.

Orientation and Practical Information

Arras is on the main Paris-Lille line. To get to the tourist office and pl. des Héros from the train station, walk straight across pl. Foch, past the fountain, and onto rue Gambetta. Turn right onto rue Ronville (opposite the post office), and turn left onto rue de la Housse, by the church of St-Jean Baptiste. The tourist office is across the square, inside the left door of the Hôtel de Ville. The Grande Place is to the right, on the other side of the pl. des Héros.

Tourist Office: pl. des Héros (tel. 21 51 26 95), in the Hôtel de Ville. City map indicates accommodations. Open Mon.-Sat. 9am-noon and 2-6pm.

Post Office: rue Gambetta (tel. 21 22 94 94), 1 block from the train station. Open Mon.-Fri. 8am-6:30pm, Sat. 8am-noon. **Postal Code:** 62000.

Trains: pl. Maréchal Foch (tel. 21 71 00 42). Station open 24 hrs. Ticket office open daily 7:15am-7:15pm. Information hotline daily 7am-9pm (tel. 21 73 50 50). To: Paris (15 per day, 1 1/2hr., 127F); Lille (frequent service, 45min., 46F); Dunkerque (10 per day, 1 1/2hr., 78F); Amiens (5 per day, 1hr., 51F).

Laundromat: Superlav, pl. Vivani, near the tourist office. **Lavomatique,** rue Frédéric de Georges. 25-30F per load. Both open daily 7am-8pm.

Hospital: 57, av. Winston Churchill (tel. 21 24 40 00).

Medical Emergency: SAMU, tel. 15.

Police: 18, bd. de la Liberté (tel. 21 24 50 17). **Emergency:** tel. 17.

Accommodations, Camping, and Food

Cheap hotels are scarce in Arras, and they fill quickly during peak season. The centrally located youth hostel provides the most practical accommodations.

Auberge de Jeunesse, 59, Grande Place (tel. 21 23 54 53). Very clean and comfortable dorm-style rooms, with nice showers and excellent kitchen facilities. Lounge with TV. Reception open May-Sept. daily 7:30-10am and 6-11pm; Oct. and March-April 7:30-10am and 5-10pm. Curfew 11pm. Members only. 43F. Showers and sheets included.

Grand Hôtel Raoul, 29, av. Michonneau (tel. 21 55 45 17). Bd. Faidherbe turns into av. Michonneau as you walk north (away from the station). Grand? Non. Comfortable? Oui. Singles 100F. Doubles 140F. Breakfast 20F. **Hôtel le Commerce,** pl. de Maréchal Foch, right near the station (tel. 21 71 10 07). Simple, clean, and well-located. Singles 120F. Doubles 220-240F. Breakfast 20F.

Camping: 166, rue du Temple (tel. 21 71 55 06), at av. Fernand Lobbedez. From the train station, turn left on rue du Docteur Brassart, then left on av. du Maréchal Leclerc. Follow this street to the campground. 10F per person, 4F per tent, 4F per car. Open April-Oct.

Inexpensive cafés skirt pl. des Héros; more elegant restaurants are found on the Grande Place. Genteel **Restaurant Montesilvano,** Grande Place, is a special treat for the cosmopolitan. For 30-40F, you can down delicious Italian pizza topped with mussels, a Flemish speciality, all in a French restaurant. (Open Sun.-Fri. noon-2pm and 7-11pm, Sat. 7-11pm.) **La Cave,** 50, Grande Place, is a popular place in—you guessed it—an old cellar. Indulge in the exquisite 60F and 90F *menus,* specializing in *choucroute* (sauerkraut) dishes and roast of duck and beef. (Open Mon. noon-3pm, Tues.-Sat. noon-3pm and 7:30-11pm.) Treat your tummy to a 72F or 135F *menu* of sole, lamb, or *foie gras* at the large old-style **Les Grandes Arcades,** 12, Grande Place. The huge **Monoprix supermarket** on rue Gambetta across from the post office defies description. (Open Mon.-Sat. 9am-12:30pm and 1:45-7pm). **Place des Héros** and adjoining squares erupt in boisterous color every Wednesday and Saturday morning from 8am-1pm during Arras's open-air **market.**

Sights

The 15th-century **Hôtel de Ville** near the marketplace acquired a new façade in the early 16th century after a fire destroyed the original. Inside this purely French beauty, ask the concierge to show you the municipal chamber, reception room, and the marriage chamber, where all marriages officially take place (a church wedding is not sufficient, and most French have both ceremonies). You can also ride the elevator to the top of the Hôtel's belfry. (Open same hours as tourist office. Admission 10F, students 4F, children 3F.) Serene **Grande Place** is surrounded by 155 homogeneous, 15th-century Flemish townhouses, whose first floors are collectively supported by 345 columns. Although barbed wire sliced this inspired Gothic masterpiece down the middle during World War I when the French and Germans occupied opposite sides, it shows few battle scars. A block away, boutiques, bars, and cafés line **place des Héros.**

Les Boves, 20km of interconnected subterranean **tunnels** built to house medieval chalk miners, stretch under the area around the town hall. The passageways have served as refuges during different wars, most recently as a shelter and hospital for British soldiers during World War I. (Tours leave from the Hôtel de Ville Tues.-Sat. 10am-noon and 2-6pm, Sun. 10am-noon and 3-6:30pm; Oct.-April Tues.-Sat. 2-6pm, Sun. 10am-noon and 3-6pm. Half-hr. tours 12F; 50-min. tours 17F, students 8F, children half price. Call 21 51 26 95 for information. Open daily 9am-noon and 2-6pm.) Next to the square, in the 18th-century **Abbaye St-Vaast,** the **Musée des Beaux Arts** assembles a collection of exquisite 18th- and 19th-century French and Dutch porcelain.

Sample a meter of beer (10 glasses arranged on a meter-long board; the 11th is free) at the raucous **Café de la Plage,** 6, bd. Faidherbe. Disco fever stays alive at **Le Pago** in the Petite Place, where the cool crowd does the Bus-Stop until dawn. (Cover 60F.)

Near Arras

Having played host to heavy fighting during World War I, the area surrounding Arras is dotted with 30 war cemeteries and countless unmarked graves. Trains depart frequently from Arras for many small towns in the region, but groups traveling to more than one site may save time and money by renting a car or hiring a cab.

Eight km northeast of Arras along the RN25 is the **Vimy Memorial**, a monument to the 75,000 Canadians killed in World War I. Tours of the trenches, tunnels, and the memorial are given by lively young Canadian guides brimming with information about the war as well as lighter subjects like Arras nightlife. The 11,285 trees planted in the park represent the number of Canadian soldiers whose final resting place is unknown. (Open daily 10am-6pm. Tours April-Nov. 15. Free.) Trains (13min., 26F round-trip) run three times per day to Vimy, but you still have to hike from the station to the memorial. **Allo Taxi** (tel. 21 58 18 17) will either deliver you to the foot of the memorial or follow a more scenic route through the area's cemeteries, but it charges 80-100F each way.

Farther west along the A26 lies **Neuville-St-Vaast,** which holds the graves of over 400,000 German soldiers. The rows of black crosses and civilian tombstones are made more sobering by the fact that each cross represents four fallen soldiers. North of Neuville on the A25 is the French cemetery, basilica, and museum of **Notre-Dame-de-Lorette.** Two hundred thousand French soldiers from World War I rest here beneath rows of white crosses. (Open May-Sept. 8am-6pm; Dec.-Jan. 9am-4:30pm, Feb.-March and Oct.-Nov. 8:30am-5pm. Museum admission 12F, children 6F.)

Twenty minutes by train from Arras is the sleepy town of **Douai** (pop. 45,000). Local excitement climaxes on the last Sunday in August to celebrate the annual **Garlic Festival.** Douai produces 80 tons of it yearly and bestows the dubious honor of "Queen Garlic" on one lucky lady who wins her weight in garlic. Oh my head! In the first week of July, the town swells to double its habitual size for the annual **Fêtes du Gayant** (Festivals of the Giant); a family of enormous mannequins parades through the streets before nightly concerts, exhibitions, and sporting events. The rest of the year, visitors will have to content themselves with Douai's more modest permanent attractions.

A former convent, the **Chartreuse,** now serves as the **Musée de Douai,** harboring works by Van Dyck, Rubens, Corot, Renoir, and Rodin. (Open Mon. and Wed.-Sat. 10am-noon and 2-5pm, Sun. and holidays 10am-noon and 3-6pm. Admission 10F, students and children 5F.) Rising out of the *Hôtel de Ville* and topped by a sculpted lion, Douai's **beffroi** (belfry) contains Europe's largest single collection of bells. In addition to pealing every half-hour, the *carillon* (bell collection) rings in concert every Saturday (10:45am-11:45pm) and holidays (11am-noon). (Open Mon.-Fri. and Sun. 10am-noon and 2:30-5:30pm; Sept.-March Sun. 2:30-5:30pm; April-June Mon.-Fri. 10am-noon and 2:30-5:30pm. Admission 8F, students 4F.) As late as the 15th century, Douai was entirely surrounded by a thick wall broken only by gates leading to roads to nearby cities. Only the **Porte d'Arras** and the more impressive **Porte de Valenciennes** remain.

Trains run to Paris-Nord (every 2hr., 2hr., 135F), Arras (every hr., 20min., 23F), and Lille (every hr., 1/2hr., 28F). The **tourist office** (tel. 27 88 26 79) is in the Hôtel du Dauphin, 70, pl. d'Armes, right next to the *Hôtel de Ville*. (Open Mon. 10am-noon and 2-6pm, Tues.-Fri. 9am-noon and 2-6pm, Sat. 2-6pm.) To reach the tourist office from the train station, cross pl. de la Gare and turn left onto av. du Maréchal Leclerc; follow this for several blocks. When you pass the **post office** on your right, turn into pl. d'Armes.

Amiens

"Of Gothic [tradition], mind you!" exulted John Ruskin about the Amiens Cathedral, "Gothic clear of Roman tradition, and of Arabian taint; Gothic pure, authoritative, unsurpassable, and inaccessible." Built to surpass the magnificence of Paris's Notre-Dame, Amiens's cathedral is undoubtedly one of the greatest Gothic specimens in Europe. Aside from its cathedral, however, Amiens (pop. 150,000) is not an especially attractive city; the capital of the Picardie region contains too many ramshackle buildings, treeless avenues, and disappointing concrete plazas. Fortunately, the ancient Quartier St-Leu on the Somme and the flourishing *hortillonages* (market gardens) offset the architectural anomie of the *centre ville*.

Orientation and Practical Information

Direct rail lines connect Amiens to Rouen, Boulogne, Arras, and Paris. To reach the center from the train station at the east end of town, head down rue de Noyon. The street changes names several times, eventually becoming rue des Trois Cailloux when it turns into pl. Gambetta. The cathedral and one of the tourist offices are to your right down rue des Sergents; rue de la République is to the left. Or take the rue des Vergueaux, which becomes rue du Marché Lanselle, and turn left onto the rue St-Germain; the tourist office is on the corner of St-Germain and rue du Chapeau des Violettes. At night, lone travelers should avoid the Cirque area.

Tourist Office: 12, rue du Chapeau des Violettes (tel. 22 91 79 28). Open Mon.-Sat. 9am-12:30pm and 2-7pm. **Branch offices** in front of the cathedral (tel. 22 91 61 74; open June to mid-Oct. Mon.-Fri. 10am-midnight, Sat.-Sun. 10am-8pm), and at the train station (tel. 22 92 65 04; open Mon.-Sat. 8am-8pm, Sun. 9:30am-7pm). The station office books hotels for free.

Post Office: 7, rue des Vergeaux, 2 long blocks from the cathedral. **Telephones.** Open Mon.-Fri. 8am-7pm, Sat. 8am-noon. **Postal Code:** 80000.

Trains: Gare du Nord, pl. Alphonse Fiquet (tel. 22 92 50 50). To: Paris (every 2-3 hr., 1 1/2hr., 90F); Calais via Boulogne (7 per day, 2 1/4hr., 110F); Lille (12 per day, 1 1/2hr., 87F); Rouen (3 per day, 1 1/2hr., 84F). **Lockers** 20-30F. Information office open Mon.-Sat. 8am-7:15pm, Sun. 9am-noon and 2-6:20pm.

Buses: Les Courriers Automobiles Picards, 6, rue de L'Oratoire (tel. 22 91 46 82). Buses leave to points in northern France from bd. d'Alsace Lorraine, adjacent to the train station. To Beauvais (4 per day, 2hr., 50F) and Croissy (1 per day, 20min., 13F). Information office open Mon.-Sat. 9am-noon and 2-6:30pm. Minimal service on Sun. **City Buses: SEMTA** (tel. 22 43 84 00). All city buses stop at pl. Alphonse Fiquet, in front of the train station.

Hospital: pl. Victor Pauchet (tel. 22 44 25 25).

Police: rue des Jacobins (tel. 22 92 08 81). **Emergency:** tel. 17.

Accommodations, Camping, and Food

Finding a room in Amiens should pose no problem. There's no youth hostel, but dorm singles are available July through September through **CROUS,** 25, rue St-Leu (tel. 22 43 38 07), across the river from the cathedral. The dormitories are near the university campus in the charming **Quartier St-Leu.** (Reserve ahead. 30F; student ID required. 15-20F meal tickets.) A few comfortable and inexpensive hotels are scattered throughout the *centre ville*. Between the cathedral and the train station, the elegant, freshly painted **Hôtel Victor Hugo,** 2, rue l'Oratoire (tel. 22 91 57 91), is run by an amiable proprietor. (Singles and doubles 105-120F, with shower 170-230F. Breakfast 20F.) **Les Touristes,** pl. Notre Dame (tel. 22 91 33 45) offers small, ho-hum rooms with the best view in town—it is directly across from the cathedral. (Singles 90-120F. Doubles 130-150F.)

Local dishes include *pâté de canard* (duck *pâté), tuiles amiénoises* (chocolate and almond macaroons), and *ficelle picarde* (a *crêpe* stuffed with mushrooms, ham, and cream). Intimate **Le Belu,** 63, rue Belu, in the Quartier St-Leu, serves regional specialties (37-55F) to students who gather at riverside tables. (Open daily noon-2pm and 6-

10:30pm. Café open daily 10am-midnight.) Farther along the canal, the **Côté St-Leu,** 4, rue des Mojots, sheltered by flowers and green shutters, serves *rocquefort* tart (38F) and big fresh salads (30-40F). (Open Mon.-Fri. noon-2pm and 7-10:30pm, Sat. 7-10pm.) The 46F *menu* at frenetic **Le Mangeoire,** 3, rue des Sergents, includes two *galettes,* a *crêpe,* and wine or cider. (Open Tues.-Sat. 11:30am-2:30pm and 5-11pm.)

Sights and Entertainment

When the leaders of Amiens decided to rebuild their **Cathédrale de Notre Dame** in 1220, they sought to outdo the achievements at Paris and Laon by making theirs even grander. By most accounts, they succeeded. By modifying classic Gothic design, they were able to incorporate taller arches, making the cathedral seem a leviathan even by French Gothic standards. Sixty years after construction began, the highest nave in France (42m) was completed. The speedy construction of the cathedral, made possible by Amiens' tremendous prosperity at this time, helps explain its remarkable stylistic homogeneity; in contrast, Notre-Dame in Paris, which took over two centuries to complete, vaunts a hodgepodge of medieval styles. The astoundingly complex west façade, with its 4000 figures enacting the episodes of the Old and New Testaments, attracted pilgrims craving Biblical lore at a time when written texts were hard to come by. (Open daily 7:30am-noon and 2-7pm. Treasury open Mon.-Sat. 10am-noon and 2-6pm. Treasury admission 10F, children 5F.) A *son et lumière* transforms the cathedral nightly from mid-April through mid-October. (Tues.-Sat. 45F. Shows available in English; check times in the information booth outside the cathedral or call 22 91 83 83.) Watch your bags while in the cathedral—the torrents of tourists draw a steady stream of pickpockets.

The **Quartier St-Leu** just north of the Somme River is the oldest section of Amiens. Built along a system of waterways and canals, its narrow winding streets and frequent galleries recall at once the simplicity of a portside community and the classic flavor of the Latin Quarter in Paris. Spread over 150 hectares of inlets created by Roman canalization of the area's marshland, the **hortillonages** (market gardens) still supply Amiens's produce and also display decorative flora. (Open spring and summer daily 10am-noon and 2-6pm.) Call the tourist office about **barge tours** (20F).

Jules Verne spent most of his life in Amiens and wrote his fantastical novels here. His home, at the corner of rue Charles Dubois and rue Jules Verne, is the brightest star in a rather dull firmament of museums. (Open Tues.-Sat. 9:30am-noon and 2-6pm.) This early science fiction writer lies 0.00046 leagues under the surface of the earth in the **Cimetière de la Madeleine.**

Amiens hosts an international **Jazz Festival** during one week in May; trumpets shout and walking basses stroll in local clubs and public plazas. Also popular are the **Cinéma Festival** in November and the **Fête d'Amiens,** a great shindig the city throws for itself one weekend in June. Call the tourist office for dates and details.

Laon

Victor Hugo mused that "tout est beau à Laon," and indeed, approaching this hill town that unexpectedly soars from the surrounding flat farmlands, you too might be inspired to such profound thoughts, even more so when you realize that this cloistered center of past prominence and current prosperity, remains aloof from the thicket of tourists. Quiet faded stone houses and steep cobblestone streets weave around a magnificent cathedral and 12th- and 13th-century buildings. To reach the *haute ville,* climb the steep public stairway straight ahead of the train station or hop on the brand-new POMA 2000 cable car system, which leaves frequently from the station (6F, round-trip 8F; *carnet* of 10 43F; bring your walking shoes after 8pm and on Sunday when service stops). The capital of France under the Carolingian kings and the birthplace of Roland, flattened folk hero and nephew of Charlemagne, Laon witnessed the construction of the **Cathédrale de Notre Dame,** beginning in 1155. The western façade tells the story of the Last Judgment in explicit Gothic detail, while the five towers display the heads of oxen in memory of the ox that miraculously appeared to bring building materials to the top of the hill. (Open daily 8am-7pm.) During guided tours, visitors may be allowed to climb the cathedral's towers. (Tours leave from the tourist office July-Sept. Sun.-Thurs. 3:30pm; Sept.-Nov. and April-July. Sat., Sun., and holidays 3:30pm. Admission 35F, students 25F.) The less fanciful **Eglise St-Martin,** at the other end of the *haute ville,* is an example of primitive Gothic architecture from the 12th and 13th centuries. To visit the interior, ask at 4, av. de la République. The abbey cloisters, to the side of the church, now house the municipal library. In July and August, expositions of contemporary prints (Robert Doisneau in 1991) hang in the library as part of **L'Eté de la Photographie.** (Open Tues.-Sat. 10am-noon and 1:30-6pm. Free.) Two blocks from Notre-Dame on rue Georges Hermant are the **Musée Municipale** (tel. 23 20 19 87), with its distinguished collection of Greek vases, and the charming, well-preserved 13th-century **Chapelle des Templiers.** Inside stand two statues of prophets that once supported the cathedral façade and the carved 14th-century "skeleton" of Guillaume de Harcigny, physician to Charles VI. (Both open Wed.-Mon. 10am-noon and 2-6pm; Oct.-March 10am-noon and 2-5pm. Admission 8F, students 5F.)

The cheapest place in town is the **Maison des Jeunes,** 20, rue du Cloître near the cathedral (tel. 23 20 27 64). A *foyer* for students and young workers, with pumpkin orange hallways leading to basic singles and doubles. The bathroom facilities have seen better days. (No curfew. 66F. Breakfast and sheets included. Call ahead.) While hotels in the *haute ville* price as high as 130F per night, several budget establishments hold out along av. Carnot by the train station. **Hôtel le Carnot,** 16, av. Carnot (tel. 23 23 02 08), has plain carpeted rooms. (Singles 95F. Doubles 120F, with shower 155F. Showers 15F. Breakfast 23F.)

If you crave local fare, look for *menus* featuring *tarte aux poireaux* (leek pie) and anything made with the locally produced cheese, *maroilles,* or liqueur, *genièvre.* **Les Chevaliers,** 3, rue Serrurier, serves excellent regional specialties for 55-70F. (Open Tues.-Fri. noon-2:30pm, Wed.-Fri. 7-9:30pm.) The **Agora Crêperie,** rue des Cordeliers at rue de la Herse, features a 42F *menu,* and *crêpes* and *galettes* for 10-24F. (Open Tues.-Fri. and Sun. 11:45am-2:30pm and 7pm-1am, Sat. 7pm-1am.)

Laon's **tourist office,** pl. du Parvis (tel. 23 20 28 62), next to the cathedral, occupies the oldest hospital in France, a frescoed 12th-century stone structure. (Open Mon.-Sat. 9am-12:30pm and 2-6:30pm, Sun. 10am-noon and 2-6:30pm.) Direct **trains** run to Paris's Gare du Nord (frequent, 1 1/2hr., 95F), Reims (5 per day, 1hr., 43F), and Amiens (6 per day, 1 1/2hr., 75F). Other destinations are only indirectly accessible. Train service is limited on Sundays. (For info call 23 79 42 44. Office open Mon.-Sat. 9am-noon and 2-6pm.)

Noyon

Dozing Noyon (pop. 15,000) intersperses its landmark historical buildings with shady parks and twisting streets. Despite Norman and Spanish invasions and occupations during both World Wars, the *noyonnais* claim an illustrious past. Charlemagne was crowned King of Neustrie here in 768, and Hugh Capet's coronation as King of France took place in Noyon in 987. John Calvin, whose teachings ignited a revolution in world thought was born in this tranquil and primarily Catholic town in 1509. **Calvin's restored birthplace,** on pl. Aristide Briand (tel. 44 44 03 59), contains pictures, engravings, and Calvin's original works on the Reformation. (Open April-Oct. Wed.-Mon. 10am-noon and 2:30-5pm; other times by appointment. Admission 8F.) Although one of the earliest and purest Gothic cathedrals, Noyon's 12th-century **Cathédrale de Notre Dame** displays renegade Romanesque elements in its second-story arches. (Open daily 9am-noon and 2-6pm; Oct. to April 9am-noon and 2-5pm.) Flanking the cathedral, the 16th-century wooden **bibliothèque** contains a 9th-century illuminated gospel and some 4000 other precious volumes. Unfortunately, only groups of at least six people qualify for the guided visits; call the tourist office at least one week in advance.

On a Sunday in early July each year, *noyonnais* gather for the bizarre **Marché aux Fruits Rouges,** a festival devoted entirely to trading recipes and selling cherries, strawberries, and currants. The highlight of the day is the question-and-answer session given by the celebrated TV horticulturist, Nicolas le Jardinier (Nicholas the Gardener), who discusses the trials and tribulations of raising and caring for red fruits.

Noyon's **tourist office,** pl. de l'Hôtel de Ville (tel. 44 44 02 97), sells 20F maps of the town and suggests daytrips. (Open Tues.-Sat. 9am-noon and 2-6pm, Sun. 10am-noon, Mon. 2-6pm; Oct.-May Mon.-Sat. only.) Ask about excursions to the majestic 12th-century ruins of the **Abbaye Notre-Dame d'Ourscamp** (tel. 44 76 98 08), 15km toward Compiègne in tiny **Chiry-Ourscamp.**

The **Hôtel le Grillon,** 37-39, rue St-Eloi (tel. 44 09 14 18), just up the street from the train station, features well-appointed rooms. (Singles with shower 140-180F. Doubles with shower from 190F. Breakfast 30F.) You can also try the **Hôtel le Balto,** 18, pl. de l'Hôtel de Ville (tel. 44 44 01 95). (Singles and doubles 82-92F, with shower 120F. Breakfast 17F. Closed several weeks in July, Aug., or Sept.) **Camping "La Montagne,"** 3, rue de Chêne (tel. 44 76 98 29), is 3km away toward Ourscamp. (8F per site, 5F per adult, 2F50 per child under 7, 3F per car. Showers 5F.)

A small group of restaurants off bd. Mony post traditional 45-55F *menus.* The **Restaurant Ganesh,** 14, pl. de la République serves a 44F lunch *menu* of southern Indian specialties (42-58F; open Tues.-Sun. noon-2:30pm and 6:30-11:30pm).

Trains run to Noyon from Compiègne (3 per day, 15min., 22F); Paris's Gare du Nord (7 per day, 1-1 1/2hr., 70F); and Laon (7 per day, change at Tergnier; 1hr., 44F). The ticket office (tel. 44 21 50 50) at the station is open Monday through Friday 5am to 8:15pm, Sunday 6:15am to 9:40pm.

Veni, Vidi, Scripsi.

Appendices

Glossary

Here you will find a compilation of some of the French terms *Let's Go* has used, along with their pronounciations. The gender of the noun is either indicated in parentheses or by the article (feminine, *la;* masculine, *le*). The glossary is followed by some phrases you might find helpful. The listed words or phrases which use the article "le" ("luh"), "la" ("lah"), "les" ("lay") indicate the pronounciation of the noun only. Eu and eue (pronounced the same) have a pronounciation in between the English "ew" and "uh." In this guide we have used "uh" to indicate this sound.

l'abbaye (f.)	abbey	lah-BAY
l'abri (m.)	shelter	lah-BREE
l'aile (f.)	wing	LEHL
l'allée (f.)	lane, avenue	lah-LAY
l'aller et retour	round-trip	lahLAY ay ruh-TOOR
l'arc (m.)	arch	LAHR
les arènes (f.)	arena	ah-REHN
l'auberge (f.)	inn, tavern	loh-BEHRZH
la banlieue	suburbs	bahn-LEEH
la baptistère	baptistery	bahp-tees-TEHR
la basse ville	lower town	bahs VEEL
le bateau	boat	bah-TOH
la bastide	walled town	bahs-TEED
le beffroi	tower	behf-WAH
la bibliothèque	library	bihb-lee-oh-TECK
le billet	ticket	bee -YAY
le bois	forest	BWAH
la bourse	stock exchange	BOORS
la calanque	cove	cah-LAHNK
le cap	cape, foreland	KAHP
la cathédrale	cathedral	kah-tay-DRAHL
la cave	cellar	KAHV
le centre ville	center	SAHN-truh VEEL
la chambre	room	SHAHM-bruh
la chambre d'hôte	rural bed and breakfast	SHAHM-bruh DOHT
le champ	field	SHAM
la chapelle	chapel	shah-PEHL
la chartreuse	charterhouse (Carthusian monastery)	shahr-TRUHZ
le château	castle	shah-TOH
le cimetière	cemetery	see-meh-TYAYR
la cité	walled city	see-TAY
le cloître	cloister	KLWAH-truh
le col	pass	KOHL
la corniche	cliff road, coastal road; cornice	kohr-NEESH
la côte	coast	KOHT
cours	tree-lined walk	KOOR
le couvent	convent	koo-VON
la croisière	cruise	kwahz-YAYR
la croix	cross	KWAH

le cru	wineyard, vintage	KRU
la dégustation	tasting	day-GOOS-tah-SYOHN
donjon	dungeon	dohn-ZHON
la douane	customs	DWAHN
l'école (f.)	school	lay-KOHL
l'église (f.)	church	lay-GLEEZ
l'escalier (m.)	stairway	lehs-kahl-YAY
l'evêché (m.)	bishop's palace; bishopric	lay-veh-SHAY
la falaise	cliff	fah-LEHZ
le faubourg	quarter	foh-BOOR
la fête	celebration	FEHT
la ferme	farm	FEHRM
les feux d'artifices	fireworks	FUH dahr-tee-FEES
la foire	fair	FWAHR
la fontaine	fountain	fohn-TEHN
la forêt	forest	foh-RAY
la gare	station	GAHR
la gare routière	station	GAHR root-YAYR
le gîte d'étape	rural lodging for non-drivers	ZHEET day-TAHP
le gîte rural	rural bed and breakfast	ZHEET roo-RAHL
la gorge	gorge; pass	GOHRZH
le gouffre	gulf; pit	GOOF-ruh
la grotte	grotto	GROHT
la halle	market hall, covered market	AHL
la haute ville	upper town	OHT VEEL
l'horloge (f.)	clock	lohr-LOHZH
l'hôtel (particulier) (m.)	mansion (town house)	loh-TEHL (pahr-tee-cool-YAY)
l'hôtel de ville (m.)	town hall	loh-TEHL duh VEEL
l'île (f.)	island	LEEL
le logis	lodging, dwelling	loh-ZHEE
la mairie	seat	meh-REE
le marché	market	mahr-SHAY
la montagne	mountain	mohn-TAHN
la mosquée	mosque	mohs-KAY
le mur	wall	MYUR
le palais	palace	pah-LAY
le parc	park	PAHR
le pic	peak	PEEK
le pilier	pillar	peel-YAY
la place	square	PLAHS
la plage	beach	PLAHZH
la pointe	headland, promontory	PWANT
le pont	bridge	POHN
la porte	gate; mountain pass	POHRT
le quartier	section (of town)	kahr-TYAY
la randonnée	hike	rahn-duh-NAY
la rencontre	meeting	rahn-COHN-truh
la roche	boulder	ROHSH
le rocher	rock; crag	roh-SHAY
la rue	street	RU
le salon	drawing or living room	sah-LOHN

le sentier	path, lane	sehn-TYAY
la tapisserie	tapestry	tah-pees-REE
le téléphérique	cable car	tay-lay-fay-REECK
les thermes (m.)	hot springs	TEHRM
le thon	tuna	TOHN
la tour	tower	TOOR
le trésor	treasure	tray-ZOHR
la trésorerie	treasury	tray-SOHR-uhree
la vallée	valley	vah-LAY
la vendange	grape harvest	vahn-DANZH
la vieille ville	old town	VYAY VEEL

Helpful Phrases

please	*s'il vous plaît*	see voo PLAY
thank you	*merci*	mehr-SEE
hello	*bonjour*	bohn-ZHOOR
good evening	*bonsoir*	bohn-SWAHR
How are you?	*Comment allez-vous?*	KOH-mehn TAH-lay VOO
I am well.	*Je vais bien.*	ZHUH VAY BYEHN
goodbye	*au revoir*	OH ruh-VWAHR
Excuse me.	*Excusez-moi.*	ehks-KOO-ZAY MWAH
Do you speak English?	*Parlez-vous anglais?*	PAHR-lay VOO zahn-GLAY
I don't understand.	*Je ne comprends pas.*	ZHUH NUH kohm-PRAHN pah
How much	*combien*	kohm-BYEHN
I'm sorry.	*Je suis désolé.*	ZHUH SWEE day-soh-LAY
who	*qui*	KEE
What?	*Comment?*	koh-MOH
how	*comment*	koh-MOH
why	*pourquoi*	poor-KWAH
when	*quand*	KAHN
What is it?	*Qu'est-ce que c'est?*	KEHS-kuh SAY
I would like	*Je voudrais*	ZHUH voo-DRAY
I need	*J'ai besoin de*	ZHAY buhz-WAN DUH
I want	*Je veux*	ZHUH VUH
I don't want	*Je ne veux pas*	ZHUH NUH VUH PAH
to rent	*louer*	loo-AY
The bill, please.	*L'addition, s'il vous plaît.*	lah-dees-YOHN, SEE VOO PLAY
Where is/are	*Où est/sont?*	OO AY/SOHN
the bathroom?	*les toilettes.*	twa-LET
the police	*la police*	po-LEES
to the right	*à droite*	ah DWAHT
to the left	*à gauche*	ah GOHSH
up	*en haut*	ahn OH
down	*en bas*	ahn BAH
straight ahead	*tout droit*	TOO DWAHT
a room	*une chambre*	oon SHAHM-bruh
double room	*une chambrepour deux*	oon SHAHM-bruh POOR DEUH
single room	*une chambre simple*	oon SHAHM-bruh SAYM-pluh
with	*avec*	ah-VECK
without	*sans*	SAHN
a shower	*une douche*	oon DOOSH
breakfast	*le petit déjeuner*	puh-TEE day-jhuh-NAY

lunch	*le déjeuner*	day-jhuh-NAY
dinner	*le dîner*	dee-NAY
shower included	*douche comprise*	DOOSH kohm-PREE
included	*compris*	kohm-PREE

Numbers

one	*un*	UHN
two	*deux*	DEUH
three	*trois*	TWAH
four	*quatre*	KA-truh
five	*cinq*	SANK
six	*six*	SEES
seven	*sept*	SEHT
eight	*huit*	WEET
nine	*neuf*	NUHF
ten	*dix*	DEES
twenty	*vingt*	VAN
thirty	trente	TRAHNT
forty	*quarante*	kah-RAHNT
fifty	*cinquante*	san-KAHNT
sixty	*soixante*	swah-SAHNT
seventy	*soixante-dix*	SWAH-sahnt DEES
eighty	*quatre-vingt*	KA-truh VAN
ninety	*quatre-vingt-dix*	KA-truh VAN DEES
one hundred	*cent*	SAHN

Menu Reader

à la	in the style of
abatis	giblets
abricot	apricot
agneau	lamb
aiguillettes	long, thin slices, usually of duck breast
ail	garlic
aile	wing
aioli	garlic mayonnaise
allemande	a white sauce with eggs
allumettes	matchstick potatoes
alsacien	with sauerkraut
amandes	almonds
ananas	pineapple
anchois	anchovies
andouillette	tripe sausage
aneth	dill
anguille	eel
apéritif	before-meal cocktail
à point	medium rare
artichaut	artichoke
asperge	asparagus
assiette de	plate of

au	in the style of
aubergine	eggplant
avec	with
avocat	avocado
baba au rhum	rich rum cake with currants
baguette	long loaf of bread, called "French bread" in the U.S.
ballotine	a roll of boned and stuffed poultry, meat, or fish
banane	banana
bar	sea bass
bardé	wrapped in fat and roasted
basilic	basil
basquais	with ham, tomatoes, and red pepper
bavarois	Bavarian cream: custard whipped with cream and gelatine
béarnaise	sauce made with egg yolks, shallots, white wine, vinegar, and tarragon
béchamel	white sauce with butter, flour, milk, onions, and herbs
beignet	fritter: deep-fried dough or fruit
bercy	with herbs and butter
betterave	beet
beurre	butter
beurre blanc	butter sauce with white wine, vinegar, and shallots
beurre à la maître d'hôtel	butter seasoned with parsley, lemon juice, salt, and pepper
beurre noir	butter with parsley and capers
bigarade	bitter sauce made with orange peel
bien cuit	well done
bière	beer
bifteck	steak
bisque	shellfish puree soup
blanc	white
blanc de volaille	breast of chicken
blanquette	stew in a white sauce with onions, mushrooms, eggs, and cream
blette	chard (white beet)
bleu	very rare, blood red
boeuf	beef
boeuf à la mode	beef marinated and braised in red wine and served with vegetables
bouef bourgignon	beef stewed in red Burgundy wine, onions, and garlic
boissons	drinks
boissons compris	drink (usually a glass of wine) included in the price
boissons non compris	drinks not included
bombe glacée	mixture of ice creams and flavored ices
bordelais	brown sauce with red wine, shallots, tarragon, and bone marrow
bouchée	filled pastry shell
boudin	sausage
boudin noir	blood sausage
bouillabaisse	Marseillaise soup with chunks of saltwater fish and sometimes shellfish, with tomatoes, garlic, saffron, herbs, and olive oil
bouilli	boiled

bourride	Provençal fish soup, with mayonnaise and bread
braisé	braised
brochette	kebab (skewer)
Bretonne, à la	with white beans
brûle	caramelized
brunoise	shredded vegetables or a mixture of vegetables
cacahouète	peanut
caille	quail
café	coffee
calamar	squid
Calvados	apple brandy
canard	duck
carneton	duckling
cannell	cinnamon
câpre	caper
carafe d'eau	tap water
carbonnade	beef stew with beer and onions
carotte	carrot
carpe	carp
carré d'agneau	rack of lamb
carte	menu
carte des vins	wine list
cassis	black currants
cassoulet	casserole of white
céleri	celery
cèpe	wild boletus mushroom
cerf	venison
cerise	cherry
cervelas	pork sausage with garlic
cervelles	brains
chair humaine	human flesh
champignon	mushroom
chanterelles	yellow mushrooms
Chantilly	whipped cream sweetened with sugar
charcuterie	prepared meats
charlotte	molded dessert, filled with cream or fruit
chasseur	sauce with wine, mushrooms, tomatoes, and shallots
chaud	hot
chèvre	goat cheese
chevreuil	venison
chiffonnafe	thin strips of lettuce or other vegetables
chocolat chaud	hot chocolate
choix	choice
chou	cabbage
chou frisée	kale
choucroute	sauerkraut with sausage and potatoes
chou-fleur	cauliflower
choux	pastry; cream puff
choux de Bruxelles	Brussels sprouts
ciboulette	chive
cidre	cider
citron	lemon

citron vert	lime
civet	stew made with red wine and blood
clafoutis	fruit pastry or crêpe
cochon	pig
cochon de lait	suckling pig
cochonnailles	platter of sausages and pâtés
coeur	heart
compote	whole fruit cooked in syrup and seasonings
concombre	cucumber
confit	duck or goose cooked and preserved in its own fat
confiture	jam
consommé	clear meat or poultry broth
contre-filet	sirloin steak
coq au vin	chicken stewed in red Burgundy wine with mushrooms
coquillages	shellfish
coquilles St-Jacques	sea scallops in a white sauce
cornichon	small pickle, served with pâtés
côte	rib or chop
cotelette	cutlet
coulis	meat juices, also a thick soup
coupe glacée	ice cream sundae
courge	squash
courgette	zucchini
court-bouillon	a flavored broth in which poultry, fish, or meat is cooked
crème caramel	caramel custard
crème fraîche	fresh heavy cream
crêpe	thin pancakes, but pancakes to die for. Served with jam, sugar, or other fillings
crêpe suzette	crêpes with fresh-squeezed orange juice and Grand-Marnier
crépinette	small, flat sausage
cresson	watercress
crevette grise	shrimp
crevette rose	prawn
croque-madame	toasted, open-faced ham and cheese sandwich, with an egg on top
croque-monsieur	toasted, open-faced ham and cheese sandwich
crôte	crust
cru	raw
crudités	raw vegetables, usually with a dressing
crustacés	crustaceans
cuisset	haunch
cuit	cooked
darne	a thick slice of fish
datte	date
daube	red-wine stew
déjeuner	lunch
digestif	after-dinner drink
dinde	turkey
dîner	dinner

duxelles	chopped mushrooms and shallots sautéed and mixed with cream
eau	water
échalote	shallot
écrevisse	crayfish
émincé	thinly sliced meat
entrecôte	rib steak
entrée	first course (appetizer)
épaule	shoulder
épices	spices
épinard	spinach
escabéche	small fish fried in olive oil, boiled and then marinated in court-bouillon, and served cold
escalope	thinly sliced meat, cutlet
escargot	snail
estouffade	beef
estragon	tarragon
étouffe	stewed
faisan	pheasant
farci	stuffed
faux-filet	tenderloin steak
fenouil	fennel
feuilleté, en	puff pastry, in
fèves	broad beans
figue	fig
fines herbes	mixture of parsley and other herbs, such as chervil, chives, and tarragon
flageolet	small kidney bean
flambé	flamed
flan	open, round tart, usually filled with custard
flétan	halibut
fleur	flower
florentine	with spinach
foie	liver
foie gras	liver of a fattened goose
forestière	with mushrooms
four, au	baked
fraise	strawberry
fraise des bois	wild strawberry
framboise	raspberry
fricassée	braised or stewed in white wine
frit	fried
frites	french fries
froid	cold
fromage	cheese
fromage blanc	sweet white cheese, served with jam
fruits de mer	seafood
fumé	smoked
galantine	cold meat, glazed in aspic
galette	thick crêpe made with buckwheat and topped with cream or eggs, nothing sweet
garni	garnished
gâteau	cake

gelée	aspic
génoise	sponge cake
gésier	gizzard
gibelotte	rabbit casserole
gigot	leg (of lamb or mutton)
girofle	clove
girolles	wild mushrooms
glace	ice cream
glacé	glazed
gratin	crust, made of bread and cheese
gratin dauphinois	potatoes boiled in milk and topped with a crust of cheese
grecque, à la	cooked in olive oil
grenouille	frog (legs)
grillé	grilled
groseille	red currant
hachis	hash
hareng	herring
haricot de mouton	mutton stew with turnips and potatoes
haricot rouge	kidney bean
haricot vert	green bean
herbes de Provence	parsley, sage, rosemary, and thyme
hollandaise	yellow sauce made of egg yolk, butter, and lemon juice or vinegar
homard	lobster
homard à l'Américaine	lobster with tomatoes, olive oil, shallots, and wine
homard Thermidor	lobster with butter, cream, brandy, and Madeira
hors d'oeuvre	appetizer
huile	oil
huître	oyster
île flottante	layered dessert of sponge cake, jam, custard, and cream
infusion	herbal tea
jambon	ham
jambon cru	raw ham, salt-cured or smoked
jambonneau	pig's knuckle
jardinière	garnish of vegetables
jeune	young
julienne	cut into strips
jus	juice
kir	aperitif with white wine and crème de cassis
kir royale	aperitif with champagne and crème de cassis
knepfen	Alsatian dumplings
lait	milk
laitue	lettuce
langouste	spiny lobster (rock lobster)
langoustine	prawn
langue	tongue
lapereau	young rabbit
lapin	rabbit
lardon	cubed bacon
léger	light

légume	vegetable
lièvre	wild hare
limande	sole
limousine, à la	with red cabbage
lotte	monkfish, angler
loup de mer	Mediterranean sea bass, similar to striped bass
lyonnaise	with onions
macédoine	mixture of raw or cooked diced fruit or vegetables
mâche	lamb's lettuce
madeleine	lemon-flavored tea cake
magret de canard	breast of fattened duck
maigre	lean
mandarine	tangerine
mange-tout	snow pea
maquereau	mackerel
marchand de vin	sauce with red wine, shallots, and meat juices
marinée	marinated
marmite	a pot; also a thick soup made in a pot
marron	chestnut
médallion	round or oval piece, usually of meat
mélange	mixture
menthe	mint
meunière	dipped in flour and cooked in butter
meurette	red wine sauce made with mushrooms, onions, bacon, and carrots, often served with fish
miel	honey
mignonette	small cubes, usually of beef; also coarsely ground peppercorns
mille feuille	"thousand-layered" pastry with cream; a Napoleon
mimosa	with chopped hard-boiled egg
mirabelle	sweet yellow plum
mirepoix	minced onions, celery, carrots, and sometimes ham simmered in butter and herbs
mixte	mixed
monégasque	with crushed walnuts, anchovies, garlic, and mustard in olive oil
mornay	béchamel sauce with cheese
moule	mussel
moule à la marinière	mussels steamed in white wine and served in broth
moule-frites	steamed mussels, served with french fries
mousse	literally "foam:" a whipped mixture containing eggs and cream
mousseline	whipped whipped cream
moutarde	mustard
mouton	mutton
mûres	blackberries
nantua	béchamel sauce with crayfish or shrimp
nature	plain
navarin	lamb or mutton stew with potatoes and turnips
navet	turnip
niçoise, à la	with tomatoes, onions, anchovies, and olives
noisette	hazelnut; slice of tender meat or potato
noix	nut

noix de coco	coconut
normande	with cream, eggs, and mushrooms or cooked in cider or Calvados
nouilles	noodles
omelet	omelette
ouef	egg
oeuf à la coque	soft-boiled egg
oeuf à brouillé	scrambled egg
oeuf dur	hard-boiled egg
ouef à la neige	beaten egg whites poached in milk, served in a custard sauce
oie	goose
oignon	onion
os	bone
oseille	sorrel
oursin	urchin
pain	bread
palourdes	clams
pamplemousse	grapefruit
panaché	mixed
pané	breaded
papillote, en	cooked in parchment paper
parfait	flavored-ice dessert
parisienne, à la	with scoops of potatoes, fried and doused in gravy
parmentier	with potatoes
pastèque	watermelon
pastis	anise (licorice-flavor) liqueur
pâté	minced and seasoned liver or meat, baked in a crust and served hot or cold. This spread without the crust is technically a terrine, but is often called a pâté.
pâté à choux	cream puff
pâté feuilletée	layered pastry
pâte	pasta
pâtisserie	pastry
pavé	thick steak (literally cobblestone), usually very rare inside
paysan, à la	with braised potatoes, vegetables and bacon
pêche	peach
pêche Melba	peach with vanilla ice cream and raspberries
perche	perch
perdreau	partridge
périgourdine, à la	with foie gras and truffles
persil	parsley
petit déjeuner	breakfast
petit-fours	tiny, bite-sized cakes
petit pain	roll
petit pain au chocolat	chocolate croissant
petit-pois	peas
pied	foot
pintade	guinea fowl
pipérade	Basque dish of scambled eggs, pepper, tomatoes, and onions and ham, grilled meat, or grilled fish

pistache	pistachio
pistou	sauce of basil, garlic, and olive oil
plat du jour	daily special
plateau	platter
poché	poached
poêlé	pan-fried
poire	pear
poireau	leek
poire belle Hélène	half-pears with vanilla ice cream and chocolate sauce
poisson	fish
poitrine	breast
poivrade	peppercorn sauce with wine and vinegar
poivre	pepper
poivron	bell pepper
pomme	apple
pomme de terre	potato
pommes frites	french fries
porc	pork
porc salé	salt pork
potage	soup
potage purée condé	red-bean soup with bacon and wine
pot-au-feu	beef boiled with vegetables in a ceramic pot
potée	rich soup with cabbage, pork, and potatoes
pouding	pudding
poularde	fattened pullet (chicken)
poulet	chicken
poulet marengo	chicken with tomatoes, mushrooms, wine, and crayfish
poulpe	octopus
poutine	french fries topped with gravy and cheese curds
pressé	pressed
profiteroles	small pastries filled with custard, cream, or ice cream and covered in chocolate sauce
provençal	with garlic, olive oil, onions, tomatoes, parsley, and white wine
pruneau	prune
quenelle	dumpling, usually with fish, sometimes with poultry or meat
raclette	melted cheese served over boiled potatoes
ragoût	stew
raie	ray (skate)
raisin	grape
râpé	grated
ratatouille	sliced eggplant, zucchini, tomatoes, peppers, and garlic fried in olive oil
ravigote	white sauce made with oil, vinegar, and several herbs
redis	radish
rémoulade	mayonnaise with mustard and herbs
rhum	rum
rillette	coarsely minced pork
riz	rice
rognon	kidney
Romanoff	(fruit) with cream and liqueur

romarin	rosemary
rosé	pink, as in meat
rôti	roast
rouget	red mullet
sabayon	custard, flavored liquor or wine
safran	saffron
saignant	rare (bleeding)
saison	season
salade niçoise	lettuce, tomatoes, green beans, tuna, black olives, potatoes, spanish onions, and anchovies
salade verte	green salad
salé	salted
sanglier	wild boar
sauce vert	mayonnaise with pickles and capers
saucisse	fresh pork sausage
saucisson	large dried sausage
sauge	sage
saumon	salmon
savoyarde	with Gruyère cheese
sel	salt
soissonaise	white-bean soup
sorbet	sherbet
soubise	white onion sauce
soupe de poisson croisiçause	fish chowder with potatoes
sucre	sugar
suprême	white, creamy sauce
suprême de volaille	chicken breast
tartare	chopped raw meat topped with a raw egg
tartare (sauce)	mayonnaise with mustard and cayenne pepper
tarte tatin	caramelized upside-down apple pie
tartine	open-faced sandwich or buttered bread
terrine	baked minced liver or meat, served cold; see pâté
thé	tea
thon	tuna
tiède	warm
timbale	anything cooked in a metal casserole
tournedos Rossini	filet mignon with foie gras, truffles, and Madeira
tortue	turtle
truite	trout
vacherin	baked merinque with ice cream
vapeur	steamed
veau	veal
velouté	"velvety" cream sauce
véronique, à la	with white grapes
viande	meat
vichyssoise	cold cream soup with leeks and potatoes
vin	wine
vinaigre	vinegar
volaille	poultry
vol au vent	pastry shell
xérès	sherry
yaourt	yogurt

INDEX

Brittany — St. Malo, Dinan.
203   207.

Sarlat   316

Ingrid —
(Flats) — (22/9/93 – OS 400 for 2 bed flat)
LASTENSTR 26

Ingrid Grubinger
Elisabethst. 8A
5020 Salzburg
Telephone – 0662 883877.